PSYCHOLOGY

THE PEARSON CUSTOM LIBRARY

Pearson Learning Solutions

New York   Boston   San Francisco
London   Toronto   Sydney   Tokyo   Singapore   Madrid
Mexico City   Munich   Paris   Cape Town   Hong Kong   Montreal

Senior Vice President, Editorial and Marketing: Patrick F. Boles
Senior Sponsoring Editor: Natalie Danner
Development Editor: Mary Kate Paris
Assistant Editor: Jill Johnson
Operations Manager: Eric M. Kenney
Production Manager: Jennifer Berry
Art Director: Renée Sartell
Cover Designer: Kristen Kiley and Sharon Treacy

Cover Art: "Chess piece" by Anton Seleznev courtesy of iStock; "Curtain and trees" by Neil Brennan courtesy of Veer Incorporated; "Couple and young girl standing in a line on a plank" and "Shadow on grass of children holding hands" courtesy of OJO Images Photography/Veer Images.

Please visit our website at *www.pearsoncustom.com.*

Attention bookstores: For permission to return any unsold stock, contact us at *pe-uscustomreturns@pearson.com.*

Pearson Learning Solutions, 501 Boylston Street, Suite 900, Boston, MA 02116
A Pearson Education Company
www.pearsoned.com

ISBN 10: 0-558-88284-6
ISBN 13: 978-0-558-88284-6

introducing psychology

brain, person, group

FOURTH EDITION

STEPHEN M. KOSSLYN

Stanford University

ROBIN S. ROSENBERG

Allyn & Bacon

Boston   Columbus   Indianapolis   New York   San Francisco   Upper Saddle River
Amsterdam   Cape Town   Dubai   London   Madrid   Milan Munich   Paris   Montreal   Toronto
Delhi   Mexico City   Sao Paulo   Sydney   Hong Kong   Seoul   Singapore   Taipei   Tokyo

To David, Justin, and Nathaniel, for showing us so much about how psychology really works.

Editorial Director: *Craig Campanella*
Editor in Chief: *Jessica Mosher*
Executive Editor: *Stephen Frail*
Project Manager, Editorial: *Judy Casillo*
Editorial Assistant: *Kerri Hart-Morris*
VP/Director of Marketing: *Brandy Dawson*
Executive Marketing Manager: *Jeanette Koskinas*
Marketing Assistant: *Craig Deming*
Managing Editor: *Maureen Richardson*
Project Manager, Production: *Shelly Kupperman*
Senior Sponsoring Editor, Custom: *Natalie Danner*
Project Manager, Custom Production: *Troy Lilly*
Senior Operations Supervisor: *Mary Fischer*
Senior Operations Specialist: *Sherry Lewis*
Senior Art Director: *Nancy Wells*
Text and Cover Designer: *Ilze Lemesis*

Manager, Visual Research: *Beth Brenzel*
Photo Researcher: *Billy Ray, Bill Smith Group*
Manager, Rights and Permissions: *Zina Arabia*
Manager, Cover Visual Research & Permissions: *Karen Sanatar*
Cover Art: *Sebastian Kaulitzki/Shutterstock Images (top); Tony West/Alamy (middle); amana images inc./Alamy (bottom)*
Director, Digital Media: *Brian Hyland*
Senior Digital Media Editor: *Paul DeLuca*
Full-Service Project Management: *Jenna Gray*
Full-Service Composition: *PreMediaGlobal*
Printer/Binder: *R.R. Donnelley & Sons*
Cover Printer: *Lehigh-Phoenix Color Corp*
Text Font: *Minion-Roman 10/12*

Credits and acknowledgments borrowed from other sources and reproduced, with permission, in this textbook appear on appropriate page within text.

Library of Congress Cataloging-in-Publication Data
Kosslyn, Stephen Michael-
   Introducing psychology : brain, person, group / Stephen M. Kosslyn, Robin S. Rosenberg. — 4th ed.
     p. cm.
   Includes bibliographical references and index.
   ISBN 978-0-205-77716-7 (alk. paper)
1. Psychology—Textbooks.   I. Rosenberg, Robin S.   II. Title.
   BF121.K586 2011
   150—dc22

2010038284

10 9 8 7 6 5 4 3 2 1

**Allyn & Bacon
is an imprint of**

www.pearsonhighered.com

Student Edition ISBN-13: 978-0-558-88284-6
ISBN-10:   0-558-88284-6
Exam Edition ISBN-13: 978-0-205-77717-4
ISBN-10:   0-205-77717-1

Acknowledgments

We want to give a heartfelt thanks to the many reviewers who read earlier versions of one or more chapters, sometimes the entire book, and helped shape this fourth edition and previous editions. This is by far a better book for their efforts.

Nancy Adler, University of California, San Francisco

Michael Todd Allen, University of Northern Colorado

Bernard J. Baars, The Neurosciences Institute

Lisa Feldman Barrett, Boston College

Marlene Behrmann, Carnegie Mellon University

Sara C. Broaders, Northwestern University

Ekaterina V. Burdo, Wright State School of Professional Psychology

Lynda Cable, Wilmington University

Charles S. Carver, University of Miami

Howard Casey Cromwell, Bowling Green State University

Patrick Cavanagh, Harvard University

KinHo Chan, Hartwick College

Jonathan D. Cohen, Princeton University

Virginia Ann Cylke, Sweet Briar College

Richard J. Davidson, University of Wisconsin, Madison

Mark Davis, University of West Alabama

Pamela Davis-Kean, University of Michigan

Douglas R. Detterman, Case Western Reserve University

Wendy Domjan, University of Texas, Austin

Dale V. Doty, Monroe Community College

Wendy L. Dunn, Coe College

Nicholas Epley, University of Chicago

Joseph R. Ferrari, DePaul University

Tierra Freeman, Kentucky State University

Albert M. Galaburda, Harvard Medical School

Justin T. Gass, The College of Charleston

Peter Gerhardstein, Binghamton University

Marilyn Gibbons-Arhelger, Texas State University—San Marcos

David T. Hall, Baton Rouge Community College

Argye Hillis, Johns Hopkins School of Medicine

Herman Huber, College of Saint Elizabeth

Alan E. Kazdin, Yale University School of Medicine

Angela Lipsitz, Northern Kentucky University

Andrea Rittman Lassiter, Minnesota State University, Mankato

Jon K. Maner, Florida State University

Rebecca Martin, South Dakota State University

Michele Mathis, University of North Carolina, Wilmington

Stuart McKelvie, Bishop's University

Richard J. McNally, Harvard University

Steven E. Meier, University of Idaho

Robin K. Morgan, Indiana University Southeast

Eric S. Murphy, University of Alaska, Anchorage

Lynn Nadel, University of Arizona

Margaret Nauta, Illinois State University

Jason Nier, Connecticut College

Matthew K. Nock, Harvard University

Kevin Ochsner, Columbia University

Kathy R. Phillippi-Immel, University of Wisconsin, Fox Valley

Heidi Pierce, Kirkwood Community College

Brad Pinter, Pennsylvania State University, Altoona

Robert Plomin, Institute of Psychiatry, London

Frank J. Provenzano, Greenville Technical College

Scott Rauch, Harvard Medical School

Patricia Sampson, University of Maryland, Eastern Shore

Lisa M. Shin, Tufts University

Jennifer Siciliani, University of Missouri, St. Louis

William C. Spears, Louisiana State University

Larry R. Squire, University of California, San Diego

Robert Stickgold, Harvard Medical School

Lisa Valentino, Seminole Community College

Tor Wager, Columbia University

J. Celeste Walley-Jean, Spelman College

Daniel T. Willingham, University of Virginia

Karen L. Yanowitz, Arkansas State University

Marvin Zuckerman, University of Delaware

About the Authors

Stephen M. Kosslyn

Stephen M. Kosslyn is professor of psychology and Director of the Center for Advanced Study in the Behavioral Sciences at Stanford University. He was formerly Chair of the Department of Psychology, Dean of Social Science, and John Lindsley Professor of Psychology in Memory of William James at Harvard University as well as Associate Psychologist in the Department of Neurology at Massachusetts General Hospital. He received his B.A. from UCLA and his Ph.D. from Stanford University, both in psychology. His research has focused primarily on the nature of visual mental imagery and visual communication, and he has published nine books and over 300 papers on these topics. For 10 years he was "head tutor" at Harvard, supervising graduate students who were teaching yearlong introductory psychology courses using the levels-of-analysis approach. While actively engaged with writing and academic pursuits, Dr. Kosslyn is currently on the editorial boards of many professional journals. In his spare time, he takes French lessons and plays bass guitar.

Robin S. Rosenberg

Robin S. Rosenberg is a clinical psychologist in private practice and has taught psychology at Lesley University and Harvard University. She is board certified in clinical psychology by the American Board of Professional Psychology and has been certified in hypnosis. She is a fellow of the American Academy of Clinical Psychology and is a member of the Academy for Eating Disorders. She received her B.A. in psychology from New York University and her M.A. and Ph.D. in clinical psychology from the University of Maryland, College Park. Dr. Rosenberg did her clinical internship at Massachusetts Mental Health Center, held a postdoctoral fellowship at Harvard Community Health Plan, and was on the staff at Newton-Wellesley Hospital's Outpatient Services. Dr. Rosenberg specializes in treating people with eating disorders, anxiety, and depression. Dr. Rosenberg also writes and speaks about how superhero stories reveal psychological phenomena. She is series editor of the *Oxford Superhero Series*, and she can sometimes be found at comic book conventions. When the opportunity arises, she also sings and plays guitar.

Contents

Source: © Leo Mason/CORBIS

> If you could identify and explain the factors that led to Tiger Woods's meteoric rise to fame and his subsequent fall from grace, you would be a very insightful psychologist.

INTRODUCTION TO THE SCIENCE OF PSYCHOLOGY

HISTORY AND RESEARCH METHODS

On a balmy April day in 2002, a young man was playing golf. Nothing unusual about that. But when this young man sank his final putt, the watching crowd let out a roar, and he looked for his parents and embraced them, fighting back tears. The occasion was the PGA Masters Tournament, and the young man was Tiger Woods. In a sport that had long been effectively closed to all but Whites, Tiger

Woods was of Asian, Black, White, and Native American ancestry. Woods then went on to dominate the sport of golf like no one before him. He has now been awarded PGA player of the year nine times (a record), and in 2008 he was the highest-paid professional athlete in the world, earning about $110 million in that year alone!

But then, at the end of the 2009, the world learned that Tiger Woods had multiple extramarital relationships, and his storybook marriage was left in shambles. He became the butt of jokes in late-night talk shows and a target of gossip in the media and around water coolers across the country. His product endorsements—which made up the bulk of his income—quickly began to disappear. How could someone who "had it all" have put his hard-won efforts and the trust of his family members at risk like this?

If you were a psychologist and could identify and explain the factors that led to Tiger Woods's meteoric rise to fame and his subsequent fall from grace, you would be a very insightful psychologist indeed. But where would you begin? To understand his ability at golf, you could look at his hand–eye coordination, his concentration and focus, and his intelligence. You could look at his personality, his religious beliefs (he was raised in his mother's faith, Buddhism), and his discipline in training. You could look at his relationships with the social world around him—his family, his competitors, and his fans.

To try to understand his personal problems, you could look at the role of sex in human motivation, you could look at his self-image and how he conceived of his role in the world, and you could look at how women behaved toward him and how he responded.

All of this is psychology. Psychologists use science to try to understand not only why people behave in abnormal or self-destructive ways but also why and how people think, feel, and behave in "normal" ways. Psychology is about the mind and behavior, both exceptional and ordinary. In this chapter, we show you how to look at and answer questions about mind and behavior by methods used in current research and (because the inquiry into what makes us tick has a history) how psychologists over the past century have approached these questions.

◙ ◙ ◙

The Science of Psychology: Getting to Know You

Virtually everything any of us thinks, feels, or does falls within the sphere of psychology. You are dealing with the subject matter of psychology when you watch people interacting in a classroom or at a party or notice that a friend is in a really terrible mood.

LOOKING AHEAD Learning Objectives

1. What is psychology?
2. What is the concept of *levels of analysis*, and how can you use it to understand psychology?

What Is Psychology?

The field you are studying in this textbook can be defined in one simple sentence: **Psychology** *is the science of the mind and behavior*. Let's look at the key words in this definition: *science, mind,* and *behavior*.

First, *science*: Science avoids mere opinions, intuitions, and guesses and instead strives to nail down facts by using objective (not influenced by an observer's feelings or interpretations) evidence. A scientist uses logic to reason about the possible causes of a phenomenon and then tests the resulting ideas by collecting additional facts that will either support the ideas or refute them.

Second, *mind*: The mind is what the brain does. Or, more accurately, the mind is what your brain does—the mental events it produces—both when you engage in "thinking" activities, such as storing memories, recognizing objects, and using language, and also when you are "feeling" something, such as when you are depressed or savoring the experience of being in love.

How can we collect objective facts about the mind, which is hidden and internal? One way, which has a long history in psychology, is to work backward, observing what people do and inferring from outward signs what is going on "inside." This basic approach is commonplace in science. For instance, astronomers have observed flames roiling on the surface of the sun and drawn inferences about the inner workings of stars. Similarly, psychologists have observed that unintended facial expressions offers a window into a person's emotional reactions and that the size of the pupils of the eyes offer a window into what a person finds interesting (the pupils are relatively large when a person is paying close attention).

Another, more recent method for studying facts about the mind does not require drawing inferences from behavior. Instead, researchers use brain-scanning techniques to take pictures of the living brain that show its physical changes as it works and then relate those physical changes to the mental events they produce. For example, a brain structure called the amygdala is activated whenever people are afraid and often when they have strong emotional reactions in general—and hence if researchers see it activated, they have grounds for drawing inferences about the accompanying mental events.

Third, *behavior*: By **behavior**, we mean the outwardly observable acts of a person, either alone or in a group. Behavior consists of physical movements—voluntary or involuntary—of the limbs, facial muscles, or other parts of the body. A particular behavior typically is preceded by mental events, such as a perception of the current situation

Psychology The science of the mind and behavior.

Behavior The outwardly observable acts of a person, alone or in a group.

What Is Psychology?

Science

Mind

Behavior

3

(for instance, how far a golf ball must travel to reach a cup) and a decision about what to do next (how forcefully to swing the club). A behavior may also be governed by the relationship between the individual and a group of people. Tiger Woods might not have performed the way he did in 2002 had he been playing in 1920, when many in the crowd would not have wanted a non-White person to win.

So there are layers upon layers: An individual's mental state depends on brain functioning, and mental events affect his or her behavior, and—at the same time—these events are affected by the surrounding group (the members of which, in turn, have their own individual minds and behaviors).

The field of psychology is dedicated to helping us understand ourselves and each other by using the tools of science. But more than that, research in the field of psychology is designed not simply to describe and explain mental events and behavior but also to *predict* and *control* them. As an individual, you'd probably like to be able to predict what kind of person would make a good spouse for you or which politician would make sound decisions in crisis situations. As a society, we all would greatly benefit by knowing how people learn most effectively, how to control addictive and destructive behaviors, and how to cure mental illness. The field of psychology can help us become masters of our own fates, to control what otherwise might seem to be inevitable consequences of human nature.

Levels of Analysis: The Complete Psychology

To answer questions about Tiger Woods's successes and failures, were you a psychologist, you would try to understand psychological phenomena at different *levels of analysis* (to use the most widely accepted terminology). To understand the idea of levels of analysis, let's begin by considering a building, say the City Hall in your city or town.

First, imagine the building and then zoom in so that all you can see are bricks, boards, cement blocks, or other basic building materials. At this level of analysis, what's important is the nature of the physical structure.

Second, imagine that you can use X ray vision so that you can see the internal organization of the building, the rooms, corridors, stairways, and so on. Now you can tell which are offices, which are waiting rooms, where the restrooms are, and so forth. The building materials are no longer key; rather, you are now considering the functions and contents of different parts of the structure.

Third, zoom out so you can see the building situated in your city or town. Now you can see how roads and electric lines lead to and from City Hall, how it is positioned relative to other structures (such as a parking lot), and so on.

In this example, you have been looking at the same thing—a building—but considering it from different levels of analysis. Notice also that characteristics evident at each of the different levels affect each other: The physical structure affects the function (for example, if the building doesn't have a steel skelton, it can't be very high—and so cannot have as much space as would be possible if steel were used), and the function affects the relation to other structures (for example, a large parking lot wouldn't be necessary if there weren't a lot of visitors). We can perform exactly the same sort of analyis when we consider psychological phenomena, as we discuss in the following sections.

Three Levels of Analysis in Psychology Psychologists often distinguish among three levels of analysis: the brain, the person, and the group (hence the subtitle of this book). Let's consider these levels one at a time and then consider how events at the different levels interact.

LEVEL OF THE BRAIN. At the **level of the brain**, psychologists focus on both the activity of the brain and the structure and properties of the organ itself—brain cells and their connections, the chemical soup in which they exist (including hormones that alter the way the brain operates), and the genes that give rise to them. (This level is analogous to considering the physical makeup of a building—its building blocks.) At the level of the brain, a psychologist might want to study the amount and type of activity in different parts of Tiger Woods's brain when he plans a shot or when he sees an attractive woman.

Level of the brain Events that involve the activity, structure, and properties of the organ itself—brain cells and their connections, the chemical solutions in which they exist, and the genes.

LEVEL OF THE PERSON. At the **level of the person**, psychologists focus on *mental events*—the *contents* and *functions* of the mind. (This level is analogous to considering the contents and functions of a building—the offices and hallways, for instance.) Unlike the level of the brain, we no longer talk about the physical characteristics of the brain; rather, we divide mental events into two types, *mental contents* and *mental processes*. **Mental contents** consist of knowledge, beliefs (including ideas, explanations, and expectations), desires (such as hopes, goals, and needs), and feelings (such as fear, sadness, joy, and guilt). **Mental processes**, in contrast, consist of sets of operations that work together to carry out a function, such as attention, perception, or memory. These operations are like the chopping, measuring, and mixing that goes into cooking, and the different mental contents are analogous to different ingredients in cooking. For example, visualize the uppercase version of the letter "n" (this is a "mental content"); now, imagine that you are rotating it 90 degrees clockwise. Can you "see" whether it's now another letter? Most people can "see" the Z in their mental image. Each step—forming the mental image, rotating the letter in the image, and recognizing the new letter—is a mental process.

Although the brain is the location and vehicle for mental contents and mental processes, the brain and the mind are not the same—any more than a computer and a love letter written on it are the same. Rather, the brain is in many ways a canvas on which life's experiences are painted. Just as we can discuss how aspects of a canvas (such as its texture) allow us to paint, we can discuss how the brain supports mental contents and mental processes. But just as we can talk about the picture itself (a portrait, a landscape, and so on) without mentioning aspects of the canvas, we can talk about mental contents and mental processes themselves. To do so, we must shift from the level of the brain to the level of the person. At the level of the person, a psychologist who is studying Tiger Woods might want to investigate the factors behind the inner calm he displays under pressure (for example, the role that his Buddhist faith might play).

LEVEL OF THE GROUP. At the **level of the group**, psychologists focus on the ways that collections of people (as few as two or as many as a society) shape the mind and behavior. "No man is an island," the poet John Donne wrote. We all live in *social environments* that vary over time and space and that are populated by our friends and acquaintances, our relatives, and the other people we have contact with in our daily lives. Our lives are intertwined with other people's lives from birth to old age. (This level is analogous to viewing the building in the context of its relation to other aspects of the city, such as nearby municipal buildings or eateries.)

Psychologists conduct two sorts of investigations at the level of the group. On the one hand, they consider how other people affect an individual's mind and behavior. For example, a researcher might want to examine the role of a supportive and enthusiastic audience in helping Tiger Woods play golf well. On the other hand, psychologists consider groups in their own right. Researchers might study the distinct identities of groups, which are based on shared beliefs and practices that are passed on to new members as *culture;* culture has been defined as the "language, beliefs, values, norms, behaviors, and even material objects that are passed from one generation to the next" (Henslin, 1999). For example, golfers as a group have certain shared beliefs and practices.

THE PHYSICAL WORLD AS BACKDROP. Events that occur at every level of analysis—brain, person, and group—are intimately tied to conditions in the physical world. All our mental events and behaviors take place within and are influenced by a specific *physical environment*. A windy day at the golf course changes the way Tiger Woods plays a shot. The group is only part of the world; to understand the events at each level of analysis, we must always relate them to the physical world that surrounds all of us.

All Together Now Events at the different levels are constantly interacting. Unlike a computer, the human brain does not act the same way when we write a love letter and when we write directions to someone's house. When you feel an emotion (at the level of the person), that experience is accompanied by changes in how your brain operates (Davidson, 2004; Sheehan et al., 2004). Events at each level modify and trigger events at

Level of the person Events that involve the function (mental processes) and content (mental content) of the mind.

Mental contents Knowledge, beliefs (including ideas, explanations, and expectations), desires (such as hopes, goals, and needs), and feelings (such as fears, guilts, and attractions).

Mental processes Sets of operations that work together to carry out a function, such as attention, perception, or memory.

Level of the group Events that involve relationships between people (such as love, competition, and cooperation), relationships among groups, and culture.

the other levels. Consider the following example: As you sit in a lecture hall, the signals among your brain cells that enable you to understand the lecture, and the new connections among your brain cells that enable you to remember it are happening because you decided to take the course (perhaps because you need it to graduate); that is, events at the level of the person (your interests or perhaps knowledge of your school's requirements) are affecting events at the level of the brain. But, as you listen to the lecture, your neighbor's knuckle cracking is really getting to you, and you're finding it hard to concentrate, which is interfering with your learning the material: Events at the level of the group are affecting events at the level of the person and the brain. Because you really want to understand this lecture (knowing that a test is coming up soon), you're wondering how to get your neighbor to cut it out, and you decide to shoot a few dirty looks his way: Events at the level of the person are affecting events at the level of the group (which, as we've seen, affect events at the level of the brain). And all of this is going on within the physical environment of the room, where the sunlight that had seemed warm and welcoming is now pretty hot, and you're getting *really* irritated, and you finally change your seat—and round and round. Events at the three levels of analysis, in a specific physical context, are constantly changing and influencing one another. To understand fully what's going on in any life situation, you need to look at events at all three levels of analysis.

The concept of levels of analysis has long held a central role in science in general (Anderson, 1998; Nagel, 1979; Schaffner, 1967), and in the field of psychology in particular (de Pinedo-Garcia & Noble, 2008; Fodor, 1968; Kosslyn & Koenig, 1995; Marr, 1982; Putnam, 1973; Saha, 2004), and for good reason: This view of psychology not only allows you to see how different types of theories and discoveries illuminate the same phenomena but also lets you see how these theories and discoveries are interconnected—and thus how the field of psychology as a whole emerges from them.

The *Looking at Levels* sections consider one aspect of psychology in detail, showing how it is illuminated when we investigate events at the three levels of analysis and their interactions. Moreover, we draw on the different levels continually as we explore different aspects of the field.

> *THINK* like a
> **PSYCHOLOGIST** In your own life, can you identify instances where events at the different levels of analysis were clearly at work?

✔●─Study and Review on
mypsychlab.com

LOOKING BACK

1. **What is psychology?** Psychology is the science of the mind and behavior. Psychology focuses on both the internal events that underlie our thoughts, feelings, and the behavior itself.

2. **What is the concept of levels of analysis, and how can you use it to understand psychology?** Any psychological phenomenon can best be understood by considering events at three levels of analysis: the brain (its structure and activity), the person (mental contents and mental processes), and the group (social interactions and cultural characteristics). All these events occur in the context of the physical world. Events at the different levels are constantly interacting, and thus it is impossible to explain the mind or behavior adequately in terms of only a single level of analysis.

Psychology Then and Now

How do you think psychologists 50 or 100 years ago might have interpreted Tiger Woods's behavior, both on and off the golf course? Would they have focused on the same things that psychologists do today? One hallmark of the sciences is that rather than casting aside earlier findings, researchers use them as stepping-stones to the next set of discoveries. Reviewing how psychology has developed over time helps us understand better where we are today. In the century or so during which psychology has taken shape as a formal discipline, the issues under investigation have changed, the emphasis has shifted from one level of analysis to another, and events at each level have often been viewed as operating separately or occurring in isolation. ●View

●─View the Psychology Timeline on
mypsychlab.com

1. How did psychology develop over time?
2. What do today's psychologists actually do?

Structuralism The school of psychology that sought to identify the basic elements of consciousness and to describe the rules and circumstances under which these elements combine to form mental *structures*.

Introspection The technique of observing your mental events as, or immediately after, they occur.

The Evolution of a Science

In one form or another, psychology has probably always been with us. People have apparently always been curious about why they and others think, feel, and behave the ways they do. In contrast, the history of psychology as a scientific field is relatively brief, spanning little more than a century. The roots of psychology lie in *philosophy* (the field that relies on logic and speculation to understand the nature of reality, experience, and values) on the one hand and *physiology* (the field that studies the biological workings of the body, including the brain) on the other.

From philosophy, psychology borrowed theories of the nature of the mind and behavior. For example, the 17th-century French philosopher René Descartes focused attention on the distinction between mind and body and the relation between the two (still a focus of considerable debate). John Locke, a 17th-century English philosopher (and friend of Sir Isaac Newton), stressed that all human knowledge arises from experience of the world or from reflection about it. Locke argued that we know about the world only via how it is represented in the mind.

From physiology, psychologists learned to recognize the role of the brain in giving rise to mental events and behavior. But more than that, psychologists acquired a scientific approach to studying brain function and how it produces mental events and behavior. And they inherited methods to investigate the mind and behavior.

These twin influences of philosophy and physiology remain in force today, shaped and sharpened by developments over time.

Early Days: Beginning to Map the Mind and Behavior The earliest scientific psychologists were not much interested in why we behave as we do. Instead, these pioneers typically focused their efforts on understanding the operation of perception (the ways in which interpret information from our eyes, ears, and other sensory organs), memory, and problem solving.

STRUCTURALISM. Wilhelm Wundt (1832–1920), usually considered the founder of scientific psychology, set up the first psychology laboratory in 1879 in Leipzig, Germany. The work of Wundt and his colleagues led to **structuralism**, the first organized "school of thought" in psychology. The structuralists sought to identify the "building blocks" of consciousness (*consciousness* is the state of being aware). Consciousness itself occurs at the level of the person, as do the mental processes that underlie and produce it—but these processes in turn rely on brain function. Part of Wundt's research led him to characterize two types of elements of consciousness: (1) *sensations*, which arise from the eyes, ears, and other sense organs, and (2) *feelings*, such as fear, anger, and love. The goal of structuralism was to describe the rules that determine how particular sensations or feelings may occur at the same time or in sequence, combining in various ways into mental *structures*. Edward Titchener (1867–1927), an American student of Wundt's, broadened the structuralist approach to apply it to the nature of concepts and thinking in general.

The structuralists developed and tested their theories partly with objective techniques, for example, by measuring the time it takes to respond to different stimuli. Their primary research tool, however, was *introspection*, which means literally "looking within." **Introspection** is the technique of observing your mental events as, or immediately after, they occur. Here is an example of introspection: Try to recall how many windows and doors are in your parents' living room. Are you aware of "seeing" the room in a mental image, of scanning along the walls and counting the windows and doors?

Considering the nature of mental images is one form of introspection, but there are many others. For example, you would use introspection to notice which factors

Margaret Floy Washburn was not only Edward Titchener's first graduate student to receive a Ph.D. but was also the first woman to earn a Ph.D. in psychology (at Cornell in 1894).

Source: Archives of the History of American Psychology - The University of Akron

Wilhelm Wundt (the man with the long gray beard standing behind one table) in his laboratory.

Source: Archives of the History of American Psychology - The University of Akron

The functionalists sought to apply knowledge of psychology and helped to improve education in the United States.

Source: North Wind Picture Archives

Functionalism The school of psychology that sought to understand how the mind helps individuals to adapt to the world around them, to *function* effectively in it.

you emphasize when making decisions (such as noticing that when you think about registering for next semester's courses, you are paying less attention to how far you will have to walk to the classroom than to how much you think you will enjoy the material). Suppose the structuralists had been asked to analyze Tiger Woods's golf success—such as how he perceives distances, fairway terrain, and wind direction. They probably would have trained him to use introspection to describe his mental contents and mental processes.

However, using introspection to study mental contents and mental processes ran into two major problems. To understand the first problem, suppose that you are able to use mental imagery as a tool to recall the numbers of windows and doors in your parents' living room, but a classmate claims that she isn't able to do the same. In fact, she denies ever having had a "mental image" and thinks that you are making up the very idea. This is the first problem: How could you prove that mental images actually exist and that objects can indeed be visualized? For the early psychologists, this was a major obstacle; there was no way to resolve disagreements about the mental events that introspection revealed. The second problem is that a considerable amount of mental contents and of mental processing cannot be accessed via introspection, which severely limits its usefulness for studying the mind. For example, people don't know how their memories or reasoning processes work or why they sometimes fail to work well.

FUNCTIONALISM. Rather than trying to chart the building blocks of the mind, as did the structuralists, the adherents of **functionalism** sought to understand how our minds help us to adapt to the world around us—in short, to *function* in it (Boring, 1950). Whereas the structuralists asked *what* the building blocks of the mind are and *how* they operate, the functionalists wanted to know *why* humans think, feel, and behave as we do. The functionalists addressed events at the level of the person and were also very interested in events at the level of the group. The functionalists, many of whom were Americans, shared the urge to gather knowledge that could be put to immediate use. Sitting in a dark room introspecting simply didn't seem worthwhile to them. The functionalists studied the methods by which people learn and also studied how goals and beliefs are shaped by environments. As such, their interests spanned the levels of the person and the group.

The functionalists were strongly influenced by Charles Darwin (1809–1882), whose theory of evolution by natural selection stressed that some individual organisms in every species, from ants to oak trees, possess characteristics that enable them to survive and reproduce more fruitfully than others. The phrase "survival of the fittest," often quoted in relation to natural selection, doesn't quite capture the key idea. (For one thing, these days "the fittest" implies the muscle-bound star of the health club, whereas in Darwin's time it meant something "fit for" or "well suited to" its situation.) The idea of natural selection is that certain inherited characteristics make particular individuals more fit for their environments, enabling them to have more offspring that survive (and inherit those characteristics), and those offspring in turn have more offspring of their own (that inherit the characteristics) and so on, until the characteristics that led the original individuals to flourish are spread through the population. Darwin called the inborn characteristics that help an organism survive and produce many offspring *adaptations*.

The functionalists applied Darwin's theory to mental characteristics. For example, William James (1842–1910), who set up the first psychology laboratory in the United States, studied the ways in which being able to pay attention can help an individual survive and adapt to an environment. The functionalists likely would have tried to discover how Tiger Woods's goals and beliefs enable him to press on in the face of adversity, such as when he lost an important match or when he tried to save his marriage. ▯●▮Read

The functionalists made several enduring contributions to psychology. Their emphasis on Darwin's theory of natural selection and its link between humans and nonhuman animals led them to theorize that human psychology—or at least some of it—is related to the psychology of animals. This insight meant that the study of animal behavior could provide clues about characteristics of the human mind and behavior. The functionalists' focus on social issues, such as improving methods of education, also spawned research that continues today.

GESTALT PSYCHOLOGY. Although their work began in earnest nearly 50 years later, the Gestalt psychologists, like the structuralists, were interested in consciousness, particularly as it arises during perception—the organizing and interpreting of sensory information (and thus Gestalt psychologists focused on events at the levels of the brain and the person). But instead of trying to dissect the elements of consciousness, **Gestalt psychology**—taking its name from the German word *Gestalt*, which means "whole"—emphasized the overall patterns of perceptions and thoughts; the members of this school stressed that "the whole is more than the sum of its parts." Initially based in Germany (but later based in the United States, after the outbreak of World War II), these scientists—led by led by Max Wertheimer (1880–1943)—noted that much of the content of our thoughts comes from what we perceive and, further, from inborn tendencies to structure what we sense in certain ways.

The Gestalt psychologists developed over 100 perceptual laws, or principles, that describe how our minds organize the world. For example, have you ever glanced up to see a flock of birds heading south for the winter? If so, you probably didn't pay attention to each individual bird but instead focused on the flock. In Gestalt terms, the flock was a *perceptual unit*, a whole formed from individual parts. Most of the Gestalt principles illustrate the dictum that "the whole is more than the sum of its parts." When you see the birds in flight, the flock has a size and shape that cannot be predicted from the size and shape of the birds viewed one at a time. To Gestalt psychologists, just as the flock is an entity that is more than a collection of individual birds, our patterns of thought are more than the simple sum of individual images or ideas. Gestaltists would want to know how Tiger Woods can take in the overall layout of each hole, or even an 18-hole course, and plan his strategy accordingly.

Today, the study of perception is a central focus of psychology, as well it should be. Perception is, after all, our gateway to the world; if our perceptions are not accurate, our corresponding thoughts and feelings will be based on a distorted view of reality. The research of the Gestaltists addressed how mental processes work, and this work in turn led to detailed studies of how the brain gives rise to such mental processes and how mental processes influence mental contents.

Psychodynamic Theory: More Than Meets the Eye Sigmund Freud (1856–1939), a Viennese physician who specialized in neurology (the study and treatment of diseases

Gestalt psychology An approach to understanding mental events that focuses on the idea that the whole is more than the sum of its parts.

▯●▮Read more about William James on mypsychlab.com

We do not see isolated individual musicians but rather a marching band. In the words of the Gestalt psychologists, "the whole is more than the sum of its parts."

Source: © Kelly Mooney Photography / CORBIS All Rights Reserved

9

Sigmund Freud, the father of psychodynamic theory.

Source: Copyright WHO

of the brain and the nervous system more generally), developed a theory that reached into all corners of human thought, feeling, and behavior (Freud, 2009).

Freud stressed the notion that the mind is not a single thing but, in fact, has separate components. Moreover, some of these components are **unconscious**; that is, they are outside our awareness and beyond our ability to bring into awareness at will. Freud believed that sexual—and sometimes aggressive—urges arise from unconscious mental contents and mental processes. Moreover, Freud also believed that a child absorbs his or her parents' and culture's moral standards, which then shape the child's (and, later, the adult's) goals and motivations. Thus, he argued, we often find our urges unacceptable and so keep them in check, hidden in the unconscious. According to Freud, these unconscious urges build up until, eventually and inevitably, they demand release as thoughts, feelings, or behaviors. This theory focuses on the level of the person but also relies on the level of the group (for example, when considering the effects of the parents' and culture's morals standards).

Freud's theory has since been called **psychodynamic theory**. From the Greek words *psyche*, or "mind," and *dynamo*, meaning "power," the term refers to the continual push-and-pull interaction among conscious and unconscious forces and specifies how such interactions affect behavior. Freud also believed that these interactions sometimes produced abnormal behaviors. For example, according to Freud, some people obsessively wash their hands until they crack and bleed as a way to ward off strong but unacceptable unconscious sexual or aggressive impulses (the "dirt" perceived on the hands) and that washing symbolically serves to remove the "dirt." To understand the reasons for Tiger Woods's multiple extramarital affairs, a Freudian would probably ask Woods about his earliest memories and experiences and try to analyze the unconscious urges that led to his behavior.

However, as intriguing as it is, the guiding principles of psychodynamic theory do not rely on results from objective scientific studies but instead rest primarily on subjective interpretations of what people say and do (and what they don't say and don't do). Moreover, over time psychodynamic theory became so intricate and complicated that it could usually explain any given observation or research result as easily as the opposite observation or result and thus became impossible to test—which is obviously a serious drawback in any science.

Nevertheless, a key idea of psychodynamic theory—that complex behavior is driven by mental processes operating on mental contents—had a crucial influence on later theories. In addition, the idea that some mental contents and processes are hidden from awareness has proven invaluable. Furthermore, psychodynamic theory focused attention on analyzing and interpreting previously ignored types of behavior and experiences, such as slips of the tongue and dreams. Attention to such behavior and experiences sparked subsequent research. And psychodynamic theory led to entirely new approaches to treating psychological problems (directed toward discovering underlying causes, not simply treating symptoms), which have since been modified and refined.

Behaviorism: The Power of the Environment

By the early part of the 20th century, a new generation of psychologists calling themselves *behaviorists* began to question a key assumption shared by their predecessors, namely that psychologists should study the mind. These researchers found theories of the nature of unconscious mental contents and processes difficult to pin down, and they argued that the methods used to study such topics lacked rigor—and hence they rejected the idea that psychology should focus on such unseen phenomena. Instead, American psychologists such as Edward Lee Thorndike (1874–1949), John B. Watson (1878–1958), Clark L. Hull (1884–1952), and B. F. Skinner (1904–1990) concluded that psychology should concentrate on understanding directly observable behavior.

The school of **behaviorism** focuses on how a specific stimulus (object, person, or event) evokes a specific response (a behavior in reaction to the stimulus); together these are sometimes referred to as *stimulus–response associations*. For instance, rather than trying to study the nature of "affection" in order to understand why someone treats dogs well ("affection" being an unobservable mental state), these behaviorists would observe

Unconscious Outside conscious awareness and not able to be brought into consciousness at will.

Psychodynamic theory A theory of mental events that specifies the continual push-and-pull interaction among conscious and unconscious thoughts and feelings and specifies how such interactions affect behavior.

Behaviorism The school of psychology that focuses on how a specific stimulus (object, person, or event) evokes a specific response (behavior in reaction to the stimulus).

when and how a person approaches dogs, protects them from harm, pets them, and otherwise treats them well. The goal of such studies would be to discover how particular responses characteristic of "affection" came to be associated with the stimulus of perceiving a dog. The later behaviorists acknowledged that mental events probably exist but argued that it was not useful for psychology to focus on them. Because of their concern with the content of stimulus–response associations, the behaviorists focus on events at the level of the person.

How might the behaviorists explain Tiger Woods's golfing success? A key idea in behaviorism is *reinforcement*, which is a desirable consequence that occurs after an individual (human or nonhuman) responds to a stimulus in a particular way. A reward, such as payment for a job, is a common type of reinforcement. If the consequence of a response is reinforcing, we are likely to repeat the response when we encounter the stimulus. Conversely, if a response produces an undesirable consequence ("punishment"), we are less likely to do it again. Behaviorists would probably argue that reinforcement is at the root of Tiger Woods's success in golf. Consider that fact that, from his earliest days, Tiger Woods received an extraordinary amount of reinforcement for playing well, at first from his father and then from an increasingly larger affirming public. Such reinforcement would have spurred him to repeat those specific acts (behaviors) that brought desirable consequences (such as hitting the ball so that it went into the cup). Reinforcement was probably also at the root of his extramarital affairs until his wife found out, at which point the consequence changed to punishment.

The behaviorists have developed many important principles that describe the conditions in which particular responses are likely to occur or not occur. Such principles explain how a history of being reinforced for making those responses has linked the stimuli to them. Moreover, the behaviorists' emphasis on controlled, objective observation has had a deep and lasting impact on psychology. Today, even studies of mental events must conform to the level of rigor established by the behaviorists. Behaviorist insights also have improved psychotherapy and education. On the other hand, many of the behaviorists' objections to the study of mental contents and processes have not stood the test of time; much subsequent research has shown that we can rigorously study mental contents (such as mental images) and mental processes (such as those used in reasoning). Moreover, consequences alone cannot account for all behavior: Children may receive positive consequences for golfing well, but most of them will not go on to become another Tiger Woods.

Humanistic Psychology Partly as a reaction to the theories of the Freudians and behaviorists, which viewed people as driven either by mental events or by external stimuli, a new school of psychological thought—*humanistic psychology*—emerged in the late 1950s and early 1960s; among the influential theorists was Abraham Maslow (1908–1970). According to **humanistic psychology**, people have positive values, free will, and deep inner creativity, which in combination can allow them to choose life-fulfilling paths to personal growth. The humanistic approach (focused on the level of the person) rests on the idea that all individuals—and their unique experiences—should be respected.

Psychologist Carl Rogers (1902–1987) developed a therapy based on the humanistic approach; Rogers used the term *client* rather than *patient*, and he called his therapy *client-centered therapy*. This form of therapy grew out of the idea that human nature leads each of us to want to develop to our fullest potential, and the therapist's job is to help us do so. (This view emerged from Maslow's theory that people have an urge to *self-actualize*—that is, to develop to their fullest potentials.) Rather than serving as an expert in a position of authority, the client-centered therapist provides an unconditionally supportive and positive environment to help the client overcome obstacles and develop to his or her full potential.

How might humanistic psychologists explain Tiger Woods's golf success? No doubt they would point to him as someone who is striving to reach his full potential. They might also suggest that his intense focus on golf did not prove entirely satisfying, which led to his subsequent personal problems as Woods sought fulfillment in other ways.

Humanistic psychology The school of psychology that assumes people have positive values, free will, and deep inner creativity, the combination of which allow them to choose life-fulfilling paths to personal growth.

Cognitive psychology The approach in psychology that attempts to characterize the mental events that allow information to be stored and operated on internally.

Humanistic psychology is important in part because of its emphasis on humans as active agents who can formulate plans and make decisions. This school continues to attract followers today and played a role in the emergence of *positive psychology*—the area of psychology that focuses on "the strengths and virtues that enable individuals and communities to thrive" (Compton, 2005; Peterson, 2006). Researchers in this field focus on psychological strengths and the factors that are associated with psychological health and fulfillment rather than on psychological weaknesses and the factors that are associated with mental illness and psychological problems. This field is just now starting to produce a body of solid research findings and may develop into a major force in psychology.

The Cognitive Revolution The tension between approaches—on the one hand, studying unobservable mental events (structuralism, functionalism, and psychodynamic psychology) and, on the other, studying only directly observable behavior (behaviorism)—was resolved by a new arrival on the scene, the computer. The *cognitive revolution* of the late 1950s and early 1960s hinged on using the computer as a model for the way the human mind works. This movement came into full flower in the mid-1970s, led by, among others, psychologists/computer scientists Herbert A. Simon and Alan Newell (Simon went on to win a Nobel Prize, in part for this work) and linguist Noam Chomsky (Gardner, 1985).

The cognitive revolution gave birth to **cognitive psychology**, which attempts to characterize the nature of human *information processing*, that is, the mental events that allow information to be stored and processed (Neisser, 1967). In this view, the mind is like the software (with stored data) on a computer, and the brain is like the hardware (the machine itself). A cognitive psychologist might analyze the way information is processed when Tiger Woods plans his shots and might even program computers to mimic the sort of information processing involved in such a complex activity (such "computer simulation models" can help generate testable predictions from a theory).

Computers showed, once and for all, why it is important that there be a science of the unobservable events that take place in the head, not just a science of directly observable behavior. Consider, for example, how a computer programmer might react if her new word-processing program produced *italics* whenever she entered the command for **boldface**. Noticing the software's "behavior" would be only the first step in fixing this error: She would need to dig deeper in order to find out where the program had gone wrong. This would involve seeing what internal events are triggered by the command and how those events affect what the machine does. So, too, for people. If somebody is acting oddly, we must go beyond the essential step of noticing the unusual behavior; we also need to think about what is happening inside and consider what is causing the problem.

Indeed, the cognitive revolution led to new ways of conceptualizing and treating mental disorders, such as depression. For example, researchers had long believed that depression led people to have negative thoughts, but psychologist Albert Ellis and psychiatrist Aaron Beck argued the reverse—namely, that negative thoughts (mental contents) caused depression. And research findings have supported this theory (for example, Abela & D'Allesandro, 2002). Once negative thoughts were identified as the cause (not the effect), therapies then were developed to help people modify such thoughts.

Computers provided a new way to conceptualize mental contents and mental processes and to develop detailed theories about them.

Source: © Philip Gendreau / CORBIS All Rights Reserved

The theories and research methods developed by cognitive psychologists have also proven crucial in the development of **cognitive neuroscience**, which blends cognitive psychology and neuroscience (the study of the brain) when attempting to specify how the brain gives rise to mental processes that store and process information. Cognitive neuroscientists hope to discover the nature, organization, and operation of mental events by studying the brain (Gazzaniga, 2009; Kosslyn & Koenig, 1995). One of the goals of cognitive neuroscience is to distinguish among different sorts of mental processes, in part by showing that different brain areas give rise to those processes. For example, researchers have found that there is more than one way to produce lies, documented by the fact that separate brain areas come into play when lies are based on previously memorized stories versus making up new stories on the spot (Ganis et al., 2003). Cognitive neuroscience is one of the most exciting areas of psychology today, in part because brain-scanning technologies have allowed researchers to observe human brains at work.

The cognitive neuroscience approach considers events at the three levels of analysis but with a primary focus on the brain. Cognitive neuroscientists seeking to explain Tiger Woods's golfing achievements would probably investigate how different parts of his brain function while he plays golf, looking specifically to discover the ways his mind processes information. For example, they might study how his brain responds to visual input when he judges the distance to the pin.

Evolutionary Psychology In the late 1980s, a new field of psychology arose, which owes a lot to the work of the functionalists and their emphasis on Darwin's theory of natural selection. According to **evolutionary psychology**, certain cognitive strategies and goals are so important that natural selection has built them into our brains. However—and this is the key innovation—instead of proposing that evolution has selected specific behaviors (as earlier evolutionary theorists, including Charles Darwin himself, believed), these theorists believe that evolution has given us certain goals (such as finding attractive mates) and cognitive strategies (such as deceiving others in order to achieve one's goals). This approach addresses events at all three levels of analysis, but primarily at the levels of the person and the group. Researchers such as Lida Cosmides and John Tooby (1996), David Buss (1994, 1999), and Steven Pinker (1994, 1997) are leaders in this field (but many others are involved, for instance, Barkow et al., 1992; Plotkin, 1994, 1997; Schmitt, 2002).

For example, consider the claim that we have the ability to lie because our ancestors who could lie successfully had an advantage: They could trick their naïve companions

Cognitive neuroscience The approach in psychology that blends cognitive psychology and neuroscience (the study of the brain) when attempting to specify how the brain gives rise to mental processes that store and process information.

Evolutionary psychology The approach in psychology that assumes that certain cognitive strategies and goals are so important that natural selection has built them into our brains.

Perhaps the best source of evidence for theories in evolutionary psychology is *cultural universals*, behaviors or practices that occur across all cultures, including playing music, dancing, lying, telling stories, gossiping, expressing emotions with facial expressions, fearing snakes, giving gifts, and making medicines (Brown, 1991).

Sources: AP Wide World Photos; Louise Gibb\The Image Works

13

into giving up valuable resources. According to evolutionary psychologists, more devious ancestors had more children who survived than did their nonlying contemporaries, and their lying children who inherited this ability in turn had more children and so on, until the *ability* to lie was inborn in all members of our species. Notice that lying is not a specific behavior; it is a strategy that can be expressed by many behaviors, all of them deceitful.

Evolutionary psychologists also compare human abilities with those of other animals, particularly nonhuman primates (Hauser, 1996). By studying other animals, researchers hope to infer the abilities of our common ancestors and develop theories about the ways our abilities may have emerged over the course of evolution. For example, by studying the way animals communicate, researchers try to infer which abilities may have been shared by our common ancestors—and hence may have formed the basis of human language. When asked about what might underlie Tiger Woods's golfing achievements, an evolutionary psychologist might note that the abilities that arose via natural selection for hunting game and avoiding predators can also be used in other ways—in playing sports, for instance. And an evolutionary psychologist might suggest that males are biologically predisposed to want to have sex with attractive women (but might also note that we are not simply slaves to such predispositions).

However, evolutionary theories are notoriously difficult to test because we don't know what our ancestors were like and how they evolved. Just because we are born with certain tendencies and characteristics does not mean that these are evolutionarily selected adaptations. As Stephen Jay Gould and Richard Lewontin (1979) pointed out, at least some of our modern characteristics are simply by-products of other characteristics that were in fact selected. For instance, your nose evolved to warm air and detect odors, and once you have a nose, you can use it to hold up your eyeglasses. And just as nobody would claim that the nose evolved to hold up glasses, nobody should claim that all the current functions of the brain resulted from natural selection.

The various schools of psychological thought are summarized in Table 1.

TABLE 1 Schools of Psychological Thought

Name	Landmark Events	Key Ideas
Structuralism	Wundt founds first psychology laboratory, 1879.	Use introspection to discover the elements of the mind and rules for combining them.
Functionalism	James's *Principles of Psychology*, published 1890.	Study why thoughts, feelings, and behavior occur, how they are adaptive.
Gestalt psychology	Wertheimer's paper on perceived movement, 1912.	Focus on overall patterns of thoughts or experience; "the whole is more than the sum of its parts."
Psychodynamic theory	Freud publishes *The Ego and the Id*, 1927.	Conflicts among conscious and unconscious forces underlie many thoughts, feelings, and behaviors.
Behaviorism	Watson's paper *Psychology as the Behaviorist Views It*, 1913; Skinner's *The Behavior of Organisms*, 1938.	Behavior is the appropriate focus of psychology, and it can be understood by studying stimuli, responses, and the consequences of responses.
Humanistic psychology	Maslow publishes *Motivation and Personality*, 1954.	Belief that people have positive values, free will, and deep inner creativity. Inspired the *positive psychology* movement.
Cognitive psychology	Neisser's book *Cognitive Psychology* gives the "school" its name, 1967.	Mental events correspond to information that is stored and processed, analogous to information processing in a computer.
Cognitive neuroscience	First issue of the *Journal of Cognitive Neuroscience* appears, 1989.	The structure of the mind can be understood by learning how mental events arise from brain function.
Evolutionary psychology	Barkow, Cosmides, and Tooby edit *The Adapted Mind*, 1992.	Key mental strategies and goals are inborn, the result of natural selection.

Note: Dates prior to Maslow are based on Boring (1950).

The State of the Union: Psychology Today Although new schools of psychology emerged over time, the earlier approaches did not simply fade away. Rather than being replaced by their descendants, the earlier schools often continued to develop and produce new and important discoveries. Moreover, the different schools began to influence each other. Today, we have a rich mix of different sorts of psychology. Here are some examples:

- Techniques in cognitive neuroscience (most notably brain scanning) are being used to understand the ways in which reasoning about people is different from other kinds of reasoning (Canessa et al., 2005) and to discover the mental processes that allow people to form stimulus–response associations (Blakemore et al., 2004).

- Research in cognitive psychology is beginning to answer questions that motivated the functionalists, particularly in the area of improving methods of education; for instance, some researchers have discovered that there are two types of "visual learners," those who learn best from seeing objects and shapes and those who learn best from graphs or other spatial patterns (Kozhevnikov et al., 2005).

- Behaviorist techniques have been used to train animals to respond only to certain visual patterns, which then has allowed scientists to discover how interactions among individual brain cells give rise to some of the Gestalt laws of organization (Merchant et al., 2003).

- Psychodynamic theory has influenced questions being asked in cognitive psychology and cognitive neuroscience, such as whether we can intentionally forget information (Anderson et al., 2004).

- Evolutionary psychology is making intriguing points of contact with modern behaviorist theories, which has produced support for the idea that animals regulate their behaviors to obey economic laws (for example, by maximizing gain while minimizing expended effort; Glimcher, 2003).

As evident in these brief glimpses into current research, the varied approaches to psychology not only coexist but also feed off one another. The result is that we are learning about the mind and behavior at an ever-increasing clip. If you are interested in psychology, these are truly exciting times in which to live! ◉─ Watch

Watch "So Much to Choose From" video on **mypsychlab.com**

The Psychological Way: What Today's Psychologists Do

If you read that Tiger Woods had seen a psychologist, would you think that he had a personal problem or that he was suffering from too much stress? This is a trick question, as neither guess would necessarily be true; psychologists do much more than help people cope with their problems. As the field of psychology developed, different schools of thought focused on different aspects of the mind and behavior—and their varying influences are felt in what today's psychologists do.

In the following sections, we consider three major types of psychologists: those who help people deal with personal problems or stress (clinical and counseling psychologists), those who teach and usually also conduct research on the mind and behavior (academic psychologists), and those who seek to solve specific practical problems, such as help athletes to perform better (applied psychologists).

Clinical and Counseling Psychology: A Healing Profession A **clinical psychologist** is trained to provide psychotherapy and to administer and interpret psychological tests. Consider Andrea, a clinical psychologist who specializes in treating people with eating disorders. Many of Andrea's clients have a disorder called *anorexia nervosa*; these patients are underweight and refuse to eat enough to maintain a healthy weight. Some of Andrea's other patients have a disorder called *bulimia nervosa*; they eat and then force themselves to vomit or take laxatives immediately afterward. Andrea sees such patients once or twice a week, for 50 minutes per session. During these sessions,

Clinical psychologist The type of psychologist who is trained to provide psychotherapy and to administer and interpret psychological tests.

Psychotherapy The process of helping people learn to change so they can cope with troublesome thoughts, feelings, and behaviors.

Counseling psychologist The type of psychologist who is trained to help people with issues that naturally arise during the course of life.

part of Andrea's job is to identify the factors that lead patients to engage in these behaviors that are so destructive in the long run but seem so desirable to them in the short run. She then helps her patients phase out the destructive behaviors and replace them with more adaptive ones—for instance, by taking a quick walk around the block to decrease the anxiety that arises with keeping food down instead of vomiting after eating (Rosenberg & Kosslyn, 2011).

Depending on the setting in which Andrea works (probably a private office, clinic, or hospital), she will spend varying portions of her day: with patients; meeting with other psychologists to discuss how to be more helpful to patients; supervising psychotherapists in training; going out into the community, perhaps lecturing about eating disorders at high school assemblies; and doing paperwork, including writing notes on each patient, submitting forms to insurance companies for payment, and reading professional publications to keep up with new findings and techniques.

Andrea has been trained to provide **psychotherapy**, which involves helping people learn to change so that they can cope with troublesome thoughts, feelings, and behaviors. She also administers and interprets psychological tests, which can help to diagnose a person's problem and to plan appropriate treatment for him or her. Some clinical psychologists work specifically with tests designed to diagnose the effects of brain damage on thoughts, feelings, and behavior and to indicate which parts of the brain are impaired following trauma. Such *clinical neuropsychologists* receive additional training, some of which involves learning about the field of neurology. Other clinical psychologists work with organizations, such as corporations, to help groups function more effectively; for example, a psychologist might advise a company about reducing stress among workers in a particular unit or might teach relaxation techniques to all employees. These psychologists generally do not administer tests or deliver psychotherapy.

Some clinical psychologists have a Ph.D. (doctor of philosophy) degree, awarded by a university after a person has completed all the requirements of a graduate program in a psychology department (graduate programs are so named because students enrolled in them must have already graduated from college). Graduate programs in psychology departments teach students not only how to do psychotherapy and psychological testing but also how to conduct and interpret psychological research. Other clinical psychologists have a Psy.D. (doctor of psychology), a graduate degree from a program that typically is housed in a private, stand-alone institute. These programs place less emphasis on research, and more emphasis on the delivery of psychotherapy. In some states, clinical psychologists with either type of degree can obtain additional training and be granted the right to prescribe medication for psychological disorders (the first state to grant this privilege was New Mexico, in 2002).

In contrast, a **counseling psychologist** is trained to help people deal with issues that arise during the course of everyday life, such as choosing a career, marrying, raising a family, and performing at work. If Andrea had been trained as a counseling psychologist, she might have provided career counseling and vocational testing to help people decide which occupations best suit their interests and abilities. These professionals sometimes provide psychotherapy, but they may have a more limited knowledge of therapeutic techniques than do clinical psychologists. They may have a

There are many kinds of psychotherapy, and different training prepares therapists in different ways. Psychiatrists, for example, typically would not treat families, but clinical psychologists and social workers—as well as other mental health professionals—might.

Source: Michael Newman\PhotoEdit Inc.

Ph.D. (often from a university-based graduate program that specifically trains people in this area) or often an Ed.D. (doctor of education) degree from a school of education.

Alternatively, Andrea could have become a **psychiatrist**, a physician with special training in treating mental disorders. If she had gone this route, her training and area of competence would have differed from those of the other mental health professionals. First, as a physician with an M.D. (doctor of medicine) degree, a psychiatrist has extensive medical training and can prescribe drugs, whereas, typically, psychologists cannot. Second, as a medical doctor, a psychiatrist (unlike a clinical psychologist) has not been trained to interpret and administer psychological tests or to conduct and understand psychological research.

Two other types of clinical mental health professionals are not psychologists: *social workers* and *psychiatric nurses*. If Andrea had become a **social worker**, she might use psychotherapy to help families and individuals or would help clients use the social service systems in their communities. In order to become a social worker who employs psychotherapy, Andrea would need to earn an M.S.W. (master of social work) degree. A **psychiatric nurse** holds a master's degree (M.S.N., master of science in nursing) as well as a certificate of clinical specialization (C.S.) in psychiatric nursing. As a psychiatric nurse, Andrea would provide psychotherapy, usually in a hospital, clinic, or in private practice, and work closely with medical doctors to monitor and administer medications; in some cases, a psychiatric nurse can prescribe medications.

Psychiatrist A physician with special training in treating mental disorders.

Social worker A mental health professional who may use psychotherapy to help families (and individuals) or help clients to use the social service systems in their communities.

Psychiatric nurse A nurse with a master's degree and a clinical specialization in psychiatric nursing who provides psychotherapy and works with medical doctors to monitor and administer medications.

Academic Psychology: Teaching and Research

James is a professor of psychology at a large state university. Most mornings he prepares lectures, which he delivers three times a week. He also has morning office hours, when students can come by to ask a wide range of questions, from guidance about which courses they should take, to advice about future career plans, to questions about the material in James's classes. Once a week he attends a committee meeting; for example, one week the committee on computer technology may discuss how best to set up a new wireless network for the department, and the next week may discuss the best way to organize the Psychology Department Help Desk. James has several other meetings on a monthly basis, such as meetings of all the professors in his department (when they may discuss new courses that need to be taught, among many other topics). His afternoons are taken up mostly with research. If James worked at a smaller college, he might spend more time teaching and less time on research; alternatively, if he worked at a hospital, he might spend the lion's share of his time doing research and very little time teaching. In fact, if James worked in a research institute (perhaps affiliated with a medical school), he might not teach at all but instead would make discoveries that might be discussed in other people's classes or textbooks.

James also must find time to write papers for publication in professional journals, and he regularly writes grant proposals requesting funding for his research (so that he can buy research materials and pay assistants—including students—to help him test the children in his studies). He also writes letters of recommendation, grades papers and tests, and reads journal articles to keep up with current research in his and related fields. James tries to eat lunch with colleagues at least twice a week to keep up-to-date on departmental events and the work going on at the university in other areas of psychology and related fields.

Developmental psychologists often take special care to prevent their presence from affecting the child's behavior in any way.

Source: LAIF\Redux Pictures

Academic psychologists Psychologists who focus on teaching and conducting research.

Applied psychologists Psychologists who use the principles, findings, and theories of psychology to improve products and procedures and who conduct research to help solve specific practical problems.

THINK like a **PSYCHOLOGIST** Do you think a president would be more effective if he or she had a chief psychologist? If so, which sort of psychologist would be most helpful? (Don't assume it would necessarily be a clinical psychologist.) Why?

Although the activities of most **academic psychologists** are similar in that most teach and many also conduct research, the kinds of teaching and research vary widely. Different types of academic psychologists focus on different types of research questions. For example, James chose to specialize in developmental psychology, the study of how thinking, feeling, and behaving develop with age and experience. His research work takes place at a laboratory preschool at the university, where he and his assistants are investigating the ways that children become attached to objects such as dolls and blankets. If James had become a *cognitive psychologist* (one who studies thinking, memory, and related topics), he might ask, "How is Tiger Woods able to figure out how to hit the ball with the appropriate force in the correct direction?" but not, "When does the audience help Woods's golfing?" If James had become a *social psychologist* (one who studies how people think and feel about themselves and other people and how groups function), he might ask the second question but not the first. And in neither case would he ask, "What aspects of Tiger Woods's character led him to have so many extramarital affairs?" That question would interest a *personality psychologist* (one who studies individual differences in preferences and inclinations).

Because psychology is a science, researchers evaluate theories on their objective merits. Theories about the mind and behavior can come from anywhere, but there is no way to know whether an idea is right or wrong except by testing it scientifically, through research. It is through research that psychologists learn how to diagnose people's problems and how to treat them; it is through research that they determine what kind of career will make good use of a particular person's talents; it is through research that they discover how to present material so that students can understand and remember it most effectively.

There are at least as many different types of academic psychologists as there are separate sections in this book. In fact, this book represents a harvest of their research. Thousands of researchers are working on the topics covered in each chapter, and it is their efforts that allow a book like this one to be written.

Applied Psychology: Better Living Through Psychology **Applied psychologists** use the findings and theories of psychology to improve products and procedures, and they conduct research to help solve specific practical problems in areas such as education, industry, and marketing. Maria is an applied psychologist; more specifically, she is a *human factors psychologist*, a professional who works to improve products so that people can use them more intuitively and effectively. An applied psychologist may have a Ph.D. or, sometimes, only a master's degree in an area of psychology (in North America, a master's degree typically requires two years of study in graduate school instead of the four to six required for a Ph.D.).

Many specialties in academic psychology also have a place in applied psychology. For example, a *developmental psychologist* may be employed by the product development department of a toy company. Using her knowledge of children, she can help design toys that will be appropriate for particular age levels; she then brings children to a playroom at the company to see how they play with the new toys. A *physiological psychologist* studies the brain and brain–body interactions and may work at a company that makes drugs or brain-scanning machines. A *social psychologist* may recommend to lawyers which potential jurors should be chosen or excluded from a given jury, depending on the defendant and the details of the case. A *personality psychologist* may design a new test to help select suitable personnel for a job. An *industrial/ organizational (I/O) psychologist* focuses on using psychology in the workplace; he or she might help an employer create a more comfortable and effective work environment in order to increase worker

Applied psychologists have many roles, one of which is to help attorneys decide which potential jurors are likely to be sympathetic or hostile to the defendant.

Source: Bob Daemmrich\The Image Works

TABLE 2 What Psychologists Do

Clinical psychologist	Administers and interprets psychological tests; provides psychotherapy; helps people function more effectively.
Clinical neuropsychologist	Administers tests to diagnose the effects of brain damage on thoughts, feelings, and behavior and to diagnose what parts of the brain are damaged.
Counseling psychologist	Helps people manage issues that arise during everyday life (career, marriage, family, work).
Developmental psychologist	Researches and teaches the development of mental contents and processes, as well as behavior, with age and experience.
Cognitive psychologist	Researches and teaches the nature of thinking, memory, and related aspects of mental contents and processes.
Social psychologist	Researches and teaches how people think and feel about themselves and other people and how groups function.
Personality psychologist	Researches and teaches individual differences in preferences and inclinations.
Physiological psychologist	Researches and teaches the nature of the brain and brain–body interactions.
Human factors psychologist	Applies psychology to improve products.
Industrial/organizational psychologist	Applies psychology in the workplace.
Sport psychologist	Applies psychology to improve athletic performance.
Educational or school psychologist	Applies psychology to improve cognitive, emotional, and social development of schoolchildren.

productivity. A *sport psychologist* works with athletes to help them improve their performance by helping them learn to concentrate better, deal with stress, and practice more efficiently (Tiger Woods has consulted a sport psychologist). An *educational* or *school psychologist* works with educators (and sometimes families) to devise ways to improve the cognitive, emotional, and social development of children at school.

The occupations of the various types of psychologists are summarized in Table 2.

The Changing Face of Psychology You may have noticed a lack of female names when we reviewed the history of psychology, and for good reason. In earlier times, few opportunities were available for women to make major contributions to this field; however, in spite of the barriers of those days, a few women did make their mark on psychology, such as Margaret Floy Washburn, who was Edward Titchener's first student to earn a Ph.D. (in 1894), and Mary Whiton Calkins, the first woman to become president of the American Psychological Association (in 1905).

As shown in Figure 1, the situation is changing: Increasing numbers of women—such as Mahzarin Banaji, Linda Bartoshuk, Laura Carstensen, Susan Carey, Nancy Kanwisher, Elizabeth Spelke, and Anne Treisman—are making major contributions in all areas of psychology. In fact, in the last major survey (National Science Foundation, 2001), fully 77% of college graduates with psychology majors were women. Thus, we can expect to see increasing representation of women in the field at large.

FIGURE 1 Women Winning the APA Award for Distinguished Scientific Contributions

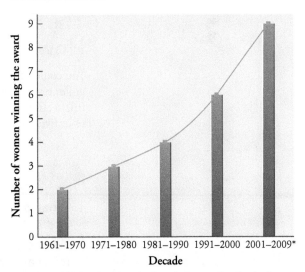

*Note: Using available data, this column is based on only nine years of awards, rather than ten years' worth of awards conveyed in each of the other columns.

Women are playing an increasingly prominent role in scientific psychology. Among American Psychological Association members in 2004, over half of the Ph.D.s in psychology were earned by women (American Psychological Association).

Source: DATA SOURCE: American Psychological Association. http://www.apa.org/pi/wpo/wapa03.pdf

✓●─┤ **Study** and **Review** on
mypsychlab.com

LOOKING BACK

1. **How did psychology develop over time?** Wundt, Titchener, and the other structuralists aimed to understand the elements of mental contents and processes and how they are organized; this approach relied in part on introspection ("looking within"), which turned out not always to produce consistent results and did not access some important mental contents and processes. The functionalists rejected this approach as disconnected from real-world concerns and focused instead on how the mind and behavior adapt to help us survive in the natural world; their pragmatic concerns led them to apply psychology to education and other social activities. In contrast, the Gestalt psychologists, who reacted to the attempt to dissect mental contents and processes into isolated elements, studied the way the mind organizes material into overarching patterns. Freud shifted the subject matter to other sorts of mental events; his psychodynamic theory was concerned largely with the operation of unconscious mental processes and urges (often related to sex and aggression) in dictating what people think, feel, and do. The behaviorists denounced the assumption, shared by all their predecessors, that the mind should be the focus of psychology; they urged psychologists to study what could be observed directly—stimuli, responses, and the consequences of responses. But this view turned out to be too limiting. The humanists developed psychotherapies that relied on respect for individuals and their potentials. Elements of the various strands came together in the cognitive revolution, which emerged in large part from treating the mind and brain as analogous to computer programs and computer hardware, respectively. Evolutionary psychology treats many cognitive strategies and goals as adaptive results of natural selection.

2. **What do today's psychologists actually do?** Clinical and counseling psychologists administer diagnostic tests and help people to cope with their problems and function more effectively academic psychologists teach and do research, and applied psychologists trained in various areas of psychology seek to solve specific practical problems, such as making better products and improving procedures in the workplace.

The Research Process: How We Find Things Out

You could probably speculate for hours about how Tiger Woods came to be such a superb golfer or why his personal life fell into such disarray. How could you find out for sure? In this section we consider the scientific method, which specifies how to answer questions objectively and definitively.

LOOKING AHEAD Learning Objectives

1. What is the scientific method, and how is it used to study the mind and behavior?
2. What scientific research techniques are commonly used to study the mind and behavior?
3. What are key characteristics of good scientific studies in psychology?
4. How are ethical principles applied to scientific studies in psychology and to psychotherapy?

The Scientific Method

Scientific method A way to gather facts that will lead to the formulation and validation (or refutation) of a theory.

Psychology is a science because it relies on a specific method of inquiry. The **scientific method** is a way to gather facts that will lead to the formulation and validation (or refutation) of a theory. It involves *systematically observing events, formulating a question, forming a* *hypothesis about the relation between variables in an attempt to answer the question, collecting new observations to test the hypothesis, using such evidence to formulate a theory, and, finally, testing the theory.* Let's take a closer look at the scientific method, one step at a time.

Step 1: Systematically Observing Events All science ultimately begins with observations. Although these observations may begin as impressions or anecdotes, to be the first step in science they must move beyond that—they must lead to systematic observations. Scientists want to know the facts, as free as possible from interpretations of their implications. Facts are established by collecting **data**, which are careful, objective descriptions or numerical measurements of a phenomenon. Data are "objective" because researchers try to eliminate distortions based on their personal beliefs, emotions, or interpretations; while data are collected, their interpretation must be set aside, saved for later. In addition, if data are systematically collected, the investigator or somebody else should be able to collect comparable data by repeating the observations; when a study is repeated, so that the data can be compared to those collected originally, the study is a called a **replication**.

Scientists often prefer quantitative data (numerical measurements), such as how many men versus women are diagnosed with depression, in part because such data are relatively easy to summarize, analyze, and report. However, many scientists—especially in the relatively early phases of an investigation—rely on systematic qualitative observations (descriptions), which may simply document that a certain event occurs or may describe specific characteristics of the event, such as which toys children play with while at their preschool.

Objectively and systematically observing events is just the first step in the scientific method because events typically can be interpreted in more than one way. For example, a smile could mean happiness, agreement, politeness, or amusement. To sort out the proper interpretation of data, researchers need to follow up observations with the additional steps described in the sections below. ✳ Explore

✳ Explore **THINK AGAIN: Research Methods** on mypsychlab.com

Step 2: Formulating a Question Most of science is about answering questions that are raised by observations. For example, a scientist might note that even as a child, Tiger Woods's abilities made him stand out from his peers. Why? Was there something different about his brain or the way he was being raised? Questions can come from many sources: For example, in addition to direct observation (which occurs when the scientist notices something that piques his or her interest), they can arise from a "secondhand" observation, reported by someone else (and often published in a journal article), or from reflection (which may even occur when the scientist is puzzling about why a certain event does not occur—such as toddlers learning to read at exactly the same time that they learn to talk).

Step 3: Forming a Hypothesis To try to answer a question, scientists make an educated guess about the answer, called a **hypothesis**. A hypothesis is a tentative idea that might explain a set of observations. Hypotheses typically specify a relationship between two or more variables (such as between the amount of time a child sleeps and his or her activity level during the day); hypotheses often propose that one variable (or set of variables) *cause* another. By the term **variable**, researchers mean an aspect of a situation that can vary; more precisely, a variable is a characteristic of a substance, quantity, or entity that is measurable. Examples of variables that could be of interest to psychologists include the amount of time someone needs to decide which reward to receive, whether or not a person was raised in a single-family household, or what part of the country a person lives in.

For example, say you decide to take golf lessons. On the golf course, you notice a particularly good player and ask her for tips. She confesses that when she's off the course, she often practices her swings mentally, visualizing herself whacking the ball straight down the fairway or out of a sand trap; she assures you that the more time she has spent doing such *mental practice*, the better her game has become. You can translate this idea into a hypothesis, speculating that there's a connection between two variables, the time spent visualizing swings and golf score. This idea appeals to you, in part because it means that you can practice at night or whenever you are bored.

But at this point all you have is a hypothesis. Before you go to the trouble of imagining yourself swinging a club, over and over and over, you want to test the hypothesis to find out whether it's correct.

Data Careful descriptions or numerical measurements of a phenomenon.

Replication Repeating the method of a study and collecting comparable data as were found in the original study.

Hypothesis A tentative idea that might explain a set of observations.

Variable An aspect of a situation that can vary, or change; specifically, a characteristic of a substance, quantity, or entity that is measurable.

Step 4: Testing the Hypothesis To test the hypothesis, you need to collect new data. But before you can do that, you must make the key concepts of the hypothesis specific enough to test. An **operational definition** defines a concept by indicating how it is measured or manipulated. For example, you could define "improvement in playing golf" in terms of the number of putts sunk or the distance the ball is driven.

In fact, much research has been conducted on mental practice, and many studies have documented that it actually does improve performance, as it is measured—operationally defined—in various ways. In a typical study, people are divided into two groups, and the performance of both groups is assessed. One group then uses mental practice for a specified period, while the other is asked to take an equal amount of time to visualize familiar golf courses (but does not imagine practicing). Then the golf performance of both groups is assessed again. Usually, the people who engage in mental practice show greater improvement (Doheny, 1993; Driskell et al., 1994; Druckman & Swets, 1988; White & Hardy, 1995; Yagueez et al., 1998).

To test hypotheses, scientists make two types of observations: (1) those that directly address the object of study, such as how many times in an hour a mother speaks to her infant or how far a golf ball traveled after being hit, and (2) those that indirectly address the object of study, which might be the nature of thoughts, motivations, or emotions. Many sorts of behavior can be used to draw inferences about mental events. For example, when people smile without really meaning it (as they often do when posing for photographs), the muscles they use are not the same ones they use when they produce a sincere smile (Ekman, 1985). By studying what's observable (the particular muscles being used), researchers can learn about the unobservable (the mental state of the smiler).

Step 5: Formulating a Theory Now we consider the aspect of the scientific method that uses "such evidence to formulate a theory." A **theory** consists of concepts or principles that explain a set of research findings. Whereas a hypothesis focuses on possible relationships among variables, a theory focuses on the *underlying reasons* why certain relationships may exist in data. In our example, the idea that mental practice leads to better performance is a hypothesis, not a theory. A theory might explain that mental practice works because the brain structures that are used to perform an action (golf) are also engaged when you mentally practice that action; thus, after practicing it mentally, the relevant brain mechanisms operate more efficiently when you perform the actual behavior later.

Step 6: Testing the Theory Finally, what do we mean by "testing the theory"? Researchers evaluate a theory by testing its predictions. It's not enough that a theory can, after the fact, explain previous observations; to be worth its salt, it has to be able to predict new ones. As illustrated in Figure 2, theories produce **predictions**, which are new hypotheses that should be confirmed if the theory is correct. For example, the theory of mental practice predicts that the parts of the brain used to produce a behavior—in our example, swinging a golf club—are activated by merely imagining the behavior. This prediction has been tested by using brain-scanning techniques to observe what happens in the brain when an individual imagines making certain movements. And, in fact, parts of the brain that are used to control actual movements are activated when the movements are only imagined (Jeannerod, 1994, 1995; Kosslyn et al., 1998; Parsons, 1987, 1994; Parsons & Fox, 1998).

Each time a theory makes a correct prediction, the theory is supported, and each time it fails to make a correct prediction, the theory is weakened. If enough of its predictions fail, the theory must be rejected and the data explained in some other way. The theorist is no doubt disappointed when his or her theory is shot down, but this is not a bad thing for science. In fact, a good theory is *falsifiable*; that is, it makes predictions it cannot "squirm out of." A falsifiable theory can be rejected if the predictions are not confirmed. Part of the problem with astrology, for example, is that its predictions are so vague and general that they are difficult to disprove.

Putting the Steps Together Now that you understand all the steps of the scientific method, you could use it to investigate an enormous range of questions. For instance, say you've heard that putting a crystal under your bed will improve your athletic

Operational definition A definition of a concept that specifies how it is measured or manipulated.

Theory Concepts or principles that explain a set of research findings.

Prediction A hypothesis that follows from a theory, which should be confirmed if the theory is correct.

FIGURE 2 The Scientific Method

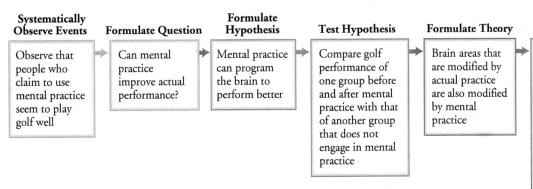

Systematically Observe Events	Formulate Question	Formulate Hypothesis	Test Hypothesis	Formulate Theory	Test Theory
Observe that people who claim to use mental practice seem to play golf well	Can mental practice improve actual performance?	Mental practice can program the brain to perform better	Compare golf performance of one group before and after mental practice with that of another group that does not engage in mental practice	Brain areas that are modified by actual practice are also modified by mental practice	(1) Identify brain areas activated during actual practice; (2) measure activation of those areas while people engage in mental practice; (3) relate the amount of activation during mental practice to the level of improved performance

Research begins by observing relevant events and then formulating a question. These events lead to a hypothesis about a possible answer to the question, which is then tested. When enough is known about the relations among the relevant variables, a theory can be formulated. The theory in turn produces predictions, which are new hypotheses and are in turn tested. If these theory-based hypotheses are confirmed, the theory is supported; if they fail to bear fruit, then the theory must be altered or simply rejected and the whole process repeated.

ability. Should you believe this? The scientific method is just what you need to decide whether to take this claim seriously! Let's walk through the steps of the scientific method, applied to the role that crystals under the bed might play in increasing athletic performance:

1. You *start with a systematic observation*. The observation might be secondhand: Let's say your friends report that they've carefully noted that they score higher when a crystal was under their beds the night before they play.

2. You *formulate a question to guide further investigation*: Can crystals under a person's bed while he or she sleeps really improve athletic performance the next day?

3. You *formulate a hypothesis about the relation between variables*: Having a crystal under someone's bed (that's one variable: the crystal is there versus not there) will lead him or her to perform better at his or her usual sport on the following day (that's another variable, the measure of performance).

4. You *test the hypothesis*: Before some of your friend's athletic games, you sneak a crystal under her bed, making sure that your friend never knows when the crystal is there and when it isn't (we'll discuss why this is important shortly); then you observe whether she plays better on days after the crystal was present.

5. If the hypothesis is supported (your friend does play better on the days after the crystal is under her bed), you need *a theory to explain the relationship between the variables* (how the crystal affects performance). For example, you might propose that the crystal focuses the magnetic field of the earth, which helps the blood circulation of people who are sleeping above it (blood has iron in it, which is affected by magnetic fields). This theory makes the prediction that putting the crystal in a magnetically shielded box while under the bed should disrupt its effects on performance.

6. Finally, you *test the theory*: You might go ahead and put the crystal in such a magnetically shielded box and see whether your friend still plays better on days after the crystal has been under the bed while she sleeps.

The Psychologist's Toolbox: Techniques of Scientific Research

Although all sound psychological investigations rely on the scientific method, researchers working in the different areas of psychology often pose different questions and try to answer them using different methods. Psychologists use a variety of research tools, each with its own advantages and disadvantages.

Would putting a crystal under his bed make him play better?

Source: AP Wide World Photos

Case study A scientific study that focuses on a single participant, examining his or her psychological characteristics (at any or all of the levels of analysis) in detail.

Descriptive Research: Tell It Like It Is Any individual researcher need not go through all of the steps of the scientific method in order to do science. In fact, he or she can focus solely on the first step, observing events systematically; some research is devoted simply to describing "things as they are." Although—as we've just seen—there is more to the scientific method than observation, it's no accident that "observing events" is a key part of the scientific method: Theorizing without facts is a little like cooking without ingredients. Researchers carry out such observations in several ways: *naturalistic observations, case studies,* and *surveys*.

NATURALISTIC OBSERVATION. As noted earlier, data are collected via careful, systematic, and unbiased observation that can be repeated by others. Researchers use *naturalistic observation* to collect such data from real-world settings, observing events as they naturally occur. For example, researchers have carefully observed how caregivers interact with young children and noted that the caregivers changed their language and speech patterns when talking to the young children. Specifically, when caregivers interacted with young children (compared to older children or adults), they used short sentences and spoke in a high-pitched voice. This modified way of speaking is known as *child-directed speech* (Liu, Tsao & Kuhl, 2009; Snow, 1991, 1999).

Naturalistic observations can lead psychologists to notice a phenomenon and are often the first step of the scientific method. Throughout this book, we invite you to use the tools of psychology (such as naturalistic observation) and the fruits of psychological research to see yourself and the world around you in a new light. We encourage you to observe, formulate questions and hypotheses, and collect data—about yourself and others. In order to help make the link between what we describe in this text and your lives, we include suggestions or questions in the margin, like the one here, that ask you to observe or introspect about how some psychological phenomena arise in your life. That is, we encourage you to *Think Like a Psychologist* (the name of this feature in the book, which may include trying specific activities that are described in the online *DO IT!* folders).

Although naturalistic observation is an essential part of science, it is only the first step of the entire method. For instance, documenting the existence of child-directed speech does not explain why caregivers use it; perhaps they think it will help children understand them, or they use it to entertain the children, or they are simply imitating other caregivers they have heard before. Naturalistic observation is difficult to use to test specific hypotheses for a finding (although this is not impossible, as any astronomer will confirm). The problem is that to test your hypothesis, you must seek out a specific situation where the relevant variables happen to be appropriate (such as, for an astronomer, might occur when the moon eclipses the sun).

CASE STUDIES. A **case study** in psychology is a scientific study that focuses on a single participant, examining his or her psychological characteristics (at any or all of the levels of analysis) in detail. For example, a researcher might study a single professional athlete, such as Tiger Woods, looking closely at his brain function, personal beliefs, and social circumstances. The goal of such a study is not to understand that one person, but rather to discover underlying principles that can be applied to all similar people. Case studies are used in many areas of psychology and often focus on a single level of analysis. For example:

- Neuropsychologists may study an individual brain-damaged patient in depth to discover which abilities are "knocked out" following certain types of damage.

- Psychologists who study mental illness might examine an usual case of bulimia in a 10-year-old to discover whether what special factors might contribute to an eating disorder in someone so young.

- Cognitive psychologists may investigate how an unusually gifted memory expert is able to retain huge amounts of information almost perfectly.

- Personality psychologists might study how a professional athlete remains motivated enough to practice for years and years with no guarantee that he or she will ever succeed.

Some scientists observe animals in the wilds of Africa, others observe sea life in the depths of the ocean, and others observe humans in their natural habitats.

Source: Dennis MacDonald\PhotoEdit Inc.

Like all other methods, case studies have their limitations. In particular, we must always be cautious about generalizing from a single case; that is, we must be careful not to assume that the findings in the case study necessarily extend to all other similar cases. Any particular person may be unusual for many reasons, and so the findings about that individual may or may not apply to similar people in general.

SURVEYS. A **survey** is a set of questions that people are asked about their beliefs, attitudes, preferences, or activities. Surveys are a relatively inexpensive way to collect a lot of data—the responses to the questions—quickly (especially when conducted over the Internet), and they are popular among psychologists who study personality and social interactions. Surveys provide data that can be used to formulate or test a hypothesis.

However, surveys have a number of limitations. For instance, some of them require the respondents to introspect about their feelings and beliefs, and, as we discussed earlier in this chapter, people may not be capable of reporting accurately all such information. In particular, we humans do not have conscious access to much of what motivates us; sometimes we aren't even aware of the beliefs that drive our behavior (for example, we may not be aware of some aspects of our attitudes about race, even though they affect how we respond to members of particular races; Phelps et al., 2000). There are no hard-and-fast rules about precisely which sorts of questions people can answer accurately in a survey, but some types of information clearly can be answered through a survey, whereas other types of information clearly cannot be answered through a survey. For example, you could use a survey to ask people how often they play golf but not to ask people how their brains work or to report subtle behaviors, such as body language, that they may engage in unconsciously.

Brain damage following an accident can cause someone to fail to name fruits and vegetables while still being able to name other objects (Hart et al., 1985). A case study would examine such a person in detail, documenting precisely what sorts of things could and could not be named. *Source:* PhotoEdit Inc.

Moreover, even if they are capable of answering a survey question, people may not always respond honestly; this is especially a problem when the survey touches on sensitive personal issues, such as sexual preferences. Furthermore, not everyone who is asked to respond does, in fact, take the survey. Because a particular factor (such as income or age) may incline some people but not others to respond, it is difficult to know whether the responses obtained are actually representative of the whole group that the survey was designed to assess.

Finally, many pitfalls must be avoided when designing surveys. Survey questions have to be carefully worded so that they don't lead the respondents to answer in a certain way and yet still get at the phenomena of interest. For instance, the question "Don't you think that it's bad to lie?" is phrased in a way that will lead most people to answer "yes," simply because it is clear that *yes* is probably the "right" answer to the question. Similarly, people tend to answer differently with different types of response scales, such as those that have relatively many or few possible choices (Schwarz, 1999). For instance, the different choices below would probably lead some people to choose different answers, depending on which of the four response scales they were given. How would you answer when given the choices in each row below the question?

Don't you think that it's bad to lie?

Yes		No		
Yes	Not Sure	No		
Always Yes	Mostly Yes		Mostly No	Always No
Always Yes	Mostly Yes	Not Sure	Mostly No	Always No

Correlational Research: Do Birds of a Feather Flock Together?

Researchers can use another method to study the relationships among variables—a method that relies on the idea of correlation. A *correlation* is a relationship in which two variables are measured for each person, group, or entity, and the variations in measurements of one variable are compared to the variations in measurements of the

Survey A set of questions that people are asked about their beliefs, attitudes, preferences, or activities.

FIGURE 3 Strength of Correlation

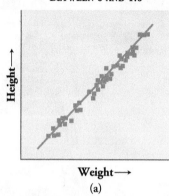

POSITIVE CORRELATION
BETWEEN 0 AND 1.0

(a)

Here, increases in one variable (height) are accompanied by increases in another (weight); this is a positive correlation, indicated by a correlation value that falls between 0 and 1.0.

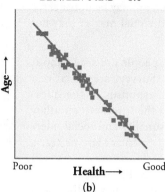

NEGATIVE CORRELATION
BETWEEN 0 AND −1.0

(b)

Here, increases in one variable (age) are accompanied by decreases in another (health); this is a negative correlation, indicated by a correlation value that is between 0 and −1.0.

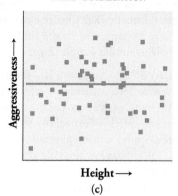

ZERO CORRELATION

(c)

A zero correlation indicates no relationship between the two variables, height and aggressiveness here; they do not vary together.

Source: From *Introduction to the Practice of Statistics* by David S. Moore and George P. McCabe. © 1989, 1993, and 1999 by W. H. Freeman and Company. Used with permission.

Researchers have found that the lower the level of a chemical called monoamine oxidase (MAO) in the blood, the more the person will tend to seek out thrilling activities (such as sky diving and bungee jumping; Zuckerman, 1995). Thus, there is a negative correlation between the two measures: As MAO levels go down, thrill seeking goes up. But this correlation doesn't indicate that low MAO levels *cause* thrill-seeking behavior.

Source: Terje Rakke/Stone/Getty Images

Correlation coefficient A number that ranges from −1.0 to 1.0 that indicates how closely interrelated two sets of measured variables are; the higher the coefficient (in either the positive or negative direction), the better the value of one measurement can predict the value of the other. Also simply called a *correlation.*

other variable. For example, height is correlated with weight: Taller people tend to be heavier than smaller people. A correlation coefficient is a number between −1 and +1 that indicates how closely related two measured variables are; the higher the coefficient (in either the positive or negative direction), the better the value of one measurement can predict the value of the other. The **correlation coefficient** is often simply referred to as a *correlation* because the coefficient is the numerical summary of the relationship between two variables.

Figure 3 illustrates three predicted correlations between variables. Figure 3a shows a positive correlation, a relationship in which increases in one variable (height) are accompanied by increases in another (weight); a positive correlation is indicated by a correlation value that falls between 0 and 1.0. Figure 3b shows a negative correlation, a relationship in which increases in one variable (age) are accompanied by decreases in another (health); a negative correlation is indicated by a correlation value that is between −1.0 and 0. The closer the correlation is to 1.0 or to −1.0, the stronger the relationship; visually, the more tightly the data points cluster around a slanted line, the higher the correlation. Finally, Figure 3c shows a zero correlation, which indicates no relationship between the two variables (height and aggressiveness); they do not vary together.

Correlations always compare two sets of measurements at a time. Sometimes several pairs of variables are compared, but each pair of measurements requires a separate correlation. Thus, correlational research has two steps:

1. Obtaining measurements of two variables (such as height and weight or age and health status);

2. Examining the way that one set of measurements goes up or down in tandem with another set of measurements—in our example, it would be the extent to which height and weight go up or down together.

The main advantage of correlational research is that it allows researchers to compare variables that cannot be manipulated directly (which is what happens in experiments, which we discuss in the following section). The main disadvantage is that correlations indicate only that the values of two variables tend to vary together, not that values of one *cause* the values of the other. For example, evidence suggests a small correlation between poor eyesight and intelligence (Belkin & Rosner, 1987; Miller, 1992; Williams et al., 1988), but poor eyesight doesn't cause someone to be smarter! Remember: *Correlation does not imply causation.*

Experimental Research: Manipulating and Measuring

Much psychological research relies on conducting *experiments*, controlled situations in which the investigator observes the effects of altering variables. Experiments provide the strongest way to test a hypothesis because they can provide evidence that changes in one variable cause changes in another.

INDEPENDENT AND DEPENDENT VARIABLES. The variables in a situation—such as "time spent mentally practicing" and "golf score"—are the aspects of the situation that can vary. In an experiment, the investigator deliberately manipulates the value of one variable, which is called the **independent variable** (so called because it can be changed independently of anything else), and measures another, called the **dependent variable** (so called because the investigator is looking to see whether the values of this variable *depend on* those of the independent variable). Going back to our mental practice of golf example, the amount of time participants in the experiment spend mentally practicing is the independent variable (it is deliberately varied), and their golf score is the dependent variable (it is measured, and it is hypothesized to depend on the amount of time spent visualizing), as illustrated in Figure 4.

By examining the link between independent and dependent variables, a researcher hopes to discover exactly which factor is causing an **effect**: the difference in the value of the dependent variable that arises from changes in the independent variable. In our mental practice example, the effect is the change in participants' golf score from the first assessment of their performance (before mental practice) to the second assessment (after mental practice).

Demonstrating that changes in an independent variable are accompanied by changes in the dependent variable usually is not enough to confirm a hypothesis: In most cases, it's relatively easy to offer more than one interpretation of a relation between an independent and a dependent variable, and hence additional research is necessary to understand what this relation means. In our example, say we had tested only one group, the one that used mental practice. The fact that these players improved would not necessarily show that mental practice improves actual golf performance. Perhaps simply playing during the first assessment (before mental practice) is enough to cause an improvement at the second assessment. Or perhaps people are simply more relaxed at the time of the second assessment, and that is why they perform better. Researchers can narrow down the explanations by testing additional groups or conducting separate experiments; only by

Independent variable The aspect of the situation that is deliberately and independently varied while another aspect is measured.

Dependent variable The aspect of the situation that is measured as the values of an independent variable are changed; in an experiment, the value of the dependent variable is expected to depend on the value of the independent variable.

Effect The difference in the value of the dependent variable that arises from changes in the independent variable.

Confound (or confounding variable) Any aspect of the situation that varies along with the independent variable (or variables) of interest and could be the actual basis for what is measured.

FIGURE 4 Relationship Between Independent and Dependent Variables

INDEPENDENT VARIABLE: Amount of time the person practices mentally

DEPENDENT VARIABLE: Subsequent performance on the golf course

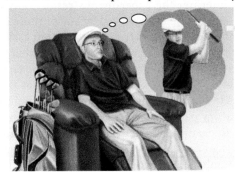

The independent variable is what is manipulated—in this example, the amount of time participants spend mentally practicing. The dependent variable, what is measured, is in this case their golf score.

FIGURE 5 Confounding Variables in Everyday Life

Professor Moret has made a startling observation: Students who slump when they sit are more intelligent than those who sit up straight. He plans to alert the college admissions office to this finding and urge them to require applicants to supply full-body photos while students are sitting. But is it intelligence that accompanies poor posture? Perhaps a strong motivation to do well leads to more intense poring over books, with hunched posture. Or is it that shy people tend both to hunch and to be more comfortable spending time alone studying? Can you think of other possible confounding variables that should make Professor Moret take pause?

Source: PhotoEdit Inc.

Experimental group A group that receives the complete procedure that defines the experiment.

Control group A group that is treated exactly the same way as the experimental group, except that the independent variable that is the focus of the study is not manipulated. The control group holds constant—"controls"—all of the variables in the experimental group.

Random assignment The technique of assigning participants randomly, that is, by chance, to the experimental and the control groups, so that members of the two groups are comparable in all relevant ways.

Experimental condition A part of a study in which participants receive the complete procedure that defines the experiment.

Control condition A part of a study in which participants receive the same procedure as in the experimental condition except that the independent variable of interest is not manipulated.

eliminating other possibilities can researchers come to know why varying the independent variable produces an effect on the dependent variable.

One particularly vexing problem in experiments is the possibility of a **confound**, or *confounding variable,* which is any other aspect of the situation (such as the anxiety that accompanies taking a test) that varies along with the independent variable (or variables) of interest and could be the actual basis for what is measured. Because more than one variable is in fact changing, you cannot tell which one is actually responsible for any observed effect. When a confound is present, varying one independent variable has the (unintended) consequence of varying one or more other independent variables—and they might in turn be responsible for changing the dependent variable. For example, if the participants were more relaxed at the time of the second assessment in the golf mental practice experiment, that would be a confound with the effects of mental practice per se—and you can't know whether both or only one of these variables are responsible for improved performance. Confounds thus lead to results that are ambiguous, that do not have a clear-cut interpretation (see Figure 5). As we discuss in the following section, researchers have developed several ways to eliminate confounds.

EXPERIMENTAL AND CONTROL GROUPS AND CONDITIONS. One way to remove the possible influence of confounds requires comparing two groups—*the experimental* and *control groups:* The **experimental group** receives the complete *treatment,* that is, the complete procedure that defines the experiment. A **control group** is treated identically to the experimental group except that the independent variable is not manipulated but rather is held constant; a good control group holds constant—or controls—all of the variables in the experimental group (and hence does not receive the manipulations of the independent variable that constitute the treatment). For example, in the mental practice experiment, the experimental group does mental practice, and the control group does not do mental practice—but is otherwise treated the same as the experimental group in every other respect, taking an equal amount of time to visualize familiar golf courses as the experimental group does in imagining practicing.

However, if the kinds of people assigned to the experimental and control groups differ markedly, say, in age, gender, relevant history, or ability to learn (or any combination of such variables), those factors would make it difficult to interpret the experiment's results; any difference in the groups' golf scores could have been caused by any of those characteristics. To eliminate these sorts of confounds, researchers rely on **random assignment**: Participants are assigned randomly, that is, by chance, to the experimental and the control groups, so that the members of the two groups are likely to be comparable in all relevant ways. Without random assignment, an experimenter might (unconsciously) assign better (or worse) golfers to the mental practice group. With random assignment, the experimenter does not use any particular characteristics to assign participants to the groups. (Indeed, in order to ensure that participants are randomly assigned to their group, researchers may assign each participant a number and then use a computer-generated list of random numbers to determine the group for each participant.)

Rather than using two different groups to disentangle confounds, researchers might have a single group but one that has two different *conditions:* an *experimental condition* and a *control condition.* The **experimental condition** is analogous to an experimental group: it is the part of a study in which participants receive the complete procedure that defines the experiment. The **control condition** is analogous a control group: it is the part of the study in which the same participants receive the same procedure as in the experimental condition except that the independent variable of interest is not manipulated. Thus, the same people are tested twice, once in each condition. For example, in an experimental condition you could put a crystal under a group of golfers' beds before they slept, and in the control condition you would do everything else the same but not put a crystal there. You would test all the golfers in both conditions. To avoid confounding the order of testing with the condition (experimental versus control), you would test half the participants in the control condition before testing them in the experimental condition and would test the other half of the participants in the experimental condition before testing them in the control condition.

Quasi-Experimental Design Like an experimental design, a *quasi-experimental design* includes independent and dependent variables and assesses the effects of different values of the independent variable on the values of the dependent variable. However, unlike true experiments, in quasi-experiments, participants are not randomly assigned to conditions and the conditions typically are selected from naturally occurring situations— that is, they are not created by the investigator's manipulating the independent variable. For example, if you wanted to study the effects of having been in an earthquake on how well people sleep at night, you would need to select and compare participants who had or had not been in an earthquake. You could not randomly assign participants to the different groups.

Quasi-experimental designs are used because it is not always possible or desirable to assign people to different groups randomly. For instance, let's say that you want to discover whether the effects of mental practice are different for people of different ages, and so you decide to test four groups of people: teenagers, college students, middle-aged people, and elderly people. Obviously, you cannot assign people to the different age groups randomly. Rather, you select groups from what nature has provided. When composing the groups, you should control for as many variables—such as health and education level—as you can in order to make the groups as similar as possible. By "control for," we mean that you should ensure that values of variables (such as education level or health) don't differ systematically in the different groups. (In fact, in the example we just gave of dividing participants into four age-groups, a variety of variables are not controlled for and so create confounds. For instance, the middle-aged and elderly participants will be more likely to have finished college than the teens and college students.) Similarly, if you want to track changes over time, it is not possible to assign people randomly to the groups because you are taking measurements only from people you have measured before.

Unfortunately, because groups can never be perfectly equated on all characteristics, you can never be certain exactly which of the differences among groups produce the observed results. And thus, you cannot draw conclusions from quasi-experiments with as much confidence as you can from genuine experiments.

Table 3 summarizes the key research methods used in psychology, along with their relative strengths and weaknesses. When thinking about the various methods, keep in mind that even though experiments are the most rigorous, they cannot always be performed—particularly

TABLE 3 **Summary of Research Methods in Psychology**

Method	Key Characteristic(s)	Advantage(s)	Disadvantage(s)
Naturalistic observation	Observed events are carefully documented	Forms the foundation for additional research by documenting the existence or key characteristics of an event or situation	Cannot control for confounding variables or change the variables to discover critical factors that underlie a phenomenon
Case study	A single participant is analyzed in depth	Can provide in-depth understanding of the particular person's abilities or deficits	Cannot assume that the findings generalize to all other similar cases
Survey	A number of participants answer specific questions	Relatively inexpensive way to collect a lot of data quickly	Limited by how the questions are stated and by what people can and are willing to report
Correlational research	Relations among different variables are documented	Allows comparison of variables that cannot be manipulated directly	Cannot infer causation
Experimental design	Participants are assigned randomly to groups, and the effects of manipulating one or more independent variables on a dependent variable are studied	Allows rigorous control of variables; is able to establish causal relations between independent and dependent variables	Not all phenomena can be studied in controlled laboratory experiments (in part, because not all characteristics can be manipulated)
Quasi-experimental design	Similar to an experiment but participants are not assigned to groups randomly and conditions are often selected, not created	Allows the study of real-world phenomena that cannot be studied in experiments	Cannot control relevant aspects of the independent variables

THINK like a **PSYCHOLOGIST** Suppose you wanted to know whether Tiger Woods's upbringing played a crucial role in leading him to become a professional golfer; how would you go about studying this? (Don't assume that it has to be a case study.) Which specific questions would you ask? What are the best methods for answering them and the drawbacks of each method?

if you are interested in studying large groups or if it is difficult (or unethical) to manipulate the independent variables. In addition, we must stress that different combinations of the methods are often used. For example, observational methods are used as part of correlational research, and observational, correlational, or experimental research can be conducted with single individuals (case studies).

Meta-Analysis **Meta-analysis** is a statistical technique that allows researchers to combine results from different studies on the same topic in order to discover whether there is a relationship among variables (Cooper, 2010). Meta-analysis is particularly useful when the results from many studies are not entirely consistent, with some showing an effect and some not. Thus, meta-analysis is not a way to collect new data by observing phenomena—it is a way of analyzing data that have already been collected.

A meta-analysis can sometimes reveal results that are not evident in all the individual studies that go into them. This is possible because studies almost always involve observing or testing a *sample* from a *population*; the **sample** is the group that is measured or observed, and the **population** is the entire set of relevant people or animals (perhaps defined in terms of age or gender). The crucial fact is that there is always variation in the population; just as people vary in height and weight, they also vary in their behavioral tendencies, cognitive abilities, emotional reactivity, and personality characteristics. Thus, samples drawn from a population will not be the same in every respect, and if samples drawn from different populations are relatively small, the luck of the draw could obscure an overall difference that actually exists between the populations. For example, if you stopped the first two males and first two females you saw on the street and measured their heights, the females might actually be taller than the males. In this example, the two populations would be all males and all females, and the samples would be the two people drawn from each population. And these samples would—by the luck of the draw—not accurately reflect the general characteristics of each of the populations.

The problem of variation in samples is particularly severe when the difference of interest—the effect—is not great and the sample sizes are small. In our example of male and female heights, if men averaged 8 feet tall and women 4 feet tall, small samples would not be a problem; you would quickly figure out the usual height difference between men and women. But if men averaged 5 feet 10 inches and women averaged 5 feet 9 inches (and the heights in both populations varied by an average of plus-or-minus 6 inches), you would need to measure many men and women before you were assured of finding the difference. By combining the samples from many studies, meta-analysis allows you to detect even subtle differences or relations among variables (Rosenthal, 1991).

Be a Critical Consumer of Psychology

No research technique is always used perfectly, so you must be a critical consumer of all science, including the science of psychology. Whenever you read a report of a psychological finding in a newspaper, a journal article, or a book (including this one), think about other ways that you could interpret the finding. In order to do this, begin by looking for potential confounds. But confounds aren't the only aspect of a study that can lead to alternative explanations; here are a few other issues that can cloud the interpretation of studies.

Reliability: Count on It! Some data should be taken more seriously than other data because data differ in their quality. One way to evaluate the quality of the data is in terms of reliability. **Reliability** means consistency. A reliable car is one you can count on to behave consistently, starting even on cold mornings. Data are reliable if you obtain the same findings each time the variable is measured. For example, an IQ score is reliable if you get the same score each time you take the test.

Validity: What Does It Really Mean? Something is said to be valid if it is what it claims to be; a valid driver's license, for example, is one that confers the right to drive because it was, in fact, issued by the state and has not expired. In research, **validity** means that a method does in fact measure what it is supposed to measure. A study may be valid (measure what it's supposed to measure) but not reliable (the results cannot be found repeatedly) or vice versa.

Meta-analysis A statistical technique that allows researchers to combine results from different studies on the same topic in order to discover whether there is a relationship among variables.

Sample A group that is drawn from a larger population and that is measured or observed.

Population The entire set of relevant people or animals.

Reliability Consistency; data are reliable if the same values are obtained when the measurements are repeated.

Validity A research method is valid if it does in fact measure what it is supposed to measure.

Bias: Playing with Loaded Dice   The outcome of a study can also be affected by what the participants or the researchers believe or expect to happen or by their habitual ways of responding to or conceiving of situations. **Bias** occurs when (conscious or unconscious) beliefs, expectations, or habits alter how participants in a study respond or affect how a researcher sets up or conducts a study, thereby influencing its outcome. Bias can take many forms. For example, **response bias** occurs when research participants tend to respond in a particular way regardless of their actual knowledge or beliefs. For example, many people tend to say "yes" more than "no," particularly in some Asian cultures (such as that of Japan). This sort of bias toward responding in "acceptable" ways is a devilish problem for survey research. For instance, even though a residents of community in Japan might not want a local, publicly funded golf course, the politician pushing the idea could take advantage of this cultural response bias by having a pollster ask residents "Do you support using public funds to build golf courses, which will increase recreational options?" Respondents would be more likely to say "yes" simply because they are more likely to answer "yes" to any question.

Another form of bias is **sampling bias**, one form of which occurs when researchers do not choose the participants at random but instead select them so that an attribute is over- or underrepresented. For example, say you wanted to know the average heights of male and females, and you went to shopping malls to measure people. You would fall victim to sampling bias if you measured males outside a toy store (and so were likely to be measuring little boys) but measured females outside a fashion outlet for tall people (and so were likely to find especially tall women). (As you've probably noticed, such bias leads to a confound—in this case between where the samples were chosen and the type of sample.)

Sampling bias isn't just something that sometimes spoils otherwise good research studies. Have you read about the U.S. presidential election of 2000? Albert Gore and George W. Bush were in a dead heat, and the election came down to the tally in a few counties in Florida. Based on surveys of voters exiting their polling places, the TV commentators incorrectly predicted that Gore would be the winner. What led them astray? In part, sampling bias. The news organizations that conducted the surveys did not ask a representative sample of the relevant population—in fact, they forgot to include absentee voters in their exit polls. In such a close election, this was an important factor because the absentee voters included many members of the armed services, who tend to be Republicans. This error in sampling produced a biased view of how the entire population of Florida had voted—and the TV commentators had to eat their words.

Experimenter Expectancy Effects: Making It Happen   Another set of problems that can plague psychological research goes by the name of experimenter expectancy effects, even though these effects can occur in all types of psychological investigations (not just experiments). **Experimenter expectancy effects** occur when an investigator's expectations lead him or her (consciously or unconsciously) to treat participants in a way that encourages them to produce the expected results. Here's a famous example, with an unusual participant: Clever Hans was a horse that lived in Germany in the early 1890s. He apparently could add (Rosenthal, 1976). When a questioner (one of several) called out two numbers to add (for example, "6 plus 4"), Hans would tap out the correct answer with his hoof. Was Hans a genius horse? Was he psychic? No. Despite appearances, Hans wasn't really adding. He seemed to be able to add, but he responded only when his questioner stood in his line of sight and knew the answer. It turned out that each questioner, who expected Hans to begin tapping, always looked at Hans's hoof right after asking the question—thereby cuing Hans to start tapping. When Hans had tapped out the right number, the questioner always looked up—cuing Hans to stop tapping. Although, in fact, Hans could not add, he was a pretty bright horse: He was not trained to do this; he "figured it out" on his own.

The story of Hans nicely illustrates the power of experimenter expectancy effects. The cues offered by Hans's questioners were completely unintentional; they had no wish to mislead (and, in fact, some of them were probably doubters). But such cues led Hans to respond in specific way. In psychological research, the cues can be as subtle as when a researcher makes eye contact with or smiles at a participant. For instance, if you were a researcher interviewing participants about their attitudes about alcohol, your own views

Bias When conscious or unconscious beliefs, expectations, or habits alter how participants in a study respond or affect how a researcher sets up or conducts a study, thereby influencing its outcome.

Response bias A tendency to respond in a particular way regardless of respondents' actual knowledge or beliefs.

Sampling bias A bias that occurs when the participants are not chosen at random but instead are chosen so that one attribute is over- or underrepresented.

Experimenter expectancy effects Effects that occur when an investigator's expectations lead him or her (consciously or unconsciously) to treat participants in a way that encourages them to produce the expected results.

Double-blind design The participant is "blind" to (unaware of) the predictions of the study (and so cannot consciously or unconsciously produce the predicted results), and the experimenter is "blind" to the group to which the participant has been assigned or to the condition that the participant is receiving (and so experimenter expectancy effects cannot produce the predicted results).

Pseudopsychology Theories or statements that at first glance look like psychology but are in fact superstition or unsupported opinion, not based in science.

could affect how you behave, which in turn affects what the participants say—for instance, if you smile whenever they mention an attitude that is similar to yours and frown when they mention an attitude that different from yours. In turn, the participants may try to please you by saying what they think (perhaps unconsciously) you want to hear.

At least for experiments, you can guarantee that experimenter expectancy effects won't occur by using a particular type of experimental arrangement called a *double-blind design*. In a **double-blind design**, the participant is "blind" to (unaware of) the predictions of the study—and hence unable consciously or unconsciously to serve up the expected result— and the experimenter is also "blind" to the group to which the participant has been assigned to or the particular condition the participant is receiving, and thus is unable to induce the expected results. Clever Hans failed when the questioner did not know the answer to the question, and his human counterparts also can't respond to cues that aren't provided.

Psychology and Pseudopsychology: What's Flaky and What Isn't?

The field of psychology—rooted in science—must be distinguished from **pseudopsychology**, which is theories or statements that at first glance look like psychology but in fact are superstition or unsupported opinion. For example, astrology—along with palm reading and tea-leaf reading and all their relatives—is not a branch of psychology but is pseudopsychology. Pseudopsychology is not psychology at all. It may look and sound like psychology, but it is not science.

Unfortunately, some people are so interested in "knowing more about themselves" or in getting help for their problems that they turn to pseudopsychology. So popular is astrology, for example, that you can get your daily horoscope delivered to your *Yahoo!* home page. And advice found in some (but not all) self-help books falls into the category of pseudoscience. For instance, at one point in history, some self-help gurus told people that screaming was good because it would "let it all out" (the "it" being anger and hurt)—but there was absolutely no evidence that such screams did any more than annoy the neighbors. In fact, research suggests that venting anger in this way sometimes may end up *increasing* your angry feelings, not diminishing them (Bushman, 2002; Lohr et al., 2007). (It's a good idea to check whether the advice dispensed in a self-help book is supported by research before you shell out your hard-earned cash and possibly waste your time reading it.)

It's not always obvious what's psychology and what's pseudopsychology. One key to distinguishing the two is the method; we've already seen what goes into the scientific method, which characterizes all science—regardless of the topic. For example, is extrasensory perception (ESP) pseudopsychology? ESP refers to a collection of mental abilities that do not rely on the ordinary senses or abilities. *Telepathy*, for instance, is the ability to read minds. This sounds not only wonderful but magical. No wonder people are fascinated by the possibility that they, too, may have latent, untapped, extraordinary abilities. But the mere fact that the topic may seem "on the fringe" does not mean that it is pseudopsychology. Similarly, the mere fact that many experiments on ESP have come up empty, failing to produce solid evidence for the abilities, does not mean that the experiments themselves are bad or "unscientific." One can conduct a perfectly good experiment—taking care to guard against confounds, bias, and expectancy effects, for instance— even on ESP.

For example, let's say that you want to study telepathy. You might arrange to test pairs of participants, with one member of each pair acting as "sender" and the other as "receiver." Both the sender and receiver would each look at different sets of the same four playing cards (say an ace, a two, a three, and a four). The

Dogbert (Dilbert's dog) is thinking scientifically about astrology. He proposes a relationship among seasonal differences in diet, sunlight, and other factors and personality characteristics. These variables can be quantified and their relationships tested. If these hypotheses are not supported by the data but Dogbert believes in astrology nevertheless, he's crossed the line into pseudopsychology.

Source: United Media/United Feature Syndicate, Inc.

sender would focus on one of the cards (say, the ace) and would "send" the receiver a mental image of the chosen card. The receiver's job would be to try to receive this image and report which card the sender is focusing on. By chance alone, with only four cards to choose from, the receiver would be right about 25% of the time. So the question is, can the receiver do better than mere guesswork? In this study, you would measure the percentage of times the receiver picks the right card and compare this to what you would expect from guessing alone.

But wait! What if the sender, like the questioners of Clever Hans, provided visible cues (accidentally or on purpose) that have nothing to do with ESP, perhaps smiling when "sending" an ace, grimacing when "sending" a two. A better experiment would have sender and receiver in different rooms, thus controlling for such possible confounds. Furthermore, what if people have an unconscious bias to prefer red over black cards, which leads both the sender and the receiver to select red cards more often than would be dictated by chance? This difficulty can be countered by including a control condition, in which a receiver guesses cards when the sender is not actually sending. Such guesses will reveal response biases (such as a preference for red cards), which exist independently of messages sent via ESP.

Just following the scientific method is not enough to ensure that a set of claims is not pseudopsychology. For instance, whether ESP can be considered a valid, reliable phenomenon will depend on the results of such studies. If they conclusively show that there is nothing to it, then people who claim to have ESP or to understand it will be trying to sell a bill of goods—and will be engaging in pseudopsychology. If proper studies are conducted, we must accept their conclusions. To persist in beliefs in the face of contradictory results would be to engage in pseudopsychology.

Ethics: Doing It Right

Let's say that Tiger Woods wants to learn how to overcome pain so that he can practice hard even when he is hurt—but practicing when injured might cause long-term damage to his body. Would it be ethical for a sport psychologist to teach Woods—or anyone else—techniques to help Woods continue to work out even in the presence of damaging pain? Or, what if Woods decided that he was "addicted to sex" and was desperate to be cured; would it be ethical for a therapist to treat him with new, unproven techniques? To address these questions, we must learn more about the ethical code that guides the research and treatment undertaken by psychologists. ⊙► Simulate

⊙► Simulate Ethics in Psychological Research on mypsychlab.com

Ethics in Research Psychologists have developed a set of rules to ensure that researchers follow sound ethical standards, especially when participants' rights may conflict with a research method or clinical treatment. Certain methods are obviously unethical: No psychologist would cause people to become addicted to drugs to see how easily they can overcome the addiction or would abuse people to help them overcome a psychological problem. But many research situations are not so clear-cut.

RESEARCH WITH PEOPLE: HUMAN GUINEA PIGS?   Some New York psychiatrists were taking fluid from the spines of severely depressed teenagers at regular intervals in order to see whether the presence of certain chemicals in the teens' bodies could predict which particular teens would attempt suicide. As required by law, the youths' parents had given permission for the researchers to draw the fluids. However, this study was one of at least ten that a court ruling brought to a screeching halt in 1996 (*New York Times*, December 5, page A1). The New York State Appeals Court found that the rules for the treatment of children and mentally ill people in experimental settings were unconstitutional because they did not properly protect these participants from abuse by researchers. However, the researchers claimed that without these studies they would never be able to develop the most effective drugs for treating serious impairments, some of which might lead to suicide. Do the potential benefits of such studies outweigh the pain they cause?

At the time of this study, New York was more lax in its research policies than many other states. California, Connecticut, Massachusetts, and Illinois have defined strict rules regarding when researchers can conduct studies in which the pain outweighs the gain or

Informed consent The requirement that a potential participant in a study be told what he or she will be asked to do and be advised of possible risks and benefits of the study before formally agreeing to take part.

Debriefing An interview after a study to ensure that the participant has no negative reactions as a result of participation and to explain why the study was conducted.

that have risks and do not benefit participants directly. In these cases, the study can be conducted *only* when the participants themselves—not family members—provide *informed consent*. **Informed consent** means that before agreeing to take part, potential participants in a study must be told what they will be asked to do and must be advised of the possible risks and benefits of the procedure. They are also told that they can withdraw from the study at any time without being penalized. Only after an individual clearly understands this information and gives consent by signature can he or she take part in a study. (Because minors, and some patients, may not be able to understand the information adequately, they might not be able legally to provide informed consent.) But not all states have such rules, and there are no general federal laws that regulate all research with human participants.

Nevertheless, a study that uses funds from the U.S. government or from most private funding sources must be approved by an *institutional review board* (IRB) at the university, hospital, or other institution that sponsors or hosts the study. The IRB monitors all research projects at that institution, not just those of psychologists. An IRB usually includes not only scientists but also physicians, clergy, and representatives from the local community. The IRB considers the potential risks and benefits of each research study and decides whether the study can be performed. These risks and benefits are considered from all three levels of analysis: effects on the brain (for example, of drugs), the person (for example, through imparting false beliefs), and the group (for example, being embarrassed in front of others or humiliated). Deceiving participants with false or misleading information is permitted only when the participants will not be harmed and the knowledge gained clearly outweighs the use of dishonesty. If there is any chance that participants might respond negatively to being in a proposed study, many universities and hospitals require researchers to discuss their proposed studies with the board, to explain in more detail what they are doing and why.

Concerns about the ethical treatment of human participants lead most IRBs to insist that participants be **debriefed**, that is, interviewed after the study to ask about their experience and to explain why it was conducted. The purposes of debriefing are to ensure that participants do not have negative reactions from participating and that they have understood the purposes of the study.

In large parts of India, animals are not eaten (some are even considered sacred). Many in that culture may believe that animal research is not appropriate.

Source: © Imagestate Media Partners Limited - Impact Photos/Alamy

RESEARCH WITH ANIMALS. Animals are studied in some types of psychological research, particularly studies that focus on understanding the brain. Animals, of course, can't give informed consent, don't volunteer, and can't decide to withdraw from the study if they experience pain or are uncomfortable. But this doesn't mean that animals lack protection. Animal studies, like human ones, must have the stamp of approval of an IRB. The IRB makes sure the animals are housed properly (in cages that are large enough and cleaned often enough) and that they are not mistreated. Researchers are not allowed to cause animals pain unless that is explicitly what is being studied—and even then, they must justify in detail the potential benefits to humans (and possibly to animals, by advancing veterinary medicine) of inflicting the pain.

Is it ethical to test animals at all? This is not an easy question to answer. Researchers who study animals argue that their research is ethical. They point out that although there are substitutes for eating meat and wearing leather, there is no substitute for the use of animals in certain kinds of research; if animals are not used, the research will not be conducted. So, if the culture allows the use of animals for food and clothing, it is not clear why animals should not be studied in laboratories if the animals do not suffer and the findings produce important knowledge. This is not a cut-and-dried issue, however, and thoughtful people disagree.

Ethics in Clinical Practice New therapies are developed continually, but only qualified therapists who have been trained appropriately or are learning the therapy under supervision can ethically provide it. For instance, imagine that Dr. Singh has developed a new type of therapy that she claims is particularly effective for patients who are afraid of some ocial situations, such as public speaking or meeting strangers. You are a therapist who has a patient struggling with such difficulties and is not responding to conventional therapy. You haven't been trained in Singh's therapy, but you want to help your patient. According to the American Psychological Association guidelines (see Table 4), you can try this therapy only if you've received training or will be supervised by someone trained in this method.

Some ethical decisions, such as not administering treatments you haven't been trained to provide, are relatively straightforward, but the ethical code can also come into conflict with the state laws under which psychologists and other psychotherapists practice. For instance, generally speaking, psychologists should obtain specific permission from the patient before they communicate about the patient with people other than professionals who are treating him or her. However, the law makes certain exceptions to the need to maintain confidentiality, such as when a life or (in some states) property is at stake.

Indeed, difficult cases sometimes cause new laws to be written. A patient at the University of California told a psychologist at the student health center that he wanted to kill someone and named the person. The campus police were told; they interviewed the patient and let him go. The patient later killed his targeted victim. The dead woman's parents sued the psychologist and the university for "failure to warn." The case eventually wound its way to California's highest court. One issue the court debated was whether the therapist had the right to divulge confidential information from therapy sessions even when someone's safety is at risk. The court ruled that a therapist is obligated to use reasonable care to protect a potential victim. More specifically, in California (and in most other states now), if a patient has told his or her mental health clinician that he or she plans to harm a specific other person, and the clinician has reason to believe the patient can and will follow through with that plan, the clinician must take steps to protect the targeted person from harm—even though doing so may violate the patient's confidentiality. Similar guidelines apply to cases of potential suicide.

Further, a therapist should not engage in sexual relations with a patient or mistreat a patient physically or emotionally. The American Psychological Association has developed many detailed ethical guidelines based on the principles listed in Table 4.

New Frontiers: Neuroethics As research in psychology continues to progress at an increasing pace, new issues have emerged that would have been in the realm of science fiction a few years ago. To address one set of these issues, a new branch of ethics,

TABLE 4 General Ethical Principles and Code of Conduct for Psychologists

Principle A: Beneficence and Nonmaleficence	"Psychologists strive to benefit those with whom they work and take care to do no harm. . . . Because psychologists' scientific and professional judgments and actions may affect the lives of others, they are alert to and guard against personal, financial, social, organizational, or political factors that might lead to misuse of their influence."
Principle B: Fidelity and Responsibility	"Psychologists uphold professional standards of conduct, clarify their professional roles and obligations, accept appropriate responsibility for their behavior, and seek to manage conflicts of interest that could lead to exploitation or harm."
Principle C: Integrity	"Psychologists seek to promote accuracy, honesty, and truthfulness in the science, teaching, and practice of psychology. In these activities psychologists do not steal, cheat, or engage in fraud, subterfuge, or intentional misrepresentation of fact. Psychologists strive to keep their promises and to avoid unwise or unclear commitments."
Principle D: Justice	"Psychologists recognize that fairness and justice entitle all persons to access to and benefit from the contributions of psychology and to equal quality in the processes, procedures, and services being conducted by psychologists."
Principle E: Respect for People's Rights and Dignity	"Psychologists respect the dignity and worth of all people, and the rights of individuals to privacy, confidentiality, and self-determination. . . . Psychologists are aware of and respect cultural, individual, and role differences, including those based on age, gender, gender identity, race, ethnicity, culture, national origin, religion, sexual orientation, disability, language, and socioeconomic status and consider these factors when working with members of such groups."

Note: This is a direct quote with portions abridged; a complete description can be found at http://www.apa.org/ethics/code/code.pdf.

The Center for Cognitive Liberty and Ethics (http://www.cognitiveliberty.org) asserts that two fundamental principles should form the core of neuroethics: First, individuals should never be forced to use technologies or drugs that alter how their brains function. Second, individuals should not be prohibited from using such technologies or drugs if they so desire, provided that such use would not lead them to harm others.

Source: Courtesy of Center for Cognitive Liberty & Ethics

called *neuroethics*, is focusing on the possible dangers and benefits of research on the brain (Farah, 2009). Still in its infancy, this field is already a hotbed of debate (a recent Google search on "neuroethics" turned up more than 165,000 hits). So far, however, neuroethicists have more questions than answers. For example, is it ethical to use brain-altering drugs to force prisoners to be docile? To scan people's brains to discover whether they are telling the truth? To require young children to take medication that helps them pay attention better in school?

Some scholars have been particularly concerned about the use of neuroscience to predict and control individual behavior (Markus, 2002). For example, suppose that the brains of murderers could be shown conclusively to have a distinctive characteristic (perhaps one region that is much smaller than normal). Should we then scan people's brains and watch them carefully if they have this characteristic? Should this characteristic be used as a criterion for parole for prisoners? These are questions that neuroethicists try to resolve.

LOOKING AT LEVELS   Graph Design for the Human Mind

Source: © Superstock; (inset) Photo Researchers, Inc.

In our earlier discussion, we did not consider the final result of successfully using the scientific method—namely, communicating new findings and theories to others. Science is a community activity, and effective communication is a key part of the practice of science. Graphs are one way to convey scientific findings without overwhelming the user (Kosslyn, 2006). But what kind of graph should be used? The answer to this question depends on what message needs to be conveyed. Bar graphs are better than line graphs when you need to convey comparisons between discrete data points (such as specific numbers of Democratic versus Republican voters in various regions), whereas line graphs are better when you need to convey trends (such as changes in the numbers of Democratic and Republican supporters in different parts of the United States over time) (Zacks & Tversky, 1999). Bars end at discrete locations, and thus it's easy to compare data points simply by comparing the heights of the bars. In contrast, bars are not as useful for conveying trends because the reader needs mentally to connect the tops of bars, creating a line in order to determine visually whether there is a trend. Hence, if that's what you want to convey, it's better to give the reader the line in the first place. But if the reader needs to compare discrete data points, a line isn't so good: Now the reader must "mentally break down" the line into specific points, which requires effort (Kosslyn, 2006).

Think about this finding from the levels-of-analysis perspective: When designing a graph, you need to respect the way the human perceptual system works (level of the brain). If you choose an inappropriate graph, you are asking the reader to work harder to understand your message—which he or she may not be willing to do. But that's not all there is to it. Researchers who focus on the level of the group argue that people use graphs both to communicate data as well as to impress others—for example, by making bars look three-dimensional, which don't convey information about the data and actually require the reader to worker harder to understand the graph (Tractinsky & Meyer, 1999).

In addition, researchers have studied events at the level of the person, such as the qualities of graphs that presenters prefer. One finding is that a presenter's preferences depend in part on the conclusions likely to be drawn from the data. For instance, participants preferred a visually elaborate three-dimensional graph when they were presenting undesirable information (such as financial losses) (Tractinsky & Meyer, 1999). Why might this be? Perhaps because the graph obscures the data? Or perhaps because a fancy graph might partly compensate for undesired findings?

As usual, events at the three levels interact: Depending on the graph you choose for a specific purpose, you will reach the readers (level of the group) more effectively if they do not have to work hard to understand the display (level of the brain), and the particular message (level of the person) may influence both the type of graph you choose as well as how motivated the readers are to understand it. Not only do events at the different levels interact, but also these events *themselves* often must be understood at the different levels. For example, what occurs in the brain when someone is "impressed"? Trying to impress someone is clearly a social event, but it relies on events at the other levels of analysis. Similarly, "communication" is more than a social event—it also involves conveying content to readers (level of the person) and, ultimately, engaging their brains. Any psychological event can be understood fully only by considering it from all three levels.

LOOKING BACK

✓●─ Study and Review on
mypsychlab.com

1. **What is the scientific method, and how is it used to study the mind and behavior?** The scientific method is a way to gather facts that will lead to the formulation and validation of a theory. This method relies on systematically observing events, formulating a question, forming a hypothesis about the relation between variables in an attempt to answer the question, collecting new observations to test the hypothesis, using such evidence to formulate a theory, and, finally, testing the theory.

2. **What scientific research techniques are commonly used to study the mind and behavior?** Psychologists use naturalistic observation, involving careful documentation of events; case studies, which are detailed analyses of a single participant; surveys, in which participants are asked sets of specific questions about their beliefs, attitudes, preferences, or activities; correlational research, in which the relations among variables are documented but causation cannot be inferred; experimental designs, assigning participants randomly to groups and studying the effects of changing the value of one or more independent variable on the value of a dependent variable; and quasi-experimental designs, which are similar to experimental designs except that participants are not randomly assigned to groups and conditions are selected from naturally occurring variations. Finally, psychologists also use meta-analysis, in which the results of many studies are considered in a single overall analysis.

3. **What are key characteristics of good scientific studies in psychology?** The measures taken must be reliable (repeatable), valid (assess what they are supposed to assess), unbiased, and free of experimenter expectancy effects (which lead participants to respond in specific ways). The studies must be well designed (eliminate confounds and use appropriate controls), and the results must be properly interpreted (alternative accounts are ruled out).

4. **How are ethical principles applied to scientific studies in psychology and in psychotherapy?** For research with humans, informed consent is necessary before a person can participate in a study (informed consent requires that the person appreciate the potential risks and benefits of taking part in a study); in the vast majority of cases, studies must be approved in advance by an Institutional Review Board (IRB); and participants must be debriefed after the study to ensure that they have no negative reactions and to confirm that they understand the purpose of the study. For research with animals, the animals must be treated humanely, animal studies must be approved in advance by an IRB, and animals cannot be caused pain or discomfort unless that is what is being studied (even then, researchers must justify the potential benefits to humans or animals). For psychotherapy, in general, strict confidentiality is observed except where the law stipulates that confidentiality should be violated, such as when a specific person may be harmed, when suicide appears to be a real possibility, or (in some states) when another's property may be damaged. Moreover, therapists should not take advantage of their special relationships with patients in any way. A new branch of ethics, called neuroethics, focuses on the potential benefits and dangers of research on the brain.

LET'S REVIEW

((•—[Listen to an audio file of your chapter on **mypsychlab.com**

I. THE SCIENCE OF PSYCHOLOGY: GETTING TO KNOW YOU

A. Psychology is the science of the mind and behavior.

B. The goals of psychology are to describe, explain, predict, and control mental events and behavior.

C. Psychology can best be understood by studying events at different levels of analysis: the levels of the brain, the person, and the group.

D. The level of the brain is where we examine the activity of brain systems, structural differences in people's brains, and effects of genes and chemicals (such as hormones) on the mind and behavior.

E. The level of the person is where we study mental events: the function (mental processes) and content (mental content) of the mind. Mental contents include knowledge, beliefs, desires, and feelings; mental processes include operations that interpret, transform, and store mental contents.

F. The level of the group includes all our social interactions, past and present.

G. Events at the different levels are interdependent and are always interacting. They are also influenced by the physical environment.

II. PSYCHOLOGY THEN AND NOW

A. Psychology grew out of philosophy and physiology and began as the study of mental contents (such as the elements of our perceptions) and mental processes (such as those that underlie perception, memory, and problem solving).

B. The structuralists tried to identify the elements of consciousness and the rules by which these elements are combined into mental structures. The primary method of the structuralists was introspection ("looking within").

C. The functionalists rejected the goal of identifying the building blocks of the mind in favor of seeking explanations for thoughts, feelings, and behavior. The functionalists were interested in how mental events adapt to help people survive in the natural world.

D. The Gestalt psychologists reacted against the structuralists' emphasis on breaking mental processes and mental contents into distinct elements. The Gestaltists studied the way the mind organizes material into overall perceptual patterns.

E. Freud developed a detailed theory of mental events. His psychodynamic theory was formulated to explain how both conscious and unconscious thoughts and feelings affect a person's behavior.

F. The behaviorists rejected the assumption that psychology should focus on the mind; they urged psychologists to study what could be observed directly—stimuli, responses, and the consequences of responses.

G. The humanists, in part reacting against Freud's theory and the psychotherapy it gave rise to, assumed that people have positive values and free will; Rogers developed a treatment for psychological problems that relied on respect for individuals and their potentials.

H. Elements of the various strands came together in the cognitive revolution, which began by conceiving of the mind by analogy to a computer program; in this view, mental processing is information processing.

I. Cognitive neuroscientists study the relation between events at all three levels of analysis, with an emphasis on how the brain gives rise to thoughts, feelings, and behavior (including social behavior).

J. Evolutionary psychology treats many cognitive strategies and goals as adaptations that are the results of natural selection.

K. The three major types of psychologists are distinguished by their training, work settings, and types of work: (1) clinical and counseling psychologists administer and interpret psychological tests, provide psychotherapy, offer career and vocational counseling, help people with specific psychological problems, and help people function more effectively; (2) academic psychologists teach and do research, in addition to helping to run their universities, colleges, or institutions; and (3) applied psychologists use the findings and theories of psychology to solve practical problems.

III. THE RESEARCH PROCESS: HOW WE FIND THINGS OUT

A. The science of psychology relies on the scientific method, which involves systematically observing events, formulating a question, forming a hypothesis about the relation between variables in an attempt to answer the question, collecting new observations to test the hypothesis, using such data to formulate a theory, and testing the theory.

B. Psychologists test hypotheses and look for relations among variables using a variety of approaches, including naturalistic observation, case studies, surveys, correlational studies, experiments, quasi-experiments, and meta-analyses.

C. Naturalistic observation involves careful observation and documentation of events.

D. Case studies are detailed investigations of a single participant.

E. In surveys, participants are asked to answer sets of specific questions.

F. In correlational studies, researchers measure the relationship between the values of pairs of variables, to determine whether the values of one variable go up or down as the values of the other go up or down. Correlational studies cannot determine whether changes in the values of one variable *cause* changes in the other.

G. In an experiment, the effect of manipulating the value of one or more independent variables on the value of a dependent variable is measured, and participants are assigned randomly to groups.

H. Quasi-experiments are like experiments, but participants are not assigned to groups randomly, and conditions are selected from naturally occurring variations.

I. In a meta-analysis, researchers combine results from different studies in order to identify a relationship among variables that cuts across the entire set of studies.

J. When reading reports of studies, you should be alert for the following: (1) evidence that the data are reliable; (2) evidence that the data are valid; (3) biases, including response bias (the tendency to respond in particular ways to everything) and sampling bias (the nonrandom selection of participants); and (4) experimenter expectancy effects.

K. Pseudopsychology differs from psychology not necessarily in its content but in its methods and whether it is supported by data.

L. Research with humans or nonhuman animals at universities, hospitals, and most institutional settings requires approval from an IRB.

M. For research with humans, the IRB will insist that the participants provide informed consent, which means that

they must be given information in advance about the possible risks and benefits of participation.

N. The IRB will also require debriefing, which is an interview after the study to ensure that the participants had no negative reactions and did, in fact, understand the purpose of the study.

O. The IRB will also rule out any deceiving of participants, unless the deception is harmless and absolutely necessary for the research (and the potential value of the research is large enough to outweigh the use of deception).

P. For research with animals, the IRB requires that the animals be treated well (for example, housed in clean cages) and that pain be inflicted only if that is what is being studied and it is justified by the benefits from the research.

Q. In clinical practice, psychotherapists must follow clear ethical guidelines, which include maintaining confidentiality except when legal mandates conflict with such guidelines, as is the case when a specific other person (or, in some states, property) is clearly in danger, or suicide is an imminent genuine concern.

R. In addition, therapists should not use techniques that they have not been trained to use or are learning but are not being properly supervised. Therapists should not engage in inappropriate personal behavior with patients.

S. A new branch of ethics, called neuroethics, focuses on the possible dangers and benefits of research on the brain.

KEY TERMS

academic psychologists	debriefing	level of the brain	random assignment
applied psychologists	dependent variable	level of the group	reliability
behavior	double-blind design	level of the person	replication
behaviorism	effect	mental contents	response bias
bias	evolutionary psychology	mental processes	sample
case study	experimental condition	meta-analysis	sampling bias
clinical psychologist	experimental group	operational definition	scientific method
cognitive neuroscience	experimenter expectancy effects	population	social worker
cognitive psychology	functionalism	prediction	structuralism
confound	Gestalt psychology	pseudopsychology	survey
control condition	humanistic psychology	psychiatric nurse	theory
control group	hypothesis	psychiatrist	unconscious
correlation coefficient	independent variable	psychodynamic theory	validity
counseling psychologist	informed consent	psychology	variable
data	introspection	psychotherapy	

PRACTICE TEST

For each of the following items, choose the single best answer.

1. Why is psychology a science?
   a. It relies on popular opinion and intuition.
   b. It examines psychological questions by considering them in detail and ensuring that all answers to those questions are based on naturalistic observations.
   c. It uses logic to reason about phenomena and then tests the resulting ideas by collecting additional facts.
   d. It is not a science, although, when it becomes more mathematical, it may develop into one.

2. At the level of the person, the psychologist focuses on
   a. mental contents and mental processes.
   b. events that involve the structure and properties of the brain—brain cells and their connections, the chemical solution in which they exist, and the genes.
   c. events that involve relationships between people, relationships among groups, and culture.
   d. directly observable variables that differentiate among people (such as weight, height, shoe size, and eye color).

3. How are conditions in the physical environment related to events at the three levels of analysis?
   a. Conditions in the physical environment are not related to events at any of the levels of analysis.
   b. Conditions in the physical environment are intimately tied to events that occur at every level of analysis.
   c. Conditions in the physical environment relate to events occurring only at the level of the brain.
   d. Conditions in the physical environment influence only occasional events at the level of the person.

4. Who is usually considered the founder of scientific psychology?
   a. Max Wertheimer
   b. Sigmund Freud
   c. Edward Titchener
   d. Wilhelm Wundt

5. An approach to understanding mental events that focuses on the idea that the whole is more than the sum of the parts is
   a. Gestalt psychology.
   b. psychodynamic theory.
   c. functionalism.
   d. structuralism.

6. Which school of psychology assumes that people have positive values, free will, and deep inner creativity?
   a. psychodynamic theory
   b. evolutionary psychology
   c. functionalism
   d. humanistic psychology

7. What type of psychologist provides psychotherapy and is trained to administer and interpret psychological tests?
   a. an applied psychologist
   b. a physiological psychologist
   c. a clinical psychologist
   d. a cognitive psychologist

8. Properly collected data can be replicated, meaning that
   a. objective observations were collected.
   b. an aspect of a situation that is liable to change was described.
   c. a control group is included, and alternative explanations for the finding are systematically ruled out.
   d. if the same observations or measurements are collected again, they will yield the same results as found previously.

9. A tentative idea that might explain a set of observations is called
   a. data.
   b. a hypothesis.
   c. replication.
   d. an operational definition.

10. A variable that is not the independent variable but nonetheless varies along with the independent variable, and that could be the actual cause of changes in the dependent variable is a
    a. dependent variable.
    b. control group.
    c. hypothesis.
    d. confound.

11. Suppose that Dr. Knight reported a correlation of 0.02 between height and income. This correlation indicates that
    a. taller people are very likely to have greater income relative to shorter people.
    b. greater height causes greater income.
    c. height and income are not very closely related.
    d. Dr. Knight used a quasi-experimental design.

12. Suppose that Dr. Blaine has been told that he needs to improve the validity of his study. To do so, he ought to make sure that his
    a. design and procedure appear to assess the variables of interest.
    b. measures assess all aspects of the phenomenon of interest.
    c. measure or procedure is comparable to several different, reliable measures or procedures.
    d. measures assess variables specified by a theory.

13. What is a double-blind design?
    a. one in which both participants and experimenters wear blindfolds
    b. one in which experimenter expectancy effects will influence the results unless deception is used to obscure the actual purposes and predictions of the study
    c. one that is based on pseudopsychology
    d. one in which the participant is unaware of the predictions of the study and the experimenter is unaware of the condition assigned to the participant

14. The interview that takes place after a study (to ensure that the participant has no negative reactions as a result of participation and understands why the study was conducted) is called
    a. informed consent.
    b. debriefing.
    c. behaviorism.
    d. unconscious.

15. Suppose Dr. Singh has developed a new type of therapy that she claims is particularly effective for patients who are afraid of some social situations. You have a patient struggling with such difficulties and not responding to conventional therapy. You haven't been trained in Dr. Singh's therapy, but you want to help. Could you try Dr. Singh's therapy?
    a. no
    b. only if your patient wants to
    c. yes, but only if you receive proper training or supervision
    d. It depends on how long Dr. Singh's therapy takes to work

Answers: 1. c 2. a 3. b 4. d 5. a 6. d 7. c 8. d 9. b 10. d 11. c 12. a 13. d 14. b 15. c

Clearly, something was wrong with the young soldier's vision, but the problem had nothing to do with his eyes; it had to do with his brain.

THE BIOLOGY OF MIND AND BEHAVIOR

THE BRAIN IN ACTION

As the hard jets of water massaged the 25-year-old soldier while he showered, colorless and odorless fumes of carbon monoxide, which are known to cause brain damage, slowly seeped into the stall. Unaware that he was being accidentally poisoned, the soldier continued his routine until he eventually passed out.

After the soldier was discovered and revived, doctors examined him. Although the young man could get around with ease (he clearly could see objects well enough to avoid bumping into them), his visual abilities definitely were not normal. He could not name objects that he saw but was able to name them as soon as he touched and handled them; he could identify things by smell and sound but could not name the colors of objects or identify a color named by someone else by pointing to it; and he had no difficulty recognizing familiar people when they spoke but couldn't identify these same people by sight alone. In fact, when he looked at his own face in the mirror, he thought he was looking at one of his doctors. When the doctors asked the soldier to inspect a picture of a nude woman and show where her eyes were, he pointed to her breasts (Benson & Greenberg, 1969).

Something was wrong with the young soldier's visual abilities, but the problem had nothing to do with his eyes; it had to do with his brain. He couldn't acquire normal amounts of knowledge by way of his sense of sight. Why? Although he retained some aspects of his vision, he had lost others—he seemed unable to recognize what he clearly could see. The fumes the soldier had inhaled had affected his brain, but how? What, exactly, had gone wrong? To consider these questions, we need to understand essential facts about how the brain works.

Events at the level of the brain can influence many aspects of behavior, in ways not immediately apparent. If you broke your hand, you would have trouble holding a pencil: The effect of the accident would be direct and mechanical. If you were in any doubt before your mishap about the role of muscle and bone in grasping and holding, you would be in no doubt afterward, when those abilities would be obviously impaired because your muscles were torn when your bones were broken. Although the brain is a body part like the hand, the brain is unique: It is ultimately responsible for our thoughts of present and past, our plans for the future, moods of despair and elation, our sense of well-being and our sense that something's wrong, our perception of the outside world and our awareness of its meaning. The effects of damage to the brain are no less real than those of a broken hand, but the nature of this damage is more difficult to understand and to document.

So, how does it work, this mysterious brain? What is it made up of; what are its building blocks, and how does understanding these building blocks provide insight into what happened to the soldier? What do different parts of the brain do? How could we find out exactly which parts of the soldier's brain were damaged? Do all of our brains respond the same way to the same environmental influences? Or, do different people, with different genetic makeups and life experiences, respond differently? Let's start finding out.

▫ ▫ ▫

Brain Circuits: Making Connections

Why did the carbon monoxide fumes that the soldier breathed cause such damage? The answer is that they interfered with his brain's ability to obtain oxygen. Ordinarily, brain cells begin to die after a few minutes without oxygen. When brain cells die, it is as if bricks in the walls of a building crumble, leaving holes in some walls and causing other walls to collapse. In both cases, the basic building blocks no longer function together as they originally did. Unfortunately, the soldier inhaled enough fumes that some of his brain cells were deprived of oxygen and died. To understand why the fumes had their effects, we need to understand the basic building blocks of the brain. In so doing, we will also gain insight into how various kinds of drugs operate.

LOOKING AHEAD Learning Objectives

1. How do neurons work?
2. How do chemicals allow neurons to communicate?

The Neuron: A Powerful Computer

The physical structure of the brain allows it to function in certain ways, just as the physical structure of a building allows it to function in certain ways—to have doors, windows, hallways, rooms, and so forth. In the case of the brain, its physical characteristics give rise to *mental contents* and *mental processes*. **Mental contents** comprise knowledge, beliefs (including ideas, explanations, and expectations), desires (such as hopes, goals, and needs), and feelings (such as fears, guilts, and attractions). In contrast, **mental processes** are sets of operations (such as shifting the focus of attention over a scene) that work together to carry out a function (such as perception, language, or memory).

The brain is arguably the most complex object in the known universe, and to begin to grasp its general structure and function, we start with the fundamental building blocks and then see how they are organized into structures that carry out particular functions. We could easily write a book about the structure or function of the brain; we present here just what you will need to know to understand material about the brain in the remainder of this book (for example, the actions of drugs that treat psychological disorders).

Just as you need to understand the characteristics of bricks before you could see how to build a wall out of them, you need to understand key properties of the cells that compose the brain before you can understand how the brain works (and why brain damage has specific effects). All brain activity hinges on the workings of specialized cells, called **neurons**, which are cells that receive signals from sense organs or other neurons, process these signals, and send the signals to muscles, organs, or other neurons. Neurons are the basic unit of the nervous system, and are located in the brain and throughout the entire nervous system (Kandel et al., 2000); the nervous system is a coordinated network of neurons and other types of cells that work with them. In many respects, neurons are like computers: They accept *inputs* (typically many thousands of signals at the same time), operate on them (as if they were running a computer program), and produce *outputs* (signals that are transmitted). (Pause to reflect on this for a moment: Your brain has about 100 *billion* neurons, each of which is like a computer!)

Neurons are classified into three types, according to what they do. **Sensory neurons** are specialized to respond to signals from sensory organs (notably the eyes, ears, the nose, the tongue, and the skin—for touch) and transmit those signals to other neurons in the brain or spinal cord. In contrast, **motor neurons** are specialized to send signals from the brain and spinal cord to muscles in order to control movement (they also send signals to bodily organs, such as glands), and **interneurons** link sensory and motor neurons—or they link other interneurons. Most of the neurons in the brain are interneurons, and most interneurons are connected to yet other interneurons.

A large number of neurons work together to accomplish any particular task; for instance, neurons work together to enable you to control what you pay attention to, allow you to catch a ball, or produce a sentence when you speak. Neurons are organized into **brain circuits**, which are sets of neurons that work together to receive input (that is, signals from other neurons or from a sensory organ), operate on it in some way, and produce specific output (that is, produce signals to other neurons or to muscles). For example, a relatively simple brain circuit might register a loud noise (the input) and cause your head to turn in that direction (the output).

THINK like a
PSYCHOLOGIST Researchers have estimated that there are more possible connections in the brain than there are atoms in the Universe (Thompson, 1993)! Why do you think the human brain is so complex? Do you think humans could have survived with less complex brains?

Mental contents Knowledge, beliefs (including ideas, explanations, and expectations), desires (such as hopes, goals, and needs), and feelings (such as fears, guilts, and attractions).

Mental processes Sets of operations that work together to carry out a function, such as attention, perception, or memory.

Neuron A cell that receives signals from sense organs or other neurons, processes these signals, and sends the signals to muscles, organs, or other neurons; the basic unit of the nervous system.

Sensory neuron A neuron that responds to signals from sensory organs and transmits those signals to the brain and spinal cord.

Motor neuron A neuron that sends signals to muscles in order to control movement (and also to bodily organs, such as glands).

Interneuron A neuron that is connected to other neurons, not to sense organs or muscles.

Brain circuit A set of neurons that work together to receive input, operate on it in some way, and produce specific output.

FIGURE 1 Major Parts of a Neuron

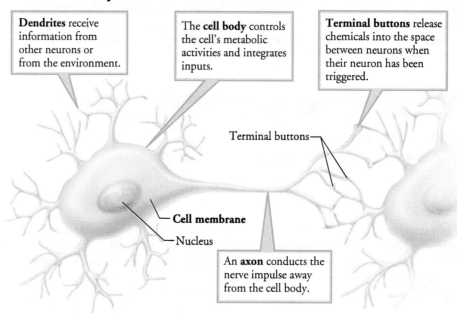

Dendrites receive information from other neurons or from the environment.

The **cell body** controls the cell's metabolic activities and integrates inputs.

Terminal buttons release chemicals into the space between neurons when their neuron has been triggered.

Terminal buttons

Cell membrane

Nucleus

An **axon** conducts the nerve impulse away from the cell body.

A neuron has many parts. The major ones are labeled here, but much of the action occurs internally where a complex dance of chemicals occurs.

Source: From Goodenough, Judith A., McGuire, Betty A., Wallace, Robert A., *Biology of Humans: Concepts, Applications and Issues,* 1st edition, © 2005, Figure 7.2. Adapted by Permission of Pearson Education, Inc., Upper Saddle River, NJ.

Cell body The central part of a neuron (or other cell), which contains the nucleus.

Cell membrane The skin that surrounds a cell.

Axon The sending end of the neuron; the long cablelike structure extending from the cell body.

Terminal button A structure at the end of the branch of an axon that can release chemicals into the space between neurons.

Dendrite The treelike part of a neuron that receives messages from the axons of other neurons.

Resting potential The negative charge within a neuron when it is at rest.

Ion An atom that has a positive or negative charge.

Structure of a Neuron: The Ins and Outs To understand psychological events and how they can be disrupted following brain damage, you need to know a few facts about the structure of the neuron. The key parts of a neuron are shown in Figure 1.

The central part of a neuron is called the **cell body**. Like all cells, a neuron contains a nucleus, which regulates the cell's functions, and a **cell membrane**, which is the skin that surrounds the cell. The sending end of the neuron is the **axon**, the long, cablelike structure extending from the cell body, along which signals travel to other neurons, muscles, or bodily organs. Although each neuron has only a single axon, most axons divide into many branches, the ends of which are called *terminals*. This branching allows each neuron to send a message to more than one place at a time. At the ends of the terminals are **terminal buttons**, little knoblike structures that can release chemicals into the space between neurons. Neurons are surrounded by fluid, and they are affected by chemicals in that fluid.

Each neuron has only one axon, but a neuron typically has many receiving ends. The receiving end of the neuron is composed of *dendrites*; their name is derived from the Greek word *dendron*, meaning "tree," which makes sense when you look at their shape. **Dendrites** receive messages from the axons of other neurons. Although axons sometimes connect directly to the cell body of another neuron, the connection is usually made from the axon of one neuron to the dendrite of another.

Neural Impulses: The Brain in Action We've noted that neurons receive inputs and produce outputs, but what, exactly, are these inputs and outputs? In short, the answer is: chemicals. To answer this question more fully, let's first examine a neuron's output and how a neuron produces it. In turn, one neuron's output can serve as the input for other neurons.

Neurons are either at rest or they are sending signals—outputs—to other neurons. When at rest, they maintain a negative charge within them; this negative charge is called the **resting potential**. This potential arises because of how ions are distributed inside and outside the cell. **Ions** are atoms that are positively or negatively charged. During rest, more positively charged ions (consisting mostly of sodium ions) are outside the neuron than

FIGURE 2 Ion Flow That Produces an Action Potential

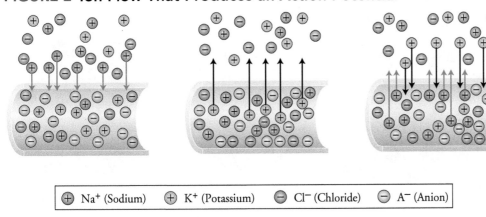

Na⁺ (Sodium) K⁺ (Potassium) Cl⁻ (Chloride) A⁻ (Anion)

Direction of action potential

Chemicals released

Na⁺ channels open after the neuron is stimulated, and Na⁺ ions rush into the cell; the inside of the cell then becomes positively charged. (Ions are not drawn to scale, but relative proportions are correct.)

The Na⁺ channels close, K⁺ channels briefly open, and K⁺ ions go outside the cell. (The K⁺ ions are pushed out because of the addition of the positively charged Na⁺ ions.)

After this, Na⁺ pumps actively push Na⁺ ions back outside, and K⁺ ions are drawn inside until the inside and outside concentrations are returned to their original levels.

When the ion exchanges reach the end of the axon, they cause chemicals to be released from the terminal buttons.

Source: From Goodenough, Judith A., McGuire, Betty A., Wallace, Robert A., *Biology of Humans: Concepts, Applications and Issues,* 1st edition, © 2005, Figure 7.5. Adapted by Permission of Pearson Education, Inc., Upper Saddle River, NJ.

are inside it, and more negatively charged ions are inside the neuron than are in the surrounding fluid.

A neuron "fires" when the dendrites (and, in some cases, the cell body) receive appropriate inputs from other neurons. When this occurs, very small pores, called *channels,* open in the membrane that covers the axon. When these channels open, a complex exchange of ions occurs, with some ions flowing into the cell from the surrounding fluid and some ions flowing from inside the cell to the surrounding fluid. This exchange of ions then changes the electrical charge inside the axon. This exchange process begins at the part of the axon that is connected to the cell body and works its way down to the end of the axon, like a line of dominoes falling, finally causing the terminal buttons to release chemicals; generally, these chemicals will then function as signals—inputs—to other neurons. The shifting change in the electrical charge that moves down the axon is known as an **action potential.** This process, which is the basis of the neural communication that in turn permits us to live in the world and respond to it, is illustrated in Figure 2. (We must also note that although the vast majority of neurons send and receive chemical signals, some—such as some of those in the eye—affect each other directly via electrical impulses; such neurons do not play a large role in psychological phenomena, and thus we will not discuss them here.)

The action potential obeys an **all-or-none law:** If adequate inputs reach the neuron, it fires—and chemicals are released from the terminal buttons. Either the action potential occurs or it doesn't. Many neurons can fire hundreds of times a second because chemical reactions reset the neurons so that they can fire again if they receive adequate input. Nevertheless, neurons require a measurable amount of time to produce action potentials, release neurotransmitters, and ultimately affect other neurons; to convince yourself that this is so, gather some friends and try the simple exercise described in Figure 3 on page 46 (developed by Rozin & Jonides, 1977).

Most axons are covered with **myelin,** a fatty substance that helps impulses efficiently travel down the axon. Myelin is a bit like the insulation around copper wires, which allows the wires to transmit electrical current more effectively. *Multiple sclerosis (MS)* is one of several disorders that illustrates the importance of myelin. In MS, the myelin has deteriorated, which makes the action potentials in those neurons "stumble" as they move down the axon. People with MS can experience impaired sensation in their limbs, loss of vision, and/or paralysis (Zajicek, 2004). MS is probably caused by an

Action potential The shifting change in charge that moves down the axon.

All-or-none law States that if the neuron is sufficiently stimulated, it fires, sending the action potential all the way down the axon and releasing chemicals from the terminal buttons; either the action potential occurs or it doesn't.

Myelin A fatty substance that helps impulses efficiently travel down the axon.

THINK like a **PSYCHOLOGIST** To do the exercise in Figure 3, use the *DO IT!* log at www.mypsychlab.com; select the *Biology of Mind and Behavior* chapter, and click on the *DO IT!* folder.

FIGURE 3 Measuring Neural Conduction Time

In the fastest neurons, impulses travel only about 120 meters per second, compared with 300,000,000 meters per second for the speed of light. Even compared with the impulses traveling in a computer, our neurons are extremely slow. You can actually measure the speed of neural processing. Here's how.

Sit in a row with some friends, with each person using his or her left hand to grasp the ankle of the person to his or her left. The person at the head of the line, the leader, says "Go" and starts a stopwatch at the same time he or she squeezes the ankle of the person to his or her left; as soon as that person feels the squeeze, he or she squeezes the ankle of the next person to the left and so on. When the last person feels the squeeze, he or she says "Done." The leader records the time.

Now repeat the exercise, but each of you should grasp not the ankle but the shoulder of the person to your left. Less time is required for the squeezes to make their way down the row when shoulders are squeezed than when ankles are squeezed. Why? Because the impulses have farther to travel when the ankle is squeezed. By subtracting the difference in times and estimating the average distance from ankle to shoulder for each person, you can actually estimate neural transmission time! This exercise should be done several times, first ankle, then shoulder, then shoulder, and then ankle; this procedure helps to control for the effects of practice in general.

FIGURE 4 The Synapse

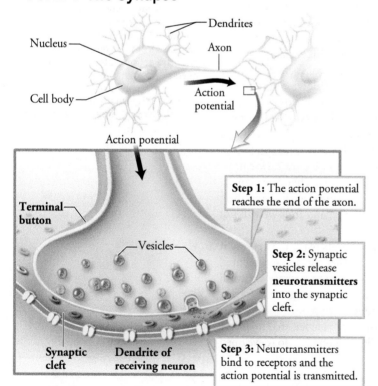

Impulses cross between neurons at the synapse. Chemicals released at the terminal buttons cross the synaptic cleft, where they bind to receptors and trigger events in the receiving neuron.

Source: From Goodenough, Judith A., McGuire, Betty A., Wallace, Robert A., *Biology of Humans: Concepts, Applications and Issues,* 1st edition, © 2005, Figure 7.7. Adapted by Permission of Pearson Education, Inc., Upper Saddle River, NJ.

autoimmune problem. Could myelin loss have caused the young soldier's problem? Probably not: His visual difficulties arose following exposure to carbon monoxide, which does not disrupt myelin.

Neurotransmitters: Bridging the Gap

Brain circuits operate properly only when the neurons that comprise them send and receive signals effectively. In this section, we consider neural communication in more detail, focusing on the site where communication between neurons occurs—the **synapse**, where an axon of one neuron sends a signal to the membrane of another neuron. The synapse has three parts: the portion of the axon that actually sends the message, the portion of the receiving neuron that receives the message, and the space between the axon and receiving neuron. That is, the sending and receiving neurons do not actually touch each other but rather are separated by a gap called the **synaptic cleft**, shown in Figure 4. Understanding the events that occur at the synaptic cleft is important because this is where brain circuits often are disrupted and is where many drugs have their effects.

Chemical Messages: Crossing the Gap As their name suggests, the chemical signals—that travel from the terminal buttons across the synaptic cleft—are the **neurotransmitter substances** (often simply called *neurotransmitters,* for short). As shown in Figure 4, the neurotransmitter molecules are contained in small sacs, called *vesicles*. Researchers have discovered many substances that act as neurotransmitters in the brain (Barañano et al., 2001). Table 1 summarizes key properties of the major neurotransmitter substances.

TABLE 1 Major Neurotransmitter Substances

Summary of the most important neurotransmitter substances, their distinguishing features, major disorders associated with them, and common drugs that modulate their effects. Many of the disorders are discussed in this and other chapters of this book. A question mark indicates that the substance may be involved in the disorder, but conclusive evidence has yet to be obtained.

Name	Distinguishing Features	Related Disorders and Symptoms	Drugs That Alter
Acetylcholine	Causes muscles to contract; memory; arousal	Alzheimer's disease, delusions (shortage); convulsions, spasms, tremors (excess)	Physostigmine (increases, used to treat Alzheimer's disease); scopolamine (blocks)
Dopamine	Motivation, reward, movement, thought, learning	Parkinson's disease, depression, attention-deficit/hyperactivity disorder (ADHD) (shortage); aggression, schizophrenia (excess)	Amphetamine, cocaine (causes release); chlorpromazine (blocks at receptors); methylphenidate (Ritalin, blocks reuptake)
Noradrenaline (norepinephrine)	Dreaming, attention	Depression, fatigue, distractability (shortage); anxiety, headache, schizophrenia (excess)	Tricyclic antidepressants such as amitriptyline (keeps more available at the synapse)
Serotonin	Primary inhibitory neurotransmitter regulating mood, sleep	Obsessive-compulsive disorder, insomnia, depression (shortage); sleepiness, lack of motivation (excess)	Fluoxetine (Prozac), tricyclic antidepressants (keeps more present at the synapse)
GABA (gamma-aminobutyric acid)	Inhibits sending neuron	Anxiety, panic (?), epilepsy, Huntington's disease (shortage); sluggishness, lack of motivation (excess)	Sedatives (such as phenobarbital), alcohol, benzodiazepines (such as Valium, Halcion) (mimics effects)
Endogenous cannabinoids	Memory, attention, emotion, movement control, appetite	Chronic pain (shortage); memory and attention problems, eating disorders, schizophrenia (?) (excess)	R141716A (blocks effects of); Tetrahydrocannabinol (THC) (mimics effects of)

Endogenous cannabinoids are a very important and very unusual neurotransmitter substances. These chemicals provide a way for the receiving neuron to provide feedback to the sending neuron. That is, **endogenous cannabinoids** are released by the *receiving* neuron (through its cell membrane, not its axon) and then influence the activity of the *sending* neuron (Wilson & Nicoll, 2002). Cannabinoids can fine-tune activity underlying learning, memory, pain perception, and attention (Katona et al., 2000; Kreitzer & Regehr, 2001; Sanudo-Pena et al., 2000; Schneider & Koch, 2002). Marijuana contains cannabinoids that affect neurons indiscriminately and promiscuously and thereby overwhelms our exquisitely tuned neural systems—disrupting memory and attention as well as other cognitive functions (Ashton, 2001; Schneider & Koch, 2002). As Barinaga (2001) put it, the chemicals introduced by marijuana eliminate the fine-tuned "local activity patterns . . . just as spilling a bottle of ink across a page obliterates any words written there" (p. 2531).

Receptors: On the Receiving End Once they cross the synaptic cleft, neurotransmitters will affect different types of receiving neurons in different ways. Each neuron has **receptors**, specialized sites on the dendrites or cell body that respond to specific neurotransmitter substances; the receptor sites are the places where neurotransmitter molecules attach themselves. And there are many types of receptors, each of which accepts only specific types of neurotransmitters. A good analogy here is an ordinary lock and key: The lock is the receptor, which is opened by the keylike action of a particular neurotransmitter.

Synapse The place where an axon of one neuron sends signals to the membrane (on a dendrite or cell body) of another neuron; the synapse includes the sending portions of an axon, the receiving portions of the receiving neuron, and the space between them.

Synaptic cleft The gap in the synapse between the axon of one neuron and the membrane of another across which communication occurs.

Neurotransmitter substance A chemical that carries a signal from the terminal button of one neuron to the dendrite or cell body of another; often referred to as a *neurotransmitter*.

Endogenous cannabinoids Neurotransmitter substances released by the receiving neuron that then influence the activity of the sending neuron.

Receptor A site on a dendrite or cell body where a neurotransmitter molecule attaches itself; like a lock that is opened by one key, a receptor receives only one type of neurotransmitter.

Reuptake The process by which surplus neurotransmitter in the synaptic cleft is reabsorbed back into the sending neuron so that the neuron can effectively fire again.

Neurotransmitters only have effects if they *bind* (become attached) to the receptors (see Figure 5). After binding, they can have one of two general types of effects. They can be *excitatory* inputs, making the receiving neuron more likely to have an action potential, or they can be *inhibitory* inputs, making the receiving neuron less likely to have an action potential. Because the typical axon divides into many branches and each neuron has many dendrites, there are many binding sites; thus, the neuron can receive thousands of different inputs from different sending neurons at the same time. The excitatory and inhibitory inputs to each receiving neuron add up or cancel one another out, and only when their sum total is large enough will an action potential be initiated.

Not all of a given neurotransmitter released by the terminal buttons is taken up by receptors; some of it remains in the gap. Special chemical reactions are required to reabsorb—or **reuptake**—the excess neurotransmitter back into the vesicles of the sending neuron.

FIGURE 5 Neurotransmitter Substances

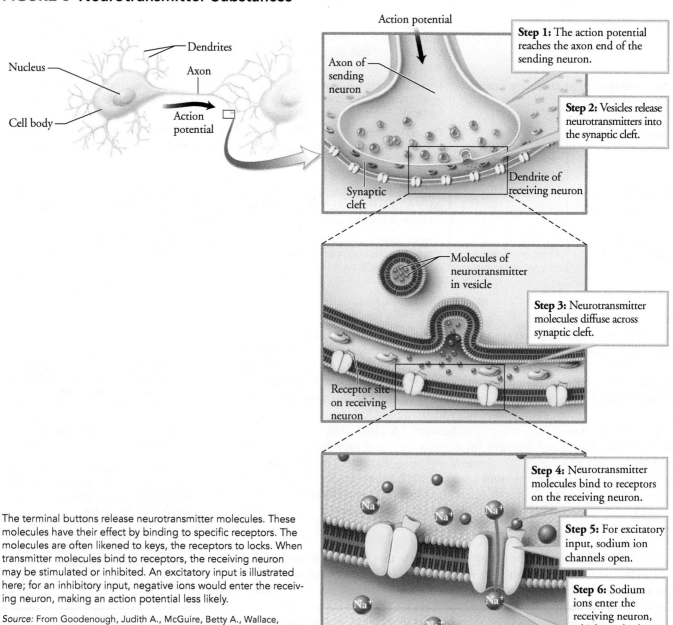

The terminal buttons release neurotransmitter molecules. These molecules have their effect by binding to specific receptors. The molecules are often likened to keys, the receptors to locks. When transmitter molecules bind to receptors, the receiving neuron may be stimulated or inhibited. An excitatory input is illustrated here; for an inhibitory input, negative ions would enter the receiving neuron, making an action potential less likely.

Source: From Goodenough, Judith A., McGuire, Betty A., Wallace, Robert A., *Biology of Humans: Concepts, Applications and Issues,* 1st edition, © 2005, Figure 7.2. Adapted by Permission of Pearson Education, Inc., Upper Saddle River, NJ.

Unbalanced Brain: Coping with Bad Chemicals By piecing together the story of how neurons communicate, scientists are not only developing a clear picture of how the brain works but are also learning how its functioning can go awry and how they can use drugs to repair it. Some of these drugs are **agonists**, which mimic the effects of a neurotransmitter substance by activating a particular type of receptor. Other drugs may actually increase the amount of a neurotransmitter in the synapse, sometimes by slowing down its reuptake. Depression, for example, is currently treated by several types of drugs that affect neurotransmitters, including **selective serotonin-reuptake inhibitors (SSRIs)**, which block the reuptake of the neurotransmitter serotonin (Reid & Barbui, 2010). (Prozac, Zoloft, and Paxil are all SSRIs.) Still other drugs interfere with the effect of a neurotransmitter. Some of these drugs are **antagonists**, which block a particular receptor. (As a memory aid, think of an "antagonist" at a party who is "blocking you" from meeting a charmer across the room.) An example of an antagonist drug is Naltrexone (also called Revia and Depade), which blocks the effects of alcohol and opiates (Roozen et al., 2006; Unterwald, 2008).

The connection between neurotransmitter substances and behavior is also evident in the devastating effects of *Parkinson's disease*, a brain disorder. Named after the British physician James Parkinson, who first described the disorder in 1817, Parkinson's afflicts about half a million Americans. People with Parkinson's disease may have hands that shake; they may move sluggishly, with a stooped posture and shuffling walk; and their limbs often seem frozen in position and resist attempts to bend them. All of these changes, physical and behavioral, are caused directly or indirectly by the death of some of the cells that produce dopamine. When patients take L-dopa, a drug that helps produce dopamine, their symptoms decrease (Marini et al., 2003), often for a long period of time. However, L-dopa becomes less effective with continued use (and sometimes produces side effects), and thus researchers are developing new dopamine agonists to treat this disorder (Barone, 2003; Jenner, 2002).

Could the young soldier whose visual abilities were so strangely disrupted have had malfunctioning neurotransmitters? Could malfunctioning neurotransmitters have produced the highly selective impairments he experienced after inhaling the carbon monoxide fumes? This scenario is unlikely: Because most neurotransmitters are used widely throughout the brain—not solely in the parts of the brain involved in visual perception—we would expect their disruption to create more widespread difficulties, such as in hearing, understanding language, walking, and other functions.

Parkinson's disease apparently can strike anyone and can interfere with a wide variety of careers. However, as actor Michael J. Fox showed, at least in some cases, medical or surgical procedures can help keep symptoms in check.

Source: © Ron Sachs/CNP/Sygma / CORBIS All Rights Reserved

Glial Cells: More Than the Neurons' Helpmates

The average human brain contains about ten times as many *glial cells* (the name comes from the Greek word for "glue") as neurons, which is a hint that these cells must have important roles. Researchers have long known that **glial cells** help neurons both to create synapses and to form appropriate connections while the brain is developing, prenatally and during childhood, and thereafter participate in the "care and feeding" of neurons. The traditional view was that glial cells physically cushion neurons, clean up the remains of dead neurons, dispose of extra neurotransmitters and ions in the fluid surrounding neurons, and provide nutrients to neurons. This view is correct, as far as it goes. But recent research has revealed that this view doesn't go far enough; glial cells are much more than just the neurons' helpmates (Halassa & Haydon, 2010).

Neurons and Glia: A Mutually Giving Relationship Neurons and glial cells influence each other in complex ways. On the one hand, neurons have synapses with glial cells, and they stimulate glial cells to release specific chemicals. On the other hand, glial cells can directly regulate how strongly one neuron affects another. Researchers now believe that glial cells coordinate the activity of vast sets of brain circuits (Halassa & Haydon, 2010; Hamilton & Attwell, 2010). In addition, glial cells can prod neurons to form additional synapses (Mauch et al., 2001; Pfrieger, 2002; Ullian et al., 2001).

Glial Networks: Another Way to Think and Feel? Glial cells do not produce action potentials; you will never hear about a glial cell "firing." Instead, these cells communicate by passing chemicals directly through their walls to adjoining glia or by

Agonist A chemical that mimics the effects of a neurotransmitter by activating a type of receptor.

Selective serotonin-reuptake inhibitor (SSRI) A chemical that blocks the reuptake of the neurotransmitter serotonin.

Antagonist A chemical that blocks the effect of a neurotransmitter.

Glial cell A type of cell that helps neurons to form both synapses and connections when the brain is developing, influences the communication among neurons, and generally helps in the "care and feeding" of neurons.

49

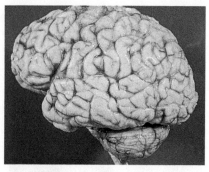

Most of your brain is water; the average brain weighs about 3 pounds, but if the water were removed, it would weigh only 10 ounces. The remaining substances (which include proteins and fats, as well as various types of ions) are the parts of the neurons, glial cells, and everything else that gives the brain a structure.

Source: Photo Researchers, Inc.

✓●─Study and Review on
mypsychlab.com

releasing (into brain fluid that surrounds the cells) molecules that affect both neurons and other glia. Chemicals released by one glial cell can induce other glial cells to release chemicals and so on, "like ripples on a pond" (Fields & Stevens-Graham, 2002). Researchers do not yet understand exactly what these glial networks do, but they have found that glia are important in a remarkably wide range of brain functions (Blalock et al., 2003; Cotter et al., 2001; Lonky, 2003; Watkins et al., 2001). For example, glial cells appear to play a role in drug addiction (Miguel-Hidalgo, 2009) and in controlling the 24-hour internal clock that governs daily night/day rhythms (Suh & Jackson, 2007).

LOOKING BACK

1. **How do neurons work?** Neurons receive input—from other neurons or from sensory organs—on either their dendrites or their cell bodies. If the sum of all the inputs is strong enough, an action potential is initiated, sending a rapid exchange of ions across the cell membrane. This exchange of ions works its way down the axon, until the terminal buttons release a neurotransmitter (a chemical signal). This neurotransmitter typically crosses the synaptic cleft to the dendrite or cell body of another neuron.

2. **How do chemicals allow neurons to communicate?** The dendrites and cell bodies of neurons have receptors, which are like locks that can be opened by certain keys; the keys are the neurotransmitters. Depending on the properties of the particular receptors, the neurotransmitters can excite the neuron to fire or inhibit it from firing. Agonists mimic the action of neurotransmitters, whereas antagonists block their effects.

The Nervous System: An Orchestra with Many Members

Consider some additional problems experienced by the young soldier who was poisoned while taking a shower. When researchers showed him a blue page on which white letters were printed, he thought he was looking at a "beach scene"—the blue was water, and the white letters were "people seen on the beach from an airplane." His doctors found that he could be trained to name a few everyday objects by sight as children are taught to recognize words by sight without actually reading them—as is encouraged on *Sesame Street*—but this training broke down when the color or size of the objects changed. For instance, the young man learned to name a red toothbrush as "toothbrush," but he couldn't properly name a green toothbrush, and when he was shown a red pencil, he called it "my toothbrush."

The results of the entire series of tests made it clear that the soldier could see and understand color and size but not shape. He had *some* sense of shape, though; he called the pencil a "toothbrush," not a "shoe" or a "basketball." To understand what had gone wrong in the soldier's brain, you need to need to know what the different parts of the nervous system do.

The nervous system has two major parts: (1) the *central nervous system* and (2) the *peripheral nervous system*. We will start with the simpler peripheral nervous system, which is crucial for getting information into and out of the brain, and then turn to a very general overview of the central nervous system, which consists of the brain and the spinal cord. ●►─Simulate

⊙►─Simulate the Organization
of the Nervous System on
mypsychlab.com

LOOKING AHEAD Learning Objectives

1. What two parts make up the peripheral nervous system, and what role does each part play?

2. How do the brain and spinal cord work together?

The Peripheral Nervous System: A Moving Story

The **peripheral nervous system (PNS)** allows the brain both to affect the organs of the body and to receive information from them. As shown in Figure 6, the PNS has two parts: the *autonomic nervous system* and the *sensory-somatic nervous system*.

The Autonomic Nervous System

The **autonomic nervous system (ANS)** controls the smooth muscles in the body and some glandular functions, as well as many of the body's self-regulating activities, such as digestion and circulation. Smooth muscles, so called because they look smooth under a microscope, are found in the heart, blood vessels, stomach lining, and intestines. Many of the activities that the ANS controls, such as digestion and circulation, usually are not under conscious control (Goldstein, 2000). The ANS has two branches—which are often referred to as "nervous systems" in their own right—the *sympathetic* and *parasympathetic nervous systems*.

THE SYMPATHETIC BRANCH OF THE ANS. The **sympathetic nervous system** readies an animal (including you and the authors of this book) to cope with an emergency, such as a near accident when you are driving in heavy traffic. When this system operates, more oxygen flows into your muscles, your vision is improved, and the rest of your body is ready to support physical exertion.

Specifically, the sympathetic nervous system speeds up the heart, increases the breathing rate to provide more oxygen, dilates the pupils for greater light sensitivity and thus sharper vision, produces a small amount of sweat (giving your hand a better grip), decreases salivation, inhibits stomach activity, and relaxes the bladder. If your heart is

Peripheral nervous system (PNS)
The autonomic nervous system and the sensory-somatic nervous system.

Autonomic nervous system (ANS)
Controls the smooth muscles in the body, some glandular functions, and many of the body's self-regulating activities, such as digestion and circulation.

Sympathetic nervous system Part of the autonomic nervous system that readies an animal to fight or to flee by speeding up the heart, increasing breathing rate to deliver more oxygen, dilating the pupils, producing sweat, decreasing salivation, inhibiting activity in the stomach, and relaxing the bladder.

FIGURE 6 Major Parts of the Nervous System

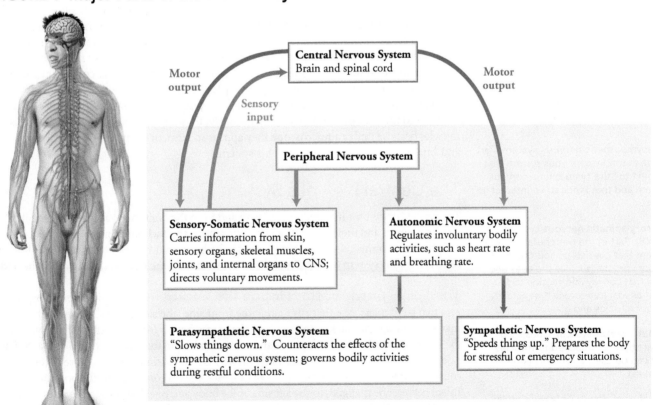

The peripheral nervous system (PNS) is composed of the sensory-somatic nervous system (SSNS) and the autonomic nervous system (ANS). The two major branches of the ANS are the sympathetic and parasympathetic nervous systems. In general, the sympathetic nervous system prepares the body to fight or flee, and the parasympathetic dampens down the sympathetic nervous system.

Source: From Goodenough, Judith A., McGuire, Betty A., Wallace, Robert A., *Biology of Humans: Concepts, Applications and Issues*, 1st edition, © 2005, Figure 8.10. Adapted by Permission of Pearson Education, Inc., Upper Saddle River, NJ.

pounding, your palms are sweaty, and your mouth is dry, it's a good bet that your sympathetic system has kicked in.

The sympathetic nervous system is often activated in *fight-or-flight* situations, in which you must decide whether to fight or flee, but these are not the only conditions that activate the sympathetic nervous system. This system also operates in circumstances that may be less extreme but nonetheless threatening or stressful, such as getting ready to give an important speech, having a conversation with an irritable authority figure, or rushing to avoid being late for an important meeting. People prone to feeling excessive amounts of anxiety tend to have sympathetic nervous systems that are overly active and get the body too revved up. Such people might hyperventilate (that is, breathe in too much oxygen), sweat profusely, or experience a pounding heart when there is no apparent threat. These and other unpleasant physical symptoms of anxiety occur whenever the sympathetic nervous system responds too strongly.

THE PARASYMPATHETIC BRANCH OF THE ANS.   The other branch of the ANS is called the **parasympathetic nervous system**; this system lies, figuratively, "next to" the sympathetic system (*para* is Greek for "next to" or "alongside") and tends to counteract its effects (see Figure 6). The sympathetic nervous system speeds things up, and the parasympathetic nervous system slows them down. For example, after you have a near collision in heavy traffic, you might pull over to the side of the road because your heart is pounding and you've broken into a sweat; it's your parasympathetic system that will allow you to calm down so that you will soon be in full control of yourself. The parasympathetic system slows heart rate, contracts the pupils, increases salivation, stimulates digestion, and contracts the bladder. Whereas the sympathetic nervous system tends to affect all the organs at the same time and can be thought of as increasing arousal in general, the parasympathetic nervous system tends to affect organs one at a time or in small groups.

The Sensory-Somatic Nervous System

To allow us to function in the world, the brain needs both to receive information from the body and the outside world and to be able to act on such information. The part of the PNS that receives such information and enables you to act on it is the **sensory-somatic nervous system (SSNS)**; the SSNS includes (a) the neurons in our sensory organs (such as the eyes and ears) that convey information to the brain and (b) neurons that trigger muscles and glands.

The SSNS includes the **somatic motor system**, which consists of nerves that are attached to muscles that can be used voluntarily; these muscles are also known as striated muscles because under a microscope they appear *striated*, or striped. If you clench your fist and "make a muscle," you are using this system.

The Central Nervous System

The largest conduit for information going to and from the brain is the **spinal cord**, the flexible rope of neurons and their connections that runs inside the backbone, or *spinal column*. In fact, so intimately connected is the spinal cord to the brain that the two together are called the **central nervous system (CNS)**. The PNS, in contrast, links the CNS to the organs of the body.

The Spinal Cord: Getting Inside the Backbone

The spinal cord is organized into two large tracts, one that runs along the front side (the side that faces forward) and one that runs along the back side (the side that faces backward). The tract that runs along the front side sends the brain's commands to the body, and the tract that runs along the back side registers information about the body (as well as information from the sense of touch) and conveys that to the brain. At each of 31 places, each tract is connected to the body by a pair of spinal nerves, one that goes to the left side of the body and one that goes to the right side.

The spinal cord isn't simply a set of cables that relays commands and information between brain and body. The spinal cord itself can initiate some aspects of our behavior, such as reflexes. A **reflex** is an automatic behavioral response to an event, an action that does not require thought. Although some reflexes (such as the kicking response that occurs when you are tapped right below your kneecap) involve only a few neurons, most reflexes require hundreds of neurons. How do reflexes work? When *sensory receptors* (which are types of cells, so named because they are activated by appropriate sensory stimulation) in

Parasympathetic nervous system Part of the autonomic nervous system that is "next to" the sympathetic nervous system and that tends to counteract its effects.

Sensory-somatic nervous system (SSNS) Part of the peripheral nervous system that consists of neurons in the sensory organs (such as the eyes and ears) that convey information to the brain as well as neurons that actually trigger muscles and glands.

Somatic motor system Consists of nerves that are attached to muscles that can be used voluntarily (striated muscles).

Spinal cord The flexible rope of neurons and their connections that runs inside the backbone (spinal column).

Central nervous system (CNS) The spinal cord and the brain.

Reflex An automatic behavioral response to an event.

the skin detect a sharp thorn, for example, they send signals that stimulate sensory neurons in the spinal cord (located at the back side of the cord). These neurons in turn are connected to interneurons in the spinal cord. When you jerk away from something that pricks you, interneurons have sent signals to motor neurons, which then cause the muscles to jerk, pulling your finger away from the source of pain. This arrangement allows you to respond immediately, bypassing the brain—it wouldn't be efficient or safe to have to think through what to do every time you encountered a harmful stimulus.

If the point of reflexes is to get things done in a hurry, why aren't the sensory neurons usually connected directly to motor neurons? Why the intermediary? Because interneurons provide a particular benefit: They allow the brain to send signals to *prevent* a reflex response. Ordinarily, if you pick up something that pricks your finger, you will jerk your hand away from it. But perhaps you are handing a beautiful red rose to a good friend as a gift and accidentally prick your finger. Instead of flinging the rose away, you grit your teeth and continue to hold it. You are able to do this because the part of your brain that is involved in formulating goals and intentions knows not to flub this gesture and sends a signal to the interneurons to stop the motor neurons from firing.

The Visible Brain: Lobes and Landmarks

As important as the spinal cord is, the brain governs the vast majority of human abilities. In this section, we turn to the other part of the central nervous system, the brain itself.

Imagine that you could see through someone's hair and scalp, even through the skull itself. The first thing you would see under the skull are the **meninges**, three protective layered membranes that cover the brain (*meningitis* is an inflammation of these membranes). Under these lies a network of blood vessels on the surface of the brain itself. Viewing the brain from above—looking down through the top of the head—you can see that the brain is divided into two halves, left and right, separated by a deep crease down the middle. Each half-brain is called a **cerebral hemisphere** (*cerebrum* is Latin for "brain") because each is shaped roughly like half a sphere. Curiously, each hemisphere receives information from, and controls the muscles of, the opposite side of the body. For example, if you are right-handed, your left hemisphere controls your right hand as you write.

As noted in Figure 7, each hemisphere is divided into four major parts, or **lobes**:

- the *occipital* lobe, at the back of the brain;
- the *temporal* lobe, below the temples, in front of the ears;

> **THINK like a PSYCHOLOGIST** Try this: Sit down on a chair or couch. Bend your knee and gently tap the lower part of your knee until a tap leads at a reflex—your lower leg lifts; your doctor may have done this to you during a check-up. This is called the patellar reflex. Once you've found the right spot, try it again, this time trying to suppress or prevent the reflex. Can you?

Meninges Three protective layered membranes that cover the brain.

Cerebral hemisphere A left or right half-brain, shaped roughly like half a sphere.

Lobes The four major parts of each cerebral hemisphere—occipital, temporal, parietal, and frontal; each lobe is present in each hemisphere.

FIGURE 7 The Lobes of the Brain

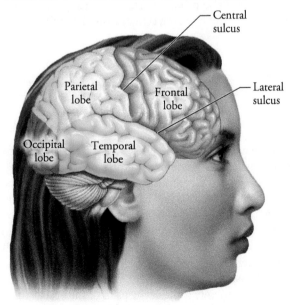

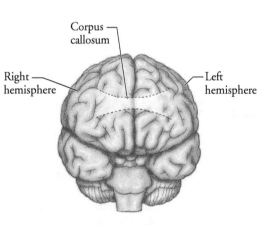

FRONTAL VIEW

The brain is divided into four major lobes—occipital, temporal, parietal, and frontal; each hemisphere has each of these four lobes. These lobes are named after the bones that cover them. The same major sulci (creases) and gyri (bulges) are evident on most brains.

- the *parietal* lobe, in the upper rear portion of the brain, above the occipital lobe; and
- the *frontal* lobe, in the front, behind the forehead.

The two halves of the brain are connected by a large bundle of axons (between 250 million and 300 million) referred to as the **corpus callosum** (some other smaller connections exist between the two halves of the brain, but they are less important).

Now, peer deeper. Immediately under the network of blood vessels on the surface of the brain is the convoluted, pinkish-gray outer layer of the brain itself: This is the **cerebral cortex** (*cortex* means "rind" or "shell" in Latin), and is where most mental processes arise. Although the cerebral cortex is only about 2 millimeters thick, it is brimming with the cell bodies of neurons, giving the cortex its characteristic color and its nickname, "gray matter." Looking directly at the surface of the brain, you can see that the cortex has many creases and bulges, as shown in Figure 7. The creases are called **sulci** (the singular is *sulcus*), and the areas that bulge up between the sulci are the **gyri** (singular, *gyrus*). The cortex, so vital to our functioning, is crumpled up so that more of it can be stuffed into the skull. **Subcortical** ("under the cortex") **structures** of the inner brain also contain gray matter and are very similar to structures in the brains of many nonhuman animals.

✔•—Study and Review on
mypsychlab.com

LOOKING BACK

1. **What two parts make up the peripheral nervous system, and what role does each part play?** The peripheral nervous system (PNS) has two parts: the autonomic nervous system (ANS) and the sensory-somatic nervous system (SSNS). The ANS controls the smooth muscles (like those of the heart) and some glands. The ANS has two branches: the sympathetic and parasympathetic nervous systems. The sympathetic nervous system readies you to cope with an emergency, whereas the parasympathetic nervous system brings you back to its normal state after having been aroused. In contrast, the SSNS deals with inputs from the world and voluntary control of muscles.

2. **How do the brain and spinal cord work together?** The brain and spinal cord together make up the central nervous system (CNS). The spinal cord is the largest conduit for information going to and from the brain. The tract on the front side of the spinal cord sends the brain's commands to the body and thus allows us to move in coordinated ways. The tract on the back side of the spinal cord conveys information about the body to the brain. The spinal cord also produces reflexes, which are triggered automatically when specific stimuli are present; however, signals from the brain often can inhibit these reflexes.

Corpus callosum The large bundle of axons that connects the two halves of the brain.

Cerebral cortex The convoluted pinkish-gray outer layer of the brain where most mental processes arise.

Subcortical structures Parts of the brain located under the cerebral cortex.

Sulcus A crease in the cerebral cortex.

Gyrus A bulge between sulci in the cerebral cortex.

Brain system A set of brain circuits that work together to accomplish a particular task.

Spotlight on the Brain: How It Divides and Conquers

Testing revealed that the soldier did not have a problem with his PNS. The neural signals from his eyes were sent on to his brain. His problem was more subtle and could be diagnosed only by considering the specific functions accomplished by different parts of the brain. Even though visual perception—how we perceive and make sense of what our eyes "see"—intuitively might seem to be a single ability, it is in fact accomplished by many separate *brain systems*; a **brain system** is a set of brain circuits that work together to accomplish a particular task. The brain is a master at the strategy of divide and conquer: It takes all complex activities and breaks them into a set of relatively simple tasks, and a different brain system usually tackles each task.

The soldier's problem arose from damage to only some of the parts of the brain, which disrupted only some aspects of his visual abilities. To understand what went wrong after his accident, we need to delve into the brain in more detail, appreciating how it divides and conquers the challenges of daily life.

1. What are the major regions of the cortex, and what do they do?
2. How do the functions of the two sides of the brain differ?
3. What parts of the brain lie under the cerebral cortex? What do these subcortical structures do?
4. What are the neuroendocrine and neuroimmune systems, and what do they have in common?

The Cerebral Cortex: The Seat of the Mind

Although the various parts of the brain typically work in concert with one another, some functions are largely carried out in particular regions. In the following sections, we consider distinct forms of mental activity that arise in each of the four lobes of the brain.

Occipital Lobes: Looking Good The **occipital lobes**, located at the back of the head, are concerned entirely with different aspects of vision. Most of the signals from the eyes arrive at these lobes (Brewer et al., 2002; Simos, 2001). If somebody were to hit you in the back of the head with a brick (an experiment we do not recommend), the "stars" you would likely see would appear because the impact triggers random firings of neurons in this area. The occipital lobes contain many separate areas that work together to characterize properties of viewed objects—such as their shape, color, and motion. Damage to these lobes results in partial or complete blindness. Because each half of the brain receives sensory information from the opposite side of space, if a surgeon has to remove the left occipital lobe (perhaps to take out a brain tumor), the patient will not be able to see things to his or her right side when looking ahead.

Because some of the neurons in the occipital lobes are highly active, they require more oxygen than other neurons—which makes them particularly vulnerable to poisoning by carbon monoxide. Carbon monoxide will take the place of oxygen in the blood, but this substance cannot be used in metabolism; thus, if someone breathes enough carbon monoxide, neurons in the occipital lobes are suffocated to death because they don't get enough oxygen. However, typically, not *all* the neurons will die after carbon monoxide poisoning, and thus the person is not completely blind but rather has highly impaired vision. Specifically, the damage makes the entire world seem fuzzy, and the victim cannot easily organize visual information. Our young soldier probably suffered damage to the occipital lobes, but this probably does not sufficiently explain all of the soldier's vision problems–if this were all there was to it, why would he confuse white letters with sunbathers on the beach?

Temporal Lobes: Up to Their Ears in Work The **temporal lobes**, which lie in front of the ears, play a key role in processing sound, entering new information into memory, storing visual memories, and comprehending language (Hart et al., 2003; Sekiyama et al., 2003; Witter et al., 2002). The soldier may have had damage in either one or both temporal lobes or in the connections from the occipital lobes to the temporal lobes. If the connections were damaged, only a small amount of information from the occipital lobe might reach the part of the temporal lobes where visual memories of shapes are stored and compared to visual signals from the eyes (allowing you to recognize stimuli). A diagnosis of damaged connections between the occipital and temporal lobes could go a long way toward explaining his problems. For example, when looking at a letter, he could not register the entire pattern at once (this would be too much information to process, given his brain damage); thus, he might look at one segment at a time (a vertical line, then a curved line, and so on), which isn't good enough to recognize the shape of a letter as a whole. The world might look to the soldier like the images in Figure 8 on the top of the next page.

Occipital lobes The brain lobes at the back of the head; concerned entirely with different aspects of vision.

Temporal lobes The brain lobes under the temples, in front of the ears; among its many functions are processing sound, entering new information into memory, storing visual memories, and comprehending language.

FIGURE 8 Shattered Vision

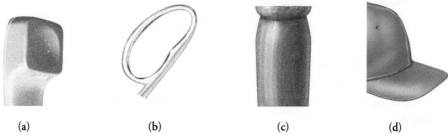

(a)	(b)	(c)	(d)

Answers: a. telephone receiver b. scissors handle c. table leg d. baseball hat

Some forms of brain damage may lead the victims to be aware of only small fragments of objects at a time, as shown here. If all you were aware of were fragments of an object, how easily do you think you could identify it? To get a sense of what such a deficit would be like, try to identify these common objects when all you have to go on are individual parts.

Parietal Lobes: Inner Space When you recall where you left your keys, how to get to a friend's house, or think about what's behind you, your **parietal lobes** are at work (Siegel et al., 2003). Right now, your parietal lobes are playing a role in allowing you to know the distance between your face and this book and to shift attention from one word to the next as you read this sentence; they are even helping control your eye movements. The parietal lobes are also involved when you do arithmetic, indicating the values of numbers by using a kind of "mental number line" to indicate quantity (Göbel et al., 2006).

The parietal lobes also play a key role in the sense of touch. Part of each parietal lobe, just behind the central sulcus (see Figure 9), is the gyrus referred to as the **somatosensory strip**. This gyrus registers the sensations on the body (rubs, scrapes, tickles, and so forth). In fact, sensations from each part of the body are registered in a specific section of this strip of cortex. Tickling your toes, for example, activates neurons in the gyrus next to the area activated by rubbing your ankle, as you can see in Figure 9. Larger areas of this gyrus

FIGURE 9 The Organization of the Somatosensory Strip

Parietal lobes The brain lobes at the top, rear of the brain; among their functions are attention, arithmetic, touch, and registering spatial location.

Somatosensory strip The gyrus immediately behind the central sulcus; it registers sensations on the body and is organized by body part.

Frontal lobes The brain lobes located behind the forehead; critically involved in planning, memory search, motor control, speech control, reasoning, and emotions.

Motor strip The gyrus immediately in front of the central sulcus; it controls fine movements and is organized by body part. It is also called *primary motor cortex*.

Split-brain patient A person whose corpus callosum has been severed for medical reasons, so that neural signals no longer pass from one cerebral hemisphere to the other.

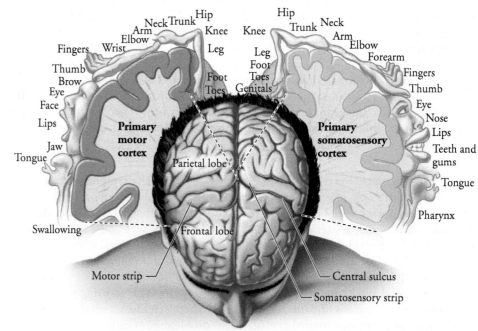

The somatosensory strip is organized so that different parts of the body are registered by adjacent portions of cortex in the gyrus; the size of the body part in this illustration indicates the amount of cortex dedicated to that part.

Source: From Goodenough, Judith A., McGuire, Betty A., Wallace, Robert A., *Biology of Humans: Concepts, Applications and Issues*, 1st edition, © 2005, Figure 8.7. Adapted by Permission of Pearson Education, Inc., Upper Saddle River, NJ.

correspond to areas of the body that are more sensitive (notice the amount of space devoted to lips and hands).

Frontal Lobes: Leaders of the Pack

The size and development of the *frontal lobes*, in conjunction with their plentiful connections to other areas, are features of the brain that make us uniquely human (Goldberg, 2001). Probably the most dramatic difference between the appearance of a human brain and a monkey brain is how much the human brain bulges out in front. The **frontal lobes**, located behind the forehead, are critically involved in planning, the search for specific memories, motor control, speech control, reasoning (including the use of memory in reasoning), and emotions. These crucial lobes each also contain the gyrus referred to as the **motor strip** (also called the *primary motor cortex*); as shown in Figure 9, it is located immediately in front of the central sulcus. The motor strip controls fine movements and, just like the somatosensory strip, is organized in terms of parts of the body. Relatively large areas of this strip of cortex are dedicated to those parts of the body that we control with precision, such as the hands and mouth.

Hints about the functions of the frontal lobes, as well as other parts of the brain, have emerged from studies of patients with brain damage. Phineas Gage, the foreman of a gang of workers building a railroad in Vermont late in the 19th century, is perhaps the most famous case of a patient with damage to the frontal lobes. The story began when Gage became distracted as he was packing blasting powder into a hole in a rock. When the metal bar he was using to pack in the powder accidentally hit the rock, it created a spark that set off the powder. The metal bar, like a spear shot from a cannon, went right through the front part of his head, flew high in the air, and landed about 30 meters behind him. Miraculously, Gage lived—but he was a changed man. Previously, he had been responsible and organized; afterward he led a disorderly life. He couldn't stick to any decision, he had little self-control, and his formerly decent language became laced with profanity (Macmillan, 1986, 1992). Like Phineas Gage, other people with damage to the frontal regions of the brain have difficulty reasoning, may have trouble controlling their emotions, and may have changed personalities.

The Dual Brain: Thinking with Both Barrels

The cortices (the plural of cortex) of the two cerebral hemispheres—left and right—play distinct roles in thinking, feeling, and behaving (Hugdahl & Davidson, 2003). What do the hemispheres do differently?

Split-Brain Research: A Deep Disconnect

The most compelling evidence to date that the two half-brains perform distinct functions has come from looking at the effects of severing the major connection between the two hemispheres—the corpus callosum. When this is done, almost no neural impulses pass from one cerebral hemisphere to the other. A patient who has undergone this surgery is called a **split-brain patient** (Zaidel & Iacoboni, 2003). Why would such drastic surgery be performed? This procedure has been used to help patients with severe, otherwise untreatable epilepsy. *Epilepsy* is a disease that causes massive uncontrolled neural firing in parts of the brain, leading to bodily convulsions; in severe form, it prevents sufferers from leading a normal life. When the epilepsy engages the entire brain and is so severe that drugs cannot control it, surgeons may cut the corpus callosum. This operation prevents the spasm of neural firing that originates in one hemisphere from reaching the other hemisphere, and thus the whole brain does not become involved in the convulsions—and their severity is thereby lessened.

Although it is easy to see how cutting the corpus callosum would decrease the severity of epileptic convulsions, to understand the full effects of this surgical procedure on mental processes, we need to understand how the eyes are connected to the brain. As shown in Figure 10, the *left half* of each eye sends signals to the left hemisphere but not to the right hemisphere; similarly, the *right half* of each eye sends signals to the right hemisphere. (Note that it's not that the left *eye* sends signals to the left hemisphere and that the right *eye* sends signals to the right hemisphere.) Thus, if you stare straight ahead, objects to the left are seen first by the right brain, and those to the right are seen first by the left brain. Normally, this information quickly crosses over to the other hemisphere, so the entire

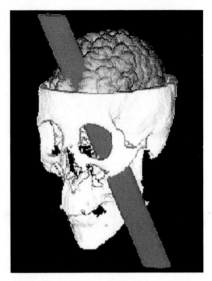

A computer-reconstructed picture of the path taken by the metal bar as it passed through Phineas Gage's skull.

Source: Damasio H, Grabowski T, Frank R, Galaburda AM, Damasio AR: The return of Phineas Gage: Clues about the brain from a famous patient. *Science*, 264: 1102–1105, 1994. Department of Neurology and Image Analysis Facility, University of Iowa.

FIGURE 10 The Eyes, Optic Nerves, and Cerebral Hemispheres

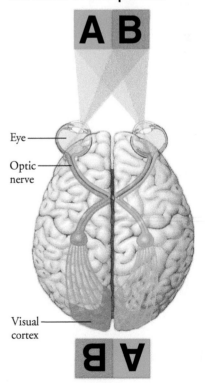

The left half of each eye is connected only to the left cerebral hemisphere, whereas the right half of each eye is connected only to the right cerebral hemisphere.

FIGURE 11 Gazzaniga and LeDoux Experiment

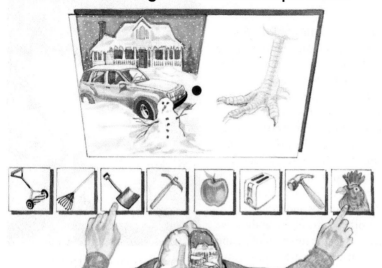

The right hemisphere of split-brain patients is capable of understanding and responding to simple stimuli but not speaking about them. Thus, the left hemisphere will sometimes make up stories to explain actions controlled by the right hemisphere.

Source: From Gazzaniga, M.S. and LeDoux, J.E., *The Integrated Mind.* New York: Plenum Press, 1978. Reprinted with kind permission from Springer Science and Business Media.

brain receives signals from both halves of each eye. However, when the corpus callosum is cut, the signal stays in the hemisphere that initially receives the information.

The two cerebral hemispheres have some different functions. One way that differences were discovered involves presenting pictures or words only to the left or right side of space when a split-brain patient was staring straight ahead. (This presentation must be done so quickly that the participant doesn't have time to move his or her eyes to look directly at the stimuli.) In a classic study of this type, illustrated in Figure 11, Gazzaniga and LeDoux (1978) presented a picture of a snow scene to the right hemisphere (which controls the left hand) and, at the same time, a picture of a chicken's claw to the left hemisphere (which controls the right hand and, usually, speech). The split-brain patient was then shown several other pictures and asked to choose which of them is related in some way to the initial set of stimuli. The patient used his right hand (controlled by the left hemisphere) to select a picture of a chicken and his left hand (controlled by the right hemisphere) to select a picture of a shovel. The investigators then asked the patient what he had seen. "I saw a claw, and I picked a chicken," he replied. Because the left hemisphere controls almost all speech, it described what the left hemisphere saw. However, the surprising result was that the patient continued, saying, "And you have to clean out the chicken shed with a shovel." The left hemisphere did not actually know what the right hemisphere had seen, so it made up a story! The left hemisphere, in right-handed people (and most left-handed people), not only controls most aspects of language but also plays a crucial role in making up stories, in interpreting the world, and in many forms of reasoning (Gazzaniga, 1995; LeDoux et al., 1977). The right hemisphere, in contrast, generally plays a larger role than the left in spatial attention and in processing nonverbal cues (such as emotional tone of voice; Voyer et al., 2009).

Hemispheric Specialization: Not Just for the Deeply Disconnected It's often said that the left brain is verbal and analytical, whereas the right brain is perceptual and intuitive. But these simple generalizations are not accurate. For example, the left brain is actually better than the right at some aspects of interpreting sensory information (such as determining whether one object is above or below another; Hellige & Michimata, 1989; Kosslyn, 2006; Kosslyn et al., 1989; Laeng et al., 2003), and the right brain is better than the left at some aspects of language (such as making the pitch of the voice rise at the end of a question or understanding humor; Bihrle et al., 1986; Brownell et al., 1984; Ellis & Young, 1987).

When the hemispheres differ in their functions, they typically differ in their abilities to perform very narrow, specific tasks (such as the one we just noted: making the pitch of the voice rise at the end of a question). If such very specific abilities were impaired by the carbon monoxide poisoning, this might underlie part of the young soldier's difficulties in recognizing shapes. The right temporal lobe, in particular, appears to play a key role in recognizing overall shapes (Ivry & Robertson, 1998). If the relevant parts of the right temporal lobe were damaged, the soldier would have had to rely on his left temporal lobe, which tends to register details only, not overall shape.

Beneath the Cortex: The Inner Brain

The *subcortical* parts of the brain, situated deep beneath the cortex, carry out many crucial tasks that affect every moment of our lives. For example, although the examiners of the young soldier did not mention it, the soldier was probably sluggish after his accident—as is typical of people who have suffered brain damage. But why would brain damage cause

FIGURE 12 Key Subcortical Brain Areas

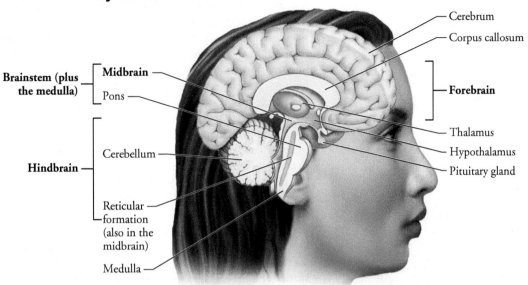

Many of the parts of the brain needed for day-to-day living are located beneath the cortex, such as those illustrated here.

Source: From Goodenough, Judith A., McGuire, Betty A., Wallace, Robert A., *Biology of Humans: Concepts, Applications and Issues,* 1st edition, © 2005, Figure 7.2. Adapted by Permission of Pearson Education, Inc., Upper Saddle River, NJ.

someone to be less vigorous? The answer lies in the connections between the cortex and inner parts of the brain that are concerned with motivation and emotion. The most important of these subcortical areas are illustrated in Figure 12.

Together with the cortex, the thalamus, limbic system, and basal ganglia are considered to be part of the **forebrain** (so called because in four-legged animals such as cats and rats, these areas are at the front); but given their great variety of function, this historical category is not very useful, and we mention it now only because the term is still occassionally used.

Thalamus: Crossroads of the Brain
The *thalamus* is often compared with a switching center, where messages are received and redirected to the appropriate destination—but it could also be likened to a airline hub where planes converge and then take off for far-flung destinations (see Figure 12). The sensory systems, such as that of vision and hearing, and the motor systems that control muscles have neural connections to the **thalamus**, which routes their signals to other parts of the brain. The thalamus is also involved in controlling sleep and in attention; as a matter of fact, at this very second, your thalamus is allowing you to fix your attention on each word you read. The thalamus plays such a critical role in daily life that if it is badly damaged, the patient will die, even if the rest of the brain remains untouched.

Hypothalamus: Thermostat and More
The **hypothalamus** sits under the thalamus, as illustrated in Figure 13. The small size of this structure shouldn't fool you: It is absolutely critical for controlling many bodily functions, such as eating and drinking; keeping body temperature, blood pressure, and heart rate within the proper limits; and governing sexual behavior (Swaab, 2003). The hypothalamus also regulates hormones, such as those that prepare an animal to fight or to flee when confronted by danger. If visual recognition is impaired, as in the case of our young soldier, the hypothalamus will not receive the information it needs to function properly. If confronted by an enemy in the field, the soldier would not be able to register the information required to cause the right chemicals to flow into his bloodstream to marshal the body's resources for fight or flight.

Hippocampus: Remember It
The **hippocampus** plays a key role in allowing us to enter new information into the brain's memory banks (Gluck & Myers, 2000; Squire & Schacter, 2002). The hippocampus looks something like a seahorse (at least to some

Forebrain According to a historical way of organizing brain structures, a unit of the brain that includes the cortex, thalamus, limbic system, and basal ganglia.

Thalamus A subcortical structure that receives signals from sensory and motor systems and plays a crucial role in attention, sleep, and other functions critical to daily life; often thought of as a switching center.

Hypothalamus A brain structure that sits under the thalamus and plays a central role in controlling eating and drinking and in regulating the body's temperature, blood pressure, heart rate, sexual behavior, and hormones.

Hippocampus A subcortical structure that plays a key role in allowing new information to be stored in the brain's memory banks.

FIGURE 13 The Limbic System

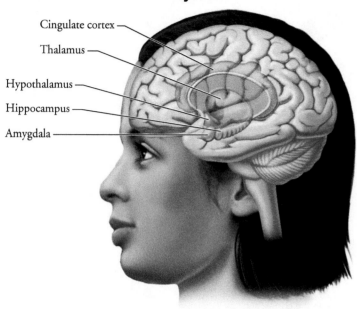

Cingulate cortex

Thalamus

Hypothalamus

Hippocampus

Amygdala

These are the key structures that make up the limbic system, which plays a role in emotion, motivation, and other psychological events.

Source: From Goodenough, Judith A., McGuire, Betty A., Wallace, Robert A., *Biology of Humans: Concepts, Applications and Issues,* 1st edition, © 2005, Figure 8.8. Adapted by Permission of Pearson Education, Inc., Upper Saddle River, NJ.

Amygdala A subcortical structure that plays a special role in fear and is involved in other types of strong emotions, such as anger.

Limbic system A set of brain areas, including the hippocampus, amygdala, hypothalamus, and other areas, that has long been thought of as being involved in key aspects of emotion and motivation, namely, those underlying fighting, fleeing, feeding, and sex.

Basal ganglia Subcortical structures that play a role in planning, learning new habits, and producing movement.

people—see Figure 13), hence its name, from the Greek *hippokampos,* a mythological "seahorse" monster. The role of the hippocampus was vividly illustrated by the case of H.M., who had his hippocampus (and nearby portions of the brain) removed in an effort to control his epilepsy. After the operation, his doctors noticed something unexpected: H.M. could no longer learn new facts (Milner et al., 1968). His memory for events that occurred a year or so before the operation seemed normal, but he was stuck at that stage of his life. In fact, he could not even remember what had happened a few minutes ago, let alone hours or days. H.M. does not seem particularly aware of his deficit, and when one of the authors of this book interviewed him years after the operation, he was in good spirits and relaxed. When asked about the meanings of words that were coined after his operation, he gamely offered definitions, suggesting, for example, that a *Jacuzzi* is a "new kind of dance." He didn't seem to notice what was missing in his life. (Perhaps this is a case of the left hemisphere telling stories to fill in gaps, as we noted when discussing the Gazzaniga and LeDoux study of a split-brain patient.)

Patients such as H.M. led researchers eventually to discover that although the hippocampus itself does not permanently store memories, it triggers processes that store new information elsewhere in the brain. The young soldier did not seem to have problems storing new information in memory, and hence his hippocampus probably operated normally.

Amygdala: Inner Feelings The **amygdala,** an almond-shaped structure (its name means "almond" in ancient Greek) near the hippocampus, plays a special role in strong emotions such as fear and anger (Morris & Dolan, 2002). It also affects whether a person can correctly interpret emotions in facial expressions (Adolphs et al., 1996). The hypothalamus and amygdala play crucial roles as bridges between the CNS and the PNS. The hippocampus, amygdala, and hypothalamus are also key components of the **limbic system,** shown in Figure 13. The limbic system has long been thought of as being involved in critical aspects of emotion and motivation, namely, those that underlie fighting, fleeing, feeding, and sex. Although each of the structures in the limbic system is involved in at least some of these four functions, each structure is now known to have additional roles that do not involve these functions (for example, the hippocampus is crucially important in storing new memories). Furthermore, other brain structures, not in the limbic system, also play important roles in emotion and motivation (LeDoux, 1996).

Basal Ganglia: More Than Habit Forming Positioned on the outer sides of the thalami (plural for thalamus—one in each hemisphere) are the **basal ganglia,** which are involved in planning and producing movement (Iansek & Porter, 1980). (Each of these structures itself has several clearly defined parts, and hence "ganglia"—the plural of "ganglion"—is used to refer to them.) The basal ganglia also play a central role in a particular type of learning: forming a habit. When you learn to put your foot on a car's brake automatically at a red light, the basal ganglia are busy connecting the neural signals produced when you see the stimulus (the light) with the parts of the brain that produce your response (moving your foot). This system is distinct from the one used to learn facts (the one that, presumably, is at work right now as you read this page). The basal ganglia rely crucially on dopamine, and hence it is not surprising that people with Parkinson's disease—which involves low levels of this neurotransmitter—often have abnormal functioning of their basal ganglia.

Dopamine is also crucial for the operation of the *nucleus accumbens,* which is sometimes considered part of the basal ganglia; the nucleus accumbens plays a key role in the brain's response to reward (Hall et al., 2001; Tzschentke & Schmidt, 2000) and in the anticipation of reward (Knutson et al., 2001; Pagnoni et al., 2002). Indeed, drugs such as cocaine, amphetamines, and alcohol have their effects in part because they engage the nucleus accumbens (Dackis & O'Brien, 2001; Robbins & Everitt, 1999; Vinar, 2001).

Brainstem: The Brain's Wake-Up Call

As illustrated in Figure 12, at the base of the brain are structures that feed into, and receive information from, the spinal cord. These structures are often collectively called the **brainstem**. The **medulla**, at the lowest part of the lower brainstem (see Figure 12), is important in the automatic control of breathing, swallowing, and blood circulation. The brainstem also contains a number of small structures, together called the **reticular formation**, which has two main parts. One part is the *reticular activating system*, which plays a key role in keeping you awake and making you perk up when something interesting happens. The soldier who suffered carbon monoxide poisoning would have been sluggish following damage to these structures. The other part of the reticular formation receives input from the hypothalamus and plays a key role in producing autonomic nervous system reactions. It is also involved in conducting impulses from muscles not under voluntary control to those under voluntary control (such as those used in swallowing and speech).

The **pons** (see Figure 12) is a bridge (*pons* is Latin for "bridge") connecting the medulla and the midbrain, and also connecting the upper parts of the brain to the cerebellum; it is involved with a variety of functions, ranging from the regulation of sleep to control of facial muscles.

Cerebellum: Walking Tall

The **cerebellum** is concerned in part with physical coordination, estimating time, and paying attention. If your cerebellum were damaged, you might walk oddly and have trouble standing normally and keeping an upright posture. If you ever see an aging prizefighter or former professional football player, look at his walk: You may notice that he seems to stumble and be unsteady. Too many blows to the head may have damaged his cerebellum, leading to a condition aptly described as being "punch-drunk." In addition, damage to some parts of the cerebellum can disrupt the ability to estimate time or to pay attention properly (Ivry & Spencer, 2004). The surface area of the cerebellum is nearly the same size as that of the entire cerebral cortex, and hence it will not be surprising if this structure turns out to be involved in many complex functions (Manto & Pandolfo, 2001).

We should also note, because you may sometimes see the terms, that the medulla, pons, cerebellum, and parts of the reticular formation have historically been grouped together as the **hindbrain** because they lie at the rear end of the brain of a four-legged animal. The remaining brainstem structures historically have been grouped to form the **midbrain**, which lies between the hindbrain and the forebrain (see Figure 12). However, this classification scheme—which also includes the forebrain, noted earlier—is now rarely used to describe the human brain.

The Neuroendocrine and Neuroimmune Systems: More Brain–Body Connections

Some of the subcortical structures we just considered play another important role: They allow the brain to communicate with the body. The brain has a total of four mechanisms that directly affect the body:

- *Somatic motor system.* As you now know, the somatic motor system affects the body by moving muscles voluntarily.
- *Autonomic nervous system.* The brain can influence the ANS, which—among other things—regulates involuntary muscles (such as those in the heart).
- *Hormones.* In addition, the brain produces hormones and controls the production of hormones elsewhere in the body.
- *Immune responses.* Finally, the brain affects our immune systems, making us more or less able to fight off the onslaught of disease and to repair damage to the body from injury.

Drugs such as cocaine, amphetamines, and alcohol have their effects in part because they engage the nucleus accumbens. This structure plays a crucial role in the brain's response to, and anticipation of, reward.

Source: Victoria Pearson/Taxi/Getty Images

Brainstem The set of structures at the base of the brain—including the midbrain, medulla, and pons—that feed into and receive information from the spinal cord.

Medulla The lowest part of the lower brainstem, which plays a central role in automatic control of breathing, swallowing, and blood circulation.

Reticular formation A collection of small structures in the brainstem, organized into two main parts: the reticular activating system and another part that is important in producing autonomic nervous system reactions.

Pons A bridge between the medulla and midbrain, which also connects the upper parts of the brain to the cerebellum.

Cerebellum A large structure at the base of the brain that is concerned in part with physical coordination, estimating time, and paying attention.

Hindbrain According to a historical way of organizing brain structures, a unit of the brain that includes the medulla, pons, cerebellum, and parts of the reticular formation.

Midbrain According to a historical way of organizing brain structures, a unit of the brain that includes parts of the reticular formation as well as the brainstem structures that lie between forebrain and hindbrain.

FIGURE 14 The Major Endocrine Glands

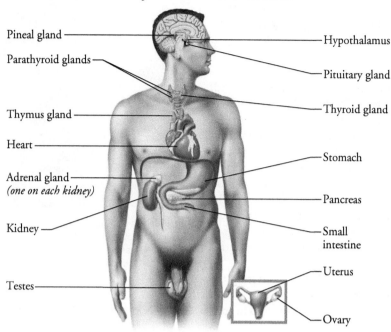

The locations of major endocrine glands in the body.

Hormone A chemical that is produced by a gland and can act as a neurotransmitter substance.

Neuroendocrine system The system that makes hormones that affect many bodily functions and that also provides the CNS with information.

Testosterone The hormone that causes males to develop facial hair and other external sexual characteristics, and to build up muscle volume.

Estrogen The hormone that causes girls to develop breasts and is involved in the menstrual cycle.

Cortisol A hormone produced by the outer layer of the adrenal glands that helps the body cope with the extra energy demands of stress.

Pituitary gland The "master gland" that regulates other glands but is itself controlled by the brain, primarily via connections from the hypothalamus.

Hypothalamic-pituitary-adrenal (HPA) axis The system of the hypothalamus, pituitary gland, and adrenal glands that is activated by stress, injury, and infection and that works to fight off infection.

We've already discussed the first two of these mechanisms; let's now consider the last two mechanisms, which rely in part on the deep brain structures just discussed.

The Neuroendocrine System: It's Hormonal! **Hormones** are chemicals that are produced by glands and can act as neurotransmitter substances, and hence they not only can affect organs of the body but also can affect thoughts, feelings, and behavior. For example, hormones released during puberty typically trigger an interest in sexuality activity. The **neuroendocrine system** makes hormones that affect many functions. The CNS not only regulates this system but also receives information from it—which in turn alters the way the CNS operates.

Figure 14 shows the locations of the major *endocrine glands*; endocrine glands secrete substances—including hormones—into the bloodstream (unlike other glands, such as sweat glands, that excrete substances outside the body). The hormones excreted by endocrine glands have numerous functions. For example, as we just noted, some hormones affect sexual development and functioning. Among these, **testosterone** causes boys to develop facial hair and other external sexual characteristics as well as to build up muscle volume. In contrast, **estrogen** causes girls to develop breasts and is involved in the menstrual cycle.

Other hormones play a crucial role in the fight-or-flight response. In particular, the outer layer of the adrenal glands (located on top of the kidneys) produces the hormone **cortisol**, which helps the body cope with the extra energy demands of stress. It does so by breaking down protein and fat and converting them to sugar (which provides energy to the body), increasing blood flow, and allowing the person to respond more vigorously and for a longer period of time. Cortisol production is triggered even by the sight of angry faces (van Honk et al., 2000).

The **pituitary gland**, located in the skull just behind the bridge of the nose, is particularly interesting because its hormones control the other endocrine glands; for this reason, it has sometimes been called the "master gland." But, master or not, this gland is still controlled by the brain, primarily via connections from the hypothalamus.

The Neuroimmune System: How the Brain Fights Disease The brain also affects our bodies in ways that help us fight disease and heal from wounds. In particular, the hypothalamus, the pituitary gland, and the adrenal glands form the **hypothalamic-pituitary-adrenal (HPA) axis**. This system is activated by infections and injury, which in turn leads it to regulate the white blood cells that are in the bloodstream, thus fighting the threat.

Psychological stress and pain also activate the HPA axis, which can backfire and actually be detrimental to health. The HPA axis operates partly by producing cortisol (via the adrenal glands), and if too much cortisol is produced, it can interfere with the immune system. Thus, being stressed out can make you more likely to catch a cold (Glaser & Kiecolt-Glaser, 1998), make you more vulnerable to bacterial infections (Bailey et al., 2003), and cause your wounds to take more time to heal (Marucha et al., 1998). Even worse than that, if cortisol is produced chronically, it can damage the brain—particularly the hippocampus. And such damage in turn will interfere with storing new information in memory. Thus, your mind affects your body and vice versa.

LOOKING AT LEVELS The Musical Brain

Source: Pablo Corral V/CORBIS All Rights Reserved; (inset) © Digital Art/ CORBIS All Rights Reserved

All human cultures have music. Why does music have its power over us? To begin to understand the psychology of music, we need to consider events at the different levels of analysis and how they interact.

First, the brain. A large network of different brain areas is activated when people listen to or play music (Baeck, 2002). For example, in one study researchers monitored brain activity while music students either played the right-hand piano part of a classical music piece or simply imagined playing the piece while keeping still (Meister et al., 2004). These researchers found very similar patterns of activation in a large part of the frontal and parietal lobes (in both hemispheres) while participants were actually playing and while imagining playing. But only during actual playing was the motor strip activated, and the parietal lobes were more strongly activated during actual playing (which probably reflects their role in specifying the spatial layout of the visible keyboard).

The appreciation and production of music arises from many different areas in the brain—and these brain areas play different roles. For example, damage to the upper parts of the temporal lobes, which process sound, can prevent people from distinguishing consonant (harmonious) from dissonant (clashing) sounds (Peretz et al., 2001). Damage to the left temporal-parietal region can disrupt the perception and production of rhythm while leaving perception and production of melody intact (Di Pietro et al., 2004). Researchers also found that in at least in one case, damage to the amygdala and a related brain area (the *insula*) led a patient to lose his emotional reactions to music; pieces that previously had sent a "shiver down his spine" no longer did so (Griffiths et al., 2004).

Music also affects events at the level of the person, including arousal level and mood. As anyone who has been to a rousing concert can attest, music clearly affects arousal— even among the elderly; when elderly participants listened to music they liked, they too felt energized (Hirokawa, 2004). Moreover, music not only can rev people up but also can reduce arousal (Pelletier, 2004) and can calm people who have experienced trauma and help them to cope with their difficulties (Baker, 2001). Music can also influence people's moods (Hunter et al., 2008; Winkelman, 2003), even people who have had brain damage (Magee & Davidson, 2002). However, these effects on mood depend in part on the nature of the music. One study, for example, found that listening to Mozart relaxed people more than did listening to New Age music (Smith & Joyce, 2004).

Further, events at the level of the group affect your preferred type of music. Consider that social factors may have led you to prefer one type of music over another: You probably have certain stereotypes about "people who like" classical music versus those who like hip-hop, heavy metal, country, or other genres of music (Rentfrow & Gosling, 2007). To the extent that you identify with the stereotypes associated with fans of one genre, you'll probably be drawn more to that type of music (Rentfrow et al., 2009). In turn, your friends probably like the type of music that you like (Miranda & Claes, 2009). Moreover, if and when you publicly express your taste in music (perhaps by wearing a T-shirt that has the name of your favorite performer), you are communicating to other people something about yourself—perhaps that you possess some of the stereotypical qualities of people who like that genre of music.

Finally, events at the different levels clearly interact. For instance, a rock concert is a social event, which can give an individual pleasure (at the level of the person), which in turn arises in part from being aroused—and arousal relies on events in the brain and body. And the thought of getting so excited may lead some people to want to attend a rock concert in the first place.

Moreover, such interactions are also present when it comes to making music. For example, if you are motivated (level of the person) to play music, perhaps because a teacher inspired you or others have appreciated your playing (level of the group), this activity may actually change your brain! Researchers have shown that part of the motor strip (in the right half of the brain, which controls the fingers of the left hand) is larger in orchestra members who play stringed instruments than in nonmusicians (Elber et al., 1995; Münte et al., 2001; Schlaug et al., 1995). In fact, professional keyboard players have more gray matter (cell bodies of neurons) in auditory and visual-spatial areas than do either amateur musicians or nonmusicians (Gaser & Schlaug, 2003)—and the more people practice, the larger the relevant areas tend to be.

In short, if you have musical talent and interest (characteristics at the level of the person) and have the opportunity to develop musical ability, your brain can be altered by the experience. And if others reward your playing (even if simply by their attention; the level of the group), you will be even more motivated to continue practicing—further changing your brain. And, once your brain is altered, your playing may improve—leading to more enjoyment and more praise from others.

✓•—Study and Review on
mypsychlab.com

LOOKING BACK

1. **What are the major regions of the cortex, and what do they do?** The major cortical regions are organized into four sets of lobes: (1) The occipital lobes are the first part of the cortex to process visual input in detail. (2) The temporal lobes receive neural signals from the occipital lobes and are the seat of visual memories. They are also involved in language comprehension, hearing, and storing new memories. (3) The parietal lobes register location in space and are also involved in attention and arithmetic. Each parietal lobe includes part of the somatosensory strip, which registers sensation from parts of the body. Different regions of the somatosensory strip register input from different parts of the body, with larger areas being devoted to more sensitive parts of the body. (4) The frontal lobes are involved in planning, memory search, motor control, speech control, reasoning, and some aspects of emotion. These lobes contain the motor strip, which controls fine motor movements; larger areas of the motor strip are devoted to parts of the body that we can control more precisely.

2. **How do the functions of the two sides of the brain differ?** The two cerebral hemispheres differ primarily in how effectively they perform very specific tasks (such as categorizing the locations of objects). However, we can make the following generalizations: The left hemisphere typically plays a larger role in language, and the right hemisphere plays a larger role in spatial attention and processing nonverbal cues. Moreover, the left half of the brain appears to play a critical role in inventing stories to make sense of the world and in many forms of reasoning.

3. **What parts of the brain lie under the cerebral cortex? What do these subcortical structures do?** The thalamus is often thought of as a switching center; it handles connections to and from distinct parts of the brain; attention, sleep, and other functions critical to daily life depend on the thalamus. The hypothalamus controls many bodily functions, such as eating, drinking, and sex. It is also critically involved in regulating hormones. The hippocampus plays a key role in storing new memories in the brain, and the amygdala is involved in fear and other strong emotions. The hippocampus, amygdala, hypothalamus, and other subcortical structures make up the limbic system, which is essential for fighting, fleeing, feeding, and sex. The basal ganglia are important in planning and producing movements as well as in learning new habits. The brainstem contains a number of structures, many of which are crucial for alertness, sleep, and arousal. The cerebellum is involved in motor control, timing, and attention.

4. **What are the neuroendocrine and neuroimmune systems, and what do they have in common?** The CNS regulates the neuroendocrine system, which in turn produces hormones. Hormones are chemicals that can act as neurotransmitter substances, which not only affect specific organs but also affect thoughts, feelings, and behavior. Stress triggers the release of the hormone cortisol, produced by the outer layer of the adrenal glands. The CNS also regulates the neuroimmune system, which helps us fight disease. Stress also affects this system. The neuroendocrine and neuroimmune systems, along with the somatic motor system and the autonomic nervous system, are the means by which the CNS influences the body (and they in turn send information back to the brain).

Probing the Brain

Having toured the major parts of the brain and noted their major functions, you can make a pretty good guess about what areas of the brain were damaged when the soldier suffered carbon monoxide poisoning. We can guess, but we cannot know for sure, given the limitations of the tests available at the time of his accident, in 1966. Today, however, doctors and researchers can obtain an impressive amount of information about the structure and functioning of human brains. Such information includes high-quality images, which can show damage to particular brain structures and can record brain activity, or the disruption of it, in specific areas.

Although strokes are a more common cause of brain damage, some people have suffered such damage from riding on roller coasters. One woman had trouble remembering things she just heard, could no longer see clearly, and even blacked out sporadically (Gilbert, 2002).

Source: ATABOY/Image Bank/Getty Images

LOOKING AHEAD Learning Objectives

1. What can researchers learn about the brain's functions by studying behavior following brain damage?
2. What techniques allow researchers to record the activity of neurons in the brain as they function?
3. What is neuroimaging?
4. How can different parts of the brain be stimulated to determine their functions?

The Damaged Brain: What's Missing?

The first evidence that different parts of the brain do different things came from accidents in which people suffered damage to the brain. Such damage typically produces a region of impaired tissue, called a **lesion**. The most frequent cause of damage is a **stroke**, which occurs when blood, with its life-sustaining nutrients and oxygen, fails to reach part of the brain (usually because a clot clogs up a crucial blood vessel), and thus neurons in the affected area die. Researchers study patients with such problems, seeking to learn which specific abilities are disrupted when particular brain structures are damaged.

Researchers also study the effects on behavior of removing specific parts of the brains of animals. But, because animals are not people, we must be cautious in generalizing from animal brains to human brains. ⊙⊢Watch

Watch the Video on Head Injury on mypsychlab.com

Recording Techniques: The Music of the Cells

Researchers can use several methods to record the activity of normal brains. To some extent, brain activity can be measured by making an electromagnetic recording. In one version of this technique, a machine called an **electroencephalograph** records electrical activity in the brain, as shown in Figure 15. When neurons fire, they produce electrical fields. When many neurons are firing together, these fields can be detected by electrodes (small metal disks that pick up electrical activity) placed on the scalp. Researchers can record electrical activity over time or in response to a particular stimulus (which produces *event-related potentials*); when recorded over time, the result is a tracing of the "brain waves" of electrical fluctuation called an **electroencephalogram (EEG)** (see Figure 15). However, the abbreviation of EEG is also used to refer to the technique itself, *electroencephalography*. Psychologists have used this technique to learn much about the brain. It is through EEGs, for example, that they learned that people go through distinct stages of sleep marked by different types of brain activity.

Another, more recent technique, **magnetoencephalography (MEG)**, records magnetic waves produced by neural activity (without electrodes). Just as running a current through a wire produces a magnetic field, neural firings produce a magnetic field. Very fast changes in neural firing can be detected with this technique. For example, this technique has been used to show that when people hear higher tones, their brain activity shifts farther along a strip of cortex in the temporal lobes—the brain uses the location on the cortex to stand for the pitch (Pantev & Lütkenhöner, 2000). However, neither EEG nor MEG is very sensitive to activity in subcortical brain structures.

Lesion A region of impaired brain tissue.

Stroke A cause of brain damage that occurs when blood (with its life-giving nutrients and oxygen) fails to reach part of the brain, and thus neurons in that area die.

Electroencephalograph A machine that records electrical activity in the brain.

Electroencephalogram (EEG) A tracing of brain waves of electrical fluctuation over time.

Magnetoencephalography (MEG) A technique for assessing brain activity that relies on recording magnetic waves produced by neural activity.

FIGURE 15 The Electroencephalogram and Electroencephalograph

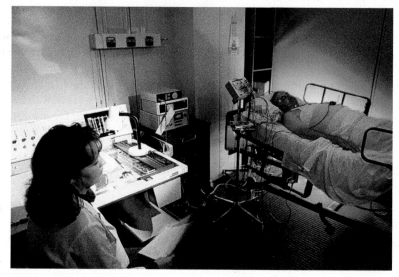

The synchronized waves evident during relaxation or rest (shown in the top electroencephalogram) are disrupted during task performance (shown in the bottom).

Electroencephalograph equipment allows researchers to record electrical activity on the scalp (which reflects electrical activity in the brain).

Source: Photo Researchers, Inc.

In a more direct and sensitive technique referred to as **single-cell recording**, tiny probes called *microelectrodes* are placed in the brain and used to record neural firing rates. A typical microelectrode is at most only 1/10 as wide as a human hair (and some are only 1/100 as wide!). Usually researchers hook up the wires from microelectrodes to amplifiers and speakers rather than to a screen so that they can hear neural activity (as clicking sounds) rather than watch a monitor; their eyes are then free to guide the placement of the electrodes. Brain surgeons sometimes put microelectrodes in human brains in order to find out what a part of the brain does before operating on it; such information helps surgeons decide which part of the cerebral cortex to avoid cutting in order to reach a subcortical brain tumor. Psychologists work with brain surgeons to chart the specific functions of parts of these patients' brains. Such studies have yielded some fascinating results. For example, when people look at words, some neurons respond to specific words but not others—such as to "luck" but not to "stay," "deny," or "carve" (Heit et al., 1988).

Neuroimaging: Picturing the Living Brain

Today, if you had an emergency like the young soldier's, you would probably be rushed to a hospital and immediately have your brain scanned. Your doctors would order procedures to determine both the structural damage (which brain areas were physically affected) and the functional deficits (which areas were performing below par). Because they yield an actual picture of the structure or functioning of regions of the brain, scanning techniques are referred to as **neuroimaging**. It is fair to say that neuroimaging techniques have transformed many facets of psychology, allowing researchers to answer questions that were hopelessly out of reach before the mid-1980s (Cabeza & Nyberg, 2000; Cappa & Grafman, 2004; Poldrack & Wagner, 2004; Posner & Raichle, 1994).

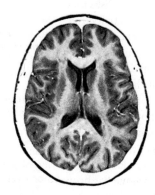

On the left, a computer-assisted tomography (CT) scan, and on the right, a magnetic resonance imaging (MRI) scan. MRI provides much higher resolution images of structures of the brain.

Source: Photo Researchers, Inc.

Visualizing Brain Structure The oldest neuroimaging techniques involve taking pictures of brain structures using X rays. The invention of the computer allowed scientists to construct machines for **computer-assisted tomography** (**CT**, formerly CAT). In this technique, a series of X rays is used to build up a three-dimensional image. More recently, **magnetic resonance imaging** (**MRI**) makes use of the magnetic properties of different atoms to take even sharper pictures of the three-dimensional structure of the brain.

Visualizing Brain Function

CT scans and MRIs give amazing views of the physical structure of the living brain, but to visualize the entire brain in action, researchers need other types of brain scans, those that track the amount of blood, oxygen, or nutrients moving to particular parts of the brain. The more frequently neurons fire, the more blood, oxygen, and nutrients they require. Thus, the amounts of these substances in a particular part of the brain indicate how vigorously neurons in that region are firing.

One of the most important techniques for measuring blood flow or energy consumption in the brain is **positron emission tomography (PET)**. Small amounts of a radioactive substance are introduced into the blood, which is then taken up into different brain areas in proportion to how vigorously the neurons in each area are firing (see Figure 16). The amount of radiation emitted at different parts of the head is recorded, and a computer uses this information to build a three-dimensional image of the brain. This technique has been used in far-reaching investigations, ranging from detecting the early signs of Alzheimer's disease (McMurtaya et al, 2008), to documenting the existence of visual mental images (Kosslyn et al., 1999), to charting differences in brain function between normal people and convicted murderers (Raine et al., 1994).

Probably the most common type of neuroimaging for psychological research today is **functional magnetic resonance imaging (fMRI)**. This type of magnetic resonance imaging charts the level of activity of portions of the brain while a person performs a particular task, and does so by detecting the amount of oxygen that is being brought to different places in the brain (the more frequently neurons fire, the more oxygen they consume). This technique has been used in research in many creative ways, such as to allow participants to "train their brains." In one such study, participants viewed a graph that indicated how strongly activated their somatosensory and motor strips were while they imagined moving; this visual feedback allowed participants to learn to "turn on" these parts of their brains voluntarily—in fact, they later could voluntarily activate this part of the brain as strongly as it was activated during actual movement (deCharms et al., 2004).

It is worth emphasizing that *all* of the neuroimaging techniques we have discussed that assess brain function suffer from a fundamental problem: They produce evidence for *correlations* between performing a task and activation of a specific brain region. They do not establish that activated brain regions play a *causal* role in producing the behavior. To make this connection, we must turn to other techniques.

Single-cell recording The technique in which tiny probes called microelectrodes are placed in the brain and used to record neural firing rates.

Neuroimaging Brain-scanning techniques that produce a picture of the structure or functioning of regions of the brain.

Computer-assisted tomography (CT) A neuroimaging technique that produces a three-dimensional image of brain structures using X rays.

Magnetic resonance imaging (MRI) A technique that uses magnetic properties of atoms to take sharp pictures of the three-dimensional structure of the brain.

Positron emission tomography (PET) A neuroimaging technique that uses small amounts of a radioactive substance to track blood flow or energy consumption in the brain.

THINK like a PSYCHOLOGIST Suppose a new, inexpensive, and portable brain-scanning technique shines very dim lasers through your head and projects an image of brain activity as it is happening. What uses for it can you think of for education or psychotherapy?

FIGURE 16 Positron Emission Tomography

Hearing words

Seeing words

Speaking words

Reading words

A positron emission tomography (PET) machine like that shown here allows researchers to observe brain activity while participants perform various tasks.

Brighter colors indicate regions of greater blood flow in the brain while the participant performed a particular task.

Source: From Goodenough, Judith A., McGuire, Betty A., Wallace, Robert A., *Biology of Humans: Concepts, Applications and Issues*, 1st edition, © 2005, Figure 8.6. Adapted by Permission of Pearson Education, Inc., Upper Saddle River, NJ.; (photo) Photo Researchers, Inc.

Stimulation: Inducing or Inhibiting Neural Activity

To come closer to discovering how brain activity actually gives rise to thoughts, feelings, and behavior, researchers can stimulate neurons in a given brain area and observe the results. Two kinds of stimulation studies have been used to find out what parts of the human brain do.

In one technique, a part of the skull is opened up, and a mild electric current is delivered directly to parts of the exposed cortex; the person is asked to report what he or she experiences while the current is being applied. Wilder Penfield and his colleagues (Penfield & Perot, 1963; Penfield & Rasmussen, 1950) pioneered this method with patients who were about to undergo brain operations. Penfield reported that people experience different images, memories, and feelings depending on the area in the brain that is stimulated. These results are sometimes difficult to interpret, however, because researchers cannot be sure whether actual memories are activated, whether new experiences are being created at the time, or even whether the participants simply are intentionally making up stories.

In other stimulation studies, instead of asking for reports, researchers observe which activities are disrupted when current is applied (Ojemann, 1983; Ojemann et al., 1989). For instance, researchers note when electrically stimulating a particular part of the brain impairs someone's ability to name pictures. However, even this method is limited because stimulating particular neurons can lead to the activation of other neurons that are connected to the stimulated ones, and these other neurons could produce the observed effects. Nevertheless, advances in *microstimulation* of nonhuman animals have allowed researchers to stimulate a few neurons at a time and observe the direct consequences on an animal's perceptions, decisions, and actions (Cohen & Newsome, 2004).

In another method, **transcranial magnetic stimulation (TMS)**, researchers stimulate parts of the human brain by pressing a coil against the scalp and creating a very brief, very strong magnetic pulse (or series of pulses). The magnetic field is so strong that it causes neurons under the coil to fire. Using this technique, for example, researchers can make a person's fingers move by shifting the coil over the parts of the motor strip that control the fingers (Pascual-Leone et al., 1997, 1998; Walsh & Pascual-Leone, 2003). When neurons are repeatedly stimulated in this way, they become temporarily unresponsive. Thus, for example, if such pulses are directed to the occipital lobe, visual perception can be temporarily impaired (Walsh & Pascual-Leone, 2003). By showing that temporarily disrupting a particular brain area in turn temporarily disrupts a particular type of behavior, this technique allows researchers to show that a brain area plays a causal role in a particular type of mental processing. As noted earlier, though, in some cases stimulation travels to other neurons that are connected to the stimulated ones, and these other neurons produce the observed effects. This possibility can be evaluated by using a combination of TMS and fMRI, where patterns of brain activation caused by TMS can be observed. ((•─Listen

In closing this section, we want to emphasize that each of these techniques for studying brain function has different strengths and weaknesses. As summarized in Table 2, some techniques can detect activity in well under a second but cannot pinpoint where the activity originates; other techniques are slower but can establish the location of activity relatively well. Some techniques can monitor only a very small part of the brain at a time, whereas others can monitor larger portions of the brain; some techniques can monitor only the cortex, and some can also monitor subcortical activity. And some techniques establish correlations among far-flung parts of the brain and behavior but cannot establish causal relations, whereas other techniques establish causal relations between specific individual brain regions and behavior but have limited scope. Some are expensive, and some are relatively inexpensive. Recognizing these trade-offs, researchers are increasingly using combinations of techniques, taking advantage of the strengths of each while compensating for their weaknesses. For example, PET scanning has revealed that the occipital lobe of the brain is activated even when people visualize with their eyes closed, and TMS has shown that this brain activity plays a *causal* role in mental imagery; when the occipital lobe is temporarily disrupted, so is the ability to visualize (Kosslyn et al., 1999).

((•─Listen to the **Podcast** on **Brain Mapping** on **mypsychlab.com**

THINK like a **PSYCHOLOGIST** Have you or someone you know ever undergone some type of neuroimaging tests? If so, based on what you have read, which technique(s) do you think it was? Why might the physician have chosen that particular type of neuroimaging technique?

TABLE 2 Key Characteristics of Various Techniques Used to Study Brain Function

Technique	Does the technique document changes that occur in less than a second?	Does the technique document functions of brain regions of 2 millimeters or less?	Is the technique only used on the cortex?	Size of brain region assessed by the technique	Expense of technique ("High" indicates at least $1,000 for each session with person)
Electrical stimulation	Yes	No	No	Small	Low
EEG	Yes	No	Yes	Large	Low
fMRI	Almost	Almost	No	Large	High
PET	No	Almost	No	Large	High
MEG	Yes	Yes	Yes	Small	Medium
Single-cell recording	Yes	Yes	No	Small	Low
TMS	Almost	Almost	Yes	Small	Low

LOOKING BACK

✓●─[Study and **Review** on
mypsychlab.com

1. **What can researchers learn about the brain's functions by studying behavior following brain damage?** By looking at altered performance after brain damage has occurred, researchers can gain hints about what functions are carried out by the particular parts of the brain that have been damaged.

2. **What techniques allow researchers to record the activity of neurons in the brain as they function?** Electroencephalographs record "brain waves"—fluctuations in electrical activity produced by the brain. Electroencephalography (EEG) involves placing electrodes on the skull to record electrical activity in response to a stimulus or over a period of time. Magnetoencephalography(MEG) records magnetic waves produced by neural activity. Researchers can also use microelectrodes to record neural activity in both humans and animals.

3. **What is neuroimaging?** Neuroimaging is a set of techniques that allow researchers to visualize the structure and function of the brain. At present, four major techniques are used: computer-assisted tomography (CT), which uses X rays to obtain a three-dimensional image of the structure of the brain; magnetic resonance imaging (MRI), which uses the magnetic properties of atoms to produce sharp pictures of the three-dimensional structure of the brain; positron emission tomography (PET), which uses small amounts of a radioactive substance to track blood flow and thus neural activity; and functional magnetic resonance imaging (fMRI), which detects the amount of oxygen brought to different places in the brain.

4. **How can different parts of the brain be stimulated to determine their functions?** Electric current can be applied to parts of the brain or, with microstimulation, to just a few neurons, and effects on perception or behavior can then be observed. Transcranial magnetic stimulation (TMS) can be used to stimulate clusters of neurons.

Genes, Brain, and Environment: The Brain in the World

Why was the brain of the young soldier vulnerable to damage from carbon monoxide fumes? Could he have done anything in advance to prepare his brain to survive such an event? Could he have done anything after the accident to speed his recovery? Let's consider the aspects of environment and heredity that shape our brains so that they operate in particular ways and not in others, and the degree to which parts of the brain can change their functions if need be.

Mendelian inheritance The transmission of characteristics by individual elements of inheritance (now known to be genes), each acting separately.

Gene A stretch of the DNA molecule that produces a specific protein.

Genotype The genetic code within an organism.

Phenotype The observable structure and behavior of an organism.

Complex inheritance The transmission of characteristics by the joint action of combinations of genes working together; also called *polygenetic inheritance*.

1. How do genes and the environment interact as the brain develops and functions?
2. What does "heritability" mean?
3. How has evolution shaped the functions of the brain?

Genes as Blueprints: Born to Be Wild?

Our genes shape us from the instant of conception and continue to affect us at every phase of our lives. The story of genetics begins in 1866, when Gregor Mendel, an Augustinian monk who lived in what is now the Czech Republic, wrote one of the most fundamental papers in all of science. In it he formulated the core ideas of what is now known as **Mendelian inheritance**, the transmission of characteristics by individual elements of inheritance (now known to be genes), each acting separately. After carefully observing characteristics of plants that he bred, Mendel made two crucial inferences: (1) For each characteristic, an offspring inherits an "element" (that is, a gene) from each parent, and (2) in some cases, one of the elements dominates the other, and that is the one whose effect is apparent. If an element is not dominant, it is recessive: The effect of a recessive element is evident only when the offspring receives two copies of it, one from each parent.

Mendel never knew what the elements actually were because he was working long before the relevant biochemistry existed; the great biochemical discovery—that the mysterious "elements" are genes—was not made until the middle of the 20th century. A **gene** is a stretch of the deoxyribonucleic acid, or DNA, molecule that produces a specific protein (which may be an enzyme). The sum total of your particular set of genes is your **genotype**, your genetic code. In contrast, the **phenotype** is the observable structure and behavior of an organism, which arises partly from the genotype and partly from the environment. Your genotype is hidden in the nucleus of each of your cells, whereas many aspects of your phenotype (such as your height and eye color) are evident to anybody who cares to look.

We must contrast Mendelian inheritance with *complex inheritance*. In Mendelian inheritance, the presence or absence of a particular gene produces qualitative variations, such as whether a pea pod is smooth or wrinkled (or whether you have attached versus unattached ear lobes). One or the other characteristic is produced. In contrast, some characteristics are produced not through Mendelian inheritance but through **complex inheritance** (sometimes called *polygenetic inheritance*), in which the characteristic is produced by the joint action of combinations of genes working together. Moreover, also unlike Mendelian inheritance, the characteristic isn't all-or-none: Instead, complex inheritance produces quantitative variations in characteristics, such as differences in height or intelligence (Plomin & DeFries, 1998; Plomin et al., 2003).

Genes both produce obvious characteristics—such as eye color—and, by affecting our brains, affect our behavior.

Tuning Genetic Programs: The Environment Matters

Genes provide the blueprints for building cells—including neurons—and govern the way the brain is wired up before birth. However, unlike a building, the brain does not have a blueprint that specifies all aspects of its structure in advance. In fact, it is critical to point out that genes *cannot* program the structure of the brain entirely in advance. Here's an example of why the genes cannot program the entire brain in advance: When you look at an object, slightly different images strike your two eyes (because they are in different locations on your head), and the differences in these images allow you to see very precisely how far away objects are. However, to use the differences in the images striking the two eyes

The far-reaching power of relatively small genetic differences can be seen dramatically by comparing chimpanzees with humans: About 99% of the genetic material in both species is identical (Wildman et al., 2002).

Source: © Karen Huntt / CORBIS All Rights Reserved

in this way, the brain must take into account how far apart the eyes are—which cannot be entirely a result of the genes. Rather, the distance between the eyes depends on bone growth, which is affected partly by both the child's diet and the mother's diet during pregnancy. The genes can't "know" about such eating habits. Hence, the genes produce many connections in the visual system that could be used to infer distances from the differences in images striking the two eyes—but only some of these connections will end up being useful for the infant, depending on how far apart his or her eyes actually are. (The signals conveyed by only some of these connections will correctly guide reaching, looking, and movement.) And the brain will eliminate the connections that turn out not to be useful. The result is that the wiring of the brain depends partly on the genes and partly on experience.

The process of eliminating neural connections that are not useful is called **pruning**, which occurs in many brain systems (not just the visual system; Cowan et al., 1984; Huttenlocher, 2002). Pruning is responsible for the fact that your brain contains far fewer connections now than it did when you were born. As you interacted with the environment, certain neural connections were used over and over again, while others were used hardly at all. Connections among neurons in parts of the brain that are used frequently are retained, while others that are not used frequently are pruned away (Huttenlocher, 2002). As the saying goes, "Use it or lose it."

Interactions with the environment not only select among connections established by the genes but can also cause new connections to form. Researchers have found that if rats are raised in enriched environments, with lots of toys and things to do, their brains actually become heavier than those of rats raised in average environments. The additional weight comes about in part because new connections are formed (Black et al., 1998; Comery et al., 1995; Diamond et al., 1972; Greenough & Chang, 1985; Greenough et al., 1987; Nelson, 1999; Turner & Greenough, 1985).

Both pruning and adding new connections are examples of the brain's **plasticity**, its ability to change as a result of experience (like plastic, the brain can be molded by external forces). The plasticity of the human brain is most evident in four circumstances: (1) during infancy and childhood, when most pruning occurs; (2) when the body changes, so that the sensory input changes (for example, after a finger has been amputated); (3) when we learn something new or store new information; and (4) as compensation after brain damage, such as occurred to healthy portions of the soldier's brain after his injury.

Although it is true that an adult's brain can learn and adapt to change, adult brains are not as plastic as are the brains of children (particulary prior to puberty). The adult brain loses plasticity with age because the functions of neurons and brain circuits become set in place with experience (Payne & Lomber, 2001). However, under certain circumstances—such as occurs during learning—even adult brains are capable of dramatic reorganization. In fact, researchers have shown that adult brains can create new neurons, at least in some regions (Gould et al., 1999; Kempermann et al., 2004).

In short, instead of determining our characteristics in detail, our genes often specify the range of what is possible, and the environment then operates to set up the brain within this range. For example, because of our genes, we humans can't grow wings and cannot learn a new language after hearing it spoken for 3 hours. But within the limits set by the genes, interactions with the environment can alter both the structure and the function of the brain, as occurs when you learn to fly a plane or spend a year learning a new language. 👁—Watch

👁—Watch **Brain Building on mypsychlab.com**

Genes and Environment: A Single System How do interactions with the environment alter the brain? Some people think of genes as blueprints, providing the instructions on how to build the various parts of the body, but—as we've just seen—this notion is not accurate. Not only do genes fail to specify the complete brain, but also—unlike blueprints that are filed away in a dusty drawer once their instructions have been followed—many genes keep working throughout your life. Their action is the reason some people go bald, others are prone to develop high cholesterol, and still others get varicose veins. Even more important, genes are not simply time bombs that are set at birth and ready to explode at the proper hour. Many genes constantly change how they operate, sometimes producing proteins and sometimes not. Psychiatrist Steven Hyman (personal communication) suggested the following illuminating example: Say you want bigger biceps, and so you go to the

Pruning A process whereby certain connections among neurons are eliminated.

Plasticity The brain's ability to change as a result of experience.

71

If you lift heavy weights, you will damage your arm muscles, which in turn causes the release of certain chemicals that *turn on* genes in the muscle cells. These genes then produce proteins, which build up the muscles. Dwayne (The Rock) Johnson has managed to turn on many of these genes, but all of us turn on genes in our brains when we expend mental effort.

Source: ALPHAVILLE/IMOHOTEPPROD/THE KOBAL COLLECTION/HAMSHERE, KEITH

gym and start lifting weights. After the first week, all you have to show for your time and sweat is aching arms. But, after a few weeks, the muscles begin to firm up and soon may even begin to bulge. What has happened? When you first lifted weights, you actually damaged the muscles, and the damage caused the release of certain chemicals. Those chemicals then—and this is the important part—*turned on* genes in the muscle cells. Here, "turned on" means that they instructed the genes to produce additional protein molecules, and these additional molecules increased the size of the muscles. If the damage—caused by lifting the heavy weights—stops, so do the chemicals that signal the genes to turn on, and the genes will no longer produce those extra proteins. So, you need to lift increasingly heavier weights to keep building more muscle. No pain, no gain.

The important point to remember is that interactions with the environment cause many genes to be turned on and off, and when they are turned on, they have specific effects on your body and brain. As you read this, for example, neurotransmitters are being released as brain activity takes place; your genes turn on to trigger the production of new neurotransmitter molecules to replace those that are broken down.

Just as interacting with the environment by lifting weights can lead to bulging muscles, interacting with the environment in various ways can set your brain to operate more or less efficiently. And, depending on how your brain is working, you behave differently. By regulating brain activity, genes affect behavior.

It is commonplace today for scientists to stress that both genes and environment are important. This is true, but, stated in that way, it misses the mark. Genes and environment cannot really be considered as separate factors; they are instead *different aspects of a single system*. In much the same way as you can focus separately on the brushstrokes, perspective, composition, and colors of a painting, you can discuss genes and the environment as discrete entities. But, as with a painting, to appreciate the "whole picture," you must consider genes and environment together (Gottlieb, 1998).

Environment and Genes: A Two-Way Street Plomin, Defries and colleagues (1997), Scarr and McCartney (1983), and others distinguish three ways that genes and environment interact:

- **Passive interaction** occurs when genetically shaped behavioral tendencies of parents or siblings produce an environment that is passively received by the child. An example: Parents with higher intelligence tend to read more and thus have more books in the house. Given that parents with higher intelligence tend to have children with higher intelligence, this means that children with higher intelligence will tend to be born into environments with more books (Plomin, 1995).

- **Evocative (or reactive) interaction** occurs when genetically influenced characteristics (both behavioral and physical) induce other people to behave in particular ways. We might call this the "blondes have more fun" effect. Having blonde hair is (often, anyway) a genetic characteristic, one that can elicit varying responses. Some people react to blondes more positively than they do to brunettes, but other people might react to blondes as if they conform to the stereotype of "intellectually challenged blonde." In either case, a genetically determined characteristic leads other people to treat a person in particular ways—and such treatment is part of the social environment.

- **Active interaction** occurs when people choose, partly based on genetic tendencies, to put themselves in situations that are comfortable for them and to avoid situations that are uncomfortable. A timid person, for instance, may avoid loud parties and amusement parks, instead seeking out peaceful settings and quiet pastimes. And by choosing the environment, a person constrains the ways that the environment can affect the genes. For example, if you avoid exciting situations, you are less likely to experience the "fight-or-flight response" than if you seek out thrills—and hence such choices will directly affect genes that produce "fight-or-flight" hormones.

Passive interaction Occurs when genetically shaped behavioral tendencies of parents or siblings produce an environment that is passively received by the child.

Evocative (or reactive) interaction Occurs when genetically influenced characteristics (both behavioral and physical) induce other people to behave in particular ways.

Active interaction Occurs when people choose, partly based on genetic tendencies, to put themselves in specific situations and to avoid others.

About 90% of the *variation* in height is controlled by the genes, and thus height is about 90% heritable. Heritability estimates assume that the environment is constant; if the environment varies (perhaps by providing a better or poorer diet), environmental factors can overshadow even very high heritability.

Source: PhotoDisc/Getty Images

Behavioral Genetics

Researchers in the field of **behavioral genetics** try to determine the extent to which the differences among people's behaviors and psychological characteristics are due to their different genetic makeups or to differences in their environments (Dick et al., 2010; Plomin, DeFries et al., 2003).

Heritability, Not Inheritability

Researchers in behavioral genetics focus on estimating the heritability of various characteristics, ranging from intelligence to personality, as they occur in specific environments. *Heritability* is a potentially confusing term. It does not indicate the amount of a characteristic or ability that is inherited. Rather, **heritability** indicates how much of the *variability* in a characteristic or ability in a population is due to genetics—given a specific environment. Let's go through an example: Height in Western countries is about 90% heritable. This statement means that 90% of the variability among the heights of people in these countries is genetically determined, not that *your* height was determined 90% by your genes and 10% by your environment. In fact, the possible differences in height that arise from differences in diet may actually be greater than the differences in height that arise from genes, but *in a specific environment* (for instance, one in which everyone has access to and eats a healthy diet), heritability indicates the relative contribution of the genes to variations in height. If the environment were different, the heritability might be different, too.

Twin Studies: Only Shared Genes?

Researchers have developed different methods to study how much genes versus the environment contribute to the development of characteristics and abilities. One such method involves the study of twins. In **twin studies**, researchers assess the contribution of genes to variations in a characteristic or ability by comparing identical and fraternal twins. Identical twins start life when a single, fertilized egg divides in two; these twins are **monozygotic** (like many scientific terms, this comes from Greek *monos*, meaning "single," and *zygotos*, meaning "yoked," as occurs when a sperm and egg are joined). Monozygotic twins have virtually identical genes. In contrast, fraternal twins grow from two separate eggs that are fertilized by two different sperm; these twins are **dizygotic**. Fraternal twins share only as many genes as any other pair of siblings—on average, half. By comparing the degree to which identical twins are similar to

Behavioral genetics The field in which researchers attempt to determine the extent to which the differences among people's behaviors and psychological characteristics are due to their different genes or to differences in their environments.

Heritability The degree to which the variability of a characteristic or ability in a population is due to genetics—given a specific environment.

Twin study A study that compares identical and fraternal twins to determine the relative contribution of genes to variability in a characteristic or ability.

Monozygotic From the same egg and having virtually identical genes.

Dizygotic From different eggs and sharing only as many genes as any pair of siblings—on average, half.

Men with a particular gene (for which they can be tested) are likely to become alcoholics if they drink at all (Goedde & Agarwal, 1987). Having this gene presents no downside, however, for men who obey the norms of a strict Muslim or Mormon culture, in which alcohol is forbidden. Genes are merely one element in a larger system, which includes the environment.

Source: Art Resource/Philadelphia Museum of Art

each other in a characteristic or ability with the degree to which fraternal twins are similar to each other in that respect, we get a good idea of the contribution of the genes—if we assume that the environment is the same for members of both sets of twins. When identical twins are more similar than are fraternal twins on a given characteristic or ability, this indicates that genes play a role in that characteristic or ability (assuming that all twins live in comparable environments).

Twin studies have shown that the amount of gray matter in the brain (where cell bodies of neurons exist) is more similar in identical twins than in fraternal twins, which suggests that the amount of gray matter is, in part, under genetic control (Plomin & Kosslyn, 2001; Thompson et al., 2001). This difference between identical and fraternal twins in the similarity of the amount of gray matter is particularly pronounced in the frontal lobes and in a part of the temporal lobe involved in language comprehension. So what? Well, the amount of such gray matter is correlated with scores on intelligence tests, and identical twins tend to have more similar scores on intelligence tests than do fraternal twins, perhaps for this reason.

Adoption Studies: Separating Genes and Environment?

Another way to gather evidence for the relative contributions of genes and environment is to compare characteristics of children adopted at birth to those of their adoptive parents or siblings versus their biological parents or siblings. Called an **adoption study**, this type of investigation is particularly powerful when twins who have been separated at birth (or shortly thereafter) grow up in different environments. Even in these cases, however, it is difficult to separate genetic from environmental influences: The environment matters, and there is no guarantee that separated twins will have different environments. For example, if the twins are cute, caregivers in both households will treat them differently than if they seem tough and fearless; if they are smart and curious, both sets of adoptive parents may be inclined to buy books and read to them. Again, we emphasize that the genes and the environment form a single system, with each factor affecting the other.

Evolution and the Brain: The Best of All Possible Brains?

The loss of consciousness and brain damage suffered by the young soldier occurred because he breathed toxic fumes and was deprived of oxygen. However, not all species would be affected by that situation the way this member of our human species was. Sperm whales, for instance, do just fine if they take a breath every 75 minutes or so. This observation leads to questions about **evolution**, the gene-based changes in the characteristics or abilities of members of a species over successive generations.

Natural Selection: Reproduction of the Fittest

Evolution occurs in part by **natural selection**, which occurs when individuals with inherited characteristics that contribute to survival have more offspring, and over time those characteristics come to be widespread in a population. (Natural selection was first described in detail in 1858 by Charles Darwin and, independently, by Alfred Russel Wallace.) In other words, individuals with characteristics helpful for survival live long enough to have many offspring. In turn, those offspring, equipped with the favorable characteristics inherited from their parents, survive to have more offspring. In this way, the "selection" of the survivors is made by "nature." An inherited characteristic that results from such selection is called an **adaptation**. The oft-used phrase "survival of the fittest" is perhaps unfortunate: The crucial point is not that organisms "survive" but rather that well-adapted organisms

Adoption study A study in which characteristics of children adopted at birth are compared to those of their adoptive parents or siblings versus their biological parents or siblings.

Evolution Gene-based changes in the characteristics or abilities of members of a species over successive generations.

Natural selection Occurs when individuals with inherited characteristics that contribute to survival have more offspring, and over time those characteristics come to be widespread in a population.

Adaptation An inherited characteristic that increases an organism's ability to survive and reproduce successfully.

reproduce themselves more often and thereby pass their selected genes on to more members of the next generation (and the same is then true for their offspring). Plomin, DeFries, and colleagues (1997) point out that the principle might better have been expressed as "reproduction of the fittest." ✳️ ⌗Explore

✳️ ⌗Explore **Charles Darwin** biographical info on mypsychlab.com

Evolution via natural selection tends to mold the characteristics of a group of organisms to the requirements of their environment. If a certain species of mammal lives near the North Pole, the members of this species with warmer fur will tend to have more babies that survive, and those individuals that are white (and thus harder for predators to spot in the snow) will tend to have more babies that survive. If these characteristics are useful enough in that environment, eventually the species as a whole will have warmer white fur.

Here's a contemporary analogy of the way natural selection works. There were two Chinese brothers; one settled in Louisiana and the other in Ohio. They both opened Chinese restaurants and began with identical menus. After the first month, the brother in Louisiana noticed that his blander dishes were not selling well, so he dropped them from the menu; in Ohio, these dishes were doing fine, so they remained. One day, the Louisiana brother accidentally knocked a jar of chili powder into a pot of chicken he was simmering. He found that he liked the taste, so this new dish became the special of the day. It sold so well that it became a standard on the menu. Hearing the tale, the brother up north in Ohio tried the chili chicken soup, but it didn't sell well. Later that year, the Ohio brother bought a lot of corn, which was on sale. He tried adding it to a traditional dish and called it the special of the day. The Ohio brother wasn't trying to achieve a particular taste, he was just experimenting. That corn dish did not sell well and so was dropped. But when he added corn to another recipe, the result was an instant hit. Both brothers continued to add new elements in their cooking, with varying degrees of success on different occasions. As shown in Figure 17, after 2 years, the brothers' menus had diverged considerably.

Two important principles of evolution are illustrated here. First, the *environment*: The hungry restaurant patrons "selected" different aspects of the menus. The diners in Louisiana, for example, apparently liked spicy food better than did those in Ohio. Second, *variation* is at the heart of the process: Without the accidents and substitutions, the

FIGURE 17 The Menu Model of Natural Selection

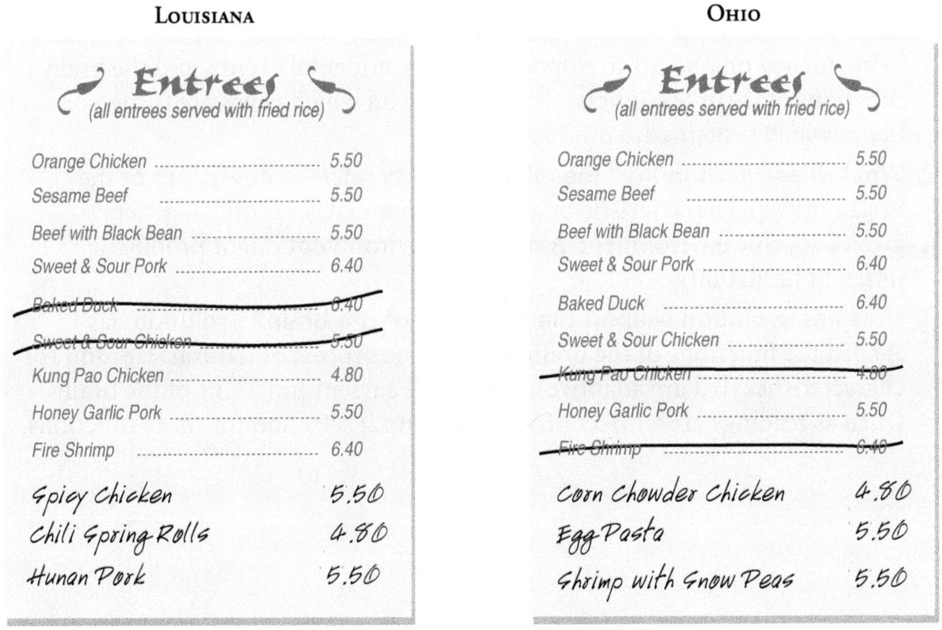

Evolution by natural selection is illustrated when variations change the menus, and features of the environment (the diners' tastes, in this analogy) "select" some of these changes. In living beings, over generations such selection of genes results in changes in the population.

process would not have worked—the menus would not have evolved over time. Natural selection in the evolution of the two menus depended on *random variation*, which provided the "options" that proved more or less adaptive. In the evolution of species, genetic mutations lead to random variation in genes, varying the "menu" of genes that different organisms possess.

So, back to the question of why we humans don't have the sperm whale's ability to go without breathing for many minutes. If our ancestors had had to go for long periods without breathing in order to survive, then only individuals who could do so would have survived and had offspring—and we lucky descendants would have inherited this ability. And the story of our young soldier might have had a happier ending.

Not Just Natural Selection A word of warning: Always exercise caution when trying to use the idea of natural selection to explain our present-day characteristics. Just because a characteristic exists doesn't mean that it is an adaptation to the environment or that it is the result of natural selection. For example, the nose originally evolved to warm air and help us detect and localize odors, but once you have a nose, you can use it to hold up your glasses (Gould & Lewontin, 1979). This use of the nose, as helpful as it is, was not a product of natural selection! As another example, once we had the brain machinery to see lines and edges, abilities that probably helped our ancestors to discern prey, the brain could allow us to learn to read. But reading itself was not a product of natural selection.

In short, some of our abilities, personality types, social styles, and so forth may have arisen from natural selection because they were useful during our evolutionary past, and others may be useful today but not because of natural selection. It is not easy to sort out which characteristics and abilities are a product of natural selection and which are not, and we should not assume that there is a sound evolutionary reason for everything people do.

THINK like a
PSYCHOLOGIST Did natural selection give rise to our ability to drive automobiles? Think about the specific skills that underlie this ability: What arguments might lead you to conclude that natural selection produced them? What arguments might lead to you to conclude that natural selection did *not* produce them?

✓•—Study and Review on
mypsychlab.com

LOOKING BACK

1. **How do genes and the environment interact as the brain develops and functions?** When the brain is developing, there are more neural connections than are later used; the process of pruning eliminates connections that are not used when the animals (or person) interacts with the environment. In addition, neurons grow more connections with use. Many genes are regularly being turned on and off in response to environmental events, and the brain functions more or less efficiently depending on which genes are turned on and hence which proteins are produced.

2. **What does "heritability" mean?** Heritability refers to how much of the variability in a characteristic or ability in a population is due to genetics—given a specific environment. A different environment might produce a different heritability.

3. **How has evolution shaped the functions of the brain?** Evolution has shaped the functions of the brain through the process of natural selection (of characteristics that are adaptive), but not all current functions of the brain (such as reading) are a direct product of natural selection for those functions.

LET'S REVIEW

((•• Listen to an audio file of your chapter on mypsychlab.com

I. BRAIN CIRCUITS: MAKING CONNECTIONS

A. The neuron is the key building block of the brain. The cell body receives inputs from the dendrites (or, sometimes, directly from axons of other neurons) and sends its output via the axon (which is connected to the dendrites of other neurons or, in some cases, their cell bodies).

B. The axon is covered with myelin, a fatty insulating material that makes neural transmission more efficient. The axon can have many branches, allowing it to affect many other neurons. The terminal buttons at the end of the axon contain neurotransmitter substances ("neurotransmitters" for short) that are released by an action potential.

C. Neurotransmitters typically cross the synaptic cleft (the gap between the end of the axon and the receiving neuron) and affect another neuron, specifically its receptors, which are like locks that are opened by the right key. Once the transmitter molecule binds to a receptor, it causes a chain of events inside the neuron.

D. In rare cases, neurotransmitters are released through the cell membrane. Endogenous cannabinoids, for example, are released by the receiving neuron and fine-tune sending neurons.

E. When the total excitatory input to a neuron sufficiently exceeds the total inhibitory input, the neuron "fires"—that is, chemical reactions work their way down the axon, and neurotransmitter substances are released at the terminal buttons. After a neuron has fired, some of the neurotransmitter substance is reabsorbed back into the sending cell, referred to as reuptake. Some drugs block this reuptake mechanism.

F. Glial cells not only participate in the "care and feeding" of neurons but also help to create synapses and form appropriate connections when the brain is developing, and influence the communication among neurons.

II. THE NERVOUS SYSTEM: AN ORCHESTRA WITH MANY MEMBERS

A. The nervous system has two major parts: the peripheral nervous system (PNS) and the central nervous system (CNS).

B. The PNS consists of the autonomic nervous system (ANS) and the sensory-somatic nervous system (SSNS). The ANS is in turn divided into the sympathetic and parasympathetic nervous systems; the sympathetic nervous system is critically involved in the "fight-or-flight" response, and the effects of this response are counteracted by the parasympathetic nervous system. The SSNS includes the somatic motor system, which connects to muscles that can be moved voluntarily.

C. The CNS consists of the spinal cord and the brain itself. In addition to sending commands from the brain to the body and passing along sensory input to the brain, the spinal cord is responsible for some reflexes. Most reflexes depend on the action of interneurons, neurons that hook up to other neurons.

D. The brain itself is organized into lobes; the brain's outer layer is the cerebral cortex, a thin layer of neurons.

E. The cerebral cortex contains many bulges (gyri) and creases (sulci), which allow a lot of cortex to be crammed into a relatively small space.

III. SPOTLIGHT ON THE BRAIN: HOW IT DIVIDES AND CONQUERS

A. The four major lobes in each hemisphere are the occipital, temporal, parietal, and frontal. The occipital lobes are concerned with aspects of vision. The temporal lobes are the seat of visual memories and are also involved in storing new information in memory, language comprehension, and processing sound. The parietal lobes register location in space and are also involved in arithmetic; each parietal lobe includes part of the somatosensory strip, which registers sensation from parts of the body. The frontal lobes are involved in planning, searching for memories, reasoning, motor control (governed in part by the motor strip), and some aspects of emotion.

B. Each lobe is duplicated, one on the left and one on the right. The left hemisphere, which plays a larger role in language for most people, appears to be better at some aspects of interpreting sensory information and is critical to the ability to invent stories. The right hemisphere plays a larger role than the left in some aspects of language, in spatial attention, in recognizing overall shapes, and in processing nonverbal cues.

C. Split-brain patients have had the two brain hemispheres surgically disconnected through severing of the corpus callosum. This rare surgery is done only for medical reasons.

D. Under the cortex, many subcortical areas play crucial roles in the brain's function. The thalamus manages connections to and from distinct parts of the brain; the hypothalamus helps to control bodily functions, such as eating, drinking, and sex; the hippocampus is involved in storing new memories; and the amygdala plays a role in fear and other strong emotions.

E. The hypothalamus, hippocampus, amygdala, and other structures constitute the limbic system, which plays key roles in emotion and motivation, particularly as involved in fighting, fleeing, feeding, and sex.

F. The basal ganglia are used in planning and producing movements as well as in learning new habits. The brainstem contains structures involved in automatic functions (such as breathing), alertness, sleep, and arousal; and the cerebellum is involved in motor control, timing, and attention.

G. The neuroendocrine system produces hormones, which not only affect the body but also affect the brain itself (for example, altering moods).

H. The neuroimmune system produces substances that affect our immunity to infection and help wounds to heal.

IV. PROBING THE BRAIN

A. The earliest method used to discover what the various parts of the brain do involved observing the effects of brain damage on behavior. Scientists also investigate the effects of removing parts of animal brains.

B. Scientists can record electrical activity produced by the firing of neurons while people and animals perform specific tasks, using either electrodes placed on the scalp for electroencephalography (EEG) or microelectrodes inserted into the brain; researchers find more vigorous activity in brain areas involved in the task than in areas that are not involved. Researchers can also record magnetic fields produced by neurons when they fire, using magnetoencephalography (MEG).

C. Various neuroimaging techniques include the following: computer-assisted tomography (CT), which uses X rays to obtain three-dimensional images of the structures of the brain; magnetic resonance imaging (MRI), which makes use of magnetic fields to produce very sharp pictures of the brain; positron emission tomography (PET), which relies on small amounts of a radioactive substance to track blood flow or energy consumption in the brain; and functional magnetic resonance imaging (fMRI), which tracks changes in the oxygen level in different parts of the brain.

D. Neurons can be stimulated with a magnetic pulse (using transcranial magnetic stimulation, TMS) to fire and the effects on behavior observed.

V. GENES, BRAIN, AND ENVIRONMENT: THE BRAIN IN THE WORLD

A. Individual genes can affect the brain and behavior (via Mendelian inheritance), or sets of genes working together can have these effects (via complex inheritance). The genes lay down the basic structure of the brain, but the environment can mold both the brain's structure and its function.

B. Genes influence how people and other animals respond to environmental effects.

C. The environment affects brain structure and function through the pruning of connections that are not being used; it also causes the brain to form new connections in response to new stimuli.

D. The genes place limits on what is possible (for example, people can't grow wings), and even small genetic changes can sometimes exert significant effects on the brain, mental processes, and behavior.

E. Many of your genes are turned on and off, depending on what you are doing; specific genes cause the manufacture of neurotransmitters and can cause neurons to make connections in new ways.

F. Behavioral genetics attempts to discover how much of the variability in a psychological characteristic or ability is due to the genes versus the environment, but such estimates apply only to the environment in which the behavior or ability is measured.

G. The relative contributions of genes and environment are sometimes investigated by comparing twins (identical versus fraternal) and by comparing people who have been adopted with their adopted and biological family members.

H. We have our present sets of genes because of evolution, partly as a consequence of natural selection (genes are passed on through the generations when the genes produce characteristics that lead to more surviving offspring who in turn have surviving offspring).

KEY TERMS

action potential
active interaction
adaptation
adoption study
agonist
all-or-none law
amygdala
antagonist
autonomic nervous system (ANS)
axon
basal ganglia
behavioral genetics
brain circuit
brainstem
brain system
cell body
cell membrane
central nervous system (CNS)
cerebellum
cerebral cortex
cerebral hemisphere
complex inheritance
computer-assisted tomography (CT)
corpus callosum
cortisol
dendrites
dizygotic

electroencephalogram (EEG)
electroencephalograph
endogenous cannabinoids
estrogen
evocative (or reactive) interaction
evolution
forebrain
frontal lobes
functional magnetic resonance imaging (fMRI)
gene
genotype
glial cell
gyrus
heritability
hindbrain
hippocampus
hormone
hypothalamic-pituitary-adrenal (HPA) axis
hypothalamus
interneuron
ion
lesion
limbic system
lobes
magnetic resonance imaging (MRI)

magnetoencephalography (MEG)
medulla
Mendelian inheritance
meninges
mental contents
mental processes
midbrain
monozygotic
motor neuron
motor strip
myelin
natural selection
neuroendocrine system
neuroimaging
neurons
neurotransmitter substance
occipital lobes
parasympathetic nervous system
parietal lobes
passive interaction
peripheral nervous system (PNS)
phenotype
pituitary gland
plasticity
pons
positron emission tomography (PET)
pruning

receptor
reflex
resting potential
reticular formation
reuptake
selective serotonin-reuptake inhibitor (SSRI)
sensory neuron
sensory-somatic nervous system (SSNS)
single-cell recording
somatic motor system
somatosensory strip
spinal cord
split-brain patient
stroke
subcortical structures
sulcus
sympathetic nervous system
synapse
synaptic cleft
temporal lobes
terminal button
testosterone
thalamus
transcranial magnetic stimulation (TMS)
twin study

PRACTICE TEST

✓●[Study and Review on mypsychlab.com

For each of the following items, choose the single best answer.

1. A neuron that sends signals to muscles to control movement is called
   a. a brain circuit.
   b. a glial cell.
   c. an interneuron.
   d. a motor neuron.

2. Each neuron has a receiving end, a sending end, and a part in the middle. The part is the middle is called
   a. the cell body.
   b. the axon.
   c. the dendrite.
   d. the resting potential.

3. If a neuron receives sufficiently more excitatory input than inhibitory input, it fires, sending an action potential all the way down the axon and releasing a neurotransmitter substance from the terminal buttons; either the action potential occurs or it doesn't. This fact is best captured by
   a. the shifting change in charge that moves down the axon.
   b. the loss of myelin.
   c. the all-or-none law.
   d. the resting potential.

4. How do neurons typically communicate?
   a. They rarely communicate directly but instead rely on glial cells to pass information.
   b. They are always hooked up physically, so that electrical charges can affect the receiving neuron.
   c. They use sound waves.
   d. Chemical signals are typically sent across the synaptic cleft.

5. Chemical M is an agonist. What does this mean?
   a. Chemical M blocks the effect of a neurotransmitter substance.
   b. Chemical M mimics the effects of a neurotransmitter substance.
   c. Chemical M is used solely in the parts of the brain involved in visual perception.
   d. Chemical M helps produce dopamine.

6. Which of the following allows the central nervous system to affect the organs of the body?
   a. the back side of the spinal cord
   b. the reflex
   c. the peripheral nervous system
   d. The central nervous system is not linked to the organs of the body.

7. What system usually comes into play in response to a threat in the environment, perhaps a near accident while you are driving in heavy traffic?
   a. the sympathetic nervous system
   b. the synaptic clefts of all neurons
   c. spinal reflexes
   d. the parasympathetic nervous system

8. The occipital lobes are concerned entirely with
   a. processing sound, entering new information into memory, and comprehending language.
   b. different aspects of vision.
   c. registering spatial location, attention, and motor control.
   d. the somatosensory strip.

9. Many aspects of language are carried out by
   a. a single hemisphere, usually the right.
   b. both hemispheres.
   c. a single hemisphere, usually the left.
   d. the somatosensory strip.

10. What brain structure sits under the thalamus and plays a central role in controlling eating and drinking and in regulating the body's temperature, blood pressure, and heart rate?
    a. the hypothalamus
    b. the hippocampus
    c. the amygdala
    d. the basal ganglia

11. One way that researchers learn about the function of the brain is by observing the effects of
    a. diets.
    b. accidents in which people suffer damage to the brain.
    c. genetic mutations that change visible characteristics, such as hair color.
    d. all of the above.

12. In general, when an inherited characteristic varies continuously, it reflects
    a. Mendelian inheritance.
    b. deoxyribonucleic acid in the occipital lobe.
    c. complex inheritance.
    d. pruning.

13. What statement best reflects current understanding of how genes that affect the brain interact with the environment?
    a. Genes don't interact with the environment; genes are destiny.
    b. Genes determine the range of what is possible, but within those limits interactions with the environment can alter both the structure and the function of the brain.
    d. Many genes stay constantly on or off, and the environment has nothing to do with the state of genes.
    e. Genes are affected by the young child's environment but thereafter are not directly affected by environmental factors.

14. The process that occurs when offspring inherit characteristics that contribute to their survival—and so they tend to live long enough to have more offspring—is referred to as
    a. acquired characteristics.
    b. variability.
    c. heritability.
    d. natural selection.

15. Evolution via natural selection
    a. is no longer considered a scientific explanation for any aspects of psychology.
    b. is rarely the way evolution works.
    c. tends to mold the characteristics of a group of organisms to the requirements of its environment.
    d. means that there is a sound evolutionary reason for everything people do.

If we cannot sense the world, then for all practical purposes, it does not exist for us; if we sense it incorrectly, our world will be bent and distorted.

SENSATION AND PERCEPTION

HOW THE WORLD ENTERS THE MIND

The Mexican painter Frida Kahlo (1907–1954) did not simply paint what she saw—she painted what she felt and understood. Kahlo's style of painting is classified as *surrealist* because with her brushstrokes she often distorted objects in order to reveal the feelings, desires, and longings that welled within her as she perceived the world (Lowe, 1995). Kahlo often injected her physical and emotional pain into her paintings.

Kahlo was all too familiar with pain. She contracted polio at the age of 6, which left her right leg thin and weak. During childhood, Kahlo embarked on an intensive program of exercise and athletics to strengthen that leg. But her physical pain did not end there. When she was 18 years old, she was in a horrendous bus accident. She spent most of the next year in bed, during which time she began to paint.

One way that she coped with her pain was to focus on the world around her: She loved watching her husband Rivera paint his giant murals; she enjoyed hearing the songs of street musicians in the local plaza; she reveled in the smells and tastes of Mexican food; she took pleasure in her husband's caresses.

Like all of us, Frida Kahlo had contact with the world only through her senses—her vision, hearing, tense of touch, and all the rest. Although she may have taken the workings of her senses for granted, the way they work is neither simple nor obvious; we experience the world around us initially when stimuli evoke sensations, which our brains then organize and interpret as perceptions. The act of sensing and perceiving stimuli of any kind, whether a song, a color-soaked canvas, or a soft caress, encompasses a remarkable series of events at the levels of the brain, the person, and the social group, all happening within the context of the physical world. The processes of sensation and perception lie at the root of our experience of feeling alive, serving as the foundation for most of what we know and do. If we cannot sense the world, then for all practical purposes it does not exist for us; if we sense it incorrectly, our world will seem bent and distorted. To understand the human mind and behavior, therefore, we must understand how our senses allow us to make contact with the world.

It is through our senses that we initially receive information about what is happening. In fact, we take in such information in two sequential sets of processes: that of *sensation* and then *perception*. **Sensation** arises from neural responses that occur after physical energy (such as light waves or sound waves) stimulates special cells in the sensing organ (such as the eyes or ears)—but before the stimulus is organized and interpreted by the brain. The special cells that are stimulated during sensation are called *receptor cells*, and they work like locks that are opened only by an appropriate key. (Note, though, that receptor cells are different than the receptors *on the dendrites of neurons*, which are activated by specific neurotransmitters in the synapse.) In vision, for instance, light serves as the key; in hearing, sound waves serve as the key. Once receptors cells are sufficiently stimulated, that physical energy is transformed to neural signals that are sent to parts of the brain for the next phase, that of perception. **Perception** arises when the information conveyed by sensory signals is organized into characteristics of objects or events (such as a particular shape of an object or a timbre of a musical note) and then interpreted (such as by identifying the object or sound).

The processes of sensation and perception allow us to see, hear, smell, taste, experience touch, and know where we are in space. In this chapter we explore how we experience the world through our senses and whether there is a sense beyond these—an "extrasensory sense"—that allows us to send and receive information mind to mind and allows us to be immediately aware of distant and future events.

◧ ◧ ◧

Vision

Frida Kahlo learned new ways to look at the world from her father, Guillermo Kahlo, who was a photographer and an amateur painter (Herrera, 1983). Kahlo's experiences watching her father work no doubt led her to develop skills that would later serve her well when she herself took up a brush to become a professional painter. Could such experiences have changed the way Kahlo saw the world? Can having specific experiences change what we see and how we interpret what we see?

Kahlo's label as a surrealist painter comes, in part, from her use of "X ray" images, allowing the viewer to see what cannot normally be perceived. This painting, *The Two Fridas*, was painted in 1939 as Kahlo was getting divorced from Diego Rivera; the Frida on the left is, literally, heartbroken.

Source: Picture Desk, Inc./Kobal Collection

LOOKING AHEAD Learning Objectives

1. What is *sensation*, and how does it differ from *perception*?
2. What is the nature of light, and how do we see color?
3. How are we able to separate figure from ground and see the world as a stable collection of objects?
4. How do we make sense of what we see?

Phases of Vision

Visual sensations are triggered when strong enough light waves cause specialized receptor cells at the back of the eye to send neural signals to the brain. These signals specify fundamental characteristics of the stimulus (such as its color); most of the processes that underlie visual sensation occur in the eye and in subcortical structures of the brain, before the neural signals reach the cerebral cortex. Perceptual processing occurs in the cerebral cortex and organizes the neural signals of sensation, deriving a particular shape, texture, and other features, and then identifies the observed object and its position in space.

Visual perception itself relies on two phases of processing (Marr, 1982; Nakayama et al., 1995):

1. *Organization into coherent units.* When you look at a scene, such as a table piled high with books and papers, you don't see isolated colored patches—you see objects, which have surfaces that are organized into shapes (such as the surfaces of the covers of several books, which are organized into rectangular oblong shapes). To get from sensations to surfaces and shapes, the brain must organize patches of color, texture, edges, and other fundamental visual characteristics into units. As part of this process, the brain must specify the sizes and locations of objects.
2. *Identifying what and where.* After the organizing phase of processing, the surfaces and shapes still don't have meaning; they are just surfaces and shapes. The processes that organize sensory signals are a prelude to the final task of perception, which is to identify what you see (the objects)—to know, for instance, that you are seeing a book and not a bed—and where the objects are, both relative to the body and relative to other objects.

Let's examine more about how we "see" the world around us; first we explore visual sensation, and then visual perception.

Visual Sensation: More Than Meets the Eye

In everyday experience, you may think you have direct contact with the world—but you don't. You know the world only as it is filtered through your senses—in the case of vision, that's your eyes—and your senses are not always accurate. The examples in Figure 1 show how far off base your experience can be.

Scientists have developed careful methods for discovering the relation between what's actually out there and what we sense and perceive, which we explore in the following sections.

Sensation The result of neural responses that occur after physical energy stimulates a receptor cell (such as those at the back of the eye, in the ear, on the skin) but before the stimulus is organized and interpreted by the brain.

Perception The result of neural processes that organize (such as by specifying a particular shape) and interpret (such as by identifying the object) information conveyed by sensory signals.

FIGURE 1 Visual Illusions

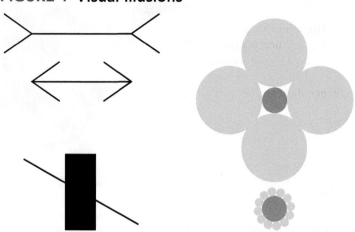

The visual system is not like a camera that accurately captures the world, as illustrated by these visual illusions. The two lines with the arrow heads and tails are in fact the same length; the diagonal line that cuts across the vertical bar is straight, not jagged; and the circles in the center of the two "flowers" are actually the same size.

Psychophysics The field in which researchers study the relation between physical events and the corresponding experience of those events.

Threshold The point at which stimuli activate receptor cells strongly enough to be sensed.

Absolute threshold The magnitude of the stimulus needed, on average, for an observer to detect it half the time it is present.

Just-noticeable difference (JND) The size of the difference in a stimulus characteristic needed for a person to detect a difference between two stimuli or a change in a single stimulus.

Weber's law The rule that the same percentage of a magnitude must be present in order to detect a difference between two stimuli or a change in a single stimulus.

Signal detection theory A theory of how people detect signals, which distinguishes between sensitivity and bias; the theory is based on the idea that signals are always embedded in noise, and thus the challenge is to distinguish signal from noise.

Psychophysics: A World of Experience

Researchers in the field of **psychophysics**, founded by German scientist Gustav Theodor Fechner (1801–1887), study the relation between physical events and the corresponding experience of those events. Researchers in psychophysics made a series of discoveries, which apply to all the senses.

THRESHOLDS: "OVER THE TOP." Much as you cross a doorway when going from one room to the next, stimuli cross a **threshold** when they activate receptor cells strongly enough to be sensed. For example, if a stereo is turned down too low, you won't hear it—it's below your threshold. An *absolute threshold* is the smallest amount of stimulation needed in order to detect that the stimulus is present. For example, if a star is too small or too far away, you won't be able to see it with the naked eye—its light is too dim. The **absolute threshold** is defined as the magnitude of the stimulus (such as the intensity of a light) needed, on average, to allow an observer to detect it half the time that it is present. For example, the absolute threshold for seeing a particular light would be the intensity level where you see it about 50 times when it's shown 100 times, and you don't see it the other 50 times; the intensity teeters right on the threshold of what's visible. If the intensity of a warning light on your car's dashboard is near the absolute threshold, you won't always notice that it's on—which could be a serious problem if the light indicates that your car's radiator is about to boil over.

Sometimes you need to distinguish among stimuli, not simply to detect the presence of a stimulus. For example, when Kahlo was painting the clouds at sunset, she needed to distinguish carefully among the subtle shades of yellow and red that she saw in the sky in order to capture what she saw on canvas. A **just-noticeable difference (JND)** is the size of the difference in a stimulus characteristic (such as the amount of yellow that is mixed with red in order to produce two different shades of orange) needed for an observer to detect a difference between two stimuli (in this case, a difference between two shades of orange) or to detect a change in a single stimulus (such as occurs when a dimmer switch is used to turn down the lights in a room gradually). A JND is a kind of threshold. The change in color might be so slight that sometimes you notice it, and sometimes you don't. This change would be defined as a JND if, on average, you noticed the difference half the time it is present.

The size of a JND depends on the overall magnitude of the stimulus. For example, if you are a thin person, a weight gain of 5 pounds would probably be noticeable at a glance, but if you are on the hefty side, a 5-pound gain might not be detected by anyone but you. Similarly, turning up the light the same amount is much more noticeable when the dimmer switch starts at a low setting than when it starts at a high setting. Why is this? Psychophysicists have an answer: **Weber's law** (named after another German researcher, Ernst Weber), which states that the same percentage of the magnitude must be present in order to detect a difference between two stimuli or a change in a single stimulus. So, the greater the magnitude of the light (or the thickness of the waist or the volume of the sound), the greater the extra amount must be in order to be detected. Weber's law is remarkably accurate except for very large or very small magnitudes of stimuli.

DETECTING SIGNALS: NOTICING NEEDLES IN HAYSTACKS. During World War II, radar operators sometimes "saw" airplanes that did not exist and sometimes missed airplanes that did. The simple fact that people make these kinds of errors led to a new way of thinking about thresholds, and led to *signal detection theory*. The key idea of **signal detection theory** is that signals are always embedded in noise, and thus the challenge is to distinguish signal from noise. *Noise*, in this sense, is extraneous information that interferes with detecting a signal; for example, if you are looking into a room through a screened window, the screen can create "visual noise," making it difficult to see what's in the room.

Such noise can arise (1) from other stimuli in the environment (such as a screen that interferes with seeing or a jackhammer that interferes with hearing a friend speak) and/or (2) from random firings of neurons; neurons are never completely "off"—even when they are not being stimulated, they nonetheless fire from time to time. The task for the brain, then, is to distinguish between neural firings that result from the signal and those that result from noise.

Two key concepts in signal detection theory explain how signals are detected or missed: *sensitivity* and *bias*. **Sensitivity** corresponds to the amount of information required to detect a signal. Having greater sensitivity means that less information is required, which means that you have a lower threshold for distinguishing between a stimulus (the "signal") and the background (the "noise"). Using an example of noise in the environment (rather than from random neural firings), some dots on a radar screen may indicate enemy aircraft, and these need to be distinguished from noise, such as the random specks that arise from pockets of moisture in the air and the specks on the screen that arise from electronic noise; if you have greater sensitivity, you can distinguish between dots indicating aircraft and dots caused by noise even with relatively small differences between the two types of dots. By trying harder to detect signals, you can increase your sensitivity—at least within limits and for a limited period of time.

In contrast, **bias** is the willingness to decide that you have detected a target stimulus (such as the willingness of a radar operator to risk identifying specks as aircraft). If you are very biased, you will be willing to decide that you have seen the target with only a minimal difference between signal and noise. For example, to a farmer gathering his herd at dusk, he may treat even a passing shadow from a wind-blown bush as a cow; in this case, his bias is very strong. In the terminology of signal detection theory, you change your bias by adjusting your *criterion*—the threshold the signal must exceed before you are willing to decide that you have seen the target; if you set the criterion too low, you will decide that you've seen the target even when it's not there because noise alone (such as shadows caused by bushes, not cows) exceeds this threshold.

Psychologists assess sensitivity and bias by comparing the occasions when people *say* a stimulus is or is not present with the occasions when the stimulus is *in fact* present or not (Figure 2; Green & Swets, 1966; MacDonald & Balakrishnan, 2002).

THINK like a
PSYCHOLOGIST Do you think "boosted," or enhanced, sensory sensitivities would be an advantage or a disadvantage? (What if you could see the dirt in the pores on a friend's face across the room?) In what ways would such superabilities be a benefit? A drawback?

FIGURE 2 Signal Detection Outcomes

	Reported Signal?	
	Yes	No
Signal Present? Yes	Hit	Miss
Signal Present? No	False alarm	Correct rejection

Suppose that you are asked to decide whether you've heard a whistle blow (the signal) during an outdoor rally (where lots of talking produces noise). As noted in this figure, your answer will correspond to one of four possible outcomes. Based on signal detection theory, psychologists use the relative frequencies of such outcomes to compute a measure of how sensitive an individual observer is to a signal and to compute a measure of how willing the observer is to decide that he or she has detected the signal.

Christopher Columbus had an intuitive grasp of signal detection theory. He offered a reward to the first sailor to spot land, but then sailors started mistaking low clouds for land. The reward not only increased sensitivity but also lowered the criterion. To adjust the criterion, Columbus announced that sailors who made false sightings would forfeit the reward. Columbus applied this higher criterion to himself and didn't wake the crew on the night he first saw a glimmer of light on a distant island.

Source: North Wind Picture Archives

Sensitivity In signal detection theory, corresponds to the amount of information required to detect a signal, with greater sensitivity indicating that less information is required.

Bias In signal detection theory, a person's willingness to decide that he or she has detected a stimulus.

How Do Objects Enter the Mind? Let There Be Light Information about an object in the world must somehow be converted to a mental specification of the object, such as an image (this is the connection between the "physics" and "psycho" of visual psychophysics). The Greek philosopher Plato, who some 2,400 years ago theorized about many aspects of existence, psychological and otherwise, offered an interesting explanation of how this process works. Plato believed that the eyes produce rays that illuminate objects and that these rays are the basis of sight. This turns out not to be the case, and Plato wasn't the only intelligent person to hold this view: Surveys of college students reveal that a surprisingly high proportion of them—fully one third—believe the same thing. In fact, researchers report that the percentage of students accepting this explanation actually doubles (to 67%) when participants were shown a computer-graphic illustration of the concept (Winer & Cottrell, 1996; Winer et al., 1996). Furthermore, two thirds of the college students who believe in such rays apparently also believe that a person whose rays fail will go blind (Winer et al., 1996). Several studies have shown that these misconceptions are remarkably difficult to change (Gregg et al., 2001; Winer et al., 2002, 2003).

To set the record straight, there are no rays that shine from your eyes; in fact, the process works the other way: Rather than producing rays, the eye registers light that is reflected from, or is produced by, objects in the line of sight. ✳ Explore

Light is a form of electromagnetic radiation. All of us swim in a sea of electromagnetic radiation. This sea has waves: some large, some small, some that come in rapid succession, some spaced far apart. The height of a wave is its **amplitude**, and the number of waves arriving each second is the **frequency**. With higher frequency, the peaks of the waves arrive more often. When more peaks arrive per second, there is less distance between them, and hence the light is said to have a shorter **wavelength**. The distance between light waves is measured in *nanometers*, or millionths of a meter. Within the electromagnetic spectrum, the human eye senses—or sees—as visible light only a narrow band of radiation. Within this narrow band, our eyes and brains are sensitive to slight differences in wavelength, which we perceive as different colors. An almost uncountable number of colors are conveyed by this light; the traditional seven we readily distinguish are red, orange, yellow, green, blue, indigo, and violet. The lower frequencies (and longer wavelengths—more nanometers) are toward the red end of the spectrum; the higher frequencies (and shorter wavelengths) are toward the violet end, as illustrated in Figure 3, which also illustrates the properties of light.

The Brain's Eye: More Than a Camera The eye converts the electromagnetic energy that is light into neural signals; this conversion process is called **transduction**. Light enters the eye through an opening called the **pupil** (see Figure 4). Surrounding the pupil is a circular muscle called the **iris**. The iris changes the size of the pupil to let in more or less light. The **cornea**—the transparent covering over the iris and pupil—focuses the light as it first enters the eye, and then the focusing is fine-tuned by the *lens*. Unlike a camera lens, the lens in a human eye flexes. In fact, muscles can adjust the lens into a more or less round shape to focus light from objects that are different distances away. **Accommodation**, the

✳ Explore **Receptive Fields** on mypsychlab.com

Amplitude The height of the peaks in a light wave or sound wave.

Frequency The number of light waves or sound waves that move past a given point per second.

Wavelength The distance between the arrival of peaks of a light wave or sound wave; shorter wavelengths correspond to higher frequencies.

Transduction The process whereby physical energy is converted by a sensory receptor cell into neural signals.

Pupil The opening in the eye through which light passes.

Iris The circular muscle that adjusts the size of the pupil.

Cornea The transparent covering over the eye, which (along with the lens) focuses light onto the back of the eye.

Accommodation The automatic adjustment of the eye for seeing at particular distances, which occurs when muscles adjust the shape of the lens so that it focuses incoming light toward the back of the eye (the *retina*).

Retina A sheet of tissue at the back of the eye containing cells that convert light to neural signals.

Fovea The small, central region of the retina with the highest density of cones and the highest resolution.

Rods Rod-shaped retinal receptor cells that are very sensitive to light but register only shades of gray.

Cones Cone-shaped retinal receptor cells that respond most strongly to one of three wavelengths of light; the combined signals from cones that are most sensitive to different wavelengths play a key role in producing color vision.

Optic nerve The large bundle of axons carrying neural signals from the retina into the brain.

FIGURE 3 The Range of Electromagnetic Radiation

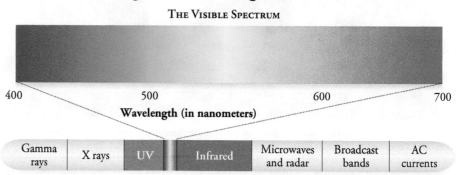

THE VISIBLE SPECTRUM

Wavelength (in nanometers)

| Gamma rays | X rays | UV | Infrared | Microwaves and radar | Broadcast bands | AC currents |

Note that only a small portion of the range comprises visible light and that the color depends on the wavelength.

automatic adjustment of the eye for seeing at particular distances, occurs when muscles change the shape of the lens so that it properly focuses incoming light from near and faraway objects into the eye. With age, the lens thickens and becomes less flexible (Fatt & Weissman, 1992), and hence it does not focus the light as effectively; this problem often causes older people to have trouble seeing nearer objects, such as reading material.

TRANSDUCTION: FROM PHOTONS TO NEURONS. The critical step in the transduction of light waves to neural signals occurs at the *retina*. The **retina** is a sheet of tissue at the back of the eye—about as thick as a piece of paper—containing receptor cells that convert light to neural signals (Wässle, 2004). The central part of the retina (where an image of a dot would fall if you were looking directly at it) contains the most densely packed receptor cells that transform light to neural signals, and this central region—called the **fovea**—gives rise to the sharpest images. The density of receptor cells drops off toward the periphery of the retina, and thus images that are transduced from peripheral portions of the retina are not as sharp as those transduced from the central region. Most of the time we notice only the images that strike the fovea, which are sharp and clear, but much of what we see is, in fact, not very sharp; the world generally appears sharp and clear because we constantly move our eyes, focusing on objects in different locations so that they each—at one moment or another—lands on the fovea. To get a sense of the dropoff in acuity for images that strike the periphery of the retina, take a moment to look up and focus on a single spot on the other side of the room; don't move your eyes, and notice how blurry things look even a short distance to either side of that spot.

Two kinds of receptor cells in the retina are particularly important for transducing light to neural signals: *rods* and *cones*. Oddly, as shown in Figure 5, these cells are at the very back of the eye, which requires light to pass through blood vessels and various other types of cells to reach them. **Rods** (which actually look like little rods) are extraordinarily sensitive to light, and because they respond to all wavelengths of light, they do not register color; rather, rods allow us to sense only black, white, and shades of gray. Each eye contains between 100 million and 120 million rods. The **cones** (which look like, yes, cones) are not as sensitive to light as are the rods, but the cones allow us to see color. The retina has three types of cones, each of which responds most vigorously to a different, particular wavelength of light—and because the different wavelengths correspond to different colors, the cones play a crucial role in allowing us to see color. Each eye contains between 5 million and 6 million cones (Beatty, 1995; Dowling, 1992). The cones are densest in the fovea, and the rods are everywhere within the retina except in the fovea. In very dim light, there isn't enough light for the less light-sensitive cones to work, so night vision is based on the firing of the rods alone. That is why a red apple looks black and an orange cat looks gray under a moonlit night sky.

The axons from rods and cones connect to *retinal ganglion cells*, which function as a kind of gathering station in each eye. The axons of these ganglion cells in turn are gathered into a single large cord called the **optic nerve**, which is about as thick as your little finger. There are no rods or cones at the place where the optic nerve exits the retina, which causes a *blind spot* in what you can see. Because an image that falls on the blind spot in one eye usually falls on another portion of the retina (which does have rods or cones) in the other eye, you are not aware of the blind spot as you look around every day. Look at Figure 6 with one eye, though, and you can discover where your blind spot is.

FIGURE 4 Anatomy of the Eye

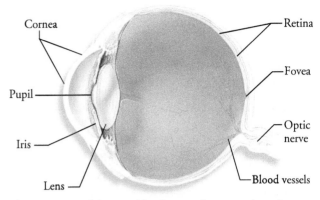

The many parts of the eye either focus an image on the retina or convert light into neural signals that are sent to the brain.

Source: From Goodenough, Judith A., McGuire, Betty A., Wallace, Robert A., *Biology of Humans: Concepts, Applications and Issues*, 1st edition, © 2005, Figure 9.4. Adapted by Permission of Pearson Education, Inc., Upper Saddle River, NJ.

FIGURE 5 Rods and Cones

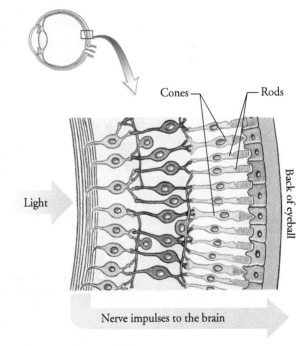

Two types of cells in the retina convert light into nerve signals that produce visual sensations. The rods allow us to see with less light but not in color; the cones allow us to see colors but are not as light sensitive as the rods.

Source: From Goodenough, Judith A., McGuire, Betty A., Wallace, Robert A., *Biology of Humans: Concepts, Applications and Issues*, 1st edition, © 2005, Figure 9.5. Adapted by Permission of Pearson Education, Inc., Upper Saddle River, NJ.

THINK like a
PSYCHOLOGIST To see best at night, look slightly to the side of what you want to examine (because of the way the rods are arranged on the retina). Try the experiment in dim light: Compare what you see when you look directly at an object versus look to the side of it. Try this with objects of different colors, too. To collect your data systematically, use the *DO IT!* log at www.mypsychlab.com; select the *Sensation and Perception* chapter and click on the *DO IT!* folder.

FIGURE 6 Finding Your Blind Spot

X

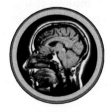

Cover your left eye and stare at the X with your right eye. Now slowly bring the book closer to you, continuing to focus on the X. When the picture on the right disappears, you have found your right eye's blind spot.

DARK ADAPTATION. When you first enter a darkened theater, you can't see a thing; you may have noticed, though, that the risk of tripping or bumping into someone is a lot less if you wait even a brief time because you soon can see much better. In fact, after about 30 minutes in the dark, you are about 100,000 times more sensitive to light than you are when you are in full daylight. The process that leads to increased sensitivity to light after being in the dark is called **dark adaptation**. Part of this increased sensitivity to what light there is arises because your pupil enlarges when you are in darkness; in fact, it can expand to let in about 16 times as much light as enters in full daylight. But letting in more light is only part of the story: In addition, darkness causes the rods to release a chemical called *rhodopsin*, which makes the rods more sensitive to light.

MORE THAN RODS AND CONES. Researchers discovered rods and cones well over 100 years ago, but only recently have they produced evidence for a third kind of receptor in the eye that also registers light. Freedman and her colleagues (1999) studied mice that had been genetically modified so that their eyes had no rods or cones. Nevertheless, these animals still shifted their *circadian behavior* when light was shined on them (circadian behavior is behavior that follows the daily pattern of light and dark, such as waking and sleeping). At the end of this study, the researchers removed the eyes—and the mice then no longer responded to light.

Clearly, animals have some way to detect light that does not depend on rods and cones, and this mechanism is in the eyes. Berson and colleagues (2002) took this research a step further and showed that this third type of light receptor is a certain type of ganglion cell in the retina (as noted earlier, ganglion cells consolidate information from rods and cones in each eye).

Color Vision: Mixing and Matching Color plays many roles in vision. For example, it allows us to tell whether a banana is ripe, helps us identify a barber's pole, and plays a key role in our appreciation of beauty. One of the remarkable aspects of human vision—which makes painting and the appreciation of painting such rich experiences—is the huge range of colors that people can use and see. Indeed, colors vary along three different dimensions:

- *Hue.* Different wavelengths of light produce sensations of different colors, as illustrated in Figure 3. This aspect of color—whether it looks red, blue, and so on—is called *hue*.

- *Saturation. Saturation* is the deepness of the color, which corresponds to how little white is mixed in with it. The more saturated the color, the less white is in it. For example, red is more saturated than pink.

- *Lightness.* The amplitude of the light waves (how much light is present) produces the perception of *lightness* (if the light is reflected from an object) or *brightness* (if the object, such as a TV or computer screen, produces light).

Different combinations of values on these three dimensions produce the incredibly rich palette of human color vision. Given the ways that color can vary and the huge range of colors we can see, you might think that complicated processes underlie our ability to see these visual properties—and you would be right. Color arises through the operation of two distinct types of processes.

Dark adaptation The process that leads to increased sensitivity to light after being in the dark.

COLOR MIXING. In the late 19th and early 20th centuries, researchers debated how humans can see color. One camp took its lead from observations reported by Thomas Young and Hermann von Helmholtz. This approach focused on phenomena such as the mixing of colors to produce new colors (for example, mixing yellow and blue paint produces green paint). These researchers, arguing by analogy to how paints are mixed, believed that we see hue when the eye combines responses to separate wavelengths. In particular, they proposed that the eye contains three kinds of color sensors, each most sensitive to a particular range of wavelengths: long (in the range we see as red), medium (in the range we see as green), and short (in range we see as blue)—and the particular mix of responses of these sensors produces the sensation of a given hue. Because these researchers proposed that the eye has three kinds of color sensors, this view was called the **trichromatic theory of color vision.**

Subsequent research has shown that, consistent with trichromatic theory, our perception of hue arises because most of us possess three different types of cones. One type of cone is most responsive to light in the wavelength seen as a shade of yellowish red, another to light in the wavelength seen as green, and another to light in the wavelength seen as bluish violet (Reid, 1999). One reason we can see many more than three hues is that although each type of cone responds maximally to a particular wavelength, it also responds to some degree to a range of similar wavelengths (De Valois & De Valois, 1975, 1993). And another reason is that the precise ratios of the responses of the three types of cones is different for different wavelengths—and it is this mixture of responses that is the crucial signal to the brain. Just as a painter can produce many hues by mixing three colors in different ways, the brain responds to the mixture of the responses from the three types of cones, not to isolated individual cones.

As if this weren't complicated enough, there's one more twist we must discuss, which concerns the difference between sensing "mixed" colors (mixtures of red, green, and/or blue) that you see on a TV or computer screen versus those that you see when you look at objects in the world. On the one hand, when you look at a TV screen or computer monitor (or any other object from which light is emitted, such as an LED photo frame), the hues of each contributing color are *added* together in each tiny spot on the screen to give rise to the experience of a single color at that spot. When looking at a screen, we "see" the color white because blue, red, and green wavelengths are all being emitted from the same small spot at the same time—and these three wavelengths activate all three types of cones.

On the other hand, when you see a "mixed" color of an object in the world, the hues of each contributing color are *subtracted* from the end result. To understand why, you need to know two facts: First, the light you see has been *reflected* (not emitted) from the object, and not all the wavelengths of light may have been reflected. What you see is wavelengths that have not been *absorbed* by each of the paints; a yellow paint, for example, absorbs all wavelengths except that which produces the sensation of seeing yellow. This wavelength is reflected, not absorbed, and so it reaches your eyes. Second, when you mix paints, the wavelengths absorbed by each type of paint contribute to what is absorbed by the mixture. So even if yellow is reflected by one type of paint, it is absorbed by other types of paint when you mix them. If you mixed red, green, and blue, you would see black: The combination of the paints absorbs all the visible wavelengths that give rise to the perception of hue. Figure 7 illustrates this difference in sensing colors that are emitted versus reflected.

A COLOR TUG-OF-WAR? The other camp in the debate about how we see hue followed the lead of German physician Ewald Hering, who worked at the end of the 19th century and the beginning of the 20th. Hering noticed that whereas some pairs of colors can be mixed to make one

Trichromatic theory of color vision The theory that color vision arises from the combinations of signals from three different kinds of sensors, each of which responds maximally to a different range of wavelengths.

FIGURE 7 Mixing Color

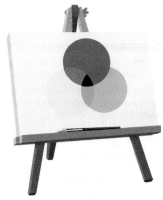

EMITTED LIGHT   REFLECTED LIGHT

The results of mixing colors depend on whether the light waves being sensed are emitted or reflected. When the light is emitted, from a TV screen, for example, the wavelengths of each contributing hue are added; when the light is reflected, from a photograph in a book, for example, the wavelengths of each contributing hue are subtracted.

color have a tinge of the other (such as yellow with a tinge of red), the same is not true of other pairs of colors: You can't mix paints to get red with a tinge of green or green with a tinge of red; if you mix red and green in any ratio, you get a shade of brown. Similarly, you can't mix paints to get a yellowish blue or a bluish yellow; if you mix yellow and blue in any ratio, you get a shade of green. This and similar observations led Hering to develop the **opponent process theory of color vision**, which states that for some pairs of colors, the presence of one inhibits our sensing the other color in the same location on the retina. In particular, red inhibits green, yellow inhibits blue, and black inhibits white (we don't see white with a tinge of black—we see gray). The reverse is also true for all pairs—green, for example, inhibits red.

FIGURE 8 Seeing Afterimages

 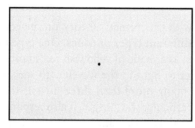

Does this flag look strange to you? Stare at the dot in the center of the flag for about 60 seconds in a bright light and then look at the blank space. You should see a brilliant afterimage of the American Flag, with red and white stripes and a blue field. This illusion arises because of the way the opponent cells work.

To see this inhibition effect in action, take a look at the strangely colored flag in Figure 8. Stare at the flag and then look at the space to its right; you should see an **afterimage**, an image left behind by a previous perception (Thompson & Burr, 2009). Furthermore, the flag should look normal in the afterimage, not strangely colored as it is printed on the page. Why are the colors of afterimages different from those of the object? You need to understand more about color vision to answer that question.

A key fact is that the cones feed into *opponent cells* in the retina and in part of the thalamus, a subcortical structure of the brain. The **opponent cells** respond to one color from a pair at a time— red versus green, yellow versus blue, or black versus white—and inhibit sensing the other color from the pair. When you gaze at a green lime, for example, your opponent cells are making it difficult for you to see the red of a delicious apple at the place where the two fruit touch. This is the sort of effect that Hering predicted, and his ideas have since been developed in more detail (Hurvich & Jameson, 1957; Nayatani, 2001, 2003).

The operation of opponent cells explains why you can't see greenish red or yellowish blue: Seeing one member of a pair inhibits seeing the other. It also explains why you see afterimages like the one illustrated by staring at Figure 8. Here's how such afterimages arise: If you stare at a color, such as red, after a while the cones that register it become adapted to that stimulus, and they stop firing. Thus, if you then look at a white or gray background (which reflects wavelengths that stimulate all three types of cones), the green cones will respond more strongly than the red ones—and these green cones thereby stimulate the red/green opponent cells more strongly than do the red cones, and hence we see green. This same process works with all three pairs of opposing hues. In short, as it turned out, both types of theories—trichromatic and opponent process—were correct, but were describing separate systems that work together.

COLOR BLINDNESS.   You may have noticed that earlier we said that "most of us" possess three different types of cones; the reason we said "most of us" is that some of us do not in fact have all three types of cones—which leads such people to be partially color blind. People who have **color blindness** either cannot distinguish two or more hues from each other (while still being able to distinguish among other hues) or, in more serious cases, cannot see hue at all. Most color blindness is genetic and present from birth (Hayashi et al., 2001; Tanabe et al., 2001). Depending on the specific population tested, as many as 8% of men but less than 0.5% of women are born color blind (Reid, 1999). People who have the most common form of color blindness cannot distinguish red from green. Normally, we distinguish red from green because the two types of cones contain differently colored substances, which filter the incoming light in different ways—thereby making the receptor cell more responsive to certain wavelengths and less responsive to others. For most people with red/green color blindness, the problem arises because their red and green cones have the same colored substance that filters the incoming light (Neitz et al., 1996). Thus, because they filter light in the same way, the two types of cones cones do not respond to different wavelengths as they should—leading two hues to appear the same. A small number of people are actually missing a type of cone. Even more severe deficits occur when more than one type of cone is affected (Reid, 1999).

Opponent process theory of color vision The theory that for some pairs of colors, if one of the colors is present, it causes cells to inhibit sensing the complementary color (such as red versus green) in that location.

Afterimage The image left behind by a previous perception.

Opponent cells Cells that respond to one color from a pair (blue/yellow, red/green, or black/white) and inhibit sensing the other color from the pair.

Color blindness An acquired (by brain damage) or inherited inability to distinguish two or more hues from each other or to sense hues at all.

People with normal color vision see the crayons as shown on the left. People with the most common form of color blindness—inability to distinguish red from green—would see the crayons as shown on the right. Before traffic lights were standardized so that red is always on the top, not being able to see colors made driving hazardous for people with red/green color blindness. In what other ways would such a disorder affect someone's life?

Source: Robert Harbison

Not all color blindness is genetic and present from birth; some people become color blind only after a particular part of their brains is damaged. When this part of the brain (located in the bottom portion of the temporal lobe) is damaged, patients can no longer distinguish hue—they see the world as if in a black-and-white photo. Losing color perception can have profound effects on a person's experience of the world. For example, in Oliver Sacks's (1995) book *An Anthropologist on Mars*, a color-blind artist describes how hard it is for him to eat certain foods, particularly red foods (such as apples and tomatoes), which appear to him to be a repulsive deep black. Nevertheless, in spite of not being able to sense color, at least some of these unfortunate people can still use wavelength variation to track moving objects and even to see shape; this remarkable ability appears to arise from the functioning of the color-opponent system (Cole et al., 2003).

Phase 1 of Visual Perception: Organizing the Visual World

Although it may seem that we perceive the world effortlessly, in—literally—the blink of an eye, a large number of mental steps actually occur between the time your brain receives neural signals from your eyes and the time you identify an object in front of you. At each of these different steps, different parts of the brain play a role in allowing you to perceive (Connor, 2002; Grill-Spector et al., 1998; Husain & Jackson, 2001; Olson, 2001; Sheinberg & Logothetis, 2001). As noted earlier, we can divide the steps of visual perception into two phases (Treue, 2003). In Phase 1, sensory information is organized into units; in Phase 2, these organized units are identified, and the position of each one is specified. In this section, we consider Phase 1, the first step of visual perception after a stimulus has been sensed, and then afterward consider Phase 2.

To get a sense of what is accomplished in the first phase of processing, take a glance at Figure 9. You should have no trouble seeing the sailboats, the buildings, and so forth. Now take a closer look. Like pictures in old comic books, this painting is composed entirely of colored dots; no lines indicate the edges of objects or their parts. Nevertheless, you see separate objects and their parts. How? Your brain effortlessly and unconsciously grouped the dots into patterns.

In fact, this sort of processing is the first step of all visual perception; the edges of most objects are not specified by continuous sharp lines that set the object apart, as in a line drawing. Instead, just as you group the dots in the painting, you group the characteristics signaled by sensory processes (Marr, 1982; Nakayama et al., 1995).

A crucial goal of Phase 1 processing is to separate *figure* from *ground*. The **figure** is a set of perceptual characteristics, such as shape, color, and texture, that typically corresponds to an object, whereas the **ground** is the background; we must distinguish between

FIGURE 9 Inserting Edges

Even though this painting has no lines indicating the edges of objects and their parts, we readily see them. Why? Because we organize the elements—colored dots, in this case—into perceptual groups.

Source: © Erich Lessing/Art Resource, NY

Figure A set of perceptual characteristics (such as shape, color, texture) that typically corresponds to an object.

Ground In perception, the background.

Can you see which animals are present? The coloring of these animals blends nicely with the background. This effect is called *camouflage*.

Source: The Greenwich Workshop, Inc.

figure and ground in order to identify an object. The task of separating figure from ground can range from being relatively easy to being very difficult—if the figure and ground are very similar. When figure and ground are very similar, the figure is said to be *camouflaged*. Note that camouflage works only because of the limitations of our perceptual systems; some other animal, with different perceptual abilities, might be able to distinguish figure from ground when we cannot.

Perceptual Organization: Seeing the Forest Through the Trees

Separating figure from ground involves organizing sensory information into shapes that are likely to correspond to objects or their parts. One facet of this process requires the brain to organize sensory information into regions of space where adjacent points have similar characteristics—as occurs, for instance, when adjacent points of brown at the same distance are organized into a vertical elongated shape (which may, for example, indicate a tree trunk).

In addition to organizing regions of common characteristics, the brain must specify the edges of objects; edges are often an important aspect of separating figure from ground—which, as we just saw, can be challenging. Edges are indicated by a series of adjacent points that separate regions that have different visual characteristics. For example, the sensory information from one region of space might specify something green, bright, and relatively close to you (perhaps these characteristics arise from the green of a tree), whereas the sensory information from another region might specify something brown, dull, and relatively far away from you (perhaps these characteristics arise from the hillside behind the tree); the change from one set of characteristics to another indicates an edge.

Neurons in the occipital lobe (part of the brain entirely devoted to vision) are organized into a set of distinct areas that work together to identify regions and edges between them. The organization of the neurons within each of these areas helps the brain accomplish the task of identifying regions and edges. Specifically, the neurons in each area are *topographically organized*, as shown in the photo: The pattern of light falling on the retina produces signals that activate a corresponding pattern on the surface of the cerebral cortex (Engel et al., 1997; Tootell et al., 1982). This layout allows neurons that are responding to nearby stimuli to communicate quickly and efficiently, indicating where changes in visual characteristics occur—which helps specify where edges are located.

When the brain detects a series of adjacent points where visual characteristics change, it specifies an edge. It does so in part by indicating the orientation of a series of small segments of the edge (such as the extent to which it is horizontal), which allow the brain to indicate precisely the slight twists and turns of edges between objects. David H. Hubel and Torsten N. Wiesel (1962, 1974) received the Nobel Prize in 1981 for discovering that certain neurons (in the first part of the cortex to process visual information—the *primary visual cortex*, in the occipital lobe) fire selectively to sections of edges that have a specific orientation. For instance, some neurons, but not most, fire when an edge is perfectly horizontal; other neurons, but not most, fire when an edge is rotated 5 degrees clockwise from horizontal, and so on. Each neuron fires most vigorously at one specific orientation.

Once regions and edges have been specified, they need to be organized into shapes. A number of well-understood principles specify how this occurs as we see in the following sections.

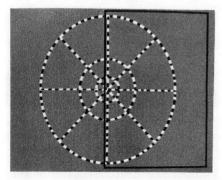

Tootell and colleagues (1982) produced this remarkable illustration of topographic organization in one area of the monkey brain. The animal looked at the figure on the left while radioactive sugar was being taken up by its brain cells. The dark lines on the right show which brain cells were working hardest when the animal viewed the figure (shown here is the left-hemisphere area, which processed the right side of the display). The spatial structure of the figure is evident on the surface of the brain.

Source: From Tootell, RBH, Silverman, MS, Switkes, E, and DeValors, RL1982. "Deoxyglucose analysis of retinotopic organization in primate striate cortex." *Science*, Vol. 218, 26, November 1982. pg. 902. © 1982 American Association for the Advancement of Science.

GESTALT LAWS OF ORGANIZATION. Gestalt psychologists discovered a set of laws that describe how the brain organizes sensory characteristics (Koffka, 1935; Wertheimer, 1923). The most important of these **Gestalt laws of organization** follow: ⊙▶ Simulate

- *Proximity*: Visual characteristics (such as patches that have a specific hue, intensity, or distance) that are near one another tend to be grouped together. So, for example, we see XXX XXX as two groups and XX XX XX as three groups, even though both sets have the same total number of Xs.
- *Continuity* (also called *good continuation*): Visual characteristics that fall along a smooth curve or a straight line tend to be grouped together. For example, we see _ _ _ _ as a single line, not four separate dashes; and we see _ _ _ _ ⁻ ⁻ ⁻ ⁻ as two separate lines because all eight of the dashes do not fall on the same plane.
- *Similarity*: Similar visual characteristics tend to be grouped together. For example, we see \\\/// as two groups.
- *Closure*: The visual system tends to fill in missing parts of a shape. For example, we will see a circle with a small section missing as a circle.
- *Good Form*: Visual characteristics that form a single shape tend to be grouped together. For example, we see [ ] as a single group, but not [_ .

⊙▶ Simulate Gestalt Laws of Perception on **mypsychlab.com**

THINK like a **PSYCHOLOGIST** We are able to perceive most emoticons—text characters that create an image—because of the Gestalt laws of organization. Try this: Which Gestalt laws help you to perceive this emoticon-like symbol as a fish? ><((((o>

AMBIGUOUS FIGURES. Sometimes a figure can be organized and perceived in more than one way. Figure 10 shows two classic *ambiguous figures*. As these figures show, sometimes you can voluntarily organize visual patterns in different ways. But even when you organize such patterns automatically, you organize them not only on the basis of their physical properties but also as a result of learning from previous experience with similar patterns. For example, have you ever thought about becoming a professional "chicken sexer"? Before you dismiss this possible career path out of hand, consider the fact that even during the Great Depression, members of this profession prospered. Why? Chicken farmers didn't want to send female chickens to be cooked in someone's pot—they were for laying eggs. It was the males that were sent to market. However, just looking at the pattern of bumps and indentations on a baby chick's bottom, it's very difficult to distinguish a male from a female. Traditionally, experts required years of practice before they could make this distinction accurately. Biederman and Shiffrar (1987) analyzed the problem and were able to teach people to make the discrimination by observing whether a particular part of the chick's bottom was convex versus concave or flat (which discriminates between the two sexes). However, even after training, these participants were not as accurate as the experts. The participants in the study, although trained, had to look carefully and think about exactly what they were trying to do. For the experts, their perceptual systems had changed so that they could detect the relevant variations in chicks' bottoms with extraordinary accuracy after glancing at a chick for half a second. After extensive practice—in chicken sexing or any other perceptual task—your visual system becomes tuned—you "build in" new processes that organize what you see in a new way (Crist et al., 2001; Olson & Chun, 2002; Vuilleumier & Sagiv, 2001).

FIGURE 10 Ambiguous Figures

In the left panel, you can see either two silhouetted faces or a vase, depending on how you organize the figure; in the right panel, you can see an old or a young woman, depending on how you organize the figure.

Perceptual Constancies: Stabilizing the World

When we look around us—literally, not metaphorically—the world appears stable, even though the images that strike our eyes are anything but stable. Imagine strapping a camera onto your head and making a video as you walk; the images would seem jerky, their sizes would change as you approached objects, the shapes of objects might change (think about seeing a bike from the side versus viewing it from above), and they would sometimes be yellowed in sunlight,

Gestalt laws of organization A set of rules describing the circumstances—such as proximity, good continuation, similarity, closure, and good form—under which visual characteristics will be grouped into perceptual units.

93

Perceptual constancy The perception that characteristics of objects (such as their shapes or colors) remain the same even when the sensory information striking the eyes changes.

Size constancy The perception that the actual size of an object remains the same even when it is viewed at different distances.

Shape constancy The perception that the actual shape of an object remains the same, even when it is seen from different points of view and so the image on the retina changes shape.

Color constancy The perception that the color of an object remains the same even when it is seen in different lighting conditions.

Binocular cues Cues to the distance of an object that arise from both eyes working together.

Notice the relative sizes and spacing of the bricks in this example of a texture gradient, which are cues that the street is receding into the distance.
Source: Bill Lyons

sometimes darkened in shadow. Nevertheless, in spite of such changes in the images that fall on our retinas, objects in the world appear to keep their size, shape, and color even when you view them in very different positions or circumstances. **Perceptual constancy** is the perception that characteristics of objects remain the same even when the sensory information striking the eyes changes. Here are examples of characteristics that have perceptual constancy:

- **Size constancy** occurs when you perceive an object (such as a car) as the same actual size even when it is seen from different distances. This is remarkable because if you took two photographs of a car—a close-up of the car and one of the car in the distance—the size of the image of the car in the second photo would be smaller than that in the first photo. Nevertheless, you don't perceive the car itself as smaller.

- **Shape constancy** occurs when you see an object as having the same shape, even when you view it from different angles. If you took new photographs of the car—this time at the same distance as the first photo but showing it from a different angle (for instance, from the side rather than the front), the car's shape in the second photo would be different than its shape in the first. Nevertheless, you will still perceive that the object itself has the same shape in the two photographs despite the differences in the photos. The fact that you perceive the same shape from different vantage points results not from processing in the eyes but rather from processing in the brain.

- **Color constancy** occurs when you see colors as constant (green as green, red as red, and so on) even when the lighting changes. For example, when Kahlo painted in her studio or bedroom, the lighting conditions were different than they are in a gallery (perhaps the lighting was dimmer in one setting than in the other); nevertheless, the colors will appear to remain the same in the painting no matter where it is viewed. Color constancy results partly from experience; when monkeys are raised in light of only a single hue, for instance, their ability to see colors as constant is later severely impaired (Sugita, 2004). Studies of the brain mechanisms of color constancy suggest that it may occur because we see the lightest thing in a scene as white (no matter what the lighting conditions) and the color of everything else is relative to that white (Land, 1959, 1977, 1983).

Knowing the Distance Establishing how far away objects are from you and how far they are from each other helps you accomplish numerous tasks, such as the following:

- *Separating figure from ground.* The shape of a figure may be a different distance from you than from the background.

- *Preserving size constancy.* We know that when objects are farther away, their images become smaller.

- *Preserving shape constancy.* We use information about the relative distance of parts of an object to help us correct for the shape of the image that falls on our retinas.

- *Guiding navigation and reaching.* For example, in order to walk between a table and chair as we cross a room or in order to reach for a mug of soda, we need to know how far away objects are from us and how far apart objects are from each other.

To accomplish these various tasks, we need to know the relative positions of objects in three-dimensional space. This requirement poses an interesting problem: Our eyes project images onto the two-dimensional surface of our retinas, but we need to see objects in three dimensions. Given that our eyes capture images in only two dimensions, how is it that we see in three? Our brains use a number of types of cues to derive three dimensions from the two-dimensional images on the retinas: *static cues*, *motion cues*, and cues that rely on *movement*.

STATIC CUES. Static (stationary) information is extracted when both you and the object are standing still; such information plays a large role in allowing us to determine how far away something is. One way that we use static information relies on **binocular cues**, which arise from both eyes working together. Because your eyes are separated, they need to swivel toward the center (as they would if you were cross-eyed) in order to focus on an object (so that the same image appears on the central, high-resolution fovea in each eye). The degree to which you swivel your eyes toward the center is called **convergence**, and this is one of the cues that your brain uses to determine distance: The more you have to cross both of your eyes, the closer the object; for example, hold a finger 2 inches from your eyes and notice the degree to which your eyes aim toward the center and compare this to when you hold your finger at arm's length.

Another static cue that your brain uses to assess distance comes from the slight differences in the images striking each of your eyes as you view an object. When you shift your eyes toward the center in order to focus on an object, the images of other objects will fall on slightly different parts of the retinas of the two eyes. For example, say you focus on a chair so that its image falls on the fovea in both eyes; if a dog is slightly in front of and to the left of the chair, the image of the dog will fall at different distances from the fovea in the right and left retinas (Qian, 1997). This difference between the images on the two retinas is called **retinal disparity** (also called *binocular disparity*), and the brain uses the amount of disparity to determine which objects are in front of and which are behind others (Fang & Grossberg, 2009; Julesz, 1971; Pinker, 1997). Retinal disparity works only up to about 10 feet; after that, the disparity is too small for the brain to detect.

Monocular (or "one-eyed") **static cues** for distance can be picked up with one eye, without movement of the object or the eye; such cues operate even for far distances. Monocular static cues are used effectively by artists (even surrealists such as Frida Kahlo) to create the illusion of distance. One of these cues is the **texture gradient**, an increase in the density of the texture of an object with increasing distance (Gibson, 1966). Look at the brick street in the photograph (or, for that matter, such a street in reality). The bricks that are closer to you, the observer, are more distinct; as they recede into the distance, their density (number per unit of space, say, a square inch on a photo) increases, and they begin to blur together—and you use this cue to determine distance.

In drawing pictures, artists also use a variety of other cues—all of which work because we use them in normal perception. For example, *linear perspective*, or *foreshortening*, makes farther-away parts of objects smaller on the paper. Artists also use *atmospheric perspective* to convey distance, taking advantage of the fact that vapor and dust in the air scatter the light, which makes far objects look hazy. They also use *occlusion cues*, in which one object partially blocks another, indicating that the obscured object is behind the other and thus farther away. Artists also make the base of an object appear higher on the horizon than the base of another object, which you take as a cue that the higher one is farther away. Figure 11 provides a good example of the power of these monocular cues.

Cross-cultural studies have shown that people are not born with the ability to interpret some monocular cues in drawings—they must learn to do so (Crago & Crago, 1983; Duncan et al., 1973; Leibowitz, 1971; Liddell, 1997; Nodelmann, 1988). For instance, in some rural parts of Africa, children's books are very rare, which probably explains why young children in such areas may not initially understand all the depth and perspective cues used in drawings (Liddell, 1997). For example, these children sometimes say that trees are on top of a house when the trees are drawn off in the distance, behind the house (Liddell, 1997). Such problems in interpretation disappear with education and experience.

MOTION CUES. **Motion cues** specify the distance of an object on the basis of its movement, and these cues work as well with one eye as with two. In fact, motion cues are so effective that Wesley Walker, blind in one eye from birth, could catch a football well enough to be the star wide receiver for the New York Jets football team (in fact, he played for them for 13 years). To notice a motion cue, try this: Hold up this book and move your head back and forth as you look at it. Note how the images of objects behind the book seem to shift.

Convergence The degree to which the eyes swivel toward the center (are crossed) when a person focuses attention on an object.

Retinal disparity The difference between the images striking the retinas of the two eyes; also called *binocular disparity*.

FIGURE 11 Size Constancy

Even though you know that the two white bars on the rails are in fact the same size, the one that appears farther away also appears larger. This figure is interesting because it violates size constancy: For an object to be perceived as the same size when it is farther away, it needs to cover a smaller area of the picture (or visual field); when objects cover the same area of a picture (or visual field), our visual system assumes that the one appearing farther away is larger.

The woman on the left is actually taller than the boy on the right. How is this possible? The woman is farther away, but this special Ames room (named after its inventor, Adelbert Ames) has been constructed to eliminate the usual monocular depth cues.

Source: Woodfin Camp & Associates, Inc.

Monocular static cues Information that specifies the distance of an object that can be picked up with one eye without movement of the object or eye.

Texture gradient An increase in the density of the texture of an object with increasing distance.

Motion cues Information that specifies the distance of an object on the basis of its movement.

As you shift your head to the left, the distant objects seem to move to the left; as you shift to the right, they shift to the right. Now focus on the background, still holding the book, and move your head back and forth; note how the image of the book seems to shift. This time the object you aren't focusing on, the book, seems to shift in the opposite direction to the way you move your head! Objects closer than the one on which you have fixated (that is, the one on which you've locked your attention) seem to move in the opposite direction to your movements, whereas those farther away than the fixation point seem to move in the same direction. And, depending on the distance, the objects will seem to shift at different speeds.

In short, the way that objects seem to shift with movement provides information about how far away they are, a cue called *motion parallax*. Motion parallax is important when you are moving, and thus it is unfortunate that alcohol intoxication disrupts the brain mechanisms for this sort of depth perception; at least some alcohol-related driving accidents may be traced to this problem (Nawrot et al., 2004).

Phase 2 of Visual Perception: Identifying Objects and Positions

Vision is more than organizing the world into shapes and specifying their locations, of course; the processes involved in Phase 2 of visual perception accomplish two major goals; they allow you to do the following:

- *Identify objects.* You need to assign meaning to the figures you have separated from ground.

- *Identify spatial relations.* You need to interpret and specify (in some cases by naming) how objects are arranged into scenes and their positions relative to you (James et al., 2003; Kosslyn, 1994, 2010; Ullman, 1996).

These two goals are attained by separate mechanisms in the brain. From the results of experiments originally conducted with monkeys, Ungerleider and Mishkin (1982) described two major neural pathways that they dubbed the *what* (properties of objects) and the *where* (spatial properties) *pathways*. As shown in Figure 12, the "what" pathway runs from the occipital lobes (the first part of cortex to receive information from the eyes) down to the bottom parts of the temporal lobes; the "where" pathway runs from the occipital lobes up to the back parts of the parietal lobes. The two pathways continue forward in the brain and come together in the frontal lobes, where information about an object's identity and position is combined and used to make decisions (such as whether to approach or avoid it; Ng et al., 2001; Rao et al., 1997).

Many forms of evidence have characterized the functions of these two visual pathways in the human brain. Some evidence comes from studies of people who have suffered brain damage. Damage in the bottom parts of the temporal lobes impairs the patient's ability to identify objects by sight, and damage in the back parts of the parietal lobes impairs the patient's ability to specify locations of objects (James et al., 2003; Lê et al., 2002; Levine, 1982; Riddoch et al., 2004). Moreover, these separate brain areas are activated during neuroimaging studies in which people without such brain damage are asked to distinguish among shapes or among locations (Bar et al., 2001; Bly & Kosslyn, 1997; Flas et al., 2002; Grill-Spector, 2003; Haxby et al., 1991, 1994, 2001; Kohler et al., 1995; Rao et al., 2003; Tsao et al., 2003; Ungerleider & Haxby, 1994). The operation of these two distinct types of processes is evident even during infancy (Mareschal & Johnson, 2003).

Identifying Objects: Knowing More Than You Can See
When you identify an object, you know more about it than what is immediately visible—for instance, when you identify an object as an apple, you know that inside this object are seeds and, maybe, a worm. For you to know these things, the final phases of perceptual processing must occur, which allow the perceptual units organized during Phase 1 to access information you've stored in memory from your prior experience. To interpret what you see, you need to compare what you are currently

FIGURE 12 Two Visual Pathways

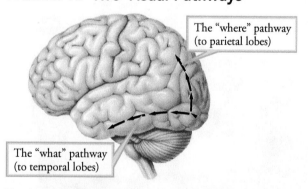

The "where" pathway (to parietal lobes)

The "what" pathway (to temporal lobes)

Visual information flows along two major pathways in the brain. The "where" pathway going from the occipital lobes up to the back parts of the parietal lobes is concerned with spatial properties (such as an object's location), whereas the "what" pathway going from the occipital lobes down to bottom parts of the temporal lobes is concerned with properties of objects (such as their shape and color).

seeing to information that you stored from previous encounters with similar objects. If a shape (with its color, textures, and other visual characteristics) matches something you've stored in memory, the information associated with that previously encountered object can be applied to the present case (and that's how you know that an apple *may* have a worm inside, even if you can't see one *this time*). If the object is *identified*, you know additional facts about it.

The Phase 1 processes that separate figure from ground sometimes organize a shape into a set of distinct parts, and in Phase 2 processing these parts can serve as the basis for identifying the object. Irving Biederman and his colleagues (Biederman, 1987; Hummel & Biederman, 1992) have suggested that

Look at these faces and then turn the book and look at them right-side up. One explanation for the peculiar lapse in noticing the parts is that when you view the entire face, you are attending to a single pattern—but to see the parts in detail, you need to attend to smaller pieces of the whole. Notice that if you focus on each part, you can see that some are upside down.

Source: Steve Azzara\CORBIS- NY

objects are represented in the brain as collections of simple shapes, with each shape's representing a part of the object, such as the head, neck, body, and legs of a dog. It is clear that we can see parts of objects individually (Hoffman & Richards, 1984). But take a look at the two photographs of Britney Spears and then turn the book around so that you can see the photos right-side up. It should also be clear that we do not always identify objects in terms of their individual parts. If that were the case, we wouldn't need to turn the book over to see how weird one of the photos is. Rather, we usually focus on the overall views of shapes and look for details only if we need them (Cave & Kosslyn, 1993).

Informed Perception: The Active Viewer The progression from sensation to organization to identification may seem to indicate a simple sequential process, but more is happening. So far, we've been dis-cussing **bottom-up processing**, which is triggered by light waves that strike the retina, which in turn leads to the events in Phase 1 processing. Bottom-up processing operates like a row of standing dominoes: When the neural equivalent of the first domino is tripped by the light waves reaching your eye, other neural signals are successively tripped, like falling dominoes, until you've understood what you're seeing.

In contrast, **top-down processing** is guided by knowledge, expectation, or belief. For example, go back to the ambiguous figure in the left of Figure 10. Can you intentionally see the two faces or the vase? Top-down processing allows you to impose what you want to see on what is actually out there. However, in most cases, top-down processing does not change how you see an object (the way it changes how you see the ambiguous figure) but instead just makes it easier to organize or interpret it (van Zoest & Donk, 2004). For example, if you are asked whether a fruit that someone points to is a Delicious apple, your brain may activate stored information about the dimples on the bottom that characterize Delicious apples, making it easier for you to see them. Simply expecting to see a particular object not only facilitates separating that figure from ground but also facilitates accessing the relevant information stored in memory.

Bottom-up and top-down processes are often in play at the same time (Corbetta & Shulman, 2002; Humphreys et al., 1997; Kosslyn & Koenig, 1995). For example, if you turn on the TV to a random channel, you will be able to understand what appears on the screen even if it's not a show that you're expecting: The processing is bottom up, from the stimulus alone, unaided by any expectation you might have. Your eyes and ears are stimulated by what's there, and your brain processes the resulting signals. However, after the first few moments of watching this randomly selected channel, even if you seem to be just another vegetating couch potato, you are, in fact, actively anticipating what will appear next and

Bottom-up processing Processing that is triggered by physical energy striking receptor cells.

Top-down processing Processing that is guided by knowledge, expectation, or belief.

Perceptual set The sum of assumptions and beliefs that lead a person to expect to perceive certain objects or characteristics in particular contexts.

using this information to help you interpret what you see—you are engaging in top-down processing. You are using your knowledge of what to expect to help you look for specific characteristics and fill in missing parts of the stimulus. Even if the picture is very blurry, should the sound track of a TV show make it clear that two people are about to kiss, you will be able to see their faces more easily than if no such audio clues were provided. Such top-down processing often helps you integrate what you see with what you hear (Ernst & Bülthoff, 2004)—which is one reason why it's disconcerting to see video clips when the sound is even slightly unsynchronized with the video.

Top-down processing can affect the way you interpret the results from bottom-up processing (Chun, 2000; Corbetta & Shulman, 2002; Humphreys et al., 1997; Kosslyn, 1994). In a classic study by John Delk and Samuel Fillenbaum (1965), for example, participants were shown stimuli that were all cut from the same orangish-red cardboard, including objects that are normally red (such as an apple and a valentine heart) as well as objects that are not normally red (such as a mushroom and a bell). The participants were asked to use a dial to adjust a sample color until they thought it matched the color of the cutouts. The results were clear: When asked to match the color of the normally red objects, the participants consistently selected a redder color than the one they chose to match the color of objects that are not normally red, such as a red mushroom and a red bell. Apparently, the knowledge of the usual color of the objects affected, via top-down processing, how participants saw the actual color.

Top-down processing can be guided by your **perceptual set**, which is the sum of the assumptions and beliefs that lead you to expect to perceive certain objects or characteristics in particular settings or circumstances. For example, when the bottom light on a traffic light is illuminated, you will see it as green even if it is, in fact, a bluish green.

Coding Space in the Brain: More Than One Way to Identify "Where"

We have so far been focusing on the "what" pathway, but researchers have also studied perceptual processing in the "where" pathway. The main goal of processing in the "where" pathway is to use the sum total of the distance cues (discussed earlier) to identify the distance and direction of objects, either relative to yourself or relative to other objects. Kosslyn (1987, 2006) proposed that the brain uses two different ways to specify spatial relations. To get a rough sense of the idea of this distinction, think of the difference between a list of directions ("go straight for two blocks, then turn right") and a map that does not include such directions (just a "picture of a territory"). The list relies on *categorical spatial relations*, which specify relative positions with categories such as "above" or "left of" or "beside." Like all categories, these group together a set of specific examples. For instance, take the simplest list of directions: Say that a friend asks you to go through the door into her bedroom to get her backpack, which she tells you is to the right of the bed. "Right of" is a categorical relation; it doesn't indicate a particular, specific spot but instead gives you a whole group of possible locations—anywhere to the right of the bed.

However, categorical spatial relations won't help very much to accomplish two main tasks of vision: providing information to guide navigation and reaching (Goodale & Milner, 1992; Milner & Goodale, 1995). Knowing that the backpack is "to the right of" (a categorical spatial relation) the bed will not allow you to walk right over to it. For instance, imagine that the electricity went out and the room was pitch black; if all you knew was that the backpack was to the right of the bed, you would have to creep carefully around, feeling your way until you happened upon it. For navigation and reaching, you need precise information about the distance and direction of objects. In contrast to categorical spatial relations, *coordinate spatial relations* specify continuous distances from your body or another object that serves as an "origin" of a coordinate space. For example, your friend might tell you that the backpack is a foot away from the right-hand corner of the head of the bed (see Figure 13). Knowing this, you could find it easily, even in the dark; as

FIGURE 13 Coding Space

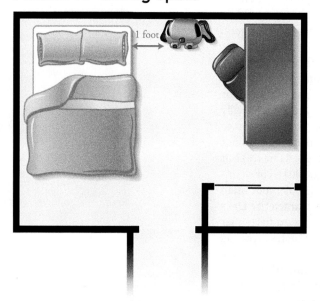

A categorical spatial relation could be used to specify that the backpack is "to the right of" the bed, which would indicate that it could be in any location in the light blue region. A coordinate spatial relation could indicate that the backpack is 1 foot to the right of the back, right-hand corner of the bed, which specifies a particular spot on the floor (shown by the red arrow). Categorical and coordinate spatial relations are useful for different purposes.

soon as you felt your way to the right-hand side of the bed, you would know exactly where to find the backpack.

One source of evidence that the brain does in fact use these two different ways to identify spatial relations comes from studies of *cerebral lateralization*—how functions are accomplished in the left hemisphere versus the right hemisphere of the brain. Kosslyn (1987) proposed that the left cerebral hemisphere may be better at identifying categorical spatial relations, which are easily named by a word or two (and thus are compatible with the left hemisphere's facility at verbal labeling). In contrast, he proposed that the right hemisphere may be better at identifying coordinate spatial relations, which are essential for navigation (and the right hemisphere typically is better at this ability; De Renzi, 1982). This hypothesis has now been supported by many different studies (Kosslyn, 2006; Laeng et al., 2003; Slotnick et al., 2001). For example, patients with damage to the left hemisphere have more difficulty using categorical spatial relations than coordinate spatial relations, whereas patients with damage to the right hemisphere have more difficulty using coordinate spatial relations than categorical spatial relations.

Attention: The Gateway to Awareness

Attention is the act of focusing on particular information, which allows that information to be processed more fully than information that is not attended to. We are aware only of what we pay attention to. Although in this part of the chapter we consider visual attention, we stress that attention operates in virtually all domains of human thought and feeling, not only in visual perception; you can pay attention to a particular instrument in a band, a nuance of a word, a feeling, a taste, a particular place, or the sensation of a ladybug walking over the back of your hand.

We pay attention to something for one of two reasons: (1) The stimulus grabs our attention (bottom-up), or (2) we are actively searching for it (top-down). For instance, if you are walking down the sidewalk the morning after a big storm, you might come across a fallen tree branch in your path (which would grab your attention) and would probably be on the lookout for puddles (which you actively search for). Research has shown that paying attention increases sensitivity (in the sense of signal detection theory, discussed earlier) to the attended events (Nakayama & Mackeben, 1989; Yeshurun & Carrasco, 1998, 1999). **Selective attention** allows you to pick out and maintain focus on a particular characteristic, object, or event, and to ignore other stimuli or characteristics of the stimuli. For instance, after the storm you could be looking specifically for puddles that are too wide to step over easily (and instead need to be circled around). ⊙▶ Simulate

Pop-Out: What Grabs Attention? Certain qualities or features of displays, such as advertisements, automatically (via bottom-up processing) come to our attention—a phenomenon psychologists refer to as *pop-out*. For example, look at the left panel of Figure 14. Is a red dot present? The red dot appears to pop out; it is immediately evident without your having to search for it. Attention is immediately drawn to this "odd man out"

◟ ⌇ ◞

THINK like a
PSYCHOLOGIST To compare categorical and continuous spatial relations, go to **maps.google.com** and obtain directions between where you are now and another destination within a mile. The left side of the screen will display categorical spatial relations (such as to turn left or right), and the right side of the screen will display a map—providing coordinate spatial relations. Are there circumstances in which you would prefer one of these ways to specify location?

⊙▶ **Simulate Selective Attention** on **mypsychlab.com**

FIGURE 14 Pop-Out Versus Search

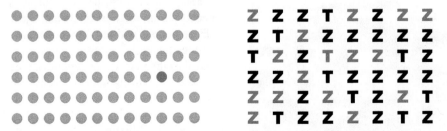

As shown in the left panel, basic features, such as color, are registered without needing an item-by-item search. When pop-out is not possible, you need to search the items one at a time. For example, notice what you do when you try to decide whether there is a red T in the right panel. In general, such a search is necessary to find a combination of features, such as the arrangements of segments or a shape with a particular color.

Attention The act of focusing on particular information, which allows it to be processed more fully than what is not attended to.

Selective attention The process of picking out and maintaining focus on a particular quality, object, or event, and ignoring other stimuli or characteristics of the stimuli.

FIGURE 15

The Stroop Effect

GREEN	RED
RED	BLUE
BLUE	GREEN
BLACK	**BLACK**
BLUE	GREEN
RED	BLUE
GREEN	**BLACK**
BLACK	RED
RED	BLUE
BLUE	GREEN

In 1935, John Ridley Stroop published a classic paper describing what is now known as the Stroop effect. Try it yourself: Name the color of the ink used to print each word in the left column (not the color named by the word); then do the same for the words in the right column. Which is easier? You cannot help both seeing the color and reading the word, and when the meaning of the word is different from the color of the ink, you experience interference.

Source: From *Psychology* by Peter Gray. © 1991, 1994, 1999, and 2002 by Worth Publishers. Used with Permission.

Pop-out The phenomenon that occurs when the perceptual characteristics of a stimulus are sufficiently different from the ones around it that it immediately comes to our attention.

(Krummenacher et al., 2002; Monnier, 2003). In general, **pop-out** occurs when a stimulus differs from other present stimuli in its perceptual qualities, such as size or color (pop-out also arises during hearing, based on frequency; for instance, you immediately hear a high-pitched flute in a band if all the other instruments are playing low notes).

Active Searching: Not Just What Grabs Attention The other reason we pay attention is that we are actively searching for a particular characteristic, object, or event (via top-down processing). In some situations, what we see and hear influences what we expect, which in turn directs our attention (Macaluso, 2010). For instance, when walking under trees after a storm, you could be listening for the sounds of branches swaying suddenly, which would lead you to watch out for a momentary deluge from water on the leaves overhead. In other situations, our initial perception of an event may not be very clear, and so we need a "second look" (or "second hear"). In these cases, our first suspicions of what we might have perceived guide top-down processes to collect more information in a very efficient way. For example, have you ever wondered whether you have actually glimpsed a friend in a crowd (or heard a familiar voice in an unexpected context)? In such circumstances, you then search for distinctive characteristics, such as someone with the shape of your friend's haircut (or the pitch of that familiar voice).

Another use of top-down processing occurs when you anticipate a particular event and thus maintain attention as you wait for it. For example, you might be watching the Olympics and rooting for your country's runners; in this case, you would wait very attentively for the starting gun. The ability to maintain attention as you anticipate an event is called *vigilance*.

However, as shown in the Stroop Effect in Figure 15, we cannot always use top-down processing to focus on one characteristic and shut out others. Bottom-up processing keeps us perceptually honest—we see what's there, not just what we want to see.

Seeing Without Awareness Some people who suffer strokes that leave them blind can nevertheless report accurately when spots of light appear—and will even know where these spots of light are located. These people are not aware of seeing the spots of light but rather simply "know" when they are present. Similarly, animals with damage to the primary visual cortex in the occipital lobe may appear to be blind at all other times, but when they are lowered onto a surface, they stick out their legs to support themselves at just the right point; some of these animals can avoid obstacles when walking, even though the primary visual cortex has been removed and therefore the usual visual perceptual processes cannot be at work (Cowey & Stoerig, 1995). This visual capacity has been called *blindsight* (Cowey, 2010; Weiskrantz, 1986). How does blindsight occur? The optic nerve branches into separate pathways, which lead to different places in the brain (Felleman & Van Essen, 1991; Zeki, 1978, 1993), and one of these pathways bypasses the primary visual cortex, which is a brain area crucial for visual consciousness—the awareness of seeing. Instead, this pathway leads directly to the parietal lobe, which allows people to know the locations of visual stimuli—even when the brain areas crucial for visual consciousness (or connections from these areas) are damaged.

Even people without brain damage will sometimes fail to be aware of what has been processed by their perceptual systems. For example, read the following sentence: A bird in the hand is worth two in the the bush. Did you notice anything odd about it? Many people miss repeated words ("the the" in this case); in fact, spotting repeated words is said to be the hardest error for a proofreader to catch. Nancy Kanwisher (1987, 1991) has dubbed this effect **repetition blindness**, and she and many others

Stimuli used in studies of change blindness.

Source: (left and right) Corel, Courtesy of Ron Rensink/Rensink, O'Regan, and Clark, 1997. *Psychological Science.* Vol. 8, No. 5, September 1997. Need for Attention to See Change.

(such as Morris & Harris, 2004) have shown that people will fail to see a second instance of a stimulus if it occurs soon after the first instance. (A similar effect, called *repetition deafness*, occurs in hearing; Soto-Faraco & Spence, 2001.) Repetition blindness appears to result because repeated stimuli are registered not as individual events but simply as a single "type" of event (Kanwisher, 1987).

In addition, people suffer from change blindness, not seeing even large alterations of features as scenes change over time if those features are not of central interest (O'Regan, 1992; Simons, 2000; Simons & Ambinder, 2005). For example, in one study, the two versions of the scenes in the photographs on the previous page were alternated every 640 milliseconds. In the pair of photos on the left, the railing changes. People had a difficult time noticing this change because it is not of central interest; participants required 16.2 alternations of the two photos, on average, to spot it. In the pair of photos on the right, the helicopter is of central interest, and participants noticed changes in its location after only 4.0 alternations, on average (Rensink et al., 1997).

A related phenomenon is the **attentional blink**, a rebound period in which a person cannot pay attention to a second stimulus after having just paid attention to a previous stimulus. In contrast to repetition blindness, the attentional blink can occur for pairs of different stimuli, not necessarily a second instance of the same or a closely related stimulus (Arnell & Jolicoeur, 1999; Chun, 1997; Jolicoeur, 1998; Luck et al., 1996; Raymond et al., 1992). Proofreaders and copy editors experience this unfortunate phenomenon all the time, missing obvious errors that happen to fall right after a large error or a string of errors. Researchers believe that the attentional blink occurs because the act of registering information in detail may "lock up" certain neural processes for a brief period (within about half a second after seeing the first stimulus), during which time attention cannot easily be reengaged (Fell et al., 2002).

Repetition blindness The inability to see the second instance of a stimulus when it appears soon after the first instance.

Attentional blink A rebound period in which a person cannot pay attention to a second stimulus after having just paid attention to another one (which need not be the same as the second stimulus).

LOOKING AT LEVELS The Essential Features of Good Looks

Source: LeLand Bobbe/Photographer's Choice/Getty Images; (inset) © Volker Steger/Photo Researchers, Inc.

As any painter can tell you, vision is used for more than identifying what objects are and where they are located; through the visual system, we also perceive what we call "beauty," including the physical attractiveness of other people. To understand the basis of how we perceive physical attractiveness, we again consider events at all three levels of analysis.

Faces are clearly an important facet of what we find attractive in other people. Psychologists have conducted many studies to discover exactly which features of faces are perceived to be attractive and have drawn the following conclusions:

- *Smooth skin.* Smooth, even-colored skin is perceived as more attractive than coarser, uneven skin tone (Fink et al., 2001).
- *Symmetry.* Symmetrical faces tend to be perceived as attractive and as healthy (Reis & Zaidel, 2001).
- *Makeup.* Makeup enhances the attractiveness of female faces (Osborn, 1996), especially makeup that darkens the region around the eyes and the mouth; however, such makeup yields precisely the opposite reaction when applied to male faces (Russell, 2003).
- *Female hormones.* Faces that show the effects of female hormones (such as a relatively small chin, full lips, and high cheekbones) are perceived as attractive, and this is true even among people from different cultures. Specifically, David Perrett and his colleagues (1998) asked Asian people (Japanese in Japan) and Caucasians (Scots in Scotland) to choose the most attractive faces from a set of photographs (which included faces from both groups), some of which had been altered to emphasize features that reflect high levels of male or female hormones (see Figure 16 on the next page). The researchers found that men and women in both national groups preferred women's faces with a female "hormone-enhanced" look to average faces. In addition, all groups of participants found even *male* faces more attractive if they showed effects of *female* hormones. Faces that showed effects of high levels of male hormones (such as having thicker brow ridges, a larger chin, and narrow lips) were rated as having high "perceived

FIGURE 16 Effects of Hormones on Good Looks

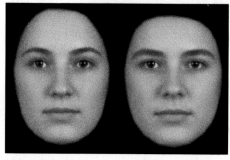

| Caucasian female, feminized | Caucasian female, masculinized | Caucasian male, feminized | Caucasian male, masculinized |

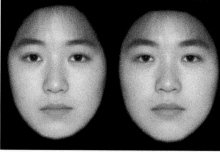
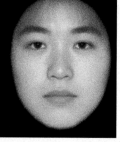
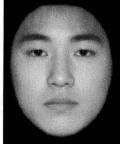

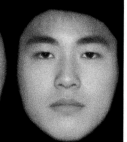

| Japanese female, feminized | Japanese female, masculinized | Japanese male, feminized | Japanese male, masculinized |

Using computer graphics techniques, facial images of Caucasian and Japanese females and males were "feminized" and "masculinized" 50% in shape. Which face in each pair do you prefer? In general, faces that reflect effects of female sex hormones are seen as more attractive.

Source: Perrett, DI, et al. (1998). *Nature*, vol. 394, August 27, 1998, pg. 885. Effects of Sexual Dimorphism on Facial Attractiveness. 884-887.

dominance," as being older, and as having less warmth, emotionality, honesty, and cooperativeness (as well as other attributes).

In fact, at the level of the brain, a specific part of the frontal lobe (the medial orbital frontal cortex [OFC], which is in the midline, behind the eyes) is more strongly activated when people look at attractive faces than when they look at less attractive faces—and is even still more strongly activated when an attractive face is smiling (O'Doherty et al., 2003). This finding is intriguing because the OFC plays a key role in specifying the "reward value" of stimuli, how valuable things are to us.

At the level of the person, we note that the effects of the variables we just considered—the attractiveness of various features—can be modified by learning. For example, take that effect of female hormones: Digitally enhancing the features to have more female characteristics affected the participants' evaluations of the faces of women in a participant's own national group more strongly than it affected participants' evaluations of the faces of women from the other national group. This effect apparently grows out of a person's familiarity with women's faces in his or her own culture.

At the level of the group, beyond feminized features, what's perceived as attractive in one society may not be the same as what's perceived as attractive in another (Jones, 1996); values and tastes develop and are taught, either explicitly (via instruction) or implicitly (via example), to the individual members of the group. In addition, appealing faces are only part of what makes someone attractive. Consider body shapes: People find bodies with a specific weight for a specific height most attractive, but the preferred body shape varies in different cultures and even subcultures (Wetsman & Marlowe, 1999; Yu & Shepard, 1998)—as you might suspect from the art of Rubens, whose plump models would never find work on today's fashion runways. For example, Ford and Beach (1951) considered what people in over 200 cultures looked at when evaluating attractiveness. The researchers found that different cultures focused on different parts and characteristics of the body (such as the size of the pelvis, pudginess, and height). Moreover, people's posture—which may differ, on average, even between countries such as Italy and the United States—plays a role in judgments of attractiveness (Osborn, 1996).

As usual, events at the different levels of analysis interact. For example, hormone levels (level of the brain) depend in part on diet (Nagata et al., 1997), which in turn is affected by events at the level of the group (the content of both a "normal" diet and an impoverished diet can be affected by cultural events, such as wars). Moreover, what an individual considers to be physically attractive (level of the person) is influenced by culture—and such individual judgments and beliefs in turn contribute to the cultural norms (level of the group).

LOOKING BACK

✔●─Study and Review on
mypsychlab.com

1. **What is sensation, and how does it differ from perception?** Sensation occurs when physical energy, such as light waves (or sound waves), stimulates receptor cells such as those at the back of the eye (or in the ear), which then send signals about characteristics of the stimulus—such as its hue—to the brain. We detect a stimulus when it activates receptor cells strongly enough to cross a threshold; stimulation must cross an absolute threshold in order for us to detect that the stimulus is present at all, or constitute a just-noticeable difference (JND) to detect a difference between two stimuli or a change in a single stimulus. Our sensitivity (amount of information required to detect a signal) to stimuli must be distinguished from our bias to classify sensory events as signal (versus treating them as noise). Perception follows sensation and itself occurs in two broad phases; in the first, the sensory characteristics are organized into units that separate figure from ground, and in the second, the figure is identified as a particular object or event and its position is determined.

2. **What is the nature of light, and how do we see color?** Light is made up of electromagnetic waves. These waves enter the pupil of the eye, and the cornea and lens focus the light on the retina. Special receptors and ganglion cells in the retina transduce the light waves into neural signals, which continue along the optic nerve to the brain. Rods are receptor cells that are very sensitive to light but indicate only shades of gray. Cones are receptor cells that are not as sensitive as rods but respond to particular wavelengths of light, which is essential for color vision. Consistent with the trichromatic theory of color vision, most people have three types of cones, with each type most responsive to a particular color: yellowish red, green, and bluish violet. The cones in turn send signals to opponent cells; consistent with the opponent process theory of color vision, opponent cells work in pairs—yellow/blue, red/green, and black/white. The activation of one color in the opponent cell pair inhibits sensing the other.

3. **How are we able to separate figure from ground and see the world as a stable collection of objects?** We perceive figures as distinct from ground in ways that are described by organizational principles, such as the Gestalt laws of organization; these principles include proximity, continuity, similarity, closure, and good form. Critical constancies include size constancy (objects appear the same size in spite of differences in the sizes of the images that fall on the retina), shape constancy (objects seem to have the same shape in spite of differences in the shapes of their images on the retina), and color constancy (colors appear the same in different lighting conditions). In addition, we use information about how far away objects are in order to separate figure from ground, to establish size and shape constancy, and to guide us when we navigate around or to objects and when we reach for objects. Various cues—from both eyes or only one, from static images or moving images—help establish distances of objects from the observer as well as distances among objects.

4. **How do we make sense of what we see?** If you have seen an object before, information about it is stored in your memory; when you see it again, you can match the stimulus to the stored information and apply the information associated with the stored object to the current example. We identify an object when associated information stored in memory is applied to the current stimulus. Once we have identified an object,

information in memory can fill in information missing from the stimulus itself. Bottom-up processing is triggered by physical energy (such as light waves or sound waves) from a stimulus, whereas top-down processing is guided by knowledge, expectation, or belief. Attention is the act of focusing on particular information and is necessary to be aware of that information.

Hearing

According to Diego Rivera's daughter, Frida Kahlo loved whistles. They were sold in stands in the market: "They came in various sizes and made different sounds. She used them to call for [the different house staff], and she created quite a stir when she did" (Rivera & Colle, 1994, p. 100). How is it that Kahlo (and everyone else nearby whose hearing was intact) could *hear* the sounds of the whistles? And how could she (and we) notice that different whistles made different sounds? And how could the staff know who, in particular, was being called by a specific whistle? We see how psychologists have gone about answering such questions in the following sections.

As we discuss hearing, we first consider auditory sensation and then move on to auditory perception. Like vision, we begin with sensory processes that transduce physical energy to signal basic auditory characteristics. And, like vision, we divide the subsequent perceptual processes into two phases, a first phase that organizes sensory characteristics (and separates figure from ground) and a second phase that identifies what the stimulus is that produces the sound and specifies where it is located.

LOOKING AHEAD Learning Objectives

1. How do the ears register auditory sensations?
2. What auditory cues allow us to organize sounds into coherent units and to locate sources?
3. How do we extract the meaning of a sound and specify its location?

Auditory Sensation: If a Tree Falls But Nobody Hears It, Is There a Sound?

Auditory sensations begin when physical energy strikes the ear, at which point that energy (in the form of waves of pressure—often referred to as either *pressure waves* or *sound waves*) is transduced into neural signals. We can understand many facts about auditory sensation by using the same psychophysical concepts that apply to vision, such as absolute threshold, JND, and so on. However, sound waves are different from light waves in key ways, and thus we must begin by considering the nature of the physical energy.

Sound Waves: Being Pressured
Sound usually arises when something vibrates, creating waves of moving air that enter our ears. However, sound can arise when any type of molecules—gas, liquid, or solid—move and create pressure waves. Thus, we can hear when we are surrounded by either air or water or when we put an ear to the ground, to a wall, or to another solid object. An old (but true) cliché of western movies is listening with an ear pressed to a rail to hear whether a train is approaching. But movies sometimes get it wrong. In outer space—where there are no molecules to be moved—we could not hear anything; the loud explosion of the demolished Death Star in the original *Star Wars* movie would, in fact, have been utterly silent.

The pressure waves that create the sensation of sound have peaks (of greater pressure) and valleys (of less pressure), and these patterns occur repeatedly; each complete shift from peak to valley is called a *cycle*. Like light waves, the pressure waves that give rise to sound have both frequency and amplitude; the frequency is the number of cycles per second, and the amplitude is the height of the peaks. We usually hear variations in frequency as differences in **pitch**—how high or low the sound seems (Yost, 2009). It probably is no coincidence that people are most sensitive to the frequencies of a baby's cry, around 2,000 to 5,000 hertz; a hertz, or

Pitch How high or low a sound seems; higher frequencies of pressure waves produce the experience of higher pitches.

Loudness The strength of a sound; pressure waves with greater amplitude produce the experience of louder sound.

Hz, is the number of cycles per second. And we hear variations in amplitude as differences in **loudness**. Loudness is measured in *decibels* (dB). The threshold for hearing is set at 0 dB. Figure 17 presents the loudness levels of some common sounds. Any sound over about 85 dB can impair your hearing if you listen to it for 8 hours straight; a sound over 140 dB can damage your hearing after a single exposure—and 160 dB will probably break your eardrums on the spot (National Institute for Occupational Safety and Health, 1998).

A question often asked in beginning philosophy classes is this: If a tree falls in the forest but nobody hears it, is there a sound? For psychologists, the answer is now clear: No. Sound is *caused* by pressure waves (a physical event), but the waves themselves are not sound. Sound is a psychological event and hence depends on a nervous system to transduce the physical energy of the waves to nerve signals. Without a brain to register the transduced physical energy, there can be no sound. But, by the same token, if you merely imagine hearing a sound (such as a song that you "hear in your head"), that's not a sound either; you need both the "psycho" and the "physical" to have a sound. (That is, the waves in "sound waves" do not themselves convey sound; rather, the waves only give rise to the sensation of sound when they are transduced by the ear, just as light waves only give rise to the sensation of light when they are transduced by the eye.)

FIGURE 17 Decibel Levels

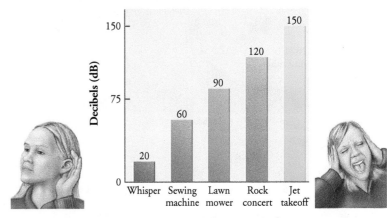

Sound is measured in terms of decibels (dB). Any sound over about 85 dB will damage hearing after 8 hours.

The Brain's Ear: More Than a Microphone The anatomy of the ear is illustrated in Figure 18. The ear has three parts: the outer ear, middle ear, and inner ear. The eardrum (the *tympanic membrane*) stretches across the inside end of the auditory canal, and everything between the eardrum and the auditory nerve is designed to convert movements of the eardrum to nerve signals that are sent to the brain. Specifically, pressure waves move the eardrum, which in turn moves three bones in the middle ear (the hammer, anvil, and stirrup; incidentally, these are the smallest bones in the human body). The three bones of the middle ear not only transfer but also amplify the vibration and cause the *basilar membrane* (which is inside the cochlea, as shown in the right side of Figure 18) to vibrate. The basilar membrane is where different frequencies of sound are transduced into the nerve signals that underlie auditory sensation. Hairs sticking up from receptor cells lining

FIGURE 18 Anatomy of the Ear

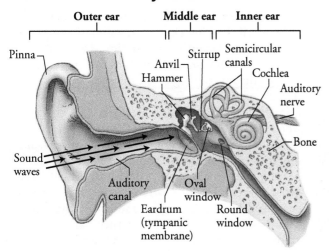 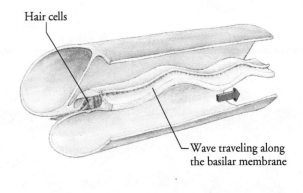

The major parts of the outer ear, middle ear, and inner ear. The semicircular canals have no role in hearing; they help us keep our balance.

If you unwound the cochlea and looked into it (as shown here), you would see the basilar membrane with its hair cells.

Source: From Goodenough, Judith A., McGuire, Betty A., Wallace, Robert A., *Biology of Humans: Concepts, Applications and Issues,* 1st edition, © 2005, Figure 9.11. Adapted by Permission of Pearson Education, Inc., Upper Saddle River, NJ.

FIGURE 19 Place Coding of Sound Frequency

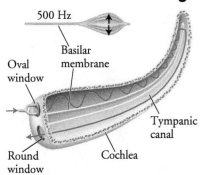

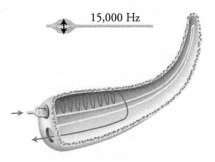

Low frequencies cause maximal vibration of the basilar membrane near one end but also vibrate the entire membrane.

Medium frequencies cause maximal vibration of the basilar membrane near the middle.

High frequencies cause maximal vibration of the basilar membrane near the other end.

Hair cells The receptor cells with stiff hairs along the basilar membrane of the inner ear; when hairs are moved, they produce neural signals that are sent to the brain and underlie auditory sensation.

Frequency theory In hearing, the theory that higher frequencies produce higher rates of neural firing.

Place theory In hearing, the theory that different frequencies activate different places along the basilar membrane.

Conduction deafness A type of deafness caused by a physical impairment of the outer or middle ear.

Nerve deafness A type of deafness that typically occurs when the hair cells are destroyed by loud sounds.

the basilar membrane—these cells are called *hair cells*—are moved by the vibrations and trigger nerve signals, which are then sent to the brain. The **hair cells** function in hearing the same way rods and cones do in vision; they produce the initial nerve signals.

Researchers have formulated two main theories about the way the basilar membrane converts pressure waves to sound sensations. **Frequency theory** holds that higher frequencies produce greater neural firing. However, this theory cannot explain the full extent of our ability to hear: Neurons can fire only about 1,000 times a second at most, so how is it that we can hear sounds produced by much higher frequencies (Gelfand, 1981)? According to **place theory**, different frequencies activate different places along the basilar membrane, as shown in Figure 19. This theory appears to be correct, at least for most frequencies. It is also possible that frequency theory is partly correct—that differences in the rate of vibration of the basilar member convey information about low tones.

The ear not only carries out bottom-up processing but also is affected by top-down processing. For example, if you hear a loud sound, the muscles in the ear reflexively tighten, which protects against damage (Borg & Counter, 1989). These muscles also contract when you talk, which protects your ears from damage by the sounds produced when you talk. Such protection is necessary because the ear is amazingly sensitive: We can hear when pressure waves move the eardrum less than 1 billionth of an inch (Green, 1976).

One study found that almost a third of a group of college students who went regularly to a dance club featuring loud music exhibited permanent hearing loss for high-frequency sounds (Hartman, 1982). Similarly, people who persistently use ear buds with iPods or other MP3 players whose volume is set too high (over 60% of the volume capacity) risk hearing loss (Norton, 2008).

Source: Mark Richards\PhotoEdit Inc.

Deafness: Hear Today, Gone Tomorrow

More than 28 million Americans have some sort of difficulty in hearing (Kochkin, 2001). One common hearing impairment is **conduction deafness**, which can result from any accident or other event that impairs the functioning of the outer ear or middle ear. A broken ear-drum, for example, can cause conduction deafness; conduction deafness can also occur when any of the small bones of the middle ear become locked in place and do not move when the eardrum is moved by sound waves. Another relatively common hearing impairment is **nerve deafness**, which typically occurs when the sound-transducing hair cells are destroyed by loud sounds—and once a hair cell is destroyed, it is gone forever. A rock band (or other kinds of bands that use electronic amplification) heard at close range can produce sounds loud enough to cause this sort of damage. Nerve deafness may impair our ability to hear only certain frequencies; in those instances, a hearing aid can amplify the remaining frequencies, improving hearing.

Phase 1 of Auditory Perception: Organizing the Auditory World

In the last year of Frida Kahlo's life, a Mexican gallery had the first-ever one-woman show of her work. The organizers scheduled a grand party on the show's opening night. Everyone wondered whether Kahlo would appear but doubted it because she had been bedridden for some time. Friends, patrons, and well-wishers crowded into the gallery, waiting to see whether she would arrive. In the distance, they heard a siren, which got louder and louder, and finally an ambulance pulled up in front of the gallery. The ambulance staff carried Kahlo, and the four-poster bed on which she lay, out of the ambulance and into the gallery where everyone was waiting. On any other opening night, the patrons probably would not have paid much attention to the sound of a siren, but on this night they waited eagerly as they heard the sound growing louder.

Like vision, we divide the steps of auditory perception into two main phases. In Phase 1, the sensory characteristics are organized as coming from distinct objects that are located in particular locations; in Phase 2, these organized units are identified or are used to guide movement (as occurs when you locate and then turn your head to watch a particular member of a band play). In this section, we consider Phase 1—the first task of auditory perception after a stimulus has been sensed.

Sorting Out Sounds: From One, Many In daily life, a complex jumble of many sounds—not individual sounds one at a time—usually assaults our ears; to make sense of what we hear, we first need to distinguish individual sounds (Carlyon, 2004), to separate auditory figure from ground. Bregman (1990, 1993) calls this process *auditory scene analysis*, which relies on processes very much like those used in vision. Indeed, the Gestalt laws of organization apply here, too. For example, people organize sounds partly based on similarity (such as by grouping sounds with the same pitch) and good continuation (such as by grouping the same pitch continued over time).

In particular, identifying speech sounds relies crucially on auditory scene analysis because the sounds of one word blend seamlessly into those of the next word; in spite of what you may think you hear, the words do not have pauses between them when we speak. Nevertheless, to communicate, people must identify individual words. This is the **speech-segmentation problem**. By analogy, *thisproblemisliketheoneyouarenowsolving* in vision.

In vision, we see continuous variations in the frequency of light not as continuous variations in hue but rather as different colors. Similarly, we hear speech sounds as members of categories of sound, such as the sounds of the syllables of words. This **categorical perception** automatically groups a range of different sounds (such as those spoken by males, females, or children missing their front teeth) into categories that correspond to the basic units of speech (Jacobsen et al., 2004). For example, we hear the sound "hear" as the same word even if someone is speaking with his or her mouth full while eating or when singing it in falsetto—even though the actual sounds being produced are very different. Such processing produces categories with remarkably sharp boundaries. For example, if a computer is programmed to vary the time between the start of a syllable (the consonant being pronounced, such as "b") and the "voiced" part of the syllable (the sound of the vowel being pronounced, such as "a"), we will hear "ba" if the voiced part starts from 0 to around 25 thousandths of a second after the consonant starts; but if the voiced part starts after a longer interval, we will hear "pa." There is very little intermediate ground; we hear one or the other (Eimas & Corbit, 1973).

Infants (Dehaene-Lambertz & Pena, 2001), as well as monkeys, chinchillas, and various other animals (Kuhl, 1989; Moody et al., 1990), engage in categorical perception; this finding suggests that the perceptual system itself does this work—not the language systems of our various cultures.

Locating Sounds: Why Two Ears Are Better Than One In vision, our brains use slight differences in the images striking the two eyes to assess the distance of an object; similarly, hearing makes use of differences in the stimuli reaching the two ears to assess the distance of a sound source (Yost & Dye, 1991). For example, a *difference in loudness* at the two ears is used as a cue for both the distance and position of the object making

Speech-segmentation problem The problem of organizing a continuous stream of speech into separate parts that correspond to individual words.

Categorical perception Automatically grouping sounds as members of distinct categories that correspond to the basic units of speech.

Barn owls and bats are adept at using sound to localize objects (Konishi, 1993; Suga, 1990). The structure of the barn owl's face has developed in a way to direct sound to its ears; this maximizes location cues. Bats produce sounds and then listen for the echoes coming back. The echoes are precise enough for the bat to discern the shapes of even small objects, in the same way that radar works (Simmons & Chen, 1989).

Source: The Image Works

THINK like a PSYCHOLOGIST Do you think that the way a musician looks or behaves when he or she is performing could influence the way the music sounds? If so, how could this occur?

Cocktail party phenomenon The effect of not being aware of other people's conversations until your name is mentioned and then suddenly hearing it.

Dichotic listening A procedure in which participants hear different stimuli presented separately to each of the two ears (through headphones) and are instructed to listen only to sounds presented to one ear.

the sound. In addition to all of their other functions, our heads are useful because they block sound, and thus the amplitude of a pressure wave is smaller when it reaches the ear on the side of the head away from the sound source. This cue is particularly effective for high-frequency sounds.

We use many different cues to locate an object on the basis of the sound it makes. Some cues depend on only one ear, not two. For example, by moving our heads and bodies, we can compare the relative volume of a sound from different vantage points, which helps us locate its source.

Phase 2 of Auditory Perception: Identifying Objects and Positions

As in vision, sounds become meaningful when they are matched to information already stored in memory, which is accomplished in Phase 2 of auditory perceptual processing. In addition to interpreting speech and music, we also know that the snap of a green bean indicates freshness, that a knock on a door means someone wants to come in, and that a cat's meowing may mean she wants to be fed.

More Than Meets the Ear Frida Kahlo's biography recounts an incident before she was bed-ridden, when she and Diego Rivera were to meet outside a movie theater, but crowds prevented them from seeing each other. In trying to find each other, "Diego whistled the first bar of the *Internationale*. From somewhere in the crowd came the second; it was unmistakably Frida. After this, the task [of finding each other] no doubt seemed easier, and the whistling continued until the couple found each other" (Herrera, 1983, p. 308). Hearing the whistle over the noise of the crowd probably was easier once they knew to listen for their whistled tune. Why would this be? Just as in vision, you can adjust your criterion for "detecting a signal," and this adjustment will be based on what you expect to hear. But also, as in vision, what you expect to hear actually influences what you do hear. A demonstration of such an effect was reported by Warren and Warren (1970), who asked people to listen to a tape-recorded sentence after part of a word had been replaced with the sound of a cough. Although part of the word was actually missing, all the participants claimed that they actually heard the entire word and denied that the cough covered part of it. In fact, the listeners were not exactly sure at what point the cough occurred. This effect, more obvious for words in sentences than for words standing alone, is called the *phonemic restoration effect* (a phoneme is the smallest segment of spoken speech, such as "ba" or "da").

This auditory filling-in effect is not limited to speech sounds, nor is it affected only by other sounds. For example, if you see someone bowing the strings of a cello at the same time as you hear the strings being plucked, the sight of the plucking is enough to alter the sound you hear (Saldana & Rosenblum, 1993). This phenomenon illustrates not only that the sound of music is affected by top-down processing but also that visual information can cross over and affect auditory processing. Indeed, neuroimaging studies have shown that vision can modify how sound is processed in the brain (Thesen et al., 2004).

Hearing Without Awareness We pick up some auditory information without being aware of it. Perhaps the most common experience of perception without awareness is auditory, namely, the **cocktail party phenomenon:** At an event like a large party, you may not be aware of other people's conversation until someone mentions your name—which you typically will hear immediately (Cherry, 1953; Conway et al., 2001). But in order to become aware of the sound of your name, you must have been tracking the conversation all along (using bottom-up processing); you simply were not aware of the conversation until that important word was spoken. In experiments she performed as an undergraduate, Anne Treisman (1964a, 1964b) showed that when people listen to different sounds presented separately to each of the two ears (through headphones) and are instructed to listen to only one ear, a procedure known as **dichotic listening** (Hugdahl, 2001), they still register some information—such as whether the voice is male or female—from the ignored ear (see Figure 20).

This discovery spawned an industry that proclaimed that people can learn in their sleep, simply by playing recordings (purchased at low, low discount prices) while sleeping. Unfortunately, it turns out that unless a person is paying attention, very little information is perceived. And even when information is perceived, it is retained very briefly; when tested hours later, people remember virtually none of the information presented outside their awareness (Greenwald et al., 1991).

Specifying Positions   The auditory and visual perceptual mechanisms that specify position have much in common. Both sorts of processing can specify the position of an object relative to the body or relative to other objects and apparently do so in similar ways: auditory spatial processes and visual spatial processes rely on the same portions of the parietal lobes (Alain et al., 2008; Klostermann et al., 2009; Salmi et al., 2007). Moreover, the two sorts of processes often work together when we note the positions of objects—indeed, people can locate a stimulus in the dark solely on the basis of the sound it emits more accurately if they move their eyes toward the source of the sound (even though they cannot "see" the source!) than if they do not (Dufour et al., 2002).

FIGURE 20 Dichotic Listening

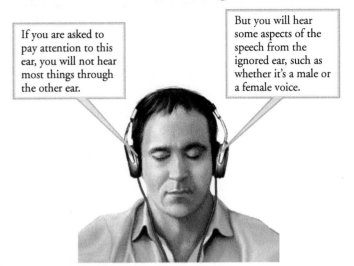

If you are asked to pay attention to this ear, you will not hear most things through the other ear.

But you will hear some aspects of the speech from the ignored ear, such as whether it's a male or a female voice.

Dichotic listening occurs when different messages are provided to each of the two ears, and the person is asked to listen only to one. Even so, some information from the ignored ear is processed.

LOOKING BACK

✓●─[Study and Review on
mypsychlab.com

1. **How do the ears register auditory sensations?** Pressure waves move the eardrum, which causes the bones of the middle ear to move, which in turn moves the hair cells of the basilar membrane, which then transduce the waves into neural signals. The frequency of the waves determines the pitch of the sound, and the amplitude determines its volume. Frequency theory may explain the conversion of pressure waves to sound at low frequencies, and place theory explains it at most frequencies, especially high ones. Conduction deafness occurs when the external or middle ear is impaired; nerve deafness occurs when the hair cells do not function properly.

2. **What auditory cues allow us to organize sounds into coherent units and to locate their sources?** We use similarity of sounds and other Gestalt principles to organize sounds into units. In addition, categorical perception allows us to hear some types of sounds—particularly those from speech—as distinct units, not as continuous variations. We use a variety of cues to localize the sources of sounds, some of which hinge on differences in the way sound is registered by the two ears.

3. **How do we extract the meaning of a sound and specify its location?** As in vision, sounds become meaningful when they are matched to information already stored in memory. Both bottom-up and top-down processes are at work in audition. Top-down processes, which produce phenomena such as the phonemic restoration effect, can fill in fragmentary information. Some of the auditory processes that allow us to identify sounds take place outside awareness and can guide attention. Finally, similar auditory and visual processes identify the position of an object on the basis of the sound it makes.

Sensing and Perceiving in Other Ways

Left to his own devices, Diego Rivera did not bathe frequently—and Frida Kahlo was not fond of his body odor. She bought him bath toys in hopes that they would motivate him to bathe more often (apparently she was successful). Kahlo's sense of smell wasn't the only other sense of which she was keenly aware; she was very aware of tastes. During several lengthy visits to the United States, Kahlo consistently complained about the blandness of American food (although she did like applesauce and American cheese). Kahlo was also

Chemical senses Smell and taste, which rely on sensing the presence of specific chemicals.

aware of the senses in her body; unfortunately, she experienced much pain (and gangrene in her right foot led to its eventual amputation). In the following sections we consider what researchers have discovered about these and other senses.

LOOKING AHEAD Learning Objectives

1. How does the sense of smell work?
2. How does the sense of taste work?
3. How do we sense our bodies?
4. Do a magnetic sense and extrasensory perception (ESP) exist?

Smell: A Nose for News?

Smell and taste are often grouped together as the **chemical senses** because both, unlike the other senses, rely on registering the presence of specific chemicals. Most people are remarkably poor at identifying odors, even though they often think they are good at it (de Wijk et al., 1995). Cain (1979) found that people could correctly identify only about half of 80 common scents; although we may know that an odor is familiar, we may be unable to identify it.

However, people differ widely in their sense of smell, or *olfaction*. Some people are 20 times more sensitive to odors than are other people (Rabin & Cain, 1986); Kahlo may simply have had a better sense of smell than Rivera and hence was more sensitive to his odor when he hadn't bathed. In fact, women are generally better than men at detecting many types of odors (Cain, 1982). Women are particularly sensitive to smell when they are ovulating—unless they take birth control pills, in which case their olfactory abilities do not fluctuate over the course of the month (Caruso et al., 2001; Grillo et al., 2001). In addition, younger adults are better at detecting odors than either children (up to 14 years old) or middle-aged adults (between 40 and 50 years old) (Cain & Gent, 1991; de Wijk & Cain, 1994; Murphy, 1986).

Distinguishing Odors: Lock and Key The most widely accepted theory of odor detection can be described using the lock-and-key metaphor: The molecules are like keys, and the receptors like locks. Specifically, molecules have different shapes, and the olfactory receptors are built so that only molecules with particular shapes will fit in particular places on the receptors (see Figure 21). When the specific molecule fits into a particular receptor, the receptor sends a signal to the brain, and we sense the odor. Just as there is not a single type of cone for each color we can see, there is not a single receptor for each odor we can smell (see Figure 22); rather, the overall pattern of receptor activity signals a particular odor (Freeman, 1991; Friedrich, 2004; Hallem et al., 2004).

Two Americans, Linda Buck and Richard Axel, won the Nobel Prize in 2004 for their work in identifying the genes that produce the individual odor receptors (Buck & Axel, 1991). They found that about 1,000 different genes (which is about 1.3% of the total that we have) are devoted to this task.

Two aspects of the neural bases of olfaction reveal that our sense of smell is tightly bound to emotions and to memories. First, two major neural pathways send signals about odor into the brain: One, connected to the limbic system, is particularly involved in emotions; the other, passing through the thalamus, is particularly involved in memory. Second, neuroimaging studies have shown that the left cerebral hemisphere plays a special role in emotional responses to odors and that the right cerebral hemisphere plays a special role in memory for odors (Royet & Plailly, 2004). The two hemispheres are connected by massive numbers of axons, and these connections explain how odors and memories tap into each other—for instance, remember the way you felt when you unexpectedly smelled a girlfriend's perfume or a boyfriend's aftershave?

FIGURE 21 Lock-and-Key Mechanism of Smell

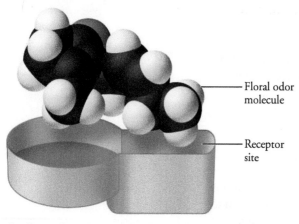

Floral odor molecule

Receptor site

The shape of a molecule is like a key, and the shape of the corresponding receptor is like a lock. When this key fits in this lock, the result is not a door opening, but instead a neural signal is sent to the brain—which gives rise to the sensation of smelling an odor.

Olfaction Gone Awry: Is It Safe to Cook Without Smell?

You may have sometimes wished you could not smell, but losing your sense of smell completely could have dire consequences. Smell serves to signal the presence of noxious substances; our brains are wired so that odors can quickly activate the *stress response*—the bodily changes that occur to help a person cope with a stressor. In addition, we use smell as a warning that something is amiss. For example, it would not be wise to ask a friend who has no sense of smell to cook dinner on a regular basis: Smell is often the only signal that meat or other food is spoiled. Fortunately, relatively few people have no olfactory sense, a deficit that can arise from brain damage or a virus (Doty et al., 1991).

Pheromones: Another Kind of Scents?

Airborne chemicals released by female animals in heat arouse the male of the species. These chemicals are examples of **pheromones**, chemical substances that serve as a means of communication. Like hormones, they modulate the functions of various organs, including the brain. Unlike hormones, pheromones are released *outside* the body, in urine and sweat.

Much to the delight of perfume manufacturers the world over, studies have shown that female pheromones can lead men to be more sexually interested in a woman. In one study (McCoy & Pitino, 2002), university women were asked at the outset to record seven social/sexual behaviors (such as having sexual intercourse or sleeping next to a partner) for 2 weeks (the baseline period). The participants then mixed a substance into their perfume that they applied daily and continued to record those behaviors; the substance was either a clear, odorless pheromone or, for the control group, an identically appearing *placebo*—a medically inactive substance that is presented as if it has medicinal effects. The study used a double-blind design—neither the investigator nor the participants knew whether a given participant received the pheromone or placebo. Participants who wore perfume containing the pheromone reported having more sexual petting (which included affectionate behavior in general), sexual intercourse, sleeping next to a partner, and formal dates—but did not report that more men had approached them, that they had more informal dates, or an increase in masturbation.

However, before male readers start to bemoan the uneven advantage female pheromones might confer, they will be interested to learn that another substance (derived from the human sex steroid compound 4,16-androstadien-3-one, known as AND for short) not only increases positive mood and decreases negative mood in women but also appears to arouse them—while at the same time it apparently relaxes men (Bensafi et al., 2004). Although AND has such effects only at high concentrations, it might have a future role in male colognes or aftershave lotions.

FIGURE 22 The Olfactory System

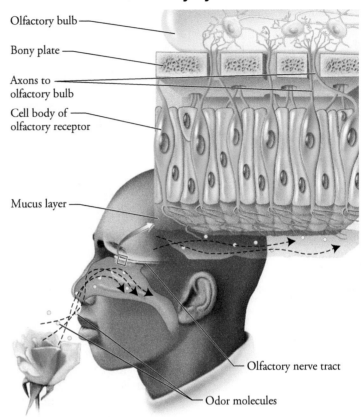

Olfactory bulb
Bony plate
Axons to olfactory bulb
Cell body of olfactory receptor
Mucus layer
Olfactory nerve tract
Odor molecules

Depending on which olfactory receptor cells are stimulated, different messages are sent to the olfactory bulb, the first part of the brain to process such signals.

Source: From Goodenough, Judith A., McGuire, Betty A., Wallace, Robert A., *Biology of Humans: Concepts, Applications and Issues*, 1st edition, © 2005, Figure 9.15. Adapted by Permission of Pearson Education, Inc., Upper Saddle River, NJ.

> **THINK like a PSYCHOLOGIST** If this finding and those about female pheromones hold up with repeated testing, do you think that people who use such substances should warn their dates? Would you use a male or female pheromone as an aphrodisiac? Why or why not?

Taste: The Mouth Has It

When scientists discuss taste, they are talking about sensing via receptor cells located in the mouth, in spite of the fact that much of the flavor we taste involves both these receptors and olfactory receptors. **Taste buds** are the receptor cells for taste, which are microscopic structures mounted on the sides of the little bumps you can see on your tongue in a mirror (see Figure 23 on the next page). You have taste buds in other places in your mouth as well, such as the back of the throat and inside the cheeks (Smith & Frank, 1993). Your taste buds die and are replaced, on average, every 10 days (McLaughlin & Margolskee, 1994).

Pheromones Chemicals that function like hormones but are released outside the body (in urine and sweat).

Taste buds The receptor cells for taste, which are microscopic structures on the bumps on the tongue surface, at the back of the throat, and inside the cheeks.

FIGURE 23 Taste Buds on the Tongue

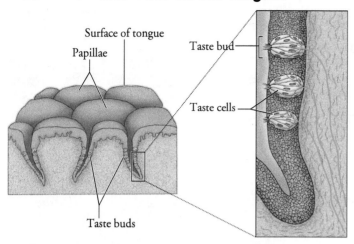

The taste buds on the tongue line the sides of the *papillae*, the visible bumps.

Source: From Goodenough, Judith A., McGuire, Betty A., Wallace, Robert A., *Biology of Humans: Concepts, Applications and Issues*, 1st edition, © 2005, Figure 9.16. Adapted by Permission of Pearson Education, Inc., Upper Saddle River, NJ.

Humans have more taste buds than some species, such as chickens, but fewer than others; some fish have taste buds spread all over their skin (Pfaffmann, 1978). Children have more sensitive taste buds than adults, and thus flavors are presumably stronger for them than for adults—which may account for children's notoriously strong likes and dislikes of foods. Nevertheless, even adults can be remarkably sensitive to slight differences in taste. When wine tasters speak of wine as having a flavor of mushrooms or cloves, they may be sensing the effects of the composition of the soil in which the vines grew.

Sweet, Sour, Salty, Bitter, and More You've seen how a wide range of colors arises from three types of cones and how patterns of odors arise from the combinations of receptors being activated; the brain uses the same sort of mixing-and-matching for taste (Konstantinidis, 2009). Until recently, researchers believed that the flavors of foods arose from combinations of four tastes: sweet, sour, salty, and bitter (Bartoshuk & Beauchamp, 1994; Scott & Plata-Salaman, 1991). A fifth taste, called *umami*, has now been identified. This taste arises from the most abundant amino acid, glutamate, which is present in many high-protein foods (such as meat and seafood). The umami taste is registered by two additional receptors, both of which respond to monosodium glutamate (MSG)—which is often used as a "taste enhancer" in Chinese restaurants (Chaudhari et al., 2000; Ruiz et al., 2003). Moreover, in addition to the five types of taste receptors, dendrites of neurons in the mouth appear to be irritated by spicy foods (Lawless, 1984), and these neurons also contribute to the flavors we experience.

Taste and Smell Most people believe that the flavor of food arises from its taste (Rozin, 1982), but, in fact, much of what we think of as taste is actually smell, or a combination of smell and taste. For example, aspartame (NutraSweet) tastes sweeter if you simultaneously smell vanilla (Sakai et al., 2001). In rats, neural signals that convey information about taste and smell converge on a region of the frontal lobes that is critical for the perception of flavor (Schul et al., 1996). The next time you have a stuffy nose, notice the flavor of your food or lack thereof—particularly when you close your eyes and eliminate top-down processing to fill in your perception of the flavor. Researchers have found that people have a much harder time detecting most flavors when smell is blocked (Hyman et al., 1979). Kahlo might have liked the idea of not being able to smell her husband's body odor, but not smelling at all would ruin the taste of everything from chocolate to chili peppers.

Somasthetic Senses: Not Just Skin Deep

The traditional five senses—sight, hearing, smell, taste, and touch—were listed and described by Aristotle more than 2,000 years ago; today, we know that there are at least nine senses, perhaps ten: sight, hearing, smell, taste, and then a collection of five (or six) senses that together are called **somasthetic senses**. These senses all have to do with perceiving the body and its position in space: *kinesthetic sense* (awareness of where the limbs are and how they move), *vestibular sense* (sense of balance), *touch*, *temperature sensitivity*, and *pain*. There may be a sixth somasthetic sense, *magnetic sense*. And, finally, some researchers have argued that there is possibly an eleventh sense: extrasensory perception, or ESP (Bem & Honorton, 1994).

Kinesthetic Sense: A Moving Sense The **kinesthetic sense** registers the movement and position of the limbs. To experience this sense in action, read this and then close your eyes and hold out your left arm in an odd position. Now, keeping your eyes closed and your left arm in place, touch your left hand with your right hand. You shouldn't

Somasthetic senses Senses that produce the perception of the body and its position in space—specifically, kinesthetic sense, vestibular sense, touch, temperature sensitivity, pain, and possibly magnetic sense.

Kinesthetic sense The sense that registers the movement and position of the limbs.

have any trouble doing this because you know where your hands are without having to see them. You know this because of your kinesthetic sense. Two types of specialized cells sense this information: One type is in the tendons (the material that connects muscles to bones) and is triggered by tension; the other is in the muscles themselves and is triggered by whether the muscle is stretched out or contracted (Pinel, 1993).

Vestibular Sense: Being Oriented

The inner ear is used not only for hearing but also for balance. The **vestibular sense**, which provides information about how the body is oriented relative to gravity, relies on an organ in the inner ear that contains three *semicircular canals* (illustrated in Figure 18). If these structures are disrupted, say, by infection or injury (or by spending too much time in weightlessness in outer space, as happens to astronauts), people have a difficult time keeping their balance.

Touch: Feeling Well

Here's a trick question: What's your body's largest organ? The lungs? The intestines? The answer is the skin. As well as protecting our bodies from the environment (such as dirt, germs, flying objects, changes in temperature), making crucial vitamins, and triggering the release of various hormones, the skin is also a massive sensory organ. Millions of eceptor cells in the skin produce neural signals when stimulated in specific ways. Moreover, once again it is the particular combination of receptors being stimulated that produces a specific sensation, such as the feeling of being stroked or poked. Because of the many ways that signals from receptors can be combined, we can feel many more types of sensations than we have types of receptors.

The vestibular and kinesthetic senses often work together. These people would be out of a job (or worse) if either sense failed. The vestibular sense lets them know how their bodies are oriented relative to gravity, and the kinesthetic sense lets them know where their limbs are relative to their bodies.

Source: John Lund/Blend Images/Alamy Images Royalty Free

In addition, receptor cells in the skin over different parts of the body send neural signals to different parts of the somatosensory cortex; somatosensory cortex preserves a map of the body, with neurons in different locations of cortex indicating that different locations of the body have been stimulated. In general, the larger the portion of somatosensory cortex devoted to a particular area of the skin, the more sensitive we are to stimulation of that area (Weinstein, 1968).

Temperature

The skin has separate systems for registering hot and cold; indeed, there are distinct spots on your skin that register *only* hot or *only* cold. These spots are about 1 millimeter across (Hensel, 1982). If a cold spot is stimulated, you will feel a sensation of cold even if the stimulus is something hot. However, people are not very good at telling exactly where a hot or cold stimulus is located, particularly if it is near the skin but not touching it (Cain, 1973).

Pain

Despite the discomfort, even the agony, pain brings, it usually serves to warn us of impending danger and it is crucial to survival. To appreciate its importance, consider the consequences of not being able to feel pain: Sternbach (1978) described children who could not feel pain and who picked off the skin around their nostrils and bit off their fingers because they didn't receive pain signals to alert them that they were harming their bodies. ◉ Watch

The sensation of pain arises primarily when either of two different neural pathways are stimulated, each of which underlies a different type of pain (Rollman, 1991). And because the two pathways differ in the speed with which they transmit signals, we can feel **double pain**: The first phase, of sharp pain, occurs at the time of the injury; the second phase, which occurs later, consists of a dull pain.

One of the ways we deal with pain is by producing substances in our brains, called **endorphins**, that have painkilling effects. Some drugs, such as morphine, bind to the same receptors that accept endorphins, which explains how those drugs can act as painkillers (Cailliet, 1993).

Pain involves more than simple bottom-up processing; it also relies on top-down processing. For example, a placebo has its effects in part on the basis of what you believe, and

◉ Watch **Brain Pain** on mypsychlab.com

Vestibular sense The sense that provides information about the body's orientation relative to gravity.

Double pain The sensation that occurs when an injury first causes a sharp pain and later a dull pain; the two kinds of pain arise from different neural pathways sending their messages at different speeds.

Endorphins Painkilling chemicals produced naturally in the brain.

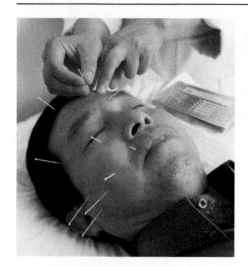

Acupuncture, the placing of small needles in the body to treat pain, may work because the needles are a counter-irritant; this idea makes sense, given the gate control of pain (Carlsson & Sjoelund, 2001; Chapman & Nakamura, 1999).

Source: TEK Image\Photo Researchers, Inc.

activates some of the same brain structures as do drugs such as morphine (Petrovic et al., 2002). In addition, top-down processing can inhibit the interneurons—neurons that are connected to other neurons—that send pain signals to the brain (Gagliese & Katz, 2000; Melzack & Wall, 1982; Wall, 2000), which explains how severely injured people may not feel any pain immediately after the injury. The mechanism that allows top-down processing to reduce pain, called **gate control**, may explain how hypnosis can influence pain (Kihlstrom, 1985); indeed, hypnosis can selectively make pain *feel* less unpleasant but leave a person still aware of the intensity of the pain. Hypnosis thus may alter processing in only some of the brain areas that register pain (Rainville et al., 1997). Inhibitory signals from the brain to neurons that send signals from the body may also occur when pain is reduced by a *counter-irritant*—a painful stimulus elsewhere in the body (Willer et al., 1990). For example, acupuncture may work because the thin needles provide such a counter-irritant, which in turn relieves other pains (Tian, 2010).

Other Senses?

Two additional senses are more controversial. One of these—magnetic sense—may not exist in humans, and one—extrasensory perception—may not exist at all.

Magnetic Sense: Only for the Birds?
Many birds migrate long distances each year, guided in part by the magnetic field of the earth. Tiny bits of iron found in crucial neurons of these birds apparently play a role in this sense (Gould, 1998; Kirschvink et al., 2001). Researchers have also documented that at least some mammals (mole rats and mice) can sense magnetic fields. For example, magnetic fields have been shown to disrupt spatial learning in mice, at least for brief periods of time (Levine & Bluni, 1994). Researchers have been able to zero in on the crucial part of the brain that underlies this effect (a subcortical structure called the *superior colliculus*; Nemec et al., 2001).

Although some researchers have shown that humans may have a weak form of this sense (Baker, 1980), the phenomenon has not yet been studied in enough detail to conclude with certainty whether we do or do not possess it.

Extrasensory Perception (ESP)
The ability to perceive and know things without using the ordinary senses is often referred to as **extrasensory perception (ESP)** but is also sometimes called *anomalous cognition* or *psi*. Many forms of ESP have been described, including *telepathy*, the ability to send and transmit thoughts directly from mind to mind; *clairvoyance*, the ability to perceive events without using the ordinary senses or reading someone else's mind; and *precognition*, the ability to foretell future events. In addition, *psychokinesis* (PK), the ability to move objects simply by willing them to move—not by manipulating them physically—has also been reported (this ability is not a form of ESP since it does not involve perception or knowing).

Most psychologists are skeptical about ESP and PK, for at least the four following reasons (Alcock, 1987, provides additional ones):

- *Failure to replicate.* When studies find evidence that suggests that ESP or PK exists, other researchers typically find that these results cannot be replicated. Some ESP researchers have argued that such failures to replicate occur because the phenomena depend on personality, details of the setting, and other variables (Brugger et al., 1990; Honorton, 1997; Watt & Morris, 1995). But as more such qualifications are added, the claims become increasingly harder to disprove; at some point, such claims can no longer be considered to be scientific hypotheses, but instead are simply assertions based on opinion and belief.

- *Lack of brain mechanism.* It is not known how the brain could *in principle* produce or pick up ESP signals or produce PK signals. Although researchers cannot at present link many abilities (such as "good judgment") directly to specific brain activity, these abilities are consistent with what we know about how the brain works; ESP and PK, on the other hand, would require some entirely new kind of mechanisms, unlike anything yet discovered.

Gate control (of pain) The mechanism that allows top-down processing to inhibit interneurons that send pain signals to the brain.

Extrasensory perception (ESP) The ability to perceive and know things without using the ordinary senses.

- *Lack of signals.* No "ESP signals" have been measured, and it is not known what form these signals might take. For example, physical energy (such as magnetic or electrical waves) typically declines in strength with increasing distance from the source, but there is no hint that the same is true for ESP or PK signals.

- *Alternative explanations.* Finally, although many recent ESP studies are well-designed, many still leave open possible avenues for the influence of other factors. For example, in a study of telepathy, simply having the "sender" (the person trying to send a message mind-to-mind) and the "receiver" (the person trying to receive such a message) in the same room leaves open the possibility of non-verbal communication, such as via sighs or the sound of the sender squirming in a chair.

One study attempted to eliminate all possible confounds and provide an extremely sensitive measure of ESP (Moulton & Kosslyn, 2008). In this study, a "receiver" in one room saw pairs of pictures and had to indicate which one was being viewed (and "transmitted") by a "sender" in another room; after each choice, the correct choice was shown. This task could be accomplished using any of three different forms of ESP: telepathy (if the sender could communicate mind-to-mind with the receiver), clairvoyance (if the receiver could perceive the picture being viewed by the sender), and precognition (if the receiver could see into the future, noting the correct answer after each choice). The receiver's brain activity was monitored by fMRI. The results were clear: There was no behavioral evidence for any of the three relevant forms of ESP, and there was no difference in brain activity when the receivers chose correctly versus when they made errors. In fact, in this study there was no evidence at all for any form of ESP. Could these negative results simply indicate that the technique was insensitive? Probably not, given that even subtle effects of other variables (such as the emotional reactions to different pictures) were clearly evident in the brain scans.

In short, in spite of many years of hard work by many dedicated scientists (Bem & Honorton, 1994; Child, 1985; Thalbourne, 1989), the weight of the evidence does not support the claim that humans have ESP or PK.

THINK like a PSYCHOLOGIST Do you think that researchers should spend time studying ESP instead of studying the nature of learning, reasoning, or the traditional five senses? What are the potential pros and cons of studying ESP rather than abilities that clearly are used by everyone every day?

✓ **Study** and **Review** on **mypsychlab.com**

LOOKING BACK

1. **How does the sense of smell work?** We are able to smell when molecules are the right shape to fit into specific olfactory receptors, which in turn triggers neural signals that are sent to the brain. As with colors, the range of possible smells arises from the combinations of signals from different receptors; we do not have a different receptor for every possible odor we can distinguish.

2. **How does the sense of taste work?** Taste is produced by receptor cells that give rise to five types of tastes (sweet, sour, salty, bitter, and that which is triggered by glutamate) and by neurons that are irritated by spicy foods; it is combinations of such signals produce specific tastes. However, what we experience as flavor, in fact, relies in part on our sense of smell.

3. **How do we sense our bodies?** We sense the positioning of our bodies via the kinesthetic and vestibular senses. The kinesthetic sense lets us know the positions of our limbs and identify body movements. An impaired vestibular sense can cause problems with keeping balance. When stimuli activate receptors on the skin, neurons convey sensations of pressure, temperature, or pain.

4. **Do a magnetic sense and extrasensory perception (ESP) exist?** Some birds definitely can sense magnetic fields, as can some rodents—but it has yet to be solidly established whether or not humans also have this ability. However, the evidence does not support claims that humans have ESP, nor is it clear how the brain would register or transmit the necessary signals.

LET'S REVIEW

((•⧉ **Listen** to an audio file of your chapter on **mypsychlab.com**

I. VISION

A. Sensation results from stimulation of receptor cells, which specify basic characteristics of an object or event, such as its color, whereas perception uses such information to separate the figure from the background and then to interpret the figure as a particular object in a particular place.

B. You detect a stimulus when it activates receptor cells strongly enough to exceed a threshold and hence be sensed. You can increase your sensitivity by paying close attention to the relevant stimulus characteristics. In addition, you can adjust your criterion so that you are more or less willing to decide whether a particular stimulus is present.

C. Vision begins when light waves enter the eye; light waves consist of physical energy of certain wavelengths.

D. The retina, a thin sheet of tissue at the back of the eye, contains types of cells that convert ("transduce") light to neural signals. These signals underlie the processes of visual sensation.

E. Rods are sensitive to light but do not register color, whereas cones register color but are not as sensitive to light. Retinal ganglion cells gather axons from rods and cones and send this information to the brain; the axons from these ganglion cells comprise the optic nerve.

F. The operation of the three types of cones (each of which responds most strongly to a different wavelength of light), in combination with the opponent cells, underlies our ability to see color.

G. The trichromatic theory of color vision focuses on the ways that separate responses to different wavelengths of light are combined, whereas the opponent process theory focuses on the ways that perception of different colors can inhibit perception of other colors.

H. Visual perception can be divided into two phases. The first takes the signals from sensory processing and organizes them into sets of perceptual units that correspond to objects and surfaces.

- The Gestalt laws of organization (such as similarity, proximity, continuity, good form, and closure) describe how the visual system organizes lines, dots, colored regions, and other visual characteristics into perceptual units.

- The distance, size, and shape of figures are also specified so that the perceptions do not vary when the object is seen from different viewpoints. Similarly, color is specified so that we perceive an object as having the same color even when viewing it in different lighting conditions.

I. During the second phase of visual perception, the "what" and "where" of stimuli are identified by separate neural pathways. In the "what" pathway, information about the stimulus is matched to information already stored in memory, which allows you to know more about the stimulus than you can see at the time. In the "where" pathway,

positions are specified, using either spatial categories or spatial coordinates.

J. Perception relies on a combination of bottom-up processes, which arise when physical energy stimulates receptor cells, and top-down processes, which are guided by knowledge, expectation, or belief.

K. Attention is the act of focusing on particular information, which allows that information to be processed more fully than information that is not attended to; attention can be guided both by stimulus properties (bottom-up) and by knowledge, expectation, or belief (top-down).

L. When a different simple feature is embedded in a set of other simple features (such as a red light in a sea of green lights), the different stimulus "pops out" and attention is not necessary for easy detection.

M. Some information can be identified outside visual awareness.

II. HEARING

A. Auditory sensation arises when auditory receptor cells are stimulated by pressure waves that move molecules (usually in air but also in liquids and solids).

B. Sounds differ in pitch (which reflects variations in the frequency of the pressure waves) and loudness (which reflects variations in the amplitude of the pressure waves).

C. Hair cells along the basilar membrane, when stimulated, produce nerve signals, which are sent to the brain. Hair cells can be impaired by exposure to loud sounds.

D. The position of maximal activity on the basilar membrane specifies a sound's frequency, but for low frequencies the rate of vibration of the basilar membrane may also indicate frequency.

E. Auditory perception can be divided into two phases. The first takes the signals from sensory processing and organizes them into sets of perceptual units and specifies the locations of those units in space. Sounds are organized using Gestalt principles (such as similarity in pitch) and are localized using a combination of cues that rely on the two ears (such as differences in loudness) and cues that rely only on a single ear (such as changes in loudness resulting from movement of the head, body, or the object).

F. The second phase of auditory perception occurs when the results from the first phase are matched to information previously stored in memory, which allows the sound to be identified. Top-down processing can actually fill in missing sounds, as occurs in the phonemic restoration effect. The position of the object relative to the body and relative to other objects is also specified in the second phase.

G. People not only understand speech sounds by accessing the appropriate stored memories but also understand environmental sounds (such as the meaning of a siren) by accessing the appropriate stored memories.

III. SENSING AND PERCEIVING IN OTHER WAYS

A. The senses of smell and taste are considered to be the chemical senses because they detect the presence of particular molecules.

B. Both smell and taste involve mechanisms in which a specific molecule triggers a specific receptor, which in turn sends neural signals to the brain. Both smell and taste rely on combinations of receptors' being activated.

C. Pheromones can influence some types of emotional reactions and sexual behavior.

D. Instead of the traditional five senses, we humans have at least nine and possibly ten: In addition to sight, hearing, smell, taste, and touch, humans have a kinesthetic sense, a vestibular sense, temperature sensitivity, the ability to feel pain, and possibly a magnetic sense.

E. The additional senses all inform you about the state of your body (where limbs are located, how the body is positioned or located, what is touching you or otherwise affecting your skin).

F. Each part of the skin is mapped out on the somatosensory cortex, with the percentage of surface in this brain area generally reflecting the relative sensitivity in the corresponding region of skin.

G. Pain is registered by two different neural pathways, which can produce the feeling of double pain. Top-down processing can affect interneurons involved in pain, allowing your beliefs and desires to affect the degree to which you feel pain.

H. Some researchers have argued that an eleventh sense, extrasensory perception (ESP), exists. However, there has yet to be a reliable demonstration that any form of ESP actually exists.

KEY TERMS

absolute threshold
accommodation
afterimage
amplitude
attention
attentional blink
bias
binocular cues
bottom-up processing
categorical perception
chemical senses
cocktail party phenomenon
color blindness
color constancy
conduction deafness
cones
convergence
cornea

dark adaptation
dichotic listening
double pain
endorphins
extrasensory perception (ESP)
figure
fovea
frequency
frequency theory
gate control (of pain)
Gestalt laws of organization
ground
hair cells
iris
just-noticeable difference (JND)
kinesthetic sense
loudness
monocular static cues

motion cues
nerve deafness
opponent cells
opponent process theory of color vision
optic nerve
perception
perceptual constancy
perceptual set
pheromones
pitch
place theory
pop-out
psychophysics
pupil
repetition blindness
retina
retinal disparity

rods
selective attention
sensation
sensitivity
shape constancy
signal detection theory
size constancy
somasthetic senses
speech-segmentation problem
taste buds
texture gradient
threshold
top-down processing
transduction
trichromatic theory of color vision
vestibular sense
wavelength
Weber's law

PRACTICE TEST

✓●─┤Study and Review on mypsychlab.com

For each of the following items, choose the single best answer.

1. When enough physical energy strikes a sense organ, its receptor cells send neural signals to the brain. What is the result?
   a. Sensations arise.
   b. Top-down processing is invariably triggered.
   c. Psychophysics is invalidated.
   d. None of the above statements is true.

2. Weber's law is
   a. always accurate.
   b. never accurate.
   c. remarkably accurate except for very large or very small magnitudes of stimuli.
   d. rarely accurate except for very large or very small magnitudes of stimuli.

3. With normal vision, why does the world appear sharp and clear?
   a. The lens in a human eye cannot flex.
   b. We are constantly moving our eyes, and what we choose to look at can quickly be moved into focus.
   c. The iris changes the size of the pupil to let in more or less light.
   d. The rays produced by the eyes automatically illuminate everything you point your eyes toward.

4. When you first enter a darkened theater, you can't see a thing; if you wait even a brief time, you can see much better. This occurs because
   a. there are no rods or cones at the place where the optic nerve exits the retina.
   b. night vision is based on the firing of the cones alone.
   c. circadian behavior changes when light is shined on the eyes.
   d. your pupil enlarges and the rods actually become more sensitive.

5. The trichromatic theory of color vision
   a. contends that if a color is present, it causes cells that register it to inhibit the perception of the complementary color.
   b. does not apply to the eye but does apply to the brain.
   c. contends that color vision arises from the combinations of neural signals from three different kinds of sensors, each of which responds maximally to a different range of wavelengths.
   d. is not accurate because most of us possess four types of cones.

6. The Gestalt law of organization that is known as _____ states that marks that form a single shape tend to be grouped together.
   a. proximity
   b. good form
   c. similarity
   d. continuity

7. Given that our eyes capture images in only two dimensions, how is it that we see in three?
   a. The Gestalt laws of organization enable us to create a third dimension, and thus we always can see in 3D even with only one eye.
   b. Perceptual constancies stabilize the world.
   c. The brain uses different types of cues to derive three dimensions from the two-dimensional images on the retinas of the eyes.
   d. If an object is *identified*, you know additional facts about it.

8. Paintings and photographs are two-dimensional, and yet they seem to portray information in three dimensions. This is possible because
   a. nearer objects partly block farther objects.
   b. progressive changes in texture signal distance.
   c. farther objects appear smaller in the picture.
   d. All of the above are correct, and additional static, monocular cues are used.

9. Top-down processing
   a. accounts for why pop-out occurs.
   b. cannot be in play at the same time as bottom-up processing.
   c. is guided by knowledge, expectation, or belief.
   d. cannot explain how you are able to recognize objects even when the visual input is degraded.

10. Relative to the right cerebral hemisphere, the left cerebral hemisphere
    a. is better at specifying categorical spatial relationships, which are easily named by a word or two.
    b. is better at specifying coordinate spatial relations, which are essential for reaching to a specific object and for navigating to a goal and avoiding hitting other objects along the way.
    c. is not involved in specifying spatial relations.
    d. can only specify information about space relative to the body.

11. In general, pop-out
    a. is a top-down process.
    b. occurs only in visual perception.
    c. has such great adaptive value that it is the only reason we pay attention.
    d. occurs when objects differ in their fundamental perceptual characteristics.

12. Sound waves are different from light waves in that
    a. only sound waves have amplitude and frequency.
    b. only light waves stimulate receptor cells.
    c. we do not perceive variations of hue on a continuum, but we do perceive variations of pitch on a continuum.
    d. greater amplitudes of sound waves can specify different sound categories.

13. If a tree falls in the forest but nobody hears it, would psychologists say that there is a sound?
    a. yes, always
    b. not unless someone later hears a recording of the sound
    c. yes, but only if the sound is caused by waves of molecules
    d. yes, but only if there are no molecules to be moved

14. The receptor cells in the basilar membrane
    a. transduce pressure waves into the sensation of touch.
    b. are only sensitive to high-frequency sounds.
    c. are called hair cells and are activated by vibrations.
    d. are activated both during hearing and when you move your body in space.

15. In general, women are
    a. less sensitive to odors than are men.
    b. particularly sensitive to smell if they take birth control pills.
    c. no better nor no worse than men at detecting odors.
    d. particularly sensitive to smell when they are ovulating—unless they take birth control pills.

Answers: 1. a 2. c 3. b 4. d 5. c 6. b 7. c 8. d 9. c 10. a 11. d 12. c 13. b 14. c 15. d

Source: Picture Desk, Inc./Kobal Collection

Learning how
to sleep standing up
was probably the
most useful thing
that school ever
taught me.

LEARNING

HOW EXPERIENCE CHANGES US

Jackie Chan, actor, director, martial arts choreographer, and stuntman, begins his autobiography, *I Am Jackie Chan* (Chan & Yang, 1999), at the moment he is 45 years old and about to jump from the 21st floor of an office building in Rotterdam, the Netherlands, for his movie *Who Am I?* The stuntmen on the film had only done the jump from the 16th floor, and Chan never asks his stuntmen to do stunts that he himself would not do. Jackie Chan did, in fact, jump from the 21st floor and land safely.

From *Introducing Psychology: Brain, Person, Group,* **Fourth Edition,** Stephen M. Kosslyn and Robin S. Rosenberg. Copyright © 2011 by Pearson Education, Inc. Published by Allyn & Bacon. All rights reserved.

Chan's kung fu training began early in his childhood: His father woke him up each morning before sunrise and required him to work out for hours as the sun rose progressively higher in the sky. Chan spent all day at home until he was about 6 years old, when he attended first grade; unfortunately, he had a hard time sitting still in the classroom. In fact, he was not promoted to second grade. As an alternative form of schooling, his parents enrolled him in Yu Jim-Yuen's Chinese Drama Academy, a residential school that trained students in the ancient art of Chinese opera.

This school was not like any acting or martial arts school with which you might be familiar. In fact, schools like this no longer exist in Hong Kong because the training methods are now considered abusive. The children rose at 5 a.m., trained in martial arts, singing, and drama, for more than 12 hours, then did chores and perhaps received a couple of hours of traditional "school" a few evenings a week. The children went to sleep at midnight, on the hard wooden floor with only a blanket, in the same room where they trained during the day. Their "day" was 19 hours long, 365 days each year. School discipline included being hit repeatedly with a cane, often past the point where blood was drawn.

As an adult, Jackie Chan no longer had to put his body—and life—under such stress. Yet he performed many dangerous stunts in his career—so dangerous that no insurance company would provide insurance on his films! Why did he put himself at such risk? According to Chan, the answer is that he wanted to please his fans; their approval is very important to him. Chan's abilities to perform stunts (and do them safely), acquire the martial arts he relies on, and direct and script films all reflect the capacity to learn—and the fact that the audience's approval is important to him also plays a key role in his learning, as we shall see.

Learning helps us to survive and underlies most of our behavior: what we eat and the way we eat it, how we dress, how we acquire the knowledge contained in books like this one, and how we live in a society with other people. And yet not all learning has positive results: Sometimes we "learn" to do things that either may not be good for us (as when someone "learns" that downing a few shots of whiskey temporarily leads to feeling relaxed) or may not be what other people wanted us to learn (such as when someone learns that yelling at other people causes them to listen and pay attention). We can learn to do things that hurt as well as help.

What do we mean by *learning*? Psychologists define **learning** as the acquisition of information or a behavioral tendency that is retained for a relatively long period of time. Learning typically changes behavior. For example, young children often work very hard, over months or even years, sometimes with great effort, to learn to read. Eventually, they can sound out new words and understand their meanings. And, once the learning has occurred, it is long term: Once children learn to read, they remember this skill for the rest of their lives. Such durability is true of all learned information and behavior, in virtually every domain of life, from learning the layout of a city to learning how to ride a bicycle.

Learning some elements of a task is not the same thing as having learned to do the task itself. For example, suppose you watch someone write your name in Chinese characters: Having seen it done, can you claim that you have learned how to do it—without actually writing it yourself? The answer is probably no.

Merely watching someone do something complex and unfamiliar on a single occasion may be enough for you to pick up some aspects of the task (such as the number of strokes in the characters) but is usually not enough to allow you to learn it. What if you are only able to *copy* the characters successfully—to look at the characters drawn by the other person and to mimic them? Can you legitimately say that you have "learned" to write your name in Chinese in this case? Even if you copy the characters correctly, the answer is still likely to be no. Just performing an action once is not enough; unless you can do it repeatedly and without assistance, you cannot claim that you have really learned to do it.

At the most basic level, psychologists group learning into two types, associative and nonassociative. *Associative learning* occurs when one object or event becomes associated with another object or event. For instance, Jackie Chan learned to associate doing risky stunts in his films with the audiences' approval of him. In contrast, just as its name suggests, *nonassociative learning* does not rely on the association between two or more objects or events but rather occurs when repeated exposure to the same stimulus alters how an animal (including a human animal!) responds to that stimulus. One type of nonassociative learning is **habituation**, which occurs when repeated exposure to a stimulus decreases responsiveness to that stimulus. For instance, if you are walking in a city and hear a car horn honk nearby, you may well be startled; however, if the horn continues to honk, you will not startle as much (if at all). Here's another example that you've probably experienced: When you first come into the presence of a strong odor—a woman wearing a lot of perfume, a man wearing a lot of cologne, an apartment in which the garbage hasn't been emptied for a week—you will notice the odor. But after a few minutes, the odor will be less noticeable because your olfactory system will have habituated to it.

Another type of nonassociative learning occurs when repeated exposure to a stimulus *increases* responsiveness; this process is called *sensitization*. Here's an example: Suppose you are trying to go to sleep and your neighbor is playing music relatively quietly (you may not have even noticed). All of a sudden, his stereo blasts for a few seconds, then quiets down to the same level it was before. You now will notice the music—at this quiet level—more than you did originally. You are sensitized to it.

Throughout the rest of this chapter, we will explore different types of associative and nonassociative learning, and we'll use to examples from Jackie Chan's life to illustrate the types of learning. For all types of learning, though, the criterion for learning is that we demonstrate that information or a behavioral tendency has been acquired and retained for a relatively long period of time. Let's begin by exploring the model of associative learning investigated not quite a hundred years ago—classical conditioning.

⊚ ⊚ ⊚

Classical Conditioning

Jackie Chan's early life was filled with adversity, often in the form of physical punishment. Within a few weeks of living at the Chinese Drama Academy, Chan received his first caning:

> Master pushed me down to the ground and told me to lie flat on my belly. I closed my eyes and gritted my teeth. I felt my pants being roughly drawn down to my knees, as my belly and thigh collapsed on the polished wooden floor. Then a whistle and a crack, a sound that I registered in my brain just a flash before the pain raged from my buttock up my spine. (Chan & Yang, 1999, p. 38)

Source: Chan & Yang, *I am Jackie Chan.* 1999. p. 38. New York: Ballantine Books.

THINK Like a **PSYCHOLOGIST** To experience habituation systematically, try the activity described in the *DO IT!* log at www.mypsychlab.com: select the *Learning* chapter, and click on the *DO IT!* folder.

Learning The acquisition of information or a behavioral tendency that persists over a relatively long period of time.

Habituation The learning that occurs when repeated exposure to a stimulus decreases an organism's responsiveness to that stimulus.

Classical conditioning A type of learning that occurs when a neutral stimulus becomes associated (paired) with a stimulus that causes a reflexive behavior, and, in time, this neutral stimulus is sufficient to elicit—draw out from the animal—that behavior.

Unconditioned stimulus (US) A stimulus that elicits an automatic response (UR), without requiring prior learning.

Unconditioned response (UR) The reflexive or automatic response elicited by a particular stimulus.

That whistling sound came to elicit fear in Chan; *elicit* means that the response (fear) is drawn out of the animal (in this case, Chan) by a stimulus (in this case, the sound). When a student received a caning (in front of the rest of the students), the entire class would cringe on hearing the sound. This fear response (which includes the cringe) is an example of classical conditioning.

In its simplest form, **classical conditioning** is a type of learning in which a neutral stimulus becomes associated (paired) with a stimulus that causes a reflexive behavior, and, in time, this neutral stimulus alone is sufficient to elicit—draw out from the animal—that behavior. A *neutral stimulus* is one that has not previously been associated with the stimulus and that does not elicit the reflexive behavior by itself; in Chan's case, the neutral stimulus was the whistling sound of the cane moving through the air. In the example with Chan, classical conditioning occurred when the whistling sound of the fast-moving cane became paired with the pain of the beating, and thereafter the whistling sound came to elicit fear (and the cringe response that is one bodily response to fear).

Classical conditioning has many facets, as we shall see in the following pages.

LOOKING AHEAD: Learning Objectives

1. What is classical conditioning? How was it discovered?
2. Can classically conditioned responses be modified?
3. What are common examples of classical conditioning in daily life?

Pavlov's Experiments

The simplest example of the way classical conditioning works is found in the famous experiments that led to the discovery of this type of learning: the work of Pavlov and his dogs. In fact, classical conditioning is also sometimes called *Pavlovian conditioning* because Ivan Pavlov (1849–1936), a Russian physiologist, was the first person to investigate systematically the variables associated with classical conditioning. Pavlov's work on conditioning began by accident. As part of his research on digestive processes, which won him a Nobel Prize, Pavlov studied salivation in dogs. To measure the amount of saliva that dogs produce when given meat powder (food), Pavlov collected the saliva in tubes attached to the dogs' salivary glands (see Figure 1). Salivation usually occurs while eating (to help the digestive processes), but Pavlov and his colleagues noticed that his dogs began to salivate even before they were fed: They would salivate simply on seeing their food bowls or on hearing the feeder's footsteps.

FIGURE 1 Pavlov's Apparatus for Measuring Salivation

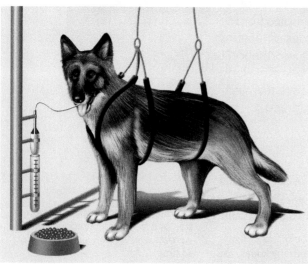

Ivan Pavlov started out measuring saliva production in dogs as part of his research on the digestive system. He went on to use this same saliva collection technique with his investigations into classical conditioning.

Phases of Classical Conditioning Intrigued, Pavlov shifted from studying digestion to studying this new phenomenon, where a previously neutral stimulus came to elicit a particular response. His basic method is still in use today (see Figure 2). Here's what Pavlov did: He sounded a tone on a tuning fork just before the food was brought into the dogs' room (that is, he paired the tone with the subsequent presentation of the food). After several occasions of hearing the tone and then receiving food, the dogs salivated when they heard the tone even when food was not presented. Because food by itself elicits salivation, Pavlov considered the food the **unconditioned stimulus (US),** which is a stimulus that elicits an automatic response that does not depend on prior learning (that's why it's called "unconditioned"). The dogs' salivation is the **unconditioned response (UR),** which is the reflexive or automatic response elicited by a US. The UR does not require learning, but it does depend on certain circumstances. For example, if an animal has just eaten and is full, it will not salivate when given food.

FIGURE 2 The Three Phases of Classical Conditioning

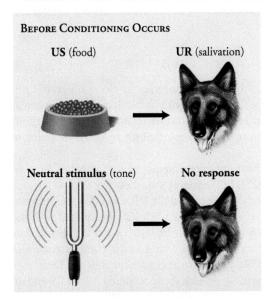

BEFORE CONDITIONING OCCURS

US (food) → UR (salivation)

Neutral stimulus (tone) → No response

1. Before conditioning occurs, the neutral stimulus (that will become the CS) does not lead to a conditioned response, but the US does.

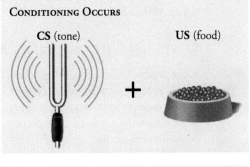

CONDITIONING OCCURS

CS (tone) + US (food)

2. Then the CS is paired with the US—here, the tone is sounded, and then the food is presented.

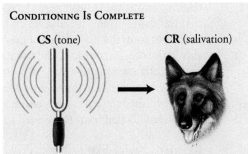

CONDITIONING IS COMPLETE

CS (tone) → CR (salivation)

3. Classical conditioning is complete when the CS elicits the conditioned response—here, the dog salivates after hearing the tone.

In Pavlov's experiment, the tone is the **conditioned stimulus (CS)**, which is a neutral stimulus that comes to produce a response evoked by a US after it has been paired enough times with that US. Pavlov's dogs, after hearing the tuning fork a number of times before they were fed, began to associate the tone with food. Thereafter, whenever the dogs heard the tone, they salivated. Salivating in response to the tone alone is thus a **conditioned response (CR)**, which—more generally—is a response that depends (is conditional) on the prior pairing of the CS with a US (Pavlov, 1927). Psychologists call the initial learning of the conditioned response **acquisition**. ◉ Watch

Watch **Rat Race** on mypsychlab.com

Variations of the Procedure In order to discover what factors affect the process of conditioning, Pavlov—and researchers after him—altered the variables involved in creating a CR. One of the first variables they examined was the timing between the CS and US. Based on Pavlov's work with dogs, researchers hypothesized that in order to create a CR, the US (the food) must immediately follow the CS (the tone). This procedure is called *forward conditioning*, which occurs when the CS begins before the US begins. And in fact, when Pavlov tried the reverse order, he did not find that conditioning occurred. This reverse procedure—where the US comes first, followed quickly by the CS—is called *backward pairing*. In Pavlov's experiments on backward pairing, he fed the dogs first and presented the tone 1, 5, or 10 seconds later. The dogs did not salivate when hearing the tone after eating the food. However, we must note that although Pavlov did not establish backward conditioning with his dogs, other researchers have since found that such conditioning can occur in some animals—but this type of conditioning is rare and only occurs in very specific circumstances (Chang et al., 2003).

Researchers have also varied the timing of the US and CS in another way, presenting the US and CS simultaneously. This procedure is called *simultaneous conditioning*. Simultaneous conditioning does not usually lead to a CR (Hall, 1984), although under some specific circumstances, such conditioning is possible (Albert & Ayres, 1997; Barnet et al., 1991). In short, forward conditioning is the procedure that is most likely to lead to classical conditioning.

Using forward conditioning, researchers have also studied whether classical conditioning can occur when there is a delay between the CS (a tone, in this example) and the US (food). The answer: generally, not very well. That is, conditioning best occurs when the US is presented immediately after the CS. However, again we must note that there are exceptions to this generalization, but in this case some of these exceptions are very important: As we

Conditioned stimulus (CS) An originally neutral stimulus that comes to produce a response evoked by a US after it has been paired enough times with that US.

Conditioned response (CR) A response that depends (is conditional) on pairing the conditioned stimulus with an unconditioned stimulus; once learned, the response to the US now occurs when the conditioned stimulus is presented alone.

Acquisition In classical conditioning, the initial learning of the conditioned response (CR).

shall see, an aversion to a particular type of food is one of the rare examples in which strong conditioning can occur when there is a relatively long interval between the presentation of the CS and the US.

Classical Conditioning: Variations on a Theme

Some types of stimuli and responses can easily be bound together by classically conditioning, whereas others cannot. Moreover, some CRs remain with us for all of our lives whereas others fade or even disappear altogether. In this section, we examine such variations, beginning with a type of classical conditioning that is important for survival—learning to avoid painful stimuli.

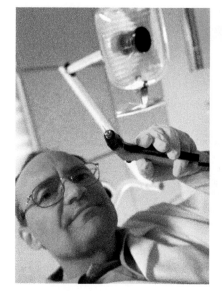

Does avoidance learning explain why some people put off going to the dentist for many years?

Source: Brand X Pictures/Anderson/Ross

While Pavlov was conducting conditioning experiments, so was another Russian researcher, Vladimir Bechterev (1857–1927). In Bechterev's studies, the US was a shock that was delivered to a metal plate under the dog's foot, and the UR was a dog's withdrawal of its foot from the plate. When a neutral stimulus such as a bell (CS) was paired with the shock, the dog learned to withdraw its foot (CR) after the bell but before the shock, thus successfully learning to avoid pain. Bechterev's findings were an important extension of Pavlov's work because they showed that CRs could also affect motor reflexes. Bechterev also established the basis for **avoidance learning**—classical conditioning with a CS and an unpleasant US that leads the animal to try to avoid the CS (Viney, 1993).

Conditioned Emotions: Getting a Gut Response One particularly powerful type of CR is called a **conditioned emotional response (CER)**, which is an emotionally charged CR elicited by a previously neutral stimulus. For instance, if you saw a cane—like the one used to beat students at the Chinese Drama Academy—leaning against a chair, chances are that it would not make you cringe or show any other signs of fear. For you, the cane would be a neutral stimulus. However, for Jackie Chan and his schoolmates, the cane that Master Yu held in his hand was no longer a neutral object or stimulus. Repeated beatings with it created a CER.

A CER was dramatically illustrated in a landmark study by psychologists John B. Watson, the founder of behaviorism, and Rosalie Rayner (Watson & Rayner, 1920). Their study illustrates not only how classical conditioning can produce a straightforward CER but also how fear can lead to a **phobia**, which is an irrational fear of a specific object or situation. Watson and Rayner classically conditioned fear and then a phobia in an 11-month-old infant—Albert B.—whom they called "Little Albert" (see Figure 3). As shown in the figure, Watson and Rayner made Albert afraid of rats; on seeing a white rat, Albert would cry and exhibit signs of fearfulness. (This study could not be done today because of the rigorous ethical principles that now govern psychological research but did not exist at the time the study was undertaken. Moreover, we don't know what became of Little Albert or whether his phobia changed with time; neither Watson nor Rayner followed up on what happened to Albert after the study because the boy and his mother moved away.)

Preparedness and Contrapreparedness Researchers initially thought that forward conditioning could cause any reflexive response to be elicited by any previously neutral stimulus (Kimble, 1981). It turns out that this idea is not correct. Animals have a **biological preparedness**, a built-in readiness for certain previously neutral stimuli to come to elicit particular conditioned responses—which means that less training is necessary to produce learning when these neutral stimuli are paired with the appropriate unconditioned responses (Domjan et al., 2004). For instance, you may learn to avoid a certain kind of cheese if the first time you eat it you become nauseated. The fact that it takes only one pairing of the cheese and the nausea for you to develop an aversion to that particular type of food is an example of biological preparedness. Similarly, research has shown that it is easier to condition a fear response to some objects than to others. For example, Öhman and colleagues (1976) used pictures as the CS and shock as the US. They found that the fear-related response of sweaty hands is more easily conditioned (and less easily lost) if the CS is a picture of a snake or a spider than if it is a picture of flowers or mushrooms. Snakes, rats, and the dark are typical objects of phobias. Some researchers have argued that the fear response to these stimuli makes sense from an evolutionary

Avoidance learning In classical conditioning, learning that occurs when a CS is paired with an unpleasant US that leads the animal to try to avoid the CS.

Conditioned emotional response (CER) An emotionally charged conditioned response elicited by a previously neutral stimulus.

Phobia An irrational fear of a specific object or situation.

Biological preparedness A built-in readiness for certain previously neutral stimuli to come to elicit particular conditioned responses, which means that less training is necessary to produce learning when these neutral stimuli are paired with the appropriate unconditioned responses.

FIGURE 3 Classical Conditioning of a Phobia: Little Albert

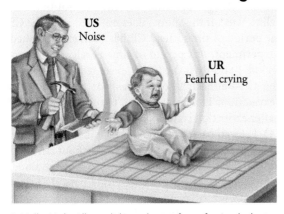

Initially, Little Albert did not show a fear of animals, but he did exhibit fear if a loud noise was made behind his back (a hammer striking a steel bar).

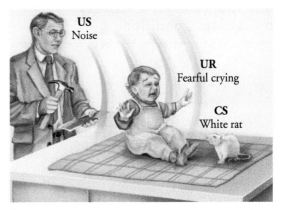

Then the researchers presented a white rat (CS) and made the loud noise (US).

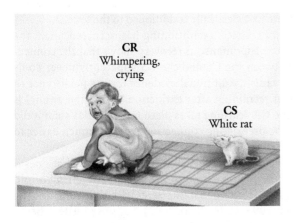

After five presentations of the CS and US, Albert developed a phobia of rats—he began whimpering and withdrawing (the conditioned emotional response) and trying to avoid the rat. After two more presentations of the CS and US, he immediately began crying on seeing the rat. "He . . . fell over on his left side, raised himself . . . and began to crawl away so rapidly that he was caught with difficulty before reaching the edge of the table" (Watson & Rayner, 1920, p. 5).

Source: John B. Watson, Rosalie Rayner, "Conditioned emotional reactions." *Journal of Experimental Psychology,* 3, 1-14. 1920

perspective—sensitivity to the presence of such possibly dangerous elements in the environment could help an animal survive (Seligman, 1971).

Exactly opposite to preparedness, **contrapreparedness** is a built-in disinclination (or even an inability) for certain stimuli to be conditioned to elicit particular conditioned responses. For example, Marks (1969) described an adult patient he was treating: When this woman was 10 years old, she was on a car trip and had to go to the bathroom. Her father pulled off the road so that she could relieve herself in a ditch. As she stepped out of the car, she saw a snake in the ditch—and at that moment her brother accidentally slammed the door on her hand. At 43, she was still deathly afraid of snakes (which reflects preparedness, as noted above), but she was not afraid of car doors—which had actually done the damage. Similarly, Bregman (1934) failed—with 15 different infants—to replicate Watson and Rayner's experiment when, instead of a rat as the CS, she used various inanimate objects, such as wooden blocks and pieces of cloth. These two examples highlight the point that certain stimuli, such as a car door and a wooden block, do not make successful conditioned stimuli for specific responses.

Extinction and Spontaneous Recovery in Classical Conditioning: Gone Today, Here Tomorrow Once a response has been classically conditioned, it will not necessarily be elicited by the CS forever. Even after a CR (such as a fear of snakes) is acquired, it is possible to reduce the CR. This weakening of the association does not happen because of forgetting, which occurs simply with the passage of time. Rather, it happens through the process of **extinction**, which occurs when the CR is gradually eliminated, or *extinguished*, by repeated presentations of the CS without the US. How would this work with Pavlov's dogs? If the tone continues to be presented, but is no longer followed by the presentation of food, after a while the dogs will no longer salivate at the tone: The CR will be extinguished.

Contrapreparedness A built-in disinclination (or even an inability) for certain stimuli to be conditioned to elicit particular conditioned responses.

Extinction (in classical conditioning) The process by which a CR comes to be eliminated through repeated presentations of the CS without the presence of the US.

FIGURE 4 Acquisition, Extinction, and Spontaneous Recovery in Classical Conditioning

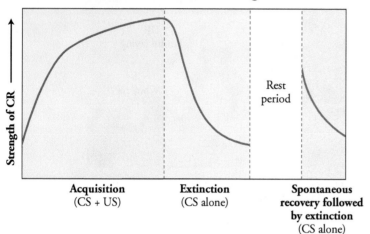

When the CS and US are paired, the animal quickly acquires the CR (left panel). However, when the CS occurs without the US, the CR quickly weakens (blue panel). After a rest period, the CR returns in response to the CS alone, but this is followed by extinction (right panel).

Spontaneous recovery (in classical conditioning) The event that occurs when the CS again elicits the CR after extinction has occurred.

Stimulus generalization A tendency for the CR to be elicited by neutral stimuli that are similar but not identical to the CS.

Stimulus discrimination The ability to distinguish among stimuli that are relatively similar to the CS and to respond only to the actual CS.

However, even after extinction—when the overt behavior is no longer present—the CR will not be completely eliminated. If the animal does not encounter the CS for some period of time after a CR has been extinguished (in an experiment, this period of time is referred to as a "rest period") and then the CS is presented, it will again elicit the CR—although sometimes not as strongly as before extinction. This restored ability of the CS to elicit the CR after extinction is called **spontaneous recovery** (see Figure 4). Let's go back to those dogs: As just noted, after the tone has been presented several times without any food forthcoming, the dogs will stop salivating to the tone alone. However, if the tone is not presented for a period of time and then is presented again, the dogs will again salivate when they hear it; the previously learned CR of salivation will return after the dogs simply hear the tone. However, although the dogs have spontaneously recovered the response, they may not salivate as much as they did when they were first classically conditioned to the tone.

Once classical conditioning has occurred, then, the existence of spontaneous recovery shows that the connection between the CS and the US apparently never completely vanish. Additional evidence for the persistence of this connection comes from studies of retraining after extinction. When the animal is retrained so that the CS again elicits the CR, learning takes place more quickly than it did during the original training period. The preexisting connection makes it much easier to condition again, after extinction, than to condition in the first place.

If extinction doesn't eliminate the connection between the CS and CR, what does it do? Research indicates that what occurs during extinction is not the forgetting of old learning but rather the production of new learning that interferes with the previous classically conditioned response (Bouton, 1993, 1994, 2000, 2002). Suppose Little Albert's fear of rats had been extinguished—that the rat had been presented without the loud noise often enough so that it failed to elicit the CR. Albert's association between the rat and the noise would *not* have disappeared, but rather new learning would have occurred "on top of" his previous learning. In this case, the new learning was that the CS (rat) does not indicate that the US (noise) was about to occur, which would mean that the CS was no longer associated with a CR but instead was associated with some other events that do not evoke fear (such as the opportunity to pet the animal). If these new associations are stronger than the old one (where the CS and CR were linked), a fear response will not occur (Bouton, 2000).

Generalization and Discrimination in Classical Conditioning: Seen One, Seen 'Em All?

Watson and Rayner wrote that 5 days after conditioning Little Albert, a rabbit, a dog, a fur coat, cotton, and a Santa Claus mask all elicited the conditioned response of fear in him. These are examples of **stimulus generalization**, a tendency for the CR to be elicited by neutral stimuli that are similar but not identical to the CS; in other words, the response generalizes to similar stimuli. In addition, the more closely the new stimulus resembles the original CS, the stronger the response; this relationship is referred to as a *generalization gradient*. Stimulus generalization can be helpful for survival because often a dangerous stimulus may not occur in exactly the same form the next time. Without stimulus generalization, we might not be afraid of lions as well as tigers.

Stimulus generalization has its limits (we don't generalize from lions to house cats), and we can learn not to generalize in certain circumstances: Animals are able to distinguish, or discriminate, among different stimuli that are relatively similar to the CS, and to respond only to the actual CS; this ability is called **stimulus discrimination**. Stimulus discrimination can be extremely helpful for survival; consider that one type of mushroom may be poisonous, but another type is food. If Albert had been shown a white ball of cotton without a loud noise's occurring (but he continued to be presented with a rat paired with the loud noise), after a while only the rat would have elicited fear. Albert would have been able to discriminate between the two similar—but not very similar—stimuli. ✳️—Explore

✳️—Explore **Process Stimulus Generalization** on mypsychlab.com

Cognition and the Conditioned Stimulus

Research indicates that numerous mental processes typically are engaged between the time of the initial presentation of the CS and its eventual ability to elicit a CR. In particular, attention to the stimuli and the expectations that arise following the CS influence the learning that occurs (Hollis, 1997; Kirsch et al., 2004). The existence of these mental processes allows us to explain some of the phenomena we've already described, such as the contrast between forward conditioning, which is very effective, with backward and simultaneous conditioning, which are rarely effective. Consider: When rats were presented with a tone (CS) immediately before being shocked (US), they quickly learned a fear response to the tone. However, when the tone is sometimes presented after the shock instead of before the shock, rats do not become conditioned to the tone (Rescorla, 1967).

Why do these differences in conditioning occur? Apparently, the CS provides *information* by heralding the upcoming US (and therefore UR), and conditioning occurs because the animal learns that relationship. The CS is an indicator that the US will occur, at least in the particular context in which the conditioning took place.

The idea that the CS provides information about the upcoming US has received much research support. For example, Kamin (1969) conditioned rats by presenting a tone and then a brief shock; the rats developed a conditioned fear response to the tone. He then added a second CS by turning on a light with the tone. Now, the rats did not develop a conditioned fear response to the light alone. Kamin hypothesized that the original pairing of tone and shock was blocking new learning: The light did not add new information and was therefore of no consequence and not worth the rats' attention. The tone was enough of an indicator that the US (the shock) would soon follow. Thus, Kamin concluded that classical conditioning takes place only if the pairing of CS and US provides useful information about the likelihood that the US will occur.

Perhaps the strongest evidence for the role of mental processes in conditioning comes from studies in which a mental image of an object—what you see in your "mind's eye" when you visualize something—functions as either a CS or a US. For instance, imagining food can lead to salivation in humans (Dadds et al., 1997). How does this work? During eating, the sight of food alone can produce salivation, where the sight of food plays the same role as the sight of the bowl in Pavlov's original experiments: Seeing the food is a CS that has been conditioned with preparing to eat it (US), and thus the salivation associated with eating (UR) has become associated with the CS (and is now a CR). Because visual mental imagery relies on most of the mental processes used during visual perception (Kosslyn et al., 2006), the conditioning that arises from perceiving a stimulus generalizes to imagining it—and hence we salivate when merely visualizing that delicious piece of cake.

Such cognitive factors can also explain how the *placebo effect* works; this effect occurs when a medically inactive substance (such as a sugar pill) comes to exert medicinal effects: The placebo has come to convey information that a future response is likely to occur, and thus the animal (which can be a human) comes to *expect*—consciously or not—that the placebo will lead to a particular response (Kirsch, 2004; Stewart-Williams & Podd, 2004). For example, suppose that you routinely take the pain reliever ibuprofen when you have a headache; you've got a headache now, and someone now gives you a pill that looks exactly like the ibuprofen pill you normally take (unbeknownst to you, though, it's a placebo pill). You've previously been conditioned so that merely swallowing the pill is enough to begin to trigger the response (which is why you usually begin to feel better well before the medicinal properties of the pill have had enough time to work). You now generalize this conditioning to the new pill because it looks and feels so much like the one you're used to taking. Thus, you *expect* relief from the pain (the response) soon after taking the pill (which acts as a CS). That placebo is likely to work—your headache pain will fade.

> **THINK like a PSYCHOLOGIST** Try this experiment with yourself: Imagine the most scrumptious food you've ever eaten (was it cake or ice cream drowning in chocolate sauce?). Imagine it in vivid detail—how it looks, smells, what it feels like when you touch it with a spoon, fork, or straw. Spend at least a minute imagining it (perhaps with your eyes closed). Did you start salivating? If not, can you think of reasons why that might be—for instance, did you eat recently so that you are full?

In one study, some rats were allowed to exercise and others were not. Both groups then heard tones that were followed by shocks. The rats that exercised showed stronger conditioning to the particular context in which the shocks occurred. Why? Exercise enhances the functioning of a brain structure called the hippocampus, which is crucially involved in learning—and plays a special role in learning the context that surrounds stimuli and responses. Thus, exercise made the rats better able to distinguish the context in which a shock was delivered (Baruch et al., 2004).

Source: Photo Researchers, Inc.

Dissecting Conditioning: Brain Mechanisms

In order to understand classical conditioning in greater depth, let's examine the brain mechanisms that underlie it.

Learning to Be Afraid

Classical conditioning is a complex activity that relies on many different neural structures working together. To understand the brain's contribution to classical conditioning, let's consider the case of a driver who has been honked at by a huge truck as it roars by and has barely missed being crushed. At the time of the incident, the driver experienced fear. As a result of this close encounter, when he later hears the sound of a horn and sees a truck drive by, he feels a twinge of fear—even if that truck, in fact, poses no danger.

Such conditioned responses are produced via the joint actions of a set of neural mechanisms. At the outset, *the stimuli are registered by the brain*. When the driver hears the sound of a horn and sees a truck drive by, the images and sounds stimulate the sensory organs (the eyes and ears, respectively), which create neural signals. These signals are sent first to brain areas that are specialized for organizing signals in a particular sensory modality (visual cortex and auditory cortex, in this case), and these brain areas in turn send signals to other parts of the brain.

Following this, *the amygdala reacts*. After the perceptual brain areas organize the input, they send signals (via direct neural connections) immediately to a part of the brain that lies beneath the surface of the temporal lobe (the lobe that lies under the temples), called the amygdala (LeDoux, 1996). The amygdala plays a crucial role in storing the stimulus–response associations that underlie fear. The result of classical conditioning is that sets of neurons in the amygdala become linked. With the honking truck, conditioning causes brain cells that respond to the stimulus to fire in tandem with cells in the amygdala that trigger the fear response. When the CS (the honking sound) later occurs, these stimulus–response associations are activated—and the amygdala sends signals to parts of the brain that actually produce the behaviors that *express* fear and conditioned fear—for example, wincing when an 18-wheeler rumbles by (Cardinal et al., 2002).

Thus, whenever the CS later occurs, the amygdala automatically triggers the CR. A crucial finding is that this linked activity never disappears entirely: Even after conditioning has been extinguished, linked neural activity remains, making it very easy for an animal (or person) to relearn a conditioned fear response. Hence, events at the level of the brain clearly affect events at the level of the person.

More Than One Type of Conditioning

Research on the neural bases of conditioning has shown that numerous types of conditioning exist, each of which relies on different mechanisms. This discovery is important because, depending on the particular characteristics of the underlying brain mechanisms, conditioning is more or less easily acquired and extinguished.

We've already discussed fear conditioning; another type of conditioning causes the eyes to blink. For example, have you ever heard a gun fired at close range? If you have, you may have noticed that you blinked. And after this experience, simply seeing someone nearby on the verge of pulling the trigger may cause you to blink. Eyeblink conditioning relies on the cerebellum, a brain structure that does not underlie fear conditioning; in fact, the cerebellum plays a key role in forming and storing the conditioned associations and also in producing the eyeblink itself.

In addition, researchers have found that other brain areas are crucial for other sorts of conditioning, such as the conditioning of pain (Kung et al., 2003). Such findings underscore the fact that, in spite of their similarities, different types of conditioning exist. In the following section we see practical reasons why understanding the nature of specific types of conditioning is important.

Classical Conditioning Applied

If the investigation of classical conditioning had ended with the study of dogs' salivation, the great psychological importance of this kind of learning might not have been recognized. But other studies of classical conditioning showed that it can play a role in our responses to drugs and medicines, in the operation of our immune systems, and in other aspects of health and illness. Even without our awareness, it contributes to our feelings about events, objects, ourselves (Baccus et al., 2004; Bunce et al., 1999; Núñez & de Vincente, 2004), and to our sexual interests (Lalumiere & Quinsey, 1998). In the sections that follow, we explore various examples of how classical conditioning can affect people's lives—even without their being aware of it.

Drug Use and Abuse Classical conditioning can sometimes play a role in deaths caused by drug "overdoses." The word *overdoses* is in quotes because often such deaths occurred after the users ingested or injected their customary quantity of a drug—but they took it in a different environment, leading the usual dose to have a greater effect. Here's how it works: A user who generally takes a drug in a particular setting—the bathroom, for instance—typically develops a CR to that place (Siegel, 1988; Siegel et al., 2000; Siegel & Ramos, 2002). As part of classical conditioning, as soon as the user walks into the bathroom, his or her body begins to compensate for the influx of drug that is soon to come—a *conditioned compensatory response* (Siegel & Ramos, 2002). This CR is the body's attempt to counteract, or dampen, the effect of the drug. When the user takes the drug in a new setting, perhaps a friend's living room, this compensatory response does not occur. Because there is no conditioned compensatory response to the new setting, the user's body does not try to counteract the effect of the drug. Hence, in this new setting, the net result—to the user's body—is a higher dose of the drug, which may be higher than the user can tolerate, leading to an overdose.

Similarly, classical conditioning also helps explain why people addicted to cocaine experience drug cravings merely from handling money (Hamilton et al., 1998; O'Brien et al., 1988). Part of the experience of using cocaine is buying it, often just before using it. Thus, handling money becomes a CS. Even virtual CSs can induce a craving: One study found that among heroin addicts, virtual reality simulations of heroin-related cues elicited a craving for the drug (Kuntze et al., 2001). In the same way, cigarette smokers may automatically reach for a cigarette when they get a phone call or have a cup of coffee, often without realizing what is happening; certain environmental stimuli are CSs and elicit a desire for a cigarette (Lazev et al., 1999).

Therapy Techniques Classical conditioning also serves as the basis for a number of treatment techniques that have been used to treat phobias (such as fear of snakes, heights, or elevators). According to classical conditioning principles, phobias are conditioned emotional responses, and thus treatment can be designed to disrupt the associations learned through classical conditioning. One such treatment is *systematic desensitization*, which is the structured and repeated presentation of a feared CS in circumstances designed to reduce anxiety. So, for instance, systematic desensitization with someone who has a phobia of elevators would reduce the phobic response in three steps. First, the therapist would train the person to become relaxed. Second, the person would then learn to continue to be relaxed even when thinking about an elevator. After mastering this step, the person would move on to the third step—to be relaxed when actually in an elevator. After the third step, the CS (elevator) no longer elicits the CR (fear).

Another treatment technique based on classical conditioning is *exposure*, which works by repeatedly presenting the patient with a fear-eliciting CS in a planned and systematic way—but without first inducing relaxation as is done in systematic desensitization. Instead, when exposed to the feared stimulus for 20 to 30 minutes, patients get a chance to learn that their fear response will decrease naturally (because of habituation), and that nothing terrible happens as a result of contact with the feared stimulus.

Advertising John B. Watson revolutionized the advertising industry when he showed how to use behavioral principles to increase sales. For instance, the use of "sex appeal" to sell products stems from Watson's ideas; sex appeal relies on

Through the obvious sex appeal of this man and woman, Polo Sport® is trying to get you to buy its swimwear. If you find the ad to have sex appeal, then classical conditioning principles suggest that your mild arousal or pleasure on seeing the ad (and thereafter on seeing the product itself, following its pairing with the attractive couple) would induce you to buy the product.

Source: Bill Aron\PhotoEdit Inc.

THINK like a
PSYCHOLOGIST Try this: Examine advertisements—on television, in magazines, online. What unconditioned stimuli do the advertisers pair with their products? *Hint*: classical conditioning generally involves reflexive responses, such as those associated with fear, salivation, and sexual arousal.

FIGURE 5 Taste Aversion Conditioning

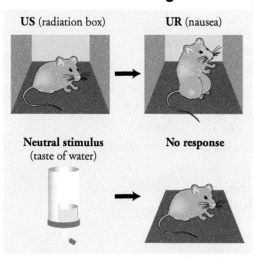

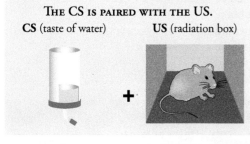

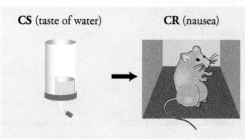

Did Garcia and Koelling (1966) inadvertently create a classically conditioned taste aversion? Yes. In their study, the US was the radiation, the CS was the taste of water in the plastic bottle in the radiation chamber, the UR and CR was becoming nauseated, and the rat's taste aversion was avoidance learning.

the US's being some type of sexually arousing stimulus—such as an attractive person in tight jeans—that elicits a UR of mild to strong sexual arousal. Sex isn't the only US that can produce a desired response—food works too; political slogans (CS), when paired with the eating of food (US), were viewed more favorably by participants (Razran, 1940).

Classical conditioning continues to be used in advertising to promote consumers' positive attitudes about products (Kim et al., 1998; Till et al., 2008; Till & Priluck, 2000). This is referred to as *evaluative conditioning*: The goal is to change your liking, or evaluation, of the CS—the product the advertisers want you to buy (De Houwer et al., 2001).

Food and Taste Aversion A **food** or **taste aversion** occurs when an unpleasant experience during or after eating (or even just tasting) a particular food leads an animal to avoid that food in the future. If you have ever had food poisoning, you may have developed such a classically conditioned food aversion. This type of classical conditioning usually involves learning after only a single experience of the CS–US pairing. Generally, the food that made you sick had some unhealthy and unwanted ingredient, such as salmonella bacteria. The bacteria are the US, and the ensuing nausea and vomiting are the UR. If the salmonella was in your dinner of broiled trout, trout might become a CS for you; whenever you eat it (or perhaps another fish similarly prepared), you become nauseated (the CR). Rather than put yourself through this experience, you are likely to avoid eating broiled trout, and a food aversion is born.

Garcia and colleagues (1966) accidentally discovered the mechanism behind taste aversion when studying the effects of radiation on rats. The rats were exposed to high enough doses of radiation that they became sick. The researchers noticed that the rats drank less water from the plastic water bottle in the radiation chamber than from the glass water bottle in their "home" cage. (The water in the plastic bottle had a slightly different taste, thanks to the plastic, than did the water in the glass bottle.) The researchers shifted their focus to discover *why* the rats drank less from the plastic than the glass bottle. Was it because the taste of the water in the plastic bottle had become associated with the radiation that made the rats sick, and thus become a CS? If so, then the radiation was the US, the taste of the water from the plastic bottle was the CS, getting sick was the UR and CR, and not drinking the water from the plastic bottle would be the avoidance learning. The researchers tested this hypothesis and found that it was correct: The taste of water in the plastic bottle was a CS, causing the rats' taste aversion (see Figure 5).

Garcia's research led to another important discovery. Continuing with experiments on conditioned taste aversion, Garcia and colleagues (1966) found that rats avoided novel-tasting water even if the nausea didn't occur until several hours after they drank. This further research showed that, at least in this case, the US doesn't need to come immediately after the CS. These findings stirred considerable controversy because they described exceptions to the "rules" of classical conditioning—in this case that the US should immediately follow the CS.

Classical conditioning often is adaptive, whether it involves an animal's (including a human's) ability to learn which foods are poisonous or which animals or objects in the environment (such as predators or guns) to fear and avoid. The more readily an animal learns these associations, the more likely that animal is to survive. Learned food aversions based on one exposure to the food can be particularly adaptive: Animals that readily learn what not to eat will probably live longer and have more offspring.

Conditioning the Immune System Classical conditioning can even affect the operation of the immune system. For example, suppose you worked day and night for a week, hardly taking the time to eat or sleep, and so severely weakened your immune system that you became very sick. During that exhausting work-filled week, you spent all of your waking hours with a laptop computer on your bed, which is covered by a bright red bedspread. After your recovery, simply sitting on that same bedspread could cause your immune system to weaken!

Robert Ader and his colleagues (Ader, 1976; Ader & Cohen, 1975) have documented exactly this kind of conditioning in rats. In one study, saccharin-flavored water was paired with injections of cyclophosphamide, a drug given to organ transplant donors that suppresses the immune system and has a side effect of nausea. Ader had intended to use this drug not for its immune-suppressing qualities, but as a way to induce nausea in a study of taste aversion. He wanted to see how long the taste aversion would last once injections of cyclophosphamide stopped, while the rats continued to drink sweetened water (the CS). Unexpectedly, a few rats died on day 45 of the experiment, and more died over the next several days.

Ader was confused by their deaths; he had done similar experiments before with a different nausea-inducing drug, and none of those animals had died. He eventually showed that the taste of the sweetened water was not only triggering nausea, but it was also suppressing the rats' immune systems (as the actual drug would do)—which eventually caused the rodents to die. Each time the rats drank the sweetened water, their immune systems were weakened—even without the immune-suppressing drug! The taste of the saccharin-sweetened water was acting as a CS, and this water was in essence a type of placebo because the inert substance (water) had a medicinal effect (immune suppression). The rats' bodies responded to the CS as if it were the US—the cyclophosphamide.

Ader's accidental discovery and his follow-up studies were noteworthy for two reasons: (1) they showed that a type of placebo response could be classically conditioned in animals, not just humans; (2) they showed that the animal doesn't have to believe that the placebo has medicinal properties in order to have a placebo response (although such beliefs may heighten a placebo effect; Waber et al., 2008). The researchers could not ask the rats what they believed would happen when they drank the sweet water, but—given their minimal intellectual abilities—we have good reason not to think that the rats "believed" it would impair their immune systems (Dienstfrey, 1991).

Ader and his colleagues reported a number of follow-up studies, all designed to rule out other explanations of their results, and their hypothesis about the conditioning of the immune system has stood up well. Indeed, another study with rats showed that conditioning could not only weaken the immune response but also boost the immune response (Gorcynski, cited in Dienstfrey, 1991). In fact, there is evidence that the placebo effect may be a conditioned immune response that occurs in humans (Voudouris et al., 1985).

LOOKING AT LEVELS Sick at the Thought of Chemotherapy

Source: Custom Medical Stock Photo, Inc.

Cancer patients undergoing chemotherapy may experience intense nausea and vomiting as side effects of the treatment. But some patients develop *anticipatory nausea*, they start feeling sick well before they receive the actual treatment. Why?

The patients developed a classically conditioned response to chemotherapy (Burish & Carey, 1986; Carey & Burish, 1988; Davey, 1992). After conditioning, a previously neutral stimulus—such as the sight of a particular flower shop seen en route to the hospital where chemotherapy is provided—can trigger nausea or vomiting. To understand this event in detail, we must consider events at the three levels of analysis. At the level of the brain, such conditioning was established when the US (the drugs used in chemotherapy) stimulated the activity of neurons that feed into the patient's immune and autonomic nervous systems and, as a side effect, induce the UR (nausea or vomiting). The US then became paired with the activity of neurons that respond to certain sights or sounds, for example, the sight of the flower shop; these sights and sounds become the CS. After enough such pairings, the two groups of neurons became functionally connected so that the activity in one group triggers activity in the other (producing a CR; LeDoux, 1996). Indeed, for some people undergoing chemotherapy, just thinking about the hospital where the treatment is given can produce nausea (Redd et al., 1993).

Some patients are more likely to develop anticipatory nausea than others—specifically, people who are generally more autonomically reactive than others (Kvale & Hugdahl, 1994).

Food aversion (taste aversion) A classically conditioned avoidance of a certain food or taste.

Classical conditioning explains why some people undergoing chemotherapy develop anticipatory nausea. Previously neutral stimuli—such as the sight of a florist shop on the way to the hospital—after being paired with nausea-inducing chemotherapy, can come to elicit nausea. Fortunately, treatments exist to prevent or minimize such conditioning.

Source: © Andreas von Einsiedel; Elizabeth Whiting & Associates / CORBIS All Rights Reserved

✔●─┤**Study** and **Review** on **mypsychlab.com**

That is, individuals who have a tendency toward a stronger sympathetic or parasympathetic responses (in their autonomic nervous systems) to given levels of stimulation are more likely to develop anticipatory nausea.

At the level of the person, this sort of adverse effect can lead to a sense of helplessness as well as physical discomfort, and can cause some chemotherapy patients to stop the treatment altogether (Siegel & Longo, 1981). (Fortunately, behavioral interventions such as relaxation training can be helpful in controlling anticipatory nausea, as can antinausea medications; Vasterling et al., 1993.)

At the level of the group, chemotherapy has a social component. It is administered by medical staff in the social setting of a hospital or clinic, and the patient may be escorted to treatment by a friend or member of the family. People who are involved in the chemotherapy treatment can become the CS, which—for example—can lead a patient to become nauseated at the sight of a particular nurse who always administers the treatment (Montgomery & Bovbjerg, 1997).

The events at the different levels interact. Autonomic reactivity influences the likelihood of developing anticipatory nausea, which can create yet another challenge for the patient, affecting how he or she sees the illness and ability to fight it, and how he or she interacts with medical staff, family, and friends. Moreover, the social interaction that occurs when a person is taught behavioral interventions for the anticipatory nausea (such as relaxation techniques) can influence events at the level of the brain and the person by helping the patient have some sense of control over the nausea.

LOOKING BACK

1. **What is classical conditioning? How was it discovered?** Pavlov discovered classical conditioning while conducting studies of dogs' salivation. Classical conditioning involves the pairing of an initially neutral stimulus (such as a tone, which then becomes the CS) with an unconditioned stimulus (US, such as food). The US reflexively elicits an unconditioned response (UR, such as salivation), and with repeated US–CS pairings, the CS will come to elicit the response evoked by the US as a conditioned response (CR, salivation).

2. **Can classically conditioned responses be modified?** Yes, they can be modified in a variety of ways, such as through extinction. Extinction is achieved by repeatedly presenting the CS without the US. However, if extinction is followed by a rest period, the CS may again elicit the classically conditioned response; this is known as spontaneous recovery. With stimulus discrimination, the animal learns to distinguish among similar stimuli so that only a particular stimulus will elicit the CR. In contrast, with stimulus generalization, a similar but nonidentical stimulus elicits the CR.

3. **What are common examples of classical conditioning in daily life?** Classical conditioning is used in advertising and treatment for phobias, and is the mechanism underlying food or taste aversions and conditioned immune responses (such as can occur with a placebo effect).

Operant Conditioning

Classical conditioning is not the only way that Jackie Chan learned; he also learned from experiences with reward and punishment. At times, Master Yu would give some of the students special rewards—extra food or a meal in a restaurant—or special punishments. Chan's classmates were also sources of rewards and punishments: Younger classmate Yuen Baio (who later acted in several of Chan's films) was a friend, providing support, camaraderie, and sometimes snacks from his parents' weekly gift of food. Moreover, Chan was honored with the most powerful reward at the school—a much desired place in the Seven Little Fortunes, a troupe of seven students who performed nightly in front of a paying audience (the income from the performances, however, went to Master Yu to pay for running the school).

How did the food treats come to be such a powerful force in Chan's life? And how did the possibility of being picked to perform in the Seven Little Fortunes exert such a powerful influence on Chan and the other students, motivating them to practice even harder and more intensely than they otherwise would have? The answer might lie in the principles of another kind of learning, **operant conditioning**, the process by which a stimulus and response become associated with the consequences of making the response.

Operant conditioning The process by which a stimulus and response become associated with the consequences of making the response.

LOOKING AHEAD: Learning Objectives

1. What is operant conditioning? How does it occur?
2. What is the difference between reinforcement and punishment?
3. How are complex behaviors learned and maintained?
4. What is the role of the neurotransmitter dopamine during operant conditioning?

The Roots of Operant Conditioning: Its Discovery and How It Works

A basic observation about behaviors and their consequences underlies the concept of operant conditioning: If a behavior is followed by a positive consequence, an animal is more likely to repeat that behavior in the future; if a behavior is followed by a negative consequence, an animal is less likely to repeat that behavior. For instance, suppose you are swamped with schoolwork, and the day before a paper is due, you ask the professor for an extension (asking for the extension is the *behavior*). If the professor gives you an extension (getting the extension is the *positive consequence*), you will probably be more likely to ask for an extension in the future. In contrast, should the professor not only refuse you but also become angry (the professor's getting angry is the *negative consequence*), you will probably be less likely to ask for an extension in the future—at least from that professor.

Unlike classical conditioning, in which the animal is largely passive, operant conditioning requires the animal to "operate" in the world, to do something. Operant conditioning is also called *instrumental conditioning* because behavior is required—is instrumental—to produce the effect. Whereas classical conditioning usually involves involuntary reflexes, such as salivating in response to seeing food, operant conditioning usually involves voluntary, nonreflexive behavior, such as singing a song, assuming a kung fu stance, or eating with chopsticks or a fork.

However, a given behavior typically occurs in response to a specific stimulus. We put our foot on the brake because a red light goes on (we don't do it randomly and not when the green light goes on), we turn up the thermostat when it's cold inside (again, we don't do it randomly and not during the heat of the summer), and we say "Thank you" when somebody has done us a favor (not randomly and not when they have disrespected us). In fact, operant conditioning is the key component of what is called "S-R Psychology" (short for "Stimulus-Response Psychology") because the consequences of making a response strengthen the *connection* between the stimulus and the response that led to the pleasant consequences.

Thorndike's Puzzle Box The scientific investigation of operant conditioning began at about the same time that Pavlov was working with his dogs, with research conducted by the American psychologist Edward L. Thorndike (1874–1949). Thorndike studied behavior by creating a puzzle box, a cage with a latched door that a cat could open by pressing down on a pedal inside the cage (see Figure 6).

FIGURE 6 Thorndike's Puzzle Box

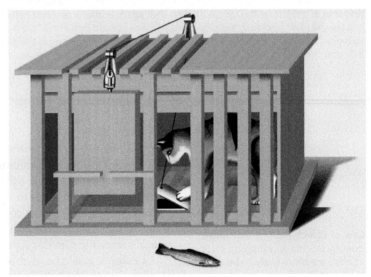

Thorndike placed a hungry cat inside the box and fish just outside the door, within the cat's sight. The cat tried many behaviors to get out of the box and to the fish, but only pressing the pedal would open the door. Eventually, the cat pressed the pedal, and the door opened. When the cat was put back inside the box, it pressed the pedal more quickly, improving each time.

FIGURE 7 The Phases of Operant Conditioning

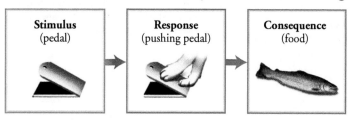

| Stimulus (pedal) | → | Response (pushing pedal) | → | Consequence (food) |

Unlike classical conditioning, operant conditioning requires the animal to produce the desired behavior, the response to the stimulus. That response is then followed by a positive or negative consequence.

Food was placed outside the cage door. Although the cat took a while to get around to pressing down the pedal (first trying to reach the food directly with a paw), once it did and the door opened, the cat was quicker to press the pedal in its subsequent sessions in the box: It had learned that pressing the pedal opened the door and enabled it to get the food (see Figure 7).

Thorndike called this type of learning "trial-and-error learning." He noted that such learning depends on getting a reward after performing a specific behavior. This finding led to his famous formulation of the **Law of Effect** (Thorndike, 1927), which lies at the heart of operant conditioning: Actions that subsequently lead to a "satisfying state of affairs" are more likely to be repeated (Thorndike, 1949, p. 14).

The Skinner Box B. F. Skinner (1904–1990), the 20th century's foremost proponent of behaviorism, is important in the history of psychology both because he most fully developed the concept of operant conditioning and because he showed how such conditioning could explain much of our daily behavior. Working mostly with pigeons and wanting to minimize his handling of the birds, he developed an apparatus that is now often referred to as a *Skinner box*. The box (see Figure 8) could feed the animals as well as record the frequency of their responses, making it easy to quantify the responses (this enormously helpful feature was, in fact, an unintended bonus of the box's design and is called a *cumulative recorder*; Skinner, 1956).

Skinner boxes became standard in laboratories that investigated animal behavior and are often used with rats. If a rat is put in a Skinner box, it learns to associate pressing the lever or bar with the likelihood of a food pellet's appearing. In this case, the lever is the stimulus, pressing the lever is the response (or behavior), and receiving the food pellet is the consequence.

FIGURE 8 Skinner Box and Cumulative Recorder

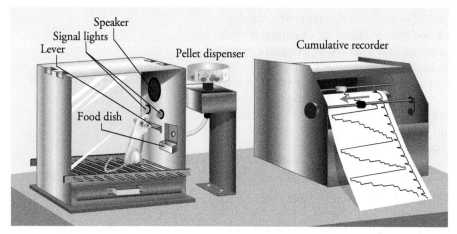

In a Skinner box, a hungry rat presses a lever (or a pigeon pecks a key). As with Thorndike's cat, the rat will produce random behaviors, eventually pressing the lever, causing a food pellet (reinforcement) to come down the chute into the food dish, increasing the likelihood of the response in the future. The rat presses the lever again, and another food pellet appears. It presses the lever (and eats) more frequently—it has learned that pressing the lever will be followed by the appearance of a food pellet. On the outside of the box is a cumulative recorder, a device that records each lever press and the time interval between presses.

Principles of Operant Conditioning

As noted earlier, operant conditioning involves two sorts of associations: between a *stimulus* and a *response* to that stimulus, and between the response and the *consequence* of that response. (In classical conditioning, the association is between a neutral stimulus and a US.) The consequence may be either *reinforcement* or *punishment*. Operant conditioning works like this: A stimulus leads to a particular response, and the association between stimulus and response is forged by the consequence of the response. **Reinforcement** is the process by which the consequences of a response increase the likelihood that the response will occur again when the stimulus is present; the response becomes associated with its consequences. An example would be when a teacher gives a young student a "gold star" or some other type of recognition for helping the teacher to clean up the bulletin board. For reinforcement to bring about learning most effectively, the reinforcement should be contingent on—conditional on—a desired response; in our example, the student should receive the gold star only after he or she finishes clearing the bulletin board, not after simply volunteering to do so. This relationship between the response and the consequence is called the

Law of Effect Actions that subsequently lead to a "satisfying state of affairs" are more likely to be repeated.

Reinforcement The process by which the consequences of a response lead to an increase in the likelihood that the response will occur again when the stimulus is present.

response contingency; it occurs when a consequence depends on the animal's producing the desired response. In contrast to the responses that are elicited in classical conditioning, responses in operant conditioning are voluntarily produced.

An example of such operant conditioning occurred in Jackie Chan's life when, as a young adult, he and many other martial arts experts were seeking work as stuntmen in the Hong Kong film industry. There were more young and inexperienced stuntmen than there were jobs, and Chan desperately needed the work in order to pay his bills. One day, a director wanted a stunt done; it was deemed so unsafe by the stunt coordinator that he refused to have any of his stuntmen do it. Chan volunteered to do it, figuring that this was the only way he'd be likely to get work. He did the dangerous stunt (twice) and *did* get more jobs after that. What Chan learned from this experience was that trying very dangerous stunts (behavior) would get him paid work (the reinforcement).

A **reinforcer** is an object or event that, when it follows a response, increases the likelihood that the animal will make that response again when the stimulus is present. In Thorndike's puzzle box and in the Skinner box, the reinforcer is food. Many different objects and events can serve as reinforcers—in fact, almost any desired object or event can play this role. What reinforcer works best for people? The answer to this question is tricky: What one person considers a "reward" might leave another person cold. Reinforcement, therefore, is in the eyes of the recipient (Raj et al., 2006; Rynes et al., 2005). For instance, for one person, a night at the ballet might be a wonderful reinforcer for thoroughly cleaning out the garage. To another, a night at the ballet might seem like punishment. Even food, which is often a reinforcer, isn't always so; when the animal or person is full, food may not work as a reinforcer. ((•—Listen

As an illustration of this fact about reinforcers, consider an account Chan provides of the filming of his first *Rush Hour* movie, when he was already considered a "star" in America:

> The studio [spared] nothing to make me feel like I'm a star. I have a beautiful rented mansion, a luxurious trailer on the set, a personal trainer, and a car standing by at all times. Even my stuntmen have their own private rooms. In my Hong Kong movies, we squeeze together, share what we have to, and eat lunch together, all out of the same big pot. I do everything and anything I want to—I'm the director, the producer, the cameraman, the prop guy, the janitor. Anything. Here, they won't let me do anything except act. They won't even let me stand around so they can check the lighting—they have a stand-in, my height, my color, wearing my clothes, come in, and they check the lighting off of him while I sit in my trailer.

Source: Chan & Yang, *I am Jackie Chan*. 1999, p. 303. New York: Ballantine Books.

The producers apparently thought that this "star treatment" would reinforce Chan for acting in American movies—but, in fact, he didn't like it and was itching to be more involved between scenes.

The fact that what constitutes a reinforcer is in the eyes of the recipient applies to parents who want to reward certain of their children's behaviors. In some cases, parents may give stickers to their child for good behavior but find that the stickers are useless—their child's behavior doesn't change (and so the child doesn't get any stickers). The problem isn't with the concept of rewarding certain of the child's behaviors. The problem is that their child doesn't consider stickers to be a reward. The parents simply need to find a reinforcer that will work for their child, increasing the likelihood that he or she will repeat a particular behavior. For instance, when the authors of this book were toilet training their children, they used reinforcers whenever the children tried to use the potty. They had asked each child to name a reinforcer, and one of the children requested black olives (an usual food for a toddler to enjoy with such a passion), which proved to be a very effective reinforcer for that child. This anecdote serves as a reminder that the proof is in the pudding—the degree to which an object or event is a reinforcer is determined by its effect on the individual animal. Just calling something a reinforcer doesn't make it so.

Like classical conditioning, operant conditioning involves cognitive processing. Simply telling people about the contingency between a behavior and its consequence can lead to behavior change (Kirsch et al., 2004), as occurs when parents or teachers explain what the child must do to earn a sticker or when supervisors announce upcoming opportunities for employees to earn bonuses through improved performance.

((•—**Listen** to the **Podcast** on **Punishment and Reinforcement** on mypsychlab.com

Response contingency The circumstance in which a consequence depends on the animal's producing the desired response.

Reinforcer An object or event that, when it follows a response, increases the likelihood that the animal will make that response again when the stimulus is present.

Positive reinforcement Occurs when a desired reinforcer is presented after a response, thereby increasing the likelihood of that response in the future.

Reinforcement: Increasing Responses There are two types of reinforcement, *positive* and *negative*. In **positive reinforcement**, a desired reinforcer is presented after a response, thereby increasing the likelihood of that response in the future (see the first row in Figure 9). The food for Thorndike's cat and black olives for the toddler during potty training are examples of positive reinforcement. Food is the usual positive reinforcer for animals; for humans, toys, money, and intangibles such as praise and attention can also be positive reinforcers, as was Jackie Chan's acceptance into the Seven Little Fortunes.

FIGURE 9 Positive and Negative Reinforcement and Punishment

POSITIVE REINFORCEMENT

Chan's behavior (a correct landing from a flying side kick) is positively reinforced; after he does the behavior correctly, he receives a treat.

NEGATIVE REINFORCEMENT

In contrast, the same behavior is negatively reinforced: the Master has a frown as Chan is going into the move (an aversive stimulus), but the aversive stimulus is removed when Chan lands from the flying side kick correctly. The Master's goal is the same in both examples—to maximize the likelihood that the behavior (a perfect flying side kick landing) will occur again.

POSITIVE PUNISHMENT

Chan's behavior (falling when landing from a flying side kick) is being positively punished: The Master gives an unpleasant consequence (a caning) so as to minimize the likelihood that the behavior (an incorrect flying side kick landing) will occur again.

NEGATIVE PUNISHMENT

Chan's behavior (falling when landing from a flying side kick) is being negatively punished: The Master removes a pleasant event (his smile at Jackie) so as to minimize the likelihood that the behavior (an incorrect flying side kick landing) will occur again.

Sometimes we inadvertently reinforce certain behaviors by paying too much attention to them (which can unintentionally provide positive reinforcement); this can happen when patients with coronary heart disease receive attention when talking about their symptoms, which leads them to talk even more about their symptoms (Itkowitz et al., 2003). Scolding children is another example: If the only time a child receives any attention at all is when he or she misbehaves, then even "bad attention," such as a scolding, can be a positive reinforcer.

In contrast, in **negative reinforcement,** an unpleasant object or event is *removed* after a response, thereby increasing the likelihood of that response in the future (see Figure 9, second row). If a rat is being mildly shocked in its cage and the shocks stop when it presses a bar, then the behavior of bar pressing is negatively reinforced. Or consider the student whose neighbor is blaring particularly aversive music, song after blasting song. This unpleasant event ends when the student knocks on the neighbor's door and asks the neighbor to turn down the volume—and the neighbor complies. Asking to have the volume lowered has been negatively reinforced. Yet another example of negative reinforcement in action is when people use substances, such as alcohol, to decrease their anxiety (Hohlstein et al., 1998; Samoluk & Stewart, 1998); because it reduces the aversive state of anxiousness, using alcohol is negatively reinforced.

Both positive and negative reinforcement are described as reinforcing because they increase the likelihood that a behavior will be repeated (see Figure 10). Negative reinforcement is *not* the same thing as punishment. Let's see why.

> **Negative reinforcement** Occurs when an unpleasant object or event is removed after a response, thereby increasing the likelihood of that response in the future.

> **Punishment** The process by which an unpleasant object or event is presented after a response, which decreases the likelihood of that response in the future.

FIGURE 10 Positive Reinforcement and Negative Reinforcement

This couple has been positively reinforced for buying a lottery ticket—they have received a large amount of money.

The nonsmoker has been negatively reinforced for pointing out the "No smoking" sign to the smoker—the aversive cigarette smoke disappears.

Punishment In **punishment**, an unpleasant object or event is presented after a response, thereby *decreasing* the likelihood of that response in the future. Punishment thus has the opposite effect of reinforcement, because both positive and negative reinforcement *increase* the likelihood that the response will be repeated.

Punishment is commonly confused with negative reinforcement, but, as noted previously, they lead to contrasting outcomes: Punishment *decreases* the likelihood that a response will be repeated, whereas negative reinforcement *increases* the likelihood that a response will be repeated (by removing an unpleasant event or circumstance after the desired response) (see Figure 11). Although we might all agree that being caned or otherwise hurt is an unpleasant event, to some extent, punishment is in the eyes of the beholder. Consider this example: When Chan was in first grade, before he began at Master Yu's school, he frequently made jokes and got into trouble. The school "punished" him—they would force him to stand in the hallway, holding a desk over his head, or wear around his neck a sign explaining the nature of his offense. But Chan describes standing out in the hall as "peaceful." The consequences the teachers put in place to decrease his behavior did not function as punishment for Chan. Therefore, he did not learn what his teachers wanted him to learn—that is, the consequences did not decrease his troublesome behavior (and so should not be considered to be punishment at all because they did not change Chan's behavior).

FIGURE 11 Negative Reinforcement Versus Punishment

Wow, what a surprise! It's nice of you to have cleaned the kitchen—and without my asking. How about if you don't have to do any more chores this week?

I didn't ask you to clean the kitchen, did I? Now I won't be able to find things when I need them. You're grounded the rest of the weekend, young man!

The boy performed the exact same behavior in both these cases, but the consequences of his behavior are different. With negative reinforcement, he is more likely to repeat the behavior. In contrast, with punishment, he is less likely to repeat the behavior.

Just as there are positive and negative forms of reinforcement, there are also positive and negative forms of punishment. In **positive punishment** (sometimes called punishment by application), a response leads to an undesired consequence, thereby decreasing the likelihood of that response in the future (see Figure 9, third row). For example, a student may be positively punished with a failing grade for plagiarizing a term paper. If this punishment is effective, she will be less likely to plagiarize a paper in the future. In **negative punishment** (sometimes called punishment by removal), a response leads a pleasant object or event to be removed, thereby decreasing the likelihood of that response in the future (see Figure 9, fourth row). Consider a boy who misbehaves: His parents might negatively punish him by temporarily taking away his MP3 player or cell phone.

Positive punishment comes in many forms, but not all aversive stimuli are positive punishment. For example, Chan and his classmates were forced to suffer through various uncomfortable activities as part of their training. They were required to do handstands for at least half an hour at a time, despite distressing physical experiences as a result of remaining upside down for so long: "after fifteen minutes, our arms would grow limp, our blood would rush to our heads, and our stomachs would begin to turn flip-flops. But we couldn't show any weakness at all. A limb that moved would receive a whack from the master's rattan cane" (Chan & Yang, 1999, p. 43). The "distressing physical experiences" weren't positive punishment. But, in this example, the whack of the cane and ensuing pain was positive punishment. To qualify as punishment, the aversive event has to be a consequence of a particular response (moving a limb, in this case).

Punishment of either type is most likely to lead to learning—that is, to decrease the likelihood of that response in the future—when it has three characteristics:

- *Punishment should be swift*, occurring immediately after the undesired behavior. The old threat "Wait till you get home!" undermines the effectiveness of the punishment.

- *Punishment must be consistent*. The undesired behavior must be punished each and every time it occurs. If the behavior is punished only sporadically, the person or animal doesn't effectively learn that the behavior will be followed by punishment, and so will not learn to stop making the response.

- *Punishment should be aversive* but not so aversive as to create problems such as high levels of fear or anxiety, injury, or new, undesired behaviors.

We must note several cautionary points about the use of punishment:

1. Although punishment may decrease the frequency of a response, it doesn't eliminate the capacity to engage in that behavior. Your little sister may learn not to push you because your mother will punish her, but she may continue to push her classmates at school because the response has not been punished in that context. Moreover, sometimes people are able to modify the response so that they can continue to perform it but avoid punishment; for example, your little sister might figure out that if she pushes you but then apologizes, she will not get punished.

2. Physical punishment, such as a spanking, may actually increase aggressive behavior by the person on the receiving end (Berlin et al., 2009; Haapasalo & Pokela, 1999; Straus et al., 1997; Taylor et al., 2010) in part because the person may "learn" that physical

Positive punishment Occurs when a response leads to an undesired consequence, thereby decreasing the likelihood of that response in the future.

Negative punishment Occurs when a response leads a pleasant object or event to be removed, thereby decreasing the likelihood of that response in the future.

aggression is an acceptable behavior (Steinberg, 2000). Such learning could account for the finding that abusive parents (and physically aggressive juvenile delinquents) tend to come from abusive families (Conger et al., 2003; Kwong et al., 2003; Straus & Gelles, 1980; Straus & McCord, 1998).

3. Through classical conditioning, the one being punished may come to fear the one doing the punishing. This may happen even with infrequent punishment. If the punishment is severe, a single instance may be enough for the person being punished to learn to live in fear of the punisher, as Chan and his classmates lived in fear of Master Yu. Constantly living in fear can make people and animals chronically stressed, and it can lead to depression (Pine et al., 2001).

Because of the disadvantages of punishment, many training programs for parents emphasize positive reinforcement for good behavior. In fact, punishment alone hasn't been found to be as effective as punishment used in combination with reinforcement. This is because punishment conveys information about what *not* to do; it doesn't convey information about what responses should be made in place of the undesired, punished responses. Consider a preschool-age boy who wants to draw, so he draws on the wall. You don't want him to ruin the wallpaper, so you punish him, and he learns not to draw on the wall. But what should he draw on—the floor, the table, or something else? If you punish the preschooler for drawing on the wall and then provide him with paper and reinforce him for drawing on the paper, he can be artistically creative without inadvertently producing a new response that would also lead to punishment.

Simply punishing someone does not provide that person with appropriate alternative behaviors. This mother clearly states an appropriate alternative to biting someone when angry—using words to express feelings.

Source: W.W. Norton & Company, Inc.

Primary and Secondary Reinforcers Researchers distinguish between two different categories of reinforcers: *primary reinforcers* and *secondary reinforcers*. **Primary reinforcers** are events or objects that are inherently reinforcing, such as food, water, and relief from pain. At the Chinese Drama Academy, the children barely had enough to eat, and food became a much sought-out and fought-over item; Master Yu rewarded the Seven Little Fortunes with a trip to a restaurant after a particularly good performance. **Secondary reinforcers** are not inherently reinforcing, but instead have acquired their reinforcing value through learning; examples of secondary reinforcers are attention, praise, money, a good grade, and a promotion. When training dolphins, trainers—such as those at the theme park Sea World—use both primary reinforcers (food) and secondary reinforcers (playtime with a favorite toy). Animals, including humans, will work very hard to receive secondary reinforcers, as Chan did.

Behavior modification is a technique in which behavior is changed through the use of secondary reinforcers. Behavior modification is used to treat individuals with behavior problems and also plays a key role in programs designed to help people with mental retardation, psychiatric patients, and prisoners. Participants in such programs earn a type of secondary reinforcer known as a "token," which can be traded for candy or for privileges such as going out for a walk or watching a particular TV show. Tokens can be earned either by exhibiting a specific desired behavior (such as doing chores) or by not exhibiting an undesired behavior (such as cursing or having a tantrum) for a specified period of time (Conyers et al., 2003). The token is thus a chit that can traded for other secondary reinforcers (such as watching a TV show) or for primary reinforcers (such as candy). Such tokens are commonly used to reward children for desired behavior change (Jason & Fries, 2004). Behavior modification techniques have also been used effectively in the workplace. When employees arrive at work on time, for instance, they receive a coupon toward a bonus; this program resulted in employees arriving late less often (Hermann et al., 1973).

A creative and important study of behavior modification with secondary reinforcers was carried out by researchers who wanted to improve nutrition among poor children in

Primary reinforcer An event or object, such as food, water, or relief from pain, that is inherently reinforcing.

Secondary reinforcer An event or object (such as attention) that is not inherently reinforcing but instead has acquired its reinforcing value through learning.

Behavior modification A technique in which behavior is changed through the use of secondary reinforcers.

Immediate reinforcement Reinforcement given immediately after the desired response is exhibited.

Delayed reinforcement Reinforcement given some period of time after the desired response is exhibited.

Generalization The ability to transfer a learned stimulus–response association to a new stimulus that is similar to the original one, making the same response to it that led to reinforcement previously.

Discrimination The ability to respond only to a particular stimulus and not to a similar one.

Choosing a delayed reinforcement over an immediate one has its advantages, but the choice is not necessarily easy. A dieter trying to obtain the delayed reinforcement of looking and feeling better sacrifices immediate reinforcement (ice cream, now!) for future personal benefits. But immediate reinforcement can be very powerful and often difficult to reject in favor of some future good. At some point, the dieter may yield to the satisfaction of eating the ice cream—or even just a normal-sized portion of dinner—instead of making yet another sacrifice for the sake of eventual slimness.

Source: Dennis MacDonald\PhotoEdit Inc.

the rural Philippines (Guthrie et al., 1982). The study was designed to discover whether reinforcement would modify mothers' nutritional care of their children more than would simply giving the mothers information about health and nutrition for children. All of the mothers were given appropriate information. Then the health clinic provided different forms of reinforcement that were contingent on increases in the children's heights and weights. Three different villages participated in the study. In one, the reinforcer was a ticket in a clinic lottery in which the prize was food; in the second village the reinforcer used was a photograph of the child; the third village was a control group, and these people received no reinforcement for height or weight gains. One year later, children in the two villages that received reinforcement grew more and had less malnutrition than did those in the third village; no differences were observed between the first and second villages.

Immediate Versus Delayed Reinforcement The interval of time between a response and its consequence can affect operant conditioning. In the Skinner box, for instance, if the rat receives a food pellet immediately after pressing the bar, it is receiving **immediate reinforcement**, reinforcement given immediately after the desired response. The association between a response (bar pressing) and the consequence (food pellet) is relatively clear. When the interval of time between the response and the consequence isn't immediate, the animal is receiving **delayed reinforcement**. In such cases, the relationship between a particular response and its consequence may be less clear. Going back to the rat in the Skinner box, if the food pellet doesn't appear immediately but comes, say, 30 seconds later, the rat may have some difficulty learning that bar pressing is followed by food. After pressing the bar but before receiving reinforcement, the rat may have sniffed some other section of the cage, scratched its ear, or done any number of things. It would be hard for the rat to "figure out" which response had produced the pellet.

Humans have an advantage over animals with regard to delayed reinforcement because we can be explicitly told about the contingent relationship. This leads us to work hard even to receive delayed reinforcement: We practice kicking the soccer ball into the goal so that we'll be able to score at the next game; we study hard in college to get into graduate school or to land a good job; we put in extra hours at work to get a promotion, raise, or bonus; and we push our bodies to the limit of what's possible to please an audience or receive a medal.

However, not everyone is equally good at modifying behavior to receive a delayed reward—but the ability to do so is associated with certain advantages: Walter Mischel and his colleagues (1989) found that among the 4-year-olds they studied, those who would pass up a small reward now for a big one tomorrow became more socially competent and were more likely to be high achievers during adolescence. In fact, the ability to delay reinforcement is thought to be a central feature of exercising self-control (Dixon et al., 2003).

Beyond Basic Reinforcement

Operant conditioning can play a powerful role in people's lives. To see how, let's look at ways in which conditioning is more than simply learning to respond when reinforcement is likely to result; let's consider how complex behaviors can be learned and maintained.

Generalization and Discrimination in Operant Conditioning Just as in classical conditioning, animals (including humans) can generalize and discriminate during operant conditioning. In operant conditioning, **generalization** is the ability to transfer a learned stimulus–response association to a new stimulus that is similar to the original one, making the same response that had previously led to reinforcement. When a child has a runny nose, most parents teach her to wipe her nose on a tissue. She may then generalize the learned behavior of wiping her nose and begin to wipe it on similar stimuli: any available soft surface—her sleeve, her parent's shirt, or her pillow.

In contrast to generalization, **discrimination** is the ability to respond only to a particular stimulus (wiping a runny nose on a tissue or handkerchief) and not to a similar one (wiping a runny nose on a shirt sleeve). The child's parents could help her make this discrimination by reinforcing her every time she wipes her nose with tissues (making sure that they are readily available) and by not reinforcing her when she wipes her nose on her sleeve or on theirs.

Discrimination depends on the ability to distinguish among different stimuli or among different situations—different contexts—in which a given stimulus may occur. Consider that animals can be trained to press a bar to get food in specific situations, such as when a tone sounds, or even when a high tone sounds (but not when a low or medium tone sounds). The technical name for the cue that signals to the animal whether a specific response will lead to the expected reinforcement is the *discriminative stimulus*. Experienced drivers react to a red light without thinking, automatically putting a foot on the brake pedal. In this situation, the red light is the stimulus, pressing the brake pedal is the response, and the reinforcement (negative, in this case) is avoiding a dangerous situation. But people don't stomp their right feet if they encounter a red light while walking on the sidewalk. Driving a moving car that is approaching the signal is the discriminative stimulus that cues the response to move the right foot when a red light appears.

Extinction and Spontaneous Recovery in Operant Conditioning: Gone Today, Back Tomorrow

As in classically conditioned responses, operantly conditioned responses can be extinguished. In **extinction (in operant conditioning)**, when an animal has learned a behavior through operant conditioning and the reinforcement stops, initially there is an increase in responding—and after this initial burst of behavior, the response lessens in intensity and frequency, dropping off until the animal no longer responds to the stimulus. For example, have you ever lost money in a vending machine? If so, does this sequence of events sound familiar? You are thirsty and pass a vending machine (the stimulus); you deposit coins in the machine and press the button for your selection (a complex set of responses) because you have learned the association between depositing money and selecting a beverage with the desired consequence of receiving that drink after it comes down the chute. When you press the button this time and no drink appears, you press the button again. Still nothing. You then have a burst of pressing the button several times (and maybe a few other buttons for good measure), and only after these responses fail to make the machine deliver the goods do you give up. When you finally give up, the response has been extinguished for that machine (at least until it has been repaired).

Just as we saw with classical conditioning, the original response that was operantly conditioned—putting money in the vending machine, for instance—isn't lost through extinction; what happens is that new learning overrides the previous learning: In the vending machine example, the new learning is that dropping coins in the slot (and then making your beverage selection) does not produce your chosen drink.

As arises with classical conditioning, **spontaneous recovery** occurs with operant conditioning: After a period of time following extinction, the original response that was reinforced will reappear. So if you don't use that vending machine for a month, you might very well put money in it again, expecting it to dispense your beverage.

Building Complicated Behaviors: Shaping Up

Operant conditioning can also explain how humans and animals acquire complex, multistep responses such as those used to drive cars, ride bikes, and use utensils for eating (to name only a few complex behaviors). Such complex responses do not occur because the person or animal just happens to behave in the complicated way and then gets reinforced for doing so. Rather, complicated responses are acquired through **shaping,** which is the gradual process of reinforcing an animal for responses that get closer and closer to the desired response. The process of shaping must be done in phases, nudging the animal closer and closer to the desired response. The final desired response can be thought of as a series of simpler, reinforced responses that, taken together, become increasingly similar to the desired complex response; these simpler responses that together build toward the final desired response are called **successive approximations.**

For example, dolphins don't naturally do high jumps, so they can't be reinforced for that behavior. Rather, as shown in Figure 12 (on the next page), shaping is used to train dolphins to do high jumps. Shaping is also the method by which Jackie Chan learned kung

Extinction (in operant conditioning) The fading out of a response following an initial burst of that behavior after reinforcement ceases.

Spontaneous recovery (in operant conditioning) The process by which an extinguished, previously reinforced response reappears if there is a period of time after extinction.

Shaping The gradual process of reinforcing an animal for responses that get closer to the desired response.

Successive approximations The series of relatively simple responses involved in shaping a complex response.

141

FIGURE 12 Shaping Dolphins at Sea World

At Sea World, training dolphins to jump requires a number of phases, each getting closer to the final goal.

The dolphin initially receives reinforcement (a food treat) after touching a target on the surface of the water.

The target is raised slightly out of the water. When the dolphin touches the target, it receives food.

The target continues to be raised until eventually the dolphin's body must come out of the water for it to touch the target. The dolphin receives a treat for doing so.

fu: His complex behaviors were gradually shaped, first by his father when he was very young, and later by Master Yu. Although shaping is key to learning complex responses, this is not its only use. Generally speaking, shaping is used when the desired response is not one that the animal would produce in the normal course of events—such as a dolphin's doing a high jump.

Reinforcement Schedules: An Hourly or a Piece Work Wage? Whether a reinforced behavior is simple or complex, Skinner's work highlighted that the frequency and spacing of reinforcement—the *schedule* on which the reinforcement is delivered—affects how frequently the response is produced (Staddon & Cerruti, 2003). Reinforcement can be given every time a desired response occurs, or it can be given less frequently. When an animal is reinforced for each desired response, it is receiving **continuous reinforcement**. When reinforcement does not occur after every response but only intermittently, the animal is receiving **partial reinforcement**.

The type of reinforcement—continuous or partial—affects both the ease of acquiring a response and extinguishing it. Acquiring a response is slower with partial reinforcement than with continuous reinforcement. For this reason, when shaping a new behavior, it is best to use continuous reinforcement until the desired behavior is stable. Thus, Sea World trainers reward a dolphin every time it touches the target on the surface of the water. In contrast, a partial reinforcement schedule is more resistant to extinction: The animal learns that it won't receive reinforcement after each response, so it doesn't stop responding right away when no reinforcement is given. Once the behavior is learned and you want the animal to continue to produce the behavior—you want the dolphin to keep doing high jumps, for instance—it can be useful to switch to a partial reinforcement schedule.

There are different types of partial reinforcement schedules; different schedules affect how easily responses are acquired and extinguished. On **interval schedules,** reinforcement is given for responses after a specified interval of time (for example, a dolphin might receive a treat every 5 minutes if the animal exhibits the desired behavior within that time interval). On **fixed ratio schedules,** reinforcement is given after a certain number of responses are produced (for example, a dolphin might receive a treat after every five jumps it makes). Ratio and interval

Continuous reinforcement Reinforcement given for each desired response.

Partial reinforcement Reinforcement given only intermittently after desired responses.

Interval schedule Partial reinforcement schedule based on time.

Ratio schedule Partial reinforcement schedule based on a specified number of responses.

Fixed interval schedule Reinforcement given for responses only when they are produced after a fixed interval of time.

Variable interval schedule Reinforcement given for responses produced after a variable interval of time.

Fixed ratio schedule Reinforcement given for responses produced after a fixed number of prior responses.

schedules can each be further classified as whether those schedules remain constant (referred to as *fixed schedules*) or whether the schedule changes over time (referred to as *variable schedules*). We consider these schedules in more detail in the following sections.

FIXED INTERVAL SCHEDULES. On a **fixed interval schedule**, the animal is given reinforcement for a response produced after a *fixed*—unchanging—interval of time. In a Skinner box, a rat on a fixed interval schedule of 10 minutes would receive reinforcement for the first bar press that occurs 10 minutes after the previous reinforcement was given but not during that 10 minutes, regardless of how many times it pressed the bar, and not after 9 minutes or 11 minutes or any other

Source: Photodisc Red/ Anderson/Ross

As a reward for working hard all week, these students see a movie every Friday afternoon; they have put themselves on a fixed interval schedule.

amount of elapsed time. The same applies for the next 10-minute interval: The rat would receive a food pellet only for the first bar press after 10 minutes since the last reinforcement.

Animals on a fixed interval schedule tend to respond less frequently right after reinforcement and pick up again right before reinforcement. A study break after every hour of studying is reinforcement on a fixed interval schedule. So is a weekly paycheck: No matter how hard you work, you will not get an additional paycheck that week. A fixed interval schedule is not necessarily the best schedule of reinforcement, depending on the specific behaviors that you want to increase and the availability of the reinforcer; for instance, for employers who want to reward employees for meeting their sales quota, promotions are usually not available at a fixed interval. As shown in Figure 13, animal responses to a fixed interval schedule produce a scalloped pattern on the graph of cumulative responses.

VARIABLE INTERVAL SCHEDULE. On a **variable interval schedule**, the animal is given reinforcement after a variable interval of time (one that is an *average* unit of time rather than after a fixed unit of time). Here's an example: If a rat were reinforced for its first response after 8 minutes, then after another response 12 minutes later, then 13 minutes later, and then 7 minutes later, it would be on a variable interval schedule

Source: Dynamic Graphics, Inc/ Inmagine, LLC

Although this teacher intends to put the appropriate star on each child's sticker chart each day, she sometimes forgets until the next day—reinforcing each child's targeted behavior on a variable interval schedule.

of 10 minutes. If you took a study break after approximately an hour of studying but sometimes after 45 minutes, sometimes after an hour and 15 minutes, sometimes after half an hour, and sometimes after an hour and a half, the average would be every hour, so you would be on a variable interval 60-minute schedule. In animals, this kind of schedule creates consistent although somewhat slow responding (see Figure 13).

FIXED RATIO SCHEDULE. On a **fixed ratio schedule,** the animal is given reinforcement after a fixed number of responses. If an animal is on a "fixed ratio 10" schedule for bar pressing, it receives a food pellet after its 10th bar press, then again after another 10 bar presses, and so on (regardless of the amount of time since the previous reinforcement). Certain types of work are compensated on a fixed ratio schedule; this type

Source: Robert Harbison

A fixed ratio schedule is used to pay those doing piecework: Workers receive money for a certain number of pieces, in this case, for a certain number of shirts. This schedule often has the highest responding rate but can be exhausting for the workers.

of work is generally referred to as *piecework*, where people are paid by the amount of work they completed. For example, in the garment industry, workers may be paid a certain amount for every 10 completed articles of clothing. On a fixed ratio schedule, workers have a good reason not to take breaks (they will not be paid for that time), so this schedule typically has a higher response rate than others. Piecework can be exhausting, whether the work is inputting data (being paid for every 100 lines of data entered), sewing garments, or assembling machinery. Thus, as people work long hours without breaks, efficiency and accuracy decline (Proctor & Van Zandt, 1994).

When the responses of animals on this schedule are graphed, they assume a steplike pattern (see Figure 13): Animals respond frequently until reinforcement is delivered, then briefly pause, and then respond frequently until the next reinforcement, and so on. This schedule usually produces a higher rate of responding than does a fixed interval schedule.

A variable ratio reinforcement schedule, often referred to as the gambling reinforcement schedule, is the most resistant to extinction. If you were playing a slot machine and didn't hit the jackpot, how long would you need to play before you might think there was a problem with the machine?

Source: PhotoEdit Inc.

VARIABLE RATIO SCHEDULE. On a **variable ratio schedule,** the animal is given reinforcement after a variable ratio of responses. If reinforcement occurs on average after every 10th response, reinforcement could be presented after 5, 18, 4, and 13 responses, or it could presented after 24, 1, 10, and 5 responses. You never really know when the reinforcement will come. This type of schedule is often called the *gambling reinforcement schedule* because most gambling relies on such unpredictable reinforcement. Slot machines, for instance, hit the jackpot on a variable ratio reinforcement schedule. You will eventually win if you play long enough (and spend enough money); unfortunately, you might spend years and tens of thousands of dollars trying to hit the jackpot.

The variable ratio schedule is the most resistant to extinction (which is part of the reason some people get hooked on gambling): Because you don't know exactly when you will be reinforced (but expect that eventually reinforcement will come), you keep responding. For example, Skinner (1953) found that when he shifted to reinforcing a pigeon on a variable, infrequent schedule, the pigeon continued to peck at a disk 150,000 times without reinforcement, as if still expecting reinforcement! Commission sales jobs are based on the same principle: The hope of an eventual sale (and therefore reinforcement in the form of the resulting commission) keeps salespeople trying their best. As shown in Figure 13, animals on a variable ratio schedule tend to respond frequently, consistently, and without long pauses.

THINK like a **PSYCHOLOGIST** Based on what you have read, if you had to hire someone to help you move, what type of reinforcement schedule would you want to use in order to get the highest rate of responding from your employee?

The Operant Brain

Studies of how operant conditioning arises in the brain have both illuminated the nature of operant conditioning and also shown how it differs from classical conditioning (Montague et al., 2004).

Operant Conditioning: The Role of Dopamine

Neurons that rely on the neurotransmitter dopamine play a crucial role in operant conditioning, and understanding the actions of these neurons has changed our conception of how operant conditioning works. At first glance, it might be tempting to think of operant conditioning as a simple mechanical activity, where stimulus–response associations are "stamped in" when reinforcement follows the response. Not so. We saw earlier that cognitive events, such as expectations, play a key role during classical conditioning, and we now see that such cognitive events play a crucial role in operant conditioning.

In particular, research on animals has shown that when a particular stimulus arises, the animals plan their response in advance, with the expectation that the response will have certain consequences (such as producing reinforcement). Operant conditioning rarely, if ever, is a one-shot affair: It occurs only after the animal comes to expect certain (positive) consequences if it makes a particular response to a stimulus. The process of building up the associations between stimulus, response, and the

FIGURE 13 Schedules of Reinforcement

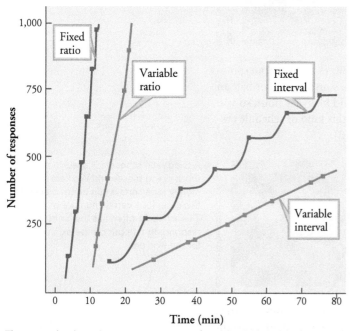

These graphs show the response patterns for rodents. Some studies with humans have found similar patterns of responding (Higgens & Morris, 1984); others have not (Lowe, 1979; Matthews et al., 1977). For both humans and rodents, however, variable reinforcement schedules induce a more consistent rate of responding than do fixed reinforcement schedules.

Source: Figure from "Teaching Machines" by B.F. Skinner, *Scientific American*, 1961. Reprinted by permission of the estate of Mary E. and Dan Todd.

expected consequences depends crucially on dopamine-releasing neurons—which together are referred to as the *dopamine reward system*. These neurons respond when positive consequences occur, and send signals to specific brain areas to strengthen the associations between the stimulus and response and between the response and its consequences (Fiorillo, 2004; Hollerman & Schultz, 1998; Waelti et al., 2001).

Variable ratio schedule Reinforcement given after a variable ratio of responses.

Classical Conditioning Versus Operant Conditioning: Are They Really Different?

We have repeatedly seen similarities between classical and operant conditioning, and there are so many similarities that researchers have wondered whether the two sorts of conditioning are really distinct. Many studies have shown that the two types of conditioning can have similar effects. For example, voluntary movements can be shaped via both classical and operant conditioning (Brown & Jenkins, 1968). Similarly, both classical and operant conditioning can help people develop some control over responses that are usually considered to be involuntary; for instance, people can learn to control blood flow to their head in order to decrease migraine headaches, and can learn to moderate their heart rate (Weiss & Engel, 1995).

The fact that similar ends can be reached with either type of conditioning, though, does not necessarily show that the means to those ends are the same. After all, bats, birds, and helicopters fly, but they do so in different ways. Table 1 presents a comparison of operant and classical conditioning. As you can see, both types of conditioning share some common features: Classical and operant conditioning are subject to extinction and spontaneous recovery, generalization, and discrimination. Moreover, in both types of conditioning, response acquisition is affected by moderating factors, especially time (in classical conditioning, the length of time between the CS and the US; in operant conditioning, the length of time between a response and reinforcement, which can be immediate or delayed). Also, for both types of conditioning, biological factors influence how easily certain behaviors can be learned. Table 1 also notes differences between the two types of conditioning; they clearly are not identical.

TABLE 1 Classical and Operant Conditioning Compared

	Classical Conditioning	Operant Conditioning
Similarities	• Learning is based on an association (in this case, between the unconditioned stimulus and the conditioned stimulus)	• Learning is based on associations (in this case, between the stimulus and response and between the response and its consequence)
	• Extinction	• Extinction
	• Spontaneous recovery	• Spontaneous recovery
	• Stimulus generalization	• Generalization
	• Stimulus discrimination	• Discrimination
	• Moderating factors can affect learning	• Moderating factors can affect learning
Differences	• The animal is passive	• The animal is active, "operating" on the world
	• Responses are reflexes (limited number of possible responses)	• Responses are voluntary behaviors (limitless possible responses)
	• Responses are elicited	• Responses are produced
	• Reinforcement doesn't play any role	• Reinforcement is contingent on the desired response

Perhaps the best evidence that the two kinds of conditioning are truly different is that different neural systems are used in each. As noted earlier, the classical conditioning of different responses relies on different brain structures, depending on the response being conditioned (Christian & Thompson, 2003; LeDoux, 1996)—but the neural systems involved in all types of classical conditioning operate in similar ways. In contrast, operant conditioning relies on neural systems that operate in fundamentally different ways than do those used in classical conditioning: Operant conditioning—and not classical conditioning—arises from parts of the brain involved in the dopamine reward system (Montague et al., 2004; Robbins & Everitt, 1998). Moreover, as its name implies, operant conditioning involves actively operating on the world, which includes planning and producing responses, and changing the responses depending on the consequences. The neural systems that underlie such activities are distinct from those used in the various forms of classical conditioning (which, by its

✓●─Study and Review on
mypsychlab.com

LOOKING BACK

1. **What is operant conditioning? How does it occur?** Operant conditioning is a process whereby a stimulus becomes associated with a response that has produced certain consequences; in contrast to classical conditioning, these responses typically are voluntary. Thorndike's work with cats in a puzzle box led him to develop the Law of Effect. Skinner's work with pigeons (and later with rats) in a Skinner box showed that operant conditioning could explain many features of everyday human behavior.

2. **What is the difference between reinforcement and punishment?** Reinforcement *increases* the likelihood that a response will recur; punishment *decreases* that likelihood. Positive reinforcement is the *presentation* of a desired reinforcer after a particular response; negative reinforcement is the *removal* of an unpleasant object or event after a particular response. Positive punishment is the presentation of an aversive object or situation after a response; negative punishment is the removal of a reinforcer after a response. Punishment by itself is not very effective. Reinforcement can be given via primary or secondary reinforcers (examples of the latter are money, praise, and good grades); behavior modification programs make use of secondary reinforcers.

3. **How are complex behaviors learned and maintained?** Complex behaviors rely on generalization and discrimination, and are subject both to extinction and spontaneous recovery. Many complex behaviors are learned through shaping, which involves reinforcing responses that are successive approximations toward the desired, complex behavior. Reinforcement schedules help maintain learned responses; the variable ratio schedule produces behaviors most resistant to extinction.

4. **What is the role of the neurotransmitter dopamine during operant conditioning?** The process of building up the associations between stimulus, response, and the expected consequences depends crucially on dopamine-releasing neurons; these neurons respond when positive consequences occur, and send signals to specific brain areas to strengthen the associations between the stimulus and response and between the response and its consequences.

nature, is essentially passive). By providing evidence that different neural systems are used in the two types of conditioning, studies of the brain show that the two are distinct.

Cognitive and Social Learning

Jackie Chan's first huge film success came with the film *Project A*, a pirate movie that deviated from the previously accepted formula for kung fu movies. Prior to *Project A*, films starring the martial arts expert and actor Bruce Lee were all the rage, and the hero he portrayed was always a "noble" man, avenging some injustice. Chan broke the mold by having the hero of *Project A* be just a regular guy, and *Project A* broke box office records in Asia. In order to understand Chan's success, we need to consider how Chan learned about movies; we must look beyond classical and operant conditioning.

When Chan was first given the opportunity to star in films and coordinate the stunts, he also began watching directors and film editors, observing what they did, how and why they included certain scenes and deleted others from the finished film. Chan's behavior was

LOOKING AHEAD: Learning Objectives

1. What is cognitive learning? How does it differ from classical and operant conditioning?
2. What is insight learning?
3. How can watching others help people learn?
4. What makes some models more effective than others?

not being changed primarily through classical or operant conditioning but rather through cognitive and social learning. Similarly, he learned how to do dangerous stunts, in part, by watching others.

Cognitive learning The acquisition of information that may not be acted on immediately but is stored for later use.

Cognitive Learning

Cognitive learning is the acquisition of information that may not be acted on immediately but is stored for later use. Information acquired through cognitive learning may be used to plan, evaluate, and in other forms of thinking, without necessarily producing any overt behavior; it may only, perhaps, be used to produce more information to be stored. Learning how to add is an example of cognitive learning, as is learning the names of the 50 states or the meaning of a new word. You are engaged in cognitive learning right now. Thus, cognitive learning is different from the types of learning that we have discussed so far, which generally focus on behavior: We know when classical conditioning has occurred because a specific behavior—the CR—has been elicited; similarly, we know when operant conditioning has occurred because a specific response is more frequent after reinforcement (or is less frequent after punishment).

Examples of Chan's cognitive learning include his learning what types of stunts underlie a successful kung fu movie (his answer: dangerous stunts without a blue screen or computer special effects) and then learning how to incorporate such stunts into a film.

Illustrating the fact that cognitive learning is more than simple associations between stimuli and responses, Tolman and Honzik (1930a, 1930b) conducted a series of classic studies with rats. In one study, one group of rats was put in a maze that led to a food box, thus receiving a food reward for completing the maze (left panel of Figure 14). In contrast, another group was also put in the maze but received no reinforcement; the rats were simply removed from the maze after a certain amount of time. Over a number of trials—occasions in the maze—the rats that were rewarded with food quickly increased their speed in the maze and decreased the number of mistakes; the speed and accuracy of the unrewarded second group did not improve very much if at all.

These people are engaged in cognitive learning: They are storing information—directions—that they will use later.

Source: Getty Images - Blend Images

This finding was consistent with what behaviorists would predict—the rats would repeat behaviors (going through the maze in a particular way) that were reinforced (with food). However, when rats in the second group began to receive a food reward on the 11th day, their performance improved dramatically; they ran much faster and made many fewer errors

FIGURE 14 Tolman and Honzik's Discovery of Latent Learning

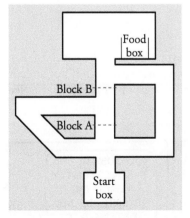

Three routes of differing lengths wind from start to finish. If two points along the most direct route are blocked, it is still possible to get to the end.

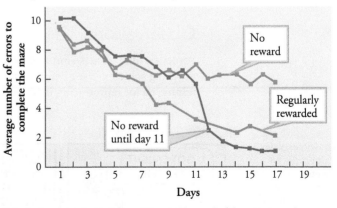

Rats that were rewarded for getting to the end of the maze made fewer "navigational" errors than rats that were not rewarded. Once rewarded (on day 11), the previously unrewarded rats made fewer mistakes, illustrating that the unrewarded rats had learned the spatial arrangement of the maze but did not apply that knowledge until reinforced.

Latent learning Learning that occurs without behavioral indicators.

Insight learning Learning that occurs when a person or animal suddenly grasps how to solve a problem or interpret a pattern of information, and incorporates that new knowledge into old knowledge.

Observational learning Learning that occurs through watching others, not through reinforcement.

⊙→ **Simulate** Latent Learning on mypsychlab.com

than before (Figure 14, right panel). These rats apparently had learned how to run the maze quickly and correctly before the 11th day, but had no reason to do so. That is, they had acquired the information about how to get to the end of the maze, but before the 11th day, they did not exhibit behaviors that indicated their learning.

Learning that occurs without behavioral indicators is called **latent learning**. Tolman reasoned that the unreinforced rats, in their wanderings around the maze, had developed a *cognitive map* of the maze, storing information about its spatial layout. However, they did not use the map until they were motivated to do so by the reinforcement. (Note that although latent learning is a form of cognitive learning, not all cognitive learning is latent learning—you can rehearse to-be-memorized words aloud and otherwise produce observable behaviors when acquiring new information.) Tolman's results—and the concept of latent learning—remind us of the important distinction between learning something and acting on that knowledge. ⊙→ **Simulate**

Insight Learning: Seeing the Connection

You may have had the following experience with a type of cognitive learning: You're trying to solve some problem—you're struggling to find the correct answer to a math problem, or you keep (re)reading the same passage in your Spanish book—but you still can't understand it. All of a sudden, things click for you, and you understand the problem and its solution. Such learning is called **insight learning** and consists of suddenly grasping how to solve a problem or interpret a pattern of information, and incorporating that new knowledge into old knowledge. It is often signaled by the phenomenon known as the "ah-ha experience," the triumphal moment when an idea becomes crystal clear. By its very nature, insight learning, unlike other types of learning, is accompanied by a sudden flash of awareness that learning has occurred.

The most famous psychological experiments regarding insight learning were reported by Wolfgang Köhler (1887–1967), a German Gestalt psychologist, with a chimpanzee named Sultan. (Yes, chimpanzees can have insight learning.) Köhler put Sultan in a cage; outside the cage and out of reach, Köhler put fruit. Also outside the cage and out of reach but closer than the fruit, he placed a long stick. Inside the cage, Köhler placed a short stick. Initially, Sultan showed signs of frustration as he tried to reach the food. Then he stopped. He seemed suddenly to have an insight into how to snag the fruit: He used the short stick to get the long one, and then used the long stick to capture the fruit. In another study, Köhler put bananas in the cage but high up, out of Sultan's reach. Also in the cage were stacks of boxes. At first, Sultan tried to jump up to grab the bananas. Eventually, he looked around at the objects in the cage and again appeared to have a flash of insight; he saw that stacking the boxes and climbing on them would enable him to reach the bananas.

Observational Learning: To See Is to Know

Some learning occurs simply by observing others; everyone has had the experience of watching someone else's behavior and then being able to reproduce it, even if not directly reinforced for reproducing it. To account for such learning, a group of psychologists, led

Observational learning explains why people may not make an effort to get to meetings on time: They see that latecomers do not suffer any negative consequences.

Source: United Media/United Feature Syndicate, Inc.

by Albert Bandura, developed *social learning theory*, which emphasizes the fact that much learning occurs in a social context. This kind of learning, which results simply from watching others and does not depend on the observing individual's receiving reinforcement, is called **observational learning**. Observational learning helps people learn how to behave in their families (Thorn & Gilbert, 1998) and in their cultures: By watching others, we learn how to greet people, eat, laugh, and tell jokes. Observational learning has helped you figure out how to behave in your classes and on campus. Do you remember your first few days at high school or college? By watching others, you learned how people talked to each other, what clothes were "fashionable," and how to interact with instructors. Similarly, Jackie Chan recounts how he learned to minimize the number of beatings he received after arriving at the Academy: "I quickly learned to watch the other children carefully. Whenever they stood up, I stood up. If they sat down, I sat down. Whatever they said, I said, and whatever they did, I did . . . it made it less likely that Master would single me out for punishment" (Chan & Yang, 1999, p. 40).

Observational learning depends on *modeling*, the process in which other people function as models, presenting a behavior to be imitated. In one of Bandura's famous studies, he showed children a Bobo doll, an inflated vinyl doll that pops back up when punched (Figure 15; Bandura et al., 1961). The children were divided into three groups: One group watched an adult beating up the Bobo doll, one group watched an adult ignoring the Bobo doll, and the third group didn't see an adult at all. After being mildly

THINK like a **PSYCHOLOGIST** Have you ever tried to learn or enhance a skill by watching a video about it? What was the skill, and do you think the video was more—or less—effective in helping you learn the skill than reading about it would have been? What types of skills and abilities do you think would be easiest to learn by observing, and what types would be harder to learn by observing?

FIGURE 15 Bandura's Study on Observational Learning

Three groups of children were tested; the groups differed only in the first part of the study.

Children in one group watched an adult abuse a Bobo doll, for example, by slamming it with a mallet, kicking it, and yelling at it.

Children in a second group watched adults play with Tinkertoys and ignore the Bobo doll.

Children in a third group never saw a model (an adult) in the playroom.

In the second part of the study, all of the children played in a room with a variety of toys, including Bobo.

Children in the first group tended to imitate what they had seen, mistreating the doll (and inventing new ways to abuse it) and being more aggressive with the other toys in the room.

Children who observed the adult ignoring the Bobo doll were even less aggressive toward it than were children in the control group!

frustrated by being placed in a room with toys but not being allowed to play with some of them, all of the children were then placed in another room with many toys, including a Bobo doll. The key finding was that children who had observed the adult behaving aggressively with Bobo were themselves more aggressive. Similar studies have found similar results, including the finding that watching a live person be aggressive has more of an impact than does watching a video of a person exhibiting the same behaviors. In turn, a realistic video has more of an impact than does a cartoon version of the same behaviors (Bandura et al., 1963).

Learning from Models

Learning from models has many advantages over other sorts of learning. By learning from models, you can avoid going through all the steps (and missteps) that learning usually requires and instead go directly to the end product. If a picture is worth a thousand words, then watching someone's movements—live or on video—is probably worth millions of words. That's why learning to cook by observing others is often easier than learning to cook by reading a cookbook. And the same is true for learning to make various types of home, car, or bike repairs. (That's why there are so many "how to" videos on YouTube.com.)

However, observational learning can produce both desired, adaptive learning and undesired, maladaptive learning. Models may say one thing and do another (such as occurs when a parent who smokes cigarettes admonishes his or her children not to smoke), and the observer learns both, saying what the model said and doing what the model did (Rice & Grusec, 1975; Rushton, 1975). Thus, the specifics of what you learn will depend on the behaviors of your models. If you are surrounded by models who exhibit adaptive behaviors, you have the opportunity to learn a lot of adaptive behaviors. But if you are surrounded by models who do not exhibit adaptive behaviors, you not only won't have that opportunity to learn certain adaptive "skills" but also may actually learn maladaptive behaviors. Thus, if adults in a family have trouble holding jobs, become explosively angry, exhibit little patience, and treat others rudely, it can be difficult for the children to learn the skills needed to maintain a job, effectively control anger, manage impatience and frustration, and treat others kindly.

Both modeling and operant conditioning are involved in learning about culture and gender. You may learn how to behave by observing others, but whether you'll actually perform a behavior repeatedly depends, in part, on the consequences that occur when you first try out the behavior. For example, imagine the following family interaction in a culture that has sex-stereotyped expectations of what constitutes appropriate play for girls and boys: A boy observes his older sister asking her parents for a new doll and sees that they buy it for her. He then asks his parents for a doll for himself and is severely punished. His request was prompted by modeling, but because it resulted in punishment, he is unlikely to make that request again.

Observational learning occurs frequently in everyday life. Observational learning is the way we learn first languages, form standards of judgment, learn to cook, and even discover ways to solve many types of problems (Bandura, 1986).

Source: © Jim Sugar / CORBIS All Rights Reserved

Researchers have discovered that several characteristics of models can make learning through observation more effective (Bandura, 1977, 1986). Not surprisingly, the more you pay attention to the model, the more you learn. And you are more likely to pay attention if the model is an expert, is good looking, has high status, or is socially powerful (Brewer & Wann, 1998). Perhaps intuitively realizing the importance of models for children's learning through observation and recognizing the high-status position of his office, cigar enthusiast President William McKinley refused to be photographed with a cigar (Seuling, 1978). However, tobacco companies are using the same principles toward other ends, through product placement in films—showing actors smoking on screen. Unfortunately, research suggests that such use of models has some success: 9- to 15-year-olds watching films with more incidents of smoking were more likely to try smoking themselves (Sargent et al., 2001—this finding has since been backed up many times, for example, by Hanewinkel, 2009, and Sargent & Hanewinkel, 2009).

Children are often participants in studies of observational learning because it is easy to find domains in which they have much to learn, and thus researchers can better control how the children acquire new information. Children are not the only ones who learn through observation, however. Consider a study (Merlo & Schotter, 2003) in which college students played a complex game in which the best strategy was not immediately obvious. Players competed for small payoffs; behind each player was another participant who simply observed the player's moves and decisions. At the end of the tournament, each player and observer were independently given the opportunity to play again for a larger payoff. Observers were more likely to play better than the players, perhaps because they had been able to discern patterns that were more difficult for players—caught up in the moment—to see. In addition, those observers who had the good fortune to watch better players tended to play better themselves than those who observed worse players, which suggests that observing someone who is good at their craft will help the observer to perform better. Even complex negotiation skills can be learned well through observation (Nadler et al., 2003).

We learn from models by seeing which of their behaviors or responses are reinforced and which are punished. We are then able to make predictions about the reactions that our own behaviors will provoke. This pattern of learning is one of the reasons many people have become increasingly concerned about the amount and type of violence, foul language, and sexuality portrayed on television. Many TV shows geared to children contain violence, which is often imitated by young viewers. Moreover, television often shows no harm to the victim as a result of violence and no negative consequences for the perpetrator.

Source: Michael Newman\PhotoEdit Inc.

LOOKING BACK

✓●─ **Study** and **Review** on
mypsychlab.com

1. **What is cognitive learning? How does it differ from classical and operant conditioning?** Cognitive learning is the acquisition of information that often is not acted on immediately but rather is stored for later use. This process contrasts with classical and operant conditioning, which involve learning specific behaviors. Latent learning (such as creating a cognitive map) is an example of cognitive learning.

2. **What is insight learning?** Learning can occur as a result of an insight—suddenly grasping what something means and incorporating that new knowledge into old knowledge. Insight learning is often accompanied by the "ah-ha experience."

3. **How can watching others help people learn?** Observational learning allows you to acquire knowledge "secondhand," without having to perform a behavior yourself. This sort of learning helps explain how children (and adults) learn their family's and their culture's rules, and the different rules that sometimes exist for men and women, boys and girls.

4. **What makes some models more effective than others?** Modeling is the process of learning a new behavior by observing others, and the more attention paid to the model, the more effective the learning will be. You are more likely to pay attention to a model who is an expert, is good looking, or has high status.

LET'S REVIEW

((•─[Listen to an audio file of your chapter on **mypsychlab.com**

I. CLASSICAL CONDITIONING

A. Classical conditioning, which was first investigated systematically by Pavlov, has four basic elements:

1. The unconditioned stimulus (US), such as food, which reflexively elicits an unconditioned response (UR).

2. The UR, such as salivation, which is automatically elicited by a US.

3. The pairing of a conditioned stimulus (CS), such as a tone, with a US, such as food, elicits a conditioned response (CR), such as salivation. (Note that salivation can be either a conditioned or an unconditioned response, depending on the stimulus that elicits it.)

4. The presentation of the CS alone then elicits the UR (the tone presented alone elicits the response of salivation, now as a CR).

B. A conditioned emotional response is involved in the development of fears and phobias, as shown by Watson and Rayner in the case of Little Albert.

C. Extinction is the unpairing of the CS and US; spontaneous recovery is the return of a classically conditioned response after a rest period following extinction.

D. In stimulus generalization, a similar, but not identical, stimulus elicits the CR.

E. In stimulus discrimination, the animal learns to distinguish among similar stimuli so that only a particular stimulus elicits the CR.

F. Classical conditioning is involved in certain bodily responses to drug abuse, certain therapy techniques, certain types of advertising, and the acquisition of food or taste aversions.

II. OPERANT CONDITIONING

A. Operant conditioning is the process whereby a stimulus and response (usually a voluntary one) become associated with the consequences of making that response. Operant conditioning has three basic elements: stimulus, response, and consequence.

B. Both negative and positive reinforcement increase the probability that the animal will respond to the stimulus the same way in the future.

C. Both positive and negative punishment decrease the probability that the animal will respond to the stimulus the same way in the future.

D. Reinforcers can be primary or secondary.

E. Extinction, spontaneous recovery, generalization, and discrimination all occur in operant conditioning.

F. Shaping makes it possible to learn, by successive approximations, responses that would otherwise not be produced.

G. Reinforcement schedules can be continuous or partial; if partial, reinforcement may be given for responses after an interval of time (interval schedule) or after a set number of responses (ratio schedule). For both these types of schedules, reinforcement can be given on a fixed or variable basis.

III. COGNITIVE AND SOCIAL LEARNING

A. Cognitive learning is the acquisition of information that may not be acted on immediately but rather is stored for later use.

B. Latent learning occurs without behavioral signs, and latent learning and insight learning (suddenly grasping what something means and incorporating that new knowledge into old knowledge) are examples of cognitive learning.

C. Observational learning is learning by watching the behavior of others, who serve as models. The more you pay attention to a model, the more you are likely to learn.

KEY TERMS

acquisition	conditioned response (CR)	extinction (in operant conditioning)	insight learning
avoidance learning	conditioned stimulus (CS)	fixed interval schedule	interval schedule
behavior modification	continuous reinforcement	fixed ratio schedule	latent learning
biological preparedness	contrapreparedness	food aversion (taste aversion)	Law of Effect
classical conditioning	delayed reinforcement	generalization	learning
cognitive learning	discrimination	habituation	negative punishment
conditioned emotional response (CER)	extinction (in classical conditioning)	immediate reinforcement	negative reinforcement
			observational learning

operant conditioning
partial reinforcement
phobia
positive punishment
positive reinforcement
primary reinforcer

punishment
ratio schedule
reinforcement
reinforcer
response contingency
secondary reinforcer

shaping
spontaneous recovery (in classical conditioning)
spontaneous recovery (in operant conditioning)
stimulus discrimination

stimulus generalization
successive approximations
unconditioned response (UR)
unconditioned stimulus (US)
variable interval schedule
variable ratio schedule

PRACTICE TEST

✓○ Study and Review on mypsychlab.com

For each of the following items, choose the single best answer.

1. Which of the following best expresses how psychologists define *learning*?
   a. the acquisition of information or a behavioral tendency that is retained for a relatively long time
   b. when repeated exposure to a stimulus decreases an organism's responsiveness
   c. as watching someone do something complex and unfamiliar on a single occasion
   d. when a neutral stimulus becomes associated, or paired, with a stimulus that causes reflexive behavior

2. In Pavlov's experiments, food by itself elicited salivation. This means that the food was
   a. a conditioned stimulus.
   b. an acquisition.
   c. an unconditioned stimulus.
   d. an unconditioned response.

3. Presenting the unconditioned stimulus and the conditioned stimulus simultaneously
   a. leads to a very strong conditioned response.
   b. does not lead to a strong conditioned response.
   c. has not been investigated.
   d. results in habituation.

4. Biological preparedness is
   a. a built-in disinclination (or even an inability) for certain conditioned stimuli to elicit particular conditioned responses.
   b. an example of avoidance learning.
   c. a built-in readiness for certain conditioned stimuli to elicit particular conditioned responses, so that less learning is necessary to produce conditioning.
   d. an irrational fear of a specific object or situation.

5. Once classical conditioning has occurred, the connection between the conditioned stimulus and the unconditioned stimulus
   a. never completely vanishes.
   b. vanishes if the conditioned stimulus and the unconditioned stimulus are not paired frequently.
   c. can vanish unexpectedly through a process known as spontaneous recovery.
   d. can be completely eliminated through repeated presentations of the unconditioned stimulus in the presence of the conditioned stimulus.

6. When animals or people have an unpleasant experience during or after eating or tasting a particular food, the animals or people
   a. are unaffected unless the unpleasant experience occurs repeatedly.
   b. may develop a classically conditioned aversion to that food or taste.

   c. always develop a conditioned response, which is nausea or vomiting.
   d. go through extinction.

7. What is true about the placebo effect?
   a. It can develop only in people and not in animals.
   b. It can develop in people only if they believe that the placebo has medicinal properties.
   c. It is an unconditioned immune response, but this response can affect attitudes and beliefs.
   d. It can be induced in both people and animals, and the organism does not have to believe that the placebo has medicinal properties in order to produce a placebo response.

8. The Law of Effect states that
   a. behavior that leads to an undesired consequence increases the likelihood of the recurrence of that behavior.
   b. actions that subsequently lead to a "satisfying state of affairs" are more likely to be repeated.
   c. an object or event that comes after a response changes the likelihood of its recurrence.
   d. classical conditioning works best if there is a long delay between the presentation of the unconditioned stimulus and the presentation of the conditioned stimulus.

9. What do psychologists know about the use of punishment?
   a. Punishment eliminates the capacity to engage in a particular behavior.
   b. Physical punishment decreases aggressive behavior in the person on the receiving end.
   c. Punishment alone is more effective than punishment used in combination with reinforcement.
   d. None of the above statements is true.

10. If a rat receives a food pellet immediately after pressing a bar, the rat is receiving
    a. delayed reinforcement.
    b. behavior modification.
    c. immediate reinforcement.
    d. positive punishment.

11. What is discrimination in operant conditioning?
    a. the ability to distinguish between the desired response and a similar but undesirable response
    b. the ability to generalize to similar stimuli
    c. the ability to generalize from a learned response to a similar response
    d. the ability to distinguish the precise stimulus that indicates whether a specific response will lead to the expected consequence

12. In a variable interval schedule of reinforcement,
    a. reinforcement is given after a variable ratio of responses.
    b. reinforcement is given for a response produced after a fixed interval of time.

c. partial reinforcement is given based on a specified number of responses.

d. reinforcement for a response is given after a variable interval of time.

13. Which statement best captures what psychologists currently know about the role of the brain in learning?
   a. The neurotransmitter acetylcholine plays a pivotal role in most every aspect of learning.
   b. An understanding of how the brain works can shed considerable light on the process of learning.
   c. The entire brain is involved in all forms of learning, but different parts may be used in different ways (depending on the nature of the stimulus).
   d. Learning is a single activity.

14. What evidence best suggests that operant conditioning and classical conditioning are essentially different?
   a. Only operant conditioning is subject to moderating factors that affect response acquisition.
   b. Biological factors influence what can be easily learned only in classical conditioning.
   c. They are not essentially different.
   d. Qualitatively distinct neural systems are used in each.

15. Learning that occurs without behavioral signs is called
   a. latent learning.
   b. insight learning.
   c. modeling.
   d. a cognitive map.

> "S. could memorize a list of words or numbers of any length, and could recall it backward or forward equally easily!"

MEMORY

LIVING WITH YESTERDAY

A Latvian newspaper reporter, known simply as "S." (short for S. V. Shereshevskii), had an almost superhuman memory. Each morning the editor of his newspaper would describe the day's stories and assignments, often providing addresses and details about the information the reporters needed to track down. The editor noticed that S. never took notes and initially thought that S. was simply not paying attention. When he called S. on the carpet for this apparent negligence, he was shocked to discover that S. could repeat back the entire briefing, word-perfect. When the editor quizzed S. about his memory, S. was surprised; he assumed that everyone could accurately remember what they had heard and seen. The editor suggested that S. visit the noted Russian psychologist Alexander Luria, who then studied him over the course of almost 30 years.

Luria soon discovered that S.'s memory "for all practical purposes was inexhaustible" (Luria, 1968/1887, p. 3). S. could memorize a list of words or numbers of any length and could recall it backward or forward equally easily! In fact, if given an item from the list, he could recall which items came immediately before it or after it. He generally made no errors. Moreover, he performed as well when he was tested years later, recalling perfectly not only the list itself but also when he learned it, where he and the examiner had been sitting, and even what the examiner had been wearing at the time.

Luria focused on unlocking the secrets behind S.'s formidable abilities. The results of this massive project are summarized in Luria's celebrated book *The Mind of a Mnemonist: A Little Book About a Vast Memory*. Luria found that S. recalled objects, events, words, and numbers by using mental imagery (mental imagery is like perception but is based on information stored in memory rather than on information coming in from sensory organs; mental images give rise to the experience of "seeing with the mind's eye," "hearing with the mind's ear," and so on for the other senses). His mental imagery was rich and complex:

> . . . I recognize a word not only by the images it evokes but by a whole complex of feelings that image arouses. . . . Usually I experience a word's taste and weight, and I don't have to make an effort to remember it—the word seems to recall itself. (p. 28)
>
> Source: *The Mind of a Mnemonist: A Little Book About a Vast Memory*, by Lynn Solotaroff and Jerome Bruner. 28, 31, 36

Sounds were accompanied by images of colored lines, puffs, *splotches*, and splashes, and these visual images could later remind him of the sound. Moreover, S. formed associations between images and concepts, which allowed the images to stand for other things. For example,

> When I hear the word green, a green flowerpot appears. . . . Even numbers remind me of images. Take the number 1. This is a proud, well-built man; 2 is a high-spirited woman; 3 a gloomy person (why, I don't know) . . . 8 a very stout woman—a sack within a sack. (p. 31)
>
> Source: *The Mind of a Mnemonist: A Little Book About a Vast Memory*, by Lynn Solotaroff and Jerome Bruner. 28, 31, 36

S. could recall items in any order because he organized his image of objects into a scene and could imagine "seeing" the imaged objects in any sequence. For example,

> I put the image of the pencil near a fence . . . the one down the street, you know. (p. 36)
>
> Source: *The Mind of a Mnemonist: A Little Book About a Vast Memory*, by Lynn Solotaroff and Jerome Bruner. 28, 31, 36

S.'s ability may sound like a dream come true, especially to a student slaving away to memorize the contents of several textbooks— but S.'s abilities had a dark side: Unlike normal people, S. could not stop himself from thinking about a flood of associations, which could overwhelm him when he tried to read. Moreover, because he always converted information to concrete images, he had trouble understanding metaphors or abstract principles (such as those used in science).

As we shall see, S. was extraordinary but not supernatural; S.'s memory, like yours, relies on three fundamental types of processing:

1. **Encoding** is the process of organizing and transforming incoming information so that it can be entered into memory, either to be stored or to be compared with previously stored information. S. was a master at encoding.
2. **Storage** is the process of retaining information in memory.
3. **Retrieval** is the process of accessing information stored in memory.

For example, have you ever seen someone you know you've met before but at first can't recall the person's name? In this situation, you get to experience the process of retrieval at work, as you struggle to bring the name to mind. S. never had such struggles, in part because his encoding and storing of information were so efficient that he could virtually always locate all of the information he sought in memory. ✳️ Explore

✳️ Explore **Encoding, Storage, and Retrieval on** mypsychlab.com

◉ ◉ ◉

Encoding Information into Memory Stores: Time and Space Are of the Essence

As he learned to use his memory, S. became a master at organizing information effectively. A key part of this activity was transforming information to make it memorable. For example, when given a complex (and meaningless) mathematical formula to recall, he generated a story that described each term. The first term was N, which he recalled by thinking of a gentleman named Neiman; the next symbol was a dot (indicating multiplication), which he thought of as a small hole where Neiman had jabbed his cane in the ground; next came a square-root sign, which he converted to Neiman's looking up at a tree that had that shape; and so on (Luria, 1887/1968, p. 49).

Such fancy mental gymnastics were useful for S. because they helped him to encode new information into memory. In this section, we begin by considering the nature of memory stores. Only after we see how the stores work can we then consider the crucial step of encoding new information into them.

LOOKING AHEAD Learning Objectives

1. What is a memory store? How do memory stores differ?
2. What factors affect whether we retain information in memory?

Types of Memory Stores

S.'s tricks required him to use different sorts of memories. Here's an example of these different sorts of memories that may be familiar to you: Until someone asks for your address, you aren't consciously aware of it—or even that you have one. But, once you are asked, the information springs to mind and is immediately accessible. This difference, between memories we are aware of and those we are not, is one sign that different types of "memory stores" are at work. A **memory store** is a set of neurons that serves to retain information over time. Notice that neurons are key; although we sometimes talk as if our "hands remember" how to shoot baskets and our "fingers remember" how to play the guitar, all memories are stored in the brain.

We can distinguish among three types of memory stores, which differ in the time span over which they operate and in the amount of information they can hold (Shiffrin, 1999). These three types of structures are known as *sensory*, *short-term*, and *long-term memory stores*. The fundamental distinctions among these types of memories were first characterized

Encoding The process of organizing and transforming incoming information so that it can be entered into memory, either to be stored or to be compared with previously stored information.

Storage The process of retaining information in memory.

Retrieval The process of accessing information stored in memory.

Memory store A set of neurons that serves to retain information over time.

FIGURE 1 The Three-Stage Model of Memory

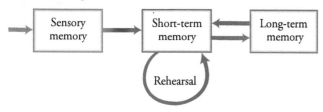

The three-stage model not only identified distinct types of memory stores but also specified how information flows among them. Later research showed that information can, in fact, move to long-term memory without necessarily passing through short-term memory. Nevertheless, this model provided the framework for many subsequent studies and theories of memory.

✳ Explore **Key Processes** on mypsychlab.com

in detail by Richard Atkinson and Richard Shiffrin (1968, 1971) and Nancy Waugh and Donald Norman (1965), as illustrated in Figure 1.

Sensory Memory: Lingering Sensations **Sensory memory (SM)** holds a large amount of perceptual information for a very brief time, typically less than 1 second. To get a sense of sensory memory at work, look at scenery rushing past the window of a moving car; even though you see literally miles and miles of landscape slipping by you, your perceptions of the trees, signs, and telephone poles leave your awareness almost as soon as you notice them. But, even so, the images linger for an instant, and this very brief retention requires a form of memory, namely, sensory memory. Sensory memory occurs without effort, arising simply because a stimulus activates perceptual areas of your brain.

George Sperling (1960) reported an experiment, now regarded as a classic, that documented sensory memory in vision (the visual form of SM is called *iconic memory*). When shown sets of many letters or digits very briefly, people can report only a handful afterward. However, even though participants cannot report all of the letters or digits that they saw, they claim that they could briefly remember all the items, but then the memory faded too quickly to retain them. Sperling was able to demonstrate that this impression is, in fact, correct. As illustrated in Figure 2, here's what he did: He flashed up rows of randomly arranged letters, leaving them visible for only a fraction of a second. These displays contained more items than the participants could report, such as three rows with four letters in each one. Immediately after the display went off, he presented one of several different tones. The pitch of the tone cued the participants to report the letters in the top, middle, or bottom row. The key result was that when the tone sounded immediately after the items were removed, the participants could report the corresponding row almost perfectly. Because the tonal cue was presented *after* the items were removed, the participants had to have retained some memory of all of the rows in order to perform so well. Moreover, if the cue was presented a mere second after the items were removed, performance dropped dramatically. This finding shows that iconic memory retains a large amount of information but that it fades very quickly.

We have a sensory memory store for each of our senses, not just for vision. For example, you can continue to hear the sound of a voice that has stopped speaking for the brief time it is still in auditory sensory memory (Cherry, 1953; the auditory form of SM is called *echoic memory*). ✳ Explore

Short-Term Memory: The Contents of Consciousness Sensory memory is the first memory store in which information is held; if a person pays attention to

FIGURE 2 The Sperling Study

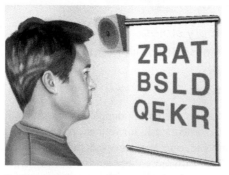

Participants saw sets of letters randomly arranged in three rows. When the letters were flashed very quickly (for less than 0.25 second), people were able to report around four or five letters, even though they claimed that they had seen more.

In another part of the study, a high, medium, or low tone was presented immediately *after* the rows of letters were flashed. Participants were to report the top row if the tone was high, the middle row if it was medium, and the bottom row if it was low. The participants could report the appropriate row almost perfectly, showing that they had briefly stored more letters than they could report aloud.

Sensory memory (SM) A memory store that holds a large amount of perceptual information for a very brief time, typically less than 1 second.

the stimulus, information about it is passed along to a different type of memory store—**short-term memory (STM)**, also called *immediate memory*, which can briefly retain a small amount of information. STM differs from SM in two key ways, in terms of its duration and capacity.

THE DURATION OF STM.   Whereas SM retains information for a very brief period of time (typically less than a second) before it fades away, STM holds relatively little information but can do so for several seconds—and that time can be prolonged (typically up to about 30 seconds) with effort. How can you prolong the time that information is in STM? By using **rehearsal**—repeating the information over and over again. When you see something you want to remember (such as the numbers on the license plate of a car involved in an accident), you can retain this information in STM by rehearsal. You are rehearsing when, after looking up a telephone number, you repeat that number until you're done pushing the appropriate numbers on your phone's keypad.

THE CAPACITY OF STM.   Whereas SM can hold a large amount of information, STM holds only a handful of separate pieces of information. For instance, do you think you would be able to keep in your STM a phone number that was 20 digits long? Unless you are like S., you'd have STM overload. How much information can ordinary people retain in STM? George Miller (1956) argued that the limits of STM should be measured in terms of *chunks*; a **chunk** is an organized unit of information, such as a digit, letter, or word. Miller claimed that STM can hold only about 7 plus-or-minus 2 (that is, from 5 to 9) "chunks" at once, but more recent research suggests that STM can in fact retain only about 4 chunks (Cowan, 2001). Generally speaking, STM can handle somewhere between 5 and 9 separate items (organized into about 4 chunks); this is why telephone numbers are fairly easy to remember; for example, even though an area code is made up of three digits, you will organize a familiar area code as a single chunk. The definition of a chunk is not precise, however, and research has shown that the amount of information STM can hold depends in part on the type of information; specifically, people need to expend more effort to hold in mind more complex patterns or concepts, and hence the capacity tends to decrease when complex material is held in STM (Luria et al., 2010). In addition, the individual's experience with specific material affects how much of it can be held in STM (Baddeley, 1994; Broadbent, 1971; Mandler, 1967); for example, if you speak French, you can organize the syllables of French words into meaningful units (that is, chunks) more easily than if you don't speak French—and thus you can retain more French words in STM than someone who doesn't speak the language. To get a sense of the importance of chunking, try the exercise in Figure 3.

STM AND CONSCIOUSNESS.   You are conscious only of information that is present in STM, and you can typically access this information more quickly than information stored in long-term memory (discussed shortly). The very fact that you are aware of information is a sure sign that it is in STM. You are aware of information in SM only because it is in the process of being transferred to STM. (So when participants in Sperling's study [see Figure 2] recalled letters, the information had moved from their SM to their STM.) But two factors conspire to prevent the entire contents of SM from being fully encoded into STM: (1) SM can retain information only very briefly, and so the relatively slow process of encoding information into STM doesn't have a chance to finish before the contents of SM have faded away, and (2) even if this weren't the case, STM can hold relatively little information, so not all of the information in SM can be fully transferred to STM.

Short-term memory (STM) A memory store that holds relatively little information for only a few seconds (but perhaps as long as 30 seconds); also called *immediate memory*.

Rehearsal The process of repeating information over and over to retain it in STM.

Chunk An organized unit of information, such as a digit, letter, or word.

FIGURE 3 Chunking in Action

A	E
7 9 1 2 8 9 8 9	5 1 8 6 1 9 2 4 7 7 7 5 5 5 8 8

B	F
1 4 2 5 9 2 2 4 4 1	9 6 5 2 4 6 3 7 9 2 2 2 2 7 7 7 7 1

C	G
9 1 3 9 2 6 4 2 4 2 4 2	1 3 8 5 2 6 2 1 7 4 3 3 5 5 9 9 4 4 2 2

D	H
6 4 1 7 6 2 8 3 3 3 8 8 5 5	7 2 5 8 3 1 8 4 3 2 1 6 2 2 5 5 8 8 1 1 6 6 3 3

Read the first row in box A, left to right, and then look up from the book and say it aloud. Check to see whether you could recall all the digits. Then read the second row in box A, left to right, and do the same. Work your way through the table, and keep going until you can't recall either of the two equal-length rows in a pair perfectly. You should find that for the shorter rows, you can remember both rows with equal ease. But for the longer ones, the second row in each pair is easier to remember than the first one. Now that you know about chunking, you know why: It's not the number of digits, it's the number of chunks that's important—and the second row of each pair is easier to organize into fewer chunks.

FIGURE 4 Working Memory

Working memory (WM) is a system that involves a central executive and two specialized short-term memory (STM) stores: one that holds pronounceable sounds (the articulatory loop) and one that holds visual or spatial patterns (the visuospatial sketchpad).

Source: Adapted from *Working Memory* by Alan Baddeley, Clarendon Press (1986). Reprinted by permission of Oxford University Press.

WORKING MEMORY: THE THINKING PERSON'S MEMORY. When S. was asked to memorize a set of meaningless sounds, he would organize the information in clever ways. The process of organizing information relies on STM but isn't the same thing as STM. Researchers soon realized that information in STM is used—operated on—in various ways. Whenever you reason something out—as you do, for example, during the game Scrabble, when you mentally rearrange letters to see whether you can form words—you are using STM (Zhang & Zhu, 2001). This observation led researchers to develop the theory of *working memory (WM),* a memory system that uses STM to reason or to solve problems.

The conception of WM differs from—and is an advance over—the original conception of STM in three ways:

1. The original conception of STM specified only one type of process (rehearsal) that operated on information in STM (as shown in Figure 1), whereas the theory of WM includes processes that transform and interpret information in STM more generally (Baddeley, 1986; Cohen et al., 1997; D'Esposito et al., 1995; Smith, 2000; Smith & Jonides, 1999). For example, while playing Scrabble you may use WM to transform sets of letters by mentally recombining them, and then you may interpret the results of such transformations by noticing whether sets of letters form a word.

2. As shown in Figure 4, the theory of WM distinguishes between different types of STM (and thus the "STM" box in Figure 1 should be divided into a set of more specialized STM boxes); specifically, we now know that STM includes distinct stores, which retain different kinds of information (Jonides et al., 2005). Alan Baddeley (1986, 1992) distinguishes between an STM that holds verbally produced sounds, which he calls the *articulatory loop,* and another STM that holds visual and spatial information, which he calls the *visuospatial sketchpad.*

3. The theory of WM includes a **central executive**, which is a set of processes that transforms and interprets information in the two STMs when you plan, reason, or solve a problem. The central executive is at work when you plan what you will say on a first date or when you think about what you would like to do tomorrow. The central executive relies in large measure on a part of the frontal lobes that is crucially involved in managing information in order to carry out specific plans (Passingham & Sakai, 2004).

In sum, **working memory (WM)** is the system that includes two specialized STMs (auditory loop and visuospatial sketchpad) and a central executive that operates on information in the STMs to plan, reason, or solve a problem. WM is so important that it is sobering to learn that people who regularly used the club drug ecstasy (also known as "e") show impaired working memory for up to 2 years after they've stopped using the drug (Morgan et al., 2002).

Long-Term Memory: Records of Experience

The central executive component of WM is guided by rules that are often retained in a third type of memory store, long-term memory. **Long-term memory (LTM)**, unlike STM, both stores a huge amount of information and stores it for a very long time, from hours to years. LTM stores the rules that can guide WM or overt behavior as well as the information that specifies the meanings of pictures, words, and objects, and the encoded memories of everything else you've ever done or learned. As we noted earlier, until you are asked for your address, you are not directly aware of that information; it has to move from LTM into STM before you are conscious of it. As an analogy, think of the difference between storing a file on your hard drive versus entering it into RAM (random-access memory), the active memory in a computer. Once information is saved on the hard drive, it can be stored indefinitely, and—unlike the information in RAM—the information saved on the hard drive will not be disrupted if the power fails. The difference between typing words into RAM and saving them on the hard drive is much like the difference between memories held in STM versus those stored in LTM.

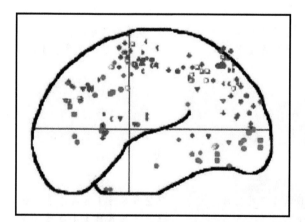

During tasks involving working memory, both the frontal lobes and perceptual areas of the brain are often activated. Different sets of areas are activated by different types of working memory tasks. The areas indicated by blue spots were activated when participants had to hold locations in mind, whereas the areas indicated by red spots were activated when participants had to hold shapes in mind (Smith & Jonides, 2000).

Source: Reprinted with permission from Smith, EE, & Jonides, J, "Storage and executive processes in the frontal lobes," *Science,* Vol. 283, 12 March 1999. pp 1657–1661. © 1999 American Association for the Advancement of Science

The storage capability of LTM is so large that researchers have yet to measure its limits. Some people don't appreciate this fact and worry about filling up their memories. A famous example is the first president of Stanford University, David Starr Jordan. President Jordan was an expert on fish, and he knew the names and habits of thousands of underwater species. At the beginning of each year, he met the new students and politely smiled as they were introduced but ignored their names. One bold student asked President Jordan if he had heard the name clearly and then repeated it. Jordan listened and realized that he had now learned the student's name. He slapped himself on the forehead and exclaimed, "Drat, there goes another fish!" He need not have worried.

LTM AND MEANING. In order for a stimulus to be *meaningful* (that is, associated with stored information that defines or situates it), it must activate relevant information in LTM. For example, you see the visual pattern "six" or the squiggle "6" as specifying a particular quantity (and not just as marks on a page) because relevant information in LTM is activated.

We access LTM not only to derive the meanings of words and digits but also to identify all types of stimuli we perceive. For example, to know that the thing you see in front of you is a cat, you need to access information about shapes of animals that you've stored in LTM. And once you match the visible shape to one you've seen before (and stored in LTM), you then automatically and unconsciously access information associated with that shape—such as its name and facts about it (including, in this case, the animal's fondness for drinking milk and sleeping during the day).

Accessing information in LTM allows us to do much more than understand the nature of objects and events we encounter. For example, accessing stored information also allows us to predict the future. This use of memory has been dubbed *prospection; retrospection* is looking behind, into the past, whereas prospection is looking ahead, into the future. In fact, neuroimaging studies have shown that the neural events that arise when we try to predict the future are very similar to those that arise when we try to recall the past—which makes sense because our views of the likely future cannot help but be based on the lessons we have learned from the past (Schacter, et al., 2007; Spreng & Grady, 2010).

INFORMATION FLOW BETWEEN STM AND LTM: A TWO-WAY STREET. Information not only goes from STM to LTM but often moves in the other direction, from LTM to STM. In fact, as noted earlier, the contents of working memory are typically drawn from LTM, not STM. For example, when you wrestle with a difficult decision, you draw on what you've learned from previous experiences to guide your reasoning—and that information is stored in LTM. (Note that sending the information temporarily to STM doesn't remove it from LTM—it continues to be in LTM even after it is accessed, just as a picture can be shown on a computer's screen even while the information used to produce it remains in the computer itself.)

In addition, most information in STM is meaningful, and it is meaningful because information in LTM has been sent to STM. For example, when you see something and recognize it as a cat, not only is information in LTM activated (as just discussed, that is where the information that conveys meaning is stored), but you also are aware of this meaning because after it was accessed in LTM, the relevant information was sent to STM. Similarly, after you access LTM, you can temporarily store in STM the meanings of words, phrases, sentences, and even paragraphs; this may seem like a lot of information to hold in STM, but remember that it's not the number of items but rather the number of chunks that defines the capacity of STM.

DISTINGUISHING BETWEEN STM AND LTM. The distinction between STM and LTM matters in everyday life, sometimes a great deal. If you see the license number of a car that has just hit a cyclist but then quickly lose that information from STM, it is gone forever. But if the information has moved into LTM, you should be able to retrieve it.

Evidence for separate STM and LTM stores has been provided by many studies. The earliest of these took place over 100 years ago, when German philosopher and pioneering memory researcher Hermann Ebbinghaus (1850–1909) undertook a series of experiments to discover the factors that affect memory. Although he didn't realize it at the time, Ebbinghaus's findings were the first solid evidence that STM and LTM are separate and operate differently. Here's what he did: To see how well he could memorize letters, digits, and

Central executive The set of processes in WM that transforms and interprets information in one or another of two specialized STMs during planning, reasoning, and problem solving.

Working memory (WM) The memory system that includes two specialized STMs (auditory loop and visuospatial sketchpad) and a central executive that operates on information in the STMs to plan, reason, or solve a problem.

Long-term memory (LTM) A memory store that holds a huge amount of information for a long time (from hours to years).

FIGURE 5 The Memory Curve

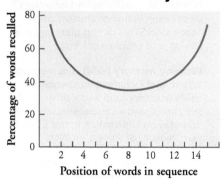

Memory is typically better for the first few and last few items in a set, producing the memory curve shown here.

Source: Adapted from M. Glanzer and A.R. Cunitz, "Two storage mechanisms in free recall," *Journal of Verbal Learning and Verbal Behavior*, 5, 351–360, 1996. Copyright © 1996, Elsevier. Used with permission.

FIGURE 6 Which Coin Is Correct?

Nickerson and Adams (1979) found that people perform poorly when asked to choose the correct image of a coin from a set of choices. Because we need only to distinguish pennies from other coins—not to notice which way Abe faces—we do not encode information about Lincoln's profile very well.

Primacy effect Increased memory for the first few stimuli in a set, reflecting storage of information in LTM.

Recency effect Increased memory for the last few stimuli in a set, reflecting storage of information in STM.

Code A particular method for specifying information (such as in words or images).

nonsense syllables (such as *cac*, *rit*, and the like, which are not words but can be pronounced), Ebbinghaus (1885/1964) composed a set of cards, with one stimulus per card; one deck had a different letter on each card, another had a different nonsense syllable on each card, and so on. He then studied the cards in the deck, one at a time and in order, and later on, he tested his memory by writing down as many of the stimuli as he could, in order. Ebbinghaus found—as many researchers have since confirmed—that the first and last items studied were more easily remembered than those in the middle. The graph in Figure 5 illustrates this *memory curve*. For example, suppose your mother asks you to "bring a few things" for her from another room and then she reads off a list of eight items; if you don't write down the list but simply trust your memory, then when you arrive at the room, you will be more likely to recall the first few items and the last few items on the list—and may need a second trip to fetch those items in the middle of the list that you forgot. The increased memory for the first few stimuli is called the **primacy effect**; as we discuss in the following section, this effect arises because this information has been stored in LTM. The increased memory for the last few stimuli is the **recency effect**, which arises because this information is still in STM.

Making Memories

We've seen how important it is to store information in LTM if you want to retain it. In this section, we examine what it means to "store" information in LTM, and then we examine several factors that determine whether such storage will occur. For example, take a look at Figure 6; do you remember which way Abraham Lincoln faces on a penny? Most people don't. Why not? You will be able to answer this question after reading what follows.

Coding: Packaged to Store
We store information in LTM using different types of codes; a **code** is a particular method for specifying information. For example, if you think of an apple, you probably have a visual mental image of that round, red, shiny fruit—but you can also use words to describe its shape and its alleged role in keeping doctors away. The image and the verbal description are different types of codes. Just as you can print letters, draw pictures, or write the dots and dashes of Morse code on a blackboard (all of these are different codes), your brain can use many types of codes.

The ability to use different codes allows us to retain information more effectively than if we had only a single code. For example, Allan Paivio (1971) not only showed that concrete words (which name objects that can be seen or touched, such as "tree" or "table") are generally remembered better than abstract words (which name intangible things, such as "spirit" and "integrity") but also made a convincing case that this difference occurs because concrete words can be stored using *dual codes*. You can visualize the object named by a concrete word and store that image along with the word itself—which gives you two chances later to find the information in LTM. But with an abstract word you can only store the word itself, and thus have fewer chances later to find the word in LTM.

WM plays a key role in encoding when the material is organized in a new way, such as by visualizing the object named by a word or verbally describing something you are seeing. The encoding process draws on portions of the frontal lobes that are used as part of WM (Buckner et al., 1999; Kelley et al., 1998; Turriziani et al., 2010). Indeed, the degree of activity in the frontal lobes when information is studied predicts how well it will later be remembered (Brewer et al., 1998; Wagner et al., 1998).

Consolidation and Reconsolidation
Simply entering information into LTM does not guarantee that it will be retained there indefinitely. For example, if you were ever in a play, you probably found that although you knew your lines well enough for the performances, a week or two after the last performance you had almost forgotten them. What happened? And what's different about the lines of a play versus facts about your hometown, which you aren't as likely to forget even if you don't think about them for months on end? In this section we consider the processes that fully encode information into LTM.

CONSOLIDATION: LODGED IN MEMORY. When information first enters LTM, it is stored in a *dynamic* form; such memories depend on continuing neural activity. To be retained indefinitely, the information must be converted from this dynamic form into a *structural* form; when information is stored in a structural form, it no longer requires ongoing neural activity to be maintained but instead is stored by connections among neurons. The process of converting memories to a structural form occurs when the brain produces proteins that help set up new connections among neurons (Ehlers, 2003), and this process takes time. Consider the following metaphor: Say you want to remember a geometric pattern that you are supposed to paint on a floor. Someone demonstrates that pattern to you by pacing it out on a lawn, and, to remember it, you walk that path over and over, repeatedly tracing its shape. This is a metaphor for *dynamic memory*; if it is not continually active, it is lost (rehearsal is one example of dynamic memory, but dynamic memory can exist in LTM even when rehearsal is not taking place in STM). However, if you walk that path over and over on the lawn, you eventually will wear through the grass, creating a dirt pathway; the corresponding kind of memory is called *structural memory*, and, like the worn path, it no longer depends on continuing activity. The process of wearing a bare pathway in a lawn is analogous to storing a memory as a new structure; this process is called *consolidation*. More precisely, **consolidation** is the process of converting information stored dynamically in LTM into a structural change in the brain.

Many studies have shown that memories are initially stored in LTM in a dynamic form and are consolidated only after considerable amounts of time (at least a couple of years—but often longer; Manns et al., 2003; McGaugh, 2000; Meeter & Murre, 2004; Squire et al., 2001). The neurons that are crucial for consolidating memories of facts and events are located in the hippocampus and related brain areas (Squire et al., 2001); after information has been consolidated, these brain areas are no longer necessary for retaining or accessing memory (Corkin, 2002).

RECONSOLIDATION: CAN RECALL MAKE MEMORIES FRAGILE? In spite of the evidence that memories become increasingly consolidated over time, researchers have discovered that after you recall information, you may need to *reconsolidate* it in order to retain it; reconsolidation is the process of stabilizing stored information again as a stored structure (Nader & Einarsson, 2010; Tronson & Taylor, 2007). Here's a metaphor: When you encode information in the first place, it is as if you have assembled pieces into a puzzle, which you then set down on a shelf. When you later retrieve the information, you need to lift that puzzle, which puts it in danger of coming undone; before putting it back on the shelf, you have to nudge the pieces and perhaps even reassemble parts of it (but this sort of reconsolidation is far different from consolidation, which was required to assemble the puzzle from scratch in the first place). Because reconsolidation is a dynamic process, memories can be altered during this process—which can disrupt them or distort them.

Researchers have shown that reconsolidation is not just consolidation all over again (Alberini, 2004). We noted earlier that proteins play a crucial role in setting up the neural connections that store information in memory (Ehlers, 2003); researchers have found that different types of proteins are critical for consolidation after information is initially encoded than are critical for reconsolidation after a previously stored memory is activated (Lee et al., 2004). This fact indicates that consolidation and reconsolidation are not accomplished by identical processes.

However, reconsolidation is not necessary every time stored information is activated (Biedenkapp & Rudy, 2004; Hernandez & Kelley, 2004). Why is reconsolidation necessary at some times but not others? To return to our metaphor, sometimes the pieces of the puzzle stick together well enough that you don't need to reassemble parts of it after you lift it. The length of time information has been retained in memory, the nature of the task, the degree to which the information was effectively stored and subsequently consolidated, the correspondence between what is expected and what actually occurs (Pedreira et al. 2004), and various other factors could affect the need for reconsolidation (Alberini, 2004).

Consolidation The process of converting information stored dynamically in LTM into a structural change in the brain.

163

Variations in Processing: Why "Thinking It Through" Is a Good Idea

S.'s memory was so good that the scientists who studied him found that there wasn't much room for improvement. You can use the same techniques that S. used, which will improve your ability to remember information. For example, if you want to remember the material in this book, you should use the *Looking Back* and *Let's Review* features as prompts to help you recall the details discussed in the text, and you should take some time to reflect on the *Think Like a Psychologist* questions and activities. These features of the book have been designed to take advantage of a fundamental fact about memory: The more you think through the associations and implications of information, the better you will remember its meaning. This finding has been interpreted in two ways, in terms of *depth of processing* and *breadth of processing*.

DEPTH OF PROCESSING: THE VIRTUE OF "GETTING TO THE BOTTOM OF IT."

Fergus Craik and Robert Lockhart (1972) hypothesized that the *depth of processing* determines whether information is stored in memory when it is encoded; **depth of processing** refers to the number and complexity of the mental operations used when you process information, with deeper processing occurring when more—or more complex—operations are used during encoding. Craik and Lockhart argued that the more deeply you process information when you first encode it, the more likely you are to remember it later. For example, if you are given a list of words and asked to judge whether each one rhymes with the sound of "tree," you are engaged in relatively shallow processing that focuses simply on the words' sounds; in contrast, if you are given a list of words and are asked whether each names a living thing, you are engaged in relatively deep processing because you have to think actively about both the meaning of the words and whether each names something alive. If you are later tested for the meanings of the words, you will be more likely to remember the words that you initially processed more deeply.

However, the ease of encoding information into memory is not solely a matter of how deeply the information is processed: The most effective processing is tailored to the reasons the material is being learned (Fisher & Craik, 1977; Morris et al., 1977; Moscovitch & Craik, 1976). Specifically, two factors are critical: ⊙▶ Simulate

1. *Attention:* What you pay attention to plays a key role in what is encoded into your memory. For example, if you are shown words and asked which ones rhyme with "tree," this forces you to pay attention to the sounds of the words. Although this is relatively shallow processing, you later will recall the *sounds* of the words better than if you were initially asked to decide which words name living objects (even though retrieving the meaning of the words is relatively deep processing).

2. *Comparability:* Knowing the ways in which you later will use stored information is critical for knowing how best to encode it. For example, if you are shown words and asked later to recall their *meanings*, you will have better recall if you initially judged whether the words named living objects than if you initially evaluated their sounds. But if you are shown words and asked later to recall their *sounds*, you will have better recall if you initially evaluated their sounds. This effect illustrates that you should direct your attention so that it is aligned with your reasons for learning the material. If you are trying to learn a formula for a chemistry test, you could either try to memorize it or you could try to understand fully the underlying concepts of the formula. If you will need to identify the formula, the first strategy may be better—but if you will need to use the formula to solve a problem, then the second strategy will be better.

Such results have led some researchers to reinterpret the effects of depth of processing. They have stressed that you will be able to remember information more easily if you use the same type of processing when you try to retrieve it as you did when you originally studied it; this is the principle of **transfer appropriate processing** (Morris et al., 1977; Rajaram et al., 1998). For example, as we just saw, encoding words in terms of their sounds makes it easier later to recall the sound, whereas encoding words in terms of their meanings makes it easier later to recall their meanings.

BREADTH OF PROCESSING: THE VIRTUE OF "REACHING OUT."

Information is encoded more effectively if it is *organized and integrated* into what you already know. This is accomplished by **breadth of processing**, which is processing that organizes and

⊙▶ Simulate the Experiment Depth of Processing on mypsychlab.com

Depth of processing The number and complexity of the mental operations used when processing; deeper processing occurs when more—or more complex—operations are used during encoding.

Transfer appropriate processing Processing used to retrieve material that is the same type as was used when the material was originally studied, which improves memory retrieval.

Breadth of processing Processing that organizes and integrates new information into previously stored information, often by making associations.

integrates information into previously stored information, often by making associations. For example, if you've ever learned a foreign language, you may have tried to learn new words by making some association between a new word—how it sounds or how it's written—with something that's related to that word. For instance, to learn the Spanish verb *correr* (which means "to run"), you might think of a courier (which sounds similar to *correr*) who runs to deliver messages.

Elaborative encoding consists of strategies that produce great breadth of processing (Bradshaw & Anderson, 1982; Craik & Tulving, 1975). For example, when you meet a new person, you could simply say her name over and over a few times, using rehearsal to try to store it in LTM; this strategy would not involve great breadth of processing. Alternatively, you could think of somebody you already know who has the same first name, visualize that person's face, and imagine that face morphing into the face of the person you've just met; this strategy would involve great breath of processing, requiring you to dig into LTM to elaborate the information you just encoded—and this strategy would result in better memory for the person's name.

Perhaps the most dramatic demonstration of the benefits of elaborative encoding involved an undergraduate student, S.F. (only his initials are used, to preserve his privacy). This young man volunteered to take part in a long-term study of memory. On the first day, he listened to a researcher read random digits to him, starting with a single digit, then two digits, then three, and so on; after each list, he was asked to repeat back the digits, in order. The researcher gave S.F. longer and longer lists until he could no longer repeat them back from memory. On that first day, the longest list he could recall was seven digits long (which, as we saw earlier, is normal). But after participating in this task for about an hour a day, 3 to 5 days a week for 20 months, S.F. could repeat back lists of 79 random digits (Ericsson et al., 1980)! How could he do it? He used elaborative encoding: S.F. was on the track team and was familiar with the times for various races and segments of races; thus, he was able to convert the numbers on the list into times, data with which he had associations. For example, he categorized the digits 3492 as "3 minutes and 49 point 2 seconds, near world-record mile time." He was able to organize the digits into chunks and then store them by integrating the information into what he already knew.

INCIDENTAL VERSUS INTENTIONAL LEARNING. One of the most remarkable discoveries in the study of memory is that it barely matters how much or how hard you try to learn something; what matters is how well you attend to, integrate, and organize the specific information you want to learn. For example, Bower (1972) describes experiments in which participants were asked to form a mental image connecting each pair of words in a list (for example, pairing "car" and "desk" by imagining a desk strapped to the roof of a car). Forming such images requires considerable breadth of processing. Some of the participants were told to use mental images to memorize the pairs of words; this kind of learning, in which you try to learn something, is called **intentional learning**. In contrast, other participants were told simply to rate the vividness of their images, and they did not try to learn the pairs of words; learning that occurs without the intention to learn is called **incidental learning**. The interesting finding was that participants who were told to rate their images later recalled the word pairs as well as those who were told to memorize them. In both cases, though, participants were asked to direct their attention, organize, and integrate the material in ways that were relevant to learn the pairs of words.

Such findings show that the effort of attending to, organizing, and integrating information is key to encoding it. But motivation to learn is important too. A person must be motivated to put in the effort to pay attention to, organize, and integrate information—and such effort is well worth the time and trouble. In the study just discussed, for instance, the participants in the incidental learning group were motivated to rate the vividness of the images, which then resulted in their learning the word pairs.

Emotionally Charged Memories As we've explored, the amount that we remember depends on how much we pay attention to, organize, and integrate the information; how much we remember also depends on the information's emotional impact: People store emotionally charged information better than they do neutral information. For instance, Bradley and colleagues (1992) showed people slides with positive, negative, and neutral images—for example, an attractive nude young man hugging an attractive nude

Elaborative encoding Encoding strategies that produce great breadth of processing.

Intentional learning Learning that occurs as a result of trying to learn.

Incidental learning Learning that occurs without the intention to learn.

young woman, a burned body, and a table lamp. The participants later remembered the emotion-inducing stimuli, both positive and negative, better than the neutral ones.

WHY DOES EMOTION BOOST MEMORY?   The neurotransmitter noradrenaline is released during strong emotion and plays a critical role in allowing emotion to boost memory. For example, consider a classic study reported by Timothy Cahill and colleagues (1994). They showed people photographs that illustrated a story. For some participants, the photos were all described in a neutral way (for example, "While walking along, the boy sees some wrecked cars in a junkyard, which he finds interesting"); for others, the photos at the beginning and end were described in a neutral way, but those in the middle were described as depicting a bloody accident ("While crossing the road, the boy is caught in a terrible accident which critically injures him"). An hour before seeing the photos, half of each set of participants were given a placebo, a medically inactive sugar pill; the other half were given a drug (propranolol) that blocks the action of noradrenaline (noradrenaline is released when people are aroused or experience stress). A week later, all of the participants were given surprise memory tests. The group that received the placebo pill showed better memory for the pictures that had an emotional context than for the neutral pictures, but the group that received the noradrenaline blocker failed to show this memory boost for emotional material.

Cahill and McGaugh suspected that the boost in memory for emotional material reflects the activity of the amygdala, which is known to play a key role in emotion and can cause more noradrenaline to be produced, which in turn enhances memory consolidation. To test this idea, Cahill and his colleagues (1996) used neuroimaging to examine the relation between activity in the amygdala and the degree to which people could recall emotionally arousing or neutral film clips. The amount of activity in the right amygdala when the participants viewed the clips later predicted remarkably well how many clips they could recall. Thus, the enhanced memory for emotional material relies on the activation of the amygdala, which in turn influences how much noradrenaline is produced.

FLASHBULB MEMORIES.   A special case of an emotionally charged memory is a **flashbulb memory**, an unusually vivid and detailed memory of a dramatic event. It is as if a flashbulb in the mind goes off at key moments, creating instant records of the events. Perhaps you have such a memory for the moment you heard about the planes crashing into the World Trade Center towers on September 11, 2001.

Roger Brown and James Kulik (1977) coined the term "flashbulb memory" and conducted the first studies of the phenomena. They polled people about a number of events, counting the recollections as flashbulb memories if respondents claimed to remember details about where they were when they learned of the event, who told them about it, and how they or others felt at the time. Most of the people these researchers polled at the time had flashbulb memories of President John F. Kennedy's assassination.

Brown and Kulik suggested that only events that have important consequences for a person are stored as flashbulb memories. Consistent with this view, they found that although three quarters of the Black Americans interviewed had flashbulb memories for the assassination of Martin Luther King Jr., fewer than one third of the White interviewees had such memories.

Researchers have found that people's ratings of how vivid their flashbulb memories are—and of how strongly they believe that the memories are accurate—do not diminish over time. Nevertheless, when these memories are objectively tested, researchers find that they often become distorted over time (Neisser & Harsch, 1992). And this distortion becomes progressively worse with the passage of time (Schmolck et al., 2000). In fact, although people believe that their flashbulb memories are more accurate than everyday memories, they are not (Talarico & Rubin, 2003). Moreover, in a study of flashbulb memories of the events of September 11, researchers showed that people actually remember non-emotional aspects of the situation (such as where they were when they first learned of the attack) better than the strong emotional reactions that accompany flashbulb memories (Hirst et al., 2009).

Women remember emotional stimuli better than men, in part because emotion boosts the brain's memory circuits more effectively in women than in men (Canli et al., 2001). It is also possible, however, that socialization has led women to pay closer attention to emotion—and thus to encode circumstances surrounding it more effectively.

Source: AP Wide World Photos

Flashbulb memory An unusually vivid and detailed memory of a dramatic event.

THINK like a PSYCHOLOGIST   Try this: if you have a flashbulb memory of some national, community, or family event, write down your memory of the event and then ask other people who were present with you what they remember of the event. How do the memories of the same event compare and why might this be?

LOOKING BACK

1. **What is a memory store? How do memory stores differ?** A memory store is a set of neurons that serves to retain information. Three types of memory stores have been identified: sensory memory (SM), which briefly stores a large amount of perceptual information; short-term memory (STM), which stores relatively little information for a few seconds (but for perhaps as long as 30 seconds); and long-term memory (LTM), which stores a large amount of information for a long time (hours to years). Only information in STM is in immediate awareness, and such information generally can be recalled faster than information in LTM. Working memory includes two specialized STMs (articulatory loop and visuospatial sketchpad) and a central executive that operates on information in the STMs.

2. **What factors affect whether we retain information in memory?** One key to effective encoding of information into LTM is to organize the information well. In addition, using two kinds of codes—verbal and visual—is more effective than using only a single code. Material must be consolidated, that is, stored as a new neural structure, which can take years to complete. In general, engaging in greater depth of processing results in more effective storage for characteristics that are attended to, as does engaging in elaborative encoding, which consists of strategies that produce great breadth of processing (which organize the new material and integrate it into previously stored material). However, different types of encoding are effective for different purposes; for example, encoding the sound of a word at the time of study is more effective than encoding the meaning of a word if the memory test requires recalling sound—but vice versa if the test requires recalling the meaning of the word. Finally, emotionally charged material is generally stored better than emotionally neutral material, in part because of the operation of the amygdala in boosting levels of noradrenaline.

Retaining Information: Not Just One LTM

S. relied heavily on mental images to help him memorize new information but he also used words and phrases as memory aids. He eventually became a professional stage performer, and people paid to see him demonstrate his amazing memory. As part of his act, he asked audience members to produce any list or set of phrases, and he would memorize them. The audiences often tried to trip him up by giving him meaningless word-like sounds or nonsense phrases. When given such verbal material to memorize, S. found it best to "break the words or meaningless phrases down into their component parts and try to attach meaning to an individual syllable by linking it up with some association" (Luria, 1887/1968, p. 43). These associations often relied on verbal knowledge, both about the meanings of words and their sounds. Here's an example that one of the authors of this book used to learn a French word: He had trouble memorizing the word "mouillé" (pronounced something like "moo-yay"), which means "wet." He was thinking about this while his children and he watched a cow being milked at a petting farm. While the farm worker milked the cow, he unexpectedly squirted one of the kids with milk, and the cow mooed at the precise moment the surprised kid yelled "yay." To remember the word, all that was necessary was to associate the sounds "moo" and "yay" (from cow and kid, respectively) with his kid's getting wet. This memory aid (which turned out to be very effective!) relied on the sounds as well as a mental image of the event to convey the meaning. Just as S. clearly relied on many different sorts of information (such as visual, auditory, verbal), so do the rest of us. In this section, we consider these different types of information that are stored in memory.

LOOKING AHEAD Learning Objectives

1. How are different types of information stored over a long period of time?
2. What role do genes play in memory?
3. How does stress affect memory?

Modality-Specific Memories: The Multimedia Brain

Humans have more than one type of LTM, and each type stores different kinds of information. You can get a sense of the different ways in which information is stored by answering some the following simple questions and noting your experiences while you do so: Which is the darker green, a pine tree or a frozen pea? What shape are Mickey Mouses's ears? Do the first three notes of "Three Blind Mice" go up or down? When answering such questions, most people report recalling visual or auditory memories, that is, "seeing" a tree and a pea, the cartoon rodent's ears, or "hearing" the nursery song. Our brains store different types of memories: Visual memories enable us to identify previously seen objects and scenes; auditory memories enable us to identify environmental sounds, words, and melodies; olfactory memories enable us to identify previously encountered scents (Gottfried & Dolan, 2003); and so on. These different types of memories are stored in **modality-specific memory stores**, each of which retains information from a single perceptual system, such as vision or audition, or from a specific processing system, such as language (Fuster, 1997; Karni & Sagi, 1993; Squire, 1987; Squire & Kandel, 1999; Ungerleider, 1995). In addition to visual, auditory, and olfactory memory stores, we have separate memory stores for touch, movement, and language.

Semantic Versus Episodic Memory

In each kind of modality-specific memory store in LTM, you can retain two types of information, *semantic* and *episodic*.

- **Semantic memories** are memories of the meanings of words (a *pine* is an evergreen tree with long needles), concepts (money is a medium of exchange), and general facts about the world (the original 13 American colonies were ruled by the British). For the most part, you don't remember specifically when, where, or how you learned the information in semantic memories. For example, the meaning of the word *memory* is, no doubt, firmly implanted in your semantic memory, but you probably have no idea when, where, or how you learned it.

- **Episodic memories** are memories of events that are associated with a particular time, place, and circumstance (when, where, and how); in other words, episodic memories include a *context*. For example, the time, place, and reasons you first began to read this book are probably in your episodic memory. And if you remember specifically where and when you first learned that the 13 original American colonies were ruled by the British, that would be an episodic memory. At first, a new word may be stored both as an episodic and as a semantic memory, but after you use it for a while, you probably don't remember when, where, or how you learned its meaning; however, even though the episodic memory may be gone, the word's meaning is retained in semantic memory.

Explicit Versus Implicit Memories

Researchers also distinguish between memories in another way, defining two broad types—*explicit and implicit*—that differ in multiple respects. **Explicit memories** can be voluntarily retrieved from LTM and brought into STM (Squire, 2004); explicit memories are also called *declarative memories*. For example, in order to answer the question about the pine tree and pea, you activated information stored in LTM to create visual mental images in STM, which you then interpreted. Explicit memories have the following characteristics:

- They can be voluntarily recalled.
- They can be stored either in episodic or semantic memory; for example, you can recall not only the relative sizes of objects (from episodic memory) but also the meaning of the word "memory" (from semantic memory).
- They can occur in any modality, such as visual or verbal.

Modality-specific memory store A memory store that retains input from a single perceptual system, such as vision or audition, or from a specific processing system, such as language.

Semantic memories Memories of the meanings of words, concepts, and general facts about the world.

Episodic memories Memories of events that are associated with a particular time, place, and circumstance.

Explicit memories Memories that can be retrieved voluntarily and brought into STM; also called *declarative memories*.

- They are what is stored after *cognitive learning* occurs, which is the acquisition of information that may not be immediately acted on but is stored for later use.

- When they are activated, they can be operated on in WM: You can think about the recalled information in different ways and for different purposes and build on it with new ideas.

In contrast, **implicit memories** are unconscious and cannot be voluntarily accessed in LTM and sent to STM; instead they predispose you to process information or behave in certain ways in the presence of specific stimuli (Roediger & McDermott, 1993; Schacter, 1987, 1996; Squire, 2004); implicit memories are also called *nondeclarative memories*. For instance, you can't explain to someone else how to balance on a bike, but nonetheless you probably have implicit memories that allow you to balance on a bike. Implicit memories guide us through the world efficiently: Think of how exhausting it would be if every time you met a friend, you had to try consciously to recall everything you knew about how people interact socially before you could have a conversation. Implicit memories have the following characteristics:

- They are unconscious and cannot voluntarily be recalled.

- They are not stored as semantic or episodic memories—they do not specify concepts, facts about the world, or information about specific events. Instead, they predispose you to process information or behave in specific ways (when in the presence of particular stimuli).

- They can occur in any modality.

- They are not stored after cognitive learning occurs, but rather arise from other types of learning.

- They cannot be reinterpreted or otherwise operated upon in WM.

The first hint that memory can be either explicit or implicit arose from the dreadful accidental consequences of one person's brain operation. A patient who is now known as H.M. suffered from such a severe case of epilepsy that nothing could control his body-wracking convulsions. Finally, in 1953, at age 27, he underwent surgery to remove his hippocampus (and related parts of the brain in the front, inside part of the temporal lobe; Corkin, 2002). His doctors, whom H.M. had met many times, were pleased that the operation lessened his epileptic symptoms, but they were bewildered when he seemed not to recognize them. He could not remember ever having met them, and every time he saw them, he introduced himself and shook hands. H.M.'s explicit memories of his doctors were gone; however, an experiment later revealed that some of his memories—his implicit memories—were at least partially intact. To discover just how thorough this memory loss was, one of the doctors is said to have repeated an experiment first reported by Claparède in 1911: The doctor concealed a pin in his hand and gave H.M. a jab during the handshake. The next day, H.M. again behaved as if he had never seen the doctor before, but, as he reached out to shake hands, he hesitated and pulled his hand back. Even though he had no conscious (explicit) memory of the doctor, his actions indicated that he had learned something about him; H.M. had acquired a type of implicit memory (Hugdahl, 1995a).

Researchers sort implicit memories into five major types: (1) classically conditioned responses, (2) memories formed through nonassociative learning, (3) habits, (4) skills, and (5) priming of perception or behavior. Let's examine each of these in turn.

Classically Conditioned Responses

The first type of implicit memory consists of *classically conditioned responses*, which are an example of associative learning; such memories are formed when a neutral stimulus is paired with a unconditioned stimulus

Implicit memories Memories that cannot be retrieved voluntarily and brought into STM but rather predispose a person to process information or behave in certain ways in the presence of specific stimuli; also called *nondeclarative memories*.

Source: David Young-Wolff\PhotoEdit Inc.

Source: Marko MacPherson/Image Bank/Getty Images

You can voluntarily recall explicit memories, such as a particularly important birthday, but you cannot voluntarily recall implicit memories, such as how to ride a bike. Implicit memories guide much of our behavior, freeing up mental processes to focus on novel or particularly important stimuli or events.

that produces an unconditioned response, which in turn leads the neutral stimulus to produce the same response as the unconditioned stimulus. For example, if you teetered on the low railing of a balcony to the point where you thought you would fall, you probably would shy away from going out on that balcony in the future. The balcony started off a neutral stimulus, the act of almost falling was the unconditioned stimulus, and the fear of falling was the unconditioned response, which then became associated with that balcony. You aren't necessarily consciously aware of the association and may not even be able to explain your aversion to the balcony (Hugdahl, 1995b).

Nonassociative Learning

Implicit memories are also formed through *non-associative learning*. In this sort of learning, the response to a stimulus itself changes—without any new associations between stimuli or between stimuli and responses being formed. For instance, if you are at a shooting range, you may be startled the first time you hear a gun being shot—but after a few shots, you will no longer be startled as much, and after a dozen shots, you probably will not startle at all. It's not that you have a new association to the sound of the gunshot but rather that the magnitude of your response has changed; this process is called *habituation*, which is the learning that occurs when repeated exposure to a stimulus decreases how responsive a person or animal is to that stimulus.

Habits

Another type of implicit memory is habits. A **habit**, as the term is defined by memory researchers, is a well-learned response that is carried out automatically (without conscious thought) when the appropriate stimulus is present. When you see the term "habit," you might think of bad habits, such as nail biting—but that's not what memory researchers mean by the term; habits include the entire gamut of automatic behaviors we engage in every day—good, bad, and neutral. When you are driving and see a red light, you automatically lift your foot from the accelerator, shift it left, and press it on the brake (we hope!); if you think a response is automatic, that's a giveaway that the action is probably being guided by a habit.

Consider an example of the habits of patient H.M. When one of the authors of this book examined him some years ago, H.M. was using a walker because he had slipped on the ice and injured himself. The walker was made of aluminum tubes, and several operations were needed to fold it properly for storage. H.M. did not remember falling on the ice (which would have been an explicit memory), but he could fold and unfold the walker more quickly than the author could—thanks to the habit he learned through using the device. He clearly had acquired a new implicit memory, even though he had no idea how he had come to need the walker in the first place. The intact ability to learn new habits—but not new episodic memories—is evidence that implicit and explicit memories are distinct from each other.

Skills: Automatic Versus Controlled Processing

A *skill* is a set of habits that can be coordinated in a range of ways. For example, riding a bike is a skill; once you've learned how to ride a bike, you coordinate balancing, pedaling, and steering—not to mention looking where you are going! After you learn to ride, each of the components is a habit, and they are coordinated in slightly different ways, depending on the situation (are you going uphill? pedal harder; are you in heavy traffic? slow down and look around more carefully).

You use a two-phase process to acquire new skills. When you first begin to acquire a skill, you use *controlled processing*. **Controlled processing** requires paying attention to each step of a task and using WM to coordinate the steps; controlled processing relies on explicit memories. Do you remember when you first learned to ride a bike (or drive a car)? It was exhausting! In contrast, after you've become highly practiced, you can perform the action without such painstaking attention. Instead, you use **automatic processing**, which is processing that allows you to carry out a sequence of steps without having to pay attention to each one or to the relations between the steps; as just discussed, such automatic processing relies on implicit memories.

According to Schneider and Chein (2003), automatic processes are distinguished from controlled processes by seven characteristics, as summarized in Table 1.

Habit A well-learned response that is carried out automatically (without conscious thought) when the appropriate stimulus is present.

Controlled processing Processing that requires paying attention to each step of a task and using working memory to coordinate the steps; relies on explicit memories.

Automatic processing Processing that allows you to carry out a sequence of steps without having to pay attention to each one or to the relations between the steps; relies on implicit memories.

TABLE 1 Automatic Processes Versus Controlled Processes

Characteristics of Automatic Processes Not Used by Controlled Processes	Examples Involving an Automatic Process
Become automatic only after extended training	Reading aloud written words
Occur without awareness and two or more can take place simultaneously	Driving (for an experienced driver) and understanding speech (in a highly familiar language)
Operate effectively even when the maximal amount of effort is required	Driving during rush hour in a very busy city
Work effectively even when a person is stressed	Reading street signs when rushing a friend to a hospital
Are difficult to alter through changes in expectations, beliefs, and goals	Once you've been burned by a hot stove, you may have difficulty forcing yourself to touch a burner—even when you know it has not been used for hours
Are difficult to adjust via learning	Changing a tennis swing after having played for many years
Depend on the importance of a stimulus, not its context	Putting the right foot on the car brake when you see a red light, even in a new city or foreign country

Priming of Perception or Behavior   **Priming** of perception or behavior occurs when having performed a task (such as recognizing a particular object) predisposes you to perform the same or an associated task more easily in the future (Schacter, 1987, 1996). Priming occurs when a preexisting memory or combination of implicit memories is activated and the activation lingers; the lingering activation itself is a kind of implicit memory. For example, if you just saw an ant on the floor, you would be primed to see other ants, and, thus primed, you would notice them in places where you might previously have missed them (such as on dark surfaces).

Priming that makes the same information more easily accessed in the future is called **repetition priming** (this is the kind of priming that enables you to see more ants). Many studies have shown that you can recognize a word or picture more quickly if you have seen it before than if it is novel. Such priming can be very long-lasting; for example, Cave (1997) found that people could name previously seen pictures faster when shown them again 48 weeks after the initial, single viewing. Your first exposure to the stimulus creates an implicit memory, which then "greases the wheels" for your later reaction to the stimulus; in fact, after priming with a familiar object, the brain areas that allow you to identify that object work less hard when you see it again than they did initially (Gabrieli et al., 1995, 1996; Henson et al., 2000; Schacter & Badgaiyan, 2001; Squire et al., 1992).

In short, the next time someone complains to you that they have a bad memory, you now know to wonder, What sort of memory? Short-term or long-term? Which modalities? Explicit or implicit? The different major types of long-term memories are summarized in Figure 7 (on the next page).

Genetic Foundations of Memory

Evidence is emerging that different genes are used when we form different types of memories, which demonstrates further that these types are, in fact, distinct. How could we tell whether different genes affect different aspects of memory? One answer comes from the study of *knockout mice*, so named because a particular gene has been "knocked out," or removed, and thus disabled. Researchers have found many examples where knocking out a specific gene impairs one sort of memory while not affecting other sorts. For example, some types of knockout mice have normal episodic memory for spatial information (remembering where to find a platform just under the surface of a pool of opaque water, a type of explicit memory) but impaired memory for conditioned fear (learning that a foot shock would follow an auditory cue, a type of implicit memory; Huynh et al., 2009). Genes affect these types of memories in part by altering the functioning of specific parts of the

Priming (of perception or behavior) Occurs when having performed a task predisposes you to perform the same or an associated task again in the future.

Repetition priming Priming that makes the same information more easily accessed in the future.

FIGURE 7 Types of Memories

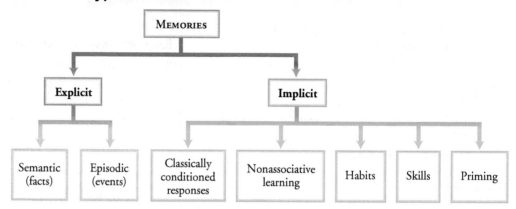

Not only are there many types of memories, as shown here, but also each type can occur in multiple modalities (visual, auditory, and so on).

Source: Adapted from L.R. Squire and S. Zola-Morgan, 1991. "The medical temporal lobe memory system." *Science, 23,* 1380–1386. Copyright © 1991 American Association for the Advancement of Science. Reprinted with permission from AAAS.

brain and in part by altering the production and functioning of key proteins and neuro-transmitters that are used when new memories are stored.

However, tracing the connection between a missing gene and a specific behavior it normally affects is easier said than done. For example, in a task often used to study memory in mice, the animals are put into a pool of opaque water and must swim around until they find a platform that's just under the surface—which allows them to rest, and so they are motivated to remember where it is (Morris, 1984). After they've located it, mice typically will swim back to it when they are moved to a different location in the pool. Using this technique, early investigators thought they had found that knocking out particular genes disrupted a mouse's ability to remember the location of the concealed platform. However, in one such study, Huerta and colleagues (1996) observed that the mice without the "remembering" gene weren't lost; they just didn't swim forward. When the researchers tickled the mice's hind feet, the animals swam and learned where the platform was located as quickly as normal mice. Their inability to find the platform wasn't caused by poor memory but rather by a lessened motivation to swim. (We have to wonder whether the researchers may have stumbled on a laziness gene!) One moral of this story is that removing a given gene can cause the animal to do poorly on a task for any number of reasons (Gerlai, 1996).

Stressed Memories

Genes also can affect your memory by producing specific chemicals when you are stressed, which in turn leads your brain to send signals to your body to prepare it for the *fight-or-flight response*—the stress response that consists of bodily changes such as increased heart rate and breathing rate—which helps you cope with the stressful stimulus. One of these signals from your brain increases the production of the hormone cortisol, which converts protein and fat into sugar, readying the body for rapid action. However, cortisol is only helpful in the short term: Robert Sapolsky and his colleagues have shown that long-term exposure to cortisol actually kills neurons in the hippocampus in rats and baboons (McEwen, 1997; Sapolsky, 1992). And the loss of hippocampal neurons disrupts the ability to encode new explicit memories.

The effects of long-term exposure to cortisol are a serious problem because this hormone is produced when animals are chronically stressed, even when they aren't stressed strongly enough to trigger the fight-or-flight response. For example, in one study, Sapolsky and his colleagues observed a troop of baboons in Africa. The baboons had a well-defined social order, with some members of the troop being "on top" (getting the first choice of food, mates, and shelter) and others "on the bottom." Those on the bottom were found to have higher levels of cortisol in their blood, which indicated that their social circumstances put them in a state of near-constant stress. When the researchers examined the brains of baboons that died, they found that those near the bottom of the social order had smaller hippocampi than those higher up that were not continually stressed. And this sad state of affairs is not limited to baboons. Magnetic resonance imaging studies of the brains of people who have undergone prolonged stress during combat have shown that they have smaller hippocampi than people who were spared these experiences, which suggests that the stress of battle caused the hippocampi to shrink (Bremner et al., 1993). Similar results have been reported for victims of childhood sexual abuse who are diagnosed with post-traumatic stress disorder (Bremner et al., 2003). Fortunately, in humans, the effects of stress on the hippocampus may be reversed if the environment changes (McEwen, 1997), and not all people who undergo stress suffer from these effects (Pederson et al., 2004; Vythilingam et al., 2004).

In addition to disrupting the structure of the hippocampus and its ability to encode new information into memory, at least some forms of stress may also affect other brain areas involved in storing and retrieving memories—including parts of the frontal lobes and amygdala (Rodrigues et al., 2009). Researchers have found that when stress hormones disrupt storage processes in the hippocampus, they also disrupt them in a pathway connecting the amygdala and frontal lobes (Maroun & Richter-Levin, 2003).

LOOKING AT LEVELS   Autobiographical Memory

Source: Royalty Free/Corbis; (inset) © GJLP/PHOTO RESEARCHERS, INC.

Episodic memories of events of your own life are called *autobiographical memories* (Conway & Rubin, 1993). For example, what is the earliest object or event from your childhood you can recall? How about your first memory of today? Such memories require a kind of "time travel," where you put yourself back into a particular moment in your past and relive what you experienced at that time. To understand autobiographical memories, we must consider events at each of the three levels of analysis and their interactions.

Let's start with the brain. Researchers have found that memories of events that occurred in your own life rely on different parts of the brain than do memories of events that you observed happening to other people. For example, in one study researchers asked undergraduate students to take photos of specific locations on campus, asking different students to photograph different places. They later brought the participants into the laboratory and showed each student some of the photos taken by others. The researchers then scanned (using functional magnetic resonance imaging) the students' brains while they looked at photos and decided which ones they themselves had taken (based on the memory of having done so), which had been taken by others but seen in the laboratory, and which had not been previously seen. The important result was that a network of brain areas was activated more strongly by the photos that corresponded to autobiographical memories than by the other photos; this network included a portion of the frontal lobes, visual regions, the hippocampus, and regions near the hippocampus (Cabeza et al., 2004). The region of the frontal lobes that was activated has been found to be activated when people think about their own characteristics but not when thinking about characteristics of other people (Johnson et al., 2002; Kelley et al., 2002; Macrae et al., 2004).

Consistent with such findings, other researchers have found that brain damage can affect memories about famous people while not affecting participants' own autobiographical memories (Joubert et al., 2003). From these and similar studies, it is clear that autobiographical memory holds a special place not only in our lives but also in our brains (Greenberg & Rubin, 2003; Levine, 2004; Levine et al., 2004).

Autobiographical memories also depend on and are affected by events at the level of the person. For example, researchers have found that when people with Alzheimer's disease lose autobiographical memories (it is a disease in which sufferers increasingly lose their memories), this loss is linked to changes in their "self-concept." Based on their results, these researchers suggest that autobiographical memories of childhood and early adulthood (which they define as the age range 16–25) are especially critical for self-identity (Addis & Tippett, 2004).

In addition, numerous events at the level of the person affect which autobiographical memories you will recall and how you will feel about them. Notably, if you felt good about an event at the time you experienced it, you are more likely to be able to recall it later. Moreover, your personal psychological characteristics (such as goals, fears, and traits) also affect the recall of autobiographical material. For example, people who are anxious in social situations tend to recall more negative and shameful autobiographical memories of social situations than do people who are not socially anxious (Field et al., 2004).

And, of course, events at the level of the group affect autobiographical memories. It's been said that a fish is the last one to find out about water (because it has always been surrounded by it and never known anything else)—and, like the fish, we may not be aware of the many and varied ways that social events shape our memories. Most notably, the cultures in which we live play an important role in how we remember events about our lives. For example, in one study, people living in the United States and people living in China were asked to recall memories of their lives. This is an interesting comparison to make because the United States is an "individualist" culture, where the focus tends to be on the individual, whereas China is a "collectivist" culture, where the focus tends to be on the family and other groups. Consistent with this type of cultural difference, people living in the United States recalled more unique, one-time events than did those living in China, and people living in China recalled more social events than did those living in the United States (Wang & Conway, 2004). In addition, studies have shown that the emotional impact of remembered autobiographical events can be reduced if people talk about these events—and this is especially the case if you have a sympathetic listener who agrees with you (Pasupathi, 2003).

Finally, as usual, events at the different levels interact. For example, we noted that if you feel good about an event when you experience it, you are more likely to be able to recall it later—and feelings also affect memory in other ways (for example, if you are depressed, you will be more likely to recall negative events; Lyubomirsky et al., 1998). Thus, feelings (level of the person) affect recall (level of the brain). But more than this, you will tend to forget negative feelings associated with autobiographical memories more quickly than you forget positive feelings. And this effect is enhanced for memories that you frequently discuss with others (level of the group)—and is even more enhanced if you talk to many different types of people, such as friends, teachers, acquaintances, and strangers (Skowronski & Walker, 2004; Skowronski et al., 2004). The social factors that influence your decision to talk about autobiographical memories not only alter your feelings, but this change in turn affects how well your brain retains information.

Study and Review on mypsychlab.com

LOOKING BACK

1. **How are different types of information stored over a long period of time?** Each modality (such as vision, audition, and touch) has a separate LTM store; separate memories also exist for motor and verbal information. Furthermore, each of these types of LTM can be divided into semantic memory (which is memory for meaning, concepts, and facts about the world) and episodic memory (which is memory for events that occur in the context of a specific time, place, and circumstance). In addition to explicit memories, which can be voluntarily brought to mind, implicit memories in each modality are triggered by specific cues and predispose us outside our awareness to process information or behave in specific ways.

2. **What role do genes play in memory?** Different genes are used when we form different types of memories. Genes affect memory in part by altering the functioning of specific parts of the brain and in part by altering the functioning of key proteins and neurotransmitters that are used when new memories are stored. Studies of knockout mice have provided evidence for the roles of genes in memory, but the results of such studies must be interpreted with caution.

3. **How does stress affect memory?** Chronic stress increases the levels of the fight-or-flight hormone cortisol, which can kill neurons in the hippocampus. Thus, stress can disrupt the encoding of new explicit memories into LTM. In addition, stress disrupts processes involved in memory retrieval.

Retrieving Information from Memory: More Than Reactivating the Past

S. was not simply adept at organizing material to be memorized; he was also expert at later digging out material from memory. No matter how well he encoded it and retained it in memory, the information would have been useless if he couldn't later retrieve it. In this section, we explore the process of retrieving information from memory.

LOOKING AHEAD Learning Objectives

1. How are memories reconstructed?
2. What role do cues play in retrieving stored memories?

The Act of Remembering: Reconstructing Buried Memories

It is tempting to think of memory as a collection of file drawers that contain assorted documents, all neat and complete in labeled folders, so that when we need to recall something, we simply open a drawer and take out what we need. But memory doesn't work this way. When we open that file drawer, we don't find well-organized folders but instead a bunch of partially torn pages that are not necessarily in order. Remembering is in many ways similar to the work archaeologists do when they find fragments of buildings, walls, furniture, and pottery and reconstruct from them a long-buried city; they fit the pieces together in a way that makes sense, and they fill in the missing parts (Neisser, 1967). We store in episodic memory only bits and pieces of a given event, and we use other stored information to fit the pieces together and fill in the gaps.

Recall Versus Recognition

All remembering involves finding fragments of information stored in LTM. We remember information in two ways, through *recall* or *recognition*. **Recall** is the act of intentionally bringing explicit information to awareness, or, put more precisely, it is the transfer of explicit information from LTM to STM. Once information is in STM, you are aware of it and can use it or communicate it. **Recognition** is the act of successfully matching an encoded stimulus to information about that stimulus that was previously stored in memory. Recognition typically allows you to identify the stimulus and thus allows you to pick out which alternative among a set of choices has a certain association; for example, if you witnessed a crime and look at the police lineup of suspects, recognition consists of picking out the person who you saw at the scene of the crime. In general, when you recognize something, you then have access to information that is associated with the object or event; for example, if you see an apple, you know that it has seeds inside—even though you cannot see them. You know this because you match the stimulus—the red, round, shiny object—to information you've previously stored about similar objects, and that information also includes the fact that there are seeds (and perhaps a worm) inside.

Methods of assessing memory rely on either recall or recognition. Essay and fill-in-the-blank questions require recall; the test taker must retrieve facts from memory and produce the required information. In contrast, true/false, multiple-choice, and matching

Recall The act of intentionally bringing explicit information to awareness, which requires transferring the information from LTM to STM.

Recognition The act of successfully matching an encoded stimulus to information about that stimulus that was previously stored in memory.

◟ ╷ ◞
THINK like a

◟ ╷ ◞
THINK like a
PSYCHOLOGIST Collect some data for yourself: Keep track of your tests scores this semester and compare how well you did on questions that require recognition versus questions that require recall. Was there a difference in how well you did? If so, why do you think that is?

Cues Stimuli, thoughts, or feelings that trigger or enhance remembering; reminders of an object or event.

questions require recognition; the test taker must recognize the correct answer among the options, picking out the alternative that has the appropriate stored associations.

All else being equal, questions that require you to recognize information tend to be easier than questions that demand recall. But recognition can become difficult if you must discriminate between similar choices. The more similar the choices, the harder it is to recognize the correct one. Why? Because similar objects or concepts have more characteristics in common than do dissimilar ones. If the choices are dissimilar, you can pick out the correct one on the basis of just a few stored features—but if the choices are similar, you must have access to many stored details in order to recognize the correct answer. Professors who want to make devilishly hard multiple-choice tests put this principle to work. If the alternative answers for each question have very similar meanings, the test taker must know more details than if the choices are very different.

Of course, you do not always know in advance which details you will need to remember to distinguish an object from other objects. Suppose S. witnessed a theft and later was asked to pick the thief from a police lineup. S., unlike the rest of us, typically remembered exactly what he saw. In the lineup, suppose both the thief and another man in the group of six are tall, are a bit overweight, and have brown hair. The major difference between them is that the thief has relatively thin eyebrows. S. would have probably noticed and remembered the thief's eyebrows and would be able to identify him. But the rest of us might not have encoded this detail at the time and thus would be hard pressed to recognize the actual culprit.

The Role of Cues: Hints on Where to Dig The key to remembering (either via recall or recognition) is to locate the appropriate pieces of stored information in LTM. The task of locating stored information is a bit like the task faced by an archaeologist who must decide where to dig to find the right bits of pottery to reconstruct a water jug. A logical place to start might be in the ruins of a kitchen. The archaeologist digs, finds bits of a typical kitchen floor from the period, and then is encouraged to continue digging in the same area. Similarly, a good *cue* directs you where to find the stored information you seek. **Cues** are stimuli, thoughts, or feelings that trigger or enhance remembering; cues are reminders of an object or event. For example, imagine running into an acquaintance in a bookstore and trying to remember his name. You might recall that when you first met him, he reminded you of someone else who had a similar hairline—and with the same name. Here the hairline is a cue, reminding you of your friend Sam and allowing you to remember that this is another person named Sam. A helpful cue directs you to relevant information stored in LTM, as illustrated in Figure 8 (Barclay et al., 1974).

FIGURE 8 Effective Cues Match Encoded Material

The man lifted the piano.

Something heavy

The man tuned the piano.

Something with a nice sound

Participants were asked to memorize two sets of sentences (as in the left column). The participants then received cues intended to help them recall the word *piano*. Because the two sentences each drew attention to a different characteristic associated with the word *piano*, which was then encoded into memory, the top cue on the right would be more effective if the participant read the top sentence, whereas the bottom cue on the right would be more effective for the bottom sentence.

Source: Adapted from Barclay et al., 1974. "Comprehension and semantic flexibility." *Journal of Verbal Learning and Verbal Behavior*, 13, 471–481.

Mental States as Cues In some cases, cues are generated by your own psychological state; in this section we consider the nature of cues that you supply yourself.

STATE-DEPENDENT RETRIEVAL: BEING IN THE RIGHT FRAME OF MIND. We remember information better if we are in the same mood or psychological state when we try to remember it as when we first learned it. For example, if you drink alcohol while studying, you will later tend to recall the information better if you are drinking when you try to remember it. This can be a sobering thought if you are preparing for an exam! This effect is called **state-dependent retrieval** (Eich, 1989): Information tends to be better remembered if recall or recognition is attempted in the same psychological state as when the information was first encoded. A closely related effect occurs with mood: If you are in a happy mood at the time you learn something, you will probably remember it better when you are feeling happy than when you are feeling sad (Bower, 1981, 1992); state-dependent retrieval also explains why, when depressed, people are more likely to remember sad, shameful, or other negative stimuli more readily than positive ones. The effects of state and mood are not always very strong, however, and they can be overshadowed by other factors, such as how well the information is organized (Eich, 1995).

Mood can affect how easily certain types of memories are recalled, and memories can influence mood: After people recall positive memories, their mood improves (Setliff & Marmurek, 2002).

Source: PhotoEdit Inc.

HYPNOSIS AND MEMORY.   S. had very vivid mental images, which apparently allowed him to recall information with ease. If someone hypnotized you and told you that any mental images you had would be especially vivid, would that hypnotically enhanced imagery ability be able to boost your recall? In some circumstances, possibly. For example, in 1976 in Chowchilla, California, a school bus was hijacked, and all of the children within were kidnapped. The bus and all those inside were buried and held for ransom. When freed, the bus driver remembered the car driven by the assailants but no other details. The bus driver agreed to be hypnotized, and, while hypnotized, he was able to recall the car's license plate, which ultimately led to the arrest of the kidnappers. Thus, in some cases hypnosis can help people recall information.

However, the effects of hypnosis in the bus hijacking case have proven to be the exception, not the rule. Using hypnosis to boost recall has two major problems:

1. In many—if not most—cases, hypnosis increases people's *confidence* in their recollections but not their actual accuracy (Sheehan, 1988; Worthington, 1979). Indeed, studies have found no overall differences in accuracy of memory between witnesses who were hypnotized and those who were interviewed without hypnosis (using techniques employed by the police; Geiselman et al., 1985).

2. Hypnosis can implant beliefs, leading the hypnotized person to believe that suggested events happened (for example, Barber, 1997; Bryant & Barnier, 1999; Green et al., 1998).

Recognizing these problems, courts in many states will not consider testimony based on recall during hypnosis.

LOOKING BACK

✓●─ **Study** and **Review** on **mypsychlab.com**

1. **How are memories reconstructed?** Recall occurs when information has been retrieved from LTM into STM. Recognition occurs when a stimulus has been matched to information about a stimulus previously stored in memory, which can allow you to identify the stimulus and access its associated characteristics. Both recall and recognition rely on activating collections of memory fragments stored in LTM.

2. **What roles do cues play in retrieving stored memories?** Memories are retrieved when they are triggered by specific stimuli, thoughts, or feelings—which serve as cues, or reminders; such cues are effective to the extent that they match material stored in LTM. Your state of mind can serve as a cue, and hence you will tend to recall information more effectively if you are in the same state of mind when you try to recall it that you were in when you first learned it. Hypnosis generally does not contribute effective memory cues.

State-dependent retrieval Memory retrieval that is better if it occurs in the same psychological state that was present when the information was first encoded.

False memories Memories of events or situations that did not, in fact, occur.

When Memory Goes Wrong— and What to do About it

S. had a near-perfect memory, but even he occasionally forgot information. When he made an error in recall, sometimes it was because of a "defect of perception," a result of the particular mental images he formed. For example, he once forgot the word "egg" in a long list. He reported, "I had put it up against a white wall and it blended in with the background. How could I possibly spot a white egg up against a white wall?" (Luria, 1968/1887, p. 36).

More often, though, S. had the opposite problem: he wanted to forget—but had trouble doing so. For example, when he performed onstage, material from a previous session could spring to mind, confusing him about the current list he was memorizing. He initially tried to imagine erasing the blackboard or burning sheets of paper on which previously memorized information had been written, but he could just as easily imagine undoing these acts or seeing the writing on the charred embers—and thus the memories persisted. Finally, S. realized that the key to forgetting was simple: He just had to want the information not to appear, and if he did not think about it, it would not return. For S., this technique worked: He could forget information, and so it did not interfere with his memorizing new material.

Could the interference of old memories cause losses and failures of memory for the rest of us? How accurate are our memories?

LOOKING AHEAD Learning Objectives

1. How can actual memories be distinguished from fictional memories?
2. Is a forgotten memory necessarily gone forever, or is it still stored but difficult to retrieve?
3. Are memories ever repressed?
4. How can you improve your memory?

False Memories

Not everything we remember actually happened. **False memories** are memories of events or situations that did not, in fact, occur. An extreme example of this sort of "memory" is illustrated in Figure 9.

Implanting Memories In general, when we remember events, we do not necessarily remember what *actually* happened but rather what we *experience* as having happened. If we (consciously or unconsciously) infer that something occurred—even if it did not—we are likely later to remember it as occurring. For example, researchers have shown that people regularly make errors of this sort (Deese, 1959; Roediger & McDermott, 1995), and you can experience it for yourself by following the instructions in Figure 10 (and then Figure 11). (If you weren't fooled by Figures 10 and 11 on page 190, read the list of words to a friend and wait 5 minutes before testing him or her; this will increase the likelihood of an error.) People tend to associate the idea of "sweet" with all of the words listed, so its representation in LTM becomes activated, and people experience it as associated with the context of the list and thus misremember having seen it.

False memories can arise from the inferences we draw and also can be directly implanted by other people. For example, consider this disturbing finding reported by psychologist Elizabeth Loftus (1993). In a study with a pair of brothers, she asked the older brother to tell his younger, 14-year-old brother about the time the younger brother had been lost in a shopping mall when he was 5 years old. This story was told as if it were fact, but it was entirely fiction. The youngster later gave every indication of having genuine memories of the event, adding rich detail to the story he had been told. For example, the boy claimed to remember the flannel shirt worn by the old man who found him, his feelings at the time, and the scolding he later received from his mother. When this study was repeated with many participants, about one quarter of them

FIGURE 9 Memories of Alien Abduction

Some people claim to remember being abducted by space aliens. Such people display the same bodily reactions when asked to remember the abduction as when they imagine other stressful events; people who do not report memories of abduction do not react as strongly when asked to imagine an alien abduction (McNally et al., 2004). Does this mean that the memories of alien abduction are genuine?

experienced such false memories (Loftus & Pickrell, 1995). Moreover, these participants clung steadfastly to their false memories, even after the procedure was explained to them and they were told that the event hadn't actually happened—participants refused to believe that the memories had been artificially created!

Similar results have been obtained many times (Loftus, 2004). Lindsay and colleagues (2004) reported especially striking results, finding that fully 65.2% of their participants could be led to believe that they had put Slime (a gooey concoction sold as a toy) in their teacher's desk when they were in first or second grade. These researchers combined the memory-inducing suggestions (of the sort used by Loftus) with showing the participants an actual photo of their class, which boosted the number of false memories (perhaps because they were able to imagine this plausible event concretely). And there was no doubt that the participants came to harbor false memories; the participants often expressed surprise and shock upon learning the truth after the study, saying things such as "No way! I remember it! That is so weird!" and "If you didn't tell me it was a false event, I would have left here thinking I did this" (p. 153).

However, some false memories are easier to create than others. Kathy Pezdek and colleagues (1997) used the same memory implanting procedure used in the earlier studies and found that whereas some participants did acquire false memories of being lost in a shopping mall, none acquired false memories of having been given a rectal enema during childhood. Strong emotions make memories more vivid, and thus people intuitively may expect that if a highly emotional event had actually happened, they would have had a very vivid memory of it—and hence if they didn't have a very vivid memory, it probably didn't happen. (The ethics of carrying out such studies might be an interesting topic for discussion.)

FIGURE 10 False Memory

Please read this list of words. Now go to Figure 11.

candy	caramel
soda pop	chocolate
honey	cake
pie	icing
fudge	cookie
cotton candy	

A twin sometimes has a false memory of an event that actually occurred to the other twin, such as being sent home from school for wearing a skirt that was too short. The same thing can happen (although less frequently) to nontwin siblings who are close in age and even among same-sex friends (Sheen et al., 2001). Roediger and his colleagues (2001) describe this phenomenon as a kind of "social contagion," where one person's recounting of memories can lead another to encode and store them.

Source: Tony Hopewell/Taxi/Getty Images

Source: Dilbert © Scott Adams/Dist. by United Feature Syndicate, Inc.

Distortions of memory have practical—and often quite serious—implications. After a crime is committed, for instance, witnesses are interviewed by the police, read newspaper stories about the crime, and perhaps see reports on TV or the Internet. This information can interfere with the witnesses' actual memories. Moreover, during a trial, the way a question is asked can influence a witness's faith in his or her recollection or even change the person's testimony altogether. Lest you think that such findings are merely of academic interest, reflect on the fact that in 2002, Larry Mayes of Indiana was the 100th person released from prison because DNA evidence proved that he was innocent. Like many others who were later released, Mr. Mayes was convicted because witnesses had faulty memories (Loftus, 2004).

Distinguishing Fact from Fiction Do any characteristics of false memories distinguish them from actual memories? Daniel Schacter and his colleagues (1996) performed the "sweet" experiment (presented in Figures 10 and 11), using similar words, while the participants' brains were being scanned. The participants were then asked which words were on the list and which words were merely implied by those listed. The hippocampus, which plays a key role in encoding new information into memory, was activated both when participants recognized actual words listed *and* when they identified associated words not on the

THINK like a
PSYCHOLOGIST Can you think of any circumstances under which implanting a false memory might be a good idea? Why might it be a good idea? If effective methods for implanting false memories are demonstrated conclusively, should they be outlawed?

FIGURE 11 True or False?

Which of these words do you remember from Figure 10?

candy   chocolate
soda pop   cake
honey   sweet
pie   icing
fudge   cookie
cotton candy

Did all of these words, including *candy*, *chocolate*, and *sweet*, appear on the list you read in Figure 10. Are you sure? In fact, the word *sweet* does not appear. If you think it did, you are not alone; most people do. This exercise shows how easily a false memory can be implanted.

Remember when you shook Mickey's hand during a childhood trip to Disneyland? Even if this never happened, seeing an advertisement that leads you to imagine this happy event will later make you more confident that it actually occurred. Researchers found that the same held true even when an ad led participants to imagine that they had shaken hands with Bugs Bunny at Disneyland, which could never have happened (Bugs is not a Disney character)—and thus the ad could not have activated an actual memory (Braun et al., 2002).

Source: © David Butow / CORBIS All Rights Reserved

Reality monitoring Paying attention to characteristics that distinguish actual from imagined stimuli.

Forgetting curve A graphic representation of the rate at which information is forgotten over time.

Encoding failure A failure to process to-be-remembered information well enough to ensure that it is fully entered into LTM.

original list. However, a different pattern of activity occurred in other brain locations, depending on whether words were or were not correctly recognized. Crucially, when words actually on the list were correctly recognized, brain areas in the temporal and parietal lobes that register the sound and meaning of spoken words also were activated. In contrast, these areas were *not* active when people encountered words not on the list.

Apparently, actual memories include stored information about the perceptual qualities of the encoded material. Because the false words were not in fact heard when the original list was read, this information was not encoded—and thus not activated when the word was later falsely recognized. The presence of associated perceptual information is thus one way that actual and false memories can be distinguished.

Although stored perceptual information is a useful sign that a memory is real, this sort of information can sometimes mislead us. Johnson and her colleagues (Johnson & Raye, 1981; Johnson et al., 1993) found that people often confuse actually having *seen* something with merely having *imagined* seeing it (which may be the basis of some false memories; Garry & Polaschek, 2000). Indeed, several studies have found that people who experience vivid mental images are more likely than people who do not have such vivid mental images to believe they saw an event when in fact they only read a description of it (Dobson & Markham, 1993; Eberman & McKelvie, 2002). S., once again, describes an extreme example of this when he commented, "To me there's no great difference between the things I imagine and what exists in reality" (p. 146).

Reality monitoring is paying attention to characteristics that distinguish actual from imagined stimuli. At the time of retrieval, reality monitoring can be improved greatly if people are led to pay attention to the amount of perceptual detail in their memories (as would occur if they tried to notice the texture of objects, other nearby objects, and shadows)—and by enhancing such reality monitoring, people are better able to distinguish actual memories from false memories (Mather et al., 1997; Norman & Schacter, 1997; Schacter et al., 2001). However, there is a limit to how well people can use perceptual cues to distinguish real from false memories; false memories produced in the "sweet" experiment, for example, are remarkably persistent, even when people are warned in advance that such false memories may occur (McDermott & Roediger, 1998).

Forgetting: Many Ways to Lose It

As first shown in 1885 by Hermann Ebbinghaus, we are not equally likely to forget each piece of information that was encoded into LTM. In particular, we humans generally recall recent events better than more distant ones, and most of our forgetting occurs soon after learning—however, as time goes on, people lose less and less additional information from LTM (Wixted & Ebbesen, 1991, 1997). Ebbinghaus discovered the **forgetting curve**, illustrated in Figure 12, which shows the rate at which information is forgotten over time.

Why do people lose information from memory? Sometimes the information was not well encoded in the first place. Remember the path traced over and over again through the grass? If the walker abandons the path before it is completely worn through to bare dirt, the pattern of the path is not stored structurally. An **encoding failure** results if you do not process information well enough to ensure that it is fully entered into LTM (Schacter, 1999).

An encoding failure causes information to be lost shortly after it is encountered, which may be one reason for the sharp drop at the beginning of the forgetting curve. But, even if information is properly encoded, it can be lost later. How? For many years, memory researchers hotly debated the fate of information that was once stored but then forgotten. One camp argued that once memories are gone, they are gone forever. According to this view, the memory decays and disappears, just as invisible ink fades until nothing is left. The other camp claimed that the memories themselves never disappear; rather, the memories remains in LTM but cannot be "found." The ink hasn't faded, but the message has been misfiled.

As researchers eventually showed, both factors—decay and problems locating stored information—contribute to forgetting. We briefly consider key evidence for both factors in the following sections.

Decay: Fade Away One theory, well-illustrated by the invisible ink metaphor, proposes that memories *decay*; that is, they degrade with time. More precisely, **decay** is the loss of memories over time because the relevant connections among neurons are lost. And in fact there is evidence that supports this theory. For example, in the sea slug, *Aplysia*, which has a relatively simple nervous system, researchers have shown that the strength of the connections among neurons established by learning fades away over time (Baily & Chen, 1989). If human neurons are similar, as seems likely, memories may, in fact, decay over time. Indeed, researchers have produced evidence both that certain genes promote stronger connections among neurons, and that other genes prevent such connections and, hence, block memory (Abel et al., 1998). When these "memory suppressor genes" are turned on, they could cause the decay of connections that store memories.

At one time, research seemed to produce compelling evidence against the decay theory. Particularly dramatic evidence seemed to come from the studies of neurosurgeon Wilder Penfield (1955). Before performing brain surgery, Penfield removed part of the patient's skull and sometimes put small electrodes directly on the surface of the brain (on the exposed cortex). These patients were fully awake (although local anesthesia was used to prevent their feeling any pain) and reported what they experienced when neurons were stimulated electrically. Penfield found that a few patients reported vivid images and memories of long-forgotten events. For example, on having a particular area of the brain stimulated, one patient said, "Yes, sir, I think I heard a mother calling her little boy somewhere. It seemed something that happened years ago." However, at least some of these reports may not have been memories but rather were auditory and visual mental images of fictional events that the patients created on the spot (Squire, 1987; Squire & Kandel, 1999). There is no strong evidence that all memories stay stored forever. In fact, Penfield obtained such results for only a minority of patients, and later work failed to reveal compelling evidence that memories are stored permanently.

Interference: Tangled Up in Memory The view that a mix-up in memory often explains forgetting has long been supported by strong direct evidence. For example, if every summer you work with a group of kids as a camp counselor, you will find that learning the names of the current crop impairs your memory of the names of last year's campers. This is an example of *interference*. **Interference** occurs when information disrupts encoding or retrieval of other information. Two types of interference can plague your memories: *retroactive* and *proactive*. ⊙▶─Simulate

1. **Retroactive interference** occurs when new learning disrupts memory for something learned earlier. For example, learning the names of the new campers can interfere with your ability to remember the names of the previous group.

2. **Proactive interference** occurs when information already stored in memory makes it difficult to learn something new. For example, your memory of the names of previous groups of campers may interfere with your learning the names on this summer's roster, particularly if some of the new names are similar to old ones.

Why does interference occur? The capacity of LTM is not the problem. You are not overloading a "memory-for-people" region in your brain; after all, some people (such as pastors and politicians) can remember the names of thousands of people with little or no difficulty. Interference probably occurs because the retrieval cues for various memories are similar, and thus a given cue may call up the wrong memory. The more similar the already-known and to-be-learned information, the more interference you get (Adams, 1967).

FIGURE 12 Ebbinghaus's Forgetting Curve

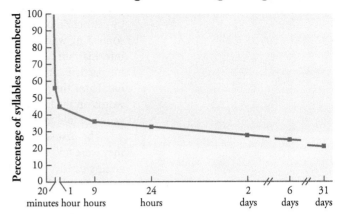

Elapsed time between learning syllables and memory test

The forgetting curve shows that information becomes harder to recall over time but that most forgetting occurs relatively soon after learning.

⊙▶ **Simulate** the Experiment on Interference on **mypsychlab.com**

Decay The loss of memories over time because the relevant connections among neurons are lost.

Interference Occurs when information disrupts encoding or retrieval of other information.

Retroactive interference Interference that occurs when new learning disrupts memory for something learned earlier.

Proactive interference Interference that occurs when information already stored in memory makes it difficult to learn something new.

Amnesia A loss of memory over an entire time span.

Intentional Forgetting: Out of Mind, Out of Sight Given that interference is one reason we forget, you might wonder whether you could improve your memory by getting rid of useless information that might interfere with important facts. Was S. onto something when he tried to clear his cluttered mind by willing himself to forget unneeded information? Can we intentionally forget? Psychologists have studied this question by asking participants to learn a list of words or other stimuli and then telling them to forget the list. Later the participants are given a surprise memory test, and their memory for the words on the list is compared to their memory for the words when they (or other people) were not told to forget the list.

The first set of findings seemed clear: People have trouble later recalling information they were told to forget (Bjork, 1972). However, later research showed that intentional forgetting doesn't make the information truly forgotten if it was successfully encoded; rather, the "forgotten" information becomes not easily accessible (Bjork & Bjork, 2003).

Intentional forgetting relies on the frontal lobes of the brain, which play a key role in organizing information during encoding and in actively searching for stored memories during retrieval. If you decide not to remember something immediately after you perceive it, your left frontal lobe will not work as hard to encode the information as it does when you are trying to store it (Reber et al., 2002). This makes sense because you don't want to store the information effectively. But what about if you've already stored it well—what happens when you later don't want to recall it? Reseachers addressed this question by asking participants first to memorize pairs of words; later, the participants saw the first word of each of the pairs while their brains were being scanned. In one condition, they were asked not to recall the second word of each pair; in another condition, they were asked to recall the second words. When they tried not to recall the second words, their frontal lobes became more active than when they tried to recall these words—which suggests that the participants were using strategies to help them ignore information (Anderson et al., 2004).

THINK like a
PSYCHOLOGIST Based on what you've read, if you were a juror and the judge instructed you to forget a comment that a witness just made, do you think that you could intentionally forget the comment? What factors do you think might make you more or less able to "forget" the comment?

Amnesia: Not Just Forgetting to Remember In some cases, information that was previously learned and stored can become entirely lost or wiped out. For instance, if you—or even S.—received a strong blow to the head, you might not recall anything that had happened to you for a period of time after the assault. Neither normal decay nor interference accounts for such unusual losses of memory. Instead, such memory failure is an example of **amnesia**, a loss of memory over an entire time span. Amnesia is not like normal forgetting, which typically affects only some of the material learned during a given period. Moreover, there are two broad sorts of amnesia:

1. *Organic amnesia*, which arises after the brain has been damaged by stroke (a loss of blood—and its life-giving oxygen and nutrients—to part of the brain, leading to cell death in that region), injury (including during surgery), or disease.

2. *Functional amnesia*, which typically arises after psychological trauma or extreme stress (Kritchevsky et al., 2004) and there is no obvious problem in the brain itself (although changes in the brain ultimately must underlie even this variety). Functional amnesia is particularly difficult to study because in some cases it may actually be *malingering*, intentional faking of the disorder (that is, the person is pretending to have amnesia; people occasionally do this in order to avoid legal or personal problems or to receive disability benefits).

In spite of its usefulness as a plot twist in novels and TV dramas, functional amnesia is very rare—and in general you would be wise to take the portrayals of amnesia in movies and TV shows with more than a single grain of salt. For example, the film "*50 First Dates* maintains a venerable movie tradition of portraying an amnesiac syndrome that bears no relation to any known neurological or psychiatric condition" (Baxendale, 2004, p. 1480). Moreover, other events portrayed in such movies—such as a second bump on the head hitting a "reset button" and curing the amnesia—have no basis in fact. (However, Baxendale notes that the main character in

Drew Barrymore, as the lead character in the movie *50 First Dates*, appears to suffer from anterograde amnesia after a car accident, but she can remember the contents of each new day—until she goes to sleep; when she wakes up, she's forgotten what happened the previous day. Her character's amnesia is not realistic; typically patients with anterograde amnesia cannot retain information for an entire day.

Source: Picture Desk, Inc./Kobal Collection

Memento and Dory the fish in *Finding Nemo* both do a reasonable job of portraying known forms of amnesia.)

Either type of amnesia typically creates problems with memories prior to the brain damage or psychological stress (*retrograde amnesia*) and/or problems with learning new information after the brain damage or psychological stress (*anterograde amnesia*) (Mayes & Downes, 1997; Parkin, 1987):

- **Retrograde amnesia** disrupts previous memories (Fast & Fujiwara, 2001). This is the sort of amnesia often popularized in soap operas and movies. Most of us are affected by a special form of retrograde amnesia called *infantile amnesia* or *childhood amnesia* (Newcombe et al., 2000): We don't remember much about our early childhood experiences, although some people apparently do remember very significant events (such as the birth of a sibling) that occurred when they were less than 2 years old (Eacott & Crawley, 1999).

- **Anterograde amnesia** leaves intact memories that were already consolidated but prevents the storing of new facts. It affects all explicit memories—that is, memories of facts that can be brought to awareness voluntarily—and produces massive encoding failure. Its manifestation is well presented in an old joke: A man runs into a doctor's office, screaming, "Doc! I've lost my memory!" The doctor asks him, "When did this happen?" The man looks at him, puzzled, and says, "When did what happen?" However, it is no joke for people with anterograde amnesia, who live as if frozen in the present moment of time. Patient H.M. had a form of anterograde amnesia.

Organic amnesia typically impairs episodic memories, such as remembering what someone just said or what happened at work last month, while leaving semantic memories almost entirely intact (Warrington & McCarthy, 1988). Most people who have an accident that causes organic amnesia have no idea what they were doing immediately before the accident, but they can remember semantic information such as their names and birth dates. However, such selective forgetting reflects not the distinction between episodic and semantic memory but instead the fact that most information in semantic memory was learned long ago—and hence is fully consolidated. Episodic memories of long-ago events are not disrupted by organic amnesia (Bayley et al., 2003).

However, depending on the location of the brain damage, organic amnesia can have the opposite effect, impairing mostly semantic memories. For example, one patient forgot the meanings of words and most characteristics of common objects. Nevertheless, she remembered details about key events in her life, such as her wedding and her father's illness (De Renzi et al., 1987). Researchers have found that semantic memories are more likely to be impaired by amnesia if they are relatively recent (for example, memories for new words that have entered everyday usage, such as "iPad"; Manns et al., 2003).

As we just saw, different forms of amnesia may arise from different types of brain damage. Often, as in the case of H.M., amnesia follows damage to the hippocampus or its connections to or from other parts of the brain (Spiers et al., 2001). In addition, amnesia can sometimes result from damage to the cortical brain areas that serve as LTM stores. One example of the selective effects of brain damage on types of memory occurs in Alzheimer's disease, a disease that disrupts neural connections (Bishop et al., 2010). In Alzheimer's disease, the amnesia typically begins with small memory deficits that become progressively worse. And depending on which specific parts of the brain are affected, Alzheimer's patients can have greater amnesia for one form of information or another; for example, some patients have worse spatial memory than verbal memory, and others show the opposite pattern (Albert et al., 1990).

Repressed Memories: Real or Imagined?

Recent years have witnessed many dramatic reports of suddenly recollected memories, often of highly emotional events such as sexual abuse during childhood; are these false memories or are they **repressed memories**, memories of actual events that were pushed into the unconscious because they are emotionally threatening, as Freud believed? (When repressed information is later recalled, this is called a *recovered memory*.) For example, some people claim to have suddenly remembered that they were sexually molested by their

Retrograde amnesia Amnesia that disrupts previous memories.

Anterograde amnesia Amnesia that leaves consolidated memories intact but prevents the storing of new facts.

Repressed memories Memories of actual events that were pushed into the unconscious because they are emotionally threatening.

Approximately 4.5 million Americans are afflicted with Alzheimer's disease, and some experts estimate that this disease will affect over 13 million Americans by 2050 (Hebert et al., 2003). But not everybody is equally susceptible. In one study, nuns who had better linguistic ability, as judged from autobiographical essays they wrote in their 20s, were less likely than nuns with poorer linguistic ability to develop Alzheimer's disease (Snowdon et al., 2000).

Source: Paul Conklin\PhotoEdit Inc.

parents decades before, when they were no more than 3 years old. Some of these reports are bizarre, such as one person's claim that as a child he had been strapped to the back of a dolphin as part of a devil worship ritual. Whether or not repressed memories exist is perhaps the most heated issue in contemporary memory research (Fivush & Edwards, 2004; Madill & Holch, 2004; McNally, 2003, 2004; Ost, 2003; Pope, 1996; Rubin, 1996; Wessel & Wright, 2004). Let's briefly examine the various positions.

On the one hand, there are plenty of examples in which recovered memories turned out to be false, ranging from a memory of having been abducted by space aliens (McNally & Clancy, 2005) to one about someone's having committed murder. For example, Eileen Franklin-Lipsker claimed that she remembered that her godfather raped Veronica Cascio and that her father then murdered Ms. Cascio. However, her father's attorneys discovered that the semen found on the victim could not have come from either her godfather or her father and that her father was definitely at a union meeting when the murder was committed (Curtius, 1996).

On the other hand, there is also evidence that traumatic memories can truly be repressed. For example, Linda Williams (1994) interviewed 129 women 17 years after each had been admitted during her childhood to a hospital emergency room for treatment of sexual abuse. Thirty-eight percent of the women had no memory of an event of sexual abuse; in fact, 12% claimed that they had never been abused. These results suggest that some people may forget traumatic memories. Could this finding simply reflect infantile amnesia, the forgetting of events that occurred in early childhood? Not likely, for two reasons:

1. Whereas 55% of the women who had been 3 years old or younger at the time of abuse had no recall, 62% of those who were between 4 and 6 years old at the time had no recall; if the forgetting were due to infantile amnesia, the women abused at a younger age should have had the poorer recall.

2. More of the women who were abused by someone they knew, as determined from independent evidence, claimed to have forgotten the incident than did the women who were abused by a stranger. Again, this difference should not have occurred if the forgetting simply reflected infantile amnesia.

Indeed, a review of 28 studies of memory for childhood sexual abuse found robust evidence that such memories can be forgotten, as well as good evidence that such memories later sometimes can be recovered (Scheflin & Brown, 1996). (In some cases, people who suddenly remembered being abused as children were then able to track down the evidence for the event; Schacter, 1996.)

There is a mystery here. As noted earlier, highly charged, emotional information is typically remembered *better* than neutral information. So, why should this particular kind of emotionally charged information be recalled poorly or forgotten for decades? One explanation is that in these cases of forgetting, the person has not really unconsciously pushed the memories out of awareness. Instead, it is as if the individual mentally went "somewhere else" during the abuse and thus has few retrieval cues for later accessing the memories. Nevertheless, the memories may be stored and may, under some circumstances and with appropriate cues, later be retrieved (Schacter, 1996). If so, it seems that people sometimes forget emotionally charged events, but sometimes—even after long periods of time—they later can come to remember them.

Improving Memory: Tricks and Tools

You can use what you've learned in this chapter about the mechanics of memory to improve both your storage and later retrieval of information. Among people without memory problems, the crucial difference between having a "good" memory and a "bad" memory lies largely in the strategies used when storing and retrieving information. The fact that memory is so dependent on such strategies explains why genes contribute very little to whether someone has a relatively good or bad memory (Nichols, 1978).

Enhancing Encoding: New Habits and Special Tricks
One way to improve your memory is to learn to encode information effectively. If you encode the information, you've won half the battle. The research results you've read about in this chapter show that you can improve your memory for information if you train yourself to engage in the following activities when you study. ◉—Watch

1. *Organize It! Organize* material so that you *integrate* it, making connections between what you want to remember and what you already know. The following techniques will help you organize and integrate effectively.

   - *Chunk it!* The first part of the organizational process requires you to form chunks—to organize the material into units. Instead of trying to remember individual facts, try to figure out how groups of facts flesh out a single underlying idea and remember the facts as different facets of this same general idea. For example, if you were learning about the functions of the frontal lobe, you might read that it's involved in producing language, in understanding grammar, in setting up plans, in working memory, and in setting up sets of movements. As soon as you noticed that all of these activities involve arranging stimuli or arranging responses into sequences, you can use that idea—that sequencing is a key general function—to organize the material into a chunk.

   - *Bundle it!* After you organize the material into chunks, organize these chunks so that they are tightly associated with each other. If you succeed in bundling the information into a tightly organized set, then when you recall one fact, the others will follow. *Hierarchical organization* is an especially effective way to improve learning and memory (Bower et al., 1969). For example, when you go shopping, you might organize your list into four main sections: baked goods, canned goods, meats, and produce. Within each category you would then have subcategories, such as fruits and vegetables for produce. And within each of these categories would you have specific instances, such as apples, bananas, and oranges for fruit and carrots and corn for vegetables. The key to thinking of ways to organize the material hierarchically is to break the big task or set of items into smaller ones, which themselves may break down into yet smaller ones.

2. *Process It!* Organization is often only the first step to improved memory; how you process that organized information makes a big difference.

   - *Think it through!* To be sure that you understand material (such as that presented in this book), the principles of *depth of processing* and *breadth of processing* imply that you need to think about the meanings and implications of facts and ideas. For instance, you can think of ways in which facts are similar and different. (Remember those compare-and-contrast essays you had to do in high school? They actually helped you learn.) In addition, you should think of examples that demonstrate statements made in the text.

   - *Match it!* In order to learn information effectively (and so succeed on tests), you should try to find out what kind of test the instructor will give: If it is an essay test, you would be better off figuring out the connections among the various facts you have read and asking yourself "why" questions about them (Pressley et al., 1995); this sort of studying will help more than simple memorization, both for success on the test and for lasting understanding. For a multiple-choice or true-or-false test that just taps knowledge of facts and figures, however, simple memorization might be quicker and do as well as the more complicated strategies designed to integrate and organize the material (but even here you probably will retain more of the relevant information if you process it deeply so that you understand it well).

   - *Distribute practice!* Just as two thin coats of paint are better than one thick coat, you will remember better if you study in distributed sessions—repeatedly, in relatively short sessions, spread out over time. Each time you study, you encode new retrieval cues and you have more chances to integrate the information into what you already know—and both factors will improve later memory. And speaking of retrieval cues, you should study in conditions as similar as possible to what you will experience when you take the test (for instance, you should not listen to music while you study).

Cramming is a good way to learn material for an exam, right? Wrong. Research has shown that people remember material much better if they rely on *distributed practice*, which takes place over a period of time, than if they rely on *massed practice*, which is crammed into one or two intense sessions.

Source: Corbis Super RF\Alamy Images Royalty Free

Mnemonic devices Strategies that improve memory, typically by effectively organizing and integrating to-be-learned information.

3. *Mnemonic Tricks: Going the Extra Mile.* In addition to developing new ways to think and study, you can improve your memory by using many of the same tricks S. developed. These tricks will improve your memory—perhaps dramatically so. A recent search for "memory improvement" books in the online bookstore Amazon.com came up with over 1,300 books—all of which provide tips on how to improve your memory and many of which emphasize memory tricks. The use of **mnemonic devices**, or strategies that improve memory (*mnemonic* is derived from the Greek word for "memory"), requires extra effort but is often well worth it: These mnemonics can easily double your recall. For example, common mnemonic devices include the following:

- *Visualize interacting objects: Images that play together, stay together.* Probably the single most effective mnemonic device is the use of *interactive images*, which involves forming mental images of interacting objects that stand for to-be-learned information. For instance, if you want to learn someone's first name, you could visualize someone else you already know who has the same name and imagine that person interacting with your new acquaintance in some way. You might envision them hugging, arguing, or shaking hands. Later, when you see the new person, you can recall this image and thus the name. As discussed earlier, forming images of interacting objects will improve memory even without any effort to learn the material (Bower, 1972; Paivio, 1971). Such interacting images can help you remember the sequences of events in a history class, the associations between meanings and sounds for foreign vocabulary, and most other types of associations.

- *Visualize "in location": Put objects in their place.* A related mnemonic device, usually called the *method of loci*, was discovered by the ancient Greek orator Simonides. He was attending a banquet one evening when he was called out of the room to receive a message. Shortly after he left, the ceiling collapsed, mangling the guests' bodies so badly that they were difficult to identify. When asked who had been at the feast, Simonides realized that he could remember easily if he visualized each person sitting at the table. This led him to develop the method of loci (*loci*, the plural of *locus*, means "places" in Latin). To use this method, first memorize a set of locations. For example, you could memorize 12 distinct places along your usual route to work, such as the first mailbox you see, a distinctive tree, a distinctive house, and so on. Later, when you want to memorize a list of objects, such as those on a shopping list, you can imagine walking or driving along the route and stopping at each location to imagine putting one object in each place. For instance, you might visualize a lightbulb leaning against the mailbox, a box of tissues nestled in a branch of the tree, a can of coffee sitting on the first step of the stairs leading to the front door of the house, and so on. When you want to recall the list, all you need to do is visualize the scene and move through it, "looking" to see what object is at each place. This method generally is very effective, but researchers have found that some types of locations are better than others; in particular, using locations along a route to work is more effective than using locations within a house, perhaps because the former locations are more distinctive (Massen et al., 2009).

To use the method of loci, pick out a set of locations on your way to work (or school), and visualize each to-be-remembered object in a different location as you mentally walk or drive along the route. To recall them, later repeat this mental journey and "see" what's in each location. You can do the same thing with locations in your house, but this won't be as effective as using locations along the route to work.

Source: © Photo Disc/Getty Images

- *Peg it: Numbered images.* The *pegword system* is similar to the method of loci, except that instead of places, you first memorize a set of objects in order. For example, you might memorize a list of rhymes, such as "One is a bun, two is a shoe, three is a tree, four is a door," and so on. Then you can treat the names of the memorized objects (bun, shoe, tree, and door) in the same way as the locations in the method of loci. You could associate the first item on your grocery list, for example, with a bun, the second with a shoe, and so on. In this case, when you want to remember the list, you remember each of the pegwords (*bun* and so on) in order and "see" what is associated with it. This method can be used to memorize all manner of lists, including those that you often find in tables in a textbook.

- *Try other mnemonic devices.* We can use many different sorts of tricks to improve our memories, not just the three discussed so far. For example, *acronyms* are pronounceable words made from the first letters of the important words in a phrase, such as "Roy G. Biv," for the order of the colors in the spectrum (red, orange, yellow, green, blue, indigo, violet). *Initialisms* are made up of the initial letters but are usually not pronounceable words, such as LSU for Louisiana State University or

STM for short-term memory. Initialisms may be easier to make up for most situations; the idea in both cases is to create a single unit that can be unpacked as a set of cues for something more complicated.

When Henry Roediger (1980) asked people to use different mnemonic devices to remember sets of words, he found that three methods—interactive imagery, the method of loci, and the pegword system—were the most effective. However, as you now know, there are many types of memory, and people differ in how well they can use various techniques. You might find some other mnemonic devices more useful.

You can use mnemonics for material throughout this book, setting up mental connections or associations from one thing to another, perhaps with the use of mental imagery. For example, to remember that the word *suppression* means "voluntarily forcing unwanted thoughts back into the unconscious," you might visualize SUPerman PRESSing down demons that are bursting out of someone's head, shoving them back inside. When you form the image, you need to remember that the first part of Superman's name and what he's doing (pressing) are critical, so make sure that the S on his cape is very vivid and visible and that he is clearly pressing with his hands. Showing you a drawing of such a scene would work almost as well, but challenging you to make up your own image has the added advantage of forcing you to process the information more thoroughly, which in and of itself improves memory.

In addition, you can remember information by stringing it into a story. For example, if you wanted to remember that in the history of psychology Freud came before the cognitivists, you can make up a story in which Freud wishes he had a computer to help him bill his patients but gets depressed when he realizes it hasn't been invented yet. Making the story a bit silly or whimsical may actually help memory (McDaniel & Einstein, 1986; McDaniel et al., 1995) and certainly makes the information more fun to think about!

As we saw when we discussed incidental learning and depth and breadth of processing, one of the fundamental facts about memory is that you will remember more material if you are actively involved when you encode it. Instead of just reading, try to find connections across areas and try to think of your own mnemonics. You won't go wrong if you form visual mental images, make up an association, invent a rhyme or a joke. You will be better off if you try to be an active learner. Although such studying involves more time and energy in the first place, you'll need less studying to brush up on the material before a final exam—and, in general, will be less likely to forget the material.

Enhancing Memory Retrieval: Knowing Where and How to Dig

Sometimes we need to remember things that we didn't expect to need or didn't have the opportunity to store effectively. Police officers are regularly faced with trying to help witnesses of crimes recall as much as they can. Moreover, the police—and the legal system—want witnesses to be as accurate as possible when recalling details surrounding a crime. Thus, researchers have developed methods to help people accurately remember after the fact. For example, Fisher and colleagues (Fisher & Geiselman, 1992; Fisher et al., 1989) used the results of laboratory studies to develop a method to help witnesses and victims of crimes recall what actually happened. Detectives trained in using their method were able to lead witnesses to recall 63% more information than was obtained with the standard police interview format. This method made use of the following memory principles and techniques:

- *Remember the context.* Recall is better when you mentally reinstate the environment in which information was learned. For example, taking a witness back to the scene of the crime can sometimes trigger memories. In fact, even visualizing or otherwise mentally re-creating the scene will help. If you want to remember something, try to think of where you were when you learned it, what the weather was like, how you felt at the time, where you were standing, and so on.

- *Structure the environment.* For certain kinds of memory retrieval, you can arrange your environment in such a way that you are reminded about what to remember. In other words, use external cues as mnemonic devices. If you are prone to forgetting your backpack, leave it by the door; if you forget to check the weather forecast before you leave home in the morning, put an umbrella on the door handle.

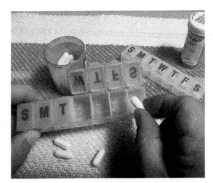

Arranging your world properly can aid memory. In this case, the pill holder makes it easy to recall whether you've taken your medication each day.

Source: PhotoEdit Inc.

THINK like a **PSYCHOLOGIST** To help implement all of these memory-enhancing strategies when you study, download the encoding and retrieval-based study guide at www.mypsychlab.com; select the *Memory* chapter and click on the *DO IT!* folder.

Study and Review on
mypsychlab.com

- *Focus.* Searching for information in LTM requires effort and is easily disrupted by other stimuli. To remember well, focus on the task, shutting out distractions.
- *Keep trying.* The more times you try to remember something, the more likely you are eventually to retrieve it (Roediger & Thorpe, 1978).
- *Seize fragments.* If you cannot recall something immediately, try to think of characteristics of the information sought. Fisher and colleagues (1989) advised detectives that if a witness could not remember a criminal's name, he or she should try to remember its length, first syllable, ethnic origin, and so on. These bits of information can serve as retrieval cues.

If you can find a method for improving retrieval that is fun and easy and that works for you, you are more likely to use it and benefit by it. As in the case of mnemonic devices, try various methods and see which suits you.

LOOKING BACK

1. **How can actual memories be distinguished from fictional memories?** Actual memories may include perceptual information from the modality in which a fact was learned—perhaps information obtained by seeing it, hearing it, or reading it—whereas false memories typically do not include this sort of information. In many circumstances, however, it is difficult to distinguish between actual and false memories.

2. **Is a forgotten memory necessarily gone forever, or is it still stored but difficult to retrieve?** Memories may be lost by decay, probably because the relevant connections between neurons are lost. However, many "forgotten" memories are, in fact, still present but are difficult to retrieve. Memories become difficult to retrieve because of retroactive interference, in which new learning disrupts previously acquired memories, or because of proactive interference, in which information already stored in memory makes it difficult to learn something new.

3. **Are memories ever repressed?** Memories have been thought to be repressed as a defense against trauma—threatening information is forced into the unconscious. At least in some situations, encoding failure or a failure to encode information that can later be used as retrieval cues could result in poorer memory for traumatic events. In general, however, strong emotion enhances, not reduces, memory—and thus "repressed memories" are not common.

4. **How can you improve your memory?** Tricks for improving memory typically involve effectively organizing and processing the information during encoding. Mnemonic devices to help you encode information include visualizing objects interacting with other objects and organizing information into larger units. In addition, you can improve memory retrieval by mentally recreating the situation in which learning occurred, focusing attention on retrieving the information, repeatedly trying to recall, and generating new cues based on partial recall. It is also possible to arrange the world—your immediate circumstances—in such a way that you are reminded of what to do.

LET'S REVIEW

I. ENCODING INFORMATION INTO MEMORY STORES: TIME AND SPACE ARE OF THE ESSENCE

A. Encoding is the process of organizing and transforming incoming information so that it can be entered into memory.

B. Psychologists distinguish among three types of memory stores: sensory memory (SM), short-term memory (STM), and long-term memory (LTM). The memory stores differ in the amount of information they can retain and how long they can retain it.

C. Working memory (WM) involves specialized STMs and a central executive, which is a set of processes that manipulates information in the short-term storage structures.

D. Memory is improved as more time is spent thinking about the material to be stored and how it relates to current knowledge. Memory is most effective if the learner focuses on the properties of the material that will be relevant later.

E. Depth of processing refers to the complexity of the mental operations used to process information. Elaborative encoding consists of strategies that produce great breadth of processing—organizing and integrating information into previously stored information, often by making associations.

F. When first encoded, information is stored in a dynamic form (by active neurons); processes that consolidate information to be stored convert it to a structural form (connections among neurons).

G. Strong emotion typically amplifies memory, not diminishes it.

H. Flashbulb memories are defined as being unusually vivid and accurate. However, although people may be very confident that flashbulb memories are accurate, such memories in fact become progressively more distorted over time.

II. RETAINING INFORMATION: NOT JUST ONE LTM

A. Multiple types of LTMs exist, each of which stores information for a different modality, such as visual and auditory.

B. Some of the information stored in each LTM is semantic, pertaining to the meanings of words, concepts, and facts about the world. Other information stored in each LTM is episodic, pertaining to events that occurred at a specific time, place, and circumstance.

C. Some memories in LTM are explicit (stored so that the information can be retrieved voluntarily into STM). Other memories in LTM are implicit (stored as tendencies to process information or behave in specific ways). Implicit memories include classically conditioned responses,

responses acquired through nonassociative learning (as occurs in habituation), habits (automatic responses to appropriate stimuli), skills, and priming (which makes it easier perform the same or an associated task in the future).

D. The process of storing new memories depends on the actions of specific genes.

E. Stress can impair memory, in part because it increases production of the hormone cortisol, which in turn impairs the functioning of the hippocampus. (Note that stress is not the same thing as emotion, which does not impair the hippocampus and can actually enhance memory.)

III. RETRIEVING INFORMATION FROM MEMORY: MORE THAN REACTIVATING THE PAST

A. Memory retrieval depends on a constructive process; episodic memory is stored in bits and pieces, and we must use other stored information to fit the pieces together and fill in the gaps. Recognition is often easier than recall, but the ease of recognition depends on the choices you must distinguish among; the more attributes the choices have in common, the harder it is to distinguish among them.

B. Effective retrieval depends on having cues, or reminders, that match part of what is in memory, allowing you to reconstruct the rest.

C. Hypnosis typically does not improve the accuracy of memory retrieval, although it may improve confidence in the accuracy of the hypnotically retrieved memories.

IV. WHEN MEMORY GOES WRONG—AND WHAT TO DO ABOUT IT

A. False memories occur when a person stores information about an event that did not happen or that did not happen in the way that is "remembered." Actual memories typically include information about the perceptual features of the stimuli involved, whereas false memories do not. Reality monitoring can be used to check for perceptual features in memory and thereby help to distinguish between actual and false memories.

B. Forgetting occurs in various ways: Encoding failure occurs when information is not effectively stored. Decay results when neural connections are weakened to the point where they are no longer functional. Retroactive interference impairs the retrieval of stored information; proactive interference impairs the encoding of new information.

C. Intentional forgetting relies in part on the operation of the frontal lobes.

D. In contrast to ordinary forgetting, amnesia wipes out memory for a span of time, not just isolated memories or aspects of memories.

E. Memories of abuse may sometimes be "repressed" if the person went "somewhere else" when experiencing the abuse and hence few retrieval cues will access the memory later.

F. Organizing information via chunking or using hierarchical organization can make the information easier to remember.

G. Extensive processing of information, especially through distributed practice, aids memory.

H. Some mnemonic devices that can help you store information effectively include interactive mental images, the method of loci, the pegword system, acronyms, and initialisms. Mental imagery is generally very effective when it is used to organize information in a meaningful way.

I. Several tricks have been shown to help people retrieve information previously stored in LTM. One technique is to provide effective retrieval cues by having people think about where they were and how they felt at the time the information was encoded. In addition, effort and persistence in trying to remember can aid retrieval. If information is still difficult to recall, then people can be asked to try to recall its characteristics or associated information (which in turn can serve as retrieval cues). Finally, sometimes just arranging external cues as reminders can be helpful.

KEY TERMS

amnesia
anterograde amnesia
automatic processing
breadth of processing
central executive
chunk
code
consolidation
controlled processing
cues
decay
depth of processing
elaborative encoding

encoding
encoding failure
episodic memories
explicit (or declarative) memories
false memories
flashbulb memory
forgetting curve
habit
implicit (or nondeclarative) memories
incidental learning
intentional learning
interference

long-term memory (LTM)
memory store
mnemonic devices
modality-specific memory stores
primacy effect
priming
proactive interference
reality monitoring
recall
recency effect
recognition
rehearsal
repetition priming

repressed memories
retrieval
retroactive interference
retrograde amnesia
semantic memories
sensory memory (SM)
short-term memory (STM)
state-dependent retrieval
storage
transfer appropriate processing
working memory (WM)

PRACTICE TEST

✓●⌐Study and Review on mypsychlab.com

For each of the following items, choose the single best answer.

1. Which of the following statements is true?
   a. Information can flow to long-term memory without necessarily passing through short-term memory.
   b. Rehearsal—repeating items over and over—is the best way to ensure that information never leaves STM.
   c. Atkinson and Shiffrin proposed the four-stage model of memory.
   d. Some memories are not stored in the brain.

2. The visual form of sensory memory
   a. is called echoic memory.
   b. stores a small amount of information but holds that information for a long time.
   c. explains why you can continue to hear the sound of a voice that has stopped speaking for a brief time.
   d. stores a large amount of information, but the information fades very quickly.

3. How much information can short-term memory hold?
   a. 4 items
   b. 4 numbers
   c. 5–9 items organized into about four chunks
   d. 5–9 chunks organized into about four items

4. Long-term memory
   a. contains information of which you are directly aware.
   b. holds a small amount of information for a long time.
   c. can be thought of as analogous to your computer's RAM.
   d. is divided into specialized components.

5. The primacy effect
   a. is increased memory for the last few stimuli in a set.
   b. reflects the storage of information in long-term memory.
   c. reflects the storage of information in short-term memory.
   d. None of the above statements is true.

6. People
   a. Do not remember a context when they recall specific events.
   b. use only short-term memory to retain information about the meanings of words.
   c. remember the context in which a specific event occurred.
   d. remember when, where, and how semantic memories were learned.

7. Neuroimaging studies have
   a. provided evidence that semantic and episodic memories are not distinct.
   b. not provided useful information about the nature of memory.
   c. revealed that when we recall semantic memories, our visual systems are always active.
   d. shown that memory relies on multiple different systems.

8. Which of the following is an implicit memory?
   a. an episodic memory
   b. a semantic memory
   c. a habit
   d. a declarative memory

9. Researchers have increasingly studied how genes affect memory. Which of the following statements is true?
   a. Genes do not affect memory.
   b. Removing a given gene always has a single effect on the organism.
   c. Genes can disrupt memory but do not affect how well the normal brain stores information.
   d. Evidence is emerging that different genes underlie different types of memory.

10. In humans, the effects of stress on the hippocampus
    a. may be reversed if the environment changes.
    b. result in a larger hippocampus.
    c. lead to better memory.
    d. are not at all similar to the effects of stress on the hippocampus in baboons.

11. When people encode new information,
    a. portions of the frontal lobes are often active.
    b. the degree of activation of the frontal lobes does not predict how well the information will be remembered later.
    c. the memories are consolidated immediately.
    d. None of the above statements is true.

12. Depth of processing refers to
    a. processing that uses associations to information that was previously stored information to retrieve new information.
    b. reliance on massed practice.
    c. learning that occurs as a result of trying to learn.
    d. the number and complexity of the operations involved in processing information.

13. Certain emotions affect noradrenaline production and memory by causing
    a. less noradrenaline to be produced, which in turn causes enhanced memory encoding.
    b. more noradrenaline to be produced, which in turn causes enhanced memory encoding.
    c. less noradrenaline to be produced, which in turn causes decreased memory encoding.
    d. more noradrenaline to be produced, which in turn causes decreased memory encoding.

14. How accurate are our memories?
    a. Misremembering occurs only when associated material is stored.
    b. Everything we remember actually happened.
    c. In general, we do not necessarily remember what actually happened but rather what we *experience* as having happened.
    d. False memories do occur, but they persist for only 2 days.

15. An encoding failure results
    a. because all memories are stored forever.
    b. because long-term memory has only a limited capacity.
    c. if the retrieval cues for various memories are similar.
    d. if you do not process information well enough to begin consolidation.

Answers 1. a 2. d 3. c 4. d 5. b 6. c 7. d 8. c 9. d 10. a 11. a 12. d 13. b 14. c 15. d

> In general, Einstein's work was marked by 'out of the box' thinking, by enormous intellectual flexibility. He did not accept the common wisdom of the day, but instead was comfortable breaking all the rules.

LANGUAGE, THINKING, AND INTELLIGENCE

WHAT HUMANS DO BEST

Albert Einstein had one of the most remarkable minds in history. He didn't simply revolutionize physics, he changed the way the human species looks at the world. Einstein is often thought of today as he was in his later years—a saintly figure, patient and benevolent, his head framed by a white halo of hair. However, as a young man, he had a rebellious streak. He hated his experiences in the rigid and authoritarian German schools—experiences so alienating that he renounced his German citizenship when he was 17 years old and remained stateless until he was granted Swiss citizenship 5 years later. Indeed, his rebellious behavior led his teachers to shun him and not to help him find employment after graduation. Einstein held only temporary jobs until he was 23 years old, when a friend's father helped him land an entry-level position at the Swiss patent office. He worked in the patent office for 7 years.

Even though he was cut off from universities and good libraries, Einstein later recounted that he was very lucky to have been working in the patent office at that point in his life (Clark, 1971). His job was to rewrite the often vague and muddled descriptions, cleaning them up so that they could be protected by law. In those days in Switzerland, hopeful inventors had to supply physical models along with their patent applications. Einstein became adept at studying such models and describing clear-cut principles that explained how devices worked. He later noted that this was good training for grasping the laws of nature. In his spare time, he thought long and hard about the fundamental properties of the universe, and he published a series of papers that shook the world.

In general, Einstein's work was marked by "out-of-the-box" thinking, by enormous intellectual flexibility. He did not accept the common wisdom of the day, but instead was comfortable breaking all the rules. He correctly reasoned that light waves are bent when they pass near a strong source of gravity (such as a star), that time isn't constant, and that mass and energy are, in fact, different facets of the same thing.

Einstein's insights often arose only after years of thought and intense work. For example, he labored for 10 years to produce his famous Special Theory of Relativity. But don't think of Einstein as a kind of supercomputer, working through problems methodically and systematically, a step at a time. Einstein's methods of thinking often resembled those of an artist. He said, "When I examine myself and my methods of thought, I come to the conclusion that the gift of fantasy has meant more to me than my talent for absorbing positive knowledge" (Clark, 1971, p. 88).

What is thinking? What is the role of language in thinking? Of mental images? How do people solve problems and reach decisions? Can you learn to think more effectively? What does it mean to be intelligent, and why are some people apparently more intelligent than others? In this chapter we consider these questions, which address some of the most fundamental ways in which we humans tower over the other animals—namely, in our language, thinking, and intelligence.

◘ ◘ ◘

Language: More Than Meaningful Sounds

Albert Einstein did not begin to talk until he was 3 years old, and by 9, his speaking still wasn't nearly as fluent as that of his peers (Clark, 1971). His language skills were so poor that his parents worried that he might be intellectually impaired! Nevertheless, he eventually learned to speak not only his native German, but also French and English. However, he mixed German with his French, and his English, learned later in life, never became very good—as countless satirists have noted, he made many grammatical mistakes and had a heavy German accent. If we judged him by his language alone, we wouldn't be impressed. Clearly, using language to communicate relies on at least some abilities that are not used in reasoning and problem solving.

LOOKING AHEAD Learning Objectives

1. What are the essential characteristics of all languages?
2. Are there differences in how first and second languages are acquired and used?

The Essentials: What Makes Language, Language?

Language serves two functions during communication: it allows us to send and to receive an almost limitless number of messages. **✳ Explore**

First, let's examine the ability to send messages. **Language production** is the ability to use words, phrases, and sentences to convey information. Perhaps the most remarkable thing about language production is that it is *generative*—we can arrange words in countless new combinations to produce novel sentences. We create, or generate, new sentences all the time; we don't simply retrieve and repeat stored sentences. The number of new sentences we can produce is astounding. Psychologist Steven Pinker (1994) estimates that we would need at least 100 trillion years to memorize all the sentences any one of us can possibly produce.

Second, let's examine the ability to receive messages: **language comprehension** is the ability to understand the messages conveyed by words, phrases, and sentences. We humans are endowed with the extraordinary ability to comprehend even fragments of speech, mispronounced words, and scrambled syntax. For example, you can probably decipher the following: "Hxmxn bxxngs arx amxzxng!" as "Human beings are amazing!" We can understand the speech of the very young, speech flavored with foreign or regional accents, and (usually) words produced around a mouthful of food—even though the actual sounds made in each of these cases are very different.

But the ability to send and receive messages is not all there is to language (Pinker & Jackendoff, 2005). If it were, your dog would be using language when it whines because it is hungry and when it sits after being told to do so. Your pet can send and receive messages, all right, but is it using language? To answer this question, think about what would happen if you tried to strike up a conversation with your pet. No doubt, this exchange would be very one-sided. A dog isn't much of a conversationalist because it—unlike you—cannot use language to produce and comprehend an almost limitless number of messages.

The key to understanding language is to appreciate that it consists of simple building blocks that can be combined in many ways according to specific rules. Four distinct types of building blocks, and the rules for combining them, distinguish language from other communicative sounds such as whines. These building blocks and rules make up the (1) *phonology*, (2) *syntax*, (3) *semantics*, and (4) *pragmatics* of a language. Let's look at each of these aspects of language in turn.

Phonology: Some Say "ToMAYto"
Phonology is the structure of the sounds of the words in a language. Part of learning to speak a language is learning to pronounce the words properly; if you can't pronounce the words well, you don't really speak the language well. Although it may not be obvious, the sounds of all words are built up from a small, fixed set of basic sounds that humans are capable of producing—these sounds are called **phonemes** (Halle, 1990; Jakobson & Hall, 1956). The words *boy* and *toy* differ in one phoneme. Humans can produce about 100 phonemes, but no single language uses all 100; English, for instance, uses about 45. Back-of-the-throat, soft French *r*'s do not exist in the world of hard American *r*'s, and Japanese has no *r*'s at all.

In English, some sounds in each word are accented (given extra emphasis). Some people say "toMAYto," and others say "toMAHto," but in both cases the second syllable is stressed. Some other languages typically do not usually stress any syllable in a word. In French, for example, each sound typically is given equal emphasis. Linguist Lisa Selkirk

✳ Explore **THINK AGAIN:** Language, Thinking, and Reasoning on mypsychlab.com

Language production The ability to use words, phrases, and sentences to convey information.

Language comprehension The ability to understand messages conveyed by words, phrases, and sentences.

Phonology The structure of the sounds of the words in a language.

Phoneme A small, basic sound from a fixed set that specifies the building blocks of speech sounds that humans are capable of producing.

(personal communication, 2002) suggests that this difference explains why French rock and roll often sounds bland: French rock artists can't synchronize the "beats" in the language with the rhythm of the music.

Syntax: The Rules of the Road We've just been considering the sounds of words, but words alone do not a language make. We string words together into sentences, and not any combination of words will do: All languages include rules for how words can be organized into sentences. For example, in English, "Kicked girl ball blue the" is not an acceptable sentence because it violates the rules. These rules are called a *grammar*, and they specify how different parts of speech—such as nouns, verbs, and adjectives—can be combined to form sentences. For instance, English grammar specifies that the adjective (e.g., "blue") usually has to come before the noun (e.g., "ball"); the rules apply to parts of speech, not to the individual words that fall into each category. In contrast, the *syntax* is the specific arrangement of words in a given sentence, and the syntax is determined by the grammar; for example, the syntax in "Kicked girl ball blue the" is not acceptable in English because English grammar does not allow that combination of those types of words (for example, a determiner, "the" in this case, cannot come at the end of a sentence). In short, the *grammar* is the set of rules that determines the proper *syntax* of sentences.

Let's examine syntax in more detail; **syntax** is the internal organization of a sentence, the arrangement of words, which is determined by the grammar of a language. Figure 1 illustrates the syntax of a simple sentence. Try the following exercise to get a sense of the syntax of sentences: Read this paragraph aloud, and notice where you pause. You will generally pause on the basis of the syntax, for example between separate phrases (which are often signaled by a comma, dash, or a connective word, such as "and" or "or"). When you read, you organize the material in terms of the syntax of the sentences.

Semantics: The Meaning Is the Message To be useful, language must convey meaning. The **semantics** of a word, phrase, or sentence is its meaning. Because we build sentences from words, many people initially think that words are the fundamental elements of semantics—but in fact **morphemes** are the smallest units of meaning in a language. The meanings of many words are determined by more than one morpheme. For example, adding the morpheme -*ing* to a verb, as in *walking, talking,* or *flirting,* creates a word that expresses a continuing state, whereas adding the morpheme -*ed* to a verb indicates a

Syntax The internal organization of a sentence, determined by a set of rules (grammar) for combining different parts of speech into acceptable arrangements.

Semantics The meaning of a word, phrase, or sentence.

Morpheme The smallest unit of meaning in a language.

FIGURE 1 The Syntax of a Sentence

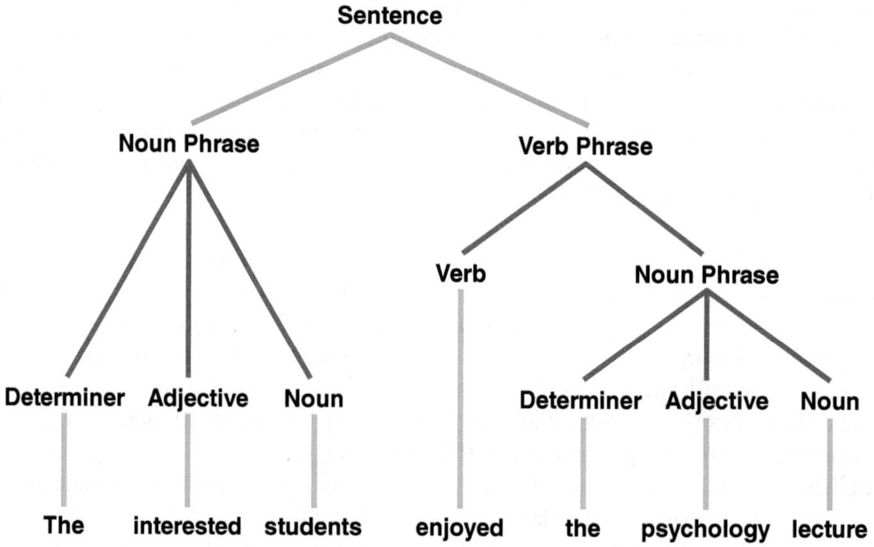

The syntax is the internal organization of a sentence, which is determined by the grammar of the language. In this illustration, we see a conventional way of showing the structure of the syntax. Note that the syntax is only concerned with parts of speech (such as nouns and verbs), not with the meanings of the particular words in the sentence.

completed state. Many jokes rely on the fact that the same spoken or written word can stand for more than one set of morphemes—that is, the word can have more than one meaning. Take, for example, the sentence: "Energizer Bunny arrested—charged with battery." In this case, the joke hinges on the fact two words each have more than one morpheme: "battery" can mean either the crime or the energy storage device, and "charged" can mean either replenishing energy or that an individual has been accused of a crime.

Moreover, just as the other elements of language are combined according to rules, so, too, with combining morphemes. We cannot add -ing at the front of a word, or mis- (another morpheme) to the end. Nevertheless, we can combine morphemes in many ways, creating many meaningful words.

HOW IS MEANING ASSIGNED TO WORDS? Meanings are often assigned arbitrarily to different sounds or written words; *dog* (both the combination of sounds and the written set of letters) could easily have been assigned to that feline we keep as a pet and *cat* to the animal that likes to bark and gnaw on bones. Specific events in the past have a lot to do with how particular words have come to have their meanings. For example, early medieval Scandinavian warriors wore bearskin shirts, for which the Old Norwegian word was *berserkr*; the ferocity of the Vikings' frenzied attacks in battle thus led to the English expression "going berserk." Sometimes the meanings of words seem to reveal deeper aspects of a culture: The Chinese character for *crisis* is composed of two other characters, one signifying "risk" and the other "opportunity."

HOW DOES SEMANTICS DIFFER FROM SYNTAX? The meaning of a sentence and its syntax are to a large extent distinct; in fact, different parts of the brain are involved in processing semantics and syntax (Gernsbacher & Kaschak, 2003; Grodzinsky & Friederici, 2006). To see how semantics and syntax differ, consider these two examples: On the one hand, the sentence "Colorless green ideas sleep furiously" has an acceptable English syntax but is meaningless (Chomsky, 1957). On the other hand, "Fastly dinner eat, ballgame soon start" has the opposite properties: It is syntactically incorrect but understandable. The wise alien Yoda of the *Star Wars* movies often uttered such sentences, probably in part to remind the audience that he was not an ordinary person. Nevertheless, although syntax and semantics are distinct, they do interact; for example, sentences are easiest to understand when named objects appear in the same order in the sentence as they do in the corresponding event (O'Grady & Lee, 2005).

Pragmatics: Being Indirect Utterances have not only a literal meaning but also an *implied* meaning. The **pragmatics** of a language specify the ways that words and sentences convey meaning indirectly, by implying rather than asserting. For example, have you ever asked a 13-year-old, "Do you know what time it is?" and gotten back the one-word response, "Yes"? You probably regarded this response as a feeble attempt at humor. Although this question can be interpreted literally (just in terms of the semantics) as an inquiry about your knowledge of time, it is usually interpreted, using pragmatics, as a request to be told the time (Grice, 1975; Lindblom, 2001).

Pragmatics plays a key role in understanding metaphors; a *metaphor* is a direct comparison of two things in which one is described as being the other (Bowdle & Gentner, 2005; Gentner & Bowdle, 2001). But metaphors do not imply that two things are identical—that they share all characteristics. In order to understand a metaphor, we actively inhibit—we suppress—the irrelevant aspects of the meaning (Glucksberg et al., 2001). For example, if someone were to say that a lawyer is a shark, he or she probably means that the attorney is vicious—and not that the lawyer can breathe under water or has pebbly skin. Like other aspects of pragmatics, understanding metaphors involves different brain mechanisms than

Curiously, the left cerebral hemisphere is primarily activated when males process phonemes, but both hemispheres are strongly activated when females process phonemes (Shaywitz et al., 1995); perhaps this is one reason females tend to be better with language than males (Halpern, 1997).

Source: © Paul Barton/CORBIS

Pragmatics The ways that words and sentences in a language convey meaning indirectly, by implying rather than asserting.

Patients with left-hemisphere damage that disrupted their ability to comprehend speech nevertheless could detect lies better than normal people (Etcoff et al., 2000). Apparently, the meanings of words can obscure other telltale features of deception, such as changes in intonation that underlie some aspects of pragmatics.

Source: Getty Images, Inc - Stockbyte Royalty Free

those used for other aspects of language. In fact, phonology, syntax, and semantics depend primarily (in right-handed people) on the left cerebral hemisphere, but the ability to understand metaphors, as well as humor, depends crucially on the brain's right hemisphere. For example, patients who have suffered damage to the right hemisphere might understand a metaphorical question such as "Can you lend me a hand?" not as a metaphor, but rather as asking literally for a hand on a platter (Brownell, 2000; Rinaldi et al., 2004).

Interlocking Mechanisms Although we've summarized the four aspects of language separately, we must stress that they constantly interact (Németh & Bibok, 2010). We typically learn to produce the sounds of words at the same time that we learn to comprehend them, and the mechanisms that produce syntactically correct sentences also help us understand them. Moreover, we use the principles of pragmatics both when producing speech (guiding our patterns of intonation and use of metaphor and humor) and when comprehending speech.

Here's a particularly compelling demonstration of interactions among the different facets of language. The sound of a cough was inserted randomly over a segment of a recorded sentence. When people later heard this modified sentence, the cough did not produce a gap between phonemes; rather, listeners reported hearing the whole word, and often weren't even sure where in the sentence the cough occurred! Their knowledge of syntax and semantics (and possibly even pragmatics, depending on the sentence) allowed them to fill in what they weren't actually hearing (Warren & Warren, 1970).

Bilingualism: A Window of Opportunity?

All people with normal language ability learn a language just by being immersed in it, and most of the people in the world learn a second language at some point in life (Fabbro, 2001); are there differences in how first and second languages are acquired and used? If having learned a language amounts to the same thing in both cases, then we would expect the same brain systems to be active when a person spoke his or her mother tongue as when he or she spoke a second language. To test this idea, Kim and his colleagues (1997) used functional magnetic resonance imaging (fMRI) to scan the brains of two groups of bilingual people while they thought about what they had done the previous day, using each of their two languages in turn. One group had learned their second language as young children, the other as adults. Although a brain area crucially involved in comprehension (located in the back part of the left temporal lobe) was activated in the same way with both languages and in both groups, other brain areas behaved very differently for those who had learned the language as young children than for those who had learned the language as adults—which is evidence that language was processed differently by those who learned it as adults.

Moreover, we gain insight into exactly how language is different for those who learned it as adults versus as children by considering precisely how their brains functioned differently: For the participants who learned the second language as an adult, but not the ones who learned the language during childhood, part of the left frontal lobe was activated when they used the second language. This finding is important because this part of the frontal lobe plays a key role in *working memory*, which holds information in short-term memory whenever a person must deliberately and consciously think through that material. Language learned during childhood is "automatic," it does not require "thinking through what you are saying," whereas language learned as an adult does require such extra effort (Ullman, 2001). ◉—Watch

In spite of the fact that languages learned as an adult generally are not as easily used as those acquired during childhood, it is remarkably easy to learn some aspects of second languages, particularly vocabulary words. For example, researchers asked third-semester college students who were taking French to read five different scenes from the script of a French movie (they also viewed the scenes preceding those five, so that they could get the story line; Dupuy & Krashen, 1993). The scenes that the students read contained many

◉—Watch **Bilingual Education** on mypsychlab.com

slang words that the students were unlikely to have seen or heard before. A surprise vocabulary test after reading showed that participants had learned almost five words per hour, without trying! This rate is remarkably close to the learning rates of children who are reading in their native languages.

Although adults can pick up vocabulary well, the same cannot be said for learning grammar and phonology. Indeed, the vast majority of people who learn a second language after puberty will—like Einstein—make grammatical errors and will speak with an accent. However, even so, there are exceptions to the rule: some adults can learn to pronounce words in another language almost flawlessly (Marinova-Todd et al., 2000; Snow, 2002). Musical ability apparently contributes to these differences: people with good musical ability can learn to pronounce words in another language better than people who do not have good musical ability (Milovanov et al., 2010). Moreover, in general, the more formal education you have and the younger you are when you start, the better you will be at learning a second language (Hakuta et al., 2003).

LOOKING BACK

1. **What are the essential characteristics of all languages?** All languages have four key characteristics: (1) *Phonology:* The sounds of the language; phonemes are the basic units of spoken speech, and they are arranged in sequences to form words; (2) *Syntax:* The internal arrangement of words in a sentence, produced by a set of rules called a grammar; a grammar governs how different words can be combined according to their parts of speech; (3) *Semantics:* The literal meaning of words and sentences; the semantics of a word arise from its morphemes, the smallest elements of meaning; and, (4) *Pragmatics:* The indirect or implied aspects of meaning; pragmatics are also involved in understanding metaphor and humor.

2. **Are there differences in how first and second languages are acquired and used?** Depending on your age when you learn it, a second language functions in the brain either in the same way as the first language or in a different way. At least for people of college age, acquiring vocabulary in a second language is remarkably easy. However, mastering the grammar and phonology (sound patterns) of a second language after puberty is difficult for most people.

Means of Thinking: The Mental Tool Kit

Einstein was a theoretical physicist. He didn't perform experiments; he didn't collect new data. Instead, he tried to put together known facts and to formulate specific principles, which in turn led to larger overarching theories. At first glance, these abilities and skills might suggest that Einstein reasoned at a very abstract level, using esoteric mathematical symbols to manipulate complex ideas. But Einstein denied that he thought in that way. Instead, he said that he relied on *mental imagery*: He would play with mental images of objects and events, "seeing" what would happen in certain circumstances. **Mental images** are mental contents like those that arise during perception (when you register information from your senses), but they arise from stored information rather than from immediate sensory input (such as from the eyes or ears). For example, you will probably experience a visual mental image if you try to recall the shape of Mickey Mouse's ears. In fact, the initial insight that led to Einstein's Special Theory of Relativity came when he imagined himself chasing a beam of light, matching its speed, and "seeing" what it would look like. He reported, "Conventional words or other signs have to be sought for laboriously only in a secondary stage," after he used mental imagery to develop the ideas (Einstein, 1945, pp. 142–143).

Thinking relies on mentally manipulating information, and information is stored in various ways. We think partly by using language, but this isn't always the case. In fact, as Einstein noted, language may come into play rather late in the mental processing that a person uses when grappling with a problem. Both inner speech ("talk" that we direct to ourselves) and mental images are manipulated in working memory, and thus they play a key role in thinking (working memory holds information in short-term memory whenever a person must deliberately and consciously think through that material). However, although language and images help us to think, they cannot themselves be the only means by which

THINK like a **PSYCHOLOGIST** If you'll learn a new foreign language while in college, based on what you've read, what aspects of the new language are likely to be the hardest to learn? How should this affect the amount of time you allocate for studying different aspects of the language?

✓○─ **Study** and **Review** on **mypsychlab.com**

Mental images Mental contents like those that arise during perception, but they arise from stored information rather than on immediate sensory input.

199

we think. To see why, let's consider the ways that language and mental images are used in thinking, and then look at another way in which information is specified in the mind.

LOOKING AHEAD Learning Objectives

1. Does language mold our thoughts?
2. How can we think with mental images?
3. What is a concept?

Words: Inner Speech and Spoken Thoughts

Many people, if asked, would say that they think with words. And, at first glance, that seems plausible: After all, to communicate with someone, we usually have to express ourselves in words, so why not use words when thinking? In fact, the founder of behaviorism, John B. Watson (1913), claimed that thinking is just talking to yourself. But Watson was wrong. Let's see why, and let's see ways in which we do use language in thinking.

Putting Thoughts Into Words There are at least three problems with the idea that thinking is just talking to yourself:

1. Words are often ambiguous, but thoughts are not. It's one thing to use an ambiguous word when speaking, when confusion may later need to be cleared up, but quite another not to know what you are thinking because you are using an ambiguous word. This does not happen: If you are thinking about "the port," you never have to stop to wonder whether you are thinking about a type of wine or about a harbor; similarly, if you realize that you found a "solution," you are never uncertain about whether you mean the answer to a problem or you mean a type of fluid. You know what you meant.

2. If thinking were just talking to yourself, why would you ever have trouble "putting a thought into words"? If thoughts were already formed in language, expressing them in language should be child's play.

3. Anyone who has owned a dog or a cat has sensed that at least some animals can think, and yet they don't use language. In fact, there is ample evidence that many animals can solve problems (Hauser, 2001); for example, even rats can successfully learn to figure out a maze in order to obtain food at the end.

Does Language Shape Thought? Even though thought is not simply talking to yourself, many people have been fascinated by the possibility that our perceptions and thoughts are shaped by the particular language we speak. The idea that language shapes our perceptions and thoughts, and thus that people who speak different languages think differently, is known as the **linguistic relativity hypothesis**. This idea was championed by Benjamin Lee Whorf (1956). For example, some have suggested that because the Inuit of northern Canada have many words for the different types of snow they recognize, they can see and think about subtle differences in snow better than can speakers of English—who have only a single word for the white stuff.

Eleanor Rosch (1973, 1975) tested the linguistic relativity hypothesis by studying the Dani, a remote tribe living in Papua New Guinea. She reasoned that if the linguistic relativity hypothesis is correct, then people who speak languages with many color words should be able to perceive more distinctions among colors than people who speak languages with few such words. As it happens, the Dani use only two words for color, corresponding to *light* and *dark*. However, Rosch found—contradicting the linguistic relativity hypothesis—that the Dani perceive variations in color and are able to learn shades of color as readily as people who speak languages with words that label many colors.

Clearly, language does not entirely shape our perceptions and thoughts. Nevertheless, we can use words as a crutch to help us think, particularly when working memory is involved. In such circumstances, we often perform relatively slow, step-by-step reasoning—for example, memorizing a series of directions and recalling them one at a time, holding

Linguistic relativity hypothesis The idea that language shapes our perceptions and thoughts, and thus people who speak different languages think differently.

them in working memory long enough to turn the right way and continue to the next landmark.

Furthermore, language can enhance memory. For example, you can remember the shapes of clouds better if you come up with a distinctive characterization for each (such as "a rabbit sticking out of a tube" or "a face without a chin") than if you use a single label for them all (such as simply "clouds"; Ellis, 1973).

Researchers produced additional evidence for the role of language in memory by conducting a variant of Rosch's study (Roberton et al., 2004). Instead of studying perception and learning, these researchers studied memory in speakers of the Himba language of Africa. This language makes fewer distinctions among colors than does English; for instance, red, orange, and pink are named with the same word. The Himba speakers made memory errors when they had to recall different colors that were named with the same word in Himba; in contrast, English speakers performed better in remembering those colors, because their language helped them to draw the necessary distinctions.

Even though the Dani have only two words for color, *light* and *dark*, they can perceive and learn shades of color as easily as people who speak languages with many terms for color.

Source: © Charles & Josette Lenars/CORBIS All Rights Reserved

Also, the written version of a language may affect thought. For example, speakers of English tend to think of time as if it were horizontal, but speakers of Mandarin Chinese think of time as if it were vertical ("Wednesday is lower than Tuesday"; Boroditsky, 2001).

In short, even if language does not determine the nature of our thoughts, it does contribute to them.

Mental Imagery: Inner Perception

If language is not the basis of thinking, what might be? Virtually all the great thinkers who considered this question, including Plato and Aristotle, and later John Locke and other British philosophers, identified thought with a stream of mental images (Kosslyn, 1980). Visual mental images give rise to the experience of "seeing with the mind's eye," an experience you probably will have if someone asks you, for example, whether the Statue of Liberty holds the torch in her left or right hand. Auditory mental images give rise to the experience of "hearing with the mind's ear," as is likely to happen if you try to decide whether the first three notes of "Three Blind Mice" go up or down in pitch.

Are mental images the basis of thought, or are they like language—used in thinking, but not themselves the fundamental form of thoughts? To answer this question, we need to understand more about the nature of mental images.

Visual Mental Imagery Because visual imagery is the most common form of imagery (Kosslyn et al., 1990, 2001, 2006; McKellar, 1965), we focus on it here. Visual mental images rely on most—as much as 92%—of the same parts of the brain as are used in visual perception (Ganis et al., 2004; Kosslyn et al., 2006). To get a rough idea of the difference between perception and mental imagery, think of perception as like the picture on a screen that's coming from a camera, whereas mental imagery is like the picture on a screen that comes from a DVD player. We can understand the properties of visual mental imagery in part because images arise in brain areas used in visual perception. Consider three properties of visual mental imagery—*spatial extent*, *limited field of view*, and *limited resolution*.

SPATIAL EXTENT. When we see an object, we see it as extending over a specific portion of space; the object is thus said to have *spatial extent*. And most people report the same experience when they form a visual mental image of an object with their eyes closed—which suggests that objects in mental images resemble actual objects.

But can we trust such reports about mental images? It is best to have evidence that objects in mental images do in fact have spatial extent. We can obtain such evidence through the process of scanning objects in images (that is, shifting visual attention across the object; Borst & Kosslyn, 2008). For example, try this: Visualize a horse as seen from the side,

FIGURE 2 Scanning Visual Mental Images

Participants memorized a map like this one, paying special attention to the locations of the seven objects.

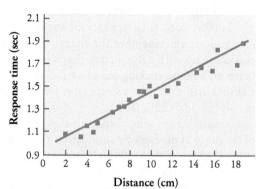

Even though their eyes were closed, the farther the participants had to scan mentally from the first object to the second, the longer it took.

Later, the participants were asked to close their eyes and focus on one location (such as the hut) and then to scan to another named location if it was on the map; they were to press one button if they found the second object and another if they could not (and the time was recorded). Participants scanned between every possible pair of objects.

Source: From Kosslyn, S.M., Ball, T.M., and Reiser, B.J., "Visual images preserved metric spatial information: Evidence from studies of image scanning," *Journal of Experimental Psychology: Human Perception and Performance*, 4, 47–60. Copyright © 1978 by the American Psychological Association. Reprinted with Permission.

and focus your mental gaze on the place where the horse's tail meets its body. Once you've focused on that part, decide whether the horse's ears stick up or flop down. To answer this question, people typically report that they scanned along the horse's body, from the tail up the neck and head, and then "looked" at the ears. Now try to answer the question when you first start by fixating not on its tail, but rather on the center of its body. And, finally, try this again, but start by fixating on its head. If we measured the time it took you to respond, we would find that the farther you had to shift your mental attention (starting from where you first fixated and going to the ears), the longer it would have taken you. And in fact, as illustrated in Figure 2, many experiments have shown that more time is required to scan greater distances across visualized objects; these results show that when you visualize an object, that object in the image has a definite *spatial extent* (Denis & Kosslyn, 1999).

How can we explain the fact that imagined objects have spatial extent? There is a puzzle here: objects aren't actually inside the brain; if you open up a brain, you won't find a tiny toy car when somebody is visualizing a car (think of how uncomfortable it would be to have little objects in your brain—and besides, who or what would look at such objects?). Rather, instead of objects in the brain there are patterns of activation among the neurons. And it is these patterns of activation that specify the shape, color, and spatial extent of objects.

We can explain the fact that imagined objects have spatial extent the same way we can explain the fact that perceived objects have spatial extent: Spatial extent is specified by patterns of activation in particular brain areas. Critically, many areas of the brain that process visual information are organized so that the images projected onto the back of the eyes are laid out as patterns of activation on the surface of the brain; these areas are said to be *topographically organized* (from the Greek *topos*, "place"). Researchers have found that when people visualize with their eyes closed, these areas in the occipital and parietal lobes usually are active (Kosslyn & Thompson, 2003; Thompson & Kosslyn, 2000). Moreover, if such areas in the occipital lobe are temporarily impaired by the effect of strong magnetic pulses, people have difficulty forming visual mental images (Kosslyn et al., 1999; Kosslyn et al., 2006).

LIMITED FIELD OF VIEW.   When you look at the scene in front of you, your field of view spans only a certain angle (spread)—you don't see objects behind your head. The same is true in visual mental imagery: We can "see" only a limited field of view. Try this demonstration: Visualize an elephant, facing to the side, 50 feet away. Now imagine that you are walking toward the elephant, mentally staring at the center of its body. Imagine walking closer and closer to it so that it looms larger in your image as you get closer, keeping your mental gaze fixed on its center. Most people report that when they are at a certain distance from the elephant, its edges seem to blur, to "overflow" their mental field of vision. Note how far away you seem to be from the elephant when its edges seem to blur (keeping your mental gaze fixated on the center of the animal's body). Now try the same exercise with a rabbit. Fixate on its center, and imagine seeing it loom up as you get closer and closer to it. When you imagine walking toward the rabbit, can you get closer to it than you could to the elephant before the edges seem to blur? When this method was used in studies, participants consistently reported that the larger the object, the farther away it seemed to be in the mental image when it began to overflow (Kosslyn, 1978). This result is just as expected if mental imagery has a limited field of view; larger objects must be "seen" from farther away to fit within it.

Why do we have a limited field of view in mental imagery? Here's a hint: Objects in visual mental images overflow at about the same spatial extent that actual objects seem to become blurred in perception (Kosslyn, 1978). This finding makes sense if imagery relies on most of the same brain systems used in perception—as the neuroimaging findings have shown. Because our eyes only have limited scope, our brains needed only to process that limited field of view—and this property also affects our mental images.

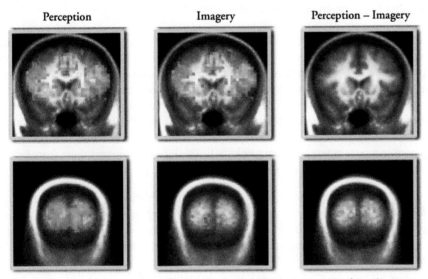

The scans in the top row are from the front parts of the brain. It is evident from these scans that activation in these brain areas was virtually identical in imagery and perception, even though the participants had their eyes closed during imagery. The scans in the bottom row are from the back parts of the brain. As is evident, these parts of the brain were more strongly activated during perception than during imagery. The greater activation during perception may be one way we know whether we are seeing or imaging.

Source: An fMRI study, Giorgio Ganis, William L. Thompson, Stephen M. Kosslyn. *Cognitive Brain Research* 20 (2004), 226–241.

LIMITED RESOLUTION.   When we see an object, we see it with a limited *resolution* (level of distinguishing fine details). In perception, if an object is too tiny, you can no longer distinguish all of its parts—and the same is true in mental imagery. Try one more mental imagery demonstration: Imagine stretching out your right arm and looking at a butterfly perched on the tip of your index finger. Can you see the color of its head? Many people find that they mentally have to "zoom in" to answer that question. Now imagine moving your finger, gently bringing the butterfly to within 10 inches from your eyes; this time, zooming probably isn't necessary to "see" its head. Studies have shown that people require more time to "see" properties of objects that are visualized at small sizes than those visualized at larger sizes (Kosslyn, 1975, 1976). When visualized very small, parts become obscured.

Just as was true for the limited field of view of images, characteristics of topographically organized brain areas can also explain why images have limited resolution: The brain areas used in perception evolved to process what the eyes send them, and our eyes have only a limited resolution (which is nowhere near as good as the resolution of an eagle's eyes). By analogy, why have a high-definition TV screen if all you have is a low-resolution TV camera? And because mental imagery shares the same brain structures with perception, the limitations of those structures also affect mental images.

Other Types of Imagery

We have many types of mental images. For example, we have auditory images, which activate brain areas involved in perceiving sounds, and have "motor images" (as occur, for example, if you imagine making a golf swing), which activate brain areas involved in controlling movement (Kosslyn et al., 2009). And we have "spatial" images, which specify where things are around you at any given moment (Mellet et al., 1998); even blind people have such spatial images (Kosslyn et al., 2006).

In addition, we can manipulate objects in our mental images. For example, if you mentally rotate the letter *N* 90° clockwise, is it another letter? Most of us can do such tasks, and such "mental rotation" mimics our actually rotating the object—we need more time to rotate the object in the image by greater amounts, just as if we were shifting the object through actual space as it rotated (Shepard & Cooper, 1982). Moreover, we can manipulate objects in images by imagining that we physically manipulate them, which actually engages parts of the brain involved in physical movement (Grèzes & Decety, 2001; Guillot & Collet, 2009; Lamm et al., 2001; Wraga et al., 2003). In all of these cases, key properties of mental imagery arise from the fact that it relies on brain mechanisms used for other purposes, specifically perception and controlling movement.

Limitations of Mental Images as Vehicles of Thought

Mental images can "stand in" for actual objects and hence can represent ("re-present") those objects. In so doing, images clearly play a role in thinking, allowing us to consider the results of possible arrangements and transformations of objects (such as imagining how best to pack up the trunk of the car when heading off to college), as well as the implications of being in certain situations (as illustrated by Einstein's "looking" at a beam of light in his mental image, or by your visualizing how easily you could move around if you rearrange the furniture in your room in a certain way). But images have limitations that prevent them from being the only means of thought. Here are some of the more striking difficulties:

1. *Abstract concepts.* Abstract concepts are not easily represented as images. Take justice, for example. How would you represent "justice" with an image? You might choose a blindfolded woman holding a pair of scales. But how would you know if that image represented the familiar statue itself or was supposed to stand for the abstract concept of justice?
2. *Ambiguity.* Images, like words, are often ambiguous. An image of a box seen from the side could just as easily be an image of a square piece of cardboard, not attached to a box.
3. *Individual differences.* Not everybody can produce good images. Approximately 2% of the population has poor visual imagery (McKellar, 1965)—but this doesn't imply that people with poor imagery are poor thinkers.

In short, like language, imagery can contribute to our thought processes, and like language, it cannot be the only means by which we think.

Concepts: Neither Images nor Words

In its most fundamental form, thought arises from the manipulation of concepts (Murphy, 2002). A **concept** is the idea that underlies the meaning of a word or image; depending on the language, some concepts may be expressed by a single word or may require a phrase or two to be fully expressed (such as "very well packed, dry powdery snow"). A concept is unambiguous and may be concrete (such as the concept of a dog or table) or abstract (such as the concept of truth or justice).

What is the relationship between concepts, words, and images? Concepts may be *expressed* by words and images, but they are not the same as either (Kosslyn, 1980; Pinker, 1994). For words, a concept is specified by morphemes, which, as we've already seen, convey the underlying idea, the meaning, of the word. The difference between words and concepts is illustrated by two observations: (1) As we've already noted, the same word

THINK like a
PSYCHOLOGIST Our senses give rise to corresponding images. To sample systematically what types of imagery you experience throughout the day, use the *DO IT!* chart at www.mypsychlab.com; select the *Language, Thinking,* and *Intelligence* chapter and click on the *DO IT!* folder.

Concept The idea that underlies the meaning of a word or image; depending on the language, some concepts can be expressed with a single word or may require a phrase or two to be fully expressed.

sometimes can convey more than one concept (for instance, the word "solution" can specify a type of fluid or an answer to a problem); (2) The same concept can sometimes be expressed by different words or phrases (for instance, "sofa," "couch," and "very wide plush chair, on which several people can sit").

By the same token, a concept specifies the underlying meaning of a mental image of an object. The difference between images and concepts is illustrated by the same two observations that apply to words: (1) The same image can sometimes express different concepts (for example, an image of an apple can express the concepts of "apple," "fruit," or even "good health"); (2) More than one image can sometimes express the same concept (for example, images of bananas and oranges can also be used to express the concept of "fruit").

Words and images play much the same role in thinking as do notes and preliminary sketches on a notepad. For example, consider the notes and sketches you might make when you are planning how to arrange the furniture in a room before you've moved in; they help you work through and organize your thoughts, and can help you manipulate information and discover connections among ideas. In all cases, however, you know the meanings of the words and images because of the concepts they express.

The Nature of Concepts Aristotle proposed the first theory of the nature of concepts, in the 4th century B.C. According to this view, a given concept is defined by a set of features. For example, for the concept "bird," the features might be "wings, feathers, a beak, and the ability to fly." The features describe characteristics (such as wings and beak) and appropriate activities (such as flight). However, Aristotle's approach to defining concepts has been discarded, for two reasons: (1) It often isn't clear what the features of a particular concept might be (think about possible features for the concept of "justice"); (2) Even when it is clear what the features are for a concept, the theory makes wrong predictions.

This last problem is crucial, so let's take a moment to examine one such prediction. This theory predicts that a concept either applies to a given object or it doesn't, period: If an object has the necessary features, the concept applies to it; if it doesn't have the features, the concept does not apply to it. But in fact, concepts are not all-or-none in this way. Rather, concepts can apply more-or-less well to a given object (Rosch, 1978). The concept of "bird," for instance, applies better to a canary and robin than to a penguin and ostrich, even though all of them qualify as being birds.

How well a concept applies depends on an entity's **typicality**—that is, how representative it is of the concept; the more typical the entity is, the better the concept applies to it. For example, you can affirm that a canary is a bird more quickly than that an ostrich is a bird, and will be more confident that a canary is a bird than that an ostrich is a bird (Garrard et al., 2001; Murphy, 2002; Smith & Medin, 1981); a canary is a typical bird, whereas an ostrich is not. To see these effects for yourself, name the objects in Figure 3 as quickly as you can; you should immediately notice the fact that it's easier to name objects

FIGURE 3 Name These Animals

Research has shown that you will name the animal in the center most quickly and accurately; and, in fact, the mutt is the most typical for the concept "dog."

Typicality The degree to which an entity is representative of a concept.

that are typical for a concept faster than objects that are not typical. This effect should not occur if Aristotle was correct, and an object is either a dog or is not a dog.

Prototypes. One way to explain these findings rests on two ideas, both of which involve the notion of a **prototype**—the most typical example of a concept:

1. A concept is specified as a set of features that describe the **prototype** (these features are like morphemes, specifying elementary aspects of meaning).

2. Only a *percentage* of those features need to be present in any particular member in order to apply the concept. So, an ostrich has enough features of birds (such as a beak, wings, and feathers) for the concept "bird" to apply, even though it doesn't fly.

It's this last idea that is an advance over Aristotle, and that allows us to explain the effects of typicality. In particular, because more of the relevant features apply to prototypical members of a concept, you can apply the concept to the object more quickly and with greater confidence (Rips et al., 1973). For example, people take a relatively long time to decide that penguins qualify as birds because relatively few bird features apply to them (they cannot fly; they are not the size of the standard bird); in contrast, we take relatively little time to decide that canaries qualify as birds because more of the features of birds, in general, apply to them.

However, not all prototypes of concepts can be specified as collections of features; instead, some prototypes are specific examples. For example, consider the concept "an odd number between 1 and 10" (Armstrong et al., 1983). Quick, think of an odd number between 1 and 10. Most people select 3, and on that basis 3 can be considered as the most typical member of this concept. But the number 3 isn't a collection of features.

SETS OF EXAMPLES AND FUNCTIONS. In addition, researchers have made the case that some types of concepts are not stored as prototypes at all, but instead are stored as sets of examples of the concept or as functions (Medin & Schaffer, 1978; Smith & Medin, 1981).

1. *Sets of examples.* In some cases, you might specify a concept by storing a collection of examples, and not a prototype. For instance, your concept of a chair might correspond to a collection of individual chairs (rocking chair, desk chair, easy chair, and so on), not a single prototype.

2. *Functions.* In other cases, you might specify a concept by storing functions. Functions would be particularly useful for specifying concepts of movement or of action, such as those labeled by verbs (for instance, whether an object can be lifted; Bird et al., 2000). For some concepts (such as the one that underlies the verb "push"), this information may be stored as commands for making movements, not as descriptions of features.

At least some concepts may be stored in multiple ways or using combinations of methods, and different methods may be used in different situations (Anderson & Betz, 2001; Medin et al., 2000; Rips, 2001; Smith et al., 1998).

How Are Concepts Organized? Concepts are organized in terms of specificity, and when classifying an object or event, we typically use a concept at what Rosch and her colleagues (1976) have called the basic level. The **basic level** of a concept is at an intermediate level of specificity; it is like the middle rung of a ladder, with more general concepts above it and more specific concepts below it. For example, "apple" is the basic level; "fruit" is on a rung above it, and "Granny Smith" on a rung below. Each more general concept includes a number of more specific concepts; for example, "apple" includes "Granny Smith," "Delicious," "McIntosh," and many more. Try this: Look at the objects in Figure 4, and name them as fast as you can. It's very likely that you named them "apple," "tree," and "dog." You probably didn't name the apple a "fruit" or a "Granny Smith" or call the tree an "oak" or the dog a "mammal" or an "animal."

Rosch offered several ways to identify the basic level. For example, one way is based on the similarity of the shapes of the members of concepts at different levels of specificity. At the most specific level, if we compare individual Delicious apples with other Delicious apples, their shapes are very similar. Moving up a rung of generality, if we compare Delicious apples with McIntosh apples, Cortland apples, and so on, their shapes are still similar. But,

Prototype The most typical example of a concept.

Basic level (of a concept) An intermediate level of specificity that is usually the most likely to be applied to an object.

FIGURE 4 Basic-Level Names

Name these objects as fast as you can. It is remarkable that most people choose the same three names, a feat no computer vision system can match.

moving up another rung, if we compare apples with other fruits, such as bananas, watermelons, or grapes, their shapes have very little in common. The "basic level" category is the one that is as general as possible, while still being limited to objects that have similar shapes ("apple", in this case).

LOOKING BACK

✓•—Study and Review on
mypsychlab.com

1. **Does language mold our thoughts?** Although some researchers have claimed that language determines thought, the evidence does not support this view. Thinking cannot rely entirely on words; for example, words are ambiguous, but thoughts are not. Nevertheless, some thinking does make use of language, language can influence some very specific aspects of thought, and being able to name something makes that object or idea easier to remember.

2. **How can we think with mental images?** Objects in images can "stand in" for the actual objects, and visual mental images rely on most of the same brain systems also used in visual perception. These shared brain systems lead objects in mental images to have spatial extent, to extend over a limited field of view, and to have limited resolution. Nevertheless, thinking cannot rely entirely on mental images; for example, such images are difficult to use to represent abstract ideas and, like words, can be ambiguous.

3. **What is a concept?** A concept is the idea that underlies a word, phrase, or image. A concept can sometimes consist of a set of unambiguous features that specify a prototype, but only a percentage of the features must apply in any given instance. Members of concepts that have more of the key features are more typical examples of the concept. Some concepts may be specified by prototypes that are not collections of features; others may be specified by sets of examples of the concept. Concepts are organized according to levels of specificity.

Problem Solving and Reasoning: From Mental Processes to Behavior

Albert Einstein's reasoning abilities were so acute that he often felt that a solution was virtually implied by the nature of a problem itself. For instance, he derived equations that explained a previously inexplicable slip of the planet Mercury from its orbit, and when his

Problem solving Devising a way to overcome an obstacle that stands between the present situation and a desired goal.

Reasoning Deciding what follows from an idea, ideas, or a situation.

Problem An obstacle that must be overcome to reach a goal.

Representation problem The challenge of how best to formulate the nature of a problem.

equations produced the correct result, he was satisfied but not exuberant, noting that "I did not for one second doubt that [my calculations] would agree with observation. There was no sense in getting excited about what was self-evident" (Clark, 1971, p. 206).

Problem solving consists of devising a way to overcome an obstacle that stands between the present situation and a desired goal. In contrast, **reasoning** consists of deciding what follows from an idea, ideas, or a situation. Reasoning plays a key role in solving problems, but is often used even when there are no obstacles to overcome—you also reason when you just want to know what are the implications of a particular idea, ideas, or situation. You reason about the mundane matters of daily life—which movie to see or which classes to take (mentally considering the advantages and disadvantages of each)—as well as such weighty matters as what you should major in, what career path to take, which person you want to make your life partner.

Humans are vastly better than other animals at both problem solving and reasoning, but even Einstein was susceptible to human foibles—as was all too evident by his signing countless petitions for all manner of causes. They say that "to err is human" for good reason, as we shall see in the following sections.

1. What methods can we use to solve problems?
2. How do people reason logically? Why do we commit reasoning errors?

FIGURE 5 The Hiking Monk Problem

A monk leaves the bottom of a mountain every Monday at 5:00 AM and walks up a winding path, climbing at a rate of 1.5 miles an hour, until he reaches the top at 4:00 PM, having taken off a half-hour for lunch. He meditates on the mountain until sundown and then goes to sleep. At 5:00 the next morning, he departs and walks down the path, going 3.5 miles an hour, until he reaches the bottom. Is there *any* point in the two journeys when he is at precisely the same location on the path at precisely the same time of day? You don't need to say what that time is, just whether there would be such a time.

How to Solve Problems: More Than Inspiration

Einstein solved many daunting problems in physics, and never shied away from proposing radically new ideas to do so (such as the idea that light can bend). A **problem** is an obstacle that must be overcome to reach a goal. Problems come in many types and can often be solved in many ways. Let's consider some of the tools at your disposal for solving a diverse range of problems, puzzles, and predicaments.

Solving the Representation Problem: It's All in How You Look at It The first step to solving any problem is figuring out how to characterize the nature of the problem itself. This fundamental challenge is called the **representation problem**. You can characterize the problem with different descriptions, with drawings, or with a combination of the two. If you hit on the right way to represent a particular problem, the solution can be amazingly simple. Here's a good example (based on Duncker, 1945): As shown in Figure 5, a monk leaves the bottom of a mountain at 5:00 AM and hikes up the mountain at 1.5 miles per hour; he spends the night at the summit and departs the next morning at 5:00 AM, walking downhill at a 3.5 miles per hour. The problem is to decide whether, *at any one time of day*, the monk would be at precisely the same spot on the path on the day he went up and on the day he came down. At first glance, this problem may seem almost impossible. If the precise specifications of departure times, speed, and so on lure you into trying to use algebra, you may work on it for hours. But if you find the right representation of the problem, solving it is easy: Imagine a mountain with a monk leaving from the top at the same time that another monk leaves from the bottom. It is clear that the two monks must pass each other at a particular point on the path, and hence they will be at precisely the same spot on the path at a specific time of day—and the same will be true if instead of two monks leaving at the same time on the same day, a single monk departs from the bottom on one morning and departs from the summit on another morning. And so the answer is simply yes.

FIGURE 6 The Candle Problem

Participants are asked to use the materials provided to mount the candle on the wall so that it can be lit. Some participants are given the materials as shown on the left; others, as shown at the right. Participants given the materials as shown at the right are more likely to solve the problem.

Source for Figures 6 and 7: From *Cognition: Exploring the Science of the Mind* by Daniel Reisberg. Copyright © 1997 by W.W. Norton & Company, Inc. Used by permission of W.W. Norton & Company, Inc.

Finding the best representation of a problem can be a challenge in part because once you think of a problem in a certain way, you may find it difficult to drop this view and try out others (Smith & Blankenship, 1989, 1991). For example, consider the problem in Figure 6 (adapted from Duncker, 1945); after you think about it, look at its solution in Figure 7. If you are like most people, when you saw the problem you thought of the box simply as a container, and not as a potential part of the solution. Becoming stuck on one interpretation of an object or aspect of a situation is called **functional fixedness** (Behrens, 2003), and it requires effort to break out of a given way of viewing a situation. Not surprisingly, neuroimaging studies have shown that extra brain activity is required when you need to inhibit one way of viewing a situation and switch to another (Konishi et al., 1999).

Algorithms and Heuristics: Getting From Here to There To solve a problem, you need a **strategy**, an approach to solving a problem, which indicates the processing steps to be tried. There are two types of strategies: *algorithms* and *heuristics*. An **algorithm** is a set of steps that, if followed methodically, will guarantee the correct solution to a problem. For example, say you hear on your local radio broadcast about a fantastic price for a buffet dinner at a restaurant in your area, but you didn't catch the name of the restaurant. You could find the restaurant if you call every eating place in your area; if you follow this procedure methodically, you will definitely locate the right restaurant. But you may not have time to call every restaurant. Instead, you might guess that the restaurant is in the part of town where many students—who are looking for cheap meals—live. In this case, you could begin by calling only restaurants located near campus, and you might find the restaurant after calling only a few. This last process reflects use of a **heuristic**, a rule-of-thumb strategy that does not guarantee the correct solution to a problem but offers a likely shortcut to it.

One common heuristic is to divide a big problem into smaller problems and solve each of them one at a time. This is a heuristic because it won't always work, but when it does work it is often faster than trying to solve the entire problem at once. For instance, if you want to go to Hawaii for spring break, you might divide the problem into three subproblems: how to obtain enough money, how to find someone to go with, and how to make the travel plans themselves (how to get there, where to stay, and so on). (You could use either an algorithm or heuristic to solve any of the subproblems.) But this overall approach—like all heuristics—may not work: For example, you might only be able to come up with enough funds if you find somebody to share an inexpensive hotel room with—and thus you need to solve all three of those subproblems together. Nevertheless, approaching each subproblem separately is likely to contribute to reaching your sun-swept goal.

Functional fixedness When solving a problem, getting stuck on one interpretation of an object or one aspect of the situation.

Strategy An approach to solving a problem, which indicates the processing steps to be tried.

Algorithm A set of steps that, if followed methodically, will guarantee the correct solution to a problem.

Heuristic A rule-of-thumb strategy that does not guarantee the correct solution to a problem but offers a likely shortcut to it.

FIGURE 7 Solution to the Candle Problem

When the box is presented as a container, functional fixedness often prevents people from imagining the box as a shelf.

Solving Problems by Analogy: Comparing Features Another heuristic that can help you solve problems requires drawing an analogy between the present problem and a previous one that you've already solved. To do this, you need to compare the features of two situations, noticing what they have in common and what's different (Gentner & Gunn, 2001; Hummel & Holyoak, 1997). For example, consider the following problem (based on Duncker, 1945): A surgeon has to remove a cancerous tumor from deep within a patient's brain. Cutting into the brain with a scalpel would cause permanent brain damage. An alternative is to use a beam of X rays to demolish the cancerous cells. However, the beam will also kill healthy cells in its path. Is there a way to reach only the cancerous cells and spare the healthy ones? The solution is to split the beam into several minibeams, each of which is so weak that it will not hurt the healthy tissue. But if each of these minibeams is directed from a different angle, so that the beams cross at the location of the tumor, their combined impact will destroy the tumor.

Most people do not find the solution to this problem (Gick & Holyoak, 1980, 1983). However, if they are first presented with an analogous problem and are told to think about how it relates to the second problem, success rates skyrocket. In this case, they first read about a problem faced by a general who wants to attack a fortress. If he advances all of his troops along a single road, mines will blow them to pieces. But smaller groups could travel on various approach roads without exploding the mines. The solution is to divide the army into smaller parties and have each take a separate road to the fortress. Once people see this solution and know it is relevant to the tumor problem, the solution to the tumor problem becomes much easier (in fact, close to 80% get the problem right).

However, to see for yourself how a previous experience can be applied to a present problem, you must recognize the similarities in the structures of the situations. For example, if the participants are not told that the army problem is relevant to the tumor one, thinking about the solution to the former does not help them much with the latter. At first glance, the two problems are unrelated. One involves soldiers and a fortress; the other, beams of radiation and a tumor. But beneath these surface differences, the problems have the same structure: Something too big is broken into parts, the parts are delivered separately, and then they are recombined. Once people appreciate the similar structures, it's clear how to draw the analogy from one problem to the other—and to draw the analogy from one solution to the other.

Various approaches to problem solving are summarized in Table 1.

TABLE 1 Approaches to Problem Solving

Approach	Definition	Example
Use a new representation of the problem	Specify the nature of the problem	Use an image of two monks starting to walk the path at the same time, one from the top and the other from the bottom
Use an algorithm	Series of steps that is guaranteed to produce a solution	Check every restaurant in the area to find the low-price buffet dinner
Use a heuristic	Short-cut, rule-of-thumb, strategy that may or may not be effective	First check restaurants near campus to find the low-price buffet dinner
Use an analogy	A type of heuristic that relies on finding points of correspondence with previously solved problems and their solutions	Realizing that a particular medical problem is like a previously encountered military problem.

Overcoming Obstacles to Problem Solving You can improve your ability to solve problems if you keep the following points in mind (Ellis & Hunt, 1993; Newsome, 2000):

1. *Represent the problem effectively.* A major challenge is to represent the problem effectively. One way to meet this challenge is to make sure that you really understand the problem. Explain the problem to somebody else; sometimes, the simple act of explaining leads to a way of representing the problem that immediately implies a solution.

2. *Focus on the problem.* Don't lose sight of what actually constitutes the problem. People sometimes tend to transform the problem—resist this. If the problem is "how to get to Hawaii for spring break," don't redefine the problem as "how to talk my parents into subsidizing the trip." This advice also applies to debates and arguments; you might be surprised at how much more effective you'll be if you keep the pertinent issue in mind and don't allow yourself to be drawn off on tangents.

3. *Don't restrict the resources.* Don't get locked into viewing your resources in only one way, which is a form of functional fixedness. See whether you can come up with more than one way of thinking about your resources. For example, instead of focusing on raising funds to rent a hotel room, perhaps through the Internet you can find someone in Hawaii who would be willing to put you up in exchange for yard work or some other exchange of services.

4. *Consider alternative types of solutions.* Don't get stuck with a certain **mental set**, an approach to solving a problem that worked for a similar problem in the past, which leads to a fixed way of thinking about how to solve a present problem. It's okay to begin by focusing on one possible type of solution, but recognize that there may be more than one happy outcome. Be willing to consider alternatives to the general problem. (Florida can be a great spring break destination, too, as can home.)

5. *Take a fresh look.* If you do get stuck, walk away from the problem for a while. A fresh look can lead to new ways of representing it or new strategies for solving it.

Logic, Reasoning, and Decision Making

As we noted earlier, reasoning is sometimes used to help solve problems—but this is not the only purpose of reasoning. Reasoning consists of deciding what follows from an idea, ideas, or situation—and we reason whenever we evaluate choices or decide to take one alternative or course of action over others. All types of reasoning rely on **logic**, which is a set of rules that determines which conclusions follow from particular assumptions. How do we humans—Einstein included—reason logically? And why do we sometimes reason incorrectly?

Are People Logical? Let's review the ways people reason and then consider some common errors in reasoning.

HOW PEOPLE REASON. We can divide reasoning into two main types, *deductive* and *inductive*. **Deductive reasoning** works from the general to the particular; the rules of logic are applied to a set of assumptions to discover what conclusions inevitably follow from those assumptions. Here's an example of deductive reasoning: "Hector is a man; all men are human; therefore Hector is a human." But note that the following is also an example of correct deductive reasoning: "Hector is a man; all men are Martians; therefore Hector is a Martian." The first two statements in each case are the *premises*, and they define the assumptions that you are working with; in deductive reasoning the only question is whether the final statement, the *conclusion*, follows logically from the premises. The *content*—the actual meaning of the premises—is irrelevant to logic; only the *form*, the sequence of what-implies-what, counts in logic. If you accept the premises, then the rules of logic dictate when you must also accept certain conclusions.

In contrast, **inductive reasoning** works from the particular case to a generalization; induction uses individual examples to discover a rule that governs them. For example, if you were to examine the European paper money (one unit of which is referred to as a euro), you might notice that the 10 euro note (the paper bill) is physically bigger than the 5 euro note and that a 100 euro note is bigger than a 50 euro note. This might lead you to induce—correctly in this case—that the more valuable the bill, the larger its physical size (and so, for example, that the 100 euro note is bigger than the 50 euro note but is smaller than the 200).

However, using the same method of inductive reasoning, if you ate two green, under-ripe apples and each was sour, you might induce that green apples in general are sour—but in this case your conclusion would be faulty: You ignored the evidence of Granny Smiths (which are sweet). All it takes is one counterexample to reject a rule. This fact leads to a problem: you rarely can consider all of the possible relevant examples—and thus, you

Mental set An approach to solving a problem that worked for a similar problem in the past, which leads to a fixed way of thinking about how to solve a present problem.

Logic A set of rules that determines which conclusions follow from particular assumptions.

Deductive reasoning Reasoning that applies the rules of logic to a set of assumptions (stated as premises) to discover whether certain conclusions inevitably follow from those assumptions; deduction goes from the general to the particular.

Inductive reasoning Reasoning that uses examples to discover a rule that governs them; induction goes from the particular (examples) to the general (a rule).

FIGURE 8 Deductive Versus Inductive Reasoning

DEDUCTIVE REASONING

| General principles (premises) |

↓

| Specific example to which principles (premises) apply |

↓

| Conclusion based on application of general principles to specific example |

INDUCTIVE REASONING

| Induction of general principles |

↑

| Notice of regularities in specific examples |

↑

| Observation of individual examples |

To remember the difference between deductive and inductive reasoning, try these mnemonics: To DEduce is to move DOWN FROM something larger; to INduce is to move INTO something larger.

FIGURE 9 Wason and Johnson-Laird's Card Task

Here is the rule presented along with these cards: "If a card has a vowel on one side, then it will have an even number on the other side." How many and which of these cards must be flipped over to decide whether this rule is true?

Affirming the consequent A reasoning error that occurs when a person assumes that a specific cause is present because a particular result has occurred.

Confirmation bias A bias to seek information that will confirm a rule and not to seek information that would refute the rule.

can easily miss the one counterexample that would disprove the rule. Nevertheless, inductive reasoning often works well (Prasada, 2000), and much of scientific discovery relies on just this kind of reasoning: Researchers formulate a general rule on the basis of a set of individual observations. But researchers try to sample from a wide range within the population, and they don't stop there: they then explore the limits on applications of the general rule, and try to formulate better rules as they move ahead.

Figure 8 schematizes the difference between deductive and inductive reasoning. Much of our reasoning involves a combination of deductive and inductive processes.

LOGICAL ERRORS. Much research has shown that humans—even extraordinary ones such as Albert Einstein—are not entirely logical, and hence sometimes reason poorly and make poor decisions. For example, people often make the error of **affirming the consequent**—that is, assuming that a specific cause is present because a particular result has occurred. Affirming the consequent occurs because we incorrectly work backward, from result to cause. For example, here is a cause–effect relation: "If it is sunny out, Hector wears a hat." In this case, "Hector wears a hat" is the consequence of the sun's being out. Given this relationship, can you assume that it is sunny out if you see Hector wearing a hat? Not necessarily. Maybe Hector's on his way to a ballgame and has put on a hat with his team's logo. Maybe after checking The Weather Channel, he has put on a rain hat. Maybe he simply thinks a particular hat looks good with his outfit. Maybe—well, there might be any number of reasons, including that it is, in fact, sunny out. But just seeing Hector wearing a hat is not enough to infer that it is sunny out. Armed with knowledge about this error, you can now tell what's wrong with the following reasoning:

1. The Japanese do not eat much fat and have fewer heart attacks than the Americans and British.

2. The French eat a lot of fat and have fewer heart attacks than the Americans and British.

3. The Japanese do not drink much red wine and have fewer heart attacks than the Americans and British.

4. Italians drink large amounts of red wine and have fewer heart attacks than the Americans and British.

5. Conclusion: Eat and drink what you like. It's speaking English that causes heart attacks.

Another common reasoning error is a **confirmation bias**, which is a bias to seek information that will confirm a rule but not to seek information that would refute it. Here's a task that lays bare this aspect of our reasoning frailties (Wason & Johnson-Laird, 1972)—look at Figure 9: What would you do? The answer is that both A and 7 must be flipped. People tend to flip A, to see whether an even number is on the other side; if not, the rule would be wrong. If there is an even number on the reverse of A, most people assume that the rule is confirmed. Very few think to turn over the 7, but this is crucial: If there is a vowel on the other side, then the rule is wrong no matter what's on the reverse of A. Most people do not think about what it would take to *disconfirm* the rule.

Heuristics and Biases: Shortcuts Sometimes Have a Cost If the rules of logic lead to inescapable conclusions, why do people make errors in reasoning? The answer is implied in the question: people do not always use the rules of logic, but instead often rely on sets of heuristics. Although heuristics—short-cut, rule-of-thumb strategies—are often useful, they sometimes steer us to the wrong conclusions (Kahneman, 2003). Amos Tversky and Daniel Kahneman performed the ground-breaking studies of such errors—which earned Kahneman a Nobel Prize in 2002 (Tversky unfortunately did not live to see his work so honored). Two heuristics that may get us into trouble are the *representativeness* and the *availability heuristics*, which we consider in the following sections.

REPRESENTATIVENESS. The **representativeness heuristic** is the strategy in which we assume that the more similar something is to a prototype stored in memory, the more likely it is to belong to the category of the prototype. To study this heuristic, Tversky and Kahneman (1974) asked participants to read this passage:

> Jack is a 45-year-old man. He is married and has four children. He is generally conservative, careful, and ambitious. He shows no interest in political and social issues and spends most of his free time on his many hobbies, including home carpentry, sailing, and mathematical puzzles.

Source: From Tversky and Kahneman, "Judgment under uncertainty: Heuristics and biases." *Science*, 185, 1974 pp. 1124–1131.

The participants were then told that Jack was selected at random from a group of 100 people, all of whom were either lawyers or engineers, and the participants were asked to decide whether Jack was a lawyer or engineer. Here's the trick: Half of the participants were told that 70 members of the group were lawyers and 30 were engineers; the other participants were told that 30 members of the group were lawyers and 70 engineers. Pause for a moment and imagine that there are 100 balls in a jug, 70 red and 30 black, randomly mixed up. Imagine shutting your eyes and drawing out one ball. Do you think you would be more likely to pluck out a red one than a black one? Sure. Now reverse the colors, so that 70 are black and 30 red. Now you would be more likely to pull out a black one. However, when asked to decide whether Jack, who was selected at random from the group, was a lawyer or an engineer, the great majority of all participants, no matter what they had been told about the constitution of the group, said he was an engineer. The description of Jack, especially his interest in mathematical puzzles, fit the participants' prototype of engineers better than it fit their prototype of lawyers, and thus they labeled Jack "engineer" because he shared more characteristics with this prototype.

The participants in Tversky and Kahneman's study used their knowledge—or assumptions—about typical properties of people in different professions to make their decision, ignoring the **base-rate rule**. This rule states that if something is chosen at random from a set, the chance that the thing will be of a particular type is directly proportional to the percentage of that type in the set. If you think back to the example with the red and black balls, it's clear that the base-rate rule is correct, but even knowing this, you probably feel a tug toward using prototypes and ignoring base rates.

Here's a different interpretation of such findings (Gigerenzer et al., 1988): People simply have trouble understanding descriptions of probabilities, and don't have difficulty reasoning logically. To evaluate this view, in one study researchers tried to ensure that the participants understood the information about the proportions of different professions; to do so, they took 10 slips of paper and wrote descriptions of one profession on seven slips and descriptions of another profession on the other three slips. The slips were then folded and put in an urn. Each participant drew out a single slip and read the description, and then guessed the profession. In this situation, the participants did well, proving themselves able to keep in mind the relative proportions of the two professions. Thus, when they clearly understand what the base-rates are, people can in fact use this information effectively during reasoning. Nevertheless, even though people have the capacity to reason correctly, in many situations they do not clearly understand base rates, or ignore them, and instead rely on the representativeness heuristic (based on how similar the situation is to a stored prototype) to guide their reasoning.

AVAILABILITY.   Another reasoning shortcut is the **availability heuristic**, which is the strategy in which we judge objects or events as more likely, common, or frequent if they are easier to retrieve from memory. For example, Tversky and Kahneman (1974) asked people to judge the relative proportions of English words that begin with the letter *k* versus words that have *k* in the third position (such as the word *baker*). What do you think? Most of the participants in the study thought that *k* occurs more often as a first letter than as a third letter, but in fact almost three times as many words have *k* in the third position as in the first one. Why this error? Because it is much easier to retrieve from memory words starting with *k* than words that have *k* in the third position. And, in accordance with the availability heuristic, the easier it is to bring to mind, the more frequent we think it is.

Similarly, when given a list that contains equal numbers of names of famous men and not-famous women, people later will mistakenly remember that there were more men than

THINK like a
PSYCHOLOGIST Can you think of times when you've fallen victim to the confirmtion bias? Do you think this bias is always a good thing (or always a bad thing)? If you wanted to fight against this bias, what could you do?

Representativeness heuristic The strategy in which we assume that the more similar something is to a prototype stored in memory, the more likely it is to belong to the prototype's category.

Base-rate rule The rule stating that if something is chosen at random from a set, the chance that the thing will be of a particular type is directly proportional to the percentage of that type in the set.

Availability heuristic The strategy in which we judge objects or events as more likely, common, or frequent if they are easier to retrieve from memory.

If you have ever budgeted time to work on a paper and then run out of hours way too soon, you may have fallen victim to the *planning fallacy*: the tendency to underestimate the time it takes to accomplish a task. This error may arise because the completion of similar tasks is more available in your memory than is their duration. Thus, the availability heuristic can lead to the planning fallacy. The good news is that the planning fallacy can be reduced by thinking carefully about how long past projects actually took to complete (Buehler et al., 1994).

Source: Getty Images Inc - Image Source Royalty Free

women on the list (or vice versa, if given names of famous women and not-famous men; McKelvie, 2000). The availability heuristic may also explain why people tend to think that infrequent but highly memorable events, such as murders and plane crashes, are more common than they really are, and that more frequent but mundane killers, such as stomach cancer and stroke, are less common.

Donald Redelmeier, Joel Katz, and Daniel Kahneman (2003) reported a particularly dramatic and compelling example of the availability heuristic at work. They asked patients to judge the pain of a colonoscopy, a medical procedure in which a monitoring instrument is inserted through the anus to observe the intestines. For half the patients they added 3 minutes of more pain at the end of the procedure (by leaving the tip of the apparatus in the rectum), but the level of this pain was reduced from that of the procedure itself; for the other half of the patients, they did not include this additional pain. The striking result was that even though adding an additional 3 minutes of reduced pain at the end of the procedure was still adding more pain, the patients judged the entire procedure to have less pain than did the patients who did not have the 3 additional minutes of reduced pain at the end. Apparently the patients were judging the overall pain on the basis of the most available part of the procedure, namely the most recent part.

The bottom line is that people use different strategies to reason in different situations—sometimes heuristics (especially when thinking about events that only happen once, such as the destruction of the World Trade Center), sometimes relative frequencies, and sometimes other kinds of information (Ayal & Hochman, 2009; Ayton & Wright, 1994; Gigerenzer, 1996; Gigerenzer & Goldstein, 1996; Kahneman & Tversky, 1996; Teigen, 1994; Vranas, 2000).

Emotions and Decision Making: A Two-Edged Sword Many people apparently think that emotion clouds reason and distorts our ability to be objective. But, in fact, researchers have found that sometimes emotion can actually help reasoning (Martinez-Miranda & Aldea, 2005). For example, one study found that people played a gambling game better if they had "hunches," even though they were not aware of the bases of the hunches (Bechara et al., 1997). The researchers determined whether a participant had hunches based on his or her skin-conductance response (which reflects how much a person is sweating). Such a response occurred when the brain signaled the body that certain choices were risky—and this typically occurred before the participant consciously realized it. Thus, emotion played a key role in reasoning in this task.

However, emotion does not always help reasoning; sometimes emotion—especially negative emotions (such as fear or anger)—can disrupt reasoning (Goel & Dolan, 2003; Gray, 1999). In particular, if you become agitated ("frazzled"), working memory is disrupted and reasoning is more difficult to accomplish (Qin et al., 2009). For example, take chess, which very much relies on reasoning. In 1997, the world champion chess player Garry Kasparov was challenged to play a match against a new computer program. Kasparov had defeated the previous version of this computer program the year before—but now the program was much better than the previous version. In the second of six games of the rematch, Kasparov became shaken by the unexpectedly strong performance of the computer and conceded the game to it when he still could have managed a tie (Chabris, personal communication, 1999). Moreover, Kasparov did not win any of the subsequent four games, which suggests that his emotional response to the newer computer program disrupted his remarkable reasoning ability.

✓●⟵**Study** and **Review** on
mypsychlab.com

LOOKING BACK

1. **What methods can we use to solve problems?** The first step is to discover how best to specify the problem, how to represent it to yourself. If you find the proper representation, the solution is sometimes obvious. To solve a problem, you can use an algorithm or a heuristic. One common heuristic is to divide a problem into a set of

smaller problems. In addition, you can search for correspondences with other situations and then use an analogy to solve a problem.

2. **How do people reason logically? Why do we commit reasoning errors?** In deductive reasoning, logic is applied to determine what specific conclusions must follow from a set of general premises. People often make errors in this kind of reasoning, for example, by affirming the consequent or by having a confirmation bias. Inductive reasoning goes in the other direction, from particulars to a generalization. Inductive reasoning is also prone to errors because we can never consider all relevant examples before inducing a general principle—and it is not always obvious what general principle is suggested by a set of examples. In addition, we often use heuristics in reasoning, which can lead to specific types of errors. The representativeness heuristic, for example, can lead us to ignore the base-rate rule. And emotion can nudge reasoning in a positive direction or disrupt reasoning, depending on the type of emotion and the circumstances.

THINK like a **PSYCHOLOGIST** Do you think it's worth teaching high school students about reasoning biases? Why or why not? Do you think the general human weakness in using logic adversely affects world politics? Why or why not?

Intelligence: What Is It and How Does It Arise?

Albert Einstein wasn't born into an extraordinarily gifted family. His father, Hermann, was not a successful businessman and spent much of his time trying to keep the family financially afloat. Nonetheless, Einstein's family influenced him in major ways. For example, the independence of mind he exhibited so often as an adult may have been a result of his parents' encouraging him to be independent, to the point of allowing him to cross streets alone when he was only 4 years old (Brian, 1996). Young Einstein was not the child of geniuses, but did have the good fortune to have intelligent, caring parents who stimulated him with interesting ideas and encouraged him to fend for himself.

Einstein is often offered as the prototype genius, but his extraordinary intellect did not apply to all areas of his life—regarding financial matters, for instance, he was not intelligent. And he was not very successful as a husband or a father.

What does it mean to say that someone is or is not intelligent? Intelligence is certainly not a concrete entity that can be quantified, like the amount of water in a jug; rather, it is a concept. Psychologists have offered many definitions of intelligence, and there is considerable disagreement about what intelligence is and whether it can be accurately measured (Gardner, 2002; Gardner et al., 1996; Sternberg, 1986b, 1990; Sternberg & Detterman, 1986). However, what most researchers in psychology mean by "intelligence" is pretty close to the standard dictionary definition: **Intelligence** is the ability to reason and solve problems well and to understand and learn complex material. Researchers sometimes also stress that a key aspect of intelligence is the ability to adapt to the environment (Cianciolo et al., 2009; Sternberg, 1985, 2009). Intelligence is often associated with mental quickness, but this need not be so; however, researchers typically do assume that "solving problems well" implies "in a reasonable amount of time." Virtually all tests of intelligence rely on the assumption that intelligent people can reason, solve problems, and understand and learn complex material relatively easily—and thus perform quickly as well as accurately.

LOOKING AHEAD Learning Objectives

1. What is IQ?
2. Is intelligence a single characteristic or a complex set of characteristics?
3. How do the environment and genetics contribute to intelligence?
4. How can we interpret group differences in IQ?
5. What does it mean to have unusually high or low intelligence?

Intelligence The ability to reason and solve problems well and to understand and learn complex material.

Wechsler Adult Intelligence Scale (WAIS) The most widely used intelligence test in the United States; it consists of four sets of subtests.

Measuring Intelligence: What Is IQ?

Let's look at exactly what IQ is. IQ stands for *intelligence quotient*. But what "quotient" is being measured, and how is it measured? In the following sections we address these questions.

A Brief History of Intelligence Testing

To understand the meaning of intelligence test scores, it will be helpful to see how intelligence testing has evolved over time.

BINET AND SIMON: TESTING TO HELP. A French physician named Alfred Binet (1857–1911) and his collaborator, Theodore Simon (1873–1961), developed the first intelligence test between 1904 and 1911 (Matarazzo, 1972). Their aim was to devise an objective way to identify children in the public schools who needed extra classroom help. They started with the idea that intelligence shows itself in a wide variety of ways, a perspective that led them to construct a test that included of many sorts of tasks. Among other things, children were asked to copy a drawing, repeat a string of numbers, recognize coins and make change, and explain why a particular statement did not make sense. Binet and Simon assumed that the children's performance on the tests reflected their educational experiences, and thus that special classes could help those who did poorly.

To develop an objective way to grade performance, Binet and Simon first gave the test to a group of "normal" children of various ages. They noted which problems were solved by most of the 6-year-olds, by most of the 10-year-olds, and so forth; then they compared the performance of other children of the same age with those "normal" scores. They used a child's performance relative to the comparison group to assign a *mental age (MA)* to the child. For example, if a child could solve ("pass") all of the problems that are solved by most 9-year-olds, but failed those passed by most 10-year-olds, the child's mental age was said to be 9. Children with a mental age lower than their *chronological age (CA)* were considered relatively slow.

TERMAN AND WECHSLER: TESTS FOR EVERYONE. Binet and Simon's test was quickly adapted to suit new purposes, in particular to assess adult intelligence. In 1916, Lewis Terman and his colleagues at Stanford University developed the Stanford-Binet Revision of the Binet-Simon test, which is still used to test people from age 2 to adulthood. In addition, David Wechsler (1958) developed another set of intelligence tests, the **Wechsler Adult Intelligence Scale (WAIS)** and the *Wechsler Intelligence Scale for Children (WISC)*. The WAIS was designed to assess adults more accurately (by expanding the range at the "top"), to test a wider range of abilities, and to improve the method of scoring and interpreting results. Today, the WAIS and WISC are the most widely used intelligence tests in the United States. Both tests are currently in their fourth revised version, denoted as WAIS-IV and WISC-IV.

Weschler believed that Binet's test relied too much on verbal skills (such as explaining why a statement doesn't make sense), and hence Wechsler originally divided his test into two major parts, a set of verbal subtests and a set of performance subtests (they are called "subtests" because they are parts of a larger, overall test). The most recent version of the WAIS, however, has four major parts, each of which assesses a different facet of intelligence. The four parts are:

- *Verbal Comprehension*, which assesses the test-taker's understanding of verbal information;
- *Perceptual Reasoning*, which assesses the test-taker's reasoning about nonverbal information;
- *Working Memory*, which assesses the test-taker's ability to hold and manipulate information in working memory;
- *Processing Speed*, which assesses the test-taker's ability to focus his or her attention and to use information quickly.

Table 2 provides summaries of the ten subtests of the WAIS-IV, as well as representative examples of the sorts of items on each subtest. The *Perceptual Reasoning* and *Processing*

The WISC-IV is administered to children individually by a trained examiner.

Source: Bob Daemmrich Photography, Inc.

TABLE 2 **WAIS-IV Subtests with Simulated Examples of Questions**

I. Verbal Comprehension Subtests

Similarities: Questions that require explaining how the concepts named by two words are similar.

Example: "How are an airplane and a car alike?"

Information: Questions that draw on literature, history, general science, and common knowledge.

Example: "Who was Martin Luther King, Jr.?"

Vocabulary: Written and spoken words that must be defined; the words are ordered in terms of increasing difficulty.

Example: "What does trek mean?"

II. Perceptual Reasoning Subtests

Block Design: Problems that require arranging blocks colored on each side—white, red, or half white and half red—to reproduce a white-and-red pattern in a fixed amount of time.

Example:

Visual Puzzles: Items that require the test-taker to determine which puzzle pieces are needed to assemble a particular design.

Example: Which of the square pieces below go together to make the puzzle?

Matrix Reasoning: Items that require the test-taker to study a progression of stimuli in a sequence from which a section is missing. The test-taker must choose which of a number of possibilities completes the sequence.

Example:

III. Working Memory Subtests

Digit Span: Lists of digits, two to nine numbers long, are presented. The test-taker repeats the digits, either in the same or reverse order.

Example: "6, 1, 7, 5, 3."

Arithmetic: Arithmetic problems, all but one presented orally (one involves using blocks); the test is timed.

Example: "If 2 men need 4 days to paint a house, how long would 4 men need?"

IV. Processing Speed Subtests

Symbol Search: The test-taker is shown a particular symbol and a set of symbols and is asked to compare the given symbol to those in the set and choose the similar one in the set; the test is timed.

Example: "Which of the following symbols is the same as this one:

å

¢ ß Δ Ω å / ø ∑"

Coding: The test-taker is given a coding key in which each of the numbers 1–9 is paired with a unique symbol. The test-taker is then shown a series of numbers and must write their corresponding symbols; the test is timed.

Example:

Shown: Fill in:

1 2 3 4   4 1 3 2

+ 2 × ÷   __ __ __ __

Note: The WAIS-IV is intended for people aged 16 to 90. The examples above are included to provide a general idea of the nature of the tasks; they are not reproduced from the actual test. Five additional tests are included as "spares," to be used if there are problems in administering the basic set summarized here.

Source: Actual WAIS test items cannot be published; part of the table was adapted from Gardner et al., *Intelligence: Multiple Perspectives.* 1996, pp. 80–81. Copyright 1996 Cengage Learning. Adapted with permission.

Speed subtests assess cognitive abilities with nonverbal tasks, such as those that require the test-taker to arrange pictures in an order that tells a story, spot the missing element in a picture, or pick out a particular symbol from among a set of symbols. Because these subtests do not rely heavily on the ability to use and manipulate words, they may be less sensitive than other subtests to the test-taker's level of education or cultural experiences.

Scoring IQ Tests: Measuring the Mind Modern intelligence tests not only include different subtests than did earlier versions, but they also are scored differently. Contemporary methods of scoring provide a much more precise assessment than was possible previously. The first big innovation came early in the twentieth century, when William Stern, a German psychologist, developed the idea of an *intelligence quotient (IQ)*.

Stern computed IQ by dividing mental age (MA) by chronological age (CA) and multiplying by 100 to avoid fractional scores:

$$IQ = (MA/CA) \times 100$$

Thus, a score of 100 meant that a person's mental age exactly matched his or her chronological age. This method refined Binet and Simon's approach; they were satisfied with simply knowing whether a child was below or at par for his or her age.

However, computing IQ scores using the MA/CA ratio has a major disadvantage: Mental age does not keep developing forever, whereas chronological age marches on—and thus test-takers cannot help but appear to become less intelligent as they age. For example, if your mental age is 25 and you are 25 years old, you would be average; but if your mental age is the same in 5 years, your IQ would drop from 100 to 83, even though you are just as smart at 30 as you were at 25. And at 40, your IQ would be about 62. But people do not actually become progressively less intelligent with advancing age. As discussed in the following section, modern intelligence tests are scored in a way that solves this problem.

COMPUTING AND INTERPRETING IQ SCORES: STANDARDIZED SAMPLES AND NORMING. Intelligence tests are no longer scored by using the MA/CA ratio. Instead, IQ is now computed by comparing a particular person to the average of other people of the same age, and a score of 100 is set as the average score. To understand what IQ scores mean, and what they don't mean, we need to look more closely at exactly how intelligence tests are now scored.

Scores can be assigned only after the test itself has been developed in a particular way. The first step is to give the test to a large **standardized sample**, which is a representative selection of people from a carefully defined population. In this sense, a *population* is defined as a group of people who share one or more specific characteristics, such as age, sex, or any other relevant attributes. Almost always, the obtained scores are spread along a normal distribution, illustrated in Figure 10; when the distribution of scores follows a normal distribution, most scores fall near the middle, with gradually fewer scores toward either extreme.

The second step is to take the distribution of scores obtained from the standardized sample and to "norm" the test to make it easy to interpret the meaning of any one test-taker's

FIGURE 10 The Normal Curve and WAIS-IV IQ Scores

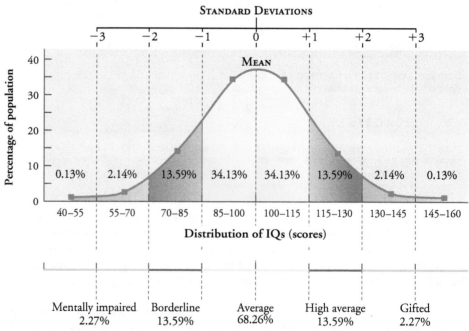

Because of its shape, the normal curve is also known as the *bell curve*. In nature, most characteristics clump around the midpoint, and progressively fewer have very high or very low measures. This diagram indicates the percentage of people who have scores on the WAIS-IV IQ test that fall within different regions of the distribution.

Standardized sample A representative selection of people, drawn from a carefully defined population.

score relative to the others. **Norming** a test involves setting the numerical values of two measures: (1) the *mean* (numerical average); the mean score for the WAIS (and virtually all other IQ tests) is adjusted so that it equals 100; and (2) the *standard deviation*, which indicates the degree to which the individual scores deviate from—spread out around—the mean. The greater the number of standard deviations from the mean, the farther above or below the score is from it. Because the IQ scores fall into a normal distribution, then by definition a certain percentage of scores are within each standard deviation from the mean, as shown in Figure 10 (each marked unit on the bottom corresponds to one standard deviation).

Here's an example of norming with which you might be more familiar: The SAT tests. Although SAT test scores are not IQ scores, the SAT and its subject tests undergo norming. Each student's raw score—the actual number of correct items—is transformed so that the numerical value of the score conveys the student's performance relative to his or her peers who took the same test. The mean score of each SAT test is always set at 500, with a standard deviation of 100 points.

For the WAIS-IV IQ test, norming results in a mean of 100 and a standard deviation of 15 points. As shown in Figure 10, about two-thirds of all people have IQs from 85 to 115 points (that is, within one standard deviation above or below the mean), but only a bit more than a quarter have IQs either between 70 and 85 or between 115 and 130 (within the second standard deviation above or below the mean). Only 4.54% of IQ scores are above 130 or below 70.

In short, the **intelligence quotient, IQ,** is a score on an intelligence test, originally based on comparing mental age to chronological age, but later based on norms and used as a measure of intelligence.

RELIABILITY AND VALIDITY.   For IQ scores to be meaningful and useful, the test must be *reliable* and it must be *valid*. A reliable test produces consistent results; that is, if you test the same group of people on two occasions, the two sets of scores will be highly positively correlated. The Wechsler intelligence tests are highly reliable.

In addition, a *valid* test measures what it is supposed to measure; in this case, the IQ test should in fact measure intelligence. Do IQ tests really measure the ability to reason and solve problems well and to understand and learn complex material? One way to find out whether IQ tests actually measure intelligence is to discover whether scores on these tests are related to measures of performance for other tasks that seem to require intelligence, which we consider next.

IQ and Achievement: IQ in the Real World   IQ scores do in fact predict performance in the real world. In the United States, people with higher IQs tend to land higher-prestige jobs and make more money; they are also more likely to enjoy stable marriages and to stay out of jail (Deary et al., 2004; Herrnstein & Murray, 1994).

However, most of the variation in job success reflects something other than IQ: Correlations between IQ and job performance show that, at most, only about a quarter of the variation in job success can be predicted by IQ (Hunter, 1983; Jensen, 1980; Schmidt & Hunter, 2004; Streufert & Swezey, 1986). What else might explain success? Several factors (in addition to IQ) have been identified:

1. The personality traits of conscientiousness and integrity predict success on the job (Schmidt & Hunter, 2004).
2. Motivation, ambition, and education also contribute to success (Gagné & St. Père, 2001; Lubinski, 2000, 2004).
3. Culture clearly plays a role. For example, Asian cultures, with their strong family bonds and emphasis on hard work, foster achievement (Stevenson et al., 1986), and Japanese Americans and Chinese Americans are more successful than IQ scores alone would predict (Flynn, 1991, 1999a, 1999b).

Norming The process of setting the mean and the standard deviation of a set of test scores, based on results from a standardized sample.

Intelligence quotient (IQ) A score on an intelligence test, originally based on comparing mental age to chronological age, but later based on norms and used as a measure of intelligence.

Achievement is only partly determined by intelligence; motivation is also important. Subcultures differ in the degree to which they value education, and thus the degree to which their members are strongly motivated to obtain education.

Source: © Owen Franken/CORBIS All Rights Reserved

219

In short, IQ plays a role in whether a person will be successful, especially in intellectually challenging jobs, but so do personality factors, motivation, ambition, education, and culture.

Analyzing Intelligence: One Ability or Many?

As we just noted, in the United States, a high IQ score predicts success in school and in life. To interpret these findings, we need to know more about what, precisely, IQ tests measure. Is there some general ability, some basic intelligence, that IQ scores reflect? And do IQ tests tap everything meant by "intelligence"?

IQ, g, and Specialized Abilities
Researchers have made great progress in figuring out just what IQ tests measure, and in the sections that follow we review how their conclusions have developed over time.

SPEARMAN'S G FACTOR. Today's IQ tests include a variety of specialized individual tests (such as the vocabulary, block design, and arithmetic subtests included in the WAIS-IV), and people who do well on one tend to do well on others. That is, scores on the different types of tests are positively correlated (Deary, 2000; Gottfredson, 1997; Jensen, 1998). This finding led British psychologist Charles Spearman (1927) to argue that the different types of mental tests tap a single underlying intellectual capacity, which he labeled *g*, for "general factor."

To find out whether *g* exists, Spearman developed a new statistical tool to analyze sets of test scores, called factor analysis. **Factor analysis** is a statistical method that uncovers the particular characteristics (factors) that make scores more or less similar. A factor analysis of the correlations among different measures of performance shows, for example, that speed of processing is one important factor in many tasks, and the amount of information that can be held in working memory is another. However, when Spearman analyzed the correlations among various test scores, he found that the first—and most important—factor underlying test performance was *g*. Subsequently, researchers have repeatedly replicated Spearman's finding, reporting that different sets of tests reflect, at least in part, an underlying common ingredient (Deary et al., 2004; Johnson et al., 2004).

But factor analysis did more than document the existence of *g*; it also provided evidence for many "specific factors," abbreviated by the letter **s**, each of which applies to a particular kind of task. The existence of *s* was implied by the pattern of correlations among test scores. That is, if intelligence is simply *g*, then the scores from the different individual tests all should be highly correlated with each other, so that scores on a given test should accurately predict scores on each of the others. This is not the case: Spearman also noted a wide variation in the sizes of the correlations, so that scores on each individual test didn't predict scores on each of the others; Spearman took this variation to reflect the influence of *s*. When you perform a task, according to Spearman, you are drawing on *g* as well as on a particular type of ability, *s*, specific to that task. For example, spelling draws on a specialized ability, which is largely independent of other abilities. Some tasks, such as being able to analyze Shakespeare, rely more on *g* than on *s*; others, such as discriminating musical tones, rely more on a particular *s* than on *g*.

Factor analysis provided evidence for the existence of specific factors and also showed that they usually are less important than *g* for predicting overall performance. In Spearman's view, IQ scores depend mostly on *g*; how intelligent you are for the most part depends on how much of this general intellectual capacity you have.

THURSTONE'S PRIMARY MENTAL ABILITIES. A second perspective on what IQ scores reflect came from Louis L. Thurstone (1938), who sought to determine the basic abilities that constitute intelligence. Thurstone devised a battery of 56 tests and then analyzed the correlations of scores on these tests using Spearman's method of factor analysis. Thurstone found that how well you can do arithmetic has little if anything to do with your other abilities, such as those that underlie how well you notice visual changes in your environment or how well you figure out the best way to get home when traffic is heavy (Thurstone & Thurstone, 1941). Thurstone's research results suggested that intelligence consists of seven separate **primary mental abilities**, fundamental abilities that are the components of intelligence and that are distinct from other abilities. Verbal comprehension and spatial visualization are two of Thurstone's primary mental abilities.

g "General factor," a single intellectual capacity that underlies the positive correlations among different tests of intelligence.

Factor analysis A statistical method that uncovers the particular characteristics (factors) that make scores more or less similar.

s "Specific factors," or aspects of performance that are particular to a given kind of processing—and distinct from *g*.

Primary mental abilities According to Thurstone, seven fundamental abilities that are the components of intelligence and are distinct from other abilities.

CATTELL AND HORN'S FLUID AND CRYSTALLIZED INTELLIGENCES. Other researchers, Raymond B. Cattell and John Horn, argued that instead of a single general capacity, *g*, people possess two general types of intelligence: *fluid* and *crystallized* (Cattell, 1971; Horn, 1985, 1986, 1989, 1994; Horn & Cattell, 1966; Horn & Noll, 1997). **Fluid intelligence** is the kind of intelligence that underlies the creation of novel solutions to problems; such intelligence hinges on the ability to reason without relying heavily on previous experience or learned procedures ("a person's mental horsepower, the ability to solve cognitive problems on the spot"; Gottfredson, 2003a, p. 350). For example, fluid intelligence would be used to figure out how to write when a pen or pencil isn't available (one clever songsmith in such straits scribbled the lyrics to a new rock tune using the heads of burnt matches). Without question, Einstein excelled at using this sort of intelligence.

In contrast, **crystallized intelligence** relies on knowing facts and having the ability to use and combine them; such intelligence hinges on using experience and on learned procedures to reason (it is the "very general skills [e.g., language] that have been developed—crystallized—from exercising fluid *g* in the past"; Gottfredson, 2003a, p. 350). This is the sort of intelligence that develops as you become an expert in an area. If you make good use of your college experience, you should boost your crystallized intelligence. Key characteristics of fluid and crystallized intelligences are summarized in Table 3.

Fluid intelligence According to Cattell and Horn, the kind of intelligence that underlies the creation of novel solutions to problems.

Crystallized intelligence According to Cattell and Horn, the kind of intelligence that relies on knowing facts and having the ability to use and combine them.

TABLE 3   Fluid Versus Crystallized Intelligence

Fluid Intelligence	Crystallized Intelligence
Ability to reason about novel situations and to solve novel problems	Ability to reason using previously learned procedures
Ability to abstract concepts on the basis of new information or procedures	Ability to use factual knowledge acquired through education and experience
Ability to use reasoning that does not depend primarily on learning and acculturation	Ability to use reasoning that is based on learning and acculturation
Ability to manipulate abstract concepts, rules, and generalizations and to use logical relations	Ability to use language to communicate

As illustrated by Einstein, the two sorts of intelligence can go together—but people can also excel at one but not the other. A variety of factors each affect fluid and crystallized intelligence differently, which is evidence that the two types of intelligence are, in fact, distinct; if there were only a single form of intelligence, such factors should show the same effects on the two sets of abilities. For example, as we age, crystallized intelligence does not suffer much, if at all, whereas fluid intelligence deteriorates; we are still able to maintain our expertise in areas of strength, but the ability to shift gears quickly to solve new problems tends to decrease (Horn, 1985, 1986, 1994; Horn & Noll, 1994; Salthouse, 1996). In addition, the two forms of intelligence develop at different rates during childhood, appear to rely on different brain structures, and are not equally influenced by genes (Horn & Masunaga, 2000; Horn & Noll, 1997). Moreover, different facets of academic achievement are predicted by the two forms of intelligence (Evans et al., 2002).

CARROLL'S THREE-STRATUM THEORY OF COGNITIVE ABILITY. John B. Carroll produced a landmark book in 1993, in which he reanalyzed massive amounts of test data (from over 450 high-quality studies). He found that the relations among test scores are neatly structured into a three-tiered hierarchy (building in part on the earlier work of Gustafson, 1984). At the top of the hierarchy is *g*, and immediately under it are eight broad cognitive abilities (which include fluid and crystallized intelligences), and under each of those broad cognitive abilities

For the veteran angler, fishing consists of well-worn routines (such as putting the bait on the hook, casting the line in the water, knowing when to yank and when to wait, reeling in the fish, and so on), and thus it relies on crystallized intelligence. But what would happen if you didn't have bait, a hook, line, and sinker? You would need fluid intelligence to figure out how to catch fish.

Source: Scottish Viewpoint\Alamy Images

Emotional intelligence (EI) The ability to understand and regulate emotions effectively.

is a set of narrow abilities. Each of the broad abilities relies on *g*, and each of the broad abilities is, in turn, drawn on by narrow abilities. Using Carroll's model then, performance on any specific task requires factors in all three tiers (Deary, 2000).

The hierarchical structure of intelligence in Carroll's *three-stratum theory* is a grand synthesis of the earlier theories, fitting them all into a single framework. For example, this structure allows us to understand fluid and crystallized intelligences by noting that they are somewhat—but not entirely—distinct. Because they have unique aspects, factors such as aging can affect them differently; but because they both draw on *g*, they are positively correlated.

Although many subsequent studies have supported Carroll's theory (Deary, 2000), two areas of debate persist: (1) Horn and his colleagues continue to maintain that fluid and crystallized intelligences sit at the top of the hierarchy, not a single *g*, as Carroll maintains. (2) Other researchers have argued that the broad cognitive abilities of the middle tier can be specified by only three categories, namely, quantitative, spatial, and verbal abilities (Lubinski, 2004; Snow, 1994, 1996).

Emotional Intelligence: Knowing Feelings The sorts of intelligence assessed by IQ tests are important, but do not fully explain differences in performance. As we saw earlier, personality characteristics (such as how conscientious you are) contribute, but this is not the whole story: Many researchers have shown that people rely on additional sorts of intelligence, which are not tapped by the standard tests. Let's consider one example of another sort of intelligence—emotional intelligence.

Emotional intelligence (EI) is the ability to understand and regulate emotions effectively (Salovey & Mayer, 1990). Salovey and Mayer argue that whether you act intelligently often depends in large part on how well you understand both your own emotions and the effects your actions have on others. We've all seen someone we *know* is generally bright do something that can only be described as incredibly "dumb"—for instance, unintentionally or uncontrollably make a remark that infuriates a friend or boss. Such behavior illustrates the distinction between the kind of cognitive intelligence we've been discussing so far and EI.

EI has two major facets, one that plays a role in reasoning, problem solving, and learning, and one that plays a role in subjective experiences and inclinations.

EI IN REASONING, PROBLEM SOLVING, AND LEARNING. This facet of EI is typically defined as having the four "branches" listed in Table 4; these branches are ordered from specific to general, from perceiving emotions (which is the most specific) to managing emotions (which is the most general). The tests for this facet of EI rely on asking test-takers to make decisions about emotion-laden situations, and the decisions are scored as right or wrong (Mayer et al., 2000, 2001a, 2001b, 2003). Because the test designers have defined right and wrong answers, these tests are often referred to as "objective tests."

TABLE 4 The Four-Branch Model of Emotional Intelligence

The four branches of emotional intelligence are ordered here from least to most general.

Branch	Description	Example
1. Perceiving emotion	Ability to identify emotions on the basis of perceptual cues	Noticing a slight frown when a friend hears someone's name, and realizing that it signals jealousy
2. Facilitating thought with emotion	Ability to harness emotional information to enhance thinking	Thinking through a planned comment to your friend, and changing the plan to avoid an anticipated rocky outcome
3. Understanding emotion	Ability to comprehend emotional information about relationships, transitions from one emotion to another, and verbal information about emotion	Understanding that your friend is jealous of someone else because of your previous relationship with that person
4. Managing emotion	Ability to manage emotions and emotional relationships	Noticing that you are becoming annoyed at your friend, and being able to take a deep breath, count to 10, and then respond calmly

EI IN SUBJECTIVE EXPERIENCES AND INCLINATIONS. The tests for this facet of EI require test-takers to rate themselves subjectively regarding relevant characteristics, such as their degree of assertiveness, empathy, tolerance for stress, and optimism (Bar-On et al., 2000). Because there is no right or wrong answer, these tests are often referred to as "subjective tests."

EVALUATING EI. In evaluating EI, the first question you might ask is whether it is distinct from IQ and measures of personality characteristics. A meta-analysis revealed that the objective measures (of the first facet of EI, the four branches) are positively correlated with *g*, but this correlation is not large—accounting for only about 10% of the differences in performance. In contrast, the subjective measures are almost entirely distinct from *g*. However, the subjective measures are correlated with some measures of personality, whereas the objective measures are barely correlated with personality measures (Dawda & Hart, 2000; Van Rooy et al., 2005b).

Another question you might ask about EI is whether the tests are valid—do they predict relevant sorts of behavior? Researchers have reported that measures of EI do in fact successfully predict relevant behavior (Bar-On & Parker, 2000; Ciarrochi et al., 2001; Joseph & Newman, 2010; Matthews et al., 2002; Roberts et al., 2001). For example, people who can more accurately read variations in other people's moods tend to be better adjusted socially (Engelberg & Sjöberg, 2004).

In addition, you might ask whether measures of EI have revealed interesting and important aspects of psychology that were not revealed by other types of measures. Such findings are being reported. For example, researchers report that women tend to score higher than men on some dimensions of EI (Carrothers et al., 2000; Van Rooy et al., 2005a), particularly those that relate to social skills (Petrides & Furnham, 2000). Nevertheless, men may (falsely) believe that they have higher EI than women do (Petrides & Furnham, 2000). In addition, members of minority groups tend to score higher than Whites, and older people tend to score higher than college students (Van Rooy et al., 2005a).

In short, this is an exciting and promising area of research, but it is still in its infancy. Researchers are just beginning to chart the utility and limits of EI for understanding human cognition and behavior.

Multiple Intelligences: More Than One Way to Shine? Some researchers have rejected the three-tier hierarchy idea, and instead argued that people possess different forms of intelligence—with no single form being more important than the others. Most of these forms of intelligence are not assessed by traditional intelligence tests. Although controversial, these alternative "multiple intelligence" perspectives have proven attractive to many, particularly to those who work in education. Let's briefly consider the two most influential of these theories.

GARDNER'S THEORY OF MULTIPLE INTELLIGENCES: SOMETHING FOR EVERYONE. Howard Gardner (1983/1993b, 1995, 1999) developed the **theory of multiple intelligences**, which holds that there are at least eight distinct forms of intelligence, with possibly a ninth form, as summarized in Table 5. **Simulate**

Theory of multiple intelligences Gardner's theory of (at least) eight distinct forms of intelligence, each of which can vary for a given individual.

Simulate Gardner's Theory of Intelligence on **mypsychlab.com**

TABLE 5 Gardner's Multiple Intelligences

Form of Intelligence	Definition	Examples of Professions in Which the Form Is Important
Linguistic	The ability to use language well	Journalism, law
Spatial	The ability to reason well about spatial relations	Architecture, surgery
Musical	The ability to compose and understand music	Audio engineering, music
Logical-Mathematical	The ability to manipulate abstract symbols	Science, computer programming
Bodily-Kinesthetic	The ability to plan and understand sequences of movements	Dance, athletics
Intrapersonal	The ability to understand yourself	Ministry
Interpersonal	The ability to understand other people and social interactions	Politics, teaching
Naturalist	The ability to observe aspects of the natural environment carefully	Forest conservation
Existential (tentative; Gardner, 1999)	The ability to address "the big questions" about existence	Philosophy professor

Linguistic intelligence is the ability to use language well, as relied on, for example, by journalists and lawyers.

Source: PhotoEdit Inc.

The best support for Gardner's theory comes from the very findings and phenomena that inspired it in the first place. Specifically, Gardner initially sought to identify brain systems associated with different individual forms of intelligence (such as spatial intelligence or musical intelligence). These brain systems are involved in "intelligence" in the sense that they play key roles in different kinds of reasoning, problem solving or learning. He further reasoned that if brain damage can disrupt some abilities while leaving others intact, this is evidence that the abilities arise from distinct brain systems. And in fact, brain damage often results in the loss of a certain ability while leaving other diverse types of abilities relatively intact. For example, language can be disrupted but the patient can still sing, or vice versa; mathematical ability can be disrupted but the patient can still speak, or vice versa; social skills can be disrupted while ordinary reasoning is unimpaired, or vice versa. Gardner considered each type of ability to reflect a distinct form of intelligence.

Gardner also considered other kinds of data when formulating his theory. He noted, for example, that although everybody learns their first language in a few years, very few people master complex mathematics so easily. If two abilities develop at different rates during childhood, he reasoned, they probably rely on different underlying processes. He also observed that some abilities, such as music and mathematics, can be extraordinarily well developed in child prodigies, whereas these same children perform at average levels in other areas. This coexistence of the extraordinary and the ordinary, Gardner believes, suggests that some intellectual capacities, such as those related to music and mathematics, are psychologically distinct from others.

According to Gardner, various combinations of forms of intelligence are needed to succeed in different professions; to be a novelist, for example, you need linguistic, intrapersonal, and interpersonal intelligence—but you don't need bodily-kinesthetic intelligence. Each person can be characterized by a *profile of intelligences*, which indicates a person's relative strengths and weaknesses regarding the various forms of intelligence (Connell et al., 2003; Walters & Gardner, 1985).

As appealing as Gardner's theory of multiple intelligences is to many, however, it has not been embraced by most researchers who study intelligence. One significant problem is that neither Gardner nor anyone else has devised rigorous ways to measure all of the separate intelligences, which makes the theory difficult to test scientifically (Hunt, 2001). Another problem is perhaps even more fundamental: Some researchers question whether the word *intelligence* is appropriate for the capacities he identifies; many of Gardner's proposed types, they say, have more to do with talents and skills than with intelligence as most of us understand the concept—and that to label those talents and skills as "intelligence" doesn't merely widen the concept of intelligence, it redefines it.

Spatial intelligence is the ability to reason well about spatial relations, as relied on, for example, by architects and surgeons

Source: Tetra Images\Alamy Images Royalty Free

STERNBERG'S ANALYTIC, PRACTICAL, AND CREATIVE INTELLIGENCES. Robert Sternberg (1985, 1988b, 2009) has also developed a theory of multiple intelligences, which he calls the *triarchic theory of successful intelligence*. According to this theory, there are three forms of intelligence: *analytic*, *practical*, and *creative*.

1. *Analytic intelligence* is the ability to learn to write clearly, do math, and understand literature. This sort of intelligence is critical for academic performance. Einstein had a high level of analytic intelligence.

2. *Practical intelligence* is the ability to do such things as fix a car or sew on a button, and it sometimes relies on learned responses and skills that guide our actions without our being aware of them; "street smarts" are a form of practical intelligence. Einstein was notoriously low in such intelligence.

3. *Creative intelligence* is the ability to formulate novel solutions to problems. Einstein was extraordinarily gifted in this respect—but only with regard to physics.

How do these three types of intelligence relate to IQ? According to Sternberg and his colleagues, IQ is a measure of only one of the three sorts of intelligence, namely analytic intelligence. They further claim that practical intelligence is largely distinct from analytic intelligence, and that measures of practical intelligence are better predictors of how well someone will do on the job than are standard measures of IQ (Sternberg & Wagner, 1993; Sternberg et al., 1993, 2001). But these claims have proven highly controversial: Other researchers have found that IQ predicts on-the-job performance better than do measures of practical intelligence (Kuncel et al., 2004).

In addition, although creative intelligence is largely distinct from IQ, people do need a certain level of IQ to be able to find creative solutions to problems or to create novel products that have specific uses (Guilford, 1967; Runco & Albert, 1986; Sternberg, 1985).

Finally, some researchers have objected to various aspects of Sternberg's theory. For one, as we noted when discussing Gardner's theory, critics have questioned whether Sternberg is treating talents and skills as "intelligence"—which redefines the concept of intelligence. In addition, some experts argue that research findings (even Sternberg's own findings) provide only weak support, if any, for his theory (Brody, 2003a, 2003b; Gottfredson, 2003a, 2003b).

Table 6 summarizes six prominent views about the nature of intelligence.

TABLE 6 **The Nature of Intelligence: Six Views**

Theorist	Key Ideas
Spearman (1927)	• g (generalized ability, contributes to all intellectual activities) • s (specialized abilities, such as spelling or distinguishing among tones) • IQ mostly reflects g.
Thurstone and Thurstone (1941)	• Seven primary mental abilities, such as verbal comprehension and spatial visualization • No g
Cattell (1971) and Horn (1985, 1986, 1989)	• Fluid intelligence (producing novel solutions to problems, such as by using burnt match heads to write) • Crystallized intelligence (using knowledge to guide reasoning)
Carroll (1993)	• Three-stratum theory • g at the top, 8 broad abilities (including fluid and crystallized intelligences) in the middle tier, and 69 specific abilities at the bottom
Gardner (1983/1993b, 1999)	• Multiple types of intelligence (at least eight) • Based on a wide variety of types of data (such as effects of brain damage, and areas in which child prodigies excel)
Sternberg (1985, 1988b, 2009)	• Three types of intelligence (analytic, practical, and creative)

Smart Genes, Smart Environment: A Two-Way Street

Gardner was undoubtedly correct in assuming that intelligence must be related—in one way or another—to the way the brain functions; it is the brain, after all—not the kidney or the big toe—that underlies reasoning, problem solving, and learning. But there's no reason to think that intelligence *must* be related to the genes. Could the genetic deck of cards that Einstein was dealt by his parents have given him a certain level of g and high levels of some specific abilities but not others? Or were his g and specific abilities mostly (or entirely) a result of his particular experiences? Or did his intelligence grow out of interactions between genetics and the environment?

Genetic Effects: How Important Are Genes for Intelligence? All theories and characterizations of intelligence acknowledge that it has many facets. Thus, we would not expect intelligence to be determined by a single gene, or even a small number of genes. And, in fact, studies (for instance, Fisher et al., 1999) have shown that multiple genes contribute to intelligence and do so in different ways. For example, a portion of DNA has been found to be associated with one type of spatial ability (Berman & Noble, 1995) but not with *g* (Petrill, Plomin, et al., 1997), and two different genes have been shown to predict nonverbal aspects (but not verbal aspects) of IQ (Tsai et al., 2002, 2004). Moreover, although researchers have been able to associate particular genes with some specific aspects of IQ, researchers have had trouble identifying individual genes that are related to *g* (Hill et al., 1999, 2002; Plomin & Spinath, 2004).

SHARED GENES VERSUS SHARED ENVIRONMENT: WHAT PREDICTS IQ?   Many scholars, biographers, and novelists have noted that intelligence seems to run in families—but they have also noted that this tendency is by no means universal. Einstein, for example, was not descended from geniuses, and his own children did not inherit his intellectual gifts. How can we begin to sort out the relative contributions to intelligence of genes and the environment? How strong is the genetic influence?

One way that researchers have tried to sort out the effects of genes versus environment is through *adoption studies.* In these studies, IQ scores of adopted children are compared to those of their adoptive and their biological relatives. The results of such studies consistently show that an adopted child's IQ correlates more highly with the biological mother's IQ score than with the adoptive mother's IQ. Moreover, although the IQ scores of an adopted child and the biological children in a family are positively correlated, by the time the children grow up, virtually no correlation remains (Plomin, 1990; Plomin, Fulker, et al., 1997; Scarr & Weinberg, 1983).

In addition, particularly compelling findings come from studies in which tests were given to twins who were separated soon after birth and adopted into different families (Bouchard et al., 1990). Because these twins were reared in different homes, any similarities between them are thought to reflect their common genetics. Consistent with the view that genes contribute strongly to intelligence, these studies have shown that the IQs of adult identical twins (who have practically the same genes; Bruder et al., 2008) who were raised apart are more similar to each other than they are to the IQs of fraternal twins (who share only half their genes) or nontwin siblings raised together (Bouchard & McGue, 1981; Bouchard et al., 1990; Plomin, 1990). These findings provide clear evidence that genes affect IQ.

Other studies have been conducted to find out exactly how large a role genes play in determining IQ. These studies compare IQs of people with different numbers of genes in common and attempt to establish how well the number of common genes accounts for the similarities in IQ. The results clearly show that the more genes in common, the higher the correlations in IQ. Moreover, the difference in correlations between identical and fraternal twins is used to estimate the heritability of IQ; *heritability* indicates what proportion of the variability in a characteristic within a population is caused by inherited factors (Bell, 1977; Lush, 1937). The usual estimate of heritability for IQ is around .50, which means that about half the variation in IQ can be attributed to heredity—to genes (Chipuer et al., 1990; Loehlin, 1989). Note that heritability estimates have no bearing on how much of any individual's personal intelligence is the result of his or her genes; a heritability estimate refers to the proportion of variation within a population, not to the proportion of the characteristic that is inherited by an individual.

BRAIN SIMILARITIES, GENETICS, AND INTELLIGENCE.   Researchers have also studied the role of genes in determining which brain areas contribute the most to IQ (Thompson et al., 2001). For example, one group of researchers used MRI to scan the brains of identical twins and fraternal twins. They then compared the gray matter (which indicates cell bodies of neurons) in the two groups of twins, which allowed them to compute the heritability of gray matter in different portions of the brain. They found high heritability for the frontal lobes and the left temporal lobe (which plays a crucial role in language comprehension). To discover which areas were related specifically to IQ, the researchers then simply correlated the IQ scores with the amount of gray matter in different brain areas, and found that IQ was highly correlated with the amount of gray matter in the frontal lobes.

Thus, there is evidence that genes shapes the brain, and in so doing, affect IQ. The frontal lobes, in particular, appear to be the region of the brain with high heritability that plays a key role in IQ. This is interesting in part because the frontal lobes play a key role in working memory, and also are critical for inhibiting emotional responses and generally regulating much of the rest of the brain.

Environmental Effects: More Real Than Apparent? Without question, the environment affects intelligence as assessed by IQ tests (Kohn & Schooler, 1973; Neisser et al., 1996). In fact, some of the effects that have been attributed to the genes may reflect effects of the environment, such as the *prenatal environment*, the environment of the *adoptive household*, the *microenvironment*, and the *ability to select environments* in which to spend time—as we discuss in the following sections.

SHARED PRENATAL ENVIRONMENT: ON BEING WOMBMATES. The environment starts to affect humans even before birth, and aspects of the prenatal environment clearly affect later IQ (Devlin et al., 1997; Jacobs et al., 2001). For instance, the developing fetuses do well when the mother eats a balanced diet, takes vitamins, and doesn't drink, smoke, or take drugs; as children, they tend to have higher IQ scores. In contrast, the developing fetuses suffer when the mother has a poor diet, takes drugs or drinks alcohol, smokes, or experiences a great deal of stress; as children, they tend to have lower IQ scores.

Moreover, the prenatal environment can affect identical twins differently than fraternal twins—and thus the similarities between twins may reflect not just their genes, but also their early environment. Specifically, about two thirds of identical twins share the same placenta and amniotic sac in the uterus (Phelps et al., 1997; see Figure 11). At first glance, you might think that sharing the same placenta and amniotic sac would make the twins more similar, but the opposite turns out to be true: These twins compete for resources; one identical twin will be in the favored position and will obtain more of the nutrients—and whatever else is in the mother's blood—than the other. Thus, these identical twins have larger disparities in weight and length at birth than do fraternal twins, and their early environment may make them less similar than their genes might otherwise lead them to be.

FIGURE 11 Fraternal and Identical Twins

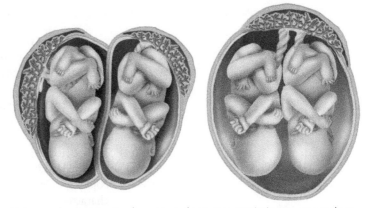

Twins can have separate placentas and separate amniotic sacs or can share a single placenta and sac; sharing results in greater competition for "environmental resources"—such as nutrients in the mother's blood—prior to birth. Virtually all fraternal twins are in separate sacs (left), whereas about two thirds of identical twins are in the same sac (right).

ADOPTIVE HOUSEHOLDS. Studies that examine IQs of twins separated at birth typically assume that the twins have been placed in very different environments, and thus any similarities reflect the contributions of genes. But it is not clear just how different the early environmental influences on twins raised in different homes really are. Families that seek to adopt a child share many characteristics, and these similarities are further enhanced by the fact that adoption agencies frown on placing children in disadvantaged conditions. Thus, separated twins are often placed in similar households. In fact, in a study that mathematically corrected for the small variations among adopting families, the estimated effects of environment on IQ was 57%, which is greater than the usual estimate for the effects of genes (Stoolmiller, 1999).

MICROENVIRONMENTS: HERE, THERE, EVERYWHERE. Estimates of heritability rest on the idea that the genes and environment are independent, but this may not in fact be the case: A person's genes can help shape aspects of his or her environment. The **microenvironment** is the environment that you create by your presence and behavior. The people around you *respond* to you, and if someone else were standing in your shoes, those same people would respond differently—in ways both obvious and subtle—to that person. People respond to the particular characteristics of whoever is filling the shoes. For example, a sluggish and overweight person will often be treated differently than a peppy and trim person. A person's physical appearance elicits particular responses from others; merely being there creates some aspects of a microenvironment. And many aspects of a person's appearance reflect their genes.

Microenvironment The environment created by a person's own presence, which depends partly on his or her appearance and behavior.

We create a part of our environments simply by the way we look and act, which influences how others treat us. This *microenvironment* is similar for twins, and their shared characteristics may, in part, reflect common aspects of their microenvironment, not the direct effects of the genes.

Source: Cleo Photography\PhotoEdit Inc.; Robert W. Ginn\PhotoEdit Inc.

Furthermore, how a person acts and responds to others also affects how people treat that individual. Take the case of a child who enjoys being read to: That child will reinforce adults for this activity—with attention, cuddling, smiles—which then leads the adults to buy or borrow more books. The child's behavior shapes the microenvironment created by his or her very presence. And a child's temperament may reflect his or her genes.

In short, genes may affect the microenvironment, which then may affect IQ. But is it the genes that are affecting IQ, via the environment, or the environment itself? Clearly, the genes and environment are not as distinct as they might at first appear to be.

SELECTING THE ENVIRONMENT.   People shape not just their microenvironments, but also other aspects of their environments (which are not a result of their physical or behavioral characteristics). In particular, people *select* aspects of the environment that appeal to them—perhaps because of personality characteristics that are partly regulated by genes. Hence, people who share the same personality characteristics may gravitate toward similar environments. For example, two children—from two different homes—who both enjoy reading may spend time in the school library, the town library, in a quiet corner for the schoolyard with a book at recess. Thus, their genes lead them to select environments, thereby allowing the environment to influence them (for example, by providing intellectual stimulation, which in turn could influence crystallized intelligence).

As people age, they are increasingly able to select their environments, and genetically influenced characteristics, such as temperament, lead people to select certain environments over others. For example, if you are temperamentally shy, you will not take a job in sales; if you are outgoing, you might enjoy managing a hotel. These observations explain why the effects of a *shared family environment* (aspects of the family setting that are present for all siblings in a household, such as the number of books in the house, Plomin, Fulker, et al., 1997) on IQ wear off by adulthood, and genetic influences become increasingly evident with age (McCartney et al., 1990; McGue et al., 1993; Plomin, 1990). As people grow older, the effects of genes and of the environment become increasingly tangled and increasingly difficult to sort out.

In short, genes may have some of their effects indirectly, by causing a person to affect or select the environment. If this is true, then changing the environment can change the individual—even if he or she has genes that ordinarily would affect the environment in a different way. For example, introducing a bookworm child to skiing could change her life (perhaps by making her more adventurous), even though she would never have sought out this activity on her own.

Group Differences in Intelligence

Researchers consistently report that some groups have lower average IQ scores than others; for example, in Israel, Jews of North African descent score about 15 points lower than Jews of European descent. But what do such findings mean?

Within-Group Versus Between-Group Differences   Most experts have concluded that about 50% of the variation in IQ can be accounted for by differences in genes, but this does not mean that differences in IQ scores between groups are largely genetic. The genetic contribution to intelligence *within* a given group cannot say anything about possible genetic differences *between* groups (Block, 1995; Lewontin, 1976a, 1976b; Plomin, 1988). To see why not, imagine that you have two orchards with the same kind of

FIGURE 12 Within-Group Differences Do Not Explain Between-Group Differences

The state of an organism is a result of interactions between genes and environment. The two groups of trees could have the same genes, but differences in the environment cause the genes to produce different characteristics. Differences among trees in the *same* environment may reflect differences in genes, but this says nothing about differences among trees in different environments.

apple trees. You make sure that each orchard receives exactly the same amounts of sunlight, fertilizer, water, and so on. If you succeed in making the environments identical, then any differences in the sizes of apples from the two orchards should arise from genetic differences among the trees. However, say the two orchards are not identical, that they have overall different conditions; in fact, say that one gets more sunshine and water than the other (see Figure 12). *Within* each orchard, differences in the sizes of the apples would reflect genetic differences (assuming that the environment is exactly the same throughout the orchard). But those differences say nothing about the differences *between* the orchards: the disadvantaged environment can override any genetic differences between the trees in the two orchards. Similarly, differences within one group cannot be used to explain differences between groups or within another group.

Researchers have shown that this analogy is not simply theoretical. For example, Eric Turkheimer and colleagues (2003) compared the IQs of identical and fraternal twins from both affluent and impoverished backgrounds. They found that genetics accounted for the bulk of the variations in IQs for the affluent twins (with a heritability of 72%), and that the shared environment accounted for little variation (15%—the remaining percentage of variation in IQ was accounted for by aspects of the environment that are not shared within a family). In striking contrast, the story was exactly the reverse for the impoverished twins: In this group, the shared environment accounted for the bulk of the variations in IQ (58%), and heritability accounted for little variation (10%). This result is clear evidence that the environment plays a more important role in affecting IQ scores for impoverished children than do the genes—which makes perfect sense if we think of each pair of twins as a mini-orchard, getting different amounts of sun and water.

Heritability estimates only tell us about the effects of genes in a *certain environment*; they say nothing about the possible effects of genes in *other environments* (Hirsch, 1971, 1997). Understanding why IQs vary for different people is analogous to understanding why an apple has its present size, which reflects the actions of genes *in a specific environment*. You have no way of knowing the range of possible sizes for that type of apple, should the tree have been raised in different circumstances.

Our genes determine the range within which the environment can mold us. For example, Japanese youth are typically much taller than their parents. Why? Same genes, but different environment (especially nutrition)—which leads the genes to operate differently. Similarly, genes for intelligence define a range of possible intelligences, and an individual's intelligence level embodies just one instance from the range of possibilities offered by the genes.

Source: Michael S. Yamashita\CORBIS- NY

Race Differences Charles Darwin long ago pointed out that the races meld seamlessly into one another, and the very concept of race is difficult to define. In fact, some researchers believe that the concept of race is a social invention, not a biological reality. Today, the idea that different races exist is highly controversial; this controversy is addressed, for example, in the pages of a special issue of the journal the *American Psychologist* (Anderson & Nickerson, 2005).

Nevertheless, many researchers have grouped people into different races, using various criteria to assign an individual's race (including simple self-identification). Such studies have documented differences among these groups—and such differences must be explained. Here we consider some key differences and explanations.

To begin, researchers have repeatedly shown that Asian Americans tend to score higher on IQ tests than do White Americans, who in turn tend to score higher than Black Americans (Neisser et al., 1996; Rushton, 1995; Suzuki & Valencia, 1997); Hispanic Americans tend to score between White and Black Americans. For decades, the relatively low IQ scores of Black Americans (which on average are 10 to 15 points lower than the scores of White Americans) have attracted attention, and controversy has flared over the claim that their scores, and their poorer achievement, are rooted in their genes (Herrnstein & Murray, 1994; Wicherts et al., 2009). But as we noted in the discussion of the size of apples from different orchards, we must consider various possible factors when we try to explain this difference (Block, 1995; Nisbett, 1996). Although we focus on White versus Black Americans in the following discussion, as has most of the research literature, keep in mind that the same issues apply to all differences among groups in IQ scores.

TEST BIAS? Some have argued that the disparity in test scores simply reflects the fact that the tests were designed for people from a White middle-class culture and thus are biased against Black Americans, who may have a different set of common experiences. This account specifically proposes that *test bias* exists, which invalidates the test; **test bias** consists of features of test items or test design that lead a particular group to perform well or poorly. Such test bias could apply to the verbal comprehension subtests of the IQ test, but what about the nonverbal subtests? The nonverbal subtests do not rely on language, and are supposed to be much less influenced by culture than are the verbal comprehension subtests. Nevertheless, the race difference in IQ scores is present even here. So a simple "biased testing" account is probably not the whole explanation for the observed differences among races (Glutting et al., 2000; Neisser et al., 1996; Sackett et al., 2001).

TEST ANXIETY? As you no doubt know from experience, taking a test of any kind, whether an achievement test (such as the SAT) or a midterm exam or an IQ test, can be anxiety provoking—and such anxiety can disrupt performance. Test stress may produce distinct physical symptoms, such as a speeded-up heart rate and sweaty palms. And as you feel literally "put to the test," your thinking may become clouded by a variety of distracting thoughts. Thus, factors unrelated to intelligence may affect IQ scores and other test scores. And it is possible that people with different backgrounds are more or less comfortable taking various sorts of tests (Serpell, 1979).

BAD ENVIRONMENTS? Others have argued that the observed IQ difference between White and Black Americans is caused by environmental differences. Black Americans typically make less money than do Whites, and children from families with less financial means are more likely to have poorer diets and may live in areas that have greater environmental hazards. Thus, financial factors could result in environmental differences that lead poorer people to score lower: Some orchards get less sun and water than others, and thus the trees tend to bear smaller fruit (Flynn, 1999b).

INFERIOR SCHOOLING? Another possibility is that Black Americans tend to have inferior schooling. In one study, researchers found that Black and White children have the same levels of intelligence when they begin kindergarten (provided that certain variables are controlled, such as age, birth weight, and number of children's books in the home). However, after 2 years of school, Blacks score notably worse than do Whites (Fryer & Levitt, 2004). The researchers considered a number of possible explanations for this

Test bias Features of test items or test design that lead a particular group to perform well or poorly and that thus invalidate the test.

finding, but only one received any support: Blacks tend to go to lower quality schools than do Whites—probably at least in part because Black children tend to live in less affluent school districts (because their parents earn less money than do Whites, as noted earlier).

The role of inferior schools might help to explain Lynn's (1998) report that the difference between Black and White intelligence scores had not changed over the years 1972–1996. Lynn assessed intelligence by looking at scores on a 10-item vocabulary test, and Blacks consistently fared worse than Whites. However, other researchers showed that Blacks do just as well as Whites on vocabulary tests *provided that they had the opportunity to learn the words* (Fagan & Holland, 2002). These researchers argue that Blacks simply haven't had "equal opportunity" to learn many of the words that are typically on vocabulary tests—which is consistent with the claim that they tend to attend inferior schools.

Nevertheless, the quality of schools is probably not the whole story. For example, one study found that parents on welfare talk to their children less than working-class and professional parents do—and when welfare parents do talk to their children, they use a smaller vocabulary (Hart & Risley, 1995/2002). Most of the welfare parents in this study were Black.

However, as intriguing as these sorts of findings are, they cannot explain why Black children adopted into White families have lower IQ scores by the time they reach adolescence than do their White siblings (Scarr & Weinberg, 1983). These Black and White children attended the same schools, and so schooling alone—or family environment alone—cannot explain the difference in their scores.

EFFECTS OF THE MICROENVIRONMENT?   Another explanation for the difference in IQ between Blacks and Whites focuses on the possible role of the microenvironment. Black Americans have darker skin, which may elicit behaviors from the White majority that are the psychological equivalent of blocking the sun and providing rocky soil in our orchards analogy. Support for this account comes from a study that examined what happens in a society in which the majority did not respond this way: Eyferth (1961) studied the IQs of German children who were fathered by White or Black American servicemen right after World War II. If the Black American fathers had lower IQs than the White fathers, which is not known but is likely given the group averages, and if this difference were a result of genes, then the children of the Black soldiers should have had a lower average IQ. But they didn't; both groups of children had the same average IQs. At that time, there were very few Blacks in Germany, and the majority Whites may not have had negative stereotypes about Blacks. Thus, the children may not have experienced negative environmental influences because of their racial background.

Finally, whatever the explanation of the observed group differences in IQ scores may turn out to be, it is crucial to realize that the distributions of scores between races overlap; plenty of Black Americans have higher IQs than plenty of Whites. Group differences do not necessarily apply to any particular individual.

Sex Differences Group differences in intelligence are often considered only in the context of race differences, but another possible group difference would have even larger consequences: Sex differences would affect fully half the population. Although some findings may suggest very small sex differences in IQ (Dai & Lynn, 1994; Held et al., 1993; Lynn & Irwing, 2004), these effects are not always found (Aluja-Fabregat et al., 2000; Jensen, 1998). Instead, researchers typically find that females, on average, are better at some specialized abilities than are males, on average, and vice versa (McGillicuddy-De Lisi & De Lisi, 2002). In general, females tend to be better than males at verbal reasoning (such as is required in the verbal comprehension subtests of the WAIS-IV), whereas males tend to be better than females at spatial reasoning (for example, in "mental rotation," discussed earlier in this chapter, and perceptual reasoning subtests on the WAIS-IV). Such differences have been found in at least 30 countries (Beller & Gafni, 1996; Halpern, 1992, 2000; Vogel, 1996).

Numerous accounts have been offered for these sex differences, and we briefly consider the major ones—*evolution, biology, health,* and *sociological factors*—in the following sections.

EVOLUTIONARY ACCOUNTS.   Some theorists have drawn on evolutionary theory to explain sex differences in spatial ability (D. M. Buss, 1995; Eals & Silverman, 1994;

Geary, 1996). The men, in this view, were out hunting, which required the ability to navigate and recall where the home cave was, whereas the women stayed home, picking berries, weaving baskets, and tending children. If so, then men who had better spatial ability would have been more successful, and presumably had more children who inherited the relevant genes.

This theory is interesting, but we really don't know much about what our distant male and female ancestors actually did—and even if these role descriptions are accurate, it isn't clear that women engaged in fewer spatial tasks: gathering berries requires remembering where they are likely to grow and how to return home, and weaving baskets certainly requires spatial processing (Halpern, 1997). Moreover, this theory is very difficult to test.

BIOLOGICAL FACTORS. At least some of the sex differences in cognitive abilities appear to arise from the effects of sex hormones (Fitch & Bimonte, 2002; Hines, 2004; Kimura, 1994). For example, one study examined women who were about to have a sex-change operation to obtain the sexual characteristics of men. As part of the procedure, the women received massive doses of male hormones, specifically testosterone. Within 3 months of this treatment, these people's spatial abilities increased and verbal abilities decreased (Van Goozen et al., 1995). Other researchers have found that a woman's spatial abilities shift during the course of her monthly cycle, as the balance of hormones changes (Hampson, 1990; Hampson & Kimura, 1988; Hausmann et al., 2000). Similarly, researchers have found that the level of male hormones affects spatial abilities in men. For instance, elderly men have low levels of male hormones, and testosterone supplements can boost their scores on spatial tests (Janowsky et al., 1994).

However, these relationships between hormone levels and behavior are not always found (Halari et al., 2005; Liben et al., 2002; Wolf et al., 2000), and the effects observed probably depend on a variety of other currently unknown factors.

HEALTH DIFFERENCES. Some researchers argue that systematic differences in men's and women's health account for at least some of the observed sex differences in cognitive abilities. For example, men tend to exercise more often than do women, and women tend to have more depressive symptoms than do men (Jorm et al., 2004). When health factors were controlled statistically, male's superior performance on certain cognitive tasks (such as being able to recite a memorized list of digits backwards) disappeared—and the female superior performance on other tasks (such as recalling a list of words) actually became even greater. As the researchers put it, "better health and health habits in males can account for their better performance on some tests, but such factors cannot account for better female performance on other tests" (Jorm et al., 2004; p. 16). However, health differences have not been shown to account for sex differences in spatial abilities.

Participating in activities that utilize spatial abilities means that the neural systems that underlie those activities are exercised. Spatial abilities can be improved by having children play certain video games, with boys and girls improving the same amount (Subrahmanyam & Greenfield, 1994). However, sex differences in spatial abilities are evident even in early childhood, and so are unlikely to be totally the result of learning (Reinisch & Sanders, 1992; Robinson et al., 1996).

Source: Getty Images Inc. RF

SOCIOLOGICAL FACTORS. At least part of the sex differences may arise from how boys and girls are expected to behave in our society. Boys and girls are encouraged to take part in "sex appropriate" activities (Lytton & Romney, 1991). This is important in part because if you do not perform activities that utilize spatial abilities, those abilities do not develop (Baenninger & Newcombe, 1989). And traditionally, girls have not been encouraged to participate in as many activities that require spatial skills, such as climbing trees and playing ball, as have boys—and hence would not develop spatial skills as well as do boys.

In addition, differences in how boys and girls are treated may affect their self-concepts and motivation (Wigfield et al., 2002), which in turn can amplify sex differences in cognitive abilities if these factors lead boys and girls to engage in different sorts of activities.

Finally, keep in mind that many females are better than many males at spatial reasoning, and many males are better than many females at verbal reasoning. Here, too, differences in the group averages say nothing about differences among particular individuals.

LOOKING AT LEVELS Stereotype Threat

Source: PhotoEdit Inc.

Researchers Claude Steele and Joshua Aronson (1995) conducted a study to investigate the possible effects of negative racial stereotypes on the test performance of Black Americans. They asked Black and White American college students to take a test that included the most difficult items from the verbal portion of the Graduate Record Examination (GRE), a test similar to the SAT, but used for admission to graduate school. The researchers tested two groups (both of which included Blacks and Whites): In one group, participants were told that the test they were about to take assesses intellectual ability; in the other group, participants were told simply that the test was for a study conducted by the laboratory. In the group that was told that the test was simply a laboratory experiment, Blacks and Whites performed comparably—but in the group that was told that the test assessed intelligence, Black students did much worse than Whites.

In another study, Steele and Aronson (1995) asked half the participants of each race to list their race immediately before taking the test and half simply to take the test—without listing their race. The test was always described as part of a laboratory study, not a test of intelligence. Blacks and Whites performed the same when they did not list their races, but the simple act of being asked to list race drastically reduced the Black students' scores.

How can we explain these findings? According to Steele (1997), asking Blacks about race activates information stored in memory about negative stereotypes of members of their race, such as that Blacks are not intelligent. If people believe that a negative stereotype addresses characteristics that are important to them, then the mere possibility that others will see them as conforming to that stereotype is threatening—even if they do not believe the stereotype or that they themselves have those characteristics. Steele terms this phenomenon **stereotype threat**. ((•⎯Listen

These sorts of findings have been replicated by many others (Croizet & Claire, 1998; Keller & Dauenheimer, 2003; Mayer & Hanges, 2003; Smith & White, 2002) and have been shown to apply not only to race but also to many other characteristics. For example, corresponding effects have been found with respect to gender (women perform worse on math tests when the negative stereotype about female math ability is activated; Cadinu et al., 2003; O'Brien & Crandall, 2003; Schmader, 2002), old age (older people have poorer memories after the negative stereotype about older adults' memory is invoked; Hess et al., 2003), homosexuality (gay men have greater anxiety when interacting with preschoolers after the negative stereotype is activated; Bosson et al., 2004), and even athletic ability (activating the stereotype that Whites have poorer "natural athletic ability" than Blacks led Whites to practice less before a sports test; Stone, 2002).

These studies dramatically illustrate interactions of events at the levels of the brain, the person, and the group. At the level of the brain, when you are threatened, a number of neurotransmitters (including dopamine and norepinephrine) are released; these neurotransmitters play crucial roles in the stress response—the fight-or-flight response. However, what may be a good response in an emergency is not good for taking a test: when confronted by an emergency, you want to act quickly and decisively, and not be lost in thought. But when taking a test, you need to be able to think things through, and don't want to act impulsively. Unfortunately, biological substances that facilitate the systems involved in the fight-or-flight response also disrupt the operation of the parts of the frontal lobes involved in working memory (Arnsten, 1998)—and working memory is crucial for reasoning, problem solving, and making plans. In fact, acute stress leads to the release of a substance called *protein kinase C*, which also disrupts working memory—and may cause a person to become distractible and impulsive, and to have impaired judgment (Birnbaum et al., 2004; Tan et al., 2004). And researchers have found clear evidence of such a stress response when participants took a nonverbal intelligence test while experiencing stereotype threat (Croizet et al., 2004), and have found evidence that stereotype threat does, in fact, disrupt working memory (Schmader & Johns, 2003).

((•⎯**Listen** to Stereotype Threat on **mypsychlab.com**

Stereotype threat Threat that occurs when people believe that a negative stereotype addresses characteristics important to them, and that others will see them as conforming to that stereotype.

At the level of the person, the effects of stereotype threat depend on the particular beliefs and sense of identity that a person holds. Stereotype threat disrupts performance more severely if a person strongly identifies with the negatively stereotyped group and thus feels more strongly threatened (Marx et al., 2005; McFarland et al., 2003; Ployhart et al., 2003; Schmader, 2002). Moreover, the effect is larger if a person feels that the stereotyped ability is important (Cadinu et al., 2003) or feels stigmatized by the stereotype (Brown & Pinel, 2003). However, events at the level of the person also can reduce the effects of stereotype threat; for example, stereotype threat is less disruptive for people who use humor to cope with their anxiety (Ford et al., 2004).

At the level of the group, social interactions can both promote and minimize the effects of stereotype threat. On the one hand, such interactions both implant stereotypes in the first place and also activate stored stereotypes. On the other hand, a social interaction can alleviate the effects of stereotype threat. For example, in one study, Aronson and colleagues (2002) report that coaching Black students (which is a social interaction) to see intelligence as "a malleable rather than fixed capacity" helped them to earn higher grades than students in control groups who were not led to adopt this perspective.

As usual, events at the different levels interact: A social invention—stereotypes about groups—can become part of an individual's knowledge (level of the person). And that knowledge in turn can be activated by social situations. When activated, the knowledge produces events in the brain (as well as in the body—pounding heart, sweaty palms, and so on), which in turn disrupt performance. And the disrupted performance can then reinforce the stereotypes. By the same token, events at the level of the group (such as coaching) can alter beliefs at the level of the person, which in turn can undermine stereotypes and thereby break this negative cycle. In fact, interactions among events at the various levels appear to be responsible for whether the effect occurs at all (Davies et al., 2005; Major & O'Brien, 2005; Ryan & Ryan, 2005); indeed, researchers do not always find that activating a negative stereotype disrupts performance on relevant tasks (Cullen et al., 2004; McKay et al., 2002; Stricker & Ward, 2004).

> **THINK like a PSYCHOLOGIST** Can you think of ways in which making all high school students take an IQ test would be potentially harmful? Potentially helpful?

Diversity in Intelligence

Einstein is often regarded as *the* example of genius, largely based on his astonishing creativity—his ability to think "outside the box" and see things in a new light. This aspect of his intelligence made him so unusual, so extreme. In this section, we consider the extreme levels of intelligence, high and low. We also consider the bases of perhaps the highest form of intelligence, creativity.

Mental Retardation: People with Special Needs
For want of a better definition, people with an IQ score of 70 or lower (that is, who fall more than two standard deviations below the mean; see Figure 10) have traditionally been considered to have **mental retardation** (also referred to as *intellectual disability*). The American Association for Mental Retardation (1992) specifies two additional criteria:

1. "significant limitations" in two or more everyday abilities, such as communication, self-care, and self-direction; and,
2. the presence of the condition since childhood.

Retardation does not imply that someone cannot learn at all. People with mild mental retardation can learn to function independently, and behavioral techniques that use explicit shaping and reinforcement can allow even people with severe retardation to master some tasks.

Although estimates vary widely, the number of Americans with mental retardation falls somewhere in the range of 4 million (Larson et al., 2001) to 7 million people (Fryers, 1993). Mental retardation affects about 100 times more people than does total blindness (Batshaw & Perret, 1992); one out of every 10 families in the United States is directly affected by mental retardation (American Association for Mental Retardation, 1992). The good news is that mild mental retardation appears to be on the decline (Howard, 2001).

Mental retardation The condition characterized by an IQ of 70 or less and significant limitations in at least two aspects of everyday life since childhood; also referred to as *intellectual disability*.

Mental retardation results when the brain fails to develop properly, which can happen in the womb or during childhood. Although hundreds of causes have now been identified, the causes of about one third of all cases are still mysteries. However, it is clear that both genetic and environmental factors can lead to retardation, as discussed in the following sections.

GENETIC INFLUENCES: WHEN GOOD GENES GO BAD. Genetics underlie many forms of mental retardation. The most common type of mental retardation (occurring in about 1 in 1,000 births) is known as **Down syndrome**, first described by British physician J. Langdon Down in 1866. Down children have an average IQ of 55, but the degree of retardation varies widely—and may disrupt everyday activities less severely than other forms of mental retardation (Chapman & Hesketh, 2000). The most frequent form of Down syndrome is caused by a genetic problem but is not inherited—the problem is that an extra chromosome (number 21) is created during conception. This genetic abnormality apparently prevents neurons from developing properly, so that action potentials (neural firings) do not operate normally (Galdzicki et al., 2001). Down syndrome is more likely to occur in births to older parents. Females are born with all the eggs (ova) they will ever have. As women get older, their eggs get older too, and so children born to older mothers are more likely to have chromosomal abnormalities. In addition, as men age, they too are more likely to pass on chromosomal abnormalities to their children, causing Down syndrome (Fisch et al., 2003).

Another relatively common cause of mental retardation is *fragile X syndrome*, so named because a particular genetic mutation makes the X chromosome likely to break when examined under laboratory conditions. The X chromosome is the female sex chromosome; the Y chromosome is the male sex chromosome. Females have two X chromosomes, whereas males have one X and one Y chromosome. Because females have a "backup" X chromosome, which may not have the mutation, Fragile X syndrome is more common in males than females; Fragile X syndrome affects about 1 in 3600 males and 1 in 4000–6000 females.

Mutations do more than produce fragile X syndrome—in fact, mutations in over 280 separate genes have each been found to lead to mental retardation (Inlow & Restifo, 2004).

ENVIRONMENTAL INFLUENCES: BAD LUCK, BAD BEHAVIOR. Various characteristics of the fetus' and young child's environment can cause mental retardation. For one, if the mother drinks alcohol heavily during pregnancy, she changes the environment of the fetus and essentially poisons her developing child—and her child can be born with **fetal alcohol syndrome**. Part of this syndrome is mental retardation (Streissguth et al., 1989, 1999).

But alcohol is not the only environmental factor that can lead to mental retardation: if a pregnant woman has malnutrition, rubella, diabetes, HIV infection, is exposed to high doses of X rays, has any of a number of infections, or takes various drugs (such as cocaine), her child may be born with mental retardation. Physical malformations of the brain during pregnancy can also lead to mental retardation.

In addition, mental retardation can arise from a host of other hazards, some of which occur at or after birth. For example, mental retardation can occur if the birth is premature or unusually difficult and the infant's brain is injured. Low birth weight can also lead to retardation. Moreover, some childhood diseases, such as whooping cough, chicken pox, and measles, can sometimes cause brain damage, as can ingesting lead or mercury, or experiencing a blow to the head or almost drowning. In addition, poverty and cultural deprivation can lead to mental retardation—by malnutrition or leading people to live in unsanitary conditions or not to have adequate health care.

The good news is that in the last half century, vaccines and other medical treatments greatly reduced the incidence of mental retardation that arise from childhood diseases (Alexander, 1991; Croen et al., 2002). In addition, people whose retardation arises from environmental factors tend not to have children with mental retardation themselves.

Genetic and environmental factors that can lead to mental retardation are summarized in Table 7 on the next page.

The Gifted   The term **gifted** commonly refers to people who have IQs over 145 (which is three standard deviations above the mean for the WAIS-IV; see Figure 10; Robinson et al., 2000; Winner, 1997). It is not known how genes and the environment, including the environment in

Down syndrome A type of mental retardation that results from the creation of an extra chromosome during conception; it is a genetic problem but not inherited.

Fetal alcohol syndrome A condition that includes mental retardation and is caused by excessive drinking of alcohol by the mother during pregnancy.

Gifted People who have IQs at least three standard deviations above the mean (which is a score of 145 on the WAIS-IV).

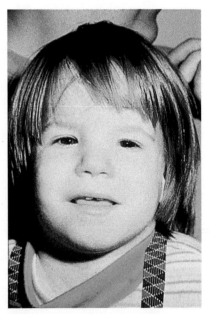

If a mother drinks alcohol heavily during pregnancy, her child can be born with fetal alcohol syndrome—one aspect of which is mental retardation and another aspect of which is the type of facial characteristics shown here.

Source: Reprinted with permission from Streissguth, A.P., Landesman-Dwyer, S., Martin, J.C., & Smith, D.W. (1980). Teratogenic effects of alcohol in humans and laboratory animals. *Science*, 209 (18): 353–362. © 1980 American Association for the Advancement of Science.

235

TABLE 7 Causes of Mental Retardation: Common Examples

Genetic conditions
- Down syndrome
- Fragile X syndrome

Problems during pregnancy
- Use of alcohol or drugs
- Malnutrition
- Rubella
- Exposure to X Rays
- Diabetes
- Infection of the mother during pregnancy
- Physical malformations of the brain
- HIV infection in the fetus

Problems at birth
- Prematurity
- Low birth weight

Problems after birth
- Childhood diseases such as whooping cough, chicken pox, and measles, which may lead to meningitis and encephalitis, which can in turn damage the brain
- Accidents such as a blow to the head or near drowning
- Lead and mercury poisoning

Poverty and cultural deprivation
- Malnutrition
- Inadequate medical care
- Environmental health hazards

Prodigies Children who demonstrate immense talent in a particular area, such as music or mathematics, but who may have only average abilities in other areas.

the womb, contribute to the condition. However, here's one intriguing hint: gifted boys tend to have lower testosterone levels than nongifted boys, whereas gifted girls may actually have higher amounts of testosterone than nongifted girls (Dohnanyiova et al., 2001; Ostatnikova et al., 2000, 2002). Such findings suggest that biological factors could predispose some people to become gifted—but this does not mean that biological factors directly cause people to become gifted. For example, perhaps lower testosterone inclines boys to avoid rough-and-tumble play and to spend more time reading instead—and this contributes to their intellectual development.

As expected from the finding that intelligence has a number of facets, children can be gifted in some domains while not being gifted in others (Winner, 2000a, 2000b). **Prodigies**, children with immense talent in a particular area, may have only average abilities in other areas; for example, mathematically gifted children often are not gifted in other domains (Benbow & Minor, 1990). One study found that over 95% of the gifted children they tested had sharply differing mathematical and verbal abilities (Achter et al., 1996).

The cognitive processes of gifted people may differ from those of people with average IQ scores in two ways:

1. *Efficient processing.* According to some researchers (such as Jackson & Butterfield, 1986), gifted children engage in the same kinds of processing as average children but simply do it more effectively. This theory is consistent with the fact that most gifted children grow up to be rather ordinary adults (Richert, 1997; Winner, 2000a, 2000b); they were ahead of the pack as children, but eventually most other people caught up with them.

2. *Different processes.* According to other researchers, the cognitive processes of gifted children are not simply more efficient, but are qualitatively different from those of other people; for example they may be able to intuit solutions to problems unusually well. As Ellen Winner (1997) notes, some gifted children "as young as three or four years of age have induced rules of algebra on their own (Winner, 1996), have memorized almost instantly entire musical scores (Feldman & Goldsmith, 1991), and have figured out on their own how to identify all prime numbers (Winner, 1996)" (p. 1071). Such accomplishments would be remarkable even for an adult.

It is possible that two sorts of gifted children exist; ones who are simply precocious and may later grow up to be ordinary adults, and ones who are like Albert Einstein—who have special gifts that distinguish them for life.

No matter what their source, intellectual gifts are sometimes bestowed with a price. Gifted children are at times socially awkward and may be treated as "geeks" and "nerds" (Silverman, 1993a, 1993b; Winner, 1996). In addition, they may tend to be solitary and introverted (Silverman, 1993b). Moreover, gifted children have twice the rate of emotional and social problems as nongifted children (Winner, 1997).

Finally, it's worth emphasizing that the gifted aren't the only ones who make extraordinary contributions to society. Many distinguished adults—Charles Darwin, for example—showed no signs of being gifted as children (Simonton, 1994). We noted earlier that IQ scores (on which the classification of "gifted" is based) do predict success in life, but they are just one of many factors that predict success. For example, many eminent adults had the help of able mentors at critical phases of their lives (Bloom, 1985; Gardner, 1993a). Having an apprentice relationship with an appropriate mentor can make a huge difference. That is one reason why graduate education in the sciences in the United States is based on apprenticeship: Students in Ph.D. programs in the sciences learn at the elbows of their supervisors, not simply from reading books or listening to lectures.

Creative Smarts: Not Just Inspiration Creativity lies at the heart of many forms of intelligence. **Creativity** is the ability to produce something original of high quality or to devise an effective new way to solve a problem. Creativity can be applied to practical problems (such as raising money), intellectual tasks (such as making new connections among various topics when writing a term paper), or artistic work (such as writing a work of fiction). Creativity necessarily involves the ability to recognize and develop a novel approach, the ability to consider a problem from multiple angles and to change points of view repeatedly, and the ability to develop a simple idea in different ways.

Creativity involves an interplay between two types of thinking, *divergent* and *convergent* (Guilford, 1967; Mumford, 2001).

1. *Divergent thinking.* This sort of thinking occurs when you come at a problem from a number of different angles, exploring a variety of approaches to a solution; your goal is to generate as many relevant ideas as possible, free from concerns about practicalities (Mednick, 1962; Reese et al., 2001). Divergent thinking leads you to fan out, to produce a lush jungle of ideas.

2. *Convergent thinking.* Following divergent thinking, you need to use convergent thinking—to prune down the possibilities, refining at least one to the point where it can be used. In the process of focusing down to a solution, convergent thinking can itself produce new ideas.

In some cases, you may cycle between the two modes, repeatedly throwing out ideas and then refining them, until you converge on a viable one.

What Makes a Person Creative? Creative people may tend to think differently than the rest of us. Creative people keep options open, do not make snap decisions about the likely outcome of an effort, and are good at seeing a problem from a new vantage point (Amabile, 1983, 1998). Similarly, when Guilford used factor analysis to discover which underlying abilities are tapped by various tests of creativity, he found that flexibility and the ability to reorganize information were key (similar conclusions were drawn by Aguilar-Alonso [1996] and Eysenck [1995]). Moreover, creative people may often think in terms of analogies (Martindale, 1989, 2001).

Creative people are different from others in more than their preferred ways of thinking; they also tend to have high intelligence, have wide interests, don't necessarily go along with traditional ways of thinking, have high self-esteem, and like to work hard (Martindale, 1989, 2001). Perhaps most importantly, creative people are often highly motivated and persistent, driven to create (Sulloway, 1996). Theresa Amabile (2001) emphasizes the role of hard work and strong motivation in creativity, and Kenneth Heilman and colleagues (2003) underscore the importance of knowledge about the relevant domain and having the skills to be able to work with that knowledge.

Another, less desirable, characteristic has sometimes been attributed to highly creative people: mental instability. It has long been believed that certain mental disorders promote creativity (Kraepelin, 1921). In particular, some have argued that bipolar (manic-depressive) disorder promotes creativity. This disorder typically includes shifts between very "high" manic moods and very "low" depressed ones, and some researchers claim that a "loosening" of thought occurs during the manic phase—which would then enhance creativity (Goodwin & Jamison, 1990; Hershman & Lieb, 1988, 1998; Jamison, 1989; Jamison et al., 1980). If so, the manic phase would spur creativity by increasing the number of possible solutions a person can formulate during the divergent thinking component of the creative process (Barrantes-Vidal, 2004). Isaac Newton, Charles Dickens, and Kurt Cobain apparently suffered from this disorder, and Andreasen (1987) found that almost half the visiting faculty in the University of Iowa Writers' Workshop, an intensive course for creative writers, had experienced it. Similar findings have been reported for other writers, particularly poets (Jamison, 1989).

Prodigies are children who have a gift in one particular area. For example, a child may be an extraordinary violinist but not so outstanding in other areas.

Source: Getty Images/Time Life Pictures

How many uses can you think of for a brick? Divergent thinking might lead you to consider bricks as doorstops, supports for bookshelves, or bookends.

Source: DK Stock

Creativity The ability to produce something original of high quality or to devise an effective new way to solve a problem.

237

In some ways, creativity is like pitching in baseball. Cy Young was the pitcher with the greatest number of wins in baseball history. The pitcher with the most losses? Cy Young. People who produce large numbers of creative works are also likely to produce large numbers of mundane works.

Source: AP Wide World Photos

✔●─Study and Review on
mypsychlab.com

However, others have claimed that mental illness is independent of creativity. Research supporting these claims shows that the quality of a creative person's work tends to be constant over their productive years; in years when a large number of particularly good works are produced, a correspondingly large number of inferior works are also produced (Dennis, 1966; Simonton, 1984, 1997). Hence, being in a manic state may simply increase the number of works produced, both good and bad.

Finally, researchers are beginning to study and theorize about the neural bases of creativity (Dietrich, 2004; Heilman et al., 2003; Ione, 2003; Zeki, 2002), but we do not yet know how the brains of creative people are special. However, we do know that differences in creativity are not strongly related to genetic differences, if at all—in sharp contrast to differences in IQ. Furthermore, and also in contrast to IQ, shared aspects of the home (such as exposure to cultural resources, home libraries, or parents' mechanical or artistic hobbies) strongly affect creativity (Canter, 1973; Nichols, 1978; Simonton, 1988).

LOOKING BACK

1. **What is IQ?** IQ (intelligence quotient) is a score on an intelligence test. IQ originally was a comparison of mental age to chronological age, but now IQ scores relate individual performance to a norm for the test. The most common tests are the Wechsler Adult Intelligence Scale (WAIS) and the Wechsler Intelligence Scale for Children (WISC). The scores are normed so that 100 is the mean, and each standard deviation is 15 points.

2. **Is intelligence a single characteristic or a complex set of characteristics?** Intelligence has many facets. Although intelligence probably involves, as Spearman theorized, a single general intellectual ability (symbolized as *g*), virtually all theorists agree that it also includes many specialized abilities. These abilities may be strong or weak, independently of *g*. Various theorists, however, disagree about the specific aspects of intelligence. Thurstone proposed that intelligence consists of seven primary mental abilities. Cattell and Horn theorized that instead of one general capacity, *g*, people possess two types of intelligence—crystallized and fluid. Carroll derived aspects of intelligence that are arranged in three levels, with *g* at the top, 8 broad abilities in the middle, and 69 specific abilities at the bottom. Gardner, in his theory of multiple intelligences, posits at least eight basic forms of intelligence ranging from linguistic, to logical-mathematical, to interpersonal. According to Sternberg, the different types of intelligence boil down to three: analytic, practical, and creative. Finally, emotional intelligence may affect the operation of all other types.

3. **How do environment and genetics contribute to intelligence?** In general, approximately 50% of the variability in IQ scores can be attributed to variations in genes. At least some of these effects may, in fact, reflect the way that the environment is regulating the genes or the way that genes in turn affect the environment (including by influencing appearance and temperament, which affect the microenvironment).

4. **How can we interpret group differences in IQ?** Although group differences definitely exist, it is impossible to sort out the relative contributions made by genes and the environment in creating such differences. Findings about the genetic contribution to within-group differences do not apply to between-group differences. In addition, all distributions of abilities within any group overlap those of other groups; for this reason, group differences cannot be applied to particular individuals.

5. **What are the extremes of intelligence, high and low?** Mental retardation is usually defined as having an IQ of 70 or less since childhood and having significant limitations in two or more everyday abilities. Researchers have identified hundreds of causes of mental retardation. Some types are caused by genetic abnormalities; others are caused by environmental events, such as childhood diseases. Gifted people are defined as those having high IQs, typically at least three standard deviations above the mean (which corresponds to an IQ of 145 on the WAIS-IV). It is not clear how the genes and environment interact to produce such high IQs. Finally, creative people are not born that way, but rather have learned certain cognitive strategies. Although creative people are typically highly motivated and driven to create, their creativity is not a by-product of mental instability.

LET'S REVIEW

((•─ Listen to an audio file of your chapter on **mypsychlab.com**

I. LANGUAGE: MORE THAN MEETS THE EAR

A. Both comprehension and production rely on four aspects of language: (1) phonology (proper speech sounds), (2) syntax (the internal structure of sentences, determined by grammatical rules that govern how different types of words can be combined), (3) semantics (meanings of words, phrases, and sentences), and (4) pragmatics (meaning that is indirect or implied).

B. Adults can learn semantics and pragmatics of a new language as well as children can, but unless people learn a second language early in life, they probably will never use it as well or as automatically as they do their first language.

II. MEANS OF THINKING: THE MENTAL TOOL KIT

A. When thinking, we use words and images as a way to keep track of thoughts, to store them effectively, and to make connections among ideas—much like making notations on a pad of paper. Language does not determine thought but may influence it in various ways.

B. Objects in visual mental images preserve many of the properties of actual objects, such as spatial extent and relative size; at least some of these properties may arise from characteristics of the brain areas that are used in both imagery and perception.

C. Thinking cannot rely solely on words or images: Both words and images are ambiguous, and thoughts are not. Moreover, if thoughts were based only on words, we would never have difficulty figuring out how to put our thoughts into words; if thoughts were based only on images, we would have trouble thinking about abstractions (such as truth and justice).

D. Thoughts arise from manipulations of concepts; a concept is the idea that underlies the meaning of a word or image.

E. Concepts are unambiguous and can be concrete (such as "bird") or abstract (such as "justice"). Some examples of a concept are better (more typical) than others.

F. Concepts are organized according to how specific or general they are.

III. SOLVING PROBLEMS AND REASONING: FROM MENTAL PROCESSES TO BEHAVIOR

A. If a problem is not specified appropriately from the outset, it will be difficult to solve.

B. People can solve problems by using algorithms (sets of steps that are guaranteed to produce the answer) and heuristics (short-cut, rule-of-thumb strategies that do not guarantee a correct answer). Analogies are a common heuristic that people use to solve problems.

C. Knowing about the obstacles to problem solving can help you to overcome them.

D. Reasoning involves both deduction (going from general premises to particular implied conclusions) and induction (going from particular instances to generalizations), as well as making decisions at pivotal points. Decision making requires you to evaluate possible outcomes and choose one alternative or course of action over the others.

E. People are not always logical; for example, we fall prey to biases, such as affirming the consequent and the confirmation bias.

F. We often rely on heuristics, such as the availability heuristic, when making decisions. Heuristics often lead us to the correct conclusion faster than we could get there with a step-by-step algorithm; however, they also sometimes lead to errors.

G. Although many people consider emotion a weakness when reasoning, emotion can in fact help us to develop useful hunches and intuitions. However, if emotion leads us to become agitated, it can disrupt reasoning.

IV. INTELLIGENCE: WHAT IS IT AND HOW DOES IT ARISE?

A. The most common measure of intelligence is the score on an intelligence test, called the intelligence quotient, or IQ. IQ scores are a composite of many different underlying abilities, and the same IQ score can arise from different mixtures of relative strengths and weaknesses.

B. The most common IQ tests are the Wechsler Adult Intelligence Scale (WAIS) and the Wechsler Intelligence Scale for Children (WISC).

C. When first devised, IQ was a measure of mental age compared to chronological age. Today, IQ scores are based on standardized norms for large samples, which are updated periodically so that the mean score on the WAIS or the WISC is always 100 and a standard deviation is 15.

D. Scores on IQ tests are positively correlated with achievement on the job and are correlated with many aspects of success in life, such as staying out of prison or having an enduring marriage.

E. There are many theories of intelligence, most of which posit a single overarching "general intelligence" (g) and a set of specific abilities. According to one theory, g may be broken down into fluid and crystallized intelligence.

F. Emotional intelligence is not assessed by standard IQ tests, but it may turn out to be important in daily life.

G. The theory of multiple intelligences posits a number of forms of intelligence. However, this theory has yet to be tested, and many researchers question whether all of the abilities are, in fact, forms of intelligence.

H. Although about 50% of the variability in scores on IQ tests can be explained in terms of genetic factors, this number is a population average and does not apply to individuals. In addition, variations in intelligence probably reflect an intimate dance between the genes and the environment.

I. Group differences in IQ have been well documented; it is impossible to sort out the relative contributions of genes and environment to such differences. Group differences may in part reflect the way in which individuals' characteristics create their microenvironments and influence the reactions of others to them.

J. All distributions of abilities within any group overlap those of other groups, and hence group differences have no applicability to particular individuals in a given group.

K. Immediate environmental effects—such as stereotype threat—can also influence how a person performs on an IQ test; when this happens, test scores are not valid indicators of ability.

L. Mental retardation (also called *intellectual disability*) is traditionally defined on the basis of overall IQ score *plus* significant difficulty with two or more everyday tasks, with both conditions existing since childhood. By this definition, someone with mental retardation cannot be gifted; giftedness is defined by a very high IQ score (typically at least three standard deviations above the mean, which is a score of 145 on the WAIS-IV).

M. Mental retardation can arise for many reasons, some genetic and some environmental. Not all of the genetic reasons reflect inherited defects; some reflect accidents during conception or environmental damage to genes.

N. Creativity leads to the production of original works of high quality or to innovative effective solutions to problems. Creative people have many characteristics, including the tendency to make loose associations and engage in divergent thinking. Creativity has a very low heritability and is strongly influenced by shared environment.

KEY TERMS

affirming the consequent
algorithm
availability heuristic
base-rate rule
basic level
category
concept
confirmation bias
creativity
crystallized intelligence
deductive reasoning
Down syndrome
emotional intelligence (EI)
factor analysis

fetal alcohol syndrome
fluid intelligence
functional fixedness
gifted
heuristic
inductive reasoning
intelligence
intelligence quotient (IQ)
language comprehension
language production
linguistic relativity hypothesis
logic
mental images

mental set
mentally retarded
microenvironment
morpheme
norming
phoneme
phonology
pragmatics
primary mental abilities
problem
problem solving
prodigies
prototype

reasoning
representation problem
representativeness heuristic
semantics
standardized sample
strategy
stereotype threat
syntax
test bias
theory of multiple intelligences
typicality
Wechsler Adult Intelligence Scale (WAIS)

PRACTICE TEST

✓•—[Study] and Review on mypsychlab.com

For each of the following items, choose the single best answer.

1. Sentences in any language contain an internal structure, an acceptable arrangement of words called
   a. syntax.
   b. phoneme.
   c. phonology.
   d. aphasia.

2. The smallest unit of meaning is
   a. a morpheme.
   b. a syntactic component.
   c. an aspect of pragmatics.
   d. found only in the English language.

3. Learning a second language as an adult leads you to use
   a. exactly the same brain areas used by your first language.
   b. the same brain areas as your first language if you learn the language by hearing it spoken.
   c. some areas involved in working memory that are not used by your first language
   d. completely different brain areas than those normally used by your first language.

4. What is wrong with the idea that thinking is just talking to yourself?
   a. Words are often ambiguous, but thoughts are not.
   b. If thoughts were already formed in language, expressing them in language should be easy.
   c. At least some animals can think, and yet they don't use language.
   d. All of the above statements identify problems with this idea.

5. Visual mental images have the perceptual property of
   a. spatial extent.
   b. limited field of view.
   c. limited resolution.
   d. all three of the above properties.

6. Visual mental images
   a. do not actually exist for most people.
   b. rely on most of the same parts of the brain that are used in visual perception.
   c. can be the only means by which we think, at least when we are thinking about objects and events we have actually seen.
   d. All of the above statements are true.

7. The basic level at which people name objects is
   a. the most typical example of a category of things.
   b. a collection of concepts that specify necessary and "optional" aspects of the particular situation.
   c. a level of specificity that is usually the most likely to be applied to an object.
   d. a grouping of objects in which the members are specific cases of a more general type.

8. You can improve your ability to solve problems if you
   a. represent the problem effectively.
   b. don't get locked into viewing your resources in only one way, which is a form of functional fixedness.
   c. don't get stuck with a certain mental set, a fixed way of viewing the kind of solution you seek, based on what has worked previously.
   d. All of the above describe ways that will help improve your ability to solve problems.

9. The reasoning error called affirming the consequent
   a. is rarely made by humans.
   b. occurs because of the assumption that if a result is present, a specific cause must also be present.
   c. occurs when people seek out information that will confirm a rule but do not seek information that might refute it.
   d. assumes that the more similar something is to a prototype stored in memory, the more likely it is that the entity belongs to the category of the prototype.

10. The intelligence quotient was originally computed by
    a. dividing mental age by chronological age and multiplying by 100.
    b. dividing chronological age by mental age and multiplying by 100.
    c. subtracting mental age from chronological age and multiplying by 100.
    d. subtracting chronological age from mental age and multiplying by 100.

11. The mean and standard deviation for the WAIS-IV IQ test are, respectively,
    a. 100 and 10.
    b. 110 and 15.
    c. 100 and 15.
    d. 100 and 12.

12. According to Raymond Cattell and John Horn, people possess
    a. one type of intelligence, g, for "general factor."
    b. two types of intelligence: crystallized and fluid.
    c. seven separate primary mental abilities.
    d. eight basic forms of intelligence.

13. Robert Sternberg proposed three types of intelligence. According to Sternberg's theory, which of the following statements is true?
    a. Analytic intelligence is what IQ tests measure.
    b. Measures of practical intelligence are worse predictors of how well someone will do on the job than are standard measures of IQ.
    c. Practical intelligence is largely the same as analytic intelligence.
    d. All of the above statements are true.

14. Intelligence
    a. is determined by a single gene.
    b. is affected by multiple genes; the heritability of IQ is around .50.
    c. is clearly not affected by genes.
    d. is determined primarily by shared family environment.

15. What do researchers know about sex differences in intelligence?
    a. In general, males tend to be better than females at tasks that require spatial reasoning.
    b. In general, females tend to be better than males at tasks that require spatial reasoning.
    c. In general, males tend to be better than females at tasks that require verbal reasoning.
    d. In general, females tend to be better than females at tasks that require all types of reasoning.

Answers: 1. a 2. a 3. c 4. d 5. d 6. b 7. c 8. d 9. b 10. a 11. c 12. b 13. a 14. b 15. a

> In disputes between management and workers, he sided with the workers and started using fasting as a political tool. He used this tool repeatedly in his career, refusing to eat until a social end was achieved.

EMOTION AND MOTIVATION

FEELING AND STRIVING

The people called him "Mahatma," or "great soul." As an adult, Mohandas Karamchand Gandhi was described as follows: "Quiet dark eyes. A small, weak man, with a thin face and big ears. Wearing a white cap as headgear, clothed in rough white material, barefoot. He feeds on rice and fruits, drinks only water, sleeps on the floor, rests little, works all the time. Nothing about him strikes more than an expression of great patience and great love. . . . Such is the man who has incited to revolt three hundred million men, has shaken the British Empire and launched the most powerful movement in the politics of mankind for almost two thousand years".

Source: Markovitz, The un-Gandhian Gandhi: The Life and afterlife of the Mahatma. London: Anthem Press 2003, p. 18

This physically slight man cast a giant shadow across the 20th century, not only changing the face of India but also inspiring Martin Luther King Jr. and the American civil rights movement.

In spite of his saintly reputation, Gandhi was a man of flesh and blood, possessed of raw emotions and strong motivations, just like the rest of us. The personal history of Gandhi provides us with a case study of the nature of emotion and its role in motivation.

By all reports, Gandhi was a shy, ordinary child who was perhaps a little more stubborn than his peers, but this tendency was noticeable only through the keen lens of hindsight. As a young man, he decided to become a lawyer, following in the footsteps of his father and grandfather before him. At age 19, he went to England to study law, over the objections of his mother. She relented when he promised not to touch alcohol, women, or meat, but other members of his caste (hereditary social class) were not so flexible: They viewed crossing the ocean as a form of "contamination" and excommunicated him for this act. Knowing this consequence in advance did not discourage him, so determined was he to reach his goal.

When he first arrived in England, Gandhi bent over backward to adapt. He adopted English dress and manners and even studied ballroom dancing and took French lessons so that he could have the same social skills as his British classmates. He soon realized the folly of trying to pretend to be something he was not, and he began to return to his roots in the Hindu faith—which provided spiritual support for him in this foreign land.

Gandhi returned to India after obtaining his law degree but was a miserable failure as a lawyer in Bombay. When rising to argue his first case in court, he was overcome with anxiety and froze, tongue-tied and speechless. Following this humiliating experience, he was happy to accept a job in South Africa, helping a group of Indian merchants with a lawsuit. This was near the end of the 19th century, a century before apartheid ended and when the social climate in South Africa was hostile to Indians, who were treated as second-class citizens—or, worse, resident aliens. Gandhi's emotional and intellectual reactions to the insults—and even beatings—he experienced gave rise to an unusually strong sense of social justice that was to stay with him the rest of his life.

Gandhi's fellow Indians living in South Africa asked him to stay and help them fight against discrimination. He agreed, and the shy lawyer gradually evolved into a charismatic leader. As part of this evolution, he abandoned Western clothes and began to dress as an Indian peasant. He reduced his needs and simplified his life, doing his own laundry, cleaning his own chamber pots (this was before flushing toilets were available), and even learning to be a midwife so that he could deliver his fourth (and last) son.

Gandhi organized the Indians living in South Africa and taught them to use nonviolent resistance to oppose oppressive new tax laws as well as a Supreme Court ruling that invalidated all Hindu and Muslim marriages. After he prevailed, he sent a gift to his main adversary, General Jan Christian Smuts—a pair of sandals he had made while in jail for leading demonstrations and civil actions. Twenty-five years later, the general wrote, "I have worn these sandals for many a summer since then even though I may feel that I am not worthy to stand in the shoes of so great a man" (Nanda, 1987).

After 20 years in South Africa, Gandhi returned to India in 1915, when it was still a colony ruled by Great Britain. He became the first person in history to lead all of India (all previous leaders had been regional), spending much time with peasants and focusing on teaching them to overcome the many fears that accompany powerlessness and poverty. In disputes between management and workers, he sided with the workers and started using fasting as a political tool. He used this tool repeatedly in his career, refusing to eat until a social end was achieved (such as the resolution of a dispute or an end to violence in a particular clash).

What emotions did Gandhi feel when confronted with the social realities of his day? How did his emotions and motivations affect him? Emotions and motivations, for Ghandi and for the rest of us, have in common the power to move us. (The root of both English words—*emotion* and *motivation*—comes from the Latin *movere*, "to move.") Our motivations and emotions are intimately interwoven: On the one hand, emotions lead to specific motivations, such as when love leads us to hug someone; on the other hand, our motivations change our emotions, such as when we finish work! on an overdue project and guilt is replaced with pride or relief. Our emotions and motivations are not always obvious; they may confuse us or compel us to do things that surprise us.

In this chapter, we consider first the nature of emotion and how it affects our behavior. This analysis leads us to consider motivation—what makes us act. Finally, we focus on two of the most important motivations: hunger and sex.

▨ ▨ ▨

EMOTION: I FEEL, THEREFORE I AM

Soon after his return to India, Gandhi called for nonviolent demonstrations to protest repressive laws. But the disobedience soon spun out of control, sparking arson and violence—and the British reacted by killing many Indian protestors. Gandhi admitted that he had made a "Himalayan blunder" (referring to the highest mountains in the world) because he had initiated a social movement before he understood how to lead it. The peasants had trouble grasping Gandhi's ideas about nonviolence, and they questioned whether he was serious about using nonviolent demonstrations to force societal change—or whether he was talking about this strategy just to confuse the British. Gandhi's views on nonviolent protest stemmed from his spiritual convictions; he believed that if people could learn to control and overcome their "internal violence" (their destructive impulses, thoughts, and goals), "external" violence would not occur. But most people did not have his degree of self-control, and their inflamed emotions sometimes led them to behave violently.

What, specifically, is an emotion? An **emotion** has four components: (1) a positive or negative subjective experience, (2) bodily arousal, (3) the activation of specific mental processes and stored information, and (4) characteristic behavior. Emotions not only help guide us to approach some things and withdraw from others, but also provide visible cues that help other people know key aspects of our thoughts and desires.

Emotion A psychological state with four components: (1) a positive or negative subjective experience, (2) bodily arousal, (3) the activation of specific mental processes and stored information, and (4) characteristic overt behavior.

1. What are the different emotions?
2. What causes emotion?
3. How do we express and regulate our emotions?
4. How do we perceive emotions in others?

Types of Emotion: What Can You Feel?

We humans have an enormous range of emotions. Think of the emotions you have experienced in your life. Fear? Guilt? Guilt tinged with fear? Love? Love mixed with joy? Some researchers who have studied emotions have argued that the brain produces many gradations and types of these experienced reactions by combining sets of simple emotions (Plutchik & Kellerman, 1980). Just as all colors can be produced by mixtures of three primary colors, researchers have claimed that all emotions, even the most complex, arise from combinations of a simple set of emotions we all possess, which, like primary colors on an artist's palette, can be blended, experienced, and presented to the world.

Basic Emotions Charles Darwin (1872/1965), for one, believed that many emotional behaviors—the outward acts that arise from our emotions—are inborn. He noticed that people of many races and cultures appear to use very similar facial expressions to signal similar emotional states. Moreover, blind people show those same expressions, even if they have never had the chance to observe the way others look when they have particular emotional reactions. Are we all born with a built-in set of emotions? If so, these emotions would be an essential part of what we call "human nature," serving as a defining characteristic of what it means to be human in every time and culture. ◉ Watch

Paul Ekman and Wallace Friesen (1971) described the results of studies that they conducted to investigate whether all humans perceive the same set of fundamental emotions (see Figure 1). Specifically, they asked whether people who had never seen White faces could identify the emotions underlying facial expressions in photographs of such faces. The researchers visited a New Guinea tribe, the Fore, who had rarely, if ever, seen White people in person or in images. Even so, when shown photos of White people, the Fore could easily identify expressions of happiness, anger, sadness, disgust, fear, and surprise. The one difficulty they had was in distinguishing the expression of fear from that of surprise, perhaps because the two are very similar emotions. Also, it is possible that in Fore culture these two emotions often go together: Many surprises in the jungle, such as the unexpected wild boar, are life threatening, and hence such surprises would induce fear.

Ekman (1984) concluded that surprise, happiness, anger, fear, disgust, and sadness are **basic emotions**, emotions that are innate and shared by all humans. Other theorists have offered slightly different lists of basic emotions. For example, Tomkins (1962) proposed surprise, interest, joy, rage, fear, disgust, shame, and anguish. Some of the apparent disagreements may be simply a matter of word choice; *joy* and *happiness*, for example, may label the same emotion (LeDoux, 1996) or versions of it (perhaps joy is more intense than happiness or comes and goes more quickly). Panksepp (1998, 2005) offers a set of "emotional systems," which guide behavior (such as sexuality-lust, nurturance-care, and joy-play). And other specific emotions, such as pride, have been proposed for the list of basic emotions (Tracy & Robins, 2004).

But, putting aside the specific list of basic emotions, the very idea that there is a fixed set of basic emotions has proven controversial. One challenge rests on the finding that some of these basic emotions are not simple. For example, Paul Rozin and colleagues (1994) distinguish among three types of disgust, each of which is signaled by a different facial expression: A nose-wrinkling expression of disgust is associated with bad smells (and, sometimes, bad tastes), an open mouth with the tongue hanging down is associated with foods perceived as disgusting (the "yech" reaction), and a raised upper lip accompanies *feelings* of disgust, such as those associated with death and filth. Similarly, positive emotions can be divided at least into five types (amusement, desire, happiness, love, and interest; Keltner & Shiota, 2003).

◉ Watch the Video on Basic Emotions on mypsychlab.com

THINK like a PSYCHOLOGIST To get a better feel for your emotions and whether certain emotions are more common for you, keep track of your emotions for 3 days with the *DO IT!* log at www.mypsychlab.com; select the *Emotion and Motivation* chapter and click on the *DO IT!* folder.

Basic emotion An innate emotion that is shared by all humans.

FIGURE 1 Recognition of Basic Emotions

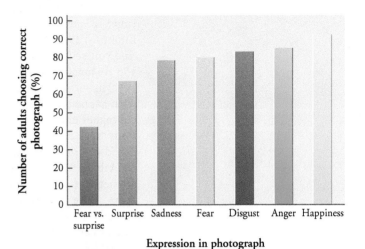

Ekman and Friesen told the participants a story and then presented three pictures of faces displaying different emotions. The participants chose the face that showed the appropriate emotion for the story.

Participants could distinguish all of the emotions, except they tended to confuse fear and surprise. (Note that chance performance would be 33.3%.)

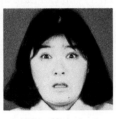

Happiness   Sadness   Fear   Anger   Surprise   Disgust

The six basic emotions that Ekman and others identified and studied. In the Ekman and Friesen (1971) study, however, all the faces were Caucasian.

Source: From Ekman & Friesen, "Constants across cultures in the face and emotion." From *Journal of Personality and Social Psychology.* Copyright © 1971, American Psychological Association. Reprinted with permission.

Another challenge to the claim that all humans have the same basic emotions focuses on the role of culture in shaping emotion. Some researchers have argued that although certain emotions are basic, in the sense that they have a consistent "signature" across cultures, other emotions are shaped by the social practices and norms of a culture (Keltner & Haidt, 2001). In fact, the ability to perceive basic emotions in others turns out not to be entirely innate; learning also plays a role, as documented by a meta-analysis of studies on the perception of emotion (Elfenbein & Ambady, 2002). The researchers looked carefully at the effects of many variables, and two of their findings are particularly illuminating:

1. They found that although people can recognize basic emotions of members of other racial groups better than would occur by chance alone, they generally recognize emotions of people from their own group better than those of people from other groups.

2. However, this effect depended on whether their own group was in the majority: Some members of a minority group may actually recognize emotions on faces of members of the majority group better than they do on faces of their own group. What matters is how often you see certain kinds of faces—the more often you see them, the easier it is to recognize emotions in them. This finding is a clear testament to the role of learning.

Thus, even with "basic" emotions, the contribution of the genes (which produce inborn tendencies) cannot be considered in isolation from events at the levels of the person (such as learning) and the group (such as whether one is a member of a specific culture).

Separate but Equal Emotions If positive and negative emotions are "opposites," then experiencing one type of emotion should mean that you can't experience the "opposite" emotion at the same time; however, research suggests that positive and negative emotions are not really opposites. Instead, positive and negative emotions appear to be independent; that is, positive and negative emotions can occur at the same time, in many combinations (Bradburn, 1969; Cacioppo et al., 1997; Diener & Emmons, 1984; Goldstein & Strube, 1994; Larsen et al., 2001). For example, you can find yourself enjoying a luscious dessert and simultaneously feeling disgusted because you are being such a glutton.

The notion that positive and negative emotions are independent is supported by what happens in the brain when people experience emotions. Richard Davidson and his colleagues have provided evidence that separate brain systems underlie *approach* emotions (such as love and happiness) and *withdrawal* emotions (such as fear and disgust; Davidson, 1992a, 1992b, 1993, 1998, 2002; Davidson et al., 2000a; Lang, 1995; Solomon & Corbit, 1974). In general, approach emotions are positive, and withdrawal emotions are negative. For example, EEG recordings show that the left frontal lobe tends to be more active than the right when people have approach emotions, whereas the right frontal lobe tends to be more active when people have withdrawal emotions (Simon-Thomas et al., 2005). Moreover, people who normally show more activation in the left frontal lobe tend to have a rosier outlook on life than do people who show more activation in the right frontal lobe. And neuroimaging has shown that clinically depressed patients have lower activity in the left frontal lobe than do people who are not depressed (Davidson, 1993, 1994, 1998; Davidson et al., 1999). However, if both the left and the right frontal lobes are active, you can have approach and withdrawal emotions simultaneously—such as might occur when you are disgusted with yourself for enjoying that dessert so much.

FIGURE 2 Four Theories of Emotion

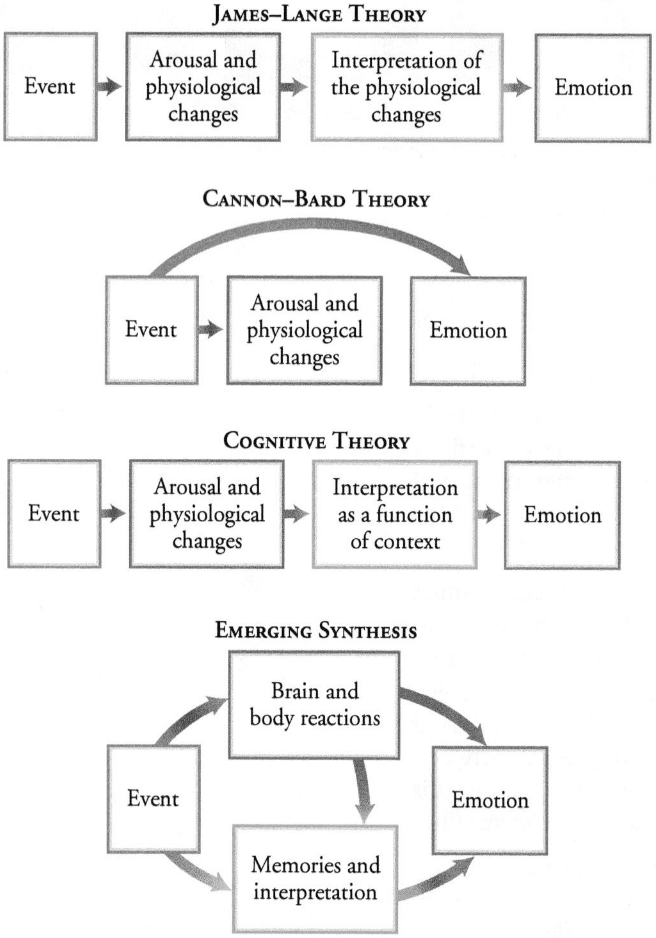

Theories of emotion differ in how they view the relationship between bodily reactions and interpretations of events.

Source: From Lester A. Lefton, *Psychology,* 7/e. Published by Allyn and Bacon, Boston, MA. © 2000 by Pearson Education. Reprinted by permission of the publisher.

What Causes Emotions?

Distinguishing among different types of emotions is a first step toward understanding them, but we also need to know what functions emotions serve and why particular emotions arise when they do. Consider Gandhi: He was not a placid person. He wrote cutting critiques of Western civilization, disparaging its values and creations (for example, he detested the scale of modern cities and the ugliness of many of their buildings). And although he used nonviolent methods, he nonetheless felt angry at times. Why did he feel angry? What possible good would such an emotion do him? The major theories of emotion provide insight into these questions.

Intuitively, it may seem as if a person has an emotion, and that emotion triggers him or her to behave in a certain way; for instance, the British soldiers would shoot at Indian demonstrators, expecting that the sight and sound of guns firing would trigger fear, and make them run away. However, researchers have shown this the commonsense idea about the relation between emotion and behavior is incorrect. But if this view is not right, then what is? Each of the following theories has succeeded in capturing at least some aspects of how emotions actually operate.

James–Lange Theory More than 100 years ago, William James (1884) argued that we feel emotions not before but *after* our bodies react (see Figure 2). For example, if you had been one of those Indian demonstrators and a soldier raised his gun the moment he saw you coming, James would say that you would first run and then feel afraid, not the other way around. The emotion of fear, according to James, arises because you sense your bodily state as you are fleeing. You are aroused, and you sense your heart speeding up, your breathing increasing, and other signs that your sympathetic nervous system is being activated. You then feel these bodily responses as fear. According to his theory, different emotions arise from different sets of bodily reactions, and that's why emotions feel different (Reisenzein et al., 1995). Carl Lange (1887), a Danish physiologist, independently developed a similar theory, and thus the theory has come to be called the *James–Lange theory* (Lang, 1994).

SUPPORT FOR THE JAMES-LANGE THEORY.   As predicted by this theory, *some* emotions are accompanied by particular patterns of heart rate, body temperature, sweating, and other reactions (Craig, 2004; B. H. Friedman, 2009; Prinz, 2008). For example, when you feel angry, your heart rate increases, and so does the temperature of your skin; and when you feel afraid, your heart rate increases, but your skin temperature decreases (Levenson et al., 1990). In addition, different bodily reactions occur in response to challenge versus threat (Quigley et al., 2002; Tomaka et al., 1997) and with positive versus negative emotions (Cacioppo et al., 2000). ⊙➤ Simulate

Moreover, so far we have treated "bodily responses" as related to arousal, such as changes in heart rate, sweat, and breathing—but other bodily changes may contribute to emotion. Specifically, changes in the muscles in your face may play a role in how you feel! At least 20 muscles in your face change your facial expressions (Fridlund, 1994), and your brain receives feedback from these muscles when you move them. According to the **facial feedback hypothesis**, you feel emotions in part because of the way your muscles are positioned in your face (Izard, 1971; Tomkins, 1962).

And in fact, researchers have found that "putting on a happy face" is more than a phrase from an old song; it can actually make you feel happier. Following up on other studies (Duclos et al., 1989; Laird, 1974, 1984), Ekman and colleagues (Ekman, 1992; Ekman et al., 1990) tested this idea by leading participants to shift parts of their faces until they held specific expressions—for example, lifting the corners of the mouth until they formed a smile and other facial expressions associated with happiness. The participants maintained these facial poses while they rated their mood. If their faces were posed in a positive expression, they rated their mood more positively than if their faces were posed in a negative expression. Clearly, feedback from the positions of the muscles affected the emotions they experienced.

PROBLEMS WITH THE JAMES–LANGE THEORY.   Aside from the general results based on the facial feedback hypothesis, the James-Lange theory has not generally fared well in the face of research results. In fact, even the facial feedback hypothesis has received mixed results. For example, putting on a happy face does not put our brains into exactly the same state as when we are genuinely happy (Ekman & Davidson, 1993). Thus, although facial feedback may affect emotions, our smiles, frowns, and glowers are not the only causes of our emotional experiences. Similarly, although some bodily differences may accompany different emotions, there is no evidence that a specific and unique bodily state underlies each of our emotions. Bodily responses contribute to some of our emotions, but differences in bodily states are not enough to explain the range of our emotions—many emotions arise from similar bodily states (Cacioppo et al., 2000).

In addition, perhaps the strongest evidence against the idea that emotions arise when people experience their own bodily states is the finding that people who have spinal cord injuries so severe that they receive no sensations from their bodies report having emotions (Bermond et al., 1991). However, it is possible that even though these patients experience emotions, they do so differently than do people with intact spinal cords. For example, one such patient described in this way what it felt like when a lit cigarette fell onto his bed: "I could have burned up right there, but the funny thing is, I didn't get all shook up about it. I just didn't feel afraid at all, like you would suppose." Speaking about another common emotion, he said, "Sometimes I act angry when I see some injustice. I yell and cuss and raise hell, because if you don't do it sometimes, I've learned people will take advantage of you, but it doesn't have the heat to it that it used to. It's a mental kind of anger" (Hohman, 1966, pp. 150–151). These quotations suggest that this man's emotions were largely rational evaluations rather than feelings in reaction to events. Nevertheless, he did have emotions—which should not occur if emotions arise solely from bodily states.

Cannon–Bard Theory   Walter Cannon (1927) claimed that the James–Lange theory focused too much on noticing bodily signals, such as heart and breathing rates. He argued against the James–Lange theory, noting that it takes many seconds for the body to become

Stick a pencil sideways (not point first) in your mouth so that as you bite down on it, the corners of your lips turn up. Simply making this motion will actually make you feel happier (Strack et al., 1988). For more dramatic results, try to make a big smile, raising your cheeks.

Source: © Author John Saul Biting Pencil / CORBIS All Rights Reserved

⊙➤ **Simulate the Experiment on Transfer of Emotions on mypsychlab.com**

Facial feedback hypothesis The idea that emotions arise partly as a result of the positioning of facial muscles.

aroused, and yet emotions are usually experienced before arousal happens. To explain how we can feel emotion before the body reacts, Cannon proposed that the brain itself is all that matters. You perceive the threat of being shot, and the results of that perception trigger the body's resources for fleeing or fighting *at the same time* that they generate an emotion. According to the *Cannon–Bard theory* (see Figure 2), formulated by Cannon and another physiologist, Philip Bard, bodily arousal and the experience of emotion arise at the same time, and neither causes the other.

SUPPORT FOR THE CANNON–BARD THEORY.   Fear is one of the best-studied emotions (LeDoux, 1996), and just as the Cannon–Bard theory predicts, the bodily reactions are triggered at the same time as the conscious experience of emotion (Öhman, 2002). Researchers have found that the amygdala plays a crucial role in producing the reactions you have when you are afraid. It sends signals to other brain areas and structures, such as the hypothalamus, that cause your heart to speed up, your muscles to freeze (as Gandhi's apparently did when he rose to plead his first case in court), and all the other autonomic reactions associated with fear.

PROBLEMS WITH THE CANNON–BARD THEORY.   Nevertheless, this theory has not generally fared well in the face of research results. For example, meta-analyses of neuroimaging data have shown that, in general, each emotion does not arise from a unique pattern of activation in the brain; rather, different emotions are associated with overlapping patterns of brain activation (Murphy et al., 2003; Phan et al., 2002, 2004; Wager et al., 2003).

In addition, according to the Cannon–Bard theory, our bodies are aroused similarly in different situations; according to this view, arousal is arousal—it occurs if you are mugged and also if you win the lottery. But, as noted above, *some* emotions (but not all) are accompanied by particular patterns of heart rate, body temperature, sweating, and other reactions (Levenson et al., 1990). And, as we noted as support for the James–Lange theory, different bodily reactions occur in response both to challenge versus threat (Quigley et al., 2002; Tomaka et al., 1997) and with positive versus negative emotions (Cacioppo et al., 2000).

Cognitive Theory An additional concern with the Cannon–Bard theory is that it does not explain how particular brain states arise; for example, why is being on a roller coaster exhilarating for one person but terrifying for another? *Cognitive theory* addresses such issues. Cognitive theory holds that an emotion arises when you interpret the situation—and the "situation" can include your bodily state in the context of everything that surrounds it. For example, the act of running and the accompanying arousal can equally well be associated with the emotion of joy (as you rush to embrace someone you love), fear (as you flee a pursuing soldier), or excitement (as you join the crowd on the field to celebrate a football victory). According to this theory, you don't react to a stimulus and then feel an emotion after the reaction (as the James–Lange theory holds), and you don't have separate bodily and emotional reactions (as the Cannon–Bard theory has it). Rather, you interpret your reactions and the general situation together—and this interpretation forms the basis of emotions. Richard Lazarus, Stanley Schachter, and Magda Arnold were pioneers in developing this view.

In general, the cognitive theory of emotion rests on the idea that, as Lazarus puts it, emotion "cannot be understood solely in terms of what happens in the person or in the brain, but grows out of ongoing transactions with the environment that are evaluated" (Lazarus, 1984, p. 124). This statement clearly embodies our by-now-familiar approach of looking at events at the levels of brain, person, and group.

SUPPORT FOR COGNITIVE THEORY.   Consider a classic experiment that convincingly documented the role of cognitive interpretation in emotion. This experiment, reported by Stanley Schachter and Jerome Singer (1962), is illustrated in Figure 3. The participants, who believed that they would be taking part in a test of vision, received an injection of what they were told was a vitamin supplement. The injection was really a shot of adrenaline (also called epinephrine), which causes general arousal. Each participant then waited in a room before beginning the "vision test." Also waiting in the room was a *confederate*— that is, someone who was posing as a participant but was, in fact, cooperating with the investigators to set up the conditions of the experiment. The experiment consisted of having the confederate act in different ways during the "waiting period" and recording the effects of his behavior on the participant. In one condition, the confederate exhibited almost manic-like behavior, playing with a hula hoop, tossing paper airplanes, and generally acting silly. In another condition, the confederate was sullen and irritable; he tried to make the participant angry, and eventually stormed out of the room. The participants who had waited with the silly confederate reported that they felt happy, whereas the participants who had waited with the irritable confederate reported that they felt angry.

Here's the important point about the results: Although these participants had the same bodily arousal induced by the drug, they experienced this arousal very differently, depending on the context in which it occurred, and this difference apparently led them to attribute different explanations for the arousal. In contrast, when participants were told in advance about adrenaline and the fact that it causes arousal, they did *not* feel differently in the different contexts; it was only when they interpreted the arousal as arising from the context that their feelings differed. In addition, participants in a control group, who did not receive an injection, experienced no effects of context; what was important was the way context affected how the participants interpreted the arousal, not simply the presence of the context itself. (It is worth noting that this study took place more than 50 years ago; giving participants drugs without their permission is now recognized to be unethical and impermissible.)

FIGURE 3 The Schachter–Singer Experiment

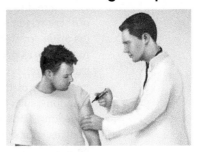

Participants received an adrenaline injection.

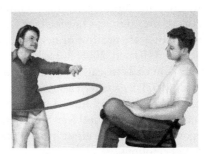

Confederates acted very differently while the participants waited.

The participants reacted very differently to the drug, depending on what the confederate was doing.

If, like the adrenaline-injected participants we just considered, you interpret signs of bodily arousal incorrectly, you would make a cognitive error called *misattribution of arousal*. The **misattribution of arousal** is the failure to interpret signs of bodily arousal correctly, which leads to the experience of emotions that ordinarily would not arise in that particular situation. For example, in one study, male participants were given false feedback about their own internal responses (Valins, 1966). They had been asked, while looking at slides of partially nude women, to listen to what they were told was their own heart beating. The heartbeats the men heard were, in fact, not their own; they were sometimes faster and sometimes slower than their actual heart rates. When the participants later were asked to rate the attractiveness of each woman, their ratings were based not just on what they saw but also on what they had heard: If they had heard a rapid heartbeat while looking at a particular picture, they rated the woman in that picture as more attractive.

PROBLEMS WITH COGNITIVE THEORY.   The main problem with cognitive theory is that not all emotions rely on cognitive interpretation. In particular, fear often operates as a kind of reflexive response, requiring no thought (LeDoux, 1996). As discussed in the following section, this observation led to a modification of cognitive theory, which also incorporates the aspects of the previous theories best supported by research.

The Emerging Synthesis   The study of emotion is particularly exciting today because researchers are formulating an overarching theory. Let's briefly consider two elements of the emerging view.

Misattribution of arousal The failure to interpret signs of bodily arousal correctly, which leads to the experience of emotions that ordinarily would not arise in the particular situation.

First, Joseph LeDoux (1996) modified the cognitive theory in an important way: he showed that different brain systems underlie different broad categories of emotions. Some of these systems operate as reflex pathways do, *independent* of thought or interpretation (as proposed by the Cannon–Bard theory), whereas others *depend* on thought and interpretation (as proposed by both the James–Lange theory and cognitive theory). Fear, for example, relies on activation of the amygdala, a small brain structure located at the front inside part of the temporal lobes, without need for cognitive interpretation. But other emotions, such as guilt, rely on cognitive interpretation and memories of previous similar situations. Thus, the emotions we feel at any moment arise from a mixture of (1) brain and body reactions (as the James–Lange theory stresses) and (2) interpretations and memories pertaining to the situation (as both the Cannon–Bard and the cognitive theories stress).

Second, other researchers are focusing on exactly how people interpret brain and bodily reactions. Some researchers claim that these reactions produce *core affect*, which consists of the "simplest raw feelings." These feelings only differ in two ways: the degree to which they are positive or negative and the degree to which they are strongly or weakly activated (Barrett, 2006; Russell, 2003). We then (unconsciously) *categorize* changes in core affect, much as we categorize ambiguous visual or auditory stimuli (Barrett, 2006; Barrett et al., 2007). By analogy, hearing firecrackers on July 4 wouldn't generally upset most of us, but hearing them on April 4 might lead us to categorize them as gunshots—which would indeed induce us to feel fear. Similarly, context and previous experience may lead us to categorize types of core affect in ways that fit the situation, leading us to feel and express different emotions.

To see why this new synthesis is useful, let's take a closer look at what has been learned about one key emotion in particular: fear.

Fear: The Amygdala and You Because it is so important for survival, many researchers have focused on understanding fear—and today it is one of the best-understood emotions. We have repeatedly referred to how fear arises and operates in the earlier discussion, and here we take a close look at what has been learned.

Fear arises from changes in the brain, in the autonomic nervous system, and in hormones. These events both produce the experience of being afraid and, at the same time, produce changes in behavior. The changes in behavior are easily assessed: When people are afraid, they tend to freeze (to be "paralyzed by fear") and they have an increased tendency to be startled, a tendency called *fear-potentiated startle* (Davis, 1992; Lang, 1995; Vrana et al., 1988). For example, as Indian demonstrators approached a line of armed soldiers, they probably became susceptible to being startled, so that they were more likely to be thrown off balance when the first gunshots rang out.

Researchers have discovered five important facts about fear from studying the brain systems that produce it:

1. *After you have learned to fear an object, fear can well up later as a kind of "emotional reflex," with no cognitive interpretation* (LeDoux, 1996). As noted, when you are afraid, your amygdalae (there are two, one in each cerebral hemisphere) send signals to other brain areas and structures (such as the hypothalamus), which in turn trigger your autonomic responses (such as speeding up your heart and making your muscles freeze). These responses are "automatic" in the sense that conscious awareness is not needed for a stimulus to trigger the amygdala into producing fear-related responses (Öhman, 2002).

2. *Once you learn to associate fear with an object or situation, you apparently will always do so.* Fear is a type of classically conditioned response where a previously neutral stimulus comes to elicit fear because that stimulus signals an aversive event. For instance, if you touch the hot part of a waffle iron when the "on" light is lit, you will soon learn to fear touching the hot part of waffle irons when that "on" light is illuminated. Such conditioned responses can be extinguished; *extinction* is the process by which a conditioned response comes to be eliminated because the stimulus no longer leads to the feared event. However, even after it has been extinguished, the neurons that were linked by the conditioned association still fire together. Thus, the *emotion* of fear is still associated with the stimulus, even though extinction has eliminated the

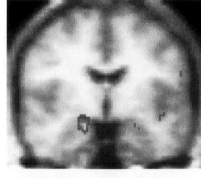

In an fMRI study, pictures of faces with angry expressions were shown so briefly to participants that they were not aware of having seen the expressions. Even so, their amygdalae responded to the angry expressions, as shown by the colored areas (Whalen et al., 1998).

Source: Whalen, P.J., et al., Masked presentations of emotional facial expressions modulate amygdala activity without explicit knowledge. *J. Neurosci.* 18:411–418. Used with permission.

behaviors associated with that emotion. Although you are not aware of the association, it is never fully lost (LeDoux, 1996).

3. *In spite of the fact that cognitive interpretation is not necessary to trigger a previously learned fear response, mental processes can alter how easily the fear response occurs.* For example, if you merely visualize yourself in a scary situation, you become susceptible to being startled (Cook et al., 1991; Lang et al., 1990; Vrana & Lang, 1990); the parts of the brain involved in mental imagery play a key role in "setting you up" to be easily startled. Moreover, you can acquire fear associations merely by watching someone else be conditioned to fear a specific stimulus (Olsson & Phelps, 2004)! For instance, if you see somebody else touch the hot part of a waffle iron when the "on" light is lit and then see that person jump back, howling with pain and sucking on his or her fingers, you will learn to fear touching the hot part of waffle irons when that "on" light is lit.

4. *The amygdala does not play a direct role in producing the emotional "feel" of fear.* By "feel" of fear, we mean how the emotion is experienced—rather than simply having the emotion. For instance, as noted earlier, people who have had spinal injuries make a distinction between whether they have the emotion of fear versus whether they have the experience of that emotion. Evidence that the amygdala is not directly involved in producing the emotion of fear comes from patients with damaged amygdalae, who report experiencing positive and negative emotions (such as fear) as often and as strongly as do people without this type of brain injury (Anderson & Phelps, 2002).

5. *In spite of the role of the amygdala in fear, neither it nor any other single brain area always gives rise to a particular emotion.* Researchers have shown that no one brain area produces any single emotion (Barrett, 2006; Barrett et al., 2007; Phan et al., 2002, 2004; Wager et al., 2003). For example, researchers have shown that the amygdala responds when we perceive or feel strong emotions in general—not just fear in particular (Davis & Whalen, 2001). In fact, researchers have found that the amygdala responds when people experience both strong positive and negative emotions (Aalto et al., 2002), when they read words that name positive and negative emotions (Hamann & Mao, 2002), and even when they think they've won or lost a simple game (Zalla et al., 2000).

In short, the three older theories of emotion all contain a grain of truth. The fact that particular biological events are associated with fear is consistent with the James–Lange theory. However, these states are not just bodily reactions; they also involve specific brain structures, in particular the amygdala—but this same brain structure gives rise to more than one emotion. Moreover, the stimuli that trigger fear produce separately both the feelings of fear and the bodily reactions, which is consistent with the Cannon–Bard theory. In addition, the fact that cognitive events can alter the fear response supports aspects of cognitive theory—but the fact that fear arises without requiring a person to interpret the events is not consistent with this theory. Taken together, the sum total of the findings is most consistent with the emerging synthesis, which includes roles for all of these factors.

Positive Emotions: More Than Feeling Good
Lest you think that psychologists have a morbid fascination with the dark side of emotions, we must note that much has also been learned about positive emotions (Biswas-Diener et al., 2004; Diener, 2000; Fredrickson, 2001; Lyubomirsky, 2001; Myers, 2000; Peterson, 2000; Ryan & Deci, 2000).

HAPPINESS. Fear and happiness differ in fundamental ways. For one, fear narrows the scope of attention and tends to restrict behavior to the small set of responses, such as behaviors related to trying to escape or to freezing in place; in contrast, happiness leads people to broaden the scope of attention and to be open to new ways of understanding and responding to events (Biswas-Diener et al., 2004). Moreover, whereas fear is a momentary state, which is easy to study in the brain, happiness is a more chronic state, which is harder to study in the brain. Instead of focusing on the brain mechanisms that underlie happiness, researchers have studied happiness largely from the levels of the person and the group. ◉─Watch

Watch the Video of Michael Cohn Interview on mypsychlab.com

Researchers have found that in 16 of 17 countries they examined (the exception was Northern Ireland), marriage is linked to greater happiness than is either being single or living with someone to whom you aren't married. This increase in happiness was comparable for both men and women (Ross, 1995; Stack & Eshleman, 1998; Weerasinghe & Tepperman, 1994). Apparently, most of the effects of marriage on happiness are indirect: increasing satisfaction with household finances and improving perceived health. However, this is not all there is to it; the simple fact of being married, all by itself, contributes to happiness when the marriage is good (Waite et al., 2009).

Source: © Ariel Skelley / CORBIS All Rights Reserved

THINK like a PSYCHOLOGIST Which of these five variables do you think leads you to be happy most frequently?

What makes us happy? There are several answers to this question.

- *Money?* A survey of happiness in 40 countries found that money *can* sometimes buy happiness, at least to some extent: People who have lived in poverty and deprivation tend to be happier when they live in better economic conditions (Diener & Biswas-Diener, 2002; Schyns, 1998). However, once a person has risen above the level of poverty and deprivation, additional material resources make little—if any—difference in happiness. Although we are happier immediately after getting a big raise or winning the lottery, the blip in happiness is short lived; before long, we are no more or less happy than we were before (Brickman & Campbell, 1971; Gilbert, 2007).

- *Life circumstances.* Life circumstances, such as how we are treated by those around us and how much time pressure we feel at work, clearly affect our happiness (Kahneman et al., 2004).

- *Realistic expectations.* In general, happy people have come to terms with their available resources (such as their income) and abilities and do not crave what is not realistically possible (Crawford Solberg et al., 2002).

- *Social support.* Social support—the degree to which a person feels that other people are willing and able to listen and help—contributes to happiness (Myers, 2000). In China, for instance, the strongest predictor of happiness is social support (Lu, 1999; Lu et al., 1997).

- *Personality.* Personality affects happiness. For example, at least in Western countries, assertive people tend to be happier than nonassertive people (Argyle & Lu, 1990). And extraverted (outgoing) people tend to be happier than introverted people. But more than that, happy people tend to perceive the world through rose-colored glasses; they interpret situations in ways that "maintain and even promote their happiness and positive self views" (Lyubomirsky, 2001, p. 241).

Although not much has been learned about the neural bases of happiness, some progress has been made. We have already noted that people whose left frontal lobes are generally more active (not only during a particular task, but in general) tend to be happier than people whose right frontal lobes are generally more active (Davidson, 1992a, 1992b, 1993, 1994, 1998, 2002). But why do people differ in these ways? One possibility lies in their genetic makeup. Researchers have reported that at least 50% of the variability in happiness arises from heredity (Lykken & Tellegen, 1996). Does this mean that if you are unhappy, you should just adjust because your genes have doomed you? No. Another way to look at this is that much of the variability in happiness arises from factors and circumstances that you can affect (such as having realistic expectations and developing social support), not from heredity. Moreover, as we see in the following section, if you adopt a positive outlook on life, striving to see the good in what has happened and in what can come, this turn of mind can affect other aspects of your life—which then can affect how happy you are.

POSITIVE PSYCHOLOGY: MORE THAN A STATE OF MIND. Being happy is one focus of what has come to be known as *positive psychology* (Linley et al., 2010; Seligman & Csikszentmihalyi, 2000; Seligman & Pawelski, 2003). Researchers have shown that positive states of mind can promote *resilience*, which is the ability to bounce back from adversity, to keep an even keel (Bonanno, 2004, 2005; Tugade & Fredrickson, 2004). In fact, positive emotions can literally boost the immune system to help us cope with disease (Rosenkranz et al., 2003; Tugade et al., 2004). Because positive emotions broaden attention and lead people to become more open and receptive, such emotions often promote effective coping strategies—adaptive strategies for handling stress. And effective coping, in turn, creates more positive emotions, which produces an "upward spiral" (Fredrickson & Joiner, 2002).

Expressing Emotions: Letting It All Hang Out?

Emotions occur in the social context of family, friends, and culture. Many of our emotions arise from social interactions, both positive (Gandhi's exhilaration when he attains a victory for social justice) and negative (his fear and anger after having been beaten by a train conductor for refusing to give up his seat to a White person). Not only do social stimuli trigger emotions, but emotions also influence social interactions, as we see in the following sections.

Culture and Emotional Expression: Rules of the Mode

The *experience* of emotion is not the same as the *expression* of emotion. In most ways, experiencing emotions is a private affair, inaccessible to others. But expressing emotions is crucial for our daily interactions with other people. According to Paul Ekman (1980), each of us learns a set of **display rules** for our culture that indicate when, to whom, and how strongly certain emotions can be shown. For example, he notes that in North America, people will find it suspicious if a man's secretary seems more upset at his funeral than does his wife. In the display rules for North American culture, the closer the relation to the deceased, the more emotion may be displayed in this circumstance. We all learn display rules within our specific cultural context; although individuals may differ in their styles, these rules reflect "the way things are done" in a particular region, class, or culture (Diefendorff & Greguras, 2009).

Ekman (1984) described a fascinating test of his theory that all people share the same basic emotions, but they sometimes express emotions differently because they follow different display rules. At the time he did the study, many Westerners believed that Asians are less emotional than Westerners. Ekman suspected that Asians are in fact just as emotional as Westerners but that their display rules lead them to conceal outward expression of their emotions. To test this hypothesis, he showed films to Americans in Berkeley, California, and to Japanese in Tokyo. Both groups saw a positive film (of pleasant scenery) and a negative film (of a surgical procedure). Participants viewed the films either alone or in the company of a white-coated scientist. The results were straightforward: Both national groups showed the same range of emotional expression (for example, smiling or wincing to the same extent) when they viewed the films in individual screenings, one person at a time. But the Japanese participants were notably more restrained when they were with company. Ekman analyzed slow-motion videotapes of the participants as they watched. The tapes revealed that a Japanese participant watching alone reacted in the same way as the Americans. But a Japanese watching with company would begin showing an emotional reaction, then quickly squelch it. According to Ekman, the initial Japanese reaction reflected the basic, innate emotions, and then display rules came to the fore, and the participants regulated their show of emotions accordingly. ◉─｢Watch

Body Language: Broadcasting Feelings

Nonverbal communication is particularly effective at conveying emotions, and "body language"—posture and body movement—is one form of nonverbal communication. Body language plays many roles, one of which is to convey sexual interest. For example, studies have shown that men and women hold their bodies differently in the presence of someone of the opposite sex if they are interested in that person than if they are not interested. However, interest is not conveyed in exactly the same way by men and women. Grammer (1990) found that when men in the United States were sexually interested in a woman, the men had "open postures" (with the legs relaxed and open) and watched the women, whereas interested women avoided eye contact, presented their body rotated slightly to the side (so that their breasts were seen in profile), and uncrossed their arms and legs. For both males and females, a closed posture conveyed lack of interest.

Culture clearly affects the nature of body language, but some of our body language may arise from innate factors. Although there has yet to be a good rigorous study of this, one anecdote is highly suggestive. In reviewing 30 studies of identical twins who were separated and raised apart, Faber (1981) wrote, "As with voice, the way the twins held themselves, walked, turned their heads, or flicked their wrists was more alike than any quantifiable trait the observers were able to measure. . . . If one twin had a limp, moist handshake, so did the other. If one had a spirited prance, so did the partner" (pp. 86–87). Given that identical twins have virtually identical genes and that if they are separated and

Emotion is conveyed not only by facial expression but also by tone of voice and body movements. People can sense happiness more accurately than other emotions from facial expressions—but they sense happiness least accurately from tone of voice. In contrast, of all the emotions, anger is most easily sensed from the tone of voice, and it is less well sensed from the face (Elfenbein & Ambady, 2002).

Source: Dwayne Newton\PhotoEdit Inc.

◉─｢Watch the Video of Shinobu Kitayama Interview on mypsychlab.com

Display rule A culture-specific rule that indicates when, to whom, and how strongly certain emotions can be shown.

raised apart they will not have identical environments, this finding suggests that genes may influence body language.

Emotion Regulation The very fact that display rules exist implies that we have at least some voluntary control over our emotional expressions. One source of evidence that we can regulate our emotions comes from studies of how the brain responds to efforts to control emotions.

REGULATING THE EMOTIONAL BRAIN Researchers have shown that we also have some ability to prolong the experience of certain emotions. For instance, in one study, participants saw neutral or negative pictures while their brains were being scanned using fMRI. The participants were told either simply to view the pictures or were asked to notice the way they responded emotionally to each picture and then to maintain this initial emotional response. The results showed that when they maintained their emotional response to the negative pictures, their amygdalae continued to be activated over a longer period of time (Schaefer et al., 2002). These results demonstrate both that we can voluntarily prolong an emotional response and also that by so doing we can voluntarily prolong the brain activity that underlies emotions.

Having just read that people can voluntarily prolong an emotional response, the natural question to ask is whether we can also voluntarily reduce our emotional reactions. Gandhi assumed that the answer to this question is "yes" and apparently trained himself to keep his emotions in check. And his assumption was justified (Lewis et al., 2010; Ochsner & Gross, 2005). In one neuroimaging study, for example, researchers showed male participants erotic videos and asked them either to respond normally or to try to inhibit sexual arousal (Beauregard et al., 2001). When the men were reacting normally, various brain areas involved in emotion were activated, such as the amygdala and hypothalamus. When the men were inhibiting their reactions, parts of the frontal lobe became activated—and the brain areas normally activated by those reactions no longer were. The frontal lobes play a key role in inhibiting processing in other parts of the brain and apparently inhibit responses in parts of the brain that underlie sexual arousal.

CONSEQUENCES OF EMOTION REGULATION. Emotion regulation is important for at least four reasons:

1. *If emotions are not regulated, the behavior that results from them may be undesirable and problematic* (such as when negative emotions produce aggression; Davidson et al., 2000b).

2. *Only suppressing behavior that arises from emotions—rather than modifying the emotions themselves—can lead temporarily to reduced cognitive abilities.* If instead of controlling your emotions you try to suppress the overt behavior that arises from those emotions, you will probably find that the effort affects some of your cognitive functions: You will impair your memory for the surrounding events (Bonanno et al., 2004; Richards & Gross, 2000), impede your ability to reason (Baumeister et al., 1998), and impair your ability to communicate clearly (Butler et al., 2003).

3. *Regulating—modifying—emotions prevents the negative cognitive effects of suppressing the emotionally driven behaviors.* You can most effectively regulate your emotions by reinterpreting the situation and your role in it (Gross, 2001, 2002; Richards, 2004; Richards et al., 2003).

4. *Different emotions selectively affect different aspects of cognition, especially working memory. Working memory* is a memory system that uses short-term memory to reason or to solve problems (J. R. Gray, 2001). Thus, regulating emotions can moderate the effects of emotion on cognition. Positive emotions facilitate verbal tasks but interfere with spatial tasks (such as remembering an object's location); negative emotions have the opposite effects. The different effects of positive and negative emotions on cognition may arise from the fact that positive emotion activates the left frontal lobe during a verbal task, whereas negative emotion activates the right frontal lobe during a spatial task (J. R. Gray et al., 2002)—and different aspects of working memory rely on different portions of the frontal lobes.

Perceiving Emotions: A Form of Mind Reading

Other people's emotional expressions and additional forms of nonverbal communication invite us to engage in a form of "mind reading." Just as we know that a dog is feeling hot when it pants and its tongue lolls out, we can read expressions and draw inferences from them about a person's emotional state. In some cases, people may direct an emotional expression toward another person as a deliberate form of communication; for example, your roommate might intentionally smile at you after you've just done him or her a favor. But in other cases, an emotional expression may simply be an unconscious sign of an internal state, such as may occur if someone droops her head because she is sad (Russell et al., 2003). We read emotions in part by interpreting such cues, and in part by imitating what we see—as discussed in the following sections.

Reading Cues We humans are remarkably good at "reading" (correctly interpreting) cues about emotion, acquiring information from even minimal bodily signs. For instance, in one study researchers attached 13 small lights to the bodies of each of two professional dancers and had them perform dances that conveyed fear, anger, grief, joy, surprise, and disgust. Undergraduate students who later watched videos of the dances were able to recognize the intended emotions, even when the dancers performed in the dark so that only the lights were visible (Dittrich et al., 1996).

The ability to read nonverbal communications is at least partly determined by experience. For example, people who grow up in different cultures differ in how sensitive they are to the emotional expressions of others (Stephan et al., 1996). If a culture has relatively strict display rules (as does Japan), then emotions will be relatively difficult to detect—and the members of the culture become more sensitive to relatively subtle emotional cues. For example, although display rules in China call for more emotional restraint than those in Australia, Chinese children can detect basic emotions more accurately than Australian children can (Markham & Wang, 1996).

Perceiving by Imitating: Making the Match "Smile and the whole world smiles along with you." This is more than a well-worn saying; researchers have found that when we perceive an emotional expression, we subtly move our muscles so that we imitate that expression (Adolphs, 2002; Niedenthal et al., 2001). Such imitation can occur even when people are not consciously aware of having seen a face displaying a specific emotion (Dimberg et al., 2000). And the feedback from moving our muscles contributes to our ability to recognize emotions in others.

LOOKING AT LEVELS Lie Detection

Source: © Stewart Cohen/Getty Images/ Stone; (inset) © Digital Art/CORBIS All Rights Reserved

Gandhi was lied to often in his long and turbulent career. In South Africa, for example, General Smuts tried to lull Gandhi with agreements that he had no intention of honoring. Gandhi no doubt would have appreciated knowing whether others were lying to him and might have appreciated a method for detecting lies. Some methods used to detect lies rely on the "lie detector" machine; although the results of using this device are not admissible evidence in court, they are still used in various investigations. What do lie detectors really "detect"?

If distinct brain and body states accompany at least some emotions, researchers have reasoned, then people might have biological "signatures" of feelings of guilt and fear when they are caught at a wrongdoing. (Even people who are usually honest sometimes lie, and thus what's at issue is detecting *when* someone lies—not trying to sort people into "liars" versus "honest" folk.) The idea that guilt and fear have a biological signature underlies a long history of attempts to detect deception objectively. One result has been machines called **polygraphs**, known misleadingly as "lie detectors." These machines don't

Polygraph A machine that is used to detect lying by monitoring the activity of the sympathetic and parasympathetic nervous systems, particularly changes in how easily the skin conducts electricity, breathing, and heart rate.

Polygraphs are used to detect changes in autonomic nervous system activity, which interviewers use to try to determine whether the person being interviewed is lying.

Source: Mark C. Burnett\Photo Researchers, Inc.

"detect lies" directly; they monitor the activity of the sympathetic and parasympathetic nervous systems—in particular, changes in how easily the skin conducts electricity (which reflects the amount of sweat in the skin), breathing, and heart rate.

In the polygraph test, the person is hooked up to sensors, and then the examiner asks the person questions and monitors the person's bodily responses. Over time, researchers and law enforcement professionals have devised four ways of asking questions, all of which are intended to make it easy to detect bodily responses associated with lying:

1. The most basic questioning technique used with a polygraph is the *relevant/irrelevant technique* (Larson, 1932). Suppose you are trying to determine whether the suspect in a crime is telling the truth. When this technique is used, the suspect is asked crime-related questions ("Did you break into Mr. Johnson's house last night?") and neutral questions ("Do you live at 43 Pleasant Street?"). The bodily responses accompanying the answers to the two types of questions are then compared. The key idea is that different bodily responses will occur when a person lies than when he or she tells the truth. However, the two types of questions clearly differ in their emotional weight. Thus, a greater bodily response to a crime-related question may reflect not guilt but simply the fact that the idea posed by the question is more arousing.

2. To avoid the possibility that bodily responses simply reflect how arousing the question is, the *control question technique* (Reid, 1947) includes comparison questions that should have an emotional weight roughly equivalent to that of the crime-related questions. For example, in addition to the two questions above, the suspect might be asked, "Did you ever do anything you were ashamed of?"

3. A more recent technique is the *guilty knowledge test* (sometimes called the *concealed information test*; Lykken, 1959, 1960). In contrast to the two earlier techniques, the guilty knowledge test does not rely on asking direct questions about the crime. Instead, this test includes indirect questions that presumably only the guilty person would be in a position to answer correctly. In addition, the guilty knowledge test relies on multiple-choice questions. So the suspect might be asked, "Was the color of the walls in Mr. Johnson's bedroom white? Yellow? Blue?" Someone who has never been in the room should have comparable responses to each of the choices, whereas someone who has guilty knowledge should respond selectively to the actual color.

4. Finally, the *guilty actions test* (Bradley & Warfield, 1984; Bradley et al., 1996) is a modification of the guilty knowledge test. This test requires the examiner to observe responses when people are given statements about actions that they may have committed.

Do these techniques work? Ben-Shakhar and Furedy (1990) report that in the laboratory, the control question technique on average correctly classifies 80% of the times when people lie—but it also incorrectly classifies as lying 37% of the times when they tell the truth. Thus, this technique unfortunately leads too often to the classification of honest responses as lies. The guilty knowledge test has a better track record; on average, lies were correctly classified 84% of the time, and the honest responses were correctly classified 94% of the time. However, the range of accuracy in the reviewed studies was from 64% to 100% for classifying lies and from 81% to 100% for classifying truthful responses. Many other researchers have reported comparable results (DeClue, 2003). (You are probably getting a sense as to why polygraph evidence is not admitted in courts of law.)

More recent techniques for detecting lies do not rely on the polygraph. Most of these techniques measure brain activity. For example, methods that rely on measuring electrical activity in the brain can sometimes have accuracy as high as 95%, but there is still enough error to cast doubt on the examiner's ability to classify individual answers as untruthful (Allen & Iacono, 1997).

Also at the level of the brain, neuroimaging studies are beginning to illuminate just why it is so difficult to detect lies. For example, Ganis and colleagues (2003) found that not all types of lies are neurologically equivalent; from a neural point of view, there is more than one way to lie. Specifically, in this study participants were asked to lie in two ways: In one condition, they lied spontaneously, making up responses "on the fly"; in the other condition, the participants first made up an "alternative reality" for a specific real incident in their lives and later used this story to make up lies about this incident. For example, if they had taken a vacation in the mountains with their family, they might make up a story where they took the vacation at the beach with a friend. And later when asked where they took the vacation, they would use the story to produce a lie. All participants' brains were scanned as they told the truth and lied. The results showed that when the participants told lies spontaneously, parts of the brain involved in working memory and in monitoring errors were very active; when they told lies on the basis of an "alternative reality" scenario, areas of the brain involved in retrieving memories were activated instead. Thus, different neural systems were involved when the participants used different methods to tell lies (Ganis, Morris, & Kosslyn, 2009; Morgan, LeSage, & Kosslyn, 2009)—there is more than one way to tell lies, which makes detecting lies complex.

And the neural basis of lying is even more complicated than this. Not only do different types of lies arise from different brain systems, but the precise actions of these brain systems vary for different people (Kozel, Padgett, et al., 2004; Kozel, Revell, et al., 2004; Morgan et al., 2009). Because the brain produces the bodily signals recorded by the polygraph, such findings may explain why polygraph results are difficult to interpret.

At the level of the person, we can ask whether people who think that they are good at detecting lies are in fact good at doing so. DePaulo and her collaborators (1997) reported a meta-analysis of studies on the relation between an individual's confidence that he or she has spotted a lie and the degree of that person's accuracy: They found essentially no relation between the two. Similarly, researchers have found that even police officers are not very accurate in spotting lies about crimes. In one study, police officers viewed video of an interview with a man who was lying about a murder (which he later confessed to committing). These officers were able to categorize only 70% of the true statements as true (making errors 30% of the time), and were even worse when they categorized false statements: In these cases, the officers were able to categorize only 57% of the lies as lies (and judged 43% of the lies as being honest responses; Vrij & Mann, 2001). Many other researchers have reported similar results (Elaad, 2003; Garrido et al., 2004; Granhag & Strömwall, 2001; Vrij, 2004).

At the level of the group, people usually observe behavioral cues—not the outputs from a polygraph—when they try to determine whether another person is lying. What cues do people use to detect whether someone is lying? Researchers have discovered that we detect lies by noting people's *microexpressions*, flickers of expressions—such as frequent eyeblinks, quick sideways glances, or downcast eyes—for as little as a tenth of a second (DePaulo et al., 2003; Ekman, 1985; Ekman & Friesen, 1975). We notice these various types of nonverbal information and can detect inconsistencies across them, such as a stiff body posture combined with trusting, direct eye contact. We are also sensitive to a variety of telltale cues, summarized in Table 1. However, we must stress that although these cues can sometimes be useful, they do not always signal that someone is lying—and people can lie without engaging in any of these behaviors (Mann et al., 2004; Strömwall et al., 2003; Vrij & Mann, 2001).

Events at the three levels of analysis do not operate in isolation but rather interact in complex ways. Perhaps the greatest problem with the polygraph is that it really detects feelings of guilt or fear (the level of the person) rather than lies. If the person being tested lies but does not *feel* guilty or afraid, the palms won't become sweaty, heart rate won't increase, and so forth; there won't be any biological cues of deceit. And because the interviewer does not have any basis for detecting the lie, this lack of biological response in turn may alter how the interviewer treats the person during the interview (a social interaction). And that treatment in turn can affect the person's reactions to the questions (level of the brain). Moreover, if the person being interviewed feels comfortable, he or she may be less likely to produce the microexpressions that some interviewers can readily detect (without any need for the machine).

TABLE 1

Some Common (Although Not Always Accurate) Signs of Deception

- Frequent eyeblinks
- Sideways glances
- Downcast eyes
- Stiff body posture combined with direct eye contact
- Larger pupil size
- Rising pitch of voice
- Exaggerated facial expressions
- Increased grammatical errors
- Slower and less fluent speech than normal
- Repetition of words and phrases

THINK like a PSYCHOLOGIST What would be the advantages and disadvantages of a machine that always detected lies and never mistook the truth for lying?

✓●─Study and Review on
mypsychlab.com

LOOKING BACK

1. **What are the different emotions?** Ekman and his collaborators offered much evidence that six emotions are "basic"—happiness, anger, sadness, disgust, surprise, and fear—but the last two are more easily confused with each other than are any of the others. Basic emotions can be combined to produce a wide range of emotions. In general, emotions can be categorized as approach or withdrawal emotions.

2. **What causes emotion?** The James–Lange theory states that emotions follow bodily reactions; the Cannon–Bard theory holds that emotions and bodily reactions occur at the same time, not in the order claimed by James and Lange; cognitive theory holds that emotions arise when bodily states are interpreted in the context of the specific situation; and, most recently, an emerging synthesis of previous theories maintains that some emotions arise reflexively from specific brain activity, whereas others depend on interpretation and memory. All the theories have captured some aspects of how emotions work. As the James–Lange theory predicts, some emotions are associated with particular bodily responses (such as heart rate and breathing rate). As the Cannon–Bard theory predicts, the events that trigger fear simultaneously produce both the experience of fear and its bodily responses. As cognitive theory predicts, how you interpret the causes of your bodily states (which often depends on the surrounding context) influences which emotion you will feel. But as the emerging synthesis predicts, some emotions (in some circumstances) rely more on cognitive interpretation than do others.

3. **How do we express and regulate our emotions?** We express our emotions through overt behavior—such as changes in facial expression, tone of voice, and posture—as well as through speech. However, our outward behavior does not always reflect our inner feelings. Cultures have different display rules, which determine when and to what degree emotions are shown. In addition, we can voluntarily regulate our expression of emotions as well as emotions themselves. The most effective way to regulate emotions relies on reinterpreting the situation and our role in it.

4. **How do we perceive emotions in others?** We can interpret even minimal cues—such as subtle differences in body language—to infer emotion. When a culture has stringent display rules, its members appear to compensate by becoming more sensitive to even very subtle emotion cues. In addition, when we perceive an emotional expression, we may imitate it, and the act of imitation provides feedback that allows us to interpret the expression better.

Motivation and Reward: More Than Feeling Good

((●─Listen to the Podcast on
Psychological Conflict on
mypsychlab.com

Gandhi eventually proved exceptionally successful as a lawyer in South Africa. Not only did he make an unusually good living, but he also had White employees—a sign of status for an Indian lawyer (Markovits, 2003). This success may have helped him become self-confident, which allowed him to behave unconventionally. For example, he adopted the dress of an Indian peasant and eventually wore only a loincloth. Why? His appearance disconcerted his upper-crust British opponents, who often had trouble reconciling his fluent English and obvious intelligence with his garb. But his motivation for dressing as he did was not simply to disconcert other people: He dressed in this way to draw attention to the sorts of clothing that could be produced locally; Gandhi wanted to promote hand spinning and hand weaving in India in order to eliminate the dependence on imported cloth that largely came from England. For him, establishing economic independence was a central part of helping India establish its dignity. He was also motivated to help India attain political independence and develop spiritually. Ghandi had many motivations—as do we all. In this section we explore the nature of motivation. ((●─Listen

LOOKING AHEAD Learning Objectives

1. What are the sources of motivation?
2. What is the difference between needs and wants, and what factors affect them?

Getting Motivated: Sources and Theories of Motivation

Motivation is the set of requirements and desires that leads an animal (including a human) to behave in a particular way at a particular time and place. Emotions motivate us both when we experience them (such as occurs when fear motivates us to avoid walking alone down a dark alley) and when we anticipate them (such as occurs when we take a long trip, anticipating the pleasure of reaching our destination). But not all motivations rely on emotions. Some *motives* (that is, specific motivations) are based on biological needs or drives (for example, the desire for food and sex), and some are based on learning (for example, the desire for a promotion). Psychologists have analyzed, classified, and identified human motives in numerous ways, developing a variety of theories of motivation. In what follows, we consider the key concepts in these theories. Keep in mind, though, that no single, widely accepted theory can explain all of human motivation.

Many different goals motivate us, ranging from getting good grades to needing to keep warm to being the object of others' attention. What goals motivate you most strongly?

Instincts: My Genes Made Me Do It Why do birds fly south for the winter and spiders make certain kinds of webs? Instinct. For many animals, instincts provide the main motivation for behaviors. An **instinct** is an inherited tendency to produce organized and unalterable responses to particular stimuli. For several decades at the beginning of the 20th century, a number of psychologists tried to explain human motivation in terms of instincts (for example, McDougall, 1908/1960); their approach is termed *instinct theory*. Much of Freud's theory of personality, for example, hinges on ideas about how we grapple with our sexual urges, which he considered to be instinctive.

But unlike many other animals, we humans are remarkably flexible in the way we can respond to any stimulus; an instinct is a fixed behavioral pattern, but one of the strengths of our species is that we are not locked into very specific responses to many stimuli. For instance, we don't just eat to satisfy hunger—we develop cuisines, which give us a huge range of ways of fulfilling this basic requirement. So, it is difficult to assign an important role to instincts in human motivation.

Evolutionary psychology has offered an alternative to instinct theory. Instead of proposing that evolution has selected specific behaviors (as earlier evolutionary theorists, including Charles Darwin himself, believed), these theorists believe that evolution has predisposed us have certain *goals* (such as finding healthy mates) and *cognitive strategies* (such as using deception to achieve one's goals; Cosmides & Tooby, 1996; Pinker, 1997, 2002; Plotkin, 1997).

However, evolutionary theories of motivation are notoriously difficult to test because we can never know for sure what our ancestors were like and how they evolved. Moreover, some goals are unlikely to be a result of heredity. For example, Gandhi valued punctuality and was almost obsessively on time. Punctuality does not seem like a good candidate for a goal that is built into our brains via evolution—but it is not clear how to decide which goals are best explained in terms of evolution and which are best explained in terms of their importance in present society.

Motivation The set of requirements and desires that leads an animal (including a human) to behave in a particular way at a particular time and place.

Instinct An inherited tendency to produce organized and unalterable responses to particular stimuli.

261

Drive An internal imbalance caused by the lack of a needed substance or condition that motivates animals (including humans) to reach a particular goal that will reduce the imbalance.

Homeostasis The process of maintaining a steady state, in which bodily substances and conditions are kept within the range in which the body functions well.

Drives and Homeostasis: Staying in Balance Instinct theory and evolutionary theory focus on identifying particular innate behaviors or goals and strategies. In contrast, *drive theory* focuses on the mechanisms that underlie such tendencies. A **drive** is an internal imbalance (caused by the lack of a needed substance or condition) that pushes you to reach a particular goal, which in turn will reduce that imbalance. For example, hunger is a drive that pushes you to get food, thirst is a drive that pushes you to obtain liquids you can drink, and being cold is a drive that pushes you find a source of warmth. Drives differ in terms of the goals to which they direct you, but all are aimed at decreasing an imbalance caused by the lack of a needed substance (such as food or drink) or condition (such as warmth).

Some drive theories link drives with reinforcement: Something is reinforcing if it reduces a drive. According to this theory, if you are thirsty, water is reinforcing because it reduces the imbalance experienced when you have the thirst drive; if you are not thirsty, water is not reinforcing.

Researchers have long tried to specify the nature of the imbalance that is reduced by reinforcement. In 1932, Walter B. Cannon published a groundbreaking book titled *The Wisdom of the Body*, in which he pointed out that for life to be sustained, certain substances and conditions of the body must be kept within a certain range, neither rising too high nor falling too low. These characteristics and substances include body temperature and the amounts of oxygen, minerals, water, and food taken in. Bodily processes such as digestion and respiration work toward keeping the levels steady. The process of maintaining a steady state is called **homeostasis**. Homeostasis works not simply to keep the body in balance—but to keep the body in balance in the range in which it functions well. The usual analogy to homeostasis is a thermostat and furnace: The thermostat turns the furnace on when the temperature drops too low and turns it off when the temperature reaches the desired level. But Cannon pointed out that in living creatures, homeostasis often involves active behavior, not simply the passive registering of the state of the environment. To stay alive, you must nourish yourself by obtaining and taking in food and water, and you must maintain body temperature by finding shelter and wearing clothing. If the homeostatic balance goes awry, an imbalance results—and you are motivated to correct the imbalance.

Arousal Theory: Avoiding Boredom, Avoiding Overload People are also motivated to maintain another kind of balance, one that has nothing to do with physiological homeostasis: Simply put, we don't like stimuli that are either too boring or too arousing; instead, we seek to maintain an intermediate level of stimulation. Berlyne (1960, 1974) showed that people like random patterns, paintings, or music best when they are neither too simple nor too complex but rather somewhere in the middle. What is classed as "simple" or "complex" depends partly on the person as well as the nature of the stimulus. For example, patterns that are complex to children typically are less so to adults.

Berlyne's findings conform to what is known as the *Yerkes–Dodson law* (Figure 4), named after the researchers who first described a similar principle. This law states that we perform best when we are at an intermediate level of arousal. If we are underaroused, we are sluggish; if we are overaroused, we can't focus and sustain attention, and our performance suffers. Intermediate levels of arousal occur when we are challenged not too much and not too little. For example, if you are rehearsing a speech alone in your room, you may be understimulated and give a lackluster presentation; if you have to speak before a large group, you may become tongue-tied because of overarousal. Moreover, people adapt to a constant set of stimuli, become bored, and then seek additional stimulation (Helson, 1964).

FIGURE 4 The Yerkes–Dodson Law

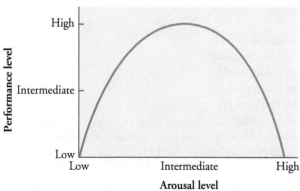

People perform best at intermediate levels of arousal.

Incentives and Reward: Happy Expectations A need to maintain homeostasis and a preference for intermediate levels of arousal are not the only factors that motivate us. Homeostasis is a useful concept for understanding thirst, hunger, and certain other drives (such as those for adequate oxygen and temperature control), and the idea that we attempt to maintain an intermediate level of arousal helps explain why people select certain activities and situations and reject others. But neither factor explains why people work so hard for money.

The prospect of being paid, along with many other goals that motivate us, is best understood in terms of **incentives**, which are stimuli or events that draw animals (including humans) to achieve a particular goal in anticipation of a reward (such as what money can buy). To see the difference between a drive and an incentive, consider the fact that hunger is a drive, which is often long gone before dessert—but dessert can nevertheless still be an incentive to keep eating (as exploited by countless parents who use dessert as an incentive to get their kids to eat their spinach).

The notion that much of motivation can best be understood in terms of incentives has led theorists to think about some aspects of motivation in terms of *expectations* of reinforcement (Wise, 2004). We tend to behave in ways that experience has shown us will produce a desirable outcome, either a positive consequence of the behavior (positive reinforcement) or the removal of a negative condition (negative reinforcement). If working 20 hours a week in a store has led to a regular paycheck, you will likely want to keep working (assuming that the check is large enough!).

In general, because we have all had different experiences and hence learned different things, it's hard to know for sure what stimuli will serve as incentives for a given person. Consider, for example, the fact that, for Gandhi, prison was "more a luxury than a punishment. He could devote more time to prayer, study and spinning [making yarn] than he could outside" (Nanda, 1987).

Learned Helplessness: Unhappy Expectations People not only can learn new strategies for coping with problems but also can learn to give up trying. Martin Seligman and his colleagues first described **learned helplessness**, which occurs when an animal has an aversive experience in which nothing it does can affect what happens to it, and so it simply gives up and stops trying to change the situation or to escape (Mikulincer, 1994). As shown in Figure 5 (Overmeier & Seligman, 1967), when dogs were put in a cage in which they could not escape shocks, they eventually gave up responding and just huddled on the floor and endured—and they continued to do so even when they were moved to a new cage in which it was easy to escape the shocks. This condition can also afflict humans who experience a lack of control over negative events: If nothing you do seems to make an abusive spouse stop tormenting you, you may eventually just give up and stop trying. Learned helplessness can lead to depression and a range of stress-related problems.

Incentive A stimulus or event that draws animals (including humans) to achieve a particular goal in anticipation of a reward.

Learned helplessness The condition that occurs after an animal has an aversive experience in which nothing it does can affect what happens to it, and so it simply gives up and stops trying to change the situation or to escape.

FIGURE 5 The Classic Learned Helplessness Experiment

An animal is placed in a cage and shocked. Initially, the animal tries to escape, but it can do nothing to stop or avoid the shocks.

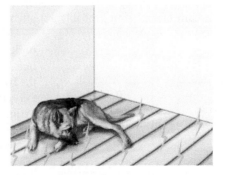

The animal eventually gives up.

When the animal is moved into a new cage in which only a small barrier separates the side where shocks are delivered from the side where no shocks occur, it does not try to escape the shock, even when the shock is signaled by a tone.

263

Need A condition that arises from the lack of a necessary substance (such as food) or condition (such as warmth); needs give rise to drives.

Want A state that arises when you have an unmet goal that does not arise from a lack of a necessary substance or condition; wants turn goals into incentives.

Deprived reward Reward that occurs when an animal (including a human) lacks a substance or condition necessary for survival and an action then produces this substance or condition.

Nondeprived reward Reward that occurs when the animal (including a human) does not lack a substance or condition necessary for survival—in other words, when you had a want but not a need.

THINK like a
PSYCHOLOGIST When you think about the activities that you plan to do during a weekend or during a break from classes, are you hoping that most of them will fulfill a need or a want?

Needs and Wants: The Stick and the Carrot

Different things motivate different people: Gandhi was not motivated to make money; the typical entrepreneur is not motivated to give away all earthly possessions and lead a social and political revolution. Moreover, you are not motivated by the same forces day in and day out; rather, your motives often shift over the course of the day (or year or life span). A particular motive comes to the fore when you have a *need* or *want*. A **need** is a condition that arises from the lack of a necessary substance (such as food) or condition (such as warmth). Needs give rise to drives, which push you to reach a particular goal that will reduce the need. A low level of nutrients creates a need; hunger is a drive that will lead you to fill that need. In contrast, a **want** is a state that arises when you have an unmet goal that does not arise from a lack of a necessary substance or condition. A want causes the goal to act as an incentive. You might *need* to eat, but you don't *need* a fancier car, although you might desperately *want* one—and the promise of a new car for working hard over the summer would be an incentive for you to put in long hours on the job. You are not necessarily aware of your needs or wants.

Is There More Than One Type of Reward?
For all needs and wants, attaining the goal reinforces the behaviors that lead to this result. But what makes attaining the goal rewarding? What is "reward"? Even the strongest needs that grow out of maintaining homeostasis—which create drives such as hunger and thirst—arise from the brain. To understand why something is rewarding, we must look more closely at the brain's response to events in the body and in the world. By looking at the brain mechanisms underlying reward, we find support for the distinction between needs and wants.

Olds and Milner (1954) found that rats that received electrical stimulation in a certain brain area acted as if they desired more of it. These researchers thought that they had identified a "pleasure center" in the brain. Later research showed that they had stumbled on a brain system that underlies reward when an animal has been deprived of the reinforcer. **Deprived reward** is reward that occurs when an animal (including a human) lacks a substance or condition necessary for survival, and an action then produces this substance or condition. Such reward arises from the brain pathway that runs from certain parts of the brain stem, through the hypothalamus, on up to specific parts of the limbic system and the frontal lobes (Baxter et al., 2000; Kalivas & Nakamura, 1999; Rolls & Cooper, 1974; Wise, 1996). Many of the neurons in this circuit use or are affected by the neurotransmitter dopamine (Wise, 2004).

There is good evidence that the brain has a second system that operates for **nondeprived reward**, reward that occurs when the rewarding stimulus or activity is not something that is necessary and lacked—in other words, when you had a want but not a need. For example, when ending a fast (which he often used as a political tool), even Gandhi probably felt pleasure in eating. In contrast, if Gandhi ate one last juicy piece of fruit at the end of the meal, even though he was no longer hungry, he was eating even though he was nondeprived (it's an open question how often Gandhi actually did eat in such circumstances—but probably not often).

The fact that different brain mechanisms underlie deprived versus nondeprived reward is one source of evidence for the distinction between the two types of reward. As noted, dopamine plays a crucial role in producing the rewarding effects of a stimulus or activity that fills a need. However, it does not play a role when you are not deprived. Instead, a key part of the brain involved in nondeprived reward is in the brain stem. Damage to this area knocks out the system that registers reward when an animal is not deprived but leaves intact the system that registers reward when the animal is deprived (Bechara & Van der Kooy, 1992; Berridge, 1996; Nader et al., 1997). Figure 6 summarizes the relation among these different facets of motivation.

FIGURE 6 Needs and Wants

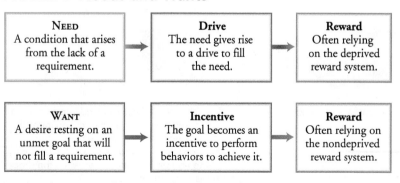

Needs and wants typically trigger different sorts of events.

Types of Needs: No Shortage of Shortages Humans have psychological needs as well as bodily needs. A *psychological need* is a condition that arises from the lack of necessary information or the lack of an opportunity to exercise specific mental processes or behave in a specific way. Such needs are not simply desires; depending on our genes and how a given person is raised, we all require certain psychological conditions in order to thrive. As one example, if young children are not spoken to, they will not develop language properly (Grimshaw et al., 1998; Pinker 1994). Many psychological needs have been identified and studied, as summarized in the following section.

Need for achievement The need to reach goals that require skilled performance or competence to be accomplished.

PSYCHOLOGICAL NEEDS. Researchers have proposed that our psychological needs include a need to be competent, to be independent (Sheldon et al., 1996), to have social approval, to be dominant or in control (Kim & Kim, 1997), to be affiliated with others, to be powerful (McClelland et al., 1989), to be autonomous (Markland & Tobin, 2010), to wrap up tasks (Kruglanski & Webster, 1996; Taris, 2000), to understand, to maintain self-esteem, and even to see the world in a positive light (Stevens & Fiske, 1995). Many studies have documented that individuals differ widely in such needs. These differences probably arise from multiple sources. For one, people vary in their temperament (such as how much social contact they prefer), and some of these differences reflect the operation of genes (Kagan, 1994); for another, people have different personal experiences, which shape their psychological needs—and such experiences include interactions with peers (J. R. Harris, 1998) and family (Sulloway, 1997, 1999).

A classic example of a psychological need is the **need for achievement** (McClelland & Atkinson, 1953), which is the need to reach goals that require skilled performance or competence to be accomplished. Many studies have documented variables that are associated with differences in the strength of this need (Neel et al., 1986; Spangler, 1992). For example, people who have a high need for achievement tend to assume that their successes are due to their personal characteristics, whereas their failures are due to environmental circumstances (Nathawat et al., 1997; Weiner & Kukla, 1970); apparently, these people tend to interpret events in a way that helps to satisfy this need.

In short, measures of many psychological needs have been associated with a wide range of types of behavior.

MASLOW'S HIERARCHY OF NEEDS. Abraham Maslow (1970) created a hierarchy of physical and emotional needs, illustrated in Figure 7. Lower-level needs are considered more essential to life and must be met before needs further up the hierarchy can be addressed and satisfied. Needs toward the top of the hierarchy are considered less basic because they arise less frequently and, if not met, do not seriously disrupt a person's life—although not achieving them will prevent a person from fully thriving. You can live without the respect of your peers but not without air or food. According to Maslow's theory, once a need is met, it becomes less important, and unmet, higher-level needs become more important. For example, if your house burned down and all your possessions were destroyed, your physiological and safety needs are likely to demand all of your attention, and you would probably care much less about how others regard you or about other "higher-level" needs at that point in time.

FIGURE 7 Maslow's Hierarchy of Needs

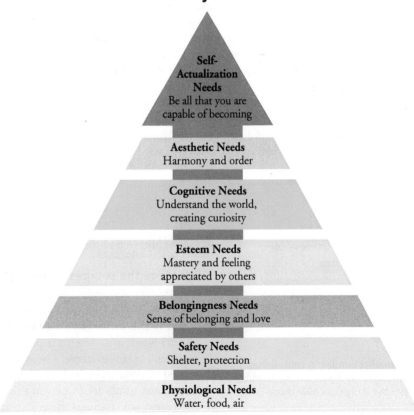

According to Maslow's theory, needs lower in the hierarchy must be met before needs higher up become the focus of concern.

Source: Maslow, Abraham (1954). *Motivation and Personality.* New York: Harper. pp. 236. originally published in A.H. Maslow, "A Theory of Human Motivation," *Psychological Review* 50(4) (1943):370–96.

What sorts of needs do you suppose motivated President Franklin Delano Roosevelt? During FDR's entire presidency (from 1933 to 1945), he could not walk without the use of metal braces or crutches (he contracted polio in 1921 and was paralyzed thereafter). However, this did not stop him from getting around the White House on his own by using his hands to crawl from one room to another.

Source: The Image Works

THINK like a

PSYCHOLOGIST If you were to have a roommate from a collectivist culture, how might you negotiate with him or her differently than if your roommate was from an individualist culture, such as that of the United States?

✓●─Study and Review on
mypsychlab.com

Individualist culture A culture that emphasizes the rights and responsibilities of the individual over those of the group.

Collectivist culture A culture that emphasizes the rights and responsibilities of the group over those of the individual.

Maslow's hierarchy of needs has had an enormous impact on how people think about motivation, particularly in the business world (Soper et al., 1995). But is this theory of motivation correct? Research has produced mixed evidence, at best, for the idea that needs are organized into a hierarchy (Wahba & Bridwell, 1976). There is no good evidence that unmet needs become more important than met needs. In fact, one study found that the more consistently a need was met, the more important it became (Hall & Nougaim, 1968). Furthermore, Maslow's theory fails to explain various phenomena—for example, why people voluntarily go to war and put themselves in the line of fire (Fox, 1982).

Maslow's hierarchy has been revised in light of evolutionary psychology (Kenrick et al., 2010). The revised theory retains basic subsistence needs at the base but replaces the higher levels with reproductive goals ("mate acquisition," "mate retention," and "parenting"). Moreover, the revised theory posits that needs are overlapping, and later ones do not replace earlier ones. Although the revised theory avoids many of the problems with the original theory, it has yet to be tested rigorously.

Needs and Wants in Individualist Versus Collectivist Cultures Many of the goals that motivate us stem from our culture, in part because the structure of a society often determines what sorts of activities will be reinforced. Cultures can be divided into two general types, and these types affect achievement motivation differently. **Individualist cultures**, such as that of the United States, emphasize the rights and responsibilities of the individual over those of the group. **Collectivist cultures**, such as that of China, emphasize the rights and responsibilities of the group over those of the individual. Although these differences are often matters of degree (and may vary for subgroups within a culture; Oyserman et al., 2002), such cultural differences have been shown to affect achievement goals. For example, Anglo-Australians (from an individualist culture) have been found to be focused more on personal success than on family or groups, whereas Sri Lankans (from a collectivist culture) are oriented more toward their families and groups (Niles, 1998). Similarly, Americans had higher achievement motivation (as measured by scales that emphasize individual achievement) than did Japanese and Hungarians, who grew up in collectivist cultures (Sagie et al., 1996). Thus, growing up in one or the other type of culture influences a person's needs and wants.

The effects of growing up in an individualist culture are not without a cost: Americans like themselves less than do Chinese (Tafarodi & Swann, 1996). Why? Collectivist cultures tend to deemphasize competition among individuals, which may lead them to like each other more (Tafarodi & Swann, 1996). This may lead to greater self-liking if we assume that self-liking is increased if others like us. In individualist cultures, on the other hand, members are raised to strive for freedom and independence, which tends to produce competition and conflict. In such cultures, there are more feelings of self-competence but fewer of self-liking.

LOOKING BACK

1. **What are the sources of motivation?** Motivation arises for many reasons, including evolutionarily shaped instincts, drives, the maintenance of homeostasis, and a desire to have an intermediate level of arousal, and incentives.

2. **What is the difference between needs and wants, and what factors affect them?** Needs arise when a requirement is not met, which creates a drive to fill the requirement (for example, a need for water leads to a drive to drink). Needs may be related to a system in the brain that provides a reward when a deprivation is satisfied. In contrast, wants arise when an animal has an unmet goal that will not fulfill a requirement, which causes the goal to act as an incentive; wants may be related to a system in the brain that provides a reward when you achieve a desired goal but are not deprived. There are many types of needs and wants, and the importance of any given one depends partly on your culture—for example, on whether it is individualist versus collectivist.

Hunger and Sex: Two Important Motivations

Metabolism The sum of the chemical events in each of the body's cells, events that convert food molecules to the energy needed for the cells to function.

Gandhi's diet centered around fresh fruit, and the amount that he ate would have broken the budget of a typical middle-class Indian household. Reflecting on his diet, a financial backer once quipped that it cost Gandhi's friends "a great deal of money to keep him in poverty" (Markovits, 2003, p. 89). However, in spite of his love of such food, Gandhi fasted many times in his life, using the threat of his starvation to force the hands of his adversaries. What led him to need to eat, and what allowed him to stop eating voluntarily?

In addition to having unusual eating habits, Gandhi had unusual attitudes toward another major source of motivation—sex. Gandhi felt that sex for pleasure was morally wrong, that sex should be engaged in only for procreation. In his later years, he urged sexual abstention so that "sexual energy" could be preserved and channeled into work that advanced worthy social causes (Markovits, 2003, p. 94).

Hunger and sex are two of the drives that are best understood, and they represent strikingly different kinds of motivation. Hunger is the classic drive that relies on the deprived reward system; by definition, to be hungry is to be deprived of food. If you don't eat, you will eventually die. Sex does not rely on this system; if you follow Gandhi's advice and don't have sex, you won't die. In spite of their differences, hunger and sex—and their satisfaction—share many characteristics and affect many aspects of our lives.

LOOKING AHEAD Learning Objectives

1. What makes you hungry and full, and what leads you to eat particular foods at particular times?
2. How is weight kept relatively constant, and why do some people become obese?
3. What is the nature of the sexual response cycle?
4. What determines whether you are attracted to the same sex or the opposite sex?

Eating Behavior: The Hungry Mind in the Hungry Body

Your life is sustained by your body's **metabolism**, the sum of the chemical events in each of your cells, events that convert food molecules to the energy needed for the cells to function. Eating is necessary to maintain your metabolism. In the sections that follow, we explore what factors determine what and when we eat.

Is Being Hungry the Opposite of Being Full?

Hunger arises from the action of two distinct brain systems; one system leads you to feel a need to eat, and the other leads you to feel full (Davis & Levine, 1977; Yeomans & Gray, 1997).

The feeling of a need to eat arises when your brain senses that the level of food molecules in your blood is too low. The brain registers the quantities of two major types of food molecules: *glucose* (a type of sugar) and *fatty acids* (M. I. Friedman, 1991; M. I. Friedman et al., 1986).

In contrast, "feeling full" does not depend on the level of food molecules in the blood: You feel full well before food is digested and food molecules enter the bloodstream. If you suspect that feeling full has something to do with the state of your stomach, you're on the right track. When food is removed with a flexible tube from the stomach of a rat that has just eaten to satisfaction, the rat will eat just enough to replace the loss (Davis & Campbell, 1973). But a

The brain system that regulates eating is surprisingly complex, as is revealed when it is disrupted by a stroke. For example, a person can develop what is known as *gourmand syndrome*, a neurological disorder that is characterized by an obsession with fine food. Such people do not report being hungry all of the time, and they may not overeat—but their entire lives become centered on food.

Source: PhotoEdit Inc.

full stomach is not enough to tell an animal to stop eating. Filling an animal's stomach with saltwater does not diminish appetite as much as filling it with milk, even if the fluids are placed directly into the stomach so that the animals cannot taste them (Deutsch et al., 1978). The stomach contains detectors that register the food value of its contents, and this information is transmitted to the brain. Signals sent by sensory neurons in the stomach to the brain tell you that you have eaten "enough" and can stop eating. Similar signals are also sent by other organs, including the upper part of the small intestine and the liver.

Appetite: A Moving Target Whether you will eat something depends in part on how it tastes. When you take the first bites of a meal or snack, you probably experience the *appetizer effect*: if those first bites taste good, your appetite is stimulated. This effect is driven in part by *opioids* in the brain; as you might suspect from their name, opioids are chemicals that behave like opium-derived drugs and cause you to experience pleasure. The opioids are released when you first eat food that tastes good (Yeomans & Gray, 1997).

As you continue to eat, your responses to food-related stimuli change. After eating a few fresh-baked cookies, for example, the smell of them doesn't seem quite as heavenly as it did before you began to eat them. If people have had their fill of a certain food, they rate its odor as less pleasant than they did before eating it (Duclaux et al., 1973). However, just having your fill of a certain food does not mean you won't keep eating: In fact, if the flavor, texture, color, or shape of a food is changed, people will eat more of the same food (Rolls et al., 1981). After you've eaten a few chocolate chip cookies, you might find yourself not interested in more of those cookies, but darker, larger cookies with big chunks of chocolate might still be appealing.

These changes in your appetite are linked to the activity of the hypothalamus. Neurons in the lateral hypothalamus initially fire when an animal sees or tastes a food and then reduce their firing after the animal has eaten its fill of that food (Burton et al., 1976). These neurons are selective: After they stop responding to one food, they can still be stimulated by another (Rolls et al., 1981). But appetite, like most psychological phenomena, is governed by a complex set of brain areas and chemical events (Blouet & Schwartz, 2010; Small et al., 2001). ✳ Explore

And appetite isn't just about the brain. To understand why you eat the amount you do, you need to consider events at the different levels of analysis. Anything that reminds you of good food you've eaten on a previous occasion—an event at the level of the person—can increase hunger. For example, if you see a photograph of a street with outdoor cafés and that reminds you a similar street where you enjoyed a huge ice cream sundae, you may find yourself suddenly feeling hungry.

In addition, when alone, you vary the size of a meal depending on its size and the length of time since your last meal—for example, you may eat less for dinner if you had a late lunch (Woods et al., 2000). But this biological mechanism doesn't work so well when you eat with others (De Castro, 1990; Herman et al., 2003). When people eat in groups, they often do not vary the size of their meals to reflect their degree of hunger. People tend to eat more when with company and may even eat a greater amount when a larger number of people are present for a meal. However, in some circumstances, people will actually eat less when eating in a group than they would when alone. You might call this the "not wanting to look like a pig" effect! It is clear that eating with other people can lead you to eat more or less than you would when alone, but the precise ways in which others exert their influence are not yet known (Herman et al., 2003).

As usual, events at the different levels of analysis interact. For example, you get hungry when reminded of good food in part because your body responds both to perceptions of food and to insulin, which is secreted by thoughts of food. **Insulin** is a hormone that stimulates the storage of food molecules in the form of fat. Insulin thereby reduces the level of food molecules in the blood, which usually increases hunger.

Why Does It Taste Good? Some of our tastes clearly are a consequence of experience. French people cannot believe that Americans actually like the taste of peanut butter, and Americans often lift an eyebrow at the thought of eating a nice, succulent snail. But beyond cultural differences, individual experience has a lot to do with what you, as

✳ Explore the Effects of the Hypothalamus on Eating Behavior on mypsychlab.com

Insulin A hormone that stimulates the storage of food molecules in the form of fat.

opposed to your friends and neighbors, happen to like to eat. Consider the following examples:

1. People can develop disgust reactions to certain foods (Rozin & Fallon, 1986), and refuse to eat those foods. Such *cognitive taste aversion* can arise from classical conditioning; for instance, if you become nauseated soon after eating rhubarb, you may associate nausea with that food and avoid it in the future (Garcia & Koelling, 1966; Garcia et al., 1966). However, classical conditioning may not always be necessary to develop food aversions (Batsell & Brown, 1998); for example, seeing somebody else react poorly to a food may be enough to make you avoid it.

2. Seeing a food in contact with something disgusting may be enough to make you avoid eating it. Paul Rozin and his colleagues (1996) have shown that people apparently believe that "once in contact, always in contact." If a neutral food was in contact with a repulsive object, the aversive properties seem to transfer. For instance, suppose someone dunked a sterilized, dead cockroach briefly in your glass of water. Would you want to take a sip? The answer is probably a resounding no!

3. The mere fact that food physically resembles something repulsive is enough to make food unappealing. For instance, if a morsel of premium chocolate fudge were molded into the shape of feces, the shape alone would make it unappealing.

4. Rozin and his colleagues have also shown that Americans harbor exaggerated beliefs about the harmful effects of some foods; in fact, many incorrectly believe that salt and fat are harmful even at trace levels (Rozin et al., 1996).

5. Beliefs also play another role in determining what we want to eat: Perhaps unconsciously, people believe that "you are what you eat." In one study, participants rated qualities of people who "ate boar" and those who "ate turtle." The boar eaters were believed to be more likely to have boarlike qualities, such as being bearded and heavyset (Nemeroff & Rozin, 1989).

Culture plays a key role in shaping our tastes in food: The French would never give up their beloved snails or frogs, Koreans find pickled snakes delicious, Filipinos enjoy unhatched chicks in the shell, Germans savor stuffed pig intestines, and Chileans eat a kind of sea anemone whose looks would qualify it to star in a science-fiction movie.

Source: © Reuters / CORBIS All Rights Reserved

Overeating: When Enough Is Not Enough

We humans like the taste of fatty foods, which is bad news because eating too much fat can lead to a variety of diseases, such as diabetes, cardiovascular disease, cancer, gallbladder disease, and—of course—obesity (Schiffman et al., 1999). Our culture places a premium on being thin, but many of us nonetheless overeat. And according to the Centers for Disease Control and Prevention (Flegal et al., 2010), 33% of Americans are obese and another 34% are overweight—and these numbers are increasing over time. In the following sections we consider why so many people find it so hard to control their weight.

Set Point: Your Normal Weight Even if you lose weight, it's difficult to retain a thinner body. Why? After you lose weight, your fat cells become less likely to give up their stored energy. In addition, receptors in your brain that are sensitive to low levels of fat then become active and make you hungry; you eat more, and thus you end up gaining weight. This mechanism reminded researchers of the way a thermostat turns on the heater when the room is too cold, bringing it back to a constant temperature. This analogy led to the notion that animals, including humans, settle at a particular body weight that is easiest to maintain; this weight is called the **set point**.

For many years, researchers thought of the set point as relatively constant, kept that way by homeostatic mechanisms (Nisbett, 1972; Stunkard, 1982). However, more recently, some researchers have argued that the body doesn't maintain the set point the way a thermostat maintains room temperature (Berthoud, 2002; Levine & Billington, 1997). Rather, although your body weight is relatively stable, it can change if your environment changes (for example, when more and fattier foods become available), your activities change (for example, you walk to work and thus exercise more often), or your emotional state changes (for example, you become depressed and listless).

It's all too easy to alter your set point so that you gain weight. Brain systems involved in decision making and reasoning (such as those in the frontal lobes) are connected to and apparently can "overpower" the systems in the hypothalamus that underlie hunger (Berthoud, 2002). Thus, we sometimes eat not because we're hungry but because we're

Set point The particular body weight that is easiest to maintain.

bored or lonely, because a piece of food just looks too good to pass by (think of the last moist brownie you saw), or simply because we think we ought to eat (perhaps because the clock says it's lunchtime). If you eat when your body doesn't need the energy, you are "overeating"; if you overeat for a prolonged time, the number of fat cells in your body increases to store the additional energy. Thus, you gain weight.

In contrast, it's much harder to alter your set point so that you weigh less. Simply eating less is not likely to work in the long run; when you lose weight, each fat cell decreases in size, but you don't lose fat cells. Instead, regular, moderately vigorous exercise is more likely to adjust your set point downward. Exercise can speed up your metabolism, leading your cells to need more energy even when you are not exercising. This is the best method of changing your balance of energy input and output and thereby of losing weight.

Obesity An obese person is defined as one who is more than 20% heavier than the medically ideal weight for that person's sex, height, and bone structure. In the following sections, we consider three theories of why people become obese.

Obese people have the same "willpower" to resist eating junk food as nonobese people.

Source: MBI\Alamy Images Royalty Free

FAT PERSONALITIES?   One theory is that obese people have weak characters that make them slaves to food. This is not the case. The personality characteristics of obese and nonobese people are similar (Nilsson et al., 1998; Poston et al., 1999).

However, if obese people do not have "weak characters," does some other aspect of their personalities lead them to overeat? According to one such theory, people who become obese eat when they feel stress, as a kind of defense. However, the evidence for this idea is mixed: Obese people do not always overeat when they feel stress—and may instead tend to overeat when aroused, positively or negatively (Andrews & Jones, 1990; McKenna, 1972).

FAT GENES?   At least some forms of obesity may have a genetic basis. In fact, these forms of obesity may not be connected to how much a person actually eats. If one identical twin is obese, the other probably is too; variations in weight may be as much as 70% heritable (Berthoud, 2002; Ravussin & Bouchard, 2000). At last count, some 58 distinct genes and portions of all chromosomes except for chromosome Y (the male sex chromosome) have been related to obesity (Rankinen et al., 2002). Claude Bouchard, a researcher in this area, notes that genes may affect weight in numerous ways: "Some affect appetite, some affect satiety [a sense of fullness]. Some affect metabolic rate" (quoted in Gladwell, 1998, p. 53).

Given how many genes appear to be involved, the genetics of obesity will not be simple to unravel—but some highlights have already been discovered. For example, the neurons in certain brain areas involved in registering satiety appear to rely on the neurotransmitter serotonin (Blundell, 1977, 1984, 1986; Blundell & Halford, 1998), and mutant mice that lack specific receptors for this neurotransmitter will keep eating until they become obese (Tecott et al., 1995). The notion that humans may act the same way is supported by the finding that people gain weight if they take medication that happens to block these receptors (Fitton & Heel, 1990); moreover, people who take drugs that activate these receptors report being less hungry, and they may actually lose weight while on the medication (Sargent et al., 1997).

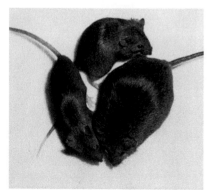

Genes can make a big difference. Researchers found that by altering a single gene, they could increase the production of substances that make a mouse obese.

Source: AP Wide World Photos

FAT ENVIRONMENT?   Genes determine the range of possibilities—called the *reaction range*—for a particular characteristic, and the environment sets individuals within that range. For example, genes set the range of possible heights for a given person, but how tall a person will grow depends in large part on his or her diet (compare young adults in Japan with their grandparents—same genes but a large difference in height). By the same token, genes set the range of possible weights for a person. When some people overeat even a small amount and do not exercise, their genes will cause them to gain weight

(Ravussin & Bouchard, 2000). Overeating is encouraged by many aspects of the American environment: Food is relatively cheap, fast foods are high in fat, snacking is all too easy and acceptable, and food portions have grown larger in the United States (but not in many parts of Europe). At the same time, we exercise less not only because most of us drive or ride to work but also because many of our amusements, such as watching television and surfing the Web, are sedentary. Moreover, in earlier eras many people were paid for work that involved significant exercise, but such jobs are now less common. In these and other ways, the environment in some cultures such as that of the United States promotes behaviors that lead to obesity. Hill and Peters (1998) suggest three approaches to "curing the environment":

1. Educate people to eat smaller portions,
2. Make tasty foods that are low in fat and calories more available, and
3. Encourage more physical activity.

Some obese people are capable of losing large amounts of weight and keeping the weight off (Tinker & Tucker, 1997). These people are able to adopt healthier eating and exercise habits. Note, however, that changes in the environment can be effective only if the genes define a relatively wide range of possible weights for the individual. If the range of possible weights set by the genes that control obesity is narrow, then people who have those genes may not be able to change how heavy they are.

Dieting Even Gandhi, famous for his fasts, liked to eat. None of us especially relishes diets that require us to eat less, and we are receptive to diets that promise weight loss while allowing us to eat like we always do. But do diets really work? The bottom line is clear: yes, for moderate weight loss. For example, a study of four popular diets found that overweight or obese people lost modest amounts of weight when following any of the diets, and that the diets were equally effective (Dansinger et al., 2005). (The study also found that at least a third of people who began a diet did not stick with it.) Furthermore, low-carbohydrate diets (such as the Atkins) do not lead obese people to shed more pounds than standard diets, such as that advocated by Weight Watchers (Foster et al., 2003). The science of dieting is clear: If you want to lose weight, eat fewer calories (Freedman et al., 2001) and exercise more.

Sexual Behavior: A Many-Splendored Thing

Eating is not the only biological function that people enjoy; sex is another good example. But your body doesn't actually need sex in the way you need food and oxygen; as we noted earlier, you won't die from celibacy. We engage in sexual activity in large part because it leads to some of the most intense of all positive emotions. Although we are "wired" to want to engage in sex, it is not exactly an instinct: Our sexual responses are not generally fixed and unalterable but rather are rich and varied. Moreover, surveys indicate that only a small minority of sexual acts in the United States, about 2%, are to procreate (Linner, 1972). In fact, sexual partners sometimes take great pains to avoid conception. (The earliest known attempts at contraception were developed 4,000 years ago by the Egyptians; they thought that dried crocodile dung would do the job.)

Because sexual behavior is so important to humans, researchers have tried to understand it. Alfred Kinsey began the first systematic surveys about human sexual behavior in the late 1940s. He and his colleagues interviewed thousands of Americans about their sex lives. Kinsey found that people frequently reported engaging in sexual practices then considered rare or even abnormal. However, attempts to study sexual behavior ran into some unique problems. As Freud (1910, p. 41) wrote, "People in general are not candid over sexual matters, they do not show their sexuality freely, but to conceal it wear a heavy overcoat of a tissue of lies, as though the weather were bad in the world of sexuality." Psychologists have had difficulty seeing through this "tissue of lies," and even today there is debate about whether we have reliable information about many facets of human sexuality.

Studies of sexual behavior often are flawed because of two types of biases—selection bias and response bias. Many studies suffer from *selection bias*, which occurs when a study has a nonrandom sample of participants. Researchers have found that not everybody is

Alfred Kinsey's life and work have received renewed interest—and generated controversy—as a result of the 2004 movie about him.

Source: AP Wide World Photos

271

THINK like a **PSYCHOLOGIST** Would you volunteer to fill in a questionnaire about your most intimate sexual activities? What sorts of people do you think would be most comfortable participating in such a study?

equally willing to report their sexual preferences and activities, and thus the data are likely to come from a biased sample. And this situation is more extreme for behavioral studies (as opposed to questionnaire studies) of sexual activity. Anthony Bogaert (1996), for example, asked undergraduate males to volunteer for a study on human sexuality. The people who volunteered to do so differed in many ways from males who volunteered for a study on personality: The former group had more sexual experience, were interested in engaging in a wider range of sexual activity, were more inclined to seek out sensation and excitement, and were less socially conforming and less likely to follow rules (Trivedi & Sabini [1998] reported similar findings).

In addition to selection bias, studies of sexual behavior often suffer from *response bias*, which occurs when people who are participating in a study do not respond to questions accurately or do not behave as they normally would. In particular, people from different cultures may respond differently when asked about their sexual and reproductive behavior: Researchers found that Hispanic American women reported less sexual activity when their interviewers were older (women), but Black American women did not display this bias as strongly (Ford & Norris, 1997). The researchers suspected that this bias arose because the Hispanic culture has traditionally frowned on premarital sex for women, leading the Hispanic women to underreport their sexual activity to older women who might disapprove.

In short, data about sex are often suspect. Sampling bias as well as response bias can distort the results.

Sexual Responses: Step-by-Step William Masters and Virginia Johnson (1966) were the first researchers who systematically studied actual sexual behavior, not just reports or descriptions of it, with a large sample of participants. Their effort was the first that provided a detailed look behind the "tissue of lies" about sex. Over the course of many years, Masters and Johnson brought thousands of men and women into their laboratory and devised ways to measure what the body does during sex. The outcome was a description of four stages the human body—male or female—passes through during sexual activity:

1. *Excitement* (during the initial phases, when the person becomes aroused),
2. *Plateau* (when the person becomes fully aroused),
3. *Orgasm* (accompanied by muscle contractions and, in men, ejaculation), and
4. *Resolution* (the release of sexual tension).

These stages meld into one another, with no sharp divisions separating them (R. S. Levin, 1980; R. J. Levin, 1994). The mountain of research they conducted led Masters and Johnson to reach four general conclusions, summarized in Table 2. Read

Read **Masters and Johnson Biography** on **mypsychlab.com**

TABLE 2 **Masters and Johnson's Conclusions**

- Men and women are similar in their bodily reactions to sex.
- Women tend to respond more slowly than men, but stay aroused longer.
- Many women can have multiple orgasms, whereas men typically have a *refractory period*, a period of time following orgasm when they cannot become aroused again.
- Women reported that penis size is not related to sexual performance unless the man is worried about it.

Others have built on Masters and Johnson's research and have developed a comprehensive description of the **sexual response cycle**: *Sexual attraction* leads to *sexual desire*, *sexual excitement* (arousal), and possibly *sexual performance* (which involves becoming fully aroused, reaching orgasm, and then experiencing resolution followed by—for men—a refractory period). More recently, researchers have proposed an alternative cycle of sexual response for females, one in which (1) sexual excitement leads to or occurs at the same time as desire, (2) sexual excitement can also amplify desire, and (3) satisfying sexual encounters do not necessarily require orgasm (Basson, 2001).

Why do we desire to engage in sexual behavior at the times and with the partners we do? Not unexpectedly, events at all three levels of analysis play crucial roles in our sexual behavior, as discussed in the following sections.

The Role of Hormones: Do Chemicals Dictate Behavior?

In 1849, German scientist Arnold Berthold wondered why castrated roosters acted like hens. Such roosters stopped crowing, mating with hens, fighting, and engaging in other typical rooster behaviors. So, Berthold castrated some roosters and then put the testes into their abdominal cavities. Shortly thereafter, the roosters started behaving like roosters again. Berthold reasoned that the testes produced their effects not because of nerves or other physical connections but because they released something into the bloodstream. We now know that what the testes release is the male hormone *testosterone*.

Hormones are chemicals that are secreted into the bloodstream (primarily by endocrine glands) and that trigger receptors on neurons and other types of cells. Hormones are controlled in large part by the pituitary gland, the brain's "master gland." The pituitary gland in turn is controlled by the hypothalamus, which plays a major role in emotion and motivation and is affected by hormones produced elsewhere in the body.

SEX HORMONES. When you are sexually aroused, hormones from the gonads (the testes and ovaries) act on the brain and genital tissue. **Androgens** are usually referred to as "male hormones" (such as testosterone), which lead the body to develop many male characteristics, such as beard growth and a low voice. **Estrogens**, usually referred to as "female hormones," lead the body to develop many female characteristics, such as breasts and the bone structure of the female pelvis. However, the labels "male hormones" and "female hormones" are not quite accurate because both types of hormones are present in both males and females—but males have more testosterone, and females have more estrogen.

Although they exert direct effects on physical characteristics, hormones don't directly dictate behavior. Rather, they lead to a tendency to *want* to behave in certain ways in the presence of particular stimuli. That is, they modify motivation.

INSENSITIVITY TO SEX HORMONES. Not everyone's body responds to sex hormones in the same way, and some people's bodies don't respond at all to certain sex hormones. As an extreme example, people who have *androgen insensitivity syndrome* have an X chromosome (the female sex chromosome) and a Y chromosome (the male sex chromosome) and so genetically they would be considered male, but a genetic mutation prevents receptors for androgens from developing properly—which prevents androgen from binding to these receptors. Thus, the lock is missing for the hormonal key, and androgens have no effects either during fetal development or afterward. People with androgen insensitivity syndrome—who ordinarily would have been boys, given the presence of the Y chromosome— instead grow into girls, but with testes tucked up in the belly and no uterus or ovaries. In spite of their genes, they develop and behave as females because androgen cannot influence their bodies or brains. In fact, adults with androgen insensitivity syndrome would in most other ways be considered female: they look exactly like women, often marry, and have normal female sex lives (which include normal orgasms during intercourse), although their vagina sometimes is too shallow and must be surgically altered later in life and they sometimes may require female hormone supplements.

HORMONES AND DESIRE. Sex hormones also influence our interest in sexual activity. In fact, changes in the level of sex hormones over the course of a woman's menstrual cycle affect the degree to which she is inclined to become sexually aroused. But more than that, researchers have reported that the nature of a woman's sexual interest may shift over the course of the menstrual cycle. For example, in one study, researchers report that when women are ovulating, they prefer "ruggedly handsome" male faces more than when they are not ovulating (Penton-Voak & Perrett, 2000). Similarly, in another study, while women were ovulating they were more likely to be interested in men who are not their spouses (Gangestad et al., 2002). However, the effects of shifting hormone levels are only tendencies, affecting different people to different degrees (Regan, 1996).

Sexual response cycle The stages the body passes through during sexual activity, including sexual attraction, desire, excitement, and possibly performance.

Androgens Sex hormones that lead the body to develop many male characteristics, such as beard growth and a low voice.

Estrogens Sex hormones that lead the body to develop many female characteristics, such as breast development and the bone structure of the female pelvis.

Although single and married men have the same levels of testosterone in the morning, by the end of the day married men have less than unmarried men; testosterone normally decreases over the course of the day but does so more sharply for married men (P. B. Gray et al., 2002). This is true whether or not the men have children.

Source: Photodisc/Getty Images

The relationship between hormones and sexual desire runs in both directions. Consider a famous study, reported by a researcher who signed his paper "Anonymous" (1970). This man was a scientist who worked on a small island and only occasionally visited the mainland, where he would have brief periods of contact with the opposite sex. He apparently had time on his hands when he was alone, as he decided to measure his beard growth every day by weighing his beard clippings after shaving. He found that his beard grew thicker as his visits to the mainland approached. Just thinking about the prospect of female companionship apparently caused his levels of androgens to increase, which in turn caused his beard to grow more quickly.

OXYTOCIN AND MOTHERLY LOVE. The so-called sex hormones aren't the only ones that affect our sex lives (Carter, 2004; Meston & Frohlich, 2000). *Oxytocin* is a hormone (produced by the pituitary gland) that increases dramatically in women immediately after they give birth and probably helps to forge the mother–infant emotional bond (Insel, 2000). For both sexes, oxytocin is also released after orgasm and may play a role in emotional bonding between sex partners.

Sexual Motivation We earlier noted that only a very small percentage of sexual acts are performed in order to reproduce. The remaining percentage, about 98% of the total, are performed for a variety of reasons. Cooper and colleagues (1998) showed that motivations for having sex can be thought of in terms of the two dimensions illustrated in Figure 8, which range from avoidance to approach (the horizontal dimension) and from self-oriented independence to social connection (the vertical dimension). For example, the lower left quadrant would include sex in abusive relationships, where a woman uses sex to try to prevent her partner from mistreating her, and the upper right quadrant would include sex intended simply for recreation. Not every sexual encounter falls squarely into only one of the quadrants, and each quadrant may be more relevant for different people at different phases of their lives.

FIGURE 8 Motives for Having Sex

	SELF	
Use sex to escape, avoid, minimize negative emotions or threats to self-esteem		Use sex to enhance positive emotions or experience
AVOIDANCE		APPROACH
Use sex to escape, avoid, minimize negative social experiences		Use sex to enhance social connections
	SOCIAL	

People engage in sex for many reasons, which Cooper and colleagues (1998) characterize as falling along two dimensions.

Source: From Cooper et al, "Motivations for sex and risky sexual behavior among adolescents and young adults: A functional perspective." From *Journal of Personality and Social Psychology,* Dec. 1, 1998. Copyright © American Psychological Association. Reprinted with permission.

Mating Preferences People are notoriously selective about their choices in sexual partners, and evolutionary psychologists have offered theories of what makes someone seem desirable as a sexual partner. Some of these theories derive from Trivers's (1972) influential concept of *parental investment.* He argued that males should be interested in having as many offspring as possible because males do not need to invest much time or energy into fathering a child—and hence males should be more interested in short-term relationships for sex and less particular about sexual partners. In contrast, because females cannot have as many children as is possible for males (if only because each one requires 9 months to develop as a fetus), they should be invested in nurturing and raising the children they do have—and hence males should be less interested in short-term relationships for sex and more particular about their sexual partners (who would influence the qualities of their children and help to raise them). However, when Pedersen and colleagues (2002) tested this idea, they found that 98.9% of men and 99.2% of women hoped eventually to have a long-term stable relationship. Very few participants of either gender reported that they were motivated by the prospect of continued short-term sexual relationships. In addition, the two genders spend comparable amounts of time and money in "short-term mating," such as trying to meet someone at a party (L. C. Miller et al., 2002).

Another evolutionary theory relies on the observation that because fertilization occurs in the privacy of a woman's fallopian tubes, a man can never be absolutely certain that a baby carries his genes; thus, according to this theory, men should be particularly alert to their mates' possible sexual infidelity. In contrast, because women value a man who will devote time, energy, and resources to her children, women should be particularly alert to their mates' becoming emotionally involved with someone else. Consistent with this prediction, when asked which would be more upsetting— their mates' falling in love with someone else or having sex with someone else—most men chose the latter and most women chose the former (Buss et al., 1992; Cramer et al., 2001–2002). However, these preferences may not be observed when participants are asked to respond on the basis of their actual experiences, not just abstract ideas (C. R. Harris, 2002). Moreover, other researchers have found that men and women value remarkably similar characteristics in a potential mate (L. C. Miller et al., 2002).

Adolescents apparently model their behavior after that of their friends and hence are more likely to have sexual relations early if their friends are having sexual relations early (DiBlasio & Benda, 1990).

Source: David Young-Wolff\PhotoEdit Inc.

To avoid methodological problems—such as the tendency to respond in ways that are considered socially desirable—that arise when participants are asked to report their sexual behavior or desires, some researchers have recorded bodily reactions to questions about sexual relationships (Buss et al., 1992; Grice & Seely, 2000). One particularly careful study of such reactions was conducted by Christine Harris (2000). She asked participants to imagine different scenarios while she recorded their blood pressure, heart rate, and skin conductivity. Men showed greater reactions to imagining their mate having sex versus being emotionally involved with someone else. But they showed the same reactions when they imagined *themselves* having sex versus being emotionally involved with their mate. Moreover, women who had been in a committed sexual relationship showed reactions very much like those of the men—which complicates the evolutionary story.

These findings do not mean that evolution had no role in shaping mate preferences, but they do show that mate selection—like all other human behavior—does not arise solely from events at a single level of analysis.

Sexual Orientation: More Than a Choice

People who are sexually attracted to the opposite sex are termed **heterosexual**, people who are sexually attracted to the same sex are termed **homosexual**, and people who are sexually attracted to both sexes are termed **bisexual**. Sexuality might best be regarded as a continuum, with most people being primarily heterosexual in their preferences and behavior and somewhere between 4% and 10% of the U.S. population being primarily homosexual in their preferences and behavior (Fay et al., 1989). Studies of bisexual men have shown that many of them tend to prefer and have sexual relationships with same-sex partners over time (Stokes et al., 1997).

For many years, homosexuality was considered either a personal choice or the result of being raised a certain way (for instance, with a weak father and an overly strict mother), but research indicates that these views are generally not correct. Moreover, programs to train homosexuals to prefer the opposite sex have failed, even those that relied on extreme techniques such as electric shock to punish homosexual thoughts or behavior (Brown [1989] offers a personal account). Homosexuality is not, at least in the vast majority of cases, either a personal choice or the result of being raised a certain way, as we discuss below. Much evidence indicates that biological events—particularly the functioning of the

Heterosexual A person who is sexually attracted to members of the opposite sex.

Homosexual A person who is sexually attracted to members of the same sex.

Bisexual A person who is sexually attracted to members of both sexes.

hypothalamus and the influence of *genes*—play a major role in determining sexual orientation, as we discuss below.

A Gay Hypothalamus?

One source of evidence for the biological foundations of sexual orientation comes from studies comparing the brains of men who are homosexual with those of men who are heterosexual. For example, LeVay (1991) carefully examined the brains of homosexual and heterosexual men (after they had died) and found that a small part of the hypothalamus, about as large as an average-sized grain of sand, was about half the size of that part of the brain in heterosexual men (Allen & Gorski [1992] report related evidence). This was interesting for two reasons: (1) The hypothalamus is the major brain structure that is activated when males see erotic stimuli that match their sexual preference (homosexual or heterosexual; Paul et al., 2008), and (2) this part of the hypothalamus is typically smaller in women than in men. However, all of the brains LeVay studied came from men who had died of AIDS, and it is possible that the disease had something to do with the structural abnormality. But when this same structure was surgically disrupted in monkeys, they displayed atypical sexual behavior (Slimp et al., 1978).

These and similar data may suggest that particular brain structures may lead some men to be homosexual (LeVay & Hamer, 1994). However, keep in mind that correlation does not prove causation: In theory, there could be something else about being homosexual that causes a part of the brain to change.

Other Biological Differences

Other findings support the idea that biological factors lead someone to be homosexual. Consider, for example, the fact that when some people hear a clicking sound, their ears immediately respond by producing a sound. Researchers have found that this response to a click is less frequent and weaker for homosexual and bisexual women than for heterosexual women—and men in general have less frequent and weaker ear responses than do heterosexual women (McFadden & Pasanen, 1999). Apparently, parts of the ear are different in women with different sexual orientations. Moreover, these results not only show a biological difference for homosexual and bisexual women but may also hint at different biological bases for male and female homosexuality.

In the Genes?

The findings of biological differences between homosexual and heterosexual people do not indicate whether the causes are hereditary (that is, genetic), the result of experiences in the womb, or the result of experiences during early childhood. Hamer and his colleagues (1993) studied 114 families that included a homosexual man and found that inheritance of homosexuality seemed to be related to homosexuality in the mother's family. This result led them to examine the X chromosome, which is the sex chromosome from the mother (females have two X chromosomes, one from the mother and one from the father; males have one X chromosome, from the mother, and one Y chromosome, from the father). These researchers concluded that a small portion of the X chromosome is related to homosexual preference and behavior. However, not all studies have supported this view (McKnight & Malcolm, 2000). Moreover, although one study with twins supported the idea that homosexuality is at least partly inherited (Bailey & Pillard, 1991), a later study failed to find this effect (Rice et al., 1999).

The mixed findings from genetic studies may mean that there is more than one way that homosexuality can arise. One intriguing possibility is suggested by the finding that homosexual men are more likely than heterosexual men to have older brothers (Blanchard, 2001; Cantor et al., 2002; Ellis & Blanchard, 2001). Why might this be? It appears that the mother's body somehow "remembers" the number of boys she bore (possibly by building up specific antibodies; Ellis & Blanchard, 2001) and alters the level of testosterone accordingly. Boys with older brothers receive proportionally more testosterone during gestation, which appears to increase the likelihood that they will be homosexual.

One intriguing—if preliminary—bit of evidence for this theory relies on the fact that the prenatal level of maternal testosterone affects testosterone levels in the fetus—which also happens to affect the relative lengths of the ring and index fingers (Kondo et al., 1997). Hence, if large amounts of testosterone were present in the womb, as predicted by the theory, then indicators of this should be evident in the relative lengths of the fingers of adult homosexuals. As predicted, some researchers have found that, on average, the relative lengths of the ring and index fingers differ for homosexual and heterosexual men (Robinson & Manning, 2000). Also consistent with the theory, additional research with a large number of participants suggests that this relation occurs only for gay men who have older brothers (Williams et al., 2000).

LOOKING BACK

✓●─[Study and Review on
mypsychlab.com

1. **What makes you hungry and full, and what leads you to eat particular foods at particular times?** Different mechanisms determine whether you feel hungry or full. Hunger occurs when the brain determines that the level of glucose or fatty acids in the bloodstream is too low. Being full depends in large part on having nutrients in your stomach. At the beginning of a meal, taste plays an especially important role in determining whether you eat. As a meal progresses, changes in the type of food will keep your appetite up, and tastes (as well as thoughts) that cause insulin to be released will increase hunger. Beliefs about the history of a food item (such as whether it was ever in contact with something repulsive) and even associations linked to the shape of a food affect how appealing it is.

2. **How is weight kept relatively constant, and why do some people become obese?** The set point operates to keep your weight constant. However, your weight can change if your environment, activity level, or emotional state changes. At least some obese people are genetically predisposed to becoming obese.

3. **What is the nature of the sexual response cycle?** According to research on sexual activity, people first experience sexual attraction, next desire, and then excitement (arousal), which may be followed by sexual performance; sexual performance involves becoming fully aroused, reaching orgasm, and finally experiencing resolution (followed by a refractory period for men). In an alternative sexual response cycle for females, sexual excitement can precede and amplify desire, and orgasm is not required for a sexual encounter to be satisfying. Hormones play a role in sexual behavior by biasing people to behave in certain ways.

4. **What determines whether you are attracted to the same sex or the opposite sex?** Biological events, either caused by the genes or occurring in the womb or during childhood, appear to play a key role in determining sexual orientation.

LET'S REVIEW

((•—Listen to an audio file of your chapter on **mypsychlab.com**

I. EMOTION: I FEEL, THEREFORE I AM

A. Ekman identified six basic emotions: surprise, happiness, anger, fear, disgust, and sadness. Research results have shown that surprise and fear are more easily confused with each other than they are with any of the other basic emotions. Basic emotions can be combined to produce many types of emotion.

B. Culture and experience influence how easily emotions can be interpreted; although humans can "read" emotions from any other human at better than chance levels, we can more accurately read emotion in members of familiar cultures.

C. Each of several widely known theories has captured an aspect of how emotions arise. The James–Lange theory holds that we feel emotion after our body reacts to a situation. The Cannon–Bard theory holds that emotions and bodily reactions occur at the same time. Cognitive theory claims that emotions arise when we interpret our bodily reactions in the context of the specific situation. The emerging synthesis of views on emotion proposes that some emotions arise from brain responses that do not involve cognitive interpretation, whereas others depend on such interpretation.

D. As the James–Lange theory predicts, some emotions may arise in part from changes in bodily reactions, such as heart rate, breathing rate, and facial expression. As the Cannon–Bard theory predicts, some emotions, such as fear, are reflexes that produce the emotional experience and the bodily reaction simultaneously. As cognitive theory predicts, how we interpret the causes of our bodily reactions does in fact influence which emotion we feel. The emerging synthesis puts all of these discoveries together, recognizing that emotions arise from a mixture of different brain systems that operate at the same time.

E. Fear is one of the strongest emotions, and the amygdala plays a role in fear and in strong emotions in general. Environmental events influence emotion; our happiness, for example, depends in part on our economic and cultural context. In addition, the emotions we feel depend on how we construe a situation; happy people tend to remain happy, in part because of how they view the world.

F. Culture shapes people's emotional reactions. It also influences how effectively they can interpret body language to determine another person's emotion.

G. We can control our emotions, both by prolonging them over time and by suppressing them; this control is directly reflected in the activation of brain systems. Culture affects the display rules we use, which determine when and how we express emotion.

H. Lies cannot be reliably detected by current techniques, in part because different types of lies arise from different brain systems.

II. MOTIVATION AND REWARD: FEELING GOOD

A. Motivations arise from: (1) evolutionarily shaped instincts, although such instincts are rare in humans (sex seems like an obvious example, but human sex is not characterized by rigid, unalterable behaviors); (2) drives, such as thirst; some drives are designed to maintain homeostasis (when we are cold, we seek warmth); (3) a preference for an intermediate level of arousal; and (4) incentives, such as the potential rewards (including money) for engaging in a behavior.

B. Animals (including humans) can developed learned helplessness if their behavior can't reduce aversive stimuli or conditions.

C. A need arises from the lack of a necessary substance (such as food) or condition (such as warmth); needs give rise to drives, which push us to reach a particular goal that will reduce the need. A want arises when we have an unmet goal that does not arise from a lack of a necessary substance or condition; a want causes the goal to act as an incentive.

D. Needs may be related to a brain system that provides an internal reward when a deprivation is satisfied (for example, by eating when we are hungry). In contrast, many wants may be related to a system that provides a reward when we are not deprived but achieve a desired goal.

E. There are many types of needs; the importance of at least some needs depends partly on culture, particularly on whether the culture is individualist or collectivist.

F. Maslow proposed a hierarchy of needs, but the evidence for his highly influential theory is mixed.

III. HUNGER AND SEX: TWO IMPORTANT MOTIVATIONS

A. The brain senses when the level of nutrients in the blood is too low and causes sensations of hunger. We often eat until signals from the stomach (and other digestive organs) indicate that we've consumed enough food.

B. The hypothalamus plays a particularly critical role in hunger. At the beginning of a meal, taste is especially important in determining whether we want to eat particular foods. As a meal progresses, changes in the type of food we are eating will keep our appetite up, and tastes (as well as thoughts) that cause insulin to be released will increase hunger.

C. Beliefs about the history of a food item (for example, whether it was ever in contact with something repulsive) and even associations with the shape of the food affect how appealing it is.

D. Overeating can cause body weight to increase, and the increase is often difficult to lose. However, weight is determined by many factors that affect metabolism and behavior, including set point, environment, types of activities, and emotional state. Brain systems involved in decision making and reasoning can override the hypothalamic system, leading us to eat when we aren't actually hungry.

E. Obese people do not have "weak characters" but rather may be genetically predisposed to becoming obese or be subject to aspects of the environment that encourage overeating. Many genes are likely to affect body weight and do so in different ways.

F. Sexual attraction can lead to sexual desire, sexual excitement (arousal), and possibly sexual performance (which involves becoming fully aroused, reaching orgasm, and then experiencing resolution followed, for men, by a refractory period).

G. Hormones play a key role in sexual development and modify motivation toward sexual behavior. Fluctuations in sex hormones affect cognition and emotion—and vice versa.

H. Mating preferences may be influenced by evolutionary characteristics, but they are not determined by them.

I. Evidence indicates that certain brain structures are different in male homosexuals than in male heterosexuals and that the operation of certain neural systems (involved in hearing) is different in female homosexuals and bisexuals than in heterosexuals. Such biological differences—and homosexuality itself—are probably caused by genes, by events in the womb, or some combination of these factors.

KEY TERMS

androgens	emotion	individualist culture	need
basic emotion	estrogens	instinct	need for achievement
bisexual	facial feedback hypothesis	insulin	nondeprived reward
collectivist culture	heterosexual	learned helplessness	polygraph
deprived reward	homeostasis	metabolism	set point
display rule	homosexual	misattribution of arousal	sexual response cycle
drive	incentive	motivation	want

PRACTICE TEST

✓●─ Study and Review on mypsychlab.com

For each of the following items, choose the single best answer.

1. Which of the following statements is true?
   a. Our emotions are not always obvious.
   b. Emotions help guide us to approach some things and withdraw from others.
   c. Emotions provide visible cues that help other people know key aspects of our thoughts and desires.
   d. All of the above statements are true.

2. There is widespread agreement that
   a. there are precisely five basic emotions.
   b. humans have a set of built-in emotions that express the most basic types of reactions.
   c. damage to the brain cannot affect emotions.
   d. blind people do not show the same facial expressions of emotion as do people with sight.

3. Davidson and his colleagues have provided evidence that there are separate systems in the brain for two broad types of human emotion. In general,
   a. approach emotions are negative, and withdrawal emotions are positive.
   b. the right frontal lobe tends to be more active than the left when people have approach emotions.
   c. clinically depressed patients have relatively diminished activity in the left frontal lobe.

   d. positive and negative emotions are really opposite sides of the same coin and cannot occur at the same time.

4. Theories of emotion differ in the relationships they assume among bodily events, interpretations of events, and distinct brain systems. Which of the following statements best represents this relationship according to the Cannon–Bard theory?
   a. Different emotions arise from different sets of bodily reactions.
   b. An emotion arises when you interpret the situation as a whole—your bodily state in the context of everything that surrounds it.
   c. The emotions we feel at any moment arise from a mixture of brain and body reactions as well as interpretations and memories pertaining to the situation.
   d. Bodily arousal and the experience of emotion arise in tandem.

5. According to the facial feedback hypothesis, "putting on a happy face"
   a. is just the lyric of an old song.
   b. leads our brains to be in exactly the same state as when we are genuinely happy.
   c. tends to result in more positive ratings of mood than when the face is posed in a negative expression.
   d. has an effect that suggests that emotions are defined only in terms of autonomic reactions.

279

6. In their classic experiment, Schachter and Singer found that
   a. bodily factors are sufficient to explain the range of feelings we have.
   b. participants who were told in advance about the drug used in the experiment and its effects felt differently in the different contexts.
   c. participants in the control group, who did not receive an injection, experienced a strong effect of context and made a cognitive error called the misattribution of arousal.
   d. None of the above statements is true.

7. From studying the brain systems that produce fear, researchers have discovered that
   a. conscious awareness is needed for a stimulus to trigger the amygdala into producing a fear response.
   b. once you learn to associate fear with an object or situation, you will always do so.
   c. people who have a gene (SLC6A4, the human serotonin transporter gene) that affects serotonin levels show decreased activation of the amygdala when they see emotional stimuli.
   d. the amygdala does not play a role in perceiving that *other* people feel fear.

8. Emotion is conveyed not only by facial expression but also by tone of voice and body language. Researchers studying nonverbal communication have determined that
   a. people cannot easily decode nonverbal cues.
   b. people do not automatically imitate expressions.
   c. the ability to *read* nonverbal communications is at least partly determined by experience.
   d. All of the above statements are false.

9. What happens in the brain when people try voluntarily to dampen down the mechanisms that underlie emotion?
   a. Nothing happens; people cannot voluntarily dampen down these mechanisms.
   b. Various brain areas involved in emotion are activated, such as the amygdala and hypothalamus.
   c. Parts of the frontal lobe become activated—and the brain areas normally activated during emotional responses are no longer activated.
   d. None of the above statements is true.

10. Deprived reward
    a. is reward that fills a biological need.
    b. occurs when an action produces a substance or condition necessary for survival.
    c. arises from a brain circuit in which many of the neurons use or are affected by dopamine.
    d. All of the above statements are true.

11. According to Abraham Maslow's hierarchy of physical and emotional needs,
    a. higher-level needs are considered more essential to life.
    b. needs lower in the pyramid must be met before needs higher in the pyramid become the focus of concerns.
    c. once a need is met, its level of importance does not change.
    d. during crises, higher needs advance to an even higher level, and lower-level needs are put on hold.

12. Which of the following statements best explains why you "feel full" when you eat?
    a. Feeling full depends on the level of food molecules in the blood.
    b. A full stomach is enough to tell an animal to stop eating.
    c. You feel full after food is digested.
    d. You know when to stop eating largely because of signals sent by sensory neurons in the stomach to the brain.

13. When you take the first bites of a tasty meal or snack,
    a. you probably experience the appetizer effect.
    b. opioids are released.
    c. neurons in the lateral hypothalamus fire.
    d. All of the above statements are true.

14. Estrogens
    a. are present in both males and females.
    b. cause many male characteristics such as beard growth and a low voice.
    c. directly dictate behavior.
    d. are released after orgasm and probably help to forge the mother–infant emotional bond.

15. Which of the following did Masters and Johnson *not* find in their research on sexual behavior?
    a. Young people enjoy sex more than middle-aged people do.
    b. Men and women have similar bodily reactions to sex.
    c. Women stay aroused longer than men do.
    d. Many women can have multiple orgasms.

Answers 1. d 2. b 3. c 4. d 5. c 6. d 7. b 8. c 9. c 10. d 11. b 12. d 13. d 14. a 15. a

> When you describe an acquaintance as 'intense,' wonder how a friend will handle a piece of bad news, or think about the type of partner you would like to have in life, personality is exerting its influence.

PERSONALITY

VIVE LA DIFFÉRENCE!

Tina and Gabe met in their introductory psychology class. They were immediately attracted to each other and started studying together. After a few conversations, they were pleased to discover that they had similar values and political views. Predictably, they began going out together. On their fourth date, though, Tina began to realize that she and Gabe weren't as much alike as she had thought; she was surprised by this because their views on so many issues were so similar. Tina sometimes had trouble "reading" Gabe because he was shy and emotionally steady,

From *Introducing Psychology: Brain, Person, Group,* Fourth Edition, Stephen M. Kosslyn and Robin S. Rosenberg. Copyright © 2011 by Pearson Education, Inc. Published by Allyn & Bacon. All rights reserved.

without many highs or lows—his manner was "mellow." She wondered why he wasn't more enthusiastic when she proposed activities she thought would be fun to do together, such as in-line skating, bungee-jumping, or biking. "Well, opposites attract, I guess," she thought. And although Gabe enjoyed Tina's spirit, her emotional vibrancy, and her interest in trying new things, now and then he asked her why she was so emotional and always in such a hurry. Tina began to worry that, even though they were strongly attracted to each other, a long-term relationship might reveal persistent differences between them that would be difficult to resolve.

Do such differences reveal something fundamental about Tina and Gabe as people? Do they reflect their personalities? And if so, are personalities set in stone?

The concept of personality infuses daily life. When you describe an acquaintance as "intense," wonder how a friend will handle a piece of bad news, or think about the type of partner you would like to have in life, personality is exerting its influence. What exactly is this quality, which is part and parcel of each of us? **Personality** is a set of emotional, cognitive, and behavioral tendencies that people display over time and across situations and that distinguish individuals from each other. In this chapter, we explore the idea of personality, the perspectives of a number of different theorists who have sought to describe and explain it, the ways that psychologists measure it, and key findings that such measurements have revealed. We also consider the ways that genes influence personality development; the influence of learning experiences, motives, and thoughts on personality; and the effects of the social environment on personality. First, we examine historical views of personality.

◨ ◨ ◨

Personality: Historical Perspectives

Tina wanted to understand why Gabe has the particular lenses through which he views the world and what might account for the way he tends to behave—or, put another way, why he had the personality he did. Tina couldn't help but notice that Gabe studied a lot—much more than Tina did. In fact, he was content to sit for much longer periods of time than was Tina. On the plus side, she learned a lot when she studied with him; but lately, when they studied together, he'd have a big bag of pistachio nuts and sit there cracking and eating nuts while he read. Tina found this very annoying, and it added to her restlessness while studying. Plus, Gabe would leave the shells lying around on the table, creating a mess. She wanted to ask him what the deal was (if he wanted nuts so badly, why didn't he just buy shelled nuts, and wasn't he distracted by the shelling process?). But she didn't feel comfortable asking him; she thought he might get defensive or hurt, or it might lead to a fight, which wasn't worth it. Tina wondered why she and Gabe were so different in so many ways while at the same time they were so similar in other ways. In this section we ask, how do our personalities develop, and why do they develop differently? Among the notable theories that attempt to answer these questions are the psychodynamic theory of Sigmund Freud and the humanistic theory of Carl Rogers, which we examine first.

LOOKING AHEAD Learning Objectives

1. What is the Freudian view of personality?
2. What is the main emphasis of humanistic theories, such as that of Carl Rogers?

Freud's Theory: The Dynamic Personality

Sigmund Freud's wide-ranging theory of personality is referred to as *psychoanalytic theory* because it is rooted in the idea that the mind can be analyzed to understand the causes of mental events and behaviors. This theory rests on his belief in **psychological determinism**, the view that all thoughts, feelings, and behavior—even something as mundane as forgetting someone's name or being late for an appointment—ultimately have an underlying psychological cause. Freud proposed that two major drives, sex and aggression, are the primary motivating forces of human behavior. Freud viewed personality as a bubbling cauldron, rocked by unconscious, irrational forces at war with one another, competing for expression and preventing the individual's exercise of free will. Moreover, he believed that tension arises when these thoughts and desires are not allowed to be expressed.

The Structure of Personality In order to understand Freud's view of personality, we must first understand his view of consciousness. Freud proposed that consciousness is not one thing but rather can be thought of as divided into three levels (see Figure 1):

- The topmost level is normal awareness, or the *conscious*, which includes thoughts, feelings, and motivations of which we are aware.

- The second level, the *preconscious*, holds information that we can easily bring into conscious awareness but we are not aware of most of the time. Information in the preconscious includes material we have learned as well as other thoughts, feelings, and motivations. Your telephone number is in your preconscious until someone asks you what it is, and at that point, it moves into your conscious (and hence you become aware of it).

- The final level is the *unconscious*, which houses the thoughts, feelings, and motivations that cannot voluntarily be brought into consciousness but that nevertheless influence our conscious thoughts, feelings, and behavior. According to Freud, a much greater proportion of our thoughts, feelings, and motivations are in the unconscious than are in the conscious.

In Freud's theory, material in the different levels of consciousness plays different roles in personality. To see how, we need to look at another aspect of his theory. Specifically, Freud proposed three mental structures—the *id*, *superego*, and *ego* (see Figure 1). These mental structures are not physical structures (such as different parts of the brain) but rather are abstract mental entities. The **id**, which exists from birth, houses the sexual and aggressive drives, physical needs such as the need to sleep and eat, and simple psychological needs such as the need for comfort; these needs and drives constantly vie for satisfaction. The id lies largely in the unconscious, and thus we are not directly aware of the drives and needs themselves—but only of the id's indirect effects. The id lives by the *pleasure principle*, wanting pleasure and the immediate gratification of its needs by a reduction in pain, hunger, discomfort, or tension, regardless of the consequences. Because of this insistent urge for immediate gratification, the id is sometimes compared with a demanding infant. Freud proposed that when the id's instincts threaten to erupt, anxiety can develop. And when that anxiety reaches a sufficiently high level, abnormal behavior and mental illness can result.

A second personality structure, the **superego**, houses the child's (and later the adult's) sense of right and wrong, based on the internalization—the "taking in"—of parental and cultural morality. By internalizing the values of the parents and the surrounding culture, the child learns a sense of right and wrong—morality. Formed during early childhood and residing largely in the unconscious (although portions lie in the other two levels), the superego tries to prevent the expression of the id's inappropriate sexual and aggressive impulses.

Depending on the parents' way of teaching right and wrong, the superego can be more or less punishing. If your superego is very harsh, you experience much anxiety and strive

FIGURE 1 Freud's View of Personality Structure

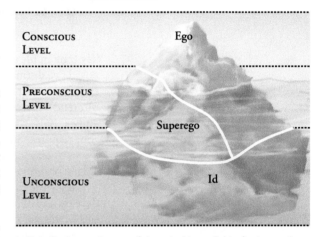

In Freud's view, only part of the mind is available for inspection and provides normal awareness (conscious level); some of the mind can voluntarily be brought into consciousness (preconscious level), and some is hidden, not available for observation (unconscious level). Repressed thoughts, feelings, and wishes are hidden from awareness.

Source: From Lester A. Lefton, *Psychology*, 8/e. Published by Allyn and Bacon, Boston, MA. © 2003 by Pearson Education. Reprinted by permission of the publisher.

Personality A set of emotional, cognitive, and behavioral tendencies that people display over time and across situations and that distinguish individuals from each other.

Psychological determinism The view that all thoughts, feelings, and behavior, no matter how mundane or insignificant, ultimately have an underlying psychological cause.

Id A personality structure, proposed by Freud, that exists at birth and houses sexual and aggressive drives, physical needs, and simple psychological needs.

Superego A personality structure, proposed by Freud, that is formed during early childhood and houses the sense of right and wrong, based on the internalization of parental and cultural morality.

Ego A personality structure, proposed by Freud, that develops in childhood and tries to balance the competing demands of the id, superego, and reality.

Psychosexual stages Freud's developmental stages based on erogenous zones; the specific needs of each stage must be met for its successful resolution.

Neurosis An abnormal behavior pattern that arises from a conflict between the ego and either the id or the superego.

for perfection. The superego can also cause feelings of *guilt*, an uncomfortable sensation of having done something wrong, which results in feelings of inadequacy. The superego's morality is responsible for the *ego ideal*, which provides the ultimate standard of what a person should be (Nye, 1992).

The third mental structure proposed by Freud is the **ego**, which tries to balance the competing demands of the id, superego, and reality. The ego develops in childhood and lies primarily in the preconscious and conscious levels. The ego is guided by the *reality principle*, which leads it to assess what is realistically possible in the world. While working within the constraints of what is possible, the ego tries to give the id enough gratification to prevent it from making too much trouble while at the same time making sure that no major moral lapses lead the superego to become too punishing. The ego attempts to make sure that the actions of the id and superego, as well as its own actions, don't create problems for the person in daily life. According to Freud's theory, the ego is also responsible for cognitive functions such as problem solving and reasoning. Although he believed that the ego develops out of the id, Freud (1937/1964) wrote late in his life that the ego's characteristics may be determined by heredity (Nye, 1992).

Personality Development: Avoiding Arrest Freud viewed childhood as the key time in life when the specific form of each individual's personality develops; he proposed five distinct stages, or phases, of development. Each of these stages has an important task that must be successfully resolved in order for a healthy personality to develop. Four of Freud's five stages involve specific *erogenous* zones—areas of the body (mouth, anus, and genitals) that can provide satisfaction of drives. Freud believed that each erogenous zone requires some form of sexual gratification and that a different zone is prominent during each stage of development. For this reason, Freud's stages are called **psychosexual stages**: oral, anal, phallic, latency, and genital (see Table 1).

If a child does not satisfy the needs and urges related to a given stage, he or she will develop a *fixation*, a state of "arrested development" in which energy is still focused on an earlier stage of development even as the child moves on to the next stage. Thus, a fixation results from incomplete resolution of an earlier stage. Because energy is still focused on an earlier stage, Freud believed that in times of stress an individual will regress to the thoughts, feelings, and behaviors of his or her fixated stage—an unhealthy state of affairs. In fact, a fixation could create a **neurosis**: an abnormal behavior pattern that arises from a conflict between the ego and either the id or the superego. According to Freud (1938), when there is sufficient conflict between the ego and reality, the result may be a *psychosis*— a break from reality. (Note that Freud's definition of psychosis differs from that currently used by most mental health clinicians, for whom psychosis is marked by the presence of hallucinations and entrenched delusional beliefs.)

Some of Freud's most provocative ideas focus on the phallic stage (see Table 1) and were inspired by the ancient Greek story of Oedipus, who unknowingly killed his father

TABLE 1 Freud's Psychosexual Stages

Psychosexual Stage	Age of Stage (years)	Locus of Pleasure	Developmental Task of Stage
Oral Stage	0–1	Mouth (sucking and biting)	Successful weaning from mother's breast or bottle
Anal Stage	1–3	Anus (retaining and expelling feces)	Successful toilet training
Phallic Stage	3–6	Clitoris or penis	Successful identification with same-sex parent
Latency Period	6 to puberty	No particular locus of pleasure; sexual impulses are repressed	Successful transformation of repressed sexual urges into socially acceptable activities
Genital Stage	Puberty onward	Vagina or penis	1. Successful formation of mature sexual love relationship 2. Successful development of interests and talents related to productive work

and married his mother. Freud believed that boys in this stage jealously love their mothers and view their fathers as competitors for their mothers' love, so they both fear and hate their fathers. Freud thus called this dynamic the *Oedipus complex*. As part of this dynamic, Freud believed that a boy unconsciously fears that, as punishment for loving his mother and hating his father, his father will cut off his penis, the primary zone of pleasure at this stage; this concern leads to the boy's **castration anxiety**. To resolve this stage successfully, a boy must renounce his passionate love for his mother and make peace with his father—he must identify with his father and accept his subordinate position instead of viewing his father as a competitor. In doing so, the boy "introjects," or internalizes, his father's morality as part of his superego.

Girls' personality development at this stage, according to Freud, is different from that of boys; girls' version of the Oedipus complex has been labeled the *Electra complex*, after the Greek myth about Electra, a girl who avenges her father's murder—committed by her mother and her mother's lover—by persuading her brother to kill their mother. Freud proposed that girls in this stage are preoccupied with the discovery that they don't have penises, which leads them to have *penis envy*—a desire to have a penis as well as a sense of being ineffectual because they don't have a penis. Another aspect of the Electra complex is that girls unconsciously struggle with feelings of anger and jealousy toward the mother: anger for neither providing a penis for her daughter nor having one herself, and jealousy because of the mother's relationship with the father. According to Freud, girls ambivalently identify with their mothers.

As a product of the Victorian era, Freud justified women's lower status in his society by explaining that girls can only partially resolve the phallic stage: Because girls do not experience castration anxiety, he wrote, they are not motivated to resolve fully their ambivalent identification with their mothers. According to Freud, girls remain fixated at the phallic stage and, as a result, have a less well-developed superego, less ego strength, and less ability to negotiate between reality and the id.

Defense Mechanisms: Protecting the Self The ego handles threatening material in part by using **defense mechanisms**, which are various unconscious processes that prevent unacceptable thoughts or urges from reaching conscious awareness—and thereby decrease anxiety (see Table 2). Freud proposed a number of defense mechanisms;

Castration anxiety A boy's fear that, as punishment for loving mother and hating father, his father will cut off his penis.

Defense mechanism The unconscious processes that prevent unacceptable thoughts or urges from reaching conscious awareness.

TABLE 2 Common Defense Mechanisms

Defense mechanisms are used by the ego to prevent threatening thoughts from entering awareness.

Denial

Threatening thoughts are denied outright. *Example*: You have a drinking problem but deny that it is a problem (and truly believe this).

Intellectualization

Threatening thoughts or emotions are kept at arm's length by thinking about them rationally and logically. *Example*: While watching a frightening part of a horror movie, you focus on the special effects, makeup, camera angles, and other emotionally nonthreatening details.

Projection

Threatening thoughts are projected onto (attributed to) others. *Example*: You accuse your partner of wanting to have an affair rather than recognizing your own conscious or unconscious wish to have one yourself.

Rationalization

Threatening thoughts or actions are justified with explanations. *Example*: You watch a football game instead of studying for a test and justify this by saying that watching the game will relax you and so you'll feel less tense when taking the test.

Reaction Formation

An unacceptable feeling is unconsciously changed into its opposite. *Example*: You harbor aggressive impulses toward your boss, but instead you experience warm, positive feelings toward him, transforming your anger about his obnoxious behavior into an appreciation of "his fairness as a manager."

Repression

Anxiety-provoking thoughts, impulses, and memories are directly blocked from entering consciousness. *Example*: After failing an exam, you "keep forgetting" to tell your parents about it.

Sublimation

Threatening impulses are directed into more socially acceptable activities. *Example*: You sublimate your unacceptable aggressive urges to engage in physical fights by playing ice hockey.

Undoing

Your actions try to "undo" a threatening wish or thought. *Example*: After having the thought of eating several slices of chocolate cake, you go to the gym and work out for an hour.

Repression A defense mechanism that occurs when the ego directly blocks threatening unconscious thoughts, impulses, and memories from entering consciousness.

⚹ Explore the Concept of Defense Mechanisms on mypsychlab.com

these were further developed by his daughter, Anna Freud (1895–1982), herself a noted psychoanalyst. Probably the most important defense mechanism is **repression**, a process in which the ego directly blocks threatening unconscious thoughts, impulses, and memories from entering consciousness. An example of repression might be "forgetting" to go to a dreaded dentist appointment. According to Freud, a person can develop a neurosis if he or she relies too much on particular defense mechanisms. ⚹ Explore

Freud's Followers Freud attracted many followers, a number of whom modified his theory of personality or added ideas of their own. Among those who expanded on Freud's work, termed *neo-Freudians*, were Carl Jung, Alfred Adler, and Karen Horney. All of his followers deemphasized sexuality and emphasized additional factors (see Figure 2). For example, Jung emphasized the *collective unconscious* (the unconscious storehouse of ideas and memories common to all humankind), Adler emphasized feelings of inferiority, and Horney emphasized parent–child interactions.

FIGURE 2 Neo-Freudians: Jung, Adler, and Horney

Source: © Hulton/Archive/Getty Images

Carl Jung (1875–1961) was a former student of Freud's whose own theory of personality focused on the *collective unconscious*—the unconscious storehouse of ideas and memories common to all humankind, including *archetypes*, the basic personality types found in all cultures and folklore.

Source: UPI\CORBIS- NY

Alfred Adler (1870–1937) focused on the importance of feelings of inferiority and helplessness in personality formation. Feelings of inferiority fuel the striving for superiority; if inferiority feelings become too severe, they can lead to an *inferiority complex*, which hampers such strivings.

Source: UPI\CORBIS- NY

Karen Horney (1885–1952) emphasized the importance of parent–child interactions, proposing that parents should show warmth, respect, and consistent interest in their children. Horney also proposed that girls did not have penis envy but *privilege envy*, the desire for the privileges that go along with having a penis.

Critiquing Freudian Theory: Is It Science? Psychoanalytic theory remains fascinating a century after Freud first conceived it, and legions of people worldwide—psychologists, writers, filmmakers, and others—have seen truth in his observations about personality. But as fascinating as Freud's theory of personality development may be, is it grounded in good science? In short, the answer is "no"—and three types of criticism highlight why not.

First, to be "good science" a theory must be testable, and many aspects of Freud's theory are difficult to test because various psychoanalytic concepts are not well defined. Freud failed to define some key concepts, changed the meaning of other concepts over time, and was often vague about when a specific concept was relevant for a specific situation. Consider this: Freud believed that many actions and objects have symbolic meanings. Thus, long, thin objects, for instance, are *phallic symbols*—they stand for a penis. However, when Freud was asked about the meaning of his sucking on a cigar (his interviewer assumed that the cigar was a phallic symbol), Freud replied, "Sometimes a cigar is only a cigar." Maybe so, but a good theory would tell us when it is and when it isn't "only a cigar." Without specific principles that indicate precisely when long, thin objects are and are not phallic symbols, researchers cannot adequately test the concepts at the heart of the theory.

A second way in which Freud's theory isn't "good science" is that it is so complicated that it can explain—or explain away—almost any observation. This characteristic makes the theory difficult to test because it does not make firm predictions—which sets it apart from all good scientific theories. For instance, when Gabe was a toddler, he had a difficult time with toilet training, which caused him frequently to be constipated. Psychoanalytic theory would seem to predict that Gabe should have a fixation at the anal stage and have an *anal-retentive personality*. According to Freud, such people are more likely to delay gratification and to be neat, methodical, miserly, and stubborn. But, if so, then how would we explain the fact that Gabe is often generous and is so messy with pistachios? Freud might counter that Gabe's generosity and messiness are an *undoing* of his desire to be selfish and orderly. Thus, any aspects of an individual's personality that are not what would be predicted by the theory are then explained (or—more accurately—explained away, after the fact) by some other aspect of the theory.

Third, Freud's theory may not generalize well to most people. He developed his theory by analyzing patients, mostly women, and by analyzing himself. And Freud's views of women, of proper parenting, and of appropriate development were all biased by his worldview and surroundings, as we are biased by ours. He and his patients were upper-middle-class or upper-class products of late 19th-century Vienna; their sensibilities were not necessarily representative of other classes, times, or cultures. We cannot assume that a theory based on a particular group of people at a particular time and place applies to other people at another time or place.

Although psychoanalytic theory as a whole does not stand up to rigorous scientific standards, some facets of the theory have received support from contemporary research (see Westen, 1998, 1999). One such facet is the influence of parents; specifically, the type of attachment we have to our parents predicts the type of attachment we will have to a partner and to our own children (Shaver & Hazan, 1994). Although not supporting Freud's specific psychosexual stages, such findings support the general idea that relationships with parents can affect aspects of later development. Another facet of his theory that is supported by research is the concept behind defense mechanisms, specifically that people have particular techniques or strategies they tend to use to cope with life's ups and downs (Bond et al., 1983; Mikulincer & Horesh, 1999; Newman et al., 1997; Silverman, 1976). More generally, the results of a variety of types of research support the broad idea that some mental processes can be unconscious—that is, occur without awareness.

Despite the difficulty in evaluating most of Freud's theory, many aspects of it have endured because it offers a truly comprehensive, interesting, and sometimes insightful view of people and of personality.

Humanistic Psychology: Thinking Positively

Partly as a reaction to Freud's theory, which in many ways draws a pessimistic picture of human nature and personality formation, the humanistic psychologists focused on people's positive aspects—their innate goodness, creativity, and free will. For example, one cornerstone of humanistic theories is that we all strive to achieve **self-actualization**, an innate drive to attain our highest emotional and intellectual potential. According to humanistic theories of personality development, people will choose to achieve self-actualization if various barriers are removed.

The work of psychologist Carl Rogers (1902–1987) represents the humanistic perspective on personality. Rogers developed both a theory of personality as well as a form of psychotherapy—*client-centered therapy*—that is grounded in his personality theory. At the center of Roger's theory is the idea of the *self-concept*—our sense of ourselves and of how others see us. According to Rogers, because our self-concept is in part a reflection of how others see us, we have a basic need for **unconditional positive regard**, acceptance without any conditions.

Rogers recognized that it is impossible to receive or provide unconditional positive regard all the time, and the socialization process requires that adults praise children for

Self-actualization An innate drive to attain the highest possible emotional and intellectual potential.

Unconditional positive regard Acceptance without any conditions.

287

behaving in accordance with societal rules. He claimed that such praise for specific behaviors leads children to learn *conditions of worth*, or "what it takes" to be treated as worthwhile. According to Rogers, some aspects of personality—such as a person's motives—can come to revolve around meeting conditions of worth in order to be accepted by others. As a result, a person will spend too much time and energy pleasing others and thus will not achieve his or her full human potential. In order to prevent such obstruction of potential and yet meet society's need for children to learn what is generally considered appropriate behavior, Rogers advised parents to make the distinction between a child's inappropriate *behavior* and his or her *worth* as a human being.

Humanistic theories appeal to many because of their emphasis on the uniqueness of each person and on free will. According to this view, how you live your life is determined not by unconscious forces but by using your conscious awareness and your freedom to choose your experiences. Critics of humanistic theory point out that, as with Freud's theory, many of the concepts are difficult to test and have received little research support. In addition, some have disagreed with the logic underlying aspects of Rogers's theory—for instance, does it really follow that just because how others regard us is important, we need unconditional positive regard all the time? Furthermore, the uplifting, positive view of human nature seems too idealistic to many people in light of the amount of intentional violence in the world.

Good or bad child? Rogers argues that a child may at times behave unsuitably, but that does not mean he or she is a bad child. Labeling children as "bad" may affect their developing self-concept or self-worth (Kamins & Dweck, 1999).

Source: PhotoEdit Inc.

✓●─[Study and **Review** on
mypsychlab.com

LOOKING BACK

1. **What is the Freudian view of personality?** Freud proposed that personality involves three different levels of consciousness (unconscious, preconscious, and conscious) and three mental structures (id, ego, and superego) in a dynamic relationship with each other. Development proceeds through five psychosexual stages (oral, anal, phallic, latency, and genital), and when resolution of a psychosexual stage is incomplete, a person's development is arrested, often creating a neurosis. Moreover, sexual and aggressive impulses can create anxiety, prompting the use of defense mechanisms. Neo-Freudians— including Carl Jung, Alfred Adler, and Karen Horney—added to or altered aspects of Freud's theory. Although Freud's theory is comprehensive and intriguing, many aspects of it are difficult to test scientifically.

2. **What is the main emphasis of humanistic theories, such as that of Carl Rogers?** Humanistic theories of personality celebrate each person's uniqueness and stress positive qualities of human nature and free will. They also emphasize self-actualization. Although uplifting, humanistic theories have many aspects that are difficult to test scientifically.

What Exactly *Is* Personality?

As Tina got to know Gabe better, she began to make certain assumptions about him, about who he was as a person. He studied hard and did well on psychology exams and quizzes, so Tina figured that he was smart, hardworking, and conscientious. (Tina did well on her psychology exams and quizzes, too, but she didn't study much. She considered herself smart but not particularly hardworking.) She was a bit surprised to discover that Gabe's apartment was a disaster area—she had assumed that he would be as orderly and neat in his personal space as he was in his approach to schoolwork. She started to wonder whether his "personality," as she thought of it, was altogether consistent. Tina also noticed that, if she suggested going to a party together, Gabe invariably declined; he didn't like parties. Tina attributed this reluctance to his shyness.

The very concept of personality implies that people have enduring, stable qualities, such as talkativeness and curiosity. These qualities are called **personality traits**, relatively consistent tendencies to think, feel, or behave in a characteristic way across a range of situations. But notice the "relatively" in the preceding sentence. Let's see just what that means.

Personality trait A relatively consistent tendency to think, feel, or behave in a characteristic way across a range of situations.

1. Does such a thing as a consistent personality really exist, or do our thoughts, feelings, and behaviors depend primarily on the situation?
2. How do psychologists group personality traits into sets of personality types?
3. What methods do psychologists use to measure personality?

Personality: Traits and Situations

Most psychologists conceive of "personality" as consisting of a set of personality traits, and conceive of each trait as falling on a continuum. For example, Gabe's shyness is a trait on the continuum of sociability; the extremes on this continuum are very sociable (outgoing) to very shy. Gabe would fall in the shy end, like this:

Very   Gabe   Very
Shy   Sociable

Typically, the name of each continuum is a variant of the name of the trait on one end of the continuum (in this case, the continuum is referred to as *sociability*), and the other end of the extreme is referred to by its antonym or opposite (in this case, the trait at the other end is related to *shyness*).

Gordon Allport (1897–1967) further refined this view when he proposed that some personality traits can be grouped as *central traits*, which are traits that affect a wide range of behavior; however, the particular traits that are central will vary from individual to individual (Allport, 1937). That is, the specific traits that are central to one person's personality may be different from the specific traits that are central to another person's personality. The particular personality traits that are Gabe's central traits may be different than those that are Tina's central traits.

However, even central personality traits aren't always accurate in *predicting* behavior (witness Gabe's domestic messiness). When traits don't predict behavior, what does? In following section we consider the power of the situation.

The Power of the Situation

The situations in which we find ourselves exert powerful influences on thoughts, feelings, and behavior. Gabe and Tina may fall on different ends of some personality trait continua and may even have different sets of central personality traits, but in certain situations—such as in a class, meeting with a professor, or attending a funeral—they are likely to behave similarly. The power of the situation in shaping behavior was illustrated in a classic study by Hartshorne and May (1928), who investigated whether the trait of honesty applies across situations. To examine this, they gave grade school children the opportunity to be honest or dishonest in various settings, such as when reporting how many push-ups they were able to do, how much work they did at home, and how much money they were given. The children believed that they could be dishonest without being caught, but the actual facts were secretly recorded. The researchers found that children who were honest in one situation were not necessarily honest in another. Although the children did show some consistency across situations, less than 10% of the differences in behavior across situations could be explained by a single, common, underlying trait of honesty.

Moreover, Hartshorne and May found that the more similar the situations, the more likely it was that each child behaved similarly across situations; for instance, lying about the number of push-ups and lying about how much work was done were correlated more highly with each other than either was with stealing, a different type of dishonest behavior.

The names of Snow White's seven dwarves fit their personalities. Imagine the personalities of dwarves named Dirty, Hungry, Shifty, Flabby, Puffy, Crabby, Awful, Doleful, all of which were on Disney Studios' list of possible names (Seuling, 1976). The final choices work so well because we view their personalities as consistent with their names; but what if Grumpy were, in fact, upbeat and easygoing?

Source: Everett Collection

Many researchers have subsequently reported that the more similar the situations, the more likely it is that a person will behave in similar ways (Magnusson, 2003; Mischel, 2004; Mischel & Shoda, 1995). Nineteen-year-old Tina behaves very differently with Gabe—drinking from his cup, sitting on his lap—than she does with her 52-year-old female economics professor. In each case, Tina's age, sex, and status relative to the other person might be said to influence her behavior. If you knew Tina only from economics class, you might be surprised by how different her "personality" seems when she is with Gabe. However, we can guess that Tina's way of interacting with her economics professor will be similar to how she interacts with other professors. And how she interacts with Gabe is probably similar to how she has interacted with past boyfriends.

In the years since Hartshorne and May's study, many other researchers have extended these findings. For example, Walter Mischel (1984) found inconsistencies in how people behave across situations that draw on the same trait—and found such inconsistencies for numerous different traits, ranging from honesty and conscientiousness to aggression and dependency. Furthermore, different measures of what should be the same trait often were only weakly correlated or not related at all. In addition, the "same" trait often is expressed in different ways. For instance, two people could score high on measures of aggression but express their aggression differently—one through put-downs and verbal abuse, the other through physical violence (Mischel, 2004). ✳ Explore

Such findings led to the theory of *situationism*, which holds that a person's behavior is mostly governed by the particular situation, not by internal traits. However, situationism has proven not to be the whole story. Although it is true that the situation can exert a powerful influence on our thoughts, feelings, and behavior, we are not simply puppets, with the situation pulling our strings. In the following section we consider how personality characteristics interact with the situation.

Interactions Between Situation and Personality The situation doesn't affect everyone in the same way; an individual's thoughts, feelings, and behavior in a given situation depend in part on his or her personality. The interaction between personality and the situation is known as *interactionism*. Interactionism arises from three major factors: First, the same "objective" situation is experienced differently by people who have different personalities (Shoda & LeeTiernan, 2002). Specifically, when different individuals are in the same situation, they differ in what they pay attention to, how they interpret the stimuli they perceive, what emotions are associated with those stimuli, and then how they respond. For instance, when a stationmaster announces to waiting passengers that the train will be 30 minutes late, the delayed passengers will have a variety of responses. Some will become agitated (they'll pace or speak angrily to train personnel), while others will relax and "go with the flow"—unfazed by the train's lateness. And how the waiting passengers behave in this situation will probably be more consistent than not with how they behave in other frustrating situations. Such differences among people in the same situation reliably reflect differences in their personality traits (Funder, 2001; Funder & Colvin, 1991; Kenrick & Funder, 1988; Roberts et al., 2001).

Second, our personalities partly *create* our situations. An aggressive person, for instance, can easily create a tense situation by words or deeds (A. H. Buss, 1995), and others will react accordingly. By the same token, a steady, calming person will affect others in a different way, creating characteristic situations in his or her wake.

Third, people often can choose their situations—their jobs, their friends, their leisure activities. Insofar as they are able, people tend to choose environments that fit their personalities. It's up to you, for instance, to decide whether to go bungee-jumping or to sunbathe at the beach when you have a day off.

Finally, it's worth noting that not only do personality traits interact with situations, but they also may interact among themselves (Ahadi & Diener, 1989). For example, if a woman is both outgoing and likes new experiences, she will behave differently than if she is outgoing but prefers routine and familiarity.

Factors of Personality: The Big Five? Three? More?

We've mentioned a variety of different personality traits in our examples; how many personality traits are there? The answer depends on how specific you want to be about a given trait. On the one hand, you could be very specific, narrowing all the way down to a

✳ Explore the Concept of Mischel's Theory of Personality on mypsychlab.com

"shy-so-only-goes-on-dates-to-dinner-and-a-movie-but-not-to-par-
ties" trait. The more precisely a trait is defined, the more accurate it is
in predicting behavior (Wiggins, 1992). Thus, saying that someone is
sociable will not predict his or her behavior at a party nearly as well
as saying that the person appears at ease when interacting with new
people. However, this finding leads to a trade-off: When traits are
defined more narrowly, they predict behavior better but they apply to
fewer situations. Indeed, traits can be defined so narrowly that the
situation itself becomes more important than the trait.

On the other hand, you could define personality traits *very*
broadly. For example, you could consider sociability—which personality psychologists call "extraversion"—as a trait. Further, you could say
that extraversion is really a combination of the more specific traits of
warmth, gregariousness, and assertiveness—each of which exists on a
continuum. In this case, you could say that extraversion is a *personality
dimension*, a set of related personality traits.

Researchers have used the statistical technique of factor analysis
to study whether specific traits are in fact associated and—together—
constitute a more general personality dimension. Factor analysis
takes a set of correlations (which indicate how strongly related two
sets of measurements are) and derives dimensions ("factors") that
underlie those correlations. Applying factor analysis to correlations
among people's scores on personality tests produces dimensions (which are sometimes
called *super-factors*). An early proponent of using factor analysis to determine personality factors was Raymond Cattell (1905–1998); he proposed 16 basic personality factors
(Cattell, 1943).

Personality dimensions, or superfactors, may be a useful way to conceptualize personality, but they have a disadvantage: They predict behavior less well than do the traits on which
they are built (Paunonen, 1998; Paunonen et al., 2003). This occurs in part because two people can score high on the same dimension but attain their high scores by being extreme on different traits that are part of that dimension; in such cases, they score high on the dimension
for different reasons (Cervone, 2005). Nevertheless, scores on such dimensions can predict
behavior in some contexts and for practical purposes may be more useful than predicting a
person's behavior based on a long list of traits that may or may not be relevant.

Many factor analytic studies have revealed that personality traits can be reduced to five
superfactors, which are listed along with their included traits in Table 3 (Digman, 1990;
McCrae & Costa, 1987). Each superfactor is on a separate continuum, with the name of the
superfactor identifying one end of that continuum. Thus, for example, at the other end of
the continuum for the superfactor neuroticism is emotional stability. These five superfactors are often referred to as the *Five-Factor Model*, or the **Big Five** (Goldberg, 1981): extraversion (versus introversion), neuroticism (also called *emotionality*, versus emotional
stability), agreeableness (versus disagreeableness), conscientiousness (also called
dependability, versus irresponsibleness), and openness to experience (versus incuriosity or
unimaginativeness) (Costa et al., 1991). One way to remember these factors is to use the

Asian Americans tend to show lower levels of assertiveness than
do White Americans on personality tests. However, according
to one study, this is true only when the people involved are
strangers (Zane et al., 1991). Thus, it isn't accurate to describe
Asian Americans as "low on the assertiveness trait." A better
characterization would be the more specific "unassertive when
among strangers."

Source: Mark Richards\PhotoEdit Inc.

TABLE 3   The Big Five Superfactors and Their Traits

Superfactor	Traits
Extraversion (also called *sociability*)	Warmth, gregariousness, assertiveness, activity, excitement seeking, positive emotions
Neuroticism (also called *emotionality*)	Anxiety, hostility, depression, self-consciousness, impulsiveness, vulnerability
Agreeableness	Trust, straightforwardness, altruism, compliance, modesty, tender-mindedness
Conscientiousness (also called *dependability*)	Competence, order, dutifulness, achievement striving, deliberation, self-discipline
Openness	Fantasy, aesthetics, feelings, actions, ideas, values

Big Five The five superfactors of personality—extraversion, neuroticism,
agreeableness, conscientiousness, and
openness—determined by factor
analysis.

Personality inventory A lengthy questionnaire for assessing personality that requires the test takers to read statements and to indicate whether each is true or false about themselves or to indicate how much they agree or disagree with each statement.

mnemonic OCEAN (Openness, Conscientiousness, Extraversion, Agreeableness, and Neuroticism).

Psychologist Hans Eysenck proposed that personality can best be captured by three—not five—superfactors, or, as he labeled them, personality dimensions: *extraversion*, *neuroticism*, and *psychoticism*. Eysenck's first two dimensions resemble the Big Five's superfactors of the same names, but the third—psychoticism—was originally thought to measure a tendency to become psychotic, that is, to lose touch with reality, as occurs in schizophrenia (Eysenck, 1992). However, although people with schizophrenia do in fact score high on this dimension, psychoticism (as defined by Eysenck) also contains traits related to social deviance (such as delinquency and the inclination toward substance addiction) and to a lack of conventional socialization (such as disrespecting rules and disregarding the feelings of others) (Costa & McCrae, 1995). For this reason, Eysenck's psychoticism includes some of the traits listed under the Big Five's superfactors of agreeableness and conscientiousness (Draycott & Kline, 1995; Saggino, 2000). (The Big Five's superfactor of openness has no direct counterpart in Eysenck's scheme.)

Some psychologists have suggested renaming Eysenck's third superfactor, calling it *nonconformity* or *social deviance*—rather than psychoticism—in order to highlight the traits of creativity and nonconformity that are also part of this dimension. Artists, for example, tend to score higher on this personality dimension than people who are truly psychotic (Zuckerman et al., 1988).

In summary, although different models may group personality traits differently, all models include some version of the broad personality characteristics of extraversion and neuroticism.

Measuring Personality: Is Grumpy Really Grumpy?

Researchers have developed various methods to understand and predict the behavior of individuals by discovering as much as possible about their personalities. Such methods are commonly used by psychologists, teachers, and employers in a wide variety of settings including mental health facilities, school, workplaces, and the military. Most methods of assessing personality measure behaviors that psychologists believe to be expressions of a given trait, and then infer the strength of the trait from the behaviors. The use of behaviors to infer personality traits is at the heart of all methods of personality assessment discussed below.

Psychologists use four methods to assess and infer personality: (1) *inventories*, which ask people to answer questions on paper-and-pencil tests; (2) *projective tests*, which ask people to characterize ambiguous stimuli; (3) *observations*, which rely on noting and recording others' behavior; and (4) *interviews*, which ask people to respond to verbal questions. Let's examine the two most commonly used methods—inventories and projective tests—in more detail.

Inventories: Check This The most common method of personality assessment is a **personality inventory**, a lengthy questionnaire that requires those being assessed to read statements and indicate whether each is true or false about themselves (with only two choices) or how much they agree or disagree with each statement along a multipoint rating scale (with three or more choices). These responses are tallied and converted into scores, one score for each trait in the inventory. In general, the results of a personality inventory provide information about many distinct traits in the form of a *personality profile*, which is often a graphical summary of the scores of the different traits that constitute someone's personality (see Figure 3). Personality inventories usually assess many different traits and contain a great number of statements, often more than 300, in order to include items that address different facets of each trait.

When "meeting" in cyberspace (for example, through a dating service), people commonly try to "assess" a potential mate's personality by looking at his or her Facebook page or finding other information on the Internet. Such information becomes the basis for inferring personality, much as we infer personality after viewing someone's bedroom or apartment (Vazire & Gosling, 2004). However, psychologists use more formal, standardized ways to assess personality.

Source: Permission given by Billy Ray

Personality inventories are used in a variety of settings and for a variety of purposes. For example, they are used by mental health professionals to assess mental illness, by research psychologists to investigate the possible reasons for differences in personality traits, and by employers to assess how personality characteristics are related to aspects of job performance (Borman et al., 1997).

Personality inventories have specific advantages and disadvantages. Key advantages are that they are easy to administer, and computer programs make it easy to score and interpret them; moreover, inventories are an easy way to compare the same personality traits among different people. Key drawbacks are: (1) that this method of assessing personality limits the type of information obtained to the specific questions on the inventory, and (2) that responses can be biased. One source of bias occurs when people check off "agree" more often than "disagree," regardless of the content of the statement. This response style, called *acquiescence*, can be reduced by wording half the items negatively. For instance, the item "I often feel shy when meeting new people" would be reworded as "I don't usually feel shy when meeting new people." Another source of bias is **social desirability**: answering questions in a way that you think makes you "look good," even if the answer is not accurate. For instance, some people might not agree with the statement "It is better to be honest, even if others don't like you for it" but think that they should agree and so respond accordingly. To compensate for this bias, many personality inventories have a scale that assesses the respondent's tendency to answer in a socially desirable manner. This scale is then used to adjust or, in the language of testing, to "correct" the scores on the part of the inventory that measures traits. ((•─|Listen

One personality inventory is Raymond Cattell's *16PF* (Cattell et al., 1970; see Figure 3). People's responses on this inventory are categorized into Cattell's 16 personality factors. Another, the **Minnesota Multiphasic Personality Inventory-2 (MMPI-2)**, is commonly used to assess psychopathology (Butcher & Rouse, 1996). The MMPI-2 has 567 questions that the test taker checks off as either true or false, and it usually takes 60 to 90 minutes to complete. (There is a short form consisting of 370 questions.) In contrast to the MMPI-2, which primarily assesses psychopathology, another personality inventory, the *NEO Personality Inventory (NEO-PI-R)*, is designed to assess 30 personality traits from the Five-Factor Model (*N* for Neuroticism, *E* for Extraversion, *O* for Openness—three of the Big Five superfactors—and *R* for Revised). The NEO-PI-R has an advantage over the other two inventories because it can be completed either by the individual whose personality is being assessed (referred to as *self-report*) or by someone close that individual, such as a spouse or roommate (referred to as *other-report*). Both the MMPI-2 and the NEO-PI-R have been used extensively and are considered to be both valid and reliable.

FIGURE 3 Personality Profiles and Employment

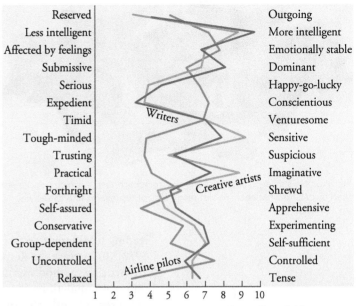

Completed personality inventories provide personality profiles of different traits. According to Cattell's personality inventory (the 16PF for its 16 personality factors), writers, creative artists, and airline pilots show different profiles.

Source: Figure depicting data relating to personality profiles for source traits for writers, artists and airline pilots and as developed by Cattell, Eber and Tatsuoka, HANDBOOK FOR THE SIXTEEN PERSONALITY FACTOR QUESTIONAIRE (16PF®, Copyright © 1970, 1988, 1992 by the Institute for Personality and Ability Testing, IPAT Inc, Champaign, IL, USA). Reproduced with permission of the copyright holder.

Projective Tests: Faces in the Clouds A **projective test** presents a person with ambiguous stimuli, such as shapeless blots of ink or drawings of people, and asks the person to make sense of the stimuli. Were you to take a projective test, you might be asked to provide the story behind each stimulus, such as "what does the inkblot look like?" or "what are the people in the drawing doing?" Because the stimuli are ambiguous, there is a lot of leeway in what you can say about each of them. The theory behind such projective tests is that people's personalities can be revealed by what they project onto ambiguous stimuli as their minds impose structure on them.

THINK like a **PSYCHOLOGIST** To get a sense of what a personality test is like, try the personality test online at www.mypsychlab.com; select the *Personality* chapter and click on the *DO IT!* folder.

((•─|Listen to audio on Personality Tests on **mypsychlab.com**

Social desirability A source of bias in responding to questions that occurs when people try to make themselves "look good" even if it means giving answers that are not accurate.

Minnesota Multiphasic Personality Inventory-2 (MMPI-2) A personality inventory used primarily to assess psychopathology.

Projective test A method used to assess personality and psychopathology that asks the test taker to make sense of ambiguous stimuli.

FIGURE 4 The Rorschach Test

This inkblot is similar to those used in the Rorschach test, in which people are asked to decide what each inkblot resembles or represents and to tell why they think so.

For example, the **Rorschach test** (see Figure 4) is a famous projective test in which the ambiguous stimuli are inkblots. Developed by Herman Rorschach (1884–1922), this projective test has 10 cards, each with a different inkblot. The ambiguous shapes of the inkblots allow people to use their imaginations as they decide what each shape might represent or resemble (for example, a bat or a butterfly) and what features of the inkblot made them think so.

A common complaint about projective tests (and the Rorschach in particular) is that they may not be valid or reliable. That is, it is not clear whether the tests assess personality (that is, whether they are *valid*) and, even if they do, whether the results are consistent (that is, whether they are *reliable*). For instance, an individual taking the test on different days may answer differently, leading to different assessments of the person's personality (Anastasi, 1988; Entwisle, 1972). To increase the Rorschach's validity and reliability, a comprehensive and systematic scoring method was developed (Exner, 1974) that has been extensively tested on different populations, yielding *norms* for these populations—the average scores, range of scores, and other information against which a given test taker can be compared. Some researchers (Exner, 2002; Meyer, 2002; Meyer & Archer, 2001) but not others (Lilienfeld et al., 2000; Wood, Lilienfeld, et al., 2001) view this scoring method as reliable and valid. Moreover, some researchers also question how truly representative the norms are, and whether someone free of psychological disorders would nonetheless appear to have psychopathology when evaluated in terms of those norms (Garb et al., 2002; Wood, Nezworski, et al., 2001).

Another projective test is the **Thematic Apperception Test (TAT)**, developed in the 1930s by Henry Murray and Christiana Morgan; it relies on the same concept as the Rorschach but uses a set of 31 detailed black-and-white drawings, often with people in them. In this test, the person is asked to tell a story about what each (ambiguous) drawing illustrates. Several criticisms are leveled at the TAT and its use, including the following: (1) Although systematic scoring systems exist, only 3% of clinicians actually use a scoring system to interpret the TAT, preferring to rely on intuitive interpretations of participants' responses (Pinkerman et al., 1993). (2) From a person's response to the cards, the test administrator cannot distinguish between how the person actually thinks, feels, and would behave versus how the person *wishes* to think, feel, and behave (Lilienfeld et al., 2000).

Defenders of the Rorschach and the TAT point out that the tests' abilities to predict future behavior depend not only on the test administrator's experience but also on the specific behavior(s) that the tests are being used to predict (Karon, 2000).

People are shown a drawing like this one from the Thematic Apperception Test (TAT) and asked to create a story to explain what is happening in the picture—what led up to it, what will happen later, and what the characters are thinking and feeling.

Source: © Lew Merrim/Photo Researchers, Inc.

✓●┤**Study** and **Review** on
mypsychlab.com

Rorschach test A projective test consisting of a set of inkblots that people are asked to interpret.

Thematic Apperception Test (TAT) A projective test consisting of a set of detailed black-and-white drawings; for each drawing, the test taker is asked to tell a story about what the drawing illustrates.

LOOKING BACK

1. **Does such a thing as a consistent personality really exist, or do our thoughts, feelings, and behaviors depend primarily on the situation?** Personality consists of a set of enduring traits that leads people to behave in specific ways. According to situationism, however, there are no enduring personality traits; rather, behavior depends on the situation. According to interactionism, enduring personality traits do exist, and the interaction of traits with the specifics of a situation determines thoughts, feelings, and behavior in that context. Research supports interactionism—that people have enduring personality traits but that the situation also influences behavior.

2. **How do psychologists group personality traits into sets of personality types?** The Big Five superfactors are described by the Five-Factor Model of personality,

which was derived through the statistical technique of factor analyzing the results of personality inventories. The five superfactors are *openness to experience, conscientiousness, extra-version, agreeableness,* and *neuroticism* (represented as the acronym OCEAN). Each superfactor is composed of a number of specific traits. Eysenck proposed three rather than five personality dimensions (his term for superfactors): *extraversion, neuroticism,* and *psychoticism.*

3. **What methods do psychologists use to measure personality?** There are four major ways to assess personality: inventories (such as the MMPI-2, which yields a personality profile), projective tests (such as the Rorschach test and the Thematic Apperception Test [TAT]), observations, and interviews. Psychologists most commonly use inventories to assess personality.

Biological Influences on Personality

As their relationship progressed, Tina began to notice a host of ways in which she and Gabe were different: She loved in-line skating, biking, dancing, and skiing, and he liked to read outdoors (weather permitting), go on long walks, and watch movies. She liked to meet new people or hang out with her friends and generally didn't enjoy being alone; Gabe had a few close friends with whom he spent time, but he was also happy spending time by himself. Tina was fairly straightforward and, up to a point, flexible; Gabe seemed less direct and more rigid. Tina was spontaneous and a bit anxious; Gabe was not very spontaneous, but he never seemed anxious, depressed, or even worried; he was totally "chill." Tina could be impatient, sometimes even snappish; Gabe was almost always kind and gentle. When Tina was finally able to drag Gabe to a party (explaining to him that it was important to her that he accompany her), she was surprised by his reaction: He stayed in a corner talking to one person for half an hour, then announced that he'd had enough and was ready to leave. Tina, on the other hand, felt like the party was just beginning when he wanted to leave. Taken together, the differences between them left Tina increasingly puzzled and wondering whether the relationship was going to work out, and how much each of them would be able to change in order to make the relationship work.

Some aspects of personality are biologically based, so personalities are partly born, not entirely made. Is Gabe shy and mellow because of his biology? Is Tina outgoing and a bit anxious because of her genes or hormones? In this section, we explore how biology contributes to personality.

LOOKING AHEAD Learning Objectives

1. What exactly is temperament?
2. What do the biologically based theories of personality have in common?
3. What does the field of behavioral genetics say about the effects of genes on personality?

Temperament: Waxing Hot or Cold

Psychologists use the term **temperament** to refer to an inclination to think, feel, or behave in particular ways; a temperament initially arises from the effects of genes and biology, and an individual's environment moderates these effects. Temperament affects not just *what* people think, feel, and do but also *how* they think, feel, and act in the ways that that do (A. H. Buss, 1995). Being "high strung" versus being "chill," for instance, reflects differences in temperament. Because temperaments initially arise from the effects of genes and biology, a person's temperament often is relatively consistent throughout the life span. In addition, unlike personality traits, temperaments are relatively consistent across situations. Although temperaments are not the same as personality traits, different temperaments can give rise to different personality traits; studies that tracked children as they grew up have found that a child's temperament at age 3 is correlated with his or her personality at age 18, as assessed by a personality inventory (Caspi, 2000; Chess & Thomas, 1996).

Temperament An inclination to engage in a certain style of thinking, feeling, or behaving; a temperament initially arises from the effects of genes and biology, and an individual's environment moderates these effects.

Your temperament—such as your preferred level of vigor for activities—and your personality traits will likely determine whether your idea of a good time at the beach (assuming you like beaches) will lead you to be physically active or inactive.

Sources: Image Source\Alamy Images Royalty Free; Fancy\Alamy Images Royalty Free

Arnold Buss and Robert Plomin (1984; A. H. Buss, 1995) propose four broad dimensions of temperament, each of which is on a continuum:

- **Sociability:** a preference for being in the company of others rather than alone (this dimension is similar to extraversion in the Big Five);
- **Emotionality:** an inclination to become aroused in emotional situations, but only when the emotions of distress, fear, or anger are involved (this dimension is similar to neuroticism);
- **Activity:** a preference for a particular activity level, which has two components: *vigor* (the intensity of activity) and *tempo* (the speed of activity);
- **Impulsivity:** a tendency to respond to stimuli immediately, without reflection or concern for consequences.

Let's examine a couple of specific, well-studied temperaments in detail.

Shyness: The Wallflower Temperament At one extreme of the sociability dimension is the type of person who enjoys other people so much that being alone is uncomfortable, and at the other extreme is the type of person who is so shy that being with people is painful. Jerome Kagan and his colleagues (1988) have asked whether such extreme shyness is innate. They began by studying aspects of temperament in infants who they thought might later become very shy or socially inhibited. Specifically, the psychologists theorized that infants whose sympathetic nervous systems are more easily aroused would later prefer situations less likely to create high arousal and hence would be inhibited. And this is exactly what they found. These researchers discovered that some babies are more reactive, or sensitive, to environmental stimuli and thus are more fussy than are other babies. These "high-reactive" infants are more likely than "low-reactive" babies to respond to a recording of a woman's voice or to a colored toy with crying, general distress, and increased motor activity, such as moving their legs. Such infants tend to have faster heart rates and higher levels of the stress hormone cortisol. These temperamental differences arise even before birth and persist over time. Babies with a fast heart rate in the womb are more likely later to become inhibited, fearful children who startle more easily (Snidman et al., 1995); in fact, the heart rates of even 2-week-old infants can predict whether the infants will become inhibited children (Snidman et al., 1995). As these inhibited children get older, they are usually the ones who hide behind their parents in a room full of adults.

Some (but not all) of these inhibited children become shy teenagers and adults—and are often extremely self-conscious. They may painfully and ruthlessly analyze their behavior after a social interaction, often (incorrectly) interpreting another person's remark or expression as "evidence" that the social interaction was unsuccessful and humiliating. This unhappy process leads the shy people to minimize interactions with others in the future because otherwise they become preoccupied with their shyness and its effects ("I can't stop imagining what they're thinking about me"). It's easy to see how the fear and distress in social situations that are common feelings for highly inhibited people can turn into extreme shyness.

In addition, the ways the family and culture react toward inhibited, shy behavior will determine how a person thinks and feels about himself or herself. For instance, American culture tends to favor outgoing people, a social bias that puts shy people at a disadvantage. In this culture, shy people are more likely to develop a negative self-concept (at least regarding their social selves), and this negative self-concept increases the likelihood of an autonomic reaction in social situations, thereby perpetuating the cycle.

Sociability A temperament dimension characterized by a preference for being in other people's company rather than alone.

Emotionality A temperament dimension characterized by an inclination to become aroused in situations in which the predominant emotions are distress, fear, or anger.

Activity A temperament dimension characterized by the preference for a particular activity level, which has two components: vigor (intensity of the activity) and tempo (speed of the activity).

Impulsivity A temperament dimension characterized by the propensity to respond to stimuli immediately, without reflection or concern for consequences.

Nevertheless, being born with a reactive temperament doesn't doom an individual to extreme shyness in adulthood—biology is not destiny, and temperaments are shaped by life experience. Not all inhibited toddlers are still inhibited at age 7, and not all inhibited children become shy adults (Kagan, 1989). The environment can play a role either in diminishing the effects of shyness or in maintaining shyness into adulthood. That's because children can develop a wide set of possible responses to novel social situations, and in so doing they can come to have more positive social experiences—which leads them to become less inhibited as they get older (Fox et al., 2005). For instance, parents can help inhibited children by recognizing their children's temperaments and supporting the children—by encouraging them to learn new responses to social situations and doing so in a way that promotes mastery rather than leads them to feel overwhelmed (Fox et al., 2005; Rubin et al., 2002; Wood et al., 2003). As one previously inhibited 7-year-old explained, "My parents introduced me to new things slowly" (Azar, 1995). However, children who are at either very extreme end of this continuum—either very inhibited or very outgoing—are the least likely to change over time (Kagan et al., 1988; Zhengyan et al., 2003).

Sensation Seeking: What's New? Another well-studied temperament, one that doesn't neatly correspond to the four temperaments described by Buss and Plomin (1984)—is that of *sensation seeking*: the pursuit of novelty or highly stimulating pursuits (such as skydiving, fast driving, or drug and alcohol use) or occupations (such as working in a hospital emergency room) (Zuckerman, 1979). People who are high on this temperament (referred to as *high sensation seekers*) are more likely to: send angry e-mails (Alonzo & Aiken, 2004); surf versus play golf (Diehm & Armatas, 2004); prefer visiting museums of modern art versus ancient art (Mastandrea et al., 2009); and, listen to punk music (Weisskirch & Murphy, 2004). High sensation seekers view a given situation as less risky than do low sensation seekers (Horvath & Zuckerman, 1993). Tina appears to have a sensation-seeking temperament, and Gabe, who actively shies away from adventurous activities, doesn't.

Biologically Based Theories of Personality

When researchers document that certain personality traits, such as shyness and sensation seeking, may have a biological basis, it is only a first step toward understanding such traits. We next need to know how biological factors can actually lead to these traits and sets of behaviors. Similarly, although the Big Five Model identifies and describes traits and superfactors, it does not take the crucial next step—it does not attempt to explain *why* these personality differences exist. In this section we consider various theories about how aspects of biology—genes, neurotransmitters, brain areas—influence temperament and personality.

Behavioral Activation and Inhibition Systems Jeffrey Gray (1982, 1987, 1991) proposes that the workings of two brain systems explain broad aspects of temperament and personality. One system, the *behavioral activation system (BAS)*, is a mechanism based on the *activation* of behavior and on the effects of reward on behavior. The BAS triggers positive feelings (such as elation or hope), but it also underlies impulsivity, and people with an easily activated BAS tend to respond readily to even minor incentives and rewards (Meyer et al., 2005). People in whom the BAS is easily activated are also more likely to have problems with substance abuse (Johnson et al., 2003). This system is associated with extraversion (both the Big Five superfactor and Eysenck's dimension).

The other system proposed by Gray, the *behavioral inhibition system (BIS)*, is a mechanism based on *inhibition* of behavior and on the effects of punishment on behavior. Whereas the BAS is activated by incentives and rewards, the BIS is activated by threat-related stimuli and punishment, which trigger anxiety and inhibit behavior. People with an easily activated BIS (such as anxious people) become distressed when confronted with even minor threats; in contrast, those with an insensitive BIS are not distressed by most threats, even when confronted with significant threats (Carver & White, 1994; Carver et al., 2000; Heponiemi et al., 2003; Mardaga & Hansenne, 2009; Meyer et al., 2005).

THINK like a **PSYCHOLOGIST** Think back to your childhood; were you inhibited or outgoing as a child? Now? Have you changed much since childhood with regard to this temperament? If so, why do you think that might be?

People who engage in highly stimulating hobbies such as hang gliding, downhill skiing, or snowboarding are more likely to be sensation seekers.

Source: Shutterstock

People who are more sensitive to, and motivated by, reward are more likely to violate traffic rules than are people less sensitive to reward (Castellà & Pérez, 2004).

Source: PhotoEdit Inc.

Many people in whom the BIS is easily activated are also anxious and depressed (Johnson et al., 2003; Kasch et al., 2002). This system is associated with neuroticism (again, both the Big Five's and Eysenck's versions).

Gray and others (Davidson, 1992a, 1992b; Fox et al., 2005; Zuckerman, 2003) argue that the properties of these systems arise from characteristics of specific brain structures and neurotransmitters, and research supports this notion. These systems thus directly affect events at all three levels of analysis, the brain (by activating certain brain systems), the person (by affecting motivation and experience), and the group (by how each individual's behavior affects and is affected by others—which in turn can produce reward or punishment).

Eysenck's Theory Eysenck proposed that biological mechanisms underlie his three personality dimensions. He conceived of a hierarchy, where the personality dimensions (at the top of the hierarchy) are composed of more specific traits. In turn, these specific traits arise from automatic responses, which are themselves based on specific, learned associations between a stimulus and response, such as what happens when you are driving a car and see a red light (stimulus)—you put your foot on the brake (response). As we discuss in what follows, there is support for some aspects of Eysenck's theory (Matthews & Gilliland, 1999; Zuckerman, 2003).

Research suggests that extraverts are more easily conditioned by reward (such as winning money), whereas introverts are more easily conditioned by punishment (such as losing money). These differences may be related to differences in brain structure or function (Gray, 1987).

Source: © Ted Soqui/CORBIS

EXTRAVERSION. Eysenck believed that the cerebral cortex of extraverts—compared to introverts—is less easily aroused by stimulation of the senses (Haier et al., 1984). His view was that it takes more stimulation to arouse or to overstimulate extraverts (Eysenck & Eysenck, 1967). That is, extraverts have a higher threshold for arousal. Extraverts thus seek out activities that are more stimulating and arousing: recreational activities such as hang gliding or occupations such as espionage. In fact, introverts and extraverts have different biological responses to caffeine, nicotine, and sedatives (Corr & Kumari, 1997; Corr et al., 1995; Stelmack, 1990), to reward and punishment, and even different patterns of brain waves (Matthews & Amelang, 1993). (In spite of such support, however, other studies of the influence of arousability of the cerebral cortex on personality—which is at the heart of Eysenck's theory—have yielded mixed results; Zuckerman, 2003.)

NEUROTICISM. People who score high on the dimension of neuroticism are easily and intensely emotionally aroused, and so are more likely to experience conditioned emotional responses—that is, emotional responses elicited by previously neutral stimuli—particularly fear (Eysenck, 1979). For example, someone who scores high on neuroticism and is stuck in an elevator is more likely to develop a fear of elevators than is someone who scores low on this dimension.

Neuroimaging data confirm that neuroticism is distinct from extraversion, as revealed by their being associated with activation in different sets of brain areas (Canli et al., 2001). However, such research is just beginning to produce solid results, and we do not yet know the neural foundations of neuroticism (Zuckerman, 2003).

PSYCHOTICISM. Eysenck viewed people high on psychoticism as having less control over their emotions, and proposed that such people may be prone to psychotic symptoms or social deviance; that is, they are likely to be aggressive, impulsive, and to engage in delinquent behavior. However, research on the relationship between psychoticism and social deviance has yielded complex results (Bruggeman & Barry, 2002; Heaven et al., 2004), and social deviance is associated with high scores of psychoticism usually only in conjunction with high scores on neuroticism and/or extraversion (Center et al., 2005; Cravens-Brown, 2003; Idemuddia, 1997; Rebollo et al., 2002). Because other personality dimensions affect the way psychoticism influences personality, it is understandable that research has not revealed specific biological underpinnings of psychoticism.

Cloninger's Theory C. Robert Cloninger and his colleagues (1993) propose that people differ on four personality dimensions:

- *Reward dependence* (a desire for socially rewarding experiences; its opposite is aloofness; it is related to Gray's BAS).
- *Harm avoidance* (pessimism, shyness, and a fear of uncertainty, an inhibition of approach behaviors and an increase in avoidance behaviors; it is related to Gray's BIS).
- *Novelty seeking* (an excited response to new situations; it is related to Gray's BAS).
- *Persistence* (the tendency to continue to seek a goal in the face of obstacles or resistance).

Cloninger further proposes that each of these dimensions corresponds to some combination of Big Five superfactors and is associated with a distinct brain system. For example, let's consider one of his dimensions in more detail: novelty seeking. Novelty seeking corresponds to a combination of a high score on extraversion and a low score on conscientiousness in the Big Five (Zuckerman, 2003). People who score higher than average on novelty seeking are "impulsive, exploratory, fickle, excitable, quick-tempered, and extravagant, whereas those who score lower than average tend to be reflective, rigid, loyal, stoic, slow-tempered, and frugal" (Ebstein et al., 1996, p. 78). In addition, Cloninger and his colleagues hypothesized that the novelty-seeking dimension is related to the dopamine-based reward system in the brain (Hansenne et al., 2002; Reif & Lesch, 2003; Wiesbeck et al., 1995; Zuckerman & Cloninger, 1996). Earlier studies with animals have shown that dopamine is involved in exploratory behavior, and a lack of dopamine in people with Parkinson's disease leads to a low level of novelty seeking (Cloninger et al., 1993).

Zuckerman's Theory Like Cloninger, Zuckerman has proposed a set of personality dimensions that is rooted in brain mechanisms; this system is known as the *alternative five*:

- *Sociability*, which is similar to extraversion.
- *Neuroticism-anxiety*, which is similar to neuroticism.
- *Impulsive sensation seeking*, which is a tendency to act impulsively. This dimension is a reconceptualization of Eysenck's psychoticism and is related to sensation seeking and Gray's BAS; it is at the opposite end of the Big Five's conscientiousness superfactor (Zuckerman, 1989; Zuckerman et al., 1999). Impulsive sensation seeking is the most studied of the alternative five; it is more typical of men than women and is associated with insensitivity to punishment or loss of reward (Zuckerman & Kuhlman, 2000). This dimension has a high genetic component (Fulker et al., 1980; Hur & Bouchard, 1997).
- *Activity*, which is a need for activity, a high energy level, a preference for challenges, and difficulty in relaxing.
- *Aggression-hostility*, which is a tendency toward antisocial behavior, verbal aggression, and vengefulness. Aggression-hostility focuses on the opposite of the Big Five's agreeableness superfactor (Zuckerman, 1994).

People with higher numbers of tattoos score higher on measures of sensation seeking (Roberti et al., 2004).

Source: The Image Works

Comparing the Biologically Based Theories The various biologically based theories are clearly similar in some ways. Although the names of the personality dimensions differ, many are variants of the same idea (see Table 4 on the next page). All four theories have a dimension related to sociability and a dimension related to anxiety or emotionality, although the theories differ in the breadth of these dimensions and in the specific traits associated with them (Ball, 2002). In addition, Cloninger's novelty seeking and Zuckerman's impulsive sensation seeking are closely related, and Cloninger's persistence and Zuckerman's activity are related (Zuckerman & Cloninger, 1996).

TABLE 4 Biologically Based Theories of Personality

Gray	Eysenck	Cloninger	Zuckerman
Behavioral activation system (BAS)	Extraversion*	Reward dependence	Sociability
Behavioral inhibition system (BIS)	Neuroticism	Harm avoidance	Neuroticism-anxiety
	Psychoticism	Novelty seeking**	Impulsive sensation seeking**
		Persistence	Activity
			Aggression-hostility

*Extraversion is also inversely related to BIS levels.

**Novelty seeking and impulsive sensation seeking are also related to BAS levels.

Genes and Personality: Born to Be Mild?

Many researchers have reported evidence that genes influence personality. In fact, a field within psychology, *behavioral genetics*, focuses on sorting out the influence of heredity versus environment on thoughts, feelings, and behavior. Some of these researchers have studied the genetics of personality, and have primarily used three methods to do so.

In the first method, researchers compare people who share different percentages of their genes. Specifically, identical twins share virtually all of their genes, and fraternal twins share 50% of their genes. In most studies of this type, the twins have been raised in the same environment. Studies find that the identical twins have more similar personalities than do the fraternal twins: The identical twins have higher correlations between their scores on personality tests than do the fraternal twins. This difference between the correlations of identical twins versus the correlations of fraternal twins is usually attributed to effects of the genes. The amount of variation in characteristics that arises from genes—such as variations in personality traits—is quantified with a number that indicates *heritability*. This number varies from 0 to 100, with higher numbers indicating that a greater percentage of the variation of a characteristic within the examined population arises from genes.

In the second method, researchers compare sets of twins (both identical and fraternal) who were separated at birth or early childhood and raised apart with sets of twins who were raised together. To the extent that twins raised apart—particularly identical twins—and twins raised together score similarly on personality tests. The assessed aspects of personality are likely to be influenced by genes. ●—Watch

In a third method by which researchers in behavioral genetics study the effects of genes on personality, scientists identify specific genes (which correspond to portions of DNA) with a personality dimension or trait. Specifically, techniques for this method typically compare the association between a personality dimension or trait with different *alleles* of a gene; alleles are the different "flavors" of the gene, which cause variations of the same characteristic (such as eye color, hair color, or aspects of behavior). These studies can document the degree to which particular alleles are associated with particular personality dimensions and traits.

Heritability of Personality Research on the genetics of personality has shown that genes influence different personality dimensions and traits more or less strongly, as shown in Figure 5 (Angleitner et al., 1995; Bouchard, 2004; Heath & Martin, 1990; Loehlin, 1992; Pederson et al., 1988).

Although there is no doubt that genes affect various aspects of personality, the precise degree of their influence is debated, and the precise findings in Figure 5 should be taken with a grain of salt. The results in this figure were obtained by studying twins, but this method has been criticized on methodological grounds (Joseph, 2001; Loehlin et al., 1981; Stoolmiller, 1999). For example, critics have pointed out that identical twins

●—Watch the Video on Twins Separated at Birth on mypsychlab.com

FIGURE 5 Heritability of Personality

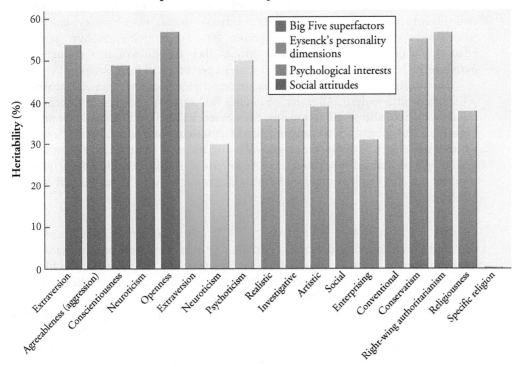

Heritability of the Big Five superfactors, Eysenck's three dimensions of personality, psychological interests, and social attitudes, based on research with twins.

typically share a more similar environment in the womb than do fraternal twins—which then influences their subsequent development.

Heritability of Specific Behaviors

Personality measures predict behavior, and thus if genes influence personality, we would expect genetic differences to predict behavior. As expected, evidence exists that genes contribute to very specific behaviors (Bergeman et al., 1990; Kendler et al., 1992; Lensvelt-Mulders & Hettema, 2001a; Lyons et al., 1993): from the amount of time spent watching television (Prescott et al., 1991) and the number of childhood accidents (Phillips & Matheny, 1995) to a tendency to marry (Johnson et al., 2004) or divorce (McGue & Lykken, 1992) and even religious attitudes (Bouchard, 2004; Waller et al., 1990). Similarly, researchers have found a substantial heritability estimate (.50; Lykken et al., 1993) for work and leisure interests, and they estimate that a subjective sense of well-being—what some might call happiness—has a heritability that's probably even higher (between .44 and .80; Lykken & Tellegen, 1996). Other researchers have found that the subjective sense of well-being has a higher heritability in women (.54) than in men (.46) (Roysamb et al., 2002); a particularly interesting implication of this study is the possibility that different genes may underlie variations in happiness for men and women.

Of course, nobody claims that the amount of time you spend watching television is explicitly coded in your genes. What some researchers do claim, however, is that genes influence characteristics such as how easily your autonomic nervous system is aroused (Lensvelt-Mulders & Hettema, 2001b; Tesser et al., 1998)—and such factors in turn influence personality traits. Indeed, even physical traits—such as how attractive and athletic you are—may indirectly reflect the influence of your genes on your personality

These identical twins were separated in infancy and adopted by different working-class families. In school, neither liked spelling, but both liked math; as adults, both worked as part-time deputy sheriffs, vacationed in Florida, had first wives named Linda and second wives named Betty, and gave their sons the same names. They both drove Chevys and liked carpentry (Holden, 1980). Moreover, their medical histories were remarkably similar, including the onset of migraine headaches at age 18. Are these similarities a result of coincidence or of the twins' shared genetics? How many similarities would any two random people have if they compared such detailed information?

Source: Bob Sacha Photography

(Olson et al., 2001). If, for instance, your activity level is both "low vigor" and "low tempo" (based on Buss and Plomin's temperament of *activity*) and you tend to be shy, you are more likely to spend time alone in sedentary pursuits (such as watching television) than if you are a gregarious person who likes vigorous, fast-paced activities. In short, genes can affect personality both *directly* (such as through their influence on temperament) and *indirectly* (such as through the types of responses a person elicits from others).

However, the finding that genes influence personality does not mean that personality is fixed from birth to death. All researchers in this field agree that other factors, such as personal experience, also shape personality. Even Eysenck (1993), who argued that much of behavior is biologically determined, proposed that the environment makes a difference in whether someone high in psychoticism will become a creative, productive researcher or artist or will be disabled by schizophrenia. As we have seen throughout this book, the environment can affect the body and the brain, which in turn leads to psychological changes (Davidson, 2001).

Genes and the Family Environment In general, researchers have found that a shared family environment does not contribute very much to personality; the shared family environment is defined as aspects of the family setting that are present for all siblings in a household, such as the number of books in the house. The exceptions are the personality traits of *social closeness*, that is, the desire for intimacy with others (Tellegen et al., 1988), and *positive emotionality*, a set of traits "characterized by an active engagement in one's environment" (p. 1037). The fact that a shared family environment minimally influences other personality traits may simply indicate that many important aspects of the family environment are not truly shared. For example:

- The same family event, such as a divorce, will be experienced differently by children of different ages and cognitive abilities (Hoffman, 1991).

- Children can elicit different responses from parents, based in part on their temperaments, which thus produces a different "family environment" for each child (Graziano et al., 1998; Jenkins et al., 2003; Plomin & Bergeman, 1991; Scarr & McCartney, 1983).

- It is also possible that some people are more susceptible than others to environmental forces during personality development (Holden, 1980).

How Do Genes Exert Their Influence? Researchers have found it difficult to map the precise set of genes that contributes to personality. Three problems have played a large role in creating the challenge:

- Most aspects of personality are affected by numerous genes that exert their influence in concert (Bouchard, 2004). In some rare cases, such as novelty seeking, a single gene influences the dimension (Ebstein et al., 1996). But this is very unusual.

- Variations in a single gene, interacting with other genes, may affect more than one aspect of personality (Ebstein et al., 2002; Livesley et al., 2003).

- The effects of any one gene are subtle; in general, variations of a single gene account for less than 10% of the genetic influence on a trait or personality dimension (Lesch, 2003; Reif & Lesch, 2003). Hence, studies that investigate the relationships between a particular gene and a trait or personality dimension often yield inconsistent results (Livesley et al., 2003).

Even if researchers succeed in identifying the sets of genes that form the basis of a personality trait or temperament, such information is of limited value by itself. Researchers want to know the mechanisms by which genes affect personality. Recent research has focused on how genes affect neurotransmitters and their activities. However, the process of discovering the relationships of genes to neurotransmitters and of neurotransmitters to personality traits and superfactors has just begun. Correlational studies sometimes find relationships between levels of a neurotransmitter by-product (in the blood, urine, or saliva) and a personality trait, but subsequent studies often fail to replicate these results. The most common explanation for such inconsistent findings is that neurotransmitters affect personality in complex ways, both direct and indirect (Zuckerman, 2003).

LOOKING BACK

✓●─Study and Review on
mypsychlab.com

1. **What exactly is temperament?** Temperament refers to an inclination to engage in a certain style of thinking, feeling, or behaving; temperaments initially arise from the effects of genes and biology, and an individual's environment moderates these effects. Four temperament dimensions are activity (which has two components, vigor and tempo), sociability, emotionality, and impulsivity. Additional temperaments include sensation seeking and shyness.

2. **What do the biologically based theories of personality have in common?** All four biologically based theories of personality (those of Gray, Eysenck, Cloninger, and Zuckerman) include a personality dimension related to sociability and another one related to anxiety or emotionality.

3. **What does the field of behavioral genetics say about the effects of genes on personality?** Based on twin studies, behavioral geneticists propose that some dimensions of personality are up to 50% heritable. Despite this high heritability, environmental factors still play an important role in personality development.

Contributions of Learning and Cognition to Personality

Tina's and Gabe's personalities may have been shaped partly by their genes, but their unique experiences also shaped their beliefs, expectations, and goals. For instance, Tina's past positive experiences with thrilling activities lead her to get excited about new stimulating activities. Similarly, Gabe may hesitate about going to parties because of previous experiences where socializing in groups was awkward and uncomfortable. How does experience build on the biological framework of our personalities, affecting our beliefs, motivations, and views of ourselves?

LOOKING AHEAD Learning Objectives

1. How do behavioral factors influence personality?
2. What is the sociocognitive view of personality?

Learning to Have Personality

Early learning theorists viewed personality as sets of behaviors that are acquired through experience (Skinner, 1953; Watson, 1913). These theorists argued that an individual's inclination to behave in consistent ways arises from classical conditioning and operant conditioning; no mental processes (or biologically based temperaments) are involved. According to this view, although people may spontaneously produce a specific behavior once or twice, they continue to engage in the behavior only because they have been conditioned to do so. Learning influences personality by creating:

- *Classically conditioned behaviors*, such as those that underlie a phobia (which leads the individual persistently to avoid a stimulus).

- *Operantly conditioned behaviors*, such as taking part in highly stimulating activities because of past reinforcement (or avoiding parties because of past "punishment" for attending).

- *Behaviors learned though observation*, such as being polite (or not saying a particular curse word after witnessing a sibling's severe punishment for saying it).

303

THINK like a **PSYCHOLOGIST** Imagine two people who have been together as a couple for 5 years. Whatever their personalities might have been like when they started dating each other, how would learning theorists explain their current personalities?

Although personality is not solely the result of conditioning, conditioning can exert an influence on personality. Here's an example: When shy children are laughed at or made the butt of pranks ("punishment"), such children will modify their social behavior and try to make themselves less likely to be such targets in the future. (And as we discuss shortly, such negative social events also lead shy children to modify their thoughts about themselves in negative ways; Fox et al., 2005.)

The Sociocognitive View of Personality

The sociocognitive approach to personality emphasizes that social interactions affect thoughts, feelings, and behaviors—and consistent thoughts, feelings, and behaviors (consistent in a given situation at least) create personality. That is, according to this view, personality develops in part via a child's thoughts, which in turn are shaped by social interactions. Consider that particular thoughts lead a person to pay attention to (or to ignore) certain stimuli. For instance, if you are worried about offending people by bumping into them, you will be particularly alert in a crowd as someone comes near to you.

Another aspect of the sociocognitive view of personality development is the role of **expectancies**: What you *expect* to happen has a powerful influence on your thoughts, feelings, and behaviors and, in turn, on your personality. Expectations, in turn, can arise from learning. For example, perhaps Gabe doesn't like parties because, from his previous experience of them, he expects that he will have a miserable time and feel socially isolated (in the language of conditioning, his prior unhappy experiences constituted punishment for attending a party). If this is what Gabe expects, one or two possible sets of events will likely transpire: (1) He will go to the party and be inclined to interpret events in ways that are consistent with his expectations (and thus feel punished for going), or (2) he will not go and will feel relieved—in which case he'll be reinforced for not going. Either way, his expectations will be strengthened. To the extent that expectancies are consistent across situations, they can be thought of as personality traits.

The sociocognitive view acknowledges the influence of biological factors on personality traits and dimensions (such as neuroticism) but emphasizes the role of the person's experiences (including social experiences), of consistent patterns of mental processing, of the self-concept, and of behavior. Moreover, the sociocognitive view of how personality develops—as indicated by the "socio" part of its name—stresses that society and culture contribute to a person's experiences and ultimately even affect biology (Mischel & Shoda, 1995). For instance, the average level of neuroticism among Americans has increased from 1963 to 1993 (Twenge, 2000), as cultural changes have led to an increase in crime and other dangers.

Locus of Control Different people have different habitual ways of interpreting events and have different expectancies, which in turn can influence their personalities. In particular, when the cause of an event is ambiguous, people differ in the extent to which they perceive that they have control over that event; specifically, **locus of control** refers to a person's perception of the source of control over life's events when the cause of events is ambiguous (Rotter, 1966). People who have an internal locus of control, called *internals*, are more likely to see control over events as coming from within themselves when the situation is ambiguous; that is, they feel personally responsible for what happens to them. For example, if you're an internal, you would feel responsible if your car breaks down—which is an ambiguous event—and you might say to yourself, "I should have taken the car in for a check up or at least had the oil changed." Similarly, Gabe's approach to studying suggests that he has an internal locus of control: If he received a poor grade, he would perceive it to reflect poor preparation on his part.

In contrast, *externals* are people with an external locus of control; these people are more likely to see control as coming from outside forces, and they feel less personal responsibility. If you are an external, you would attribute the car's breakdown to the bad roads or shoddy workmanship by your mechanic, and you might say to yourself, "I had the car tuned up last year, it shouldn't be having problems this soon; the mechanic must have done a poor job." Similarly, because Tina does well in her classes without

Expectancies Expectations that have a powerful influence on thoughts, feelings, and behaviors and, in turn, on personality.

Locus of control A person's perception of the source of control over life's events when the cause of events is ambiguous.

studying much, she chalks up her good grades to easy tests. She feels less personally responsible for her academic success than does Gabe and seems to have more of an external locus of control.

Just as the average level of neuroticism has changed over the decades, so too has locus of control. Research on the locus of control among college students between 1960 and 2002 found that, over time, college students are becoming increasingly external in their locus of control; that is, they tend to feel that their lives are out of their personal control (and therefore that they are less responsible). An average college student in 2002 had a more external locus of control than did 80% of college students in the 1960s (Twenge & Campbell, 2008; Twenge et al., 2004).

Locus of control is an important aspect of personality in part because internals and externals have different responses to success and failure. Internals are more likely to increase their expectancies after experiencing success and to lower their expectancies after failure. Externals are likely to do the opposite, lowering their expectancies after success (because how often will chance smile upon them?) and raising them after failure (because anybody can have bad luck, but a run of bad luck isn't very likely). In both cases, what a person expects for future situations depends on whether he or she attributes consequences to his or her own behavior or to outside forces. Gabe, as an internal, has lowered expectations about his experience at future parties because of what he sees as his failures at past ones. Tina, as an external, doesn't fully expect to maintain her high grades because she doesn't feel completely responsible for them in the first place.

Self-Efficacy People also differ with respect to **self-efficacy**, the sense of having the ability to follow through and produce desired behaviors (Bandura, 1977). Individuals with high self-efficacy believe that they will be able to behave in a specific way if they want to do so (Ajzen, 2002). Self-efficacy is distinct from locus of control, which focuses on inferring an internal or external cause of an ambiguous situation.

Albert Bandura (2004) hypothesized that self-efficacy helps people believe in themselves and in their ability to change or perform behaviors previously viewed as difficult or impossible. For instance, those with high self-efficacy persist more than people with low self-efficacy when working on difficult problems (Brown & Inouye, 1978). Both Gabe and Tina have high self-efficacy, a correspondence that partly accounts for the initial sense they had of being a lot alike.

LOOKING BACK

✔ Study and Review on
mypsychlab.com

1. **How do behavioral factors influence personality?** Personality can be viewed as a set of behaviors that are acquired through learning. Classical and operant conditioning, as well as observational learning, help to establish such behaviors.

2. **What is the sociocognitive view of personality?** The sociocognitive approach stresses the effects of expectancies on people's thoughts, feelings, and behaviors: What you expect to happen will influence personality development. Expectancies arise in part from locus of control, the source we perceive as exerting control over our life events, and are also affected by self-efficacy, the sense that we have the ability to follow through and produce the behaviors we would like to perform.

Sociocultural Influences on Personality

Tina wondered whether she and Gabe might be different because they grew up in very different environments. Gabe was an only child; Tina was the youngest of three, with two older brothers. Gabe grew up in a rural part of the United States and, before college, had lived in the same town his whole life. Tina, an Air Force "brat," had lived in half a dozen countries before she was 12.

As we will explore in this section, Tina was onto something. Various aspects of the environment affect personality, including birth order, gender differences, and culture.

Self-efficacy The sense of being able to follow through and produce specific desired behaviors.

1. To what extent does birth order shape personality?
2. Do social factors produce gender differences in personality?
3. Do different cultures produce different types of personalities?

Birth Order: Are You Number One?

Many researchers have proposed that birth order contributes to personality. At first glance, this seems plausible; the experience of a child who is the oldest sibling in a family is different from that of the child who is the youngest sibling in that family; the oldest sibling may feel responsible for—and annoyed by—the younger siblings, whereas the youngest sibling may feel like the baby of the family, even into adulthood. An early theory about how birth order influences personality was proposed by Alfred Adler (1933/1964), a colleague of Freud's. Adler was the first among Freud's colleagues to focus on the role that siblings play in a child's developing personality. (Adler's theory had its roots in his own experience—he was a younger sibling, raised in the shadow of a high-achieving older brother.) In spite of the appeal of such ideas, research initially did not find clear-cut evidence that birth order influences personality development (Ernst & Angst, 1983). However, birth order research after the 1980s, using the statistical technique of meta-analysis, has found consistent and interesting results.

Science historian Frank Sulloway (1996) made an important contribution to our understanding of the role in birth order in personality. He used meta-analyses to show that at least one aspect of personality—openness to experience (one of the Big Five superfactors)—is shaped by birth order. But Sulloway was careful to point out that birth order alone is not as big a factor as is birth order in combination with other factors, such as the number of children in a family and the level of conflict between each child and his or her parents. Moreover, additional factors, such as a person's sex (and that of his or her siblings), the number of years between siblings, temperament, social class, and loss of a parent, can also influence the effects of birth order on personality.

Sulloway studied birth order because he wanted to explain why, throughout history, some people have supported scientific and political revolutions, whereas others have insisted on maintaining the status quo—the way things are. He was particularly struck by the observation that such opposite views occur within the same family. From available information about the lives of historical figures, Sulloway proposed that, in general, first-borns—because of their place in the birth order—are more likely to support parental authority, see things the way their parents do, and be less open to new ideas and experiences. Younger siblings—because they must find a different niche in the family and in the world around them—are more likely to be open to new ideas and experiences. In their personalities, "only" children are similar to firstborn children.

Not all psychologists agree with Sulloway's conclusions about the effects of birth order on personality development (Modell, 1996), and not all subsequent research has supported his claims (Freese et al., 1999; Skinner, 2003)—but some studies have supported such views (Michalski & Shackelford, 2002; Zweigenhaft, 2002). Moreover, Sulloway and others have extended and replicated his results with over 5,000 adults and across different countries (Rohde et al., 2003).

In addition, other research on birth order has focused particularly on the role of middle-born children; these studies reveal that middle-borns are less likely to define their self-identities by their families than are both their elder or younger siblings (Salmon, 1998, 1999; Salmon & Daly, 1998). For instance, when hearing political speeches, middle-borns responded more positively to the speeches when the speakers used the term *friends* than when they used the terms *brothers* and *sisters*. In contrast, firstborns and last-borns responded more positively to speeches in which family terms were used (Salmon, 1998). Further, when asked to define themselves, middle-borns were least likely to define themselves by their last names, that is, their family names (Salmon & Daly, 1998). Another study found middle-borns to be more rebellious and impulsive and less conscientious than their siblings (Saroglou & Fiasse, 2003). Table 5 summarizes these research results on birth order.

THINK like a
PSYCHOLOGIST What is your birth order? Do the personality traits described for your birth position seem to apply to you? If not, what factors in your life may have led birth order to have less of an influence—or a different influence—on your personality?

TABLE 5 Typical Effects of Birth Order on Personality

Firstborns and Only Children	Middle-Borns	Later-Borns
• More responsible, ambitious, organized, academically successful, energetic, self-disciplined, conscientious • More temperamental, more anxious about their status • More assertive, dominant (Sulloway, 1996)	• More rebellious and impulsive • Less closely identified with family • Less conscientious • Less likely to ask for parental help in an emergency • Less likely to report having been loved as a child • Compared with siblings, more likely to live farther from parents and less likely to visit parents (Salmon, 1999; Salmon & Daly, 1998; Saroglou & Fiasse, 2003)	• More agreeable and warmer • More idealistic, easygoing, trusting, accommodating, altruistic • More adventurous, prone to fantasy, attracted by novelty, untraditional • More sociable, affectionate, excitement seeking, fun loving • More self-conscious (Saroglou & Fiasse, 2003; Sulloway, 1996)

In sum, birth order does appear to exert an influence on personality. However, its specific effects have not been found consistently across all studies, which may suggest that other factors may temper the ways in which it shapes a given individual.

Sex Differences in Personality: Nature and Nurture

A person's sex is another variable that researchers hypothesized might influence personality and researchers have found consistent sex differences on some traits (Feingold, 1994). Women tend to score higher on traits reflecting *social connectedness*, which is a focus on the importance of relationships (Gilligan, 1982), and also score higher on measures of neuroticism (Costa et al., 2001; Goodwin & Gotlib, 2004; Lynn & Martin, 1997; Zuckerman et al., 1988). Similarly, women tend to be more empathic than men (Lennon & Eisenberg, 1987) and report more nurturing tendencies (Feingold, 1994).

In contrast, men tend to score higher on traits reflecting *individuality* and *autonomy*, which reflect a separateness from others and self-sufficiency. Men also generally score higher than women on measures of anger and aggression (Archer, 2004; Shields, 1987) and assertiveness (Costa et al., 2001; Feingold, 1994). However, the sex difference in assertiveness has diminished over time (Twenge, 2001b).

The finding of sex differences in these personality traits doesn't tell us *why* they exist—what the roles of biological and cultural factors might play (sex differences caused by cultural factors are sometimes referred to as *gender differences*). In the following section we consider how such differences might arise from sociocultural factors.

Sociocultural Explanations Cultural and social theories attempt to explain the personality differences between men and women by pointing to the different traditional social roles for males and females. One such explanation is *social role theory*, which proposes that boys and girls learn different skills and develop different beliefs based on the social roles of males and females. According to this theory, these beliefs and skills become so ingrained that they cut across situations and thus lead individuals to think, feel, and act in consistent ways across a variety of situations. For example, in Western society, girls typically have been taught to attend to social interactions and concern for others, and are taught that getting along is more important than winning. In contrast, boys have typically been taught the importance of being competitive, of sticking up for oneself, and of working hard to get ahead.

Expectancy effects can also play a role in gender differences in personality: Through direct interaction with their environments, boys and girls come to expect different responses to behaviors that are seen as appropriate or inappropriate for typical gender roles (Henley, 1977). For example, if a girl raises her voice in a class, she may be perceived as domineering and pushy—whereas if a boy does the same thing, he may instead be seen as self-confident and appropriately assertive. In turn, teachers and fellow classmates may respond differently to a girl who raises her voice than to a boy who raises his voice. After a

Some researchers propose that gender differences in personality are caused by social roles, whereby boys and girls are socialized to learn different skills and develop different beliefs, which in turn lead them to think, feel, and act in ways that conform to their gender role. For instance, although the boy in this photograph could learn to braid hair from observing his mother, because of social roles, he is unlikely to braid people's hair as frequently as is his sister.

Source: PhotoEdit Inc.

few experiences using a loud voice, a child typically will adjust his or her behavior according to the responses of other people—and hence girls and boys will come to develop different ways of behaving, which will in turn be incorporated into their personalities.

Finally, researchers who focus on social and cultural explanations are quick to point out that sex (biologically based) and gender (culturally based) differences often depend on the specific context in which they are measured. In fact, the importance of context has raised the question of whether examining sex differences in personality is valid—especially since different situations can produce contradictory findings (Eagly, 1987, 1995; Lott, 1996). For example, one study found differences between men and women when participants interacted with same-sex friends (males were more dominant, and females were more friendly), but those differences disappeared when the interactions were between opposite-sex strangers (Moskowitz, 1993). Thus, although differences between men's and women's personalities have been observed, they do not necessarily arise in all—or even most—situations.

Biological Explanations Although culture and context shape gender differences, biological factors can also help to explain at least several of the observed sex differences in personality. Some of these explanations rely on the effects of different levels of male versus female hormones. For example, one such explanation attributes sex differences in aggression to the fact that men have higher levels of the "male" hormone testosterone (Berenbaum, 1999; Dabbs et al., 1997, 2001).

Another type of biological explanation rests of evolutionary theory. According to this view, men and women have evolved differently because of differences in mate selection and parenting strategies (D. M. Buss, 1995), which give rise to the sex difference in social connectedness. Specifically, women have a greater investment in their offspring because they cannot have as many children as men can. This greater investment, along with their caretaker role, supposedly leads women to become more strongly attached to their children, which has an evolutionary advantage: Highly attached mothers are more likely to have children who survive into adulthood and have children themselves.

Note that we don't need to pit the various sociocultural and biological explanations of sex difference in personality against one another. It's possible that both types of factors contribute to sex differences.

Finally, we must note that a large, 26-country meta-analysis using results from the NEO-PI-R (the personality inventory based on the Big Five) found that, in general, differences between men and women are not as large as differences within each sex. If sex (or gender) exerts a large role on personality, then larger differences between men and women—beyond those related to individuality and social connectedness—should have been observed. However, this was not the case (Costa et al., 2001). In fact, some researchers in the field have proposed that it is counterproductive to look for sex differences in personality, arguing that the context in which behavior takes place has a larger role in personality development (Lott, 1996). For example, there are no notable sex differences in social anxiety, locus of control, or impulsiveness (Feingold, 1994). Nevertheless, as noted above, some sex differences in personality have been found—and these differences must be explained.

From what we know of Tina and Gabe, we cannot say with certainty whether their different personalities reflect more general sex differences. Although Gabe prefers to be alone more often than Tina does, he has close friends; their contrasting preferences could reflect a difference in gender, in social connectedness and individuality, in temperament, or in what they've learned through experience.

Culture and Personality

Researchers have found consistent differences in people's personality traits (and superfactors) *over time* and *across countries*—which further attest to the influence the environment can have on personality development. In the sections that follow we explore these environmental influences in more detail.

Personality Changes Within a Culture, Over Time The personality characteristics of Americans have shifted over the decades. We noted earlier that researchers have found that, over time, college students are increasingly reporting an external locus of control and increasing levels of neuroticism (Twenge, 2000; Twenge et al., 2004). In addition, anxiety has increased significantly from 1963 to 1993; in fact, the average anxiety reported by American children in the 1980s was equivalent to the amount reported by children who were psychiatric patients in the 1950s (Twenge, 2000; Twenge & Campbell, 2008)! Furthermore, the degree of extraversion has increased over time (Twenge, 2001a), and personality traits typically considered consistent with gender roles have decreased for both sexes (Twenge, 1997).

These cultural shifts in personality traits indicate the powerful influence of environmental factors. Such shifts are thought to reflect factors such as increasing fear of crime, terrorism, and other dangers (leading to increased anxiety, neuroticism, and external locus of control) and an increasing cultural emphasis on (and value of) traits related to extraversion and decreasing emphasis on (and value of) personality traits related to sex roles (Twenge, 1997, 2000, 2001a, 2001b; Twenge et al., 2004).

Culture and Personality Differences Members of one culture can, on average, manifest different personality traits than members of another culture. In the following sections, we consider ways in which culture affects personality.

THE BIG FIVE IN DIFFERENT CULTURES. Personality measures reveal the same Big Five personality superfactors in many, but not all, cultures (Heine & Buchtel, 2009; Katigbak et al., 1996, 2002; McCrae & Costa, 1997; McCrae et al., 1998; Paunonen & Ashton, 1998; Paunonen et al., 2000). The failure to find the same Big Five superfactors in all cultures initially was thought to reflect problems in translating the tests, but different findings have been obtained even with personality measures developed in the native language of a culture (Katigbak et al., 2002). For example, Chinese college students were asked to rate other people on qualities described by Chinese adjectives (not English adjectives translated into Chinese); five personality factors were identified, but they were not the same as the Big Five found with English-language tests (Yang & Bond, 1990); these result suggest that culture affects personality development.

Providing solid proof that cultural socialization shapes personality, after Chinese immigrants move to North America, their personality profiles begin to resemble those of native-born North Americans—and the longer they have lived in North America, the more similar the profiles (McCrae et al., 1998).

INDIVIDUALIST AND COLLECTIVIST PERSONALITIES. Culture also affects personality in a more general way: People from collectivist cultures have different personalities than do people from individualist cultures. **Collectivist cultures** typically emphasize the rights and responsibilities of the group over those of the individual; that is, the needs of the group are viewed more important than those of the individual. For instance, these cultures tend to value humility, honoring the family, and efforts to maintain the social order (Triandis et al., 1990), and people raised in them are more likely to care about others, even strangers (Hui & Triandis, 1986). Asian, African, Latin American, and Arab cultures tend to have this orientation (Buda & Elsayed-Elkhouly, 1998). In contrast, **individualist cultures** emphasize the rights and responsibilities of the individual over those of the group; that is, individual freedom, equality, and enjoyment are viewed as more important than the needs of the group. The United States, Great Britain, Canada, and Australia, for example, have individualist cultures. Children in a given culture tend to be socialized according to that culture's values and thus are more likely to exhibit personality traits valued by the culture (Hofstede & McCrae, 2004).

Collectivist culture A culture that emphasizes the rights and responsibilities of the group over those of the individual.

Individualist culture A culture that emphasizes the rights and responsibilities of the individual over those of the group.

People in collectivist cultures tend to define themselves as part of a group, are very attached to the group, and see their personal goals as secondary to the group's goals. In contrast, people from individualist cultures define themselves as individuals, are less attached to the group, and see their personal goals as more important than the group's goals (Triandis et al., 1988).

Source: DDB Stock Photography, LLC

THINK like a **PSYCHOLOGIST** What might be two possible explanations for regional personality differences that have been found between "mellow" Californians and "fast-paced" northeasterners? (Hint: Genetic? Environmental?)

This collectivist-individualist distinction between types of cultures has been used to explain why crime rates are lower in collectivist cultures: Collectivist cultures exert more social control over the individual, and criminals' actions reflect not only on themselves but also on their families. In fact, as the global economy leads people in collectivist cultures to shift their work habits and values to those of individualist countries, crime rates and other social ills often increase (Strom, 2000).

Not surprisingly, the self-concept of people from individualist cultures differs from that of people from collectivist cultures: People from individualist cultures characterize the "self" as a composite of traits, independent from the group, whereas those from collectivist cultures actually incorporate other people into the definition of the "self" and they see themselves in relation to specific situations and contexts (Markus & Kitayama, 1991). Traits in general may thus be less useful for predicting behavior in collectivist cultures (Church & Katigbak, 2000).

LOOKING AT LEVELS Attachment

Source: © Myrleen Ferguson Cate/PhotoEdit; (inset) © Digital Art/Corbis

In our closest relationships, we develop deep attachments to other people. But people differ in their *attachment style*—their way of relating to significant others. Before we can understand why such differences arise, we must consider some key facts about attachment.

One crucial finding is that an adult's attachment style with a partner—his or her "love style"—stems from the way that that person interacted with his or her parents (or other primary caregivers) during infancy (Waller & Shaver, 1994). In those earliest of interactions—in the intimate choreography between parent and infant—a parent may be consistently responsive and empathic toward the infant, be neglectful or abusive, or be inconsistent. According to John Bowlby (1973), these interaction patterns between parent and infant mold an internal *working model* about relationships. The working model—which continues to operate throughout life—rests on beliefs and expectations about relationships and influences how relationship-related stimuli are perceived, remembered, and responded to. For instance, the working model leads a person to feel, react, and behave in particular ways when a romantic partner no longer seems 100% committed. The model leads a person to appraise the situation as no big deal, to ruminate about it, to become anxious, to have a "big talk" with the partner, or to pull away.

Cindy Hazan and Phillip Shaver (1987) developed three categories of adult attachment style: *secure, anxious,* and *avoidant* (see Table 6). Studies suggest that a majority of Americans have a secure style (Hazan & Shaver, 1987); other studies indicate that an anxious style is more common in Japan and Israel, and an avoidant style more common in Germany (Shaver & Hazan, 1994).

We can best understand attachment styles—how they arise and exert their influence—from a levels-of-analysis perspective. Attachment style clearly reflects events at the *level of the group*: It arises from interactions of caregivers and infants, and goes on to affect a person's relationships with his or her partners in adulthood. For example, infants who attend poor-quality day care, with few caregivers for many infants, are more likely to develop insecure attachments styles (Sagi et al., 2002). Similarly, consistent parental abuse or neglect during childhood is unlikely to engender a secure type of attachment (O'Connor et al., 2003). But our attachment styles are not fixed in stone: The relationships we have as adults can change our attachment style (Shaver & Hazan, 1994).

At the *level of the person*, attachment style influences what you pay attention to and how you process sensory information (Jerome & Liss, 2005), how you interpret what you perceive, and how you characteristically respond to those stimuli. For instance, when Paula Niedenthal and colleagues (2002) examined the effect of attachment style on adults' perception of small changes in facial expressions, they found that people with different attachment styles process such stimuli differently.

TABLE 6 Secure, Anxious, and Avoidant Attachment Styles

Adult Attachment Style	Percentage of an American Sample Having This Style	First-Person Description
Secure Attachment Style: These adults seek closeness and interdependence in relationships and are not worried about the possibility of the relationship's ending.	59%	"I find it relatively easy to get close to others and am comfortable depending on them and having them depend on me. I don't often worry about being abandoned or about someone getting too close to me."
Anxious Attachment Style: These adults want but simultaneously fear a close relationship.	11%	"I find that others are reluctant to get as close as I would like. I often worry that my partner doesn't really love me or won't want to stay with me. I want to merge completely with another person, and this desire sometimes scares people away."
Avoidant Attachment Style: These adults are uncomfortable with intimacy and closeness, and hence structure their daily lives to avoid closeness (Tidwell et al., 1996).	25%	"I am somewhat uncomfortable being close to others. I find it difficult to trust them completely, difficult to allow myself to depend on them. I am nervous when anyone gets too close, and often love partners want me to be more intimate than I feel comfortable being."

Also at the level of the person, attachment style relates to how people manage their emotions. As the word implies, people with an avoidant attachment style tend to avoid emotional aspects about relationships. Consider these findings about avoidantly attached people (compared to those with other attachment styles):

- They pay less attention to emotional events (Collins, 1996; Fraley & Shaver, 1997; Fraley et al., 2000).
- They tend to require more time to recall sad and anxious occasions (Mikulincer & Orbach, 1995).
- Although consciously denying that they feel distressed when remembering stressful family events, their bodily reactions suggest that they feel anxiety and stress while remembering such events (Dozier & Kobak, 1992).
- They store in memory less information when listening to someone speaking about relationship issues (Fraley et al., 2000).

Attachment styles also lead people to manage their emotions in particular ways after a relationship breaks up: Those with an anxious attachment style are most likely to report distress, cognitive preoccupations, and anger, and to use drugs or alcohol to cope; those with an avoidant style are most likely to exhibit self-reliance and distance themselves from the relationship. In contrast, those with a secure style rely on family and friends for support (Davis et al., 2003).

At the *level of the brain*, researchers have examined whether attachment style is related to facets of temperament. One study of women found that attachment style and BIS and BAS are related: Women who had an easily activated BIS tended to have an anxious attachment style, whereas women who had an easily activated BAS tended not to have an avoidant attachment style (Meyer et al., 2005; Muris & Meesters, 2002). Furthermore, the women with a responsive BAS preferred to confront their partners when their relationship was strongly threatened but not when the relationship was only mildly threatened.

In addition, the infant's temperament (determined in part by genes) can be compatible or incompatible with the caregiver's temperament (and the caregiver's attachment style; Sagiet al., 1997), which will contribute to how securely the infant becomes attached. Researchers have also found that infants tend to develop an attachment style like their mother's (Siegel, 1999). For instance, if the mother has an anxious style, her child will

Simulate Attachment Classifications in the Strange Situation on **mypsychlab.com**

likely have that style as well (van Ijzendoorn, 1995). At first glance, this finding might seem to reflect shared genes between mother and child. But studies of adult twins show otherwise: When adult twins were tested on six scales that measured different aspects of love styles in romantic relationships, little evidence of heritability of styles was found (Waller & Shaver, 1994). Moreover, a twin study of adult attachment styles found that unique environmental factors—rather than genetic factors—have the greatest influence on adult attachment styles (Brussoni et al., 2000). As psychologist Robert Plomin and his colleagues (1997, p. 205) put it, "Perhaps love *is* blind, at least from the DNA point of view." Even if this literally isn't true of love, at least attachment is blind from a DNA point of view. **Simulate**

Events at each level are not isolated from one another: It is primarily the caregiver's behavior with the infant (level of the group) that gives rise to the infant's—and with time, the adult's—internal working model of relationships (level of the person). And the caregiver's attachment style is partly related to BAS and BIS activity (level of the brain). Moreover, the adult's attachment style affects his or her relationships (level of the group). And adult relationships can change attachment style; events at the level of the group can change events at the level of the person.

Study and Review on **mypsychlab.com**

LOOKING BACK

1. **To what extent does birth order shape personality?** From studying historical figures, Sulloway suggests that birth order, along with other factors such as the number of children in a family and the level of conflict between parents and children, can influence openness to experience. Further research has found additional differences between first-, middle-, and later-borns. Specifically, firstborns generally are less open to new experiences and are more conscientious, middle-borns identify less closely with family, and later-borns are more easygoing and more open to new experiences.

2. **Do social factors produce gender differences in personality?** Although women and men exhibit few broad personality differences, they do tend to differ in social connectedness (versus individuality) and in neuroticism (high versus low). Social role theory provides one explanation for these differences. However, gender may not predict behavior as well as characteristics of the situation.

3. **Do different cultures produce different types of personalities?** Culture shapes personality in various respects. For example, native-born citizens of countries that emphasize the needs of the group tend to have personalities that reflect a collectivist orientation. In contrast, the native-born citizens of countries that emphasize individualism tend to have personalities that reflect an individualist orientation.

LET'S REVIEW

((•─ Listen to an audio file of your chapter on mypsychlab.com

I. PERSONALITY: HISTORICAL PERSPECTIVES

A. People's motives, thoughts, and feelings are at the heart of Freud's psychodynamic theory, which focuses on three structures of personality (id, ego, and superego) and their dynamic relationships at three levels of awareness (unconscious, preconscious, and conscious), as well as sexual and aggressive drives, defense mechanisms, and psychosexual stages (oral, anal, phallic, latency, and genital).

B. According to Freud, when the major task of a psychosexual stage has not been fully resolved, development is arrested, often creating a neurosis. Moreover, sexual and aggressive impulses can create anxiety, which leads a person to use defense mechanisms.

C. Humanistic theories (such as that of Rogers) also address motives, feelings, and the self, but they focus on each person's uniqueness, stress positive qualities of human nature and free will, and emphasize self-actualization.

II. WHAT EXACTLY IS PERSONALITY?

A. Personality is a consistent set of emotional, cognitive, and behavioral tendencies that people display over time and across situations and that distinguish individuals from each other.

B. People do not behave in the same manner in all situations: The situation influences the way people behave, but people also can influence the situation.

C. Many researchers have found that personality traits can be statistically grouped into five superfactors (extraversion, neuroticism, agreeableness, conscientiousness, and openness) or, according to Eysenck, three personality dimensions (extraversion, neuroticism, and psychoticism).

D. Personality can be measured by observation, interviews, inventories (such as Cattell's 16PF or the MMPI-2), and projective tests (such as the Rorschach test and the Thematic Apperception Test, or TAT). Personality inventories are the most commonly used method.

III. BIOLOGICAL INFLUENCES ON PERSONALITY

A. Temperament is an inclination to engage in a certain style of thinking, feeling, or behaving; tem-peraments initially arise from the effects of genes and biology, and are relatively consistent over the life span and across different situations. Temperament may differ along various dimensions, including sociability, emotionality, activity, and impulsivity. Two well-studied temperaments are shyness and sensation seeking.

B. Gray proposed two basic brain systems that underlie many aspects of temperament and personality: the behavioral activation system (BAS) and the behavioral inhibition system (BIS).

C. Eysenck proposed that each of his three personality dimensions (extraversion, neuroticism, and psychoticism) has a corresponding biological basis. Aspects of this theory have been supported by neuroimaging and other biological research.

D. Cloninger proposed four personality dimensions, each of which arises from a distinct biological system: reward dependence, harm avoidance, novelty seeking, and persistence.

E. According to Zuckerman, biological systems give rise to five personality dimensions: sociability, neuroticism-anxiety, impulsive sensation seeking, activity, and aggression-hostility.

F. Some psychologists and behavioral geneticists estimate that genes account for as much as 50% of the variation in personality, although some traits appear to be more heritable than others.

IV. CONTRIBUTIONS OF LEARNING AND COGNITION TO PERSONALITY

A. Classical conditioning, operant conditioning, and observational learning all can influence personality.

B. The sociocognitive view of personality emphasizes that social interactions affect thoughts, feelings, and behaviors—and consistent thoughts, feelings, and behaviors (consistent in a given situation at least) create personality. This approach often focuses on the effects of expectancies: What we expect to happen will influence the ways our personalities develop.

C. Personality differences related to expectancies are exhibited in our locus of control (the source we perceive as exerting control over life events) and our self-efficacy (the sense that we have the ability to follow through and produce the behaviors we would like to perform).

V. SOCIOCULTURAL INFLUENCES ON PERSONALITY

A. Birth order, along with various moderating factors (such as the number of children in a family and the level of conflict between parents and children), can influence openness to experience and other aspects of personality.

B. Women and men differ in social connectedness versus individuality and in high versus low neuroticism, but in general such differences tend to be small, and it is not clear whether they arise from biological or sociocultural factors or a combination of such factors. Sociocultural explanations for these differences include social role theory. Context may predict personality better than does sex or gender.

C. Personality differences have also been found between people raised in cultures that are collectivist as opposed to individualist; people in each type of culture tend to have personality traits that are more valued in their culture.

D. Attachment style is influenced by the person's working model of relationships; such a model develops dynamically through interactions with caregivers, through temperament, and through the specific ways that children and adults perceive and process the world around them.

KEY TERMS

activity	id	personality inventory	self-efficacy
Big Five	impulsivity	personality trait	sociability
castration anxiety	individualist culture	projective test	social desirability
collectivist culture	locus of control	psychological determinism	superego
defense mechanism	Minnesota Multiphasic Personality	psychosexual stages	temperament
ego	Inventory-2 (MMPI-2)	repression	Thematic Apperception Test (TAT)
emotionality	neurosis	Rorschach test	unconditional positive regard
expectancies	personality	self-actualization	

PRACTICE TEST

✓●─[Study] and Review on mypsychlab.com

For each of the following items, choose the single best answer.

1. Sigmund Freud believed in psychological determinism; that is, he contended that
   a. all behavior, no matter how mundane or insignificant, has a psychological cause.
   b. people have an innate motivation to fulfill the highest possible emotional and intellectual potential.
   c. people need unconditional acceptance.
   d. expectancies have a powerful influence on thoughts, feelings, and behavior and, in turn, on personality.

2. According to Freud, what developmental task occurs during the phallic stage?
   a. Successful weaning from the mother's breast or bottle
   b. Successful identification with the same-sex parent
   c. Successful toilet training
   d. Transformation of sexual urges into more culturally acceptable, nonsexual behaviors

3. Defense mechanisms are used by the ego, Freud proposed, to prevent threatening thoughts from entering awareness. With the defense mechanism of projection,
   a. threatening thoughts are attributed to others.
   b. threatening thoughts or emotions are kept at arm's length by thinking about them logically and rationally.
   c. threatening impulses are directed into more socially acceptable activities.
   d. anxiety-provoking thoughts, impulses, and memories are forced to enter consciousness.

4. According to Rogers, people
   a. need to satisfy lower-level needs before needs further up the hierarchy can be satisfied.
   b. whose lives revolve around meeting conditions of worth will achieve their full human potential.
   c. whose lives revolve around meeting conditions of worth will not achieve their full human potential.
   d. need to receive conditional positive regard to develop a healthy self-concept.

5. What is interactionism?
   a. A view of personality that regards behavior as mostly a function of the situation, not of internal traits
   b. A view of personality in which both traits and situations are believed to affect thoughts, feelings, and behaviors
   c. The relationship among the five superfactors of personality
   d. A method for assessing personality that requires test takers to read statements and indicate whether each is true or false about themselves

6. Many factor analytic studies have revealed that traits
   a. form 16 personality factors.
   b. all form a single factor called social deviance.
   c. can be captured by five superfactors.
   d. explain and thereby predict all human behavior.

7. Someone who scores high on the personality dimension of neuroticism most likely
   a. enjoys people and social situations.
   b. is easily and intensely emotionally aroused.
   c. has difficulty learning not to engage in particular behaviors.
   d. has decreased sensitivity of the amygdala.

8. Suppose that Dr. Lopez wants to minimize the effect of acquiescence in her personality inventory; that is, she is worried that
   a. people will respond to questions in a way they think will make themselves look good.
   b. people will skip difficult questions.
   c. some people will be more likely to check off "agree" than "disagree," regardless of the content of the statement.
   d. the reading level of the personality inventory is not appropriate for his or her population of interest.

9. A projective test is a(n)
   a. personality inventory primarily used to assess social deviance.
   b. bias in responding to questions that arises because people try to make themselves "look good."
   c. observational test used by employers to measure people's behavior and infer their personalities.
   d. method used to assess personality and psychopathology that involves asking the test taker to make sense of an ambiguous stimulus.

10. According to psychologists Buss and Plomin, temperament has the following dimensions:
    a. behavioral activation and behavioral inhibition.
    b. psychotism, agreeableness, and nonconformity.
    c. activity, sociability, emotionality, and impulsivity.
    d. specific response level, habit response level, trait level, and type level.

11. Gray's behavioral activation system (BAS) is most similar to
    a. Eysenck's neuroticism.
    b. Cloninger's persistence.
    c. Zuckerman's sociability.
    d. Buss and Plomin's vigor.

12. What effect does having a highly reactive autonomic nervous system have on a child?
    a. The child will necessarily become an outgoing adult who enjoys social interactions.
    b. The child will become a shy adult only if he or she is a firstborn or only child.
    c. The child will have a tendency toward shyness, and the responses of others will determine how the child thinks and feels about himself or herself.

    d. The child will most likely prefer stimulating situations that create high arousal, which in turn will lead him or her to take on challenges and become innovative and creative.

13. The family environment contributes to a child's personality in the following way:
    a. The family environment strongly influences personality traits.
    b. The family environment does not influence any personality traits.
    c. The family environment strongly affects agreeableness and does not affect the personality traits of social closeness and positive emotionality.
    d. The family environment is generally not a large contributor to personality traits; the exceptions are social closeness and positive emotionality.

14. In general, what personality differences exist between females and males?
    a. Males tend to score higher on traits reflecting social connectedness.
    b. Females tend to score lower on measures of neuroticism.
    c. There are none.
    d. None of the above statements is true.

15. People in collectivist cultures tend to
    a. engage in repression.
    b. see their personal goals as more important than the group's goals.
    c. define themselves as part of a group.
    d. have no personality differences with people in individualist cultures.

Answers 1. a 2. b 3. a 4. c 5. b 6. c 7. b 8. c 9. d 10. c 11. c 12. c 13. d 14. d 15. c

> In many ways, Spielberg's films, like the rest of his life, are shaped by his childhood.

PSYCHOLOGY OVER THE LIFE SPAN

GROWING UP, GROWING OLDER, GROWING WISER

Some of his classmates called him "Spielbug." Girls thought he was nerdy and unattractive. His social development was hindered by the fact that his father, Arnold—a pioneer in the use of computers in engineering—was hardly ever around; to make matters worse, Arnold frequently uprooted the family, moving from Ohio to New Jersey, to Arizona, and finally to Northern California. Steven Spielberg was a perpetual new kid on the block. He was also, by all accounts, an unusual child, both in his appearance (he had a large head and protruding ears) and in his fearful and awkward behavior (McBride, 1999). Spielberg himself has said that he "felt like an alien" throughout his childhood. He desperately wanted to be accepted, but didn't fit in. So, at age 12, he began making films, "little 8mm things. I did it to find something that, for me, could be permanent" (Sullivan, 1999, p. 66). Spielberg continued to make movies as a teenager, often casting his three sisters in roles. He discovered that making movies was one way to win his peers' acceptance, as well as some small measure of power—for he sometimes induced his worst enemies to appear in his films.

When he was 16, Spielberg's parents divorced, which made Spielberg unhappy; he blamed his father's constant traveling for the breakup. His unhappiness only deepened when his father remarried, to a woman Spielberg couldn't stand. At the same time that he withdrew from his father, Spielberg continued to have a close relationship with his mother, Leah, a concert pianist and artist. The split with his father lasted some 15 years.

In many ways, Spielberg's films, like the rest of his life, are shaped by his childhood. Spielberg himself has said about *E.T., The Extra-Terrestrial*, "The whole movie is really about divorce. . . . Henry's [the main character's] ambition to find a father by bringing E.T. into his life to fill some black hole—that was my struggle to find somebody to replace the dad who I felt had abandoned me" (Sullivan, 1999, p. 68). Many of Spielberg's other films feature children who are separated from their parents (such as the girl in *Poltergeist* and the boy in *Close Encounters of the Third Kind*). And *Back to the Future* might represent his longings to change the past, if he could. Only when he turned 40 did his films turn to adult contexts. As he matured, Spielberg's identification with oppressed people in general (not just oppressed children) led him to make movies such as *The Color Purple*, *Schindler's List*, and *Amistad*.

Steven Spielberg married and had a child but eventually divorced his first wife, actress Amy Irving. His own experiences made him extremely sensitive to the effect of the divorce on his son, Max, and he made every attempt to ensure that Max did not feel abandoned. When he married again, he became deeply involved with his family (which includes seven children, some of them adopted). There was a happy development in the previous generation's father–son relationship as well: Arnold became a well-loved grandfather and a regular presence in the Spielberg household.

Spielberg's journey is one version of the universal story of human development: A skinny kid beset by fears and with few friends becomes one of the most powerful figures in the global entertainment industry; from a fragmented family life develops a man's resolve to make the best possible life for and with his own family; across generations, a father and a son come to like each other, now as a grandfather and a father, after 15 years of estrangement. *Developmental psychologists* study exactly these sorts of events in our lives—the fascinating and varied process of human development over the life span. In this chapter, we begin by considering prenatal development and the newborn, and we see that even here genes and environment are intimately intertwined. We next turn to infancy and childhood and observe the interplay between maturation and experience in shaping a child's physical, mental, emotional, and social development. Then we consider adolescence, a crucial time in development, bridging childhood and adulthood. And finally, we discuss adulthood and aging, gaining insights that help us understand developmental forces during adulthood that might have led Spielberg to reconcile with his father.

◉ ◉ ◉

In the Beginning: From Conception to Birth

Steven Spielberg has been celebrated as one of the most successful moviemakers of all time. He just seemed to have a natural bent for making movies (he never attended film school). Where did his talent come from? In this section, we begin at the beginning and think about the foundations of our skills and abilities.

LOOKING AHEAD Learning Objectives

1. How does development progress in the womb?
2. What are the capabilities of newborns?

Prenatal Development: Nature and Nurture From the Start

For each of us, life began with the meeting of two cells, a sperm and an ovum (which in Latin means "egg"); these specialized cells are sex cells, or *gametes*. The egg is a supercell, the largest in the female human body. Even so, it is barely the size of a pinprick, and sperm are much smaller (about 1/500 of an inch). But despite their small sizes, within the egg and sperm reside all the machinery necessary to create a new life. A new life is initiated when the sperm penetrates the egg, and the genetic material of the sperm combines with that of the egg. The egg is not a passive partner in this dance of life; the sperm is drawn to the egg by chemical reactions on its surface. And when a sperm has been accepted within the egg, other reactions prevent additional sperm from penetrating. As we discuss in the following, even at this earliest stage of development, *genes (nature)* and the *environment (nurture)* are intimately intertwined.

From Zygote to Birth: Getting a Start in Life
The genetic heritage of every normal human being is 23 pairs of chromosomes, one member of each pair coming from an egg and the other from a sperm. A *chromosome* is a strand of *DNA (deoxyribonucleic acid)* in the nucleus of the cell. Each strand is shaped like a twisted ladder—the famous double helix—in which the "rungs" are formed by the bonds between pairs of chemicals. Each *gene* on the chromosome is a series of particular rungs. All cells in the human body except the eggs and sperm contain all 23 pairs of chromosomes; each sperm and egg contains only a single member of each of these 23 chromosome pairs. In an egg, one of these 23 is a chromosome known as X; in a sperm, the corresponding chromosome is either an X chromosome or a shorter one called a Y chromosome.

IN THE BEGINNING. From the beginning, the effects of genes and environment interact. Much of early development is determined primarily by **maturation**, the process that produces genetically programmed changes in the body, brain, or behavior with increasing age; nevertheless, the environment plays a crucial role even during the earliest phases of development. For example, sperm actually "surf" on subtle muscle contractions in the uterus (which is the environment for the sperm on its way to the egg), and the nature of these contractions influences whether sperm ever reach an egg; these waves usually move in the correct direction in fertile women, but in some women with fertility problems the

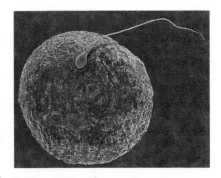

At the moment of conception, a sperm penetrates an egg (ovum). The egg, however, is not a passive recipient; by changing its surface properties, it actively regulates the behavior of the sperm.

Source: Photo Researchers, Inc.

Maturation The developmental process that produces genetically programmed changes in the body, brain, or behavior with increasing age.

waves either move in the wrong direction or are weak (Kunz et al., 1997; Lyons & Levi, 1994). In addition, the fluid in the uterus must be the right consistency and must have the right chemical composition for the sperm to complete their journey (Mori et al., 1998; Shibahara et al., 1995; Singh, 1995).

When a sperm fertilizes an egg, a new cell is created, called a **zygote,** which initiates the process of creating a new human being. The chromosomes from the egg and from the sperm pair up so that the zygote contains the full complement of 23 pairs of chromosomes. If the sperm contributes an X chromosome (which occurs roughly half the time—half the sperm have an X chromosome, half a Y), the offspring will be female (XX); if the sperm contributes a Y chromosome, the offspring will be male (XY). The Y chromosome contains a gene (the *SRY gene,* for "sex-determining region of the Y chromosome") that produces a chemical substance that ultimately causes the zygote to develop into a male; if this substance is not present, genes on the X chromosome will produce other substances that cause the zygote to be female (Goodfellow & Lovell-Badge, 1993; Hawkins, 1994).

DANCE OF THE CHROMOSOMES. Our wonderful human variety arises in part from the ways that the chromosomes from the mother and father are recombined. The two members of each pair of chromosomes (other than the XY pair in males) are similar—but they are not identical. For example, the gene for the shape of your earlobes is on the same spot on both chromosomes, but because of its particular chemical composition, the gene on one chromosome may code for an attached earlobe (one that connects the bottom part of the ear directly to the side of the head) and the gene on the other for an unattached earlobe (one that has a separate curved portion, hanging down at the bottom of the ear). (For some genes, only the version on one chromosome is active; for other genes, versions on both chromosomes are active and can produce "compromises"—such a pink color in a snapdragon flower, if one version codes for red and the other for white.) Each parent can pass on either version of a gene to his or her offspring: In the course of creating each egg and sperm, the chromosomal deck of cards is shuffled so that pieces of the chromosomes in each pair in the parent cell are exchanged, as shown in Figure 1, to form new combinations of genes.

FIGURE 1 The Long Road to a Zygote

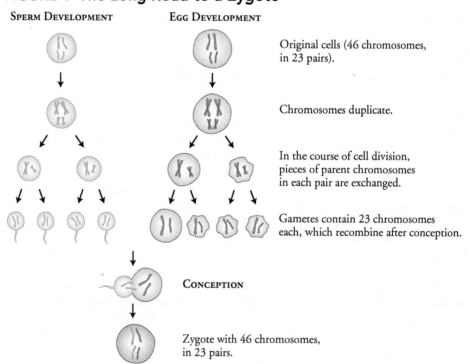

SPERM DEVELOPMENT   EGG DEVELOPMENT

Original cells (46 chromosomes, in 23 pairs).

Chromosomes duplicate.

In the course of cell division, pieces of parent chromosomes in each pair are exchanged.

Gametes contain 23 chromosomes each, which recombine after conception.

CONCEPTION

Zygote with 46 chromosomes, in 23 pairs.

The chromosomes in eggs and sperm are not simply copies of those of the parent but rather unique combinations of the material in the two chromosomes in each pair of the parent's chromosomes. The sperm and egg combine to form the basis of a unique individual.

Zygote A fertilized egg (ovum).

FROM CONCEPTION TO FETUS: A TALE OF THREE TRIMESTERS. The interactions between maturation and the environment in the uterus gradually build a human being. This process is divided into *trimesters*, three equal periods of 3 months each. The first trimester itself is divided into three stages: The developing baby starts off as a zygote, becomes an **embryo** when a tube that specifies the head-to-toe axis of the body is present (about 2 weeks after conception), and then becomes a **fetus** when all major body structures are present (about 8 weeks after conception; thereafter, the developing baby is called a fetus until birth). The nervous system is crucial for a functioning body, and the great bulk of the neurons are in place by the end of the second trimester (Nowakowski, 1987; Rakic, 1975;

The developing fetus at 8 weeks (left) and 20 weeks (right).

Source: Getty Images/Digital Vision

Rodier, 1980). However, neural development does not stop at the end of the second trimester—in fact, researchers have found that new neurons can be produced even in adult brains (Gould et al., 1999). ✳ Explore

✳ Explore **Life Stages and Approximate Ages on** mypsychlab.com

Learning and Behavior in the Womb Fetuses are active nearly from the start, at first with automatic movements, such as the heart beating, and then with large-scale coordinated behaviors. (That popular image of the fetus floating peacefully asleep in the womb is misleading!) As the fetus develops, the heart rate slows down, but also becomes more variable, the fetus moves less often but more vigorously when it does stir, and the heart rate and movement patterns become coordinated. Some researchers have even reported sex differences in behavior in the womb, with male fetuses more active than females (Almli et al., 2001; DiPietro et al., 1996).

In addition to coordinating their movements, fetuses become sensitive to both sound and light after 20 to 25 weeks of gestation (Nilsson & Hamberger, 1990; Pujol et al., 1990). How do we know this? Because when fetuses are examined by a special light-emitting instrument called a *fetoscope*, as is sometimes medically necessary, they will actually move their hands to shield their eyes. By 28 weeks, fetuses respond by changing their movements when they are stimulated externally (such as when pregnant women sit down abruptly). A bit later, their heart rates change when their mothers are startled (DiPietro et al., 1996; Kisilevsky & Low, 1998), and sometime between 25 and 34 weeks, fetuses can distinguish between human speech and other sorts of sounds (Cheour-Luhtanen et al., 1996; Zimmer et al., 1993). Furthermore, researchers have found that fetuses older than 33 weeks pay more attention to music than to nonmusical sounds (Kisilevsky et al., 2004).

Researchers have also found that fetuses can learn. For example, in a classic study (DeCasper & Fifer, 1980), pregnant women read the story *The Cat in the Hat* aloud twice each day during the 6 weeks before their babies were born. A few hours after birth, the babies were tested. The researchers put earphones on the babies' little heads and a special pacifier-like device in their mouths. Sucking faster or slower on this device changed what was played to the infants. Two results are critical: First, when the speed of sucking allowed them to hear either their mother's voice or another woman's voice reading the story, the infants sucked at the speed that produced their own mother's voice. Second, and perhaps even more impressive, the researchers also gave the infants the opportunity to choose between hearing their mother read *The Cat in the Hat* or another story—and the infants preferred the story their mother had read aloud before they were born!

Moreover, the way fetuses behave in the womb predicts children's behavior after birth. For example, fetuses that had more variable heart rates later developed into more linguistically able toddlers and demonstrated more sophisticated forms of play (Bornstein et al., 2002). Apparently, the genes and environmental events (such as a pregnant woman's diet) that influence behavior in the womb continue to influence

Embryo A developing baby from the point where the major axis of the body is present until all major structures are present, spanning from about 2 weeks to 8 weeks after conception.

Fetus A developing baby during the final phase of development in the womb, from about 8 weeks after conception until birth.

behavior after birth—even though the precise types of behavior before and after birth may differ markedly.

Teratogens: Negative Environment Events

A **teratogen** is an external agent, such as a chemical, virus, or type of radiation, that can cause damage to the zygote, embryo, or fetus. Because they develop at different rates, different organs are vulnerable to teratogens at different periods during development. In what follows we consider some of the more common teratogens and their consequences. ⊙▸ Simulate

⊙▸ Simulate Teratogens and Their Effects on **mypsychlab.com**

MATERNAL ILLNESS.   Unfortunately, the central nervous system is vulnerable at virtually every phase of prenatal development. For example, the development of the brain can be disrupted if the mother catches a virus, such as chicken pox or rubella (3-day German measles); more than half the babies born to mothers who contract rubella will have mental retardation if the baby was an embryo at the onset of the disease. In addition, a mother who is HIV-positive can pass the virus on to the baby during gestation or birth (but only about one third of these babies contract the virus). The HIV virus causes brain damage in fetuses, leading the children subsequently to have problems in concentration, attention, memory, movement control, and the ability to reason (Clifford, 2000; Grant et al., 1999).

ALCOHOL AND DRUGS.   Another potential teratogen is alcohol; if a woman drinks alcohol, it can damage her eggs before fertilization (Kaufman, 1997) as well as affect her developing baby throughout pregnancy, starting with the embryo phase. If the woman drinks enough alcohol during pregnancy, the baby may be born with *fetal alcohol syndrome* (a key component of what is now called *fetal alcohol spectrum disorder*); part of this syndrome is impaired mental functioning, such as problems with aspects of reasoning that involve working memory (the ability to use information being held in an active state) (Kodituwakku, 2009; Streissguth et al., 1989, 1999).

The pregnant woman's drinking alcohol is not the only way her behavior can disrupt her developing baby. In particular, her use of heroin or cocaine during pregnancy can cause a host of subsequent problems in the newborn: physical defects (Singer et al., 2002b), irritability, difficulties sleeping, and attentional problems (Fox, 1994; Miller et al., 1995; Vogel, 1997). Moreover, prenatal exposure to cocaine may have long-lasting consequences—some of which may become more marked as the child gets older (Chapman, 2000; Lester, 2000; Singer et al., 2002a).

In addition, the problem is not restricted to the mother's behavior. For example, cocaine can affect the father's sperm; upon penetrating the egg, an affected sperm apparently can transport the drug into the mother's egg and subsequently impair the growing fetus and developing child (Yazigi et al., 1991).

CAFFEINE AND SMOKING.   Major diseases, alcohol, and drugs are not the only threats to healthy prenatal development. Excessive amounts of caffeine (three or more cups of coffee a day, according to one study) can lead to miscarriage or low birth weight, significant irritability in newborns, and other symptoms (Eskenazi, 1993; Eskenazi et al., 1999).

In addition, smoking during pregnancy doesn't only affect the mother's lungs and health, it also affects the fetus: it is correlated with higher rates of miscarriage, lower birth weights, smaller head size, stillbirth, and infant mortality, and it can cause attentional difficulties in the infant (Cornelius & Day, 2000; Floyd et al., 1993; Fried & Makin, 1987; Fried & Watkinson, 2000). A mother's smoking may even damage the fetus's genes (de la Chica et al., 2005). Moreover, a mother's smoking during pregnancy may increase the chance that her baby will die from *sudden infant death syndrome* (SIDS; Pollack, 2001); such smoking alters the way the infant's autonomic nervous system operates, which may contribute to SIDS (Browne et al., 2000).

Teratogen Any external agent, such as a chemical, virus, or type of radiation, that can cause damage to the zygote, embryo, or fetus.

DIET AND POLLUTION.   A mother's poor diet can lead her infant to have fewer brain cells than normal (Morgane et al., 1993) and can increase the risk that the child will develop a host of psychological disorders—including schizophrenia (Susser et al., 1996).

Furthermore, the lack of even a single important vitamin or mineral during pregnancy can impair the developing embryo or fetus. For example, insufficient folic acid (a type of vitamin B) can disrupt the early development of the central nervous system (Nevid et al., 1998) and thereby cause birth defects. Most important, if the mother does not have enough folic acid, the infant can be born without the top of the skull or with *spina bifida*, which occurs when the vertebrae (the bones of the spine) are not fully closed at the base of the spine. Spina bifida requires immediate surgery and can lead to problems in bladder and bowel control (and can even prove fatal). Folic acid is also essential for producing the iron-containing protein needed to form red blood cells. ◉─|Watch

◉─|Watch the Video Brain Development and Nutrition on mypsychlab.com

A mother's diet can also impair her unborn child if she eats fish from polluted waters. In particular, if the mother eats fish with high levels of a chemical called methylmercury, this can cause the infant to be born deaf or to have visual problems; it may also impair auditory processing (Murata et al., 1999). (Pregnant women are often told not to eat certain types of fish for just this reason.)

Furthermore, other environmental pollutants, as well as X rays and similar types of radiation, can produce birth defects and cancer as well as behavioral difficulties (such as in paying attention). And, in other animals at least, these effects can be passed on to the third generation, to the offspring of the offspring (Friedler, 1996).

MATERNAL STRESSORS.   The fetus can also be impaired if the mother experiences too much stress. If stress during pregnancy is severe enough, after birth the infants may experience attentional difficulties, be unusually anxious, and exhibit unusual social behavior (Weinstock, 1997). In fact, stress directly affects behavior in the womb: fetuses with mothers of lower socioeconomic status, who are often more stressed than mothers of higher socioeconomic status, move less often and less vigorously and show other differences from fetuses whose mothers are better off financially (Pressman et al., 1998).

Maternal stress may affect the fetus by altering various biological factors, such as the following:

1. *Maternal blood flow.* When the mother is stressed, less of her blood flows to her uterus and more of her blood flows to parts of her body (such as the limbs and heart) that are affected by the fight-or-flight response—the bodily response to stress. And thus less oxygen and nutrients are available for the fetus.

2. *Increased maternal cortisol levels.* When stressed, the mother produces hormones such as cortisol, which slow down the operation of genes that guide prenatal development of the brain, suppressing brain growth (Brown, 1999). Consistent with this observation, babies born to stressed mothers tend to have smaller heads than those born to unstressed mothers—which may be related to the poorer behavioral functioning scores observed for such babies (Lou et al., 1994).

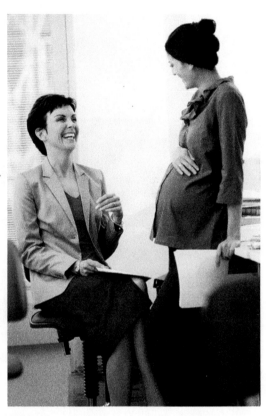

A particularly powerful example of interactions among events at the different levels of analysis is the fact that social interactions with friends and family can lead to healthier babies being born to stressed mothers (McLean et al., 1993). Social support presumably helps to reduce the mother's stress, which in turn keeps her from the fight-or-flight state and its accompanying unfortunate consequences for the developing baby.

Source: Getty Images/Digital Vision

Positive Environmental Events: The Earliest Head Start   The previous paragraphs might seem to suggest that our species would be better off if maturation alone controlled prenatal development and environmental events had no impact on the fetus—but some prenatal experiences actually help the fetus (Berghella et al., 2010). For example, consider the tantalizing report that mothers who ate chocolate every day during pregnancy later rated their 6-month-old babies as having more positive temperaments than did mothers who did not eat chocolate so regularly (Räikkönen et al., 2004). However, as interesting as this finding is, it's easy to come up with multiple interpretations for it.

Other findings show more conclusively that the prenatal environment can play a positive role in development. Consider a study by Lafuente and colleagues (1997): Each of 172

THINK like a PSYCHOLOGIST   Can you think of two interpretations for the finding that mothers who ate chocolate every day during pregnancy later rated their 6-month-old babies as having more positive temperaments?

pregnant women was randomly assigned to an experimental or control group. The participants in the experimental group were given a waistband with a tape recorder and small speakers on which they played tapes of violin music for an average of 70 hours, starting at about 28 weeks after conception and continuing until the birth of the baby. The participants in the control group did not play music to their unborn children. After the babies were born, the researchers tracked the babies' development for 6 months and found that those whose mothers were in the experimental group were more advanced than those whose mothers were in the control group. For example, they had better motor control (in psychology, *motor control* means control of movements, not something to do with engines) and better vocal abilities of the sort that precede language. Steven Spielberg's mother played the piano frequently while she was pregnant; could these prenatal concerts have had long-term positive effects on him?

The Newborn: A Work in Progress

The human brain is not fully developed at birth—perhaps because the baby's head would not fit through the birth canal if he or she had a full-size adult brain—and hence much human brain development continues after birth (M. H. Johnson, 2001). Thus, the newborn's abilities to think, feel, and behave differ from those of older children and adults. For example, unlike older children and nonhuman animals, newborns cannot be classically conditioned to associate a tone with an air puff that causes them to blink (Naito & Lipsitt, 1969; Sommer & Ling, 1970); in rats, researchers have shown that this ability emerges only after key parts of the cerebellum have matured during infancy (Freeman & Nicholson, 2001; Rush et al., 2001), and the same is probably true for humans.

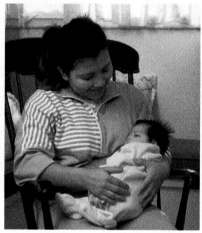

In many ways, the human infant compares unfavorably with the young of some other species. A kitten is able to walk on its own and explore its environment at only 6 weeks, an age when no human infant can even crawl.

Sources: Renee Lynn/Stone/Getty Images; PhotoEdit Inc.

Nevertheless, although the typical infant may seem thoroughly incompetent—capable of eating, sleeping, cooing, crying, drooling, and not much else—such an assessment is off the mark. A baby is not a blank slate, waiting for learning or maturity to take hold. On the contrary, babies come equipped with a surprising range of abilities and capacities.

Sensory Capacities and Reflexes Even at the earliest phases of development, babies have the beginnings of sophisticated sensory capabilities. They are born sensitive to the range of frequencies of women's voices (Hauser, 1996) and have a relatively sensitive sense of smell (as witnessed by the fact that even babies who are fed by bottle prefer the odor of a woman who is breast-feeding another infant to that of a woman who is not breast-feeding; Porter et al., 1992).

Infants also come equipped with a wide range of reflexes. A *reflex* is an inborn and automatic response to a stimulus, an action that does not require thought. Some reflexes shown by infants, such as sucking in response to a touch on the lips, have obvious survival value, and some, such as the *Moro reflex* (in which the startled baby throws its arms wide, as if to grab hold of someone), may have had survival value for our ancestors. Other reflexes, such as the *Babinski reflex* (in which the baby's big toe flexes while the other toes fan out when the sole of his or her foot is stroked), are less obviously useful. Interestingly, many of the reflexes that babies have at birth disappear as the baby develops.

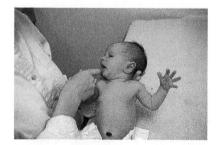

Until about 3 to 4 months of age, babies produce a *rooting reflex* when their cheek is stroked lightly: They turn their head toward the stimulus and start trying to suck.

Source: © Paul Conklin/PhotoEdit

Temperament: Instant Personality From their earliest hours, babies show the makings of individual personalities. In particular, they demonstrate differences in *temperament*, in their inclinations to engage in a certain style of behavior (such as being anxious versus calm, or being sociable versus shy). Differences in temperament are evident in many ways. For example, some babies are considered "easy" in that they do not cry often and are not demanding, whereas others are "difficult" in that they are fussy and demand a lot of attention. Babies also differ in particular aspects of their temperaments. For example, some babies may be inclined toward "approach," others toward "withdrawal" (Thomas & Chess, 1996): Infants who tend to show an approach response generally react positively to new situations or stimuli, such as a new food, toy, person, or place. Infants who tend to show a withdrawal response typically react negatively to new situations or stimuli by crying, fussing, or otherwise indicating their discomfort (Chess & Thomas, 1987).

Some aspects of temperament tend to remain stable over the course of development. Moreover, these aspects of temperament may arise not from innate predispositions but from early nurturing experiences. Probably the most compelling evidence for this idea comes from research with nonhuman animals. Michael Meaney and his colleagues (Anisman et al., 1998; Liu et al., 1997; Meaney et al., 1991; Zaharia et al., 1996) have shown that simply handling rat pups during the first 10 days after their birth has enormous effects on the way the animals later respond to stressful events. As adults, these animals don't become as nervous as other rats when put in a large open field (as reflected by fewer feces, less "freezing" responses, and more exploration), and their bodies do not react as strongly to stress (as indicated by lower levels of the stress hormone cortisol). They are also less prone to learned helplessness, which occurs when animals simply give up trying to cope with stress because their previous attempts were unsuccessful (Costela et al., 1995). Such positive effects of handling are also evident for young rats after the mother rat licks her pups and nurses them with her back arched (so the pups are directly under her; Liu et al., 1997; Weaver et al., 2004). There is good reason to believe that similar effects extend to humans: Gently touching infants not only can enhance their growth and development, but also can reduce the EEG activation in the right frontal lobe that is associated with depression (even in 1-month-old infants!) and can boost immune function (Field, 1998; Field et al., 1986; Jones et al., 1998).

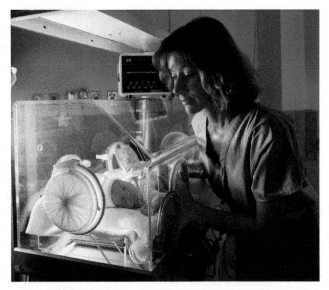

Social interactions can help babies who are born prematurely. Field and her colleagues (1986) found that premature infants who were touched three times a day (moving the babies' limbs, stroking their bodies), in 15-minute sessions, grew 50% faster, developed more quickly behaviorally, were more alert and active, and were discharged from the hospital sooner than other premature infants who were not touched three times a day.

Source: Woodfin Camp & Associates, Inc.

LOOKING BACK

✓•—Study and Review on
mypsychlab.com

1. **How does development progress in the womb?** Your mother's genes and your father's genes each recombined when their gametes (egg or sperm) were formed, and you received half of your genes from your mothers egg and half from your father's sperm; thus, you have a unique combination of genes. Prenatal development is affected by both the genes and events in the womb (such as the available nutrients in the mother's blood) and unfolds in an orderly progression through a series of stages as the zygote becomes first an embryo, then a fetus. The developing fetus is active and becomes increasingly coordinated over time. Moreover, the fetus is capable of some forms of learning and can detect human speech, preferring the mother's voice. The developmental processes can be disrupted by teratogens or enhanced by certain environmental events, such as those that reduce the level of stress experienced by the mother.

2. **What are the capabilities of newborns?** Newborns have a relatively sensitive sense of smell and are equipped with a host of inborn reflexes, such as sucking and the Moro reflexes. Many of these reflexes often disappear as the child grows and develops. In addition, aspects of temperament that are present at birth may persist as the child matures.

Infancy and Childhood: Taking Off

Steven Spielberg has repeatedly noted that his ability to make movies that appeal to children and to "the child inside adults" stems from the fact that he'd not grown up himself. He may have retained some childlike characteristics, but the filmmaker has indeed matured. That is, his motor, perceptual, cognitive, and even social abilities have long outstripped those of even a preadolescent child. In this section, we see the remarkable changes that occur during infancy and childhood, and trace the paths of these developments through the rest of this chapter.

LOOKING AHEAD Learning Objectives

1. How does the ability to control the body develop during infancy and childhood?
2. What perceptual, linguistic, and cognitive abilities emerge over the course of infancy and childhood?
3. How do social and emotional development occur during infancy and childhood?

Physical and Motor Development: Getting Control

Developmental psychologists have spent many years studying the precise ways in which babies' movements change as they grow. Two of the early pioneers, Arnold Gesell (Gesell & Thompson, 1938) and Myrtle McGraw (1943), described a series of milestones that all babies, from all races and cultures, pass through in an orderly progression. Figure 2 presents average age ranges for major motor developments (but keep in mind that various factors—such as the opportunities to use specific muscles—affect these ages). In general, control progresses from the head down the trunk to the arms and finally to the legs; at the same time, control extends out from the center of the body to the periphery (hands, fingers, toes). By the age of 2, the typical child has good control over all the limbs. However, fine motor control—of the sort needed to play piano or type on a keyboard—develops more slowly.

FIGURE 2 Typical Ages for Developmental Motor Milestones

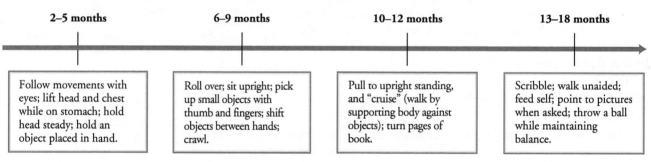

Motor abilities emerge at different times. Keep in mind, however, that the ages given in this figure are averages and may not apply to a particular child.

Source: Based on LaRossa (2000).

In spite of their limitations in actually making movements, infants have sophisticated brain systems that control movement. In particular, at an early age infants can plan their movements based the requirements of a task. For example, when reaching for a ball in order to toss it into a tub on the floor, 10-month-old infants reach more quickly than if they are going to drop the ball down a tube (which requires planning more precise movements than does tossing it into a tub)—which shows that they are planning the pair of movements in tandem (Claxton et al., 2003).

The early theorists believed that the consistent and universal order of motor development implies that such development is entirely *maturational*—it is entirely a result of genetic programs that unfold over time. However, later studies of motor control showed that this view cannot be correct (Thelen & Ulrich, 1991). For example, consider the unanticipated consequences of having infants sleep on their backs in an effort to reduce the chances of SIDS (this is advocated by the "Back to Sleep" movement, which has helped to reduce SIDS in the United States by about 30% since 1994; Association of SIDS and Infant Mortality Programs, 2002). Researchers found that premature infants who slept on their backs had more difficulty holding their heads up and lowering them with control than did infants who slept on their bellies (Ratliff-Schaub et al., 2001). Moreover, full-term back-sleeping babies took longer to roll from their backs to bellies, sit up, creep, crawl, and pull themselves to a standing position compared to full-term babies who slept on their bellies (Davis et al., 1998). However, both groups of children walked at the same age. In fact, since babies have begun sleeping on their backs, some never learn to crawl. "It was an occasional phenomenon before, and now about a third of babies skip the step of crawling and go right to walking," says Dr. Karen Dewling (quoted by Seith, 2000). Thus, developing some aspects of motor control involves more than maturation; it also involves the specific opportunities to learn about the body and the world (Adolph, 2000; Thelen, 1995).

Perceptual and Cognitive Development: Extended Horizons

A parent probably would not tell as elaborate a story to a 3-year-old as to a 10-year-old. The reason is obvious: The younger child not only has a shorter attention span and understands fewer concepts about objects and events but also can grasp only simple concepts about relations between objects and events (such as that one object can physically cause another to move). Where do concepts—simple or complex—come from? In part from: (1) perception—the organization and identification of information received through the senses; (2) reflection and reasoning, which change with cognitive and memory development; and, (3) the social environment.

Perceptual Development: Opening Windows on the World

Along with the rest of the body, the sensory organs develop with age. For example, young infants view the world blurrily, as if through thick gauze; with age, their visual acuity increases, in part because of developments in the eye, particularly in the lens and the retina (Banks & Bennett, 1988).

INFANT VISUAL PERCEPTION. Psychologists who study visual perception have developed a number of clever techniques to learn about the visual abilities of infants. For example, to determine depth perception, infants are placed on a level sheet of glass that at first lies directly on a floor but then extends over a part of the floor that has been stepped down. In this *visual cliff* experiment, researchers have found that even 6-month-old infants don't want to crawl out on the glass over the "deep end"—even when coaxed by their mothers—thus demonstrating that they can perceive depth before they can talk (Gibson & Walk, 1960).

But the visual cliff crawling task is of no use with babies who are not yet able to crawl, so it is possible that even younger babies can see depth. How can we tell? In one study, researchers measured infants' heart rates when they were placed on the shallow or deep end of the visual cliff and found that 2-month-old babies had slower heart rates on the deep side (Campos et al., 1970); slower heart rates indicate that the infants are paying closer attention, which suggests that they could in fact tell the difference between the two depths.

Other techniques for examining infants' visual perception measure the amount of time they spend looking at stimuli. For example, the *habituation technique* (also sometimes called the *looking time technique*), illustrated in Figure 3 on the next page, is based on the fact that all animals—including humans of all ages—*habituate* to a stimulus: If a baby looks at a particular shape long enough, he or she will no longer find it interesting—and thus will prefer to look at something new (Colombo & Mitchell, 2009). This technique can be used to discover what babies can perceive as "different." If you simply showed a copy of the same stimulus that was just habituated, it would be no more interesting than the original—the infant has to perceive it as different to find it interesting. By varying how two stimuli differ (in shape, distance, color, pattern of movement, and so on) and noting the circumstances in which babies prefer a new stimulus after habituating to a previous one, it is possible to discover what differences they can detect. Habituation techniques have

In the "visual cliff" test (invented by Gibson & Walk, 1960), babies are placed on the sheet of glass over a floor that appears to be directly under the glass. A short distance ahead, the floor drops down (although the glass remains level). If the baby can perceive depth, he or she will be reluctant to crawl on the part of the glass that is over the "deep end."

Source: Mark Richards/PHOTOEDIT

FIGURE 3 The Habituation Technique

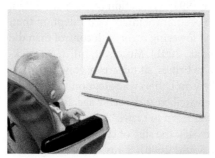

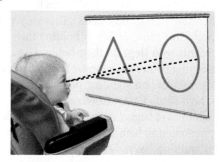

In the habituation task, the baby is first shown one stimulus and allowed to look at it until he or she is bored with it (has habituated to it).

After habituation, the baby is shown the original stimulus along with another stimulus. The baby prefers to look at something new. This technique can be used to determine what shape differences babies see and whether they see depth or other physical properties.

shown that babies can detect depth between 2 and 3 months of age. In fact, 8-week-old babies can see depth as represented by sets of points flowing on a screen, the way we do when we see a spaceship whizzing through a cloud of meteors in a movie—and infants of this age can even see shapes that are depicted three-dimensionally by sets of flowing points (Arterberry & Yonas, 2000).

In some situations looking time can be used to assess what an infant notices even without habituation. For example, newborns aren't very attentive companions, but they will notice you if you make direct eye contact with them; in fact, even infants 2 to 5 days old prefer to look at faces that look directly at them rather than faces in which the eyes are averted (Farroni et al., 2002). Other discoveries that rely on such techniques reveal that newborn infants only notice individual portions of objects; within about 2 or 3 months, they can perceive overall shapes (Spelke et al., 1993) and, when shown drawings, can even organize separate line fragments into portrayals of three-dimensional forms (Bhatt & Bertin, 2001). By about 6 months of age, they can see a set of objects as forming a group (Feigenson & Halberda, 2004; Quinn et al., 2002) and can mentally fill in when their view of a moving object is briefly obstructed (S. L. Johnson et al., 2003). Furthermore, as they grow older, babies need less information about stimuli to recognize patterns. It is tempting to speculate that their enjoyment of playing "peekaboo" may reflect this developing ability, in that they can use their knowledge about objects to infer a whole from a part.

INFANT AUDITORY PERCEPTION. Compared with visual perception, auditory perception appears to be more fully developed at an earlier age. For example, American researchers played to 4-month-olds sequences of tones that were sometimes consonant (pleasant-sounding to Western ears) and sometimes dissonant (harmonically jarring). When the sequence was consonant, the infants looked longer at the audio speakers than when it was dissonant. Not only did they look away when the stimulus was dissonant, but they were more physically active. The researchers suggested that infants innately find consonance more pleasing than dissonance (Zentner & Kagan, 1998). We can infer, then, that humans must learn to appreciate the sound of dissonant music, but such learning either is not required to appreciate consonant music or takes place very early in life (perhaps even in the womb).

AFTER THE FIRST YEAR. Perceptual development continues beyond the first year of life. When, for instance, toddlers (2- and 3-year-olds) are shown an array of objects and asked whether it includes a specific object, they look haphazardly from place to place (Vurpillot, 1968). In contrast, 6- to 9-year-olds will search the array systematically, left to right, then top to bottom, as if they were reading a page. In general, by about age 11, children have perceptual abilities that are similar to (although often slower than) those of adults (Lobaugh et al., 1998; Piaget, 1969; Semenov et al., 2000), but some aspects of perceptual processing that are used in organizing complex patterns probably continue to develop until late adolescence (Sireteanu, 2000).

Language Development: Out of the Mouths of Babes

One of the hallmarks of language is that normal human children will learn the language being spoken around them without needing to be taught. As kids, we are linguistic sponges. But what do we learn, and how do we absorb it?

HOW IS LANGUAGE ACQUIRED? One of the most obvious facts about language is that people in France grow up speaking French, people in Japan grow up speaking Japanese, and people in Greece grow up speaking Greek. Obvious or not, how this occurs is not clear; there has long been a debate about how language is acquired, and three different perspectives have emerged.

- *Behaviorist theories.* Behaviorists, following the lead of B. F. Skinner, believe that language is entirely the result of learning. According to this theory, children acquire words and combinations of words through imitation; such utterances then are reinforced, and thus language is learned according to the same principles of learning that apply to all other materials. Few scholars today subscribe to this view because it fails to explain key facts about language (Chomsky, 1959).

- *Nativist theories.* In contrast to the behaviorist view, many linguists believe that the crucial aspects of language are innate (inborn), not learned. This theory is rooted in the school of philosophy known as **nativism**, which takes the view that people are born with some knowledge. Linguist Noam Chomsky (1972) has championed the nativist approach to language acquisition, theorizing that we are all born with an internal **language acquisition device** (**LAD**), which contains a set of grammatical rules common to all languages (for example, which specify the roles played by different parts of speech, such as nouns and verbs) and thus allows children to acquire the particular language to which they are exposed.

- *Interactionist theories.* Interactionist theories call on both learning and innate knowledge to explain how language is acquired. These theories hold that language acquisition relies on social events, such as the interactions between a caregiver and child (where the caregiver does in fact teach some aspects of language), and that it draws on relatively general cognitive abilities, such as those used in motor control (to produce sounds) and perception (to organize speech; Dick et al., 2001; Dominey & Dodane, 2004; Elman et al., 1996). However, even these theorists assume that at least some language abilities are built in, part of our genetic heritage.

FOUNDATIONS OF LANGUAGE: ORGANIZING THE LINGUISTIC WORLD. We humans are innately gifted with the ability to acquire language: The fact that virtually all normally developing humans come to speak a language, even without formal instruction, is evidence that there is something special about the way our brains are constructed that allows us to acquire and use language. But this doesn't mean that we acquire language all at once; many genetically influenced characteristics do not appear full blown at birth—for example, consider baldness. Language ability develops in an orderly progression.

To help the child learn language, caregivers (typically mothers) intuitively adjust their speech so that the baby receives clear messages. The language that caregivers use to talk to babies, dubbed **child-directed speech (CDS),** is characterized by short sentences with clear pauses between phrases, careful enunciation, and exaggerated intonation that is spoken in a high-pitched voice (Bornstein et al., 1992; Cameron-Faulkner et al., 2003; R. P. Cooper et al., 1997; Fernald et al., 1989). A similar pattern has been observed in the sign language caregivers use to communicate with deaf infants: They make signs more slowly, often repeat a sign, and use

Nativism (approach to language) The view that people are born with some knowledge.

Language acquisition device (LAD) An innate mechanism, hypothesized by Chomsky, that contains the grammatical rules common to all languages and allows language acquisition.

Child-directed speech (CDS) Speech by caregivers to babies that relies on short sentences with clear pauses, careful enunciation, exaggerated intonation, and a high-pitched voice.

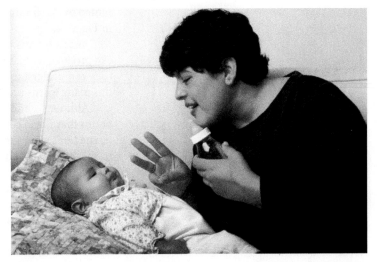

Sign language resembles spoken language in crucial ways. For example, when communicating with infants, speakers or signers slow down and exaggerate their vocalizations or their hand and arm movements in order to communicate more clearly.

Source: Michael Newman\PhotoEdit Inc.

Overextension An overly broad use of a word to refer to a new object or situation.

exaggerated movements (Masataka, 1996); babies attend more closely to such signing than to the more rapid, fluent signing used between adults.

Infants are surprisingly sophisticated in their ability to draw distinctions among spoken sounds. The simplest distinction between two spoken words (such as that between "ga" and "ba") is called a *phoneme*. Although adults have difficulty distinguishing between phonemes that are not used in their language (for instance, English speakers often have trouble distinguishing between two slightly different "wah" sounds used in French), babies have no such difficulty (Jusczyk, 1995). Moreover, infants appear to make such distinctions effortlessly; for example, at 2 to 3 months old, infants can register in less than half a second that a syllable has been changed ("ga" to "ba"; Dehaene-Lambertz & Dehaene, 1994).

However, this general facility with drawing distinctions is only temporary. After about 6 months of age, infants start to ignore distinctions among sounds that are not used in the language spoken around them (Kuhl et al., 1992). By ignoring unused distinctions, infants focus in on just the sounds in the surrounding language—which allows them to acquire words in that language. At around 8 months, infants can use patterns of sound regularity to identify individual words even when the actual sounds run together into a single continuous stream, which is the auditory equivalent of whatyoucandowiththesewords (Saffran, 2001).

Infants can discriminate and organize sounds much better than they can produce them. The process of producing speech begins with babbling; all babies, even deaf ones, begin by babbling at around 6 months of age (Stoel-Gammon & Otomo, 1986). Initial babbling includes the sounds made in all human languages. However, as the child is exposed to speaking adults, the range of sounds narrows; at about 1 year, the child's babbling begins to have adultlike intonation patterns (Levitt & Wang, 1991). The first words that children (in all languages) say grow directly out of their babbles, such as "ma-ma" and "da-da."

Deaf children do not develop the more advanced types of babbling, the types that start to sound more like the surrounding language. However, if they are exposed to sign language, their hand and arm motions develop in corresponding ways—beginning with a wide range of motions and eventually narrowing down to those used in the sign language they see around them (Petitto & Marentette, 1991).

GETTING THE WORDS. The number of words children learn changes as they get older. Most children say their first words when they are about a year old. By age 2, children are learning words at a rapid pace and can learn words even when the object or action being named is not present (Akhtar & Tomasello, 1996). And 3-year-olds can often learn the meanings of words or facts about objects after hearing them only a single time (Carey, 1978; Markson & Bloom, 1997). By the time they are 6 years old, children know approximately 10,000 words (Anglin, 1993). The rate of learning is affected by various factors, which may include hormones or sex roles—as hinted by the finding that the rate of learning differs for boys and girls, as shown in Figure 4.

FIGURE 4 The Number of New Words Understood During the First 2 Years of Life

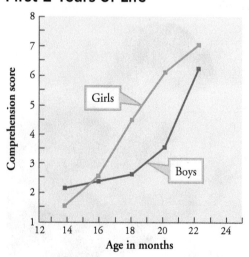

Notice the difference in comprehension rates for boys and girls.

Source: Adapted from Reznick, J. S. & Goldfield, B. (1992). "Rapid change in lexical development in comprehension and production." *Developmental Psychology, 28,* 406–413. Copyright © 1992. American Psychological Association. Adapted with permission.

Just as infants can discriminate and organize sounds much better than they can produce them, toddlers understand far more words than they can say. Indeed, they can understand about 50 words at about 13 months of age but cannot say this many words until about 18 months (Menyuk et al., 1995).

Although children in different cultures learn similar types of words, such as nouns that name common objects, culture does affect which particular words are learned initially (Tardif et al., 2008). For example, whereas children who learned to speak English initially learned more nouns than verbs, the opposite was true for children who learned to speak Mandarin Chinese. Similarly, in Vietnam, children learn the respectful pronouns used to refer to elders before learning the words for many objects (Nelson, 1981).

For most words, children do not learn the entire meaning of the word all at once, but rather initially grasp only a core aspect of what the word means. This tendency leads them to make **overextensions**—to use words overly broadly when referring to new objects or situations. They might use "dog" to refer to a dog and a cat and a horse and even a sawhorse. This makes sense if their initial idea of the meaning of "dog" is anything with four legs. Over the course of additional learning, they discover which features—in the case of a dog, more than just four-leggedness—restrict the appropriate use of the word (Clark, 1983, 1993).

Children sometimes also make **underextensions**, using words too narrowly. For example, a child may use "animal" to refer only to dogs. This may occur because an adult uses a superordinate term (such as "animal") when referring to a typical member of the category (a dog), and the child does not encounter the term being used more broadly for other members of the category (Kay & Anglin, 1982; White, 1982). However, as children hear the word used in different contexts, they broaden the underlying concept (for instance, learning that "animal" also applies to cats, birds, and turtles), which eventually eliminates underextensions.

GRAMMAR: NOT FROM SCHOOL. The heart of any language is its **grammar**, the set of rules that allows users of the language to combine words into an infinite number of acceptable sentences. Traditionally, the term *grammar* has focused on *syntax*, which is the internal organization of a sentence that is determined by a set of rules for combining different parts of speech. For example, in English you can say "John read the book" but not "The read book John"—the grammar won't let us put words in that order (for example, determiners such as "the" cannot come before verbs, such as "read"). Some scholars also include aspects of *semantics*—the meaning of words and sentences—as part of grammar, such as aspects of word meaning that must be in agreement in a sentence (for example, using a plural verb with a plural subject). However, it is clear that not all aspects of language are part of grammar. For example, *pragmatics* are indirect or implied meanings—as occurs when a question, for instance "Can you open the window," is actually a request.

Grammar, like other aspects of language, is acquired in a series of steps. By looking at the patterns of sounds to which babies became habituated, Marcus and colleagues (1999) showed that even 7-month-old babies can grasp grammarlike rules. However, only at about age 2 do children typically start putting words together into the simplest sentences, two-word utterances such as "Go dog." These utterances are called **telegraphic speech** because, like the telegrams of days gone by (and the text messages people send to cell phones today), they pack a lot of information into a few highly informative words (Bochner & Jones, 2003). Words such as *the*, *a*, and *of* are left out. By about 3 years of age, children who speak English start to use sentences that follow the sequence of subject–verb–object ("Dog chase cat"). The particular sequence of the parts of speech depends on the language being learned, but all children at this stage start to make sentences with words in the appropriate order (de Villiers & de Villiers, 1992).

Adults do not teach grammatical rules to children or even systematically correct grammatical errors (de Villiers & de Villiers, 1992; Pinker, 1994), but 4-year-olds typically have mastered such rules and generalize from them (Berko, 1958). This is true even when sentences contain nonsense words. For example, a 4-year-old can usually provide the missing word in the following:

This is a wug. Now there is another one. Now there are two _____.

One of the reasons children can grasp the rules of grammar is that most verbs in a language are *regular*, following an easily derived rule for changes in tense: *play* becomes *played*; *work* becomes *worked*. But the most frequently used verbs in a language are often *irregular*; for example, *eat* becomes *ate*. Children may start off using irregular verbs properly but then begin to make mistakes such as *runned* instead of *ran*. The same thing happens with plurals; a child who could use *feet* correctly last week may suddenly start saying, "Mommy, my feets are tired." These are **overregularization errors**, mistakes that occur in speech when the child applies a newly learned rule even to cases where it does not apply (Pinker, 1999).

Two major theories have been offered to explain the regularity in the major milestones of language acquisition (which occur for children exposed to any language), shown on the next page in the time line in Figure 5 (on the next page). On the one hand, some researchers claim that language progresses because other cognitive abilities, such as the capacity of working memory, increase as the brain matures. On the other hand, other researchers claim that language has an internal "logic," and children must learn certain aspects of a language (such as nouns that name objects) before they can learn other aspects that make use of them (such as adjectives, which modify nouns). This debate was settled by studies of international adoption, where older children (mostly from China and Russia) moved to the United States and learned English (Snedeker et al., 2007). As predicted by the

Underextension An overly narrow use of a word to refer to a new object or situation.

Grammar The set of rules that determines how words can be organized into an infinite number of acceptable sentences in a language.

Telegraphic speech Speech that packs a lot of information into a few highly informative words, typically omitting words such as *the*, *a*, and *of*.

Overregularization error A mistake that occurs in speech when the child applies a newly learned rule even to cases where it does not apply.

331

FIGURE 5 Major Milestones in Language Acquisition

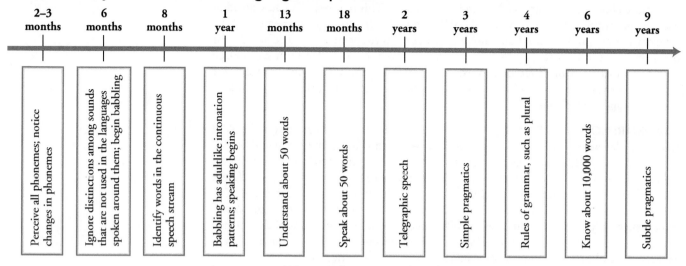

Language acquisition typically progresses through a series of orderly steps, as shown here.

second theory, these children—in spite of their advanced cognitive capacities—acquired the new language by going through the same steps as children learning their first language. The adopted children went through these steps faster than younger children, which probably does reflect their increased cognitive abilities, but the important point is that they still went through the same steps; this is exactly as expected if each step sets the foundations for the next one.

Finally, some children never progress through these milestones at all. In particular, there have been reports of children who grew up in the wild, never exposed to human language. When such cases occur, they provide a key test of the theory that language can be learned only during a narrow window of time called the **critical period**. By analogy, there may be times of the year when the climate and weather conditions are perfect for planting a particular crop—and if the farmer misses planting the crop then, it will be very difficult (if not impossible) to grow it during that year. Careful studies have shown that children who are not exposed to language before puberty never grasp the rules of grammar fully; there does seem to be a critical period for acquiring grammar (Grimshaw et al., 1998; Pinker, 1994).

Long-Term Memory Development: Living Beyond the Here and Now
Language acquisition relies in part on memory; if we could not retain information, we could not learn it. But memory is important for more than language acquisition—it is crucial for all learning, ranging from motor skills, to other skills (such as those involved in learning how to make movies), to facts about the world and our interactions in it. In the following sections we consider the development of memory—specifically, *explicit*, *implicit*, and *verbal memory*.

INFANT EXPLICIT MEMORY. Many studies have documented that even 3-month-old infants can store *explicit memories*, which are memories that can be voluntarily recalled and used in different contexts; memory for facts is a type of explicit memory (Rovee-Collier, 1997). For example, in one study of infants' ability to store information, researchers attached one end of a ribbon to an infant's foot and the other to a mobile that hung over the crib. The mobile was decorated with plus marks of a particular size. The infants soon learned that kicking would move the mobile, which they liked—and hence they kicked at a higher rate. The researchers waited a day and then showed the infants either the identical mobile or one with plus marks that were either larger or smaller than on the original. The infants kicked at a higher rate only when the plus marks were the original size; they apparently remembered that kicking would move that mobile and so kicked—but they did not recognize the other mobiles and so did not kick as vigorously (Gerhardstein et al., 2000).

Critical period A narrow window of time when a certain type of learning or some aspect of development is possible.

INFANT IMPLICIT MEMORY.   In addition to explicit memory, animals (including humans) can store *implicit memories*, which are tendencies to perceive or behave in specific ways in specific contexts (implicit memories cannot be voluntarily recalled). For example, if you learn to press the brake pedal of a car when you see a red light and do this over and over, eventually the relationship between seeing a red light and making the response will become an implicit memory—you won't need to think about it consciously.

To test whether even 3-month-old infants can store implicit memories, the same researchers used the kicking test just described, but now waited 2 weeks before retesting; infants have explicit memories for only about 6 to 8 days after testing, and thus at the time of this later testing, they no longer could recall that kicking moves the mobile. Each infant watched while the researcher held the ribbon attached to the mobile and tugged it, moving the mobile at about the same rate that the infant had moved the mobile before. This event was sufficient to reactivate the memory of the relationship between kicking and moving the mobile. However, the explicit memory—how the plus sign of a specific size was associated with the mobile—was not activated: Now infants increased their kicking when they saw mobiles that had all sizes of plus marks, not just when the plus marks were the original size (Gerhardstein et al., 2000).

In summary, studies such as this have shown that even 3-month-old infants have the ability to store both explicit memories and implicit memories.

VERBAL MEMORIES.   A major change in explicit memory occurs after children master language, which becomes increasingly important in memory as children get older. For example, in one study, Simcock and Hayne (2002) asked young children to learn to operate a machine that apparently shrank the sizes of toys. Six months or a year later, the researchers tested the children's memory for this "incredible shrinking toy" event. They found that in recalling various aspects of the event, the children used only words that they knew at the time when they initially experienced it; that is, no words learned in the intervening period were used. This finding suggested to the researchers that the "children's verbal reports of the event were frozen in time, reflecting their verbal skill at the time of encoding, rather than at the time of test" (p. 229). (*Encoding* is the process of organizing and transforming incoming information so that it can be entered into memory, either to be stored or to be compared with previously stored information.) This finding may help to explain why adults have remarkably poor memory for events that occurred during early childhood, when they had very few language skills.

Stages of Cognitive Development: Piaget's Theory

Thinking is more than perceiving and remembering; it also involves reasoning. It's obvious that babies don't have the mental capacity of adults, and the gradual transition from infant to adult mental capacity is known as *cognitive development*. The great Swiss psychologist Jean Piaget (1896–1980) developed a far-reaching and comprehensive theory of cognitive development. Interest in Piaget's theory helped generate other lines of research that have focused on how the gradual improvement in information processing, the maturation of the brain, and the social environment contribute to cognitive development.

Piaget was originally trained in biology, but early in his career, he worked in Paris with Alfred Binet's collaborator, Theodore Simon, helping to standardize Binet's newly developed intelligence tests for children. Piaget was curious about the types of reasoning mistakes children made. This new interest connected with his long-term fascination with biology and the nature of the mind, leading him to investigate the reasoning processes of children at various ages.

Piaget believed that babies begin with very simple, innate **schemas**, mental structures that organize sensory and perceptual input and connect it to the appropriate responses. For the youngest infant, such schemas organize and connect the sensation of hunger, the perception of a bottle or breast, and the act of grasping and sucking at the nipple. According to Piaget, the process of

Schema In Piaget's theory, a mental structure that organizes sensory and perceptual input and connects it to the appropriate responses.

In this study, kicking moves the mobile, which the infant likes to do. Infants kick more vigorously when the marks on the mobile are the same over repeated sessions, showing that they remember what happened last time they kicked when that stimulus was present. Gerhardstein and colleagues (2000) used this sort of apparatus to study both explicit and implicit memory.

Source: Carolyn Rovee-Collier

Piaget was an extraordinarily sensitive observer of children's behavior.

Source: Bill Anderson\Photo Researchers, Inc.

Assimilation In Piaget's theory, the process that allows the use of existing schemas to organize and interpret new stimuli and respond appropriately.

Accommodation In Piaget's theory, the process that results in schemas' changing or the creation of new schemas, as necessary to cope with a broader range of situations.

Object permanence The understanding that objects continue to exist when they cannot be immediately perceived.

assimilation allows the infant to use existing schemas to organize and interpret new stimuli and respond appropriately. For example, the schema for sucking a breast can also be used for sucking a bottle or a thumb. In contrast, the process of **accommodation** results in schemas' changing or in the creating of new schemas, as necessary to cope with a broader range of situations. For example, a schema for sucking may give rise to two separate schemas, one for sucking on a nipple and one for drinking from a straw.

According to Piaget, these two processes—assimilation and accommodation—together are the engine that powers cognitive development. Piaget's theory of development hinges on what results when assimilation and accommodation work together, which he claimed produces a system of rules—in Piaget's terms, a "logic"—that guides the child's thoughts. Thus, according to Piaget, the child's thinking changes systematically over time as new schemas develop.

Piaget described four major *periods* of cognitive development, as shown in Table 1; each period is governed by a different type of logic (in Piaget's sense of the word "logic") and includes many stages, each with key characteristics. The periods overlap slightly, and they may occur at different ages for different children; thus, the ages given in the table are only approximate. The crucial idea is that each period paves the way for the next, and thus the order of periods (and the stages within them) remains constant, even if different children may reach the different periods at slightly different ages. We now turn to examine the four major periods.

TABLE 1 Piaget's Periods of Cognitive Development

Period	Age	Essential Characteristics
Sensorimotor	0–2 years	The child acts on the world as perceived and is not capable of thinking about objects in their absence.
Preoperational	2–7 years	Words, images, and actions are used to represent information mentally. Language and symbolic play develop, but thought is still tied to perceived events.
Concrete operations	7–11 years	Reasoning is based on a logic that is tied to what can be perceived. The child is capable of organizing information systematically into categories and can reverse mental manipulations.
Formal operations	11 years (at the earliest)	Reasoning is based on a logic that includes abstractions, which leads to systematic thinking about hypothetical events.

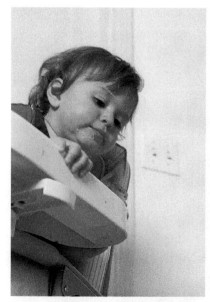

Only after an infant has object permanence does he or she understand that objects continue to exist after they are no longer being perceived.

Source: PhotoEdit Inc.

SENSORIMOTOR PERIOD. The infant's experience begins in the *sensorimotor period*, which extends from birth to approximately 2 years of age. According to Piaget's theory, infants initially conceive of the world solely in terms of what they can perceive and what they can do. In this period, infants lack the ability to think about an object in its absence. Piaget characterized this inability to be able to think about objects in their absence as a failure to have **object permanence**, the understanding that objects (including people) continue to exist when they cannot be immediately perceived. For example, a rattle dropped by an infant over the side of the high chair is quickly forgotten—and more than forgotten: Out of sight means not just out of mind but out of existence! Piaget claimed that by the end of the sensorimotor period, by about age 2, the toddler understands that objects exist even when they are no longer being perceived.

In addition, because at the outset of the sensorimotor period the infant cannot think about objects or events in their absence, he or she cannot imitate a previously perceived event (such as waving bye-bye or making a sound just like one heard earlier). Piaget claimed that a second major achievement during the sensorimotor period—at around 9 months of age—is the ability to imitate.

PREOPERATIONAL PERIOD. Once out of the sensorimotor period, the toddler enters the *preoperational period*, from roughly age 2 until age 7. Children in the preoperational period can use words, images, or actions as *mental representations*, ways of storing and recalling information; mental representations allow children in the preoperational period to think about objects and events that are not immediately present. As a result, the child can engage in symbolic play, when an object or motion stands for something else.

For example, whereas the infant might play with a bar of soap in the bath by squeezing it and watching it pop up (which involves no symbolism), the preoperational child, performing the same actions, might think of the soap as a submerged submarine that is breaking the surface (which is symbolic play).

The preoperational child still has many cognitive limitations, most of which result from his or her thinking in terms of specific mental images. For example, consider this joke: A cook asks two boys who have just ordered a large pizza, "How many slices do you want me to cut your pizza into, 8 or 12?" One boy immediately answers, "Please cut it into 12 pieces, because I'm very hungry!" This is a joke for older children and adults (who understand that cutting it into more pieces doesn't increase how much pizza there is), but not for preoperational children, who typically reason on the basis of appearances. Children in this period do not yet have a "logic" for manipulating, or *operating* on, mental representations (and this is why the name of the period is "preoperational"—before mental "operations" are available).

One of Piaget's important discoveries is that during the preoperational period children do not understand **conservation**, the principle that properties such as amount or mass remain the same even when the appearance of the material or object changes, provided that nothing is added or removed. Many studies have documented that preoperational children do not conserve, and so they do not realize that cutting a pizza into 12 pieces instead of 8 does not increase the total amount of pizza. A classic example, illustrated in Figure 6, is that preoperational children do not understand that pouring liquid from a short wide glass into a tall thin glass does not alter the amount of liquid. Similarly, they typically think that flattening a ball of clay decreases the amount of clay. Perhaps most remarkably, they believe that spreading the objects in a row farther apart changes the number of objects in the row (this is called a lack of "conservation of number").

THINK like a
PSYCHOLOGIST   If a parent gives you permission to play a quick game with their child who is 3 to 5 years old, you can see for yourself the lack of conservation in preschool-age children. Use the *DO IT!* instructions: Log on to www.mypsychlab.com; select the *Psychology Over the Lifespan* chapter, and click on the *DO IT!* folder.

FIGURE 6 Conservation of Liquids

In the classic conservation of liquids test, the child is first shown two identical glasses with water at the same level.

The water is poured from one of the short, wide glasses into the tall, thin one.

When asked whether the two glasses have the same amount or if one has more, the preoperational child replies that the tall, thin glass has more. This is a "failure to conserve" liquids.

In addition, both sensorimotor and preoperational children show **egocentrism**, which does not mean "selfishness" in the ordinary sense of the word but instead refers to the inability to take another's point of view. For example, children in this period will hold a picture they've drawn up to the telephone, to "show" it to a grandparent. They mistakenly assume that others see the same things they do.

CONCRETE OPERATIONS PERIOD.   The *period of concrete operations* is Piaget's third period of cognitive development, which takes place roughly between the ages of 7 and 11. At the beginning of this period, children develop the ability to take another person's perspective. For example, in one study researchers put the erasure end of a pencil in a 5-year-old child's palm and the point in the investigator's palm (holding the pencil between the two of them) and asked the child what the investigator felt. The response from preoperational children? "A soft rubbery thing"—not "a sharp point." In contrast, after the child enters the concrete operations period, he or she responds as would an adult.

Conservation The Piagetian principle that certain properties, such as amount or mass, remain the same even when the appearance of the material or object changes, provided that nothing is added or removed.

Egocentrism In Piaget's theory, the inability to take another person's point of view.

Concrete operation In Piaget's theory, a (reversible) manipulation of the mental representation of an object that corresponds to an actual physical manipulation.

Formal operation In Piaget's theory, a reversible mental act that can be performed even with abstract concepts.

This ability to take another person's perspective is linked to the fact that children can now perform **concrete operations**, manipulating mental representations in much the same way as they can manipulate the corresponding objects. For example, in the pencil study just described, children in this period can imagine rotating the pencil around and feeling its other end.

Concrete operations allow the child to reason logically, partly because this mode of conceptualizing is *reversible*; that is, it can be used to make or undo a transformation. For example, having seen the liquid being poured into a tall thin glass, the child can mentally reverse the process and imagine the liquid being poured back into the original container. Seeing that no liquid has been added or subtracted in the process, the child realizes that the amount in both glasses must be the same. In addition, children in this period are able to use these mental tools to begin to classify objects and their properties; to grasp concepts such as length, width, volume, and time; and to understand various mental operations such as those involved in simple arithmetic.

FORMAL OPERATIONS PERIOD. The *period of formal operations* is Piaget's final period of cognitive development, which can begin as early as age 11. During this period the child can reason about abstract concepts (such as "justice" or "infinity"), which—by definition—cannot be grasped by children in the concrete operations period. For example, children in the period of concrete operations cannot explain why adding 1 to an even number will always produce an odd number—but people in the formal operations period can explain this. To be able to reason abstractly, Piaget said, requires that the child be capable of **formal operations**, reversible mental acts that can be performed even with abstract concepts.

Rather than simply understanding the logic of "what is," as occurs with concrete operations, Piaget claimed that the emerging adolescent is now able to imagine the possibilities of "what could be." Formal operations allow children to think about "what-would-happen-if" situations, to formulate and test theories, and to think systematically about the possible outcomes of an act by being able to list alternatives in advance and consider each in turn. For example, formal operations permit a person to think about how best to spend his or her money and to weigh the benefits and drawbacks of each possible budget decision.

The Child's Concepts: Beyond Piaget Piaget's theory provides a clear story about how cognitive development proceeds, but it is tied to specific testing methods. Although Piaget employed very clever tasks (such as those used to assess conservation), those tasks typically assessed only easily observable aspects of behavior. When more subtle measurements are taken, evidence sometimes emerges that although the ordering of milestones is as Piaget claimed, children can show competence well before the ages that Piaget reported.

In particular, researchers have shown that infants have capacities beyond those claimed by Piaget. For example, Andrew Meltzoff and his colleagues (Meltzoff & Moore, 1977) have found that 2- to 3-week-old infants can show true imitation, and others have found that even 2-day-old infants can imitate happy and sad facial expressions (Field et al., 1982). And there is evidence that 9-month-old infants can add and subtract (McCrink & Wynn, 2004). Moreover, given what's been learned about infant memory, you won't be surprised that other researchers have shown that babies as young as 3 months old can have object permanence—they know that previously seen objects continue to exist after they are removed from sight (Baillargeon, 1993, 2004; Spelke et al., 1992). In addition, when tested with sensitive methods, children as young as 3 years show that they understand some aspects of the principles involved in the conservation of amount or mass (Gelman, 1972).

Moreover, Piaget's theory sometimes underestimates the sophistication of young children's conceptions of the world. Infants demonstrate an understanding of some aspects of physical laws even before they have developed the kinds of perceptual-motor schemas that Piaget claimed are the foundations of such knowledge. For example, even

Very young infants can imitate some facial expressions, as shown in these photos from Meltzoff and Moore's study.

Source: Reprinted with permission from A.N. Meltzoff & M.K. Moore, 1977. Imitation of facial and manual gestures by human neonates. *Science*, 198, p. 75 © 1977 American Association for the Advancement of Science.

4-month-old infants are aware of time intervals, showing surprise when a predictable sequence of flashing lights is interrupted (Colombo & Richman, 2002). Furthermore, from experiments using looking-time methods of the sort discussed earlier (in the section on studies of infant's perceptual abilities), researchers have concluded that even young infants realize that objects need to be physically supported or they will tumble down (Figure 7), that objects can't move *through* other objects, and that objects don't flit from place to place but shift along connected paths (Spelke, 1991; Spelke et al., 1992).

In addition, a serious challenge to the theory is the finding that children do not master all abilities that should require the same logical operations at the same age. For example, children conserve number before they can conserve liquids. If the logic of conservation is present, and allows conservation of number, why doesn't it also allow conservation of liquids? Although Piaget recognized this phenomenon, he never adequately explained it.

Moreover, the theory does not address the fact that many children do not enter the period of formal operations until high school, and some individuals never enter it at all (F. H. Hooper et al., 1984; Lunzer, 1978).

Nevertheless, many aspects of Piaget's theory have been supported; most strikingly, children's performance does change qualitatively in some types of tasks as they age. Piaget must also be credited with discovering many counterintuitive phenomena, such as failure to conserve and egocentrism, that all subsequent theories of cognitive development must be able to explain.

Information Processing and Neural Development

Efforts to explain the findings sparked by Piaget's theory have looked at specific changes in the way children process information and at how their brains mature. The brain develops dramatically from birth to about 3 years of age, and it continues to show substantial growth until the early teens (Giedd, 2008; Tsekhmistrenko et al., 2004). The *information-processing approach* is based on the idea that perception and cognition rely on a host of distinct processes in the brain, and hence these capacities develop as the relevant parts of the brain develop.

A particularly important reason why young children may perform more poorly than older children is that their working memory does not stack up well against that of older children or adults. Working memory capacity increases with age throughout childhood (Case, 1977, 1978); as working memory capacity increases, a child becomes able to perform tasks that were previously beyond reach.

The finding that working memory increases with age explains many of the phenomena documented by Piaget, such as the out-of-sight/out-of-mind behavior that he took to stem from a lack of object permanence (Baird et al., 2002). In this case, a *quantitative* change in capacity (the increase in the size of working memory) can lead to a *qualitative* change in performance (the transition to a new stage; Case, 1992a; Pascual-Leone, 1970). It's like the straw that broke the camel's back: A quantitative change (that is, adding more straws) led to a qualitative change (that is, breaking the back). Here's another analogy, which involves performance: If your phone does not have much built-in memory, it can show text but not graphics on Web pages. If you add memory, it can gain the ability to show graphics on Web pages as well as text. A quantitative change in memory leads to a qualitative change in performance.

Maturation of key brain areas probably accounts for the improvements in a child's working memory with age. The brain undergoes rapid growth spurts around the ages that Piaget identified as marking transitions to new periods (Epstein, 1980). Some of this growth with age may arise from *myelination* (the laying down of myelin, a fatty substance that serves as an insulator, on the axons of neurons), which increases the speed and efficiency of neural transmission. In addition, some of this growth may arise from larger numbers of synapses and long-distance connections (Case, 1992b; Thatcher, 1994; Thompson et al., 2000). Such changes would both increase the speed of information processing (Demetriou et al., 2002) and allow more information to be activated at the same

FIGURE 7 Early Perception of Possible Events

POSSIBLE EVENT

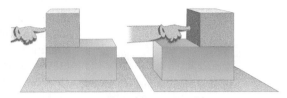

This panel shows a possible event: A box on top of another box is slid over to the edge, but it is still fully supported.

IMPOSSIBLE EVENT

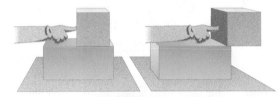

This panel shows an impossible event: The top box is slid so far over that only 15% of it is supported, and yet it does not fall (it is specially rigged). Between 3 and 6½ months, babies realize that one box must rest on top of the other to be supported.

Source: From Renee Baillargeon, "How do infants learn about the physical world?" *Current Directions in Psychological Science*, 3, 5, 133–140, 1994. Reprinted with permission from Wiley/Blackwell.

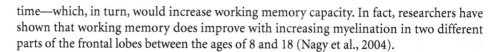

Attachment An emotional bond that leads a person to want to be with someone else and to miss him or her when separated.

Children in different cultures master different skills; for example, middle-class North Americans often master the visual-motor skills needed to play computer games, whereas street children in Brazil may master the kinds of arithmetic needed to bargain with tourists over the prices of goods (Saxe, 1988).

Source: © Nik Wheeler/CORBIS All Rights Reserved

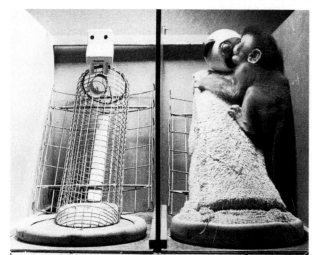

Baby monkeys were separated from their mothers shortly after birth and were raised with two substitute "mothers." One was wire and held the baby bottle, and each young monkey needed to climb on this one to be fed. The other was covered with terry cloth and did not provide food. Baby monkeys preferred to cling to the fuzzy "mother," even though it never provided food.

Source: Harlow Primate Laboratory/University of Wisconsin

time—which, in turn, would increase working memory capacity. In fact, researchers have shown that working memory does improve with increasing myelination in two different parts of the frontal lobes between the ages of 8 and 18 (Nagy et al., 2004).

Vygotsky's Sociocultural Theory: Outside/Inside Appreciating the importance of events at different levels of analysis leads us to look beyond any single source to explain psychological events. Thus, it isn't surprising that at least some aspects of cognitive development reflect social interactions. Russian psychologist Lev S. Vygotsky (1896–1934) emphasized the role of social interactions during development (Vygotsky, 1934/1986, 1978). Whereas Piaget believed that the child constructs mental representations of the world in the course of experiencing it firsthand, Vygotsky believed that the child constructs representations of the world by first learning the rules and customs of his or her culture; these rules and customs of the culture, as represented in the child's mind, then serve to guide behavior (Beilin, 1996; Kitchener, 1996).

According to Vygotsky, adults also promote cognitive development by guiding and explicitly instructing children about the world and their culture. Language plays a crucial role in this process; not only do adults use language to convey specific instruction, but they also use it to convey culture (such as by teaching children the rules of politeness in their society). In fact, according to Vygotsky, language itself is partly a cultural creation; although the capacity for language is innate, the particular language spoken is created by a culture. Thus, by helping the child learn to use a particular language in thinking, the culture influences both the content and form of the child's thinking (Cole & Wertsch, 1996; Karpov & Haywood, 1998).

It might be tempting to consider culture as one influence on cognitive development and the brain as an entirely separate additional influence. But this would be an error. The two factors interact: Culture affects the brain and vice versa. For example, culture determines which language or languages you learn, which in turn affects how your brain processes sounds (as discussed earlier, infants come to filter out sounds not in the language spoken around them). By the same token, the characteristics of the brain affect culture; for example, we don't have customs that require more working memory capacity than the brain provides.

Social and Emotional Development: The Child in the World

The psychological development of a child includes more than the improvement in mental processing and the acquisition of knowledge and beliefs. Equally impressive development occurs in the child's social interactions, such as the ability to form relationships.

Attachment: More Than Dependency In our closest relationships, we develop deep attachments to other people. **Attachment** is an emotional bond that leads us to want to be with someone and to miss him or her when we are separated. The tendency to form such an emotional bond begins during infancy, when normal infants become attached to their primary caregivers.

ORIGINS OF ATTACHMENT. Researchers have studied why infants become attached to their primary caregivers, and have developed and evaluated several theories. Decades ago, a prominent theory—sometimes called the "cupboard theory" because it centered on food—held that infants become attached because their caregivers feed them and thus become associated with positive feelings (Sears et al., 1957). However, classic experiments by Harry Harlow and his collaborators disproved this and similar theories (Harlow, 1958). These researchers found that baby monkeys became much more attached to a terrycloth-covered model of a mother monkey than to another model of a mother monkey that was constructed of metal and wire, even though the latter was the only one from which the baby monkeys received food. The preference to seek comfort from something soft is an innate rather than a learned characteristic of mammals.

British psychoanalyst John Bowlby (1969) developed a theory of attachment that has become widely accepted among developmental psychologists. According to Bowlby, children go through phases during the development of attachment. Just as in Piaget's stages, the order of the phases is thought to be determined biologically, but the precise ages of the transitions depend on experience. A major shift in the nature of attachment, usually occurring between 6 months and 2 years, is characterized by **separation anxiety**, which is fear of being away from the primary caregiver.

Separation anxiety Fear of being away from the primary caregiver.

The emergence of separation anxiety may be a consequence of a transition in cognitive development—specifically, infants can now think about and remember objects (including the primary caregiver) for relatively long periods when the objects are no longer present.

TYPES OF ATTACHMENT. Not all babies become attached to their caregivers in the same way. Mary Ainsworth and her colleagues (1978) developed a way to assess different types of attachment using a scenario they called the *Strange Situation*. The setup involves a staged sequence of events designed to discover how a child reacts when left with a stranger or alone in an unfamiliar situation. Studies using the Strange Situation revealed four types of attachment:

- *Secure attachment* (seen in about 60% to 70% of American babies) is evident if babies venture away from the mother, are upset when she leaves and not well comforted by a stranger, but calm down quickly when the mother returns.

- *Avoidant attachment* (seen in about 15% to 20% of American babies) is evident if babies don't seem to care very much whether the mother is present or absent and are equally comfortable with her and a stranger; when she returns, they do not immediately gravitate to her.

- *Resistant attachment* (seen in about 10% to 15% of American babies) is evident if babies do not use the mother as a base of operations for exploration (as occurs with secure attachment) but rather stay close to her and become angry when she leaves; some of these babies may go so far as to hit the mother when she returns, and they do not calm down easily thereafter.

- *Disorganized/disoriented attachment* (seen in 5% to 10% of American babies) is evident if the babies become depressed and have periods of being unresponsive along with spurts of sudden emotion at the end of the testing session.

However, subsequent analyses of large amounts of data from the Strange Situation have shown that differences in attachment style are often a matter of degree, and there are intermediate types (Fraley & Spieker, 2003). Various factors influence the kind of attachment an infant will show. For example, if the mother was a heavy user of cocaine or other illicit drugs while pregnant, her infant is more likely at age 18 months to have disorganized/disoriented attachment (Swanson et al., 2000). In contrast, mothers who are more sensitive to their babies' moods and behaviors had more securely attached infants (Tarabulsy et al., 2005). Moreover, the children of mothers who are economically disadvantaged are less securely attached than those of mothers who are economically advantaged, which may reflect the adverse effects of poverty on a mother's ability to remain highly sensitive to her child (Bakermans-Kranenburg et al., 2004).

The type of early attachment can have long-lasting effects. Infants with secure attachment who were later studied at age 11 were found to have closer friendships and better social skills than children who had not been securely attached as infants (Shulman et al., 1994). In fact, the type of attachment determines how some genes operate: At least in monkeys, certain genes that underlie aggression and excessive drinking of alcohol are only activated (and thus only have their effects) in monkeys that had an insecure early attachment—not in those that experienced secure attachment (Suomi, 2003). Furthermore, secure attachment can lead a child to be more comfortable with exploring, which leads to better learning and can lead to more intimate love relationships later in life (Sroufe & Fleeson, 1986; Weiss, 1986).

We know that at least some aspects of attachment are learned because infants in different cultures become attached differently. For example, American infants show less resistant attachment than do Japanese infants. In Japan, many more women are full-time caregivers for their children than in the United States, and their children are not used to being left with other adults (Takahashi, 1990).

Source: Woodfin Camp & Associates, Inc.

Knowledge of your appearance is part of your self-concept.

Source: PhotoEdit Inc.

Self-Concept and Identity: The Growing Self

A critical aspect of social development is the emerging sense of how a person defines himself or herself. Psychologists use the term **self-concept** to refer to the beliefs, desires, values, and attributes that define a person to himself or herself. A key part of Steven Spielberg's self-concept as a child was his many fears, both large and small (McBride, 1999).

For young children, the self-concept is necessarily grounded in the child's level of cognitive development. Thus, preschoolers think of themselves in very concrete terms, in terms of behaviors and physical appearance (Keller et al., 1978). However, researchers have argued that the roots of the self-concept are present even during infancy. In particular, Bahrick and her collaborators (1996) found that even 3-month-olds prefer to look at the face of another child of the same age rather than at their own face, which suggests that they are already familiar with the appearance of their own face.

The self-concept includes more than an understanding of physical appearance—it also rests on a conception of a person's own psychological characteristics. This aspect of the self-concept is clearly emerging by 3 years of age, when children begin to appreciate that they have distinct psychological characteristics such as being happy in certain situations and not in others (Eder, 1989). However, it is not until age 8 to 11 that children begin to describe themselves in terms of personality traits, perhaps as "energetic" or "musical."

But a complete self-concept is not possible until the child has the ability to characterize how his or her psychological characteristics affect his or her relationships with other people and vice versa. This ability depends on aspects of reasoning that develop during Piaget's period of formal operations. Thus, around age 11 most children also describe themselves in terms of social relations (Rosenberg, 1979), such as the relationships they have with their siblings and friends.

THE DEVELOPMENT OF GENDER ROLES. Another aspect of social development centers on learning *gender roles*. **Gender roles** are the culturally determined appropriate behaviors for males versus females. It is one thing to identify yourself as male or female, but something else entirely to understand what behaviors are appropriate for your gender (Martin & Ruble, 2004). Gender roles vary in different cultures, social classes, and time periods; for example, a proper woman in Victorian England (or, perhaps, 19th-century

Boys and girls play in characteristic ways, partly because of biological differences and partly because of social influences.

Sources: Elizabeth Crews\Elizabeth Crews Photography; Elizabeth Crews\Elizabeth Crews Photography

America) would probably be very surprised to learn that in the 21st century, some senators and presidents of major corporations are women.

A child's understanding of gender roles develops early. Indeed, by age 2, children have apparently learned about gender role differences (Caldera & Sciaraffa, 1998; Witt, 1997). Moreover, children soon come to associate different values with different gender roles; for example, some preschool boys apparently believe that if they play with cross-gender toys (say, dolls instead of tools), their fathers will think that is "bad" (Raag & Rackliff, 1998).

Children clearly develop gender roles with experience. Freud argued that children identify with the same-sex parent, and that this is the main way in which gender roles develop. But psychologist Eleanor Maccoby maintains that identification with the same-sex parent may be the *result* of gender role development, not the cause. In Maccoby's view, peer-group interactions are key to learning gender roles. It is in the peer group, she argues, that boys first learn about how to gain and maintain status in the hierarchy and that girls learn a style of interaction that focuses on relationships (Maccoby, 1990, 1991). And the peer group is largely composed of same-sex children. In fact, Maccoby and Jacklin (1987) found that 4-year-old children spent triple the amount of time playing with same-sex peers as with opposite-sex peers, and this proportion shot up to 11 times more when the children were 6 years old. According to Maccoby (1990, p. 514), "Gender segregation . . . is found in all the cultural settings in which children are in social groups large enough to permit choice."

Maccoby (1988) suggests that gender segregation may occur in part because of biological, particularly hormonal, differences. Boys play more aggressively than do girls, and their orientation toward competition and dominance may be aversive to many girls. However, shifting from the level of the brain to the level of the person, Maccoby (1990) also notes that girls may not like playing with boys because they believe that boys are too difficult to influence; the polite manner in which girls tend to make suggestions apparently doesn't carry much weight with boys. Girls find this response (or lack of response) frustrating and retreat to the company of other girls. Thus, Maccoby's account rests on events at all three levels of analysis and also depends in part on interactions among those events.

Moral Development: The Right Stuff

A key aspect of social development is the emergence of more complex ideas of morality, which center on the ability to tell right from wrong. As children grow older, their developing cognitive abilities allow them to consider more subtle aspects of a situation. The young child may feel that a girl who knocks over a lamp and breaks it is equally to blame whether she smashed it intentionally, bumped it by accident while horsing around, or fell against it accidentally when the dog jumped on her. An older child is able to make clear distinctions among the three cases, seeing decreasing blame for each in turn. Piaget was a pioneer in the study of moral as well as cognitive development. His studies often involved telling children stories in which he varied the intentions of the characters and the results of their actions, and then asking the children to evaluate the characters' morality. Lawrence Kohlberg extended Piaget's approach and developed an influential theory of moral development.

KOHLBERG'S THEORY. Kohlberg theory is based on findings from his studies of how men and boys responded to **moral dilemmas**, situations in which there are moral pros and cons for each of a set of possible actions (see Figure 8). He asked participants to decide what the characters should do and to explain why. Here is the famous dilemma that confronted Heinz (Puka, 1994):

> In Europe, a woman was near death from a special kind of cancer. There was one drug that the doctors thought might save her. It was a form of radium that a druggist in the same town had recently discovered. The drug was expensive to make, but the druggist was charging 5 times what it cost him to make the drug. He paid $400 for the radium, and charged $2,000 for a small dose of the drug. The sick woman's husband, Heinz, went to everyone he knew to borrow the money, but he could only get together about $1,000, half of what it cost. He told the druggist that his wife was dying, and asked him to sell it cheaper or let him pay later. But the druggist said, "No, I discovered the drug and I'm going to make money from it, so I won't let you have it unless you give me $2,000 now." So Heinz got desperate and broke into the man's store to steal the drug for his wife.
>
> Should Heinz have done that? Why?

Self-concept The beliefs, desires, values, and attributes that define a person to himself or herself.

Gender roles The culturally determined appropriate behaviors for males versus females.

Moral dilemma A situation in which there are moral pros and cons for each of a set of possible actions.

FIGURE 8 A Moral Dilemma

Can you imagine circumstances in which breaking into a store would not only be acceptable but would actually be the right thing to do? If you were in a situation where you had to decide whether such an action was justified, you would be facing a moral dilemma.

Kohlberg was not so much interested in *what* the participants decided as in their *reasons* for their particular decisions. Kohlberg interviewed the participants at length, and from their responses he identified three general levels of moral development (Kohlberg, 1969; Rest, 1979), which are ordered as follows:

- The *preconventional level*, which focuses on the role of an authority figure who defines what correct action is; good behaviors are rewarded and bad ones are punished. A preconventional response to the Heinz dilemma might be, "If you let your wife die, you will get in trouble" (this and the following examples are adapted from Kohlberg [1969] and Rest [1979]).

- The *conventional level*, which focuses on the role of rules that maintain social order and allow people to get along. A child reasoning at this level wants to be viewed as a "good person" by friends and family and tries to follow the Golden Rule ("Do unto others as you would have them do unto you"). Morality is still closely tied to individual relationships ("If he lets his wife die, people would think he was some kind of heartless lizard").

- The *postconventional level* (also called the *principled level*), which focuses on the role of abstract principles that govern the decision to accept or reject specific rules. In the most advanced stage at this level, principles are adopted that are believed to apply to everyone. ("Human life is the highest principle, and everything else must be secondary. People have a duty to help one another to live").

EVALUATING KOHLBERG'S THEORY. Researchers have challenged Kohlberg's theory on various grounds. For one, some have questioned the generality of Kohlberg's levels. In particular, Carol Gilligan (1982) argued that because Kohlberg's research involved interviews only with boys and men, his conclusions might not apply equally well to the moral development of girls and women. Based on her replication of Kohlberg's research with female participants, Gilligan argued that females tend to focus on an *ethic of care*, a concern and responsibility for the well-being of others. In contrast, Kohlberg's higher levels of moral development focus on abstract rights and justice, which Gilligan saw as a male-oriented perspective.

However, later studies have shown that differences in how males and females reason about moral issues do not reflect inherent fundamental differences in moral reasoning. Although there is evidence that males and females do emphasize different principles in their moral reasoning (Wark & Krebs, 1996), this difference seems to be more a reflection of their daily activities (and the assumptions and general orientations that result from such activities) than a gender difference per se. And in fact, if people are presented with dilemmas that feature concerns about raising children, men and women reason in the same ways (Clopton & Sorell, 1993). In addition, other researchers have found that males and females score comparably on Kohlberg's tests, and both sexes reveal concerns with both caring and justice (Jadack et al., 1995; Walker, 1995).

Another criticism of Kohlberg's theory of moral reasoning focuses on the consistency of reasoning in a specific way across different situations. Some researchers have claimed that the different types of reasoning are not like traits, which characterize a person in most situations. Rather, people may use different types of moral reasoning, depending on the details of the dilemma (Trevethan & Walker, 1989).

Furthermore, other researchers have pointed out that making decisions about moral dilemmas may be governed not simply by abstract reasoning but also by various aspects of a person's character. An example of such an aspect of character is a person's *conscience*, which leads him or her to appreciate what is morally correct and to feel obligated to follow this path. A conscience may develop far earlier than abstract moral reasoning. For instance, Grazyna Kochanska and her colleagues (1994) have found that conscience typically develops at about age 3. In addition, conscience is not the only aspect of character that can direct moral behavior. Another is the capacity to feel *empathy*, the ability to put yourself in another person's situation and feel what that person is likely to feel. Indeed, Martin Hoffman (2000) showed that by early adolescence most children have sophisticated abilities to feel and act on empathy in a wide range of moral situations. For example,

Differences in how men and women reason about moral issues may reflect the concerns that arise in their daily activities rather than inherent differences between the genders.

Source: Pacific Stock

young teens understand the unfairness of another person's not receiving a just reward for his or her efforts.

In short, many factors affect how people think about and behave in moral situations, and some of these factors develop much earlier than does the ability to reason logically about morality. Our behavior is a result both of how we reason and of who we are.

LOOKING BACK

✓●─Study and Review on
mypsychlab.com

1. **How does the ability to control the body develop during infancy and childhood?** In general, control progresses from the head down the trunk to the arms and, finally, to the legs; at the same time, control extends out from the center of the body to the periphery (hands, fingers, and toes). Developing motor control involves more than maturation; it also involves learning about the body and the world.

2. **What perceptual, linguistic, and cognitive abilities emerge over the course of infancy and childhood?** As perception develops, the child can make finer discriminations, needs less stimulus information to recognize objects, and can search more systematically. In addition, very young children learn to ignore the distinctions in sounds that are not used in their language, and young children typically overextend words and overregularize rules of grammar. Research findings suggest that to master the grammar of a language, we must learn it during a critical period, prior to puberty. Piaget proposed that during cognitive development the child moves through a series of major periods, each subdivided into stages, but researchers have since found that children have at least the rudiments of many abilities far earlier than Piaget's theory would predict. Cognitive development arises in part from improved information processing, particularly more efficient working memory, which in part probably reflects brain development. Finally, as Vygotsky pointed out, culture and instruction from adults also play a role in cognitive development.

3. **How do social and emotional development occur during infancy and childhood?** Children become attached to their primary caregivers but may end up being attached in different ways. The self-concept begins to develop during very early infancy and, in turn, affects and is affected by social interactions, including those that convey information about gender roles. People may move through a series of stages in the way they tend to reason about moral issues, and males and females may tend to reason slightly differently at the higher levels—but any divergence reflects their different concerns in daily life, not a difference between the genders per se.

Adolescence: Between Two Worlds

Steven Spielberg's adolescence was different from that of many of his peers in numerous ways; nonetheless, the challenges he faced in those years—forming friendships, testing limits, and coming to terms with changes in his body—are essentially universal. Because his family had moved so often, none of his friends from early childhood were still with him in high school; most of his classmates, in addition, had firmly established circles of friends. Spielberg wanted to be accepted by his classmates and used his newfound love of moviemaking and storytelling as a way to engage them. Nevertheless, his obsession with movies and his lack of interest in the usual teenage pursuits of dating and sports continued to set him apart.

Not surprisingly, Spielberg's adolescence was not an easy time for him or, sometimes, for those around him. On one occasion, he and some friends spent 3 hours throwing rocks through plate-glass windows at a shopping mall, causing about $30,000 worth of damage (McBride, 1999). His "difficult" behavior was not a one-time occurrence. For example, he later said that his film *Poltergeist* was "all about the terrible things I did to my younger sisters" (McBride, 1999, p. 89). Moreover, he fought his father's wishes for him to study math and science, declaring that someday he was going to be a famous movie director and didn't need to know those kinds of things (McBride, 1999). Extreme behavior, yes. Adolescent behavior, yes.

Puberty The time when hormones cause the sex organs to mature and secondary sexual characteristics, such as breasts for women and a beard for men, to appear.

Adolescence The period between the onset of puberty and, roughly, the end of the teenage years.

LOOKING AHEAD Learning Objectives

1. How does puberty affect the body?
2. How do thought processes change in adolescence?
3. Does adolescence always lead to emotional upheaval?

Physical Development: In Puberty's Wake

Adolescence begins at **puberty**, the time when hormones cause the sex organs to mature and secondary sexual characteristics, such as breasts for women and a beard for men, to appear. These changes are gradual and typically begin between ages 8 and 14 for girls and between ages 9 and 15 for boys. **Adolescence** is the period between the onset of puberty and, roughly, the end of the teenage years. Figure 9 summarizes pubertal events in girls and boys.

FIGURE 9 **Pubertal Events in Boys and Girls**

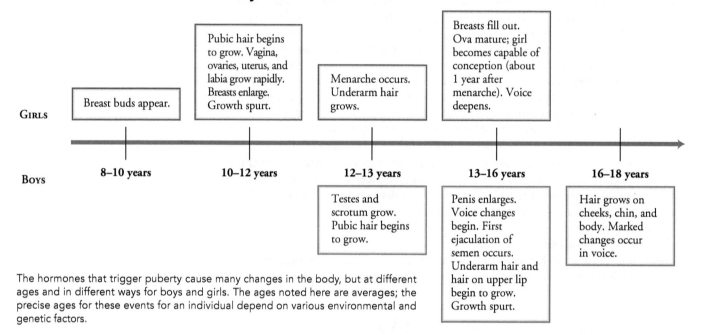

The hormones that trigger puberty cause many changes in the body, but at different ages and in different ways for boys and girls. The ages noted here are averages; the precise ages for these events for an individual depend on various environmental and genetic factors.

Although girls usually experience their first period (*menarche*) about 2 years after the onset of puberty, typically between 12 and 13 years of age today (Chumlea et al., 2003), various factors influence when this occurs. In fact, in the mid-19th century, girls had their first period at about 17 years of age. In recent years, the age of puberty has declined—for both girls and boys—throughout the developed and developing world, including the United States (Finlay et al., 2002; Herman-Giddens et al., 2001), Europe (de Muinck Keizer-Schrama & Mul, 2001), China (Huen et al., 1997), and Brazil (Kac et al., 2000), which suggests a general trend in society (Toppari & Juul, in press). In addition, American boys of various ethnic backgrounds are taller and heavier today than in previous generations, and these boys also develop pubic hair and their genitalia mature at a younger age than was previously considered the norm (Herman-Giddens et al., 2001).

Many factors have been proposed to explain the trend for puberty to occur at an earlier age today than previously:

1. *Nutrition.* Studies have shown that overweight girls tend to experience their first periods before those who are not overweight (Kaplowitz et al., 2001), which suggests a link between diet and the age of onset of puberty.

2. *Stress*, at least in girls who have a certain gene in combination with having an absent father (Comings et al., 2002).

3. *Additives* in food, such as hormones added to animal feed and then passed on to human consumers (Teilmann et al., 2002).

4. *Chemical pollutants* in the environment, such as polybrominated biphenyls (PBBs; Blanck et al., 2000).

In spite of all the hypotheses, the reason or reasons underlying the trend toward earlier puberty are still not understood.

Physical development during adolescence also, of course, includes growth. Such growth is strongly influenced by the effects of sex hormones, which cause the hips of young girls to grow large relative to their shoulders and vice versa for boys. In addition, rapid growth of the hands, feet, and legs is followed by growth of the torso (Wheeler, 1991). Do you remember when you stopped needing larger shoe sizes but still needed larger shirts and coats? That's why. The uneven growth during adolescence can lead to an awkward, gawky look, which doesn't do wonders for a teen's sense of self-confidence.

Boys and girls have growth spurts at different ages. At age 11, girls typically are taller and heavier than boys because their major growth spurt starts about 2 years before that of boys. By age 14, however, boys' heights and weights have taken off, whereas girls have stopped growing or have begun to grow more slowly. American girls typically stop growing at around age 13 (although some may continue to grow until about age 16), but American boys usually continue to grow until about their 16th birthdays (and some may continue growing until they are almost 18 years old; Malina & Bouchard, 1991; Tanner, 1990).

THINK like a **PSYCHOLOGIST** What advantages and disadvantages to children and to society might there be from earlier puberty?

Girls tend to mature faster than boys.

Source: Jeff Greenberg\The Image Works

Cognitive Development: Getting It All Together

As Piaget noted, the adolescent's ability to reason can become dramatically more powerful. But even so, their reasoning may be plagued with biases and distortions.

More Reasoned Reasoning? The major cognitive development of adolescence, achieved by some but not all adolescents, is the ability to reason abstractly. Piaget's period of formal operations describes the cognitive achievements of these adolescents. According to Piaget, formal operational thinking allows a person to think systematically about abstract concepts and possible scenarios. In one of his experiments, now regarded as a classic, Piaget gave a child a set of weights, string that could be attached to the weights, and a bar to which the string could be attached, allowing a weight to swing like a pendulum. The child was asked to vary both the weight and the length of the string in order to discover what factors would make a weight swing most quickly. Adolescents in the formal operational period can figure out the possibly relevant variables (size of weight, length of string, how high the weight is raised before being let go, and the force with which it is pushed). But more than that, adolescents also understand that they must alter only one thing at a time in order to discover the role of each variable. These adolescents have grasped the very essence of scientific experimentation: holding everything else constant while systematically changing one variable at a time. Hence, all the cognitive machinery necessary to think scientifically can be present by about 11 or 12 years of age. But not all adolescents develop these abilities this early, and some never do.

The ability to think systematically about abstractions allows people to reason about a host of topics, ranging from concepts such as justice and politics, to relationships and the causes of human behavior, to the rules that underlie algebra and geometry. In fact, there's evidence that the adolescent brain is better prepared to learn algebra than is the adult brain! Researchers found that adolescents and adults used parts of the frontal and parietal lobes when they first learned rules of algebra and used those rules to solve equations—but after practice, adolescents' parietal lobes stopped being activated, which suggests that the rules became "automatic." In contrast, adult brains don't make this transition; those brain areas in adults continued to be activated, which suggests that adults are expending more effort to use these rules (Luna, 2004; Qin et al., 2004).

Although it may be temping to conclude that the ability to think abstractly and logically emerges because working memory develops (it does not function at adult levels until about 19 years of age; Luna et al., 2004), assuming that events at any one level alone could account for such a sweeping change would be rash indeed. Cole (1990) has found that in many traditional African societies, even the adults cannot use the kinds of abilities described by Piaget's idea of formal operations, but there is no indication that their brains have failed to develop fully. Learning must play a role, perhaps when culture shapes the developing child's thought, as Vygotsky theorized.

But thinking is more than using logic or knowing how to grapple with abstractions; emotion is often involved in our reasoning (Damasio, 1994; Salzman & Fusi, 2010). For example, emotions can lead people to be appropriately cautious and can even underlie some aspects of intuition and "good judgment" (which involves weighing alternatives against each other, considering the impact of the likely consequences of each, and making decisions based on such considerations). Such processing relies in part on the lower middle part of the frontal lobes. Evidence suggests that this brain area continues to develop well into adulthood, and thus emotions (such as those that prod one to be cautious!) may not guide teenagers' thinking effectively (C. J. Hooper et al., 2004). We can speculate that this maturational lag contributes to a lack of "good judgment" during this stage of life.

Adolescent Egocentrism: It's All in Your Point of View
The enhanced cognitive abilities of adolescents allow them to take other points of view easily—and allow them to see themselves as they imagine others see them. Theorists have claimed that these improved abilities can lead to two kinds of distortions in adolescents' conceptions of how others view them (Greene et al., 2002):

1. The *imaginary audience* is a belief sometimes held by adolescents in which they view themselves as actors and everyone else as the audience (Elkind, 1967; Elkind & Bowen, 1979). This view can lead teenagers to be extremely self-conscious and easily embarrassed; a pimple feels like a beacon, not unlike Rudolph's nose. Although many adolescents do not succumb to such cognitive distortions (Vartanian, 2001), those who do—perhaps because they believe others may be watching them—are less likely to engage in risky behaviors (Galanaki, 2001).

    However, some researchers argue that often there is nothing "imaginary" about the audience and adolescents may have realistic concerns about others' opinions (Bell & Bromnick, 2003).

2. Some teenagers have a *personal fable*, which is a story in which they are the star and, as the star, have extraordinary abilities and privileges. One reason why teenagers may have unprotected sex and drive recklessly is that they believe that they are immune to the possible consequences (Lapsley, 1990; Lapsley et al., 1988).

Who is the imaginary audience?

Source: Alamy Images Royalty Free

Social and Emotional Development: New Rules, New Roles

As a bridge between childhood and adulthood, adolescence is a time of transition. An adolescent must adjust his or her identity as he or she negotiates new relationships and roles in the world (Marica, 1993).

"Storm and Stress": Raging Hormones?
Some adolescents respond to the challenges of this transitional period with wild emotional swings and by engaging in risky and impulsive behavior. This response has led some to describe adolescence as a period of "storm and stress," characterized by a tendency to have three sorts of problems (Arnett, 1999):

1. Adolescents tend to have conflicts with their parents (Laursen et al., 1998). The *frequency* of the conflicts is greatest in early adolescence, whereas the *intensity* of the conflicts is greatest in midadolescence (Laursen et al., 1998).

2. Adolescents tend to experience extreme mood swings (Buchanan et al., 1992; Larson & Richards, 1994; Petersen et al., 1993), and by the middle of the teen years, as many as about one third of adolescents are seriously depressed (Petersen et al., 1993)—and such depression is associated with increased levels of delinquency (Beyers & Loeber, 2003). Adolescents also often report feeling lonely and nervous.

3. Adolescents may be prone to taking risks and may have a tendency to commit crimes, drive recklessly, and have high-risk sex (Arnett, 1992; Gottfredson & Hirschi, 1990; Johnston et al., 1994). In addition to the possible role of having a personal fable, such behaviors are related to problems in regulating emotions (M. L. Cooper et al., 2003), and they tend to peak in late adolescence.

Not all adolescents have these problems; rather, as Arnett (1999) documents, such problems are simply "more likely to occur during adolescence than at other ages" (p. 317). But why do they occur at all? Many people assume that these problems are an unavoidable result of the hormonal changes that accompany puberty. In fact, the hormonal changes that go along with puberty do make the adolescent prone to emotional swings (Brooks-Gunn et al., 1994; Buchanan et al., 1992). But hormones only predispose, they do not cause; environmental events trigger the emotional reactions (Dodge & Pettit, 2003).

In sum, adolescents are more likely than people of other ages to experience "storm and stress," which arises in part from the workings of hormones. However, not all adolescents experience such problems, and the degree to which an adolescent does experience such turmoil depends on personal and cultural circumstances.

Evolving Peer Relationships Many kinds of life experiences affect whether a young man or woman will develop intimate relationships. For example, perhaps counterintuitively, military service can enhance the ability to form intimate relationships (for example, by helping someone learn to trust and rely on others; Dar & Kimhi, 2001). In addition, both young men and women who have a more positive relationship with their mothers later have more positive intimate relationships with others (Robinson, 2000).

Most adolescents develop predominantly same-gender networks of friends, and women's friendships tend to be stronger than men's (Roy et al., 2000). However, not all relationships are positive, and the negative ones can be as powerful as the friendships. For example, as portrayed in countless Hollywood "mean girls" and "nerd" films, some adolescents can be rejected by their peers. In particular, girls can effectively use indirect aggression (for example, by spreading false rumors) to exclude other girls from their circle (Owens et al., 2000). Hurt pride or lowered self-esteem is not always the only result of such rejection; in some cases, the victims may go so far as to commit suicide.

Gay adolescents often have different experiences with peers than do their heterosexual counterparts. In particular, gay young men tend to have more female than male friends, and gay young men typically tend to be less emotionally attached to their love interests than are heterosexual young men (Diamond & Dube, 2002). Moreover, many gay or bisexual students report being victimized at school, which apparently contributes to their being at risk for suicide and substance abuse and for their engaging in high-risk behaviors (Bontempo & D'Augelli, 2002).

Finally, although many aspects of adolescents' behaviors are influenced in large part by their peers, an adolescent's basic values and goals are influenced primarily by his or her family (Brown et al., 1986a, 1986b). ◉ Watch

Watch the Video *Changes in Friendship with Age* on mypsychlab.com

Teenage Pregnancy In general, American teenage girls engage in about the same amount of sexual activity as girls in other industrialized societies, but American teens do not use contraception as effectively. However only 23% of unmarried mothers in 2007 were teenagers—compared to 50% in 1970 (Ventura, 2009). The teenagers most likely to become pregnant typically are poor and do not have clear career plans—and their father is likely to be absent (Ellis et al., 2003). Maynard (1996) reports that a third of the teenagers who become pregnant drop out of school even before they become pregnant. Further, over half of teenage mothers were living in poverty when they had their children. For many of these young women, having a baby is part of "coming of age" and is in many ways equivalent to a career choice (Burton, 1990; Merrick, 1995). Unfortunately, when the children of teen mothers later become adults, they are likely to have dropped out of school, be unemployed, and be in trouble with the law for violent offences—and they themselves tend to become parents at an early age (Jaffee et al., 2001).

However, the specific consequences of a teen mother's having a child depend on the mother's subsequent behavior and social group. In particular, Black Americans appear to suffer the fewest negative economic consequences of having given birth as a teenager. Apparently, in many cases Black American teenage mothers live at home, continue school, and benefit from the assistance of members of their families (Burton, 1990, 1996; Rosenheim & Testa, 1992).

✓●─[Study and Review on
mypsychlab.com

LOOKING BACK

1. **How does puberty affect the body?** Hormones are responsible for the fact that the extremities (arms and legs) grow rapidly, with the trunk lagging behind, a pattern that can produce a gawky appearance. During this period, the body grows pubic hair and acquires other secondary sex characteristics.

2. **How do thought processes change in adolescence?** Many adolescents become capable of reasoning logically. In addition, if the adolescent reaches the period of formal operations, he or she can reason about abstract concepts systematically—and thus becomes capable of scientific thought. The enhanced cognitive abilities that can appear during adolescence can lead to the distorting creations of an imaginary audience and a personal fable.

3. **Does adolescence always lead to emotional upheaval?** Although hormones do predispose adolescents to experience more conflicts with parents as well as to have major mood swings and be prone to taking risks, these tendencies are neither certain nor necessarily severe. Many kinds of experiences and characteristics (especially gender) influence the way peer relationships develop during adolescence.

Adulthood and Aging: The Continuously Changing Self

Steven Spielberg was an unhappy teenager and—in some aspects of life—a spectacularly successful young adult. But being successful in his chosen career did not mean that he was successful in all aspects of life. His first marriage ended, his relationship with his father was strained, and he was concerned that he himself would not measure up as a father (several of his movies deal with difficult relationships between fathers and sons). When he had children of his own, he realized that he needed to be a parent for them; he—and his relationships—had to change, and they did.

Famous filmmaker or not, the grown-up Steven Spielberg is in a very different phase of life than his children are; he is also in a very different phase of life than his father is. To understand the developmental issues of Steven Spielberg as he is today, we must explore the stages of adult development.

LOOKING AHEAD Learning Objectives

1. How do changes in the body affect adults as they age?
2. How does aging during adulthood affect perception, memory, and intelligence?
3. What is the course of social and emotional development during adulthood?

The Changing Body: What's Inevitable, What's Not

Adolescence is a time of change, in body, mind, and behavior—but by your early 20s, it is unlikely that you will grow taller, and for the next several decades, changes in your body should be relatively minor. True, you may gain a bit of weight, you may come to need bifocals, and your hair may begin to gray or to thin. But the basic bodily systems continue to function well. However, after age 50 or so, noticeable changes in the body begin to occur (Lemme, 1995).

Aging has two aspects: changes that are programmed into the genes and changes that arise from environmental events (Busse, 1969; Rowe & Kahn, 1998). Many changes that come with aging arise not from inevitable processes but rather from various deficiencies, such as a lack of the following:

1. *Adequate nutrition,* which can produce fragile bones, such as those that result from osteoporosis-related calcium deficiency;

2. *Exercise*—or a lack thereof—which can lead some older adults to become obese, others to become frail, and others to become sluggish and develop poor health (Brach et al., 2004);

3. *Meaningful activities,* which can lead to feelings of helplessness or apathy (Avorn & Langer, 1982; Langer & Rodin, 1976; Rodin & Langer, 1977; Rowe & Kahn, 1998).

By the same token, environmental events—such as taking calcium supplements or lifting appropriate weights—can help to counter or diminish such problems.

One of the inevitable age-related changes in women is *menopause,* the gradual ending of menstruation that typically occurs between the ages of 45 and 55; following menopause, eggs are no longer released, and normal pregnancy is not possible (Wise et al., 1996). Hormonal changes that accompany menopause can lead to various bodily sensations, such as "hot flashes". On one hand, the knowledge that childbearing is no longer possible, along with the decline in youthful appearance, can adversely affect a woman's self-concept and self-esteem. On the other hand, for many women, the physical discomforts of menopause are slight, if present at all, and the idea of sexual intercourse without the threat of an unwanted pregnancy provides new pleasure. Some women feel "postmenopausal zest" and are reinvigorated by this change and the freedom it represents.

For men, after about age 40, sperm production begins to fall off—but unlike the cessation of egg production after menopause, men never fully lose the ability to produce sperm. Men do experience declining vigor (strength and energy) with age, which can affect sexual performance.

It's not just diet that can help prevent osteoporosis; behavior can also play a role. Lifting weights helps the bones retain calcium.

Source: Steven Peters\Getty Images Inc. - Stone Allstock

Perception and Cognition in Adulthood: Taking the Good with the Bad

Because aging affects the brain, it affects perception and cognition. Moreover, as we see in the following sections, it also affects two central contributors to cognition: memory and intelligence.

Perception: Through a Glass Darkly? Changes in the sensory organs (especially the eyes and ears) and the brain can markedly impair perception in older adults. During early and middle adulthood, worsening vision can usually be corrected with eyeglasses, but later in life more severe visual difficulties may emerge. For example, more than half of people aged 65 and older have *cataracts,* a clouding of the lenses of the eyes. Cataracts are especially troublesome because the pupil (the opening of the eye through which light enters) cannot open as widely in older people as it does in younger people. Surgery can remove cataracts and result in greatly improved vision. But when cataract surgery has not been performed, moderate optical difficulties cause many older people to need greater contrast to see differences in lighting (Fozard, 1990). Contrasts between lit and unlit surfaces, such as shadows caused by steps, can define differences in depth; if older people cannot perceive such definition, they are more likely to stumble over a step. Simply providing more light will not necessarily help people with cataracts to see well; because of

the clouding of the lenses, more light causes more glare. Thus, the best level of illumination is a compromise between what produces the best contrast and the least glare.

Some declines in visual perception have nothing to do with the physical condition of the eyes but rather reflect changes in how the brain functions. For instance, older adults have difficulty shifting attention rapidly, which can cause problems in driving (Baldock et al., 2008). In addition, they do not classify the identities of faces as well as younger people do—but they can classify facial expressions as well as younger people do and thus can be at least as sensitive as younger people to nonverbal cues during personal interactions (Kiffel et al., 2005).

Hearing is also affected by age. After age 50 or so, people have increased difficulty hearing high-frequency sounds (Botwinick, 1984; Lemme, 1995). Because consonants (such as *k*, *c*, *p*, and *t*) are produced with higher-frequency sounds than are vowels, older people often have trouble distinguishing between words that differ by a single consonant, such as *kill* and *pill*. Older people also have more difficulty shutting out background noise, a problem that may actually be worsened by hearing aids, which boost the loudness of both irrelevant background sounds and relevant sounds.

Memory: Difficulties in Digging It Out Memory tends to become poorer during older adulthood (Schacter, 1996). At least some of this difficulty arises because parts of the brain that produce the neurotransmitter acetylcholine become impaired with age (Albert & Moss, 1996; Smith et al., 1999); this neurotransmitter is crucial for the proper functioning of the hippocampus, which plays a key role in storing new explicit memories (the type of memories that can be recalled voluntarily). In fact, the hippocampus and related brain structures are smaller in older adults, and the sizes of these structures are correlated with recall ability (Rosen et al., 2003).

Even so, aging affects some aspects of memory more than others, and many aspects of memory are relatively intact in the older adults. In particular, *semantic memory* (memory for facts, words, meanings, and other information that is not associated with a particular time and place) remains relatively intact into very old age (Light, 1991), and older adults are able to store new *episodic memories* (memory for specific events) relatively effectively. Older adults are often able to access information if asked to recognize stimuli. For example, people in their 70s and 80s do fairly well when they are asked to study a list of words and then later are asked to pick out these words from a longer list that also contains other words (Craik & McDowd, 1987). Moreover, older adults have good implicit memory (the type of memory that biases perception or behavior; Fleischman et al., 2004), and they can recall the gist of a description and its implications at least as well as younger people (Radvansky, 1999).

However, older adults have difficulty when they must actively recall *specific* episodic memories: For example, they do poorly when they are given a list of common words to remember and later asked to recall them—versus recognize them from a list of words (Craik & McDowd, 1987). Tasks that require the recall of specific information appear to rely on the frontal lobes to dig the information out of memory, and processes accomplished there are not as efficient in older adults as they are in younger people.

Impaired frontal lobe functioning is probably also responsible for difficulties older adults have with tasks involving working memory and strategizing (De Beni & Palladino, 2004). Such deficits are especially evident when older adults must hold information in mind while doing something else at the same time (Craik et al., 1995). Similarly, older adults can have difficulty when strategies are needed to perform a task (such as figuring out the most efficient way to move through a store to collect different items; Gabrieli, 1996; Li et al., 2001). This problem is made even worse because older adults are actually more likely than younger people to use strategies that rely more on their frontal lobes because they attempt to compensate for less efficient processing in other parts of the brain (Gutchess et al., 2005).

Cognition: Slowly and Less Surely Cognitive abilities remain relatively stable through most of adulthood, but signs of a decline in some abilities begin to appear by age 50. This decline in abilities is related to changes in the brain. Aging not only leads the brain to have less gray matter (cell bodies of neurons), but also impairs

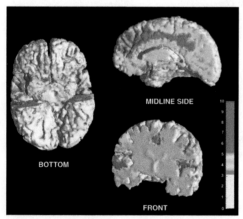

The frontal lobes are among the brain areas that lose the most gray matter in old age (Raz et al., 1997; Resnick et al., 2003), which may be one factor that affects the ability to recall information easily. In these MRI scans, the brighter the color, the more gray matter was lost with aging: *bottom*, a view from the bottom, looking up; *midline side*, a midline side view of the inside regions; *front*, a slice viewed from the front.

Source: Resnick, S.M., Pham, D.L., Kraut, M.A., Zonderman, A.B., Davatzikos, C.: Longitudinal magnetic resonance imaging studies of older adults: A shrinking brain. *J. Neurosci.* 23(8): 3295–3301, 2003. © 2003 by the Society for Neuroscience.

communication among neurons, possibly by disrupting neurotransmitter functioning (Li et al., 2001) or by breaking down the myelin that insulates axons, thereby impairing the transmission of neural signals (Guttmann et al., 1998). These changes in the brain will eventually lead a person to perform more slowly and be more prone to making errors. Indeed, by age 60, people perform most cognitive tasks more slowly than do younger people (Birren et al., 1962; Cerella, 1990; Salthouse, 1991b). The harder the task, the larger the difference in the time taken by older adults as compared to young adults. (We hasten to add that older adults compensate for the decline in their cognitive abilities by adopting better strategies, and thus their overall performance on most tasks generally remains as good—and sometimes even better—than it was in early adulthood; we discuss this point shortly.)

Shortly before death, however, some people exhibit *terminal decline* (Kleemeier, 1962). Their performance on a wide range of cognitive tasks takes a dramatic turn for the worse (Berg, 1996). This decline appears most dramatically in those who will die from cerebrovascular diseases, such as strokes and heart attacks, and it may be related to such disease states (Small & Bäckman, 2000). More common is a gradual degradation in cognitive performance in the years leading up to death (Johansson et al., 2004; Small et al., 2003).

Many herbs, vitamins, and other medicinal remedies promise to reverse the negative cognitive effects of aging. For example, the herb *Ginkgo biloba* has been reported to improve blood flow to the brain (Dean et al., 1993), but there is no evidence that it prevents cognitive decline with aging (Kuller et al., 2010; Snitz et al., 2009). *Source:* PhotoEdit Inc.

Intelligence and Specific Abilities: Different Strokes for Different Folks
Although a person's overall level of intelligence is remarkably stable from age 11 to age 78 (Deary et al., 2004), age affects different aspects of intelligence in different ways—as discussed in the following sections.

CHANGES IN FLUID AND CRYSTALLIZED INTELLIGENCE. Investigators have examined the effects of age on two types of intelligence: (1) *fluid intelligence*, which involves reasoning in novel ways and the ability to figure out new solutions, and (2) *crystallized intelligence*, which involves using previously stored knowledge as a basis of reasoning in familiar ways. These two types of intelligence have been assessed in **longitudinal studies**, which test the same group of people repeatedly, at different ages. These findings suggest that both types of intelligence are stable until somewhere between the mid-50s and the early 70s, when both decline (Hertzog & Schaie, 1988).

However, the very strength of longitudinal studies—the continuing participation of the same group—also leads to a weakness: The participants become familiar with the type of testing, and this familiarity can influence their performance on later assessments. **Cross-sectional studies** involve testing different groups of people, with each group composed of individuals of a particular age. The major weakness of such studies is that the groups may differ, and thus the key challenge is to try to equate them on all possible measures other than age (such as sex, educational level, and health status). Such studies have led most researchers to conclude that fluid intelligence begins to decline as early as the late 20s (Salthouse, 1991a), whereas crystallized intelligence may actually increase with age and decline only late in life (Baltes, 1987; Li et al., 2004; McArdle et al., 2002).

Crystallized intelligence does not decline dramatically until very late in life, which allows the elderly to tell interesting and informative stories. *Source:* PhotoEdit Inc.

CHANGES IN SPECIFIC ABILITIES. Crystallized intelligence, rooted in experience, may be thought of as underlying much of what we mean by "wisdom." The ability to draw on such intelligence may explain why researchers found that older adults were rated as telling more interesting, higher-quality, and more informative stories than younger adults (James et al., 1998). This should be cheering news for Steven Spielberg, who plans to keep telling stories as long as he can.

Moreover, in some respects, older adults think more systematically than do young people. For example, in one study, researchers asked young and old participants to indicate their preferences when given either two or three alternatives—such as chocolate or vanilla ice cream versus chocolate, vanilla, or strawberry ice cream. Young people were inconsistent, perhaps choosing vanilla when only two choices were offered but chocolate when strawberry was included. Older adults were much more consistent and "logical" in their choices (Tentori et al., 2001).

Longitudinal study A study in which the same group of people is tested repeatedly, at different ages.

Cross-sectional study A study in which different groups of people are tested, with each group composed of individuals of a particular age.

Psychosocial development The result of maturation and learning on personality and relationships.

Social and Emotional Development During Adulthood

The phrase "growing up" might seem to imply that psychological development is like height: After a certain age, you reach a plateau, and that's where you stay. Not so. At least in mentally healthy people, psychological development continues throughout the life span. In discussing Steven Spielberg's 15-year split with his father, an expert on father–son relationships, James Levine, commented, "In such a split, you don't recognize that under the anger is sadness. There's denial: pretending it's not important to heal the rift. But a split in the father–child relationship always has an effect" (quoted in Sullivan, 1999, p. 67). Still, as in Spielberg's case, relationships change and evolve over time.

After a 15-year split, Steven Spielberg developed a new relationship with his dad.

Source: Timothy Greenfield-Sanders

Read **Erik Erikson** Biography on mypsychlab.com

Theories of Psychosocial Stages in Adulthood Some theorists, Freud included, believed that personality is largely formed by the end of childhood. But Erik Erikson (1921–1994) proposed three stages of adult **psychosocial development**, which is the result of maturation and learning on personality and relationships. These three adult stages occur after five stages of psychosocial development through childhood and adolescence, as summarized in Table 2. Read

Erikson defined the three adult stages in terms of issues that adults are most likely to confront and need to resolve:

- In the first adult stage, *intimacy versus isolation*, the young adult must develop deep and intimate relations with others and avoid becoming socially isolated. Steven Spielberg had serious difficulty being intimate with people, which may be one reason why his first marriage dissolved (McBride, 1999).

- In the second adult stage, characterized by *generativity versus self-absorption*, middle-aged men and women must think about the future and decide what their contributions will be for their children and for society at large. People who are highly generative agree with the African proverb "The world was not left to us by our parents. It was lent to us by our children" (which is inscribed on a wall in the UNICEF office in New York). People who fail at the task of this stage will be faced with a sense of meaninglessness in life. Steven Spielberg not only cares for his own

TABLE 2 **Erikson's (1950) Psychosocial Stages**

Issue to Be Resolved	Average Age	Summary
Basic trust vs. mistrust	0–1 year	Depending on how well they are treated by caregivers, infants either develop a basic trust that their needs will be met or fail to develop such a basic trust
Autonomy vs. doubt	1–3 years	The child either is allowed to choose and make independent decisions or is made to feel ashamed and full of self-doubt for wanting to do so
Initiative vs. guilt	3–6 years	The child either develops a sense of purpose and direction or is overly controlled by the parents and made to feel constrained or guilty
Industry vs. inferiority	6–11 years	The child either develops a sense of competence and ability to work with others or becomes beset with feelings of incompetence and inferiority
Identity vs. role confusion	Adolescence	The adolescent either successfully grapples with questions of identity and future roles as an adult or becomes confused about possible adult roles
Intimacy vs. isolation	Young adulthood	The young adult either develops deep and intimate relations with others or is socially isolated
Generativity vs. self-absorption	Middle adulthood	The adult in the "prime of life" must look to the future and determine what to leave behind for future generations; failing this task leads to a sense of meaninglessness in life
Integrity vs. despair	Older adulthood	In reflecting back on life, a person either feels that life was worthwhile as it was lived or feels despair and fears death

children but also makes it a point to help young directors who are just starting out; such altruistic behavior is another type of generativity.

- In the third adult stage, characterized by *integrity versus despair*, older adults must be able to reflect back on life and feel that it was worthwhile; if they successfully navigate this stage, they avoid feelings of despair and fear of death.

Many researchers have picked up where Erikson left off (Gould, 1978; Havinghurst, 1953; Vaillant, 1977). Some have focused on one aspect of Erikson's theory—generativity. For example, McAdams and his colleagues developed ways to assess generativity (McAdams & de St. Aubin, 1992), and they found that adults who are concerned about providing for future generations tend to be more satisfied with their own lives (McAdams et al., 1993) and to view life optimistically—believing that even bad events will eventually have a happy outcome (McAdams et al., 2001).

Continued Personality Development We must distinguish between the changes in *perspective*—such as viewing life more optimistically—that can arise from adult psychosocial development versus changes in *personality*; evidence indicates that personality does not change substantially during adulthood (Costa et al., 2000; W. Johnson et al., 2005; Schaie et al., 2004). In fact, Paul Costa and Robert McCrae (1988) tested more than a thousand adults, both men and women, using standardized measures (not interviews) of the *Big Five personality dimensions* (which include factors such as openness to experience, conscientiousness, and agreeableness). The participants ranged in age from 21 to 96 years. In addition to asking the participants to complete the measures, the researchers also asked 167 spouses to fill in the measures about the participants. Eighty-nine men and 78 women were tested twice, 6 years apart; thus, both cross-sectional and longitudinal data were collected. The results were clear: There were very few differences in any of the dimensions of personality over the years, and when such differences were found, they were very small. Moreover, personality was equally stable over time for men and women.

Costa and McCrae (1988) concluded that "aging itself has little effect on personality. This is true despite the fact that the normal course of aging includes disease, bereavement, divorce, unemployment, and many other significant events for substantial portions of the population" (p. 862). Moreover, objective tests have shown that even when a person feels that his or her personality has changed (over the course of 6–9 years) during middle age, it usually has not (Herbst et al., 2000). However, this is not to say that personality is frozen in time: Although the structure of personality (particularly its organization into five major factors) remains constant with increasing age during adulthood, researchers found that older adults generally have higher scores on traits of agreeableness and conscientiousness than do younger adults (Allemand et al., 2008).

For the most part, apparent changes in personality over time probably reflect not so much changes in the person as changes in the life challenges that he or she is confronting at the time: For many people, aging is accompanied by changes in marital status, parenting, and job-related factors. Such major life changes often become less frequent or severe as a person grows older (except for death of a spouse), which could explain the finding that people become increasingly consistent in the degree to which they can be described by particular traits until around age 50, and thereafter are stable (Roberts & DelVecchio, 2000). Traits could become stable, at least in part, because a person settles into a niche in life and thus restricts the range and variety of situations he or she encounters.

Mature Emotions The poet Robert Browning wrote, "Grow old along with me! / The best is yet to be / The last of life, for which the first is made." He may have been more right than he realized. In one study, people of different ages were prompted to report their emotions at various times over the course of a week (Carstensen et al., 2000). The researchers found that older adults tend to experience extended periods of highly positive emotions and have fewer spells of enduring negative emotions than do younger people.

But the news is even better than this. Older people are, well, more "mature" in their emotional responses. With age, people become better able to regulate emotions (Gross et al., 1997). For example, in one study this ability to regulate emotions effectively led older adult Americans of European and Chinese ethnic backgrounds to have smaller changes in heart rate when watching emotional films than did younger adults (Tsai et al., 2000).

353

THINK like a
PSYCHOLOGIST Which sorts of jobs require a person to regulate emotions well? Could these jobs be performed well by older adults because they can regulate emotions better than younger people?

Adult Relationships: Stable Changes Perhaps as a result of their increased ability to grapple with emotions, older people tend to change their outlook on life. Laura Carstensen and her collaborators have developed the *socioemotional selectivity theory*, which rests on the idea that older adults come to focus on the limited time they have left, which in turn changes their motivations (Carstensen & Charles, 1998; Lang & Carstensen, 2002). Consistent with this theory, these researchers find that as people age, they come increasingly to value emotionally fulfilling relationships. This leads older people to prefer the company of those with whom they are emotionally close. The same findings hold true both for White and Black Americans (Fung et al., 2001).

In general, as people age, they interact with fewer people, but these interactions tend to be more intimate (Carstensen, 1991, 1992)—older people don't miss the broader social networks that they had when they were young (Lansford et al., 1998). Relationships during young adulthood tend to include more friends than relatives, but with age the mix reverses, with more time spent with relatives than with friends. This pattern is even more pronounced among Latinos than Americans of European descent (Levitt et al., 1993). However, this is not to say that relationships with friends disappear. In fact, in later life, a relationship long dormant can be picked up and reestablished with minimal effort (Carstensen, 1992); after young adulthood, personality variables are relatively stable, which makes it easy to "know" someone again even after a long lapse.

In addition, the nature of relationships with both friends and relatives changes as people move into older adulthood. During young adulthood, people are concerned that their relationships are equitable—that neither party gives more than he or she receives (Lemme, 1995; Walster et al., 1978). As people age, such concerns recede into the background. In successful marriages, the members of the couple think of themselves as a team, not separate people who are in constant negotiations (Keith & Schafer, 1991). Because they are in it for the long haul, people trust that the balance of favors and repayment will even out over time. One result of this change in perspective is that older couples resolve their differences with less negative emotion than do younger couples (Carstensen et al., 1995).

At one point, approximately 2,500 people well over 100 years old were reported to be living in countries comprising the former Soviet Union. One purportedly 168-year-old gentleman, who was still walking half a mile daily and gardening, attributed his longevity to the fact that he didn't marry until he was 65. Remarriage after the death of a spouse is common among older adults.

Source: The Image Works

LOOKING AT LEVELS Keeping the Aging Brain Sharp

Source: © David Young-Wolff/ PhotoEdit; (inset) © Volker Steger/Photo Researchers, Inc.

In older adulthood, particularly in the years just before death, many people do not function as well mentally as they did earlier in life, even if they are physically healthy (Small & Bäckman, 2000). We all have relatives who are older adults—and someday we will be the same ourselves. Thus, we all have an interest in understanding why older adults have poorer mental functioning and what can be done about it.

Why does the problem arise? In addition to the changes in the brain already discussed, this problem may occur in part because the brain receives less blood as people age—which means that it is sustained by fewer nutrients and less oxygen (Ivy et al., 1992). The blood supply to the brain decreases with age because the blood vessels themselves become smaller.

But focusing on the brain alone is not enough. At the level of the person, people (at least in the United States) have "ageist" stereotypes about older adults—and these stereotypes apparently not only can affect mental functioning of older adults but also can affect their attitudes and behavior. For example, consider the effects of aging on attitudes about coping with serious illness. In one study, young and older adults were shown positive or negative words concerning old age; the words were presented too briefly to be seen consciously—but could still affect unconscious mental processing. The older adult participants were more likely to say that they would reject treatment for serious illness after they were shown such negative words than they were after they were shown positive words; the negative words apparently activated stored negative concepts about aging. For the young participants, the type of words made no difference (Levy et al., 1999–2000).

To understand the mental decline in healthy older adults, we must also consider events at the level of the group. Social interactions, particularly social support, clearly can help older (as well as younger) people cope with stress (Krause, 2004), which in turn can reduce the stress response; unfortunately, older people cannot function as well cognitively after they lose social support (Aartsen et al., 2004).

By performing live concerts in their 60s, Mick Jagger and fellow rockers in The Rolling Stones show that many roles are open to us as we age, despite stereotypes to the contrary!

Source: David J. Phillip\AP Wide World Photos

And events at the different levels interact. It is tempting to speculate that one reason less blood flows to the brain is that the brain cells are not working as hard, so they need less blood—which in turn leads the vessels to adjust (Ivy et al., 1992). This would be a catch-22: The neurons don't work as effectively because they receive fewer blood-borne nutrients and less oxygen, but the reason they don't receive as much is that they haven't been functioning as effectively as they did before. If so, you could hypothesize that if you managed to engage older adults in more challenging tasks, you could literally increase the blood supply to their brains. And by increasing blood flow to the brain, you would improve their thinking abilities—which would in turn affect their attitudes as well as social interactions. This hypothesis is plausible because researchers have found that "mental workouts" can enhance cognitive function in older adults (Rowe & Kahn, 1998); in fact, training over the course of only 10 sessions can substantially improve memory, reasoning, and speed of processing in older adults (Ball et al., 2002).

Moreover, neurons' dendrites continue to grow normally even into old age (Coleman & Flood, 1986), and as neurons die, new connections can be formed to compensate for losses (Cotman, 1990). In one study, when old rats were moved from their standard cages into a rat playpen full of toys and other rats, they developed heavier brains with more extensive connections among neurons. Furthermore, other researchers have found that mice that live in an enriched environment (complete with lots of attractive toys, other mice to play with, and opportunities to explore and exercise) retain more neurons as they age (Kempermann et al., 1998).

Thus, if your otherwise healthy parents or grandparents are understimulated by their surroundings (as occurs in some nursing homes as well as in many home environments), this could affect their brains. The changes in their brains could in turn lead them to avoid mental challenge and engagement, which in turn could lead to changes in self-concept and level of self-esteem. These changes then may lead them to become lethargic and to avoid social interaction. And not interacting with others could lead to even less effective neural functioning and so on. Clearly, there is ample opportunity for events at all three levels to interact.

Research with mice suggests that it's not the pure amount of stimulation that boosts brain function but rather the amount of novelty that's encountered (Kempermann & Gage, 1999). If this result generalizes to humans, travel may truly broaden the mind, even for older adults!

Source: David Young-Wolff\PhotoEdit Inc.

However, it is unlikely that all of the functions that are impaired with age can be helped simply by getting older adults to use their brains more or even by changing negative stereotypes or attitudes about what it means to be elderly. MRI scans of more than 3,600 apparently normal older adults (aged 65–97) revealed that slightly over one third had small holes in their brains (Bryan et al., 1997). These holes affected both the cerebral cortex and the white matter (which consists of myelinated axons) that connects parts of the brain to each other (Koga et al., 2002). At present, the cause of these holes is not clear, and without knowing their cause (such as brain injury or disease) we cannot know whether events at the other levels of analysis could help to deter them—but this possibility is plausible, and researchers will no doubt evaluate it.

✔●─Study and Review on
mypsychlab.com

LOOKING BACK

1. **How do changes in the body affect adults as they age?** Most adults experience little physical decline or change in early and middle adulthood, until around age 50. At about this point, women experience menopause, and both men and women may find that they have less energy. Older adults can cope with many of the changes in their bodies with dietary supplements (such as calcium for bone weakness) or changes in activities (such as increased exercise).

2. **How does aging during adulthood affect perception, memory, and intelligence?** With age the lenses of the eyes cloud and the pupils dilate less, which leads to difficulty in seeing light–dark contrasts; older adults also have difficulty hearing high-frequency sounds, including consonants. With advancing old age, working memory operates less effectively, and people sometimes have difficulty recalling information. Although intelligence declines with advanced age for many people, fluid intelligence generally is more affected than crystallized intelligence.

3. **What is the course of social and emotional development during adulthood?** Many theorists, especially Erikson, have proposed that people pass through psychosocial stages as they age; these stages may reflect particular issues that need to be resolved. After age 30, a person's personality does not change much, if at all. Relationships among older adults focus on fewer people (often relatives) and tend to be stable over long periods of time.

LET'S REVIEW

((●─Listen to an audio file of your chapter on mypsychlab.com

I. IN THE BEGINNING: FROM CONCEPTION TO BIRTH

A. New combinations of genes arise both when an egg and sperm are created and then when an egg and sperm are joined at conception; a baby receives half of his or her genes from the mother's egg and half from the father's sperm. The development of both the brain and the body relies on the activation of specific genes, which is regulated in part by environmental events.

B. Prenatal development progresses in order through a series of stages; in the first trimester (3 months), the zygote becomes an embryo, then a fetus.

C. The developing fetus is active and becomes increasingly coordinated over time. The fetus can detect human speech and prefers the mother's voice.

D. Maturational processes can be disrupted by teratogens or enhanced by certain environmental events, such as those that reduce the level of stress experienced by the mother.

E. Newborns have a relatively good sense of smell and can learn that different stimuli tend to occur together. They have the sensory capacities needed to organize sounds into words and recognize objects. Newborns are equipped with a host of inborn reflexes, such as the sucking and Moro reflexes. These reflexes often disappear during the course of development.

F. Some aspects of temperament, such as a tendency to become anxious easily, may be evident early in life and persist for many years to come.

II. INFANCY AND CHILDHOOD: TAKING OFF

A. In general, motor development progresses from the head, down the trunk to the arms, and finally to the legs; at the same time, it proceeds out from the center of the body to the periphery (hands, fingers, and toes).

B. As perception develops, the child can make finer discriminations, needs less information about an object or event in order to recognize it, and can search more systematically.

C. Young children learn language without explicit instruction. Language is acquired gradually over time, but there appears to be a critical period for learning grammar.

D. Even 3-month-old infants have both implicit and explicit memory. Verbal memories reflect the child's language abilities at the time he or she encountered an event, and are not revised when the child's linguistic abilities subsequently improve.

E. Piaget believed that each child moves through a series of major periods of cognitive development. However, the age at which children enter each period is not fixed, and many abilities are evident at earlier ages than originally believed. Researchers have since found that children have at least the rudiments of many cognitive abilities far earlier than Piaget's theory would predict.

F. Cognitive development arises in part from improved information processing, particularly more efficient working memory—which probably in part reflects neural development. However, as Vygotsky stressed, culture and instruction also play a role in cognitive development.

G. Children become attached to their caregivers but may develop different attachment styles.

H. The self-concept begins to develop during very early infancy, and it probably arises in part from many types of social interactions, including those that convey information about gender roles.

I. People may move through a series of stages in the way they tend to reason about moral decisions, and males and females may tend to reason slightly differently about such decisions—but this is most likely a result of their different concerns in daily life, not something intrinsic to their genders. The conscience contributes to moral behavior and develops early in life (at around 3 years old).

III. ADOLESCENCE: BETWEEN TWO WORLDS

A. The extremities (arms and legs) grow rapidly during adolescence, with the trunk lagging behind, a pattern that can produce a gawky appearance. During this period, pubic hair and other secondary sexual characteristics appear. Puberty occurs earlier today in developed and developing nations than it did in previous eras.

B. If the adolescent reaches Piaget's period of formal operations, he or she can reason about abstract concepts systematically—and thus becomes capable of true scientific thought. This enhanced reasoning ability affects all aspects of thinking, including conceptions of self.

C. Enhanced cognitive capacities during adolescence allow the teenager to think about relationships in more sophisticated ways, but adolescents are also affected by their perceptions of an imaginary audience and a personal fable.

D. Hormonal changes can lead the adolescent to experience more conflicts with parents as well as to have mood swings and to tend to take risks, but these tendencies are not universal.

E. Most adolescents develop strong same-gender friendships, but these bonds tend to be stronger among young women than young men.

IV. ADULTHOOD AND AGING: THE CONTINUOUSLY CHANGING SELF

A. Until about age 50, most adults experience little physical decline or charge. At about this age, women experience menopause, and both men and women may begin to become less vigorous. Older adults can address many of the changes in their bodies with dietary supplements (such as calcium for bone weakness) or changes in activities (such as increased exercise, which can reduce obesity and strengthen bones).

B. For many people, as they age the lens of the eye clouds, and the pupil doesn't open as much as it did before, leading to difficulty in seeing contrast. Many older adults also have difficulty hearing higher-frequency sounds.

C. With advancing old age, working memory typically operates less effectively, and memory retrieval becomes more difficult.

D. Although intelligence may decline with advanced age, fluid intelligence may be more affected than crystallized intelligence. In some respects, however, older adults can think more systematically than younger adults.

E. Many theorists, especially Erikson, have proposed that people pass through psychosocial stages as they age. These stages reflect particular issues that need to be resolved. For most people, personality remains substantially the same throughout adulthood.

F. Older adults focus on closer involvement with fewer people (often relatives) and tend to have relationships that are stable over long periods of time. Older adults tend to have greater emotional control than younger people.

G. In older adulthood, the brain may not function as well as it did before, perhaps in part because the person is no longer being intellectually challenged; enrichment of the environment apparently can in part reverse this decline.

KEY TERMS

accommodation	cross-sectional study	longitudinal study	puberty
adolescence	egocentrism	maturation	schema
assimilation	embryo	moral dilemma	self-concept
attachment	fetus	nativism	separation anxiety
child-directed speech (CDS)	formal operation	object permanence	telegraphic speech
concrete operation	gender roles	overextension	teratogen
conservation	grammar	overregularization error	underextension
critical period	language acquisition device (LAD)	psychosocial development	zygote

PRACTICE TEST

For each of the following items, choose the single best answer.

1. At the moment of conception,
   a. a sperm penetrates an egg.
   b. a zygote becomes a gamete.
   c. the egg is a passive recipient.
   d. the egg changes its surface properties and activates the sperm.

2. Human development in the womb is divided into trimesters. At the end of the second trimester,
   a. the zygote becomes an embryo when the major axis of the body is present.
   b. the embryo becomes a fetus when all major body structures are present.
   c. the great bulk of the neurons each individual possesses are in place and are completely fixed.
   d. the great bulk of the neurons each individual possesses are in place, but they are not completely fixed.

3. As fetuses develop,
   a. their heart rates speed up.
   b. their heart rates become less variable.
   c. they move less often but more vigorously when they do stir.
   d. they become sensitive to both sound and light after 2 weeks of gestation.

4. Babies
   a. are born sensitive to the range of frequencies of women's voices.
   b. have a relatively sensitive sense of smell.
   c. prefer the odor of a woman who is breast-feeding another infant to that of a women who is not breast-feeding.
   d. All of the above statements are true.

5. Compared to infants who sleep on their bellies, those who sleep on their backs
   a. have an increased chance of sudden infant death syndrome (SIDS).
   b. are more likely to crawl at an earlier age.
   c. are more likely to walk at an earlier age.
   d. are more likely to skip the step of crawling and go right to walking.

6. At the approximate age of 2 months, babies
   a. roll over, sit upright, and pick up small objects with the thumb and fingers.
   b. have slower heart rates when they are put on the "deep" side of the "visual cliff"
   c. turn pages of a book and "cruise" (walk by supporting their body against objects).
   d. All of the above statements are true.

7. Infants who are 3 months old
   a. cannot store information implicitly.
   b. cannot store information explicitly.
   c. have completed their perceptual development.
   d. can see three-dimensional shapes instead of isolated line fragments.

8. An example of an overregularization error children make is
   a. saying *runned* instead of *ran*.
   b. calling a sawhorse a "dog."

c. only referring to dogs with the word "animal."
d. leaving out words such as *the, a,* and *of.*

9. According to Piaget's theory of cognitive development, during the preoperational period,
   a. the child tends to be between 7 and 11 years old.
   b. the child is not capable of thinking about objects in their absence.
   c. language and symbolic play develop, but thought is still tied to perceived events.
   d. the child can reverse mental manipulations.

10. To be able to reason abstractly, Piaget said, the child must
    a. be capable of concrete operations.
    b. be capable of formal operations.
    c. be capable of egocentrism.
    d. not understand conservation.

11. In studies using the Strange Situation, babies with resistant attachment
    a. have periods of unresponsiveness along with spurts of sudden emotion at the beginning of the procedure.
    b. are equally comfortable with the mother and a stranger.
    c. may go so far as to hit the mother when she returns.
    d. calm down quickly when the mother returns.

12. Girls
    a. who are overweight tend to experience their first periods before those who are not overweight.
    b. who are overweight tend to experience their first periods after those who are not overweight.
    c. typically are shorter and lighter at age 11 than boys at that age because girls' major growth spurt starts about 2 years after that of boys.
    d. typically stop growing at around age 18.

13. There is a normal tendency for adolescents to
    a. have conflicts with their parents.
    b. experience extreme mood swings.
    c. be prone to taking risks.
    d. All of the above statements are true.

14. After age 50 or so,
    a. people tend to exhibit terminal decline.
    b. people perform all cognitive tasks substantially more slowly than do younger people.
    c. people have increased difficulty hearing high-frequency sounds.
    d. more than half the population has cataracts.

15. Costa and McCrae found that as adults age, dimensions of personality
    a. change dramatically, with very large differences.
    b. are more stable over time for men than they are for women.
    c. are more stable over time for women than they are for men.
    d. remain equally stable over time for men and women.

Answers: 1. a 2. d 3. c 4. d 5. d 6. b 7. d 8. a 9. c 10. b 11. c 12. a 13. d 14. c 15. d

> His new office was cramped, noisy, and generally unpleasant. He had trouble concentrating, and he knew his work was suffering, which made him even more concerned that he'd be fired.

STRESS, HEALTH, AND COPING

DEALING WITH LIFE

Lisa, a college sophomore, was becoming worried about her father, Al. He was only 54 years old, but he always seemed exhausted, regardless of the time of day or the amount of work he'd been doing. Whenever Lisa asked him why he was so tired, he answered in generalities: "Oh, work's crazy and I haven't slept enough. That's all, honey." He'd also been coughing a lot, and when Lisa asked about this, he'd reply, "I've been sick more than usual—it's just been a bad winter."

Lisa used to look forward to her visits home and her telephone conversations with her father, but now she dreaded talking to him because he always sounded so tired and dejected. Lisa suggested that he see his doctor, exercise, maybe learn some type of relaxation technique. Al finally told her the real reason he was so tense and tired: His company had laid off several of his colleagues, and he was afraid he'd be next. The layoffs meant that Al's department was now responsible for more work with fewer staff members. In addition, as part of the downsizing, the company had moved to smaller premises. His new office was cramped, noisy, and generally unpleasant. He had trouble concentrating and trouble sleeping, and he knew his work was suffering, which made him even more concerned that he'd be fired. There was a possibility of a job offer from another company, but at a substantially lower salary.

Lisa, listening to his story, understood that he had tried to protect her by not telling her. If he was fired or took the other job, he wouldn't be able to help with her college expenses, and she was already working 25 hours a week. If Al's fears materialized, she would probably have to leave school, at least for a while, or take out very large loans. He was worried about his own situation and worried about his daughter; Lisa understood the burden of those worries, which she now shared. She worried, too, about his persistent cough—was it just from lots of winter colds, or was it something more?

Al's situation produced stress in both father and daughter. Just what is "stress"? Can it affect our health? How can we deal with stress? Such questions—and the search for answers—are in the field of **health psychology,** the area of psychology concerned with the promotion of health and the prevention and treatment of illness as it relates to psychological factors.

◉ ◉ ◉

What Is Stress?

Often, as he worked at his desk, Al felt as if he'd just finished running a race—heart beating, palms sweating, breath coming hard—but without any accompanying sense of relief or accomplishment that comes with finishing a race. He was simply exhausted all of the time—partly because he didn't sleep well—and he felt as if his heart wasn't pumping his blood fast enough for his body's needs. He began to be seriously worried about his health as well as his ability to perform his job.

In contrast, Maya, a colleague who so far had also survived at the company, didn't seem to be stressed out by the changes happening around them. Maya had two children and, like Al, needed her job, but she seemed to be taking this difficult situation in stride. Al didn't understand how Maya was able to stay so calm—didn't she understand what was going on?

And what about Al's daughter's response to pressures? Lisa had been managing the demands of college and her job well, but after her father explained his situation at work and the possible repercussions for both of them, she noticed physical symptoms in herself—sweaty palms, racing heart—even while studying or taking class notes. Al and Lisa were responding to stress.

LOOKING AHEAD Learning Objectives

1. What exactly is stress?
2. What is the biology of stress?
3. What role does the perception of control play in stress?
4. What are common sources of stress?

Stress: The Big Picture

Today, even third graders complain of feeling "stressed out," and adults take courses to help them better "manage" their stress. To psychologists, **stress** is the general term that describes the psychological and physical response to a stimulus that alters the body's equilibrium (Lazarus & Folkman, 1984). A stimulus that throws the body's equilibrium out of balance is called a **stressor**; for instance, if you got a puncture wound after stepping on a piece of glass while walking barefoot, the puncture wound would be a stressor. Similarly, if you were walking down a dark alley at night and heard the sound of footsteps rapidly approaching behind you, you would probably interpret that sound as a potential threat—for example, a mugger—and so the footsteps would be a stressor. The bodily response to a stressor—be it physical or psychological—is the **stress response**, also called the *fight-or-flight response*; this response consists of the bodily changes that occur to help cope with the stressor. If you get a puncture wound (or some other injury), as part of the stress response your body may produce chemicals called *endorphins* and *enkephalins*, its own versions of painkillers, and cause white blood cells to congregate at the site of the injury to fight off infection. After the emergency has passed, the stress response works to reestablish *homeostasis*—which is the equilibrium of bodily processes that normally exists (such as adjusting the heart rate to be appropriate for the amount of blood that the brain and body normally require).

The list of possible stressors is long; psychologists classify stressors along a number of dimensions: As noted in Table 1, stressors can be short-term (**acute stressor**) or long-term (**chronic stressor**); the stimulus that is the stressor can be physical, psychological (which affect events at the level of the person), or social (or, of course, some combination, as in our example of a potential mugger—which involves events at all three levels of analysis). In general, specific physical stressors, such as not eating for 2 days, apply to most people, whereas it is an individual's *perception* of (that is, the way he or she organizes and interprets) a psychological or social stimulus that determines whether it will elicit the stress response, not necessarily the objective nature of the stimulus itself. For example, the identical sound of footsteps approaching will be interpreted differently in a dark alley at night versus in a hallway in a secured building when you are expecting the arrival of your coworker. Moreover, what constitutes psychological and social stressors can vary from person to person. Going to a dance club for hours can be a party animal's idea of a great time or a shy person's nightmare.

Health psychology The area of psychology concerned with the promotion of health and the prevention and treatment of illness as it relates to psychological factors.

Stress The general term that describes the psychological and physical response to a stimulus that alters the body's equilibrium.

Stressor A stimulus that throws the body's equilibrium out of balance.

Stress response The bodily response to a stressor that occurs to help a person cope with the stressor; also called the *fight-or-flight response*.

Acute stressor A stressor that has a short-term duration.

Chronic stressor A stressor that has a long-term duration.

TABLE 1 **Examples of Types of Stressors**

TYPE OF STRESSOR	DURATION OF STRESSOR	
	Acute	Chronic
Physical	Being injured in a car crash	Being underfed; having high blood pressure
Psychological (level of the person)	Being given a new assignment and informed that it must be completed by the next day—a tight deadline	At work, routinely feeling unable to meet the expectations of the job
Social	Being laughed at after making a serious comment at a meeting	Living in an overcrowded home or with someone who is physically or emotionally abusive

Stress is not always a bad thing, however. Stress—or more accurately, stressors—can also lead to positive change and growth (Linley & Joseph, 2004; Peterson et al., 2008). Consider that college students reported that their most stressful experience during the previous 6 months had led to their personal growth (Park & Fenster, 2004).

To understand more about stress, when it is good and bad, and how to cope with bad stress effectively, we first need to understand the biological underpinnings of stress.

FIGURE 1 Selye's Three-Stage Stress Response

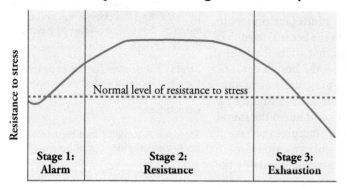

Stage 1: Alarm	Stage 2: Resistance	Stage 3: Exhaustion
The body mobilizes its resources to fight or flee.	The body mobilizes its resources to achieve homeostasis in the presence of the stressor.	Continued efforts to achieve homeostasis lead to exhaustion and damage of the body.

Time

Hans Selye proposed that the body's response to prolonged stress has three stages: alarm, resistance, and exhaustion.

Source: from *The Stress of Life*, 2nd ed., by Hans Selye, p. 476, 1976. New York: McGraw Hill. Reprinted by permission of The McGraw Hill Companies, Inc.

The Biology of Stress

The modern scientific study of stress began in earnest when Austrian-born researcher Hans Selye (1907–1982) established that the brain and body generally respond to stressors in predictable ways (Selye, 1976). He called the overall stress response the **general adaptation syndrome (GAS)** and made the case that it has three distinct phases: *alarm*, *resistance*, and *exhaustion* (Figure 1).

The Alarm Phase: Fight or Flight

The **alarm phase** consists of perceiving a stressor, which then triggers the fight-or-flight response. As we noted earlier, the perceived stressor might be a physical threat, such as a piece of glass stuck in the foot; a psychological one, such as working against a deadline; or a social one, such as a conflict with another person. As part of the fight-or-flight response, the body is mobilized to fight or to flee from the stressor.

The bodily mobilization during the alarm phase—after you perceive a threat—consists of a cascade of the following events:

1. A set of brain areas, referred to as the *hypothalamic-pituitary-adrenal axis* (the HPA axis), responds to the threat by doing the following:

    a. Initiating the release of a group of hormones called **glucocorticoids**. *Cortisol*, the most important glucocorticoid, both increases the production of energy from glucose and has an anti-inflammatory effect that helps restore the body's equilibrium after physical injury. Cortisol also affects neurotransmitter functioning, and thus it can affect cognition and emotion (Erickson et al., 2003), which may account for the common experience of increased alertness and the ability to put emotions aside when confronted by an acute and severe stressor (Reuter, 2002).

    b. Activating the sympathetic nervous system (and inhibiting the parasympathetic nervous system).

2. The sympathetic nervous system in turn releases certain neurotransmitters and hormones, such as epinephrine and norepinephrine (also referred to as adrenaline and noradrenaline, respectively).

3. Epinephrine and norepinephrine then cause changes in the body that make strenuous physical activity easier. Specifically, these chemicals help the body to fight the (perceived) threat or to flee from it. These changes: (a) affect heart rate (to pump more blood to the muscles); (b) affect breathing (to put more oxygen in the blood); (c) cause the pupils to dilate (to allow more light to enter for better vision); and, (d) cause the palms to sweat slightly (for better gripping). The cascade of neurotransmitters and hormones can also alter immune system functioning (Madden, 2003), as we discuss later in this chapter.

In the short run, all of the changes brought about by the stress response sharpen the senses, improve some qualities of memory (Sapolsky, 1997), and make it easier to fight or flee. Although the stress response occurs with all stressors, the speed of its action and the amount of each hormone that is produced can differ, depending on the particular type of stressor (Goldstein, 1995; Henry, 1977; Pacak & Palkovits, 2001; Romero & Sapolsky, 1996).

Bodily changes that are part of the fight-or-flight response may have worked well for our distant ancestors (for whom many, if not most, threats required immediate physical action, such as fighting or fleeing a hungry bear), but most of us now rarely experience such threats. Taking a final exam requires sitting in a chair, not running or climbing away from an enemy. Nonetheless, our bodies may still react to the test-taking situation with the fight-or-flight response; we can get all revved up but with nowhere to go. Thus, the

General adaptation syndrome (GAS) The overall stress response that has three phases: alarm, resistance, and exhaustion.

Alarm phase The first phase of the GAS, in which a stressor is perceived and the fight-or-flight response is activated.

Glucocorticoids A group of hormones that are released when the stress response is triggered.

stress response can be distracting and can actually interfere with successful coping in many situations.

If the stressor is quickly addressed and is no longer a threat, the effects of the stress response will ebb, and the body will return to its normal state; however, if the stressor is not eliminated, various bodily processes arise as part of the next two phases of the response. ((•─Listen

((•─Listen to the Podcast General Adaptation Syndrome on mypsychlab.com

The Resistance Phase If the stressor—the threat—continues (for instance, if running behind the tree didn't solve your problem with the bear), the brain and body mobilize resources to adapt to the continued presence of the stressor. The resulting changes in your body are collectively referred to as the **resistance phase** (also known as the *adaptation phase* because the brain and body are adapting to the new situation).

During the resistance phase, various bodily functions are disrupted. In particular, digestion, growth, sex drive, and reproductive processes are slowed. In women, menstruation may stop or may occur irregularly; in men, sperm and testosterone levels may decrease. These changes make sense as a matter of survival: Why waste energy on these processes when it is needed elsewhere? This is especially important because no new energy is stored during the stress response—which means that chronic stress leads to a lack of any reserve of energy to repair bodily damage, producing a sense of fatigue.

In addition, during the resistance phase, cortisol is produced, which helps the body return to a more normal state despite the stressor (McEwen & Schmeck, 1994). The more extreme the stressor, the more cortisol is produced. Cortisol levels reach their peak within 20 to 40 minutes after the onset of the acute stressor, and they generally return to their normal levels up to 1 hour after the acute stressor is gone (Dickerson & Kemeny, 2002). However, if the stressor is chronic, cortisol levels may not return to normal levels. And if cortisol levels remain high, they can damage the brain during the final phase of the response, the *exhaustion phase*—which we discuss next.

The Exhaustion Phase Selye proposed that, with a sustained stressor, the body eventually becomes exhausted because its limited resources for dealing with stress are depleted; Selye thus called the final phase of the GAS the *exhaustion phase*. However, more recent research has found that during the **exhaustion phase**, the continued stress response begins to damage the body, leading to an increased risk of stress-related diseases—medical problems and conditions that are exacerbated by stress—such as high blood pressure and some digestive problems. (Thus, the final phase of the GAS is misnamed; a more accurate name might be the *damage phase*.)

Only in the past couple of decades have scientists discovered that the exhaustion phase can also damage the brain. Specifically, continued release of cortisol can damage the hippocampus, decreasing the number of neurons as well as the amount of branching of some of their dendrites (McEwen, 2003). Such changes impair learning and memory (Newcomer et al., 1999; Sapolsky, 1992).

From Stressor to Allostatic Load: Multiple Stressors and Their Time Course The term *allostasis* (from the Greek *allo*, meaning "other," and *stasis*, meaning "stability") refers to the multiple biological changes that allow you to adapt to a stressor or a set of stressors in the short run so that your body functions within a comfortable range. However, the biological changes necessary to maintain homeostasis within a comfortable range have a cost—the cumulative wear and tear on the body necessary to maintain homeostasis in the face of stressors, referred to as the **allostatic load** (McEwen, 1998, 2000; McEwen & Wingfield, 2003). As the number or intensity of stressors rises, so does the allostatic load.

Here's an analogy: Say you have a wooden seesaw of the sort you see in playgrounds the world over. If two 40-pound children are on it—one on each side—it's in balance, and there's relatively little load. But what if two 400-pound gorillas were to sit on the ends? Although the seesaw could still be in balance, it would be under much greater stress. And just as the probability that the seesaw will break increases when it is put under greater stress, so too with the body; greater allostatic load increases the risk of medical and psychological problems (Goldstein & McEwen, 2002).

Resistance phase The second phase of the GAS, in which the body mobilizes its resources to adapt to the continued presence of the stressor; also called the *adaptation phase*.

Exhaustion phase The final stage of the GAS, in which the continued stress response itself becomes damaging to the body.

Allostatic load The cumulative wear and tear on the body necessary to maintain homeostasis in the face of stressors.

When you must fight or flee, more demands are made on your body than during calmer times; chronic demands (leading to high allostatic load) will produce biological wear and tear, reduce the brain and body's ability to respond appropriately, and possibly lead to disease or illness (Karlamangla et al., 2002; T. E. Seeman et al., 1997). And just as the seesaw would be in greater jeopardy if those gorillas played on it for an hour instead of a minute, chronic stressors take more toll on your body than do time-limited stressors (Evans, 2003).

It's How You Think of It: Interpreting Stimuli as Stressors

We've noted several times that it is the *perception* of a stimulus or an event that determines whether the event is a stressor; many psychological, social, and even physical stimuli are stressors only if you perceive them to be stressful (Lazarus & Folkman, 1984). Consider these questions: Is a new relationship stressful? How about writing a term paper? Hearing a baby cry? Being stuck in a traffic jam? The answer to all of these is maybe, maybe not—it depends on how you perceive each of these stimuli. In this section, we examine more about how an individual's perception of stimuli helps to determine whether they function as stressors.

Appraisal: Stressors in the Eyes of the Beholder The subjective and varying nature of stressors is particularly evident for psychological and social stimuli. For instance, Al's colleague Maya is not bothered about the recent firings because she wants to spend more time with her children. In some respects, she wouldn't mind being out of work—and collecting unemployment—so that she could stay home for a while; between savings and her husband's paycheck, the family could get by for a few months. So, for Maya—unlike for Al—the threat of being fired does not function as a stressor (at least not at the moment; after her children are grown and some of her salary goes to pay the bulk of her children's college tuition bills, she might feel differently).

In contrast to psychological and social stressors, physical stressors tend to be more objectively defined; for instance, most people would find having a piece of glass stuck in their foot a stressor. However, even with a physical stimulus, the individual's perception of it can determine whether it is a stressor: You might not view having a needle plunged into your skin as a stressor if this experience were part of acupuncture treatment for pain.

The importance of the role perception in determining whether a stimulus is a stressor was demonstrated in a classic study by Joseph Speisman and colleagues (1964); the results of this study demonstrated that varying how a film was perceived could alter the degree to which participants experienced the stress response. In this study, the participants were asked to watch a silent black-and-white film of an Aboriginal tribal ritual in which tribal elders use stones to make crude genital incisions on teenage boys. Participants in one group heard a "trauma" soundtrack for the film in which the narrator emphasized the pain experienced by the teens undergoing the rite. Another group heard a "denial" soundtrack, in which the narrator emphasized the positive aspects of the ritual and minimized the experience of pain. A third group heard an "intellectualization" soundtrack, in which the narrator described the ceremony in a detached, clinical manner. Participants in either the denial or the intellectualization group had less of a stress response to the film and reported being less upset than those in the trauma group—in spite of the fact that all participants viewed the same video (but not audio) portion of the film.

Even among college students, what is considered stressful differs, depending on whether the student is traditional (went to college straight from high school) or nontraditional (took some time off between high school and college, or has multiple roles, such as student and parent or employee). Social activities have a larger impact on traditional students, whereas nontraditional students are more likely to enjoy doing homework and going to classes and to worry less about how they are doing academically (Dill & Henley, 1998).

Source: PhotoEdit Inc.

A two-stage process, referred to as *cognitive appraisal* (see Figure 2), leads psychological and social (and sometimes physical) stimuli to function as stressors:

1. You assess a stimulus for the likelihood of danger; this stage is called the *primary appraisal*.

2. Then you determine the resources you have to deal with the stimulus; this stage is called the *secondary appraisal*.

FIGURE 2 Cognitive Appraisal of a Stimulus

Cognitive appraisal of a stimulus, in this case a snake, is a two-stage process: (1) determining whether a stimulus is dangerous and, if so, (2) determining what can be done to prevent or minimize the danger.

In other words, the question "Am I in danger?" (primary appraisal) is followed by the question "What can I do about it?" (secondary appraisal) (Bishop, 1994). (Note that such appraisals can happen without conscious awareness; Smith & Kirby, 2000.) After the secondary appraisal, assuming that the stimulus *is* a stressor, comes **coping**—namely, taking action to address a stressor or to counteract effects of a stressor.

Depending on your cognitive appraisal of a stimulus, you will experience different emotions, and your body will react in different ways (Maier et al., 2003). For instance, should you determine that you have the resources—emotional, financial, and/or practical—to cope with a stressor, you will likely treat the stressor as a challenge, not a threat. In contrast, should you determine that you do not have the resources to cope, you probably will treat the stressor as a threat (Blascovich & Tomaka, 1996). Consider: If you lost your cell phone but have insurance that covers the entire cost of a new one and it's convenient for you to pick up a new phone, you're not likely to experience the lost phone as a big deal—and so you are unlikely to have a stress response. In contrast, if you don't have phone insurance, you're almost broke, it's a huge hassle to get a new phone and you need to have a phone, you're likely to have a stress response.

In addition, when your cognitive appraisal leads you to conclude that a stimulus is a threat, you're also likely to have negative emotions—and these emotions then become a part of the problem that you must address (Folkman & Moskowitz, 2004). So, in addition to losing your cell phone and not being able to replace it, you'll also have to manage whatever emotions you experience: frustration, anxiety, guilt, and/or anger.

Perceived Control In some cases, your perception of whether you can control a stimulus determines whether it functions as a stressor. Ask yourself these questions: How would you feel if your boss regularly changed the start time and end time of your work shifts (and you really need the job, so you can't quit)? Do you think you would experience less stress if *you* had decided to make the same changes to your start and end times? What if your boss, unbeknownst to you, had actually made the decision about the changes but gave you the impression that you controlled the changes—for instance, saying that you had requested these changes weeks ago? Even though the schedule changes are the same in all of these cases, if you're like most people, you'd probably feel less stress if you were

THINK like a PSYCHOLOGIST Think of a recent occasion when you felt "stressed"; during primary appraisal, what was the stimulus that you determined was the stressor? During secondary appraisal, what resources did you identify to help you manage the stressor? To assess your cognitive appraisals more systematically, use the Cognitive Appraisal Log at www.mypsychlab.com; select the *Stress, Health, and Coping* chapter and click on the *DO IT!* folder.

Coping Taking action to address a stressor or to counteract effects of a stressor.

Cultural factors can affect people's perception of control. Western cultures, particularly that of the United States, emphasize active control of yourself and mastery of your environment. Some other cultures emphasize adaptation—accepting yourself and your circumstances (Shapiro et al., 1996), such as when a train is very late.

Source: The Image Works

the one who made the decision—or if you simply believed that you had made the decision. In fact, research has shown that actual control is not important; what is important is whether you perceive a sense of control (Shapiro et al., 1996). Perceiving that you don't have control over a stimulus can turn that stimulus into a stressor.

Moreover, when you perceive that you don't have control over the stressor, you may give up trying to cope actively with it. For example, in one classic study, caged animals could not escape being shocked. At first they jumped and tried to get out of their cages. But after a while, when these efforts failed to relieve the shocks, the animals gave up and huddled in their cages, enduring the shocks. And they continued to huddle and endure even after the cages were opened, so they could have escaped. This phenomenon is called *learned helplessness* (Overmeier, 2002). Learned helplessness may be analogous to the depressive response in humans that arises when we feel unable to control or escape from an aversive situation; for instance, some victims of domestic abuse perceive that they cannot control the abuse and at the same time feel that they cannot escape the situation—and as a result, they give up trying to cope actively and simply try to endure.

Stress does not arise only because an event is beyond our control; it may also arise because an aversive event is unpredictable. For example, you have no control over whether you take the math quizzes your professor hands out (at least, not if you want to pass the course), but you'll probably find that announced quizzes are less stressful than surprise quizzes. If quizzes are announced, you can relax—at least about math quizzes—on the days when none are scheduled; in contrast, the possibility of surprise quizzes means that you may feel stressed (and have a stress response) at the beginning of every math class as you wait to learn your fate. However, if surprise quizzes are a frequent occurrence in a course, they will no longer be so unpredictable, and so you will not view them to be as great a stressor—even though you might nonetheless view them as unpleasant.

Sources of Stress

Although the specific stimuli that function as stressors vary from person to person, certain types of psychological and social stimuli generally are likely to lead all of us to have a stress response. In particular, we will tend to feel stress when stimuli lead to *internal conflict* or *frequent daily hassles*. In the sections that follow, we examine these types of psychological and social events and how they can lead to stress.

Internal Conflict
Stress can be caused by **internal conflict**, which is the emotional predicament that people experience when they make difficult choices. That is, even when people can control upcoming events in their lives, that control brings with it choices that can cause stress. And stress-inducing choices—such as who you should live with next year, which job you should take, or whether to break up with your romantic partner—may involve competing goals, actions, impulses, or situations, which in turn lead to internal conflict. Internal conflict can be classified according to three categories (N. E. Miller, 1959), depending on whether each choice is desirable or undesirable:

Internal conflict The emotional predicament that people experience when making difficult choices.

Approach–approach conflict The internal conflict that occurs when competing alternatives are equally positive.

1. **Approach–approach conflict** arises when competing alternatives are equally positive. Although this kind of conflict can be stressful, it is not necessarily experienced as unpleasant because both options are pleasing. For instance, if you had to choose between two very good job offers and wanted both jobs about equally, you would be facing an approach–approach conflict. Even such happy circumstances can lead to stress (a fact often overlooked).

2. **Avoidance–avoidance conflict** arises when competing alternatives are equally unpleasant. In such circumstances, making a choice can be very stressful. For instance, faced with the choice of either taking a job you really don't want or being unemployed (but needing to pay back college loans), you would experience an avoidance–avoidance conflict.

3. **Approach–avoidance conflict** arises when a single possible course of action has both positive and negative aspects and thus produces *both* approach *and* avoidance. If you are offered a job that you want but it would require you to move to a city in which you don't want to live, you would experience approach–avoidance conflict.

Thus, although you have control over the stimulus, or perceive that you do, you can nonetheless experience having to make a choice as a stressor.

Avoidance–avoidance conflict The internal conflict that occurs when competing alternatives are equally unpleasant.

Approach–avoidance conflict The internal conflict that occurs when a course of action has both positive and negative aspects.

Life's Hassles Stress can also arise from *daily hassles*—which are the "little things" and ongoing concerns that plague daily life, such as worrying about the health of someone in your family, having too many things to do and keep track of, and trying to lose weight. Although each hassle, on its own, may be minor, together they can increase allostatic load and create stress (McIntyre et al., 2008).

If we think of frequent daily hassles as lots of small weights added to the allostatic seesaw, the total "weight" of daily hassles may be more than that of the heavy gorillas, and this "weight" on the seesaw is chronic because the hassles occur regularly. The effects of such increased allostatic load are wide ranging: For example, researchers have found that people who report more daily hassles also report more psychological problems (D'Angelo & Wierzbicki, 2003; Kanner et al., 1981; Mroczek & Almeida, 2004) and more physical symptoms (DeLongis et al., 1982), and they are likely to have higher cholesterol levels (Twisk et al., 1999) and problems with their immune system (Bosch et al., 1998; Martin & Dobbin, 1988; M. L. Peters et al., 2003).

Life's daily hassles—such as waiting in lines—can be significant stressors, leading to psychological and physical symptoms.

Source: PhotoEdit Inc.

Some daily hassles may seem so minor that it's difficult to appreciate that they contribute to stress. For example, simply being interrupted while engrossed in a task can increase stress (which is different than being interrupted when you are procrastinating, when you may welcome a knock on the door, the ping of a text message or email, or the ring of your phone). Think of how you feel when you're engrossed in studying or writing a paper and are repeatedly interrupted by visitors or by phone calls (even if you don't take the call, you may stop what you're doing to check who the call is from). If your reaction is to feel more "stressed out," you're not alone. Interruptions during a mentally challenging task can be stressful enough to cause large increases in cortisol levels (Earle et al., 1999; Suarez et al., 1998). Note that email "interruptions" may not feel as stressful because you choose—that is, control—when to check your email.

THINK like a **PSYCHOLOGIST** When you're concentrating on a task (for instance, writing a paper or studying for a test), what type of interruptions do you find most annoying? How might you go about decreasing that type of interruption or at least minimizing how much such interruptions intrude into your awareness (and thereby decrease your allostatic load)?

✓●⎯ **Study** and **Review** on **mypsychlab.com**

LOOKING BACK

1. **What exactly is stress?** Stress is the general term that describes the psychological and physical response to a stimulus that alters the body's equilibrium. A stressor is a stimulus that throws the body's equilibrium out of balance. Stressors can be acute or chronic in duration and physical, psychological, or social in nature.

2. **What is the biology of stress?** The stress response consists of changes in the activity of the HPA axis and the sympathetic and parasympathetic nervous systems that prepare the body for physical effort and repair injury. These include changes in heart and respiration rates and the release of epinephrine, norepinephrine, and glucocorticoids. These changes occur during the alarm phase of the general adaptation syndrome (GAS). If the stressor continues, the body tries to attain homeostasis during the resistance (adaptation) phase. During the exhaustion phase, the stress response itself begins to cause damage, leading to a risk of stress-related diseases.

3. **What role does the perception of control play in stress?** An individual's cognitive appraisal of a given stimulus determines whether he or she will perceive the stimulus as a stressor, and thus whether the stress response will occur. However, in general, some stimuli are more likely function as stressors than are others. A perceived lack of control over the stimulus can lead to higher levels of stress.

4. **What are common sources of stress?** Factors that are likely to lead to a stress response include unpredictability, internal conflict, and daily hassles.

Stress, Disease, and Sleep

Al was clearly experiencing a great deal of stress, and his being sick so often only made matters worse. He'd had to miss work some days, which didn't help his sense of control over his situation. Sometimes he'd cough so much that he would have trouble sleeping, and then he'd lie awake worrying that he had lung cancer. He had started smoking again, after having quit 5 years before, so it was hard to know whether he was coughing from the cigarettes or whether he had picked up a respiratory illness. He'd been having a few more drinks than usual, too, and he stopped exercising because he felt he didn't have the time or the energy. He also worried that if he resumed exercising, he'd bring on a heart attack. In short, Al wasn't doing very well, and he knew it.

The stress response is a good thing, very useful when the stressor is acute, such as a piece of glass in the foot. But too strong a stress response for too long a time—too great a chronic allostatic load—can lead to stress-related illness.

LOOKING AHEAD Learning Objectives

1. How can stress affect the immune system and make illness more likely?
2. Are stress and cancer related?
3. Can stress cause a heart attack or heart disease?
4. What is the relationship between sleep and stress?

The Immune System: Catching Cold

We've already mentioned that stress—and the body's response to it—adversely affects the immune system, but how does it do this? In order to understand the relationship between stress and the immune system, we first need to examine how the immune system functions generally.

The *immune system* defends the body against infection and disease. Critical to the immune system are two classes of white blood cells: **B cells**, which mature in the bone marrow ("B" is for bone marrow), and **T cells**, which mature in the thymus ("T" is for thymus), an organ located in the chest. One type of T cell is the **natural killer (NK) cell**, which detects and destroys damaged or altered cells, such as precancerous cells before they become tumors.

Here is a key piece of information: Glucocorticoids (which are released when the stress response is triggered) hinder the formation of NK cells and some other types of white blood cells and kill yet other types of white blood cells (Cohen & Herbert, 1996; McEwen et al., 1997). In turn, the body becomes more vulnerable to infection and tumor growth.

Because of the effect of glucocorticoids on white blood cells, many studies that investigate the relationship between stress and the immune system measure the number of circulating white blood cells, such as NK cells. People who exhibit greater sympathetic nervous system responses to stress also have the most changes in immune system functioning (Bachen et al., 1995; Manuck et al., 1991); this relationship indicates that changes in the immune system are moderated by changes in the sympathetic nervous system.

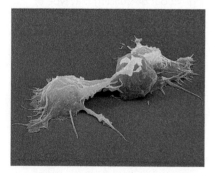

The release of glucocorticoids (as occurs during stress) suppresses the functioning of the immune system, making it more difficult for the body to fight the invaders and leaving the body more vulnerable to infection. This photo shows two natural killer (NK) cells (yellow) attacking a leukemia cell (red). The NK cells have made contact and are beginning to engulf and destroy the leukemia cell.

Source: © Eye of Science/Photo Researchers, Inc.

Thoughts and feelings—our expectations, motives, and emotions—also affect our immune systems; the field of study that focuses on the ways in which thoughts and feelings affect the immune system is called *psychoneuroimmunology*. Researchers in this field have uncovered fascinating examples of how people's psychological states affect their health. For example, it turns out that traditional elderly Chinese who are ill are more likely to die right after the Harvest Moon festival, an important event in their culture, than just before it, whereas orthodox Jews show no difference in mortality rates during this period of time. However, the pattern is exactly reversed among ill, religious elderly Jews around the time of the Jewish High Holy Days (the most important days in the Jewish calendar): These Jews are more likely hold on to life until the holidays are over, and the elderly Chinese are unaffected during those dates (D. P. Phillips & Smith, 1990; D. P. Phillips et al., 1992). What do these findings have to do with the immune system? Researchers theorize that the sick, elderly people "make it through" their important holiday because the importance of their holiday to them in turns leads their brains to boost the immune system, allowing it to fight off more effectively whatever ailment is killing them; after the holiday is over, when their motivation and will to live ebb, the illness—and the stress of living with it—takes its toll on the immune system.

Psychoneuroimmunology researchers have also investigated how psychological states affect the immune system in another way: Because stress can impair the functioning of the white blood cells, it can play a role in the length of time it takes a wound to heal. Research reveals that the wounds of women who experienced a high level of stress by caring for a relative with Alzheimer's disease (a progressive disease in which sufferers gradually lose their memory and control over their bodies) took 9 days longer to heal than the wounds of

women of similar age and economic status who were not engaged in such caregiving (Kiecolt-Glaser et al., 1995). In another study, dental student participants received slight mouth wounds on two different occasions (3 days before a major test and during summer vacation). The wounds given before exams, when, presumably, the students were experiencing more stress, took 40% longer to heal (Marucha et al., 1998). Moreover, stress can increase the risk of infection after receiving a wound (Rojas et al., 2002).

It isn't only daily stressors that affect the immune system; traumatic stressors such as surviving a disaster (a devastating earthquake or hurricane) or being victimized (as occurs when robbed or raped) can similarly impair the immune system. However, as we noted when we discussed cognitive appraisal, the perception of the severity of the stressor—not its objective characteristics—determines the body's response. For example, among people living in Florida who sustained equivalent losses from Hurricane Andrew in 1992, those who perceived their losses to be more severe had fewer NK cells than those who perceived their losses to be less severe (Ironson et al., 1997).

Traumatic events, such as experiencing the devastation of a hurricane, can produce psychological symptoms, such as anxiety and depression, and also impair the immune system.

Source: © Jason Reed/Reuters / CORBIS All Rights Reserved

B cell A type of white blood cell that matures in the bone marrow.

T cell A type of white blood cell that matures in the thymus.

Natural killer (NK) cell A type of T cell that detects and destroys damaged or altered cells, such as precancerous cells.

Stress and Cancer

Although stress doesn't cause cancer, the effect of stress on the immune system can affect the growth of some cancerous tumors. How can this happen? One way that stress is associated with at least some types of cancers is that when the immune system is suppressed, NK cells do not work as well to prevent the spread of tumor cells. For instance, lower levels of NK cell activity were found in people who perceived that they didn't have enough social support and who felt distressed, fatigued, and little joy (Levy et al., 1985, 1987, 1988; Varker et al., 2007). Such negative psychological experiences in turn can weaken the immune system, thereby leaving people more vulnerable to the growth of cancerous tumors.

Atherosclerosis A medical condition characterized by the buildup of plaque on the inside walls of the arteries.

Although stress can affect the immune system, these findings should be interpreted with caution. With certain types of cancer and with specific biological factors related to the progression of the disease, psychological factors affect tumor growth much less—if at all (Compas et al., 1998; Grossarth-Maticek et al., 2000)—especially in the final stages of the disease (Cohen & Herbert, 1996). Moreover, some people apparently have immune systems that function either so well or so poorly that psychological factors do not affect them very much. Such differences in the immune system arise in part from genes: Data on twins reared together and apart suggest that, on average, identical twins have more key antibodies in common (seven out of a possible nine) than do fraternal twins (four out of a possible nine) (Kohler et al., 1985).

Stress and Heart Disease

Stress can also lead, indirectly, to heart disease. Let's examine how.

How Stress Affects the Heart

By inducing the fight-or-flight response, chronic stress can increase blood pressure, which in turn promotes **atherosclerosis**: The buildup of plaque (fatty deposits, composed of cholesterol and other substances) on the inside walls of the arteries (Figure 3). Here's how it works:

1. Increased blood pressure creates a pounding on the artery walls and causes damage to the walls.

2. As the body tries to repair the damage, the damaged spots become a place where plaques accumulate and harden (leading to *hardening of the arteries*).

3. Accumulating plaques cause the arteries to narrow—which makes the heart have to work even harder to meet the body's need for nutrients and oxygen. Working harder means pumping the blood with more power, creating more damage to the arteries, and a vicious cycle is created.

FIGURE 3 Stress on the Arteries

CUT SECTION THROUGH BRANCHING ARTERY

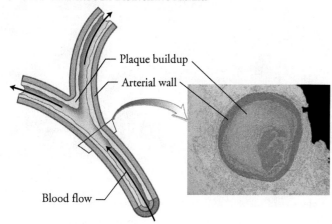

Plaque buildup
Arterial wall
Blood flow

Stressors increase heart rate and blood pressure by activating the sympathetic nervous system, and also cause hormones to be released during the fight-or-flight response; these hormones cause blood vessels to constrict, which has the net effect of increasing blood pressure even more. And when blood pressure increases, the branching points of arteries are at risk for damage. With rapidly increased blood pressure, the circulating blood can create a slight tear of the arterial wall, creating a place for plaque to attach itself to the artery wall. Once this occurs, the artery gets narrower and narrower (as plaque builds and builds). This atherosclerosis makes the work of pumping blood through the body even harder for the heart and can lead to a heart attack or stroke.

This chronic wear and tear on the cardiovascular system can lead to heart damage, which can lead to sudden death from inadequate blood supply to the heart muscle or from irregular electrical firing of the muscle, preventing coordinated heartbeats.

In addition, stress can have negative effects for people who have atherosclerosis. When a person who has atherosclerosis experiences a strong stressor, his or her body's response may cause a piece of plaque to break off (Strike et al., 2004). The loosened plaque may then block an artery going to the heart, preventing or limiting blood flow to that organ, which leads to a heart attack. Similarly, the loosened plaque may block the blood supply to the brain, which leads to a *stroke*, which occurs when brain cells die because they don't get enough oxygen. For someone who already has heart disease, even extremely positive states of stress—such as joy or orgasm—can precipitate a stroke and cause sudden death.

Some people, perhaps because of a history of heart disease or an overly responsive HPA axis, are more vulnerable to calamitous aftereffects of stress. For these people, even relatively small amounts of stress can increase the risk of a heart attack; for example, for such a person, working under a tight deadline can increase the risk of heart attack (Moller et al., 2005), as can being stuck in traffic (Peters et al., 2004).

Stress, Emotions, and Heart Disease

Researchers have found that heart disease is more likely to arise when stress is accompanied by negative emotions—such as fear, anger, sadness, and helplessness—than when it is accompanied by positive emotions.

Negative emotions can produce a rise in heart rate that lasts longer than does the rise following positive emotions (Brosschot & Thayer, 2003). When the stressors are chronic, they can lead to helplessness, depression, and despair.

DEPRESSION AND HEART DISEASE.   One particular negative emotion that is associated with a greater likelihood of heart disease is depression (Barth et al., 2004; Ferketich et al., 2000; Kiecolt-Glaser & Glaser, 2002; Rosengren et al., 2004). People who have had an episode of depression have a higher risk of developing heart problems, and once having had a heart attack, those who are depressed are more likely to have further health problems (Cuomo, 2009; Frasure-Smith et al., 1999; Parker et al., 2009). Indeed, depressed people have a faster heartbeat even when they are at rest (Moser et al., 1998), and they tend to have high blood pressure (Carney et al., 1999). When the depression is treated, however, these stress-related responses subside, and heart rate and blood pressure decrease (Kolata, 1997).

ANXIETY, FEAR, AND HEART DISEASE.   Other emotions, notably anxiety and fear, are also associated with heart disease (Goodwin et al., 2009; Kubzansky & Kawachi, 2000). Scientists don't yet know with certainty why these emotions are linked to heart disease, but one possibility is that some people may cope with their anxieties and fears by engaging in unhealthy behaviors, such as smoking or drinking. A second possibility is that the biological changes that arise with recurrent or chronic anxiety and fear—such as increased blood pressure—affect the heart or circulatory system adversely (Geiser et al., 2008).

HOSTILITY AND HEART DISEASE.   Some people seem to experience stress more than others, regardless of their environment or circumstances. At one point, researchers believed that people with "Type A" personalities were prone to stress and heart disease (Hecker et al., 1988), but it turned out that the most important component of the so-called Type A personality in predicting heart disease is **hostility**, a personality trait characterized by mistrust, expecting to be harmed or provoked by others, and having a cynical attitude (Hart & Hope, 2004; Knox et al., 2004; Kop, 2003; T. Q. Miller et al., 1996). For instance, investigators found that medical students who scored in the top 20% on a hostility scale were more than four times as likely to develop heart disease 25 years later than were their low-hostility peers. Those same high-hostility doctors were seven times more likely than their low-hostility peers to die of any cause by age 50 (Barefoot et al., 1983). Further research found similar results among lawyers: Those most likely to die at a younger age were more hostile—they were likely to have a cynical, mistrustful view of people, to experience negative emotions in personal interactions, and to express anger and aggression overtly in the face of difficulties or frustration (Barefoot et al., 1989).

Hostile people are more likely to perceive stressors in situations in which nonhostile people do not perceive stressors (Hardy & Smith, 1988; Suarez & Williams, 1989).

Source: © Getty Images/image100

The negative effects of having a lot of hostility may arise because such people have a relatively high heart rate and high blood pressure throughout the day, no matter what their mood; in contrast, people low in hostility have cardiac changes only when they are in a negative mood (Davis et al., 2000; Räikkönen et al., 1999). The high heart rate and blood pressure for males who have a lot of hostility become even more extreme when these men are interrupted while concentrating on a task—in one study, such interruptions led highly hostile men to have elevated heart rates, blood pressure, and cortisol production (as well as exhibiting other changes associated with a negative mood, such as anger) compared to men low in hostility (Suarez et al., 1998). Moreover, researchers have also found that men are higher in hostility than women (G. E. Miller et al., 1999; Räikkönen et al., 1999) and that men's blood pressure is more affected by their hostility than is women's (Räikkönen et al., 1999).

Hostility The personality trait associated with heart disease and characterized by mistrust, an expectation of harm and provocation by others, and a cynical attitude.

Lifestyle Can Make a Difference The good news is that treatment programs for people high in hostility can help reduce hostility (Beck & Fernandez, 1998), anger (DiGiuseppe & Tafrate, 2003), and their anger-related stress responses and blood pressure increases (Gidron et al., 1999). Another bit of good news is that people can counter the effects of stress on heart disease by changing their lifestyles. A study of people with severe heart disease found that intensive changes in diet, exercise, and social support, as well as the use of stress management techniques (such as meditation) helped to halt the narrowing of the arteries and in some cases even reversed the atherosclerosis and minimized further damage to the heart (Ornish et al., 1998). Other studies confirm the positive effects of such intensive lifestyle changes (Lisspers et al., 2005).

In sum, although stressors can induce negative emotions and lay the groundwork for heart disease (through increased blood pressure and plaques), various lifestyle changes can reduce the effects of stressors.

Sleep

Al was having a difficult time sleeping, and it wasn't only because of his cough. Even after a bout of coughing stopped, he would often remain awake; he'd feel tired but be unable to fall asleep. Some of those times he'd be worrying, but other times he wasn't and he desperately wanted to fall asleep. It could take hours until he'd nod off. Or he'd fall asleep but wake up hours before his alarm and be unable to go back to sleep. What was going on? Could stress be affecting his sleep? Yes, stress and health problems can prevent Al—and the rest of us—from getting a good night's sleep. In addition, not getting enough sleep— experiencing *sleep deprivation*—can affect health and the ability to cope. To understand the relationships between sleep, stress, and psychological functioning, we need to know more about sleep.

Stages of Sleep: Working Through the Night
Sleep, the naturally recurring experience during which normal consciousness is suspended, is not a single state. Rather, the electroencephalograph (which creates recordings of brain activity called *electroencephalograms,* or EEGs) has revealed several different types of sleep. Moreover, these types of sleep occur in five stages during the night, and these stages cycle throughout the night (Hobson, 1995). Everyone proceeds through these stages, but people differ in how much time they spend in each stage (Anch et al., 1988).

STAGE 1. The initial sleep stage, sometimes referred to as **hypnogogic sleep,** marks the transition from relaxed wakefulness to sleep and lasts approximately 5 minutes. When you are in Stage 1 sleep, your breathing becomes deeper and more regular, and the EEG registers brain waves that are less regular and of lower amplitude (height of the wave) than those that mark the waking state (see Figure 4). You can be awakened relatively easily from Stage 1 sleep, and if you are, you do not feel as if you have been asleep at all. When in this stage, you may experience a gentle falling or floating sensation, or your body may jerk suddenly and rather violently in a movement called a *hypnic jerk*.

STAGE 2. Once you are clearly asleep, your EEG pattern begins to record *sleep spindles*— brief bursts of brain activity (see Figure 4)—and single high-amplitude waves. You are now more relaxed and less responsive to your environment, although it's still relatively easy for others to wake you. If you are awakened during this stage, you will most likely report that you have been asleep. This stage lasts for approximately 20 minutes.

STAGES 3 AND 4. Stages 3 and 4 are sometimes referred to collectively as *slow-wave sleep* (SWS) because your brain produces *delta waves*—recorded as slow, high-amplitude waves on an EEG; notice in Figure 4 how the waves of Stages 3 and 4 are higher and more spread out compared to those of wakefulness and Stages 1 and 2. In Stage 3, 20% to 50% of EEG-recorded brain activity is in the form of delta waves; in Stage 4, the proportion is greater than 50%. In Stage 3, your heart rate and body temperature decrease, and you are no longer easily awakened. By the time you reach Stage 4, you are in a very deep sleep

Sleep The naturally recurring experience during which normal consciousness is suspended.

Hypnogogic sleep The initial stage of sleep, which lasts about 5 minutes and can include the sensation of gentle falling or floating or a sudden jerking of the body; also referred to as *Stage 1 sleep.*

FIGURE 4 Brain Waves During the Stages of Sleep

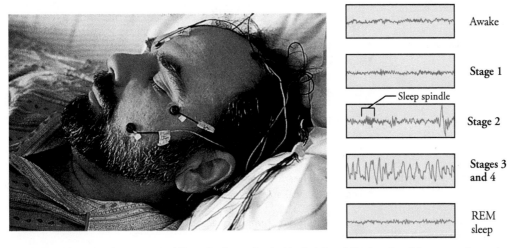

Recordings show that brain waves differ in both amplitude (the height of the wave) and frequency (how often the waves occur). By examining individuals' EEG patterns when asleep, which differ from their EEG patterns when awake, researchers have identified five phases of sleep, each with its own EEG pattern.

Source: Woodfin Camp & Associates, Inc.

indeed—so deep that attempts by a friend (or an alarm clock) to wake you won't readily succeed. If you do wake up directly from this stage, you are likely to be disoriented briefly. During Stage 4 sleep, your heart rate, blood pressure, breathing, and body temperature slow down; all are at their lowest ebb.

REM SLEEP.   About an hour after going to sleep, you begin to reverse the sleep cycle, going from Stage 4 through Stages 3 and 2. But instead of going all the way to Stage 1, you now enter a state of sleep characterized by *rapid eye movement (REM)* under the lids; at the same time, as shown in Figure 4, your EEG registers marked brain activity—similar to when you are awake. It is during this stage of sleep that you are likely to have dreams vivid enough to remember. During **REM sleep**, your breathing and heart rate are fast and irregular, and your genitals may show signs of arousal (men may have an erection, and women may have increased genital blood flow and vaginal lubrication). These events occur in REM sleep regardless of the content of the sleeper's dreams, unless a dream is particularly anxiety provoking, in which case the genitals may not be aroused (Karacan et al., 1966). During REM sleep, your muscles are relaxed and unresponsive; in fact, your voluntary muscles (except those in your eyes) are so paralyzed that you could not physically enact the behaviors in your dreams. That's why when you dream that you're running, your actual body doesn't get out of bed and start doing laps around the block. However, your involuntary muscles continue to move so that your heart can beat, you can breathe, and other systems necessary for life can keep working.

Table 2 on the next page summarizes key aspects of each stage of sleep.

SLEEP CYCLES.   After a period of REM sleep, you go through at least some of the other stages and then return to REM, as shown in Figure 5 (on the next page). Each cycle through the stages takes about 90 minutes; typically, people have four or five cycles each night. However, the time you spend in each stage varies over the course of the night, with slow-wave sleep occurring predominantly in the early hours of sleep and REM sleep occurring primarily in the later hours of sleep.

Sleep also varies over the course of a lifetime. Infants sleep longer than adults (13–16 hours per night in the first year) and have a higher percentage of REM sleep. They often enter REM immediately after falling asleep and cycle through the stages frequently. With age, the pattern of your sleep stages changes and you sleep less: When you enter your 40s, the amount of time spent in deep, slow-wave sleep begins to decrease (Van Cauter et al., 2000). With less slow-wave activity, your sleep is shallower and more fragmented, you wake more easily, and the sleep you do get is less satisfying (Hobson, 1995; Klerman et al., 2004). As you move from middle age to older adulthood, you spend

REM sleep Stage of sleep characterized by rapid eye movements, marked brain activity, and vivid dreaming.

TABLE 2   Key Aspects of Sleep Stages

Stage of Sleep	EEG Features	Key Aspects
Stage 1 (*hypnogogic sleep*)	Less regular, lower amplitude than waking state	• Can be readily awakened • If awakened, won't feel that has been asleep • May experience hypnic jerk • Lasts about 5 minutes
Stage 2	Sleep spindles and single high-amplitude waves	• Can still readily be awakened • More relaxed and less responsive to the environment than during Stage 1 sleep
Stage 3	20% to 50% of EEG activity is delta waves (slow-wave sleep—SWS)	• Decreased heart rate and body temperature • Less easily awakened than in Stages 1 and 2
Stage 4	More than 50% of EEG activity is delta waves (slow-wave sleep—SWS)	• Lowest heart rate, breathing, and body temperature of all sleep stages • Very deep sleep—difficult to awaken
REM Sleep	Brain activity similar to that of wakeful state	• Eyes move rapidly under closed lids • Fast and irregular heart rate and breathing • Voluntary muscles are paralyzed and unresponsive • Vivid dreams that are memorable if awakened during this sleep stage • May have genital arousal

FIGURE 5   The March of Sleep Cycles

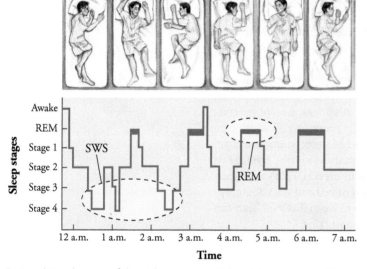

During the earlier part of the night, more time is spent in Stages 3 and 4 (slow-wave sleep—SWS), but later in the night, REM periods lengthen and Stages 3 and 4 shorten, eventually disappearing.

Source: From *Sleep* by J. Allan Hobson. Copyright © 1989 by J. Allan Hobson. M.D. Reprinted by permission of Henry Holt and Company, LLC.

less time sleeping, particularly in lighter sleep (Stages 1 and 2) and REM sleep (Van Cauter et al., 2000).

Given Al's age (54), it is natural that his sleep is less satisfying. But his difficulties sleeping started soon after his company began downsizing; such a rapid change in his sleep (and in response to such a clear-cut and chronic stressor) suggests that Al's sleep problems are more than the normal changes in sleep that arise with age.

Sleep Deprivation: Is Less Just as Good?

When Al reflected on how badly he was sleeping, he consoled himself by remembering how almost everyone he knew complained about not getting enough sleep. In fact, a 2009 survey by the National Sleep Foundation found that 70% of American adults are not getting enough sleep (defined as approximately 8 hours), and 20% of survey participants get less than 6 hours each night—indeed, the average number of hours slept on a typical workday was 6 hours and 40 minutes (National Sleep Foundation, 2009). Even children under the age of 11 are not getting enough sleep (National Sleep Foundation, 2005). However, in one sleep survey, over seven times as many people 65 and older than people under 65 reported that they got enough sleep each night (McKnight-Ely et al., 2009).

If you are like many students, you may have almost fallen asleep in a dull class; if so, it may be cold comfort to know that "boredom doesn't cause sleepiness, it merely unmasks it" (Dement, as cited in Brody, 1998). But being sleep deprived isn't simply an inconvenience; as we'll explain, it adversely affects your ability to cope with stressors—and the effects of sleep deprivation can themselves become stressors.

REM rebound The higher percentage of REM sleep that occurs following a night lacking the normal amount of REM.

REM REBOUND.   If you don't get enough REM sleep, a higher percentage of your next night's sleep will be REM sleep (Brunner et al., 1990); this phenomenon is called **REM rebound.** You can become REM deprived by not getting enough sleep at either end of the night (going to bed late or waking up early) or as a result of drinking alcohol or taking certain sleep medications, which suppress REM sleep. In fact, some people who have been deeply traumatized (victims of rape or assault, for example) and thereafter have disturbing dreams or nightmares use alcohol or drugs before sleep specifically to prevent dreams (Inman et al., 1990). If these substances are used habitually and then discontinued suddenly, dreams during REM rebound can be so vivid, bizarre, and generally unpleasant that people resume using these substances to suppress dreaming. In such cases, REM rebound becomes a stressor. Unfortunately, using a sleep medication doesn't solve the problem of REM rebound—it merely delays it.

THINK like a PSYCHOLOGIST Before you read on, if you get less than 8 hours of sleep a night, do you think that it has any negative effect on your mental process, your emotions, or your body? If so, in what ways? Now compare your answer to the information below about the effects of sleep deprivation.

SLEEP DEPRIVATION: WHAT HAPPENS WHEN YOU SKIMP ON SLEEP? Al thinks that his poor sleep is affecting his performance at work, and if you're sleep deprived, the same could be happening to you. Even if the quality of your sleep is good (unlike Al's), you can experience sleep deprivation simply by not allowing yourself enough hours of sleep, as occurs if you stay up late (studying or partying) and then wake up relatively early the next morning (or if you go to bed at a reasonable hour but wake up very early in order to accomplish some task). You may be like the 40% of adults who claim to be so sleepy during the day that their mood and daily activities are affected (National Sleep Foundation, 2002). Indeed, those who sleep less than 6 hours each weekday night—compared to people who sleep more than 6 hours per night—are more likely to report being impatient or aggravated when faced with common minor frustrations, such as being stuck in traffic or having to wait in line, and they are more dissatisfied with life in general (National Sleep Foundation, 2002, 2008).

Self-reports about sleep are interesting and a good place to start, but objective investigations allow us to learn more than can be revealed by such reports. One way that researchers objectively investigate the function of sleep is to interfere with participants' sleep—or with certain stages of sleep—and study what happens as a result of sleep deprivation. As we discuss in the following sections, even after 2 or 3 nights of restricted sleep, volunteers had problems in at least four important psychological functions— attention, performance, and learning—as well as an increased stress response (Dinges et al., 1997).

Attention and Performance. When you're sleep deprived, you're likely to have problems sustaining your attention and performing visual-motor tasks (such as driving a car). Visual-motor tasks in the laboratory typically require participants to detect a change in a particular stimulus. and then to respond as quickly as they can after they perceive the change by pressing a button (Dinges et al., 1997). Performance on such tasks declines after only 2 nights of restricted sleep. And performance is worse for more complex tasks (which require more sustained or careful attention or more intricate performance). When sleep deprived, you may be able to perform normally on simple, brief mental tasks—such as making sure you received the correct change after you paid for your lunch—but if a task requires sustained attention and a motor response, your performance will suffer.

Learning. Sleep deprivation also disrupts learning in two ways. First, chronically increased cortisol levels can cause memory deficits (Sapolsky, 1996). Second, as we shall explore in more detail later, REM and slow-wave sleep facilitate the learning information that was encountered during the day (Walker & Stickgold, 2004).

Stress Response. People who are sleep deprived perceive more stressors in their lives than do those who are not sleep deprived. In fact, the loss of even a single night's sleep can increase the next day's level of cortisol (Leproult,

Requiring medical interns and residents to stay awake for days and nights of round-the-clock duties can have detrimental effects on their cognitive processes (Landrigan et al., 2004; Lockley et al., 2004) and even increase the risk of their getting into car accidents (Barger et al., 2005). In response, some states are restricting the number of consecutive hours doctors can work.
Source: © Jose Luis Pelaez, Inc / CORBIS All Rights Reserved

Copinschi, et al., 1997). As mentioned earlier in this chapter, cortisol helps the body meet the increased demands imposed by stress. However, chronic stressors—including chronic sleep deprivation—can change the cortisol level, which in turn alters other biological functions, such as decreased immune system functioning (Kiecolt-Glaser et al., 1995), and can create an increased risk for diabetes.

A Vicious Cycle. The effects of sleep deprivation on attention, performance, and learning in turn can create additional stressors because these effects make work tasks more challenging and emotions more difficult to manage. In a vicious cycle, these effects can make people too keyed up to go to sleep promptly, which then deprives them of sleep. How can you minimize the effects of sleep deprivation? Take breaks to rest (not necessarily naps); such breaks can help counter fatigue and enhance performance (Tucker, 2003).

THE EFFECTS OF ALL-NIGHTERS. And what about a series of all-nighters, when you get no sleep at all, as might occur during finals period? Getting no sleep for even one night can interfere with certain types of learning, such as learning to make perceptual discriminations (Cajochen et al., 2004; Mednick et al., 2003). What about even more extended periods of sleep deprivation—akin to all-nighters throughout the entire exam period or longer? Volunteers who have gone without sleep for long stretches (finally sleeping after staying awake anywhere from 4 to 11 days) report profound psychological changes, including hallucinations, anxiety, paranoia, and feelings of losing control or going crazy (Coren, 1996). Moreover, going without sleep alters the normal daily patterns of changes in temperature, metabolism, and hormone secretions (Leproult, Van Reeth, et al., 1997).

The Function of Sleep

We know that doing without sleep has adverse effects on attention, performance, mood, and learning. But why do we sleep? What purpose or purposes does it serve? Researchers have offered a number of answers to these questions, as summarized below.

CONSERVES ENERGY. One theory of the function of sleep is that it provided an evolutionary advantage—sleep (and its associated biological changes) allows energy conservation because the body's temperature lowers and caloric demands decline. Although interesting, there is no evidence that sleep evolved to serve this function.

RESTORES THE BODY. Another theory of the function of sleep is that it helps the body repair the wear and tear from the day's events (Hobson, 1989); that is, it reduces the bodily effects of stressors and other stimuli. Support for this view comes from research on sleep deprivation and the adverse effects of lack of sleep noted earlier.

FACILITATES LEARNING. Yet another theory about the function of sleep is that it facilitates the learning of material encountered during the day (Walker & Stickgold, 2004). When participants were deprived of the different stages of sleep (by being awakened as soon as they entered a particular stage, as evident in an EEG), two types of sleep deprivation led to poorer memory for previously learned visual material: deprivation of slow-wave sleep in the first quarter of the night and of REM sleep in the last quarter of the night (Stickgold, 1998; Stickgold, Whidbee, et al., 2000).

Why Do We Dream?

We noted that dreams occur primarily during REM sleep. Dreams can temporarily relieve stress by offering a pleasant respite from the daily grind—or they can create stress by bringing us a nightmare. Researchers and nonresearchers alike have long sought to understand why we dream. In the sections that follow, we explore key theories of dreaming.

FREUD: WISH FULFILLMENT. Sigmund Freud (1900/1958) proposed the first modern theory of dreaming. According to Freud, dream content originates in the unconscious—outside our conscious awareness; he considered dreams to be the "royal road to the unconscious." Further, he proposed that dreams allow us to fulfill unconscious desires. Such *wish fulfillment* may not always be apparent from the **manifest content** of a dream, that is, its obvious, memorable content. We have to dig to find the **latent content** of the dream, its symbolic content and meaning, which, according to Freud, might reflect sexual or aggressive themes associated with an inner conflict.

Although dream interpretation can be interesting and fun, it is unclear whether any meaning you or anyone else might make of the content of a dream is accurate.

ACTIVATION-SYNTHESIS HYPOTHESIS. Freudians find dreams brimming over with meaningful, albeit disguised, content; the opposite view is at the heart of the **activation-synthesis hypothesis**, which contends that dreams arise from random bursts of nerve cell activity. These bursts may affect brain cells involved in hearing and seeing, as well as storing information, and the brain's response—which produces the experience of dreaming—is to try to make sense of the hodge-podge of stimuli (Hobson & McCarley, 1977). This theory would explain why dreams sometimes seem so bizarre and unrelated: Robert Stickgold and colleagues (1994) asked people to write down their dreams and then literally cut their reports in half. They asked other people to reassemble each dream, deciding which half came first. This proved a very difficult task, a result that is understandable if dreams are merely attempts to interpret random activity and have no cohesive story line.

EDITING VERSUS STRENGTHENING NEURAL CONNECTIONS. Francis Crick, the co-discoverer of the structure of DNA, believed that dreams are used to edit out unnecessary or accidental brain connections formed during the day (Crick & Mitchison, 1983, 1986). Other theories of dreaming focus on the reverse notion: that dreams are used to *strengthen* useful connections. Sleep does appear to play a role in strengthening useful connections, but it is not clear that dreaming per se is important (Stickgold, 1998; Stickgold, Whidbee, et al., 2000).

GOALS/DESIRES AND AROUSAL/INHIBITION. The largest and most systematic study of the neurological bases of dreaming was reported by Mark Solms (1997) of the London Hospital Medical College. Solms interviewed more than 350 patients about the changed nature of their dreams after they suffered brain damage. Perhaps Solms's most intriguing discovery was that dreaming stopped completely if a patient had damage that disconnected parts of the frontal cortex from the brainstem and the limbic system. These connections coordinate brain areas involved in curiosity, interest, and alert involvement with goals in the world (Panksepp, 1985, cited in Solms, 1997). Solms speculates that dreaming may occur in response to any type of arousal that activates brain structures involved in motivation (Goode, 1999).

In sum, although we cannot yet definitively answer *why* we dream, we do know something about *how* we dream. We know that dreaming is a neurological process, involving brain activity that cycles through particular stages. We don't know whether dreams represent deep desires and conflicts, random bursts of nerve cell activity, the editing of unneeded neural connections, or the strengthening of neural connections. But it is interesting that all of these theories, despite their differences, agree that in some way the day's events—or the neural connections they instigate—affect dreams.

In some societies, such as the Maya, telling dreams to others can provide a way to communicate feelings or solve problems (Degarrod, 1990; Tedlock, 1992).

Source: © Jeremy Horner / CORBIS All Rights Reserved

Circadian Rhythms Whether we're pulling all-nighters, getting 5 hours of sleep, or getting plenty of sleep each night, our brain activity and internal chemistry vary in time to the daily cycling of light and dark in a pattern called **circadian rhythms** (*circadian* means "about a day"). Daily fluctuations governed by circadian rhythms occur with blood pressure, pulse rate, body temperature, blood sugar level, hormone levels, and metabolism. Every one of us has an internal clock that coordinates these fluctuations; this clock is regulated by a small part of the hypothalamus just above the optic chiasm, called the

Manifest content The obvious, memorable content of a dream.

Latent content The symbolic content and meaning of a dream.

Activation-synthesis hypothesis The theory that dreams arise from random bursts of nerve cell activity that may affect brain cells involved in hearing and seeing; the brain attempts to make sense of this hodgepodge of stimuli, resulting in the experience of dreams.

Circadian rhythms The body's daily fluctuations in response to the cycle of dark and light.

FIGURE 6 The Suprachiasmatic Nucleus (SCN) and the Optic Chiasm

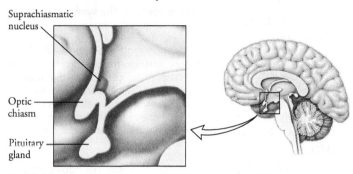

Suprachiasmatic nucleus

Optic chiasm

Pituitary gland

This illustration of a human brain shows the proximity of the SCN to the optic chiasm, which relays signals about light and dark from the eyes to the brain. Given the SCN's role in regulating circadian rhythms, it is not surprising that it is so close to the optic chiasm.

Many cultures have a rest time in the afternoon, perhaps related to the dip in energy during that part of the day that is part of our circadian rhythms.

Source: © David Lees / CORBIS All Rights Reserved

suprachiasmatic nucleus (SCN), which is illustrated in Figure 6. Through photoreceptors in the retina, the SCN registers changes in light, which lead it to produce hormones that set the body's clock and regulate various bodily functions (Berson et al., 2002).

LARKS AND OWLS. People differ in their circadian rhythms, which means that performing in the morning can be stressful for some people but not others, and vice versa for performing at night. As you have probably noticed, some people are energetic and alert early in the morning, whereas others do not perk up until late morning or afternoon. Morning people, or "larks," experience peak body temperature, alertness, and efficiency in the morning; evening people, or "owls," peak at night (Luce, 1971). Normally you are not aware of your circadian rhythms until you try to function well at your nonpeak time. If you're a night owl, for example, how do you feel when faced with a 9 a.m. class?

Regardless of the time of day that finds you most alert, though, most people have a late-afternoon dip in energy level and attention. Reflecting this late afternoon dip, more industrial and traffic accidents occur between 1 and 4 p.m. than at any other time of day (Klinkenborg, 1997).

WORKING AGAINST YOUR RHYTHMS. If you are forced to perform when your rhythms would have you asleep, you will likely develop a bad mood. For instance, Boivin and colleagues (1997), who studied mood and circadian rhythms, found that bad moods occurred during times of day when the participants' circadian clocks said they should be asleep. These results suggest that even minor alterations in sleep schedules can have a noticeable effect on mood after awakening. Thus, if you go to bed later and sleep later on weekends, you are, in a sense, putting yourself in another time zone for the weekend, so when Monday morning rolls around, you are hit with jet lag. Even fifth-grade children are affected by having to wake up earlier to go to school (Epstein et al., 1998).

Troubled Sleep Al's tiredness during the day was starting to wear him down, and drinking before bed didn't seem to help him sleep soundly. He craved a good night's sleep. Feeling tired during the day or having difficulty sleeping may be caused either by *insomnia* or *sleep apnea.*

INSOMNIA. **Insomnia** is characterized by repeated difficulty falling asleep or staying asleep or waking too early. Insomnia can be caused by stress, and it can create stress. If you suffer from this disorder, you are certainly not alone. Half the adults in the United States experience occasional insomnia. Occasional insomnia may be related to environmental factors such as stress associated with family, school, or work, or finances (Bastien et al., 2004; National Sleep Foundation, 2009).(Note: Insomnia refers to difficulty falling asleep or staying asleep before you must get out of bed. Insomnia can lead to sleep deprivation, but being sleep deprived doesn't necessarily mean that the person has insomnia. For instance, someone can sleep soundly each night but get only 5 or 6 hours sleep nightly because that's all the time the person allots for sleeping.)

Suprachiasmatic nucleus (SCN) A small part of the hypothalamus just above the optic chiasm that registers changes in light, leading to production of hormones that regulate various bodily functions.

Insomnia Repeated difficulty falling asleep, difficulty staying asleep, or waking up too early.

When sleep does not occur rapidly, the stressed person can become frustrated, which can cause increased sympathetic nervous system activity which then makes sleep difficult. Unfortunately, for many Americans insomnia is a way of life, and they can become desperate for a good night's sleep. The desperation—and frustration with being unable to fall asleep or remain asleep—serves to increase arousal, compounding the problem. As we discuss in the following sections, treatment for insomnia usually involves medication, psychological treatments, or a combination of the two. ⊙⊸⌐Watch

⊙⊸⌐Watch the Video Nightsleep on mypsychlab.com

Medication for Insomnia. One common—but not generally the most effective—treatment for insomnia is sleeping pills, specifically, a class of medications referred to as *barbiturates*. This type of medication has three significant drawbacks: (1) it suppresses REM sleep (and thus deprives the individual of this important stage of sleep); (2) it is addictive—people who use this type of medication regularly will develop tolerance to this medication, requiring larger and larger dosages to get the same effect; and (3) when the medication is stopped abruptly, the individual may experience unpleasant REM rebound.

Another type of sleep medication for short-term use (up to 1–4 weeks) is *benzodiazepines* (such as Ativan, Xanax, and Valium). These drugs suppress REM sleep less—and are less likely to be addictive with short-term use—than barbiturates; however, long term use of benzodiazepines can cause tolerance and addiction (Arana & Rosenbaum, 2000).

A third type of medication prescribed for sleep is *nonbenzodiazepines*; one medication of this type is zolpidem (*Ambien*). Drawbacks of this type of drug include the following: (1) regular use can lead to tolerance; (2) it can induce sleepwalking while the drug is in the person's system. In such cases, the person may perform daily tasks and appear to be awake to others but is in fact asleep; some people using this medication have, while sleeping, driven their cars, which obviously raises concerns about the safe use of this medication (Food and Drug Administration, 2007); (3) when regular users stop the medication without medical supervision, they may experience serious withdrawal symptoms, such as seizures, or become delirious; and (4) when the medication is stopped, the individual may experience unpleasant REM rebound and other side effects.

If you have insomnia, lying in bed should only be associated with actually going to sleep, not with watching television or reading when you are unable to fall asleep. If he can't sleep, the man in the photograph should sit in a chair or sofa while watching television.

Source: CORBIS All Rights Reserved

Psychological Treatments for Insomnia. Psychological treatments for the problem address the sleep-related thoughts and behaviors that can contribute to insomnia (Bastien et al., 2004). Such techniques are likely to be more effective than medication for insomnia over the long term, in part, because they don't have adverse side effects (Hobson, 1995; Jacobs et al., 2004; Lacks & Morin, 1992; Maas, 1998).

If you have insomnia, you should try any or all of the following techniques, all of which have been shown to be effective (at least for some people, some of the time):

- *Restrict your sleeping hours* to the same nightly pattern. Keep regular sleeping hours. Avoid sleeping later in the morning on some days, napping longer than an hour, or going to bed earlier than usual, all of which will throw you off schedule and create even more sleep difficulties later. And try to get up at the same time every day, even on weekends or days off.

- *Control bedtime stimuli* so that your bed is associated only with sleep or sex, not with the frustration of insomnia; don't read or watch TV in bed in a reclining position. If you can't fall asleep within 10 minutes, get out of bed or sit up and do something else.

- *Avoid ingesting substances known to interfere with sleep.* Don't smoke cigarettes, eat large quantities of chocolate, or drink beverages with alcohol or caffeine in the evening. After drinking alcohol you may be able to fall asleep, but it has a rebound effect so that you may find yourself wide awake in the middle of the night.

379

✓— Study and Review on
mypsychlab.com

- Don't drink large quantities of liquid close to bedtime; getting up to use the bathroom can contribute to poor sleep.
- *Try meditation or relaxation techniques.* Either of these techniques can help insomnia. Similarly, regular aerobic exercise four times a week may be a long-term solution, but it can take up to 16 weeks for the effect on insomnia to be evident (King et al., 1997).

In some cases, chronic insomnia may stem from underlying psychological disorders, such as anxiety and depression; when the underlying disorder is treated successfully, the insomnia may fade.

SLEEP APNEA.   Snoring can be a nuisance—or even lead to sleep problems—for those sharing a room with a snorer. To the snorer, though, it can be a sign of a more significant problem—one that affects sleep, restfulness, and health; chronic snoring may be a sign of *sleep apnea.* **Sleep apnea** is a disorder characterized by a temporary cessation of breathing during sleep, usually preceded by a period of difficult breathing accompanied by loud snoring. In fact, while sleeping the individual may stop breathing for up to 70 seconds, get startled by the lack of oxygen, and then shift into a lighter state of sleep. Sleep apnea results when muscles at the base of the throat relax (most likely during deeper states of sleep) so much that they don't keep the airway open. This in turn restricts oxygen intake and interrupts the normal sleep cycle; the person may be deprived of both sleep in general and REM sleep in particular. This ailment, which affects 18 million Americans (National Sleep Foundation, 2005), involves many such events each hour. Sleep apnea—and the ensuing poor sleep and reduced oxygen—can lead to heart disease and high blood pressure as well as poor mood and poor memory.

Because of the adverse effects of sleep apnea, treatment is essential. Treatments include: (1) the nightly use of a device called *Continuous Positive Airway Pressure (CPAP),* which delivers compressed air through a mask that covers the nose (the pressurized air forces the airway to remain open while the person sleeps); (2) surgery to shave off some of the tissue in the throat that obstructs airflow. One study examining the effects of surgery on cognitive abilities found that surgery led patients to have better learning, memory, and decision-making abilities compared to before the surgery. Moreover, the researchers found that the more effective the treatment was in eliminating the apnea, the larger the improvement in these abilities (Dahloef et al., 2002); and (3) for obese patients, weight loss. A significant portion of people with sleep apnea are obese (Centers for Disease Control, 2009), and in such people, weight loss can help reduce the breathing obstruction.

LOOKING BACK

1. **How can stress affect the immune system and make illness more likely?** Stress increases the production of glucocorticoids, which can depress the immune system, including the formation and functioning of white blood cells such as natural killer (NK) cells. A depressed immune system makes the body more vulnerable to infection and tumor growth and also slows healing.

2. **Are stress and cancer related?** Although stress does not cause tumors to develop, increased glucocorticoid production (part of the stress response) can depress the level of tumor-fighting NK cells. Conversely, decreasing the stress response can increase the NK cells' ability to fight tumors. However, not all cancers are equally affected by these factors.

3. **Can stress cause a heart attack or heart disease?** The stress response increases blood pressure and injures artery walls. These two events can promote atherosclerosis, the buildup of plaque in the arteries, which in turn requires the heart to work even harder to supply blood to the body and can lead to coronary heart disease. The factors that underlie heart disease can be improved by psychological and social interventions, such as stress management and social support. Some people are more stress prone than others: Hostile people are more likely than others to view social situations as stressors.

Sleep apnea A disorder characterized by a temporary cessation of breathing during sleep, usually preceded by a period of difficult breathing accompanied by loud snoring.

4. **What is the relationship between sleep and stress?** Stress can impair the ability to get a good night's sleep by causing either temporary or chronic insomnia. Also, sleep deprivation can create stress by impairing attention, performance, mood, and learning.

Strategies for Coping

Al realized that he was in bad shape and that his drinking was getting out of control. In fact, Al finally recognized that he needed to take action or he would spiral downward even further. But how could he handle his stress any better? He looked around the office to see how other people were doing—how they were handling the stress of the difficult situation at work. He paid particular attention to Maya, who didn't seem ruffled by the unsettled atmosphere and the layoffs. Al was puzzled by her reaction—or apparent lack of one—and he talked to Lisa about it. She suggested that perhaps Maya had particularly effective ways of dealing with stress. Lisa, having taken some psychology classes, explained to her father that the effects of stress depends not only on your view of a situation, but also on the conscious actions you take in response to the stressors. We earlier defined "coping" as "taking action to address a stressor or to counteract effects of a stressor"; in general, a **coping strategy** is a specific approach or technique that is employed to handle stress. Some of these techniques may "come naturally," arising partly from temperament; others can be learned. In this section, we examine coping and coping strategies. **⊙▸ Simulate**

⊙▸ Simulate the Experiment
How Healthy Are You? on
mypsychlab.com

LOOKING AHEAD Learning Objectives

1. What are the different types of coping strategies?
2. How do relationships affect stress and health?
3. What are mind–body interventions?
4. Do gender and culture play a role in coping?

Coping Strategies: Approaches and Tactics

Different people tend to use different coping strategies, and whether they use a particular strategy may depend on the situation and the emotions aroused by it (Folkman & Moskowitz, 2004). In the sections that follow, we first examine two basic ways of coping—*problem-focused* and *emotion-focused coping*—then examine some specific coping strategies that are often less effective than others: *thought suppression, aggression,* and *using drugs and alcohol.*

Problem-Focused and Emotion-Focused Coping Some coping strategies address external circumstances that give rise to stressors, whereas others address a person's reaction to stressors (Carver et al., 1989). **Problem-focused coping** consists of strategies that focus on addressing external circumstances, altering either the environment itself or the way in which the person and the environment interact (see Table 3 on the next page). Coping strategies of this type are more common when people believe that their actions can affect the stressor (Park et al., 2004), and tend to be used by people who are generally very conscientious (Watson & Hubbard, 1996). In contrast, **emotion-focused coping** consists of strategies that change a person's emotional response to the stressor (see Table 3), which typically decreases emotional and physiological arousal. People are more likely to adopt emotion-focused coping strategies when they do not think that their actions can affect the stressor itself, and so they must alter their perception of, or response to, the stressor.

Typically, people use more than one strategy in response to a given stressor. How effective a particular strategy is depends in part on how accurately a person assesses whether the environment can, in fact, be changed. For example, suppose Al's daughter, Lisa, assumes that if she gets straight As in the spring term, she can probably get a scholarship to cover next year's tuition. In this case, Lisa is approaching the need to pay for her education with the problem-focused coping strategy of *planning*: She is coping with a

Coping strategy A specific approach or technique that is employed to handle stress.

Problem-focused coping Coping focused on changing the environment itself or the way the person interacts with the environment.

Emotion-focused coping Coping focused on changing the person's emotional response to the stressor.

TABLE 3 Problem-Focused and Emotion-Focused Coping Strategies

Strategy	Description
Problem-Focused Strategies	
Active coping	Actively tries to remove or work around stressor or to ameliorate its effects
Planning	Thinks about how to manage stressor
Instrumental social support	Seeks concrete advice, assistance, information
Suppression of competing activities	Puts other activities on hold in order to concentrate on and cope with stressor
Restraint coping	Waits to act until the appropriate time
Emotion-Focused Strategies	
Emotional social support	Seeks encouragement, moral support, sympathy, and understanding from others
Venting emotions	Focuses on and talks about distressing feelings
Positive reinterpretation/growth	Reinterprets the stressor or situation in a positive way or as a challenge
Behavioral disengagement	Reduces efforts to deal with the stressor (as occurs with learned helplessness)
Mental disengagement	Turns to other activities to distract attention from the stressor

Source: From Carber, C.C., Scheier, M.F., and Weintraub, J.K., "Assessing Coping Strategies," *Journal of Personality and Social Psychology*, 56, 267–83, 1989. Copyright © 1989 by the American Psychological Association. Adapted with permission.

THINK like a PSYCHOLOGIST Think back to a time when you felt overwhelmed by stressors (that is, your allostatic load was high); what type of coping strategies did you use—more emotion- or problem-focusing coping strategies? Looking back, do you think your assessment of how much control you had was accurate, and if so, were your strategies helpful? Based on what you have learned, how might you be better off coping the next time your allostatic load is high?

stressor by thinking about how to manage it (see Table 3). Moreover, if she executes her plan and works hard all spring and carefully rations her social time, Lisa is using two additional problem-focused strategies: *active coping* and *suppression of competing activities.*

Although trying to adopt problem-focused coping in the face of stressors is adaptive, this approach is ultimately effective only when applied to factors that are, in fact, controllable. Accurate information and appraisal are important to determine whether this is the case. For example, Lisa doesn't know that the financial aid office awards all of next year's scholarships before the end of the spring term, so her efforts for top grades—and her sense that she is actively working toward her goal—will not help her actually achieve her goal of a scholarship.

The allostatic load—the nature and number of stressors in a person's life—affects the type of coping strategies he or she is likely to use. The more stressors a person faces, the more likely he or she is to use emotion-focused coping strategies that decrease the focus on the stressors and increase the focus on other matters (Ingledew et al., 1997). Examples of such coping strategies are behavioral and mental disengagement. With *behavioral disengagement*, people reduce their efforts to deal actively with the stressor (Table 3). In its extreme form, this type of disengagement can lead to a sense of helplessness. With *mental disengagement*, people turn to other activities to distract their attention from the stressor.

Behavioral and mental disengagement are examples of *avoidant* coping strategies, which can be adaptive when nothing can be done to change a stressor (Folkman & Moskowitz, 2004). Studies (with male participants) have indicated that those perceiving less control over events are less likely to use problem-focused coping strategies (which involve direct action) and more likely to use emotion-focused strategies (David & Suls, 1999). If Al thinks that nothing he does at work will ultimately affect whether he gets laid off, he is less likely to use problem-focused coping strategies.

Another type of emotion-focused coping strategy is *venting* (see Table 3)—that is, focusing on and talking about the stressor. In a study on venting, James Pennebaker (1989) asked a group of college students to write for 20 minutes a day for 4 consecutive days; they were told that their writing samples would remain confidential. Pennebaker gave half of them the following instructions:

> During each of the 4 writing days, I want you to write about the most traumatic and upsetting experiences of your whole life. You can write on different topics each day or on the same topic for all 4 days. The important thing is that you write about your deepest thoughts and feelings. Ideally, whatever you write about should deal with an event or experience that you have not talked about with others in detail.

Source: Pennebaker (1989). "Confession, inhibition and disease." In L. Berkowitz (Ed.), *Advances in experimental social psychology* (Vol. 22, pp. 211–244). New York: Academic Press.

Another group of students, serving as a control, was asked to write each day about superficial topics. In this study and many variants of it, students who were asked to write about an emotional topic (but not superficial topics) had more positive overall moods by the end of the school year, although they were more likely to report negative moods immediately after writing (Pennebaker et al., 1990). Moreover, those who wrote about traumatic events were less likely to get sick (as measured by visits to the student health center) in the months following the expressive writing. Similar results were reported by Pennebaker and Francis (1996) and were found even when the writing occurred via email (Sheese et al., 2004) or over different time periods (Chung & Pennebaker, 2008).

Writing in detail about upsetting or difficult experiences can enhance immune system functioning and can lead to better moods.

Source: Marc Romanelli/Image Bank/Getty Images

The positive effects of writing about traumatic and unsettling experiences probably result from more than just venting. Writing about a traumatic event allows the writer to work through and come to terms with the experience, which involves *positive reinterpretation*; in turn this process appears to reduce the negative effects of stress on the immune system. This interpretation of how such expressive writing confers beneficial effects is buttressed by the results of other studies that assessed the relationships between writing and (1) immune function (Petrie et al., 1995, 1998), (2) absenteeism from work (Francis & Pennebaker, 1992), and (3) specific medical problems (Smyth et al., 1999). It appears, however, that writing only briefly—say, just a 3-minute outline of a traumatic experience—doesn't provide enough emotional expression to confer the benefits; the participants must actively process their experiences by writing about them in detail (Páez et al., 1999).

These studies suggest that focusing on and "working through" feelings about a traumatic experience have positive effects, although it may take a while for these effects to appear. Note, though, that the positive effects require more than solely venting; by definition, making sense of and making peace with emotional events requires positive reinterpretation.

Thought Suppression Another avoidant emotion-focused coping strategy is **thought suppression**—intentionally trying not to think about something that is emotionally arousing or distressing (Wegner et al., 1987). Suppose Al and Lisa used thought suppression. Each would try not to think about Al's work situation and all that depended on it. Does this seem like it might be effective when they have no control over the stressor? It turns out that it's very hard to do. Research has shown that trying *not* to think about something can have the paradoxical effect of causing that "suppressed" thought to pop into consciousness more than it does when you are not trying to suppress it—a type of rebound effect (Wegner, 1989).

And when an individual's allostatic load is high, such a rebound effect is more likely to occur. In fact, because of the rebound effect, the subsequent increase in thoughts about the stressor may lead to excessive focus on the stressor and to depression (Beevers & Meyer, 2004; Koster et al., 2003; Wenzlaff & Luxton, 2003).

In general, research has revealed that the act of suppressing emotionally charged thoughts—such as those related to fear, anger, and joy—typically magnifies both the intensity of the thoughts and the autonomic reactions to those thoughts (Clark et al., 1991; Gross & Levenson, 1997; Wegner et al., 1987).

Aggression: Coping Gone Awry For good or ill, one way to cope with stressors is through **aggression**, which is behavior that is intended to harm another living being who does not wish to be harmed (Baron & Richardson, 1994). Not everyone behaves aggressively as a way to cope with stress, and various factors are associated with whether a person will use aggression in this way. As we discuss below, factors associated with using aggression as a coping strategy include the *hostile attribution bias, narcissism, gender differences,* and adverse external and internal "*background noise.*"

HOSTILE ATTRIBUTION BIAS. The **hostile attribution bias** is the tendency to misread the intentions of others as negative (Dodge & Newman, 1981; Nasby et al., 1979). If a person has this bias, he or she will tend to respond aggressively in stressful situations

Thought suppression The coping strategy that involves intentionally trying not to think about something emotionally arousing or distressing.

Aggression Behavior that is intended to harm another living being who does not wish to be harmed.

Hostile attribution bias The tendency to misread the intentions of others as negative.

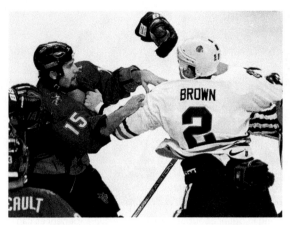

Some people are more aggressive than others. For example, hockey players who scored higher on a test of aggressiveness (administered before the hockey season began) spent more time in the penalty box for aggressive penalties, but not for nonaggressive penalties (Bushman & Wells, 1998).

Source: AP Wide World Photos

On April 20, 1999, Littleton, Colorado's Colombine High School students Dylan Klebold and Eric Harris killed 15 people (including themselves). It was reported that Eric Harris would get enraged at the smallest slight (Lowe, 1999). Before the rampage, Harris had received several rejections, including a rejection for entry into the Marine Corps 5 days before the killings. Could this rejection have threatened an unrealistically high sense of self-esteem?

Source: MARK LEFFINGWELL/Agence France Presse/Getty Images

(Anderson & Bushman, 1997). For example, if Al had this bias, he might yell at Lisa when she suggests that he get more sleep; he might assume that she just wanted him to spend more time in bed so that he would be less likely to bother her.

But this is not the whole story—not everyone who has a hostile attribution bias copes by using aggression, and not everyone who uses aggression as a coping strategy has a hostile attribution bias. We must consider other factors in order to understand why some people respond to stress by using aggression.

NARCISSISM AND SELF-ESTEEM.   Conventional wisdom, at least in the United States, has been that aggression is more likely to be perpetrated by people who feel bad about themselves—that is, who have low self-esteem—and that their aggression toward others is a way of bolstering their view of themselves. But, contrary to conventional wisdom, research results indicate that most aggressors are people who think exceedingly well of themselves (that is, have high self-esteem) and experience an insult as a threat to their positive self-view (Baumeister et al., 1996; Bushman, 1998). Their aggression is a response to a perceived threat (Bushman, 1998; Thomaes et al., 2008).

Not *all* people with high self-esteem are likely to be more aggressive, however; the aggressors are a subset of this group called *narcissists*, whose positive view of themselves may be either overinflated (that is, it doesn't correspond to reality) or unstable (that is, changing significantly from day to day; Baumeister et al., 1996; Morf & Rhodewalt, 2001). Here's how researchers think the process works: A threat to their positive self-image can lead to a drop in self-esteem, so narcissists defend against this drop (and the ensuing negative emotions) by behaving aggressively with anyone who threatens their positive self-image (Bushman et al., 2001; Twenge & Campbell, 2003). This is more likely to happen among men than women because men are more narcissistic, as indicated by well-developed measures of narcissism (Bushman, 1998).

To get a sense of how this research is conducted, let's consider one study of narcissism and aggression: Imagine that you agreed to participate in a psychological study and, as part of the study, wrote an essay on some topic. You get the essay back with this comment: "This is the worst essay I've ever read." Later, you are competing with the person who wrote this comment on a reaction time test, a test in which the winner sets the loudness and duration of a buzzer that goes off each time the other player loses. How would you respond if you won? How obnoxious would you let the sound be? Brad Bushman (1998) hypothesized that people who score high on measures of narcissism would be more likely to behave aggressively than those who score low, and indeed that is what he found. For these narcissists, a poor evaluation apparently endangered their view of themselves, and was enough to elicit aggression toward the person doing the evaluating. In contrast, participants who scored low on narcissism apparently were less likely to perceive a negative evaluation of their essays as a threat, and they were less aggressive. Not only was Bushman correct in his prediction, but he also found that the narcissistic participants were more likely to be aggressive *even if their essays were positively received*; a negative evaluation simply increased their aggressive behavior. For narcissists, then, it appears that *any* evaluation is a stressor that threatens their view of themselves. Further research on male narcissists reveals that they, in contrast to other men, are less likely to feel empathic toward rape victims and, when rebuffed by women, are more likely to retaliate in some way (Bushman et al., 2003).

GENDER DIFFERENCES IN AGGRESSION.   If aggression is defined by physical acts, then without question males are more aggressive than females. But not all forms of aggression are physical—nonphysical aggression can take a variety of forms, including that of *relational aggression*: intentionally damaging relationships or injuring others psychologically, such as by socially excluding them or gossiping about them (Crick & Grotpeter, 1995). However, in general, females are less likely than males to be aggressive if they think the aggression will physically harm another person, backfire on themselves, or cause them to feel considerable guilt or shame (Eagly & Steffen, 1986).

ADVERSE "BACKGROUND NOISE."   Certain types of stressors can create "background noise" that increases an individual's allostatic load, and can increase it to the point where he or she copes by lashing out aggressively. Such elements of background noise can be external (in the environment) or internal (mental contents). External factors that can spark aggression include noise and heat (Berkowitz & Harmon-Jones, 2004), and the targets of the aggression are often innocent people who happen to be in the line of fire.

Internal factors that contribute to background noise and can spark aggression in some people include depression and pain (Berkowitz, 1998). These internal states can lead to aggression when they predispose people to interpret a stimulus (particularly ambiguous or neutral stimuli) in a negative light. In essence, these adverse factors create a temporary hostile attribution bias (or for people already prone to this bias, exacerbate the bias).

SUMMING UP.   We are all, at one time or another, confronted by stressors that can elicit aggression; Thornton Wilder has written, "We have all murdered, in thought." Why do only some of us act on our aggressive thoughts? One answer may lie in the difficulty aggressive people have in regulating, or controlling, themselves (Baumeister & Boden, 1998). In turn, the ability to control themselves and their aggressive impulses is related to a host of factors, including community standards, the perceived likelihood of punishment, their ability to monitor their behavior, their estimate of whether aggressive behavior will make them feel better (Bushman et al., 2001), and a conscious decision *not* to control themselves (as occurs when people, knowing that the likely outcome will be physical aggression, still decide to drink or use drugs).

Drugs and Alcohol   Some people cope with life's stressors by consuming drugs and alcohol. For example, Al hadn't been much of a drinker before the downsizing began at work, but once the layoffs at work started, his drinking increased. Moreover, soon after his sleep problems developed, he began to drink alcohol to help him sleep. Now, he drinks whiskey nightly, downing his first drink when he gets home from work because he feels it helps him unwind from the stress and anxiety of the day. As Al's drinking illustrates, using drugs and alcohol as a way to cope is a form of mental disengagement. Although such *substance use* may change the perception of the stressor or the reaction to the stressor while someone is under the influence of the substance, substance use as a coping strategy does not typically change the stressor itself, nor does it provide any lasting change in how the individual views or reacts to the stressor. Thus, any relief that substance use provides is temporary. Moreover, some of the effects of drug and alcohol use can create their own stressors.

At some point such a coping strategy becomes problematic and maladaptive. But it is not always easy to determine this point. For example, is there a problem if a woman drinks heavily, but only over the weekend, and she never misses work because of it? Is she an alcoholic? How about the man who smokes marijuana at the end of the day to feel relaxed, or the student who downs four cups of caffeinated coffee each evening while studying? Have these people crossed some biological or psychological line between use and abuse?

One set of guidelines that determines when substance use crosses the line into abuse can be found in the *Diagnostic and Statistical Manual of Mental Disorders* (4th ed., text revision, often referred to by the initials DSM-IV-TR; American Psychiatric Association, 2000); DSM-IV-TR is the most frequently used classification system for psychiatric disorders, including disorders of substance use. DSM-IV-TR specifies three main criteria for identifying when substance use has crossed the line into **substance abuse**:

1. a pattern of substance use that leads to significant distress or difficulty functioning in major areas of life (for instance, at home, work, or school, or in relationships),

2. substance use that occurs in dangerous situations (for instance, while or before driving a car), or

3. substance use that leads to legal difficulties.

Substance abuse Drug or alcohol use that causes distress or trouble with functioning in major areas of life, occurs in dangerous situations, or leads to legal difficulties.

385

TABLE 4 The Seven Criteria for Substance Dependence

1. Tolerance.
2. Withdrawal.
3. Larger amounts of substance taken over a longer period of time than intended.
4. Unsuccessful efforts or a persistent desire to decrease or control the substance use.
5. Much time spent in obtaining the substance, using it, or recovering from its effects.
6. Important work, social, or recreational activities given up as a result of the substance.
7. Despite knowledge of recurrent or ongoing physical or psychological problems caused or exacerbated by the substance, continued use of substance.

Note: The criteria are from the *Diagnostic and Statistical Manual* (4th ed., text revision; DSM-IV-TR); according to the DSM-IV-TR, to be diagnosed with substance dependence, an individual must have three or more of these seven symptoms within a 12-month period.

Source: Reprinted with permission of the American Psychiatric Association, from the *Diagnostic and Statistical Manual of Mental Disorders, Fourth Edition, Text Revision,* (Copyright 2000); permission conveyed through Copyright Clearance Center, Inc.

Substance dependence Chronic substance use that is characterized by at least three out of seven symptoms, the two most important being tolerance and withdrawal.

Tolerance The condition of requiring more of a substance to achieve the same effect, because the usual amount provides a diminished response.

Withdrawal symptoms The onset of uncomfortable or life-threatening effects when the use of a substance is stopped.

Depressants A class of substances (including barbiturates, benzodiazepines, and alcohol), that depress the central nervous system, thereby decreasing the user's behavioral activity and level of awareness; also called *sedative-hypnotic drugs.*

Chronic substance abuse can lead to **substance dependence**, which is characterized by a minimum of three out of the seven symptoms listed in Table 4, the two most important of which are *tolerance* and *withdrawal* (American Psychiatric Association, 2000). **Tolerance** is the condition, resulting from repeated use, in which the same amount of a substance produces a diminished effect (and, thus, more of the substance is required to achieve the same effect). Tolerance typically occurs with the use of alcohol, barbiturates (which are sometimes used for insomnia, as we noted earlier), amphetamines, and opiates such as morphine and heroin. *Withdrawal* is the cessation of using a substance; **withdrawal symptoms** are the uncomfortable or life-threatening effects that may be experienced during withdrawal.

Substance abuse and dependence are detrimental to society as a whole as well as to the individual: In the United States, the costs of crime, drug treatment, medical care, social welfare programs, and time lost from work total an estimated $67 billion per year (National Institute on Drug Abuse, 2003).

In the sections that follow, we examine different types of substances that individuals may abuse to cope with life's stressors: *depressants* (such as alcohol), *stimulants* (such as cocaine and crack), *narcotic analgesics* (such as heroin), and *hallucinogens* (such as LSD and marijuana).

DEPRESSANTS: FOCUS ON ALCOHOL. Depressants (also called *sedative-hypnotic drugs*) are substances that depress the central nervous system, thereby decreasing behavioral activity and awareness; depressants include barbiturates and benzodiazepines (sometimes used to treat anxiety or insomnia, as discussed earlier) and alcohol. Drugs in this category tend to slow a person down. We focus on alcohol here because of its prevalence and the fact that so much is known about its effects.

Approximately 60% of adults in the United States reported that they drank alcohol within the previous year (Blazer & Wu, 2009; Pleis et al., 2009); 8% of adults in the United States (17 million people) are considered to have either alcohol abuse or dependence (Grant et al., 2004). In addition, the younger people are when they start drinking, the more likely they are to use alcohol as a coping strategy and so develop alcohol abuse or dependence (Grant & Dawson, 1997; Odgers et al., 2008).

Psychological Effects of Alcohol. The effects of alcohol depend on the dosage and the length of time since drinking; it takes about an hour for alcohol to be fully absorbed into the blood (as measured by blood alcohol levels), but drinkers can feel an effect within a few minutes:

- At low doses, alcohol can cause a sense of decreased awareness and increased relaxation, and the drinker may become talkative or outgoing. People who overuse alcohol as a coping strategy may do so, at least partly, to obtain these effects; because of tolerance that comes with regular use, though, more and more alcohol is needed to obtain these effects.

- At moderate doses, alcohol slows reaction time and impairs judgment. In addition, at these doses alcohol also impairs motor coordination. Not only is there a "drunkard's walk," characterized by stumbling and lack of balance, but hand–eye coordination is also impaired—which is why drinking and driving don't mix.

- At higher doses, alcohol impairs cognition, self-control, and self-restraint, and the drinker may become emotionally unstable or overly aggressive. "Barroom brawls" often occur because a drunk patron misinterprets a casual remark that otherwise might have passed without incident. As the effects of the alcohol take hold, the drinker's responses are more likely to be out of proportion to the situation.

- At very high doses, alcohol can diminish the sense of cold, pain, and discomfort (which is why some people drink to cope with pain). At these high doses, alcohol causes dilation of the peripheral blood vessels, which increases the amount of blood circulating through the skin and makes the drinker both feel warmer and lose heat faster. Thus, heavy drinking in the cold increases the chance of hypothermia (that is, decreased body temperature) and frostbite. Such high doses can bring on respiratory arrest, coma, or death.

Alcohol creates these effects by depressing the nervous system. It inhibits excitatory neurons, leading them to fire less often (Goldstein, 1994; Grilly, 1994); alcohol also can inhibit the action of inhibitory neurons, causing other neurons to fire that otherwise would be inhibited from firing. Because of this "release" effect, this inhibition of inhibitory neurons is called **disinhibition**.

Alcohol Myopia. One particularly significant psychological effect of drinking alcohol is **alcohol myopia**, "a state of shortsightedness in which superficially understood, immediate aspects of experience have a disproportionate influence on behavior and emotion" (Steele & Josephs, 1990, p. 923). Alcohol myopia arises, in part, because alcohol impairs attention so that the drinker is less likely to notice many cues in the environment, such as in people's expressions or tone of voice (Washburne, 1956; Giancola et al., 2010); moreover, after drinking alcohol, people are slower to make sense of the cues they do pay attention to (Curtin et al., 2001; Pihl et al., 2003; Tarter et al., 1971). Such problems in turn impair a person's ability to understand ambiguous social situations, such as occasions when someone's words and body language are contradictory. For example, suppose friends have gone out drinking and now are all drunk. One of them might announce that he is sick but laugh about it. The others might not understand that their friend really *is* sick and needs medical care.

Alcohol myopia can lead a drinker incorrectly to interpret someone else's clenched fist as a threatening aggressive act rather than as an indicator of that person's nervousness or anxiety.

Source: CORBIS All Rights Reserved

Alcohol myopia can also lead to aggressive behavior (Bushman & Cooper, 1990). Aggression can result from misreading a situation, as in the barroom brawl example: Stimuli that elicit aggression (such as someone's clenched fists) loom larger than stimuli that require more thought (such as considerations that the aggressive behavior may be immoral, illegal, or unnecessary).

Drinking—and the alcohol myopia it creates—can lead to a particular form of aggression: date rape. More than 50% of on-campus date rapes occur when men are under the influence of alcohol (Muehlenhard & Linton, 1987; Ouimette, 1997). Researchers have set out to determine exactly how drinking might be involved. In one study (Johnson et al., 2002), they asked male volunteers to drink different levels of alcohol and then to watch one of two videos of a woman on a blind date. In one video, she exhibited friendly, cordial behavior; in the other, she was unresponsive. The men were then asked how acceptable it would be for a man to be sexually aggressive toward his date (see Figure 7, on the next page). Among the men who viewed the video with the unresponsive woman, alcohol intake made no difference in the men's answers. However, alcohol intake did make a difference for the men who viewed the video of the friendly woman: Those men who had more to drink thought that sexual aggression toward a friendly date was acceptable. The alcohol impaired the men's ability to understand that the friendliness the woman showed did not mean that it was acceptable for a man to force her to have sex. To reason about this social situation appropriately, a person needs to be able think beyond the most immediate cues in the environment and to think about the situation from different points of view, identifying underlying principles and consequences of possible actions. Such functions are impaired by drinking alcohol.

Chronic Abuse: More Than a Bad Habit *Alcoholics* are people who drink alcohol compulsively, which leads to alcohol abuse or dependence; alcoholics come from all socioeconomic classes. Historically, more males than females are alcoholics, and this pattern continues today, although the gap is narrowing (Nelson et al., 1998; Pleis et al., 2009). Chronic alcohol abuse can cause additional stressors that must be coped with, including difficulties with abstract reasoning, problem solving, and visual motor tasks. In addition, alcoholics can have severe memory deficits—some so severe that they become **blackouts**, periods of time for which the alcoholic has no memory of events that occurred while he or she was intoxicated.

Disinhibition The inhibition of inhibitory neurons, which makes other neurons (the ones that are usually inhibited) more likely to fire and which usually occurs as a result of depressant use.

Alcohol myopia The disproportionate influence of immediate experience on behavior and emotion due to the effects of alcohol use.

Blackout A period of time for which an alcoholic has no memory of events that transpired while he or she was intoxicated.

FIGURE 7 Alcohol and Sexual Aggression

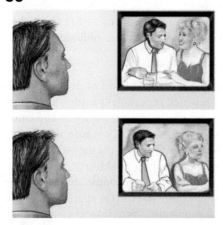

Male participants were assigned to one of four alcohol consumption groups: *moderate alcohol intake*, *low alcohol intake*, *placebo alcohol intake* (alcohol rubbed on the rim of glasses holding nonalcoholic drinks), and *control group* (drank ice water). The three alcohol groups did not know the strength of their drinks.

Half of each group of men watched a video about a blind date in which the woman was very friendly; the other half of each group watched a video about a blind date in which the woman was unresponsive and cold.

Regardless of alcohol intake, the participants who watched the unresponsive date did not find sexual aggression by the man acceptable, and attributed any responsibility for aggression to *him*. In contrast, there was clear alcohol myopia in those who watched the friendly date: The more alcohol they drank, the more the men accepted the idea of sexual aggression toward the woman, and the more they attributed any aggression by the man as being the *woman's* responsibility (Johnson et al., 2000).

STIMULANTS: FOCUS ON COCAINE. In contrast to depressants, **stimulants** excite the central nervous system, stimulating behavioral activity and heightened arousal. *Cocaine* is a powerful stimulant that can enhance a user's sense of physical and mental capacity while at the same time reduce his or her appetite; these effects are also typical of other stimulants. Chronic cocaine users develop tolerance and withdrawal as well as paranoia, teeth grinding, and repetitive behaviors; they may also experience visual disturbances (such as seeing snow), or may feel that insects ("cocaine bugs") are crawling on their skin. This latter sensation arises from the spontaneous firing of sensory neurons, caused by the cocaine.

Cocaine exerts its effects by inhibiting the reuptake of dopamine and norepinephrine, which means that these neurotransmitters are not reabsorbed into the sending neuron and so they remain in the synaptic cleft (Figure 8). In turn, the increased presence of these neurotransmitters in the synaptic cleft leads to a pleasurable, even euphoric, feeling. With continued use of cocaine, the drug becomes the main trigger that activates the reward system in the brain, leading other sources of pleasure, such as food or sex, to have little or no effect (Koob & Le Moal, 2008; National Institute on Drug Abuse, 1998). When cocaine and alcohol are taken together, the human liver (which metabolizes the substances) creates a third substance, called *cocaethylene*, which intensifies cocaine's effects while at the same time increases the risk of sudden death (National Institute on Drug Abuse, 2004).

FIGURE 8 Action of Stimulants on Neurotransmitters

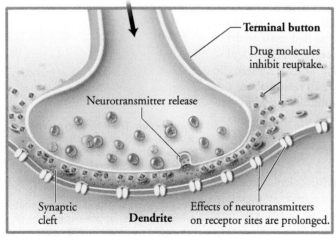

Cocaine and other stimulants have their stimulating effects by blocking reuptake—that is, by preventing the normal reabsorption into the terminal button—of some norepinephrine and dopamine molecules at the synaptic cleft. The net effect is that more of these neurotransmitters remain in the synaptic cleft.

Source: From Goodenough, Judith A., McGuire, Betty A., Wallace, Robert A., *Biology of Humans: Concepts, Applications, and Issues*, 1st edition, © 2005, Figure 7.7. Adapted by permission of Pearson Education, Inc.

Crack. **Crack** is cocaine in crystalline form, which is usually smoked in a pipe ("freebasing") or rolled into a cigarette. The user experiences a feeling of euphoria, perceived clarity of thought, and increased energy; users of crack may rapidly come to abuse it and become dependent on it. Crack is faster acting and has more intense effects than cocaine powder that is inhaled through the nostrils; however, because the effects of crack last for only a few minutes, the user tends to take greater amounts of crack than of powdered cocaine.

Crack increases heart rate and blood pressure and constricts blood vessels—which can lead to sudden death, even among occasional users. After the drug wears off, the user experiences a massive "crash," with intense depression and a strong craving for more crack.

Other Stimulants. Many other stimulants, both natural and synthetic, exist. For example, **amphetamines**—such as Benzedrine and Dexedrine—are one type of synthetic stimulant; they are usually taken in pill form or injected. With high doses, the user can suffer *amphetamine psychosis*, which is similar to paranoid schizophrenia: Symptoms include delusions (entrenched false beliefs), hallucinations, and paranoia. Chronic use of amphetamines can cause long-term neural changes that produce impaired memory and motor coordination (Volkow et al., 2001) and is associated with violent behaviors (Leccese, 1991).

Another synthetic stimulant is *MDMA* (also known as ecstasy, or "e"), which causes the neurotransmitter serotonin—and to a lesser extent dopamine—to be released from certain neurons (Colado et al., 2004; Green et al., 1995). Research on animals indicates that MDMA, used even once, can permanently damage neurons that release serotonin, which impairs memory, learning, sleep, and appetite (Fischer et al., 1995; National Institute on Drug Abuse, 2007).

Finally, some people cope with stress or insomnia by using the legal stimulants *caffeine* and *nicotine*. Caffeine is present in coffee, tea, chocolate, and colas, among other beverages and foods. It causes increased alertness, raises pulse and heart rate, and can produce insomnia, restlessness, and ringing in the ears. Chronic ingestion of caffeine will lead to tolerance; regular users can experience withdrawal headaches if they miss their customary morning dose of caffeine. Nicotine, present in tobacco in any form, can lead users to feel alert, but can also make them feel irritable and can cause increased blood pressure, stomach pains, dizziness, emphysema, and heart disease. Nicotine is addictive and causes some level of tolerance as well as withdrawal symptoms when users stop ingesting it.

Caffeine and nicotine are both stimulants, and people who regularly smoke or drink may experience tolerance and, when they skip their usual coffee or cigarette, symptoms of withdrawal.

Source: Alamy Images

NARCOTIC ANALGESICS: FOCUS ON HEROIN. **Narcotic analgesics** make up a class of strongly addictive drugs that relieve pain and dull the senses. These medications can also lessen diarrhea, protracted coughing, and troubled sleep. Examples of narcotic analgesics are heroin, morphine, codeine, Percodan, Demerol, Vicodin, and Oxycodone. Heroin, an illegal drug, is one of the stronger narcotic analgesics. Like morphine, from which it is derived, heroin is an **opioid** (or *opiate*), produced from the opium poppy.

Like other opioids, heroin is a central nervous system depressant. It reduces neural activity in various areas of the brain, including in brainstem areas responsible for respiration and coughing. When heroin is in the body, the user's pupils may constrict, and he or she may experience slower breathing and lethargy. Heroin can bring about a feeling of relaxation and euphoria, but these effects are very short lived and are followed by negative changes in mood and behavior. Tolerance and withdrawal symptoms occur with repeated use; withdrawal usually involves periods of yawning, chills, hot flashes, restlessness, diarrhea, and goose bumps on the skin, followed by up to 12 hours of sleep.

In the brain, heroin and other opioids create a negative feedback loop:

1. Initially these substances produce pleasure by activating the dopamine-based reward system and binding to opioid receptors, where the body's endorphins (opioids produced in the body) usually bind.

2. With repeated use, the body comes to produce less endorphins, which leaves the user without natural means to relieve pain.

3. More heroin is thus needed to achieve pleasure and the analgesic effect.

When the user tries to quit, endorphins do not kick in to alleviate the withdrawal symptoms, thus heightening the discomfort—and making it difficult to quit.

Stimulants A class of substances that excite the central nervous system, leading to increases in behavioral activity and heightened arousal.

Crack Cocaine in crystalline form, usually smoked in a pipe (freebasing) or rolled into a cigarette.

Amphetamines A class of synthetic stimulants.

Narcotic analgesics A class of strongly addictive drugs, such as heroin, that relieve pain and dull the senses.

Opioid A narcotic, such as morphine, derived from the opium poppy; also referred to as *opiates*.

HALLUCINOGENS.   Another category of drugs that people use, abuse, or become dependent on (sometimes in an effort to cope) is **hallucinogens**—substances that induce *hallucinations*, which are experiences in which people perceive something that is not actually present. Hallucinogens include mescaline, peyote, psilocybin, lysergic acid diethylamide (LSD), phencyclidine (PCP), ketamine ("Special K"), and marijuana. In general, all but marijuana can cause visual hallucinations at moderate dosages; much higher dosages are needed before marijuana will do so. In this section, we focus on LSD, marijuana, and ketamine.

LSD is a synthetic substance that distorts perception, partly by inducing hallucinations. The visual hallucinations experienced by users often include geometric shapes, vivid colors, and violent movement. Moreover, users may feel as if they are becoming part of whatever they observe. Auditory hallucinations include hearing invented words, languages, or symphonies. Such hallucinations may last several hours and can be shaped by what the user expects to happen after taking LSD.

LSD can produce highly stressful, frightening experiences ("bad trips"). A user may panic during a bad trip and need to be "talked down," repeatedly reminded that the frightening experience is in fact a drug-induced state that will wear off. Occasionally, suicide or murder takes place in the course of a user's hallucination. In addition, long after the user has taken the drug, hallucinations can recur in the absence of subsequent drug use; these spontaneous, perhaps alarming, **flashbacks** can happen weeks, even years, afterward (Abraham, 1983).

The most commonly used hallucinogen in the United States is marijuana (National Center for Health Statistics, 2009); its active ingredient is tetrahydrocannabinol (THC), which is chemically similar to the naturally occurring neurotransmitters in the body called *cannabinoids*. Receptors for cannabinoid molecules exist throughout the body and brain, including brain areas involved in memory, attention, time and sensory perception, pleasure, and movement control; cannabinoids thus can affect learning and memory, appetite, and pain (Gruber et al., 2003; Wilson & Nicoll, 2001).

The effects of marijuana vary in multiple ways. First, they typically depend on the user's mood, expectations, and environment: For example, if alone, the user may experience drowsiness and go to sleep; if with others, the user may feel euphoric. Second, the effects can vary from person to person: Some people may experience anxiety and panic after using the substance (Dannon et al., 2004; Patel et al., 2005), whereas others may experience subtle perceptual alterations in which sights and sounds seem more vivid. Distortions of space and time are also common, and perceptual motor skills may be impaired, making driving unsafe (Petersen, 1977, 1979; Sterling-Smith, 1976).

Although marijuana is less powerful than most other hallucinogens, every year approximately 230,000 Americans attend treatment centers in an effort to stop using it (National Admissions to Substance Abuse Treatment Services, 2001). Long-term use of marijuana can lead to withdrawal symptoms (Budney et al., 2004; Haney et al., 1999).

Finally, the substance *ketamine*, similar to PCP, is legally used as an anesthetic for animals; use by humans can induce hallucinations, anesthesia, and stimulation of the cardiovascular and respiratory systems. Ketamine use is also associated with violence, a loss of contact with reality, and impaired thinking (White & Ryan, 1996). Users are likely to develop tolerance and dependence.

Coping and Social Support

Using—and abusing—substances is one way that people cope with stressors. Another way that people cope is through **social support**, the help and support gained through interacting with others. Social support can buffer the adverse effects of stress (Taylor, 2007). Social support emerges from positive relationships, such as being in a good marriage, having positive contact with friends and family, participating in group activities, and being involved in a religious organization. The simple fact of having such connections can increase life expectancy as much as being a nonsmoker or being physically active (House et al., 1988). Consider the following findings related to social support:

Hallucinogen A substance that induces hallucinations.

Flashback A hallucination that occurs without drug use, often long after the user has taken a drug.

Social support The help and support gained through interacting with others.

- In a study of over 4,000 men and women in Alameda County, California, the death rate for socially isolated people was twice that for people with strong social ties (Berkman & Syme, 1979).
- The benefits of social support can be gained simply from holding hands or making some other kind of physical contact (Sapolsky, 1997).
- For those undergoing a painful and frightening surgical procedure, just talking with their doctor the night before surgery positively affects recovery (Egbert et al., 1964).
- In a study of people with severe coronary heart disease, half of the group without social support died within 5 years, three times the rate for those who had a close friend or spouse (Williams et al., 1992). Other researchers have reported similar results (Dornelas, 2008; Rutledge et al., 2004).
- Among college students experiencing high levels of stress, those reporting high levels of social support were less likely to be depressed than those reporting lower levels of social support (Pengilly & Dowd, 1997).

A confounding variable influences the association between social support and longevity among heart patients: Although couch potatoes report less social support, it may be their sedentary behavior, not the diminished social support, that accounts for their shorter life spans (Brummett et al., 2005).

Source: © Getty Images/Stockbyte

Social support is also associated with better immune system functioning (R. E. Seeman et al., 1994). For example, in one study, researchers found that participants who had a wide range of acquaintances (friends, neighbors, relatives, work colleagues, people from social or religious groups, and so forth) were half as likely to catch a cold as those who were socially isolated (Cohen et al., 1997). The key was not the total number of supportive relationships but rather their variety. But not just any kinds of relationships will do: Demanding and critical kinds of relationships are associated with stress-related symptoms (T. E. Seeman, 2000).

When determining the effects of social support, psychologists sometimes make a distinction between *perceived* versus *enacted social support*, which have different effects. **Perceived social support** is the subjective sense that support is available should it be needed; it is distinct from the actual size and variety of the person's social network. In contrast, **enacted social support** is the specific support that is provided to the person—such as a friend's bringing you a meal when you are ill. Research has shown that perceived support, not enacted support, generally provides the buffer against stress (Cohen & Wills, 1985). In fact, the perception of support is unrelated to actual support (Lakey & Heller, 1988).

The person dressed in yellow is receiving enacted social support. However, she may not necessarily have the sense that support is available when she needs it (perceived social support) because these two aspects of social support are not correlated.

Source: © Network Productions/The Image Works

Mind–Body Interventions

When people know that they can't change a stressor, they may seek to cope by changing their response to the stressor—through emotion-focused coping—thereby minimizing the stress response. Taking drugs or alcohol is one strategy for altering the perception of a stressor or the body's response to it. However, there are other, more effective ways to achieve this end—*mind–body interventions*, which engage the mind in particular ways in order to influence the body's functioning. As noted in Table 5 on the next page, a number of mind–body interventions are commonly used to help people cope with stressors.

The National Institutes of Health has a special branch, the National Center for Complementary and Alternative Medicine (NCCAM), which is devoted to determining whether such techniques are effective. NCCAM provides funding to researchers who study how mind–body interventions can be used to treat specific diseases and pain and to maintain health (Berman & Straus, 2004). Mind–body techniques are increasingly used by people from many walks of life, such as medical patients, athletes (Ryska, 1998), managers, teachers (Anderson et al., 1999), and law school students (Sheehy & Horan, 2004), to cope with a variety of stressors.

Perceived social support The subjective sense that support is available should it be needed.

Enacted social support The specific supportive behaviors provided by others.

TABLE 5 Common Mind–Body Interventions

Intervention	Description
• Hypnosis	A focused awareness on imagined experiences and decreased awareness of the external environment, which together make a person more receptive to suggestions. Typically this state is achieved as a result of a *hypnotic induction*, a technique in which the participant is encouraged to relax and focus his or her awareness in a particular way, often with closed eyes.
• Meditation	A sense of deep relaxation and loss of self-awareness that typically is brought on by focusing on a single stimulus.
• Yoga	A form of meditation that typically combines physical postures, breathing techniques, and meditation or relaxation techniques.
• Biofeedback	A technique that uses auditory and visual feedback to allow a person to monitor a particular bodily function; such feedback helps people learn to control that function. Biofeedback is often used to teach people to learn to relax specific muscle groups.r
• Visual mental imagery	Using visualization ("seeing with the mind's eye") to construct relaxing or positive scenarios.
• Cognitive therapy	A form of therapy that alters the pattern of an individual's stress-inducing thoughts.
• Stress management/ relaxation induction	A set of techniques that promotes physical relaxation.
• Prayer	A form of addressing God.
• Tai chi	A type of martial art that combines gentle body movements with deep breathing.

The Effects of Mind–Body Interventions Mind–body interventions don't change a stressful stimulus; rather, they allow you to adapt to the stimulus by altering heart and breathing rates, hormone secretion, and brain activity. Even sitting quietly with your eyes closed for a few minutes can decrease your pulse rate (Forbes & Pekala, 1993).

One line of research on stress and mind–body interventions has examined whether different stress-reduction techniques can boost the immune system. In one study, researchers examined medical students during the period leading up to their exams (Kiecolt-Glaser et al., 1986); half of the participants were taught hypnosis and relaxation techniques and were encouraged to practice at home; the other half were taught nothing. The students in the hypnosis-and-relaxation group did in fact have better immune functioning during the exams than did the students in the control group.

For people who are physically ill, mind–body interventions may provide specific ways to cope, a method to decrease arousal and increase perceived control, and—for those learning or using mind–body techniques in a medical setting—a supportive environment in which to address fears about the illness (Andersen, 1997). These interventions have been found to confer the following benefits:

- improved mood and immune system functioning (Fawzy et al., 1990; Zakowski et al., 1992);
- increased lung functioning in people with asthma (Hockemeyer & Smyth, 2002);
- improved control of pain (NIH Technology Assessment Panel, 1996);
- decreased levels of reported stress, emotional distress, and poor coping strategies (Tacón et al., 2004; Timmerman et al., 1998); and
- fewer subsequent heart problems (Blumenthal et al., 2002).

However, although mind–body interventions can be beneficial, they do not guarantee health or stave off death (Claar & Blumenthal, 2003).

Stress management techniques can improve aspects of health. In one study, collegiate rowers were randomly assigned to either a stress management program or a control group; those in the stress management group had fewer illnesses and injuries and fewer medical visits to the student health center than did those in the control group (Perna et al., 2003).

The Placebo Effect as a Mind–Body Intervention *Placebos* are medically inactive substances that come to have medicinal effects; placebos can be effective in decreasing stress and arousal—which illustrates yet another the link between mind and body. Simply believing that you are receiving a remedy (even if it has no medicinal ingredients) can enhance the immune system and alleviate pain (Wager et al., 2004). Moreover, placebos often affect the same brain areas as do actual painkillers. For example, in one neuroimaging study participants received an intensely hot stimulus and then were given either a placebo or a fast-acting opioid painkiller; the placebo activated the same brain areas as did the opioid. Moreover, participants who were more responsive to the pain medicine were also more responsive to the placebo (Petrovic et al., 2002).

In general, characteristics of the placebo itself and the way it is dispensed can make it more or less effective. For instance, placebo injections are more effective than placebos taken orally, capsules are more effective than pills, more placebo pills work better than fewer placebo pills, and placebo pills that are more expensive work better than those that are less expensive (Waber et al., 2008). The color of the capsule can also make a difference: Blue capsules work best as tranquilizers, and yellow, pink, and red capsules work best as stimulants (Buckalew & Ross, 1981).

In addition, if the person dispensing the treatment is friendly and sympathetic and shows an interest in the patient's problems, the placebo is more likely to be effective (Shapiro & Morris, 1978). Even the clinician's own view of a placebo's effectiveness can make a difference: If the treatment provider has high expectations for the treatment, it is more likely to be effective (Roberts et al., 1993; Shapiro, 1964).

Gender, Culture, and Coping

In previous sections, we've noted some differences between males and females in how they perceive stressors (such as gender differences in level of hostility) and in coping (such as types of aggression employed and the use of alcohol). In the following sections, we discuss how men and women may be subject to different sorts of stressors and may cope differently, as may people from different cultures. ◉─Watch

◉──Watch the Video Gender Differences in Stress Vulnerability on mypsychlab.com

Gender Differences in Stress and Coping In Western cultures, women typically experience more stress than do men. A survey of 2,500 Swedes, for instance, found that women, particularly younger women, reported feeling more hassled, depressed, anxious, and hostile than did men (Scott & Melin, 1998). Some women may experience at least one type of stress more severely than do men—juggling their multiple roles: employee, wife, daughter, and mother (traditionally, it is women who are the primary caregivers of children and of elderly parents; Edwards, 2007; Stephens et al., 2009). The effects of having multiple roles can be both positive and negative. On the negative side, women report more conflict among their different roles than do men, more stress as a result of these multiple roles, and that they are less able to unwind at home (Clay, 1995). Women employed outside the home generally do more work than men during their "second shift" at home: cooking, cleaning, and shopping (Hochschild, 1989; Phillips & Imhoff, 1997). On the positive side, these multiple roles can also confer advantages: increased feelings of self-esteem and control (Norton et al., 2005; Pietromonaco et al., 1986), financial gain, social support from colleagues (Brannon, 1996), and decreased psychological stress (Abrams & Jones, 1994). In addition, having financial and familial resources and control over the job (S. W. Taylor et al., 1997; Tingey et al., 1996), as well as a sense of mastery at work (K. A. Christensen et al., 1998), can reduce the stress women feel as a result of multiple roles.

Men and women also tend to cope differently with stressors: Women tend to use emotion-focused coping strategies (such as seeking social support), whereas men tend to use problem-focused coping strategies that directly address the cause of the stress (Luckow et al., 1998; S. E. Taylor et al., 2000, 2002).

Cultural Differences in Coping Regardless of your gender, the culture in which you were raised: (1) influences whether you perceive a stimulus as a stressor,

393

and (2) how you cope with stressors. That is, different cultures lead their members to view different stimuli as stressors, and lead their members to believe that they have more or less control over particular stressors. Take the stimulus of crowding as an example. In different cultures, different levels of *density* (the number of people in a given space) produce the perception of *crowding* (the subjective experience created by density). Members of Asian cultures experience less stress than Westerners would in high-density living conditions; Asians have developed ways of creating a sense of privacy in the midst of density, thereby providing a sense of control (Werner et al., 1997).

Culture also plays a role in defining which coping strategies are socially appropriate (Aranda & Knight, 1997; Morling et al., 2003; O'Connor & Shimizu, 2002; Patterson et al., 1998). For instance, students in India prefer emotion-focused coping strategies more than do students in Canada (Sinha et al., 2000).

LOOKING AT LEVELS — Voodoo Death and the Nocebo Effect

Source: © Henning Christoph/DAS FOTOARCHIVE/PETER ARNOLD; (inset) Digital Art/Corbis

In some cultures, people claim that after a shaman (religious leader) puts a curse on someone, he or she soon dies; this phenomenon is known as *voodoo death* (Cannon, 1942). Although there is some debate as to whether voodoo death actually occurs (Hahn, 1997), research has shown that when people expect to become ill, they are in fact more likely to become ill. For example, among American women enrolled in a study of the risk factors for heart disease, those who believed that they were more likely to die of a heart attack were, in fact, 3.7 times more likely to die of a heart attack than other women in the study—even after researchers statistically controlled for known risk factors for heart disease (Eaker et al., 1992).

Such effects can arise from the **nocebo effect**, which is like the placebo effect except that a negative expectation produces a negative outcome. (*Placebo* in Latin means "I will please"; *nocebo* means "I will harm.") Voodoo death represents an extreme example of the nocebo effect. For other examples, consider the following findings:

- Patients who were told that a medicine was a stimulant (when it was, in fact, a muscle relaxant) reported more muscle tension than those who were told that the medicine was a relaxant (Flaten et al., 1999).
- After patients with food allergies received an injection of a saline solution and were told that it contained the substance to which they were allergic, they subsequently developed allergic symptoms (Jewett et al., 1990).
- Healthy volunteers were told that they would receive mild electric current through their heads and that such current could produce mild headaches; 70% reported headaches, even though the current was never turned on (Schweiger & Parducci, 1981).
- At least 20% to 25% of people taking placebo medications report unpleasant side effects (Dhume et al., 1975; Drid et al., 1995; Rosenzweig et al., 1993; Shepherd, 1993; Tangrea et al., 1994). Such effects include drowsiness, nausea, fatigue, insomnia, poor concentration, and gastrointestinal problems.

Nocebo effects also can arise as side effects from actual (not simply placebo) medications. Although side effects from drugs often arise from the ingredients in the medicine, some people experience side effects that do not arise directly from medicinal properties. Such reactions are called *nonspecific side effects*, and they can be uncomfortable enough

Nocebo effect A variation of the placebo effect in which a negative expectation produces a negative outcome.

that they lead people to stop taking the medication; the particular nonspecific side effects vary among people taking the same medication. The results from numerous studies suggest that nonspecific side effects are, in fact, nocebo effects (Barsky et al., 2002).

Three factors can explain how the nocebo response can give rise to such nonspecific side effects (Barsky et al., 2002):

1. *Classical conditioning.* Some people may have nonspecific side effects because they've become classically conditioned, perhaps by their past experiences with side effects from other medicines, which then generalize.
2. *Expectations.* People who expect negative side effects from a new medication (perhaps because they've heard of such effects from it) may then experience them.
3. *Attributions.* Once people take a medication, they may come to attribute any uncomfortable bodily symptoms to it. Thus, some people may attribute to the medication the normal but uncomfortable aches and twinges we all have from time to time: A study of healthy college students found that 81% experienced at least one physical symptom (such as an ache or twinge) within a 3-day stretch (Gick & Thompson, 1997). People who are most likely to develop nonspecific side effects attribute these brief disturbances to the medication.

These factors may all operate, in any combination, to give rise to nonspecific side effects.

Let's examine these three factors from a levels-of-analysis perspective. At the level of the brain, classical conditioning plays a role in the development of certain nocebo—and placebo—responses. An example of a conditioned nocebo effect is found in cancer patients who, as a result of chemotherapy, experience intense nausea: After experiencing such nausea a few times, the simple act of *preparing* to have the chemotherapy (such as by entering the room where it is administered) can induce nausea—a conditioned nocebo effect.

At the level of the person, the *expectation* of a negative outcome leads an individual to be hypervigilant for any bodily changes and to *attribute* such changes to the medication (the nocebo) instead of to some other stimulus (Barsky et al., 2002). Expectation of a negative response can increase pain, and expectation of a positive response can diminish pain (Benedetti et al., 2003). For those people who experience frequent nonspecific side effects, events at the level of the person include their beliefs about what such symptoms mean, as well as the ways individuals assess whether a bodily sensation constitutes a "side effect" (Hahn, 1999).

At the level of the group, expectations about a specific nocebo can arise after one person directly *tells* another about negative effects (Benedetti et al., 2003), which creates expectations of negative effects and increases the likelihood that any uncomfortable bodily sensation will be attributed to the medication. Sometimes expectations (and subsequent attributions) are communicated through stories, warnings, or written prohibitions. For instance, beliefs about a medicine can be shaped by advertisements, information on the Internet, friends' recountings of their experiences with the medication, or a doctor's admonition about side effects. In addition, each culture promotes somewhat different ideas and expectations about sickness and health (Hahn, 1995). ⊙⌐Watch

Watch the Video Internet Health Information on mypsychlab.com

Events at these three levels of analysis interact. For example, at the levels of the brain and the person, people high in the personality dimension of *neuroticism* (characterized by being emotional reactive) are more likely to experience nonspecific side effects through classical conditioning (C. Davis et al., 1995). In addition, culture and social interactions (level of the group) provide the context for the people whose pain responses are affected by their expectations (Benedetti et al., 2003). Such group-level events, in part, lead these people to have beliefs about the "medication" they are taking and lead them to be hypervigilant (level of the person) for their physical response (level of the brain). In turn, all these events lead people to interpret the bodily changes in particular ways (level of the person).

✓●─[Study and Review on
mypsychlab.com

LOOKING BACK

1. **What are the different types of coping strategies?** Coping strategies are the ways in which people handle stress. They can be classified into two general categories: problem-focused and emotion-focused. Problem-focused coping attempts to alter either the environment itself or the way the person and the environment interact; such coping is helpful when the person can affect the stressor. Emotion-focused coping attempts to change the emotional response to a stressor, and can be particularly helpful when the stressor itself cannot be changed. Whether either type of coping strategy will be effective depends on an accurate assessment of the possibility of changing the environment. One example of emotion-focused coping is taking drugs or alcohol; this coping strategy may be effective temporarily, but it is ineffective in the long term. Moreover, regular substance use often creates additional stressors.

2. **How do relationships affect stress and health?** Positive relationships can provide social support, which can buffer the negative effects of stress and boost the immune system. Perceived social support is effective in buffering stress, even though it can be unrelated to enacted support.

3. **What are mind–body interventions?** Some coping strategies (such as relaxation and meditation) take advantage of how the mind and body interact; these interventions use psychological tools to change psychological and bodily states.

4. **Do gender and culture play a role in coping?** Although a woman may experience more stress because of multiple roles, these multiple roles also can provide a buffer against stress and depression; the financial, self-esteem, and collegial benefits of the employee role can outweigh the increased daily stress. Culture in part determines whether a stimulus is perceived to be a stressor, and also plays a role in defining which coping strategies are socially acceptable.

LET'S REVIEW

((•─Listen to an audio file of your chapter on **mypsychlab.com**

I. WHAT IS STRESS?

A. Stress is the general term that describes the psychological and physical response to a stimulus that alters the body's equilibrium. The stress response of the autonomic nervous system increases heart rate and blood pressure.

B. Continued stressors can lead the body's response to stress to become harmful. A higher allostatic load increases the risk for medical and psychological problems.

C. The perception of stress plays a key role in determining what constitutes a stressor. Common sources of stress include internal conflicts, daily hassles, a perceived lack of control and a lack of predictability.

II. STRESS, DISEASE, AND HEALTH

A. Frequent activation of the stress response can impair the immune system, which can make the stressed person vulnerable to contracting a cold or can promote the growth of some types of existing tumors.

B. Stress can induce cardiovascular changes and can contribute to heart disease by increasing blood pressure.

C. The personality trait of hostility is associated with increased stress, heart rate, blood pressure, and cortisol production. Men are generally more hostile than are women.

D. Stress can also impair sleep, and sleep deprivation can create stress through impaired performance and producing poor mood, and increased cortisol level.

III. STRATEGIES FOR COPING

A. A realistic appraisal of whether your actions can affect a stressor will help you to determine what coping strategies will be effective.

B. Emotion-focused coping strategies work best when the situation can't be changed, and problem-focused strategies work best when it can.

C. Substance use is *not* effective as a long-term coping strategy because it does not change the stressor nor lead to enduring changes in the person's response to the stressor. Substance use merely changes the person's perception of the stress while he or she is under the influence of the substance. Substance abuse often creates additional stressors.

D. Social support (particularly perceived social support) can help decrease the experience of stress.

E. Mind–body interventions, such as relaxation training, meditation, and hypnosis, can decrease the effects of stress.

F. Culture can affect both the appraisal of a stimulus as a stressor and influence the choice of coping strategies for managing the stressor.

G. Both placebo and nocebo effects reflect interactions between mind and body, and both effects arise from the actions of events at the levels of brain, person, and group.

KEY TERMS

activation-synthesis hypothesis	coping	hostility	sleep
acute stressor	coping strategy	hypnogogic sleep	sleep apnea
aggression	crack	insomnia	social support
alarm phase	depressants	internal conflict	stimulants
alcohol myopia	disinhibition	latent content	stress
allostatic load	emotion-focused coping	manifest content	stress response
amphetamines	enacted social support	narcotic analgesic	stressor
approach–approach conflict	exhaustion phase	natural killer (NK) cell	substance abuse
approach–avoidance conflict	flashback	nocebo effect	substance dependence
atherosclerosis	general adaptation syndrome (GAS)	opioid	suprachiasmatic nucleus (SCN)
avoidance–avoidance conflict	glucocorticoids	perceived social support	T cell
B cell	hallucinogen	problem-focused coping	thought suppression
blackout	health psychology	REM rebound	tolerance
chronic stressor	hostile attribution bias	REM sleep	withdrawal symptoms
circadian rhythms		resistance phase	

PRACTICE TEST

✓ ● Study and Review on mypsychlab.com

For each of the following items, choose the single best answer.

1. Perception of a stressor triggers the _____, which is characterized by the fight-or-flight response.
   a. alarm phase
   b. resistance phase
   c. adaptation phase
   d. exhaustion phase

2. With continued stressors,
   a. the brain becomes exhausted because its limited resources in fighting stress become depleted.
   b. the continued stress response begins to damage the body, leading to a risk of stress-related diseases.
   c. cortisol improves learning and memory to better address the stressors.
   d. All of the above statements are true.

3. What is the order in which coping and the phases of cognitive appraisal occur?
   a. coping, primary appraisal, and secondary appraisal
   b. secondary appraisal, primary appraisal, and coping
   c. primary appraisal, secondary appraisal, and coping
   d. coping, secondary appraisal, and primary appraisal

4. Which of the following statements about control and stress is true?
   a. Actual control is not very important; what is important is whether you *perceive* a sense of control.
   b. When people don't feel that have control over a stressor, they may give up trying to cope effectively with it.
   c. For stressors that people can't control, if they are predictable they are generally less stressful than if they are unpredictable.
   d. All of the above statements are true.

5. High hostility is
   a. a trait characterized by a desire to hurt other people.
   b. paradoxically more likely in women than in men.
   c. associated with a higher heart rate and blood pressure throughout the day.
   d. associated with a decreased risk of heart disease.

6. The natural killer (NK) cell
   a. is a type of T cell.
   b. matures in the thymus, an organ located in the chest.
   c. destroys damaged or altered cells, such as precancerous cells.
   d. All of the above statements are true.

7. Which of the following statements is true about the relationship between stress and cancer?
   a. Stress can cause cancer.
   b. Stress cannot affect the growth of cancerous tumors.
   c. Stress can depress the level of tumor-fighting NK cells.
   d. The type of cancer and biological factors related to its progression never outweigh psychological factors in tumor growth.

8. Sleep
   a. is a single state.
   b. comprises five stages that occur in cycles during the night.
   c. has an initial stage, lasting approximately 5 minutes, called REM sleep.
   d. All of the above statements are true.

9. During REM sleep, your
   a. breathing and heart rate are fast and irregular.
   b. brain shows similar amounts of activity as when you are awake.
   c. muscles are relaxed and unresponsive.
   d. All of the above statements are true.

10. Sleep deprivation
    a. affects at least three important psychological areas: attention, mood, and performance.
    b. improves mood.
    c. does not affect tasks that require sustained attention and a motor response.
    d. leads to decreases in the next day's level of cortisol.

11. Sleep apnea
    a. is a disorder characterized by a temporary cessation of breathing during sleep.
    b. results when muscles at the base of the throat relax and consequently block the airway.
    c. can be fatal.
    d. All of the above statements are true.

12. The act of trying to suppress distressing thoughts
    a. decreases the intensity of the thoughts.
    b. can result in a rebound effect.
    c. is not associated with changes in the functioning of the sympathetic nervous system or immune system.
    d. decreases the autonomic reactions to those thoughts.

13. Alcohol use
    a. excites the central nervous system through its net effect on excitatory neurotransmitters.
    b. in high doses causes constriction of blood vessels in the brain.
    c. facilitates aggressive behavior.
    d. All of the above statements are true.

14. Enacted social support
    a. provides the best buffer against stress.
    b. is the specific supportive behaviors provided by others.
    c. is the subjective sense that support is available should it be needed.
    d. is closely related to the perception of support.

15. Mind–body interventions
    a. rest on the idea of altering the body's response to a stressor.
    b. have been found to have no effect on the immune system.
    c. include yoga, prayer, taking vitamins, and exercise.
    d. are a form of controlling the stressor.

Answers: 1. a; 2. b; 3. c; 4. d; 5. c; 6. d; 7. c; 8. b; 9. d; 10. a; 11. d; 12. b; 13. c; 14. b; 15. a

Van Gogh reported that he had 'attacks' during which he would hear voices; at times, he believed he was being poisoned.

PSYCHOLOGICAL DISORDERS

MORE THAN EVERYDAY PROBLEMS

Museum-goers worldwide throng to see exhibits of the works of Vincent van Gogh, one of the most influential painters of the 19th century. Born in Holland in 1853, van Gogh created extraordinary art and took much joy in painting, but his life is a tale of misery. The son and grandson of Protestant ministers, van Gogh was the second of six children. A memoir by his sister-in-law records, "As a child he was of difficult temper, often troublesome and self-willed" (Roskill, 1963, p. 37). According to his parents, when punished, Vincent became more difficult. During his childhood, he showed no particular awareness of his great gifts; however, on two occasions, once when he modeled a clay elephant and again when he drew a cat, he destroyed his creations when he felt a fuss was being made about them (Roskill, 1963).

Van Gogh worked as a clerk in an art gallery, starting when he was 16 years old, but his long, moody silences and irritability isolated him from his coworkers. After 4 years, he was transferred to the gallery's office in London, where he fell in love with his landlady's daughter, Ursula. They spent many months together, until she revealed her engagement to a previous tenant, and rejected van Gogh. Feeling utterly defeated, he found it difficult to concentrate at work. He frequently argued with his coworkers and was soon fired.

Van Gogh next decided on a career in the ministry but could not master the Greek and Latin necessary for the entrance exams. Instead, he became a lay pastor, preaching to miners in the Borinage, a coal-mining area in Belgium. He went without bathing, and he slept in a hut on bare planks, as the miners did. But the miners feared this unkempt, wild-looking man, and the church elders dismissed him. Increasingly, van Gogh found comfort in painting and drawing—but his life continued to be marked by instability.

After he left the Borinage, he lived in and out of his parents' home and wandered around the country. Whereas once his interest in religion had been intense, if not obsessional, he now turned his back on religion. He developed a relationship with a pregnant prostitute, Sien, but their liaison ended after about a year and a half. As his life was unraveling, he reported that he had "attacks" during which he would hear voices; at times, he believed he was being poisoned. Despite all this, he continued painting.

When he was 35, van Gogh convinced fellow painter Paul Gauguin to share a house with him in Arles, France. As was true for all of van Gogh's relationships, he and Gauguin frequently quarreled. According to Gauguin, after one particularly violent argument, van Gogh approached him threateningly with an open razor, but Gauguin stared him down. Van Gogh then ran to their house, where he cut off his earlobe, which he then sent to a local prostitute (not Sien). The next day he was found at home, bleeding and unconscious; he was taken to a hospital, where he remained for 2 weeks. His brother Theo spent time with him in the hospital and found Vincent in great spiritual anguish.

After his release from the hospital in January 1889, van Gogh's behavior became increasingly bizarre, so much so that within 2 months the residents of Arles petitioned that he be confined, and he again stayed for a time in the hospital. In May of that year, van Gogh moved to the asylum at Saint-Remy, not far from Arles, where he lived on and off for the next year and a half and where he produced many paintings. Shortly after his last release from the asylum, less than 2 years after the incident with Gauguin, he purposefully ended his anguish and his life by going out into a field with a gun and shooting himself in the stomach. Yet, a few weeks before his death, he could say, "I still love art and life very much indeed" (Roskill, 1963).

Questions of art aside, van Gogh's experiences focus our attention on psychological disorders: What defines a psychological disorder? Who establishes criteria for determining what is abnormal behavior? What are the symptoms and origins of some specific disorders?

◙ ◙ ◙

Identifying Psychological Disorders: What's Abnormal?

At one point in his life, van Gogh was obsessed with religious ideas and believed in ghosts. And later in his life he exhibited unusual behaviors (such as cutting off part of his ear). Are these signs of psychological disturbance? What distinguishes merely unusual behaviors from behaviors that are symptoms of a psychological disorder? Mental health professionals—clinically trained psychologists, social workers, and psychiatrists—face questions such as these every day. In this section, we explore how formulations of and findings about psychological disorders suggest answers to those questions.

LOOKING AHEAD Learning Objectives

1. How is psychological abnormality defined?
2. How are psychological disorders classified?
3. How are psychological disorders explained?

Defining Psychological Abnormality

Psychological disorders—also referred to as psychiatric disorders, mental disorders, or, less systematically, mental illness—are difficult to define because they can encompass many aspects of thoughts, feelings, behavior, and bodily functioning. However, a good working definition is that a **psychological disorder** is a mental condition characterized by cognitive, emotional, and behavioral symptoms that: create significant distress; impair work, school, family, relationships, or daily living; or lead to significant risk of harm. This definition centers on three factors: distress, impairment, and risk of harm.

Distress People with psychological disorders may experience *distress*. Some forms of distress are immediately evident to others, and some are not. For example, repeatedly bursting into tears and expressing hopelessness about the future are obvious forms of distress—even to a casual observer—whereas chronic worrying or feeling sad for long periods of time may not be evident even to friends and family members.

Impairment People with psychological disorders may have a *disability* or *impairment* in some aspect of life. Examples include a police officer who becomes so anxious that he cannot perform his job, or a person (such as van Gogh) whose emotional outbursts drive others away. A person's impairment—such as hearing voices when no one is speaking—may not necessarily cause him or her distress but can be maladaptive nonetheless.

Risk of Harm *Risk of harm* can occur when a psychological disorder causes a person to put life (his or her own, or another's) at risk, either intentionally or accidentally. For instance, severe depression may lead someone to attempt suicide; similarly extreme paranoia may provoke someone to attack other people, or a parent's disorder may be sufficiently severe that the children's safety is put at risk. This happened when Andrea Yates suffered so severely from depression that she lost touch with reality and drowned her five young children in 2001—thinking that she was rescuing them from Satan's grasp.

> **THINK** like a **PSYCHOLOGIST** Can you think of other examples of distress that are not always easily observed by others?

Psychological disorder A mental condition characterized by cognitive, emotional, and behavioral symptoms that: create significant distress; impair work, school, family, relationships, or daily living; or lead to significant risk of harm.

Van Gogh's painting of the church at Auvers is unusual because of its unconventional perspective, use of color, and brushstrokes. Do these differences reflect a psychological disorder or just a different way of seeing or conveying impressions of the structure and its surroundings?

Source: Musee d'Orsay, Paris, France/Art Resource, N.Y.

Cultural and Social Influences Culture and the social context influence whether "unusual" thoughts, feelings, or behaviors are considered abnormal. Picture someone hopping on one leg, thumb in mouth, trying to sing the French national anthem during a hockey game. You would probably consider this behavior abnormal, but what if the behavior was part of a fraternity initiation ritual or a new kind of performance art? A behavior that is bizarre or inappropriate in one context may be entirely appropriate in another. To be considered "disordered," it is not enough for a behavior or a set of behaviors to be deviant from the mainstream culture. Being unconventional or different in religious, political, or sexual arenas does not qualify as abnormal.

In fact, both what is considered "unconventional" and what is considered "deviant" changes from generation to generation, as cultural norms shift over time. For example, in 1851, Dr. Samuel Cartwright of Louisiana wrote an essay in which he declared that slaves' running away was evidence of a serious mental disorder that he called *drapetomania* (Eakin, 2000). Also, homosexuality was officially considered a psychological disorder in the United States until 1973, when it was removed from the *Diagnostic and Statistical Manual of Mental Disorders* (the manual used by mental health professionals to classify psychological disorders).

To some extent, what is considered deviant also varies from culture to culture. If someone in the United States persistently shouts, laughs, and hits his or her head against a wall, such behavior would probably be considered symptoms of a psychological disorder. However, in some North African and Middle Eastern cultures, this collection of behaviors could reflect *zar*, or spirit possession; an experience of *zar* is not considered abnormal in the cultures in which it more commonly occurs (American Psychiatric Association, 2000).

Nevertheless, throughout the world, certain sets of thoughts, feelings, and behaviors—in specific contexts—are likely to cross the line and be classified as abnormal rather than as simply unusual or deviant. The line between normal and abnormal behavior is perhaps easiest to draw in the case of **psychosis**, which is a severely impaired ability to perceive and comprehend events accurately, combined with grossly disorganized behavior. Psychosis is usually indicated by either (or both) of two types of symptoms:

1. **hallucinations**, which are mental images—in any sensory modality (but mainly visual or auditory)—so vivid that they seem real (such as hearing voices when no one is speaking), or

2. **delusions**, which are unshakable but false beliefs that are often bizarre (such as a person's belief that he or she is being controlled by aliens).

Psychosis: A severely impaired ability to perceive and comprehend events accurately, combined with grossly disorganized behavior.

Hallucinations Mental images so vivid that they seem real.

Delusions Unshakable but false beliefs that are often bizarre.

Mathematician John Nash (left), whose life was the basis for the movie *A Beautiful Mind*, starring Oscar-winning actor Russell Crowe (right), had delusions that aliens were communicating with him. Although the movie portrayed Nash as having both hallucinations and delusions, in real life he did not have hallucinations.

Sources: © John Forbes Nash/CORBIS All Rights Reserved; © Reuters/CORBIS All Rights Reserved

However, hallucinations or delusions should not be considered abnormal if they are an accepted part of the culture. For example, in some religious groups, such as Pentecostals, it is not considered abnormal to hear voices, especially the voice of God (Cox, personal communication, 2000).

Psychological disorders directly affect large numbers of people. The World Health Organization (2008) estimates that 450 million people suffer from psychological disorders worldwide. In the United States, approximately 25% of Americans have symptoms that meet the criteria for a psychological disorder (Kessler, Chiu, et al., 2005). These numbers are daunting because psychological disorders can reduce people's ability to care for themselves and can impair their relationships and their ability to function on the job. In fact, for every 10 workers, an average of 3.7 days of work is lost each month because the workers are less productive or absent because of a psychological disorder (Kessler & Frank, 1997).

Categorizing Psychological Disorders: Is a Rose Still a Rose by Any Other Name?

Once a mental health clinician determines that a person's mental condition leads to significant distress, impairment, and/or risk of harm, the clinician must then determine the specific nature of the person's problems. For example, suppose that a man comes to a clinical psychologist's office complaining that he feels he is going crazy and that he has a strong sense of impending doom. How would the clinical psychologist determine the nature of this man's difficulties and determine out how best to help him? What questions should the psychologist ask? The *Diagnostic and Statistical Manual of Mental Disorders*, known to its users simply as the *DSM*, was developed to respond to such concerns. The *DSM* helps mental health clinicians diagnose the nature of a person's problems, which then helps guide treatment for those problems. **⊙▸ Simulate**

History of the *DSM* The *DSM* has evolved over time, partly in response to increased scientific knowledge about the nature of psychological disorders. The American Psychiatric Association published the first edition of the *DSM* in 1952; this was the first manual of mental disorders designed primarily to help clinicians diagnose and treat patients. This manual was based on psychodynamic theory (largely on the theories of Sigmund Freud), which was at the time the most well-accepted theory explaining mental disorders. In later editions of the manual, its developers did not rely on any one theory of the causes of disorders and instead characterized disorders on the basis of specific behaviors, determined by a growing body of scientific research.

Since the third edition, the *DSM* has described five *axes*, or five types of information that should be considered when assessing a person's problems:

- *Axis I* is used to specify most clinical disorders, such as anxiety disorders or schizophrenia.
- *Axis II* is used to specify *personality disorders* (which involve rigid and maladaptive personality traits) and *mental retardation*. These disorders have symptoms that are presumed to arise during childhood, persist throughout life, and can affect how symptoms of other disorders are expressed.
- *Axis III* is used to note any medical conditions that might be relevant to a diagnosis on Axis I or II, such as significant food allergies in a person with an eating disorder, or a recent broken hip in someone who refuses to leave the house.
- *Axis IV* is used to note social and environmental problems, such as marital problems or homelessness.
- *Axis V* is used to note the patient's highest level of functioning in major areas of life within the past year.

In addition, an appendix to the manual outlines aspects of the patient's cultural context that clinicians should take into account when making a diagnosis. However, most of the manual is devoted to describing disorders; the most recent edition of the manual, called the *DSM-IV-TR* (*IV* stands for *fourth edition*, and *TR* stands for *text revision*), defines 17 major categories of psychological problems, described in Table 1 on the next page.

THINK like a **PSYCHOLOGIST** In what specific ways might psychological disorders lead people to be less productive at work or at school?

⊙▸ Simulate the Overview of Clinical Assessment Tools on **mypsychlab.com**

TABLE 1   The 17 Major Categories of Disorders in the *DSM-IV-TR*

Major Category of Disorders	Explanation
Disorders usually first diagnosed in infancy, childhood, or adolescence	Disorders that are usually first evident early in life, but some adults are newly diagnosed with one of these disorders, such as *attention-deficit/hyperactivity disorder*
Delirium, dementia, and amnestic and other cognitive disorders	Disorders of consciousness and cognition, such as *dementia*
Mental disorders due to a general medical condition	Disorders in which mental and psychological symptoms are judged to be due to a medical condition that is noted on Axis III, such as anemia (which can lead to fatigue and a lack of energy) in someone who is depressed
Substance-related disorders	Disorders of substance dependence and abuse (as well as disorders induced by a substance, such as when someone becomes psychotic after taking a drug)
Schizophrenia and other psychotic disorders	Disorders related to psychoses, such as *schizophrenia*
Mood disorders	Disorders of mood, such as *depression*
Anxiety disorders	Disorders of anxiety, such as *obsessive-compulsive disorder*
Somatoform disorders	Disorders in which physical/medical complaints have no known medical origin (or the symptoms are not proportional to a medical condition) and so are thought to be psychological in nature, such as *hypochondriasis*
Factitious disorders	Disorders in which the person intentionally fabricates symptoms of a medical or psychological disorder, but not for external gain (such as disability claims)
Dissociative disorders	Disorders in which there is a disruption in the usually integrated functions of consciousness, memory, or identity, such as *dissociative identity disorder*
Sexual and gender identity disorders	Disorders of sexual function (such as *premature ejaculation*), of the object of sexual desire (such as *fetishism*), or of gender identity (*gender identity disorder*)
Eating disorders	Disorders related to eating, such as *bulimia nervosa*
Sleep disorders	Disorders related to sleep, such as *insomnia*
Impulse-control disorders not elsewhere classified	Disorders related to the ability to contain impulses, such as *kleptomania*
Adjustment disorders	Disorders related to the development of distressing emotional or behavioral symptoms in response to identifiable stress
Personality disorders	Disorders related to personality traits that are inflexible and maladaptive, and that cause distress or difficulty with daily functioning, such as *narcissistic personality disorder*
Other conditions that may be a focus of clinical attention	A problem that is the focus of treatment and for which no psychological disorder described in the manual applies or for which the symptoms do not meet the criteria for any disorder, such as *bereavement*

Source: Reprinted with permission from the *Diagnostic and Statistical Manual of Mental Disorders, Fourth Edition, Text Revision,* (Copyright 2000). American Psychiatric Association.

Disadvantages and Advantages of the *DSM* The number and breadth of disorders in the *DSM* has grown with each successive edition, and some researchers and clinicians have criticized this trend; they note the following:

- Previously normal problems (such as bereavement) are now considered to be abnormal and are included in the *DSM*.
- As the *DSM* has evolved, it introduced categories that define medical problems as psychological disorders. For example, a new diagnosis in the *DSM-IV* was "breathing-related sleep disorder" (one cause of which is sleep apnea, which arises when the throat muscles and surrounding tissues relax too much during sleep and obstruct the airway). Thus, the *DSM-IV-TR* created a *psychological* or *psychiatric* disorder for a medical problem.
- Some of the criteria of the different disorders overlap substantially, and thus the different disorders are not clearly distinct from one another (Blais et al., 1997; Tucker, 1998).

Despite these criticisms, one advantage of the *DSM-IV-TR* is that it sidesteps disputes about which theory best accounts for the cause(s) of psychological disorders; in general, the *DSM-IV-TR* does not explain why disorders arise or the best way to treat them. Another advantage of the current *DSM* is that it includes standards that can be used to ensure *reliability* (consistency) in diagnosis: If two people with similar symptoms and mental health histories are seen in two different cities by two different mental health clinicians who are using the *DSM-IV-TR* to guide their diagnosis, the odds are that those people will be diagnosed with the same disorder. Because of these advantages, the *DSM-IV-TR* is the predominant means of categorizing psychological disorders in the United States. Our exploration of psychological disorders in this chapter uses the *DSM-IV-TR* system of categorization.

Explaining Psychological Abnormality

No matter how psychological disorders are categorized, the explanations for disorders have changed with the times, and each culture's explanations reflect the values of and knowledge present in that culture. For instance, in ancient Greece, abnormal behaviors and medical problems both were thought to arise from imbalances of the body's four fluids, or "humors": yellow bile, phlegm, blood, and black bile. Too much phlegm, for instance, made you phlegmatic, or sluggish and slow; too much black bile made you melancholic. In 17th-century New England, abnormality was thought to be the work of the devil. In the middle of the 20th century, Sigmund Freud's work was influential, and psychodynamic theory led people to understand abnormality as a result of unconscious conflicts.

Currently, when psychologists and other mental health professionals explain psychological disorders, they appeal to multiple factors, which range from the level of the brain (neurological and other biological factors), to the level of the person (mental content, such as beliefs and feelings, and mental processes, such as attention and reasoning), to the level of the group (social factors, such as relationships, family environments, and culture writ large). In the sections that follow we provide a brief overview of how these three types of factors contribute to our understanding of psychological disorders. Then we discuss two models of how these three types of factors interact—the *diathesis-stress model* and the *biopsychsocial model*.

The Brain: Genes, Neurotransmitters, and Brain Structure and Function
Psychological disorders can increasingly be explained as arising in part from genetics, abnormal neurotransmitter function, and abnormal structure and functioning of the brain. For example, van Gogh's family history suggests that genes may have contributed to his psychological problems. Consider: Van Gogh's brother Theo was often depressed and anxious, and he committed suicide within a year after Vincent's suicide; his sister Wilhelmina exhibited a long-standing psychosis; and his youngest brother Cor is thought to have committed suicide. Although this family history does not prove that van Gogh inherited a vulnerability to a psychological disorder (something about the shared environment could be the culprit rather than genes), researchers are finding increasing evidence that genes can predispose some people to develop some disorders.

Genes exert their effects in part by affecting neurotransmitters and other aspects of brain function as well as by affecting the structure of the brain itself. Thus, we must consider these sorts of brain-related factors when explaining psychological disorders. For instance, with regard to neurotransmitters, depression arises in part because of abnormal serotonin levels. And, with regard to brain structure and function, an irrational fear of spiders (a type of *phobia*) arises in part because of an overreactive amygdala (a subcortical brain structure that plays a key role in the detection and expression of strong emotions, such as fear). Altered brain structure and function can also arise for reasons other than genes, as we discuss shortly.

The Person: Maladaptive Learning, Maladaptive Thoughts and Biases
Although events at the level of the brain can contribute to a psychological disorder, they are only a part of the picture. For example, genes may *predispose* someone to develop a disorder, but they do not *dictate* that the person will in fact develop it. Other factors, such as those at the level of the person, play key roles in determining whether someone—even someone with a genetic predisposition—will in fact develop a disorder.

LEARNING MALADAPTIVE BEHAVIORS. One factor at the level of the person that can help explain how and why psychological disorders arise is the nature of learning—in particular, the nature of *classical conditioning* and *operant conditioning*. **Classical conditioning** is the type of learning that occurs when an unconditioned stimulus (such as a loud noise) that

Classical conditioning A type of learning that occurs when a neutral stimulus becomes associated (paired) with a stimulus that causes a reflexive behavior and, in time, this neutral stimulus is sufficient to produce that behavior.

Operant conditioning The process by which a stimulus and response become associated with the consequences of making the response.

Diathesis–stress model An explanation for how psychological disorders develop, in which a predisposition to a given disorder (diathesis) and specific factors (stress) combine to trigger the onset of the disorder.

causes a reflexive behavior (such as a fear or startle response) is associated with a neutral stimulus (such as a white rat); over time this neutral stimulus (rat) is sufficient to produce the behavior that is reflexively elicited by the unconditioned stimulus (a fear response, in this example). Classical conditioning can explain why some people become afraid of heights: If they had an experience in which they almost fell (or believed that they might almost fall) from a high place, just being far off the ground in the future could—through classical conditioning—come to elicit fear.

The other type of learning that might help to explain psychological disorders is **operant conditioning** (the process by which a stimulus and response become associated with the consequences of making the response). People come to learn maladaptive behaviors when those behaviors—which are a response to some stimulus—are intentionally or inadvertently reinforced. That is, the behaviors are followed by desired consequences, which in turn increase the likelihood that the behaviors will occur again in response to the stimulus. For example, if chewing on your fingernails until your fingers bleed relieves your anxiety, you would be reinforced for chewing on them—and would come to do so again (and again) when you are anxious.

MALADAPTIVE THOUGHTS AND BIASES. In addition to learning principles, certain mental events are associated with psychological disorders. Specifically, certain mental events can:

- *Bias what a person tends to pay attention to.* For instance, a person can become hypervigilant for certain stimuli that are viewed as threatening—such as spiders.

- *Influence the pattern of a person's thoughts.* For instance, a person can come to think of him- or herself as incompetent and worthless: "Nothing ever turns out right for me; I don't deserve anything better so what's the point in trying?"

- *Affect the attributions that a person makes about the causes of positive and negative events.* For instance, a person can come to attribute negative events to him- or herself rather than circumstances: "It's all my fault; I can't do anything right".

The Group: Social and Cultural Factors Factors at the level of the group—involving the family, peers, or the culture at large—can also play a role in developing and maintaining psychological disorders. For example, a social event—such as a relationship breakup or getting fired from a job—triggered an episode of depression for almost three-fourths of people with that disorder (American Psychiatric Association, 2000; Tennant, 2002).

Interacting Factors As noted earlier, factors at the levels of the brain, person, and group each can help to explain psychological disorders—and, although each separate explanation may be valid, it is incomplete. Psychological abnormality does not arise from any single type of factor acting in isolation. Instead, the factors interact, and it is the net effect of these factors that ultimately gives rise to a disorder. Two frameworks have been developed to capture the ways that different types of factors interact: the *diathesis–stress model* and the *biopsychosocial approach*. We consider each in turn.

When something falls, do you attribute the mishap to some outside factor or to yourself? Do you dwell on negative things or do you tend to put them out of your mind? Some thought patterns can create a diathesis for a particular disorder.

Source: PhotoEdit Inc.

DIATHESIS–STRESS MODEL. The first general approach that specified how multiple types of factors contribute to psychological disorders was the **diathesis–stress model** (*diathesis* means a predisposition to a disorder). According to this model, illustrated in Figure 1, "for a given disorder, there is both a predisposition to the disorder (a *diathesis*) and specific factors (*stress*) that combine with the diathesis to trigger the onset of the disorder" (Rende & Plomin, 1992, p. 177).

According to the diathesis–stress model, the diathesis is typically a genetic or brain-based predisposition, and stress typically involves psychological and social factors. This model has two major implications:

- Even if a person has the genes, neurotransmitter activity and/or brain structure or function associated with a disorder, without strong enough psychological or social stress, the disorder will not be likely to develop.

- When people experience stress those who are not genetically or neurologically vulnerable for a given disorder are unlikely to develop that disorder.

From this perspective, the sum total of the different factors and their interactions is crucial; no single event or factor alone is likely to lead to a psychological disorder. For instance, genes can play a role in causing schizophrenia (a disorder typically characterized by symptoms of psychosis, discussed shortly), but even when an identical twin has schizophrenia, the other twin in the pair develops the disorder only about half the time.

A drawback of the diathesis–stress model is that all types of stress are typically grouped together, which can lead researchers and clinicians to overlook or minimize important differences among the various types of stress. Another drawback is that, as shown in Figure 1, the diatheses and the stress are typically viewed as distinct factors that do not affect one another. However, research increasingly reveals that what counts as psychological or social stress itself depends in part on a person's predispositions; for instance, if a person has an "anxious temperament," which can be in part a result of genetic factors, he or she might perceive an announced 1% increase in the crime rate as stressful—whereas someone who is not so anxious might not be stressed by such a small increase.

THE BIOPSYCHOSOCIAL APPROACH.   Reflecting a growing number of research findings, many researchers and clinicians today believe that psychological disorders can best be explained by considering all three types of factors—at the levels of the brain, person, and group—separately, as well as by understanding their influences on each other. This approach is generally known as the *biopsychosocial model*.

The biopsychosocial model has been further refined in that the brain is the crucial piece of biology for understanding psychological disorders (Rosenberg & Kosslyn, 2011). Following the emergence of neuroimaging and various sophisticated techniques in neuroscience, enough is now known about the brain to begin to understand in detail how neurological abnormalities contribute to psychological disorders (Rosenberg & Kosslyn, 2011). In the rest of this chapter, we will discuss such neurological alterations as part of how to understand psychological disorders. We will consider genetics, neurotransmitters, and brain structure and function (level of the brain); learning principles, thought patterns, and emotions (level of the person); relationships, and familial and cultural factors (level of the group); and the interactions among these various types of factors.

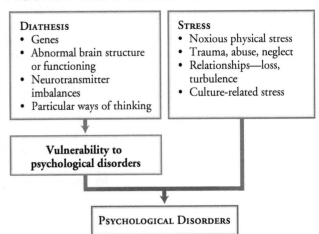

FIGURE 1 The Diathesis–Stress Model

Most mental health researchers and professionals believe that both diathesis and stress together cause psychological disorders.

LOOKING BACK

1. **How is psychological abnormality defined?** Psychological abnormality is defined in the *DSM-IV-TR* by taking into account three factors—subjective distress, significant disability or impairment, and risk of harm to self or others—as well as the culture and context in which the apparent abnormality arises. Merely deviating from a cultural norm is not sufficient for thoughts, feelings, or behavior to be diagnosed as a psychological disorder.

2. **How are psychological disorders classified?** In the *DSM-IV-TR*, psychological disorders are classified along one of two axes: Most clinical disorders are specified on Axis I, and personality disorders and mental retardation are specified on Axis II. The other three axes are provided to allow mental health clinicians to note medical factors that can affect the disorders (Axis III), the psychosocial or environmental aspects of the problem (Axis IV), and the highest level of functioning previously attained (Axis V).

3. **How are psychological disorders explained?** Psychological disorders can be explained by factors at the levels of the brain (such as genes and neurotransmitters), person (such as maladaptive learning and thought patterns), and group (such as social stress).

The diathesis–stress model regards psychological disorders as arising from neurological and other factors that make some people more vulnerable to developing particular disorders, which are then triggered by stress. The biopsychosocial model regards psychological disorders as arising from interactions among biological, psychological, and social factors.

Axis I: An Overview of Selected Disorders

Vincent van Gogh's history suggests that he met the *DSM-IV-TR* broad criteria for having a psychological disorder: He was greatly distressed, he was at times impaired by his psychological difficulties, and he was clearly at risk of harming himself and others. From what type of disorder might he have suffered? Let's examine several categories of Axis I disorders and see whether we can better understand van Gogh's difficulties.

LOOKING AHEAD Learning Objectives

1. What are mood disorders? What causes them?
2. What are the main types of anxiety disorders? What are their symptoms and causes?
3. What are the symptoms and causes of schizophrenia?
4. What are the symptoms and causes of eating disorders?

Mood Disorders

We cannot diagnose someone from a distance, but we know enough about van Gogh's life and behavior to make some educated guesses about the nature of his moods and emotional turmoil. He spoke frequently of feeling sad; still, he said, "I prefer feeling my sorrow to forgetting it or becoming indifferent" (Lubin, 1972, p. 22). Painting was the one thing that drove away his sadness, and sometimes he painted in a frenzy. He had bouts of irritability, had difficulty concentrating, and was frequently quarrelsome. People described him as odd, argumentative, very sensitive, and unpredictable. He had frequent thoughts of suicide, and in the end, at the age of 37, he died after intentionally shooting himself (Lubin, 1972).

Some of these accounts of van Gogh's behavior are consistent with the presence of a *mood disorder*. **Mood disorders** are characterized by persistent or episodic disturbances in emotion that interfere with normal functioning in at least one realm of life. Among the most common mood disorders are *major depressive disorder*, *dysthymia* (a less intense but longer lasting form of depression), and *bipolar disorder* (formerly known as manic-depressive disorder). In the following sections, we consider each disorder in turn.

Major Depressive Disorder: Not Just Feeling Blue When people feel sad or blue, they may say they are "depressed," but generally they do not mean that they are suffering from a psychological disorder. In contrast, when mental health professionals use the term *depression*, they are usually referring to **major depressive disorder (MDD)**, which is characterized by at least 2 weeks of depressed mood or loss of interest in nearly all activities, along with altered patterns of sleep or of eating, loss of energy, and feelings of hopelessness, as described in Table 2 (American Psychiatric Association, 2000). Thus, major depression affects a person's "ABCs":

- *affect* (mood),
- *behavior* (actions), and
- *cognition* (thoughts).

Some people with MDD may experience only one episode of depression; others experience recurrent episodes that may be frequent or be separated by years. For still others, depression may become chronic (Judd et al., 1998). An 11-year study of over 300

Mood disorders A category of disorders characterized by persistent or episodic disturbances in emotion that interfere with normal functioning in at least one realm of life.

Major depressive disorder (MDD) A mood disorder characterized by at least 2 weeks of depressed mood or loss of interest in nearly all activities, along with sleep or eating disturbances, loss of energy, and feelings of hopelessness.

TABLE 2 *DSM-IV-TR* Diagnostic Criteria for Major Depressive Disorder

During a period of at least 2 weeks, five or more of the following symptoms have occurred and represent a change in functioning:

- Depressed mood most of the day, almost daily (based on subjective report or observations by others).
- Markedly diminished interest or pleasure in nearly all daily activities (based on subjective or objective reports).
- Significant weight loss (not through intentional dieting), weight gain, or persistent change in appetite.
- Daily insomnia or hypersomnia (sleeping a lot).
- Daily psychomotor agitation (intense restlessness) or retardation (physical sluggishness).
- Daily fatigue, or loss of energy.
- Almost daily feelings of worthlessness or inappropriate or excessive guilt.
- Almost daily diminished ability to think, concentrate, or make decisions (based on subjective or objective reports).
- Recurrent thoughts of death or suicide with or without a specific plan.

Source: Reprinted with permission from the *Diagnostic and Statistical Manual of Mental Disorders, Fourth Edition, Text Revision,* (Copyright 2000). American Psychiatric Association.

people diagnosed with major depressive disorder found that more than one-third of the participants had only one episode of depression without a recurrence (Solomon et al., 2000).

MDD is the most common psychological disorders in the United States, and it is found among all cultural and ethnic groups as well as among people of all socioeconomic groups—rich and poor alike (Kessler et al., 2003; Weissman et al., 1991). As many as one in five people in the United States will experience MDD at some point during their lifetimes (American Psychiatric Association, 2000; Kessler et al., 2003). Indeed, according to one survey, 12% of college students reported that they had been diagnosed with depression (American College Health Association, 2008).

In developing countries, the *prevalence* (that is, the number of people who have the disorder) of MDD is estimated to be about the same for men and for women (Culbertson, 1997), but in the United States and other developed countries, the prevalence rate for women is two to three times higher than that for men (American Psychiatric Association, 2000; Culbertson, 1997; Gater et al., 1998; Kuehner, 2003).

In the workplace, MDD is the leading cause of both absenteeism and "presenteeism," which occurs when a depressed person is present in body but is not mentally engaged—and hence the person doesn't perform his or her job effectively (Druss et al., 2001; Stewart et al., 2003). If current trends continue, by 2020, depression may well be the second most disabling disease in the United States, after heart disease (Schrof & Schultz, 1999).

Major Depressive Disorder: WHAT IT'S LIKE

The experience of depression is captured in words by Elizabeth Wurtzel, author of *Prozac Nation:*

In my case, I was not frightened in the least bit at the thought that I might live because I was certain, quite certain, that I was already dead. The actual dying part, the withering away of my physical body, was a mere formality. My spirit, my emotional being, whatever you want to call all that inner turmoil that has nothing to do with physical existence, were long gone, dead and gone, and only a mass of the most . . . god-awful excruciating pain . . . was left in its wake.

Source: Elizabeth Wurtzel, *Prozac Nation* 1995, p. 22.

Artist Kate Monson, who experienced depression, describes her painting as a reflection of her depression.

Source: Sarah Thorne Mentock

Elizabeth Wurtzel's description of her depression captures the essence of the painful, extremely disturbing quality of many of the MDD symptoms. In some cases, severely depressed people also have psychotic symptoms—delusions or hallucinations. Often these symptoms involve themes of guilt, deserved punishment, and personal inadequacy; the auditory hallucinations of psychotically depressed people may include voices declaring that the depressed person is worthless. In addition, people with MDD often develop another psychological disorder, most commonly a disorder that involves excess anxiety (Kessler et al., 2003).

CULTURAL DIFFERENCES IN HOW DEPRESSION IS EXPRESSED. People in other cultures who are depressed may have different symptoms than those described in the *DSM-IV-TR*. People from Zimbabwe who are depressed, for instance, often complain of headache and fatigue (Patel et al., 2001), as do people in Latin and Mediterranean cultures. They do not necessarily report sadness and guilt. In Asian cultures, people with major depression are likely to report weakness, tiredness, a sense of "imbalance," or other bodily symptoms (Parker et al., 2001).

MDD AND SUICIDE. The hopelessness that is part of depression can lead depressed people to consider or attempt suicide: One estimate is that over 31,000 depressed people in the United States commit suicide every year, making it the eleventh leading cause of death in the country (Arlas et al., 2003). Several common misconceptions about suicide are listed in Table 3. Test yourself to see whether your views about suicide are accurate. ((•—Listen

((•—Listen to the audio file on Suicide on **mypsychlab.com**

TABLE 3 **Common Misconceptions of Suicide**

- *If you talk about suicide, you won't really do it.* (False: Most people who commit suicide gave some clue or warning. Threats or statements about suicide should not be ignored.)
- *People who attempt suicide are "crazy."* (False: Suicidal people are not "crazy"; they *are* likely to be depressed or upset or to feel hopeless.)
- *Someone determined to commit suicide can't be stopped.* (False: Almost all suicidal people have mixed feelings about living and dying up until the last moment. Moreover, most suicidal people don't want to stop living; they want their pain to stop. And the suicidal impulse often passes.)
- *People who commit suicide weren't willing to seek help.* (False: Studies have shown that more than half of suicide victims sought medical help within the 6 months before death.)
- *Talking about suicide could give someone the idea, so you shouldn't talk or ask about it.* (False: Discussing suicide openly can be helpful to someone who is suicidal.)

Bipolar Disorders: Going to Extremes In contrast to depression, the key characteristic of *bipolar disorders* is the presence of symptoms of mania. Specifically, a **manic episode** is a period of at least 1 week during which an abnormally elevated, expansive, or irritable mood persists. Being manic is not just having an "up" day. During a manic episode, the sufferer may be euphoric and enthusiastic about everything, may start conversations with strangers, and make grandiose plans. A milder form of a manic episode is *hypomania*, the symptoms of which are less likely to interfere with the ability to function. According to the *DSM-IV-TR*, **bipolar disorders** are a set of mood disorders characterized either by one or more manic episodes or by alternating episodes of hypomania and depression. Approximately 1% of Americans have this disorder (Regier & Kaelber, 1995).

Manic episode A period of at least 1 week during which an abnormally elevated, expansive, or irritable mood persists.

Bipolar disorders A set of mood disorders characterized either by one or more episodes of mania, or by alternating episodes of hypomania and depression.

Bipolar Disorder: WHAT IT'S LIKE

Psychologist Kay Redfield Jamison describes her personal experience with mania:

There is a particular kind of pain, elation, loneliness, and terror involved in this kind of madness. When you're high, it's tremendous. The ideas and feelings are fast and frequent like shooting stars, and you follow them until you find better and brighter ones.

Shyness goes, the right words and gestures are suddenly there, the power to captivate others a felt certainty. There are interests found in uninteresting people. Sensuality is pervasive and the desire to seduce and be seduced irresistible. Feelings of ease, intensity, power, well-being, financial omnipotence, and euphoria pervade one's marrow. But, somewhere, this changes. The fast ideas are far too fast, and there are far too many; overwhelming confusion replaces clarity. Memory goes. Humor and absorption on friends' faces are replaced by fear and concerns. Everything previously moving with the grain is now against—you are irritable, angry, frightened, uncontrollable, and enmeshed totally in the blackest caves of the mind. You never knew those caves were there. It will never end, for madness carves its own reality.

Source: Kay Jamison, *An unquiet mind: A memoir of moods and madness.* 1995, p. 67.

Manic or hypomanic episodes are often preceded or followed by episodes of depression, and the time period between moods typically is a year or more. However, some people may have more frequent shifts in mood, with four or more shifts in mood within a year—referred to as *rapid cycling*.

If left untreated, mood swings often become more frequent over time, leading to a poorer *prognosis*; the prognosis is the likely course of the disorder. Jamison, like many people with bipolar disorder, had difficulty recognizing that she had a psychological disorder, and she resisted attempts at treatment for a number of years.

Explaining Mood Disorders Although bipolar disorder and major depressive disorder are considered to be distinct disorders, research suggests that they may in fact arise from a set of common underlying neurological and psychological factors (Akiskal, 1996; Angst, 1998). In the following sections, we consider how events at the three levels of analysis and their interactions contribute to mood disorders.

LEVEL OF THE BRAIN IN MOOD DISORDERS. Both depression and bipolar disorder arise in part from events at the level of the brain.

The Level of the Brain in Depression. Three sorts of factors at the level of the brain affect whether someone will develop depression, including genes, neurotransmitter function, and brain activity. We briefly consider each factor in what follows.

1. *Genes play a role in predisposing someone to develop depression.* This conclusion is supported by the finding that depression tends to run in families (Weissman et al., 2005). In addition, if one identical twin has major depression, the co-twin (who has in common virtually all the genes of the other twin) is four times more likely to have depression than is the co-twin of an affected fraternal twin (who has in common only half the genes of the other twin; Bowman & Nurnberger, 1993; Kendler et al., 1999). However, the effects of genes may be relatively weak, as indicated by studies that rely on adopted children and their family members, which have not always shown the same clear-cut evidence for a genetic role as have studies of twins (Eley et al., 1998; Wender et al., 1986).

2. *Some neurotransmitters do not function normally in depressed people.* However, it is not yet clear which neurotransmitters are most involved in depression; indeed, it is not even clear whether the problem is having too much or too little of those substances. Rather, the problem is probably related to complex interactions among different neurotransmitters, specifically, serotonin, norepinephrine, and dopamine (Booij & Van der Does, 2007; Nutt, 2008), and perhaps other, as yet, unidentified neurotransmitters.

3. *Depressed people have unusually low activity in one area of the left frontal lobe that has direct connections to many brain areas involved in emotion,* such as the amygdala (Davidson et al., 2002; Liotti et al., 2002). This part of the frontal lobe also has connections to brain structures that produce serotonin, norepinephrine, and dopamine.

The Level of the Brain in Bipolar Disorder. As noted earlier, research indicates that bipolar disorder and depression have at least some common underlying factors. One of those

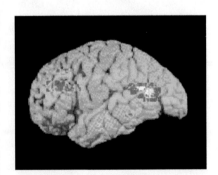

This PET scan shows brain activity of a depressed individual. Red and yellow indicate brain areas with low activity: part of the frontal lobes (at left) and the parieto-temporal area (at right). Individuals who are not depressed show higher levels of activity in these brain areas.

Source: © WDCN/Univ. College London/Photo Researchers, Inc.

Attributional style A person's characteristic way of explaining life events.

factors is genetics: Some of the same genes may predispose a person to develop either bipolar or depressive mood disorders. For example, if an identical twin has bipolar disorder, the co-twin has an 80% chance of developing a type of mood disorder, which could be either depression or bipolar disorder (Karkowski & Kendler, 1997; Vehmanen et al., 1995).

Despite the evidence that the same genes may make a person vulnerable for depression and bipolar disorder, neuroimaging studies have shown that people with bipolar disorder have differences in brain structure and function that are not generally present in people with depression who do not have bipolar disorder:

- People with bipolar disorder are likely to have an enlarged amygdala (Altshuler et al., 1998; Strakowski et al., 2002). This finding is consistent with the role of the amygdala in regulating mood and accessing emotional memories (LeDoux, 1996).
- When manic, people with bipolar disorder have shifts in the activity of their temporal lobes that do not occur during other mood states (Altshuler et al., 2005; Gyulai et al., 1997).

LEVEL OF THE PERSON IN MOOD DISORDERS. Researchers have discovered many events at the level of the person that contribute to depression, but relatively little is known about how such events contribute to bipolar disorder.

FIGURE 2 Beck's Negative Triad

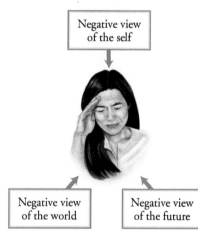

The Level of the Person in Depression. One way that depressed people differ from people who are not depressed is in the contents of their thoughts. Specifically, Aaron Beck (1967) describes a *negative triad of depression* that characterizes the thoughts of depressed people. As shown in Figure 2, this triad consists of:

1. a negative view of the world,
2. a negative view of the self, and
3. a negative view of the future.

Among people who are depressed, Beck's triad of distorted, negative thinking about the world, the self, and the future add up to produce a negative view of life. However, these cognitive distortions can be corrected.

Beck proposes that these negative views arise in people with depression because they've developed *cognitive distortions*—systematic biases in how they think about events and people, including themselves. For instance, a man who is depressed is likely to think that the presentation he just gave at work was poor—and that he is bad at his job—simply because one of his coworkers asked follow-up questions. Because of his cognitive distortions, he interprets the coworkers' questions as confirmation that he is bad at his job (and will always be bad at his job—he is beyond hope). These cognitive distortions not only give rise to but also perpetuate his negative view—which then contributes to his depressed feelings and related behaviors.

For some depressed people, the cognitive distortions may be based on early learning experiences, such have having been significantly criticized during childhood. Such people then came to believe the negative things about themselves that they were told, and so they then tell themselves similar negative (and unrealistic) criticisms. Research on how people view themselves and the world has revealed multiple ways that such views can influence whether they develop depression. In particular, a person's characteristic way of explaining life events—his or her **attributional style**—affects the risk of depression. Specifically, people who take personal responsibility for negative events, attributing them to their own actions ("I deserved to be fired ... I wasn't as good at my job as other people"), are more likely to become depressed than are people who attribute negative events to external factors ("I was laid off because I didn't have enough seniority") (Monroe & Depue, 1991). This is true even when the attributions are not accurate or appropriate (Abramson et al., 1978).

Research has found that at the beginning of a semester, college students whose attributional style led them to blame internal—as opposed to external—causes are more likely to develop symptoms of depression after receiving a bad grade. These students are more likely to attribute a bad grade to their lack of ability rather than to the difficulty of the test, poor teaching, or other external factors (Peterson & Seligman, 1984).

Source: Asia Images Group Pte Ltd\Alamy Images Royalty Free

The Level of the Person in Bipolar Disorder. Surprisingly little is known about how events at the level of the person contribute to bipolar disorder. About all we can say with confidence is that people with bipolar disorder have a depressive attributional style when in a depressed phase of the disorder (Lyon et al., 1999; Scott et al., 2000).

LEVEL OF THE GROUP IN MOOD DISORDERS. Although much is known about how events at the level of the group contribute to depression, less is known about how such events contribute to bipolar disorder.

The Level of the Group in Depression. A variety of social and environmental factors are associated with depression:

- *Stressful life events.* Stressful life events, such as a relationship breakup, experience with prejudice and discrimination, or socioeconomic stress, contribute to depression (T. Field et al., 2006; Mills et al., 2004). As shown in Figure 3, teenagers who experience three or more stressful life events within a year are more likely subsequently to develop depression than are their peers who experience fewer life stresses. In addition, the more such events experienced, the more severe the depression is likely to be (Lewinsohn et al., 1999).

- *Social isolation.* Because depressed people tend to spend more time alone, they have less opportunity for social reinforcement—to have a good time with other people—which in turn worsens the depression (MacPhillamy & Lewinsohn, 1974).

- *"Punishing" social relationships.* People's work or home lives may be stressful or even aversive if they are regularly criticized, yelled at, or belittled in other ways, which in turn increases the risk for depression.

- *Cultural factors.* Culture may influence the type of events that are likely to lead to depressed mood. For instance, among Malaysian students in a British university, depressed mood was more likely to follow negative social events, whereas among British students, depressed mood was more likely to follow negative academic events (such as a poor grade; Tafarodi & Smith, 2001). These results "are consistent with the different cultural values: Malaysian culture (and other Asian cultures) emphasizes concern for others, whereas British culture (and that of other English speaking countries) emphasizes individual achievement.

- *Sex differences.* Sex differences in depression may result in part from cultural factors. Research has shown that: (1) women in developed countries are two or three times as likely as men to experience depression (Kessler et al., 2003), and that (2) people in developed countries who *ruminate* about (persistently ponder or dwell on) their depressed mood are more likely to have longer periods of depression (Nolen-Hoeksema & Morrow, 1993; Vajk et al., 1997). Given these two findings, it's not surprising that women ruminate more frequently than do men.

Susan Nolen-Hoeksema (1987, 2000) proposes that the sex difference in developed countries arises because boys and girls are taught to respond differently to stress, and that they carry these response styles with them into adulthood. Specifically, she claims that boys are encouraged to deemphasize feelings and to use distraction and action-oriented coping strategies, whereas girls are encouraged to think about themselves—their emotions and thoughts—and not to take action. Rumination is known to promote depression, whereas action and distraction can protect against depression. In fact, research indicates that when depressed college students learn to use strategies of distraction more often and to ruminate less often, their mood improves (Nolen-Hoeksema & Morrow, 1993).

FIGURE 3 Stressful Life Events and Depression Among Teenagers

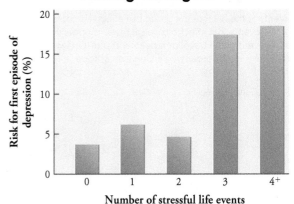

The risk of a first episode of depression almost quadruples among those teenagers who experienced three or more stressful life events in the previous year (Lewinsohn et al., 1999). After the first depressive episode, subsequent depressive episodes are triggered more easily by fewer stressful events.

Source: From Peter M. Lewinsohn, Nicholas B. Allen, John B. Seeley, and Ian H. Gotlib, "First onset versus recurrence of depression: Differential processes of psychosocial risk." *Journal of Abnormal Psychology,* 108, 483-489. Copyright © 1999, American Psychological Association. Reprinted with permission.

THINK like a PSYCHOLOGIST Next time you watch a television show or film, pay attention to how males and females cope with stress. Did the show or film portray a sex difference in how the male and female characters coped with adversity? You can assess this systematically with the log at www.mypsychlab.com; select the *Psychological Disorders* chapter and click on the *DO IT!* folder.

Events at the level of the group can affect the course of bipolar disorder. Events that affect biological rhythms or daily schedules, such as frequent plane travel or repeated changes in work schedules, can make the disorder worse (Johnson & Roberts, 1995; Post, 1992).

Source: Getty Images, Inc. - Getty News

The Level of the Group in Bipolar Disorder. Stressful life events affect the development and recurrence of mood episodes of bipolar disorder. The first episode of bipolar disorder is typically preceded by significant stress—often social stress, such as the death of a parent (Goodwin & Ghaemi, 1998; Tsuchiya et al., 2005). And stressful life events can also impede recovery after hospitalization for bipolar disorder (Johnson & Miller, 1997). One type of stress that may trigger an episode of bipolar disorder—but has not been found to play a role in triggering other psychological disorders—is activities that disrupt the daily social rhythm of life, such as going to sleep and waking at different times on weekends versus weekdays, and flying across time zones (which can lead to jet lag and a change in sleeping, waking, and eating times) (Frank et al., 2006).

INTERACTING LEVELS: DEPRESSION IS AS DEPRESSION DOES. Let's examine how events at the three levels of analysis interact in complex and subtle ways to give rise to depression. One example is found in James Coyne's (1976; Coyne & Downey, 1991) *interactional theory of depression.* He theorizes the following type of process:

1. The depressed person—who may be genetically vulnerable to depression (level of the brain)—has depressive thoughts and feelings (level of the person).

2. In turn, these thoughts and feelings lead the person to act in ways that alienate other people who might otherwise provide support (level of the group) (Katz & Joiner, 2001; Nolan & Mineka, 1997). Actions that alienate others include (Katz & Joiner, 2001)

   - seeking excessive reassurance,
   - seeking out negative feedback, and
   - being irritable or aggressive.

3. These actions then lead others to reject the depressed person (level of the group), confirming that person's negative view of himself or herself (level of the person). Such rejections and criticisms increase the likelihood of negative future events (Casbon et al., 2005).

4. The depressed person may then continue to seek out feedback from others, perhaps attempting to determine whether such negative feedback was a fluke or to elicit reassurance from others (level of the group), which perpetuates the cycle.

But this isn't all there is to the interactions among events at the different levels: Depressed mood can be contagious (level of the group), so that relatives and friends of a depressed person may find themselves feeling and acting somewhat depressed (Coyne et al., 1987). For example, Thomas Joiner (1994) found that college students who spent time with depressed roommates over a period of 3 weeks themselves became more depressed. (Indeed, anger, anxiety, and sadness have also been found to be contagious; Coyne, 1976; Hsee et al., 1990; Joiner, 1994; Katz et al., 1999; Segrin & Dillard, 1992; Sullins, 1991.) How does this sort of contagion work? Unlike a cold, no virus or germs are involved. Instead, those who develop depression are more likely to behave in ways that create stress in those around them, which in turn can trigger the onset of depression in the other people (McGuffin et al., 1988; Rende & Plomin, 1992). Thus, your roommate's or family member's depression can lead you to feel depressed, perhaps changing your brain and bodily functioning (level of the brain). In turn, the newly depressed friend or family member may be less able to help the person originally depressed.

Does a mood disorder best describe van Gogh's problems? We know that van Gogh suffered from bouts of depression, at times had poor hygiene, narrowed his activities severely, and took pleasure only in painting. MDD seems like a possible diagnosis. Van Gogh's attempted assault on Gauguin, as well as his cutting off part of his own ear, might be explained by MDD "with psychotic features": He said he heard voices (auditory hallucinations) that told him to kill his friend; these hallucinations might have been symptoms of severe depression.

Although a diagnosis of MDD could explain the majority of these symptoms, it is not the only possible diagnosis. Bipolar disorder is another. Van Gogh's episodes of frenzied painting might have been manic episodes (although they could also have been an intense restlessness that can occur with depression). Moveover, his "attacks" (which became more frequent over time) might have been episodes of mania that became psychotic.

Anxiety Disorders

Anxiety is a sense of dread or foreboding, usually about a possible future threat. Could van Gogh have had an anxiety disorder? He was considered to be nervous and had concentration problems—signs of anxiety. Moreover, we know that van Gogh had what he called "attacks"; perhaps these were related to anxiety. Can we recognize a pattern of anxiety in these symptoms? To answer these questions, we must first explore what anxiety is and what anxiety disorders are.

Anxiety often involves elements of anticipation and physical arousal. For example, people might feel anxious about upcoming exams, a date with someone new, or a job interview—and fidget, pace, or tap their fingers on a tabletop in anticipation. Anxiety (and the arousal that is part of it) is not necessarily always bad; sometimes anxiety is helpful because it can motivate people to act in appropriate and important ways—for example, to study for an exam, to take care with their dress and grooming, or to prepare for a job interview. However, too much anxiety and arousal can lead people to feel emotionally overwhelmed and unable to take appropriate action.

Some people get very anxious and aroused, typically about possible encounters with specific stimuli, such as snakes, dirt or disorder, or speaking in front of a group of people. Understandably, these people try to avoid or minimize their exposure to the stimuli that make them anxious. These are symptoms of **anxiety disorders**: A category of disorders characterized by intense or pervasive anxiety or fear—out of proportion to the situation—and/or extreme attempts to avoid these feelings. Such anxiety, and the person's reactions to it, can interfere with the ability to function normally.

In the sections that follow, we explore four types of anxiety disorders: *panic disorder*, *phobias*, *obsessive-compulsive disorder*, and *posttraumatic stress disorder*. Before we discuss these disorders, we must mention another anxiety disorder—**generalized anxiety disorder**—that is different from these other disorders in that it involves excessive anxiety and worry that is not consistently related to a specific object or situation. Approximately 3% of Americans have generalized anxiety disorder (American Psychiatric Association, 2000).

Panic Disorder The critical element of *panic disorder* is recurrent **panic attacks**, which are episodes of intense fear, anxiety, or discomfort accompanied by physical and psychological symptoms such as heart palpitations, breathing difficulties, chest pain, nausea, sweating, dizziness, fear of going crazy or doing something uncontrollable, fear of impending doom, or a sense of unreality. These symptoms reach their peak within a few minutes after an attack begins, and can last from minutes to hours. Panic attacks typically are triggered by a specific situation or object, such as feeling overheated, or being amidst a crowd of people. But some people have panic attacks that are not associated with a specific situation or object and may even seem to occur randomly; when panic attacks do not have an apparent trigger, they are referred to as *uncued attacks*. One study of college students found that 12% of the participants experienced uncued panic attacks while they were in college or in the years leading up to college (Telch et al., 1989).

A person is said to have **panic disorder** only if he or she endures frequent, unexpected panic attacks or fears additional panic attacks and thus changes aspects of his or her life in hopes of avoiding them. Internationally, approximately 3% of all people will experience panic disorder during their lives (Rouillon, 1997; Somers et al., 2006). For some people with panic disorder, the panic attacks occur in waves, with years between them; for others, the panic attacks occur frequently, without long periods between them.

Anxiety disorders A category of disorders characterized by intense or pervasive anxiety or fear, or extreme attempts to avoid the feelings.

Generalized anxiety disorder An anxiety disorder characterized by excessive anxiety and worry that is not consistently related to a specific object or situation.

Panic attack An episode of intense fear, anxiety, or discomfort accompanied by physical and psychological symptoms such as heart palpitations, breathing difficulties, chest pain, fear of impending doom or of doing something uncontrollable, and a sense of unreality.

Panic disorder An anxiety disorder characterized by frequent, unexpected panic attacks or fear and avoidance of such attacks.

Panic attacks can interfere with everyday functioning. Food Network chef Paula Deen suffered from panic disorder for many years before she sought professional help to keep her panic attacks under control.

Source: Newscom

415

Agoraphobia A condition in which people fear or avoid places that might be difficult to leave should panic symptoms occur.

Panic Disorder: WHAT IT'S LIKE

Here is one person's description of a panic attack:

My breathing starts getting very shallow. I feel I'm going to stop breathing. The air feels like it gets thinner. I feel the air is not coming up through my nose. I take short rapid breaths. Then I see an image of myself gasping for air and remember what happened in the hospital. I think that I will start gasping. I get very dizzy and disoriented. I cannot sit or stand still. I start pacing. Then I start shaking and sweating. I feel I'm losing my mind and I will flip out and hurt myself or someone else. My heart starts beating fast and I start getting pains in my chest. My chest tightens up. I become very frightened. I get afraid that these feelings will not go away. Then I get really upset. I feel no one will be able to help me. I get very frightened I will die. I want to run to some place safe but I don't know where.

Source: Aaron T. Beck, Anxiety disorders and phobias: A cognitive perspective. 1985, p. 107.

Typically, people with panic disorder worry constantly about having more attacks, and they often change their behavior to avoid or minimize panic attacks. They may go to great lengths to try to avoid panic attacks: quitting their jobs, and avoiding places (such as hot, crowded rooms or events) or activities that increase their heart rate (such as exercise, sex, or watching suspenseful movies or sporting events).

Some people fear or avoid places that might be difficult to leave (such as being in a plane or a shopping mall) should symptoms of panic arise; this condition is called **agoraphobia**, literally, "fear of the marketplace." Agoraphobia can restrict daily life and be disabling: some people with agoraphobia completely avoid leaving home (Bouton et al., 2001) or will do so only with a close friend or relative. As presented in the *DSM-IV-TR*, someone can be diagnosed as having agoraphobia *without* panic attacks when that person avoids many places and so does not have panic attacks; however, he or she may still experience less severe but still distressing symptoms of panic.

LEVEL OF THE BRAIN IN PANIC DISORDER. Several factors at the level of the brain contribute to whether someone will develop panic disorder. Once again, genes play a role; a person can inherit a vulnerability for panic (Crowe et al., 1983; Torgersen, 1983; van den Heuvel et al., 2000). Such a genetic predisposition has its effects in part by affecting the brain. In particular, results from animal studies suggest that panic attacks may arise from having an excessively sensitive *locus coeruleus*, a small group of cells deep in the brainstem (Gorman et al., 1989; see Figure 4). The locus coeruleus is the seat of an "alarm system" that triggers an increased heart rate, faster breathing, and sweating, which are components of the *fight-or-flight* response (the body's initial response to stress, which involves increased arousal of the autonomic nervous system). These normal bodily symptoms can lead to panic symptoms in some people.

Consistent with the idea that people with panic disorder have a disrupted alarm system, researchers have found that breathing-related changes are associated with this disorder. Specifically, some people with panic disorder are unusually sensitive to changes in the amount of carbon dioxide in their respiratory system (carbon dioxide levels usually change when people are afraid or anxious and hyperventilate) (Beck et al., 1999; Papp et al., 1993, 1997). For such people, changes in carbon dioxide levels then can elicit panic, perhaps through a "suffocation alarm" in the brain that has an abnormally low threshold for firing (Coplan et al., 1998; Klein, 1993).

LEVEL OF THE PERSON IN PANIC DISORDER. Various events at the level of the person contribute to whether someone develops a panic attack, and whether a single panic attack remains an isolated incident or becomes one of many and hence leads to panic disorder. Of particular note is the role of *anxiety sensitivity,* which is the belief that bodily arousal can have harmful consequences (Schmidt et al., 1997). People who have anxiety sensitivity are

FIGURE 4 Panic Disorder: Locus Coeruleus and the Alarm System

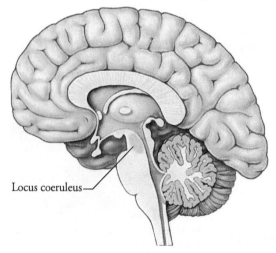

Locus coeruleus—

The locus coeruleus is a group of cells in the brainstem that serves as an alarm system. When the alarm is activated, the body responds with the fight-or-flight response, including increased heart and respiration rates.

more likely to experience uncued panic attacks than are people who do not have anxiety sensitivity (Plehn & Peterson, 2002; Schmidt et al., 1999).

Anxiety sensitivity may contribute to panic disorder in a four-step process:

1. It leads people to become frightened by changes in their heart rate or breathing rate.
2. In turn, their fear causes the fight-or-flight response (which in turn increases heart rate and breathing rate).
3. People with anxiety sensitivity then become afraid of the bodily sensations that intensify with fear—what psychologists refer to as a *fear of fear* (or more accurately, a fear of the bodily sensations associated with fear).
4. When people have a fear of fear, they become hypervigilant for the bodily signals that have previously led to panic in the past. Thus, in a vicious cycle, these people are more likely to become anxious that they *might* have a panic attack, which in turn increases the fight-or-flight response (including increased heart rate and breathing changes), which then triggers panic.

LEVEL OF THE GROUP IN PANIC DISORDER. Cultural changes are a factor at the level of the group that apparently contributes to a vulnerability to panic disorder. In the years since 1990, physicians in the United States have diagnosed increasing numbers of people with panic disorder (Skaer et al., 2008). However, it could be that this change reflects greater awareness of the disorder (and so more accurate diagnosis) and not an actual increase in the number of cases. Supporting the view that the increased diagnosis of panic disorder reflects an actual increase in the number of cases, studies reveal that today's "normal" children (children without a psychological disorder) are more prone to anxiety—and more likely to develop an anxiety disorder later—than were children in the 1950s who had a psychological disorder (Twenge, 2000). Such changes over time may reflect increased dangers in the environment—such as the rising crime rate since the 1950s—and fewer supportive social connections among people (Twenge, 2000).

Phobias: Social and Specific

A **phobia** is an exaggerated, irrational fear of a specific object, activity, or situation that leads the person to go to extreme lengths to avoid the feared stimulus—so much so that his or her avoidance of the stimulus interferes with everyday life. By avoiding the objects, activities, or situations that trigger anxiety, the sufferer avoids the fear and the anxiety or panic that the stimuli might elicit. In the *DSM-IV-TR*, phobias are sorted into two disorders, based on the stimulus that is feared: *social phobia* and *specific phobia*.

Social phobia (or *social anxiety disorder*) is the fear of public embarrassment or humiliation, which in turn leads the person to avoid social situations likely to arouse this fear (Kessler et al., 1998). People with this disorder might try to avoid eating, speaking, or performing in public or using public restrooms or dressing rooms. When unable to avoid these situations, they invariably experience anxiety or panic. This is among the most common psychiatric diagnoses (American Psychiatric Association, 2000). Approximately 12% of Americans will experience social phobia during their lives (Ruscio et al., 2008).

In contrast, a **specific phobia** is focused on a specific type of object or nonsocial situation, such as those listed in Table 4 on the next page. People may have phobias about flying, heights, spiders, or dental work that lead them to avoid such objects, activities, or situations. Usually people with a phobia recognize that their fears are excessive and irrational, but they continue to have the fears nonetheless. A unique type of specific phobia—referred to in the *DSM-IV-TR* as *blood-injury-injection* phobia—arises in people who faint when seeing blood (because

Phobia An exaggerated, irrational fear of a specific object, activity, or situation that leads the person to go to extreme lengths to avoid the feared stimulus.

Social phobia Fear of public embarrassment or humiliation, which leads the person to avoid situations likely to arouse this fear.

Specific phobia Persistent and excessive or unreasonable fear triggered by a specific object or nonsocial situation, along with attempts to avoid the feared stimulus.

A social phobia involves fear of public embarrassment or humiliation, whereas a specific phobia involves a fear of a particular object or nonsocial situation.

Sources: © Getty Images/Stockdisk; Ingo Arndt\Nature Picture Library

417

TABLE 4 Five Subtypes of Specific Phobias

Phobia Subtype	Examples (Fear of ...)
Animal type	Snakes, rats, insects
Blood–injection–injury type	Seeing blood or receiving an injection
Natural environment type	Storms, heights, the ocean
Situation type	Public transportation, tunnels, bridges, elevators, dental work, flying
Miscellaneous type cued by stimuli not already mentioned	Choking, vomiting, contracting an illness, falling down

of an extreme drop in blood pressure), and so they become afraid of situations that might involve seeing blood or injections; such people may thus avoid getting appropriate treatment for medical problems (Kleinknecht & Lenz, 1989).

LEVEL OF THE BRAIN IN PHOBIAS.   Events at the level of the brain predispose some people to develop phobias. Studies with twins suggest that genes play a role in whether someone will develop a phobia (Kendler et al., 1992, 2001, 2002; Li et al., 2001). Genes have this effect, in part, by leading the amygdala, as well as other fear-related brain structures, to react too strongly to certain stimuli (LeDoux, 1996). Genes may also account for the finding that humans are biologically *prepared* to develop phobias of certain stimuli—such as snakes or heights—and not others, such as flowers or pieces of furniture. One theory proposes that our ancestors who had certain fears—such as of snakes and heights—had an evolutionary advantage over their contemporaries who did not have such fears (Poulton & Menzies, 2002); according to this view, having such fears led our ancestors to keep their distance from poisonous snakes and the edges of cliffs, and so they were more likely to survive to have children, who in turn inherited these same fears and were more likely to survive, and so on.

However, genes are not destiny: Not all identical twins are phobic when their co-twin is phobic, so other sorts of factors must play a role.

LEVEL OF THE PERSON IN PHOBIAS.   Researchers have hypothesized that learning can contribute to whether a person develops a specific phobia. In particular, classical and operant conditioning can lead to some phobias (Mowrer, 1939).

Classical conditioning can produce an association between a stimulus and fear. For instance, with 11-month-old Little Albert, a white rat (the *conditioned stimulus*) was paired with a loud noise (the *unconditioned stimulus*) that led Albert to develop a fear of the rat (and of white furry things more generally); such a classically conditioned fear is referred to as a *conditioned emotional response.*

Operant conditioning—through negative reinforcement—can lead a person to avoid a stimulus. (*Negative reinforcement* occurs when a behavior leads to the removal of an unpleasant stimulus, making that behavior more likely to recur; negative reinforcement is not the same thing as punishment.) Fear and anxiety are reduced by avoiding a feared stimulus, and thus when someone avoids the feared stimulus, the subsequent relief reinforces the act of avoiding that stimulus.

Although both sorts of conditioning, in principle, could contribute to whether a person develops a phobia, evidence is mixed about whether such learning plays a major role. These mixed findings may reflect the difficulty of doing ethical experiments on these topics, as well as reflect the difficulty of clearly identifying such learning in natural settings.

LEVEL OF THE GROUP IN PHOBIAS.   Another sort of learning that may play a role in whether someone develops a phobia is observational learning—a type of learning that is fundamentally social in nature. Such learning may help explain the finding that women are more likely than men to be afraid of snakes and insects (and some other stimuli): Boys are more likely to observe other males who interact with these potentially fearful objects—who play with spiders or insects, for instance—and imitate them. In the process of interacting with the objects, they are exposed to such stimuli—and such exposure would, based on learning principles, decrease fear of these stimuli (Antony & Barlow, 2002). Girls, in contrast, are less likely to see other females interact with snakes and insects and, in turn, would be less likely to have direct exposure to these stimuli in a way that would eliminate or reduce the fears.

Obsessive-Compulsive Disorder

Obsessive-compulsive disorder (OCD) is characterized by the presence of *obsessions*, either alone or with *compulsions*. **Obsessions** are recurrent and persistent thoughts, impulses, or images that feel intrusive and inappropriate and that are difficult to suppress or ignore. Obsessions are more than excessive worries about real problems, however, and they may cause significant anxiety and distress. Common obsessions involve:

- thoughts of *contamination* ("Will I become contaminated by shaking her hand?"),
- repeated *doubts* ("Did I lock the door? Did I turn off the stove?"),
- the need to have things in a certain *order* (such as a perfect alignment of cans of food in a cupboard), or
- aggressive or horrific *impulses* (such as the urge to shout an obscenity in church).

Research indicates that having obsessions is common (when newly in love, for instance, people typically obsess about their new partner; Weissman et al., 1994), but the obsessions of people with OCD are distinct—they feel intrusive and inappropriate.

Compulsions are repetitive behaviors or mental acts that a person feels compelled to perform, usually in response to an obsession. Examples of compulsions are:

- *washing* in response to thoughts of contamination (washing the hands repeatedly until they are raw),
- *checking* (such as repeatedly checking that the stove is turned off or the windows are closed—so that it can take hours to leave the house),
- *ordering* (putting objects in a certain order or in precise symmetry—a task that may take hours until perfection is attained), and
- *counting* (such as counting to 100 after each obsessive thought).

Some people with OCD believe that a dreaded event will occur if they do not perform their ritual of checking, ordering, and so on—but the particular compulsion is not realistically connected to what they are trying to ward off, at least not in the frequency and duration with which the compulsion occurs. Worldwide, approximately 2% to 3% of people suffer from OCD at some point in their lives (Horwath & Weissman, 2000). ◉─Watch

Obsessive-compulsive disorder (OCD) An anxiety disorder characterized by the presence of obsessions and sometimes compulsions.

Obsession A recurrent and persistent thought, impulse, or image that feels intrusive and inappropriate and is difficult to suppress or ignore.

Compulsion A repetitive behavior or mental act that a person feels compelled to perform, usually in response to an obsession.

◉─Watch the Video on Obsessive-Compulsive Disorder on mypsychlab.com

Obsessive-Compulsive Disorder: WHAT IT'S LIKE

One woman with OCD describes the ordeal of grocery shopping:

Once I have attained control of the car, I have the burden of getting into it and getting it going. This can be a big project some days, locking and unlocking the doors, rolling up and down the power windows, putting on and off the seat belts, sometimes countlessly. . . . Sometimes while driving I must do overtly good deeds, like letting cars out of streets in front of me, or stopping to let people cross. These are things everyone probably should do, but things I must do. . . . My trip in the car may take us to the grocery store. Inside I have certain rituals I must perform. I am relatively subtle about how I do them to avoid drawing attention to myself. Certain foods must have their packages read several times before I am allowed to purchase them. Some things need to be touched repetitively, certain tiles on the floor must be stepped on by myself and my family. I'll find myself having to go from one end of an aisle to the other and back again, just to make everything all right. I fear being accused of shoplifting sometimes because of the way I behave and the way I am always looking around to see if people have noticed my actions.

Source: Gail Steketee and Kerrin White, *When once is not enough: Help for obsessive-compulsives.* Oakland, CA: New Harbinger. 1990, pp. 12–13.

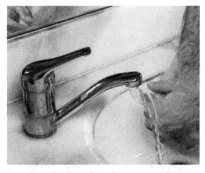

People with a hand-washing compulsion may spend hours washing their hands so much that they become raw.

Source: PhotoStock-Israel\Alamy Images Royalty Free

Researchers are beginning to understand OCD by investigating events at the three levels of analysis and their interactions.

LEVEL OF THE BRAIN IN OCD. As with the other disorders we have considered, genes may predispose someone to develop OCD. However, the relevant genes apparently do not underlie OCD in particular but rather contribute to anxiety disorders more broadly. Specifically, studies of families have shown that if one member of a family has OCD, others are more likely to have some type of anxiety disorder—but not necessarily OCD itself (Black et al., 1992; Pato et al., 2002; Torgersen, 1983).

Researchers have made progress in understanding the brain circuits that are disrupted in OCD, relating obsessions and compulsions to neural activity that occurs in the basal ganglia (Breiter et al., 1996; Jenike, 1984; Rauch et al., 1994). Specifically, the obsessions of a person with OCD can arise when part of this brain structure does not do its normal job of "turning off" recurrent thoughts about an object or situation, which leads to a repeating loop of brain activity. This loop may be temporarily turned off when the person carries out a compulsion, although the brain activity begins anew soon thereafter (Insel, 1992; Jenike, 1984; Modell et al., 1989; Saxena & Rauch, 2000).

LEVEL OF THE PERSON IN OCD. Events at the level of the person contribute to the onset of OCD and to its maintenance over time. First, regarding its onset: OCD can arise when someone interprets his or her thoughts as conveying something fundamentally negative about himself or herself or as otherwise unacceptable (such as an urge to shout an obscenity), and then tries to suppress the offending thought. The effort to suppress the thought has the paradoxical effect of making it an obsession (Ferrier & Brewin, 2005; Rachman, 1997; Salkovskis et al., 2002): The thought recurs, and thus the person must continually try to suppress it—and he or she becomes vigilant, alert for the thought, which creates the obsession.

Second, regarding maintenance: As with other anxiety disorders, operant conditioning may play a role in maintaining OCD behavior over time. In this case, the compulsive behavior can momentarily relieve the anxiety created by obsessions—and this relief is a form of negative reinforcement that thereby reinforces the behavior, making it more likely to recur.

LEVEL OF THE GROUP IN OCD. Although the prevalence of OCD is similar across different countries (Horwath & Weissman, 2000), culture plays a role in the particular symptoms that sufferers display (Weissman et al., 1994). For example, religious obsessions and praying compulsions are more common among Turkish men with OCD than among French men with OCD (Millet et al., 2000).

Posttraumatic Stress Disorder After experiencing a traumatic event such as war, physical or sexual abuse, terrorism, or a natural disaster, some people develop *posttraumatic stress disorder*. According to the *DSM-IV-TR*, the diagnosis of **posttraumatic stress disorder (PTSD)** is made when three conditions are met:

1. The person experiences or witnesses an event that involves actual or threatened serious injury or death.
2. The traumatized person responds to the situation with fear and helplessness.
3. The traumatized person then has three sets of symptoms:
   a. persistent reexperiencing of the traumatic event, which may take the form of intrusive, unwanted, and distressing recollections, dreams, or nightmares of the event or may involve flashbacks that can include illusions, hallucinations, and a sense of reliving the experience;
   b. persistent avoidance of anything associated with the trauma and a general emotional numbing; and
   c. heightened arousal, which can cause people with PTSD to startle easily (Shalev et al., 2000), have difficulty sleeping, or be in a constant state of hypervigilance.

Posttraumatic stress disorder (PTSD)
An anxiety disorder experienced by some people after a traumatic event, and characterized by persistent reexperiencing of the trauma, avoidance of stimuli associated with the trauma, and heightened arousal.

Although most people who experience trauma never develop PTSD (Breslau et al., 1998; Koren et al., 2005; Resnick et al., 1993; Shalev et al., 1998; Yehuda, 2002b), when the symptoms do appear, they do not always arise immediately after the traumatic event. Once they emerge, though, they can persist for months or even for years.

Posttraumatic Stress Disorder: WHAT IT'S LIKE

Mr. E, age 65, complained that ever since World War II he experienced extreme nervousness that was somewhat alleviated by chewing tobacco. . . . After this wartime nervousness—consisting of subjective feelings of anxiety, itching, and shaking—developed. [It got to the point where he experienced] eight such episodes in the month before he came to the hospital.

During the war Mr. E manned a landing craft that transported soldiers to the beaches. He was particularly distraught about an experience in which he felt something underfoot on a sandy beach and discovered that he was stepping on the face of a dead GI. He also described an incident in which his ship had been torpedoed and several crewmen killed. He experienced intense survivor guilt about this incident.

Source: Robert H. Hierholzer, Jan Munson, Carol Peabody, and John Rosenberg, "Clinical Presentation of PTSD in World War II Combat Veterans" in *Hospital Community Psychiatry* 43: 816-820 (1992), p. 818.

Some soldiers develop posttraumatic stress disorder.

Source: David Turnley\CORBIS- NY

The type of trauma influences whether a person will develop the disorder. For example, one study found that women were more likely to develop PTSD when their traumas resulted from being a victim of crime rather than from being in a natural disaster (Resnick et al., 1993), and other studies corroborate this finding (Breslau et al., 1998). Additional factors that affect whether PTSD will arise after a trauma can be found in the events at each level of analysis, as well as their interactions.

LEVEL OF THE BRAIN IN PTSD. Three sorts of events at the level of the brain can predispose someone to develop PTSD after a trauma:

1. Genes lead some people to be vulnerable (Shalev et al., 1998; True et al., 1993).

2. Childhood trauma can enhance the fight-or-flight response, making it both easier to trigger and more pronounced (Vermetten & Bremner, 2002). This enhanced fight-or-flight response may arise because of changes in the levels of hormones that are related to the stress response. Researchers hypothesize specifically that people who are vulnerable to developing PTSD have lower levels of the glucocorticoid hormone *cortisol* and, when stressed, may not produce the high levels that typically occur with the fight-or-flight response (Yehuda, 2002a). Cortisol normally helps provide energy for the body, has an anti-inflammatory effect, and helps restore the body's equilibrium after physical injury.

Firefighter-trainees were asked to listen to loud bursts of noise while their tendency to be startled (indicated by blinking of the eyes) was assessed. The researchers measured this tendency before the trainees experienced any fire-related trauma in their work. The researchers later reassessed this tendency within 4 weeks after the trainees experienced such trauma. The trainees who were more reactive before a trauma were more likely to develop PTSD symptoms after a trauma (Guthrie & Bryant, 2005).

Source: The Image Works

3. Various brain structures could be abnormal (in part because of genes but also possibly because of environmental effects); these abnormalities include:

- an overly reactive locus coeruleus (as occurs with panic disorder);

- a limbic system (including the amygdala) that is more easily activated by mental imagery of traumatic events than that of nontraumatic events, which in turn may occur because part of the frontal lobe doesn't do as good a job of inhibiting the amygdala (Rauch et al., 1996, 2000; Shin et al., 1997, 2004); and

- unusually small hippocampi (the brain area most responsible for memory), which may help to explain why people with PTSD have intrusive memories (Bremner et al., 2003; Yehuda, 2002b).

LEVEL OF THE PERSON IN PTSD. Events at the level of the person also influence whether an individual will develop this disorder. In particular, people who develop PTSD tend to have certain psychological characteristics before, during, and after a trauma (Ehlers et al., 1998; Ozer et al., 2003). Such psychological characteristics include:

- a prior history of social withdrawal or of depression,
- a sense of not being able to control stressful events (Joseph et al., 1995),
- believing that the person's life is at risk during the traumatic event or that he or she has no control over the situation (regardless of the actual threat) (Foa et al., 1989),
- a prior belief that the world is a dangerous place (Keane et al., 1985; Kushner et al., 1992), and
- a lower IQ, which entails having fewer cognitive resources for coping with the trauma and its aftermath (Macklin et al., 1998; McNally & Shin, 1995).

As with other anxiety disorders, classical and operant conditioning may help to explain some aspects of PTSD, in particular why people with PTSD avoid objects or situations associated with the trauma: Those objects or situations were paired with the trauma, which could lead them to act as conditioned stimuli, eliciting the same responses as the trauma itself. And hence, the person with PTSD avoids such stimuli.

LEVEL OF THE GROUP IN PTSD.   Whether trauma will lead to PTSD also depends, in part, on events at the level of the group. Support from friends, family members, or counselors immediately after a trauma may help decrease the likelihood that PTSD will develop (Kaniasty & Norris, 1992; Kaniasty et al., 1990). For people who were exposed to trauma as part of military service, social support after coming back home can reduce the risk of PTSD (King et al., 1998).

Did van Gogh likely suffer from an anxiety disorder? Although he was anxious and irritable, we do not know enough about what happened during one of his self-reported "attacks" to know whether these episodes were panic attacks or something else. In any event, panic disorder alone would not account for his symptoms of depressed mood, irritability, and impulsiveness or his bizarre behavior (such as cutting off part of his ear). He does not appear to have had symptoms that suggest any of the other anxiety disorders.

Schizophrenia

In the last years of his life, van Gogh apparently had increasing difficulty distinguishing between his internal experiences and external reality. For instance, he would become disoriented and not know who he was, and he had delusions of being poisoned and attacked. Gauguin claimed that van Gogh referred to himself as a ghost before cutting off part of his ear. When van Gogh was asked about the assault on Gauguin, during a period of mental clarity he said that he was given to hearing voices and that he had heard voices telling him to kill Gauguin. Then he explained that he'd remembered the biblical injunction "If thine own eye offend thee, pluck it out." His ear had offended him by "hearing" the voice that suggested he kill Gauguin, so he cut off part of it as penance for his sin against Gauguin (Lubin, 1972).

These details about van Gogh's life and behavior suggest the possibility that he may have had schizophrenia. The word *schizophrenia* is derived from two Greek words, *schizo*, meaning "to split" or "to cut," and *phren*, meaning "mind" or "reason." Books and movies sometimes portray schizophrenia as if it meant having a "split personality," but schizophrenia is characterized by a split from *reality*, not a split between different aspects of oneself. **Schizophrenia** is a disorder that is characterized by symptoms of psychosis that profoundly alter affect, behavior, and cognition, particularly the pattern or form of thought.

Symptoms: What Schizophrenia Looks Like   In the *DSM-IV-TR* the symptoms of schizophrenia are organized into two groups—*positive symptoms* and *negative symptoms*. **Positive symptoms** involve an excess or distortion of normal functions; an example is hallucinations. They are called positive not because they indicate something desirable but because they mark the *presence* of certain unusual behaviors. **Negative symptoms**, on the other hand, involve a *lessening* or *loss* of normal functions; an example is a restricted

Schizophrenia A disorder that is characterized by symptoms of psychosis that profoundly alter the patient's affect, behavior, and thoughts.

Positive symptom An excess or distortion of normal functions, such as a hallucination.

Negative symptom A diminution or loss of normal functions, such as a restricted range of emotional expression.

range of emotional expression, referred to as *flat affect*. Let's explore in more detail the two types of symptoms of schizophrenia. ✳️—[Explore

✳️—[Explore the Concept with Schizophrenia Overview on mypsychlab.com

POSITIVE SYMPTOMS OF SCHIZOPHRENIA. Positive symptoms include the following:

- *delusions* (distortions of thought), which can be complex and usually center on a particular theme, as described below:
  - delusions of *persecution* (beliefs that are paranoid in nature—that others are out to "get" you),
  - delusions of *grandeur* (beliefs that you are an important person),
  - delusions of *reference* (beliefs that normal events have special meaning directed toward you),
  - delusions of *control* (beliefs that your feelings, behaviors, or thoughts are controlled by others).
- *hallucinations*, which typically are auditory; hearing voices is a common symptom.
- *disorganized behavior*, which typically consists of inappropriate, childlike silliness or unpredictable agitation. People with disorganized behavior may have difficulty with everyday tasks such as organizing shopping and meals, maintaining hygiene, and selecting appropriate clothes (they might wear two overcoats in the summer).
- *disorganized speech*, as in the following example: "I may be a 'Blue Baby' but 'Social Baby' not, but yet a blue heart baby could be in the Blue Book published before the war" (Maher, 1966, p. 413).

NEGATIVE SYMPTOMS OF SCHIZOPHRENIA. Negative symptoms include the following:

- *Flat affect*, which is a general failure to express or outwardly respond to emotion. There may be occasional smiles or warm manner, but usually the facial expression, eye contract, and body language are minimal.
- *Alogia*, or "poverty of speech," is characterized by brief, slow, empty replies to questions; someone with alogia speaks less than others and doesn't use words as freely. Alogia is not the same as being reluctant to speak; rather, the thoughts behind the words seem slowed down.
- *Avolition*, an inability to initiate or persist in goal-directed activities. Someone exhibiting avolition may sit for long periods without engaging in any behavior or social interaction.

DIAGNOSING SCHIZOPHRENIA. Not all of the positive and negative symptoms are present in everyone who is diagnosed with schizophrenia. According to the *DSM-IV-TR*, a diagnosis of schizophrenia requires that the person displays two or more of the symptoms (positive and/or negative) for at least a week, and displays other signs of socially inappropriate behavior for at least 6 months.

The average age of onset—the age of first diagnosis—of schizophrenia is the 20s, although in some people (particularly women) onset does not occur until later in life. Symptoms usually emerge gradually, beginning with a *prodromal phase*; a prodromal phase is the period immediately before the symptoms fully emerge. With schizophrenia, the prodromal phase is characterized by slowly deteriorating functioning, along with outbursts of anger, withdrawal from other people, and poor hygiene (Heinssen et al., 2001). Eventually, the person enters the *active phase* of the disorder (sometimes referred to as a *psychotic episode*), in which full-blown positive and/or negative symptoms arise.

Approximately 1% of people worldwide will develop schizophrenia during their lives (Kulhara & Chakrabarti, 2001; Tandon et al., 2008). The course of schizophrenia is variable: 25% of people diagnosed with schizophrenia have only one psychotic episode and recover relatively completely, 25% improve enough to live independently, 25% improve but not enough to live independently, 15% do not improve and are the "chronic" cases, and 10% commit suicide (Torrey, 1988).

Subtypes of Schizophrenia People with schizophrenia display only some of the full range of possible symptoms, and these symptoms tend to cluster into groupings. Based on these groupings, mental health professionals and researchers have identified subtypes of schizophrenia. The *DSM-IV-TR* specifies four subtypes of schizophrenia (see Table 5): paranoid, disorganized, catatonic, and undifferentiated.

TABLE 5 Four Subtypes of Schizophrenia

Paranoid

Prominent delusions of persecution; intellectual functioning and affect are relatively intact, but auditory hallucinations are common. This type has the best prognosis.

Disorganized

Prominent disorganized speech and behavior and flat affect or inappropriate emotional expression. This type has the worst prognosis.

Catatonic

Prominent catatonic motor symptoms—such as holding bizarre postures for hours.

Undifferentiated

Symptoms that do not clearly fall into any of the above three subtypes.

Source: Reprinted with permission from the *Diagnostic and Statistical Manual of Mental Disorders, Fourth Edition, Text Revision,* (Copyright 2000). American Psychiatric Association.

Paranoid Schizophrenia: WHAT IT'S LIKE

Jeffrey DeMann describes his first hospitalization for schizophrenia at the age of 27:

I recall vividly the delusion of believing my mother was to take my place in the shock treatments. Then I was to be quietly murdered and placed in an acid bath grave, which would dissolve any physical evidence of my existence. At this time, auditory hallucinations also were present. I could actually hear the slamming of my mother's body on the table while being administered the deadly shock. I truly believed my mother was now dead in my place. I also recall curling up on an old wooden bench and repeatedly chanting the words "Die quickly now."

Source: Jeffrey DeMann, "First person account: The evolution of a person with schizophrenia." *Schizophrenia Bulletin,* 20, 579–582. (1994), p. 580.

Why Does This Happen to Some People but Not Others? The reasons why only some people develop schizophrenia involve events at the three levels of analysis and their interactions.

LEVEL OF THE BRAIN IN SCHIZOPHRENIA. A number of factors at the level of the brain predispose someone to develop schizophrenia, namely, *genetics*, *abnormal brain structure* and *function*, and *hormonal* and *neurotransmitter activity*.

Genetic Factors in Schizophrenia. Twin, family, and adoption studies show that genes can affect whether someone will develop schizophrenia (Gottesman, 1991; Kendler & Diehl, 1993; Tiernari, 1991). People who have relatives with schizophrenia have an increased risk of developing the disorder, and the more genes they have in common, the greater the risk. Thus, identical twins—who have the most genes in common—have the highest risk if a co-twin has the disorder, followed by parents and siblings, then relatives in the extended family, such as cousins.

However, it is important to note that although genes can play a role in developing schizophrenia, they are clearly not the only factor. Even for people who have a close relative with schizophrenia, the actual incidence is still relatively low. More than 80% of people who have a parent or sibling diagnosed with schizophrenia do *not* have the disorder themselves (Gottesman & Moldin, 1998). Even in the case of the highest level of genetic resemblance—pairs of identical twins—the co-twin of a twin with schizophrenia has only a 48% chance of developing schizophrenia him- or herself. If the disease were entirely genetic, there should be a 100% correspondence in its incidence in pairs of identical twins. And a fraternal co-twin of a person with schizophrenia has only a 17% likelihood of developing the disorder (Gottesman, 1991). Other factors—at the levels of brain, person, and group—play a role (Šagud et al., 2008).

Structural Brain Abnormalities in Schizophrenia. Evidence from autopsies and neuroimaging studies suggests that schizophrenia often involves abnormalities in brain structures. Compared to people without the disorder, a person with schizophrenia is more likely to have enlarged *ventricles*, cavities in the center of the brain filled with cerebrospinal fluid. Increased ventricle size means the other parts of the brain are smaller, including the frontal cortex (Goldstein et al., 1999), which plays a central role in abstract thinking and planning.

These and other brain abnormalities can reflect a basic miswiring of brain circuits, so that brain areas are connected to each other in abnormal ways. As a result of this faulty brain circuitry, neural activity doesn't occur in the way it is supposed to (Andreasen et al., 1999; Walker et al., 2004).

Researchers have suggested various ways in which these brain abnormalities might arise and have come to focus on the fetus's developing brain—specifically, on how normal brain development might go awry during pregnancy and later lead to schizophrenia. Possibilities include:

- maternal malnourishment during pregnancy (Brown et al., 1999; Wahlbeck et al., 2001),

- maternal illness during pregnancy (Buka et al., 1999; Brown et al., 2001; Ellman, 2008),

- maternal stress (and higher levels of glucocorticoids, such as cortisol) during pregnancy (Weinstock, 1997; Welberg & Seckl, 2001), and

- prenatal or birth-related medical complications that lead to fetal oxygen deprivation (Cannon, 1997; Geddes & Lawrie, 1995; McNeil et al., 2000; Zornberg et al., 2000).

Elevated Levels of Stress-Related Hormones. Cortisol, a stress-related hormone, appears to play a role in schizophrenia; among people with schizophrenia, those with higher levels of cortisol tend to have more severe symptoms (Walder et al., 2000). Some researchers suggest that the increased biological changes and stress of adolescence lead to higher levels of stress-related hormones, and the increased levels of hormones may somehow trigger the disorder in people who are vulnerable to develop schizophrenia; this hypothesis fits the fact that prodromal symptoms of schizophrenia typically begin to emerge during adolescence.

Neurotransmitters. High levels of stress-related hormones are thought to affect activity of the neurotransmitter dopamine, and abnormalities in the functioning of this neurotransmitter have been implicated in schizophrenia (Walker & Diforio, 1997). In addition, abnormalities in other neurotransmitters are also evident in schizophrenia (Goff & Coyle, 2001; Laruelle et al., 2003; Tsai & Coyle, 2002; Walker & Diforio, 1997; Walker et al., 2004).

In summary, researchers now agree that some people are genetically vulnerable to developing schizophrenia and that prenatal and birth complications play a role in whether a person develops the disorder. These prenatal factors have their effects, at least in part, by creating abnormalities in how the neurotransmitter dopamine functions and in brain structure and function, particularly in the frontal lobe. Such abnormalities may then predispose the person to develop the disorder when certain other events occur: The hormonal changes during adolescence are one possible triggering event, but others exist—including those at the level of the person, which we consider in the following section.

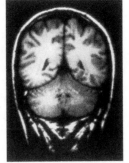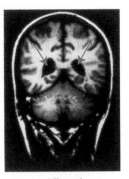

Well   Affected

28-year-old males

People with schizophrenia have larger ventricles, smaller amounts of frontal and temporal lobe cortex, and a smaller thalamus. This decreased cortical volume probably accounts for some of the cognitive deficits found in people with this disorder (Andreasen et al., 1986, 1992).

Source: National Institute of Mental Health

Despite odds of one in six, all four of these identical quadruplets—from oldest to youngest, Nora, Iris, Myra, and Hester—went on to develop schizophrenia. The physical stress experienced by their mother while pregnant with the quads may have contributed to their developing the disorder. However, each of their symptoms and the onset and course of the illness differed. Hester and Iris were more disabled than were their sisters.

Source: Edna Morlok

LEVEL OF THE PERSON IN SCHIZOPHRENIA.   Although not part of the *DSM-IV-TR* diagnostic criteria, people with schizophrenia often have many types of cognitive difficulties—which probably emerge as a result of their brain abnormalities. They can have problems processing and responding to sensory stimuli (Green et al., 1999, 2000; Krieger et al., 2001), such as the sights and sounds around them. In turn, these problems can lead to unusual sensory experiences, creating hallucinations—such as seeing inanimate objects move of their own accord. People with such information-processing problems may feel bombarded by the stimuli around them and have trouble focusing on and making sense of those stimuli, leading to additional problems in organizing what they perceive and experience.

People with schizophrenia are also likely to have difficulties interpreting the meaning of stimuli and using information appropriately in various contexts (Green et al., 2000; Kuperberg & Heckers, 2000; Walker et al., 2004). Such people may:

- not be able to sort out important from unimportant information (Hemsley, 1994) or to distinguish relevant from irrelevant stimuli (Cornblatt et al., 1997; Nuechterlein, 1991),
- lose the "big picture" or be unable to keep track of the overall goal in a multistep task,
- have difficulty understanding social cues and therefore respond inappropriately (Penn et al., 1997), or
- not realize that they are having problems (referred to as a *lack of insight*).

(You, like many researchers in the field, might wonder why these cognitive deficits are not among the *DSM-IV-TR* criteria for schizophrenia. The short answer is that it is only relatively recently that researchers have identified these cognitive deficits. In fact, many researchers suggest that the next edition of the *DSM* should include these symptoms as part of the criteria for the disorder.)

Such cognitive difficulties create stress, and as noted above, the stress response—and cortisol in particular—may play a role in triggering the disorder. Consistent with this possibility, researchers have shown that at least some of these cognitive problems exist prior to the disorder's developing (Grimes & Walker, 1994; Walker et al., 1993). Thus, it is possible that pre-existing cognitive problems may influence whether a person develops the disorder. That said, once a person actually develops the disorder, the cognitive problems become more severe.

LEVEL OF THE GROUP IN SCHIZOPHRENIA.   Social stress also plays a role in whether someone develops schizophrenia, particularly in whether symptoms recur after a psychotic episode (Gottesman, 1991; Ventura et al., 1989). Studies of demographic variables have produced one type of evidence that social stress contributes to the onset or recurrence of schizophrenia: A higher rate of schizophrenia is found in urban areas and in lower socioeconomic classes (Freeman, 1994; Mortensen et al., 1999). Why might this be? Two factors appear to play a role: *social selection* and *social causation* (Dauncey et al., 1993):

- **Social selection**, also called *social drift*, refers to the "drifting" to lower socioeconomic classes of people who have become mentally disabled (Mulvany et al., 2001). This often happens to those who are no longer able to work and who lack family support or care (Dohrenwend et al., 1992).
- **Social causation** refers to the view that chronic psychological and social stress from living in an urban environment, particularly for the poor, may trigger the disorder in persons who are vulnerable (Freeman, 1994).

In addition, family interactions affect whether a family member with schizophrenia has a recurrence of the disorder. In particular, certain ways that family members express emotion are associated with the likelihood that the family member with schizophrenia will have a relapse. Specifically, such families are critical, hostile, and overinvolved, and this style of interaction is referred to as having **high expressed emotion** (Butzlaff & Hooley, 1998; Kavanagh, 1992).

Social selection The tendency of the mentally disabled to drift to the lower economic classes; also called *social drift*.

Social causation The view that chronic psychological and social stresses from living in an urban environment may lead to an increase in the rate of schizophrenia (especially among the poor).

High expressed emotion An emotional style in families in which members are critical, hostile, and overinvolved.

It is plausible that the "high expressed emotion" interaction style *causes* the symptoms to worsen, but it is also possible that the direction of causality runs the other way: Perhaps families with high expressed emotion are responding to a relative with schizophrenia whose behavior is more bizarre or disruptive, and families with low expressed emotion include a relative with schizophrenia whose symptoms are less extreme. And it is possible that the influences run in both directions.

INTERACTING LEVELS IN SCHIZOPHRENIA. Events at the three levels of analysis interact: Walker and Diforio (1997) propose a specific diathesis–stress model to explain how stress can worsen schizophrenic symptoms. People with a diathesis for the disorder have a different biological response to stress than do people without a diathesis (level of the brain). Specifically, people who are vulnerable for developing schizophrenia have higher-than-normal levels of cortisol as part of their stress response and, according to Walker and Diforio's theory, the increased cortisol leads to an increased release of dopamine. In turn, the increased dopamine worsens symptoms of schizophrenia. The researchers further propose that the negative symptoms of schizophrenia—such as social withdrawal—are attempts to reduce stress (levels of person and group). Thus, genetic, prenatal, or birth factors increase a susceptibility to stress, and stress (which emerges in part from social factors) aggravates schizophrenic symptoms.

If van Gogh did suffer from schizophrenia, a diagnosis of the paranoid subtype would seem to fit him best because his intellectual functioning and expression of emotion did not appear to be impaired. However, beyond the single reported hallucination (which led him to cut off part of his ear), he did not appear to have had any symptoms of schizophrenia—paranoid or otherwise. Moreover, that diagnosis would not account for his lengthy bouts of depression.

A higher rate of schizophrenia is found in urban areas and lower socioeconomic classes. One explanation (referred to as *social drift*) is that people who become mentally disabled from schizophrenia are unable to work; another explanation (referred to as *social causation*) is that the stresses of urban life and financial hardship trigger the disorder in people who are vulnerable.

Source: © Ashley Cooper / CORBIS All Rights Reserved

Eating Disorders: You Are How You Eat?

For most of his life as a painter, van Gogh had very little money, and he had to choose whether to spend what money he had on painting supplies or food; he frequently chose the former (Auden, 1989). At times, van Gogh ate only breakfast and a dinner of coffee and bread, which we assume was a result of his poverty. However, some of his eating habits appear to reflect something other than poverty: While in the hospital during the last year of his life, he would eat only meager dinners of half-cooked chickpeas or bread and a little soup (Auden, 1989). Were van Gogh to be seen by mental health professionals now, they would undoubtedly ask more about these restricted and bizarre eating habits and wonder whether they might be symptoms of an eating disorder. In this section, we consider eating disorders.

To begin to understand eating disorders, consider these questions about people you know: If you have friends who are on a diet,

- Do they want to lose more weight, even if others tell them that they are too thin?
- If they eat more than they want, do they feel that they must exercise, even if they are tired or sick?
- Is their view of themselves on a given day dependent on whether they exercise that day?
- Do they eat as little as possible during the day and then find themselves "losing control" with food in the afternoon or evening?

A "yes" response to these questions does not necessarily indicate that a person has a disorder, but it does indicate a preoccupation with food, body image, and weight. These preoccupations are typical of people with **eating disorders**, a category of disorders that involves severe disturbances in eating. Although more than 90% of people diagnosed with eating disorders are females, males are increasingly suffering from these disorders, too. The *DSM-IV-TR* lists two eating disorders: *anorexia nervosa* and *bulimia nervosa*.

Eating disorders A category of disorders that involves severe disturbances in eating.

Anorexia Nervosa: You Can Be Too Thin
Anorexia nervosa is a potentially fatal eating disorder characterized by a refusal to maintain even a low normal weight, along with an intense fear of gaining weight. Someone with anorexia nervosa (often referred to

Anorexia nervosa An eating disorder characterized by the refusal to maintain even a low normal weight, along with an intense fear of gaining weight.

simply as *anorexia*) is focused on being thin regardless of the consequences—physical, psychological, social, or medical. Of people hospitalized with anorexia nervosa, 10% will eventually die of causes related to the disorder (American Psychiatric Association, 1994).

Anorexia Nervosa: WHAT IT'S LIKE

People with anorexia nervosa have irrational and unhealthy beliefs about food, as recounted by one woman:

Yesterday . . . I had a grapefruit and black coffee for breakfast, and for dinner I had the . . . salad I eat every night. I always skip lunch. I had promised myself that I would only eat three-quarters of the salad since I've been feeling stuffed after it lately—but I think I ate more than the three-quarters. I know it was just lettuce and broccoli but I can't believe I did that. I was up all night worrying about getting fat.

Source: Michele Siegel, Judith Brisman, Margot Weinshel, *Surviving an eating disorder: Strategies for family and friends.* New York: Harper and Row. 1988, p. 17.

FIGURE 5 Body Image Distortion

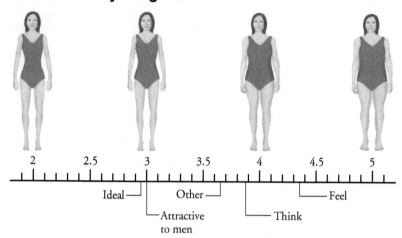

Many women, not only those with anorexia nervosa, have distorted body images. "Ideal" is the average of women's ratings of the ideal figure. "Attractive to men" is the average rating of the figure women believe is most attractive to men. "Other" is the average actual selection of the female figure that men find most attractive. "Think" is the average figure women think best matches their figure. "Feel" is the average figure women feel best matches their figure.

Source: Adapted from Thompson, J.K., *Body Image Disturbance: Assessment and Treatment* (p. 11) © 1990. Reproduced by permission of Pearson Education, Inc.

Included in the list of symptoms required for a diagnosis of anorexia are:

- distortions of how a person views his or her body ("body image"; see Figure 5),
- an intense fear of gaining weight or becoming fat,
- a refusal to maintain a healthy weight, and
- among females, *amenorrhea* (the cessation of menstruation), which usually occurs because of low weight.

People with anorexia commonly "know" that they are underweight, but they "see" fat that is not there when they look in the mirror, or they generally overestimate the body size (Smeets et al., 1997). They are often obsessed by thoughts of food, and these thoughts are usually based on irrational or illogical thinking (such as what constitutes "good" and "bad" foods). They often deny that their low weight is a problem—or even that they have a problem.

Some symptoms of anorexia nervosa may vary from culture to culture. For example, half of young Chinese women with this disorder are not afraid of being fat, as are North Americans, but instead explain their restricted diet as a distaste for food or as a result of bodily discomfort when they eat (S. Lee, 1996).

The *DSM-IV-TR* specifies two types of anorexia nervosa: (1) the classic *restricting type*, in which weight loss is achieved primarily by undereating, and (2) *binge-eating/purging type*, which involves periodic episodes of *binge eating* (eating substantially more food within a certain time period than most people would eat in similar circumstances) and/or *purging* (getting rid of unwanted calories by vomiting or misusing laxatives, diuretics, or enemas). To be diagnosed with the restricting type, the individual must not binge eat or purge.

Bulimia Nervosa **Bulimia nervosa** is characterized by recurrent episodes of binge eating followed by attempts to prevent weight gain (this disorder is often referred to simply as *bulimia*). When such attempts are made through purging (by vomiting or by using laxatives), the diagnosis of bulimia nervosa is further specified as *purging type.* People with bulimia may also try to restrict weight gain by using other methods, such as fasting or excessive exercise, and when this is the case, the disorder is specified as the *nonpurging type.* As with anorexia, females are most commonly diagnosed with bulimia; however, unlike anorexia, people with this disorder typically are of normal weight or even overweight (and thus women with this disorder often continue to menstruate).

Bulimia nervosa An eating disorder characterized by recurrent episodes of binge eating, followed by attempts to prevent weight gain.

Bulimia Nervosa: WHAT IT'S LIKE

Some people with bulimia purge even when their eating does not constitute a binge:

> If I had one bite of bread, just one, I felt as though I blew it! I'd stop listening to whomever was talking to me at the table. I'd start thinking, How can I get rid of this? I'd worry about how fat I'd look, how I couldn't fit into my clothes. My head would be flooded with thoughts of what to do now. . . . I had to undo what I'd done. The night was blown. I was a mess.

Source: Michele Siegel, Judith Brisman, Margot Weinshel, *Surviving an eating disorder: Strategies for family and friends.* New York: Harper and Row. 1988, p. 18.

Although most people with bulimia do not realize it, in the long run, purging does not usually eliminate all the calories ingested because the body can begin absorbing calories even while food is in the mouth. Purging is, in fact, a poor method for losing weight (Garner, 1997).

Explaining Eating Disorders Why do people—typically females—develop eating disorders? To answer this question, we explore factors at the levels of the brain, person, and group.

LEVEL OF THE BRAIN IN EATING DISORDERS. Research findings show that genes can predispose someone to develop an eating disorder, but the heritability of the disorders varies widely across studies: from 28% to 88%. *Heritability* indicates how much of the variability in a characteristic in a population in a specific environment is a result of genes. This large range of heritability suggests that factors other than genes play a significant role (Bulik, 2005; Jacobi et al., 2004).

Eating disorders are also associated with abnormalities in the functioning of the neurotransmitter serotonin (Kaye, 2008). But researchers have yet to discover whether such abnormalities cause, or are caused by, an eating disorder—or even whether these abnormalities are related not to the eating disorder but instead are related to personality traits or some other variable that is associated with eating disorders. What researchers do know is that weight loss (which occurs with anorexia nervosa) and malnutrition (which can occur with both eating disorders) are associated with impaired functioning of serotonin receptors. This neurotransmitter is also involved in obsessive-compulsive disorder, and the obsessional thinking about food and pathological eating behavior of anorexia may be related to changes in serotonin functioning (Barbarich, 2002; Kaye, 1995). Serotonin also helps to create a feeling of *satiety*—the sense of having eaten enough—and so altered serotonin functioning may affect the ability to feel satisfied after eating, which potentially predisposes a person to develop, or perpetuates, an eating disorder (Halmi, 1996; Kaye, 2008).

The biological effects of dieting can also make women vulnerable to developing bulimia nervosa: Some, though not all, studies indicate that dieting sometimes precedes the onset of bulimia (Garner, 1997); dieting may change serotonin functioning in some people.

LEVEL OF THE PERSON IN EATING DISORDERS. Numerous personality-related characteristics and irrational beliefs have been linked with eating disorders. Consider these findings about people with eating disorders:

- They tend to be perfectionists and have unusually high levels of anxiety (Bulik et al., 2003; Forbush et al., 2007; Tyrka et al., 2002).

- They often have irrational beliefs and inappropriate expectations about their bodies, jobs, relationships, and themselves (Fairburn et al., 2003; Garfinkel et al., 1992; Striegel-Moore, 1993). They tend to engage in dichotomous, black-or-white thinking: Fruit is "good"; pizza is "bad."

- As shown in Figure 6 on the next page, when examining photographs of themselves, women with eating disorders spend more time looking at their "ugly" body parts than at their "beautiful" parts; in contrast, when they look at photos of other women, they spend more time looking at those women's "beautiful" body parts than at their "ugly" parts. Women who do not have an eating disorder devote equal

FIGURE 6 Gazing at Body Parts: Women with and without Eating Disorders

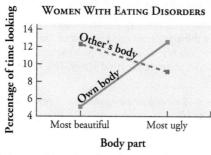

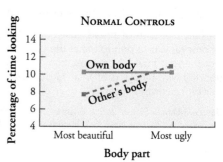

Women with eating disorders spend more time looking at their "most ugly" body parts than at their "most beautiful" parts; women without eating disorders spend equal amounts of time looking at both types of their own body parts. When looking at photos of other women, those with eating disorders look at the "most beautiful" parts more than the "most ugly" parts, and this pattern is reversed for women who do not have eating disorders (Jansen et al., 2005).

Source: From Anita Jansen, Chantal Nederkoom, Sandra Mulkens, "Selective visual attention for ugly and beautiful body parts in eating disorders." *Behaviour Research and Therapy,* 43, 183-196. Copyright © 2005, Elsevier. Reprinted by permission.

time to looking at their own "beautiful" and "ugly" parts and when looking at photos of other women spend more time looking at their "ugly" parts than at their "beautiful" parts (Jansen et al., 2005).

Moreover, people with these characteristics (personality traits, irrational beliefs, and inappropriate expectations) are likely to be reinforced by the behaviors associated with eating disorders (Blackburn et al., 2006). Purging may temporarily relieve the anxiety created by overeating, and preoccupations with food can distract the person from unpleasant work or dealing with family conflicts or social problems. And the restricted eating may lead people to gain a sense of increased control—over food and over life in general—although such feelings of mastery are often short lived as the disorder takes over (Garner, 1997).

Cultural pressure on women to be thin and to attain an "ideal" body shape can contribute to eating disorders. Such pressure explains why there is a higher incidence of eating disorders now than 60 years ago, as the ideal figure has changed from the generous proportions of Marilyn Monroe to the rail-thin silhouette of today's runway models (Andersen & DiDomenico, 1992; A. E. Field et al., 1999; Nemeroff et al., 1994).

Sources: Everett Collection; The Image Works

LEVEL OF THE GROUP IN EATING DISORDERS. The family and the larger culture also can contribute to a person's developing an eating disorder, in large part by encouraging her or him to be focused on weight and appearance (Crowther et al., 2002; Thompson & Stice, 2001). For instance, children have an increased risk of developing eating disorders if their families are overly concerned about appearance and weight (Stein et al., 2006; Strober, 1995). Moreover, symptoms of eating disorders tend to increase among immigrants from less weight-conscious cultures (such as the Chinese and the Egyptian) as they assimilate to American culture (Bilukha & Utermohlen, 2002; Dolan, 1991; A. M. Lee & Lee, 1996; Stark-Wroblewski et al., 2005).

In fact, culture can exert its effects via film, television, and other media, which can expose people the world over to the ideal thin body shape for women in Western societies. One study in Fiji found that with the advent of television (and Western television shows) in that country in 1995, Fijian girls' feelings about their bodies began to shift: Whereas before watching Western television shows, they felt comfortable having a large body—the ideal body shape in their culture—after viewing such shows, 75% of girls felt too fat or big at least some of the time (Becker et al., 2002). A similar process appears to happen to women in Western cultures as they strive to meet the culture's ideal of feminine appearance—namely, thinness (Kim & Lennon, 2007; Striegel-Moore, 1993). Moreover, it is not only females who are susceptible: Eating disorders are increasing among men who regularly take part in appearance- or weight-conscious activities, such as modeling and wrestling (Brownell & Rodin, 1992).

Van Gogh had abnormal eating habits; could he have had an eating disorder? It is unlikely; although he often ate sparingly and peculiarly, he did not appear to be preoccupied with weight gain or body image, and no information suggests that he purged in any way.

LOOKING AT LEVELS Binge Eating

Source: Photodisc/Getty Images; (inset) © Volker Steger/Photo Researchers, Inc.

You have learned what eating disorders are and explanations of why they might occur. Let's consider in detail a core aspect of bulimia nervosa—binge eating. Why do some people chronically binge eat?

At the level of the brain, dieting—food restriction—triggers both neurological and bodily responses that make people more likely to binge eat; after binging, people typically respond by dieting again—so they end up alternating between periods of restricted eating and binge eating (Fairburn et al., 2005; Polivy & Herman, 1993; Stice et al., 2002). Moreover, after a binge/purge episode, the brain may trigger a cascade of hormones called *endorphins*—which bring about a feeling of well-being, and thus reinforce the binge/purge episode. (Endorphins are also released after sustained physical exercise and cause the pleasant state among runners known as a *runner's high*.) As one woman with bulimia reported, "I go to never-never land. Once I start bingeing, it's like being in a stupor, like being drunk ... I'm like a different person. It's very humiliating—but not then, not while I'm eating. While I'm eating, nothing else matters" (Siegel et al., 1988, p. 20).

At the level of the person, people with bulimia—in their efforts to be "in control" of food when not bingeing—generally consume fewer calories than would be in a normal meal. Their restricted eating sets the stage for later binge eating because they are hungry and have food cravings. And then, when they (over)eat, they physically feel better—after all, they no longer feel as if they're starving! Thus, bingeing is reinforced. In addition, the dichotomous thinking typical of people with eating disorders leads them to view themselves as either "good" (when dieting or restricting food intake) or "bad" (when eating "forbidden foods" or feeling out of control while eating). This type of thinking sets the stage for bingeing after any small amount of forbidden food is eaten: A bite of a candy bar is followed by a thought like this: "Well, I shouldn't have eaten *any* of the candy bar, but since I did, I might as well eat the whole thing, especially since I really shouldn't have a candy bar again." This line of reasoning is part of the *abstinence violation effect* (Polivy & Herman, 1993; Urbszat et al., 2002), the sense of letting go of self-restraint after breaking a self-imposed rule about food. The person thinks, "Once I violate the rule, why not go all the way?".

At the level of the group, the cultural ideal of thinness may lead some people to feel inadequate (with the feelings occurring at the level of the person); they can't possibly achieve that ideal, so why bother? They may then turn to the comfort of (over)eating to make themselves feel better.

Events at the different levels interact: Cultural pressure to be thin (level of the group) leads vulnerable people (levels of the brain and person) to try to restrict their food intake. The hunger caused by this undereating may trigger a binge. (A binge may also be triggered by various types of stress; Polivy & Herman, 1993; Stice et al., 2002; Vanderlinden et al., 2001.) Bingeing can then temporarily lead to positive states (such as relief from hunger or distraction from an uncomfortable feeling or thought). This immediate reinforcement (level of the person) may feel more powerful than the distress, impaired functioning, or risk of medical problems or death that are the chronic or long-term consequences of eating disorders.

✔●─ **Study** and **Review** on
mypsychlab.com

LOOKING BACK

1. **What are mood disorders? What causes them?** Mood disorders include major depressive disorder (MDD) and bipolar disorder, both of which may have psychotic features. MDD is characterized by depressed mood, loss of pleasure, fatigue, weight loss, poor sleep, a sense of worthlessness or guilt, and poor attention and concentration. Bipolar disorder is characterized either by one or more episodes of mania or by alternating episodes of hypomania and depression. These disorders can arise in part because of genes and brain abnormalities, but events at the levels of the person and group play a role in onset or relapse.

2. **What are the main types of anxiety disorders? What are their symptoms and causes?** The anxiety disorders include panic disorder (with or without agoraphobia), specific and social phobias, obsessive-compulsive disorder (OCD), and posttraumatic stress disorder (PTSD). Regarding symptoms: Panic symptoms include breathing difficulties, nausea, dizziness, heart palpitations, and a fear of doing something crazy or uncontrollable. Phobias involve avoiding a feared object or situation that would cause anxiety or panic if encountered. OCD involves obsessions and often compulsions. PTSD occurs in response to traumatic events; it involves symptoms of panic as well as a reliving of the trauma. Anxiety disorders are caused by the interaction of events at the levels of the brain, the person, and the group.

3. **What are the symptoms and causes of schizophrenia?** Schizophrenia is characterized by two types of symptoms: positive and negative. Positive symptoms include delusions, hallucinations, and disorders of behavior and speech. Negative symptoms include flat affect, alogia, and avolition. A person can be vulnerable to developing schizophrenia because of genes, prenatal maternal illness, or prenatal or birth complications; all these factors may lead to brain abnormalities. The biological changes and increased stress of adolescence can play a role in the onset of schizophrenia, and environmental factors, such as living with high expressed emotion families or being a member of a lower socioeconomic class, increase with the risk of relapse.

4. **What are the symptoms and causes of eating disorders?** Symptoms of anorexia nervosa include a distorted body image, a fear of weight gain or becoming fat, a refusal to maintain a healthy weight, and (among females) amenorrhea. Symptoms of bulimia nervosa include recurrent binge eating, followed by attempts to prevent weight gain. Eating disorders appear to be caused by an interaction of biological factors, rigid thinking about food and appearance, and family and cultural messages about weight.

THINK like a **PSYCHOLOGIST** Suppose someone you know, someone whose sharp style of dress and confident manner you admire, starts looking unkempt and acting tired, nervous, and fidgety. Would this change suggest a psychological disorder? Why or why not? If so, what type of disorder do you think would be most likely and why? Would a psychological disorder be the only explanation for these changes in behavior?

Axis II: Focus on Personality Disorders

Vincent van Gogh was more than just unconventional; his difficulties in life went beyond his attacks, his hallucinations, and his periods of depression. Van Gogh's relationships with other people were troubled, and they often followed a pattern: He initially felt positively toward someone new in his life (such as happened with Gauguin and Sien), and this invariably was followed by a turbulent phase in his relationship with that person, then an eventual falling out. Throughout his life, he had emotional outbursts that sooner or later caused others to withdraw their friendship. His relationship with his brother Theo is the only one that endured. Does such a pattern of turbulent relationships suggest that he may have had a *personality disorder*?

LOOKING AHEAD: Learning Objectives

1. What are personality disorders?
2. What is antisocial personality disorder?

Axis II Personality Disorders

A **personality disorder** is a set of relatively stable personality traits that are inflexible and mal-adaptive, causing distress or difficulty with daily functioning. As noted earlier, personality disorders are noted on Axis II of the *DSM-IV-TR*. A personality disorder may be a person's only diagnosis, or it may be accompanied by diagnoses on Axis I. In the *DSM-IV-TR*, personality disorders are regarded as distinct from Axis I disorders: Whereas the symptoms of Axis I disorders typically are experienced as superimposed on top of the person's normal personality (that is, the symptoms lead them to feel that they are "not themselves"), the symptoms of Axis II disorders are integral to the person's personality. The maladaptive traits of personality disorders cause distress or difficulty with daily functioning in school, work, social life, or relationships. However, they can be so subtle as to be unnoticeable in a brief encounter; it is only after getting to know the person over time that a personality disorder may become evident.

As shown in Table 6, personality disorders are organized into three clusters in the *DSM-IV-TR*, with each grouping based on common types of symptoms:

- Cluster A—odd, eccentric behaviors,
- Cluster B—emotional or dramatic behaviors,
- Cluster C—anxious or fearful behaviors or symptoms.

TABLE 6 *DSM-IV-TR* Axis II Personality Disorders

Disorder	Description
Cluster A	*Odd, eccentric behaviors*
Paranoid personality disorder	A pattern of suspiciousness and distrust of others; other people are inferred to have ill-intentioned motives. However, unlike the paranoid subtype of schizophrenia, delusions or hallucinations are not present.
Schizoid personality disorder	A pattern of detachment from social relationships and a narrow range of displayed emotion.
Schizotypal personality disorder	A pattern of extreme discomfort in close relationships, odd or quirky behavior, and cognitive or perceptual distortions (such as sensing the presence of another person or spirit).
Cluster B	*Emotional or dramatic behaviors*
Antisocial personality disorder	A pattern of disregard for, or violation of, the rights of others.
Borderline personality disorder	A pattern of instability in relationships, self-image, and feelings, and pronounced impulsivity (such as in spending, substance abuse, sex, reckless driving, or binge eating). Relationships are often characterized by rapid swings from idealizing another person to devaluing him or her. Recurrent suicidal gestures, threats, or self-mutilation, such as nonlethal cuts on the arm, are common, as are chronic feelings of emptiness.
Histrionic personality disorder	A pattern of excessive attention seeking and expression of emotion.
Narcissistic personality disorder	A pattern of an exaggerated sense of self-importance, need for admiration, and lack of empathy.
Cluster C	*Anxious or fearful behaviors or symptoms*
Avoidant personality disorder	A pattern of social discomfort, feelings of inadequacy, and hypersensitivity to negative evaluation.
Dependent personality disorder	A pattern of clingy, submissive behavior that results from an extreme need to be taken care of.
Obsessive-compulsive personality disorder	A pattern of preoccupation with perfectionism, orderliness, and control (but no obsessions or compulsions, as occur with obsessive-compulsive disorder).

Source: Reprinted with permission from the *Diagnostic and Statistical Manual of Mental Disorders, Fourth Edition, Text Revision,* (Copyright 2000). American Psychiatric Association.

Personality disorders A category of disorders in which relatively stable personality traits are inflexible and maladaptive, causing distress or difficulty with daily functioning.

433

Some researchers argue that the combinations of traits currently defined as personality disorders should not be called "disorders" at all, for two reasons:

1. Defining such traits as disorders treats normal variations in personality—such as the desire for perfection and orderliness—as pathological, as is the case with obsessive-compulsive personality disorder, and

2. Doing so creates separate Axis II categories for some conditions that could be part of an Axis I clinical disorder, such as the extreme shyness of avoidant personality disorder, the symptoms of which overlap substantially with those of social phobia. The set of symptoms of avoidant personality may be best conceived of as a variant of social phobia rather than as a distinct personality disorder (Hyman, personal communication, 1998; Livesley, 1998).

Van Gogh's pattern of turbulent relationships is similar to that of people with borderline personality disorder. However, in order to diagnose him as having a personality disorder, a mental health professional would need more specific information about his relationship difficulties and impulsivity.

Antisocial Personality Disorder

The most intensively studied personality disorder is **antisocial personality disorder (ASPD)**, a personality disorder characterized by a long-standing pattern of disregard for others to the point of violating their rights (American Psychiatric Association, 2000). The *DSM-IV-TR* specifies that people with this disorder typically commit illegal acts, lie, are impulsive and irresponsible, are physically aggressive, recklessly disregard the safety of others, and seem indifferent to other people's suffering. People with this disorder may talk a good line, but they know how to manipulate others and don't care how another person feels.

John Wayne Gacy, convicted serial killer, saw himself as a victim; he shared this feature with other people who have antisocial personality disorder.

Source: Getty Images, Inc.

Antisocial Personality Disorder: WHAT IT'S LIKE

A common feature among people with ASPD is that they see *themselves* as the real victims. While discussing the many and horrible murders he had committed, the serial killer John Wayne Gacy portrayed himself as the 34th victim:

I was made an asshole and a scapegoat . . . when I look back, I see myself more as a victim than a perpetrator. . . . I was the victim; I was cheated out of my childhood. . . . [He wondered whether] there would be someone, somewhere who would understand how badly it had hurt to be John Wayne Gacy.

Source: Robert Hare, *Without conscience: The disturbing world of the psychopaths among us.* New York: Pocket Books. 1993 p. 43.

ASPD occurs three times more frequently in men than in women, and although only 1% to 2% of Americans are diagnosed with this disorder, 60% of males in U.S. prisons are estimated to have it (Moran, 1999). Cross-cultural studies have found a similar pattern of symptoms in both Western and non-Western cultures (Zoccolillo et al., 1999).

Understanding Antisocial Personality Disorder

What causes ASPD? As is true for other psychological disorders, this one is best understood by examining events at the three levels of analysis and their interactions.

Level of the Brain in Antisocial Personality Disorder Several types of events at the level of the brain contribute to ASPD. Genes predispose a person to develop this disorder, as shown by twin and adoption studies (Nigg & Goldsmith, 1994). Moreover, adoption studies show that the effects of the genes in ASPD depend on the specific environment: If a child's biological parents were criminals, boys adopted into a family of law-abiding people are only slightly more likely to become criminals

Antisocial personality disorder (ASPD) A personality disorder characterized by a long-standing pattern of disregard for other people to the point of violating their rights.

than boys whose biological parents were not criminals. However, there was a whopping increase in criminal behavior when children whose biological parents were criminals were adopted into a family of criminals. If the biological parents were not criminals, the adopted child's later criminal behavior was the same whether he or she grew up in a law-abiding or a criminal family (Mednick et al., 1984). Criminal behavior provides a clear example of how genes and environment can interact: The genes predispose; the environment triggers.

One proposed explanation for *how* the genes predispose is that they cause the autonomic nervous system (the part of the central nervous system involved in the fight-or-flight response) to be underresponsive, so that such people are understimulated by "normal" behaviors. In turn, this might lead people with such genes to seek out highly arousing, thrilling activities, such as criminal acts (Jang et al., 2001; Quay, 1965).

Level of the Person in Antisocial Personality Disorder Research suggests that people with ASPD have difficulty controlling their impulses and their anger (Silverstein, 2007; Zlotnick, 1999). In addition, they have difficulty understanding how others feel, which explains their lack of empathy (Kagan & Reid, 1986).

Level of the Group in Antisocial Personality Disorder People with this personality disorder are more likely than other people to have had an *insecure attachment* to their primary caregiver. This type of attachment is characterized by the expectation that the caregiver (and later, others in the person's life) will not be available to provide support and nurturance (Ogloff, 2006). Insecure attachment can arise in children who were abused, neglected, or were disciplined only inconsistently (Gabbard, 1990; Patterson et al., 1989; Pollock et al., 1990).

Interacting Levels in Antisocial Personality Disorder Events at the three levels of analysis interact to give rise to ASPD. To begin with, an underresponsive autonomic nervous system (level of the brain) can lead people to be relatively unaffected by mild punishment or social rejection (level of the group), which would ordinarily lead a person to become anxious and motivated to change his or her behavior in order to avoid these negative consequences in the future (level of the person). In other words, because of the underresponsive autonomic nervous system, the normal social and legal consequences of inappropriate behavior don't have the usual effect of deterring similar behavior in the future. In fact, one classic study found that inmates who had ASPD had difficulty learning to avoid shocks; that is, negative consequences (shocks) that followed a specific behavior by the inmates' did not lead the inmates to change their behavior so as to avoid shocks in the future. But when the inmates were injected with adrenaline so that their level of arousal was increased (and their autonomic nervous system functioned at a more normal level), the inmates learned to avoid shocks at the same rate as other people (Schachter & Latané, 1964).

The underresponsiveness of the nervous system may also contribute to the insecure attachment with caregivers (level of the group) because normal levels of stimulation provided by caregivers may not have been enough to engage children with an underresponsive autonomic system. Moreover, as these children grew up, punishment for misbehavior would have been less effective, which might then cause their caregivers to be more abusive (or to give up and neglect the children) (level of the group); thus, the path to ASPD arises from the different events at the three levels of analysis.

THINK like a **PSYCHOLOGIST** Your new neighbor seemed like a nice guy until you got to know him better. He borrows money for an "emergency" but never repays you. When your friends come by, he seems to stick his head out the door and charms them. Would you suspect that he might have ASPD? Why?

✓●─Study and Review on **mypsychlab.com**

LOOKING BACK

1. **What are personality disorders?** Personality disorders are characterized by relatively stable personality traits (such as being impulsive) that are inflexible and maladaptive, causing distress or difficulty with daily functioning.

2. **What is antisocial personality disorder?** The hallmark of antisocial personality disorder (ASPD) is a long-standing pattern of disregard for others, to the point of violating their rights. It occurs more frequently in men than in women.

A Cautionary Note About Diagnosis

The events of Vincent van Gogh's life present an opportunity to explore the ways in which the human psyche can be troubled and the ways in which the mental health field presently classifies disorders. But that is not the same as proposing a diagnosis of someone who we cannot assess firsthand to make an accurate diagnosis.

No mental health clinician can really know with certainty from what, if any, specific disorder or disorders van Gogh suffered. MDD and schizophrenia are possibilities, as is bipolar disorder (Jamison, 1993); it is possible that he had more than one psychological disorder. Moreover, van Gogh went through periods when he drank significant quantities of alcohol, which could have affected his mental state and behavior—and some of his attacks and hallucinations might have been symptoms of *delirium tremens* (the "DTs"), caused by withdrawal from alcohol. (However, these diagnoses would not explain why van Gogh had attacks even during lengthy periods of sobriety; Lubin, 1972.)

It is also possible that van Gogh may have suffered from a medical disorder, in particular a form of epilepsy, in which case his "attacks"—at least some of them—were seizures. (Seizures might also have been induced by the extremely potent alcoholic drink, *absinthe*, that was in vogue among artists at the time; Blumer, 2002; Hughes, 2005.) Moments before an epileptic seizures victims are sometimes overcome with religious feelings and delusions. The possibility that van Gogh might have suffered from epilepsy—a neurological disorder, not a psychological one—highlights that mental health professionals should ensure that patients are also assessed medically to determine whether they have a medical disorder that can cause psychological symptoms. Only after ruling out medical illnesses can the mental health clinician or researcher have confidence in a diagnosis of a psychological disorder.

After reading this chapter, it may be tempting to use the knowledge you acquired to diagnose friends, family members, or yourself. However, the information in this chapter is only a brief introduction to the topic of psychological disorders. The ability to diagnose accurately requires detailed knowledge and extensive training, just as with medical disorders. If you suspect that you or someone close to you may have a psychological disorder, consult with a mental health professional.

LET'S REVIEW

((•─ Listen to an audio file of your chapter on **mypsychlab.com**

I. IDENTIFYING PSYCHOLOGICAL DISORDERS: WHAT'S ABNORMAL?

A. A psychological disorder is characterized by a set of cognitive, emotional, and behavioral symptoms that create significant distress, impairment, and risk of harm.

B. Behaviors that are merely deviant from the mainstream culture should not be considered to reflect a disorder.

C. Psychological disorders are best understood as arising from the interactions of events at the levels of the brain, the person, and the group.

D. The *DSM-IV-TR* classifies psychological disorders into 17 different categories. This diagnostic manual allows clinicians and researchers to use five axes to specify diagnoses and relevant information.

II. AXIS I: AN OVERVIEW OF SELECTED DISORDERS

MOOD DISORDERS

A. Major depressive disorder (MDD) is characterized by depressed mood and loss of interest or pleasure, along with sleep or eating disturbances, loss of energy, and feelings of hopelessness. Bipolar disorder involves episodes of mania, or episodes of hypomania that alternate with depression.

B. Some people are genetically vulnerable to developing these disorders. Genes have their effects in part by disrupting how neurotransmitters function. Genes are implicated in both MDD and bipolar disorder, although the exact mechanisms of their influence are not yet understood.

C. Cognitive distortions, based on the negative triad of depression, also contribute to whether a person develops MDD, as does his or her attributional style. Operant conditioning and the available rewards or punishments in the social environment also may play a role in whether someone develops or continues to have depression; stressful life events are associated with the first episode of depression and with the severity of the disorder.

D. Women in developed countries experience depression more often than do men. This difference may occur because, as children, girls are taught to be introspective and not to take action, which can promote depression.

E. Depressed people, through their actions, may inadvertently alienate others, who then reject those depressed people, who, in turn, view the rejection as confirmation of their negative views of themselves.

ANXIETY DISORDERS

A. Anxiety disorders include panic disorder, specific and social phobias, obsessive-compulsive disorder (OCD), and posttraumatic stress disorder (PTSD).

B. People with panic disorder may avoid places or activities in order to minimize the possibility of additional panic attacks; when such avoidance restricts daily life, it is referred to as agoraphobia.

C. Genes can make people vulnerable to develop panic disorder. Moreover, an anxiety sensitivity can increase the risk for panic disorder, in part because it leads people to misinterpret certain bodily sensations.

D. Genes can also predispose people to develop social and specific phobias. Although conditioning can contribute to these disorders, it is unclear to what extent it does so.

E. Neural activity in the caudate nucleus is related to OCD. Compulsions may momentarily relieve the anxiety that obsessions cause, thereby reinforcing the compulsions.

F. Not everyone who experiences a traumatic event goes on to develop PTSD. The type of trauma, the person's response to it, and other factors can increase or decrease the risk of developing PTSD.

SCHIZOPHRENIA

A. Schizophrenia involves a markedly restricted range of affect, odd or disorganized thoughts and behaviors, and delusions or hallucinations; it is characterized by positive and/or negative symptoms. The DSM-IV-TR specifies four subtypes of schizophrenia—paranoid, disorganized, catatonic, and undifferentiated—each with a different set of symptoms and prognosis.

B. Research findings on schizophrenia document genetic and neurological abnormalities in those affected, including abnormal functioning of dopamine, enlarged ventricles, and a decrease in the size of the frontal cortex. Such abnor-malities may arise during fetal development as a result of maternal illness, malnutrition, or stress during pregnancy or may arise from prenatal or birth-related complications.

C. People with schizophrenia may have cognitive deficits, including a lack of insight.

D. People with schizophrenia who have high expressed emotion families are more likely to suffer a recurrence. However, this association could arise because the high expressed emotion is a cause of the relapse or is a result of having a family member who is likely to relapse.

E. Social selection and social causation may account for the higher rates of schizophrenia in urban areas and in lower socioeconomic classes.

F. Eating disorders (anorexia nervosa and bulimia nervosa) are characterized by preoccupations with weight and body image, as well as abnormal eating (such as restriction, binges, and purges).

G. Symptoms of anorexia nervosa include a refusal to maintain a healthy weight, a fear of becoming fat, a disturbed body image, and amenorrhea (in women). Symptoms of bulimia include recurrent binge eating episodes, followed by attempts to prevent weight gain.

H. Genes can influence whether someone develops an eating disorder, but environmental factors—specifically the cultural emphasis on thinness—can also play a large role.

I. Biological factors related to dieting (food restriction) and binge eating can also influence whether someone develops an eating disorder.

III. AXIS II: FOCUS ON PERSONALITY DISORDERS

A. Personality disorders are sets of inflexible and maladaptive personality traits that cause distress or difficulty in work,

school, or other social spheres. Such traits may not be evident in a brief encounter and may only reveal themselves over time.

B. In contrast to Axis I disorders, which seem to the sufferer to be inflicted from the outside, Axis II disorders are experienced as integral to the personality itself.

C. Antisocial personality disorder is the most intensively studied personality disorder; the key symptom is a long-standing pattern of disregard for others to the point of violating their rights.

D. Antisocial personality may be related to an under-responsive autonomic nervous system. For those who are genetically vulnerable, the environment in which they are raised can influence whether they later engage in criminal behavior.

KEY TERMS

agoraphobia
anorexia nervosa
antisocial personality disorder (ASPD)
anxiety disorders
attributional style
bipolar disorder
bulimia nervosa
classical conditioning
compulsion

delusions
diathesis–stress model
eating disorders
generalized anxiety disorder
hallucinations
high expressed emotion
major depressive disorder (MDD)
manic episode
mood disorders
negative symptom

obsession
obsessive-compulsive disorder (OCD)
operant conditioning
panic attack
panic disorder
personality disorders
phobia
positive symptom

posttraumatic stress disorder (PTSD)
psychological disorder
psychosis
schizophrenia
social causation
social phobia
social selection
specific phobia

PRACTICE TEST

✓— Study and Review on mypsychlab.com

For each of the following items, choose the single best answer.

1. Many researchers and clinicians today believe that psychological disorders can best be explained
   a. not solely by neurological events.
   b. by the fact that unconventional behavior is always abnormal.
   c. by biological factors alone.
   d. by imbalances of the body's four fluids, or "humors."

2. Several factors at the level of the person play a role in psychological disorders. These factors include
   a. culture.
   b. genetic factors, abnormal neurotransmitter functioning, and abnormal brain structure.
   c. classical conditioning and operant conditioning.
   d. None of the above statements is true.

3. Since the third edition, the *DSM* has described five axes. Axis III allows clinicians to note
   a. clinical disorders.
   b. personality disorders and mental retardation.
   c. psychosocial and environmental problems.

   d. any general medical conditions that might be relevant to a diagnosis on Axis I or II.

4. Which of the following statements is true about major depressive disorder (MDD)?
   a. Major depressive disorder is the most common psychological disorder in the United States.
   b. American women are diagnosed with depression two to three times more frequently than American men.
   c. The overall rate of depression is increasing in the United States.
   d. All of the above statements are true.

5. Consider a person suffering from bipolar disorder. If left untreated, his or her mood swings will probably
   a. stop occurring.
   b. become less frequent over time.
   c. become more frequent over time, leading to a poorer prognosis.
   d. become more frequent over time, leading to a better prognosis.

6. Mood disorders can best be understood by considering events
   a. at the level of the brain only.
   b. at the levels of the brain and person only.
   c. at the level of the group only.
   d. at the levels of the brain, the person, and the group, and their interactions.

7. The hallmark of panic disorder is
   a. a fear and avoidance of an object, activity, or situation extreme enough to interfere with everyday life.
   b. the presence of obsessions, either alone or in combination with compulsions, which interfere with everyday life.
   c. the experience of episodes of intense fear or discomfort accompanied by physical and psychological symptoms.
   d. at least 2 weeks of depressed mood or loss of interest in nearly all activities.

8. Which of the following statements is true about the relationship between trauma and posttraumatic stress disorder (PTSD)?
   a. The majority of people who experience trauma do not go on to experience PTSD.
   b. The type of trauma experienced makes a difference in the outcome.
   c. Women are more likely to develop PTSD when their trauma results from a crime rather than from a natural disaster.
   d. All of the above statements are true.

9. Avolition, a negative symptom of schizophrenia, refers to
   a. brief, slow, empty replies to questions.
   b. an inability to initiate or persist in goal-directed activities.
   c. a general failure to express or respond to emotion.
   d. inappropriate, childlike silliness.

10. If one twin has schizophrenia, the risk of the co-twin developing schizophrenia is
    a. higher when the twins are identical rather than fraternal, but only 48% for identical twins.
    b. the same, regardless of whether the twins are fraternal or identical.
    c. zero when the twins are identical, provided that they have been raised in different environments.
    d. higher when the twins are fraternal than when they are identical, if they have been raised in the same environment.

11. Which of the following statements is true about schizophrenia?
    a. People who develop schizophrenia experience more stressful life events than people who do not develop the disorder.
    b. People who develop schizophrenia have higher baseline levels of cortisol.
    c. People who develop schizophrenia have lower baseline levels of cortisol.
    d. Antipsychotic medications increase cortisol levels in people with schizophrenia.

12. The nonpurging type of bulimia nervosa is characterized by
    a. vomiting or the misuse of laxatives, diuretics, or enemas.
    b. a failure to maintain even a low normal weight.
    c. a failure to menstruate.
    d. fasting or excessive exercise.

13. Which of the following statements is true about eating disorders?
    a. The malnutrition and weight loss that occur with anorexia nervosa lead to changes in neurotransmitters, particularly serotonin.
    b. Symptoms of eating disorders decrease among immigrants from less weight-conscious cultures as they assimilate to American culture.
    c. Genes, rather than the environment, play the most significant role in both anorexia nervosa and bulimia nervosa.
    d. None of the above statements is true.

14. A pattern of being preoccupied with perfection, orderliness, and control (but without obsessions or compulsions) describes
    a. avoidant personality disorder.
    b. obsessive-compulsive disorder.
    c. obsessive-compulsive personality disorder.
    d. borderline personality disorder.

15. Antisocial personality disorder
    a. occurs three times more frequently in women than in men.
    b. is estimated to occur in 60% of male prisoners in the United States.
    c. does not frequently co-occur with drug or alcohol abuse.
    d. is characterized by a relatively overly responsive autonomic nervous system.

Answers: 1. a 2. c 3. d 4. d 5. c 6. d 7. c 8. d 9. b 10. a 11. b 12. d 13. a 14. c 15. b

> With each quiz or test that she couldn't finish, with each paper that required more concentration than she could summon, she felt herself spiraling downward, helpless. She had no hope that the situation would change by itself . . .

TREATMENT

HEALING ACTIONS, HEALING WORDS

At 2 A.M., Beth sat hunched over her textbook and notes, studying for her midterm exam. She was having a hard time concentrating and had to struggle to make sense of the words before her eyes. She'd read the same page four times and still couldn't remember what it said. She tried to give herself a pep talk ("Okay, Beth, read it one more time, and then you'll understand it"), but her upbeat words would be drowned out by a different, negative internal monologue ("Well, Beth, you've really done yourself in this time, and there's no way out of it. You're going to fail, get kicked out of school, never be employed, end up destitute, homeless, hopeless, talking to yourself on the street").

From Introducing Psychology: Brain, Person, Group, Fourth Edition, Stephen M. Kosslyn and Robin S. Rosenberg. Copyright © 2011 by Pearson Education, Inc. Published by Allyn & Bacon. All rights reserved.

Beth was 21 years old, a junior in college. She'd already had to walk out of two midterm exams because she couldn't answer most of the questions, although she had understood the material after studying. But during the exams, her thoughts had been jumbled, and she'd had a hard time organizing her answers to the questions.

She'd always been nervous before a test or class presentation, but this semester her anxiety had spun out of control. When she took the first quiz of the semester, she simply drew a blank as she tried to answer the questions. Since then, she'd become more anxious and depressed as well. With each quiz or test that she couldn't finish, with each paper that required more concentration than she could summon, she felt herself spiraling downward, helpless. She had no hope that the situation would change by itself, and no amount of good intentions or resolutions or even effort seemed to make a difference.

In the last couple of weeks, she began cutting classes and spent much of her time in bed; she had no interest in doing anything with her friends because she felt she didn't deserve to have fun. She'd put off saying anything to her professors; at first she figured things would get better, and then she was too embarrassed to face them. But she knew that eventually she'd have to talk to them or else she'd definitely fail her courses.

She finally did talk to her professors. Several of them suggested that she seek treatment, or at least go to the campus counseling center, but she didn't want to do that. Taking that step, she felt, would be admitting to herself and to the world both that something was wrong with her and that she was too weak to deal with it herself.

Beth was reluctant to seek help partly because she knew that when her mother was her age, her mother had experienced bouts of depression severe enough to be hospitalized—several times. Beth recognized that she, too, was becoming depressed, and she was afraid that if she went to see a therapist, she'd end up in the hospital.

Beth eventually confided in a family friend, Nina, who had been the school nurse at Beth's elementary school. Nina told Beth that people with problems like hers often felt much better after psychotherapy and that her problems were not severe enough to warrant hospitalization. Nina also pointed out that there were many forms of therapy available to Beth that were not as readily available to her mother 30 years earlier. Modern treatments, Nina explained, ranged from psychologically based approaches, such as cognitive and behavioral therapies, to biologically based treatments such as medication. Research has revealed that, for a given problem, some treatments may be more effective than others, and for Beth's problems, there were a number of potentially helpful treatments. Beth agreed to see a therapist but didn't know where to begin to find one. The campus counseling center could be useful, Nina said, but Beth might also explore other ways to find a therapist who would be right for her needs, such as the Internet and referral organizations.

In this chapter, we'll make a similar exploration: We will examine different types of therapy, how they work, and what research has to say about how effective they are. First, though, let's examine historical influences on psychotherapy.

Insight-Oriented Therapies

Beth didn't know much about psychotherapy, and she made an appointment with a psychotherapist she found on the Internet. One type of therapist with whom Beth might meet is someone who offers **insight-oriented therapy**, in which the therapist aims to remove distressing symptoms by leading the person to understand the psychological causes of his or her symptoms, through deeply felt personal insights. If she had an appointment with an insight-oriented therapist, chances are that the therapist would ask Beth about her past, her relationships with family members, how she felt about her family, and her feelings about different aspects of life; the therapist would likely ask surprisingly little about her current anxiety or her depression.

The key idea underlying insight-oriented therapy is that once someone truly understands the psychological causes of distressing symptoms, the symptoms themselves will diminish. In the following sections, we consider the two most important insight-oriented therapies—psychoanalysis (and the more common, modified version of it, psychodynamic therapy) and client-centered therapy. ◉─Watch

◉─Watch the **Video** on Building Confidence on **mypsychlab.com**

LOOKING AHEAD Learning Objectives

1. What is the focus of treatment in psychoanalysis and psychodynamic therapy? What are their main techniques?
2. What is the focus of treatment in client-centered therapy? What are its main techniques?

Psychoanalytically Inspired Therapies

Developed by Sigmund Freud, **psychoanalysis** is a type of therapy that is directly connected to Freud's theory of personality; it is based on the idea (explained in detail shortly) that psychological difficulties are caused by unconscious conflicts. Although some therapists do provide psychoanalysis, it is not a common type of treatment today. Instead, a less intensive form of therapy based on psychoanalysis, called **psychodynamic therapy,** is today more common than psychoanalysis. Psychodynamic therapy grew out of Freud's theory, and shares some of the techniques of psychoanalysis. In the following sections, we first consider key features of psychoanalytic theory (which are at the root of both psychoanalysis and psychodynamic therapy). Next we consider the theory that underlies both psychoanalysis and psychodynamic therapy, and then we turn to the actual techniques used in psychoanalysis and psychodynamic therapy. Finally, we compare psychoanalysis with psychodynamic therapy.

Key Features of Psychoanalytic Theory
Freud's theory holds that psychological difficulties are caused by conflicts among the three psychic structures of the mind: the *id*, the *superego*, and the *ego*. (Note that these are not actual physical structures.) According to Freud, the **id** is the personality structure that exists at birth and houses sexual and aggressive drives, physical needs, and simple psychological needs. The **superego** is the personality structure that is formed during early childhood and houses the sense of right and wrong, based on the internalization of parental and cultural morality. The **ego** is the personality structure that develops in childhood and tries to balance the competing demands of the id, superego, and reality.

According to Freud, the three personality structures are constantly, dynamically interacting with one another and with the external world: The id strives for immediate gratification of its needs, the superego tries to impose its version of morality, and the ego attempts to mediate among the demands of id, superego, and external reality. These unconscious competing demands can create anxiety and other symptoms.

To see how this theory can be used to analyze psychological problems, let's apply it to Beth. Her anxiety and depression might reflect two competing desires. On the one hand, Beth wants to be different from her mother. Doing well in school and going on to graduate school represent a path different from that taken by her mother, who, although she ultimately

Insight-oriented therapy A type of therapy in which the therapist aims to remove distressing symptoms by leading the person to understand the psychological causes of his or her symptoms through deeply felt personal insights.

Psychoanalysis An intensive form of therapy that is directly connected to Freud's theory of personality and based on the idea that psychological difficulties are caused by unconscious conflicts.

Psychodynamic therapy A less intensive form of psychoanalysis.

Id A personality structure, proposed by Freud, that exists at birth and houses sexual and aggressive drives, physical needs, and simple psychological needs.

Superego A personality structure, proposed by Freud, that is formed during early childhood and houses the sense of right and wrong, based on the internalization of parental and cultural morality.

Ego A personality structure, proposed by Freud, that develops in childhood and tries to balance the competing demands of the id, superego, and reality.

did well enough in college, did not pursue a graduate degree. Beth hoped that by making different choices in her own life, she could avoid the intermittent depressions that had plagued her mother. On the other hand, Beth loves her mother, and the idea of academically passing a parent by—in essence, what feels like abandoning her mother—causes Beth to feel guilty about her accomplishments. Although Beth's current anxiety and depression are upsetting and debilitating, part of her may (unconsciously) feel relief that those symptoms prevent her from "leaving her mother behind." Psychodynamic theory would say that Beth is "acting out" her ambivalent feelings, by blanking out during tests or when writing papers, and that her anxiety and depression arise because of unconscious conflicts between competing goals.

Theory of Psychoanalysis and Psychodynamic Therapies The therapies that stem from psychoanalytic theory rest on the idea that only after true understanding—that is, insight—is attained can people choose more adaptive, satisfying, and productive behaviors; if a person's motivations and feelings remain unconscious, those forces are more likely to shape his or her behavior in undesirable ways. In Beth's case, for example, bringing her ambivalence and conflicting views into her consciousness would, in theory, allow her to gain control over her choices—which would thereby eliminate the reason why she was blanking out; moreover, this should also reduce her anxiety and depression. Freud did not believe that psychoanalysis is a cure but rather that it could transform an individual's abject misery into ordinary unhappiness.

A goal of psychoanalysis and psychodynamic therapy therefore is to bring unconscious impulses and conflicts into awareness. Such therapies are designed to link the patient's current difficulties with past experiences and relationships. In addition, the patient's relationship with the therapist is an integral part of treatment. Given the importance of relationships, the therapy relationship can provide a "corrective emotional experience"—that is, a new, positive experience of relationships, which can lead to changes in symptoms, behavior, and personality (Alexander & French, 1946).

Techniques of Psychoanalysis and Psychodynamic Therapies Although Freud initially used hypnosis with his patients, over time he developed a revolutionary new approach, one in which patients talk about their problems, and the therapist—in psychoanalysis, referred to as the *psychoanalyst*—tries to infer the root causes of the problems. This was revolutionary because in Europe before Freud, most people's psychological problems were treated with bed rest, baths, or some type of medication.

Freud's "talking cure" relies on a number of distinct techniques; in what follows we summarize the major techniques that are used in psychoanalysis and psychodynamic therapy:

1. **Free association**, which occurs when the patient says whatever comes into his or her mind. The resulting train of thought reveals to the analyst or therapist the issues—perhaps unconscious ones—that concern the patient as well as the way he or she handles them.

2. **Dream analysis**, which requires the analyst or therapist to analyze the reported content of the patient's dreams in order to gain access to the patient's unconscious. Because Freud (1900/1958) viewed dreams as the "royal road to the unconscious," he paid particular attention to reports of dreams.

3. **Interpretation**, which consists of deciphering the patient's words and behaviors (perhaps through free association and dream interpretation) and assigning unconscious motivations to them. Through the therapist's or analyst's interpretations, the patient becomes aware of his or her motives and the potential conflicts within the unconscious. (The patient's own interpretations are not considered as accurate as those of the therapist because they are biased by the patient's conflicts.)

Through interpretation, patients are made aware of their *defense mechanisms*, unconscious processes that prevent unacceptable thoughts or urges from reaching conscious awareness. Sometimes unconscious thoughts or urges slip out verbally, in the form of slips of the tongue—so-called *Freudian slips*—which are interpreted by the therapist as having unconscious meanings. For example, should Beth tell her therapist that her mother recommended that she come to therapy (instead of her mother's friend, Nina, which was the case and what she meant to say), the therapist might interpret this as Beth's wish that her mother would take care of her by suggesting that she seek therapy.

Free association A technique used in psychoanalysis and psychodynamic therapy in which the patient says whatever comes to mind, and the train of thought reveals to the therapist or psychoanalyst the patient's issues and ways of handling them.

Dream analysis A technique used in psychoanalysis and psychodynamic therapy in which the therapist examines the content of dreams to gain access to the unconscious.

Interpretation A technique used in psychodynamic therapies in which the therapist deciphers the patient's words and behaviors, assigning unconscious motivations to them.

4. **Resistance**, which occurs when a patient is reluctant or refuses to cooperate with the analyst or therapist. Such resistance can range from unconscious forgetting (for instance, of a therapy appointment) to outright refusal to comply with the therapist's request. Resistance can occur as the patient explores or remembers painful feelings or experiences. Thus, if Beth comes late to a therapy session, a psychodynamic therapist might interpret this behavior as resistance: Perhaps Beth does not want to work on the issues currently being explored or is concerned about something that she doesn't want to share with her therapist.

5. **Transference**, which occurs when patients come to relate to their therapist as they did to someone who was important in their lives, perhaps a parent. For example, if Beth began a therapy session by asking how the therapist is feeling, or if Beth started to talk less about her own distressing feelings because she worried that the therapist might become upset, Beth would be "transferring" onto her therapist her usual style of relating with her mother, in which she views her mother as fragile and needing protection. The therapeutic value of transference is that patients can talk about what they are experiencing during therapy (which they may very well have been unable to do with the parent) to heighten understanding. Moreover, the therapist's acceptance of uncomfortable or shameful feelings helps patients accept those feelings in order to choose whether to act on them. A psychodynamic therapist would probably interpret Beth's questions about the therapist's well-being as transference. Beth and her therapist would then talk about what it was like for Beth to feel so protective toward and careful with her mother; in doing so, Beth would come to understand her feelings and unconscious motives and recognize that she didn't need to treat the therapist as she would her mother. Resistance is an aspect of the patient–therapist relationship that can allow the therapist to provide the patient with a new, positive experience of relationships.

Resistance A reluctance or refusal to cooperate with the therapist, which can range from unconscious forgetting to outright refusal to comply with a therapist's request.

Transference The process by which patients may relate to their therapists as they did to some important person in their lives.

Psychoanalysis Versus Psychodynamic Therapies

Psychoanalysis and psychodynamic therapy grew out of the same theory of personality, but the two types of treatment differ in two important ways:

1. *The intensity of the treatment.* Psychoanalysis usually takes place four or five times each week (for approximately 50 minutes per session); the average patient remains in psychoanalysis for at least four years—and typically engages in 835 sessions before completing psychoanalysis (Voth & Orth, 1973). Some patients who begin psychoanalysis never complete it. In contrast, psychodynamic therapy typically takes place once or twice a week, and patients engage in as few as 12 sessions (in short-term forms of the treatment; Bloom, 1997; Crits-Christoph, 1992; Leichsenring, 2009; Sifneos, 1992) to many years of weekly treatment;

Psychoanalysis usually takes place 4 or 5 days a week for a number of years. Psychodynamic therapy typically takes place once or twice a week. In psychoanalysis, the patient lies on a couch and the analyst sits in a chair behind the couch, out of the patient's range of sight so that the patient can better free associate without seeing the analyst's reactions to his or her thoughts. In psychodynamic therapy, the client and therapist sit in chairs facing each other.

Sources: David Young-Wolff\PhotoEdit Inc.; Alamy Images

2. *Modified goals.* Psychodynamic therapy typically focuses on current rather than past relationships (J. R. Greenberg & Mitchell, 1983; Kohut, 1977; Sullivan, 1953; Winnicott, 1958), whereas psychoanalysis spends proportionately more time focusing on past relationships.

Psychoanalysis has become less popular and less common over the past several decades. This shift has occurred because: (**1**) Psychoanalysis is expensive and time intensive; (**2**) Psychoanalysis is rarely paid for by health insurance; (**3**) Studies generally have not found that psychoanalysis effectively treats various disorders.

Humanistic Therapy: Client-Centered Therapy

Whereas psychoanalysis and psychodynamic therapy focus on bringing a patient's unconscious conflicts and motives into awareness, humanistic therapy emphasizes free will, personal growth, self-esteem, and mastery. One of the early proponents of humanistic psychology was Carl Rogers, who developed a therapeutic approach that came to be called **client-centered therapy,** which focuses on people's potential for growth and the importance of an empathic therapist. Instead of using the term "patient," a medical term that suggests treating a person with an illness, Rogers used the term "client," which is the term that we will generally use in the rest of this chapter. ◉─Watch

⊙─Watch the Video on Role of a Therapist on mypsychlab.com

Theory Underlying Client-Centered Therapy
Rogers believed that a person's distressing symptoms grow out of a blocked potential for personal growth; the goal of client-centered therapy is to dismantle that block so that clients can reach their full potential. Within Rogers's framework, an individual develops psychological problems because he or she lacks a coherent, unified sense of self. One reason for a lack of a coherent, unified sense of self is a mismatch, or **incongruence**, between the real self (who you actually are) and the ideal self (who you would like to be). By helping clients to develop realistic "ideal selves" and then help them become more like their ideal selves, client-centered therapy reduces the incongruence, and the clients feel better.

Based on the theory underlying client-centered therapy, Beth's problems may stem from the disparity between her real self (a self that has to work hard for good grades and feels shame and guilt about the imperfections that remind her of her mother's depression) and her ideal self (a self that always does the right thing and never experiences sadness, hopelessness, or anxiety). The tension between her real and ideal selves creates incongruence, which drains Beth's time and energy; these different parts of herself are in conflict with each other and prevent her from reaching her full potential.

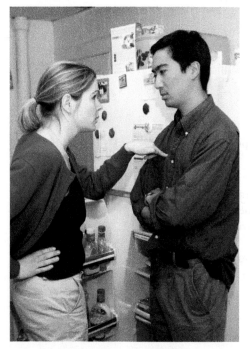

Being rejected by a partner can leave a person feeling bad about himself or herself. Client-centered therapy makes a distinction between the person's actions in the relationship and the fact he or she is still a worthwhile, good person.

Source: PhotoEdit Inc.

Techniques of Client-Centered Therapy
The techniques of client-centered therapy are intended to help the client build a coherent, unified sense of self and to reduce the incongruence between the real and ideal selves. Client-centered therapy relies on two techniques: The therapist must empathize with the client and must provide *unconditional positive regard* toward the client. To be effective, the client-centered therapist should be warm, open, receptive, and able to see the world as the client does while implementing the client-centered techniques. Let's examine these two techniques in more detail.

EMPATHY. To convey empathy, the client-centered therapist reflects back the thrust of what the client has said. The therapist must not simply parrot the client's words or phrases but rather must show accurate and genuine empathy. Such empathy allows the client to know that he or she is really being understood. If the therapist does not accurately reflect what the client says or is not genuinely empathic, the therapist's intervention will fail.

UNCONDITIONAL POSITIVE REGARD. The therapist must also provide *unconditional positive regard*; that is, he or she must convey positive feelings for the client regardless of the client's thoughts, feelings, or actions. To accomplish this, the therapist must continually

Client-centered therapy A type of insight-oriented therapy that focuses on people's potential for growth and the importance of an empathic therapist.

Incongruence According to client-centered therapy, a mismatch between a person's real self and his or her ideal self.

demonstrate to the client that he or she is inherently worthy as a human being; for instance, the therapist must persistently show positive interest in the feelings and experiences that the client is ashamed of as well as those that the client is proud of. According to the theory that underlies client-centered therapy, genuine empathy and unconditional positive regard will help the client to decrease the incongruence between the real and ideal selves.

Let's consider how these techniques would be used to help Beth were she in this type of therapy: Although Beth was not able to take some of her exams (real self), a therapist's empathy and unconditional positive regard would allow Beth to see that she nevertheless is smart (ideal self) and that everyone sometimes has negative, uncomfortable feelings (thus leading to a more realistic ideal self). The client-centered therapist provides both genuine empathy and unconditional positive regard by making a distinction between the client as a person and the client's behaviors; the therapist could dislike a client's behaviors but still would view the client as a good person. This therapeutic approach could help Beth see her real and ideal selves in a different light and allow her to think of herself more positively. If Beth were seeing a client-centered therapist, a therapy session might focus on what it was like for Beth during her mother's bouts of depression. A session might include this exchange:

Beth: I was so disappointed and ashamed when I'd come home from school and she'd still be in bed, wearing her bathrobe.

Therapist: Yes, it must have caused you to feel ashamed, anxious, and worried when you came home and found your mother still in bed.

Beth: And I felt that it was my fault, that I wasn't doing enough to make her feel better.

Therapist: Although you felt that it was your fault, you did all that you possibly could.

Beth: And now I spend most of the day in bed and don't bother to get dressed . . . am I becoming like my mother?

Therapist: You and your mother are two separate individuals. Although you may have some things in common, and right now that may include depression, that doesn't mean that your path in life is identical to hers.

The therapist repeatedly emphasizes the worthiness of the client until the client comes to accept this valuation and is able to reach his or her potential by making different, healthier choices and decisions.

Evaluating Insight-Oriented Therapies

Insight-oriented therapies are appealing to many people because they appear to provide self-knowledge—but do they effectively treat psychological problems? In this section we consider the results of research on whether such therapies are effective.

Evaluating Psychodynamic Therapies
Psychodynamic therapies are difficult to evaluate, for several reasons:

1. Until recently, there has not been much research on treatment; most articles have been about psychodynamic theory, not about systematic research on the outcome of psychodynamic therapy (Tillman et al., 2010).

2. Research on psychodynamic therapy has generally focused on case studies of single patients, which limits the reliability and generalizability of the findings (Roth & Fonagy, 2005).

3. A therapist's interpretations—considered to be a crucial component of the treatment—may or may not be correct, and it is difficult to test the accuracy of a therapist's interpretations. Moreover, research suggests that interpretations may not, in fact, be helpful to the treatment (Henry et al., 1994).

Some studies find that short-term psychodynamic therapy may be as effective as, but not superior to, other short-term treatments (Knekt et al., 2008; Leichsenring, 2001, 2009; Leichsenring et al., 2004, 2009). Psychodynamic therapy appears to be most effective with patients who are able to articulate their feelings and want to understand their unconscious mental processes (and who have the time and money for lengthy treatment). However, researchers have not extensively investigated whether short-term psychodynamic therapy can be more effective than other types of therapy for specific psychological problems.

Evaluating Client-Centered Therapy Rogers not only developed the first comprehensive insight-oriented alternative to psychodynamic therapy but also tape-recorded therapy sessions—which makes them accessible to researchers. Research results have not shown that client-centered therapy is better than other forms of therapy. Nevertheless, almost all forms of therapy incorporate Rogers's view that the therapist's warmth, empathy, and positive regard for the client are fundamental for a working relationship between client and therapist (Lambert, 1983; Roth & Fonagy, 2005). However, although client-centered therapy was the first major type of therapy to focus on assessing whether the treatment is effective, it can be difficult to measure whether clients have achieved their potential.

In summary, although there are differences among the types of insight-oriented therapies, the people most likely to benefit from these treatments are relatively healthy, articulate individuals who are interested in knowing more about their own motivations rather than seeking to modify specific symptoms, such as the fear of panic symptoms that are a key part of panic disorder. In the subsequent sections, we examine treatments that, according to research results, are likely to be more effective with a wider range of patients and problems than are insight-oriented therapies.

THINK like a **PSYCHOLOGIST** If a friend tells you that he or she is in insight-oriented therapy, what can you assume about the therapy? What can't you assume?

✔•—Study and Review on
mypsychlab.com

LOOKING BACK

1. **What is the focus of treatment in psychoanalysis and psychodynamic therapy? What are their main techniques?** Psychoanalysis and psychodynamic therapy are designed to help patients become aware of their unconscious conflicts and motivations, which according to psychoanalytic theory can cause psychological symptoms. Thus, once patients have insight, they can choose whether to respond to those unconscious forces. At some point in the treatment, patients typically experience transference to the therapist and resistance, which then provide opportunities for therapeutic analyses. Therapeutic techniques also include free association, dream analysis, and interpretation.

2. **What is the focus of treatment in client-centered therapy? What are its main techniques?** Client-centered therapy focuses on helping clients dismantle a blocked potential for personal growth so that they can reach their full potential. One type of block arises from an incongruence between their real and ideal selves. The therapist should be warm, empathic, and genuine and should show unconditional positive regard toward clients.

Cognitive–Behavior Therapy

Suppose that Beth's therapist (chosen from listings on the Internet) starts asking questions not about her family and her relationships, but about what she currently believes about herself and her abilities. Suppose the therapist also inquires about her behaviors: What does she do before she sits down to study or take an exam? What, in detail, does she do during the day? Has she ever tried any relaxation techniques? These are questions about thoughts and behaviors. Odds are that Beth has contacted a *cognitive–behavior therapist*.

Cognitive–behavior therapy (CBT) is a type of therapy designed to help patients both to reduce problematic behaviors and irrational thoughts and to develop new, more adaptive behaviors and beliefs to replace the old, maladaptive ones. CBT utilizes techniques from *behavior therapy* and *cognitive therapy*. We begin by discussing behavior and cognitive therapies separately so that you can understand the unique focus of each approach.

Cognitive–behavior therapy (CBT) A type of therapy that is designed to help patients both to reduce problematic behaviors and irrational thoughts and to develop new, more adaptive behaviors and beliefs.

1. What is the focus of behavior therapy? What are some of its techniques?
2. What are the goals of cognitive therapy? What techniques are used?
3. How does cognitive-behavior therapy grow out of behavior and cognitive therapies?

Behavior Therapy and Techniques

Behavior therapy focuses on modifying observable, measurable behavior. In general, behavior therapy rests on well-researched principles of two sorts of learning: classical conditioning and operant conditioning (Skinner, 1953; Wolpe, 1997).

1. *Classical conditioning* is the type of learning that occurs when a neutral stimulus (such as an elevator) becomes associated with an unconditioned stimulus (such as the jerking that occurs when an elevator stops abruptly) that causes a reflexive behavior (such as a fear or startle response); the pairing of the neutral stimulus (elevator) with the unconditioned stimulus can lead the neutral stimulus to elicit the behavior (fear response), in this case giving rise to a fear of being in elevators.

2. *Operant conditioning* is the process by which a stimulus and response become associated with the consequences of making the response. For example, people with substance abuse who are in treatment programs may receive various types of "rewards" (such as vouchers for local shops) after a surprise drug test comes back negative; in such cases the stimulus could be hanging around friends who are using drugs, the response would be *abstaining* from drug use, and the consequence would be the voucher.

The fact that behavior therapy pioneers focused solely on modifying problematic behaviors, and were not interested in discovering an unconscious "root cause" for them, was revolutionary at the time this therapy was developed.

Theory of Behavior Therapy To a behavior therapist, distressing symptoms are taken to be the result of learning. Clients can change unwanted behaviors by learning new, more adaptive ones. The behavior therapist is interested in the ABCs of the client's maladaptive behavior:

- its *antecedents* (what is the stimulus that triggers the problematic behavior?),
- the problematic *behavior* itself, and
- its *consequences* (what is reinforcing the behavior?). (The ABCs of Beth's anxiety are noted in Table 1.)

TABLE 1 **The ABCs of Beth's Anxiety**

The possible antecedents and consequences of Beth's problematic behaviors related to anxiety and fear.

Antecedents	(Problematic) Behavior	Consequences
The antecedents for Beth's anxiety might include the act of sitting down to study for an exam or waiting in class to receive her exam booklet.	The behavior is the conditioned emotional response of fear and anxiety, evidenced by her sweating hands and racing heart rate and her inability to do her work.	The consequences might include negative reinforcement (the uncomfortable symptoms go away) when skipping an exam, reinforcement of related nonacademic avoidant behaviors (such as sleeping through an exam), and subsequent social isolation, leading to a loss of pleasant activities and opportunities for social reinforcement, which, in turn, can lead to depression.

Techniques of Behavior Therapy The therapist takes an active, directive role in treatment, and "homework"—between-session tasks that the client works on—is an important component of the treatment. The success of behavior therapy typically is assessed by whether the client experiences less frequent or less intense symptoms—or behaves in more adaptive ways—during and after therapy. In the following sections we look in detail at how classical and operant conditioning are used in behavior therapy.

TECHNIQUES BASED ON CLASSICAL CONDITIONING. Techniques based on classical conditioning include *exposure* (and its variant, *exposure with response prevention*), *stimulus control*, and *systematic desensitization*.

1. *Exposure.* Exposure is a technique commonly used to treat anxiety disorders; **exposure** is based on the principle of habituation whereby through repeated encounters with a stimulus, the person becomes less responsive to that stimulus. Specifically, when implementing this technique, clients are asked to *expose* themselves to feared stimuli in a planned and (usually) gradual way. In general, exposure and habituation do not occur in the natural course of events for people with an anxiety disorder because they avoid the feared stimulus. People can be exposed to the feared stimulus in any of three ways:

 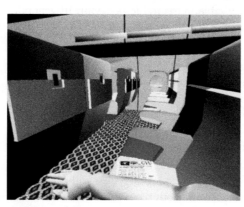

With virtual reality (left photo), clients virtually experience the stimulus or situations that make them afraid, suchas flying (right photo). Virtual reality exposure appears to work as well as actual exposure for fears of flying and heights (Emmelkamp et al., 2001, 2002; Rothbaum et al., 2001, 2002, 2006).

Sources: Bob Mahoney\The Image Works; Bob Mahoney\The Image Works

- *imaginal exposure,* during which they visualize or otherwise imagine the feared stimulus;

- *in vivo exposure,* during which they perceive (usually by seeing or touching) the actual feared stimulus; or

- *virtual reality exposure,* during which they use virtual reality techniques to encounter a virtual version of the stimulus.

Exposure, like all other behavioral and cognitive therapy techniques, is directed primarily at the levels of the person and group; however, such techniques also affect events at the level of the brain. Consider a neuroimaging study of people with a spider phobia who had exposure treatment (Paquette et al., 2003). Before treatment, fMRI scans indicated that when these people saw pictures of spiders, a set of brain areas (including part of the frontal lobes) was activated that was not activated when people who did not have such a phobia saw these pictures. After successful exposure therapy, another round of fMRI scans was done. The results were dramatically different for people treated for their phobia: Now, when the people saw the pictures of spiders, the key brain areas were no longer activated. Exposure had "rewired" brain circuits that apparently had been involved in the phobia.

2. *Exposure with response prevention. Exposure with response prevention* is a planned, programmatic procedure that requires the client to encounter the anxiety-provoking object or situation but prevents—or, more accurately, has the client abstain from making—his or her usual maladaptive response. For instance, clients with the type of obsessive-compulsive disorder (OCD) that compels them to wash their hands repeatedly would, during treatment that makes use of exposure with response prevention: (1) intentionally get their hands dirty during a therapy session and then, (2) with the guidance and support of the therapist, stop themselves from washing their hands immediately afterward. In this way, they would habituate to the anxiety-producing stimuli. Researchers have found that exposure with response prevention is as effective as medication for OCD; moreover, this treatment can have longer-lasting benefits than medication (Foa et al., 2005; Marks, 1997). However, because this technique requires clients to experience significant anxiety temporarily, not all people who have OCD are willing to use this technique (Stanley & Turner, 1995).

The technique of exposure with response prevention has also been used to treat people with bulimia nervosa. In such cases, the response that is to be prevented could be induced vomiting after eating a "forbidden food" (such as a dessert). Here's the procedure: After eating a previously forbidden food, the client does not throw up, or at least delays doing so for as long as possible. In addition, before using exposure with response prevention, the client and therapist develop strategies that the client can use while trying not to engage in the maladaptive behavior, such as taking a walk around

Exposure A therapeutic technique whereby through repeated encounters with a stimulus the person becomes less responsive to that stimulus.

the block, watching a movie, or, when the procedure is done during a therapy session, talking to the therapist.

3. *Stimulus control.* **Stimulus control** has the client control how often he or she encounters a stimulus that elicits a conditioned response, with the goal of decreasing or increasing the frequency of the response. For instance, a woman with bulimia who binges on donuts would exert stimulus control by buying only a single donut rather than a dozen.

4. *Systematic desensitization.* **Systematic desensitization** is a procedure in which people are taught to be relaxed in the presence of a feared object or situation. This technique, developed for treating phobias, grew out of the idea that an individual cannot be both fearful (and hence anxious) and relaxed at the same time. Systematic desensitization involves two steps. The first step uses **progressive muscle relaxation**, a relaxation technique whereby the client alternates tensing and relaxing muscles sequentially from one end of the body to the other, usually from feet to head. (Although progressive muscle relaxation is used in systematic desensitization, it can be used by itself to induce relaxation.)

If an alcoholic drinks to excess only when in a bar, limiting or eliminating the occasions of going to a bar would be an example of stimulus control.

Source: Getty Images/Digital Vision

The second step of systematic desensitization involves contact with the feared stimulus; the therapist and client begin by constructing a hierarchy of real or imagined activities related to the feared object or situation—such as a fear of elevators. This hierarchy begins with the least fearful activity, such as standing in a hallway and pressing an elevator call button, and progresses through to the most fearful, such as being stuck in a stopped elevator. Over the course of a number of sessions, the client works on becoming relaxed and then maintaining the relaxed state when he or she imagines doing increasingly anxiety-provoking activities in the hierarchy.

THINK like a **PSYCHOLOGIST** To try progressive muscle relaxation yourself, obtain instructions at www.mypsychlab.com; select the *Treatment* chapter, and click on the *DO IT!* folder.

TECHNIQUES BASED ON OPERANT CONDITIONING. Techniques based on operant conditioning use *reinforcement, extinction, self-monitoring,* and—less commonly—*punishment.* These techniques are used as part of **behavior modification**, which consists of using operant conditioning principles to change specific behaviors. Behavior modification can be provided to individuals or groups, as summarized below:

1. *Reinforcement* and *punishment.* Some behavioral techniques rely on *positive reinforcement* (which occurs when something desirable is presented after a behavior) or *negative reinforcement* (which occurs when something undesirable is removed after a behavior). For instance, reinforcement might be used with boy who is afraid to ride the bus to school: The therapist might arrange with the parents that for each day the boy successfully rides the bus, he receives a desired object—some special food, book, or toy. In some cases, treatment may use the technique of *punishment* (which occurs when something undesirable is presented or something desirable is taken away after a behavior).

When using reinforcement or punishment, the therapist and client typically begin by setting appropriate *response contingencies*—the specific behaviors that will earn reinforcement (or, less commonly, be followed by punishment). For instance, a teenager with bulimia might earn reinforcement of additional minutes on her cell phone plan for not throwing up after eating part of a dessert.

2. *Extinction.* *Extinction* is a process that eliminates a behavior by not reinforcing it. For instance, some people with depression ruminate about how "bad" they are and share with others this negative view of themselves; when this "sharing" behavior is identified as a problem, the therapist may seek to extinguish this behavior. Specifically, the therapist may meet with a depressed woman and her husband and suggest that the husband ignore the wife's self-deprecating comments—that is, not respond to them at all.

Stimulus control A behavior therapy technique that has the client control how often he or she encounters a stimulus that elicits a conditioned response, with the goal of decreasing or increasing the frequency of the response.

Systematic desensitization A behavior therapy technique in which people are taught to be relaxed in the presence of a feared object or situation.

Progressive muscle relaxation A relaxation technique whereby the person alternates tensing and relaxing muscles sequentially from one end of the body to the other.

Behavior modification Therapeutic techniques that use operant conditioning principles to change behavior.

3. *Self-monitoring.* *Self-monitoring techniques* lead the client to become aware of instances of a problematic behavior, usually through written logs. **Self-monitoring techniques** help clients notice and record a problematic behavior as well the antecedents and consequences of a problematic behavior. That is, self-monitoring techniques help clients to identify the problematic behavior as well as what led up to it and what followed it. Self-monitoring can clarify how behavior modification may be best achieved. Daily logs are used to help treat a variety of problems, including depressed mood, anxiety, overeating, smoking, sleep problems, and compulsive gambling.

Therapists also use behavior modification techniques in group settings, such as inpatient psychiatric units. For instance, behavior modification—specifically, reinforcement—can be used to increase the frequency of desired behaviors, such as eating normal-sized meals for people with the eating disorder anorexia nervosa.

Some behavior modification programs make use of *secondary reinforcers*, which are positive reinforcers that are learned and don't inherently satisfy a biological need (for example, money is a secondary reinforcer, whereas food is a primary reinforcer because it inherently satisfies the biological need of hunger). Secondary reinforcers are used in treatment programs not only with psychiatric patients but also with children and adults with mental retardation; prisons also make use of secondary reinforcers. **Token economies** are behavior modification programs that use secondary reinforcers (tokens) to change behavior. In these treatment programs, patients or others must earn *tokens* (which are secondary reinforcers) by behaving appropriately; these tokens then can be traded for small items such as cigarettes or candy at a "token store" or for privileges such as going out for a walk or watching a particular TV show.

Token economies can be used to mold social behavior directly by modifying what patients say to one another and to nonpatients. For instance, using a token economy, hospitalized patients with schizophrenia can learn to talk more appropriately to others, answer questions, or eat more normally after such behaviors have been reinforced through tokens. Although token economies can be effective, their use is declining because of ethical and moral questions about depriving patients and clients of secondary reinforcers if they do not earn them through behavior change (Glynn, 1990).

If Beth and her therapist used behavior modification techniques, they would seek to establish response contingencies for Beth to behave in desired new ways, such as allowing her to go back to bed after successfully taking an exam (but not allowing her to do so if she didn't successfully take the exam).

Cognitive Therapy and Techniques: It's the Thought That Counts

The so-called cognitive revolution in psychology in the 1950s and 1960s led researchers to study not just behavior, but also mental events. In addition, this shift in focus led therapists to examine the mental events that contribute to behavior, not simply the physical stimuli that trigger it. When therapists investigated the role that mental events might play in psychological disorders, they soon realized that people's thoughts (cognitions), not just their learning histories or unconscious conflicts, influence their feelings and behavior—and do so in many ways (Beck, 1967; Ellis, 1957). For instance, just thinking about a past positive experience with love can put you in a good mood, and thinking about an unhappy love experience can have the opposite effect (Clark & Collins, 1993). A cognitive therapist would focus on Beth's thoughts and the way in which one thought leads to another, contributing to her experience of anxiety and depression.

Theory of Cognitive Therapy
Two key ideas underlie cognitive therapy: (1) our *interpretations* of any stimulus or event determine our responses to it, and (2) when we persistently interpret stimuli or events in irrational and incorrect ways, we can develop psychological problems and disorders. **Cognitive therapy** is designed to help clients think

Self-monitoring techniques Behavioral techniques that help the client identify a problematic behavior as well as its antecedents and consequences.

Token economy A behavior modification program that uses secondary reinforcers (tokens) to change behavior.

Cognitive therapy A type of therapy that is designed to help clients think realistically and rationally in order to reinterpret events that otherwise would lead to distressing thoughts, feelings, and/or behaviors.

realistically and rationally in order to reinterpret stimuli and events that otherwise would lead to distressing thoughts, feelings, and/or behaviors.

Two particularly important contributors to cognitive therapy were Albert Ellis and Aaron Beck. (We must note that although both pioneered cognitive therapy, their treatments also rely in part on aspects of behavior theory and therapy.)

THE COGNITIVE THERAPY OF ALBERT ELLIS. Albert Ellis (1913–2007) was a clinical psychologist who in the 1950s developed a treatment called *rational-emotive behavior therapy (REBT)*. REBT: (1) encourages clients to engage in rational, logical thinking; and (2) assumes that distressing feelings or symptoms are caused by faulty beliefs or illogical thoughts. For instance, according to REBT, Beth's thought that she needs to do well in school is based on a dysfunctional, irrational belief that in order to be a lovable, deserving human being, she must earn good grades; if she does not, she believes that she will be unlovable and worthless. People may develop illogical or irrational thoughts as a result of their experiences, and never consider whether these thoughts are valid. They elevate irrational thoughts to "godlike absolutist musts, shoulds, demands, and commands" (Ellis, 1994b, p. 103).

Ellis (1994b) identified three processes that he believed interfere with healthy functioning:

1. *self-downing*, or being critical of oneself for performing poorly or being rejected;
2. *hostility and rage*, or being unkind to or critical of others for performing poorly; and
3. *low frustration tolerance*, or blaming everyone and everything for "poor, dislikable conditions."

REBT focuses on creating more rational thoughts. In Beth's case, these might be, "I may be disappointed or disappoint others if I don't do well this semester, but they will still love and care about me." This more rational thinking should then reduce the problematic behavior, allowing her to choose more rational courses of action. Moreover, like behavior therapy, REBT is oriented toward *solving* problems directly (as opposed to insight-oriented therapies, which—in theory—solve problems indirectly by helping a client attain appropriate insight about the underlying nature of the problem). The REBT therapist encourages self-acceptance and a new way of thinking; self-blame is viewed as counterproductive because it involves faulty beliefs. Shortcomings or failures are viewed simply as part of life, not as signs of moral weakness or as personal failings.

THE COGNITIVE THERAPY OF AARON BECK. Psychiatrist Aaron Beck (b. 1921) developed a form of cognitive therapy that, like REBT, rests on the premises that (1) automatic irrational thoughts are the root cause of psychological problems, and that (2) recognizing their irrationality and adopting more realistic, rational thoughts reduces psychological problems. According to Beck's theory, persistent irrational thoughts arise from **cognitive distortions**, which are systematic biases in the way a person thinks about events and people, including oneself. An example of a cognitive distortion is the belief that if you tell your friend you are mad at her, she will reject you; several common distortions are presented in Table 2 on the next page. Cognitive distortions and automatic negative thoughts (or faulty beliefs and illogical thoughts, in the vocabulary of REBT) are learned and maintained through reinforcement.

Unlike REBT, which relies on the therapist's attempts to persuade the client that his or her beliefs are irrational, Beck's version of cognitive therapy encourages the client to view beliefs as hypotheses to be tested. Thus, interactions with the world provide opportunities for clients to perform "experiments" to discover whether their beliefs are accurate (Hollon & Beck, 1994); in Beth's case, for instance, such experiments might include having Beth keep track of occasions when she's met her obligations at least adequately—in order to assess whether her negative view of herself is a reflection of reality or is a result of a mental filter. Beck and his colleagues have approached treatment scientifically, developing measures to assess depression, anxiety, and other problems and to evaluate the effectiveness of treatment.

Cognitive distortions Systematic biases in the way a person thinks about events and people, including oneself.

TABLE 2 Five Common Cognitive Distortions

Distortion	Description	Example
Dichotomous thinking	Also known as black-and-white thinking, which allows nothing in between the extremes; you are either perfect or a piece of garbage.	Beth thinks that if she doesn't get an A on a test, she has failed in life.
Mental filter	Magnifying the negative aspects of something while filtering out the positive.	Beth remembers only the things she did that were below her expectations and doesn't pay attention to or remember the things she did well.
Mind reading	Believing that you know exactly what other people are thinking, particularly as it relates to you.	Beth believes that she *knows* her professors think less of her because of what happened on the exams (when in fact they don't think less of her but are concerned about her).
Catastrophic exaggeration	Thinking that your worst nightmare will come true and that it will be intolerable.	Beth's fear is that she'll be kicked out of school and end up homeless; a more likely reality is that she may have to take some courses over again.
Control beliefs	Believing either that you are helpless and totally subject to forces beyond your control or that you must tightly control your life for fear that, if you don't, you will never be able to regain control.	Until talking to her family friend, Nina, Beth thought that there was nothing she could do to change the downward spiral of events.

Source: Adapted from Aaron T. Beck. *Depression: Causes and Treatment* (1967), pp 199–210, with permission of the University of Pennsylvania Press.

Techniques of Cognitive Therapy Some of the same techniques are used in REBT and Beck's cognitive therapy, but each approach also relies on its own distinctive techniques.

REBT TECHNIQUES. The REBT therapist helps the client identify his or her irrational beliefs, then tries to persuade the client of the irrationality of those beliefs (Hollon & Beck, 1994); client and therapist accomplish this work through a sequence of techniques that can be remembered by the alphabetical sequence ABCDEF: Distressing feelings exist because an *activating event* (A), which, along with the person's *beliefs* (B), lead to a highly charged emotional *consequence* (C). It is not the event itself that created the problem, but rather the beliefs attached to the event that led to a problematic consequence. Thus, changing the beliefs will lead to a different consequence. This is done by helping the client *dispute* (D) the irrational beliefs and perceive their illogical and self-defeating nature. Such disputes lead to an *effect* (E; also called an *effective new philosophy*), a new way of feeling and acting. Finally, clients may need to take *further action* (F) to solidify the change in beliefs.

Each therapy session addresses a specific aspect of the client's problem; typically at the outset of each session, the client and therapist discuss a problem and determine the effect the client wants to attain. For instance, Beth and an REBT therapist might agree on what the effect should be when she studies—namely, less anxiety—and go through the ABCDEF procedure to achieve that effect. Figure 1 illustrates the ABCDEF techniques applied to Beth's anxiety.

FIGURE 1 The ABCDEF Technique Applied to Beth's Anxiety

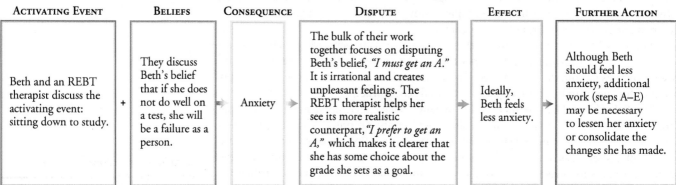

ACTIVATING EVENT		BELIEFS		CONSEQUENCE		DISPUTE		EFFECT		FURTHER ACTION
Beth and an REBT therapist discuss the activating event: sitting down to study.	+	They discuss Beth's belief that if she does not do well on a test, she will be a failure as a person.	▸	Anxiety	▸	The bulk of their work together focuses on disputing Beth's belief, *"I must get an A."* It is irrational and creates unpleasant feelings. The REBT therapist helps her see its more realistic counterpart, *"I prefer to get an A,"* which makes it clearer that she has some choice about the grade she sets as a goal.	▸	Ideally, Beth feels less anxiety.	▸	Although Beth should feel less anxiety, additional work (steps A–E) may be necessary to lessen her anxiety or consolidate the changes she has made.

Rational-emotive behavior therapy makes use of the ABCDEF technique. Here we see how the technique would be applied to Beth's problem of test anxiety.

In addition, the REBT therapist sometimes argues with the client to help him or her confront (and dispute) the faulty cognitions that contribute to his or her distress. The therapist may also use role playing to help the client practice new ways of thinking and behaving (Ellis, 1994a).

REBT can be helpful with anxiety, unassertiveness (Haaga & Davison, 1989), and unrealistic expectations; it is generally not successful with psychotic disorders.

BECK'S COGNITIVE THERAPY TECHNIQUES. This therapy relies on **cognitive restructuring**, the process of helping clients view their situations in a new light, which then allows them to shift their thinking from automatic, distorted, negative thoughts (referred to as "automatic thoughts") to more realistic ones. A therapist who adopts this approach often asks clients to make use of a *daily record of dysfunctional thoughts* (see Figure 2). As part of this daily record, clients are asked to: (1) identify the situation in which the automatic negative thoughts occurred, (2) rate their emotional state, (3) write down the automatic thoughts and the cognitive distortions involved, (4) develop rational responses to those thoughts (comparable to the REBT "dispute"), and (5) then rate their emotional state again ("Outcome"). When the technique is effective, clients should rate their emotional state as improved after going through this process. Although this technique appears straightforward, it can be difficult to use because the client has believed the "truth" of the automatic thought for so long that it doesn't seem to be distorted or irrational.

FIGURE 2 Daily Record of Dysfunctional Thoughts

Situation	Emotion(s)	Automatic Thought(s)	Rational Response	Outcome
Actual event or stream of thoughts	Rate (1–100%)	ATs that preceded emotion Rate belief in ATs (1–100%)	Write rational response to ATs Rate belief in rational response (1–100%)	Rerate AT (1–100%)
1. Sit down to study	Anxious 70%	I won't be able to do as well on the test as I would like. —100% (Dichotomous thinking)	I might not be able to do as well as I want, but that doesn't mean that I will necessarily fail. —50%	Anxious 50%
2. In bed in the morning	Sad 80%	There's no point in getting out of bed—the day will be awful. I fail at everything I try. —90% (Mental filter)	Although I may not "succeed" in the goals I set for myself, it is possible that my expectations are too high, that I have too many expectations, or that I only notice the goals I don't attain, and don't notice the ones I do. —70%	Sad 6%

In a daily record of dysfunctional thoughts, clients like Beth are asked to identify the situation in which their automatic negative thoughts occurred, rate their emotional state (Emotions column), write down the automatic thoughts and cognitive distortions, their rational response to the automatic negative thoughts, and then rerate their emotional state (Outcome column).

Source: Format adapted from Aaron T. Beck, *Cognitive Therapy of Depression* (1979). Appendix. New York, NY: Guilford Press. Reprinted by permission of Guilford Press.

To bring about cognitive restructuring, a cognitive therapist does the following:

1. Teaches the client how to use the daily record of dysfunctional thoughts;
2. Helps the client identify his or her automatic negative thoughts;
3. Has the client examine and assess whether the automatic thoughts are accurate and whether the client's habitual ways of viewing himself or herself and the world are on the mark;
4. Helps the client search for alternative interpretations to refute those automatic thoughts.

Cognitive therapy also makes use of **psychoeducation**, which involves educating clients about therapy and research findings pertaining to their disorders or problems. This knowledge is then used to help clients develop a more realistic, undistorted view of their problems. For instance, Beth was afraid to seek treatment because she was afraid that she would be hospitalized; a cognitive therapist might explain to her the criteria for a hospital admission so that this fear wouldn't become the basis for developing irrational automatic thoughts.

Cognitive restructuring The process of helping clients view their situation in a new light, which then allows them to shift their thinking from the focus on automatic, distorted, negative thoughts to more realistic ones.

Psychoeducation The process of educating clients about therapy and research findings pertaining to their disorders or problems.

Cognitive–Behavior Therapy

The distinction between behavior therapy and cognitive therapy is to some extent a matter of emphasis; these forms of therapy are not categorically distinct. We've already noted that cognitive therapy implicitly involves behavior change. Similarly, behavior therapy involves changing cognitions: For instance, during exposure treatment, clients with anxiety disorders learn that the feared consequences (irrational or faulty beliefs) do not, in fact, come to pass. That is, through exposure, they discover that the catastrophic events they believed would happen don't actually happen when using an elevator (for someone with an elevator phobia) or that touching dirt (for someone with OCD) won't lead to a catastrophe or fatal illness (Emmelkamp, 2004).

In the final quarter of the 20th century, therapists began to combine cognitive and behavioral techniques within the same treatment; this merging of therapies grew out of the recognition that cognitions and behaviors affect each other, and both affect feelings: Cognitive techniques change thoughts, which then affect feelings and behaviors; behavioral techniques change behaviors, which, in turn, lead to new experiences, feelings, and ways of relating, which then change how people think about themselves and the world. CBT is appropriate for a wide range of clients and disorders, and provides the opportunity for clients to learn new coping strategies and master new skills. As shown in Table 3, CBT combines the goals and specific techniques of both behavior and cognitive therapies.

THINK like a **PSYCHOLOGIST** If you heard that someone was being treated with CBT for pyromania (compulsive fire setting), what type of techniques do you think that treatment might include and why? Do you think that CBT would be effective if a client was not motivated to change? Why or why not?

TABLE 3 The Focus, Goals, and Techniques of Cognitive–Behavior Therapy

Although cognitive–behavior therapy (CBT) addresses clients' symptoms and focuses on symptom relief as a goal in and of itself, cognitive and behavioral techniques have different foci and goals. CBT combines the goals and techniques listed below.

Type of Techniques	Focus	Goal(s)	Specific Techniques
Behavioral techniques	Maladaptive behavior	Change the behavior, its antecedents, or its consequences	Relaxation techniques, systematic desensitization, exposure (with or without response prevention), stimulus control, behavior modification
Cognitive techniques	Automatic thoughts; cognitive distortions; faulty beliefs and irrational thoughts	Change dysfunctional, unrealistic thoughts and beliefs to more realistic ones; recognize the relationships among thoughts, feelings, and behaviors	Cognitive restructuring or Ellis's ABCDEF technique, psychoeducation, role playing

✔●─**Study** and **Review** on
mypsychlab.com

LOOKING BACK

1. **What is the focus of behavior therapy? What are some of its techniques?** The theory underlying behavior therapy is that a problematic behavior is caused by previous learning; behavior therapy is designed to change distressing or abnormal behavior through techniques based on learning principles. Such techniques include systematic desensitization, exposure, exposure with response prevention, stimulus control, and behavior modification programs.

2. **What are the goals of cognitive therapy? What techniques are used?** The theory underlying cognitive therapy is that thoughts influence feelings and behaviors. According to this theory, someone who has distressing symptoms, such as depression, has automatic negative thoughts or irrational beliefs that affect feelings and behavior. The goal of cognitive therapy is to reduce these irrational cognitive distortions via cognitive restructuring, disputes, and psychoeducation.

3. **How does cognitive-behavior therapy grow out of behavior and cognitive therapies?** Cognitive-behavior therapy (CBT) grew out of the recognition that cognitions and behaviors affect each other, and thus the two types of techniques could be effectively combined.

Biologically Based Treatments

Thinking about her mother's depression led Beth to wonder whether medication might help her own anxiety and depression. Ten years earlier, Beth's mother had participated in a research study on treatment for depression; her mother received both antidepressant medication and CBT. Although Beth's mother had tried medication many years before, it hadn't helped. But now the newer medication she took helped a great deal. Could medications or other biologically based treatments help Beth feel better? With recent advances in knowledge about the brain have come advances in biologically based treatments of many disorders. ✳️⎯Explore

✳️⎯Explore the Concept Genetic Counseling on mypsychlab.com

LOOKING AHEAD Learning Objectives

1. What are the different types of medications that can be used to treat psychological disorders?
2. What is electroconvulsive therapy, and what disorders does it help alleviate?
3. When is transcranial magnetic stimulation used as a treatment?

Psychopharmacology

In the past two decades, the number and types of medications used to treat psychological disorders have multiplied. As scientists learn more about the brain, researchers are able to develop new medications to target symptoms and the underlying brain alterations more effectively or with fewer side effects. Thus, for any given disorder, there are more medication options than in previous decades. The use of medication to treat psychological disorders and problems is known as **psychopharmacology**.

Schizophrenia and Other Psychotic Disorders The most common type of medication used to treat schizophrenia and other psychotic disorders is **antipsychotic medication** (also called *antipsychotics* or *neuroleptic medication*), which generally reduces psychotic symptoms—but does not cure the disorder. Antipsychotic drugs have long been known to reduce the positive symptoms of schizophrenia, such as hallucinations. Increasing numbers of research findings indicate that clients have better long-term outcomes if they take antipsychotics soon after the first psychotic episode rather than waiting until they've had additional episodes (Wyatt et al., 1997).

Antipsychotic medications typically are divided into two groups: *first-generation* and *second-generation* antipsychotics:

- *First-generation antipsychotics* (also referred to as *traditional antipsychotics*) are the first wave of medications developed to treat schizophrenia and other psychotic disorders; such medications include Thorazine and Haldol. Unfortunately, long-term use of these medications can cause **tardive dyskinesia**, which is an irreversible movement disorder in which the affected person involuntarily smacks his or her lips, display facial grimaces, and exhibits other symptoms.

- *Second-generation antipsychotics* (sometimes referred to as *atypical antipsychotics*) are a newer group of drugs that affect the neurotransmitter dopamine (as does first-generation antipsychotic medication) as well as other neurotransmitters. For instance, the second-generation antipsychotic medication Risperdal cuts down on the amount of dopamine and serotonin available in the brain, which affects the ease with which some neural signals cross synapses. Reducing the amount of these neurotransmitters can reduce positive symptoms, which in turn can allow psychotherapy to be more effective (Ballus, 1997). Second-generation anti-psychotics have different side effects than first-generation antipsychotic medication—specifically, the newer medications can cause hyperglycemia (high blood sugar) and diabetes but do not generally lead to tardive dyskinesia.

Psychopharmacology The use of medication to treat psychological disorders and problems.

Antipsychotic medication Medication that reduces psychotic symptoms.

Tardive dyskinesia An irreversible movement disorder in which the person involuntarily smacks his or her lips, displays facial grimaces, and exhibits other symptoms.

457

Studies have shown that the herbal remedy St. John's wort may be effective in treating mild to moderately severe depression (Szegedi et al., 2005).

Source: © Michael P. Gadomski/Photo Researchers, Inc.

Mood Disorders Many medications are now available to treat mood disorders.

MEDICATIONS FOR DEPRESSION. Effective pharmacological treatment for depression began in earnest in the 1950s with the discovery of **tricyclic antidepressants (TCAs)**, named for the three rings in their chemical structure. Elavil is an example of this class of drug. For decades, TCAs were the only effective antidepressant medication readily available, but common side effects include constipation, dry mouth, blurred vision, and low blood pressure. These medications affect serotonin levels, and they can take weeks to work.

Another type of antidepressant medication, **monoamine oxidase inhibitors (MAOIs)**, was discovered before TCAs, but MAOIs have never been as widely prescribed as TCAs, for two major reasons: (1) MAOIs require users not to eat or drink anything that contains the substance *tyramine* (which is present in foods such as cheese and wine) because of potentially fatal changes in blood pressure, and (2) they are less effective with typical symptoms of depression, although they are more effective with atypical depression—marked by increased appetite and increased need for sleep (Prien & Kocsis, 1995).

A third type of antidepressant medication, **selective serotonin reuptake inhibitors (SSRIs)** such as Prozac, Zoloft, and Paxil, was developed in the 1980s. These medications generally have fewer side effects than other antidepressants (they only work on *selective* serotonin receptors) and are generally as effective as the other classes of antidepressant medications, and thus people are less likely to stop taking them (Agency for Health Care Policy and Research, 1999; Anderson, 2000; Geddes et al., 2000). Although SSRIs have fewer side effects than other antidepressants, they still have side effects; one common side effect is decreased sexual interest or difficulty in achieving orgasm. In addition, many people experience a "Prozac poop-out" after taking the drug for a while—no longer attaining the same benefit from what had previously been an effective dose. More seriously, by 2004, researchers discovered that SSRIs have a very significant drawback for children and adolescents—an increased risk of suicide (Martinez et al., 2005). This increased suicide risk with SSRIs (compared to other antidepressants) has not been found among adults (Barbui et al., 2009; Fergusson et al., 2005; Gunnell et al., 2005).

Finally, some newer antidepressants (such as Serzone, Effexor, and Remeron) don't fall into the existing categories of antidepressants; these drugs affect both the serotonin and the norepinephrine systems and are referred to as **serotonin/norepinephrine reuptake inhibitors (SNRIs)**. In addition, another medication for depression that does not fall into the three previously described classes and that does not require a prescription is the extract from the flowering plant *St. John's wort.* This medication can be effective as a short-term treatment for mild to moderately severe depression (Gaster & Holroyd, 2000; Szegedi et al., 2005).

ANTIDEPRESSANT EFFECT AS PLACEBO EFFECT? The *placebo effect* occurs when a medically inactive substance nevertheless has medicinal effects (Lin, 2010); antidepressant medications appear to work, at least in part, through a placebo effect. Consider that studies have shown that about 75% to 80% of the beneficial effects of antidepressant medications can be achieved with a placebo. That is, only about 25% of the positive response to an antidepressant arises from the active ingredients in the medication. This placebo effect is particularly strong for mild or moderate, rather than severe, depression (Fournier et al., 2010). Moreover, the power of the placebo effect is even stronger when clients are given a placebo that mimics the side effects of antidepressants (such as causing dry mouth—as do TCAs—so that clients are more likely to think they are taking the antidepressant and not a placebo; R. P. Greenberg & Fisher, 1989). Thus, among those helped by an antidepressant, much—if not most—of the positive response arises from their *expectations* that symptoms will get better (Kirsch & Lynn, 1999; Kirsch & Sapirstein, 1998; Kirsch et al., 2002; Walach & Maidhof, 1999).

Neuroimaging studies have compared the brains of depressed people who received antidepressants (typically an SSRI) to those of depressed people who received a placebo; results showed that both groups of people—those who take an SSRI and those who take a placebo medication—had similar changes in brain functioning (Leuchter et al., 2002).

Tricyclic antidepressant (TCA) A type of antidepressant medication named for the three rings in its chemical structure.

Monoamine oxidase inhibitor (MAOI) A type of antidepressant medication that requires strict adherence to a diet free of tyramine.

Selective serotonin reuptake inhibitor (SSRI) A type of antidepressant medication that affects only selective serotonin receptors.

Serotonin/norepinephrine reuptake inhibitor (SNRI) A newer type of antidepressant that affects both serotonin and norepinephrine neurotransmitter systems.

These findings indicate that someone's expectations about what will happen after taking antidepressant medication (level of the person) affect what happens in the brain, which, in turn, affects the person's interactions with others as the individual becomes less depressed (level of the group).

Note that these findings do *not* mean that people taking antidepressants should stop taking their medication. Taking a medication—whether a placebo or an antidepressant—is *not* the same as not taking any medication. The act of taking a (placebo) medication promotes biological changes that would not otherwise occur were the person not taking any medication; moreover, the actual medications do contribute to the overall benefit, just not as strongly as initially believed.

MEDICATIONS FOR BIPOLAR DISORDER. Treatment for people with bipolar disorder typically includes taking medication for the rest of their lives. The main type of medication is a class referred to as *mood stabilizers*, which includes *lithium* (technically, lithium carbonate) and *anticonvulsant medications*. Lithium can minimize the risk of a recurrence of both manic and depressive episodes; however, up to half of people with bipolar disorder either are not helped substantially by lithium or cannot tolerate its side effects, which include gastrointestinal problems, increased thirst, and trembling. Such people may instead be given anticonvulsant medication—such as Depakote, Tegretol, and Lamictal—which also can stabilize mood and minimize the recurrence of manic episodes.

In addition to a mood stabilizer, some people with bipolar disorder may also be prescribed antidepressants for depressive symptoms. In such cases, however, people should take antidepressants for as brief a time as possible because antidepressants can sometimes induce a manic episode in people with bipolar disorder (Rosenbaum et al., 2005). When people with bipolar disorder become manic, doctors often prescribe antipsychotics or antianxiety medications until the mania has subsided.

Anxiety Disorders

People with anxiety disorders (including panic disorder, phobias, and posttraumatic stress disorder [PTSD]) may be prescribed *benzodiazepines* and/or *antidepressants*. **Benzodiazepines** are a type of antianxiety medication that reduces symptoms of panic from an hour up to 36 hours. Examples of benzodiazepines are Xanax and Valium. However, this type of medication can cause drowsiness and is potentially lethal when taken with alcohol. In addition, a person taking benzodiazepines for months or years can develop tolerance and dependence and can experience withdrawal reactions. For these reasons, drugs of this class are often prescribed for only short periods of time, such as during a particularly stressful period of a person's life.

Antidepressants (in particular, TCAs, SSRIs, or SNRIs) may be prescribed as a long-term treatment for anxiety disorders, although the dosage may be lower or higher than that used to treat depression, depending on the specific anxiety disorder (Gorman & Kent, 1999; Kasper & Resinger, 2001; Rivas-Vazques, 2001). Unlike benzodiazepines, however, antidepressants must be taken for several weeks before anxiety symptoms are noticeably reduced.

Electroconvulsive Therapy

Medication is not the only type of biologically based treatment for psychological disorders. Another type of biologically based treatment is **electroconvulsive therapy (ECT)**, which consists of using an electric current to induce a controlled brain seizure. The patient is given a muscle relaxant before each ECT treatment and is under anesthesia during the procedure; because of the anesthesia, ECT is administered in a hospital and generally requires a hospital stay. Treatment with ECT usually requires 6 to 12 sessions, and sessions occur two or threetimes a week over several weeks (Husain et al., 2004; Shapira et al., 1998; Vieweg & Shawcross, 1998)

The main side effect of ECT is that patients may experience memory loss for events right before, during, or after each treatment (Kho et al., 2006). During the past 50 years, changes in the way ECT is administered have significantly reduced the memory problems that can arise after ECT.

Benzodiazepine A type of antianxiety medication that reduces symptoms of panic within 36 hours and does not need to be taken for more than a week to be effective.

Electroconvulsive therapy (ECT) A treatment in which an electric current induces a controlled brain seizure.

459

THINK like a **PSYCHOLOGIST** Suppose your best friend's mother has bipolar disorder. What biologically based treatment(s) would probably be given to her? Why? Suppose instead that your friend's father has schizophrenia; what biologically based treatment(s) might he receive?

Who receives ECT? ECT is given to people who have disabling psychological disorders (typically psychotic depression, manic episodes of bipolar disorder, or—less commonly—schizophrenia) and for whom medication either has not been effective or is not recommended (Lehman & Steinwachs, 1998; Maletzky, 2004). Since the 1980s, the use of ECT has increased (Glass, 2001). The increase in use of ECT reflects the fact that it effectively treats some disorders (as it is now administered) and the reality that not all people with severe symptoms of depression, mania, or schizophrenia can take medication or find it helpful. In fact, over 80% of people who receive ECT suffer from depression and were not sufficiently helped by psychotherapy or medication (Eranti & McLoughlin, 2003; Lam et al., 1999; Sackeim et al., 1995). In such cases, ECT can reduce the symptoms—but researchers have yet to discover exactly why ECT can be effective.

Transcranial Magnetic Stimulation

A newer biologically based treatment is *transcranial magnetic stimulation (TMS)*, a procedure in which an electromagnetic coil on the scalp transmits pulses of high-intensity magnetism to the brain in short bursts lasting 100 to 200 microseconds. TMS is given to people who have not improved with medication, and it can reduce symptoms of some psychological disorders—particularly depression—although it is not yet known exactly how TMS alters brain activity to produce beneficial effects.

The precise effects of TMS depend on the exact location of the coil on the head and the frequency of the pulses. Placebo studies of TMS (in which the procedure of TMS is administered, but the coil is placed at an angle that does not affect the brain) have found that actual TMS is more effective than the placebo (George et al., 1999; Klein et al., 1999). Studies of people with depression who have not responded to medication have revealed that patients' depressive symptoms decrease after TMS (Epstein et al., 1998; Figiel et al., 1998; Klein et al., 1999). Moreover, some studies have found that severely depressed people who receive TMS respond as well as those receiving ECT (Dannon et al., 2002; Janicak et al., 2002).

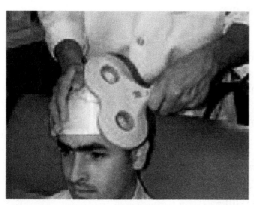

Unlike someone undergoing ECT, the person receiving transcranial magnetic stimulation is awake and does not need anesthesia or to be hospitalized.

Source: Julian Paul Keenan PhD

✓●—**Study** and **Review** on **mypsychlab.com**

TMS offers two significant advantages over ECT: (1) It is easier to administer (it requires neither anesthesia nor hospitalization), and (2) it has minimal side effects. The most common short-term side effect, experienced by 5% to 20% of patients, is a slight headache.

LOOKING BACK

1. **What are the different types of medications that can be used to treat psychological disorders?** Antipsychotic medication can help people with schizophrenia and other psychotic disorders, antidepressants can help people with depression and anxiety, mood stabilizers can help people with bipolar disorder, and benzodiazepines as well as antidepressants can help people with anxiety disorders.

2. **What is electroconvulsive therapy, and what disorders does it help alleviate?** Electroconvulsive therapy (ECT) is a procedure that induces a controlled brain seizure. ECT can reduce symptoms in people who remain severely depressed, manic, or psychotic after other types of treatments have failed to reduce their symptoms significantly.

3. **When is transcranial magnetic stimulation used as a treatment?** Transcranial magnetic stimulation (TMS) is a procedure in which pulses of high-intensity magnetism are transmitted to the brain. It is typically given to people who have mood disorders that have not improved with medication.

Treatment Variations and Issues

After a number of therapy sessions, Beth began to feel better. Moreover, her behavior changed: She was going to class more often and studying and preparing for tests more effectively. She wanted to know what it was about the therapy that was helping her and why her therapist used specific techniques at certain times. Her treatment had not included medication, and she still wondered whether she would be feeling even better—or worse—if she had taken medication. She also wondered whether her therapy would be as effective for other people in her situation. If her best friend went to see Beth's therapist for anxiety and depression, would her friend fare as well as Beth?

LOOKING AHEAD Learning Objectives

1. What are other forms, or "modalities," of therapy besides individual therapy?
2. What are recent innovations in psychotherapy?
3. What key issues should be kept in mind when reading research studies on psychotherapy?
4. What are good ways to find a therapist?

Modalities: When Two or More Isn't a Crowd

Many of the types of treatments we've described in this chapter can be implemented in a variety of **modalities**, or forms. **Individual therapy**—therapy in which one client is treated by one therapist—is a modality. Other modalities have one or more therapists working with a family or with a group of people who have a common characteristic, such as a diagnosis of agoraphobia. Each theoretical orientation described earlier in the chapter can be employed in various modalities in addition to the individual therapies discussed previously: specifically, *group therapy*, *family therapy*, and *self-help therapy*.

Group Therapy

Clients with similar needs or goals who meet together with a therapist are engaging in **group therapy**. The course of treatment in group therapy can range from a single session (usually an educational session) to ongoing treatment lasting for years. Some groups are for members who have in common a particular problem or disorder, such as divorce or PTSD. These groups may offer emotional support, psychoeducation, and/or concrete strategies for managing the problem or disorder. Other groups have members who do not share any specific problem or disorder but rather who want to learn more about the maladaptive or inappropriate ways in which they interact with other people; a therapy group of this type provides members with an opportunity to learn about themselves and change their undesired patterns of behavior.

In general, group therapy offers information, support, and (if the group has a cognitive–behavioral orientation) between-session homework assignments, and it also provides something that individual therapy cannot—interaction with other people. The group experience can decrease the sense of isolation and shame that clients sometimes feel. In revealing their own experiences and hearing about the experiences of others, clients often come to see their own lives and difficulties in a new light. Also, because some clients' problems relate to how they interact with other people, group therapy provides a safe opportunity for clients to try out new ways of interacting.

Group therapy can help reduce shame and isolation and can provide support and an opportunity to interact in new ways with other people.

Source: Jon Bradley\Getty Images Inc. - Stone Allstock

Family Therapy

In **family therapy**, the therapist treats the family as a whole or some of its members, such as a couple. A "family" is often defined as consisting of those who think of themselves or function as a family; thus, blended families created by marriage and other configurations of nontraditional families may be seen in family therapy.

Most family therapists provide **systems therapy,** which is a type of therapy in which a client's symptoms are viewed as occurring within a larger context or system (that of the family and subculture), and a change in one part of the system affects the rest of the system. With systems therapy, the client is referred to as the "identified patient," and the system (the couple or the family) is considered the "patient" that is to be treated.

Modality A form of therapy.

Individual therapy A therapy modality in which an individual client is treated by a single therapist.

Group therapy A therapy modality in which a number of clients with compatible needs or goals meet together with a therapist.

Family therapy A therapy modality in which a family (or certain members of a family) is treated.

Systems therapy A type of therapy in which a client's symptoms are viewed as occurring in a larger context or system, and a change in one part of the system affects the rest of the system.

Self-help group A group in which members focus on a specific problem or disorder and that does not usually have a clinically trained leader; also called a *support group*.

Systems therapy was originally used exclusively with families; in fact, some of the pioneers in systems therapy would refuse to see individuals without their families. Because of its history, systems therapy is sometimes referred to as "family therapy," although this name is misleading. Some family therapists treat entire families, but not necessarily from a systems approach; instead, these therapists may use a psychodynamic or behavioral approach. Similarly, some systems therapists see individuals without any other family members, but the therapy makes use of systems theory and techniques.

Systems therapy—whether with an individual client or a family—typically focuses on (1) a family's structure, (2) who in the family has power and how it is used, and (3) ways that family members communicate with each other. Initially, a systems therapist takes a family history to discover which members of the family are close to one another or angry with one another; the therapist then seeks to determine how anger, sadness, and other feelings or issues are generally handled within the family. In some cases, one parent may be underinvolved and the other overinvolved; treatment would be directed to encourage the underinvolved parent to be more involved and the overinvolved parent to be less involved. Moreover, because conflict between parents can affect their children's emotional states and behavior, the therapy may focus on improving the parents' relationship with each other (Kitzmann, 2000).

A systems therapist may consider the identified patient's symptoms as attempts by him or her to "solve" a problem within the family. For instance, in a family in which the parents fight a lot, an adolescent boy's rebelliousness may serve to unite his parents in their anger and frustration at him. The systems therapist might explain to the family that their son is intentionally being rebellious to keep his parents united—for fear of what could happen to the parents' relationship if he wasn't causing them problems. In such a situation, the systems therapist might praise the son for his efforts at keeping his parents together and even urge him not to stop rebelling until his parents have learned how to relate to each other without fighting.

Self-Help Therapies

Self-help therapies are available both in groups and individually.

HELPING GROUPS. Someone with a psychological problem or disorder may attend a **self-help group** (sometimes referred to as a *support group*)—a group in which members focus on a specific problem or disorder and that does not usually have a clinically trained leader. Self-help groups may be a person's only form of "treatment," or he or she may also receive psychotherapy and/or medication.

Alcoholics Anonymous (AA) was the first self-help program and is based on 12 steps toward recovery; these 12 steps can be found on AA's website (www.aa.org). These steps have been adapted by self-help programs that address other problems, such as drug addiction; such programs are referred to as *12-step programs*. Most 12-step programs promote a belief in a Higher Power (for most people, God) as crucial to recovery. Whether or not participants are religious, however, 12-step programs can be helpful when participants attend regularly: Weekly attendance in group meetings is associated with drug or alcohol abstinence, whereas less-than-weekly attendance is not (Fiorentine, 1999; Winzelberg & Humphreys, 1999).

Not all self-help programs are based on the 12-steps of AA. For instance, *Smart Recovery* is a self-help organization for overcoming drug or alcohol abuse that is based on cognitive–behavioral principles rather than the 12-steps. Another self-help organization that is not based on the 12-steps is the *Depressive and Bipolar Support Alliance*, which helps people with bipolar disorder or depression as well as their families and friends.

A newer vehicle for self-help is the Internet, which may provide chat room "support groups" and psychoeducation. However, beware: Information on a Web site may not be accurate, and people in an online support group may not be who they claim to be (Finn & Banach, 2000; Waldron et al., 2000).

Source: The Image Works

HELPING YOURSELF. Self-help can also be used by individuals, without the participation of others in a group. The past several decades have witnessed a proliferation of self-help books—as well as audio and video information—that address a wide range of problems; the use of such materials is sometimes referred to as **bibliotherapy**. Many of these materials incorporate techniques of the therapies discussed in this chapter, and therapists often suggest to clients that they read particular books or access specific Web sites (Adams & Pitre, 2000; Starker, 1988). Researchers have found that such material can help people who have depression or anxiety (Febbraro, 2005; Febbraro & Clum, 2008; Floyd et al., 2004; Gregory et al., 2004). Moreover, research findings indicate that at least some Internet-based self-help programs can be as effective as face-to-face therapy (Barak et al., 2008). ((•─ Listen

((•─ Listen to the audio file on eTherapy on **mypsychlab.com**

Innovations in Psychotherapy

Treatments for psychological disorders change over time not only because researchers learn which therapies and techniques are particularly effective for specific disorders but also because of technological innovations and the changes in health insurance coverage for treatment of psychological disorders. In the sections that follow, we explore ways in which treatment is changing over time: an increase in *eclectic therapists*, the increasing use of *therapy protocols* and *brief therapy*, and *incorporating technology into therapy*.

Eclectic Therapists: Mixing and Matching
Today, most therapists do not necessarily have a single theoretical orientation or employ a set of techniques based on a single theoretical orientation. Instead, many therapists are *eclectic*—they employ a variety of theoretical approaches and types of techniques. For example, a therapist using an eclectic approach may draw on ideas from psychodynamic theory, systems therapy, and CBT to understand a client's problems; based on the client's specific problems and goals of treatment, the therapist will employ techniques from one or more theoretical approaches. An eclectic therapist treating a teenager with bulimia, for instance, may use exposure with response prevention to address the symptoms and may also use systems therapy techniques to address family issues that contribute to the client's disorder. Thus, two clients with the same diagnosis may receive different treatments from the same therapist, based on factors other than the diagnosis—such as family issues, a client's preference for a certain theoretical approach or set of techniques, and other concerns.

Time and Therapy: Therapy Protocols and Brief Therapy
Recent decades have seen a rise in the use of *therapy protocols*, detailed session-by-session manuals that provide specific procedures and techniques to treat a particular disorder from a certain theoretical orientation (such as behavior therapy for panic disorder or cognitive therapy for depression). These manual-based treatments were created, in part, to ensure that when a research study assesses a given therapy (for example, CBT), all the therapists use the same techniques in the same way. Manual-based treatment ensures that clients who are supposed to receive CBT actually receive CBT and that clients who are supposed to receive psychodynamic treatment actually receive that type of treatment; thus, when researchers compare the effects of one type of treatment with those of another type of treatment, they can be more confident that clients received the intended type of treatment.

A manual-based treatment usually addresses a given disorder and most commonly employs cognitive and/or behavioral techniques. For instance, manuals have been developed to provide behavior therapy for various anxiety disorders and to provide CBT for depression, anxiety disorders, and eating disorders (Elkin et al., 1989; Linden et al., 2005; Wilson & Fairburn, 2002).

Another type of manual-based treatment is **interpersonal therapy (IPT)**, which helps clients to understand how aspects of current relationships can affect their mood and behavior. IPT techniques help clients explore the consequences of their actions in their relationships and facilitate better personal communication, in part by encouraging clients to convey more directly their feelings about and desires for the relationship. This type of therapy arose from theories about the importance of interpersonal relationships (Sullivan, 1953) and was developed in the late 1970s for a research study examining various treatments of depression. The goal of IPT is to help the client's relationships work better and become more satisfying, and in so doing—according to the

Bibliotherapy The use of self-help books and audio and video information for therapeutic purposes.

Interpersonal therapy (IPT) A type of manual-based treatment that helps clients to understand how aspects of current relationships can affect their mood and behavior.

IPT for depression was adapted to a group format and administered in 30 randomly selected rural villages in Uganda. Compared to depressed people in "control villages" (who received no treatment), depressed people who received group IPT became less depressed and functioned better in their daily lives (Bolton et al., 2003).

Source: The Image Works

Technological gadgets such as this iPhone are at the cutting edge of brief CBT; they have applications that can help participants monitor their thoughts, feelings, and behavior.

Source: Brigette Sullivan/Outer Focus Photos\Alamy Images

Outcome research Research that addresses whether, after psychotherapy, clients feel better, function better, live more independently, or experience fewer symptoms.

underlying theory—certain psychological problems will diminish. IPT for depression, for instance, rests on the assumption that if the relationships are functioning better, the depression will lessen. IPT techniques have been adapted to treat people with bulimia nervosa (Arcelus et al., 2009; Mitchell et al., 2002) and PTSD (Bleiberg & Markowitz, 2005).

Many manual-based treatments provide *brief therapy*, which takes place over 12 to 20 sessions. Research indicates that people with recent, focused problems in one sphere of life (such as work) receive more benefit from brief therapy than do people who have difficulties in multiple spheres or who have long-standing problems (Barkham & Shapiro, 1990; Klosko et al., 1990; Roth & Fonagy, 2005).

Incorporating Technology Into Therapy: High-Tech Treatment Therapists are increasingly using technology in treatment, and researchers are studying its effects. For example, therapists may use virtual reality as part of exposure techniques. In addition, clients may make use of personal digital assistants (PDAs), smartphones, computer programs, and Internet sites to help with self-monitoring as well as communicate with the therapist via email or videoconferencing over the Internet.

Such technologies are used in various ways, such as:

1. *Self-monitoring.* PDAs or smartphones may assist in self-monitoring by having an alarm goes off (at set or random times during the day), signaling the client to assess mood, hunger, anxiety, or some other relevant variable.

2. *Reminding.* These devises can signal the client to employ a previously learned technique, such as muscle relaxation.

3. *Delivering therapy.* Some treatment programs—such as one for the treatment of bulimia nervosa—are entirely electronic; they use Internet-based cognitive–behavioral programs that are supplemented through emails with clinicians (Pretorius et al., 2009). However, at least for treatment of panic disorder, although both face-to-face CBT and an Internet-based CBT program helped decrease symptoms, the face-to-face form of treatment helped clients better understand the information and tasks (Kiropoulos et al., 2008).

Issues in Psychotherapy Research

Research studies indicate that, overall, people with psychological problems or disorders improve more after they have received therapy than they do if they don't receive any treatment. However, although hundreds of types of psychological therapy are currently available (Garfield & Bergin, 1994), researchers have investigated only a small percentage of them. Research is crucial for determining how well a type of therapy treats a particular problem: It is easy to claim that a new therapy is a wonder cure but harder to back up that claim with solid data.

Research that addresses whether clients feel better, function better, live more independently, or have fewer symptoms after treatment is called **outcome research**. Researchers evaluating the success of a therapy must consider a number of issues when designing and conducting their studies; key issues include the following:

1. *What to measure.* It can be tricky to determine whether clients feel better, function better, live more independently, or have fewer symptoms after treatment: Depending on how you define "outcome," you will measure different variables. For example, you could have clients rate their thoughts, their feelings, or their behaviors—and these

three types of data are not necessarily highly correlated with each other. Researchers might obtain different results depending on which types of data they obtained (Kazdin, 1994).

2. *When to assess.* Researchers must also decide how long after the end of treatment to assess outcome (Roth & Fonagy, 2005): Immediately afterward? A month later? A year later?

3. *Appropriate control group.* Even if you find that clients' symptoms are better after treatment, how can you know that the clients' improvement occurred because of the treatment itself and not simply because of the passage of time? One way to assess whether improved symptoms are caused by treatment is to use an experimental research design, in which clients are randomly assigned to one of two groups: (1) those who received treatment (the "experimental group" or "treatment group") and (2) those who did not (the control group). Typically, the control group consists of participants who are on a waiting list for treatment but have not yet received the treatment; this group is referred to as a *wait-list control group.* The members of the control group must be as similar as possible to those in the treatment group (for instance, have the same average age, severity of symptoms, and education level).

Table 4 lists questions that researchers should address when designing studies of psychotherapy and that mental health clinicians should keep in mind when evaluating such studies.

TABLE 4 Questions About Psychotherapy Research

1. Are the participants randomly assigned to experimental and control groups?
2. Are the members of the experimental and control groups comparable on relevant dimensions?
3. Is a specific disorder being treated?
4. Is the treatment based on a manual? If not, how can researchers ensure that therapists are providing the type of therapy being investigated?
5. What types of outcome measures are selected, who is assessing the outcome (for instance, is the client or the therapist—or both—evaluating the success of the treatment?), and how is "success" defined?
6. Is a follow-up assessment planned, and, if so, at what interval of time after the end of treatment?

Source: Based on Kazdin (1994).

Therapy, Medication, or Both?

Given the variety of modalities and treatments available, clinicians and clients want to know whether some treatments are most effective for a given disorder. Research has shown that no one type of treatment is always better across all disorders; instead, different treatments (and techniques) are most effective for different disorders (Roth & Fonagy, 2005). In the sections that follow, we discuss specific treatments for particular disorders and also note relevant comparisons with medication. ⊙► Simulate

⊙► Simulate the exercise Ineffective Therapies on mypsychlab.com

Depression According to many research studies, CBT and IPT effectively reduce symptoms of depression (Blatt et al., 2000; TADS Team, 2007; Talbot & Gamble, 2008). However, the specific techniques used in a given type of therapy (such as cognitive restructuring or facilitating better communication) appear to be less important in treating depression than the factors that are common to all types of therapy—such as offering hope, a new way of thinking about problems, and a caring listener (Emmelkamp, 2004).

Medication also alleviates depression for many people; why, therefore, might someone choose psychotherapy over medication? Medication for depression—compared to various types of psychotherapy for depression—has two main drawbacks: (1) If after taking medication a person's depression lifts, at some point he or she may stop taking the medication. But depression has a high relapse rate, and hence it is likely to return after medication is stopped—a fact that has led some doctors to recommend continued use of medication for people at risk for additional depressive episodes (American Psychiatric Association, 2000). (2) Most antidepressants have side effects (as summarized earlier), and these side effects can lead people to discontinue the medication even if it does reduce their depression, which increases the risk of relapse.

CBT and IPT provide similar benefits to medication but without the side effects of drugs (Antonuccio et al., 1995; DeRubeis et al., 2005). Moreover, CBT and IPT can reduce the likelihood of relapse (Hollon & Shelton, 2001; Hollon et al., 2005) because the skills and tools learned as part of these treatments typically remain after treatment stops. Similarly, people who receive both antidepressants and CBT are less likely to relapse than people who receive only medication (Otto et al., 2005).

Although medication can work to treat social phobia, such as a fear of public speaking, symptoms often return after medication is stopped. In contrast, the benefits of CBT usually last after treatment ends.

Source: David Young-Wolff\PhotoEdit Inc.

Anxiety Disorders The behavioral techniques of exposure and exposure with response prevention are especially helpful for treating most anxiety disorders that involve fear or avoidance of specific stimuli; these techniques can reduce the symptoms of panic and avoidance. In fact, studies reveal that CBT provides as much, if not more, long-term relief of anxiety symptoms as do medications (Gould et al., 1995; Otto et al., 2005). In the treatment of panic disorder, for instance, although medication and CBT work about equally well, CBT does a better job of preventing symptom relapse because the skills gained from treatment endure after the treatment ends (Chambless & Gillis, 1993; Otto et al., 1994).

Other Disorders The effects of different types of treatments have also been studied for many other disorders; in what follows, we provide a brief overview of major findings for treatment of eating disorders and of schizophrenia and bipolar disorder.

EATING DISORDERS. For the treatment of bulimia nervosa, CBT and IPT have been shown to be effective. Moreover, numerous studies have shown that CBT is superior to medication for people with bulimia nervosa (Whittal et al., 1999; Wilson & Fairburn, 2007). For adolescents with anorexia, family-based treatments are particularly effective (Eisler et al., 2007).

SCHIZOPHRENIA AND BIPOLAR DISORDER. For both schizophrenia and bipolar disorder, medication is superior to psychotherapy in reducing psychotic and manic symptoms, respectively, and in lowering the risk of relapse (Thase & Jindal, 2004). However, psychotherapy—in conjunction with medication—can address three important functions for people with these disorders:

1. It can help them to accept the need to take medication (Colom et al., 1998; Tohen & Grundy, 1999).
2. It can provide an opportunity to learn new relationship skills after the medication has helped them to be more stable.
3. It can help to identify triggers of the psychotic, manic, or depressive episodes, which in turn can help to prevent relapses (Buchkremer et al., 1997; Goldstein, 1992).

Finally, we note that CBT can also reduce positive symptoms of schizophrenia in people who are not helped by medication, and can also decrease the likelihood of relapse (Malik et al., 2009; Sensky et al., 2000; Wykes et al., 2008).

Caveat We must end this section with a caveat: As with all research that examines groups of people, the research findings on outcomes of various types of treatments do not necessarily apply to a particular individual. Thus, for any particular person with a given disorder, one type of psychotherapy may be more effective than another, which in turn may be more effective than medication. And the opposite may be true for someone else with apparently identical symptoms.

Treatment for an Ethnically Diverse Population

Therapists—and the treatments they employ—must not only take into account a client's goals and preferred types of treatment but also be sensitive to a client's cultural and ethnic background as well as demographic factors that might influence treatment. According to the 2000 census, for instance, 30% of the population of the United States are members of an ethnic minority, and this proportion continues to grow (Zane et al., 2004). As the composition of the American population changes, so too does the composition of the population seeking mental health services.

An example of why it is important to understand a symptom's cultural context can be found in *ataques de nervios* (Spanish for "attack of nerves"), which some Puerto Rican women experience. This condition is a physical expression of strong emotions and includes trembling, heart palpitations, numbness, difficulty breathing, loss of consciousness, and an overly reactive state (Rivera-Arzola & Ramos-Grenier, 1997). If seen in a Caucasian woman with no familiarity with Puerto Rican customs, such symptoms would likely cause friends, family, and therapists to be extremely concerned; the same symptoms in a woman from Puerto Rico would be interpreted differently. In Puerto Rico, women are likely to endure great hardships, have little real power, and are actively discouraged from expressing anger. *Ataque de nervios* provides a culturally sanctioned way for them to express an inability to cope with their current situation and to receive support (Rivera-Arzola & Ramos-Grenier, 1997).

Therapists try to be aware of unique ethnic and cultural factors that can play a role in treatment, such as the stressors related to being an immigrant, a refugee, or a member of a minority group.

Source: Woodfin Camp & Associates, Inc.

It is clear that the most effective therapist is one who is aware of demographic, cultural, and familial contexts of a client's disorder. It is part of a therapist's responsibility to be aware of issues that can affect diagnosis, the process of the therapy, and its goals (Helms & Cook, 1999; Ramirez, 1999). The therapist should inquire about the client's understanding of the meaning of the problem so that therapist and client can discuss and come to agreement on the nature of the problem, the interventions to be used, and the expected goals (Higgenbotham et al., 1988; Kleinman, 1978).

But being sensitive to these characteristics and issues does not imply that the therapist must be from the same group as the client. In general, when the therapist and client are not of the same sex, ethnic group, or approximate ages, treatment is equally as effective as when patient and therapist have such demographic factors in common (Beutler et al., 1994; Lam & Sue, 2001). However, research suggests one exception: Some Asian Americans prefer a therapist from their own ethnic group, and matching such clients with an Asian American therapist leads to better outcomes for these clients (Sue et al., 1994).

THINK like a PSYCHOLOGIST Suppose you're designing a treatment program for an ethnically diverse set of depressed clients. What would you want to know about these clients, and how would you use that information?

How to Pick a Therapist and a Type of Therapy

Suppose you, like Beth, decide to seek psychotherapy. How do you pick a therapist? Keep several factors in mind when trying to find someone who could most effectively help you:

1. If your problem can be clearly identified (such as depression or anxiety), it's a good idea to see someone who has experience in treating people with that problem. You can find the names of such therapists by contacting state and national referral agencies and professional associations, such as the American Psychological Association, the National Association of Social Workers, and the American Psychiatric Association. Regional organizations, such as the Multiservice Eating Disorders Association in Massachusetts or the Depression and Bipolar Support Alliance of Boston (DBSA-Boston), can also provide referrals for specific problems. These organizations all have national associations that can also supply the names of therapists with expertise in treating specific problems.

2. If a certain type of therapy seems to be a good fit with your problem, you might want to obtain referrals for a therapist who has experience providing that type of treatment. National organizations such as those listed in Table 5 may be able to refer you to therapists in your local area.

TABLE 5 National Organizations for Specific Types of Therapy

- Albert Ellis Institute
- American Association for the Advancement of Behavior Therapy
- American Association for Marriage and Family Therapy
- American Institute for Cognitive Therapy
- American Psychoanalytic Association
- Beck Institute for Cognitive Therapy and Research
- International Society for Interpersonal Psychotherapy

3. If possible, obtain the names of *several* appropriate therapists because any one therapist may not have convenient office hours, location, or available times. You can also ask friends, family members, teachers, and religious leaders for recommendations, as well as the counseling center at your college or university. Many insurance companies will authorize or reimburse treatment only if the provider is on their list of authorized mental health clinicians. Thus, it's best to tell the therapists who you are considering seeing what insurance coverage you have and ask whether their services are reimbursed by that company; if they don't know, call the insurance company and check. Alternatively, another approach is to call your insurance company and ask for referrals to a therapist who is experienced in helping people with your problem or in a particular type of therapy.

4. It is important that you feel comfortable with your therapist. If you don't, you may be less likely to talk about what's on your mind or about how you are really doing. And if you aren't able to talk about these things, the therapy can't be as helpful. It's also important to feel that the therapist is trustworthy—if the therapist doesn't have your trust, you will find it easy to discount what he or she says if it is something that you don't want to hear. If after one or two sessions you realize that you just don't feel comfortable, make an appointment with someone else and see whether the situation feels different with a different therapist. Therapists are used to this initial "tryout" period, and you shouldn't worry about possibly hurting their feelings by switching to someone else.

LOOKING AT LEVELS — Treating Obsessive-Compulsive Disorder

Source: © Amy Etra/PhotoEdit; (inset) © Digital Art/CORBIS All Rights Reserved

Researchers have shown repeatedly that both behavior therapy and medication help people with obsessive-compulsive disorder (OCD), a disorder characterized by intrusive, illogical thoughts and overpowering compulsions to repeat certain acts, such as hand washing to get rid of feared germs. Do behavior therapy and medication act in a similar way to treat OCD? To answer this question, we must consider events at the levels of the brain, person, and group, and the interactions among them.

At the level of the brain, researchers used PET scanning to monitor the brains of people with OCD both before and after they received behavior therapy that included exposure with response prevention (Baxter et al., 1992). The researchers also scanned the brains of other people with OCD before and after they received the SSRI Prozac, which reduces some of the symptoms of OCD. The PET scans revealed that behavior therapy and Prozac both decreased activity in a crucial brain area—the right caudate (the caudate is part of the basal ganglia, a brain structure involved in automatic behaviors), which is too active in people with OCD. But only the drug affected other brain areas—the anterior cingulate and thalamus, both of which are involved in attention (these effects could be related to some of the side effects of the medication). Additional studies have found similar results, such as those in Figure 3 (Schwartz et al., 1996) and that reported by Nakatani and colleagues (2003).

But simply knowing that behavior therapy affects the brain cannot tell us the complete story. For the participants who received behavior therapy, events at the level of the person give rise to the brain changes: Researchers have shown that when people with OCD refrain from their compulsive behaviors, they end up testing the truth of automatic thoughts—and they discover that their fears of catastrophe don't come to pass. So, for instance, when clients refrain from washing their dirty hands or from rechecking that the front door is locked, they modify their thoughts of catastrophe. They can then replace their old, maladaptive thoughts and behaviors with more adaptive ones; these positive events then provide the clients with a sense of mastery and hope and lead them to resist performing the compulsive

FIGURE 3 Brain PET Scans Before and After Behavior Therapy

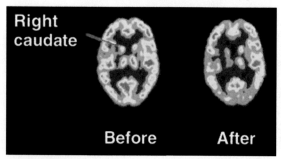

Right caudate

Before   After

These PET scans show the brain of someone with OCD before (left) and after (right) 2 months of behavior therapy. (Note: The images are from the perspective of looking up from the bottom of the brain.) Note the changes in the right caudate after successful treatment (Schwartz et al., 1996).

Source: Baxter et al., 1992

behaviors (Emmelkamp, 2004). Thus, these events at the level of the person affect events at the level of the brain—the functioning of specific brain circuits.

Events at the level of the group are also involved: It is partly the interactions with another person—the therapist—that help to change the thoughts, feelings, and behaviors of the individual with OCD. And another event at the level of the group plays a role—the family style of communication: People with OCD whose family members express hostile criticism are more likely to relapse (Chambless & Steketee, 1999; Emmelkamp et al., 1992). Moreover, one study found that clients in behavior therapy for OCD were six times more likely to drop out of treatment if relatives provided hostile criticism (versus constructive criticism or support; Chambless & Steketee, 1999). Thus, although the technique of exposure with response prevention can be very helpful, events at the level of the group can influence whether clients relapse after the treatment—or even stick with the treatment.

Given that family members can sometimes play such an important role, treatment for OCD may also target events at the level of the group—such as changing family members' responses to the client's symptoms and to his or her newly learned strategies (Van Noppen & Steketee, 2003). Consider that, prior to treatment, family members may have gone along with the client's wishes, for example, by not touching certain "contaminated" objects; such accommodation to the client's symptoms can inadvertently reinforce his or her maladaptive beliefs and behaviors. Alternatively, family members may become (understandably) angry and frustrated by such behavior, which leads them to be hostile and critical; such a response usually increases the client's anxiety and symptom severity. To address these types of family interaction patterns, the family members may receive psychoeducation, family therapy, or behavior therapy. And changing the family can in turn lead them to support the client's efforts with exposure with response prevention. Such family participation can help reduce the OCD symptoms (Grunes et al., 2001; Van Noppen & Steketee, 2003).

Thus, as usual, events at the level of the person affect the brain, and events at the level of the group affect events at both other levels. And, of course, when brain circuits function differently, the person's behavior is likely to change—which in turn will affect his or her experiences and beliefs (level of the person) and interactions with others (level of the group).

LOOKING BACK

✓●─[Study and **Review** on
mypsychlab.com

1. **What are other forms, or "modalities," of therapy besides individual therapy?** Other modalities of therapy include group therapy (often a group of people with similar problems), family therapy (and the therapist may use a systems approach), and couples therapy. People may also make use of self-help groups and bibliotherapy.

2. **What are recent innovations in psychotherapy?** Many therapists today are eclectic and use multiple theoretical orientations and types of techniques. Moreover, therapists are increasingly using manual-based and brief treatments and are incorporating technology into treatment.

3. **What key issues should be kept in mind when reading research studies on psychotherapy?** Overall, people with psychological problems or disorders are better off after psychotherapy than if they did not receive any treatment. However, the specific ways that a study is designed, the variables assessed, and when they are assessed affect what conclusions we can draw from outcome research. Therapists should consider demographic and cultural factors that may affect the treatment.

4. **What are good ways to find a therapist?** Individuals can choose a therapist by obtaining a referral from a counseling center, from family and friends, or from self-help organizations, professional associations, and/or insurance companies. The therapist should be someone with whom the client feels comfortable; if the client does not feel comfortable with a therapist, he or she should seek a different one.

LET'S REVIEW

((•—Listen to an audio file of your chapter on mypsychlab.com

I. INSIGHT-ORIENTED THERAPIES

A. Insight-oriented therapies rest on the idea that psychological problems are caused by unconscious emotional forces.

B. Such treatments focus on helping people gain insight into their problems and rest on the assumption that such insight will lead to changes in thoughts, feelings, and behavior.

C. Examples of insight-oriented therapies are psychoanalysis, psychodynamic therapy, and client-centered therapy.

D. Psychoanalysis and psychodynamic therapy differ in the intensity of the treatment and in the scope of the treatment's goals.

E. Psychoanalysis and psychodynamic therapy focus on unconscious conflicts and sexual and aggressive drives. The goal of these treatments is to make unconscious conflicts conscious.

F. Psychoanalytic and psychodynamic techniques include free association, dream analysis, interpretation, and the use of transference.

G. Client-centered therapy focuses on each client's unique experiences and potential for growth; the goal of the therapy is to unblock the client's potential for growth.

H. Client-centered techniques include having the therapist convey empathy for, and unconditional positive regard toward, the client.

II. COGNITIVE–BEHAVIOR THERAPY

A. Behavior therapy rests on the idea that psychological problems are a product of a client's learning history. Treatment is designed to help the client develop more adaptive behaviors.

B. Behavioral techniques based on classical conditioning include exposure (with and without response prevention), stimulus control, and systematic desensitization (which includes progressive muscle relaxation).

C. Behavioral techniques based on operant conditioning include behavior modification and self-monitoring.

D. Cognitive therapy rests on the idea that psychological problems are caused by faulty beliefs or dysfunctional automatic thoughts. Cognitive techniques help the client develop more realistic, rational thoughts.

E. Rational-emotive behavior therapy (REBT) involves a sequence of techniques (ABCDEF) to persuade the client to give up his or her faulty beliefs.

F. Beck's cognitive therapy involves helping the client to identify dysfunctional automatic thoughts and cognitive distortions and then to replace them with more rational thoughts.

G. Both REBT and Beck's cognitive therapy generally focus on current problems and often assign between-session homework.

III. BIOLOGICALLY BASED TREATMENTS

A. One type of biologically based treatment for psychological disorders is medication—to treat schizophrenia, mood and anxiety disorders, and other disorders.

B. For schizophrenia and other psychotic disorders, first-generation antipsychotic medications reduce positive symptoms but can cause serious side effects. Second-generation antipsychotic medications reduce positive symptoms and have less serious side effects.

C. TCAs, MAOIs, SSRIs, and SNRIs can be used to treat depression. Mood stabilizers such as lithium and anticonvulsants can help reduce symptoms of bipolar disorder.

D. Benzodiazepines may be used as a short-term treatment for anxiety disorders. For longer-term medication treatment, antidepressants may be prescribed.

E. Electroconvulsive therapy (ECT) is typically used with people who are severely depressed, manic, or psychotic and for whom other treatments have failed.

F. Transcranial magnetic stimulation (TMS) may be used instead of ECT to treat depression; TMS is easier to administer and has fewer side effects than ECT.

IV. TREATMENT VARIATIONS AND ISSUES

A. Psychological treatment can be provided in a variety of modalities: individual, family, and group therapy; people with psychological disorders may also make use of self-help resources such as self-help groups and bibliotherapy.

B. Systems therapy rests on the belief that a client's symptoms can best be understood as occurring within a larger context, such as the family; systems therapy reduces symptoms in the "identified patient" by changing the system (typically the family).

C. Therapy protocols (manual-based therapies) and brief therapy have been more widely used in recent years.

D. Research on psychotherapy shows that, overall, people who receive some type of psychotherapy fare better than those who don't receive any treatment.

E. The benefits of CBT and IPT tend to endure after treatment ends, but the same is not generally true of treatment with medication.

F. Research shows that certain types of therapy and techniques are more effective with certain disorders than with others; for example, exposure with response prevention is a particularly effective treatment for OCD.

G. Therapists should try to understand the ethnic and cultural factors related to a client's problems and goals.

KEY TERMS

antipsychotic medication
behavior modification
behavior therapy
benzodiazepine
bibliotherapy
client-centered therapy
cognitive–behavior therapy (CBT)
cognitive distortions
cognitive restructuring
cognitive therapy
dream analysis
ego

electroconvulsive therapy (ECT)
exposure
family therapy
free association
group therapy
id
incongruence
individual therapy
insight-oriented therapy
interpersonal therapy (IPT)
interpretation
modality

monoamine oxidase inhibitor
    (MAOI)
outcome research
progressive muscle relaxation
psychoanalysis
psychodynamic therapy
psychoeducation
psychopharmacology
resistance
selective serotonin reuptake
    inhibitor (SSRI)
self-help group

self-monitoring techniques
serotonin/norepinephrine
    reuptake inhibitor (SNRI)
superego
stimulus control
systematic desensitization
systems therapy
tardive dyskinesia
token economy
transference
tricyclic antidepressant (TCA)

PRACTICE TEST

✓●[Study and Review on mypsychlab.com

For each of the following items, choose the single best answer.

1. During psychoanalysis,
   a. the patient lies on a couch.
   b. the analyst sits in a chair behind the couch, out of the patient's range of sight.
   c. the analyst uses the technique of free association, in which the patient says whatever comes into his or her mind.
   d. All of the above statements are true.

2. Client-centered therapy
   a. emphasizes the past, mental mechanisms, and the working through of conflictual impulses and feelings.
   b. assumes that problems arise because of a lack of a coherent, unified sense of self.
   c. focuses on the process of transference, in which patients may relate to therapists as they did to some important person in their lives.
   d. emphasizes that the therapist must provide conditional positive regard and unfocused empathy.

3. Behavior therapy
   a. focuses on changing observable, measurable behavior.
   b. emphasizes an unconscious "root cause."
   c. views depressive thoughts as producing depressive feelings and behaviors.
   d. uses a technique called *exposure* that relies on operant conditioning principles.

4. Exposure with response prevention
   a. is a planned, programmatic procedure that exposes the client to the anxiety-provoking object but prevents the usual maladaptive response.
   b. is as effective as medication for obsessive-compulsive disorder (OCD).
   c. can have longer-lasting benefits than medication for OCD.
   d. All of the above statements are true.

5. According to Albert Ellis, one process that interferes with healthy functioning is *low frustration tolerance*, in which a person
   a. is unkind to or critical of others for performing poorly.
   b. blames everyone and everything for "poor, dislikable conditions."

   c. is highly self-critical for "performing poorly or being rejected."
   d. develops logical and rational thoughts as a result of experiences.

6. Beth thinks that if she doesn't get an A on a test, she has failed in life. This is an example of the cognitive distortion called
   a. dichotomous thinking.
   b. mental filtering.
   c. control beliefs.
   d. mind reading.

7. The use of medication to treat psychological disorders and problems is known as
   a. psychopharmacology.
   b. tardive dyskinesia.
   c. cognitive restructuring.
   d. systematic desensitization.

8. Newer antipsychotic drugs, such as Risperdal,
   a. increase the amount of free serotonin and dopamine available in the brain.
   b. have fewer side effects than first-generation antipsychotic medications.
   c. have more side effects than first-generation antipsychotic medications.
   d. cause tardive dyskinesia.

9. The tricyclic antidepressants (TCAs)
   a. affect serotonin levels and can take weeks to work.
   b. lead to decreased sexual interest as their most common side effect.
   c. are not as effective as the selective serotonin reuptake inhibitors (SSRIs) for treating depression.
   d. require users not to eat foods with tyramine (such as cheese and wine).

10. Electroconvulsive therapy (ECT)
    a. is most often used to treat anxiety disorders (including panic disorder and the panic symptoms of phobias).
    b. cures schizophrenia but is not a recommended treatment when medication does not work.

c. is particularly helpful in treating certain mood disorders, specifically psychotic depression and manic episodes of bipolar disorder.

d. is now less frequently administered to affluent patients than to those in publicly funded hospitals.

11. A person receiving transcranial magnetic stimulation
   a. requires anesthesia.
   b. needs to be hospitalized.
   c. receives pulses of low-intensity magnetism in the brain in long bursts lasting 5 to 10 minutes.
   d. may develop a slight headache, which is the most common short-term side effect.

12. Today, most therapists
   a. have a single theoretical orientation and use only the techniques derived from that orientation.
   b. provide long-term psychotherapy, with the average treatment lasting about 1 year.
   c. are eclectic in theoretical approach and the techniques that they use.
   d. use the 12-step approach.

13. What does research have to say about the effectiveness of cognitive–behavior therapy (CBT) versus medication for the treatment of panic disorder?
   a. CBT is much more effective than medication.
   b. Medication is generally more effective than CBT.

c. Medication and CBT work about equally well, but CBT is better at preventing relapse.

d. Medication is more effective and does a better job of preventing symptom recurrence than does CBT.

14. Which of the following statements best expresses the relationship between ethnicity and therapy outcome?
   a. Ethnicity plays a systematic role in therapy outcomes generally.
   b. Some people prefer a therapist from their own ethnic group, and such matching leads to better outcomes for these people.
   c. There is clear-cut evidence that matching therapist and client by ethnicity results in better outcomes for most ethnic groups.
   d. None of the above statements is true.

15. Behavior therapy and medication for obsessive-compulsive disorder
   a. affect the same sets of brain areas.
   b. affect only events at the level of the brain.
   c. work best in combination.
   d. each influence and are influenced by events at the levels of brain, person, and group.

Answers: 1. d 2. b 3. a 4. d 5. b 6. a 7. a 8. b 9. a 10. c 11. d 12. c 13. c 14. c 15. d

> People, Black and White, developed attitudes toward and stereotypes about the sisters, and some discriminated against them—because they were Black, because they were women, or simply because they were Delanys.

Source: Getty Images/Time Life Pictures

SOCIAL PSYCHOLOGY

MEETING OF THE MINDS

In 1993, Sarah Delany, known as Sadie, and her younger sister Elizabeth, called Bessie, published their first book, *Having Our Say* (Delany et al., 1993). What's remarkable about these authors is that they were 104 and 102 at the time of publication. Their book recounts the story of their lives, their experiences as Black children and then as Black women during a century of American history. It was during their childhood that the South's Jim Crow laws came into effect, legalizing separate facilities—separate schools, separate water fountains, separate seats on the bus, separate toilets—for Blacks and Whites; it was during their adulthood that these laws were struck down.

Sadie and Bessie were part of a large, tight-knit family. Their father, Henry, had been born a slave but was freed by emancipation. He became vice principal of St. Augustine's School (now St. Augustine's College), a Black college in Raleigh, North Carolina. Their mother, Nanny James, who had both Black and White grandparents, was light-skinned; she served as an administrator of the college, overseeing many of its daily functions. Sadie and Bessie had eight siblings; the Delany children were educated at "St. Aug's," where their father also taught.

All 10 Delany children became college-educated professional men and women—a remarkable feat for anyone of that era, regardless of race or sex. Sadie earned both a bachelor's and a master's degree from Columbia University and became a teacher. In 1926, she became the first Black woman appointed to teach home economics at the high school level in New York City. Bessie went to dental school at Columbia in 1923, where she was the only Black woman, and she went on to become the second Black woman licensed to practice dentistry in New York City.

The Delany family was well known in Black society in North Carolina and in New York City's Harlem neighborhood; the family was considered to be part of an elite group of educated Blacks. But the road was not easy for the sisters. People—Black and White—developed attitudes toward and stereotypes about the sisters, and some discriminated against them, because they were Black, because they were women, or because they were from the South.

Like the Delanys, we are all targets of other people's attitudes and stereotypes, and we have attitudes and stereotypes of our own about other people. Moreover, like the Delanys, we all feel pressure from others to behave in certain ways, and we exert pressure on others to behave in certain ways. How we think about other people and interact in relationships and groups is the focus of the area of psychology called **social psychology**. By definition, social psychology is about our relationships with other people. It focuses on two general topics: the way we perceive and think about others (*social cognition*) and the way we act toward them, individually and in groups (*social behavior*).

Many of the phenomena psychology seeks to understand—sensation, learning, and memory, to name just a few—take place primarily at the levels of the brain and the person but are influenced by the environment and the social world, as shown in the *Looking at Levels* discussions in this book. In this chapter, the central emphasis is the level of the group. Research has revealed many psychological principles that underlie the ways we think about and behave toward other people, as we explore in this chapter. First we'll examine the principles that underlie *social cognition*, and then we'll explore the principles that underlie *social behavior*.

◉ ◉ ◉

Social Cognition: Thinking About People

Mr. and Mrs. Delany (Bessie and Sadie's parents) worked hard to protect their children as much as possible from prejudice, discrimination, and intimidation. They also tried to instill in their children a sense of dignity, self-respect, and respect for others.

They encouraged their children to think about the world and their places in it in specific ways. For example, their parents called each other *Mr.* and *Mrs. Delany* in front of others, including their children. This was a conscious decision. It was common for Whites to call Blacks by their first names in instances in which they would use surnames for other Whites; therefore, Mr. and Mrs. Delany deliberately chose to use formal titles to convey respect for each other and the expectation of respect from others.

In part, Mr. and Mrs. Delany tried to shape how each of their children thought about other people—about the social world around them. As we already noted, psychologists use the term *social cognition* when discussing how people think about other people—"cognition" because it is about how we think, and "social" because the thoughts involve other people and the social world in general. **Social cognition** consists of the ways that people perceive the social world and how they attend to, store, remember, and use information about other people and the social world. In this section, we summarize key findings and theories about social cognition.

Social psychology The area of psychology that focuses on how people think about other people and interact in relationships and groups.

Social cognition The ways that people perceive the social world and how they attend to, store, remember, and use information about other people and the social world.

Attitude An overall evaluation of some aspect of the world—people, issues, or objects.

LOOKING AHEAD Learning Objectives

1. What is the relationship between people's attitudes and their behaviors?
2. What are stereotypes? Why do people have them? What is prejudice?
3. How do we determine responsibility for events and behavior?

Attitudes and Behavior: Feeling and Doing

Your attitudes affect your interpretations of everyday events; an **attitude** is an overall evaluation of some aspect of the world—people, issues, or objects (Petty & Wegener, 1998). This evaluation has three components: affective, behavioral, and cognitive, summarized by the acronym ABC (Breckler, 1984):

- *Affective* refers to your feelings about people, issues, or objects. For instance, your attitude about Blacks will determine how you *feel* about Blacks, which will, in turn, affect how you feel when you read about the Delanys. And in your own circle, if a friend tells you that she's had an abortion, your attitude about abortion will influence your feelings about your friend.

- *Behavioral* refers to your predisposition to act in a particular way toward people, an issue, or an object (note that this component refers not to an actual behavior but to an *inclination* to behave in a certain way). As part of your attitude about Blacks, for instance, you will have a tendency to behave in certain ways toward people who are Black. Similarly, based on your attitude about abortion, you will predisposed to behave in specific ways toward a friend who you learn has had an abortion.

- *Cognitive* refers to what you believe or know about people, issues, or objects. Your attitude about abortion, for instance, will include a set of beliefs about the topic (which may or may not be true).

The interplay between attitudes and behavior can be seen in Sadie's father's comment to her: "Daughter, you are college material. You owe it to your nation, your race, and yourself to go. And if you don't go, then shame on you" (Delany et al., 1993, p. 91). His remarks reflect the components of his attitude toward higher education for Blacks: He was passionately positive about it (affective), he was

The same issue—for instance, whether the U.S. military should intervene in a foreign war—can evoke strong negative or strong positive attitudes in different people.

Sources: AP Wide World Photos; Reuters/Mike Segar\CORBIS- NY

inclined to promote higher education (behavioral), and he believed in the power of education to elevate the position of Blacks in American society (cognitive).

Attitudes and Cognitions Attitudes play an important role in how we process information and remember events (Eagly & Chaiken, 1998). Particularly in ambiguous social situations, our attitudes determine what information we pay attention to, process, and remember. This is one reason why people in the same social situation can come away with different interpretations of what occurred.

In particular, our attitudes guide us as we evaluate information; generally, we find information that is contrary to our attitudes to be unconvincing, and we may even try to disprove the information (Eagly & Chaiken, 1998). As an example, consider the effect of socioeconomic class in the workplace (Gerteis & Savage, 1998): If you think that someone from a lower socioeconomic class will make a bad colleague, you will look for any evidence of shoddy work. You may not notice your colleague's well-performed tasks, but if you do notice them, you make up reasons that discount or discredit your colleague's abilities—perhaps, you say, those are easy tasks.

When an event is ambiguous, our attitudes can influence our cognitive processing of the event. A study of Princeton and Dartmouth students who watched the same motion picture of a controversial Princeton–Dartmouth football game found that students from the different schools described different events, such as which team started rough play (Hastorf & Cantril, 1954).

Source: © Bettmann/CORBIS All Rights Reserved

THINK like a PSYCHOLOGIST To learn more about your own attitudes, you can take an Implicit Attitude Test online. Go to www.mypsychlab.com and search for "Implicit Attitude Test" in the *Social Psychology* chapter.

Predicting Behavior Your attitudes influence your behavior, but they do not always lead you to behave in ways that are consistent with them. Several factors determine how likely it is that an attitude will lead to a corresponding behavior. An attitude is more likely to shape behavior when it is (Eagly & Chaiken, 1998):

- strong,
- relatively stable,
- directly relevant to the behavior,
- important, or
- easily accessed from memory.

For instance, suppose that you strongly dislike eating Moroccan food, which is an attitude. Against your better judgment, you went to a Moroccan restaurant recently—and ended up only picking at the food. If a friend invites you today to a meal at a Moroccan restaurant, you are likely to suggest another place to go: Your attitude about Moroccan food is strong, stable, directly relevant to your behavior, and easily accessed from memory. But if you haven't eaten this type of food in years, don't feel that strongly about it now, and have almost forgotten why you ever disliked it, you would be less likely to object to your friend's choice of a Moroccan restaurant (Sanbonmatsu & Fazio, 1990).

Behavior Affects Attitudes The relationship between attitudes and behavior isn't a one-way street: Behavior can also affect attitudes. For instance, suppose a professor assigned an essay on a topic about which you didn't have very strong feelings (let's say, supporting curbside recycling versus recycling at a local center). Do you think writing the essay would influence your subsequent views? Research has shown that it can: When people are asked repeatedly to champion an attitude on a given topic—which makes it easier to access that attitude subsequently—they are more likely later to behave in ways consistent with that attitude (compared with people who did not repeatedly express the attitude; Fazio et al., 1982; Powell & Fazio, 1984). In fact, repeatedly asserting an attitude can make the attitude stronger (Downing et al., 1992).

Cognitive Dissonance However, attitudes and behavior don't always go hand in hand; for instance, people who smoke cigarettes don't necessarily have a positive attitude about smoking. Generally, though, people prefer that their attitudes, beliefs, and behaviors are consistent (Snyder & Ickes, 1985). When an attitude and behavior—or two related attitudes, beliefs, or behaviors—are inconsistent, this can lead to **cognitive dissonance**, which is an uncomfortable state that arises from a discrepancy between two attitudes, beliefs, or behaviors. Cognitive dissonance is accompanied by heightened arousal, and people are motivated to reduce this dissonance by resolving the conflict. (Losch & Cacioppo, 1990).

To get a sense of cognitive dissonance, ask yourself these questions: Do you think that giving to charity—donating either money or time—is a good thing? Do you think that homeless people should be helped? If you answered "yes" to these questions, when was the last time you donated time or money to help a homeless person? Do you ignore homeless people on the street? You may feel uncomfortable after answering these questions, particularly if you didn't give as much time or money as you think you should have. These feelings arise from the contradiction—the dissonance—between your attitudes about helping the homeless and your behavior related toward them. ✳️⎡Explore

Cognitive dissonance The uncomfortable state that arises from a discrepancy between two attitudes, beliefs, or behaviors.

✳️⎡Explore **Cognitive Dissonance and Attitude Change** on mypsychlab.com

DISSONANCE REDUCTION.   Leon Festinger and J. Merrill Carlsmith (1959) devised a now-classic study of cognitive dissonance. They found, counterintuitively, that participants who were paid less to tell someone that a boring task was enjoyable reported afterward that they enjoyed the task more than those who were paid a greater amount (see Figure 1). How can we understand this? By the effects of cognitive dissonance reduction. The participants who were paid less, only $1, could not have justified reporting that they enjoyed the task for that amount. To reduce the dissonance between their behavior (telling someone that a boring task was enjoyable) and their attitude about the task (it was boring), they appear to have convinced themselves, unconsciously, that they really *did* enjoy the task—so much that they were willing to say that they enjoyed it even though they received little reimbursement. That is, to reduce the cognitive dissonance between their initial attitude and their behavior, they changed their attitude about the task so they did not view it as boring. In contrast, the participants who were paid more money felt no such cognitive dissonance; the money they received, they apparently felt, adequately compensated them for telling someone that they liked the task.

In general, research has shown that the less reason a person has to engage in a behavior that is counter to an attitude, the stronger the dissonance. However, cognitive dissonance does not occur with every inconsistency; it is experienced only when people believe that they have a choice and that they are responsible for their course of action and thus for any negative consequences (Cooper, 1998; Goethals et al., 1979).

FIGURE 1 Cognitive Dissonance

In Festinger and Carlsmith's (1959) classic study, participants were asked to perform a very boring, repetitive task: putting spools on a tray, then dumping them out, and starting all over again.

Participants were given either $1 or $20 (a lot of money in those days) and were then asked to tell another person that the task was, in fact, quite interesting.

After telling the other person about the task, the participants were asked to rate how much they liked the task. Participants who were paid $1 to tell the other person that they liked the task reported actually liking the task more than those paid $20 to do so!

Cognitive dissonance can occur when our attitudes, beliefs, or behaviors, are inconsistent.

Source: DILBERT: © Scott Adams/Dist. by United Feature Syndicate, Inc.

METHODS OF REDUCING DISSONANCE. Cognitive dissonance can be reduced by using any of three methods:

1. *Indirect strategies,* such as trying to feel good about ourselves in other areas of life.
2. *Direct strategies,* which involve actually changing our attitude or behavior.
3. We can *trivialize an inconsistency* between two conflicting attitudes (or between an attitude, belief, or behavior) as being unimportant and thereby make it less likely to cause cognitive dissonance (Simon et al., 1995).

For example, suppose you really believe in and talk about the issue of homelessness and the need to help homeless people. Then a friend points out that you talk about this issue repeatedly but don't do anything about it. This observation would probably induce cognitive dissonance in you. To reduce it, you could: (1) use an indirect strategy, such as by telling yourself what a good person you are, (2) use a direct strategy that has an impact on homelessness, such as volunteering to work in a shelter, or (3) trivialize the observation, perhaps simply saying, "Well, my heart's in the right place." As noted in Table 1, such ways of reducing dissonance can also explain why people who are not generally immoral may act immorally (Tsang, 2002).

TABLE 1 Immoral Actions and Cognitive Dissonance

When generally moral people commit immoral acts, they are likely to feel cognitive dissonance and will use various strategies to decrease that dissonance, such as the indirect strategies listed here (Bandura, 1999; Tsang, 2002).

Indirect Way to Minimize Cognitive Dissonance About an Immoral Behavior of Cheating on Taxes	**Example:** Otherwise upstanding citizens who cheat on their taxes may tell themselves that it's not really cheating because they . . .
Change how they understand their immoral act in order to see it as having a higher moral purpose or as being less immoral than what some other people do.	*view their lessened tax payment as a protest against a government policy.*
Minimize their responsibility for it.	*argue that it's not really their fault, they need the money because the cost of living is so high.*
Disregard the negative consequences (by avoiding knowledge of the results or minimizing the harm).	*claim that the government collects so much money that the small amount they don't pay is totally inconsequential.*
Blame and dehumanize the victims.	*blame the President or members of Congress for imposing "such a high income tax" while giving themselves high salaries, lots of perks, and tax breaks.*

Attitude Change: Persuasion Attitudes are not set in stone and can change based on experience or additional information. When one person tries to change your—or another person's—attitude, he or she engages in **persuasion**. We are bombarded by attempts to change our attitudes (sometimes in the hopes that it will change our behavior)—through advertisements, editorials, blogposts, and even conversations with friends and family members. Here's an example that might be familiar to you: Walking to class, have you ever been approached by someone offering you a leaflet about an upcoming event, a political candidate, or a new product? If so, someone (or some company) probably was trying to encourage you to shift your attitude: support a candidate, champion a cause, or become interested in a product. In the following sections, we discuss persuasion in more detail—specifically how persuasion works, and what makes a person or a message persuasive.

After Katie Couric's colonoscopy was televised live into millions of homes in 2000, 20% more colonoscopy screenings were performed (Dobson, 2002). This televised event persuaded people using both central and peripheral routes.

Source: Mario Tama/Staff/Getty Images, Inc.

ROUTES TO PERSUASION. According to the *elaboration likelihood model* of attitude change, you can be persuaded via two possible routes—*central* and *peripheral* (Petty & Cacioppo, 1986). You are affected by the *central route* when you pay close attention to the content of the argument—when you carefully read the leaflet to decide whether to support the candidate, champion the cause, or become interested in the product. (If you already hold the opposite view from that expressed in the leaflet, you will probably be persuaded only by very strong arguments.)

But people who try to persuade us know that we don't always have the time, energy, or expertise to make use of the central route, and therefore they may try to persuade us via the *peripheral route*—persuasion attempts based on the following:

- The attractiveness and/or expertise of the source (as in celebrity endorsements; Hovland & Weiss, 1951; Kiesler & Kiesler, 1969);

- The number of arguments presented (although not necessarily how "strong" we think they are);

- Information about how other people respond to the message (for example, "People rave about . . .").

Thus, in contrast to the central route, the peripheral route does not rely on the content of an argument.

Political campaigns often use the peripheral route to try to persuade people to vote for a candidate—often through the **mere exposure effect**: The change—generally favorably—in an attitude that results simply by becoming familiar with something or someone. Political campaigns try to capitalize on the mere exposure effect when they place their candidate's name in as many places as possible (through ads, bumper stickers, pins, placards, or news coverage), hoping that when voters see the name frequently, they will develop a more positive attitude toward the candidate (and then, they hope, will vote for that candidate). That is, they will be *persuaded* to vote for the candidate.

PERSUASIVE PEOPLE. Certain characteristics of the person doing the persuading can make us more likely to be swayed, notably the following:

1. *Identity.* An attractive person or an expert can be persuasive via the peripheral route.
2. *Fast talking.* People who speak quickly are generally more persuasive than people who speak slowly (N. Miller et al., 1976).
3. *Seems honest.* Persuasive people are perceived as being honest (Priester & Petty, 1995).

PERSUASIVE MESSAGE. If an attempt at persuasion arouses strong emotions in you, particularly fear, it is more likely to work—especially if it includes specific advice about what you can do to bring about a more positive outcome (Leventhal et al., 1965). This technique is used in public service messages that try to scare people into behaving differently, such as ads that graphically describe how someone contracted AIDS by not using a condom and then strongly recommend condom use. However, although fear tactics may persuade us, they may not necessarily bring about long-term changes in behavior (Ruiter et al., 2001).

THINK like a PSYCHOLOGIST Try the mere exposure effect yourself. Look to see what is being advertised on billboards, on buses, and in television ads and notice which ads have very little content (and so can't be trying to persuade you through the central route). What specific methods of persuasion are these ads using?

Persuasion Attempts to change people's attitudes.

Mere exposure effect The change—generally favorable—in an attitude that results from simply becoming familiar with something or someone.

Social cognitive neuroscience The area of psychology that attempts to understand social cognition by specifying the cognitive mechanisms that underlie it and by discovering how those mechanisms are rooted in the brain.

▶ Watch the Video *Becoming a Detective of Social Influence* on mypsychlab.com

Whether a message is persuasive also depends on when and where the message is delivered. If you are not paying full attention to an attempt at persuasion, you are less likely to be persuaded by a rational argument that requires you to think deeply but more likely to be persuaded by a simplistic argument; this comes about at least in part because your inattention makes you less able to develop a counterargument (Allyn & Festinger, 1961; Romero et al., 1996). So, if you are watching a typical TV commercial while sorting the laundry or cooking, you are more likely to be persuaded by the commercial than if your attention was fully focused on it. ▶ Watch

Tapping Into the Social Brain Attitudes reflect mental events that are often unconscious and therefore can be difficult to measure. One way to approach this thorny measurement problem is to examine the brain itself. Researchers in **social cognitive neuroscience** attempt to understand social cognition both by specifying the underlying mental events (such as those involved in memory, attention, and perception) and by discovering how the mental events are rooted in the brain (Blakemore et al., 2004; Gilbert, 2002; Heatherton, 2004; Ochsner & Lieberman, 2001).

For example, researchers in social cognitive neuroscience have asked whether people need to be consciously aware of cognitive dissonance in order to be motivated to reduce it. Traditionally, social psychologists believed that people do in fact need to be aware of the causes of cognitive dissonance in order to reduce this uncomfortable feeling. However, this question had never actually been addressed by research.

Matthew Lieberman and colleagues (2001) used a social cognitive neuroscience method to address this question. They studied patients with amnesia caused by brain damage; these patients could not consciously recall anything they had recently experienced. If you met the most severely affected of these patients, talked to him for 3 hours, and then left the room for 10 minutes, he would have no idea who you were when you returned (Schacter, 1996). Lieberman and colleagues realized that if cognitive dissonance reduction depends on consciously recalling the events that led to the dissonance, then the patients with amnesia should not experience dissonance reduction.

These researchers induced cognitive dissonance by using a classic task: If someone gives you two objects that you like almost to the same degree and requires you to decide which one you like better, you will end up liking the one you chose even more than you did at first (and disliking the rejected one; Brehm, 1956). Because the two objects are in fact so similar, you can find reasons for liking either one. Yet when forced to choose, you need to reduce the dissonance that arises from rejecting one that you do in fact like—but a hair less than the other—by exaggerating the differences between them.

By the end of the study, the researchers could answer the question, "Would such dissonance reduction operate even if a person could not consciously remember having to make the choice?" The conclusion was yes: Even amnesic patients—who immediately forgot having to make the choice—became more positive about the chosen object and more negative about the rejected one. That is, their attitudes toward the objects shifted even though these patients had no conscious memory of ever having chosen between the two almost equivalent objects! Thus, these findings challenge the traditional view; you don't need to be consciously aware of the causes of cognitive dissonance in order to try to reduce it.

When lawyers select people for a jury, they try to have certain potential jurors excluded because of stereotypes about how individuals of a certain race, sex, age, or profession are likely to view the case. But one study found that lawyers' stereotype-based expectations of whether jurors would be likely to convict a defendant were often incorrect (Olczak et al., 1991).

Source: John Neubauer\PhotoEdit Inc.

Stereotypes and Prejudice: Seen One, Seen 'Em All

In the social world we inhabit, we could easily be overwhelmed by the torrent of information conveyed by other people. This information comes from other people's words, postures, gestures, and facial expressions, which allow us in turn to make inferences about their attitudes and goals. In many cases, we also have information about them that comes from other sources—details and impressions recounted by other people. The world is overflowing with social information and stimuli, and if we had no way of organizing this enormous quantity of information, we would live in chaos. Some of the information that bombards our senses is organized by perceptual processes in our brains—but we're still left with an overload of social information.

To avoid drowning in this sea of social information, we create *stereotypes*, which organize information about people in useful ways (Allport, 1954; Gilbert & Hixon, 1991; Macrae et al., 1994). A **stereotype** is a belief (or set of beliefs) about people from a particular category; the category can be defined by race, sex, social class, religion, ethnic background, hair color, sport, hobby, or many other characteristics. A stereotype may be positive (such as "women are nurturing"), neutral (such as "Mexicans eat spicy food"), or negative (such as "soccer fans are too aggressive"). As we see in the following sections, stereotypes sometimes can lead us astray.

Stereotypes as Cognitive Shortcuts Because stereotypes assign social information to a category, they can serve as useful cognitive shortcuts. Here's an example of how this sort of shortcut works. Suppose that you have a positive stereotype of New Englanders, believing them to be punctual and hardworking. When you meet a woman from Maine, your "New Englander" stereotype is activated; you'll respond to her membership in that category ("New Englander"), not to her actual characteristics as a person. So, you'll be likely to assume that your new acquaintance is punctual and hardworking.

But stereotypes are caricatures—not reasoned formulations of people's character—and they are sometimes incorrect. When we make judgments about people based on our stereotypes, the stereotypes can mislead us. In particular, we are less likely to attend to—and therefore to encode or remember—information inconsistent with our stereotypes (Johnston & Macrae, 1994), and, in fact, we may deny the truth of such information (O'Sullivan & Durso, 1984).

Thus, because of how stereotypes work, we are *less likely* to process information that is inconsistent with our stereotypes: We may not notice such information, and if we do notice, we're less likely to remember it. Rather than process such inconsistent information and revise our stereotype, we tend to discard the information and preserve our stereotype. For example, after meeting the woman from Maine, you'll be more likely to notice aspects of her behavior that are consistent with your stereotype, and in thinking about her, you will be more likely to remember those aspects. You may not notice when she comes in late, or you will come up with plausible excuses for her tardiness and see it as the exception to the rule. In addition, the stereotype lives on and can shape your future thinking, in part, because you can recall faster information relevant to the stereotype than unrelated information (Dovidio et al., 1986).

Sometimes the discrepancy between a stereotype and the actual characteristics of someone from the stereotyped group is too great to be ignored. However, rather than change the stereotype, people typically create a new subtype within it (Anderson, 1983; Anderson et al., 1980). For example, if your New England acquaintance's chronic lateness and laziness are too obvious to ignore, you might create a subtype—"New Englander having a hard time coping"—that will apply to her. This allows you to preserve your original, overall stereotype of New Englanders as punctual and hardworking. Because of this psychological phenomenon—creating subtypes in order to preserve a stereotype—stereotypes can be extremely difficult to change or eliminate.

Fortunately, however, you are not a captive of your stereotypes, and they are not set in stone. If you are motivated to be accurate—and willing to exert extra cognitive effort—you can minimize the impact of stereotypes by not assuming that a stereotype applies to a particular person (Wyer et al., 2000). Moreover, you can change stereotypes when you think that the person's behavior results from his or her characteristics, not from the situation, and that the person is typical of his or her group (Wilder et al., 1996).

Stereotypes and Prejudice: Prejudging and Discriminating Another unfortunate consequence of stereotypes is **prejudice**, which is an attitude, generally negative, toward members of a group (Arkes & Tetlock, 2004). Prejudice includes two components: (1) a cognitive component (such as beliefs and expectations about the group) and (2) an emotional component (generally negative feelings toward the group). For instance, simply thinking about members of a disliked group can produce strong feelings about

Stereotype A belief (or set of beliefs) about people from a particular category.

Prejudice An attitude (generally negative) toward members of a group.

Discrimination Negative behavior toward individuals from a specific group that arises from unjustified negative attitudes about that group.

them (Bodenhausen et al., 1994). As is the case with attitudes and stereotypes in general, information inconsistent with a prejudice is less likely to be attended to and remembered accurately than is information consistent with a prejudice, making prejudice self-perpetuating.

Prejudice and Discrimination Prejudice often leads to **discrimination**, which is negative behavior toward individuals from a specific group that arises from unjustified negative attitudes about that group (Dovidio, 2000). Here's an example of how prejudice can lead to discrimination: When Bessie Delany was in dental school, a White professor failed her on some work that she knew was good. A White girlfriend, also a dental student, offered to hand in Bessie's work as her own to see what grade the work would be given this time. Bessie's friend passed with the same work that had earned Bessie a failing grade. This professor discriminated against Bessie because of his prejudice against her race—her membership in a particular social category.

As with stereotypes, discrimination may be based on just about anything that distinguishes groups: gender, race, social class, hair color, religion, college attended, height, weight, and on and on. As with prejudice, discrimination may be subtle. Nonetheless, most Americans believe that discrimination is wrong; when their own discriminatory behavior is pointed out to them, they are uncomfortable and may experience cognitive dissonance (Devine & Monteith, 1993)—and they may subsequently refrain from such behavior (Monteith, 1996), thereby reducing cognitive dissonance.

Why Does Prejudice Exist? The effects of prejudice are limiting, damaging, and painful. Why then does prejudice exist? Explanations include *realistic conflict, social categorization,* and *social learning,* as we discuss below. ✳️Explore

✳️Explore the Origins of Prejudice on mypsychlab.com

REALISTIC CONFLICT. According to the *realistic conflict theory* (Bobo, 1983; Sherif et al., 1961), prejudice exists because of competition for scarce resources such as good housing, jobs, and schools. As groups compete for these resources, they develop increasingly negative views of the other groups; these negative views eventually become prejudice.

A classic experiment, the Robber's Cave study, showed how easily competition can lead to prejudice (see Figure 2; Sherif et al., 1961). At an overnight camp called Robber's Cave, a set of 11-year-old boys was divided into two groups, Eagles and Rattlers. The two groups competed for valued prizes such as pocket knives and medals. Conflict between the two groups quickly escalated into prejudice and discrimination, with boys from competing

FIGURE 2 The Creation and Dissolution of Prejudice: The Robber's Cave Study

Phase 1: Eleven-year-old boys at a special overnight summer camp (called the Robber's Cave) were the participants in this study. In the initial 1-week phase of the study, the boys were randomly divided into two groups. During this time, activities fostered a sense of cohesion in each group.

Phase 2: For 2 weeks the two groups competed for highly desired prizes such as pocket knives and medals. Conflict between the two groups quickly escalated from name-calling to direct acts (destroying personal property). Negative attitudes as well as negative behavior developed, with each group's labeling members of the other with pejorative terms such as "coward."

Phase 3: The two groups were brought together to work on a number of shared goals, such as restoring the camp's water supply. Tensions between the groups dissolved by the sixth day of this phase.

groups sometimes calling each other names and even destroying each other's property. However, such attitudes and behavior stopped when the two groups no longer competed for resources and instead needed to cooperate for larger, mutually beneficial goals such as restoring the camp's water supply. The Robber's Cave study (and subsequent research on realistic conflict; Jackson, 1993) illustrates how prejudice can both develop and dissipate (Sherif et al., 1961).

SOCIAL CATEGORIZATION.   The Robber's Cave study supports the view of realistic conflict theory that competition between groups for scarce resources can produce prejudice. But scarcity and competition are not necessary to produce prejudice. For example, recall the different grades that Bessie's paper received when it was handed in by her and by a White student; the professor was not in competition with Bessie. Thus, realistic conflict theory can't be the only explanation for prejudice.

Social categorization provides another explanation for how prejudice arises when scarcity and competition aren't relevant: **Social categorization** leads people to sort others automatically into categories of "us" versus "them." You meet a new person, and automatically classify him or her as similar to you in some way ("us") or different ("them"). According to *social identity theory*, social categorization is important in part because people usually think of their own group—the **ingroup**—favorably and usually think about the other group—the **outgroup**—unfavorably. In fact, people not only dislike members of the outgroup but also assume that they possess more undesirable traits (Brewer & Brown, 1998; Fiske, 1998; Lambert, 1995; Rustemli et al., 2000; Tajfel, 1982). We are more inclined to like, trust, help, and cooperate with other ingroup members than we are to like, trust, help, and cooperate with outgroup members (Brewer & Brown, 1998).

Social categorization can lead to discrimination in two distinct ways: (1) The ingroup is actively favored, and (2) the outgroup is actively disfavored (DeSteno et al., 2004; Feather, 1996; Fiske, 2002; Perdue et al., 1990). In the case of Bessie's paper, we can speculate that the Professor viewed Whites as the ingroup (of which he was a member) and Blacks as the outgroup.

Social categorization is efficient because once we've made an "us" versus "them" distinction, we can then use our stereotypes about "us" and "them" to interpret people's behavior. We are thus spared the effort of paying close attention to other people and of actively processing our observations of their behavior. Unfortunately, the shortcuts that make social categorization efficient perpetuate a skewed picture of other people; significant effort may be required to notice when their behavior doesn't conform to our stereotypes, and so we (mis)perceive that they behave as we expect them to.

Social categorization can also *perpetuate* prejudice because once we classify an individual as a member of an outgroup, we induce that person to act according to our stereotypes about the outgroup (Bargh et al., 1996). How does this work? We may behave in ways that elicit behavior from an outgroup member that is consistent with that stereotype, even if he or she wouldn't otherwise behave that way (Major & O'Brien, 2005; Snyder, 1984, 1992). This process thus becomes a self-fulfilling prophecy: His or her elicited behavior confirms our stereotype, and we regard the outgroup member's behavior as "proof" of the validity of our prejudices (Fiske, 1998).

For example, suppose that Andre, who is an honors student, holds the stereotype that football players are not particularly smart (that is, Andre holds the "dumb jock" stereotype). In his chemistry class, Andre's assigned lab partner is Matt, the college's quarterback. When Andre talks

Social categorization The cognitive operation that leads people to sort others automatically into categories of "us" versus "them."

Ingroup A person's own group.

Outgroup A group other than a person's own.

According to social identity theory, members from both of these high school groups may view their own group as superior to the other, and these views (conscious or not) may lead to prejudicial behavior against those in the other group.

Sources: PhotoEdit Inc.; Stephen Simpson/Taxi/Getty Images

Recategorization A means of reducing prejudice by shifting the categories of "us" and "them" so that the two groups are no longer viewed as distinct entities.

to Matt, he makes sure not to use "big words" because he thinks Matt wouldn't understand. When performing their lab experiments, Andre also acts a bit like a professor, questioning Matt about what Matt is doing, "Why are you doing that, Matt? What do you expect to happen?" In turn, Matt becomes both angry at being treated like a child and nervous about making a mistake. For fear of making a mistake (and being humiliated by Andre), Matt tries to say and do as little as possible. In turn, Andre views Matt's minimal lab participation as "proof" that Matt is just a dumb jock and can't pull his weight in the partnership.

SOCIAL LEARNING. Once a prejudicial attitude is in place, *social learning theory* explains how it can be spread and passed through generations as a learned stereotype. Parents, peers, television, movies, and other aspects of the culture provide models of prejudice and discriminatory behavior that children learn and imitate (Pettigrew, 1969). Consider what children in Bosnia have been taught about Gavrilo Princip, the man who started World War I by assassinating Archduke Ferdinand D'Este of Austria-Hungary in 1914: Textbooks in the Serb-controlled part of Bosnia called the act "heroic," whereas textbooks in the Croatian-controlled part of Bosnia referred to Princip as an "assassin trained and instructed by the Serbs to commit this act of terrorism"—and a Muslim textbook referred to him as "a nationalist" and said that the resulting anti-Serbian rioting "was only stopped by police from all three ethnic groups" (Hedges, 1997).

In sum, scarce resources, competition, social categorization, and social learning may all contribute to the development and maintenance of prejudice.

Changing Prejudice: Easier Said Than Done Research has shown us how prejudice develops and deepens. At least as important, research can show us how to reduce prejudice. Prejudice can be reduced through *increased contact* between ingroup and outgroup members, *recategorization*, and *mutual interdependence*.

INCREASED CONTACT. One way to decrease prejudice is described by the *contact hypothesis*, which holds that increased contact between different groups will decrease prejudice between them (Pettigrew, 1981). Increased contact serves several purposes:

1. People in both groups are more likely to become aware of similarities between the groups, which can deemphasize group differences and enhance mutual attraction, thereby decreasing prejudice (Brewer & Miller, 1984).

2. Even though stereotypes resist change, when faced with enough inconsistent information or exceptions to the stereotypes (based on the personal experiences created through increased contact), people can change the stereotypes that give rise to their prejudice (Kunda & Oleson, 1995).

3. Increased contact between groups can shatter the illusion that the outgroup is homogeneous; such increased contact leads people in an ingroup to see differences among the people in the outgroup (Baron & Byrne, 1997).

In these ways, increased contact can reduce prejudice (Emerson et al., 2002), particularly under certain conditions, such as when people are working toward a shared goal and all of the people involved are deemed to be equal.

Many science fiction stories rely on recategorization to shift the animosity from country against country to a united Earth defending against a common enemy—aliens from space. Recategorization may decrease prejudice toward the new members of the ingroup, but some outgroup will undoubtedly still be thought of negatively (Tajfel, 1982). In the movie *Men in Black*, humans are allied with some aliens—a new definition of "us"—against a different type of alien.

Source: Everett Collection

RECATEGORIZATION. Another way to decrease prejudice is through **recategorization**—that is, shifting the categories of "us" and "them" so that the two groups are no longer viewed as distinct entities (Gaertner et al., 1993). The identity of "us" and "them" changes so that the distinction between the ingroup and outgroup blurs, and together they become seen as a single group. This is what happened in the final phase of the Robber's Cave study when, instead of being

Eagles or Rattlers, all boys became simply campers who had no running water. Recategorization is a staple of science fiction books and films: Different nations (previously categorized as ingroups and outgroups) come together to save the planet from aliens; when confronted by aliens, the shared group (category) of *human* becomes more important than the national groups.

MUTUAL INTERDEPENDENCE.   Social psychologist Eliot Aronson and his colleagues devised another way to decrease prejudice—the *jigsaw classroom*, which is a cooperative learning technique that requires students to depend on each other; this technique has been used in many American classrooms (Aronson & Osherow, 1980; Aronson & Patnoe, 1997). The technique proceeds in three steps:

STEP 1: Integrated groups of five or six students from different backgrounds are formed and given an assignment, such as learning about the American War of Independence (see Figure 3). Each member of a jigsaw group researches a different aspect of the project (such as military strategy, George Washington's actions, or women's roles);

STEP 2: After completing their individual research, the students researching the same topic form a new group—an *expert* group—composed of one member from each jigsaw group. For instance, all students researching George Washington will meet together after doing their research; this is the "George Washington" expert group. These expert groups meet to share information and rehearse presentations;

STEP 3: The expert groups then disband, and each member writes a report and reads it to his or her original jigsaw group.

The only way that jigsaw group members can learn about all of the topics is to pay close attention to everyone's reports; as with a jigsaw puzzle, each member's contribution is a piece of the whole, and each person depends on the others. The jigsaw classroom decreases prejudice (Aronson & Osherow, 1980; Walker & Crogan, 1998) in ways similar to other techniques: by increasing contact between individuals from different "groups" and creating new, integrated groups that require interdependence in order to achieve a larger goal.

> **THINK like a PSYCHOLOGIST** Suppose that you're living in an apartment or dorm where there's significant tension between two of your roommates; you think the tension is based on prejudices the two roommates have toward each other. Based on what you've read, which methods would you first use to decrease that tension and the underlying prejudices?

FIGURE 3 The Jigsaw Classroom

Step 1: The classroom is divided into groups of five or six children from different backgrounds (jigsaw groups), and each group studies the same general subject. The general subject has five or six separate research topics, and each group member is assigned a different topic to research.

Step 2: After each student does his or her research, the students reconfigure into expert groups, where one member from each jigsaw group meets with his or her counterparts from the other groups. Expert groups discuss the results of their research and practice their presentations. Above is the "George Washington" expert group.

Step 3: Each member of the jigsaw group presents his or her research to the rest of the group. Every student is tested on all of the information, so students must listen closely to every presentation. This method fosters interdependence and mutual respect and reduces prejudice.

Attributions: Making Sense of Events

When you read about the Delany sisters, how did you explain their successes? Did you say to yourself, "The sisters worked hard and persevered" or "They were lucky"? Whatever your reaction, it reflects a confluence of your attitudes, stereotypes, and prejudices—as well as the attributions you make. **Attributions** are explanations for the causes of events or behaviors.

What Is the Cause? In most cases, events and actions have many possible causes. An unreturned telephone call or text message from a friend might indicate that your friend is very busy, is annoyed at you, or is simply having problems with the phone. Similarly, if a politician you admire changes position on an issue, do you explain the change as a sincere change of heart, a cave-in to heavy campaign contributors, or a calculated attempt to appeal to new supporters?

The particular attributions people make are of two broad types: *internal* and *external*. **Internal attributions** (also called *dispositional attributions*) explain a person's behavior in terms of that person's beliefs, goals, or other characteristics. For instance, if a friend leaves a math lecture very confused, you could attribute his confusion to internal factors: "I guess he's not very good at math." **External attributions** (also called *situational attributions*) explain a person's behavior in terms of the situation (Kelley, 1972; Kelley & Michela, 1980). If you make an external attribution for your friend's confusion, you might say, "The professor gave a really bad lecture today." Table 2 provides examples of both types of attributions—about oneself and about others.

TABLE 2 **Examples of Types of Attributions**

	Internal Attributions	External Attributions
Attributions About Oneself	*Positive*: I did a good job because I'm smart.	*Positive*: I did a good job because the task was easy.
	Negative: I did a bad job because I'm inept.	*Negative*: I did a bad job because the time allotted for the task was too short.
Attributions About Others	*Positive*: She did a good job because she's smart.	*Positive*: She did a good job because the task was easy.
	Negative: She did a bad job because she's inept.	*Negative*: She did a bad job because the time allotted for the task was too short.

Attribution An explanation for the cause of an event or behavior.

Internal attribution An explanation of someone's behavior that focuses on the person's beliefs, goals, or other characteristics; also called *dispositional attribution*.

External attribution An explanation of someone's behavior that focuses on the situation; also called *situational attribution*.

Attributional bias A tendency to make certain types of attributions; this sort of bias generally occurs outside of conscious awareness.

Fundamental attribution error The strong tendency to interpret other people's behavior as arising from internal causes rather than external ones; also referred to as the *correspondence bias*.

Taking Shortcuts: Attributional Biases Like stereotypes, **attributional biases** are tendencies to make certain types of attributions; such biases are generally outside of our awareness. And like stereotypes, attributional biases function as shortcuts: they help us reduce the cognitive load required to make sense of the world—but they can lead us to make errors that have implications for social relationships, the legal system, and social policy. Let's examine some attributional biases: the *fundamental attribution error*, the *self-serving bias*, and the bias known as the *belief in a just world*.

THE FUNDAMENTAL ATTRIBUTION BIAS. The most important attributional bias is the **fundamental attribution error** (also called the *correspondence bias*; Ross et al., 1977), which is the strong tendency to interpret other people's behavior as arising from internal causes rather than external ones. This error is at work when the sight of a homeless man on a bench leads us to assume that his plight reflects an internal trait such as laziness rather than external factors such as a run of bad luck, a high unemployment rate, or a lack of affordable housing. The fundamental attribution error is at work when a driver cuts in front of you on the road, and you attribute his lack of road etiquette to his despicable personality traits rather than situational factors, such as that he's late for an appointment and so in a rush or that he accidentally drank coffee instead of the decaf he ordered before he got behind the wheel (Baxter et al., 1990). The fundamental attribution error is even at work when we attribute to an actor the personality characteristics of the character he or she played in a television show (Tal-Or & Papierman, 2007).

The fundamental attribution error affects many facets of our lives. For example, suppose you are a member of a jury and hear that the defendant confessed to the crime. It turns out that the confession was extracted after many hours of tough, coercive questioning by police. The judge then throws out the confession, striking it from the record, and tells you, the jury, to ignore it. Would you? Could you? Not likely—because of the fundamental attribution bias, jurors would probably interpret the confession as evidence of guilt (an internal attribute) rather than coercion (an external attribute). In fact, researchers using mock juries found that jurors in this situation assume that the confession was heartfelt and vote guilty more often than jurors who do not hear about a confession (Kassin & Wrightsman, 1981). Jurors can't just erase their attributions from their memories.

In addition, the fundamental attribution error helps perpetuate discrimination because we attribute fault to the person, not his or her circumstances. Moreover, once the fundamental attribution error affects your understanding of why a person behaved a certain way, you are likely to continue to make internal rather than external attributions and to ignore situational factors that give rise to future behavior. Thus, the effect of the initial error is multiplied.

Finally, as you read this, you probably think more about how this error is likely to apply to *other* people than to yourself: The fundamental attribution error is likely to lead you to assume that other people fall prey to the fundamental attribution error more than you do (van Boven et al., 2003)!

SELF-SERVING BIAS. Related to the fundamental attribution error is the **self-serving bias** (Brown & Rogers, 1991; M. G. Miller & Ross, 1975), which is the inclination to attribute your own failures to external causes and your successes to internal ones, but to attribute other people's failures to internal causes and their successes to external causes (see Table 3). As a result, you consider the negative actions of others as arbitrary and unjustified but perceive your own negative actions as understandable and justifiable (Baumeister et al., 1990). You are angry and slam things around because you've had a terrible day, but your roommate throws tantrums because he or she has an awful temper. (Note that when depressed, people typically make attributions that are the opposite to those related to the self-serving bias; Beck, 1967.)

Self-serving bias A person's inclination to attribute his or her own failures to external causes and own successes to internal causes, but to attribute other people's failures to internal causes and their successes to external causes.

Belief in a just world An attributional bias that assumes that people get what they deserve.

TABLE 3 Self-Serving Bias and Attributions

	Success	Failure
Your . . .	Internal attribution	External attribution
Others' . . .	External attribution	Internal attribution

A culture, ethnic group, or nation as a whole may engage in the self-serving bias, attributing positive values and traits to its own group and negative values and traits to other groups, thereby sustaining ethnic or cultural conflict (Rouhana & Bar-Tal, 1998). However, not all cultures exhibit these biases to the same degree. Just as different cultures value different personality traits, cultures also lead people to use attributional biases somewhat differently. For example, accounts of crimes in Chinese-language newspapers are more likely to give external explanations for the criminals' behavior, whereas for the same offense, English-language newspapers are more likely to emphasize internal factors (Morris & Peng, 1994).

BELIEF IN A JUST WORLD. Attributions can also be influenced by the bias known as a **belief in a just world** (Lerner, 1980), the assumption that people get what they deserve. The belief in a just world contrasts with the assumption that adverse events can happen randomly and "justice" may not always prevail. Consider this line of reasoning, caused by the belief in a just world bias: Because most Americans are richer than most Egyptians, Colombians, or Bulgarians, Americans must also be smarter or work harder. Similarly, if you have this type of bias, you're likely to think that if you get what

Because of the self-serving bias, you are likely to believe that you are kinder, more generous, and more selfless than other people. Research suggests that you probably overestimate your own generosity rather than underestimate that of other people (Epley & Dunning, 2000).

Source: The Image Works

487

you deserve, you must have done something to deserve what you get—notice the circular reasoning here!

The belief in a just world affects a variety of attitudes and behaviors. It can shape people's reactions to violent crime, particularly rape (Aguilar et al., 2008; Karuza & Carey, 1984), and can contribute to the practice of blaming the victim. For example, those who strongly believe in a just world are more likely than others to view AIDS among gay men as a deserved punishment for homosexual behavior (Glennon & Joseph, 1993) and to view the plight of a disadvantaged group, such as the homeless, as deserved (Dalbert & Yamauchi, 1994). Such beliefs can maintain discriminatory behaviors (Hafer & Choma, 2009; Lipkus & Siegler, 1993).

✓●─[Study and Review on
mypsychlab.com

LOOKING BACK

1. **What is the relationship between people's attitudes and their behaviors?** Attitudes affect how we process, encode, and remember information about the social world; brain-based methods can help us understand the unconscious mental events that give rise to attitudes. Attitudes that are strong, stable, relevant, important, and readily accessible are most likely to affect behavior. Attitudes and future behavior can change as a result of cognitive dissonance and persuasion. You are more likely to be persuaded via the central route by strong arguments, and via the peripheral route by the mere exposure effect and by a pursuader who is an expert, is attractive, speaks quickly, or is perceived as honest.

2. **What are stereotypes? Why do people have them? What is prejudice?** Stereotypes are beliefs or sets of beliefs about people in a particular social category; these beliefs help us to organize the large amount of information in the social world, but this organization may sometimes be misleading. Thus, although stereotypes can function as cognitive shortcuts, they may lead us to make mistakes; in addition, stereotypes may be outside our awareness and resistant to change. Prejudice is an attitude that contains a generally negative view toward members of a group. Prejudice can arise from negative feelings or from the absence of positive feelings and can give rise to discrimination. Social categorization and other cognitive operations can account for the perpetuation of prejudice. Prejudice can be decreased through increased contact, recategorization, and mutual interdependence.

3. **How do we determine responsibility for events and behaviors?** Attributions are ways we explain the cause of events or behaviors. There are two types of attributions: internal (dispositional) and external (situational). The fundamental attribution error, the self-serving bias, and the belief in a just world can lead to incorrect attributions.

Social Behavior: Interacting with People

The Delanys had very definite beliefs and attitudes about how they should and should not behave when they interacted with other people. For instance, they both wanted careers, but women of that era often had to choose between a career and marriage. Hence, relatively early in their lives, Sadie and Bessie decided not to marry. Moreover, they believed that they should be self-reliant and not depend on other people, based in part on specific advice from their parents. As an example, Sadie's father advised her not to take a scholarship from Columbia University because she might then feel indebted to the people who offered it. He encouraged her to pay for her own education. From their parents, they also learned to help others, regardless of skin color; the family motto was "Your job is to help someone."

The Delanys stuck by such beliefs and attitudes, even when others did not agree. Bessie recounted a time she vacationed in Jamaica with a darker-skinned Jamaican-born friend. There, Bessie learned that there were two official classes of Jamaican Negroes: "White Negroes," who had more privileges in society, and "Black Negroes," who were considered to be in a lower social class. The young women stayed with the family of Bessie's friend, who was a "Black Negro." "White Negroes" extended invitations to Bessie (a lighter-skinned

Black woman) and ignored her friend. Bessie refused all invitations until her friend was invited as well.

These examples illustrate *social behavior*. Whereas social cognition pertains to individuals' perceptions of and thoughts about the social world, social behavior pertains to the wide range of behaviors—from intimate relationships to obedience to others—that occur in and are affected by social situations.

LOOKING AHEAD Learning Objectives

1. What psychological principles explain why we like certain people and not others?
2. Why do all social groups have rules for social behavior and organization?
3. Why do we sometimes "go along with" or obey others even when we don't want to? Conversely, what makes us able to refuse?
4. Does being part of a group change our behavior? How do groups make decisions?
5. Are some people more helpful than others? What makes us likely to help other people?

Relationships: Having a Date, Having a Partner

Sadie and Bessie's White maternal great-great-grandmother had a liaison with a slave while her husband was away fighting in the War of 1812. This relationship produced two daughters who were half-sisters to the seven children she had already had with her husband. When her husband returned home, he adopted the two girls as his own. No one knew exactly what happened to her lover, although it was rumored that he ran away on the husband's return. The affair between the Delanys' great-great-grandmother and biological great-great-grandfather would appear to have been based on more than a passing interest, given that the relationship spanned a number of years. Why were these people attracted to each other? Why are we attracted to certain people but not others? Why do we like particular people, and love others?

As the Delanys ancestors undoubtedly experienced two centuries ago, and you may experience now, relationships are strong stuff. They can lead to our most positive emotions and can help us cope with events outside the relationship (Berscheid & Reis, 1998). Unfortunately, they can also be the source of negative emotions because of specific types of interactions, such as conflicts or disappointments (Ford et al., 2007; Ilies et al., 2009; Parkinson & Simons, 2009).

Liking: To Like or Not to Like Even though Sadie and Bessie decided not to marry, they did have boyfriends. Why did they like certain men but not others? As we discuss, *physical attraction*, *repeated contact*, and *similarity* can lead them—and you—to like someone.

PHYSICAL ATTRACTION. *Physical attraction* is a major factor that can lead you to like someone (Collins & Zebrowitz, 1995; Hatfield & Sprecher, 1986). Why? Because our stereotypes about attractive people—for instance, that they are smarter and happier—lead us to want to be around them. Although the stereotype that people who are physically more attractive possess more desirable attributes is found in many cultures, what constitutes "more desirable attributes" differs across cultures. For instance, in Korea, attractive people are thought to have greater integrity and concern for other people than do less attractive people (Wheeler & Kim, 1997).

REPEATED CONTACT. *Repeated contact* plays a role in whether you'll like someone. Typically, the more contact you have with someone, the more likely you are to think positively about that person (Moreland & Zajonc, 1982; Zajonc, 1968). You may have experienced this

Recent research recognizes that physical distance may no longer be as important as it once was for defining "repeated contact": Internet chat rooms and interest groups make it possible for a couple to "meet" and have a relationship without any physical contact (Bargh et al., 2002; McKenna et al., 2002; Parks & Roberts, 1998).

Source: © Alex Segre/Alamy

yourself: After repeatedly chatting with a neighbor or classmate, you find yourself increasingly drawn to the person, even if you weren't at your first meeting. Repeated contact probably explains, in part, how the relationship between the Delany's biological great-great-grandparents came to be something more than slave and slave owner. The Delany sisters recount that a lot of "racial mixing, especially after slavery days, was just attraction between people, plain and simple, just like happened in our family, on Mama's side. You know, when people live in close proximity, they can't help but get attracted to each other" (Delany et al., 1993, p. 76).

SIMILARITY. *Similarity* is a third factor that influences who you will like. New acquaintances can be similar to you in a variety of ways. One type of similarity is based on attitudes: The more similar the new acquaintance's attitudes are to your own, the more likely you are to be attracted to him or her (Montoya & Horton, 2004; Tesser, 1993). Thus, the adage "opposites attract" has *not* been borne out by research. Increased attraction and liking can also arise if you and another person prefer to engage in similar activities (Lydon et al., 1988) and even if you and another person use similar ways to communicate nonverbally (Dew & Ward, 1993). In general, the greater the similarity, the more probable it is that your liking for another person will endure (Byrne, 1971).

Loving: How Do I Love Thee? Psychologists have examined the variations in how and why we love as well as the components, styles, and fate of love over time. One key finding is that love isn't simply very strong liking; it's a qualitatively different feeling (Rubin, 1970). Moreover, attitudes about and experiences with love are similar across cultures as diverse as those of Russia, Japan, and the United States (Sprecher et al., 1994). Let's explore more about the psychological aspects of love relationships as we focus on *types* of love, *dimensions* of love, and *attachment styles*.

TYPES OF LOVE. People talk about "loving" many sorts of things in many sorts of ways. You might say that you love a pet, a friend, a parent, a mate, and pizza with anchovies; obviously you don't mean quite the same thing in each case. Although many distinctions have been drawn among types of love, when psychologists focus on love that involves another person, they distinguish between *companionate* and *passionate* love.

Companionate love is an altruistic type of love characterized by expending time, attention, and resources on behalf of another person (Fehr et al., 2008). Companionate love is described in many religions and is also what parents typically feel for their children. In contrast, **passionate love** is the intense, often sudden feeling of being "in love," and it typically involves sexual attraction, a desire for mutual love and physical closeness, arousal, and a fear that the relationship will end (Berscheid, 2006; Hatfield & Sprecher, 1986).

FIGURE 4 Sternberg's Triangular Model of Love

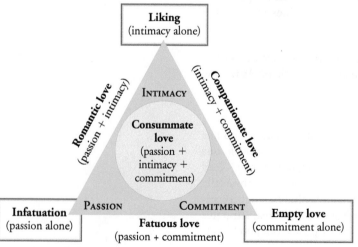

According to Sternberg's triangular theory of love, passion, intimacy, and commitment form three points of a triangle. Any given relationship may have only one component (at a point), two components (one of the sides of the triangle), or all three components (the center of the triangle).
Source: From *The Triangle of Love*, by Robert J. Sternberg. Reprinted by permission of Robert Sternberg.

DIMENSIONS OF LOVE. Not all romantic or sexual relationships are characterized by passionate love; according to the **triangular model of love**, romantic or sexual relationships can be thought of as having three dimensions (Sternberg, 1986, 1988):

1. *passion* (including sexual desire),
2. *intimacy* (emotional closeness and sharing), and
3. *commitment* (the conscious decision to be in the relationship).

Particular relationships and types of love reflect different proportions of each dimension (as shown in Figure 4), in amounts that are likely to vary over the course of a relationship. According to Sternberg's theory, most types of love relationships involve two of the three components; only consummate love has passion, intimacy, *and* commitment.

LOVE: ATTACHMENT STYLES. *Attachment style*—the manner of behaving with and thinking about a partner—is another way of conceptualizing or classifying different kinds of love relationships. Psychologists have found that the attachment style you exhibit with a partner stems from the interaction pattern you had with your parent or other primary caregiver when you were a child (Waller & Shaver, 1994). Adult attachment styles can be grouped into three types:

1. *Secure attachment style*, in which adults seek closeness and interdependence in relationships and are not worried about possibly losing the relationship because they feel secure in it. About 59% of an American sample are said to have this attachment style (Mickelson et al., 1997).

2. *Avoidant attachment style*, in which adults are uncomfortable with intimacy and closeness. About 25% of an American sample have this style and structure their daily lives in order to avoid closeness (Tidwell et al., 1996).

3. *Anxious-ambivalent style*, in which adults want but simultaneously fear a relationship (Hazan & Shaver, 1990). About 11% of an American sample have this style.

Although studies indicate that a majority of Americans have a secure attachment style (Hazan & Shaver, 1987), an anxious–ambivalent style is more common in Japan and Israel than in the United States, and an avoidant style more common in Germany than in the United States (Shaver & Hazan, 1994).

Mating Preferences: Your Cave or Mine? Finding someone attractive and liking—or even loving—that person is different from choosing him or her as a mate; we may date people we wouldn't necessarily want to marry. Why do we view certain people and not others as potential mates? According to evolutionary theory, our ancestors who were more closely bonded to their mates were more likely to have offspring who survived (Trivers, 1972). But what characteristics led people to choose mates to whom they became closely bonded? In the sections that follow, we explore this topic—*mate selection*—in more detail.

EVOLUTIONARY REASONS FOR MATE SELECTION. David Buss (1989) asked people in 37 countries to rank 18 different characteristics in order of how important they are in ideal mates. In most respects, men and women valued the characteristics similarly; everybody agreed, for example, that kindness and intelligence are of paramount importance and that emotional stability, dependability, and a good disposition are important (also found by Cramer et al., 1996; Li et al., 2002). Respondents also valued mutual attraction and love.

However, the specifics varied somewhat for men and women: Men tended to value and focus on a woman's physical attractiveness, whereas women tended to focus on a man's wealth and power. Other research expands on these findings: Men are attracted by women who have a well-proportioned body and symmetrical features, which—according to evolutionary theory—signal a woman's fertility and health (Thornhill & Gangestad, 1993). This view is supported by research with identical female twins (although such twins look alike, they their faces usually have minor differences); the twin whose face was more symmetrical was rated as more attractive (Mealey et al., 1999).

Do women view these same characteristics as attractive in men? Not to the same degree as do men; instead, women are attracted to men who appear to be able to protect and nourish them and their children. In modern society, researchers translate this characteristic as having good earning potential—men who seem like they will be good providers (Buss, 1989, 1999; Sprecher et al., 1994; Trivers, 1972, 1985).

MATE SELECTION: NOT JUST FOR EVOLUTIONARY REASONS. Not all studies support the evolutionary view, however. For example, researchers Ann Speed and Steven Gangestad (1997) asked members of a sorority and a fraternity to indicate which other members had a high degree of specific qualities, such as physical attractiveness and likelihood of financial success. The investigators then examined which of these characteristics predicted how frequently the members were asked out on dates. Perhaps the most interesting results concerned the men. As expected, romantically popular men were seen by their peers as confident, outgoing, and "trend-setting." However, contradicting evolutionary theory, these men were not seen as likely to succeed

Companionate love An altruistic type of love characterized by expending time, attention, and resources on behalf of another person.

Passionate love The intense, often sudden feeling of being "in love," which typically involves sexual attraction, a desire for mutual love and physical closeness, arousal, and a fear that the relationship will end.

Triangular model of love The theory that love has three dimensions: passion, intimacy, and commitment.

Evolutionary theorists propose that women are attracted to men who will be good providers and that men are attracted to women who have physical attributes associated with fertility. However, not all research supports this view: As women gain more economic power, they become more interested in a man's physical attractiveness.

Source: Woodfin Camp & Associates, Inc.

What constitutes an "attractive" body type differs over time and across cultures. Women who today would be considered overweight or even obese in the United States have a body type that has been and continues to be attractive in some other cultures.

Source: Art Resource, N.Y.

financially, nor were they rated as the best leaders—characteristics that would seem to reflect the qualities that evolution is supposed to favor in males.

Most importantly, other studies have shown that when women achieve economic power, their preference in mates becomes more similar to men's—that is, physical attractiveness becomes more important (Eagly & Wood, 1999; Gangestad, 1993). Women's preference for men who make good providers may reflect women's historic economic dependence on men rather than a true biological preference. Moreover, in general, the sex differences are more pronounced in situations in which women have less economic power and in studies that use self-reports than in ones that measure actual behavior (Feingold, 1990).

Culture also plays an important role in shaping mate preferences: What is deemed an attractive body type changes with generations (Wolf, 1991): In previous generations, the ideal female body shape apparently was full-figured and what we would now consider a bit overweight; in contrast, the current Western cultural ideal body shape for women is thin and muscular. Similarly, the characteristics that make a man a good provider depend in part on the culture and subculture and the man's role in it; the traits that make a man a good rancher are not necessarily those of a good stockbroker. In short, it would be an error to assume that what people find attractive or unattractive in a potential mate can be entirely explained by analyses of what might have been useful for mating among our distant ancestors.

Social Organization: Group Rules, Group Roles

It's not easy to define what, exactly, constitutes a "group." If you live with other people, in the same apartment or on the same dorm floor, you might agree that the people in your living unit constitute a group, even if you don't get along. But if you live in a building with a number of apartments or in a residence hall with many floors, would everyone living there be considered part of a group, even if they don't all know one another?

Social psychologists have defined what constitutes a group in a number of different ways, but certain commonalities cut across the various definitions. Specifically, a **group** is a social entity characterized by regular interaction among members, some type of social or emotional connection with one another, a common frame of reference, and a degree of interdependence (Levine & Moreland, 1998). In a group, each of us may feel, think, and act less from the point of view of an individual and more from the point of view of a group member. Military training during boot camp is a dramatic example of a situation that promotes the shift from feeling like an individual to feeling like a group member: Loyalties and actions may no longer be driven by individual goals but rather by group goals.

Norms: The Rules of the Group
The Delany sisters recount that in their hometown of Raleigh, North Carolina, even strangers passing on the street would nod and say good morning or good evening. However, when Sadie and Bessie moved to New York City, they discovered that courteous behavior toward strangers did not always bring about

Group A social entity characterized by regular interaction among members, some emotional connection, a common frame of reference, and a degree of interdependence.

a pleasant exchange, and they had to learn a new way of behaving in their new social context. Perhaps you, like them on their arrival in New York, have at one time or another been the "new kid on the block"—in school or college, in a new neighborhood, or in an already established group of people. Chances are you didn't know the "rules"—how people were supposed to behave toward one another, and especially how you, a new member, were supposed to behave. Once you figured things out by watching other people (Gilbert, 1995)—an obvious case of observational learning—you probably felt more comfortable in the group. And, in fact, groups create such rules and structures to help the group function.

The rules that implicitly or explicitly govern members of a group are called **norms**. They are, in essence, guides for behavior that are enforced through the group's use of *sanctions*, or penalties (Cialdini & Trost, 1998). Norms pervade our everyday experience, defining the behaviors that make us good family members, friends, neighbors, partners, employees, employers, students, teachers, and so on. Norms guide us in what we say and do—and don't say and don't do—even in virtual groups such as chat rooms and listserves (Bargh & McKenna, 2004).

Norms can affect all kinds of behavior, including a cold sufferer's willingness to wear a surgical mask when out in public. This Japanese woman is behaving according to one of her culture's norms: It is frowned on for a cold sufferer to go outside without a mask and spread cold germs to others.

Source: © Burbank/The Image Works

Although norms can endure over time, even if the members of the group change (Jacobs & Campbell, 1961), norms can also change. For example, when the term "Ms." was first introduced as a form of address, people thought that it would be used only by radical feminists. Now, however, it is much more widely used and positively viewed (Crawford et al., 1998). Another example of changing norms is found among adolescents in India who watch TV shows made in Western cultures (and derive from them what they perceive of as Western norms). Their attitudes about drugs, alcohol, and sex have changed to reflect Western values, leading them to reject the restrictive social norms of Indian society and become more Western (Varma, 2000).

Roles: Expected Behaviors

Within a group, **roles** are the behaviors that members in different positions in the group are expected to perform. Whereas norms are rules that apply to most members of a group, roles are rules that apply only to those who occupy specific positions within the group. Roles help a group to define both responsibility *within* the group (how you are supposed to interact with other members) and also responsibility *to* the group (what you are supposed to accomplish for the group). Groups often create different roles to fulfill different group functions. Sometimes roles are assigned officially, such as occurs when a group votes for a leader; sometimes roles are filled informally, without a specific election or appointment.

When Roles Become Reality: The Stanford Prison Experiment

In some circumstances, we can slip into a role without intending to do so, as indicated by a classic study by Philip Zimbardo and colleagues known as the *Stanford Prison Experiment* (Haney et al., 1973; Haney & Zimbardo, 1976; Zimbardo et al., 2000). Here's what happened: Zimbardo placed the following ad in the local newspaper, the *Palo Alto Times*: "Male college students needed for psychological study of prison life. $15 per day for 1–2 weeks. . . ." Some 70 people applied, and the 24 judged to be most healthy and "normal" (having no history of psychological problems or past problems with the police or drugs) were selected. Half of these students were randomly assigned (by flipping a coin) to be guards and half to be prisoners; the prisoners were kept in makeship prison cells in the basement of the psychology building. Of these, nine students actually played guards, and nine played prisoners; the others were backups, in case they were needed later.

Student prisoners received prison uniforms, stayed in cells, and were referred to only by a number—all of which served as regular reminders of their new roles. The guards, on the other hand, were given guard uniforms, handcuffs, keys, whistles, and billy clubs. The guards had offices, which—unlike the prisoners' cells—they were free to enter and leave as they pleased. The guards habitually wore mirrored sunglasses, which were intended to disorient the prisoners by cutting them off from common social cues such as seeing the full facial expressions of the guards. The students playing the role of guards were not given any

Norm A rule that implicitly or explicitly governs members of a group.

Role The behaviors that a member in a given position in a group is expected to perform.

493

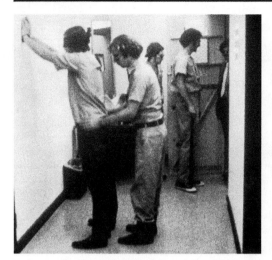

In the Stanford Prison Experiment, student guards fell into their roles easily, exploring their power. Student prisoners, in turn, reacted to their new roles by staging a rebellion.

Source: Philip G. Zimbardo, Inc., Department of Psychology, Stanford University

specific training or instructions other than to maintain "law and order" and to behave in a way that would command the respect of the prisoners.

The purpose of the experiment was to observe how the relationships between prisoners and guards developed over time. In remarkably short order, prisoners behaved passively, as if they realized that because they had no control over what happened to them, they should stop trying. In contrast, the guards began to act as if they had genuine power over the prisoners and to explore the limits of that power. Some, but not all, of the guards taunted the prisoners and harassed them (such as by sliding their billy clubs across the bars, causing a click-clacking repetitive slapping sound). After a while, the prisoners became active, staging a rebellion. The guards responded with force and put the rebellion's leaders in solitary confinement.

Zimbardo later reported that he was shocked at how quickly and deeply the prisoners and guards slipped into opposing roles. He was so disturbed by the turn of events that he terminated the experiment early; the expected 2-week duration of the study shrank to only 6 days. The participants in this study were ordinary, middle-class, healthy students who were randomly assigned to the different roles. The situation alone seems to have transformed not only their perceptions and behavior but also aspects of their characters. Assuming a role within a group can have profound effects.

Zimbardo (2004) attributes the atrocities committed by American military guards to Iraqi prisoners at Abu Ghraib prison in 2004 to the same situational factors that were at work during his Stanford experiment—roles and norms. Others, however, point out that personality factors were probably also at work at Abu Ghraib, and these factors did not play a role in the Stanford Prison Experiment: Zimbardo's participants had been carefully screened to exclude those with a history of aggression, legal, substance, or psychological problems. Abu Ghraib's guards had no such screening, and one guard, at least, had several restraining orders against him by his ex-wife because of his history of violence (Saletan, 2004).

Yielding to Others: Going Along With the Group

Part and parcel of human interactions is "going along to get along"—agreeing to people's requests in order to minimize conflict or to achieve goals. The Delany sisters were no exception. Nevertheless, in some situations the sisters did not simply comply with requests. For example, in Raleigh when the Jim Crow laws were in effect, Black customers in a White-owned shoe store were supposed to sit in the back of the store to try on shoes. On one occasion when Sadie Delany shopped for shoes, she was asked by the White owner, Mr. Heller, to sit in the back. Sadie asked, 'Where, Mr. Heller?' And he gestured to the back saying, 'Back there.' And I would say, 'Back where?' . . . Finally, he'd say, 'Just sit anywhere, Miss Delany.' And so I would sit myself down in the White section, and smile".

Source: Sarah L. Delany, Annie E. Delany, and Amy Hearth, *Having Our Say.* Kodansha America, 1993, p. 84.

What made Sadie able to resist Mr. Heller's request—or his order, backed by law? What made Mr. Heller give up his attempt to have Sadie comply with the law and social convention? What made him call her "Miss Delany" and not "Sadie"? These questions lead us to focus on three types of circumstances: conformity (we go along with the group), compliance (complying with a request), and obedience (obeying orders). We discuss each topic in turn.

Conformity and Independence: Doing What's Expected Social norms tell us how we ought to behave, and sometimes we change our behavior in order to follow these norms. This change in behavior in order to follow a group's norms is known as **conformity**. For example, immigrants must decide how much to conform to the norms of their new country and how much to retain the ways of their homeland (Lorenzo-Hernandez, 1998). More examples: suppose you are working in a study group that is trying to solve a complex engineering problem or that you are part of a medical team trying to agree on a diagnosis of a particularly perplexing case. The majority of other members of the group agree on an answer that doesn't seem right to you. What would make you more likely to go along with the majority view? Two types of social influence—*informational* and *normative*—can lead you to conform. ◉—Watch

▶Watch the Video Social Influence on mypsychlab.com

Conformity A change in behavior in order to follow a group's norms.

INFORMATIONAL SOCIAL INFLUENCE. *Informational social influence* occurs when we conform to others because we believe that their views are correct or their behavior is appropriate for the situation (Cialdini & Goldstein, 2004). This type of conformity is most likely to occur when:

- *the situation is ambiguous* (so that you are not confident of a "correct" answer or action),
- *there is a crisis* (so that quick action is crucial, and there isn't time to deliberate about the correctness of the view or action),
- *the task is very difficult* (which makes you less sure of yourself), or
- *other people are experts* (and so you are more likely to assume that they are correct).

NORMATIVE SOCIAL INFLUENCE.   *Normative social influence* occurs when we conform because we want to be liked or thought of positively. This sort of conformity was powerfully demonstrated in pioneering research by Solomon Asch (1951, 1955). If you had been a participant in Asch's original study, you would have found yourself in a group with five to seven others and been asked to perform a task of visual perception. You are all shown a target line and asked to say which of three other lines matches the length of the target line. Each person gives an answer aloud; you are next to last. This sounds like an easy task, as you can see in Figure 5, but it soon becomes perplexing. For 12 of the 18 times you are shown the lines, everyone else gives what seems to you to be clearly the wrong answer! Will you agree with the answer everyone else is giving?

In fact, in Asch's experiment, only one person in the group was the actual participant; the others were confederates (people who were enlisted to help carry out the study) playing a role. Seventy-six percent of the actual participants went along with the confederates at least once, and approximately one third of participants' total responses conformed with the obviously wrong majority.

Why would these people conform with the norm established by the group? Variations on Asch's original experiment showed that characteristics of the situation are part of the answer: Participants want the sense of belonging to the group, and don't like to contradict other group members publicly. In a modified version of the study, when participants *wrote* their answers instead of announcing them to the group (participants did not know what answers other people gave), participants gave the correct response 98% of the time.

FIGURE 5 Asch's Conformity Study

Participants in Asch's classic study on conformity were shown lines similar to these (at left) and asked the following type of question: Here are three lines of different lengths and a fourth target line. Which of the three lines matches the target line?

Only two people have yet to give their opinions, but everyone else has given the same incorrect answer. Which would you say was the correct line if you were next to answer? Asch (1951, 1955) created this situation by including confederates who were told in advance how to respond; the true participant was the next-to-last person. Although 76% of participants conformed to the incorrect group response at least once, over the entire experiment, approximately two thirds of responses were independent of the majority and did not conform.

Compliance A change in behavior brought about by a direct request rather than by social norms.

Foot-in-the-door technique A technique that achieves compliance by beginning with an insignificant request, which is then followed by a larger request.

SOCIAL SUPPORT. *Social support* (the assistance and psychological comfort provided by others) also influences conformity: If another group member openly disagrees with the group consensus, conformity then decreases (Morris & Miller, 1975). When Asch had one confederate disagree—that is, give the correct answer—before it was the participant's turn to answer, 91% of the actual participants also did not conform with the majority (incorrect) answer.

Were the people in Asch's study typical? All were men, but the results of later studies with women as participants were similar (Eagly & Carli, 1981). However, Asch's original participants may have been influenced by their culture. His experiment has been repeated by many researchers in many countries, and studies in countries with a more *collectivist* orientation (which emphasize the rights and responsibilities of the group over those of the individual) found higher levels of conformity than did those in *individualistic* countries (which emphasize the rights and responsibilities of the individual over those of the group; Bond & Smith, 1996). Moreover, the findings of conformity studies over the years suggest that conformity has decreased since Asch's original work was done (Bond & Smith, 1996). Thus, characteristics of the individual, characteristics of the group, and of the larger culture can all affect conformity and independence.

Compliance: Doing What You're Asked

Even if you don't want to conform to a group's norms, you may be willing to comply with a direct request, as occurs when someone asks, "Could you please tell me how to get to the library?" **Compliance** is a change in behavior brought about by a direct request rather than by social norms. When the driver of the car in the next lane gestures to you, asking to be let into your lane in front of you, you either will or will not comply.

PRINCIPLES OF COMPLIANCE. Skill at getting people to comply is a key to success in many occupations, from sales and advertising to lobbying, politics, and health prevention programs. Without realizing it, you are a target of multiple requests for compliance each day, from a variety of sources including TV and Internet ads, emails, and chat rooms. Psychologist Robert Cialdini decided to find out from "compliance professionals"—people in jobs such as advertising, fund-raising, and door-to-door sales—exactly what they know about the subject. He inferred that the essence of effective compliance techniques lies in six principles (Cialdini, 1994; Cialdini & Goldstein, 2004):

1. *Friendship/liking.* People are more likely to comply with a request from a friend than from a stranger.
2. *Commitment/consistency.* People tend to be more likely to comply when the request is consistent with an idea or goal that they've previously embraced. For instance, if you decide to buy something using a coupon (that is, you've committed to the purchase) but find out at checkout that the coupon has expired, you're still more likely to follow through and make the purchase.
3. *Scarcity.* People are more likely to comply with requests related to a limited, short-term opportunity ("Buy now, limited time offer") rather than open-ended opportunities.
4. *Reciprocity.* People tend to comply with a request that comes from someone who has previously provided a favor. For instance, you're more likely to comply with your neighbor's request to look after her cat for the weekend if she's taken in packages for you while you were away.
5. *Social validation.* People are more likely to comply if they think that many others—particularly those similar to themselves—have complied or would comply. For instance, you're more likely to stop buying bottled water and use tap water when you think that many people in your neighborhood are doing that.
6. *Authority.* People tend to comply with a request if it comes from someone who appears to be in authority.

THINK like a **PSYCHOLOGIST** Have you ever tried to get others to comply with your wishes by applying any of these principles? If so, which one(s)? Were you successful? Based on what you've read, can you think of ways that you could resist attempts by others to lead you to comply with their wishes?

COMPLIANCE TECHNIQUES. To see these principles at work, let's examine a few of the techniques most often used to win compliance. The commitment/consistency principle underlies a common compliance technique, the **foot-in-the-door technique**: first you make an insignificant request; if the person complies, you follow up with a larger request. Consider the classic study by Freedman and Fraser (1966), who had a male investigator phone housewives, asking what brand of soap they used. Three days later, the same man telephoned and asked if five or six people could perform a 2-hour inventory of everything in the housewife's cupboards, drawers, and closets. Fifty-three percent of the housewives who had agreed to the simple first request agreed to this much larger second request. In contrast, when housewives did not receive the first request but were asked to allow the inventory, only 22% complied. The foot-in-the-door technique appears to work, at least in part, because people want to appear consistent (Guadagno et al., 2001). If you agree to the first request, you are being a nice person; declining the second request would call this self-perception into question.

The commitment/consistency principle also explains the success of an unethical sales technique, the **lowball technique**, which consists of first getting someone to make an agreement and then increasing the cost of that agreement. Suppose you see an advertisement for some shoes you've been eyeing—for a very low price. You go the store and are told that the shoes are no longer available at that price but that you can get them for a somewhat higher (although still discounted) price. What do you do? Many people would comply with the request to buy the shoes at the higher price.

Car salespeople are notorious for using the lowball technique; however, some carmakers have changed to a nonnegotiable pricing policy so that there is less opportunity for the lowball technique.

Source: Jeremy Green\Alamy Images

Reversing the foot-in-the-door procedure also works; this is the **door-in-the-face technique**. You begin by making a very large request; when it is denied, as expected, you make a smaller request—for what you actually wanted in the first place. For instance, in one study (Cialdini et al., 1975), college students were stopped on campus and asked to serve as unpaid counselors to a group of juvenile delinquents for 2 hours a week for 2 years. Not surprisingly, no one agreed. Then the same students were asked to take the group on a 2-hour field trip, and 50% agreed. In contrast, when students were asked only to make the field trip without the larger, first request, only 17% agreed. The door-in-the-face technique is a staple of diplomacy and labor–management negotiations. Why does it work? The reciprocity principle may hold the answer. If your first request is denied and you then make a smaller one, you appear to be making concessions, and the other party tries to reciprocate.

Obedience: Doing as You're Told If people can be so obliging in response to a polite request, what happens when they receive an order? **Obedience** refers to compliance with an order. The nature of obedience attracted intense study in the United States after World War II, when the world heard about Nazi atrocities—brutal murders, horrific medical experiments, and torture—some apparently committed by people who said they were obeying an order.

THE MILGRAM STUDY. The most famous study of obedience was carried out by Stanley Milgram (1963). Milgram expected that Americans would not follow orders to inflict pain on innocent people. In testing this hypothesis, his challenge was to design a procedure that appeared to inflict pain without actually doing so. He devised the following procedure: At the outset, you would be a volunteer in a study of memory. You arrive at the laboratory and are asked to act the part of "teacher" (see Figure 6 on the next page). You are paired with a "learner" (a confederate), who, you are told, was asked to memorize a list of pairs of common words. You, the teacher, are to present one word from each pair and keep track of how well the learner does in correctly remembering the other word. If the learner makes a mistake, you are to administer an electric shock, increasing the voltage with each successive mistake. Although the shock generator is a phony and no shock at all is administered, you do not know this.

By prearrangement, when the teacher flips the switch for 120 volts, the learner shouts that the shocks are becoming too painful. At 150 volts, the learner asks to stop. At 180, he screams that he can't stand the pain. At 300, he pounds on the wall and demands to be set free. At 330 volts, there is only silence—an "incorrect response," which requires delivering an even stronger jolt according to the directions of the experimenter, who stands beside the teacher.

How far would you go in obeying the experimenter's instructions, increasing the intensity of the shock with each mistake? If you are like the participants in Milgram's study, when the

Lowball technique A compliance technique that consists of getting someone to make an agreement and then increasing the cost of that agreement.

Door-in-the-face technique A compliance technique in which someone makes a very large request and then when it is denied (as expected) makes a smaller request—for what is actually desired.

Obedience Compliance with an order.

FIGURE 6 The Milgram Obedience Study

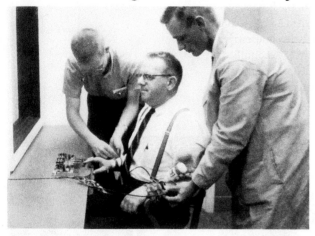

Each participant was paired with another man; the participant was always designated as, the "teacher." The "learner" was always the same 47-year-old accountant who was a confederate in the study. The man who introduced himself as the experimenter was an actor. The teacher was to present a list of pairs of common words, keep track of how well the learner memorized the word pairs, and punish the learner for incorrect responses. The teacher watched as the learner was brought to a cubicle where the experimenter asked him to sit down and strapped him in a chair to "prevent excess movement." The experimenter attached shock electrodes to his wrist. Throughout the remainder of the study, the teacher could not see the learner, and all communication took place via an intercom.

The teacher was seated in front of the shock generator. The generator had 30 switches labeled in 15-volt increments from 15 to 450 volts. A description below each switch ranged from "Slight Shock" to "Danger: Severe Shock." The labels under the last two switches were ominous: "XXX." At the outset, the teacher was given a sample shock of 45 volts so that he could know what it felt like.

Source: Both photos: Copyright 1968 by Stanley Milgram. Copyright Renewed 1993, Alexander Milgram. From the film OBEDIENCE, distributed by Penn State Media Sales

THINK like a PSYCHOLOGIST Have you ever had the experience of being ordered to do something that made you uncomfortable? If so, based on what you have read, what factors may have contributed to your willingness to obey or disobey the order?

learner cries out in pain or refuses to go on, you would turn to the experimenter for instructions, who would reply that the experiment had to proceed and that he would take full responsibility. Would you obey? When Milgram described the experiment to a group of psychiatrists, they predicted that only a "pathological fringe" of at most 2% of the population would go to the maximum shock level. In fact, much to Milgram's surprise, 65% of the participants went to the highest level. Some of the participants, but apparently not all, felt terrible about what they were doing. Yet they still continued to administer the shocks.

UNDERSTANDING MILGRAM'S RESULTS. Many people were disturbed by the fact that so many of Milgram's participants were willing to obey orders to hurt others. Was there something distinctive about Milgram's participants that could explain the results? In the original studies, the participants were all men. Later studies, however, found similar results with women (Milgram, 1965, 1974), as well as with people in Jordan, Germany, and Australia and with children (Kilham & Mann, 1974; Shanab & Yahya, 1977).

Why did so many participants obey orders to hurt someone else? Were there particular characteristics of the situation that fostered obedience? Compliance research suggests two ways in which the study's design increased the likelihood of obedience: (1) Milgram's experiment applied something like the foot-in-the-door-technique: Participants were first ordered to give a trivial amount of shock before going on to give apparently harmful ones. When participants were allowed to set the punishment voltage themselves, none ever went past 45 volts; (2) people become more likely to comply with a request if it comes from someone in authority; the same holds true for obedience (Bushman, 1984, 1988). In a variant of the study (Milgram, 1974), when a college student was the one who gave a fellow student the order to shock, instead of an older, white-coated experimenter, obedience fell to only 20%. When the experimenters were two authority figures who disagreed with each other, no participants administered further shocks. It appears that the more authoritative the person who gives the order, the more likely it is that he or she will be obeyed; when someone in authority gives an order, the person obeying can deny responsibility for his or her actions.

Later variations of Milgram's original study identified other characteristics of the situation that have an important influence on obedience, such as how near the teacher is to the learner. When teachers saw the learners while they were being shocked—and even held an electrode directly on the learner's skin (with a "special insulating glove")—30% of participants progressed to the maximum voltage, compared with 65% in the original design. And how near the teacher is to the experimenter also matters: When the experimenter telephoned his commands to the teacher instead of giving face-to-face instructions, obedience dropped to 21%.

In general, Milgram found that most people would obey orders to inflict pain. However, as disturbing as Milgram's results were, it is important to remember that not all participants obeyed the experimenter—and in some conditions the great majority did not obey; it is the specifics of the situation (such as proximity to the learner) that influence whether an individual will obey an order to hurt someone else (Blass, 1999; Gibson, 1991; A. G. Miller et al., 1995).

Performance in Groups: Working Together

Most people spend much of their daily lives with other people. When Sadie and Bessie went to New York City, they moved into their brother Hubert's apartment, along with another brother and sister; five Delanys lived in a three-room apartment. In such tight quarters, it helped to be very organized and to have clear rules and clear roles. Even though the apartment was Hubert's and they all participated in making decisions, Sadie would have the final say because she was the oldest. But groups don't always work this way, or this smoothly. What methods typically are used by groups to reach decisions? What are the advantages and disadvantages of working as a group? To answer these questions, we'll explore what psychologists have learned about *decision making in groups*, *social loafing*, and *social facilitation*.

Decision Making in Groups: Paths to a Decision

After living in Hubert's apartment for a while, Sadie and Bessie got a place of their own in New York, and their mother came to live with them. However, their mother's health began to fail, and it was no longer safe for her to be home alone all day while her daughters were at work. The situation required that one of the sisters leave her job to stay home with Mrs. Delany (it never occurred to them to hire someone to stay at home with their mother while they were out at work). How did they decide who would stay home? This question faces many families today, and the path to a solution often involves group decision making. Such decision making also occurs in other contexts: Political parties, military planners, and teams at work must decide on strategies and tactics; clinical groups must decide who receives what medical treatment and for how long; juries must decide on a verdict; and college admissions officers together decide who is accepted and who is not. How are decisions made in groups?

In general, if a group is not initially unanimous in favor of a particular decision, the view favored by the majority typically will prevail (Levine & Moreland, 1998). The larger the majority, the more likely it is that their choice will "win." This route to a decision is known as the *majority-win rule*, and it works well when the decision involves judgments or opinions and there is no objectively correct answer (Hastie & Kameda, 2005).

However, there are occasions—you may have been present at some—when what began as the minority position eventually "wins," which can arise when there is an objectively correct answer; this route to a decision is known as the *truth-win rule*, and it typically arises when the inherent correctness of a minority position is eventually recognized by the group (Kirchler & Davis, 1986).

Group Polarization

If there is no objectively correct answer (and sometimes even if there is), group decision making does not always lead to the best decision. The opinion of a powerful member can shift others' opinions by might rather than right. One process that leads groups to make a bad decision is **group polarization**, the tendency of group members' opinions to become more extreme (in the same direction as their initial opinions) after group discussion (Isenberg, 1986; Levine & Moreland, 1998).

Group polarization can occur for several reasons:

1. When some members of the group give many very compelling reasons for their initial views. In listening to these reasons, members who are in general agreement may become more convinced of the correctness of that initial assessment and become more extreme in their views (Burnstein, 1982). This route to group polarization is more likely to occur when an intellectual issue is at stake or when the group is deciding about a task to be undertaken (Kaplan, 1987).

2. After members come to see an emerging consensus, some members try to increase their standing in the group (and improve their view of themselves) by taking that consensus position to an extreme (Goethals & Zanna, 1979). This route to group polarization is likely to occur when the issue involves making a judgment call or when the group is more focused on group harmony than on correctness (Kaplan, 1987).

3. When group members who have more extreme positions take more turns in the discussion and spend more time talking (Van Swol, 2009).

Groupthink

Another means by which group decision making can go awry is through **groupthink**, which occurs when people who try to solve problems together accept one another's information and ideas without subjecting them to critical analysis. Members of the group convince each other that they are right and never stop to examine the solution critically. Members of a group are most likely to fall into groupthink when the group is cohesive (the members like and value each other), which then deters members from voicing

Group polarization The tendency of group members' opinions to become more extreme (in the same direction as their initial opinions) after group discussion.

Groupthink The group process that arises when people who try to solve problems together accept one another's information and ideas without subjecting them to critical analysis.

dissenting opinions or raising questions that can lead to conflict (Janis, 1982). In such instances, rather than objectively thinking through a problem and the advantages and disadvantages of possible solutions, members are more concerned with agreeing with one another. Groupthink has been used to explain many real-life disasters, such as why NASA launched the space shuttle *Challenger* (which crashed into the ocean, killing all aboard) despite widespread concerns about its booster rockets. (The failure of the booster rockets ended up causing the shuttle to crash.)

Although the evidence that groupthink leads to bad decisions is mixed (Aldag & Fuller, 1993), groups tend to make poorer decisions when they are isolated from outside guidance, when the group leader is vocal about his or her opinion and expects others to go along, and when the members like each other and have a sense of shared identity (Whyte, 2000). In such circumstances, the members want to cooperate and so refrain from asking questions or making comments that might lead to conflict or controversy. However, without constructive questioning, the group's discussion is less productive and can lead to poor decisions. Groups that have a norm of coming to consensus are more vulnerable to groupthink than those that encourage dissent and questioning (Postmes et al., 2001).

When a group as a whole is responsible for a task, some members may work less hard than they would if they were individually responsible for the task.

Source: The Image Works

Social Loafing *Social loafing* is another problem that can affect groups—in this case when the responsibility for a task is spread among its members; **social loafing** occurs when some members don't contribute as much to a shared group task as do others and instead let other members work proportionally harder than they do (Latané et al., 1979). If you've lived with other people, you may have experienced the effects of social loafing: When dishes pile up in the sink or the bathroom goes uncleaned for weeks, one household member eventually cleans while the rest do some social loafing, waiting for somebody else to do the work.

One way to prevent social loafing is to instill a sense of importance and responsibility in each person, even if the work is boring or if the member's contribution is anonymous (Harkins & Petty, 1982; Rynes et al., 2005). Another way is to make each member of the group clearly responsible for a particular task. Making the task attractive also reduces social loafing, as does knowing that individual as well as group performance will be evaluated (Harkins & Szymanski, 1989; Hoeksema-van Orden et al., 1998; Karau & Williams, 1993).

Social Facilitation: Everybody Loves an Audience Sometimes being part of a group or just being in the presence of other people can increase a person's performance; this effect is called **social facilitation**. However, social facilitation usually occurs only when the individual performs well-learned, simple tasks; on complicated, less well-learned tasks, the presence of others can hinder performance (Guerin, 1993)—even when the other people are "virtual others" in a virtual reality environment (S. Park & Catrambone, 2007). Both effects, helping and hindering performance, can be explained by the same process: The presence of others appears to increase arousal, which then facilitates how well people perform a well-learned, simple task (Schmitt et al., 1986; Seta & Seta, 1992) but disrupts how well people perform recently learned or complicated tasks. Hence, at a concert, a musician may perform a previously learned and well-practiced song better than a newer one, whereas when practicing at home that same day, she probably could play them both equally well.

Social loafing The group process that occurs when some members don't contribute as much to a shared group task as do others, and instead let other members work proportionally harder than they do.

Social facilitation The increase in performance that can occur simply as a result of being part of a group or in the presence of other people.

Altruism The motivation to increase another person's welfare.

Helping Behavior: Helping Others

When Bessie Delany began her dentistry practice in 1923, both teeth cleanings and extractions were $2 each, and a silver filling cost $5. When she retired in 1950, she charged the same rates and was proud of it. In fact, she treated people regardless of their ability to pay. The Delany family ethic was to help others. This quality is called **altruism**, the motivation to increase another person's welfare (Batson, 1998, 2010). What made Bessie so willing to help others? Why do we help other people? What circumstances encourage altruism? In the following sections, we explore specific aspects of helping behavior: *prosocial behavior* and *bystander intervention*.

Prosocial Behavior

Acting altruistically, called **prosocial behavior**, includes sharing, cooperating, comforting, and helping (Batson, 1998). A number of factors affect whether we help someone, including characteristics of the helper, characteristics of the person being helped, and characteristics of the situation—as summarized below.

CHARACTERISTICS OF THE HELPER. You are more likely to help others if you score highly on the personality dimension of *agreeableness* (which is characterized by a tendency to be accommodating and good-humored; Carlo et al., 2005; Graziano et al., 2007) or you have certain other personality traits or characteristics (Batson et al., 1986; Eisenberg et al., 1989, 2002), such as:

- a high need for the approval of others,
- a predisposition to taking personal and social responsibility,
- a tendency to feel concerned for others,
- a belief that the world is just, and
- relatively less concern for your own welfare (Bierhoff et al., 1991).

Bessie Delany seemed to feel a sense of personal and social responsibility toward others and could empathize with their plights. She also appeared to have less concern for her own welfare: When she was in dental school, a White girl born with syphilis (back then, untreatable and contagious by mouth) came to the dental clinic—only Bessie volunteered to help her.

A variety of other factors about the helper will influence whether he or she is willing to help. We are more likely to help another person if: (1) we've been reinforced for helping or punished for not helping (Grusec et al., 2002); (2) we've observed parents, teachers, and others helping others; and/or (3) we're in a good mood (Guéguen & De Gail, 2003).

CHARACTERISTICS OF THE PERSON BEING HELPED. A person in need of assistance is more likely to be helped if he or she has certain characteristics; we are more likely to help someone who:

- *we view as similar to ourselves* (J. H. Park & Schaller, 2005). We are more likely to help a person who is a member of our group (compared to someone who is not a member of our group; Hewstone et al., 2002; Stürmer et al., 2005). Consider an experiment in which Americans in three foreign cities asked for directions: Residents of those cities who were similar in age to the Americans were more likely to give directions (Rabinowitz et al., 1997).
- *is a friend or someone we like.*
- *we believe is not responsible for his or her predicament, or who gives a socially acceptable justification for his or her plight* (Weiner, 1980). In fact, the more justification the requester gives, the more likely he or she is to receive help (Bohm & Hendricks, 1997).

CHARACTERISTICS OF THE SITUATION IN WHICH A PERSON NEEDS HELP. We are more likely to help in situations in which: (1) the cost of helping is relatively low (Perlow & Weeks, 2002), (2) the "rewards" of helping are relatively high (Guéguen & De Gail, 2003), or (3) there appears to be an increased "cost" of *not* helping (Dovidio et al., 1991), such as a heightened sense of shame and guilt (Penner et al., 2005).

In sum, various factors about our own personality, about the person needing help, and about the situation all make us more or less likely to help others.

Bystander Intervention

A great deal has been learned about a specific type of prosocial behavior—*bystander intervention*—as a result of research inspired by one dreadful incident. At about 3 a.m. on March 13, 1964, a 28-year-old woman named Catherine Genovese—known to her neighbors as Kitty—was brutally murdered in Queens, a part of

New York City's firefighters displayed their altruism in September 2001, both when going into the burning World Trade Center towers to rescue people inside and when searching through the burning rubble for survivors.

Source: © SHANNON STAPLETON/REUTERS/ Landov

Prosocial behavior Acting altruistically, which includes sharing, cooperating, comforting, and helping others.

Bystander effect The decrease in offers of assistance that occurs as the number of bystanders increases.

New York City, only minutes from her own apartment building. She was coming home from her job as a manager of a bar. When her attacker first caught and stabbed her, she screamed for help. The lights came on in several apartments overlooking the scene of the crime, and a man yelled down to her attacker to leave her alone. Her attacker briefly stopped and walked away. The apartment lights went out. The attacker returned and stabbed her again, and she screamed again, to no avail, although lights again came on in the surrounding apartments. The attacker left in a car, and Kitty Genovese dragged herself to the lobby of an apartment building near her own. The attacker returned again, and this time he kept stabbing her until she died. The gruesome ordeal took some 35 minutes, and at least part of it was heard by no less than 38 neighbors. Only one person called the police (Rosenthal, 1964).

John Darley and Bibb Latané (1968) hypothesized that if only a few of those 38 neighbors had heard the attack, those few would have been more likely to help Kitty Genovese. This relationship is known as the **bystander effect**: As the number of bystanders increases, offers of assistance decrease. To test this relationship, Darley and Latané, with the aid of confederates, created the following situation. Imagine yourself as a participant in a study, taking part in an audio conference about campus life with a number of others who are in the same building. Each participant speaks without interruption, and when everyone has spoken, the first person gets to speak again and so on. Suppose another participant mentions that when stressed, he gets seizures; then you hear that person stutter, start to choke, and ask for help. Would you get help?

If you were like most participants in Darley and Latané's (1968) study (see Figure 7) and you believed that there were only two people in the telephone conference—you and the person with seizures—you would be very likely to seek help. But if you had been told that there were three participants, you would be less likely to seek help and even less likely with a total of six participants. In short, attempts to help dropped as the number of apparent bystanders increased: When participants thought that they were the only one aware of the "emergency," 85% of them left the cubicle and got the experimenter within the first minute. When they thought there was one other bystander, 65% helped within the first minute. When participants thought there were four other bystanders (six participants in the group), only 25% helped within the first minute. At the end of 4 minutes, all in the smallest group helped, as did 85% of those in the midsized group but only 60% in the largest group.

FIGURE 7 Bystander Intervention

Participants thought they were involved in a study of campus life. They went into a private cubicle, and were told that they could all hear one another, but only one student would be able to speak during any 2-minute period; when all had spoken, the cycle would start again. They were also told that the experimenter would not be listening. Participants were led to believe that their group consisted of a total of six, three, or two participants. In fact, there was only one true participant at a time; the rest of the voices on the intercom were prerecorded tapes.

Participants became bystanders to an emergency: The crisis came after one (prerecorded) voice confessed to having seizures in stressful situations. This person subsequently seemed to be having a seizure and asked for help.

Would participants leave their cubicles to get help? Their responses depended on how many bystanders they thought there were. The great majority of participants went to get help when they thought they were the only ones aware of the problem, but they helped less often the more bystanders they thought were aware of the problem.

From this and other studies, Darley and Latané (1970) described five steps, or "choice points," in bystander intervention (see Figure 8). At each step, various factors, such as the number of bystanders and characteristics of the bystanders, influence the likelihood that someone will help. For example, consider Step 2, perceiving the event as an emergency. If a situation is ambiguous, which leaves you uncertain about whether the emergency is real, you may hesitate to offer help. If other bystanders are present, your hesitancy may be increased by *evaluation apprehension*—a fear that you might be embarrassed or ridiculed if you try to intervene because there may be no emergency after all. The number of bystanders also influences Step 3, assuming responsibility. The more bystanders there are, the less responsible each one feels for offering help, creating a **diffusion of responsibility**. Fortunately, once people have learned about the bystander effect, they are subsequently more likely to intervene (Beaman et al., 1978). ((•—[Listen

Diffusion of responsibility The diminished sense of responsibility to help that each person feels as the number of bystanders grows.

((•—[Listen to the **Podcast**
Bystander Apathy on **mypsychlab.com**

FIGURE 8 The Five Choice Points of Bystander Intervention

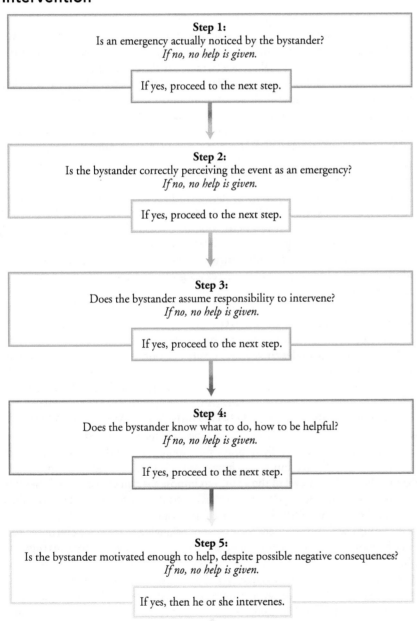

Step 1:
Is an emergency actually noticed by the bystander?
If no, no help is given.

If yes, proceed to the next step.

Step 2:
Is the bystander correctly perceiving the event as an emergency?
If no, no help is given.

If yes, proceed to the next step.

Step 3:
Does the bystander assume responsibility to intervene?
If no, no help is given.

If yes, proceed to the next step.

Step 4:
Does the bystander know what to do, how to be helpful?
If no, no help is given.

If yes, proceed to the next step.

Step 5:
Is the bystander motivated enough to help, despite possible negative consequences?
If no, no help is given.

If yes, then he or she intervenes.

LOOKING AT LEVELS Cults

Source: © Ariel Skelley/CORBIS All Rights Reserved; (inset) © GJLP/Photo Researchers, Inc.

In 1997, 39 members of the Heaven's Gate cult killed themselves in order to ascend to an alien spaceship that they believed was hidden behind the Hale–Bopp Comet; they believed that the spaceship would take them to the next level of existence. Clearly, this cult had a powerful influence on its members—but how? We can best understand how cults function by looking at the phenomenon from the three levels of analysis and their interactions.

At the level of the brain, cults typically require new recruits to engage in activities such as hours of chanting or listening to music, staying awake long hours (and thus becoming sleep deprived), and eating only certain foods at certain times; such activities alter their brain functioning and induce a meditative or hypnotic-like state. Once in this state, recruits usually cannot rationally evaluate what they are being told (Walsh, 2001).

At the level of the person, in many cults the initial immersive activities for new recruits are designed to eliminate members' sense of individuality (West, 1980; Williams, 2003). In the Heaven's Gate group, for instance, each day was structured down to the minute in order to minimize individual choice (which has the effect of decreasing the recruits' sense of individuality). Moreover, recruits were told that they could not trust their own judgment (in order to decrease their sense of autonomy; Bearak, 1997). New members were not allowed to be alone, even in the bathroom.

These measures can induce a sense of *depersonalization* (the experience of observing oneself as if from the outside) and *derealization* (the sense that familiar objects have changed or seem unreal; Singer, 1995). Such changes allow cult leaders to influence and control the new recruits' attitudes, beliefs, and behavior (Gesy, 1993; Richmond, 2004).

At the level of the group, recruits are often asked to engage in behaviors that they would normally refuse to do (such as beg for money or have sexual relations with the leader), but cults may use the foot-in-the-door compliance technique, starting with small requests and progressing to the larger, more outrageous, ones (T. W. Miller et al., 1999). In addition,the norms and practices of a cult typically create a strong ingroup (with the rest of the world's being the outgroup), which increases group cohesion (Almendros et al., 2007). In turn, such cohesion can lead to groupthink.

Once recruits conform, comply, obey, and behave in ways they otherwise would not, these actions affect events at all three levels. At the level of the person, for instance, recruits then probably develop cognitive dissonance. Such cognitive dissonance can be reduced by the recruits' changing their attitudes to be more positive about the behavior and their reasons for agreeing to do it (Galanter, 2000). Moreover, recruits receive enormous amounts of attention and reinforcement (level of the group), sometimes called "love-bombing," for behaving in desired ways—in other words, for conforming to their expected role and to group norms, complying with requests, and obeying orders (T. W. Miller et al., 1999).

Furthermore, the repetitive and exhausting activities that the established members of the group impose on new recruits alter their brain functioning and induce a meditative or hypnotic-like state in which the recruits are no longer critical, which then leads them to be receptive to the members' efforts (level of the group) to impose the cult's belief system (level of the person). As part of setting the stage for this process, recruits are often separated from their families and friends (Richmond, 2004; Singer & Lalich, 1995) and are only with other cult members (level of the group), which strengthens their sense of belonging to the cult (level of the person). Moreover, being asked to do something they don't want to do not only produces cognitive dissonance but also produces anxiety—which is reduced by the positive response of group members after recruits comply with the requests or obey the orders (level of the group). Such negative reinforcement (level of the person) leads to changes in self-concept and heightens the importance of and dependence on the group (Almendros et al., 2007; Galanter, 2000). Clearly, interactions among such events can exert a powerful influence over beliefs and behavior.

LOOKING BACK

✓●─[Study and Review on
mypsychlab.com

1. **What psychological principles explain why we like certain people and not others?** Repeated contact, similarity to ourselves, and physical attraction all tend to incline us to like specific other people. Liking is not the same as loving, which can be passionate or companionate. According to Sternberg's triangular theory, love has three dimensions: passion, intimacy, and commitment. Relationships reflect different proportions of each dimension, and those proportions change over time. People's attachment styles—secure, avoidant, or anxious–ambivalent—also affect the pattern of relationships they will develop.

2. **Why do all social groups have rules for social behavior and organization?** Social norms help a group function, defining appropriate and inappropriate behavior for some or all members; they also help new members learn how to function in the group.

3. **Why do we sometimes "go along" with or obey others even when we don't want to? Conversely, what makes us able to refuse?** If we hold a minority position, we may come to doubt the correctness of our view and conform to the majority position. We may also conform to the majority view when the task at hand is difficult. Furthermore, as Asch's studies showed, we are more likely to conform to the majority view when we are part of a cohesive group. In contrast, we are less likely to conform to the majority view if at least one other person dissents or if we have a strong desire to retain a sense of individuality. Compliance with a request can be maximized when the person making the request is a friend, someone who has provided a favor in the past, or someone in authority. We are also more likely to comply if we think that people similar to ourselves would comply. A number of persuasion techniques make use of compliance principles, including the foot-in-the-door technique, the lowball technique, and the door-in-the-face technique. Obedience to an order to harm someone is more likely when the person issuing the order is authoritative and nearby. However, not everyone obeys such orders, and the specifics of the situation help determine the level of obedience.

4. **Does being part of a group change our behavior? How do groups make decisions?** Groups can make decisions according to the majority-win rule or the truth-win rule; the latter is more likely when one answer is objectively correct. Group decision making can go awry because of group polarization and groupthink. When in a group some people do less than their share (social loafing). Being in the presence of others can increase someone's performance of well-learned or relatively simple tasks (social facilitation) but can have the opposite effect on newly learned or complex tasks.

5. **Are some people more helpful than others? What makes us likely to help other people?** People with certain personality traits—including a high need for approval and a feeling of social responsibility—are more likely to help others. In addition, we are more likely to help: people who seem similar to ourselves, people we like, or people who have a socially justifiable reason for needing help. We are less likely to help others when there are more bystanders (diffusion of responsibility) or when the situation is ambiguous.

A Final Word: Ethics and Social Psychology

The researchers who conducted many of the classic studies described in this chapter did not tell participants about the true nature of the experiments at the outset, and several used confederates. In a few cases, participants in some of these studies were distressed by the procedure and by their own behavior; the researchers did not intend to upset the participants. For instance, Milgram initially did not expect participants to be willing to shock learners at higher "voltage" levels, and thus he was not prepared for any distress that participants might feel after administering shocks. (However, Milgram did continue to perform variants of this study after he knew the results of the first one.) These classic studies and the responses of some participants led psychologists to establish rigorous ethical guidelines to ensure that the people who participate in research are not harmed in any way.

It is easy to require that studies not harm (physically or psychologically) the participants but less easy to dictate that studies never deceive participants. Some psychological phenomena are extremely difficult, if not impossible, to study if the participant knows the true nature of the experiment. For example, could you think of a way to design a study on conformity *without* using deception? Thus, rather than banning deception, rules have been put in place to govern its use. In particular, before an Institutional Review Board approves a study that deceives participants about the true hypothesis or the procedure (such occurs when participants are not told that a hidden camera is filming them), researchers must show that: (1) the deception is absolutely necessary (that the information could not be ascertained without deception); (2) the information is valuable and the deception minimal; and, (3) at the conclusion of the study, the investigators will fully explain to the participants the nature of the study and the reasons for deception.

LET'S REVIEW

((•▬ Listen to an audio file of your chapter on mypsychlab.com

I. SOCIAL COGNITION: THINKING ABOUT PEOPLE

A. Attitudes and stereotypes help us reduce cognitive effort by simplifying and organizing the complex social world. Our attitudes, stereotypes, and attributions affect how we process, encode, and remember information.

B. Our attitudes can affect our behavior and are especially likely to do so when they are strong, stable, relevant, important, and/or easily accessible.

C. Conflict between an attitude and our behavior (or between two attitudes) can lead to cognitive dissonance, which we are then driven to reduce.

D. Attempts to persuade us often focus on trying to change our attitudes. Central routes to persuasion require the recipient to devote more time and energy to the message than do peripheral routes.

E. Research in social cognitive neuroscience has helped reveal that cognitive dissonance and other social cognitive phenomena can occur outside conscious awareness.

F. The process of categorizing objects (including people) leads to stereotypes, and our stereotypes of others affect our behavior and can lead to prejudice and discrimination.

G. Because our stereotypes create biases in the way we process information, the stereotypes often seem more accurate than they really are and thus are difficult to change.

H. Although we are driven to make attributions to understand events or behavior, our reasoning about the causes of these phenomena may be colored by attributional biases, such as the fundamental attribution error, the self-serving bias, and the belief in a just world. Such biases can lead us to understand people's behavior inaccurately.

II. SOCIAL BEHAVIOR: INTERACTING WITH PEOPLE

A. In our intimate relationships, we are more likely to be attracted to and to like people we view as similar to ourselves or with whom we have repeated contact.

B. We can examine different types of love by using Sternberg's triangular model of love (three dimensions) and by considering different attachment styles.

C. All groups have norms and roles, which guide members' behaviors. Zimbardo's prison study provides an example of the power of norms and roles within a group.

D. Conformity is affected by informational and normative social influences, depending on the situation. Asch's conformity experiment illustrates normative social influence.

E. The foot-in-the-door, lowball, and door-in-the-face techniques are used to increase compliance.

F. Obedience to an order can be affected by various factors, including the status and proximity of the person giving the order.

G. The style of a group's decision making depends on the group's goals and composition and on the ways in which members articulate their views to the group.

H. Being in a group can help or harm a given individual's performance, depending on a variety of factors.

I. Prosocial behavior is affected by characteristics of the helper, the person being helped, and the situation. Psychological principles, such as the bystander effect and the related diffusion of responsibility, also determine when and whom we help.

KEY TERMS

altruism	discrimination	lowball technique	role
attitude	door-in-the-face technique	mere exposure effect	self-serving bias
attribution	external attribution	norm	social categorization
attributional bias	foot-in-the-door technique	obedience	social cognition
belief in a just world	fundamental attribution error	outgroup	social cognitive neuroscience
bystander effect	group	passionate love	social facilitation
cognitive dissonance	group polarization	persuasion	social loafing
companionate love	groupthink	prejudice	social psychology
compliance	ingroup	prosocial behavior	stereotype
conformity	internal attribution	recategorization	triangular model of love
diffusion of responsibility			

PRACTICE TEST

✓— Study and Review on mypsychlab.com

For each of the following items, choose the single best answer.

1. The *affective* component of an attitude refers to
   a. your predisposition to act in a particular way toward the object or issue.
   b. your feelings about a person, object, or issue.
   c. what you believe or know about the object or issue.
   d. your perception of the "objective" social world.

2. A stereotype
   a. is a prejudiced attitude.
   b. is always wrong.
   c. is a negative set of beliefs.
   d. is a cognitive shortcut.

3. Cognitive dissonance
   a. is an uncomfortable state that arises when an attitude and behavior—or two attitudes—are inconsistent.
   b. is accompanied by decreased arousal.
   c. occurs with every inconsistency and is experienced by people who do not believe that they have a choice.
   d. All of the above statements are true.

4. The mere exposure effect
   a. cannot change attitudes.
   b. can change attitudes through the central route to persuasion.
   c. can change attitudes through the peripheral route to persuasion.
   d. works only if close attention is paid to the content of the argument.

5. If a researcher gives you two stimuli that you like almost to the same degree and requires you to decide which one you like better, then
   a. you later will end up liking the one you chose even more than you did at the outset.
   b. you later will end up liking the one you chose much less than you did at the outset.
   c. you later will end up disliking the rejected one much less than you did at the outset.
   d. None of the above statements is true.

6. Prejudice
   a. cannot arise if someone does not have negative feelings toward a group.
   b. is discriminatory behavior toward a member of a group.
   c. is a generally negative attitude toward a member of a group.
   d. does not include an emotional component.

7. Methods of decreasing prejudice include
   a. increased contact, particularly under certain conditions, such as when working toward a shared goal and when all participants are deemed to be equal.
   b. recategorization—that is, shifting the categories of "us" and "them" so that the two groups are no longer viewed as two distinct entities.
   c. the jigsaw classroom, a cooperative learning technique.
   d. All of the above are methods that can decrease prejudice.

8. The self-serving bias
   a. is a type of external attribution.
   b. leads you to attribute your failures to external causes.
   c. leads you to attribute your failures to internal causes.
   d. leads you to attribute other people's failures to external causes.

9. Why are you attracted to some people and not others?
   a. The adage "opposites attract" has been borne out by research, so we're attracted to people who are different than we are.
   b. Repeated contact usually leads to a more negative evaluation of someone.
   c. We're attracted to people with similar attitudes to our own.
   d. People are attracted to men and women who have different, but stimulating, attitudes than their own.

10. According to Sternberg's triangular model of love, the dimensions of love are
    a. sexual excitement, intellectual contact, and emotional warmth
    b. passion, intimacy, and commitment
    c. arousal, reflection, and acceptance
    d. infatuation, appreciation, and acceptance

11. Speed and Gangestad found that romantically popular men were seen by their peers as
    a. confident and outgoing.
    b. the best leaders.
    c. likely to succeed financially.
    d. unlikely to be "trend-setting."

12. Norms
    a. are based on stereotypes.
    b. exist only in military groups.
    c. are enforced by law.
    d. guide people's behavior in groups.

13. A member of a group is less likely to conform if
    a. another group member openly disagrees with the majority of the group.
    b. participants in the group announce their answers to the group rather than writing them down anonymously.
    c. the task is more difficult; the harder the task, the less likely members are to conform.
    d. the group is more cohesive—that is, members have more attraction and commitment toward it.

14. The essence of effective compliance techniques lies in six principles. According to the principle of _____, people are more likely to comply with requests related to limited, short-term—rather than open-ended—opportunities.

    a. reciprocity
    b. scarcity
    c. social validation
    d. commitment/consistency

15. Sometimes being part of a group, or just being in the presence of other people, can increase performance. This effect
    a. is called social loafing.
    b. decreases arousal.
    c. enhances performance only on well-learned, simple tasks.
    d. enhances performance only on complicated, less well-learned tasks.

Answers: 1. b 2. d 3. a 4. c 5. a 6. c 7. d 8. b 9. c 10. b 11. a 12. d 13. a 14. b 15. c

APPENDIX

PART A – STATISTICS

To understand and evaluate reports of psychological research, you need to know a few basics about statistics. Statistics are numbers that summarize or indicate differences or patterns of differences in measurements. Statistics can be illuminating, but they also can be a mixed blessing—or even a problem. Focusing on the latter possibility, Mark Twain once said that there are three kinds of lies: "Lies, damn lies, and statistics." Twain's point was that statistics can be used to obscure the facts as easily as to illuminate them. For instance, although the divorce rate in the United States is about 50%, this does not necessarily mean that only 5 out of every 10 couples will stay married. If 3 of those 10 couples divorce and remarry, and all 3 of those second marriages end in divorce, that makes 6 divorces out of 13 marriages; and if one of those ex-partners remarries a third time and divorces again, we now have 14 marriages and 7 divorces: a 50% divorce rate, even though 7 of the original 10 couples stayed married from the start.

There are two major types of statistics: One type describes or summarizes data, whereas the other indicates which differences or patterns in the data are worthy of attention. This is the distinction between *descriptive statistics* and *inferential statistics*. **Descriptive statistics** are concise ways of summarizing properties of sets of numbers. You're already familiar with such statistics: They are what you see plotted in bar graphs, line graphs, and pie charts and presented in numerical tables. Descriptive statistics include measures of *central tendency*, such as the familiar arithmetic average (also called the *mean*). But descriptive statistics are not limited to graphs and tables. For example, in financial news, the Dow Jones Industrial Average is a descriptive statistic, as is the unemployment rate.

Inferential statistics, in contrast, are the results of tests that reveal whether differences or patterns in measurements reflect true differences in the population or just chance variations. For instance, if you toss a coin 10 times and it lands heads up 7 times instead of the 5 you would expect purely by chance, does this mean that it is a "trick coin" or that an edge is worn away, or could this outcome also arise just from chance? Inferential statistics address the question of whether patterns in a set of data are random (that is, arise from chance) or whether they reflect a true underlying phenomenon.

In this appendix, we consider both types of statistics; we start with descriptive statistics and the nature of variables and data, and then turn to an overview of key inferential statistics. We conclude by exploring how statistics can be used to deceive you, both in printed numbers and in graphs, and how you can use statistics in everyday life.

Descriptive Statistics

You already know a lot about descriptive statistics, but you may not be aware you know it—and you may not be familiar with the technical vocabulary scientists use to discuss such statistics. This section provides a review of the essential points of descriptive statistics.

Statistics Numbers that summarize or indicate differences or patterns of differences in measurements.

Descriptive statistics Concise ways of summarizing properties of sets of numbers.

Inferential statistics Results of tests that reveal which differences or patterns in the measurements reflect actual differences in a population, as opposed to those that merely reflect chance variations.

Variable An aspect of a situation that can vary, or change; specifically, a characteristic of a substance, quantity, or entity that is measurable.

Independent variable The aspect of the situation that is deliberately and independently varied while another aspect is measured.

Dependent variable The aspect of the situation that is measured as the values of an independent variable are changed.

Data Careful descriptions or numerical measurements of a phenomenon.

Continuous variables Variables that have values that can fall anywhere along the measurement scale.

Categorical variables Variables that assign measurements to discrete classes.

Frequency distribution The frequency of each value of the independent variable (for continuous variables) or of each type of case (for categorical variables) that was observed in a set of data.

Variables and Data

First, we discuss variables and data—what they are, how researchers obtain data, and how they use the data to answer the questions posed in their research.

A **variable** is an aspect of a situation that can vary, or change; specifically, a variable is a characteristic of a substance, quantity, or entity that is measurable. Variables can be divided into two types: **Independent variables** are aspects of the situation that are deliberately and independently varied while other aspects are measured, and **dependent variables** are the aspects of the situation that are measured as the values of an independent variable are changed; in an experiment, the value of the dependent variable is expected to depend on the value of the independent variable. For example, researchers might give different drugs (the independent variable) to people with memory problems, and measure changes in performance on memory tests (the dependent variable).

Dependent variables define the type of thing that is measured, such as golf scores, and **data** are the careful descriptions or numerical measurements of a phenomenon—such as specific golf scores. In other words, in an experiment, data are the measurements, the values of the dependent variable as it varies. Examples of dependent variables used in psychological research are response times (how fast it takes to press a button after perceiving a stimulus), scores on an intelligence test, and ratings of the severity of depression.

Values of variables can be described in two ways: as points on a continuous scale or as categories. **Continuous variables** have values that can fall anywhere along the measurement scale, just as measures of length can fall anywhere along a ruler. Continuous variables allow you to perform mathematical operations such as adding or subtracting two or more values. For example, suppose you developed a drug that you think boosts memory. If your drug works as promised, it would be in great demand—from students in language-learning schools to brokers in Wall Street firms. To test the effectiveness of your drug, you ask people to learn a set of words either after taking the drug or, on another day, after taking a placebo. You are interested in whether the participants can later recall more words if they've taken your drug than if they took the placebo; the condition—drug versus placebo—is the independent variable, and the number of words recalled is the dependent variable. Half the participants get the drug first, and half get an identical-looking and -tasting placebo first. You put the pills in coded envelopes so that your assistant doesn't know when she's giving the drug versus the placebo (nor do the participants because you've used a *double-blind design*). The comparison, easily accomplished with values from a continuous scale, is expressed as the number of words remembered following the drug minus the number following the placebo. Ten participants' scores in each condition are shown in Table A.1.

In contrast, **categorical variables** assign measurements to discrete classes. Such variables do not change gradually from one to the other, and you can't perform mathematical operations on them. Sex, race, location, and political party are commonly used categorical variables; stage of sleep (Stage 2, 3, 4, or REM) is another example. Moreover, note that continuous measurements can also be classified, which converts them into categorical variables—such as occurs when an IQ score (a continuous variable) is assigned to categories: To convert the continuous measure of IQ score into a categorical measure, you would put ranges of scores into groups, perhaps based on differences of 15 IQ points above or below the mean (which is 100). For example, IQs above 145 could be labeled "gifted," and those below 70 could be labeled "intellectually disabled." If you were an educator who was designing intellectual enrichment programs, such categories could be helpful in guiding you to think about how to tailor the programs to the students' needs.

Frequency Distributions

Sometimes it is useful to consider how scores are distributed in a sample. The most common way to do this is to tabulate how frequently different value of the independent variable occurred. A **frequency distribution** indicates the frequency of each value of the independent variable (for continuous variables) or of each type of case (for categorical variables) observed in a set of data. For example, you could consider how frequently IQ scores occur for each value of the scale or the number of people who voted in the last election in each state of the union.

TABLE A.1 Fictional Participant Data from Drug and Placebo Conditions

Number of Words Remembered	
Placebo	Memory Drug
15	27
12	34
18	21
21	17
22	31
38	47
28	31
15	23
14	40
17	19

Measures of Central Tendency

Descriptive statistics are used to summarize characteristics of a set of *raw data*; raw data are the individual measurements themselves (Table A.1 presents raw data). Transforming raw data into statistical terms makes the data useful, allowing you to illustrate the relationships among the values or scores. One important type of descriptive statistic is the **central tendency** of the data: the clustering of the most characteristic values or scores for a particular group or sample. Central tendency can be expressed three ways:

1. *The mean.* The most common measure of central tendency, and probably the one with which you are most familiar, is the arithmetic average, or **mean**, of the scores or values. You calculate a mean by adding up the values in the group or sample, then dividing that sum by the total number of entries you summed. As shown in Table A.2, the mean for the placebo condition is 20 words remembered, and the mean for the drug condition is 29 words remembered.

Central tendency A descriptive statistic that indicates the clustering of the most characteristic values or scores for a particular group or sample.

Mean A measure of central tendency that is the arithmetic average of a set of scores or values.

Median A measure of central tendency that is the midpoint score of the values for the group or sample; half the values fall above the median, and half fall below the median.

Mode A measure of central tendency that is the most frequently occurring value in a group or sample.

Skewed distribution A distribution of a set of data in which many scores are near one extreme value and away from the center.

Normal distribution The frequency distribution in which most values fall in the midrange of the scale, and scores are increasingly less frequent as they taper off symmetrically toward the extremes; when graphed, this type of distribution is a bell-shaped curve.

TABLE A.2 Calculating the Mean

Number of Words Remembered

Placebo condition Total: 200   Memory drug condition Total: 290

Mean = Total number of words remembered ÷ Number of participants

Mean: 200 ÷ 10 = 20   Mean: 290 ÷ 10 = 29

2. *The median.* The **median** is the score that is the midpoint of the values for the group or sample; half the values fall above the median, and half fall below the median. It is easier to find the median if the data are arranged in order, as shown in Table A.3. The median in the placebo condition is 17.5, halfway between 17 and 18, the fifth and sixth ordered scores. In the memory drug condition, the median is 29.0, halfway between the fifth and sixth ordered scores of 27 and 31.

3. *The mode.* The **mode** is the value that appears most frequently in the group or sample. The mode can be any value, from the highest to the lowest. The mode in Table A.3 is 15 for the placebo condition and 31 for the memory drug condition. In addition, you can also use a mode for categorical scales, where the mode would be the most frequent category, such as "children" among all viewers of *Sesame Street* or "Saturday night" as the evening most people go to bed the latest.

The different measures are more or less sensitive to extreme values or scores. The mean is the measure of central tendency that is most sensitive to extreme values or scores; if you add a few values at the extreme end of the scale, the mean would change much more than the median (which often will not change at all). The mode does not generally change in response to an extreme score. For example, if you changed the last score in Table A.3 in the placebo condition from 38 to 50, the mean would change from 20 to 21.2, but the median and mode would remain the same.

When a set of data has many scores near one extreme value and away from the center, it is said to have a **skewed distribution**. When a set of data has a skewed distribution, the median is often a more appropriate measure of central tendency than the mean (see Figure A.1 on the next page).

However, the three measures of central tendency generally yield similar results; this is especially likely as the number of observations (data points) becomes larger and if the data follow a normal distribution. The **normal distribution** is the familiar bell-shaped curve, in which most values fall in the midrange of the scale and scores are increasingly less

TABLE A.3 Fictional Data from Drug and Placebo Conditions, Arranged in Order

Number of Words Remembered

Placebo condition	Memory drug condition
12	17
14	19
15	21
15	23
17	27
——Median 17.5	——Median 29.0
18	31
21	31
22	34
28	40
38	47
Mode* = 15	Mode* = 31

*Mode = Value that appears most frequently.

FIGURE A.1 Skewed Distributions

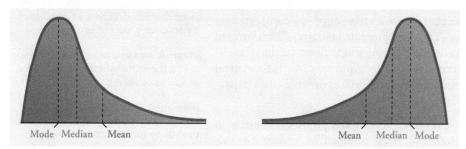

In a positively skewed distribution, the bulk of the scores cluster on the low end of the graph and tail off on the high end.

In a negatively skewed distribution, the bulk of the scores cluster on the high end of the graph and tail off on the low end.

FIGURE A.2 A Normal Distribution

A NORMAL DISTRIBUTION

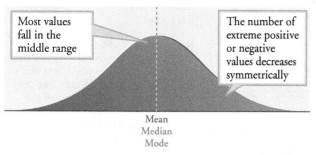

Most values fall in the middle range

The number of extreme positive or negative values decreases symmetrically

Mean
Median
Mode

Because of its shape, the normal distribution is also known as the *bell curve*. In nature, most characteristics clump around the midpoint, and progressively fewer have very high or very low measures.

Range The difference obtained by subtracting the smallest score in a set of data from the largest; the simplest measure of variability.

Standard deviation A descriptive statistic that provides a kind of "average variability" in a set of measurements.

frequent as they taper off symmetrically toward the extremes (see Figure A.2). Normal curves occur many places in nature. For example, look at stone stairs in a very old building: You can usually see that they are worn more deeply in the center and then less so as you move toward the sides. (If the building isn't old enough, you will see the beginnings of a normal curve, which over the generations will become deeper in the center until it resembles the shape of Figure A.2 upside down.) Or picture your classmates lined up according to height. Probably there are a few very tall or very short students on either end, with most clumping at an intermediate height. The same is true for many psychological qualities, such as scores on intelligence and personality tests.

Measures of Variability

Whereas measures of central tendency convey information about the most common values or scores, measures of *variability* convey information about the spread of the scores. The simplest measure of variability is the **range**, which is the difference obtained when you subtract the smallest score in a set of data from the largest. For the data in Table A.3, for example, the range of scores in the placebo condition is $38 - 12 = 26$. The range of scores for the drug condition is $47 - 17 = 30$. The range is the measure of variability most sensitive to extreme values, and the range does not tell you how variable the scores are in general (it just indicates how variable two of the scores are, namely, the highest and lowest). Suppose you have developed two different drugs for improving memory, and participants who are given either drug remember anywhere from 30 to 40 words; thus, both drugs have a range of 10. However, this measure of variability does not tell you that most participants who took drug A remember between 37 and 39 words, whereas most of those who received drug B remember between 31 and 34 words.

Another way to assess variability is the **standard deviation**, which is a kind of "average variability" in a set of measurements. The standard deviation is very common and is important for understanding many psychological findings, such as results on IQ tests. Let's walk through how this important measure is computed:

Step 1: Calculate how much each score differs from the mean of the scores, as shown in Table A.4, Step 1, in parentheses. Following this, it might be tempting to try to obtain an "average difference score" directly by simply computing the average of the differences from the mean. But if you do this, you will get an average score of zero (each difference above the mean will be compensated by one below the mean; otherwise, it wouldn't be the mean!). Instead, before taking the average of the deviations from the mean, you square them, which eliminates the plus or minus signs.

Step 2: Find the total of these squared values. This number is often referred to as the *sum of squares*, or *SS*. As shown in Table A.4, the SS for the placebo condition data recorded in Table A.3 is 556.

Step 3: Divide the sum of squares by the total number of deviation scores that contributed to this sum. The resulting value is the mean of the squared differences, which is called the *variance*. The variance for the placebo condition is 55.6.

Step 4: Finally, because the difference scores were squared in the first step, you need to "unsquare" variance to get a number that conveys meaningful information about the average variability of the scores. The square root of the variance is the *standard deviation*. The standard deviation of the placebo condition is 7.46.

Standard deviations in a normal distribution always have certain properties, which makes them easy to interpret. For example, IQ scores occur in a normal distribution, and thus it is clear how to interpret the relative standing of a score that is a certain number of standard deviations above or below the mean. Specifically, for values that are normally distributed, the standard deviation will tell you the percentage of values that fall at different points on the distribution. For instance, about 68% of values fall between one standard deviation below the mean and one standard deviation above the mean; as illustrated in Figure A.3, in an IQ test, the mean is 100, and the standard deviation is 15 points—and thus, because the scores are distributed according to a normal curve, 68% of people will have IQ scores between 85 and 115. And about 95% of the values fall between two standard deviations below the mean and two standard deviations above the mean. Because 99.7% of values fall between three standard deviations below the mean and three standard deviations above the mean, you know that any value greater than three standard deviations is *really* different from the other values.

For instance, let's go back to the earlier example of the placebo condition, which had a standard deviation of 7.46 words (for simplicity's sake, we'll round this down to 7 words). What this means is that with the placebo condition's mean of 20 words, roughly 68% of the participants in the placebo condition will remember somewhere between 13 and 27 words (20 − 7 to 20 + 7). At two standard deviations from the mean, roughly 95% of participants will remember between about 6 and 34 words.

Finally, it is well worth being familiar with the concept of a *confidence interval*, which is a measure of variability used with means of samples. To understand the confidence interval you first need to understand the difference between a sample and a population. A *sample* is the particular group of people or animals that was assessed, producing the set

TABLE A.4 Computing the Standard Deviation from the Placebo Condition Data in Table A.3

Step 1:

(Number of words remembered − Mean)^2 = Deviation score^2

$(12 - 20)^2 = -8^2 = 64$	$(18 - 20)^2 = -2^2 = 4$
$(14 - 20)^2 = -6^2 = 36$	$(21 - 20)^2 = 1^2 = 1$
$(15 - 20)^2 = -5^2 = 25$	$(22 - 20)^2 = 2^2 = 4$
$(15 - 20)^2 = -5^2 = 25$	$(28 - 20)^2 = 8^2 = 64$
$(17 - 20)^2 = -3^2 = 9$	$(38 - 20)^2 = 18^2 = 324$

Step 2: Sum of squares (SS) = Sum of squared deviation scores = 556

Step 3: Variance = SS ÷ Number of deviation scores = 556 ÷ 10 = 55.6

Step 4: Standard deviation = Square root of the variance = $\sqrt{55.6}$ = 7.46

FIGURE A.3 The Normal Curve: A Closer Look

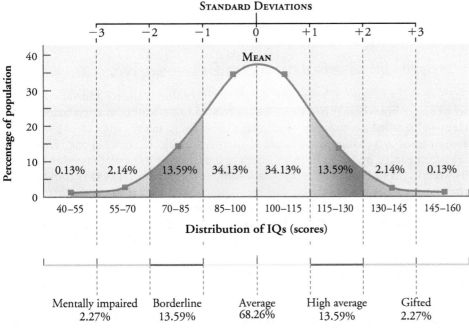

IQ, illustrated here, is a good example of a characteristic that is distributed according to a normal curve.

of measurements you have; in contrast, the population is the entire set of every single relevant member of the group of people or animals. For example, you might assess a sample of 20 6-year-olds, and the population would be all the 6-year-olds in the world. The distinction between a sample and a population is relevant to confidence intervals because this measure of variability tells you where the mean of the population is likely to be, given the measurements for a particular sample. Specifically, the **confidence interval** specifies the range above and below the mean of a sample within which the mean of the population is likely to fall. You are probably already familiar with this concept, having heard it referred to in news broadcasts as the "margin of error" that accompanies poll results. For example, you might hear that "Smith is preferred by 51% of the voters and Jones by 47%, with a margin of error of 4—which puts them in a dead heat." A margin of error of 4 is a way of saying "plus or minus 4." That is, Smith is preferred by somewhere between 47% and 55% of the voters—51% plus or minus 4%. The confidence intervals can be set more or less stringently. For example, the most common confidence interval, set at 95%, means that 95% of the time the mean of the population would fall within the range of the upper and lower ends of that confidence interval.

Relative Standing

Sometimes you want to know where a particular score stands relative to other scores, and various methods have been devised to specify such information. One way to convey this information is in terms of measures of variability. For example, you could specify how many standard deviations a score is from the mean. (This is the way IQ scores are set up, with 15 points as a standard deviation for the WAIS IQ test.) However, this isn't very useful if you are interested in the specific number or percentage of other cases that fall above or below a particular one. Another way of conveying information about a value relative to other values in a set of measurements is to use a **percentile rank**: a number indicating the percentage of data that have values at or below a particular value. A score converted to a percentile rank of 50, for example, instantly tells you that 50% of the scores in a sample fall at or below that particular score; the median is a percentile rank of 50. *Quartiles* are percentile ranks that divide the group into fourths (25th, 50th, 75th, and 100th percentiles); a score that is at the third quartile signifies that 75% of the group fall at or below that score. *Deciles* are percentile ranks that divide the group into tenths; a score at the sixth decile indicates that 60% of the scores fall at or below that value. When you received your SAT or ACT scores, you also received your percentile rank.

Inferential Statistics

So far we have focused on descriptive statistics. But you now have the tools to understand common inferential statistics.

Correlation: The Relationship Between Two Variables

Suppose that you want to know not just about the central tendency and variability of a set of scores but whether two variables are related to each other. A **correlation coefficient**—also called a *correlation*—indicates that a change in the values of one variable is accompanied by a change in the values of another variable. Increases in one variable that are accompanied by increases in another are indicated by a correlation value that falls between 0 and +1.0, and hence this relationship is referred to as a *positive correlation*. In contrast, increases in one variable that are accompanied by decreases in another are indicated by a correlation that is between 0 and −1.0, and hence this relationship is referred to as a *negative correlation*. So, for instance, you may read that people who exercise moderately don't get as severely depressed as people who don't exercise at all; if this information is based on a correlation, it would be a negative correlation: Increasing exercise is associated with less severe depression. A correlation of zero indicates that there is no relationship between the two variables—they do not vary together. The closer the correlation is to 1.0 or −1.0, the stronger the relationship.

Crucially, a correlation shows only that two variables vary together, not that a change in one *causes* a change in the other. For example, concluding that exercise helps prevent

Confidence interval The range above and below the mean of a sample within which the mean of a population is likely to occur.

Percentile rank A number indicating the percentage of data that have values at or below a particular value.

Correlation coefficient A number that ranges from -1.0 to 1.0 that indicates how closely interrelated two sets of measured variables are; the higher the coefficient (in either the positive or negative direction), the better the value of one measurement can predict the value of the other. Also simply called a *correlation*.

severe depression (exercise *causes* less severe depression) based on that correlation would be a mistake: Perhaps people who are severely depressed don't have the energy to exercise. If that is true, the direction of causation would go the other way (more severe depression *causes* less exercise). Or perhaps another variable, such as poor diet, affects both depression and the amount of exercise. With correlation, we know only that two variables are related, either positively or negatively, not the direction of causality; it is always possible that some third variable (in this case, such as poor diet) affects the other two variables.

To think about how the correlation value is calculated, go back to the idea of a standard deviation. But now, instead of computing the deviations relative to the mean of all the numbers, imagine that you have a line running through the data points (Figure A.4). The *method of least squares* is a way to fit a line to a cloud of points. Again, squared numbers are used to eliminate the signs of the difference values. This method positions the line to minimize the square of the distance of each point from the slanted line. The closer the correlation is to 1.0 or to −1.0, the stronger the relationship; visually, the more tightly the data points cluster around a slanted line, the higher the correlation.

FIGURE A.4 Strength of Correlation

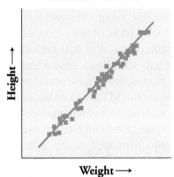

POSITIVE CORRELATION BETWEEN 0 AND 1.0

Here, increases in one variable (height) are accompanied by increases in another (weight); this is a positive correlation, indicated by a correlation value that falls between 0 and +1.0.

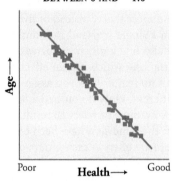

NEGATIVE CORRELATION BETWEEN 0 AND −1.0

Here, increases in one variable (age) are accompanied by decreases in another (health); this is a negative correlation, indicated by a correlation value that is between 0 and −1.0.

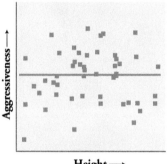

ZERO CORRELATION

A zero correlation indicates no relationship between two variables, height and aggressiveness here; they do not vary together.

Correlations and other types of inferential statistics can be *significant* or *not significant*. What does "significant" mean? In statistics, it does not mean "important." Rather, it means that the measured relationship does not arise simply from chance variations. Chance variations are always present, and thus if you correlate any two randomly selected sets of measurements, it is likely that the correlation will not be precisely zero. Say you took a sample of 10 people, correlated IQ score with ear size, and found a correlation of 0.10. Should you pay attention to this correlation, developing a grand theory to explain it? The size of a correlation needed for statistical significance, to be taken as more than just chance variation, depends on the number of pairs of values analyzed (each represented by a data point in Figure A.4). As a general rule, the more observations considered when computing the correlation, the smaller the correlation value needs to be to achieve statistical significance. Why? The more observations you have, the more opportunities there are for chance variations in one direction to cancel out chance variations in the opposite direction. For example, imagine that a machine were randomly throwing darts into a rectangular corkboard on the wall. It is possible that the first few on the left would be lower than those on the right. But as the machine tossed more and more darts, those initial quirks would be balanced out by quirks later in the process, so after 100 darts, there would no longer be any discernible pattern.

Statistical significance is expressed in terms of the probability (p) that a value (such as the size of a correlation) could have arisen from chance variations. For example, $p < .05$ means that the probability that the correlation value (for instance, a correlation of 0.10) was simply due to chance is less than 5 in 100; $p < .001$ means that the probability that it was due to chance is less than 1 in 1,000. By convention, any value with $p < .05$ or smaller is considered statistically significant—not likely to be a result simply of chance variation in the data. You can look up a correlation value in a table to determine its significance, but most computer programs that compute correlation do this for you automatically.

Samples Versus Populations in Inferential Statistics

Back to the memory-enhancing drug study—how can you tell whether the drug worked? If you had measured every person on the planet, all you would need to do is look at the descriptive statistics. Either the drug resulted in better remembering than the placebo, or it didn't. But such all-inclusive testing isn't practical. Virtually all research in psychology relies on studying data from a sample (which, as noted earlier, is a group drawn from the population at large), and the goal is to "generalize from" (extend) the findings with the sample to the larger population. Inferential statistics let you *infer* that the difference found between your samples does, in fact, reflect a difference in the corresponding populations.

Here's a simple example: Say you wanted to know whether seniors are generally friendlier than first-year students (you theorize that as students gain confidence and a sense of independence, they *do* become friendlier). To find out, you administer a questionnaire your professor has just designed and validated to measure friendliness. If you administered the questionnaire to five first-year students and five seniors, you would probably find a difference. But suppose that if instead of five first-year students and five seniors, you had ten students from a single year and randomly assigned them to two groups of five—you would very likely also find a difference between the groups! This difference would arise because of chance variations, which had an effect because of how you happened to assign students to groups. But no matter how you assigned those students to groups, the groups would probably be different. Only if you had a large number of students would randomly assigning them to two groups be likely to result in groups that were very similar; when enough students from the same class have been tested, those who score particularly high or low will be assigned equally often to each group, on average, and thus their disproportionate contributions will cancel out.

Because of the fact that random variation will affect the group, when you compare first-year students and seniors you can't know for sure whether you've got enough participants so that any difference between them is "real"—reflecting actual differences between the two classes in general—or arises from *sampling error*. **Sampling error** is a difference that arises from the luck of the draw, not because two samples are, in fact, representative of different populations. In this example, if differences between first-year students and seniors arise from sampling error, the two classes of students are not actually different; in such a case, the differences in the samples would not reflect differences in the underlying populations. (There are statistical tests that can indicate whether a difference between two samples probably arises from sampling error or probably reflects a real difference in the underlying populations. For example, some tests compare the difference in the sample means to a measure of how much the numbers that went into each mean varied, asking whether the difference between the means is greater than would be expected by chance, where the estimate of chance is based on the variability of the numbers going into the means. The details about such tests are beyond the scope of this appendix.)

Generalizing from the Results

To be useful, the results of a study should extend beyond the sample tested or examined in the study to the relevant population. For example, say that a research study found that exercise by itself really does ward off severe depression. Does that mean that *you* should start exercising when you feel yourself getting depressed? Not necessarily. Generalizing from the results of a study should be done with caution. Consider the following questions before applying the results of this or any study to yourself or anyone else:

1. Are the results *valid*? If the study was an experiment (see Chapter 1), were the participants randomly assigned? If the results relied on correlations, are the study authors implying that one variable causes another? If so, that conclusion isn't supported by

Sampling error A difference that arises by chance, not because the samples are representative of different populations.

the data. Do you think the researchers appropriately assessed the variables they claimed to have assessed? For instance, if they measured depression by simply comparing how slowly participants spoke at the end of the study with their speech speed at the beginning, would that be a valid assessment of depression?

2. If the study involved a new treatment or method to improve some aspect of life, was this method compared with a control group, such as a group given a placebo?

3. Did the researchers try to control for possible confounds?

4. Was the study performed with a wide cross section of people and a large sample? If not, be cautious in generalizing from its results. For instance, if a positron emission tomography study found that people with attention-deficit/hyperactivity disorder had unusual activity levels in a particular part of the brain, you would want to ask the following questions before concluding that the findings generalize beyond the participants in the study: How many participants were involved? (If very few, be cautious.) What was the gender of the participants? (If only one gender was tested, be cautious about generalizing to the other.) Are there other factors about the participants that make it difficult to generalize to you, to North Americans, or to all people? If a study is restricted to people of a certain geographic region, ethnic group, or age or those with a particular medical, psychological, or social history, it may not be appropriate to generalize the results, depending on the variable(s) being assessed.

Lying with Statistics

Statistics can be used or misused. In a famous book titled *How to Lie With Statistics*, Derrell Huff (1954) demonstrated many ways that people use statistics to distort the pattern of results. His book played a valuable role in inoculating many people against these deceptive techniques, and some of its high points are summarized here. Be on the lookout for these manipulations whenever you see statistics.

Selective Reporting

Because different types of statistics convey different information, the same data can be manipulated to "say" different things. Look at Figure A.5 and Table A.5, which present fictitious data for the results of a new type of talk therapy for people with acrophobia—a fear of heights. Before the therapy, participants reported a mean of 9 symptoms, with a median of 9.5 symptoms. After the therapy, the mean number of symptoms was 4.85, the median was 3.5, and the mode

FIGURE A.5 Number of Symptoms After Therapy for Acrophobia

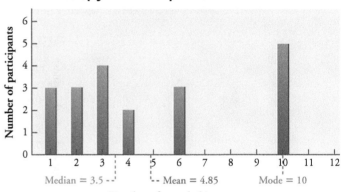

was 10. Proponents of the new therapy make the following claims: On average, symptoms decreased by almost half (based on the mean), and more than 50% of participants had substantial symptom reduction (based on the median). Opponents, however, convey the data differently. When she promotes the superiority of her company's medication, a spokeswoman from the pharmaceutical company that manufactures a medication to treat acrophobia makes the following claims about this new talk therapy: The number of symptoms most frequently reported was 10, which shows that the therapy actually made people *more* symptomatic (based on the mode). Also, the therapy achieved mixed results, as indicated by the fact that the number of symptoms after treatment ranged from 1 to 10.

As you can see, both supporters and detractors of the new treatment are correct. They are just presenting different aspects of the data. It's a little like the blind men who are feeling different parts of the elephant, with one reporting that it's like a tree trunk, another that it's like a fire hose, and so forth—but in this case they are showing you just one part at a time. To get the complete picture, you need to see all the relevant measures of central

TABLE A.5 Fictional Results of Therapy for Acrophobia

Mean number of symptoms after therapy for acrophobia
= Total number of symptoms ÷ Total number of participants
= 1 + 1 + 1 + 2 + 2 + 2 + 3 + 3 + 3 + 3 + 4 + 4 + 6 + 6 + 6 + 10 + 10 + 10 + 10 + 10
= 97 ÷ 20 = 4.85
Median = 3.5
Mode = 10

tendency and variability. Specifically, when hearing or reading about research or survey results, you should ask several questions before taking the results too seriously:

1. What is the distribution of the scores or data points? If they are normally distributed, the three measures of central tendency will be similar. If the distribution is skewed, however, the measures of central tendency will convey different information, and the one provided will be the one that conveys the information the presenter wants you to know. Do the other measures of central tendency paint a different picture of the results?

2. How variable are the data? Is the variability so great that the results may not apply to many members of the sample?

Lying with Graphs

Many results are presented in graph form. Graphs work largely because of a single principle: *More is more* (Kosslyn, 2006). Larger bars, higher lines, or bigger wedges all stand for greater amounts than smaller bars, lower lines, or smaller wedges. Our tendency to see more on the page as standing for more of a substance can lead us astray if graphs are constructed to deceive. Be alert to the following tricks:

• *Shortening the Y (vertical) axis to exaggerate a difference.* As you can see in the right-hand graph of Figure A.6, the Y axis can be drawn so that it starts at a high value and is stretched out so that it covers only a small part of the scale. Doing this makes what is in fact a small difference look like a large one. If a difference is statistically significant, it should look that way (and thus shortening the axis may be appropriate). But if it's not, then shortening the axis to exaggerate the difference is deception.

FIGURE A.6 Shortening the Y Axis Can Mislead

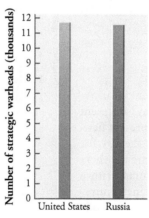 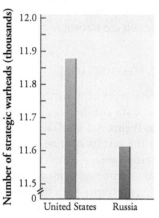

The graph on the left presents the actual numbers in a neutral way; the graph on the right exaggerates the difference.

Source: From *Graph Design for the Eye and Mind,* by Stephen Kosslyn (2006): pp. 203–204, Figures 8.1 and 8.2. By Permission of Oxford University Press, Inc.

• *Using an inappropriately large range of values to minimize amounts and differences.* The flip side of the coin is illustrated in the right-hand graph of Figure A.7, in which the total amount—as well as the difference—is made to appear smaller by using a large range in values on the Y axis.

• *Using three-dimensional graphics to exaggerate size.* As shown in Figure A.8, a designer can take advantage of our tendency to impose size constancy, which leads us to see a bar that appears farther away as larger than it would seem when it is drawn so that it appears closer. Even if an actual difference exists, this technique can exaggerate its magnitude.

FIGURE A.7 Lengthening the Y Axis Can Mislead

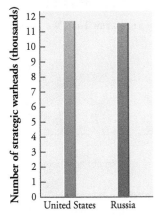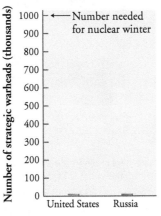

The graph on the left presents the actual numbers in a neutral way; the graph on the right minimizes the total number (as well as the difference).

Source: From *Graph Design for the Eye and Mind,* by Stephen Kosslyn (2006): pp. 209, 211. By Permission of Oxford University Press, Inc.

FIGURE A.8 Size Constancy Can Exaggerate Three-Dimensional Bar Size

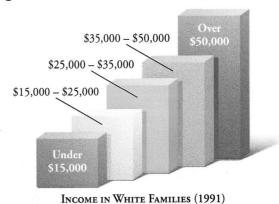

INCOME IN WHITE FAMILIES (1991)

Size constancy leads us to see the bars that are farther away as larger than they are, thereby exaggerating a difference.

Source: From *Graph Design for the Eye and Mind,* by Stephen Kosslyn (2006): p. 219. Data from Hacker, "Apartheid, American Style" in Newsweek, March 23, 1992, p. 61. By Permission of Oxford University Press, Inc.

- *Transforming the data before plotting.* Transforming the data can also distort it. Compare the two graphs in Figure A.9. The left-hand one shows the size of the stock market in three countries over 3 years; the right-hand one shows the percentage increase over two 5-year periods. If you saw only the graph on the right, you wouldn't realize that the increases in the size of the U.S. stock market were actually much greater , in dollars, than those in Japan. If the presenter is trying to sell Japanese stocks, you can bet which display will be preferred.

FIGURE A.9 Transforming Data Can Distort the Conclusions

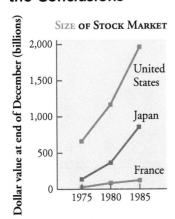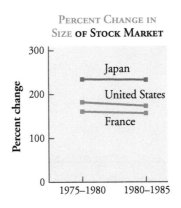

The graph on the left shows the actual dollar figures, and the one on the right shows the percentage change. Clearly, the message conveyed by the two displays is different. Which one is "more honest" depends on the purpose for which the graph is used.

Source: From *Graph Design for the Eye and Mind,* by Stephen Kosslyn (2006): p. 205. Data from Morgan Stanley Capital International, cited in *The Economist World Atlas and Almanac,* 1989, p. 90. By Permission of Oxford University Press, Inc.

- *Changing width along with height.* Changing the width along with the height gives a much larger impression of amount than is conveyed by changing height alone. As shown in Figure A.10, our visual system does not register height and width separately; instead, we see them simultaneously, as specifying area.

FIGURE A.10 Changing Width with Height Exaggerates Size

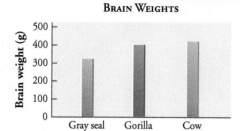

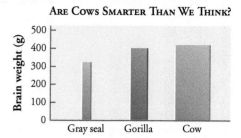

Expanding the bar width for taller bars conveys the impression that a greater quantity is being represented than is conveyed when the width is kept constant.

Source: From *Graph Design for the Eye and Mind,* by Stephen Kosslyn (2006): p. 207. Data from Weisberg, 1980, cited in Chambers et al., 1983, p. 371. By Permission of Oxford University Press, Inc.

Statistics in Daily Life

You can see that there is nothing magical or mysterious about statistics. Whenever you see a graph in the newspaper, you are seeing statistics; when you hear that a poll is accurate to "plus or minus 3 points," you know that you are being supplied with a confidence interval. The crucial ideas are that there are measures of central tendency (mean, median, and mode), measures of variability (range and standard deviation), and statistical tests that tell you the likelihood that a measured difference arises from chance alone. What you've learned here is enough to enable you to read and understand many reports of original research in psychology.

PART B – HOW TO THINK ABOUT RESEARCH STUDIES

The QALMRI Method in Action: An Example

You will find it useful to approach reading—and writing—research reports armed with the QALMRI method. This method ties directly into the steps of the scientific method itself, which we discuss in the chapter *Introduction to the Science of Psychology,* and is a vehicle for understanding the meaning of a research study in the literature—and for reporting your own research. This method will help you become clear about what question is being asked, how the researchers have tried to answer it, and whether the results really do support the preferred answer (the hypothesis).

In what follows, we first explain how to use the QALMRI method when reading a research report, we next consider how to use it when writing your own reports, and we then provide an example of the method in action. You will get the most out of this if you first read *Introduction to the Science of Psychology* and Appendix A, both of which provide useful background.

Reading Research Reports: The QALMRI Method

When you read a research report, try to identify the following components—which together make up the QALMRI method.

Q Stands for the Question   All research begins with a question, and the point of the research is to answer it.

The first few paragraphs of the Introduction section should tell the reader what question the research study addresses. In addition, the context provided by the Introduction's review of previous studies should explain why the question is important. In some cases, the question is important for practical reasons; in others, it is important as a way to test a theory (and, in some cases, it is important for both practical and theoretical reasons).

A Stands for Alternatives   A good report describes at least two possible answers to the question and explains why both are plausible. After describing the question that is being addressed, the Introduction should explain what alternatives are being considered. When reading the Introduction, try to identify the question and then the alternative answers that are being considered. If the alternatives are not spelled out, try to infer what they might be; if the study is simply seeking to confirm a theory's prediction, try to get a sense of whether other theories (or just common sense) would make the same prediction (if all of the theories make the same prediction, it probably isn't worth testing).

L Stands for the Logic of the Study   The goal of a study is to discriminate among the alternatives, and the logic is the general idea behind the study—the way the study will distinguish among the alternatives. The logic is typically explained toward the end of the Introduction section, after the question and alternative possible answers have been summarized. The logic has the following structure: **If** alternative #1 (and not the other alternatives) is correct, **then** when a particular variable is manipulated, the participant's behavior should change in a

521

specific way. For example, the logic of a study of whether a particular drug enhances memory might be: "If the drug enhances memory (and the placebo doesn't), then people should recall more test words after taking the drug than after taking the placebo."

M Stands for the Method   The details of what the researcher did are found in the Method section. A good Method section should described the details of what was done so well that the reader could replicate the study, doing exactly the same thing as the original investigators. The Method section has the following parts:

PARTICIPANTS: Look to see how the participants were selected. Are they a representative sample of the population of interest? If no particular population is specified, then the sample should be representative of the population in general. If the study involves more than one group, they should be equivalent on all important variables, such as age and education. Depending on the study, variables such as level of depression, number and type of medications used previously, or experience in noisy magnetic resonance imaging machines can be relevant. Try to think of all possible confounds that could make the groups different in ways that might affect the study's outcome.

MATERIALS: If questionnaires are used in the study, they should have been shown to be valid (that is, they should measure what they are supposed to measure). And they should be reliable (that is, they should produce consistent results). In addition, materials used in different parts of the study should not differ except as required to answer the research question.

APPARATUS: The apparatus delivers stimuli or defines the experimental situation. If a computer is used, the research report should describe exactly how it presented the stimuli. It also should describe in detail any other physical props that were used. Think about how the apparatus looked to the participants and whether it could have distracted them or allowed them to pick up inappropriate cues.

PROCEDURE: The procedure is the step-by-step process that the researchers followed to carry out the study. Try to picture yourself in the study; is it clear precisely what the participants did? Were participants given appropriate instructions (clear, but not leading them on)? Was it clear that the participants did in fact understand the instructions? Could the investigators have unintentionally treated participants in different groups differently?

R Stands for the Results   The outcome of the study is described in detail in the Results section. First, look for measures of central tendency (means, medians, modes) and some measure of the sampling variability (commonly, standard deviations). (Measures of central tendency and sampling variability are descriptive statistics; see Appendix Part A for a discussion of descriptive statistics.) The actual results—what the researchers found—are summarized by such descriptive statistics and often are presented in a graph or table. Second, not all differences and patterns in the results should be taken seriously; some differences are simply quirks that arise from chance. Inferential statistics (see Appendix Part A for a discussion of inferential statistics) should be reported to indicate which patterns of variation are unlikely to have arisen from chance. Look for the p values that document differences; if the p value is less than .05 (indicating that the observed difference in the data would have arisen from chance less than 5% of the time), you can be reasonably certain that the difference found in the sample reflects an actual difference in the population as a whole.

I Stands for Inferences   Given the obtained results, the researchers and you should be able to infer the answer to the question asked at the beginning of the paper—or at least infer that some of the possible alternative answers can be ruled out. Decide whether the researchers convincingly answered the question they posed at the outset. The Discussion section usually contains the inferences the researchers want to draw from their results. If the study was well designed (the logic sound and the method rigorous), the results should allow you to eliminate at least one of the alternatives and ideally should be most consistent with only one of the alternative answers to the question.

At this point in reading an article, take a step back and think about potential confounds that could have led to the results. Were any alternative explanations not ruled out? For example, perhaps participants in different groups were treated differently by the investigators, or perhaps they were tested at different times of day or at different periods in the semester (closer or farther from anxiety-inducing exams). And consider any loose ends—what else would you want to know about the phenomena?

In sum, the QALMRI method helps you focus on the "big picture": what a study is about and why it's important, what the researchers actually did, what they found, and what the results actually mean. The single most important bit of advice you need to remember about reading a research report is to be an active reader: Think about what the researchers are claiming—and about whether these claims make sense given the information provided in the article.

Writing Your Own Research Papers

The same principles apply to writing your own research papers. Write the Introduction section so that the reader can clearly understand the question you are addressing and why it is important. Your question can be important because:

- you've spotted a hole in the existing scientific literature and aim to fill it by obtaining new information,
- you've identified a variable that might invalidate the results of (or inferences drawn from) a previous study,
- you want to document a new phenomenon,
- you are testing a theory (a previous one or a new one of your own).

When you review other studies and theories in the published literature, only include those that help you explain why your question is important—that put it in context.

How long should your Introduction be? Abraham Lincoln was once asked how long a man's legs should be, and he replied, "Long enough to reach the ground." The same principle applies to Introductions: When writing up your results for publication, don't include any more or less material than you need to put your question in context. (If you're writing up your results for a class project, though, some professors may provide minimum or maximum page lengths, which might affect the length of your Introduction.)

The Introduction should also explain the alternative possible answers to the question that you will consider—including, in most cases, your preferred one, which is called the "hypothesis." You need to explain why each alternative is plausible, usually by referring to previously published findings and theories. Finally, the Introduction should end with a clear statement of the logic of your study, the basic idea underlying what you did.

In the Method section, be sure to include enough detail to allow another researcher to repeat exactly what you did. Explain what sort of participants were tested and how you ensured that participants in different groups were comparable in terms of important variables. In addition, you need to describe the materials in detail, and you also need to describe the apparatus and the procedure as precisely as possible.

In the Results section, start with the most important findings, which are those that bear directly on your question and the alternative answers. Don't fall prey to the temptation to present the most statistically "significant" results first. Being "statistically significant" only means that the result is not likely to have occurred by chance alone—it does not mean that the result is important (the word "significant" is ambiguous here). The most *important* results address the question being asked—even if these results are not as striking as some of the other findings. If your Introduction is clear, the reader is focused like a laser beam on the question you are asking and on which alternative answer is supported by the results (or which alternative answers you have definitively ruled out). Don't keep the reader in suspense; present the results that speak to the question at the outset of the Results section.

First present measures of central tendency and variability that directly bear on the question being asked; such measures are often best presented in a graph or table. You should also present inferential statistics along with the results so that the reader will know which differences and patterns in the data to take seriously. After you present the most important results, present anything else that you may have found.

Finally, in the Discussion section, return to the question and alternative answers and discuss exactly what you can infer from your results. Have you shown that some of the alternatives must be discarded? Is only one viable? What should future research focus on to propel the field even further ahead?

When writing a research report, always put yourself in the place of an intelligent reader. If a report has been written clearly, the reader will glide through it effortlessly, understanding why the research was conducted in a particular way, what the discoveries were, and why the results are interesting and important.

The QALMRI Method in Action: An Example

Let's now look at an example of using the QALMRI method to understand research. In this example, we'll focus on mental practice, the ability to rehearse an activity mentally, without actually making the movements associated with the activity. For example, many golfers claim that when they are off the course, they can practice by imagining themselves whacking the ball straight down a fairway or out of a sand trap. Players regularly claim that such mental practice improves their game. Well, maybe. The only way we can find out whether mental practice really works is by conducting a scientific study, and many such studies have been reported. Let's now consider one of them.

Question Can mental practice change subsequent golf putting? Woolfolk and colleagues (1985) asked whether mentally rehearsing golf putts can help or hurt sub-sequent performance.

Alternatives (1) Mental practice improves putting when participants imagine successfully tapping the ball into the hole, but it actually hurts performance when they imagine tapping the ball so that it misses the hole. (2) Mental practice can improve putting but not hurt it. (3) Mental practice can hurt putting but not improve it. (4) Mental practice does not have any effect at all.

Logic If alternative #1 is correct and the other alternatives are not, then when people imagine rehearsing the right kind of movements for a successful putt, their performance should later improve—but if they imagine rehearsing the wrong kinds of movements, then their performance should actually get worse.

Method The researchers first asked 30 college students to putt golf balls into a hole and assessed how well they could do so. After performing 20 putts (from 8.5 feet away), equal numbers of students of comparable skill were randomly assigned to each of three groups. The researchers then gave each group different instructions. They asked students in the positive imagery group to imagine making a "gentle but firm backswing" and then seeing the ball "rolling, rolling, right into the cup" (p. 338). Students in the negative imagery group received the identical instructions but were told to imagine the ball "rolling, rolling, toward the cup, but at the last second narrowly missing." Finally, they asked students in the control group to imagine putting, with no specific instructions about how to imagine the ball. The students then followed the instructions given to their group. After this, the researchers again asked the students to do actual putting and again assessed how well they could do it.

Results As shown in Figure B.1 on the next page, the students in the positive imagery group performed about 30% better after mental practice than they had when tested initially. In contrast, students in the negative imagery group actually got worse, scoring about 21% poorer than they had earlier. Finally, students in the control group improved a bit (by about 10%).

Inferences The authors concluded that mental practice depends on the specific movements you imagine. If the movements are appropriate to the goal, mental practice will help later performance—but if the movements are not appropriate to the goal, mental practice will actually hurt later performance. Many other studies have found that such appropriate mental practice improves subsequent performance (Doheny, 1993; Driskell et al., 1994; Druckman & Swets, 1988; Prather, 1973; Vieilledent et al., 2003; White & Hardy, 1995), and the present results begin to suggest why it might work.

FIGURE B.1 Effects of Mental Practice on Putting Performance

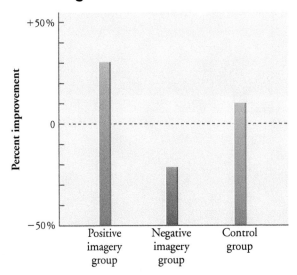

Results of Woolfolk et al. (1985), showing that mentally practicing putting improves actual performance.

Source: Source data from Woolfolk et al., 1985.

Glossary

Absolute threshold: The magnitude of the stimulus needed, on average, for an observer to detect it half the time it is present.

Academic psychologists: Psychologists who focus on teaching and conducting research.

Accommodation (in the eye): The automatic adjustment of the eye for seeing at particular distances, which occurs when muscles adjust the shape of the lens so that it focuses incoming light toward the back of the eye (the retina).

Accommodation (in Piaget's theory): The process that results in schemas' changing or the creation of new schemas, as necessary to cope with a broader range of situations.

Acquisition: In classical conditioning, the initial learning of the conditioned response (CR).

Action potential: The shifting change in charge that moves down the axon.

Activation-synthesis hypothesis: The theory that dreams arise from random bursts of nerve cell activity that may affect brain cells involved in hearing and seeing; the brain attempts to make sense of this hodgepodge of stimuli, resulting in the experience of dreams.

Active interaction: Occurs when people choose, partly based on genetic tendencies, to put themselves in specific situations and to avoid others.

Activity: A temperament dimension characterized by the preference for a particular activity level, which has two components: vigor (intensity of the activity) and tempo (speed of the activity).

Acute stressor: A stressor that has a short-term duration.

Adaptation: An inherited characteristic that increases an organism's ability to survive and reproduce successfully.

Adolescence: The period between the onset of puberty and, roughly, the end of the teenage years.

Adoption study: A study in which characteristics of children adopted at birth are compared to those of their adoptive parents or siblings versus their biological parents or siblings.

Affirming the consequent: A reasoning error that occurs when a person assumes that a specific cause is present because a particular result has occurred.

Afterimage: The image left behind by a previous perception.

Aggression: Behavior that is intended to harm another living being who does not wish to be harmed.

Agonist: A chemical that mimics the effects of a neurotransmitter by activating a type of receptor.

Agoraphobia: A condition in which people fear or avoid places that might be difficult to leave should panic symptoms occur.

Alarm phase: The first phase of the GAS, in which a stressor is perceived and the fight-or-flight response is activated.

Alcohol myopia: The disproportionate influence of immediate experience on behavior and emotion due to the effects of alcohol use.

Algorithm: A set of steps that, if followed methodically, will guarantee the correct solution to a problem.

All-or-none law: States that if the neuron is sufficiently stimulated, it fires, sending the action potential all the way down the axon and releasing chemicals from the terminal buttons; either the action potential occurs or it doesn't.

Allostatic load: The cumulative wear and tear on the body necessary to maintain homeostasis in the face of stressors.

Altruism: The motivation to increase another person's welfare.

Amnesia: A loss of memory over an entire time span.

Amphetamines: A class of synthetic stimulants.

Amplitude: The height of the peaks in a light wave or sound wave.

Amygdala: A subcortical structure that plays a special role in fear and is involved in other types of strong emotions, such as anger.

Androgens: Sex hormones that lead the body to develop many male characteristics, such as beard growth and a low voice.

Anorexia nervosa: An eating disorder characterized by the refusal to maintain even a low normal weight, along with an intense fear of gaining weight.

Antagonist: A chemical that blocks the effect of a neurotransmitter.

Anterograde amnesia: Amnesia that leaves consolidated memories intact but prevents the storing of new facts.

Antipsychotic medication: Medication that reduces psychotic symptoms.

Antisocial personality disorder (ASPD): A personality disorder characterized by a long-standing pattern of disregard for other people to the point of violating their rights.

Anxiety disorders: A category of disorders characterized by intense or pervasive anxiety or fear, or extreme attempts to avoid the feelings.

Applied psychologists: Psychologists who use the principles, findings, and theories of psychology to improve products and procedures and who conduct research to help solve specific practical problems.

Approach–approach conflict: The internal conflict that occurs when competing alternatives are equally positive.

Approach–avoidance conflict: The internal conflict that occurs when a course of action has both positive and negative aspects.

Assimilation: In Piaget's theory, the process that allows the use of existing schemas to organize and interpret new stimuli and respond appropriately.

Atherosclerosis: A medical condition characterized by the buildup of plaque on the inside walls of the arteries.

Attachment: An emotional bond that leads a person to want to be with someone else and to miss him or her when separated.

Attention: The act of focusing on particular information, which allows it to be processed more fully than what is not attended to.

Attentional blink: A rebound period in which a person cannot pay attention to a second stimulus after having just paid attention to another one (which need not be the same as the second stimulus).

Attitude: An overall evaluation of some aspect of the world—people, issues, or objects.

Attribution: An explanation for the cause of an event or behavior.

Attributional bias: A tendency to make certain types of attributions; this sort of bias generally occurs outside of conscious awareness.

Attributional style: A person's characteristic way of explaining life events.

Automatic processing: Processing that allows you to carry out a sequence of steps without having to pay attention to each one or to the relations between the steps; relies on implicit memories.

Autonomic nervous system (ANS): Controls the smooth muscles in the body, some glandular functions, and many of the body's self-regulating activities, such as digestion and circulation.

Availability heuristic: The strategy in which we judge objects or events as more likely, common, or frequent if they are easier to retrieve from memory.

Avoidance learning: In classical conditioning, learning that occurs when a CS is paired with an unpleasant US that leads the animal to try to avoid the CS.

Avoidance–avoidance conflict: The internal conflict that occurs when competing alternatives are equally unpleasant.

Axon: The sending end of the neuron; the long cablelike structure extending from the cell body.

B cell: A type of white blood cell that matures in the bone marrow.

Basal ganglia: Subcortical structures that play a role in planning, learning new habits, and producing movement.

Base-rate rule: The rule stating that if something is chosen at random from a set, the chance that the thing will be of a particular type is directly proportional to the percentage of that type in the set.

Basic emotion: An innate emotion that is shared by all humans.

Basic level (of a concept): An intermediate level of specificity that is usually the most likely to be applied to an object.

Behavior: The outwardly observable acts of a person, alone or in a group.

Behavior modification: A technique in which behavior is changed through the use of secondary reinforcers.

Behavior modification: Therapeutic techniques that use operant conditioning principles to change behavior.

Behavior therapy: A type of therapy, based on well-researched learning principles, that focuses on modifying observable, measurable behaviors.

Behavioral genetics: The field in which researchers attempt to determine the extent to which the differences among people's behaviors and psychological characteristics are due to their different genes or to differences in their environments.

Behaviorism: The school of psychology that focuses on how a specific stimulus (object, person, or event) evokes a specific response (behavior in reaction to the stimulus).

Belief in a just world: An attributional bias that assumes that people get what they deserve.

Benzodiazepine: A type of antianxiety medication that reduces symptoms of panic within 36 hours and does not need to be taken for more than a week to be effective.

Bias (in research studies): When conscious or unconscious beliefs, expectations, or habits alter how participants in a study respond or affect how a researcher sets up or conducts a study, thereby influencing its outcome.

Bias (in signal detection theory): A person's willingness to decide that he or she has detected a stimulus.

Bibliotherapy: The use of self-help books and audio and video information for therapeutic purposes.

Big Five: The five superfactors of personality—extraversion, neuroticism, agreeableness, conscientiousness, and openness—determined by factor analysis.

Binocular cues: Cues to the distance of an object that arise from both eyes working together.

Biological preparedness: A built-in readiness for certain previously neutral stimuli to come to elicit particular conditioned responses, which means that less training is necessary to produce learning when these neutral stimuli are paired with the appropriate unconditioned responses.

Bipolar disorders: A set of mood disorders characterized either by one or more episodes of mania, or by alternating episodes of hypomania and depression.

Bisexual: A person who is sexually attracted to members of both sexes.

Blackout: A period of time for which an alcoholic has no memory of events that transpired while he or she was intoxicated.

Bottom-up processing: Processing that is triggered by physical energy striking receptor cells.

Brain circuit: A set of neurons that work together to receive input, operate on it in some way, and produce specific output.

Brain system: A set of brain circuits that work together to accomplish a particular task.

Brainstem: The set of structures at the base of the brain—including the midbrain, medulla, and pons—that feed into and receive information from the spinal cord.

Breadth of processing: Processing that organizes and integrates new information into previously stored information, often by making associations.

Bulimia nervosa: An eating disorder characterized by recurrent episodes of binge eating, followed by attempts to prevent weight gain.

Bystander effect: The decrease in offers of assistance that occurs as the number of bystanders increases.

Case study: A scientific study that focuses on a single participant, examining his or her psychological characteristics (at any or all of the levels of analysis) in detail.

Castration anxiety: A boy's fear that, as punishment for loving mother and hating father, his father will cut off his penis.

Categorical perception: Automatically grouping sounds as members of distinct categories that correspond to the basic units of speech.

Categorical variables: Variables that assign measurements to discrete classes.

Cell body: The central part of a neuron (or other cell), which contains the nucleus.

Cell membrane: The skin that surrounds a cell.

Central executive: The set of processes in WM that transforms and interprets information in one or another of two specialized STMs during planning, reasoning, and problem solving.

Central nervous system (CNS): The spinal cord and the brain.

Central tendency: A descriptive statistic that indicates the clustering of the most characteristic values or scores for a particular group or sample.

Cerebellum: A large structure at the base of the brain that is concerned in part with physical coordination, estimating time, and paying attention.

Cerebral cortex: The convoluted pinkish-gray outer layer of the brain where most mental processes arise.

Cerebral hemisphere: A left or right half-brain, shaped roughly like half a sphere.

Chemical senses: Smell and taste, which rely on sensing the presence of specific chemicals.

Child-directed speech (CDS): Speech by caregivers to babies that relies on short sentences with clear pauses, careful enunciation, exaggerated intonation, and a high-pitched voice.

Chronic stressor: A stressor that has a long-term duration.

Chunk: An organized unit of information, such as a digit, letter, or word.

Circadian rhythms: The body's daily fluctuations in response to the cycle of dark and light.

Classical conditioning: A type of learning that occurs when a neutral stimulus becomes associated (paired) with a stimulus that causes a reflexive behavior, and, in time, this neutral stimulus is sufficient to elicit—draw out from the animal—that behavior.

Client-centered therapy: A type of insight-oriented therapy that focuses on people's potential for growth and the importance of an empathic therapist.

Clinical psychologist: The type of psychologist who is trained to provide psychotherapy and to administer and interpret psychological tests.

Cocktail party phenomenon: The effect of not being aware of other people's conversations until your name is mentioned and then suddenly hearing it.

Code: A particular method for specifying information (such as in words or images).

Cognitive dissonance: The uncomfortable state that arises from a discrepancy between two attitudes, beliefs, or behaviors.

Cognitive distortions: Systematic biases in the way a person thinks about events and people, including oneself.

Cognitive learning: The acquisition of information that may not be acted on immediately but is stored for later use.

Cognitive neuroscience: The approach in psychology that blends cognitive psychology and neuroscience (the study of the brain) when attempting to specify how the brain gives rise to mental processes that store and process information.

Cognitive psychology: The approach in psychology that attempts to characterize the mental events that allow information to be stored and operated on internally.

Cognitive restructuring: The process of helping clients view their situation in a new light, which then allows them to shift their thinking from the focus on automatic, distorted, negative thoughts to more realistic ones.

Cognitive therapy: A type of therapy that is designed to help clients think realistically and rationally in order to reinterpret events that otherwise would lead to distressing thoughts, feelings, and/or behaviors.

Cognitive–behavior therapy (CBT): A type of therapy that is designed to help patients both to reduce problematic behaviors and irrational thoughts and to develop new, more adaptive behaviors and beliefs.

Collectivist culture: A culture that emphasizes the rights and responsibilities of the group over those of the individual.

Color blindness: An acquired (by brain damage) or inherited inability to distinguish two or more hues from each other or to sense hues at all.

Color constancy: The perception that the color of an object remains the same even when it is seen in different lighting conditions.

Companionate love: An altruistic type of love characterized by expending time, attention, and resources on behalf of another person.

Complex inheritance: The transmission of characteristics by the joint action of combinations of genes working together; also called polygenetic inheritance.

Compliance: A change in behavior brought about by a direct request rather than by social norms.

Compulsion: A repetitive behavior or mental act that a person feels compelled to perform, usually in response to an obsession.

Computer-assisted tomography (CT): A neuroimaging technique that produces a three-dimensional image of brain structures using X rays.

Concept: The idea that underlies the meaning of a word or image; depending on the language, some concepts can be expressed with a single word or may require a phrase or two to be fully expressed.

Concrete operation: In Piaget's theory, a (reversible) manipulation of the mental representation of an object that corresponds to an actual physical manipulation.

Conditioned emotional response (CER): An emotionally charged conditioned response elicited by a previously neutral stimulus.

Conditioned response (CR): A response that depends (is conditional) on pairing the conditioned stimulus with an unconditioned stimulus; once learned, the response to the US now occurs when the conditioned stimulus is presented alone.

Conditioned stimulus (CS): An originally neutral stimulus that comes to produce a response evoked by a US after it has been paired enough times with that US.

Conduction deafness: A type of deafness caused by a physical impairment of the outer or middle ear.

Cones: Cone-shaped retinal receptor cells that respond most strongly to one of three wavelengths of light; the combined signals from cones that are most sensitive to different wavelengths play a key role in producing color vision.

Confidence interval: The range above and below the mean of a sample within which the mean of a population is likely to occur.

Confirmation bias: A bias to seek information that will confirm a rule and not to seek information that would refute the rule.

Conformity: A change in behavior in order to follow a group's norms.

Confound (or confounding variable): Any aspect of the situation that varies along with the independent variable (or variables) of interest and could be the actual basis for what is measured.

Conservation: The Piagetian principle that certain properties, such as amount or mass, remain the same even when the appearance of the material or object changes, provided that nothing is added or removed.

Consolidation: The process of converting information stored dynamically in LTM into a structural change in the brain.

Continuous reinforcement: Reinforcement given for each desired response.

Continuous variables: Variables that have values that can fall anywhere along the measurement scale.

Contrapreparedness: A built-in disinclination (or even an inability) for certain stimuli to be conditioned to elicit particular conditioned responses.

Control condition: A part of a study in which participants receive the same procedure as in the experimental condition except that the independent variable of interest is not manipulated.

Control group: A group that is treated exactly the same way as the experimental group, except that the independent variable that is the focus of the study is not manipulated. The control group holds constant—"controls"—all of the variables in the experimental group.

Controlled processing: Processing that requires paying attention to each step of a task and using working memory to coordinate the steps; relies on explicit memories.

Convergence: The degree to which the eyes swivel toward the center (are crossed) when a person focuses attention on an object.

Coping: Taking action to address a stressor or to counteract effects of a stressor.

Coping strategy: A specific approach or technique that is employed to handle stress.

Cornea: The transparent covering over the eye, which (along with the lens) focuses light onto the back of the eye.

Corpus callosum: The large bundle of axons that connects the two halves of the brain.

Correlation coefficient: A number that ranges from -1.0 to 1.0 that indicates how closely interrelated two sets of measured variables are; the higher the coefficient (in either the positive or negative direction), the better the value of one measurement can predict the value of the other. Also simply called a correlation.

Cortisol: A hormone produced by the outer layer of the adrenal glands that helps the body cope with the extra energy demands of stress.

Counseling psychologist: The type of psychologist who is trained to help people with issues that naturally arise during the course of life.

Crack: Cocaine in crystalline form, usually smoked in a pipe (freebasing) or rolled into a cigarette.

Creativity: The ability to produce something original of high quality or to devise an effective new way to solve a problem.

Critical period: A narrow window of time when a certain type of learning or some aspect of development is possible.

Cross-sectional study: A study in which different groups of people are tested, with each group composed of individuals of a particular age.

Crystallized intelligence: According to Cattell and Horn, the kind of intelligence that relies on knowing facts and having the ability to use and combine them.

Cues: Stimuli, thoughts, or feelings that trigger or enhance remembering; reminders of an object or event.

Dark adaptation: The process that leads to increased sensitivity to light after being in the dark.

Data: Careful descriptions or numerical measurements of a phenomenon.

Debriefing: An interview after a study to ensure that the participant has no negative reactions as a result of participation and to explain why the study was conducted.

Decay: The loss of memories over time because the relevant connections among neurons are lost.

Deductive reasoning: Reasoning that applies the rules of logic to a set of assumptions (stated as premises) to discover whether certain conclusions inevitably follow from those assumptions; deduction goes from the general to the particular.

Defense mechanism: The unconscious processes that prevent unacceptable thoughts or urges from reaching conscious awareness.

Delayed reinforcement: Reinforcement given some period of time after the desired response is exhibited.

Delusions: Unshakable but false beliefs that are often bizarre.

Dendrite: The treelike part of a neuron that receives messages from the axons of other neurons.

Dependent variable: The aspect of the situation that is measured as the values of an independent variable are changed.

Depressants: A class of substances (including barbiturates, benzodiazepines, and alcohol), that depress the central nervous system, thereby decreasing the user's behavioral activity and level of awareness; also called sedative-hypnotic drugs.

Deprived reward: Reward that occurs when an animal (including a human) lacks a substance or condition necessary for survival and an action then produces this substance or condition.

Depth of processing: The number and complexity of the mental operations used when processing; deeper processing occurs when more—or more complex—operations are used during encoding.

Descriptive statistics: Concise ways of summarizing properties of sets of numbers.

Diathesis–stress model: An explanation for how psychological disorders develop, in which a predisposition to a given disorder (diathesis) and specific factors (stress) combine to trigger the onset of the disorder.

Dichotic listening: A procedure in which participants hear different stimuli presented separately to each of the two ears (through headphones) and are instructed to listen only to sounds presented to one ear.

Diffusion of responsibility: The diminished sense of responsibility to help that each person feels as the number of bystanders grows.

Discrimination (in perception): The ability to respond only to a particular stimulus and not to a similar one.

Discrimination (toward others): Negative behavior toward individuals from a specific group that arises from unjustified negative attitudes about that group.

Disinhibition: The inhibition of inhibitory neurons, which makes other neurons (the ones that are usually inhibited) more likely to fire and which usually occurs as a result of depressant use.

Display rule: A culture-specific rule that indicates when, to whom, and how strongly certain emotions can be shown.

Dizygotic: From different eggs and sharing only as many genes as any pair of siblings—on average, half.

Door-in-the-face technique: A compliance technique in which someone makes a very large request and then when it is denied (as expected) makes a smaller request—for what is actually desired.

Double pain: The sensation that occurs when an injury first causes a sharp pain and later a dull pain; the two kinds of pain arise from different neural pathways sending their messages at different speeds.

Double-blind design: The participant is "blind" to (unaware of) the predictions of the study (and so cannot consciously or unconsciously produce the predicted results), and the experimenter is "blind" to the group to which the participant has been assigned or to the condition that the participant is receiving (and so experimenter expectancy effects cannot produce the predicted results).

Down syndrome: A type of mental retardation that results from the creation of an extra chromosome during conception; it is a genetic problem but not inherited.

Dream analysis: A technique used in psychoanalysis and psychodynamic therapy in which the therapist examines the content of dreams to gain access to the unconscious.

Drive: An internal imbalance caused by the lack of a needed substance or condition that motivates animals (including humans) to reach a particular goal that will reduce the imbalance.

Eating disorders: A category of disorders that involves severe disturbances in eating.

Effect: The difference in the value of the dependent variable that arises from changes in the independent variable.

Ego: A personality structure, proposed by Freud, that develops in childhood and tries to balance the competing demands of the id, superego, and reality.

Egocentrism: In Piaget's theory, the inability to take another person's point of view.

Elaborative encoding: Encoding strategies that produce great breadth of processing.

Electroconvulsive therapy (ECT): A treatment in which an electric current induces a controlled brain seizure.

Electroencephalogram (EEG): A tracing of brain waves of electrical fluctuation over time.

Electroencephalograph: A machine that records electrical activity in the brain.

Embryo: A developing baby from the point where the major axis of the body is present until all major structures are present, spanning from about 2 weeks to 8 weeks after conception.

Emotion: A psychological state with four components: (1) a positive or negative subjective experience, (2) bodily arousal, (3) the activation of specific mental processes and stored information, and (4) characteristic overt behavior.

Emotional intelligence (EI): The ability to understand and regulate emotions effectively.

Emotionality: A temperament dimension characterized by an inclination to become aroused in situations in which the predominant emotions are distress, fear, or anger.

Emotion-focused coping: Coping focused on changing the person's emotional response to the stressor.

Enacted social support: The specific supportive behaviors provided by others.

Encoding: The process of organizing and transforming incoming information so that it can be entered into memory, either to be stored or to be compared with previously stored information.

Encoding failure: A failure to process to-be-remembered information well enough to ensure that it is fully entered into LTM.

Endogenous cannabinoids: Neurotransmitter substances released by the receiving neuron that then influence the activity of the sending neuron.

Endorphins: Painkilling chemicals produced naturally in the brain.

Episodic memories: Memories of events that are associated with a particular time, place, and circumstance.

Estrogen: The hormone that causes girls to develop breasts and is involved in the menstrual cycle.

Evocative (or reactive) interaction: Occurs when genetically influenced characteristics (both behavioral and physical) induce other people to behave in particular ways.

Evolution: Gene-based changes in the characteristics or abilities of members of a species over successive generations.

Evolutionary psychology: The approach in psychology that assumes that certain cognitive strategies and goals are so important that natural selection has built them into our brains.

Exhaustion phase: The final stage of the GAS, in which the continued stress response itself becomes damaging to the body.

Expectancies: Expectations that have a powerful influence on thoughts, feelings, and behaviors and, in turn, on personality.

Experimental condition: A part of a study in which participants receive the complete procedure that defines the experiment.

Experimental group: A group that receives the complete procedure that defines the experiment.

Experimenter expectancy effects: Effects that occur when an investigator's expectations lead him or her (consciously or unconsciously) to treat participants in a way that encourages them to produce the expected results.

Explicit memories: Memories that can be retrieved voluntarily and brought into STM. Also called declarative memories.

Exposure: A therapeutic technique whereby through repeated encounters with a stimulus the person becomes less responsive to that stimulus.

External attribution: An explanation of someone's behavior that focuses on the situation; also called situational attribution.

Extinction (in classical conditioning): The process by which a CR comes to be eliminated through repeated presentations of the CS without the presence of the US.

Extinction (in operant conditioning): The fading out of a response following an initial burst of that behavior after reinforcement ceases.

Extrasensory perception (ESP): The ability to perceive and know things without using the ordinary senses.

Facial feedback hypothesis: The idea that emotions arise partly as a result of the positioning of facial muscles.

Factor analysis: A statistical method that uncovers the particular characteristics (factors) that make scores more or less similar.

False memories: Memories of events or situations that did not, in fact, occur.

Family therapy: A therapy modality in which a family (or certain members of a family) is treated.

Fetal alcohol syndrome: A condition that includes mental retardation and is caused by excessive drinking of alcohol by the mother during pregnancy.

Fetus: A developing baby during the final phase of development in the womb, from about 8 weeks after conception until birth.

Figure: A set of perceptual characteristics (such as shape, color, texture) that typically corresponds to an object.

Fixed interval schedule: Reinforcement given for responses only when they are produced after a fixed interval of time.

Fixed ratio schedule: Reinforcement given for responses produced after a fixed number of prior responses.

Flashback: A hallucination that occurs without drug use, often long after the user has taken a drug.

Flashbulb memory: An unusually vivid and detailed memory of a dramatic event.

Fluid intelligence: According to Cattell and Horn, the kind of intelligence that underlies the creation of novel solutions to problems.

Food aversion (taste aversion): A classically conditioned avoidance of a certain food or taste.

Foot-in-the-door technique: A technique that achieves compliance by beginning with an insignificant request, which is then followed by a larger request.

Forebrain: According to a historical way of organizing brain structures, a unit of the brain that includes the cortex, thalamus, limbic system, and basal ganglia.

Forgetting curve: A graphic representation of the rate at which information is forgotten over time.

Formal operation: In Piaget's theory, a reversible mental act that can be performed even with abstract concepts.

Fovea: The small, central region of the retina with the highest density of cones and the highest resolution.

Free association: A technique used in psychoanalysis and psychodynamic therapy in which the patient says whatever comes to mind, and the train of thought reveals to the therapist or psychoanalyst the patient's issues and ways of handling them.

Frequency: The number of light waves or sound waves that move past a given point per second.

Frequency distribution: The frequency of each value of the independent variable (for continuous variables) or of each type of case (for categorical variables) that was observed in a set of data.

Frequency theory: In hearing, the theory that higher frequencies produce higher rates of neural firing.

Frontal lobes: The brain lobes located behind the forehead; critically involved in planning, memory search, motor control, speech control, reasoning, and emotions.

Functional fixedness: When solving a problem, getting stuck on one interpretation of an object or one aspect of the situation.

Functional magnetic resonance imaging (fMRI): A type of magnetic resonance imaging that detects the amount of oxygen being brought to particular places in the brain, which indicates how active those neurons are.

Functionalism: The school of psychology that sought to understand how the mind helps individuals to adapt to the world around them, to function effectively in it.

Fundamental attribution error: The strong tendency to interpret other people's behavior as arising from internal causes rather than external ones; also referred to as the correspondence bias.

g: "General factor," a single intellectual capacity that underlies the positive correlations among different tests of intelligence.

Gate control (of pain): The mechanism that allows top-down processing to inhibit interneurons that send pain signals to the brain.

Gender roles: The culturally determined appropriate behaviors for males versus females.

Gene: A stretch of the DNA molecule that produces a specific protein.

General adaptation syndrome (GAS): The overall stress response that has three phases: alarm, resistance, and exhaustion.

Generalization: The ability to transfer a learned stimulus–response association to a new stimulus that is similar to the original one, making the same response to it that led to reinforcement previously.

Generalized anxiety disorder: An anxiety disorder characterized by excessive anxiety and worry that is not consistently related to a specific object or situation.

Genotype: The genetic code within an organism.

Gestalt laws of organization: A set of rules describing the circumstances under which visual characteristics (such as patches that have a specific hue, intensity, or distance) will be grouped into perceptual units.

Gestalt psychology: An approach to understanding mental events that focuses on the idea that the whole is more than the sum of its parts.

Gifted: People who have IQs at least three standard deviations above the mean (which is a score of 145 on the WAIS-IV).

Glial cell: A type of cell that helps neurons to form both synapses and connections when the brain is developing, influences the communication among neurons, and generally helps in the "care and feeding" of neurons.

Glucocorticoids: A group of hormones that are released when the stress response is triggered.

Grammar: The set of rules that determines how words can be organized into an infinite number of acceptable sentences in a language.

Ground: In perception, the background.

Group polarization: The tendency of group members' opinions to become more extreme (in the same direction as their initial opinions) after group discussion.

Group therapy: A therapy modality in which a number of clients with compatible needs or goals meet together with a therapist.

Group: A social entity characterized by regular interaction among members, some emotional connection, a common frame of reference, and a degree of interdependence.

Groupthink: The group process that arises when people who try to solve problems together accept one another's information and ideas without subjecting them to critical analysis.

Gyrus: A bulge between sulci in the cerebral cortex.

Habit: A well-learned response that is carried out automatically (without conscious thought) when the appropriate stimulus is present.

Habituation: The learning that occurs when repeated exposure to a stimulus decreases an organism's responsiveness to that stimulus.

Hair cells: The receptor cells with stiff hairs along the basilar membrane of the inner ear; when hairs are moved, they produce neural signals that are sent to the brain and underlie auditory sensation.

Hallucinations: Mental images so vivid that they seem real.

Hallucinogen: A substance that induces hallucinations.

Health psychology: The area of psychology concerned with the promotion of health and the prevention and treatment of illness as it relates to psychological factors.

Heritability: The degree to which the variability of a characteristic or ability in a population is due to genetics—given a specific environment.

Heterosexual: A person who is sexually attracted to members of the opposite sex.

Heuristic: A rule-of-thumb strategy that does not guarantee the correct solution to a problem but offers a likely shortcut to it.

High expressed emotion: An emotional style in families in which members are critical, hostile, and overinvolved.

Hindbrain: According to a historical way of organizing brain structures, a unit of the brain that includes the medulla, pons, cerebellum, and parts of the reticular formation.

Hippocampus: A subcortical structure that plays a key role in allowing new information to be stored in the brain's memory banks.

Homeostasis: The process of maintaining a steady state, in which bodily substances and conditions are kept within the range in which the body functions well.

Homosexual: A person who is sexually attracted to members of the same sex.

Hormone: A chemical that is produced by a gland and can act as a neurotransmitter substance.

Hostile attribution bias: The tendency to misread the intentions of others as negative.

Hostility: The personality trait associated with heart disease and characterized by mistrust, an expectation of harm and provocation by others, and a cynical attitude.

Humanistic psychology: The school of psychology that assumes people have positive values, free will, and deep inner creativity, the combination of which allow them to choose life-fulfilling paths to personal growth.

Hypnogogic sleep: The initial stage of sleep, which lasts about 5 minutes and can include the sensation of gentle falling or floating or a sudden jerking of the body; also referred to as Stage 1 sleep.

Hypothalamic-pituitary-adrenal (HPA) axis: The system of the hypothalamus, pituitary gland, and adrenal glands that is activated by stress, injury, and infection and that works to fight off infection.

Hypothalamus: A brain structure that sits under the thalamus and plays a central role in controlling eating and drinking and in regulating the body's temperature, blood pressure, heart rate, sexual behavior, and hormones.

Hypothesis: A tentative idea that might explain a set of observations.

Id: A personality structure, proposed by Freud, that exists at birth and houses sexual and aggressive drives, physical needs, and simple psychological needs.

Immediate reinforcement: Reinforcement given immediately after the desired response is exhibited.

Implicit memories: Memories that cannot be retrieved voluntarily and brought into STM but rather predispose a person to process information or behave in certain ways in the presence of specific stimuli; also called nondeclarative memories.

Impulsivity: A temperament dimension characterized by the propensity to respond to stimuli immediately, without reflection or concern for consequences.

Incentive: A stimulus or event that draws animals (including humans) to achieve a particular goal in anticipation of a reward.

Incidental learning: Learning that occurs without the intention to learn.

Incongruence: According to client-centered therapy, a mismatch between a person's real self and his or her ideal self.

Independent variable: The aspect of the situation that is deliberately and independently varied while another aspect is measured.

Individual therapy: A therapy modality in which an individual client is treated by a single therapist.

Individualist culture: A culture that emphasizes the rights and responsibilities of the individual over those of the group.

Inductive reasoning: Reasoning that uses examples to discover a rule that governs them; induction goes from the particular (examples) to the general (a rule).

Inferential statistics: Results of tests that reveal which differences or patterns in the measurements reflect actual differences in a population, as opposed to those that merely reflect chance variations.

Informed consent: The requirement that a potential participant in a study be told what he or she will be asked to do and be advised of possible risks and benefits of the study before formally agreeing to take part.

Ingroup: A person's own group.

Insight learning: Learning that occurs when a person or animal suddenly grasps how to solve a problem or interpret a pattern of information, and incorporates that new knowledge into old knowledge.

Insight-oriented therapy: A type of therapy in which the therapist aims to remove distressing symptoms by leading the person to understand the psychological causes of his or her symptoms through deeply felt personal insights.

Insomnia: Repeated difficulty falling asleep, difficulty staying asleep, or waking up too early.

Instinct: An inherited tendency to produce organized and unalterable responses to particular stimuli.

Insulin: A hormone that stimulates the storage of food molecules in the form of fat.

Intelligence: The ability to reason and solve problems well and to understand and learn complex material.

Intelligence quotient (IQ): A score on an intelligence test, originally based on comparing mental age to chronological age, but later based on norms and used as a measure of intelligence.

Intentional learning: Learning that occurs as a result of trying to learn.

Interference: Occurs when information disrupts encoding or retrieval of other information.

Internal attribution: An explanation of someone's behavior that focuses on the person's beliefs, goals, or other characteristics; also called dispositional attribution.

Internal conflict: The emotional predicament that people experience when making difficult choices.

Interneuron: A neuron that is connected to other neurons, not to sense organs or muscles.

Interpersonal therapy (IPT): A type of manual-based treatment that helps clients to understand how aspects of current relationships can affect their mood and behavior.

Interpretation: A technique used in psychodynamic therapies in which the therapist deciphers the patient's words and behaviors, assigning unconscious motivations to them.

Interval schedule: Partial reinforcement schedule based on time.

Introspection: The technique of observing your mental events as, or immediately after, they occur.

Ion: An atom that has a positive or negative charge.

Iris: The circular muscle that adjusts the size of the pupil.

Just-noticeable difference (JND): The size of the difference in a stimulus characteristic needed for a person to detect a difference between two stimuli or a change in a single stimulus.

Kinesthetic sense: The sense that registers the movement and position of the limbs.

Language acquisition device (LAD): An innate mechanism, hypothesized by Chomsky, that contains the grammatical rules common to all languages and allows language acquisition.

Language comprehension: The ability to understand messages conveyed by words, phrases, and sentences.

Language production: The ability to use words, phrases, and sentences to convey information.

Latent content: The symbolic content and meaning of a dream.

Latent learning: Learning that occurs without behavioral indicators.

Law of Effect: Actions that subsequently lead to a "satisfying state of affairs" are more likely to be repeated.

Learned helplessness: The condition that occurs after an animal has an aversive experience in which nothing it does can affect what happens to it, and so it simply gives up and stops trying to change the situation or to escape.

Learning: The acquisition of information or a behavioral tendency that persists over a relatively long period of time.

Lesion: A region of impaired brain tissue.

Level of the brain: Events that involve the activity, structure, and properties of the organ itself—brain cells and their connections, the chemical solutions in which they exist, and the genes.

Level of the group: Events that involve relationships between people (such as love, competition, and cooperation), relationships among groups, and culture.

Level of the person: Events that involve the function (mental processes) and content (mental content) of the mind.

Limbic system: A set of brain areas, including the hippocampus, amygdala, hypothalamus, and other areas, that has long been thought of as being involved in key aspects of emotion and motivation, namely, those underlying fighting, fleeing, feeding, and sex.

Linguistic relativity hypothesis: The idea that language shapes our perceptions and thoughts, and thus people who speak different languages think differently.

Lobes: The four major parts of each cerebral hemisphere—occipital, temporal, parietal, and frontal; each lobe is present in each hemisphere.

Locus of control: A person's perception of the source of control over life's events when the cause of events is ambiguous.

Logic: A set of rules that determines which conclusions follow from particular assumptions.

Longitudinal study: A study in which the same group of people is tested repeatedly, at different ages.

Long-term memory (LTM): A memory store that holds a huge amount of information for a long time (from hours to years).

Loudness: The strength of a sound; pressure waves with greater amplitude produce the experience of louder sound.

Lowball technique: A compliance technique that consists of getting someone to make an agreement and then increasing the cost of that agreement.

Magnetic resonance imaging (MRI): A technique that uses magnetic properties of atoms to take sharp pictures of the three-dimensional structure of the brain.

Magnetoencephalography (MEG): A technique for assessing brain activity that relies on recording magnetic waves produced by neural activity.

Major depressive disorder (MDD): A mood disorder characterized by at least 2 weeks of depressed mood or loss of interest in nearly all activities, along with sleep or eating disturbances, loss of energy, and feelings of hopelessness.

Manic episode: A period of at least 1 week during which an abnormally elevated, expansive, or irritable mood persists.

Manifest content: The obvious, memorable content of a dream.

Maturation: The developmental process that produces genetically programmed changes in the body, brain, or behavior with increasing age.

Mean: A measure of central tendency that is the arithmetic average of a set of scores or values.

Median: A measure of central tendency that is the midpoint score of the values for the group or sample; half the values fall above the median, and half fall below the median.

Medulla: The lowest part of the lower brainstem, which plays a central role in automatic control of breathing, swallowing, and blood circulation.

Memory store: A set of neurons that serves to retain information over time.

Mendelian inheritance: The transmission of characteristics by individual elements of inheritance (now known to be genes), each acting separately.

Meninges: Three protective layered membranes that cover the brain.

Mental contents: Knowledge, beliefs (including ideas, explanations, and expectations), desires (such as hopes, goals, and needs), and feelings (such as fears, guilts, and attractions).

Mental images: Mental contents like those that arise during perception, but they arise from stored information rather than on immediate sensory input.

Mental processes: Sets of operations that work together to carry out a function, such as attention, perception, or memory.

Mental retardation: The condition characterized by an IQ of 70 or less and significant limitations in at least two aspects of everyday life since childhood; also referred to as intellectual disability.

Mental set: An approach to solving a problem that worked for a similar problem in the past, which leads to a fixed way of thinking about how to solve a present problem.

Mere exposure effect: The change—generally favorable—in an attitude that results from simply becoming familiar with something or someone.

Meta-analysis: A statistical technique that allows researchers to combine results from different studies on the same topic in order to discover whether there is a relationship among variables.

Metabolism: The sum of the chemical events in each of the body's cells, events that convert food molecules to the energy needed for the cells to function.

Microenvironment: The environment created by a person's own presence, which depends partly on his or her appearance and behavior.

Midbrain: According to a historical way of organizing brain structures, a unit of the brain that includes parts of the reticular formation as well as the brainstem structures that lie between forebrain and hindbrain.

Minnesota Multiphasic Personality Inventory-2 (MMPI-2): A personality inventory used primarily to assess psychopathology.

Misattribution of arousal: The failure to interpret signs of bodily arousal correctly, which leads to the experience of emotions that ordinarily would not arise in the particular situation.

Mnemonic devices: Strategies that improve memory, typically by effectively organizing and integrating to-be-learned information.

Modality: A form of therapy.

Modality-specific memory store: A memory store that retains input from a single perceptual system, such as vision or audition, or from a specific processing system, such as language.

Mode: A measure of central tendency that is the most frequently occurring value in a group or sample.

Monoamine oxidase inhibitor (MAOI): A type of antidepressant medication that requires strict adherence to a diet free of tyramine.

Monocular static cues: Information that specifies the distance of an object that can be picked up with one eye without movement of the object or eye.

Monozygotic: From the same egg and having virtually identical genes.

Mood disorders: A category of disorders characterized by persistent or episodic disturbances in emotion that interfere with normal functioning in at least one realm of life.

Moral dilemma: A situation in which there are moral pros and cons for each of a set of possible actions.

Morpheme: The smallest unit of meaning in a language.

Motion cues: Information that specifies the distance of an object on the basis of its movement.

Motivation: The set of requirements and desires that leads an animal (including a human) to behave in a particular way at a particular time and place.

Motor neuron: A neuron that sends signals to muscles in order to control movement (and also to bodily organs, such as glands).

Motor strip: The gyrus immediately in front of the central sulcus; it controls fine movements and is organized by body part. It is also called primary motor cortex.

Myelin: A fatty substance that helps impulses efficiently travel down the axon.

Narcotic analgesics: A class of strongly addictive drugs, such as heroin, that relieve pain and dull the senses.

Nativism (approach to language): The view that people are born with some knowledge.

Natural killer (NK) cell: A type of T cell that detects and destroys damaged or altered cells, such as precancerous cells.

Natural selection: Occurs when individuals with inherited characteristics that contribute to survival have more offspring, and over time those characteristics come to be widespread in a population.

Need: A condition that arises from the lack of a necessary substance (such as food) or condition (such as warmth); needs give rise to drives.

Need for achievement: The need to reach goals that require skilled performance or competence to be accomplished.

Negative punishment: Occurs when a response leads a pleasant object or event to be removed, thereby decreasing the likelihood of that response in the future.

Negative reinforcement: Occurs when an unpleasant object or event is removed after a response, thereby increasing the likelihood of that response in the future.

Negative symptom: A diminution or loss of normal functions, such as a restricted range of emotional expression.

Nerve deafness: A type of deafness that typically occurs when the hair cells are destroyed by loud sounds.

Neuroendocrine system: The system that makes hormones that affect many bodily functions and that also provides the CNS with information.

Neuroimaging: Brain-scanning techniques that produce a picture of the structure or functioning of regions of the brain.

Neuron: A cell that receives signals from sense organs or other neurons, processes these signals, and sends the signals to muscles, organs, or other neurons; the basic unit of the nervous system.

Neurosis: An abnormal behavior pattern that arises from a conflict between the ego and either the id or the superego.

Neurotransmitter substance: A chemical that carries a signal from the terminal button of one neuron to the dendrite or cell body of another; often referred to as a neurotransmitter.

Nocebo effect: A variation of the placebo effect in which a negative expectation produces a negative outcome.

Nondeprived reward: Reward that occurs when the animal (including a human) does not lack a substance or condition necessary for survival—in other words, when you had a want but not a need.

Norm: A rule that implicitly or explicitly governs members of a group.

Normal distribution: The frequency distribution in which most values fall in the midrange of the scale, and scores are increasingly less frequent as they taper off symmetrically toward the extremes; when graphed, this type of distribution is a bell-shaped curve.

Norming: The process of setting the mean and the standard deviation of a set of test scores, based on results from a standardized sample.

Obedience: Compliance with an order.

Object permanence: The understanding that objects continue to exist when they cannot be immediately perceived.

Observational learning: Learning that occurs through watching others, not through reinforcement.

Obsession: A recurrent and persistent thought, impulse, or image that feels intrusive and inappropriate and is difficult to suppress or ignore.

Obsessive-compulsive disorder (OCD): An anxiety disorder characterized by the presence of obsessions and sometimes compulsions.

Occipital lobes: The brain lobes at the back of the head; concerned entirely with different aspects of vision.

Operant conditioning: The process by which a stimulus and response become associated with the consequences of making the response.

Operational definition: A definition of a concept that specifies how it is measured or manipulated.

Opioid: A narcotic, such as morphine, derived from the opium poppy; also referred to as opiates.

Opponent cells: Cells that respond to one color from a pair (blue/yellow, red/green, or black/white) and inhibit sensing the other color from the pair.

Opponent process theory of color vision: The theory that for some pairs of colors, if one of the colors is present, it causes cells to inhibit sensing the complementary color (such as red versus green) in that location.

Optic nerve: The large bundle of axons carrying neural signals from the retina into the brain.

Outcome research: Research that addresses whether, after psychotherapy, clients feel better, function better, live more independently, or experience fewer symptoms.

Outgroup: A group other than a person's own.

Overextension: An overly broad use of a word to refer to a new object or situation.

Overregularization error: A mistake that occurs in speech when the child applies a newly learned rule even to cases where it does not apply.

Panic attack: An episode of intense fear, anxiety, or discomfort accompanied by physical and psychological symptoms such as heart palpitations, breathing difficulties, chest pain, fear of impending doom or of doing something uncontrollable, and a sense of unreality.

Panic disorder: An anxiety disorder characterized by frequent, unexpected panic attacks or fear and avoidance of such attacks.

Parasympathetic nervous system: Part of the autonomic nervous system that is "next to" the sympathetic nervous system and that tends to counteract its effects.

Parietal lobes: The brain lobes at the top, rear of the brain; among their functions are attention, arithmetic, touch, and registering spatial location.

Partial reinforcement: Reinforcement given only intermittently after desired responses.

Passionate love: The intense, often sudden feeling of being "in love," which typically involves sexual attraction, a desire for mutual love and physical closeness, arousal, and a fear that the relationship will end.

Passive interaction: Occurs when genetically shaped behavioral tendencies of parents or siblings produce an environment that is passively received by the child.

Perceived social support: The subjective sense that support is available should it be needed.

Percentile rank: A number indicating the percentage of data that have values at or below a particular value.

Perception: The result of neural processes that organize (such as by specifying a particular shape) and interpret (such as by identifying the object) information conveyed by sensory signals.

Perceptual constancy: The perception that characteristics of objects (such as their shapes or colors) remain the same even when the sensory information striking the eyes changes.

Perceptual set: The sum of assump-tions and beliefs that lead a person to expect to perceive certain objects or characteristics in particular contexts.

Peripheral nervous system (PNS): The autonomic nervous system and the sensory-somatic nervous system.

Personality: A set of emotional, cognitive, and behavioral tendencies that people display over time and across situations and that distinguish individuals from each other.

Personality disorders: A category of disorders in which relatively stable personality traits are inflexible and maladaptive, causing distress or difficulty with daily functioning.

Personality inventory: A lengthy questionnaire for assessing personality that requires the test takers to read statements and to indicate whether each is true or false about themselves or to indicate how much they agree or disagree with each statement.

Personality trait: A relatively consistent tendency to think, feel, or behave in a characteristic way across a range of situations.

Persuasion: Attempts to change people's attitudes.

Phenotype: The observable structure and behavior of an organism.

Pheromones: Chemicals that function like hormones but are released outside the body (in urine and sweat).

Phobia: An exaggerated, irrational fear of a specific object, activity, or situation that leads the person to go to extreme lengths to avoid the feared stimulus.

Phoneme: A small, basic sound from a fixed set that specifies the building blocks of speech sounds that humans are capable of producing.

Phonology: The structure of the sounds of the words in a language.

Pitch: How high or low a sound seems; higher frequencies of pressure waves produce the experience of higher pitches.

Pituitary gland: The "master gland" that regulates other glands but is itself controlled by the brain, primarily via connections from the hypothalamus.

Place theory: In hearing, the theory that different frequencies activate different places along the basilar membrane.

Plasticity: The brain's ability to change as a result of experience.

Polygraph: A machine that is used to detect lying by monitoring the activity of the sympathetic and parasympathetic nervous systems, particularly changes in how easily the skin conducts electricity, breathing, and heart rate.

Pons: A bridge between the medulla and midbrain, which also connects the upper parts of the brain to the cerebellum.

Pop-out: The phenomenon that occurs when the perceptual characteristics of a stimulus are sufficiently different from the ones around it that it immediately comes to our attention.

Population: The entire set of relevant people or animals.

Positive punishment: Occurs when a response leads to an undesired consequence, thereby decreasing the likelihood of that response in the future.

Positive reinforcement: Occurs when a desired reinforcer is presented after a response, thereby increasing the likelihood of that response in the future.

Positive symptom: An excess or distortion of normal functions, such as a hallucination.

Positron emission tomography (PET): A neuroimaging technique that uses small amounts of a radioactive substance to track blood flow or energy consumption in the brain.

Posttraumatic stress disorder (PTSD): An anxiety disorder experienced by some people after a traumatic event, and characterized by persistent reexperiencing of the trauma, avoidance of stimuli associated with the trauma, and heightened arousal.

Pragmatics: The ways that words and sentences in a language convey meaning indirectly, by implying rather than asserting.

Prediction: A hypothesis that follows from a theory, which should be confirmed if the theory is correct.

Prejudice: An attitude (generally negative) toward members of a group.

Primacy effect: Increased memory for the first few stimuli in a set, reflecting storage of information in LTM.

Primary mental abilities: According to Thurstone, seven fundamental abilities that are the components of intelligence and are distinct from other abilities.

Primary reinforcer: An event or object, such as food, water, or relief from pain, that is inherently reinforcing.

Priming (of perception or behavior): Occurs when having performed a task predisposes you to perform the same or an associated task again in the future.

Proactive interference: Interference that occurs when information already stored in memory makes it difficult to learn something new.

Problem: An obstacle that must be overcome to reach a goal.

Problem solving: Devising a way to overcome an obstacle that stands between the present situation and a desired goal.

Problem-focused coping: Coping focused on changing the environment itself or the way the person interacts with the environment.

Prodigies: Children who demonstrate immense talent in a particular area, such as music or mathematics, but who may have only average abilities in other areas.

Progressive muscle relaxation: A relaxation technique whereby the person alternates tensing and relaxing muscles sequentially from one end of the body to the other.

Projective test: A method used to assess personality and psychopathology that asks the test taker to make sense of ambiguous stimuli.

Prosocial behavior: Acting altruistically, which includes sharing, cooperating, comforting, and helping others.

Prototype: The most typical example of a concept.

Pruning: A process whereby certain connections among neurons are eliminated.

Pseudopsychology: Theories or statements that at first glance look like psychology but are in fact superstition or unsupported opinion, not based in science.

Psychiatric nurse: A nurse with a master's degree and a clinical specialization in psychiatric nursing who provides psychotherapy and works with medical doctors to monitor and administer medications.

Psychiatrist: A physician with special training in treating mental disorders.

Psychoanalysis: An intensive form of therapy that is directly connected to Freud's theory of personality and based on the idea that psychological difficulties are caused by unconscious conflicts.

Psychodynamic theory: A theory of mental events that specifies the continual push-and-pull interaction among conscious and unconscious thoughts and feelings and specifies how such interactions affect behavior.

Psychodynamic therapy: A less intensive form of psychoanalysis.

Psychoeducation: The process of educating clients about therapy and research findings pertaining to their disorders or problems.

Psychological determinism: The view that all thoughts, feelings, and behavior, no matter how mundane or insignificant, ultimately have an underlying psychological cause.

Psychological disorder: A mental condition characterized by cognitive, emotional, and behavioral symptoms that: create significant distress; impair work, school, family, relationships, or daily living; or lead to significant risk of harm.

Psychology: The science of the mind and behavior.

Psychopharmacology: The use of medication to treat psychological disorders and problems.

Psychophysics: The field in which researchers study the relation between physical events and the corresponding experience of those events.

Psychosexual stages: Freud's developmental stages based on erogenous zones; the specific needs of each stage must be met for its successful resolution.

Psychosis: A severely impaired ability to perceive and comprehend events accurately, combined with grossly disorganized behavior.

Psychosocial development: The result of maturation and learning on personality and relationships.

Psychotherapy: The process of helping people learn to change so they can cope with troublesome thoughts, feelings, and behaviors.

Puberty: The time when hormones cause the sex organs to mature and secondary sexual characteristics, such as breasts for women and a beard for men, to appear.

Punishment: The process by which an unpleasant object or event is presented after a response, which decreases the likelihood of that response in the future.

Pupil: The opening in the eye through which light passes.

Range: The difference obtained by subtracting the smallest score in a set of data from the largest; the simplest measure of variability.

Ratio schedule: Partial reinforcement schedule based on a specified number of responses.

Reality monitoring: Paying attention to characteristics that distinguish actual from imagined stimuli.

Reasoning: Deciding what follows from an idea, ideas, or a situation.

Recall: The act of intentionally bringing explicit information to awareness, which requires transferring the information from LTM to STM.

Recategorization: A means of reducing prejudice by shifting the categories of "us" and "them" so that the two groups are no longer viewed as distinct entities.

Recency effect: Increased memory for the last few stimuli in a set, reflecting storage of information in STM.

Receptor: A site on a dendrite or cell body where a neurotransmitter molecule attaches itself; like a lock that is opened by one key, a receptor receives only one type of neurotransmitter.

Recognition: The act of successfully matching an encoded stimulus to information about that stimulus that was previously stored in memory.

Reflex: An automatic behavioral response to an event.

Rehearsal: The process of repeating information over and over to retain it in STM.

Reinforcement: The process by which the consequences of a response lead to an increase in the likelihood that the response will occur again when the stimulus is present.

Reinforcer: An object or event that, when it follows a response, increases the likelihood that the animal will make that response again when the stimulus is present.

Reliability: Consistency; data are reliable if the same values are obtained when the measurements are repeated.

REM rebound: The higher percentage of REM sleep that occurs following a night lacking the normal amount of REM.

REM sleep: Stage of sleep characterized by rapid eye movements, marked brain activity, and vivid dreaming.

Repetition blindness: The inability to see the second instance of a stimulus when it appears soon after the first instance.

Repetition priming: Priming that makes the same information more easily accessed in the future.

Replication: Repeating the method of a study and collecting comparable data as were found in the original study.

Representation problem: The challenge of how best to formulate the nature of a problem.

Representativeness heuristic: The strategy in which we assume that the more similar something is to a prototype stored in memory, the more likely it is to belong to the prototype's category.

Repressed memories: Memories of actual events that were pushed into the unconscious because they are emotionally threatening.

Repression: A defense mechanism that occurs when the ego directly blocks threatening unconscious thoughts, impulses, and memories from entering consciousness.

Resistance: A reluctance or refusal to cooperate with the therapist, which can range from unconscious forgetting to outright refusal to comply with a therapist's request.

Resistance phase: The second phase of the GAS, in which the body mobilizes its resources to adapt to the continued presence of the stressor; also called the adaptation phase.

Response bias: A tendency to respond in a particular way regardless of respondents' actual knowledge or beliefs.

Response contingency: The circumstance in which a consequence depends on the animal's producing the desired response.

Resting potential: The negative charge within a neuron when it is at rest.

Reticular formation: A collection of small structures in the brainstem, organized into two main parts: the reticular activating system and another part that is important in producing autonomic nervous system reactions.

Retina: A sheet of tissue at the back of the eye containing cells that convert light to neural signals.

Retinal disparity: The difference between the images striking the retinas of the two eyes; also called binocular disparity.

Retrieval: The process of accessing information stored in memory.

Retroactive interference: Interference that occurs when new learning disrupts memory for something learned earlier.

Retrograde amnesia: Amnesia that disrupts previous memories.

Reuptake: The process by which surplus neurotransmitter in the synaptic cleft is reabsorbed back into the sending neuron so that the neuron can effectively fire again.

Rods: Rod-shaped retinal receptor cells that are very sensitive to light but register only shades of gray.

Role: The behaviors that a member in a given position in a group is expected to perform.

Rorschach test: A projective test consisting of a set of inkblots that people are asked to interpret.

s: "Specific factors," or aspects of performance that are particular to a given kind of processing—and distinct from g.

Sample: A group that is drawn from a larger population and that is measured or observed.

Sampling bias: A bias that occurs when the participants are not chosen at random but instead are chosen so that one attribute is over- or underrepresented.

Sampling error: A difference that arises by chance, not because the samples are representative of different populations.

Schema: In Piaget's theory, a mental structure that organizes sensory and perceptual input and connects it to the appropriate responses.

Schizophrenia: A disorder that is characterized by symptoms of psychosis that profoundly alter the patient's affect, behavior, and thoughts.

Scientific method: A way to gather facts that will lead to the formulation and validation (or refutation) of a theory.

Secondary reinforcer: An event or object (such as attention) that is not inherently reinforcing but instead has acquired its reinforcing value through learning.

Selective attention: The process of picking out and maintaining focus on a particular quality, object, or event, and ignoring other stimuli or characteristics of the stimuli.

Selective serotonin reuptake inhibitor (SSRI): A type of antidepressant medication that blocks reuptake of serotonin only at selective serotonin receptors.

Self-actualization: An innate drive to attain the highest possible emotional and intellectual potential.

Self-concept: The beliefs, desires, values, and attributes that define a person to himself or herself.

Self-efficacy: The sense of being able to follow through and produce specific desired behaviors.

Self-help group: A group in which members focus on a specific problem or disorder and that does not usually have a clinically trained leader; also called a support group.

Self-monitoring techniques: Behavioral techniques that help the client identify a problematic behavior as well as its antecedents and consequences.

Self-serving bias: A person's inclination to attribute his or her own failures to external causes and own successes to internal causes, but to attribute other people's failures to internal causes and their successes to external causes.

Semantic memories: Memories of the meanings of words, concepts, and general facts about the world.

Semantics: The meaning of a word, phrase, or sentence.

Sensation: The result of neural responses that occur after physical energy stimulates a receptor cell (such as those at the back of the eye, in the ear, on the skin) but before the stimulus is organized and interpreted by the brain.

Sensitivity: In signal detection theory, corresponds to the amount of information required to detect a signal, with greater sensitivity indicating that less information is required.

Sensory memory (SM): A memory store that holds a large amount of perceptual information for a very brief time, typically less than 1 second.

Sensory neuron: A neuron that responds to signals from sensory organs and transmits those signals to the brain and spinal cord.

Sensory-somatic nervous system (SSNS): Part of the peripheral nervous system that consists of neurons in the sensory organs (such as the eyes and ears) that convey information to the brain as well as neurons that actually trigger muscles and glands.

Separation anxiety: Fear of being away from the primary caregiver.

Serotonin/norepinephrine reuptake inhibitor (SNRI): A newer type of antidepressant that affects both serotonin and norepinephrine neurotransmitter systems.

Set point: The particular body weight that is easiest to maintain.

Sexual response cycle: The stages the body passes through during sexual activity, including sexual attraction, desire, excitement, and possibly performance.

Shape constancy: The perception that the actual shape of an object remains the same, even when it is seen from different points of view and so the image on the retina changes shape.

Shaping: The gradual process of reinforcing an animal for responses that get closer to the desired response.

Short-term memory (STM): A memory store that holds relatively little information for only a few seconds (but perhaps as long as 30 seconds); also called immediate memory.

Signal detection theory: A theory of how people detect signals, which distinguishes between sensitivity and bias; the theory is based on the idea that signals are always embedded in noise, and thus the challenge is to distinguish signal from noise.

Single-cell recording: The technique in which tiny probes called micro-electrodes are placed in the brain and used to record neural firing rates.

Size constancy: The perception that the actual size of an object remains the same even when it is viewed at different distances.

Skewed distribution: A distribution of a set of data in which many scores are near one extreme value and away from the center.

Sleep apnea: A disorder characterized by a temporary cessation of breathing during sleep, usually preceded by a period of difficult breathing accompanied by loud snoring.

Sleep: The naturally recurring experience during which normal consciousness is suspended.

Sociability: A temperament dimension characterized by a preference for being in other people's company rather than alone.

Social categorization: The cognitive operation that leads people to sort others automatically into categories of "us" versus "them."

Social causation: The view that chronic psychological and social stresses from living in an urban environment may lead to an increase in the rate of schizophrenia (especially among the poor).

Social cognition: The ways that people perceive the social world and how they attend to, store, remember, and use information about other people and the social world.

Social cognitive neuroscience: The area of psychology that attempts to understand social cognition by specifying the cognitive mechanisms that underlie it and by discovering how those mechanisms are rooted in the brain.

Social desirability: A source of bias in responding to questions that occurs when people try to make themselves "look good" even if it means giving answers that are not accurate.

Social facilitation: The increase in performance that can occur simply as a result of being part of a group or in the presence of other people.

Social loafing: The group process that occurs when some members don't con-tribute as much to a shared group task as do others, and instead let other members work proportionally harder than they do.

Social phobia: Fear of public embarrassment or humiliation, which leads the person to avoid situations likely to arouse this fear.

Social psychology: The area of psychology that focuses on how people think about other people and interact in relationships and groups.

Social selection: The tendency of the mentally disabled to drift to the lower economic classes; also called social drift.

Social support: The help and support gained through interacting with others.

Social worker: A mental health professional who may use psychotherapy to help families (and individuals) or help clients to use the social service systems in their communities.

Somasthetic senses: Senses that produce the perception of the body and its position in space—specifically, kinesthetic sense, vestibular sense, touch, temperature sensitivity, pain, and possibly magnetic sense.

Somatic motor system: Consists of nerves that are attached to muscles that can be used voluntarily (striated muscles).

Somatosensory strip: The gyrus immediately behind the central sulcus; it registers sensations on the body and is organized by body part.

Specific phobia: Persistent and excessive or unreasonable fear triggered by a specific object or nonsocial situation, along with attempts to avoid the feared stimulus.

Speech-segmentation problem: The problem of organizing a continuous stream of speech into separate parts that correspond to individual words.

Spinal cord: The flexible rope of neurons and their connections that runs inside the backbone (spinal column).

Split-brain patient: A person whose corpus callosum has been severed for medical reasons, so that neural signals no longer pass from one cerebral hemisphere to the other.

Spontaneous recovery (in classical conditioning): The event that occurs when the CS again elicits the CR after extinction has occurred.

Spontaneous recovery (in operant conditioning): The process by which an extinguished, previously reinforced response reappears if there is a period of time after extinction.

Standard deviation: A descriptive statistic that provides a kind of "average variability" in a set of measurements.

Standardized sample: A representative selection of people, drawn from a carefully defined population.

State-dependent retrieval: Memory retrieval that is better if it occurs in the same psychological state that was present when the information was first encoded.

Statistics: Numbers that summarize or indicate differences or patterns of differences in measurements.

Stereotype threat: Threat that occurs when people believe that a negative stereotype addresses characteristics important to them, and that others will see them as conforming to that stereotype.

Stereotype: A belief (or set of beliefs) about people from a particular category.

Stimulants: A class of substances that excite the central nervous system, leading to increases in behavioral activity and heightened arousal.

Stimulus control: A behavior therapy technique that has the client control how often he or she encounters a stimulus that elicits a conditioned response, with the goal of decreasing or increasing the frequency of the response.

Stimulus discrimination: The ability to distinguish among stimuli that are relatively similar to the CS and to respond only to the actual CS.

Stimulus generalization: A tendency for the CR to be elicited by neutral stimuli that are similar but not identical to the CS.

Storage: The process of retaining information in memory.

Strategy: An approach to solving a problem, which indicates the processing steps to be tried.

Stress: The general term that describes the psychological and physical response to a stimulus that alters the body's equilibrium.

Stress response: The bodily response to a stressor that occurs to help a person cope with the stressor; also called the fight-or-flight response.

Stressor: A stimulus that throws the body's equilibrium out of balance.

Stroke: A cause of brain damage that occurs when blood (with its life-giving nutrients and oxygen) fails to reach part of the brain, and thus neurons in that area die.

Structuralism: The school of psychology that sought to identify the basic elements of consciousness and to describe the rules and circumstances under which these elements combine to form mental structures.

Subcortical structures: Parts of the brain located under the cerebral cortex.

Substance abuse: Drug or alcohol use that causes distress or trouble with functioning in major areas of life, occurs in dangerous situations, or leads to legal difficulties.

Substance dependence: Chronic substance use that is characterized by at least three out of seven symptoms, the two most important being tolerance and withdrawal.

Successive approximations: The series of relatively simple responses involved in shaping a complex response.

Sulcus: A crease in the cerebral cortex.

Superego: A personality structure, proposed by Freud, that is formed during early childhood and houses the sense of right and wrong, based on the internalization of parental and cultural morality.

Suprachiasmatic nucleus (SCN): A small part of the hypothalamus just above the optic chiasm that registers changes in light, leading to production of hormones that regulate various bodily functions.

Survey: A set of questions that people are asked about their beliefs, attitudes, preferences, or activities.

Sympathetic nervous system: Part of the autonomic nervous system that readies an animal to fight or to flee by speeding up the heart, increasing breathing rate to deliver more oxygen, dilating the pupils, producing sweat, decreasing salivation, inhibiting activity in the stomach, and relaxing the bladder.

Synapse: The place where an axon of one neuron sends signals to the membrane (on a dendrite or cell body) of another neuron; the synapse includes the sending portions of an axon, the receiving portions of the receiving neuron, and the space between them.

Synaptic cleft: The gap in the synapse between the axon of one neuron and the membrane of another across which communication occurs.

Syntax: The internal organization of a sentence, determined by a set of rules (grammar) for combining different parts of speech into acceptable arrangements.

Systematic desensitization: A behavior therapy technique in which people are taught to be relaxed in the presence of a feared object or situation.

Systems therapy: A type of therapy in which a client's symptoms are viewed as occurring in a larger context or system, and a change in one part of the system affects the rest of the system.

T cell: A type of white blood cell that matures in the thymus.

Tardive dyskinesia: An irreversible movement disorder in which the person involuntarily smacks his or her lips, displays facial grimaces, and exhibits other symptoms.

Taste buds: The receptor cells for taste, which are microscopic structures on the bumps on the tongue surface, at the back of the throat, and inside the cheeks.

Telegraphic speech: Speech that packs a lot of information into a few highly informative words, typically omitting words such as the, a, and of.

Temperament: An inclination to engage in a certain style of thinking, feeling, or behaving; a temperament initially arises from the effects of genes and biology, and an individual's environment moderates these effects.

Temporal lobes: The brain lobes under the temples, in front of the ears; among its many functions are processing sound, entering new information into memory, storing visual memories, and comprehending language.

Teratogen: Any external agent, such as a chemical, virus, or type of radiation, that can cause damage to the zygote, embryo, or fetus.

Terminal button: A structure at the end of the branch of an axon that can release chemicals into the space between neurons.

Test bias: Features of test items or test design that lead a particular group to perform well or poorly and that thus invalidate the test.

Testosterone: The hormone that causes males to develop facial hair and other external sexual characteristics, and to build up muscle volume.

Texture gradient: An increase in the density of the texture of an object with increasing distance.

Thalamus: A subcortical structure that receives signals from sensory and motor systems and plays a crucial role in attention, sleep, and other functions critical to daily life; often thought of as a switching center.

Thematic Apperception Test (TAT): A projective test consisting of a set of detailed black-and-white drawings; for each drawing, the test taker is asked to tell a story about what the drawing illustrates.

Theory: Concepts or principles that explain a set of research findings.

Theory of multiple intelligences: Gardner's theory of (at least) eight distinct forms of intelligence, each of which can vary for a given individual.

Thought suppression: The coping strategy that involves intentionally trying not to think about something emotionally arousing or distressing.

Threshold: The point at which stimuli activate receptor cells strongly enough to be sensed.

Token economy: A behavior modification program that uses secondary reinforcers (tokens) to change behavior.

Tolerance: The condition of requiring more of a substance to achieve the same effect, because the usual amount provides a diminished response.

Top-down processing: Processing that is guided by knowledge, expectation, or belief.

Transcranial magnetic stimulation (TMS): A technique in which the brain is stimulated from outside by putting a coil on a person's head and delivering a magnetic pulse (or series of magnetic pulses); the magnetic fields are so strong that they make neurons under the coil fire.

Transduction: The process whereby physical energy is converted by a sensory receptor cell into neural signals.

Transfer appropriate processing: Processing used to retrieve material that is the same type as was used when the material was originally studied, which improves memory retrieval.

Transference: The process by which patients may relate to their therapists as they did to some important person in their lives.

Triangular model of love: The theory that love has three dimensions: passion, intimacy, and commitment.

Trichromatic theory of color vision: The theory that color vision arises from the combinations of signals from three different kinds of sensors, each of which responds maximally to a different range of wavelengths.

Tricyclic antidepressant (TCA): A type of antidepressant medication named for the three rings in its chemical structure.

Twin study: A study that compares identical and fraternal twins to determine the relative contribution of genes to variability in a characteristic or ability.

Typicality: The degree to which an entity is representative of a concept.

Unconditional positive regard: Acceptance without any conditions.

Unconditioned response (UR): The reflexive or automatic response elicited by a particular stimulus.

Unconditioned stimulus (US): A stimulus that elicits an automatic response (UR), without requiring prior learning.

Unconscious: Outside conscious awareness and not able to be brought into consciousness at will.

Underextension: An overly narrow use of a word to refer to a new object or situation.

Validity: A research method is valid if it does in fact measure what it is supposed to measure.

Variable: An aspect of a situation that can vary, or change; specifically, a characteristic of a substance, quantity, or entity that is measurable.

Variable interval schedule: Reinforcement given for responses produced after a variable interval of time.

Variable ratio schedule: Reinforcement given after a variable ratio of responses.

Vestibular sense: The sense that provides information about the body's orientation relative to gravity.

Want: A state that arises when you have an unmet goal that does not arise from a lack of a necessary substance or condition; wants turn goals into incentives.

Wavelength: The distance between the arrival of peaks of a light wave or sound wave; shorter wavelengths correspond to higher frequencies.

Weber's law: The rule that the same percentage of a magnitude must be present in order to detect a difference between two stimuli or a change in a single stimulus.

Wechsler Adult Intelligence Scale (WAIS): The most widely used intelligence test in the United States; it consists of four sets of subtests.

Withdrawal symptoms: The onset of uncomfortable or life-threatening effects when the use of a substance is stopped.

Working memory (WM): The memory system that includes two specialized STMs (auditory loop and visuospatial sketchpad) and a central executive that operates on information in the STMs to plan, reason, or solve a problem.

Zygote: A fertilized egg (ovum).

References: Introduction to the Science of Psychology

Abela, J. R. Z., & D'Allesandro, D. U. (2002). Beck's cognitive theory of depression: The diathesis-stress and causal mediation components. *British Journal of Clinical Psychology, 41,* 111–128.

Anderson, M. C., Ochsner, K. N., Kuhl, B., Cooper, J., Robertson, E., Gabrieli, S. W., et al. (2004). Neural systems underlying the suppression of unwanted memories. *Science, 303,* 232–235.

Anderson, N. B. (1998). Levels of analysis in health science: A framework for integrating sociobehavioral and biomedical research. In S. M. McCann, J. M. Lipton, et al. (Eds.), *Annals of the New York Academy of Sciences: Vol. 840. Neuroimmunomodulation: Molecular aspects, integrative systems, and clinical advances* (pp. 563–576). New York: New York Academy of Sciences.

Barkow, J. H., Cosmides, L., & Tooby, J. (Eds.). (1992). *The adapted mind: Evolutionary psychology and the generation of culture.* New York: Oxford University Press.

Belkin, M., & Rosner, M. (1987). Intelligence, education, and myopia in males, *Archives of Opthamology, 105,* 1508–1511.

Blakemore, S., Winston, J., & Frith, U. (2004). Social cognitive neuroscience: Where are we heading? *Trends in Cognitive Sciences, 8,* 216–222.

Boring, E. G. (1950). *A history of experimental psychology* (2nd ed.). New York: Appleton-Century-Crofts.

Brown, D. E. (1991). *Human universals.* Philadelphia, PA: Temple University Press.

Bushman, B. J. (2002). Does venting anger feed or extinguish the flame? Catharsis, rumination, distraction, anger and aggressive responding. *Personality and Social Psychology Bulletin, 28,* 724–731.

Buss, D. M. (1994). *The evolution of desire: Strategies of human mating.* New York: Basic Books.

Buss, D. M. (1999). *Evolutionary psychology: The new science of the mind.* Boston: Allyn & Bacon.

Canessa, N., Gorini, A., Cappa, S. F., Piattelli-Palmarini, M., Danna, M., Fazio, F., et al. (2005). The effect of social content on deductive reasoning: An fMRI study. *Human Brain Mapping, 26,* 30–43.

Compton, W. C. (2005). *An introduction to positive psychology.* Belmont, CA: Wadsworth.

Cooper, H. (2010). *Research synthesis and meta-analysis: A step-by-step approach (4th ed.).* Thousand Oaks, CA, US: Sage Publications

Cosmides, L., & Tooby, J. (1996). Are humans good intuitive statisticians after all? Rethinking some conclusions from the literature on judgment under uncertainty. *Cognition, 58,* 1–73.

Davidson, R. J. (2004). What does the prefrontal cortex "do" in affect: Perspectives on frontal EEG asymmetry research. *Biological Psychology, 67,* 219–233.

de Pinedo-Garcia, M., & Noble, J. (2008). Beyond persons: Extending the personal/subpersonal distinction to non-rational animals and artificial agents. *Biology and Philosophy, 23,* 87–100.

Doheny, M. (1993). Effects of mental practice on performance of a psychomotor skill. *Journal of Mental Imagery, 17*(3–4), 111–118.

Driskell, J., Copper, C., & Moran, A. (1994). Does mental practice enhance performance? *Journal of Applied Psychology, 79*(4), 481–492.

Druckman, D., & Swets, J. A. (Eds.). (1988). *Enhancing human performance: Issues, theories, and techniques.* Washington, DC: National Academies Press.

Ekman, P. (1985). *Telling lies: Clues to deceit in the marketplace, marriage, and politics.* New York: Norton.

Farah, M. J. (2009). Neuroethics. In V. Ravitsky, A. Fiester, & A. L. Caplan (Eds) *The Penn Center guide to bioethics.* (pp. 71–83). New York, NY, US: Springer Publishing Co

Fodor, J. A. (1968). *Psychological explanation: An introduction to the philosophy of psychology.* New York: Random House.

Fodor, J. A. (1983). *The modularity of mind.* Cambridge, MA: MIT Press.

Freud, S. (2009). The works of Sigmund Freud (with active table of contents) (Kindle Edition). San Francisco: Douglas Editions.

Ganis, G., Kosslyn, S. M., Stose, S., Thompson, W. L., & Yurgelun-Todd, D. (2003). Neural correlates of different types of deception: An fMRI investigation. *Cerebral Cortex, 13,* 830–836.

Gardner, H. (1985). *The mind's new science: A history of the cognitive revolution.* New York: Basic Books.

Gazzaniga, M. S. (Ed.). (2009). *The cognitive neurosciences, 4th edition.* Cambridge, MA: MIT Press.

Glimcher, P. (2003). *Decisions, uncertainty, and the brain: The science of neuroeconomics.* Cambridge, MA: MIT Press.

Gould, S. J., & Lewontin, R. C. (1979). The spandrels of San Marco and the Panglossian paradigm: A critique of the adaptationist programme. *Proceedings of the Royal Society of London, Series B, 205,* 581–598.

Hart, J., Berndt, R. S., & Caramazza, A. (1985). Category-specific naming deficit following cerebral infarction. *Nature, 316,* 439–440.

Hauser, M. (1996). *The evolution of communication.* Cambridge, MA: MIT Press.

Henslin, J. M. (1999). *Sociology: A down-to-earth approach* (4th ed.). Needham Heights, MA: Allyn & Bacon.

Jeannerod, M. (1994). The representing brain: Neural correlates of motor intention and imagery. *Behavioral and Brain Sciences, 17,* 187–245.

Jeannerod, M. (1995). Mental imagery in the motor context. *Neuropsychologia, 33,* 1419–1432.

Kosslyn, S. M. (2006). *Graph design for the eye and mind.* New York: Oxford University Press.

Kosslyn, S. M., Digirolamo, G. J., Thompson, W. L., & Alpert, N. M. (1998). Mental rotation of objects versus hands: Neural mechanisms revealed by positron emission tomography. *Psychophysiology, 35,* 151–161.

Kosslyn, S. M., & Koenig, O. (1995). *Wet mind: The new cognitive neuroscience.* New York: Free Press.

Kozhevnikov, M., Kosslyn, S. M., & Shephard, J. M. (2005). Spatial versus object visualizers: A new characterization of visual cognitive style. *Memory and Cognition, 33*(4), 710–726.

Liu, H.-M., Tsao, F.-M., & Kuhl, P. K. (2009). Age-related changes in acoustic modifications of Mandarin maternal speech to preverbal infants and five-year-old children: A longitudinal study. *Journal of Child Language, 36,* 909–922.

Lohr, J. M., Olatunji, B. O., Baumeister, R. F., & Bushman, B. J. (2007). The psychology of anger venting and empirically supported alternatives that do no harm. *The Scientific Review of Mental Health Practice, 5,* 53–64.

Looren de Jong, H. (1996). Levels: Reduction and elimination in cognitive neuroscience. In C. W. Tolman, F. Cherry, et al. (Eds.), *Problems of theoretical psychology* (pp. 165–172). North York, ON, Canada: Captus Press.

Markus, S. J. (2002). *Neuroethics: Mapping the field.* New York: Dana Press.

Marr, D. (1982). *Vision: A computational investigation into the human representation and processing of visual information.* New York: Freeman.

Merchant, H., Battaglia-Mayer, A., & Georgopoulos, A. P. (2003). Functional organization of parietal neuronal responses to optic-flow stimuli. *Journal of Neurophysiology, 90,* 675–682.

Miller, E. M. (1992). On the correlation of myopia and intelligence. *Genetic, Social and General Psychology Monographs, 118,* 361–383.

Morgan, J. L., & Demuth, K. D. (1996). *Signal to syntax: Bootstrapping from speech to grammar in early acquisition.* Hillsdale, NJ: Erlbaum.

Nagel, E. (1979). *The structure of science: Problems in the logic of scientific explanation* (2nd ed.). Indianapolis: Hackett.

National Science Foundation. (2001). *National survey of recent college graduates.* Washington, DC: National Science Foundation, Division of Science Resources Statistics.

Neisser, U. (1967). *Cognitive psychology.* New York: Appleton-Century-Crofts.

Parsons, L. M. (1987). Imagined spatial transformation of one's body. *Journal of Experimental Psychology: General, 116,* 172–191.

Parsons, L. M. (1994). Temporal and kinematic properties of motor behavior reflected in mentally simulated action. *Journal of Experimental Psychology: Human Perception and Performance, 20,* 709–730.

Parsons, L. M., & Fox, P. T. (1998). The neural basis of implicit movements used in recognising hand shape. *Cognitive Neuropsychology, 15,* 583–615.

Peterson, C. (2006). *A primer in positive psychology.* New York: Oxford University Press.

Phelps, E. A., O'Connor, K. J., Cunningham, W. A., Funayama, S., Gatenby, J. C. Gore, J.C., et al. (2000). Performance on indirect measures of race evaluation predicts amygdala activation. *Journal of Cognitive Neuroscience, 12,* 729–738.

Pinker, S. (1994). The language instinct: How the mind creates language. New York: Morrow.

Pinker, S. (1997). *How the mind works.* New York: Norton.

Plotkin, H. (1994). *The nature of knowledge: Concerning adaptations, instinct and the evolution of intelligence.* New York: Allen Lane/Viking Penguin.

Plotkin, H. (1997). *Evolution in mind: An introduction to evolutionary psychology.* Cambridge, MA: Harvard University Press.

Putnam, H. (1973). Reductionism and the nature of psychology. *Cognition, 2,* 131–146.

Rosenberg, R. S., & Kosslyn, S. M. (2010). *Abnormal psychology.* New York. Worth Publishers.

Rosenthal, R. (1976). *Experimenter effects in behavioral research.* New York: Irvington.

Rosenthal, R. (1991). *Meta-analytic procedures for social research.* Beverly Hills, CA: Sage.

Saha, L. J. (Ed.). (2004). Levels of analysis in the social psychology of education [Editorial]. *Social Psychology of Education, 7,* 253–255.

Schaffner, K. F. (1967). Approaches to reduction. *Philosophy of Science, 34,* 137–147.

Schmitt, D. P. (2002). How shall I compare thee? Evolutionary psychology viewed as a psychological science. *Psychology, Evolution and Gender, 4,* 219–230.

Schwarz, N. (1999). Self-reports: How the questions shape the answers. *American Psychologist, 54,* 93–105.

Sheehan, T. P., Chambers, R. A., & Russell, D. S. (2004). Regulation of affect by the lateral septum: Implications for neuropsychiatry. *Brain Research Reviews, 46,* 71–117.

Snow, C. E. (1991). The language of the mother–child relationship. In M. Woodhead & R. Carr (Eds.), *Becoming a person* (pp. 195–210). London: Routledge.

Snow, C. E. (1999). Social perspectives on the emergence of language. In B. MacWhinney (Ed.), *The emergence of language* (pp. 257–276). Mahwah, NJ: Erlbaum.

Tractinsky, N., & Meyer, J. (1999). Chartjunk or goldgraph? Effects of presentation objectives and content desirability on information presentation. *MIS Quarterly, 23,* 397–420.

White, A., & Hardy, L. (1995). Use of different imagery perspectives on the learning and performance of different motor skills. *British Journal of Psychology, 86*(2), 169–180.

Williams, S. M., Sanderson, G. F., Share, D. L., & Silva, P. A. (1988). Refractive error, IQ and reading ability: A longitudinal study from age seven to 11. *Developmental Medicine and Child Neurology, 30,* 735–742.

Yaguez, L., Nagel, D., Hoffman, H., Canavan, A., Wist, E., & Hoemberg, V. (1998). A mental route to motor learning: Improving trajectoral kinematics through imagery training. *Behavioral and Brain Research, 90,* 95–106.

Zacks, J., & Tversky, B. (1999). Bars and lines: A study of graphic communication. *Memory and Cognition, 27,* 1073–1079.

Zuckerman, M. (1995). Good and bad humors: Biochemical bases of personality and its disorders. *Psychological Science, 6,* 325–332.

References: The Biology of Mind and Behavior

Adolphs, R., Damasio, H., Tranel, D., & Damasio, A. R. (1996). Cortical systems for the recognition of emotion in facial expressions. *Journal of Neuroscience, 16,* 7678–7687.

Ashton, C. H. (2001). Pharmacology and effects of cannabis: A brief review. *British Journal of Psychiatry, 178,* 101–106.

Baeck, E. (2002). The neural networks of music. *European Journal of Neurology, 9,* 449–456.

Bailey, M., Engler, H., Hunzeker, J., & Sheridan, J. F. (2003). The hypothalamic-pituitary-adrenal axis and viral infection. *Viral Immunology, 16,* 141–157.

Baker, F. (2001). The effects of live, taped, and no music on people experiencing posttraumatic amnesia. *Journal of Music Therapy, 38,* 170–192.

Barañano, D. E., Ferris, C. D., & Snyder, S. H. (2001). Atypical neural messengers. *Trends in Neurosciences, 24,* 99–106.

Barinaga, M. (2001). How cannabinoids work in the brain. *Science, 291,* 2530–2531.

Barone, P. (2003). Clinical strategies to prevent and delay motor complications. *Neurology, 61,* S12–S16.

Benson, D. F., & Greenberg, J. P. (1969). Visual form agnosia: A specific deficit in visual recognition. *Archives of Neurology, 20,* 82–89.

Bihrle, A. M., Brownell, H. H., Powelson, J. A., & Gardner, H. (1986). Comprehension of humorous and non-humorous materials by left and right brain-damaged patients. *Brain and Cognition, 5,* 399–411.

Black, J. E., Jones, T. A., Nelson, C. A., & Greenough, W. T. (1998). Neuronal plasticity and the developing brain. In N. E. Alessi, J. T. Coyle, S. I. Harrison, & S. Eth (Eds.), *Handbook of child and adolescent psychiatry: Vol. 6. Basic psychiatric science and treatment* (pp. 31–53). New York: Wiley.

Blalock, E. M., Chen, K., Sharrow, K., Herman, J. P., Porter, N. M., Foster, T. C., et al. (2003). Gene microarrays in hippocampal aging: Statistical profiling identifies novel processes correlated with cognitive impairment. *Journal of Neuroscience, 23,* 3807–3819.

Brewer, A. A., Press, W. A., Logothetis, N. K., & Wandell, B. A. (2002). Visual areas in Macaque cortex measured using functional magnetic resonance imaging. *Journal of Neuroscience, 22,* 10416–10426.

Brownell, H. H., Potter, H. H., Michelow, D., & Gardner, H. (1984). Sensitivity to lexical denotation and connotation in brain-damaged patients: A double dissociation. *Brain and Language, 22,* 253–265.

Cabeza, R., & Nyberg, L. (2000). Imaging cognition II: An empirical review of 275 PET and fMRI studies. *Journal of Cognitive Neuroscience, 12,* 1–47.

Cappa, S. F., & Grafman, J. (2004). Neuroimaging of higher cognitive function. *Cortex, 40,* 591–592.

Cohen, M. R., & Newsome, W. T. (2004). What electrical microstimulation has revealed about the neural basis of cognition. *Current Opinion in Neurobiology, 14,* 169–177.

Comery, T. A., Shah, R., & Greenough, W. T. (1995). Differential rearing alters spine density on medium-sized spiny neurons in the rat corpus striatum: Evidence for association of morphological plasticity with early response gene expression. *Neurobiology of Learning and Memory, 63,* 217–219.

Cotter, D. R., Pariante, C. M., & Everall, I. P. (2001). Glial cell abnormalities in major psychiatric disorders: The evidence and implications. *Brain Research Bulletin, 55,* 585–595.

Cowan, W. M., Fawcett, J. W., O'Leary, D. D. M., & Stanfield, B. B. (1984). Regressive events in neurogenesis. *Science, 225,* 1258–1265.

Dackis, C. A., & O'Brien, C. P. (2001). Cocaine dependence: A disease of the brain's reward centers. *Journal of Substance Abuse Treatment, 21,* 111–117.

deCharms, R. C., Christoff, K., Glover, G. H., Pauly, J. M., Whitfield, S., & Gabrieli, J. D. (2004). Learned regulation of spatially localized brain activation using real-time fMRI. *Neuroimage, 21,* 436–443.

Diamond, M. C., Rosenzweig, M. R., Bennett, E. L., Lindner, B., & Lyon, L. (1972). Effects of environmental enrichment and impoverishment on rat cerebral cortex. *Journal of Neural Biology, 3,* 47–64.

Dick, D. M., Riley, B., & Kendler, K.S. (2010). Nature and nurture in neuropsychiatric genetics: where do we stand? *Dialogues in Clinical Neuroscience, 12,* 7–23.

Di Pietro, M., Laganaro, M., Leemann, B., & Schnider, A. (2004). Receptive amusia: Temporal auditory processing deficit in a professional musician following a left temporo-parietal lesion. *Neuropsychologia, 42,* 868–877.

Elber, T., Pantev, C., Wienbruch, C., Rockstroh, B., & Taub, E. (1995). Increased cortical representation of the fingers of the left hand in string players. *Science, 270,* 305–307.

Ellis, A. W., & Young, A. W. (1987). *Human cognitive neuropsychology.* Hillsdale, NJ: Erlbaum.

Fields, R. D., & Stevens-Graham, B. (2002). New insights into neuron-glia communication. *Science, 298,* 556–562.

Gaser, C., & Schlaug, G. (2003). Brain structures differ between musicians and non-musicians. *Journal of Neuroscience, 23,* 9240–9245.

Gazzaniga, M. S. (1995). Consciousness and the cerebral hemispheres. In M. S. Gazzaniga (Ed.), *The cognitive neurosciences* (pp. 1391–1400). Cambridge, MA: MIT Press.

Gazzaniga, M. S., & LeDoux, J. E. (1978). *The integrated mind.* New York: Plenum.

Gilbert, S. (2002, June 25). When brain trauma is at the other end of the thrill ride. *New York Times,* p. D5.

Glaser, R., & Kiecolt-Glaser, J. K. (1998). Stress-associated immune modulation: Relevance to viral infections and chronic fatigue syndrome. *American Journal of Medicine, 105,* 35S–42S.

Gluck, M., & Myers, C. (2000). *Gateway to memory: An introduction to neural network modeling of the hippocampus and learning.* Cambridge, MA: MIT Press.

Göbel, S. M., Calabria, M., Farnè, A., & Rossetti, Y. (2006). Parietal rTMS distorts the mental number line: Simulating "spatial" neglect in healthy subjects. *Neuropsychologia, 44,* 860–868.

Goedde, H. W., & Agarwal, D. P. (1987). Aldehyde hydrogenase polymorphism: Molecular basis and phenotypic relationship to alcohol sensitivity. *Alcohol and Alcoholism* (Suppl. 1), 47–54.

Goldberg, E. (2001). *The executive brain: Frontal lobes and the civilized mind.* New York: Oxford University Press.

Goldstein, D. S. (2000). *The autonomic nervous system in health and disease.* New York: Marcel Dekker.

Gottlieb, G. (1998). Normally occurring environmental and behavioral influences on gene activity: From central dogma to probabilistic epigenesis. *Psychological Review, 105,* 792–802.

Gould, E., Tanapat, P., Hastings, N. B., & Shors, T. J. (1999). Neurogenesis in adulthood: A possible role in learning. *Trends in Cognitive Sciences, 3,* 186–192.

Gould, S. J., & Lewontin, R. C. (1979). The spandrels of San Marco and the Panglossian paradigm: A critique of the adaptationist programme. *Proceedings of the Royal Society of London, Series B, 205,* 581–598.

Greenough, W. T., Black, J. E., & Wallace, C. S. (1987). Experience and brain development. *Child Development, 58,* 539–559.

Greenough, W. T., & Chang, F.-L. F. (1985). Synaptic structural correlates of information storage in mammalian nervous systems. In C. W. Cotman (Ed.), *Synaptic plasticity* (pp. 335–372). New York: Guilford Press.

Griffiths, T. D., Warren, J. D., Dean, J. L., & Howard, D. (2004). "When the feeling's gone": A selective loss of musical emotion. *Journal of Neurology, Neurosurgery and Psychiatry, 75,* 344–345.

Halassa, M.M., & Haydon, P.G. (2010). Integrated brain circuits: astrocytic networks modulate neuronal activity and behavior. *Annual Review of Physiology, 72,* 335–355.

Hall, J., Thomas, K. L., & Everitt, B. J. (2001). Cellular imaging of *zif268* expression in the hippocampus and amygdala during contextual and cued fear memory retrieval: Selective activation of hippocampal CA1 neurons during the recall of contextual memories. *Journal of Neuroscience, 21,* 2186–2193.

Hamilton, N.B., & Attwell, D. (2010). Do astrocytes really exocytose neurotransmitters? *Nature Reviews Neuroscience, 11,* 227–238.

Hart, H. C., Palmer, A. R., & Hall, D. A. (2003). Amplitude and frequency-modulated stimuli activate common regions of human auditory cortex. *Cerebral Cortex, 13,* 773–781.

Heit, G., Smith, M. E., & Halgren, E. (1988). Neural encoding of individual words and faces by the human hippocampus and amygdala. *Nature, 333,* 773–775.

Hellige, J. B., & Michimata, C. (1989). Categorization versus distance: Hemispheric differences for processing spatial information. *Memory and Cognition, 17,* 770–776.

Hirokawa, E. (2004). Effects of music listening and relaxation instructions on arousal changes and the working memory task in older adults. *Journal of Music Therapy, 41,* 107–127.

Hugdahl, K., & Davidson, R. J. (Eds.). (2003). *The asymmetrical brain.* Cambridge, MA: MIT Press.

Hunter, P. G., Schellenberg, E. G., & Schimmack, U. (2008). Mixed affective responses to music with conflicting cues. *Cognition and Emotion, 22,* 327–352.

Huttenlocher, P. (2002). *Neural plasticity.* Cambridge, MA: Harvard University Press.

Iansek, R., & Porter, R. C. (1980). The monkey globus pallidus: Neuronal discharge properties in relation to movement. *Journal of Physiology, 301,* 439–455.

Ivry, R. B., & Robertson, L. C. (1998). *The two sides of perception.* Cambridge, MA: MIT Press.

Ivry, R. B., & Spencer, R. M. C. (2004). The neural representation of time. *Current Opinion in Neurobiology, 14,* 225–232.

Jenner, P. (2002). Pharmacology of dopamine agonists in the treatment of Parkinson's disease. *Neurology, 58,* S1–S8.

Kandel, E. R., Schwartz, J. H., & Jessell, T. M. (2000). *Principles of neural science.* New York: McGraw-Hill/Appleton & Lange.

Katona, I., Sperlagh, B., Magloczky, Z., Santha, E., Kofalvi, A., Czirjak, S., et al. (2000). GABAergic interneurons are the targets of cannabinoid actions in the human hippocampus. *Neuroscience, 100,* 797–804.

Kempermann, G., Wiscott, L., & Gage, F. H. (2004). Functional significance of adult neurogenesis. *Current Opinion in Neurobiology, 14,* 186–191.

Knutson, B., Adams, C. M., Fong, G. W., & Hommer, D. (2001). Anticipation of increasing monetary reward selectively recruits nucleus accumbens. *Journal of Neuroscience, 21,* RC159, 1–5.

Kosslyn, S. M. (2006). You can play 20 questions with nature and win: Categorical versus coordinate spatial relations as a case study. Neuropsychologia, 44, 1519-1523.

Kosslyn, S. M., Koenig, O., Barrett, A., Cave, C. B., Tang, J., & Gabrieli, J. D. E. (1989). Evidence for two types of spatial representations: Hemispheric specialization for categorical and coordinate relations. *Journal of Experimental Psychology: Human Perception and Performance, 15,* 723–735.

Kosslyn, S. M., Pascual-Leone, A., Felician, O., Camposano, S., Keenan, J. P., Thompson, W. L., et al. (1999). The role of area 17 in visual imagery: Convergent evidence from PET and rTMS. *Science, 284,* 167–170.

Kreitzer, A. C., & Regehr, W. G. (2001). Cerebellar depolarization-induced suppression of inhibition is mediated by endogenous cannabinoids. *Journal of Neuroscience, 21,* RC174.

Laeng, B., Chabris, C. F., & Kosslyn, S. M. (2003). Asymmetries in encoding spatial relations. In K. Hugdahl & R. J. Davidson (Eds.), *The asymmetrical brain* (pp. 303–339). Cambridge, MA: MIT Press.

LeDoux, J. E. (1996). *The emotional brain: The mysterious underpinnings of emotional life.* New York: Simon & Schuster.

LeDoux, J. E., Wilson, D. H., & Gazzaniga, M. S. (1977). A divided mind: Observations on the conscious properties of the separated hemispheres. *Annals of Neurology, 2,* 417–421.

Lonky, M. L. (2003). Human consciousness: A systems approach to the mind/brain interaction. *Journal of Mind and Behavior, 24,* 91–118.

Macmillan, M. B. (1986). A wonderful journey through skull and brains: The travels of Mr. Gage's tamping iron. *Brain and Cognition, 5,* 67–107.

Macmillan, M. (1992). Inhibition and the control of behavior: From Gall to Freud via Phineas Gage and the frontal lobes. *Brain and Cognition, 19,* 72–104.

Magee, W. L., & Davidson, J. W. (2002). The effect of music therapy on mood states in neurological patients: A pilot study. *Journal of Music Therapy, 39,* 20–29.

Manto, M., & Pandolfo, M. (Eds.). (2001). *Cerebellum and its disorders.* New York: Cambridge University Press.

Marini, P., Ramat, S., Ginestroni, A., & Paganini, M. (2003). Deficit of short-term memory in newly diagnosed untreated Parkinsonian patients: Reversal after L-dopa therapy. *Neurological Sciences, 24,* 184–185.

Marucha, P. T., Kiecolt-Glaser, J. K., & Favagehi, M. (1998). Mucosal wound healing is impaired by examination stress. *Psychosomatic Medicine, 60,* 362–365.

Mauch, D. H., Nägler, K., Schumacher, S., Göritz, C., Müller, E. C., Otto, A., et al. (2001). CNS synaptogenesis promoted by glia-derived cholesterol. *Science, 294,* 1354–1357.

McMurtaya, A. M., Lichta, E., Yeoa, T., Krisztala, E., Saula, R. E., & Mendeza, M. F. (2008). Positron emission tomography facilitates diagnosis of early-onset Alzheimer's disease. *European Neurology, 59,* 31–37.

Meister, I. G., Krings, T., Foltys, H., Boroojerdi, B., Müller, M., Töpper, R., et al. (2004). Playing piano in the mind—An fMRI study on music imagery and performance in pianists. *Cognitive Brain Research, 19,* 219–228.

Mello, C. V., Vicario, D. S., & Clayton, D. F. (1992). Song presentation induces gene expression in the songbird forebrain. *Proceedings of the National Academy of Sciences of the United States of America, 89,* 6818–6822.

Miguel-Hidalgo, J. J. (2009). The role of glial cells in drug abuse. *Current Drug Abuse Reviews, 2,* 72–82.

Milner, B., Corkin, S., & Teuber, H. L. (1968). Further analysis of the hippocampal amnesic syndrome: 14-year followup study of H. M. *Neuropsychologia, 6,* 215–234.

Miranda, D., & Claes, M. (2009). Music listening, coping, peer affiliation and depression in adolescence. *Psychology of Music, 37,* 215–233.

Morris, J., & Dolan, R. (2002). The amygdala and unconscious fear processing. In B. de Gelder, E. de Haan, & C. Heywood (Eds.), *Out of mind: Varieties of unconscious processes* (pp. 185–204). London: Oxford University Press.

Münte, T. F., Kohlmetz, C., Nager, W., & Altenmüller, E. (2001). Superior auditory spatial tuning in conductors. *Nature, 409,* 580.

Nelson, C. A. (1999). Human plasticity and human development. *Current Directions in Psychological Science, 8,* 42–45.

Ojemann, G. A. (1983). Brain organization for language from the perspective of electrical stimulation mapping. *Behavioral and Brain Sciences, 6,* 189–230.

Ojemann, G. A., Ojemann, J., Lettich, E., & Berger, M. (1989). Cortical language localization in left, dominant hemisphere. *Journal of Neurosurgery, 71,* 316–326.

Pagnoni, G., Zink, C. F., Montague, P. R., & Berns, G. S. (2002). Activity in human ventral striatum locked to errors of reward prediction. *Nature Neuroscience, 5,* 97–98.

Pantev, C., & Lütkenhöner, B. (2000). Magnetoencephalographic studies of functional organization and plasticity of the human auditory cortex. *Journal of Clinical Neurophysiology, 17,* 130–142.

Pascual-Leone, A., Grafman, J., Cohen, L. G., Roth, B. J., & Hallett, M. (1997). Transcranial magnetic stimulation: A new tool for the study of higher cognitive functions in humans. In J. Grafman & F. Boller (Eds.), *Handbook of neuropsychology* (Vol. 11). (pp. 267–290). Amsterdam: Elsevier.

Pascual-Leone, A., Tormos, J. M., Keenan, J., Tarazona, F., Cañete, C., & Catalá, M. D. (1998). Study and modulation of human cortical excitability with trans-cranial magnetic stimulation. *Journal of Clinical Neurophysiology, 15,* 333–343.

Payne, B. R., & Lomber, S. G. (2001). Reconstructing functional systems after lesions of cerebral cortex. *Nature Reviews Neuroscience, 2,* 911–919.

Pelletier, C. L. (2004). The effect of music on decreasing arousal due to stress: A meta-analysis. *Journal of Music Therapy, 41,* 192–214.

Penfield, W., & Perot, P. (1963). The brain's record of auditory and visual experience. *Brain, 86,* 595–696.

Penfield, W., & Rasmussen, T. (1950). *The cerebral cortex of man: A clinical study of localization of function.* New York: Macmillan.

Peretz, I., Blood, A. J., Penhune, V., & Zatorre, R. (2001). Cortical deafness to dissonance. *Brain, 124,* 928–940.

Pfrieger, F. W. (2002). Role of glia in synapse development. *Current Opinion in Neurobiology, 12,* 486–490.

Plomin, R. (1995). Genetics and children's experiences in the family. *Journal of Child Psychology and Psychiatry, 36,* 33–68.

Plomin, R., & DeFries, J. C. (1998). The genetics of cognitive abilities and disabilities: Investigations of specific cognitive skills can help clarify how genes shape the components of intellect. *Scientific American, 278,* 40–47.

Plomin, R., DeFries, J. C., Craig, I. W., & McGuffin, P. (Eds.). (2003). *Behavioral genetics in the postgenomic era.* Washington, DC: APA Books.

Plomin, R., DeFries, J. C., McClearn, G. E., & Rutter, M. (1997). *Behavioral genetics* (3rd ed.). New York: Freeman.

Plomin, R., Fulker, D. W., Corley, R., & DeFries, J. C. (1997). Nature, nurture, and cognitive development from 1 to 16 years: A parent-offspring adoption study. *Psychological Science, 8,* 442–447.

Plomin, R., & Kosslyn, S. M. (2001). Genes, brain and cognition. *Nature Neuroscience, 4,* 1153–1155.

Poldrack, R. A., & Wagner, A. D. (2004). What can neuroimaging tell us about the mind? Insights from prefrontal cortex. *Current Directions in Psychological Science, 13,* 177–181.

Posner, M. I., & Raichle, M. (1994). *Images of mind.* New York: Freeman.

Raine, A., Buchsbaum, M. S., Stanley, J., Lottenberg, S., Abel, L., & Stoddard, J. (1994). Selective reductions in prefrontal glucose metabolism in murderers. *Biological Psychiatry, 15,* 365–373.

Reid, S., & Barbui, C. (2010). Long term treatment of depression with selective serotonin reuptake inhibitors and newer antidepressants. *BMJ,* Mar 26;340:c1468. doi: 10.1136/bmj.c1468.

Rentfrow, P. J., & Gosling, S. D. (2007). The content and validity of music-genre stereotypes among college students. *Psychology of Music, 35,* 306–326.

Rentfrow, P. J., McDonald, J. A., & Oldmeadow, J. A. (2009). You are what you listen to: Young people's stereotypes about music fans. *Group Processes and Intergroup Relations, 12,* 329–344.

Robbins, T. W., & Everitt, B. J. (1999). Interaction of the dopaminergic system with mechanisms of associative learning and cognition: Implications for drug abuse. *Psychological Science, 10,* 199–202.

Roozen, H. G., de Waart, R., van der Windt, D. A. W. M., van den Brink, W., de Jong, C. A. J., & Kerkhof, A. J. F. M. (2006). A systematic review of the effectiveness of naltrexone in the maintenance treatment of opioid and alcohol dependence. *European Neuropsychopharmacology, 16,* 311–323.

Rozin, P., & Jonides, J. (1977). Mass reaction time: Measurement of the speed of the nerve impulse and the duration of mental processes in class. *Teaching of Psychology, 4,* 91–94.

Sanudo-Pena, M., Tsou, K., Romero, J., Mackie, K., & Walker, J. M. (2000). Role of the superior colliculus in the motor effects of cannabinoids and dopamine. *Brain Research, 853,* 207–214.

Scarr, S., & McCartney, K. (1983). How people make their own environments: A theory of genotype environment effects. *Child Development, 54,* 424–435.

Schlaug, G., Jancke, L., Huang, Y., & Steinmetz, H. (1995). In vivo evidence of structural brain asymmetry in musicians. *Science, 267,* 699–701.

Schneider, M., & Koch, M. (2002). The cannabinoid agonist WIN 55,212-2 reduces sensorimotor gating and recognition memory in rats. *Behavioural Pharmacology, 13,* 29–37.

Sekiyama, K., Kanno, I., Miura, S., & Sugita, Y. (2003). Auditory-visual speech perception examined by fMRI and PET. *Neuroscience Research, 47,* 277–287.

Siegel, A. M., Andersen, R. A., Freund, H., & Spencer, D. D. (Eds.). (2003). *The parietal lobes.* Philadelphia: Lippincott Williams & Wilkins.

Simos, P. G. (2001). *Vision in the brain.* Amsterdam: Swets & Zeitlinger.

Smith, J. C., & Joyce, C. A. (2004). Mozart versus New Age music: Relaxation states, stress, and ABC Relaxation Theory. *Journal of Music Therapy, 41,* 215–224.

Squire, L. R., & Schacter, D. L. (Eds.). (2002). *Neuropsychology of memory* (3rd ed.). New York: Guilford Press.

Suh, J., & Jackson, F. R. (2007). Drosophila Ebony activity is required within glia for the circadian regulation of locomotor activity. *Neuron, 55,* 435–447.

Swaab, D. F. (2003). *The human hypothalamus: Basic and clinical aspects. Part 1: Nuclei of the human hypothalamus.* Amsterdam: Elsevier.

Thompson, P. M., Cannon, T. D., Narr, K. L., van Erp, T., Poutanen, V. P., Huttunen, M., et al. (2001). Genetic influences on brain structure. *Nature Neuroscience, 12,* 1253–1258.

Thompson, R.F. (1993). *The brain, a neuroscience primer.* New York: W.H. Freeman.

Turner, A. M., & Greenough, W. T. (1985). Differential rearing effects on rat visual cortex synapses. I. Synaptic and neuronal density and synapses per neuron. *Brain Research, 329,* 195–203.

Ullian, E. M., Sapperstein, S. K., Christopherson, K. S., & Barres, B. A. (2001). Control of synapse number by glia. *Science, 291,* 657–661.

Unterwald, E. M. (2008). Naltrexone in the treatment of alcohol dependence. *Journal of Addiction Medicine, 2,* 121–127.

van Honk, J., Tuiten, A., van den Hout, M., Koppeschaar, H., Thijssen, J., de Haan, E., et al. (2000). Conscious and preconscious selective attention to social threat: Different neuroendocrine response patterns. *Psychoneuroendocrinology, 25,* 577–591.

Vinar, O. (2001). Neurobiology of drug dependence. *Homeostasis in Health and Disease, 41,* 20–34.

Voyer, D., Bowes, A., & Soraggi, M. (2009). Response procedure and laterality effects in emotion recognition: implications for models of dichotic listening. Neuropsychologia, 47, 23 – 29.

Walsh, V., & Pascual-Leone, A. (2003). *Transcranial magnetic stimulation: A neurochronometrics of mind.* Cambridge, MA: MIT Press.

Watkins, L. R., Milligan, E. D., & Maier, S. F. (2001). Glial activation: A driving force for pathological pain. *Trends in Neuroscience, 24,* 450–455.

Wildman, D. E., Grossman, L. I., & Goodman, M. (2002). Functional DNA in humans and chimpanzees shows they are more similar to each other than either is to other apes. In M. Goodman & A. S. Moffat (Eds.), *Probing human origins* (pp. 1–10). Cambridge, MA: American Academy of Arts and Sciences.

Wilson, R. I., & Nicoll, R. A. (2002). Endocannabinoid signaling in the brain. *Science, 296,* 678–682.

Winkelman, M. (2003). Complementary therapy for addiction: "Drumming out drugs." *American Journal of Public Health, 93,* 647–651.

Witter, M. P., Wouterlood, F., & Witter, M. (2002). *The parahippocampal region: Organization and role in cognitive functions.* New York: Oxford University Press.

Zaidel, E., & Iacoboni, M. (2003). *The parallel brain: The cognitive neuroscience of the corpus callosum.* Cambridge, MA: MIT Press

Zajicek, J. (2004). Primary progressive multiple sclerosis. *Cognitive Neuropsychology, 21,* 2784–2785.

References: Sensation and Perception

Alain, C., He, Y., & Grady, C. (2008). The contribution of the inferior parietal lobe to auditory spatial working memory. *Journal of Cognitive Neuroscience, 20,* 285–295.

Alcock, J. E. (1987). Parapsychology: Science of the anomalous or search for the soul? *Behavioral and Brain Sciences, 10,* 553–565.

Arnell, K. M., & Jolicoeur, P. (1999). The attentional blink across stimulus modalities: Evidence for central processing limitations. *Journal of Experimental Psychology: Human Perception and Performance, 25,* 630–648.

Baker, R. R. (1980). Goal orientation by blindfolded humans after long-distance displacement: Possible involvement of a magnetic sense. *Science, 210,* 555–557.

Bar, M., Tootell, R. B., Schacter, D. L., Greve, D. N., Fischl, B., Mendola, J. D., et al. (2001). Cortical mechanisms specific to explicit visual object recognition. *Neuron, 29,* 529–535.

Bartoshuk, L. M., & Beauchamp, G. K. (1994). Chemical senses. *Annual Review of Psychology, 45,* 419–449.

Beatty, J. (1995). *Principles of behavioral neuroscience.* Dubuque, IA: Brown & Benchmark.

Bem, D. J., & Honorton, C. (1994). Does psi exist? Replicable evidence for an anomalous process of information transfer. *Psychological Bulletin, 115,* 4–18.

Bensafi, M., Tsutsui, T., Khan, R., Levenson, R. W., & Sobel, N. (2004). Sniffing a human sex-steroid derived compound affects mood and autonomic arousal in a dose-dependent manner. *Psychoneuroendocrinology, 29,* 1290–1299.

Berson, D. M., Dunn, F. A., & Takao, M. (2002). Phototransduction by retinal ganglion cells that set the circadian clock. *Science, 295,* 1070–1073.

Biederman, I. (1987). Recognition-by-components: A theory of human image understanding. *Psychological Review, 94,* 115–147.

Biederman, I., & Shiffrar, M. M. (1987). Sexing day-old chicks: A case study and expert systems analysis of a difficult perceptual-learning task. *Journal of Experimental Psychology: Learning, Memory, and Cognition, 13,* 640–645.

Bly, B. M., & Kosslyn, S. M. (1997). Functional anatomy of object recognition in humans: Evidence from PET and fMRI. *Current Opinion in Neurology, 10,* 5–9.

Borg, E., & Counter, S. A. (1989). The middle ear muscles. *Scientific American, 261,* 74–80.

Bregman, A. S. (1990). *Auditory scene analysis: The perceptual organization of sound.* Cambridge, MA: MIT Press.

Bregman, A. S. (1993). Auditory scene analysis: Hearing in complex environments. In S. McAdams & E. Bigand (Eds.), *Thinking in sound: The cognitive psychology of human audition* (pp. 10–36). New York: Oxford University Press.

Brugger, P., Landis, T., & Regard, M. (1990). A "sheep-goat effect" in repetition avoidance: Extrasensory perception as an effect of subjective probability? *British Journal of Psychology, 81,* 455–468.

Buck, L., & Axel, R. (1991). A novel multigene family may encode odorant receptors: A molecular basis for odor recognition. *Cell, 65,* 175–187.

Cailliet, R. (1993). *Pain: Mechanisms and management.* Philadelphia: Davis.

Cain, W. S. (1973). Spatial discrimination of cutaneous warmth. *American Journal of Psychology, 86,* 169–181.

Cain, W. S. (1979). To know with the nose: Keys to odor identification. *Science, 203,* 467–470.

Cain, W. S. (1982). Odor identification by males and females: Predictions and performance. *Chemical Senses, 7,* 129–141.

Cain, W. S., & Gent, J. F. (1991). Olfactory sensitivity: Reliability, generality, and association with aging. *Journal of Experimental Psychology: Human Perception and Performance, 17,* 382–391.

Carlsson, C. P. O., & Sjoelund, B. H. (2001). Acupuncture for chronic low back pain: A randomized placebo-controlled study with long-term follow-up. *Clinical Journal of Pain, 17,* 296–305.

Carlyon, R. P. (2004). How the brain separates sounds. *Trends in Cognitive Sciences, 8,* 465–471.

Caruso, S., Grillo, C., Agnello, C., Maiolino, L., Intelisano, G., & Serra, A. (2001). A prospective study evidencing rhinomanometric and olfactometric outcomes in women taking oral contraceptives. *Human Reproduction, 16,* 2288–2294.

Cave, C. B., & Kosslyn, S. M. (1993). The role of parts and spatial relations in object identification. *Perception, 22,* 229–248.

Chapman, C. R., & Nakamura, Y. (1999). A passion of the soul: An introduction to pain for consciousness researchers. *Consciousness and Cognition, 8,* 391–422.

Chaudhari, N., Landin, A. M., & Roper, S. D. (2000). A metabotropic glutamate receptor variant functions as a taste receptor. *Nature Neuroscience, 3,* 113–119.

Cherry, E. C. (1953). Some experiments on the recognition of speech with one and two ears. *Journal of the Acoustical Society of America, 25,* 975–979.

Child, I. L. (1985). Psychology and anomalous observations: The question of ESP in dreams. *American Psychologist, 40,* 1219–1230.

Chun, M. M. (1997). Types and tokens in visual processing: A double dissociation between the attentional blink and repetition blindness. *Journal of Experimental Psychology: Human Perception and Performance, 23,* 738–755.

Chun, M. M. (2000). Contextual cueing of visual attention. *Trends in Cognitive Sciences, 4,* 170–177.

Cole, G. G., Heywood, C., Kentridge, R., Fairholm, I., & Cowey, A. (2003). Attentional capture by colour and motion in cerebral achromatopsia. *Neuropsychologia, 41,* 1837–1846.

Connor, C. E. (2002). Reconstructing a 3D world. *Science, 298,* 376–377.

Conway, A. R. A., Cowan, N., & Bunting, M. F. (2001). The cocktail party phenomenon revisited: The importance of working memory capacity. *Psychonomic Bulletin and Review, 8,* 331–335.

Corbetta, M., & Shulman, G. L. (2002). Control of goal-directed and stimulus-driven attention in the brain. *Nature Reviews Neuroscience, 3,* 201–215.

Cowey, A. (2010). The blindsight saga. *Experimental Brain Research, 200,* 3–24.

Cowey, A., & Stoerig, P. (1995). Blindsight in monkeys. *Nature, 373,* 247–249.

Crago, M., & Crago, H. (1983). *Prelude to literacy.* Carbondale: Southern Illinois University Press.

Crist, R. E., Li, Wu, & Gilbert, C. D. (2001). Learning to see: Experience and attention in primary visual cortex. *Nature Neuroscience, 4,* 519–525.

Dehaene-Lambertz, G., & Pena, M. (2001). Electrophysiological evidence for automatic phonetic processing in neonates. *Neuroreport, 12,* 3155–3158.

Delk, J. L., & Fillenbaum, S., (1965). Difference in perceived color as a function of characteristic color. *American Journal of Psychology, 78,* 290–293.

De Renzi, E. (1982). *Disorders of space exploration and cognition.* New York: Wiley.

De Valois, R. L., & De Valois, K. K. (1975). Neural coding of color. In E. C. Carterette & M. P. Friedman (Eds.), *Handbook of perception* (pp. 117–166). New York: Academic Press.

De Valois, R. L., & De Valois, K. K. (1993). A multi-stage color model. *Vision Research, 33,* 1053–1065.

de Wijk, R. A., & Cain, W. S. (1994). Odor identification by name and by edibility: Life-span development and safety. *Human Factors, 36,* 182–187.

de Wijk, R. A., Schab, F. R., & Cain, W. S. (1995). Odor identification. In F. R. Schab & R. G. Crowder (Eds.), *Memory for odors* (pp. 21–37). Mahwah, NJ: Erlbaum.

Doty, R. L., Bartoshuk, L. M., & Snow, J. B., Jr. (1991). Causes of olfactory and gustatory disorders. In T. V. Getchell, R. L. Doty, L. M. Bartoshuk, & J. B. Snow Jr. (Eds.), *Smell and taste in health and disease* (pp. 449–462). New York: Raven.

Dowling, J. E. (1992). *Neurons and networks: An introduction to neuroscience.* Cambridge, MA: Harvard University Press.

Dufour, A., Després, O., & Pebayle, T. (2002). Visual and auditory facilitation in auditory spatial localization. *Visual Cognition, 9*(6), 741–753.

Duncan, H. F., Gourlay, N., & Hudson, W. (1973). *A study of pictorial perception among Bantu and White primary school children in South Africa.* Johannesburg, South Africa: Witwatersrand University Press.

Eimas, P. D., & Corbit, J. D. (1973). Selective adaptation of linguistic feature detectors. *Cognitive Psychology, 4,* 99–109.

Engel, S. A., Glover, G. H., & Wandell, B. A. (1997). Retinotopic organization in human visual cortex and the spatial precision of functional MRI. *Cerebral Cortex, 7,* 181–192.

Ernst, M. O., & Bülthoff, H. H. (2004). Merging the senses into a robust percept. *Trends in Cognitive Sciences, 8,* 162–169.

Fang, L., & Grossberg, S. (2009). From stereogram to surface: how the brain sees the world in depth. *Spatial Vision, 22,* 45-82.

Fatt, I., & Weissman, B. A. (1992). *Physiology of the eye: An introduction to the vegetative functions* (2nd ed.). Boston: Butterworth-Heinemann.

Fell, J., Klaver, P., Elger, C. E., & Guillén, F. (2002). Suppression of EEG Gamma activity may cause the attentional blink. *Consciousness and Cognition, 11,* 114–122.

Felleman, D. J., & Van Essen, D. C. (1991). Distributed hierarchical processing in the primate cerebral cortex. *Cerebral Cortex, 1,* 1–47.

Fink, B., Grammer, K., & Thornhill, R. (2001). Human (*Homo sapiens*) facial attractiveness in relation to skin texture and color. *Journal of Comparative Psychology, 115,* 92–99.

Flas, W., Dupont, P., Reynvoet, B., & Orban, G. A. (2002). The quantitative nature of a visual task differentiates between ventral and dorsal stream. *Journal of Cognitive Neuroscience, 14,* 646–658.

Ford, C. S., & Beach, F. (1951). *Patterns of sexual behavior.* New York: Harper & Row.

Freedman, M. S., Lucas, R. J., Soni, B., von Schantz, M., Muñoz, M., David-Gray, Z., et al. (1999). Regulation of mammalian circadian behavior by non-rod, non-cone, ocular photoreceptors. *Science, 284,* 502–504.

Freeman, W. J. (1991). The psychology of perception. *Scientific American, 264,* 78–85.

Friedrich, R. W. (2004). Odorant receptors make scents. *Nature, 430,* 511–512.

Gagliese, L., & Katz, J. (2000). Medically unexplained pain is not caused by psychopathology. *Pain Research and Management, 5,* 251–257.

Gelfand, S. A. (1981). *Hearing.* New York: Marcel Dekker.

Gibson, J. J. (1966). *The senses considered as perceptual systems.* Boston: Houghton Mifflin.

Goodale, M. A., & Milner, A. D. (1992). Separate visual pathways for perception and action. *Trends in Neurosciences, 15,* 20–25.

Gould, J. L. (1998). Sensory bases of navigation. *Current Biology, 8,* R731–R738.

Green, D. M. (1976). *An introduction to hearing.* Hillsdale, NJ: Erlbaum.

Green, D. M., & Swets, J. A. (1966). *Signal detection theory and psychophysics.* New York: Wiley.

Greenwald, A. G., Spangenberg, E. R., Pratkanis, A. R., & Eskenazi, J. (1991). Double-blind tests of subliminal self-help audiotapes. *Psychological Science, 2,* 119–122.

Gregg, V. R., Winer, G. A., Cottrell, J. E., Hedman, K. E., & Fournier, J. S. (2001). The persistence of a misconception about vision after educational interventions. *Psychonomic Bulletin and Review, 8,* 622–626.

Grillo, C., La Mantia, I., Triolo, C., Scollo, A., La Boria, A., Intelisano, G., et al. (2001). Rhinomanometric and olfactometric variations throughout the menstrual cycle. *Annals of Otology, Rhinology and Laryngology, 110,* 785–789.

Grill-Spector, K. (2003). The neural basis of object perception. *Current Opinion in Neurobiology, 13,* 159–166.

Grill-Spector, K., Kushnir, T., Hendler, T., Edelman, S., Itzchak, Y., & Malach, R. (1998). A sequence of object-processing stages revealed by fMRI in the human occipital lobe. *Human Brain Mapping, 6,* 316–328.

Hallem, E. A., Ho, M. G., & Carlson, J. R. (2004). The molecular basis of odor coding in the *Drosophila* antenna. *Cell, 117,* 965–979.

Hartman, B. J. (1982). An exploratory study of the effects of disco music on the auditory and vestibular systems. *Journal of Auditory Research, 22,* 271–274.

Haxby, J. V., Gobbini, M. I., Furey, M. L., Ishai, A., Schouten, J. L., & Pietrini, P. (2001). Distributed and overlapping representations of faces and objects in ventral temporal cortex. *Science, 293,* 2425–2430.

Haxby, J. V., Grady, C. L., Horowitz, B., Ungerleider, L. G., Mischkin, M., Carson, R. E., et al. (1991). Dissociation of object and spatial visual processing pathways in human extrastriate cortex. *Proceedings of the National Academy of Sciences of the United States of America, 88,* 1621–1625.

Haxby, J. V., Horowitz, B., Ungerleider, L. G., Maisog, J. M., Pietrini, P., & Grady, C. L. (1994). The functional organization of human extrastriate cortex: A PET-rCBF study of selective attention to faces and locations. *Journal of Neuroscience, 14,* 6336–6353.
Hayashi, T., Yamaguchi, T., Kitahara, K., Sharpe, L. T., Jägle, H., Yamade, S., et al. (2001). The importance of gene order in expression of the red and green visual pigment genes and in color vision. *Color Research and Application, 26,* S79–S83.
Hensel, H. (1982). *Thermal sensations and thermoreceptors in man.* Springfield, IL: Thomas.
Herrera, H. (1983). *Frida: Biography of Frida Kahlo.* New York: Harper and Row.
Hoffman, D. D., & Richards, W. A. (1984). Parts of recognition. *Cognition, 18,* 65–96.
Honorton, C. (1997). The Ganzfeld novice: Four predictors of initial ESP performance. *Journal of Parapsychology, 61,* 143–158.
Hubel, D. H., & Wiesel, T. N. (1962). Receptive fields, binocular interaction and functional architecture in the cat's visual cortex. *Journal of Physiology, 160,* 106–154.
Hubel, D. H., & Wiesel, T. N. (1974). Sequence regularity and orientation columns in the monkey striate cortex. *Journal of Comparative Neurology, 158,* 295–306.
Hugdahl, K. (2001). *Psychophysiology: The mind-body perspective* (2nd ed.). Cambridge, MA: Harvard University Press.
Hummel, J. E., & Biederman, I. (1992). Dynamic binding in a neural network for shape recognition. *Psychological Review, 99,* 480–517.
Humphreys, G. W., Riddoch, M. J., & Price, C. J. (1997). Top-down processes in object identification: Evidence from experimental psychology, neuropsychology and functional anatomy. *Philosophical Transactions of the Royal Society of London, 352,* 1275–1282.
Hurvich, L. M., & Jameson, D. (1957). An opponent-process theory of color vision. *Psychological Review, 64,* 384–404.
Husain, M., & Jackson, S. R. (2001). Vision: Visual space is not what it appears to be. *Current Biology, 11,* R753–R755.
Hyman, A., Mentzer, T., & Calderone, L. (1979). The contribution of olfaction to taste discrimination. *Bulletin of Psychonomic Society, 13,* 359–362.
Jacobsen, L. K., Mencl, W. E., Pugh, K. R., Skudlarski, P., & Krystal, J. H. (2004). Preliminary evidence of hippocampal dysfunction in adolescent MDMA ("ecstasy") users: Possible relationship to neurotoxic effects. *Psychopharmacology, 173,* 383–390.
James, T. W., Culham, J., Humphrey, G. K., Milner, A. D., & Goodale, M. A. (2003). Ventral occipital lesions impair object recognition but not object-directed grasping: An fMRI study. *Brain, 126,* 2463–2475.
Jolicoeur, P. (1998). Modulation of the attentional blink by on-line response selection: Evidence from speeded and unspeeded Task 1 decisions. *Memory and Cognition, 26,* 1014–1032.
Jones, D. (1996). *Physical attractiveness and the theory of sexual selection: Results from five populations.* Ann Arbor, MI: Museum of Anthropology.
Julesz, B. (1971). *Foundations of cyclopean perception.* Oxford: University of Chicago Press.
Kanwisher, N. G. (1987). Repetition blindness: Type recognition without token individuation. *Cognition, 27,* 117–143.
Kihlstrom, J. F. (1985). Hypnosis. *Annual Review of Psychology, 36,* 385–418.
Kirschvink, J. L., Walker, M. M., & Diebel, C. E. (2001). Magnetite-based magnetoreception. *Current Opinion in Neurobiology, 11,* 462–467.
Klostermann, E. C., Loui, P., & Shimamura, A. P. (2009). Activation of right parietal cortex during memory retrieval of nonlinguistic auditory stimuli. *Cognitive, Affective, and Behavioral Neuroscience, 9,* 242–248.
Kochkin, S. (2001). MarkeTrak VI: The VA and direct mail sales spark growth in hearing aid market. *The Hearing Review, 8,* 16–24, 63–65.
Koffka, K. (1935). *Principles of Gestalt psychology.* New York: Harcourt Brace.
Kohler, S., Kapur, S., Moscovitch, M., Winocur, G., & Houle, S. (1995). Dissociation of pathways for object and spatial vision: A PET study in humans. *Neuroreport, 6,* 1865–1868.
Konishi, M. (1993). Listening with two ears. *Scientific American, 268,* 66–73.
Konstantinidis, I. (2009). The taste peripheral system. *B-ENT, 5,* 115–121.
Kosslyn, S. M. (1987). Seeing and imagining in the cerebral hemispheres: A computational approach. *Psychological Review, 94,* 148–175.
Kosslyn, S. M. (1994). *Image and brain: The resolution of the imagery debate.* Cambridge, MA: MIT Press.
Kosslyn, S. M. (2006). You can play 20 questions with nature and win: Categorical versus coordinate spatial relations as a case study. *Neuropsychologia, 44,* 1519–1523.
Kosslyn, S. M. (2010). Where is the spatial hemisphere? In P. A. Reuter-Lorenz, K. Baynes, G. R. Mangun, & E. A. Phelps (Eds.), *The cognitive neuroscience of mind: A tribute to Michael S. Gazzaniga.* Cambridge, MA: MIT Press. (pp. 39–58).
Kosslyn, S. M., & Koenig, O. (1995). *Wet mind: The new cognitive neuroscience.* New York: Free Press.
Krummenacher, J., Müller, H. J., & Heller, D. (2002). Visual search for dimensionally redundant pop-out targets: Parallel-coactive processing of dimensions is location specific. *Journal of Experimental Psychology: Human Perception and Performance, 28,* 1303–1322.
Kuhl, P. K. (1989). On babies, birds, modules, and mechanisms: A comparative approach to the acquisition of vocal communication. In R. J. Dooling & S. H. Husle (Eds.), *The comparative psychology of audition: Perceiving complex sounds* (pp. 379–419). Hillsdale, NJ: Erlbaum.
Laeng, B., Chabris, C. F., & Kosslyn, S. M. (2003). Asymmetries in encoding spatial relations. In K. Hugdahl & R. J. Davidson (Eds.), *The asymmetrical brain* (pp. 303–339). Cambridge, MA: MIT Press.
Land, E. H. (1959). Experiments in color vision. *Scientific American, 200,* 84–99.
Land, E. H. (1977). The retinex theory of color vision. *Scientific American, 237,* 108–128.
Land, E. H. (1983). Recent advances in retinex theory and some implications for cortical computations: Color vision and the natural image. *Proceedings of the National Academy of Sciences of the United States of America, 80,* 5163–5169.
Lawless, H. T. (1984). Oral chemical irritation: Psychophysical properties. *Chemical Senses, 9,* 143–155.
Lê, S., Cardebat, D., Boulanouar, K., Hénaff, M., Michel, F., Milner, D., et al. (2002). Seeing, since childhood, without ventral stream: A behavioural study. *Brain, 125,* 58–74.
Leibowitz, H. W. (1971). Sensory, learned and cognitive mechanisms of size perception. *Annals of the New York Academy of Sciences, 188,* 47–62.
Levine, D. N. (1982). Visual agnosia in monkey and man. In D. J. Ingle, M. A. Goodale, & R. J. W. Mansfield (Eds.), *Analysis of visual behavior* (pp. 629–670). Cambridge: MIT Press.
Levine, R. L., & Bluni, T. D. (1994). Magnetic field effects on spatial discrimination learning in mice. *Physiology and Behavior, 55,* 465–467.
Liddell, C. (1997). Every picture tells a story—Or does it? Young South African children interpreting pictures. *Journal of Cross-Cultural Psychology, 28,* 266–282.
Lowe, S. M. (1995). Essay. In F. Kahlo, *The diary of Frida Kahlo: An intimate self-portrait* (pp. 25–29). New York: Abradale Press.
Luck, S. J., Vogel, E. K., & Shapiro, K. L. (1996). Word meanings can be accessed but not reported during the attentional blink. *Nature, 383,* 616–618.
Macaluso, E. (2010). Orienting of spatial attention and the interplay between the senses. *Cortex, 46,* 282–297.
MacDonald, J. A., & Balakrishnan, J. D. (2002). Signal detection theory. *Encyclopedia of Cognitive Science.* New York: Nature Publishing.
Mareschal, D., & Johnson, M. H. (2003). The "what" and "where" of object representations in infancy. *Cognition, 88,* 259–276.
Marr, D. (1982). *Vision: A computational investigation into the human representation and processing of visual information.* New York: Freeman.
McCoy, N. L., & Pitino, L. (2002). Pheromonal influences on sociosexual behavior in young women. *Physiology and Behavior, 75,* 367–375.
McLaughlin, S., & Margolskee, R. F. (1994). The sense of taste. *American Scientist, 82,* 538–545.
Melzack, R., & Wall, P. D. (1982). *The challenge of pain.* New York: Basic Books.
Milner, A. D., & Goodale, M. A. (1995). *The visual brain in action.* New York: Oxford University Press.
Monnier, P. (2003). Redundant coding assessed in a visual search task. *Displays, 24,* 49–55.
Moody, D. B., Stebbins, W. C., & May, B. J. (1990). Auditory perception of communication signals by Japanese monkeys. In W. C. Stebbins & M. A. Berkley (Eds.), *Comparative perception: Complex signals* (pp. 311–343). New York: Wiley.
Morris, A. L., & Harris, C. L. (2004). Repetition blindness: Out of sight or out of mind? *Journal of Experimental Psychology: Human Perception and Performance, 30,* 913–922.
Moulton, S. T., & Kosslyn, S. M. (2008). Using neuroimaging to resolve the psi debate. *Journal of Cognitive Neuroscience, 20,* 182–192.
Murphy, C. (1986). Taste and smell in the elderly. In H. L. Meiselman & R. S. Rivlin (Eds.), *Clinical measurement of taste and smell* (pp. 343–371). New York: Macmillan.
Nagata, C., Kabuto, M., Kurisu, Y., & Shimizu, H. (1997). Decreased serum estradiol concentration associated with high dietary intake of soy products in premenopausal Japanese women. *Nutrition and Cancer, 29,* 228–233.
Nakayama, K., He, Z. J., & Shimojo, S. (1995). Visual surface representation: A critical link between lower-level and higher-level vision. In S. M. Kosslyn & D. N. Osherson (Eds.), *Visual cognition: An invitation to cognitive science* (Vol. 2, 2nd ed., pp. 1–70). Cambridge, MA: MIT Press.
Nakayama, K., & Mackeben, M. (1989). Sustained and transient components of focal visual attention. *Vision Research, 29,* 1631–1647.
National Institute for Occupational Safety and Health. (1998). *Criteria for a recommended standard: Occupational noise exposure.* Cincinnati: Author.
Nawrot, M., Nordenstrom, B., & Olson, A. (2004). Disruption of eye movements by ethanol intoxication affects perception of depth from motion parallax. *Psychological Science, 15,* 858–865.
Nayatani, Y. (2001). Some modifications to Hering's opponent-colors theory. *Color Research and Application, 26,* 290–304.
Nayatani, Y. (2003). A modified opponent-colors theory considering chromatic strengths of various hues. *Color Research and Application, 28,* 284–297.
Neitz, J., Neitz, M., & Kainz, P. M. (1996). Visual pigment gene structure and the severity of color vision defects. *Science, 274,* 801–804.
Nemec, P., Altmann, J., Marhold, S., Burda, H., & Oelschläger, H. H. A. (2001). Neuroanatomy of magnetoreception: The superior colliculus involved in magnetic orientation in a mammal. *Science, 294,* 366–368.
Ng, V. W. K., Bullmore, E. T., de Zubicaray, G. I., Cooper, A., Suckling, J., & Williams, S. C. R. (2001). Identifying rate-limiting nodes in large-scale cortical networks for visuospatial processing: An illustration using fMRI. *Journal of Cognitive Neuroscience, 13,* 537–545.
Nodelmann, P. (1988). *Words about pictures.* Athens: University of Georgia Press.
Norton, A. (2008). "Teens turn deaf ear to risks of MP3 players." *Reuters.* March 26. Retrieved January 10, 2010, from http://www.reuters.com/article/idUSLAU68250020080327
O'Doherty, J., Winston, J., Critchley, H., Perrett, D., Burt, D. M., & Dolan, R. J. (2003). Beauty in a smile: The role of medial orbitofrontal cortex in facial attractiveness. *Neuropsychologia, 41,* 147–155.
Olson, C. R. (2001). Object-based vision and attention in primates. *Current Opinion in Neurobiology, 11,* 171–179.
Olson, I. R., & Chun, M. M. (2002). Perceptual constraints on implicit learning of spatial context. *Visual Cognition, 9,* 273–302.
O'Regan, J. K. (1992). Solving the "real" mysteries of visual perception: The world as an outside memory. *Canadian Journal of Psychology, 46,* 461–488.
Osborn, D. R. (1996). Beauty is as beauty does? Makeup and posture effects on physical attractiveness judgments. *Journal of Applied Social Psychology, 26,* 31–51.
Perrett, D. I., Lee, K. J, Penton-Voak, I., Rowland, D., Yoshikawa, S., Burt, D. M., et al. (1998). Effects of sexual dimorphism on facial attractiveness. *Nature, 394,* 884–887.
Petrovic, P., Kalso, E., Petersson, K. M., & Ingvar, M. (2002). Placebo and opioid analgesia—Imaging a shared neuronal network. *Science, 295,* 1737–1740.

Pfaffmann, C. (1978). The vertebrate phylogeny, neural code, and integrative processes of taste. In E. C. Carterette & M. P. Friedman (Eds.), Handbook of perception (pp. 51–123). New York: Academic Press.

Pinel, J. P. J. (1993). Biopsychology (2nd ed.). Boston: Allyn & Bacon.

Pinker, S. (1997). How the mind works. New York: Norton.

Qian, N. (1997). Binocular disparity and the perception of depth. Neuron, 18, 359–368.

Rabin, M. D., & Cain, W. S. (1986). Determinants of measured olfactory sensitivity. Perception and Psychophysics, 39, 281–286.

Rainville, P., Duncan, G. H., Price, D. D., Carrier, B., & Bushnell, M. C. (1997). Pain affect encoded in human anterior cingulate but not somatosensory cortex. Science, 277, 968–971.

Rao, H., Zhou, T., Zhuo, Y., Fan, S., & Chen, L. (2003). Spatiotemporal activation of the two visual pathways in form discrimination and spatial location: A brain mapping study. Human Brain Mapping, 18, 78–89.

Rao, S. C., Rainer, G., & Miller, E. K. (1997). Integration of what and where in the primate prefrontal cortex. Science, 276, 821–834.

Raymond, J. E., Shapiro, K. L., & Arnell, K. M. (1992). Temporary suppression of visual processing in an RSVP task: An attentional blink? Journal of Experimental Psychology: Human Perception and Performance, 18, 849–860.

Reid, R. C. (1999). Vision. In M. J. Zigmond, F. E. Bloom, S. C. Landis, J. L. Roberts, & L. R. Squire (Eds.), Fundamental neuroscience (pp. 821–851). New York: Academic Press.

Reis, V. A., & Zaidel, D. W. (2001). Brain and face: Communicating signals of health in the left and right sides of the face. Brain and Cognition, 46, 240–244.

Rensink, R. A., O'Regan, J. K., & Clark, J. J. (1997). To see or not to see: The need for attention to perceive changes in scenes. Psychological Science, 8, 368–373.

Riddoch, M. J., Humphreys, G. W., Jacobson, S., Pluck, G., Bateman, A., & Edwards, M. (2004). Impaired orientation discrimination and localisation following parietal damage: On the interplay between dorsal and ventral processes in visual perception. Cognitive Neuropsychology, 21, 597–623.

Rivera, S., & Colle, M.-P. (1994). Frida's fiestas: Recipes and reminiscences of life with Frida Kahlo (K. Krabbenhoft, Trans.). New York: Clarkson N. Potter.

Rollman, G. B. (1991). Pain responsiveness. In M. A. Heller & W. Schiff (Eds.), The psychology of touch (pp. 91–114). Hillsdale, NJ: Erlbaum.

Royet, J., & Plailly, J. (2004). Lateralization of olfactory processes. Chemical Senses, 29, 731–745.

Rozin, P. (1982). "Taste-smell confusions" and the duality of the olfactory sense. Perception and Psychophysics, 31, 397–401.

Ruiz, C. J., Wray, K., Delay, E. R., Margolskee, R. F., & Kinnamon, S. C. (2003). Behavioral evidence for a role of α-gustducin in glutamate taste. Chemical Senses, 28, 573–579.

Russell, J. A. (2003). Core affect and the psychological construction of emotion. Psychological Review, 110, 145–172.

Sacks, O. (1995). An anthropologist on Mars: Seven paradoxical tales. New York: Knopf.

Sakai, N., Kobayakawa, T., Gotow, N., Saito, S., & Imada, S. (2001). Enhancement of sweetness ratings of aspartame by a vanilla odor presented either by orthonasal or retronasal routes. Perceptual and Motor Skills, 92, 1002–1008.

Saldana, H. N., & Rosenblum, L. D. (1993). Visual influences on auditory pluck and bow judgments. Perception and Psychophysics, 54, 406–416.

Salmi, J., Rinne, T., Degerman, A., Salonen, O., & Alho, K. (2007). Orienting and maintenance of spatial attention in audition and vision: Multimodal and modality-specific brain activations. Brain Structure and Function, 212, 181–194.

Schul, R., Slotnick, B. M., & Dudai, Y. (1996). Flavor and the frontal cortex. Behavioral Neuroscience, 110, 760–765.

Scott, T. R., & Plata-Salaman, C. R. (1991). Coding of taste quality. In T. V. Getchell, R. L. Doty, L. M. Bartoshuk, & J. B. Snow, Jr. (Eds.), Smell and taste in health and disease (pp. 345–368). New York: Raven.

Seuling, B. (1976). The loudest screen kiss and other little-known facts about the movies. New York: Doubleday.

Sheinberg, D. L., & Logothetis, N. K. (2001). Noticing familiar objects in real world scenes: The role of temporal cortical neurons in natural vision. Journal of Neuroscience, 21, 1340–1350.

Simmons, J. A., & Chen, L. (1989). The acoustic basis for target discrimination by FM echo-locating bats. Journal of the Acoustical Society of America, 86, 1333–1350.

Simons, D. J. (2000). Current approaches to change blindness. Visual Cognition, 7, 1–15.

Simons, D. J., & Ambinder, M. S. (2005). Change blindness. Current Directions in Psychological Science, 14, 44–48.

Slotnick, S. D., Moo, L. R., Tesoro, M. A., & Hart, J. (2001). Hemispheric asymmetry in categorical versus coordinate spatial processing revealed by temporary cortical deactivation. Journal of Cognitive Neuroscience, 13, 1088–1096.

Smith, D. V., & Frank, M. E. (1993). Sensory coding by peripheral taste fibers. In S. A. Simon & S. D. Roper (Eds.), Mechanisms of taste transduction (pp. 295–338). Boca Raton, FL: CRC Press.

Soto-Faraco, S., & Spence, C. (2001). Spatial modulation of repetition blindness and repetition deafness. Quarterly Journal of Experimental Psychology: Human Experimental Psychology, 54, 1181–1202.

Sternbach, R. A. (1978). Psychological dimensions and perceptual analyses, including pathologies of pain. In E. C. Carterette & M. P. Friedman (Eds.), Handbook of perception (pp. 231–261). New York: Academic Press.

Suga, N. (1990). Biosonar and neural computation in bats. Scientific American, 262, 60–68.

Sugita, Y. (2004). Experience in early infancy is indispensable for color perception. Current Biology, 14, 1267–1271.

Tanabe, S., Ichikawa, K., Hukami, K., & Nakashima, S. (2001). A family with protanomaly and deuteranomaly. Color Research and Application, 26, S93–S95.

Thalbourne, M. A. (1989). Psychics and ESP: A reply to Grimmer and White. Australian Psychologist, 24, 307–310.

Thesen, T., Vibell, J. F., Calvert, G. A., & Österbauer, R. A. (2004). Neuroimaging of multisensory processing in vision, audition, touch, and olfaction. Cognitive Processing, 5, 84–93.

Thompson, P., & Burr, D. (2009). Visual aftereffects. Current Biology, 19, R11–14.

Tian, L.F. (2010). A survey on acupuncture treatment of trigeminal neuralgia. Journal of Traditional Chinese Medicine, 30, 68–76.

Tootell, R. B. H., Mendola, J. D., Hadjikhani, N. K., Ledden, P. J., Liu, A. K., Reppas, J. B., et al. (1997). Functional analysis of V3A and related areas in human visual cortex. Journal of Neuroscience, 17, 7060–7078.

Tootell, R. B., Silverman, M. S., Switkes, E., & de Valois, R. L. (1982). Deoxyglucose analysis of retinotopic organization in primate striate cortex. Science, 218, 902–904.

Treisman, A. M. (1964a). Monitoring and storage of irrelevant messages in selective attention. Journal of Verbal Learning and Verbal Behavior, 3, 449–459.

Treisman, A. M. (1964b). Selective attention in man. British Medical Bulletin, 20, 12–16.

Treue, S. (2003). Climbing the cortical ladder from sensation to perception. Trends in Cognitive Sciences, 7, 469–471.

Tsao, D. Y., Freiwald, W. A., Knutsen, T. A., Mandeville, J. B., & Tootell, R. B. H. (2003). Faces and objects in macaque cerebral cortex. Nature Neuroscience, 6, 989–995.

Ullman, S. (1996). High-level vision. Cambridge: MIT Press.

Ungerleider, L. G., & Haxby, J. V. (1994). "What" and "where" in the human brain. Current Opinion in Neurology, 4, 157–165.

Ungerleider, L. G., & Mishkin, M. (1982). Two cortical visual systems. In D. J. Ingle, M. A. Goodale, & R. J. W. Mansfield (Eds.), Analysis of visual behavior (pp. 549–586). Cambridge, MA: MIT Press.

van Zoest, W., & Donk, M. (2004). Bottom-up and top-down control in visual search. Perception, 33, 927–937.

Vuilleumier, P., & Sagiv, N. (2001). Two eyes make a pair: Facial organization and perceptual learning reduce visual extinction. Neuropsychologia, 39, 1144–1149.

Wall, P. (2000). Pain: The science of suffering. New York: Columbia University Press.

Warren, R. M., & Warren, R. P. (1970). Auditory illusions and confusions. Scientific American, 223, 30–36.

Wässle, H. (2004). Parallel processing in the mammalian retina. Nature Reviews Neuroscience, 5, 747–757.

Watt, C. A., & Morris, R. L. (1995). The relationship among performance on a prototype indicator of perceptual defence/vigilance, personality, and extrasensory perception. Personality and Individual Differences, 19, 635–648.

Weinstein, S. (1968). Intensive and extensive aspects of tactile sensitivity as a function of body part, sex, and laterality. In D. R. Kenshalo (Ed.), The skin senses (pp. 195–218). Springfield, IL: Thomas.

Weiskrantz, L. (1986). Blindsight: A case study and implications. New York: Oxford University Press.

Wertheimer, M. (1923). Untersuchungen zur Lehre von der Gestalt, II (Laws of organization in perceptual forms, II). In W. D. Ellis (Ed.), A source book of Gestalt psychology (pp. 71–88). London: Routledge & Kegan Paul.

Wetsman, A., & Marlowe, F. (1999). How universal are preferences for female waist-to-hip ratios? Evidence from the Hadza of Tanzania. Evolution and Human Behavior, 20, 219–228.

Willer, J. C., Le, B. D., & De, B. T. (1990). Diffuse noxious inhibitory controls in man: Involvement of an opioidergic link. European Journal of Pharmacology, 182, 347–355.

Winer, G. A., & Cottrell, J. E. (1996). Does anything leave the eye when we see? Extramission beliefs of children and adults. Current Directions in Psychological Science, 5, 137–142.

Winer, G. A., Cottrell, J. E., Gregg, V., Fournier, J. S., & Bica, L. A. (2002). Fundamentally misunderstanding visual perception: Adults' belief in visual emissions. American Psychologist, 57, 417–424.

Winer, G. A., Cottrell, J. E., Gregg, V., Fournier, J. S., & Bica, L. A. (2003). Do adults believe in visual emissions? American Psychologist, 58, 495–496.

Winer, G. A., Cottrell, J. E., Karefilaki, K. D., & Gregg, V. R. (1996). Images, words and questions: Variables that influence beliefs about vision in children and adults. Journal of Experimental Child Psychology, 63, 499–525.

Yeshurun, Y., & Carrasco, M. (1998). Attention improves or impairs visual performance by enhancing spatial resolution. Nature, 396, 72–75.

Yeshurun, Y., & Carrasco, M. (1999). Spatial attention improves performance in spatial resolution tasks. Vision Research, 39, 293–306.

Yost, W. A. (2009). Pitch perception. Attention, Perception, and Psychophysics, 71, 1701–1715.

Yost, W. A., & Dye, R. H. (1991). Properties of sound localization by humans. In R. A. Altschuler, R. P. Bobbin, B. M. Clopton, & D. W. Hoffman (Eds.), Neurobiology of hearing: The central auditory system (pp. 389–410). New York: Raven.

Yu, D. W., & Shepard, G. H. (1998). Is beauty in the eye of the beholder? Nature, 396, 321–322.

Zeki, S. M. (1978). Functional specialisation in the visual cortex of the rhesus monkey. Nature, 274, 423–428.

Zeki, S. M. (1993). Vision of the brain. London: Blackwell.

Zihl, J., von Cramon, D., & Mai, N. (1983). Selective disturbance of movement vision after bilateral brain damage. Brain, 106, 313–340.

References: Learning

Ader, R. (1976). Conditioned adrenocortical steroid elevations in the rat. *Journal of Comparative and Physiological Psychology, 90,* 1156–1163.

Ader, R., & Cohen, N. (1975). Behaviorally conditioned immunosuppression. *Psychosomatic Medicine, 37,* 333–340.

Albert, M., & Ayres, J. J. B. (1997). One-trial simultaneous and backward excitatory fear conditioning in rats: Lick suppression, freezing, and rearing to CS compounds and their elements. *Animal Learning and Behavior, 25,* 210–220.

Baccus, J. R., Baldwin, M. W., & Packer, D. J. (2004). Increasing implicit self-esteem through classical conditioning. *Psychological Science, 15,* 498–502.

Bandura, A. (1977). *Social learning theory.* Englewood Cliffs, NJ: Prentice Hall.

Bandura, A. (1986). *Social foundations of thought and action: A social-cognitive theory.* Englewood Cliffs, NJ: Prentice Hall.

Bandura, A., Ross, D., & Ross, S. A. (1961). Transmission of aggression through imitation of aggressive models. *Journal of Abnormal and Social Psychology, 63,* 575–582.

Bandura, A., Ross, D., & Ross, S. A. (1963). Imitation of film-mediated aggressive models. *Journal of Abnormal and Social Psychology, 66,* 3–11.

Barnet, R. C., Arnold, H. M., & Miller, R. R. (1991). Simultaneous conditioning demonstrated in second-order conditioning: Evidence for similar associative structure in forward and simultaneous conditioning. *Learning and Motivation, 22,* 253–268.

Baruch, D. E., Swain, R. A., & Helmstetter, F. J. (2004). Effects of exercise on Pavlovian fear conditioning. *Behavioral Neuroscience, 118,* 1123–1127.

Berlin, L. J., Ispa, J. M., Fine, M. A., Malone, P. S., Brooks-Gunn, J., Brady-Smith, C., et al. (2009). Correlates and consequences of spanking and verbal punishment for low-income white, African American, and Mexican American toddlers. *Child Development, 80,* 1403.

Bouton, M. (1993). Context, time and memory retrieval in the interference paradigms of Pavlovian conditioning. *Psychological Bulletin, 114,* 80–99.

Bouton, M. (1994). Context, ambiguity and classical conditioning. *Current Directions in Psychological Science, 3,* 49–52.

Bouton, M. E. (2000). A learning theory perspective on lapse, relapse, and the maintenance of behavior change. *Health Psychology, 19,* 57–63.

Bouton, M. E. (2002). Context, ambiguity, and unlearning: Sources of relapse after behavioral extinction. *Biological Psychiatry, 52,* 976–979.

Bregman, E. O. (1934). An attempt to modify the emotional attitudes of infants by the conditioned response technique. *Journal of Genetic Psychology, 45,* 169.

Brewer, K. R., & Wann, D. L. (1998). Observational learning effectiveness as a function of model characteristics: Investigating the importance of social power. *Social Behavior and Personality, 26,* 1–10.

Brown, P. L., & Jenkins, H. M. (1968). Auto-shaping of the pigeon's key peck. *Journal of the Experimental Analysis of Behavior, 68,* 503–507.

Bunce, S. C., Bernat, E., Wong, P. S., & Shevrin, H. (1999). Further evidence for unconscious learning: Preliminary support for the conditioning of facial EMG to subliminal stimuli. *Journal of Psychiatric Research, 33,* 341–347.

Burish, T. G., & Carey, M. P. (1986). Conditioned aversive responses in cancer chemotherapy patients: Theoretical and developmental analysis. *Journal of Counseling and Clinical Psychology, 54,* 593–600.

Cardinal, R. N., Parkinson, J. A., Hall, J., & Everitt, B. (2002). Emotion and motivation: The role of the amygdala, ventral striatum, and prefrontal cortex. *Neuroscience and Biobehavioral Reviews, 26,* 321–352.

Carey, M. P., & Burish, T. G. (1988). Etiology and treatment of the psychological side effects associated with cancer chemotherapy: A critical review and discussion. *Psychological Bulletin, 104,* 307–325.

Chan, J., & Yang, J. (1999). *I am Jackie Chan.* New York: Ballantine Books.

Chang, R. C., Blaisdell, A. P., & Miller, R. R. (2003). Backward conditioning: Mediation by the context. *Journal of Experimental Psychology: Animal Behavior Processes, 29,* 171–183.

Christian, K. M., & Thompson, R. F. (2003). Neural substrates of eyeblink conditioning: Acquisition and retention. *Learning and Memory, 10,* 427–455.

Conger, R. D., Neppl, T., Kim, K. J., & Scaramella, L. (2003). Angry and aggressive behavior across three generations: A prospective, longitudinal study of parents and children. *Journal of Abnormal Child Psychology, 31,* 143–160.

Conyers, C., Miltenberger, R., Romaniuk, C., Kopp, B., & Himle, M. (2003). Evaluation of DRO schedules to reduce disruptive behavior in a preschool classroom. *Child and Family Behavior Therapy, 25,* 1–6.

Dadds, M. R., Bovberg, D. H., Redd, W. H., & Cutmore, T. R. H. (1997). Imagery in human classical conditioning. *Psychological Bulletin, 122,* 89–103.

Davey, G. C. L. (1992). Classical conditioning and the acquisition of human fears and phobias: A review of synthesis of the literature. *Advances in Behavior Research and Therapy, 14,* 29–66.

De Houwer, J., Thomas, S., & Baeyens, F. (2001). Associative learning of likes and dislikes: A review of 25 years of research on human evaluative conditioning. *Psychological Bulletin, 127,* 853–869.

Dienstfrey, H. (1991). *Where the mind meets the body.* New York: HarperCollins.

Dixon, M. R., Rehfeldt, R. A., & Randich, L. (2003). Enhancing tolerance to delayed reinforcers: The role of intervening activities. *Journal of Applied Behavior Analysis, 36,* 263–266.

Domjan, M., Cusato, B., & Krause, M. (2004). Learning with arbitrary versus ecologically conditioned stimuli: Evidence from sexual conditioning. *Psychonomic Bulletin and Review, 11,* 232–246.

Fiorillo, C. D. (2004). The uncertain nature of dopamine. *Molecular Psychiatry, 9,* 122–123.

Garcia, J., Ervin, F. R., & Koelling, R. A. (1966). Learning with prolonged delay of reinforcement. *Psychonomic Science, 5,* 121–122.

Garcia, J., & Koelling, R. (1966). Relation of cue to consequence in avoidance learning. *Psychonomic Science, 4,* 123–124.

Guthrie, G. M., Guthrie, H. A., Fernandez, T. L., & Esterea, N. O. (1982). Cultural influences and reinforcement stratifies. *Behavior Therapy, 13,* 624–637.

Haapasalo, J., & Pokela, E. (1999). Child-rearing and child abuse antecedents of criminality. *Aggression and Violent Behavior, 4,* 107–127.

Hall, J. F. (1984). Backward conditioning in Pavlovian type studies: Reevaluation and present status. *Pavlovian Journal of Biological Science, 19,* 163–168.

Hamilton, M. E., Voris, J. C., Sebastian, P. S., Singha, A. K., Krejci, L. P., Elder, I. R., et al. (1998). Money as a tool to extinguish conditioned responses to cocaine in addicts. *Journal of Clinical Psychology, 54,* 211–218.

Hanewinkel, R. (2009). Cigarette smoking and perception of a movie character in a film trailer. *Archives of Pediatric and Adolescent Medicine, 163,* 15–18.

Hermann, J. A., deMontes, A. I., Dominguez, B., Montes, F., & Hopkins, B. L. (1973). Effects of bonuses for punctuality on the tardiness of industrial workers. *Journal of Applied Behavior Analysis, 4,* 267–272.

Higgens, S. T., & Morris, E. K. (1984). Generality of free-operant avoidance conditioning to human behavior. *Psychological Bulletin, 96,* 247–272.

Hohlstein, L. A., Smith, G. T., & Atlas, J. G. (1998). An application of expectancy theory to eating disorders: Development and validation of measures of eating and dieting expectancies. *Psychological Assessment, 10,* 49–58.

Hollerman, J. R., & Schultz, W. (1998). Dopamine neurons report an error in the temporal prediction of reward during learning. *Nature Neuroscience, 1,* 304–309.

Hollis, K. L. (1997). Contemporary research on Pavlovian conditioning: A "new" functional analysis. *American Psychologist, 52,* 956–965.

Itkowitz, N. I., Kerns, R. D., & Otis, J. D. (2003). Support and coronary heart disease: The importance of significant other responses. *Journal of Behavioral Medicine, 26,* 19–30.

Jason, L. A., & Fries, M. (2004). Helping parents reduce children's television viewing. *Research on Social Work Practice, 14,* 121–131.

Kamin, L. (1969). Predictability, surprise, attention and conditioning. In B. A. Campbell & R. M. Church (Eds.), *Punishment and aversive behavior.* (pp. 279–296). New York: Appleton-Century-Crofts.

Kim, J., Lim, J., & Bhargava, M. (1998). The role of affect in attitude formation: A classical conditioning. *Journal of the Academy of Marketing Science, 26,* 143–152.

Kimble, G. A. (1981). Biological and cognitive constraints of learning. In L. T. Benjamin Jr. (Ed.), *The G. Stanley Hall Lecture Series* (Vol. 1). (pp. 11–60). Washington, DC: American Psychological Association.

Kirsch, I. (2004). Conditioning, expectancy, and the placebo effect: Comment on Stewart-Williams and Podd (2004). *Psychological Bulletin, 130,* 341–343.

Kirsch, I., Lynn, S. J., Vigorito, M., & Miller, R. R. (2004). The role of cognition in classical and operant conditioning. *Journal of Clinical Psychology, 60,* 369–392.

Kosslyn, S. M., Thompson, W. L., & Ganis, G. (2006). *The case for mental imagery.* New York: Oxford University Press.

Kung, J., Su, N., Fan, R., Chai, S., & Shyu, B. (2003). Contribution of the anterior cingulate cortex to laser-pain conditioning in rats. *Brain Research, 970,* 58–72.

Kuntze, M. F., Stoermer, R., Mager, R., Roessler, A., Mueller-Spahn, F., & Bullinger, A. H. (2001). Immersive virtual environments in cue exposure. *CyberPsychology and Behavior, 4,* 497–501.

Kvale, G., & Hugdahl, K. (1994). Cardiovascular conditioning and anticipatory nausea and vomiting in cancer patients. *Behavioral Medicine, 20,* 78–83.

Kwong, M. J., Bartholomew, K., Henderson, A. J. Z., & Trinke, S. J. (2003). The intergenerational transmission of relationship violence. *Journal of Family Psychology, 17,* 288–301.

Lalumiere, M. L., & Quinsey, L. (1998). Pavlovian conditioning of sexual interests in human males. *Archives of Sexual Behavior, 27,* 241–252.

Lazev, A. B., Herzog, T. A., & Brandon, T. H. (1999). Classical conditioning of environmental cues to cigarette smoking. *Experimental and Clinical Psychopharmacology, 7,* 56–63.

LeDoux, J. E. (1996). *The emotional brain: The mysterious underpinnings of emotional life.* New York: Simon & Schuster.

Lowe, C. F. (1979). Determinants of human operant behaviour. In M. D. Zeiler & P. Harzem (Eds.), *Advances in analysis of behavior: Vol. 1. Reinforcement and the organization of behavior.* New York: Wiley.

Marks, I. M. (1969). *Fears and phobias.* New York: Academic Press.

Matthews, B. A., Shimoff, E., Catania, A. C., & Sagvolden, T. (1977). Uninstructed human responding: Sensitivity to ratio and interval contingencies. *Journal of the Experimental Analysis of Behavior, 27,* 453–467.

Merlo, A., & Schotter, A. (2003). Learning by not doing: An experimental investigation of observational learning. *Games and Economic Behavior, 42,* 116–136.

Mischel, W., Shoda, Y., & Rodriguez, M. L. (1989). Delay of gratification in children. *Science, 244,* 933–938.

Montague, P. R., Hyman, S. E., & Cohen, J. D. (2004). Computational roles for dopamine in behavioural control. *Nature, 431,* 760–767.

Montgomery, G. H., & Bovbjerg, D. H. (1997). The development of anticipatory nausea in patients receiving adjuvant chemotherapy for breast cancer. *Physiology & Behavior, 61,* 737–741.

Nadler, J., Thompson, L., & van Boven, L. (2003). Learning negotiation skills: Four models of knowledge creation and transfer. *Management Science, 49,* 529–540.

Núñez, J. P., & de Vincente, F. (2004). Unconscious learning. Conditioning to subliminal visual stimuli. *Spanish Journal of Psychology, 7,* 13–28.

O'Brien, C. P., Childress, A. R., McLellan, A. T., Ehrman, R., & Ternes, J. W. (1988). Types of conditioning found in drug-dependent humans. (NIDA Research Monograph 84). Washington, DC: U.S. Department of Health and Human Services, National Institute on Drug Abuse.

Öhman, A., Fredrikson, M., Hugdahl, K., & Rimmo, P.-A. (1976). The premise of equipotentiality in human classical conditioning: Conditioned electrodermal responses to potentially phobic stimuli. *Journal of Experimental Psychology: General, 105,* 313–337.

Pavlov, I. P. (1927). *Conditioned reflexes* (G. V. Anrep, Trans.). London: Oxford University Press.

Piaget, J. (1962). *Play, dreams, and imitation in childhood.* New York: Norton.

Pine, D. S., Cohen, P., & Brook, J. (2001). Adolescent fears as predictors of depression. *Biological Psychiatry, 50,* 721–724.

Proctor, R. W., & Van Zandt, T. (1994). *Human factors in simple and complex systems.* Boston: Allyn & Bacon.

Raj, J. D., Nelson, J. A., & Rao, K. S. P. (2006). A study on the effects of some reinforcers to improve performance of employees in a retail industry. *Behavior Modification, 30,* 848–866.

Razran, G. H. S. (1940). Conditioned response changes in rating and appraising sociopolitical solutions. *Psychological Bulletin, 37,* 481.

Redd, W. H., Dadds, M. R., Futterman, A. D., Taylor, K. L., & Bovbjerg, D. J. (1993). Nausea induced by mental images of chemotherapy. *Cancer, 72,* 629–636.

Rescorla, R. A. (1967). Pavlovian conditioning and its proper control procedures. *Psychological Review, 74,* 71–80.

Rice, M. E., & Grusec, J. E. (1975). Saying and doing: Effects on observer performance. *Journal of Personality and Social Psychology, 32,* 584–593.

Robbins, T. W., & Everitt, B. J. (1998). Motivation and reward. In M. J. Zigmond, F. E. Bloom, S. C. Landis, J. L. Roberts, & L. R. Squire (Eds.), *Fundamental neuroscience* (pp. 1245–1260). New York: Academic Press.

Rushton, J. P. (1975). Generosity in children: Immediate and long-term effects of modeling, preaching, and moral judgement. *Journal of Personality and Social Psychology, 31,* 459–466.

Rynes, S. L., Gerhart, B., & Parks, L. (2005). Personnel psychology: Performance evaluation and pay-for-performance. *Annual Review of Psychology, 56,* 561–600.

Samoluk, S. B., & Stewart, S. H. (1998). Anxiety sensitivity and situation-specific drinking. *Journal of Anxiety Disorders, 12,* 407–419.

Sargent, J. D., Beach, M. L., Dalton, M. A., Mott, L. A., Tickle, J. J., Ahrens, M. B., et al. (2001). Effect of seeing tobacco use in films on trying smoking among adolescents: Cross sectional study. *British Medical Journal, 323,* 1394–1397.

Sargent, J. D., & Hanewinkel, R. (2009). Comparing the effects of entertainment media and tobacco marketing on youth smoking in Germany. *Addiction, 104,* 815–823.

Seligman, M. E. P. (1971). Phobias and preparedness. *Behavior Therapy, 2,* 307–320.

Seuling, B. (1978). *The last cow on the White House lawn and other little-known facts about the presidency.* New York: Doubleday.

Siegel, J. L., & Longo, D. L. (1981). The control of chemotherapy induced emesis. *Annals of Internal Medicine, 95,* 352–359.

Siegel, S. (1988). State dependent learning and morphine tolerance. *Behavioral Neuroscience, 102,* 228–232.

Siegel, S., Baptista, M. A. S., Kim, J. A., McDonald, R. V., & Weise-Kelly, L. (2000). Pavlovian psychopharmacology: The associative basis of tolerance. *Experimental and Clinical Psychopharmacology, 8,* 276–293.

Siegel, S., & Ramos, B. M. C. (2002). Applying laboratory research: Drug anticipation and the treatment of drug addiction. *Experimental and Clinical Psychopharmacology, 10,* 162–183.

Skinner, B. F. (1953). *Science and human behavior.* New York: Macmillan.

Skinner, B. F. (1956). A case history in scientific method. *American Psychologist, 11,* 221–233.

Staddon, J. E. R., & Cerruti, D. T. (2003). Operant conditioning. *Annual Review of Psychology, 54,* 115–144.

Steinberg, L. (2000). Punishment: Developmental perspectives. In A. E. Kazdin (Ed.), *Encyclopedia of psychology* (Vol. 6, pp. 484–487). Washington, DC: American Psychological Association; Oxford University Press.

Stewart-Williams, S., & Podd, J. (2004). The placebo effect: Dissolving the expectancy versus conditioning debate. *Psychological Bulletin, 130,* 324–340.

Straus, M. A., & Gelles, R. J. (1980). *Behind closed doors: Violence in the American family.* New York: Anchor/Doubleday.

Straus, M. A., & McCord, J. (1998). Do physically punished children become violent adults? In S. Nolen-Hoeksema (Ed.), *Clashing views on abnormal psychology: A Taking Sides custom reader* (pp. 130–155). Guilford, CT: Dushkin/McGraw-Hill.

Straus, M. A., Sugarman, D. B., & Giles-Sims, J. (1997). Spanking by parents and subsequent antisocial behavior of children. *Archives of Pediatrics and Adolescent Medicine, 151,* 761–767.

Taylor, C (2010). Mothers' spanking of 3-year-old children and subsequent risk of children's aggressive behavior. *Pediatrics,* doi:10.1542/peds.2009–2678.

Thorn, B. L., & Gilbert, L. A. (1998). Antecedents of work and family role expectations of college men. *Journal of Family Psychology, 12,* 259–267.

Thorndike, E. L. (1927). The law of effect. *American Journal of Psychology, 39,* 212–222.

Thorndike, E. L. (1949). The law of effect. In *Selected writings from a connectionist's psychology* (pp. 13–26). New York: Appleton-Century-Crofts. (Original work published 1933)

Till, B. D., & Priluck, R. L. (2000). Stimulus generalization in classical conditioning: An initial investigation and extension. *Psychology and Marketing, 17,* 55–72.

Till, B. D., Stanley, S. M., & Priluck, R. (2008). Classical conditioning and celebrity endorsers: An examination of belongingness and resistance to extinction. *Psychology and Marketing, 25,* 179–196.

Tolman, E. C., & Honzik, C. H. (1930a). Degrees of hunger, reward and non-reward, and maze learning in rats. *University of California Publications in Psychology, 4,* 241–256.

Tolman, E. C., & Honzik, C. H. (1930b). Introduction and removal of reward, and maze performance in rats. *University of California Publications in Psychology, 4,* 257–275.

Vasterling, J., Jenkins, R. A., Tope, D. M., & Burish, T. G. (1993). Cognitive distraction and relaxation training for the control of side effects due to cancer chemotherapy. *Journal of Behavioral Medicine, 16,* 65–80.

Viney, W. (1993). *A history of psychology: Ideas and context.* Needham Heights, MA: Allyn & Bacon.

Voudouris, N. J., Peck, C. L., & Coleman, G. (1985). Conditioned placebo responses. *Journal of Personality and Social Psychology, 48,* 47–53.

Waber, R. L., Shiv, B., Carmon, Z., & Ariely, D. (2008). Research letter: Commercial features of placebo and therapeutic efficacy. *Journal of the American Medical Association, 299,* n.p.

Waelti, P., Dickinson, A., & Schultz, W. (2001). Dopamine responses comply with basic assumptions of formal learning theory. *Nature, 412,* 43–48.

Watson, J., & Rayner, R. (1920). Conditioned emotional reactions. *Journal of Experimental Psychology, 3,* 1–14.

Weiss, T., & Engel, B. T. (1995). Operant conditioning of heart rate in patients with premature ventricular contractions. In A. M. Eward, J. E. Dimsdale, B. T. Engel, T. Bernard, D. R. Lipsitt, D. Oken, et al. (Eds.), *American Psychosomatic Society, Toward an integrated medicine: Classics from "Psychosomatic Medicine," 1959–1979* (pp. 191–219). Washington, DC: American Psychiatric Association.

References: Memory

Abel, T., Martin, K. C., Bartsch, D., & Kandel, E. R. (1998). Memory suppressor genes: Inhibitory constraints on the storage of long-term memory. *Science, 279,* 338–341.

Adams, J. (1967). *Human memory.* New York: McGraw-Hill.

Addis, D. R., & Tippett, L. J. (2004). Memory of myself: Autobiographical memory and identity in Alzheimer's disease. *Memory, 12,* 56–74.

Alberini, C. (2004). Mechanisms of memory destabilization: Are consolidation and reconsolidation similar or distinct processes? *Trends in Neuroscience, 28,* 51–56.

Albert, M. S., Duffy, F. H., & McAnulty, G. B. (1990). Electrophysiologic comparisons between two groups of patients with Alzheimer's disease. *Archives of Neurology, 47,* 857–863.

Anderson, M. C., Ochsner, K. N., Kuhl, B., Cooper, J., Robertson, E., Gabrieli, S. W., et al. (2004). Neural systems underlying the suppression of unwanted memories. *Science, 303,* 232–235.

Atkinson, R. C., & Shiffrin, R. M. (1968). Human memory: A proposed system and its control processes. In K. W. Spence & J. T. Spence (Eds.), *The psychology of learning and motivation: Advances in research and theory* (Vol. 2, pp. 89–195). New York: Academic Press.

Atkinson, R. C., & Shiffrin, R. M. (1971). The control of short-term memory. *Scientific American, 225,* 82–90.

Baddeley, A. (1986). *Working memory.* Oxford: Clarendon Press.

Baddeley, A. (1992). Working memory: The interface between memory and cognition. *Journal of Cognitive Neuroscience, 4,* 281–288.

Baddeley, A. (1994). The magical number seven: Still magic after all these years? *Psychological Review, 101,* 353–356.

Baily, C. H., & Chen, M. (1989). Time course of structural changes at identified sensory neuron synapses during long-term sensitization in Aplysia. *Journal of Neuroscience, 9,* 1774–1781.

Barber, J. (1997). Hypnosis and memory: A cautionary chapter. In G. A. Fraser (Ed.), *The dilemma of ritual abuse: Cautions and guides for therapists* (pp. 17–29). Washington, DC: American Psychiatric Press.

Barclay, J. R., Bransford, J. D., Franks, J. J., McCarrell, N. S., & Nitsch, K. (1974). Comprehension and semantic flexibility. *Journal of Verbal Learning and Verbal Behavior, 13,* 471–481.

Baxendale, S. (2004). Memories aren't made of this: Amnesia at the movies. *British Medical Journal, 329,* 1480–1483.

Bayley, P. J., Hopkins, R. O., & Squire, L. R. (2003). Successful recollection of remote autobiographical memories by amnesic patients with medial temporal lobe lesions. *Neuron, 38,* 135–144.

Biedenkapp, J. C., & Rudy, J. W. (2004). Context memories and reactivation: Constraints on the reconsolidation hypothesis. *Behavioral Neuroscience, 118,* 956–964.

Bishop, N. A., Lu, T., & Yankner, B. A. (2010). Neural mechanisms of ageing and cognitive decline. *Nature, 464,* 529–535.

Bjork, E. L., & Bjork, R. A. (2003). Intentional forgetting can decrease residual influences of to-be-forgotten information. *Journal of Experimental Psychology: Learning, Memory, and Cognition, 29,* 524–531.

Bjork, R. A. (1972). Theoretical implications of directed forgetting. In A. W. Melton & E. Martin (Eds.), *Coding processes in human memory* (pp. 217–235). Washington, DC: Winston.

Bower, G. H. (1972). Mental imagery and associative learning. In L. Gregg (Ed.), *Cognition and learning and memory* (pp. 51–88). New York: Wiley.

Bower, G. H. (1981). Mood and memory. *American Psychologist, 36,* 129–148.

Bower, G. H. (1992). How might emotions effect learning? In S.-Å. Christianson (Ed.), *The handbook of emotion and memory: Research and theory* (pp. 3–31). Hillsdale, NJ: Erlbaum.

Bower, G. H., Clark, M. C., Lesgold, A. M., & Winzenz, D. (1969). Hierarchical retrieval schemes in recall of categorized word lists. *Journal of Verbal Learning and Verbal Behavior, 8,* 323–343.

Bradley, M. M., Greenwald, M. K., Petry, M. C., & Lang, P. J. (1992). Remembering pictures: Pleasure and arousal in memory. *Journal of Experimental Psychology: Learning, Memory, and Cognition, 18,* 379–390.

Bradshaw, G. L., & Anderson, J. R. (1982). Elaborative encoding as an explanation of levels of processing. *Journal of Verbal Learning and Verbal Behavior, 21,* 165–174.

Braun, K. A., Ellis, R., & Loftus, E. F. (2002). Make my memory: How advertising can change our memories of the past. *Psychology and Marketing, 19,* 1–23.

Bremner, J. D., Stienberg, M., Southwick, S. M., Johnson, D. R., & Charney, D. S. (1993). Use of the structured clinical interview for DSM-IV dissociative disorders for systemic assessment of dissociative symptoms in post-traumatic stress disorder. *American Journal of Psychiatry, 150,* 1011–1014.

Bremner, J. D., Vythilingam, M., Vermetten, E., Southwick, S. M., McGlashan, T., Nazeer, A., et al. (2003). MRI and PET study of deficits in hippocampal structure and function in women with childhood sexual abuse and posttraumatic stress disorder. *American Journal of Psychiatry, 160,* 924–932.

Brewer, J. B., Zhao, Z., Desmod, J. E., Glover, G. H., & Gabrielli, J. D. E. (1998). Making memories: Brain activity that predicts how well visual experience will be remembered. *Science, 281,* 1185–1187.

Broadbent, D. E. (1971). The magic number seven after fifteen years. In A. Kennedy & A. Wilkes (Eds.), *Studies in long-term memory* (pp. 2–18). New York: Wiley.

Brown, R., & Kulik, J. (1977). Flashbulb memories. - *Cognition, 5,* 73–99.

Bryant, R. A., & Barnier, A. J. (1999). Eliciting autobiographical pseudomemories: The relevance of hypnosis, hypnotizability, and attributions. *International Journal of Clinical ad Experimental Hypnosis, 47,* 267–283.

Buckner, R. L., Kelley, W. M., & Petersen, S. E. (1999). Frontal cortex contributes to human memory formation. *Nature Neuroscience, 2,* 311–314.

Cabeza, R., Prince, S. E., Daselaar, S. M., Greenberg, D. L., Budde, M., Dolcos, F., et al. (2004). Brain activity during episodic retrieval of autobiographical and laboratory events: An fMRI study using a novel photo paradigm. *Journal of Cognitive Neuroscience, 16,* 1583–1594.

Cahill, L., Haier, R. J., Fallon, J., Alkire, M. T., Tang, C., Keator, D., et al. (1996). Amygdala activity at encoding correlated with long-term free recall of emotional information. *Proceedings of the National Academy of Sciences of the United States of America, 93,* 8016–8021.

Cahill, L., Prins, B., Weber, M., & McGaugh, J. L. (1994). Adrenergic activation and memory for emotional events. *Nature, 371,* 702–704.

Canli, T., Zhao, Z., Desmond, J. E., Kang, E., Gross, J., & Gabrieli, J. D. E. (2001). An fMRI study of personality influences on brain reactivity to emotional stimuli. *Behavioral Neuroscience, 115,* 33–42.

Cave, C. B. (1997). Very long-lasting priming in picture naming. *American Psychological Society, 8,* 322–325.

Cherry, E. C. (1953). Some experiments on the recognition of speech with one and two ears. *Journal of the Acoustical Society of America, 25,* 975–979.

Cohen, J. D., Peristein, W. M., Braver, T. S., Nystrom, L. E., Noll, D. C., Jonides, J., et al. (1997). Temporal dynamics of brain activation during a working memory task. *Nature, 386,* 604–608.

Conway, M. A., & Rubin, D. C. (1993). The structure of autobiographical memory. In A. F. Collins, S. E. Gathercole, M. A. Conway, & P. E. Morris (Eds.), *Theories of memory* (pp. 103–137). Hillsdale, NJ: Erlbaum.

Corkin, S. (2002). What's new with the amnestic patient H. M.? *Nature Reviews Neuroscience, 3,* 153–160.

Cowan, N. (2001). The magical number 4 in short-term memory: A reconsideration of mental storage capacity. *Behavioral and Brain Sciences, 24,* 87–114.

Craik, F. I. M., & Lockhart, R. S. (1972). Levels of processing: A framework for memory research. *Journal of Verbal Learning and Verbal Behavior, 11,* 671–684.

Craik, F. I. M., & Tulving, E. (1975). Depth of processing and the retention of words in episodic memory. *Journal of Experimental Psychology: General, 104,* 268–294.

Curtius, M. (1996, July 3). Man won't be retried in repressed memory case murder: Prosecutor says there is not enough evidence to re-convict him of crime daughter recalled years later. *Los Angeles Times,* p. 1.

Deese, J. (1959). On the prediction of occurrence of particular verbal intrusions in immediate recall. *Journal of Experimental Psychology, 58,* 17–22.

De Renzi, E., Liotti, M., & Nichelli, P. (1987). Semantic amnesia with preservation of autobiographic memory. A case report. *Cortex, 23,* 575–597.

D'Esposito, M., Detre, J. A., Alsop, D. C., Shin, R. K., Atlas, S., & Grossman, M. (1995). The neural basis of the central executive system of working memory. *Nature, 378,* 279–281.

Dobson, M., & Markham, R. (1993). Imagery ability and source monitoring: Implications for eyewitness memory. *British Journal of Psychology, 32,* 111–118.

Eacott, M. J., & Crawley, R. A. (1999). Childhood amnesia: On answering questions about very early life events. *Memory, 7,* 279–292.

Ebbinghaus, H. (1885/1964). *Memory: A contribution to experimental psychology.* New York: Dover.

Eberman, C., & McKelvie, S. J. (2002). Vividness of visual imagery and source memory for audio and text. *Applied Cognitive Psychology, 16,* 87–95.

Ehlers, M. D. (2003). Activity level controls postsynaptic composition and signaling via the ubiquitin-proteasome system. *Nature Neuroscience, 6,* 231–242.

Eich, E. (1989). Theoretical issues in state dependent memory. In H. L. Roediger III & F. I. M. Craik (Eds.), *Varieties of memory and consciousness: Essays in honour of Endel Tulving* (pp. 331–354). Hillsdale, NJ: Erlbaum.

Eich, E. (1995). Searching for mood dependent memory. *Psychological Science, 6,* 67–75.

Ericsson, K. A., Chase, W. G., & Faloon, S. (1980). Acquisition of a memory skill. *Science, 208,* 1181–1182.

Fast, K., & Fujiwara, E. (2001). Isolated retrograde amnesia. *Neurocase, 7,* 269–272.

Field, A. P., Psychol, C., & Morgan, J. (2004). Post-event processing and the retrieval of autobiographical memories in socially anxious individuals. *Journal of Anxiety Disorders, 18,* 647–663.

Fisher, R. P., & Craik, F. I. M. (1977). The interaction between encoding and retrieval operations in cued recall. *Journal of Experimental Psychology: Human learning and Perception, 3,* 153–171.

Fisher, R. P., & Geiselman, R. E. (1992). *Memory enhancing techniques for investigative interviewing: The cognitive interview.* Springfield, IL: Charles C. Thomas.

Fisher, R. P., Geiselman, R. E., & Amador, M. (1989). Field test of the cognitive interview: Enhancing the recollection of actual victims and witnesses of crime. *Journal of Applied Psychology, 74,* 722–727.

Fivush, R., & Edwards, V. J. (2004). Remembering and forgetting childhood sexual abuse. *Journal of Child Sexual Abuse, 13,* 1–19.

Fuster, J. M. (1997). Network memory. *Trends in Neuroscience, 20,* 451–459.

Gabrieli, J. D. E., Desmond, J. E., Demb, J. B. Wagner, A. D., Stone, M. V., Vaidya, C. J., et al. (1996). Functional magnetic resonance imaging of semantic memory processes in the frontal lobes. *Psychological Science, 7,* 278–283.

Gabrieli, J. D. E., Fleischman, D. A., Keane, M. M., Reminger, S. L., & Morrell, F. (1995). Double dissociation between memory systems underlying explicit and implicit memory in the human brain. *American Psychological Society, 6,* 76–82.

Garry, M., & Polaschek, D. L. L. (2000). Imagination and memory. *Current Directions in Psychological Science, 9,* 6–10.

Geiselman, R. E., Fisher, R. P., MacKinnon, D. P., & Holland, H. L. (1985). Eyewitness memory enhancement in the police interview. *Cognitive Journal of Applied Psychology, 70,* 401–412.

Gerlai, R. (1996). Gene-targeting studies of mammalian behavior: Is it the mutation of the background genotype? *Trends in Neuroscience, 19,* 177–181.

Gottfried, J. A., & Dolan, R. J. (2003). The nose smells what the eye sees—Crossmodal visual facilitation of human olfactory perception. *Neuron, 39,* 375–386.

Green, J. P., Lynn, S. J., & Malinoski, P. (1998). Hypnotic pseudomemories, prehypnotic warnings, and malleability of suggested memories. *Applied Cognitive Psychology, 12,* 431–444.

Greenberg, D. L., & Rubin, D. C. (2003). The neuropsychology of autobiographical memory. *Cortex, 39,* 687–728.

Hebert, L. E., Scherr, P. A., Bienias, J. L., Bennett, D. A., & Evans, D. A. (2003). Alzheimer disease in the US population: Prevalence estimates using the 2000 census. *Archives of Neurology, 60,* 1119–1122.

Henson, R., Shallice, T., & Dolan, R. (2000). Neuroimaging evidence for dissociable forms of repetition priming. *Science, 287,* 1269–1272.

Hernandez, P. J., & Kelley, A. E. (2004). Long-term memory for instrumental responses does not undergo protein synthesis-dependent reconsolidation upon retrieval. *Learning and Memory, 11,* 748–754.

Hirst, W., Phelps, E. A., Buckner, R. L., Budson, A. E., Cuc, A., Gabrieli, J. D., et al. (2009). Long-term memory for the terrorist attack of September 11: flashbulb memories, event memories, and the factors that influence their retention. *Journal of Experimental Psychology: General, 138,* 161–176.

Huerta, P. T., Scearce, K. A., Farris, S. M., Empson, R. M., & Prusky, G. T. (1996). Preservation of spatial learning in fyn tyrosine kinase knockout mice. *Neuroreport, 7,* 1685–1689.

Hugdahl, K. (1995a). Classical conditioning and implicit learning: The right hemisphere hypothesis. In R. J. Davidson & K. Hugdahl (Eds.), *Brain asymmetry* (pp. 235–267). Cambridge, MA: MIT Press.

Hugdahl, K. (1995b). *Psychophysiology: The mind-body perspective.* Cambridge, MA: Harvard University Press.

Huynh, D. P., Maalouf, M., Silva, A. J., Schweizer, F. E., & Pulst, S. M. (2009). Dissociated fear and spatial learning in mice with ceficiency of Ataxin-2. *PLoS ONE, 4*(7): e6235. doi:10.1371/journal.pone.0006235

Johnson, M. K., Hashtroudi, S., & Lindsy, D. S. (1993). Source monitoring. *Psychological Bulletin, 114,* 3–28.

Johnson, M. K., & Raye, C. L. (1981). Reality monitoring. *Psychological Review, 88,* 67–85.

Johnson, S. C., Leslie, C., Baxter, L. C., Lana S., Wilder, L. S., Pipe, J. G., et al. (2002). Neural correlates of self-reflection. *Brain, 125,* 1808–1814.

Jonides, J., Lacey, S. C., & Nee, D. E. (2005). Processes of working memory in mind and brain. *Current Directions in Psychological Science, 14,* 2–5.

Joubert, S., Barbeau, E., Walter, N., Ceccaldi, M., & Poncet, M. (2003). Preservation of autobiographical memory in a case of pure progressive amnesia. *Brain and Cognition, 53,* 235–238.

Karni, A., & Sagi, D. (1993). The time course of learning a visual skill. *Nature, 365,* 250–252.

Kelley, W. M., Macrae, C. N., Wyland, C. L., Caglar, S., Inati, S., & Heatherton, T. F. (2002). Finding the self? An event-related fMRI study. *Journal of Cognitive Neuroscience, 14,* 785–794.

Kelley, W. M., Miezin, F. M., McDermott, K. B., Buckner, R. L., Raichle, M. E., Cohen, N. J., et al. (1998). Hemispheric specialization in human dorsal frontal cortex and medial temporal lobe for verbal and nonverbal memory encoding. *Neuron, 20,* 927–936.0

Kritchevsky, M., Chang, J., & Squire, L. R. (2004). Functional amnesia: Clinical description and neuropsychological profile of 10 cases. *Learning and Memory, 11,* 213–226.

Lee, J. L. C., Everitt, B. J., & Thomas, K. L. (2004). Independent cellular processes for hippocampal memory consolidation and reconsolidation. *Science, 304,* 339–343.

Levine, B. (2004). Autobiographical memory and the self in time: Brain lesion effects, functional neuroanatomy, and lifespan development. *Brain and Cognition, 55*(1), 54–68.

Levine, B., Turner, G. R., Tisserand, D., Hevenor, S. J., Graham, S. J., & McIntosh, A. R. (2004). The functional neuroanatomy of episodic and semantic autobiographical remembering: A prospective functional MRI study. *Journal of Cognitive Neuroscience, 16,* 1633–1646.

Lindsay, S., Hagen, L., Read, J. D., Wade, K. A., & Garry, M. (2004). True photographs and false memories. *Psychological Science, 15,* 149–154.

Loftus, E. F. (1993). The reality of repressed memories. *American Psychologist, 48,* 518–537.

Loftus, E. F. (2004). Memories of things unseen. *Current Directions in Psychological Science, 13,* 145–147.

Loftus, E. F., & Pickrell, J. E. (1995). The formation of false memories. *Psychiatric Annals, 25,* 720–725.

Luria, A. R. (1968/1887). *The mind of a mnemonist: A little book about a vast memory* (L. Solotaroff, Trans.). Cambridge, MA: Harvard University Press.

Luria, R., Sessa, P., Gotler, A., Jolicoeur, P, & Dell'Acqua R. (2010). Visual short-term memory capacity for simple and complex objects. *Journal of Cognitive Neuroscience, 22,* 496–512.

Lyubomirsky, S., Caldwell, N. D., & Nolen-Hoeksema, S. (1998). Effects of ruminative and distracting responses to depressed mood on retrieval of autobiographical memories. *Journal of Personality and Social Psychology, 75,* 166–177.

Macrae, C. N., Moran, J. M., Heatherton, T. F., Banfield, J. F., & Kelley, W. M. (2004). Medial prefrontal activity predicts memory for self. *Cerebral Cortex, 14,* 647–654.

Madill, A., & Holch, P. (2004). A range of memory possibilities: The challenge of the false memory debate for clinicians and researchers. *Clinical Psychology and Psychotherapy, 11,* 299–310.

Mandler, G. (1967). Organization in memory. In K. W. Spence & J. T. Spence (Eds.), *The psychology of learning and motivation* (Vol. 1, pp. 327–372). San Diego, CA: Academic Press.

Manns, J. R., Hopkins, R. O., & Squire, L. R. (2003). Semantic memory and the human hippocampus. *Neuron, 38,* 127–133.

Maroun, M., & Richter-Levin, G. (2003). Exposure to acute stress blocks the induction of long-term potentiation of the amygdala-prefrontal cortex pathway in vivo. *Journal of Neuroscience, 23,* 4406–4409.

Massen, C., Vaterrodt-Plünnecke, B., Krings, L., & Hilbig, B.E. (2009). Effects of instruction on learners' ability to generate an effective pathway in the method of loci. *Memory, 17,* 724–731.

Mather, M., Henkel, L. A., & Johnson, M. K. (1997). Evaluating characteristics of false memories: Remember/ know judgments and memory characteristics questionnaire compares. *Memory and Cognition, 25,* 826–837.

Mayes, A. R., & Downes, J. J. (Eds.). (1997). *Theories of organic amnesia.* Hove, England: Psychology Press/Erlbaum (UK) Taylor & Francis.

McDaniel, M. A., & Einstein, G. O. (1986). Bizarre imagery as an effective memory aid: The importance of distinctiveness. *Journal of Experimental Psychology: Learning, Memory, and Cognition, 12,* 54–65.

McDaniel, M. A., Einstein, G. O., DeLosh, E. L., & May, C. P. (1995). The bizarreness effect: It's not surprising, it's complex. *Journal of Experimental Psychology: Learning, Memory, and Cognition, 21,* 422–435.

McDermott, K. B., & Roediger, H. L., III. (1998). Attempting to avoid illusory memories: Robust false recognition of associates persists under conditions of explicit warnings and immediate testing. *Journal of Memory and Language, 39,* 508–520.

McEwen, B. S. (1997). Possible mechanisms for atrophy of the human hippocampus. *Molecular Psychiatry, 2,* 255–262.

McGaugh, J. L. (2000). Memory—A century of consolidation. *Science, 287,* 248–251.

McNally, R. J. (2003). *Remembering trauma.* Cambridge, MA: Harvard University Press.

McNally, R. J. (2004). Is traumatic amnesia nothing but psychiatric folklore? *Cognitive Behaviour Therapy, 33,* 97–101.

McNally, R. J., & Clancy, S. A. (2005). Sleep paralysis, sexual abuse, and space alien abduction. *Transcultural Psychiatry, 42,* 113–122.

McNally, R. J., Lasko, N. B., Clancy, S. A., Macklin, M. L., Pitman, R. K., & Orr, S. P. (2004). Psychophysiological responding during script-driven imagery in people reporting abduction by space aliens. *Psychological Science, 15,* 493–497.

Meeter, M., & Murre, J. M. J. (2004). Consolidation of long-term memory: Evidence and alternatives. *Psychological Bulletin, 130,* 843–857.

Miller, G. A. (1956). The magical number seven, plus or minus two: Some limits on our capacity for processing information. *Psychological Review, 63,* 81–97.

Morgan, M. J., McFie, L., Fleetwood, L. H., & Robinson, J. A. (2002). Ecstasy (MDMA): Are the psychological problems associated with its use reversed by prolonged abstinence? *Psychopharmacology, 159,* 294–303.

Morris, C. D., Bransford, J. D., & Franks, J. J. (1977). Levels of processing versus transfer-appropriate processing. *Journal of Verbal Learning and Verbal Behavior, 16,* 519–533.

Morris, R. (1984). Developments of a water-maze procedure for studying spatial learning in the rat. *Journal of Neuroscience Methods, 11,* 47–60.

Moscovitch, M., & Craik, F. I. M. (1976). Depth of processing, retrieval cues, and uniqueness of encoding as factors in recall. *Journal of Verbal Learning and Verbal Behavior, 15,* 447–458.

Nader, K., Einarsson, E.O. (2010). Memory reconsolidation: an update. *Annals of the New York Academy of Science, 1191,* 27–41.

Neisser, U. (1967). *Cognitive psychology.* New York: Appleton-Century-Crofts.

Neisser, U., & Harsch, N. (1992). Phantom flashbulbs: False recollections of hearing news about *Challenger.* In E. Winograd & U. Neisser (Eds.), *Affect and accuracy in recall: Studies of "flashbulb memories"* (pp. 9–31). Cambridge: Cambridge University Press.

Newcombe, N. S., Drummey, A. B., Fox, N. A., Lie, E., & Ottinger-Alberts, W. (2000). Remembering early childhood: How much, how, and why (or why not). *Current Directions in Psychological Science, 9,* 55–58.

Nichols, R. C. (1978). Twin studies of ability, personality, and interests. *Homo, 29,* 158–173.

Nickerson, R. S., & Adams, M. J. (1979). Long-term memory for a common object. *Cognitive Psychology, 1,* 287–307.

Norman, K. A., & Schacter, D. L. (1997). False recognition in younger and older adults: Exploring the characteristics of illusory memories. *Memory and Cognition, 25,* 838–848.

Ost, J. (2003). Seeking the middle ground in the "memory wars." *British Journal of Psychology, 94,* 125–139.

Paivio, A. (1971). *Imagery and verbal processes.* New York: Holt, Rinehart & Winston.

Parkin, A. J. (1987). *Memory and amnesia: An introduction.* Oxford: Blackwell.

Passingham, D., & Sakai, K. (2004). The prefrontal cortex and working memory: Physiology and brain imaging. *Current Opinion in Neurobiology, 14,* 163–168.

Pasupathi, M. (2003). Emotion regulation during social remembering: Differences between emotions elicited during an event and emotions elicited when talking about it. *Memory, 11,* 151–163.

Pederson, C. L., Maurer, S. H., Kaminski, P. L., Zander, K. A., Peters, C. M., Stokes-Crowe, L. A., et al. (2004). Hippocampal volume and memory performance in a community-based sample of women with posttraumatic stress disorder secondary to child abuse. *Journal of Traumatic Stress, 17,* 37–40.

Pedreira, M. E., Perez-Cuesta, L. M., & Maldonado, H. (2004) Mismatch between what is expected and what actually occurs triggers memory reconsolidation or extinction. *Learning and Memory, 11,* 579–585.

Penfield, W. (1955). The permanent record of the stream of consciousness. *Acta Psychologica, 11,* 47–69.

Pezdek, K., Finger, K., & Hodge, D. (1997). Planting false childhood memories: The role of event plausibility. *Psychological Science, 8,* 437–441.

Pope, K. S. (1996). Memory, abuse, and science: Questioning claims about the false memory syndrome epidemic. *American Psychologist, 51,* 957–974.

Pressley, M., Brown, R. El-Dinary, P. B., & Allferbach, P. (1995). The comprehension instruction that students need: Instruction fostering constructively responsive reading. *Learning Disabilities Research and Practice, 10,* 215–224.

Rajaram, S., Srinivas, K., & Roediger, H. L., III (1998). A transfer-appropriate processing account of context effects in word fragment completion. *Journal of Experimental Psychology: Learning, Memory, ad Cognition, 24,* 993–1004.

Reber, P. J., Siwiec, R. M., Gitleman, D. R., Parrish, T. B., Mesulam, M. M., & Paller, K. A. (2002). Neural correlates of successful encoding identified using functional magnetic resonance imaging. *Journal of Neuroscience, 22,* 9541–9548.

Rodrigues, S.M., LeDoux, J.E., & Sapolsky, R.M. (2009). The influence of stress hormones on fear circuitry. *Annual Review of Neuroscience, 32,* 289–313.

Roediger, H. L., III. (1980). Memory metaphors in cognitive psychology. *Memory and Cognition, 8,* 231–246.

Roediger, H. L., III, & McDermott, K. B. (1993). Implicit memory in normal human subjects. In F. Bohler & J. Grafman (Eds.), *Handbook of neuropsychology* (Vol. 8, pp. 63–131). Amsterdam: Elsevier.

Roediger, H. L., III, & McDermott, K. B. (1995). Creating false memories: Remembering words not presented in lists. *Journal of Experimental Psychology: Learning, Memory, and Cognition, 21,* 803–814.

Roediger, H. L., III, Meade, M. L., & Bergman, E. T. (2001). Social contagion of memory. *Psychonomic Bulletin and Review, 8,* 365–371.

Roediger, H. L., III, & Thorpe, L. A. (1978). The role of recall time in producing hypermnesia. *Memory and Cognition, 6,* 296–305.

Rubin, L. J. (1996). Childhood sexual abuse: False accusations of "false memory"? *Professional Psychology Research and Practice, 27,* 447–451.

Sapolsky, R. M. (1992). *Stress, the aging brain, and the mechanisms of neuron death.* Cambridge, MA: MIT Press.

Schacter, D. L. (1987). Implicit memory: History and current status. *Journal of Experimental Psychology: Learning, Memory, and Cognition, 13,* 501–518.

Schacter, D. L. (1996). *Searching for memory: The brain, the mind, and the past.* New York: Basic Books.

Schacter, D. L. (1999). The seven sins of memory: Insights from psychology and cognitive neuroscience. *American Psychologist, 54,* 182–203.

Schacter, D. L., Addis, D. R., & Buckner, R. L. (2007). Remembering the past to imagine the future: The prospective brain. *Nature Reviews Neuroscience, 8,* 657–661.

Schacter, D. L., & Badgaiyan, R. D. (2001). Neuroimaging of priming: New perspectives on implicit and explicit memory. *Current Directions in Psychological Science, 10,* 1–4.

Schacter, D. L., Cendan, D. L., Dodson, C. S., & Clifford, E. R. (2001). Retrieval conditions and false recognition: Testing the distinctiveness heuristic. *Psychonomic Bulletin and Review, 8,* 827–833.

Schacter, D. L., Reiman, E., Curran, T., Yun, L. S., Bandy, D., McDermott, K. B., et al. (1996). Neuroanatomical correlates of veridical and illusory recognition memory: Evidence from positron emission tomography. *Neuron, 2,* 267–274.

Scheflin, A., & Brown, D. (1996). Repressed memory or dissociative amnesia: What science says. *Journal of Psychiatry and Law, 24,* 143–188.

Schmolck, H., Buffalo, E. A., & Squire, L. R. (2000). Memory distortions develop over time: Recollections from the O. J. Simpson trial verdict after 15 and 32 months. *Psychological Science, 11,* 39–45.

Schneider, W., & Chein, J. M. (2003). Controlled and automatic processing: Behavior, theory, and biological mechanisms. *Cognitive Science, 27,* 525–559.

Setliff, A. E., & Marmurek, H. H. C. (2002). The mood regulatory function of autobiographical recall is moderated by self-esteem. *Personality and Individual Differences, 32,* 761–771.

Sheehan, P. W. (1988). Memory distortion in hypnosis. *International Journal of Clinical Experimental Hypnosis, 36,* 296–311.

Sheen, M., Kemp, S., & Rubin, D. (2001). Twins dispute memory ownership: A new false memory phenomenon. *Memory and Cognition, 29,* 779–788.

Shiffrin, R. M. (1999). 30 years of memory. In C. Izawa (Ed.), *On human memory: Evolution, progress, and reflections on the 30th anniversary of the Atkinson-Shiffrin model* (pp. 17–33). Hillsdale, NJ: Erlbaum.

Skowronski, J. J., Gibbons, J. A., Vogl, R. J., & Walker, W. R. (2004). The effect of social disclosure on the intensity of affect provoked by autobiographical memories. *Self and Identity, 3,* 285–309.

Skowronski, J. J., & Walker, W. R. (2004). How describing autobiographical events can affect autobiographical memories. *Social Cognition, 22,* 555–590.

Smith, E. E. (2000). Neural bases of human working memory. *Current Directions in Psychological Science, 9,* 45–49.

Smith, E. E., & Jonides, J. (1999). Storage and executive processes in the frontal lobes. *Science, 283,* 1657–1661.

Snowdon, D. A., Greiner, L. H., & Markesbery, W. R. (2000). Linguistic ability in early life and the neuropathology of Alzheimer's disease and cerebrovascular disease: Findings from the nun study. *Annals of the New York Academy of Sciences, 903,* 34–38.

Sperling, G. (1960). The information available in brief visual presentations. *Psychological Monographs, 74,* 1–29.

Spiers, H. J., Maguire, E. A., & Burgess, N. (2001). Hippocampal amnesia. *Neurocase, 7,* 357–382.

Spreng, R. N., & Grady, C. L. (2010). Patterns of brain activity supporting autobiographical memory, prospection, and theory of mind, and their relationship to the default mode network. Journal of Cognitive Neuroscience, 22, 1112–1123.

Squire, L. R. (1987). *Memory and the brain.* New York: Oxford University Press.

Squire, L. R. (2004). Memory systems of the brain: A brief history and current perspective. *Neurobiology of Learning and Memory, 82,* 171–177.

Squire, L. R., Clark, R. E., & Knowlton, B, J. (2001). Retrograde amnesia. *Hippocampus, 11,* 50–55.

Squire, L. R., & Kandel, E. R. (1999). *Memory: From mind and molecules.* New York: Scientific American Books.

Squire, L. R., Ojemann, J. G., Miezin, F. M., Petersen, S. E., Videen, T. O., & Raichle, M. E. (1992). Activation of the hippocampus in normal humans: A functional anatomical study of memory. *Proceedings of the National Academy of Sciences of the United States of America, 89,* 1837–1841.

Squire, L. R., & Zola-Morgan, S. (1991). The medial temporal lobe memory system. *Science, 253,* 1380–1386.

Talarico, J. M., & Rubin, D. C. (2003). Confidence, not consistency, characterizes flashbulb memories. *Psychological Science, 14,* 455–461.

Tronson, N, C, & & Taylor, J. R. (2007). Molecular mechanisms of memory reconsolidation. *Nature Reviews Neuroscience, 8,* 262–275.

Turriziani, P., Smirni, D., Oliveri, M., Semenza, C., & Cipolotti, L. (2010) The role of the prefrontal cortex in familiarity and recollection processes during verbal and non-verbal recognition memory: An rTMS study. *NeuroImage, 52,* 348-357.

Ungerleider, L. G. (1995). Functional brain imaging studies of cortical mechanisms for memory. *Science, 270,* 769–775.

Vythilingam, M., Vermetten, E., Anderson, G. M., Luckenbaugh, D., Anderson, E. R., Snow, J., et al. (2004). Hippocampal volume, memory, and cortisol status in major depressive disorder: Effects of treatment. *Biological Psychiatry, 56,* 101–112.

Wagner, A. D., Schacter, D. L., Rotte, M., Koutstaal, W., Maril, A., Dale, A. M., et al. (1998). Building memories: Remembering and forgetting of verbal experiences as predicted by brain activity. *Science, 281,* 1188–1191.

Wang, Q., & Conway, M. A. (2004). The stories we keep: Autobiographical memory in American and Chinese middle-aged adults. *Journal of Personality, 72,* 911–938.

Warrington, E. K., & McCarthy, R. A. (1988). The fractionation of retrograde amnesia. *Brain and Cognition, 7,* 184–200.

Waugh, N. C., & Norman, D. A. (1965). Primary memory. *Psychological Review, 72,* 89–104.

Wessel, I., & Wright, D. B. (2004). Emotional memory failures: On forgetting and reconstructing emotional experiences. *Cognition and Emotion, 18,* 449–455.

Williams, L. M. (1994). Recall of childhood trauma: A prospective study of women's memories of child sexual abuse. *Journal of Consulting and Clinical Psychology, 62,* 1167–1176.

Wixted, J. T., & Ebbesen, E. B. (1991). On the form of forgetting. *Psychological Science, 2,* 409–415.

Wixted, J. T., & Ebbesen, E. B. (1997). Genuine power curves in forgetting: A quantitative analysis of individual subject forgetting functions. *Memory and Cognition, 25,* 731–739.

Worthington, T. S. (1979). The use in court of hypnotically enhanced testimony. *International Journal of Clinical and Experimental Hypnosis, 27,* 402–416.

Zhang, Q., & Zhu, Y. (2001). The relationship between individual differences in working memory and linear reasoning. *Journal of Psychology in Chinese Societies, 2,* 261–282.

References: Language, Thinking, and Intelligence

Achter, J., Lubinski, D., & Benbow, C. P. (1996). Multipotentiality among the intellectually gifted: "It was never there and already it's vanishing." *Journal of Counseling Psychology, 43,* 65–76.

Aguilar-Alonso, A. (1996). Personality and creativity. *Personality and Individual Differences, 21,* 959–969.

Alexander, D. (1991). Keynote address. In *President's Committee on Mental Retardation, Summit on the National Effort to Prevent Mental Retardation and Related Disabilities.*

Aluja-Fabregat, A., Colom, R., Abad, F., & Juan-Espinosa, M. (2000). Sex differences in general intelligence defined as *g* among young adolescents. *Personality & Individual Differences, 28,* 813–820.

Amabile, T. M. (1983). *The social psychology of creativity.* New York: Springer-Verlag.

Amabile, T. M. (1998, September–October). How to kill creativity. *Harvard Business Review,* pp. 76–87.

Amabile, T. M. (2001). Beyond talent: John Irving and the passionate craft of creativity. *American Psychologist, 56,* 333–336.

American Association for Mental Retardation (1992). *Mental retardation: Definition, classification, and systems of supports* (9th ed.). Washington, DC: Author.

Anderson, J. R., & Betz, J. (2001). A hybrid model of categorization. *Psychonomic Bulletin & Review, 8,* 629–647.

Anderson, N. B., & Nickerson, K. J. (2005). Genes, race, and psychology in the genome era. *American Psychologist, 60,* 5–8.

Andreasen, N. C. (1987). Creativity and mental illness: Prevalence rates in writers and their first-degree relatives. *American Journal of Psychiatry, 144,* 1288–1292.

Armstrong, S. L., Gleitman, L. R., & Gleitman, H. (1983). What some concepts might not be. *Cognition, 13,* 263–308.

Arnsten, A. F. T. (1998) The biology of being frazzled. *Science, 280,* 1711–1712.

Aronson, J., Fried, C. B., & Good, C. (2002). Reducing the effects of stereotype threat on African American college students by shaping theories of intelligence. *Journal of Experimental Social Psychology, 38,* 113–125.

Ayal, S., & Hochman, G. (2009). Ignorance or integration: The cognitive processes underlying choice behavior. *Journal of Behavioral Decision Making, 22,* 455–474.

Ayton, P., & Wright, G. (1994). Subjective probability: What should we believe? In G. Wright & P. Ayton (Eds.), *Subjective probability* (pp. 163–183). New York: Wiley.

Baenninger, M., & Newcombe, N. (1989). The role of experience in spatial test performance: A meta-analysis. *Sex Roles, 20,* 327–344.

Bar-On, R., & Parker, J. (Eds.) (2000). *The handbook of emotional intelligence.* San Francisco: Jossey-Bass.

Bar-On, R., Brown, J. M., Kirkcaldy, B. D., & Thome, E. P. (2000). Emotional expression and implications for occupational stress: An application of the emotional quotient inventory (EQ-i). *Personality and Individual Differences, 28,* 1107–1118.

Barrantes-Vidal, N. (2004). Creativity & madness revisited from current psychological perspectives. *Journal of Consciousness Studies, 11,* 58–78.

Batshaw, M., & Perret, Y. (1992). *Children with disabilities: A medical primer.* Baltimore: Brookes.

Bechara, A., Damasio, H., Tranel, D., & Damasio, A. R. (1997). Deciding advantageously before knowing the advantageous strategy. *Science, 275,* 1293–1294.

Behrens, R. R. (2003). Thinking outside of the box: On Karl Duncker, functional fixedness, and the adaptive value of engaging in purposely deviant acts. *Gestalt Theory, 25,* 63–70.

Bell, A. E. (1977). Heritability in retrospect. *Journal of Heredity, 68,* 297–300.

Beller, M., & Gafni, N. (1996). The 1991 international assessment of educational progress in mathematics and sciences: The gender differences perspective. *Journal of Educational Psychology, 88,* 365–377.

Benbow, C. P., & Minor, L. L. (1990). Cognitive profiles of verbally and mathematically precocious students: Implications for identification of the gifted. *Gifted Child Quarterly, 34,* 21–26.

Berman, S. M., & Noble, E. P. (1995). Reduced visuospatial performance in children with the D2 dopamine receptor A1 allele. *Behavior Genetics, 25,* 45–58.

Bird, H., Howard, D., & Franklin, S. (2000). Why is a verb like an inanimate object? Grammatical category and semantic category deficits. *Brain & Language, 72,* 246–309.

Birnbaum, S. G., Yuan, P. X., Wang, M., Vijayraghavan, S., Bloom, A. K., Davis, D. J., et al. (2004). Protein kinase C overactivity impairs prefrontal cortical regulation of working memory. *Science 306,* 882–884.

Block, N. (1995). How heritability misleads about race. *Cognition, 56,* 99–128.

Bloom, B. S. (1985). Generalizations about talent development. In B. S. Bloom (Ed.), *Developing talent in young people* (pp. 507–549). New York: Ballantine Books.

Borst, G., & Kosslyn, S. M. (2008). Visual mental imagery and visual perception: Structural equivalence revealed by scanning processes. *Memory and Cognition, 36,* 849-862.

Bosson, J. K., Haymovitz, E. L., & Pinel, E. C. (2004). When saying and doing diverge: The effects of stereotype threat on self-reported versus non-verbal anxiety. *Journal of Experimental Social Psychology, 40,* 247–255.

Bouchard, T. J., & McGue, M. (1981). Familial studies of intelligence: A review. *Science, 212,* 1055–1059.

Bouchard, T. J., Jr., Lykken, D. T., McGue, M., Segal, N. L., & Tellegen, A. (1990). Sources of human psychological differences: The Minnesota Study of Twins Reared Apart. *Science, 250,* 223–228.

Bowdle, B. F., & Gentner, D. (2005). The career of metaphor. *Psychological Review, 112,* 193–216.

Brian, D. (1996). *Einstein: A life.* New York: John Wiley & Sons.

Brody, N. (2003a). Construct validation of the Sternberg triarchic abilities test: Comment and reanalysis. *Intelligence, 31,* 319–329.

Brody, N. (2003b). What Sternberg should have concluded. *Intelligence, 31,* 339–342.

Brown, R. P., & Pinel, E. C. (2003). Stigma on my mind: Individual differences in the experience of stereotype threat. *Journal of Experimental Social Psychology, 39,* 626–633.

Brownell, H. (2000). Right hemisphere contributions to understanding lexical connotation and metaphor. In Y. Grodzinsky, L. P. Shapiro, P. Lewis & D. Swinney (Eds.), *Language and the brain: Representation and processing* (pp. 185–201). San Diego, CA: Academic Press.

Bruder, C. E., Piotrowski, A., Gijsbers, A. A., Andersson, R., Erickson, S., de Ståhl, T.D.,... Dumanski, J. P. (2008). Phenotypically concordant and discordant monozygotic twins display different DNA copy-number-variation profiles. *American Journal of Human Genetics, 82,* 763–771.

Buehler, R., Griffin, D., & Ross, M. (1994). Exploring the "planning fallacy": Why people underestimate their task completion times. *Journal of Personality and Social Psychology, 67,* 366–381.

Buss, D. M. (1995). Psychological sex differences: Origins through sexual selection. *American Psychologist, 50,* 164–168.

Cadinu, M., Maass, A., Frigerio, S., Impagliazzo, L., & Latinotti, S. (2003). Stereotype threat: The effect of expectancy on performance. *European Journal of Social Psychology, 33,* 267–285.

Cahan, S., & Cohen, N. (1989). Age versus schooling effects on intelligence development. *Child Development, 60,* 1239–1249.

Canter, S. (1973). Personality traits in twins. In G. Claridge, S. Canter, & W. I. Hume (Eds.). *Personality differences and biological variations* (pp. 21–51). New York: Pergamon.

Carroll, J. (1993). *Human cognitive abilities: A survey of factor-analytic studies.* New York: Cambridge University Press.

Carrothers, R. M., Gregory, S. W., Jr., & Gallagher, T. J. (2000). Measuring emotional intelligence of medical school applicants. *Academic Medicine, 75,* 456–463.

Cattell, R. B. (1971). *Abilities: Their structure, growth, and action.* Boston: Houghton Mifflin.

Ceci, S. J. (1991). How much does schooling influence general intelligence and its cognitive components? A reassessment of the evidence. *Developmental Psychology, 27,* 703–722.

Ceci, S. J., & Williams, W. M. (1997). Schooling, intelligence, and income. *American Psychologist, 52,* 1051–1058.

Chapman, R. S., & Hesketh, L. J. (2000). Behavioral phenotype of individuals with Down syndrome. *Mental Retardation & Developmental Disabilities Research Reviews, 6,* 84–95.

Chipuer, H. M., Rovine, M. J., & Plomin, R. (1990). LISREL modeling: Genetic and environmental influences on IQ revisited. *Intelligence, 14,* 11–29.

Chomsky, N. (1957). *Syntactic structures.* Mouton: The Hague.

Cianciolo, A. T., Grigorenko, E. L., Jarvin, L., Gil, G., Drebot, M. E., & Sternberg, R. J. (2009). Practical intelligence and tacit knowledge: Advancements in the measurement of developing expertise. In J. C. Kaufman, E. L. Grigorenko, & R. J. Sternberg (Eds.), *The essential Sternberg: Essays on intelligence, psychology, and education.* (pp. 119-144). New York, NY, US: Springer Publishing Co.

Ciarrochi, J., Forgas, J. P., & Mayer, J. D. (2001). Emotional intelligence in everyday life. Philadelphia: Psychology Press.

Clark, R. W. (1971). *Einstein: The life and times.* New York: World Publishing.

Connell, M. W., Sheridan, K., Gardner, H., & Sternberg, R. J. (Eds.) (2003). *The psychology of abilities, competencies, and expertise.* New York: Cambridge University Press.

Croen, L. A., Grether, J. K., Hoogstrate, J., & Selving, S. (2002). The changing prevalence of autism in California. *Journal of Autism & Developmental Disorders, 32,* 207–215.

Croizet, J. C., & Claire, T. (1998) Extending the concept of stereotype and threat to social class: The intellectual underperformance of students from low socioeconomic backgrounds. *Personality & Social Psychology Bulletin, 24,* 588–594.

Croizet, J., Després, G., Gauzins, M., Huguet, P., Leyens, J., & Méot, A. (2004). Stereotype threat undermines intellectual performance by triggering a disruptive mental load. *Personality & Social Psychology Bulletin, 30,* 721–731.

Cullen, M. J., Hardison, C. M., & Sackett, P. R. (2004). Using SAT–grade and ability–job performance relationships to test predictions derived from stereotype threat theory. *Journal of Applied Psychology, 89,* 220–230.

Dai, X. Y., & Lynn, R. (1994). Gender differences in intelligence among Chinese children. *The Journal of Social Psychology, 134,* 123–125.

Davies, P. G., Spencer, S. J., & Steele, C. M. (2005). Clearing the air: Identity safety moderates the effects of stereotype threat on women's leadership aspirations. *Journal of Personality & Social Psychology, 88,* 276–287.

Dawda, D., & Hart, S. D. (2000). Assessing emotional intelligence: Reliability and validity of the Bar-On Emotional Quotient Inventory (EQ-i) in university students. *Personality and Individual Differences, 28,* 797–812.

Deary, I. J. (2000). *Looking down on human intelligence: From psychometrics to the brain.* Oxford, UK: Oxford University Press.

Deary, I. J., Whiteman, M. C., Starr, J. M., Whalley, L. J., & Fox, H. C. (2004). The impact of childhood intelligence on later life: Following up the Scottish mental surveys of 1932 and 1947. *Journal of Personality & Social Psychology, 86,* 130–147.

Denis, M., & Kosslyn, S. M. (1999). Scanning visual images: A window on the mind. *Current Psychology of Cognition, 18,* 409–465.

Dennis, W. (1966). Goodenough scores, art experience, and modernization. *Journal of Social Psychology, 68,* 211–228.

Devlin, B., Daniels, M., & Roeder, K. (1997). The heritability of IQ. *Nature, 388,* 468–471.

Dietrich, A. (2004). The cognitive neuroscience of creativity. *Psychonomic Bulletin & Review, 11,* 1011–1026.

Dohnanyiova, M., Ostatnikova, D., & Laznibatova, J. (2001). Spatial imagery, testosterone and anthropometric characteristics in intellectually gifted and control children. *Homeostasis in Health & Disease, 41,* 53–55.

Duncker, K. (1945). On problem solving. *Psychological monographs, 58* (No. 270).

Dupuy, B., & Krashen, S. D. (1993). Incidental vocabulary acquisition in French as a foreign language. *Applied Language Learning, 4,* 55–63.

Eals, M., & Silverman, I. (1994). The hunter-gatherer theory of spatial sex differences: Proximate factors mediating the female advantage on recall of object arrays. *Ethology and Sociobiology, 15,* 95–105.

Einstein, A. (1945). A testimonial from Professor Einstein (Appendix II). In J. Hadamard, *An essay on the psychology of invention in the mathematical field* (pp. 142–143). Princeton, NJ: Princeton University Press.

Ellis, H. C. (1973). Stimulus encoding processes in human learning and memory. In G. H. Bower (Ed.), *The psychology of learning and motivation* (Vol. 7, pp. 124–182). New York: Academic Press.

Ellis, H. C., & Hunt, R. R. (1993). *Fundamentals of cognitive psychology* (5th ed.). Dubuque, IA: Brown Communications.

Engelberg, E., & Sjöberg, L. (2004). Emotional intelligence, affect intensity, and social adjustment. *Personality and Individual Differences, 37*, 533–542.

Etcoff, N. L., Ekman, P., Magee, J. J., & Frank, M. G. (2000). Lie detection and language comprehension. *Nature, 405*, 139.

Evans, J. J., Floyd, R. G., McGrew, K. S., & Leforgee, M. H. (2002). The relations between measures of Cattell-Horn-Carroll (CHC) cognitive abilities and reading achievement during childhood and adolescence. *School Psychology Review, 31*, 246–262.

Eyferth, K. (1961). Ein Vergleich der Beurteilung projektiver Tests durch verschiedene Berteiler [A comparison of judging projective tests by different judges]. *Zeitschrift fuer Experimentelle und Angewandte Psychologie, 8*, 329–338.

Eysenck, H. J. (1995). *Genius: The natural history of creativity*. Cambridge, England: Cambridge University Press.

Fabbro, F. (2001). The bilingual brain: Bilingual aphasia. *Brain & Language, 79*, 201–210.

Fagan, J. L., & Holland, C. R. (2002). Equal opportunity and racial differences in IQ. *Intelligence, 30*, 361–387.

Feldman, D. H., & Goldsmith, L. T. (1991). *Nature's gambit: Child prodigies and the development of human potential*. New York: Teachers College Press.

Fisch, H., Hyun, G., Golden, R., Hensle, T., Olsson, C., & Liberson, G. (2003). The influence of paternal age on Down syndrome *The Journal of Urology, 169*, 2275–2278.

Fisher, P. J., Turic, D., Williams, N. M., McGuffin, P., Asherson, P., Ball, D., et al. (1999). DNA pooling identifies QTLs on Chromosome 4 for general cognitive ability in children. *Human Molecular Genetics, 8*, 915–922.

Fitch, R. H., & Bimonte, H. A. (2002). Hormones, brain, and behavior: Putative biological contributions to cognitive sex differences. In A. McGillicuddy-De Lisi & R. De Lisi (Eds.), *Biology, society, and behavior: The development of sex differences in cognition* (pp. 55–91). Westport, CT: Ablex.

Flynn, J. R. (1991). *Asian Americans: Achievement beyond IQ*. Hillsdale, NJ: Erlbaum.

Flynn, J. R. (1999a). Massive IQ gains in fourteen nations: What IQ tests really measure. *Psychological Bulletin, 101*, 171–191.

Flynn, J. R. (1999b). Searching for justice: The discovery of IQ gains over time. *American Psychologist, 54*, 5–20.

Ford, T. E., Ferguson, M. A., Brooks, J. L., & Hagadone, K. M. (2004). Coping sense of humor reduces effects of stereotype threat on women's math performance. *Personality & Social Psychology Bulletin, 30*, 643–653.

Fryer, R. G., & Levitt, S. D. (2004). Understanding the Black-White test score gap in the first two years of school. *The Review of Economics and Statistics, 86*, 447–464.

Fryers, T. (1993). Epidemiological thinking in mental retardation: Issues in taxonomy and population frequency. In N. W. Bray (Ed.), *International review of research in mental retardation* (Vol. 19). Novato, CA: Academic Therapy Publication.

Furnham, A., Shahidi, S., & Baluch, B. (2002). Sex and culture differences in perceptions of estimated multiple intelligence for self and family: A British-Iranian comparison. *Journal of Cross-Cultural Psychology, 33*, 270–285.

Gagné, F., & St Père, F. (2001). When IQ is controlled, does motivation still predict achievement? *Intelligence, 30*, 71–100.

Galdzicki, Z., Siarey, R., Pearce, R., Stoll, J., & Rapoport, S. I. (2001). On the cause of mental retardation in Down syndrome: Extrapolation from full and segmental trisomy 16 mouse models. *Brain Research Reviews, 35*, 115–145.

Gandour, J., & Baum, S. R. (2001). Production of stress retraction by left- and right-hemisphere-damaged patients. *Brain & Language, 79*, 482–494.

Ganis, G., Thompson, W. L., & Kosslyn, S. M. (2004). Brain areas underlying visual imagery and visual perception: An fMRI study. *Cognitive Brain Research, 20*, 226–241.

Gardner, H. (1993a). *Creating minds: An anatomy of creativity as seen through the lives of Freud, Einstein, Picasso, Stravinsky, Eliot, Graham, and Gandhi*. New York: Basic Books.

Gardner, H. (1993b). *Frames of mind: The theory of multiple intelligences*. New York: Basic Books. (Original work published 1983)

Gardner, H. (1995, November). Reflections on multiple intelligences: Myths and messages. *Phi Delta Kappan*, pp. 200–209.

Gardner, H. (1999). *Intelligence reframed: Multiple intelligences for the 21st century*. New York: Basic Books.

Gardner, H. (2002). Three distinct meanings of intelligence. In R. J. Sternberg, J. Lautrey, & T. I. Lubart (Eds.), *Models of intelligence: International perspectives* (pp. 43–45). Washington, DC: American Psychological Association.

Gardner, H., Kornhaber, M. L., & Wake, W. K. (1996). *Intelligence: Multiple perspectives*. Ft. Worth, TX: Harcourt Brace.

Garrard, P., Lambon, R. M. A., Hodges, J. R., & Patterson, K. (2001). Prototypicality, distinctiveness, and intercorrelation: Analyses of the semantic attributes of living and nonliving concepts. *Cognitive Neuropsychology, 18*, 125–174.

Geary, D. C. (1996). Sexual selection and sex differences in mathematical abilities. *Behavioral and Brain Sciences, 19*, 229–284.

Gentner, D., & Bowdle, B. F. (2001). Convention, form, and figurative language processing. *Metaphor & Symbol, 16*, 223–247.

Gentner, D., & Gunn, V. (2001). Structural alignment facilitates the noticing of differences. *Memory & Cognition, 29*, 565–577.

Gernsbacher, M.A., & Kaschak, M.P. (2003). Neuroimaging studies of language production and comprehension. *Annual Review of Psychology, 54*, 91-114.

Gick, M. L., & Holyoak, K. J. (1980). Analogical problem solving. *Cognitive Psychology, 12*, 306–355.

Gick, M. L., & Holyoak, K. J. (1983). Schema induction and analogical transfer. *Cognitive Psychology, 15*, 1–38.

Gigerenzer, G. (1996). On narrow norms and vague heuristics: A reply to Kahneman & Tversky (1996). *Psychological Review, 103*, 592–596.

Gigerenzer, G., & Goldstein, D. G. (1996). Reasoning the fast and frugal way: Models of bounded rationality. *Psychological Review, 103*, 650–669.

Gigerenzer, G., Hell, W., & Blank, H. (1988). Presentation and content: The use of base rates as a continuous variable. *Journal of Experimental Psychology: Human Perception and Performance, 14*, 513–525.

Glucksberg, S., Newsome, M. R., & Goldvarg, Y. (2001). Inhibition of the literal: Filtering metaphor-irrelevant information during metaphor comprehension. *Metaphor & Symbol, 16*, 277–293.

Glutting, J. J., Oh, H. J., Ward, T., & Ward, S. (2000). Possible criterion-related bias of the WISC-III with a referral sample. *Journal of Psychoeducational Assessment, 18*, 17–26.

Goel, V., & Dolan, R. J. (2003). Explaining modulation of reasoning by belief. *Cognition, 87*, B11–B22.

Goodwin, F. K., & Jamison, K. R. (1990). *Manic-depressive illness*. New York: Oxford University Press.

Gottfredson, L. (1997). Why "g" matters: The complexity of everyday life. *Intelligence, 24*, 79–132.

Gottfredson, L. S. (2003a). Dissecting practical intelligence theory: Its claims and evidence. *Intelligence, 31*, 343–397.

Gottfredson, L. S. (2003b). Discussion: On Sternberg's "Reply to Gottfredson." *Intelligence, 31*, 415–424.

Gray, J. R. (1999). A bias toward short-term thinking in threat-related negative emotional states. *Personality and Social Psychology Bulletin, 25*, 65–75.

Grézes, J., & Decety, J. (2001). Functional anatomy of execution, mental simulation, observation, and verb generation of actions: A meta-analysis. *Human Brain Mapping, 12*, 1–19.

Grice, H. P. (1975). Logic and conversation. In P. Cole & J. L. Morgan (Eds.), *Syntax and semantics: Vol. 3, Speech acts* (pp. 41–58). New York: Seminar Press.

Grodzinsky, Y., & Friederici A. D. (2006). Neuroimaging of syntax and syntactic processing. *Current Opinion in Neurobiology, 16*, 240–246.

Guilford, J. P. (1967). *The nature of human intelligence*. New York: McGraw-Hill.

Guillot, A., & Collet, C. (Eds.) (2009), *The neural foundations of mental and motor imagery*. Oxford, UK: Oxford University Press.

Gustafsson, J. E. (1984). A unifying model for the structure of mental abilities. *Intelligence, 8*, 179–203.

Hakuta, K., Bialystok, E., & Wiley, E. (2003). Critical evidence: A test of the critical-period hypothesis for second-language learning. *Psychological Science, 14*, 31–38.

Halari, R., Hines, M., Kumari, V., Mehrotra, R., Wheeler, M., Ng, V., & Sharma, T. (2005). Sex differences and individual differences in cognitive performance and their relationship to endogenous gonadal hormones and gonadotropins. *Behavioral Neuroscience, 119*, 104–117.

Halle, M. (1990). Phonology. In D. N. Osherson & H. Lasnik (Eds.), *An invitation to cognitive science: Vol. 1, Language* (pp. 43–68). Cambridge, MA: MIT Press.

Halpern, D. F. (1992). *Sex differences in cognitive ability*. Hillsdale, NJ: Erlbaum.

Halpern, D. F. (1997). Sex differences in intelligence: Implications for education. *American Psychologist, 52*, 1091–1102.

Halpern, D. F. (2000). *Sex differences in cognitive abilities* (3rd ed.). London: LEA.

Hampson, E. (1990). Estrogen-related variations in human spatial and articulatory motor skills. *Psychoneuroendocrinology, 15*, 97–111.

Hampson, E., & Kimura, D. (1988). Reciprocal effects of hormonal fluctuations on human motor and perceptual-spatial skills. *Behavioral Neuroscience, 102*, 456–459.

Hart, B., & Risley, T. R. (1995/2002) *Meaningful differences in everyday parenting and intellectual development in young American children*. Baltimore: Paul H. Brookes.

Hauser, M. D. (2001). *Wild minds: What animals really think*. New York: Holt.

Hausmann, M., Slabbekoorn, D., Van Goozen, S. H. M., Cohen-Kettenis, P. T., & Guenteurkuen, O. (2000). Sex hormones affect spatial abilities during the menstrual cycle. *Behavioral Neuroscience, 114*, 1245–1250.

Heilman, K. M., Nadeau, S. E., & Beversdorf, D. O. (2003). Creative innovation: Possible brain mechanisms. *Neurocase, 9*, 369–379.

Held, J. D., Alderton, D. L., Foley, P. P., & Segall, D. O. (1993). Arithmetic reasoning gender differences: Explanations found in the Armed Services Vocational Aptitude Battery. *Learning and Individual Differences, 5*, 171–186.

Herrnstein, R. J., & Murray, C. (1994). *The bell curve: Intelligence and class structure in American life*. New York: Free Press.

Hershman, D. J., & Lieb, J. (1988). *The key to genius/manic-depression and the creative life*. New York: Prometheus Books.

Hershman, D. J., & Lieb, J. (1998). *Manic depression and creativity*. New York: Prometheus Books.

Hess, T. M., Auman, C., Colcombe, S. J., & Rahhal, T. A. (2003). The impact of stereotype threat on age differences in memory performance. *Journals of Gerontology: Series B: Psychological Sciences & Social Sciences, 58*, P3–P11.

Hill, L., Chorney, M. J., Jubinski, D., Thompson, L. A., & Plomin, R. (2002). A quantitative trait locus not associated with cognitive ability in children: A failure to replicate. *Psychological Science, 13*, 561–562.

Hill, L., Craig, I. W., Asherson, P., Ball, D., Eley, T., Ninomiya, T., et al. (1999). DNA pooling and dense marker maps: A systematic search for genes for cognitive ability. *Neuroreport, 10*, 843–848.

Hines, M. (2004). *Brain gender*. New York: Oxford University Press.

Hirsch, J. (1971). Behavior-genetic analysis and its biosocial consequences. In R. Cancro (Ed.), *Intelligence: Genetic and environmental influences* (pp. 88–106). New York: Grune & Stratton.

Hirsch, J. (1997). The triumph of wishful thinking over genetic irrelevance. *Cahiers de Psychologie Cognitive/Current Psychology of Cognition, 16*, 711–720.

Horn, J. (1985). Remodeling old models of intelligence. In B. B. Wolman (Ed.), *Handbook of intelligence* (pp. 267–300). New York: Wiley.

Horn, J. (1989). Models of intelligence. In R. L. Linn (Ed.), *Intelligence: Measurement, theory, and public policy* (pp. 29–73). Urbana: University of Illinois Press.

Horn, J. L. (1986). Intellectual ability concepts. In R. J. Sternberg (Ed.), *Advances in the psychology of human intelligence* (Vol. 3, pp. 35–77). Hillsdale, NJ: Erlbaum.

Horn, J. L. (1994). Theory of fluid and crystallized intelligence. In R. J. Sternberg (Ed.), *The encyclopedia of human intelligence* (Vol. 1, pp. 443–451). New York: Macmillan.

Horn, J. L., & Masunaga, H. (2000). New directions for research into aging and intelligence: The development of expertise. In T. J. Perfect & E. A. Maylor (Eds.), *Models of cognitive aging* (pp. 125–159). Oxford, UK: Oxford University Press.

Horn, J. L., & Noll, J. (1994). A system for understanding cognitive capabilities: A theory and the evidence on which it is based. In D. K. Detterman (Ed.), *Current topics in human intelligence, Vol. 4: Theories of intelligence.* Norwood, NJ: Ablex.

Horn, J. L., & Noll, J. (1997). Human cognitive capabilities: Gf-Gc theory. In D. P. Flanagan, J. L. Genshaft, & P. L. Harrison (Eds.), *Contemporary intellectual assessment: Theories, tests and issues* (pp. 53–91). New York: Guilford Press.

Horn, J., & Cattell, R. B. (1966). Refinement and test of the theory of fluid and crystallized general intelligences. *Journal of Educational Psychology, 57,* 253–270.

Howard, R. W. (2001). Searching the real world for signs of rising population intelligence. *Personality & Individual Differences, 30,* 1039–1058.

Hummel, J. E., & Holyoak, K. J. (1997). Distributed representations of structure: A theory of analogical access and mapping. *Psychological Review, 104,* 427–466.

Hunt, E. (2001). Multiple views of multiple intelligence. *Contemporary Psychology, 46,* 5–7.

Hunter, J. E. (1983). A casual analysis of cognitive ability, job knowledge, job performance, and supervisor ratings. In F. Landy, S. Zedeck, & J. Cleveland (Eds.), *Performance measurement and theory* (pp. 257–266). Hillsdale, NJ: Erlbaum.

Inlow, J. K., & Restifo, L. L. (2004). Molecular and comparative genetics of mental retardation. *Genetics, 166,* 835–881.

Ione, A. (2003). Examining Semir Zeki's "Neural concept formation and art: Dante, Michelangelo, Wagner." *Journal of Consciousness Studies, 10,* 58–66.

Jackson, N., & Butterfield, E. (1986). A conception of giftedness designed to promote research. In R. J. Sternberg & J. E. Davidson (Eds.), *Conceptions of giftedness* (pp. 151–181). New York: Cambridge University Press.

Jacobs, N., Van Gestel, S., Derom, C., Thiery, E., Vernon, P., Derom, R., & Vlietinck, R. (2001). Heritability estimates of intelligence in twins: Effect of chorion type. *Behavior Genetics, 31,* 209–217.

Jakobson, R., & Halle, M. (1956). *Fundamentals of language.* The Hague: Mouton.

Jamison, K. R. (1989). Mood disorders and patterns of creativity in British writers and artists. *Psychiatry, 52,* 125–134.

Jamison, K. R., Gerner, R. H., Hammen, C., & Padesky, C. (1980). Clouds and silver linings: Positive experiences associated with primary affective disorders. *American Journal of Psychiatry, 137,* 198–202.

Janowsky, J. S., Oviatt, S. K., & Orwoll, E. S. (1994). Testosterone influences spatial cognition in older men. *Behavioral Neuroscience, 108,* 325–332.

Jeannerod, M., & Frak, V. (1999). Mental imaging of motor activity in humans. *Current Opinion in Neurobiology, 9,* 735–739.

Jensen, A. R. (1980). *Bias in mental testing.* New York: Free Press.

Jensen, A. R. (1998). *The g factor: The science of mental ability.* Westport, CT: Praeger.

Johnson, W., Bouchard, T. J., Jr., Krueger, R. F., McGue, M., & Gottesman, I. I. (2004). Just one *g*: Consistent results from three test batteries. *Intelligence, 32,* 95–107.

Jorm, A. F., Anstey, K. J., Christensen, H., & Rodgers, B. (2004). Gender differences in cognitive abilities: The mediating role of health state and health habits. *Intelligence, 32,* 7–23.

Joseph, D. L., & Newman, D. A. (2010). Emotional intelligence: An integrative meta - analysis and cascading model. *Journal of Applied Psychology, 95,* 54–78.

Kahneman, D. (2003). A perspective on judgment and choice. *American Psychologist, 58,* 697–720.

Kahneman, D., & Tversky, A. (1996). On the reality of cognitive illusions: A reply to Gigerenzer's critique. *Psychological Review, 103,* 582–591.

Keller, J., & Dauenheimer, D. (2003). Stereotype threat in the classroom: Dejection mediates the disrupting threat effect on women's math performance. *Personality & Social Psychology Bulletin, 29,* 371–381.

Kim, K. H. S., Relkin, N. R., Lee, K., & Hirsch, J. (1997). Distinct cortical areas associated with native and second languages. *Nature, 388,* 171–174.

Kimura, D. (1994). Body asymmetry and intellectual pattern. *Personality and Individual Differences, 17,* 53–60.

Kohn, M. L., & Schooler, C. (1973). Occupational experience and psychological functioning: An assessment of reciprocal effects. *American Sociological Review, 38,* 97–118.

Konishi, S., Nakajima, K., Uchida, I., Kikyo, H., Kameyama, M., & Miyashita, Y. (1999). Common inhibitory mechanism in human inferior prefrontal cortex revealed by event-related functional MRI. *Brain, 122,* 981–991.

Kosslyn, S. M. (1975). On retrieving information from visual images. In R. Schank & B. Nash-Webber (Eds.), *Theoretical issues in natural language processing.* Arlington, VA: Association for Computational Linguistics.

Kosslyn, S. M. (1976). Can imagery be distinguished from other forms of internal representation? Evidence from studies of information retrieval times. *Memory and Cognition, 4,* 291–297.

Kosslyn, S. M. (1978). Measuring the visual angle of the mind's eye. *Cognitive Psychology, 10,* 356–389.

Kosslyn, S. M. (1980). *Image and mind.* Cambridge, MA.: Harvard University Press.

Kosslyn, S. M., & Thompson, W. L. (2003). When is early visual cortex activated during visual mental imagery? *Psychological Bulletin, 129,* 723–746.

Kosslyn, S. M., Ganis, G., & Thompson, W. L. (2001). Neural foundations of imagery. *Nature Reviews Neuroscience, 2,* 635 –642.

Kosslyn, S. M., Ganis, G., & Thompson, W. L. (2009). Multimodal images in the brain. In A. Guillot & C. Collet (Eds.), *The neurophysiological foundations of mental and motor imagery* (pp. 3–16). London, UK: Oxford University Press,.

Kosslyn, S. M., Pascual-Leone, A., Felician, O., Camposano, S., Keenan, J. P., Thompson, W. L., et al. (1999). The role of area 17 in visual imagery: Convergent evidence from PET and rTMS. *Science, 284,* 167–170.

Kosslyn, S. M., Segar, C., Pani, J., & Hillger, L. A. (1990). When is imagery used in everyday life? A diary study. *Journal of Mental Imagery. 14,* 131–152.

Kosslyn, S. M., Thompson, W. L, & Ganis, G. (2006). *The case for mental imagery.* New York: Oxford University Press.

Kraepelin, E. (1921). Ueber Entwurtzelung [Depression]. *Zietschrift fuer die Gasamte Neurologie und Psychiatrie, 63,* 1–8.

Kuncel, N. R., Hezlett, S. A., & Ones, D. S. (2004). Academic performance, career potential, creativity, and job performance: Can one construct predict them all? *Journal of Personality and Social Psychology, 86,* 148–161.

Lamm, C., Windischberger, C., Leodolter, U., Moser, E., & Bauer, H. (2001). Evidence for premotor cortex activity during dynamic visuospatial imagery from single-trial functional magnetic resonance imaging and event-related slow cortical potentials. *NeuroImage, 14,* 268–283.

Larson, S. A., Lakin, K. C., Anderson, L., Kwak, N., Lee, J., & Anderson, D. (2001). Prevalence of mental retardation and developmental disabilities: Estimates from the 1994/1995 National Health Interview Survey Disability Supplements. *American Journal on Mental Retardation, 106,* 231–252.

Lee, E. S. (1951). Negro intelligence and selective migration: A Philadelphia test of the Klineberg hypothesis. *American Sociological Review, 16,* 227–233.

Lewontin, R. C. (1976a). Further remarks on race and the genetics of intelligence. In N. J. Block & G. Dworkin (Eds.), *The IQ controversy* (pp. 107–112). New York: Pantheon Books.

Lewontin, R. C. (1976b). Race and intelligence. In N. J. Block & G. Dworkin (Eds.), *The IQ controversy* (pp. 78–92). New York: Pantheon Books.

Liben, L. S., Susman, E. J., Finkelstein, J. W., Chinchilli, V. M., Kunselman, S., Schwab, J., et al. (2002). The effects of sex steroids on spatial performance: A review and an experimental clinical investigation. *Developmental Psychology, 38,* 236–253.

Lindblom, K. (2001). Cooperating with Grice: A cross-disciplinary metaperspective on uses of Grice's cooperative principle. *Journal of Pragmatics, 33,* 1601–1623.

Loehlin, J. C. (1989). Partitioning environmental and genetic contributions to behavioral development. *American Psychologist, 44,* 1285–1292.

Lopes, P. N., Salovey, P., & Straus, R. (2003). Emotional intelligence, personality, and the perceived quality of social relationships. *Personality and Individual Differences, 35,* 641–658.

Lopes, P. N., Salovey, P., Côté, S., & Beers, M. (2005). Emotion regulation abilities and the quality of social interaction. *Emotion, 5,* 113–118.

Lubinski, D. (2000). Scientific and social significance of assessing individual differences: Sinking shafts at a few critical points. *Annual Review of Psychology, 51,* 405–444.

Lubinski, D. (2004). Introduction to the special section on cognitive abilities: 100 years after Spearman's (1904) " 'General intelligence,' objectively determined and measured." *Journal of Personality and Social Psychology, 86,* 96–111.

Lush, J. L. (1937). *Animal breeding plans.* Ames, IA: Collegiate Press.

Lynn, R. (1998). Has the black-white intelligence difference in the United States been narrowing over time? *Personality and Individual Differences, 25,* 999–1002.

Lynn, R., & Irwing, P. (2004). Sex differences on the progressive matrices: A meta-analysis. *Intelligence, 32,* 481–498.

Lytton, H., & Romney, D. M. (1991). Parents' differential socialization of boys and girls: A meta-analysis. *Psychological Bulletin, 109,* 267–296.

Major, B., & O'Brien, L. T. (2005). The social psychology of stigma. *Annual Review of Psychology, 56,* 393–421.

Marinova-Todd, S., Marshall, D., & Snow, C. (2000). Three misconceptions about age and L2 learning. *TESOL Quarterly, 34,* 9–34.

Martindale, C. (1989). Personality, situation, and creativity. In J. A. Glover, R. R. Ronning, & C. R. Reynolds (Eds.), *Handbook of creativity* (pp. 211–228). New York: Plenum.

Martindale, C. (2001). Oscillations and analogies: Thomas Young, M.D., F.R.S., genius. *American Psychologist, 56,* 342–345.

Martínez-Miranda, J., & Aldea, A. (2005). Emotions in human and artificial intelligence. *Computers in Human Behavior, 21,* 323–341.

Marx, D. M., Stapel, D. A., & Muller, D. (2005). We can do it: The interplay of construal orientation and social comparisons under threat. *Journal of Personality & Social Psychology, 88,* 432–446.

Matarazzo, J. D. (1972). *Wechsler's measurement and appraisal of adult intelligence.* Baltimore: Williams & Wilkins.

Matthews, G., Zeidner, M., & Roberts, R. D. (2002). *Emotional intelligence: Science and myth.* Cambridge, MA: MIT Press.

Mayer, D. M., & Hanges, P. J. (2003). Understanding the stereotype threat effect with "culture-free" tests: An examination of its mediators and measurement. *Human Performance, 16,* 207–230.

Mayer, J. D., Caruso, D. R., & Salovey, P. (2000). Emotional intelligence meets traditional standards for an intelligence. *Intelligence, 27,* 267–298.

Mayer, J. D., Salovey, P., & Caruso, D. (2001a). *The Mayer-Salovey-Caruso Emotional Intelligence Test* (MSCEIT). Toronto: Multi-Health Systems.

Mayer, J. D., Salovey, P., Caruso, D. R., & Sitarenios, G. (2001b). Emotional intelligence as a standard intelligence. *Emotion, 1,* 232–242.

Mayer, J. D., Salovey, P., Caruso, D. R., & Sitarenios, G. (2003). Measuring emotional intelligence with the MSCEIT V2.0. *Emotion, 3,* 97–105.

McCartney, K., Harris, M. J., & Bernieri, F. (1990). Growing up and growing apart: A developmental meta-analysis of twin studies. *Psychological Bulletin, 107,* 226–237.

McFarland, L. A., Lev-Arey, D. M., & Ziegert, J. C. (2003). An examination of stereotype threat in a motivational context. *Human Performance, 16,* 181–205.

McGillicuddy-De Lisi, A., & De Lisi, R. (Eds.) (2002). *Biology, society, and behavior: The development of sex differences in cognition.* Westport, CT: Ablex.

McGue, M., Bouchard, T. J., Jr., Iacono, W. G., & Lykken, D. T. (1993). Behavioral genetics of cognitive ability: A life-span perspective. In R. Plomin & G. E. McClearn (Eds.), *Nature, nurture & psychology* (pp. 59–76). Washington, DC: American Psychological Association.

McIntyre, R. B., Paulson, R. M., & Lord, C. G. (2003). Alleviating women's mathematics stereotype threat through salience of group achievements. *Journal of Experimental Social Psychology, 39,* 83–90.

McKay, P. F., Doverspike, D., Bowen-Hilton, D., & Martin, Q. D. (2002). Stereotype threat effects on the Raven Advanced Progressive Matrices scores of African-Americans. *Journal of Applied Social Psychology, 32,* 767–787.

McKellar, P. (1965). The investigation of mental images. In S. A. Bartnet & A. McLaren (Eds.), *Penguin science survey B (biological sciences)* (pp. 79–94). New York: Penguin.

McKelvie, S. J. (2000). Quantifying the availability heuristic with famous names. *North American Journal of Psychology, 2,* 347–356.

Medin, D. L., & Schaffer, M. M. (1978). A context theory of classification learning. *Psychological Review, 85,* 207–238.

Medin, D. L., Lynch, E. B., & Solomon, K. O. (2000). Are there kinds of concepts? *Annual Review of Psychology, 51,* 121–147.

Mednick, S. (1962). The associative basis of the creative process. *Psychological Review, 69,* 220–232.

Mellet, E., Petit, L., Mazoyer, B., Denis, M., & Tzourio, N. (1998). Reopening the mental imagery debate: Lessons from functional neuroanatomy. *NeuroImage, 8,* 129–139.

Milovanov, R., Pietilä, P., Tervaniemi, M., & Esquef, P. A.A. (2010). Foreign language pronunciation skills and musical aptitude: A study of Finnish adults with higher education. *Learning and Individual Differences.*

Mumford, M. D. (2001). Something old, something new: Revisiting Guilford's conception of creative problem solving. *Creativity Research Journal, 13,* 267–276.

Murphy, G. L. (2002). *The big book of concepts.* Cambridge, MA, US: MIT Press. (2002).

Németh T., E., & Bibok, K. (2010). Interaction between grammar and pragmatics: The case of implicit arguments, implicit predicates and co-composition in Hungarian. *Journal of Pragmatics,* 42, 501–524.

Neisser, U., Boodoo, G., Bouchard, T. J., Jr., Boykin, A. W., Brody, N., Ceci, S. J., et al. (1996). Intelligence: Knowns and unknowns. *American Psychologist, 51,* 77–101.

Newsome, G. L., III. (2000). A review of some promising approaches to understanding and improving thinking skills. *Journal of Research & Development in Education, 33,* 199–222.

Nichols, R. C. (1978). Twin studies of ability, personality, and interests. *Homo, 29,* 158–173.

Nisbett, R. E. (1996). Race, genetics, and IQ. In C. Jencks & M. Phillips (Eds.), *The black-white test score gap* (pp. 86–102). Washington, DC: Brookings Institution.

O'Brien, L. T., & Crandall, C. S. (2003). Stereotype threat and arousal: Effects on women's math performance. *Personality & Social Psychology Bulletin, 29,* 782–789.

O'Grady, W., & Lee, M. (2005). A mapping theory of agrammatic comprehension deficits. *Brain & Language, 92,* 91–100.

Ostatnikova, D., Laznibatova, J., Putz, Z., Mataseje, A., Dohnanyiova, M., & Pastor, K. (2000). Salivary testosterone levels in intellectually gifted and non-intellectually gifted preadolescents: An exploratory study. *High Ability Studies, 11,* 41–54.

Ostatnikova, D., Laznibatova, J., Putz, Z., Mataseje, A., Dohnanyiova, M., & Pastor, K. (2002). Biological aspects of intellectual giftedness. *Studia Psychologica, 44,* 3–13.

Petrides, K. V., & Furnham, A. (2000). Gender differences in measured and self-estimated trait emotional intelligence. *Sex Roles, 42,* 449–461.

Petrill, S. A., Plomin, R., McClearn, G. E., Smith, D. L., Vignetti, S., Chorney, M. J., et al. (1997). No association between general cognitive ability and the A1 allele of the D2 dopamine receptor gene. *Behavior Genetics, 27,* 29–31.

Phelps, J. A., Davis, J. O., & Schartz, K. M. (1997). Nature, nurture, and twin research strategies. *Current Directions in Psychological Science, 6,* 117–121.

Pinker, S. (1994). *The language instinct: How the mind creates language.* New York: Morrow.

Pinker, S., & Jackendoff, R. (2005). The faculty of language: What's special about it? *Cognition, 95,* 201–236.

Plomin, R. (1988). The nature and nurture of cognitive abilities. In R. J. Sternberg (Ed.), *Advances in the psychology of human intelligence* (Vol. 4, pp. 1–33). Hillsdale, NJ: Erlbaum.

Plomin, R. (1990). *Nature and nurture: An introduction to human behavioral genetics.* Pacific Grove, CA: Brooks/Cole.

Plomin, R., & Spinath, F. M. (2004). Intelligence: Genetics, genes and genomics. *Journal of Personality and Social Psychology, 86,* 112–129.

Plomin, R., Fulker, D. W., Corley, R., & DeFries, J. C. (1997). Nature, nurture, and cognitive development from 1 to 16 years: A parent-offspring adoption study. *Psychological Science, 8,* 442–447.

Ployhart, R. E., Ziegert, J. C., & McFarland, L. A. (2003). Understanding racial differences on cognitive ability tests in selection contexts: An integration of stereotype threat and applicant reactions research. *Human Performance, 16,* 231–259.

Prasada, S. (2000). Acquiring generic knowledge. *Trends in Cognitive Science, 4,* 66–72.

Qin, S., Hermans, E. J., van Marle, H. J., Luo, J., & Fernández, G. (2009). Acute psychological stress reduces working memory-related activity in the dorsolateral prefrontal cortex. *Biological Psychiatry, 66,* 25–32.

Redelmeier D.A., Katz, J., & Kahneman, D. (2003). Memories of colonoscopy: A randomized trial. *Pain, 104* , 187–194.

Redelmeier, D. A., & Kahneman, D. (1996). Patients' memories of painful medical treatments: Real-time and retrospective evaluations of two minimally invasive procedures. *Pain, 66,* 3–8.

Reese, H. W., Lee, L. J., Cohen, S. H., & Puckett, J. M., Jr. (2001). Effects of intellectual variables, age, and gender on divergent thinking in adulthood. *International Journal of Behavioral Development, 25,* 491–500.

Reinisch, J. M., & Sanders, S. A. (1992). Prenatal hormonal contributions to sex differences in human cognitive and personality development. In A. A. Gerall, H. Moltz, & I. I. Ward (Eds.), *Sexual differentiation: Vol. II. Handbook of behavioral neurobiology* (pp. 221–243). New York: Plenum.

Richert, E. S. (1997). Excellence with equity in identification and programming. In N. Colangelo & G. A. Davis (Eds.), *Handbook of gifted education* (2nd ed., pp. 75–88). Boston: Allyn & Bacon.

Rinaldi, M. C., Marangolo, P., & Baldassarri, F. (2004). Metaphor comprehension in right brain-damaged patients with visuo-verbal and verbal material: A dissociation (re)considered. *Cortex, 40,* 479–490.

Rips, L. (2001). Necessity and natural categories. *Psychological Bulletin, 127,* 827–852.

Rips, L. J., Shoben, E. J., & Smith, E. E. (1973). Semantic distance and the verification of semantic relations. *Journal of Verbal Learning and Verbal Behavior, 12,* 1–20.

Roberson, D., Davidoff, J., Davies, I. R. L., & Shapiro, L. R. (2004). The development of color categories in two languages: A longitudinal study. *Journal of Experimental Psychology: General, 133,* 554–571.

Roberts, B. W., Caspi, A., & Moffitt, T. E. (2001). The kids are alright: Growth and stability in personality development from adolescence to adulthood. *Journal of Personality & Social Psychology, 81,* 670–683.

Robinson, N. M., Abbott, R. D., Berninger, V. W., & Busse, J. (1996). The structure of abilities in math-precocious young children: Gender similarities and differences. *Journal of Educational Psychology, 88,* 341–352.

Robinson, N. M., Zigler, Z., & Gallagher, J. J. (2000). Two tails of the normal curve: Similarities and differences in the study of mental retardation and giftedness. *American Psychologist, 55,* 1413–1424.

Rosch, E. (1973). Natural categories. *Cognitive Psychology, 4,* 328–350.

Rosch, E. (1975). The nature of mental codes for color categories. *Journal of Experimental Psychology: Human Perception and Performance, 1,* 303–322.

Rosch, E. (1978). Principles of categorization. In E. Rosch, & B. B. Lloyd (Eds.), *Cognition and categorization* (pp. 27–48). Hillsdale, NJ: Erlbaum.

Rosch, E., Mervis, C. B., Gray, W. D., Johnson, D. M., & Boyes-Braem, P. (1976). Basic objects in natural categories. *Cognitive Psychology, 8,* 382–439.

Runco, M. A., & Albert, R. S. (1986). The threshold theory regarding creativity and intelligence: An empirical test with gifted and nongifted children. *Creative Child & Adult Quarterly, 11,* 212–218.

Rushton, J. P. (1995). *Race, evolution and behavior: A life-history perspective.* New Brunswick, NJ: Transaction.

Ryan, K. E., & Ryan, A. M. (2005). Psychological processes underlying stereotype threat and standardized math test performance. *Educational Psychologist, 40,* 53–63.

Sackett, P. R., Schmitt, N., Ellingson, J. E., & Kabin, M. B. (2001). High-stakes testing in employment, credentialing, and higher education: Prospects in a post-affirmative-action world. *American Psychologist, 56,* 302–318.

Salovey, P., & Mayer, J. D. (1990). Emotional intelligence. *Imagination, Cognition, and Personality, 9,* 185–211.

Salthouse, T. A. (1996). The processing-speed theory of adult age differences in cognition. *Psychological Review, 103,* 403–428.

Scarr, S., & Weinberg, R. A. (1983). The Minnesota Adoption Studies: Genetic differences and malleability. *Child Development, 54,* 260–267.

Schmader, T. (2002). Gender identification moderates stereotype threat effects on women's math performance. *Journal of Experimental Social Psychology, 38,* 194–201.

Schmader, T., & Johns, M. (2003). Converging evidence that stereotype threat reduces working memory capacity. *Journal of Personality & Social Psychology, 85,* 440–452.

Schmidt, F. L., & Hunter, J. (2004). General mental ability in the world of work: Occupational attainment and job performance. *Journal of Personality and Social Psychology, 86,* 162–173.

Serpell, R. (1979). How specific are perceptual skills? A cross-cultural study of pattern reproduction. *British Journal of Psychology, 70,* 365–380.

Shaywitz, B. A., Shaywitz, S. E., Pugh, K. R., Constable, R. T., Skudlarski, P., Fulbright, R. K., et al. (1995). Sex differences in the functional organization of the brain for language. *Nature, 373,* 607–611.

Shepard, R. N., & Cooper, L. A. (1982). *Mental images and their transformations.* Cambridge, MA: MIT Press/Bradford Books.

Silverman, L. K. (1993a). Counseling families. In L. K. Silverman (Ed.), *Counseling the gifted and talented* (pp. 43–89). Denver: Love.

Silverman, L. K. (1993b). A developmental model for counseling the gifted. In L. K. Silverman (Ed.), *Counseling the gifted and talented* (pp. 51–78). Denver, CO: Love.

Simonton, D. K. (1984). *Genius, creativity, and leadership: Historiometric inquiries.* Cambridge, MA: Harvard University Press.

Simonton, D. K. (1988). Creativity, leadership, and chance. In R. J. Sternberg (Ed.), *The nature of creativity* (pp. 386–436). New York: Cambridge University Press.

Simonton, D. K. (1994). *Greatness: Who makes history and why.* New York: Guilford.

Simonton, D. K. (1997). Creative productivity: A predictive and explanatory model of career trajectories and landmarks. *Psychological Review, 104,* 66–89.

Smith, E. E., & Medin, D. L. (1981). *Categories and concepts.* Cambridge, MA: Harvard University Press.

Smith, E. E., Patalano, A. L., & Jonides, J. (1998). Alternative strategies of categorization. *Cognition, 65,* 167–196.

Smith, J. L., & White, P. H. (2002). An examination of implicitly activated, explicitly activated, and nullified stereotypes on mathematical performance: It's not just a woman's issue. *Sex Roles, 47,* 179–191.

Smith, S. M., & Blankenship, S. E. (1989). Incubation effects. *Bulletin of the Psychonomic Society, 27,* 311–314.

Smith, S. M., & Blankenship, S. E. (1991). Incubation and the persistence of fixation in problem solving. *American Journal of Psychology, 104,* 61–87.

Snow, C. E. (2002). Second language learners' contributions to our understanding of languages of the brain. In A. M. Galaburda, S. M. Kosslyn, & Y. Christen (Eds.), *Languages of the brain* (pp. 151–165) Cambridge, MA: Harvard University Press.

Snow, R. E. (1994). A person-situation interaction theory of intelligence in outline. In A. Demetriou & A. Efklides (Eds.), *Intelligence, mind, and reasoning: Structure and development* (pp. 11–28). Amsterdam: Elsevier.

Snow, R. E. (1996). Aptitude development and education. *Psychology, Public Policy, and Law, 3/4,* 536–560.

Spearman, C. (1927). *The abilities of man.* New York: Macmillan.

Steele, C. M. (1997). A threat in the air: How stereotypes shape intellectual identity and performance. *American Psychologist, 52,* 613–629.

Steele, C. M., & Aronson, J. (1995). Stereotype threat and the intellectual test performance of African Americans. *Journal of Personality & Social Psychology, 69,* 797–811.

Sternberg, R. J. (1985). *Beyond IQ: A triarchic theory of human intelligence.* Cambridge, England: Cambridge University Press.

Sternberg, R. J. (1985). *Beyond IQ: A Triarchic Theory of Intelligence.* Cambridge: Cambridge University Press.

Sternberg, R. J. (1986b). *What is intelligence?* Norwood, NJ: Ablex.

Sternberg, R. J. (1988b). *The triarchic mind: A new theory of human intelligence.* New York: Viking.

Sternberg, R. J. (1990). *Metaphors of mind: Conceptions of the nature of intelligence.* New York: Cambridge University Press.

Sternberg, R. J. (2003a). Issues in the theory and measurement of successful intelligence: A reply to Brody. *Intelligence, 31,* 331–337.

Sternberg, R. J. (2003b). Our research program validating the triarchic theory of successful intelligence: Reply to Gottfredson. *Intelligence, 31,* 399–413.

Sternberg, R. J. (2009). The theory of successful intelligence as a basis for new forms of ability testing at the high school, college, and graduate school levels. In J. C. Kaufman (Ed), *Intelligent testing: Integrating psychological theory and clinical practice.* (pp. 113-147). New York, NY, US: Cambridge University Press.

Sternberg, R. J., & Detterman, D. K. (Eds.) (1986). *What is intelligence? Contemporary viewpoints on its nature and definition.* Norwood, NJ: Ablex.

Sternberg, R. J., & Wagner, R. K. (1993). The g-ocentric view of intelligence and job performance is wrong. *Current Directions in Psychological Science, 2,* 1–5.

Sternberg, R. J., Nokes, C., Geissler, P. W., Prince, R., Okatcha, F., Bundy, D. A., & Grigorenko, E. L. (2001). The relationship between academic and practical intelligence: A case study in Kenya. *Intelligence, 29,* 1–18.

Sternberg, R. J., Wagner, R. K., & Okagaki, L. (1993). Practical intelligence: The nature and role of tacit knowledge in work. In J. M. Puckett, H. W. Reese, et al. (Eds.), *Mechanisms of everyday cognition.* Hillsdale, NJ: Erlbaum.

Stevenson, H., Lee, S., & Stigler, J. (1986). Mathematics achievement of Chinese, Japanese, and American children. *Science, 231,* 693–699.

Stone, J. (2002). Battling doubt by avoiding practice: The effects of stereotype threat on self-handicapping in white athletes. *Personality & Social Psychology Bulletin, 28,* 1667–1678.

Stoolmiller, M. (1999). Implications of the restricted range of family environments for estimates of heritability and nonshared environment in behavior-genetic adoption studies. *Psychological Bulletin, 125,* 392–409.

Streissguth, A. P., Barr, H. M., Bookstein, F. L., Sampson, P. D., & Olson, H. C. (1999). The long-term neurocognitive consequences of prenatal alcohol exposure: A 14-year study. *Psychological Science, 10,* 186–190.

Streissguth, A. P., Barr, H. M., Sampson, P. D., Darby, B. L., & Martin, D. C. (1989). IQ at age 4 in relation to maternal alcohol use and smoking during pregnancy. *Developmental Psychology, 25,* 3–11.

Streufert, S., & Swezey, R. W. (1986). *Complexity, managers, and organizations.* Orlando, FL: Academic Press.

Stricker, L. J., & Ward, W. C. (2004). Stereotype threat, inquiring about test takers' ethnicity and gender, and standardized test performance. *Journal of Applied Social Psychology, 34,* 665–693.

Subrahmanyam, K., & Greenfield, P. M. (1994). Effect of video game practice on spatial skills in girls and boys. *Journal of Applied Developmental Psychology, 15* (special issue), 13–32.

Sulloway, F. J. (1996). *Born to rebel: Birth order, family dynamics, and creative lives.* New York: Vintage.

Suzuki, L. A., & Valencia, R. R. (1997). Race-ethnicity and measured intelligence: Educational implications. *American Psychologist, 52,* 1103–1114.

Tan, H., Zhong, P., & Yan, Z. (2004). Corticotropin-releasing factor and acute stress prolongs serotonergic regulation of GABA transmission in prefrontal cortical pyramidal neurons. *Journal of Neuroscience, 24,* 5000–5008.

Teigen, K. H. (1994). Variants of subjective probabilities: Concepts, norms, and biases. In G. Wright & P. Ayton (Eds.), *Subjective probability.* New York: Wiley.

Thompson, J. K., & Stice, E. (2001). Thin-ideal internalization: Mounting evidence for a new risk factor for body-image disturbance and eating pathology. *Current Directions in Psychological Science, 10,* 181–183.

Thompson, W. L. and Kosslyn, S. M. (2000). Neural systems activated during visual mental imagery: A review and meta-analyses. In: A. W. Toga and J. C. Mazziotta (Eds.), *Brain Mapping: The Systems.* Academic Press, San Diego. pp. 535-560.

Thurstone, L. L. (1938). *Primary mental abilities.* Chicago: University of Chicago Press.

Thurstone, L. L., & Thurstone, T. G. (1941). *Factorial studies of intelligence.* Chicago: University of Chicago Press.

Tsai, S. J., Hong, C. H., Yu, W. Y. Y., & Chen, T. J. (2004). Association study of a brain-derived neurotrophic factor (BDNF) Val66Met polymorphism and personality trait and intelligence in healthy young females. *Neuropsychobiology, 49,* 13–16.

Tsai, S. J., Yu, Y. W. Y., Lin, C. H., Chen, T. J., Chen, S. P., & Hong, C. J. (2002). Dopamine D2 receptor and N-methyl-D-aspartate receptor 2B subunit genetic variants and intelligence. *Neuropsychobiology, 45,* 128–130.

Turkheimer, E., Haley, A., Waldron, M., D'Onofrio, B., & Gottesman, I. I. (2003). Socioeconomic status modifies heritability of IQ in young children. *Psychological Science, 14,* 623–628.

Tversky, A., & Kahneman, D. (1974). Judgment under uncertainty: Heuristics and biases. *Science, 185,* 1124–1131.

Ullman, M. T. (2001). The neural basis of lexicon and grammar in first and second language: The declarative/procedural model. *Bilingualism: Language & Cognition, 4,* 105–122.

Van Goozen, S. H. M, Cohen-Kettenis, P. T., Gooren, J. J. G., Frijda, N. H., & Van De Poll, N. E. (1995). Gender differences in behaviour: Activating effects of cross-sex hormones. *Psychoneuroendocrinology, 20,* 343–363.

Van Rooy, D. L., Alonso, A., & Viswesvaran, C. (2005a). Group differences in emotional intelligence scores: theoretical and practical implications. *Personality and Individual Differences, 38,* 689–700.

Van Rooy, D. L., Viswesvaran, C., & Pluta, P. (2005b). A meta-analytic evaluation of construct validity: What is this thing called emotional intelligence? *Human Performance, 18,* 445–462.

Vogel, G. (1996). School achievement: Asia and Europe top in the world, but reasons are hard to find. *Science, 274,* 1296.

Vranas, P. B. M. (2000). Gigerenzer's normative critique of Kahneman and Tversky. *Cognition, 76,* 179–193.

Walters, J., & Gardner, H. (1985). The development and education of intelligences. In F. Link (Ed.), *Essays on the intellect* (pp. 1–21). Washington, DC: Curriculum Development Association/Association for Supervision and Curriculum Development.

Wason, P. C., & Johnson-Laird, P. N. (1972). *Psychology of reasoning: Structure and content.* Cambridge, MA: Harvard University Press.

Watson, J. B. (1913). Psychology as a behaviorist views it. *Psychological Review, 20,* 158–177.

Wechsler, D. (1958). *The measurement and appraisal of adult intelligence* (5th ed.). Baltimore: Williams & Wilkins.

Whorf, B. (1956). *Language, thought, and reality.* Cambridge, MA: MIT Press.

Wicherts, J. M., Borsboom, D., & Dolan, C. V. (2009). Why national IQs do not support evolutionary theories of intelligence. *Personality and Individual Differences, 47,* 535-540.

Wigfield, A., Battle, A., Keller, L. B., & Eccles, J. S. (2002). Sex differences in motivation, self-concept, career aspiration, and career choice: Implications for cognitive development. (pp. 93–124) In A. McGillicuddy-De Lisi & R. De Lisi (Eds.), *Biology, society, and behavior: The development of sex differences in cognition.* Westport, CT: Ablex.

Winner, E. (1996). *Gifted children: Myths and realities.* New York: Basic Books.

Winner, E. (1997). Exceptionally high intelligence and schooling. *American Psychologist, 52,* 1070–1081.

Winner, E. (2000a). Giftedness: Current theory and research. *Current Directions in Psychological Science, 9,* 153–156.

Winner, E. (2000b). The origins and ends of giftedness. *American Psychologist, 55,* 159–169.

Wolf, O. T., Preut, R., Hellhammer, D. H., Kudielka, B. M., Schuermeyer, T. H., & Kirschbaum, C. (2000). Testosterone and cognition in elderly men: A single testosterone injection blocks the practice effect in verbal fluency, but has no effect on spatial or verbal memory. *Biological Psychiatry, 47,* 650–654.

Wraga, M. J., Thompson, W. L., Alpert, N. M., & Kosslyn, S. M. (2003). Implicit transfer of motor strategies in mental rotation. *Brain and Cognition, 52,* 135–143.

Zeki, S. (2002). Neural concept formation and art: Dante, Michelangelo, Wagner. *Journal of Consciousness Studies, 9,* 53–76.

References: Emotion and Motivation

Aalto, S., Naatanen, P., Wallius, E., Metsahonkala, L., Stenman, H., Niem, P. M., et al. (2002). Neuroanatomical substrata of amusement and sadness: A PET activation study using film stimuli. *Neuroreport: For Rapid Communication of Neuroscience Research, 13,* 67–73.

Adolphs, R. (2002). Neural systems for recognizing emotion. *Current Opinion in Neurobiology, 12,* 169–177.

Allen, J. J. B., & Iacono, W. G. (1997). A comparison of methods for the analysis of event-related potentials in deception detection. *Psychophysiology, 34,* 234–240.

Allen, L. S., & Gorski, R. A. (1992). Sexual orientation and the size of the anterior commissure in the human brain. *Proceedings of the National Academy of Sciences of the United States of America, 89,* 7199–7202.

Anderson, A. K., & Phelps, E. A. (2002). Is the human amygdala critical for the subjective experience of emotion? Evidence of intact dispositional affect in patients with amygdala lesions. *Journal of Cognitive Neuroscience, 14,* 709–720.

Andrews, H. B., & Jones, S. (1990). Eating behaviour in obese women: A test of two hypotheses. *Australian Psychologist, 25,* 351–357.

Anonymous. (1970). Effects of sexual activity on beard growth in man. *Nature, 226,* 867–870.

Argyle, M. L., & Lu, L. (1990). Happiness and social skills. *Personality and Individual Differences, 11,* 1255–1261.

Bailey, J. M., & Pillard, R. C. (1991). A genetic study of male sexual orientation. *Archives of General Psychiatry, 48,* 1089–1096.

Barrett, L. F. (2006). Solving the emotion paradox: Categorization and the experience of emotion. *Personality and Social Psychology Review, 10,* 20–46.

Barrett, L. F., Ochsner, K. N., & Gross, J. J. (2007). On the automaticity of emotion. In J. Bargh (Ed.), *Social psychology and the unconscious: The automaticity of higher mental processes. Frontiers of social psychology* (pp. 173–217). New York: Psychology Press.

Basson, R. (2001). Using a different model for female sexual response to address women's problematic low sexual desire. *Journal of Sex and Marital Therapy, 27,* 395–403.

Batsell, W. R., Jr., & Brown, A. S. (1998). Human flavor-aversion learning: A comparison of traditional aversions and cognitive aversions. *Learning and Motivation, 29,* 383–396.

Baumeister, R. F., & Boden, J. M. (1998). Aggression and the self: High self-esteem, low self-control, and ego threat. In R. G. Geen & E. Donnerstein (Eds.), *Human aggression: Theories, research, and implications for social policy* (pp. 111–137). San Diego, CA: Academic Press.

Baxter, M. G., Parker, A., Lindner, C. C. C., Izquierdo, A. D., & Murray, E. A. (2000). Control of response selection by reinforcer value requires interaction of amygdala and orbital prefrontal cortex. *Journal of Neuroscience, 20,* 4311–4319.

Beauregard, M., Levesque, J., & Bourgouin, P. (2001). Neural correlates of conscious self-regulation of emotion. *Journal of Neuroscience, 21,* 6993–7000.

Bechara, A. & Van der Kooy, D. (1992). A single brain stem substrate mediates the motivational effects of both opiates and food in nondeprived rats but not in deprived rats. *Behavioral Neuroscience, 106,* 351–363.

Ben-Shakhar, G., & Furedy, J. J. (1990). *Theories and applications in the detection of deception: A psychophysiological and international perspective.* New York: Springer-Verlag.

Berlyne, D. E. (1960). *Conflict, arousal, and curiosity.* New York: McGraw-Hill.

Berlyne, D. E. (Ed.). (1974). *Studies in the new experimental aesthetics: Steps toward an objective psychology of aesthetic appreciation.* Washington, DC: Hemisphere.

Bermond, B. N., Fasotti, L., & Schuerman, J. (1991). Spinal cord lesions, peripheral feedback, and intensities of emotional feelings. *Cognition and Emotion, 5,* 201–220.

Berridge, K. C. (1996). Food reward: Brain substrates of wanting and liking. *Neuroscience and Biobehavioral Reviews, 20,* 1–20.

Berthoud, H. R. (2002). Multiple neural systems controlling food intake and body weight. *Neuroscience and Biobehavioral Reviews, 26,* 393–428.

Biswas-Diener, R., Diener, E., & Tamir, M. (2004). The psychology of subjective well-being. *Daedalus, 133,* 18–24.

Blanchard, R. (2001). Fraternal birth order and the maternal immune hypothesis of male homosexuality. *Hormones and Behavior, 40,* 105–114.

Blouet, C., & Schwartz, G. J. (2010). Hypothalamic nutrient sensing in the control of energy homeostasis. *Behavioural Brain Research, 209,* 1–12.

Blundell, J. E. (1977). Is there a role for 5-hydroxytryptamine in feeding? *International Journal of Obesity, 1,* 15–42.

Blundell, J. E. (1984). Serotonin and appetite. *Neuropharmacology, 23,* 1537–1551.

Blundell, J. E. (1986). Serotonin manipulations and the structure of feeding behaviour. *Appetite, 7,* 39–56.

Blundell, J. E., & Halford, J. C. G. (1998). Serotonin and appetite regulation: Implications for the pharmacological treatment of obesity. *CNS Drugs, 9,* 473–495.

Bogaert, A. F. (1996). Volunteer bias in human sexuality research: Evidence for both sexuality and personality differences in males. *Archives of Sexual Behavior, 25,* 125–140.

Bonanno, G. A. (2004). Loss, trauma, and human resilience: Have we underestimated the human capacity to thrive after extremely aversive events? *American Psychologist, 59,* 20–28.

Bonanno, G. A. (2005). Clarifying and extending the construct of adult resilience. *American Psychologist, 60,* 265–267.

Bonanno, G. A., Papa, A., Lalande, K., Westphal, M., & Coifman, K. (2004). The importance of being flexible: The ability to both enhance and suppress emotional expression predicts long-term adjustment. *Psychological Science, 15,* 482–487.

Bradburn, N. M. (1969). *The structure of psychological well-being.* Chicago: Aldine.

Bradley, M. T., MacLaren, V. V., & Carle, S. B. (1996). Deception and nondeception in Guilty Knowledge and Guilty Actions Polygraph Tests. *Journal of Applied Psychology, 81,* 153–160.

Bradley, M. T., & Warfield, J. F. (1984). Innocence, information, and the Guilty Knowledge Test in the detection of deception. *Psychophysiology, 21,* 683–689.

Brickman, P., & Campbell, D. T. (1971). Hedonic relativism and the good society. In M. H. Appley (Ed.), *Adaptation-level theory: A symposium* (pp. 215–231). New York: Academic Press.

Brown, R. (1989). Roger Brown. In G. Lindzey (Ed.), *A history of psychology in autobiography* (Vol. 8, pp. 37–60). Stanford, CA: Stanford University Press.

Burton, M. J., Rolls, E. T., & Mora, F. (1976). Effects of hunger on the responses of neurons in the lateral hypothalamus to the sight and taste of food. *Experimental Neurology, 51,* 668–677.

Buss, D. M., Larsen, R. J., Western, D., & Semmelroth, J. (1992). Sex differences in jealousy: Evolution, physiology, and psychology. *Psychological Science, 3,* 251–255.

Butler, E. A., Egloff, B., Wilhelm, F. H., Smith, N. C., Erickson, E. A., & Gross, J. J. (2003). The social consequences of expressive suppression. *Emotion, 3,* 48–67.

Cacioppo, J. T., Berntson, G. G., Larsen, J. T., Poehlmann, K. M., & Ito, T. A. (2000). The psychophysiology of emotion. In R. Lewis & J. M. Haviland-Jones (Eds.), *The handbook of emotion* (2nd ed., pp. 173–191). New York: Guilford Press.

Cacioppo, J. T., Gardner, J. T., & Berntson, W. L. (1997). Beyond bipolar conceptualizations and measures: The case of attitudes and evaluative space. *Personality and Social Psychology Review, 1,* 3–25.

Cannon, W. B. (1927). The James-Lange theory of emotions: A critical examination and an alternative theory. *American Journal of Psychology, 39,* 106–124.

Cannon, W. B. (1932). *The wisdom of the body.* New York: Norton.

Cantor, J. M., Blanchard, R., Paterson, A. D., & Bogaert, A. F. (2002). How many gay men owe their sexual orientation to fraternal birth order? *Archives of Sexual Behavior, 31,* 63–71.

Carter, C. S. (2004). Oxytocin and the prairie vole: A love story. In J. T. Cacioppo & G. G. Berntson (Eds.), *Essays in social neuroscience* (pp. 53–63). Cambridge, MA: MIT Press.

Centers for Disease Control and Prevention. (2004). *Health, United States, 2004: With chartbook on trends in the health of Americans.* Washington, DC: U.S. Department of Health and Human Services.

Cook, E. W., III, Hawk, L. W., Davis, T. L., Stevenson, V. E. (1991). Affective individual differences and startle reflex modulation. *Journal of Abnormal Psychology, 100,* 5–13.

Cooper, M. L., Shapiro, C. M., & Powers, A. M. (1998). Motivations for sex and risky sexual behavior among adolescents and young adults: A functional perspective. *Journal of Personality and Social Psychology, 75,* 1528–1558.

Cosmides, L., & Tooby, J. (1996). Are humans good intuitive statisticians after all? Rethinking some conclusions from the literature on judgment under uncertainty. *Cognition, 58,* 1–73.

Cramer, R. E., Abraham, W. T., Johnson, L. M., & Manning-Ryan, B. (2001–2002). Gender differences in subjective distress to emotional and sexual infidelity: Evolutionary or logical inference explanation? *Current Psychology: Developmental, Learning, Personality, Social, 20,* 327–336.

Crawford Solberg, E., Diener, E., Wirtz, D., Lucas, R. E., & Oishi, S. (2002). Wanting, having, and satisfaction: Examining the role of desire discrepancies in satisfaction with income. *Journal of Personality and Social Psychology, 83,* 725–734.

Craig, A. D. (2004). Human feelings: Why are some more aware than others? *Trends in Cognitive Sciences, 8,* 239–241.

Dansinger, M. L., Gleason, J. A., Griffith, J. L., Selker, H. P., & Schaefer, E. J. (2005). Comparison of the Atkins, Ornish, Weight Watchers, and Zone diets for weight loss and heart disease risk reduction: A randomized trial. *Journal of the American Medical Association, 293,* 43–53.

Darwin, C. (1872/1965). *The expression of the emotions in man and animals.* Chicago: University of Chicago Press.

Davidson, R. J. (1992a). Emotion and affective style: Hemispheric substrates. *Psychological Science, 3,* 39–43.

Davidson, R. J. (1992b). A prolegomenon to the structure of emotion: Gleanings from neuropsychology. *Cognition and Emotion, 6,* 245–268.

Davidson, R. J. (1993). Parsing affective space: Perspectives from neuropsychology and psychophysiology. *Neuropsychology, 7,* 464–475.

Davidson, R. J. (1994). Honoring biology in the study of affective style. In P. Ekman & R. J. Davidson (Eds.), *The nature of emotion: Fundamental questions* (pp. 321–328). New York: Oxford University Press.

Davidson, R. J. (1998). Affective style and affective disorders: Perspectives from affective neuroscience. *Cognition and Emotion, 12,* 307–330.

Davidson, R. J. (2002). Anxiety and affective style: Role of prefrontal cortex and amygdala. *Biological Psychiatry, 51,* 68–80.

Davidson, R. J., Abercrombie, H., Nitschke, J. B., & Putnam, K. (1999). Regional brain function, emotion and disorders of emotion. *Current Opinion in Neurobiology, 9,* 228–234.

Davidson, R. J., Jackson, D. C., & Kalin, N. H. (2000a). Emotion, plasticity, context, and regulation: Perspectives from affective neuroscience. *Psychological Bulletin, 126,* 890–909.

Davidson, R. J., Putnam, K. M., & Larson, C. L. (2000b). Dysfunction in the neural circuitry of emotion regulation—A possible prelude to violence. *Science, 289,* 591–594.

Davis, J. D., & Campbell, C. S. (1973). Peripheral control of meal size in the rat: Effects of sham feeding on meal size and drinking rate. *Journal of Comparative and Physiological Psychology, 83,* 379–387.

Davis, J. D., & Levine, M. W. (1977). A model for the control of ingestion. *Psychological Review, 84,* 379–412.

Davis, M. (1992). The role of the amygdala in conditioned fear. In J. P. Aggleton (Ed.), *The amygdala: Neurobiological aspects of emotion, memory, and mental dysfunction* (pp. 255–306). New York: Wiley-Liss.

Davis, M., & Whalen, P. J. (2001). The amygdala: Vigilance and emotion. *Molecular Psychiatry, 6,* 13–34.

De Castro, J. M. (1990). Social facilitation of duration and size but not rate of the spontaneous meal intake of humans. *Physiology and Behavior, 47,* 1129–1135.

DeClue, G. (2003). The polygraph and lie detection. *Journal of Psychiatry and Law, 31,* 361–368.

DePaulo, B. M., Charlton, K., Cooper, H., Lindsay, J. J., & Muhlenbruck, L. (1997). The accuracy-confidence correlation in the detection of deception. *Personality and Social Psychology Review, 1,* 346–357.

DePaulo, B. M., Lindsay, J. J., Malone, B. E., Muhlenbruck, L., Charlton, K., & Cooper, H. (2003). Cues to deception. *Psychological Bulletin, 129,* 74–118.

Deutsch, J. A., Young, W. G., & Kalogeris, T. J. (1978). The stomach signals satiety. *Science, 201,* 165–167.

DiBlasio, F. A., & Benda, B. B. (1990). Adolescent sexual behavior: Multivariate analysis of a social learning model. *Journal of Adolescent Research, 5,* 449–466.

Diefendorff, J. M., & Greguras, G. J. (2009). Contextualizing emotional display rules: Examining the roles of targets and discrete emotions in shaping display rule perceptions. *Journal of Management, 35,* 880–898.

Diener, E. (2000). Subjective well-being: The science of happiness and a proposal for a national index. *American Psychologist, 55,* 34–43.

Diener, E., & Biswas-Diener, R. (2002). Will money increase subjective well-being? *Social Indicators Research, 57,* 119–169.

Diener, E., & Emmons, R. A. (1984). The independence of positive and negative affect. *Journal of Personality and Social Psychology, 47,* 1105–1117.

Dimberg, J., Thunberg, M., & Elmehed, K. (2000). Unconscious facial reactions to emotional facial expressions. *Psychological Science, 11,* 86–89.

Dittrich, W. H., Troscianko, T., Lea, S., & Morgan, D. (1996). Perception of emotion from dynamic point-light displays represented in dance. *Perception, 25,* 727–738.

Duclaux, R., Feisthauer, J., & Cabanac, M. (1973). The effects of eating on the pleasantness of food and non-food odors in man. *Physiology and Behavior, 10,* 1029–1033.

Duclos, S. E., Laird, J. D., Schneider, E., Sexter, M., Stern, L., & Van Lighten, O. (1989). Emotion-specific effects of facial expressions and postures on emotional experience. *Journal of Personality and Social Psychology, 57,* 100–108.

Ekman, P. (1980). Biological and cultural contributions to body and facial movement in the expression of emotion. In A. O. Rorty (Ed.), *Explaining emotions.* Berkeley: University of California Press.

Ekman, P. (1984). Expression and the nature of emotion. In K. R. Scherer & P. Ekman (Eds.), *Approaches to emotion* (pp. 319–343). Hillsdale, NJ: Erlbaum.

Ekman, P. (1985). *Telling lies: Clues to deceit in the marketplace, marriage, and politics.* New York: Norton.

Ekman, P. (1992). Facial expressions of emotion: New findings, new questions. *Psychological Science, 3,* 34–38.

Ekman, P., & Davidson, R. J. (1993). Voluntary smiling changes regional brain activity. *Psychological Science, 4,* 342–345.

Ekman, P., Davidson, R. J., & Friesen, W. V. (1990). The Duchenne smile: Emotional expression and brain psychology II. *Journal of Personality and Social Psychology, 58,* 342–353.

Ekman, P., & Friesen, W. (1971). Constants across cultures in the face and emotion. *Journal of Personality and Social Psychology, 17,* 124–129.

Ekman, P., & Friesen, W. V. (1975). *Unmasking the face.* Englewood Cliffs, NJ: Prentice Hall.

Elaad, E. (2003). Effects of feedback on the overestimated capacity to detect lies and the underestimated ability to tell lies. *Applied Cognitive Psychology, 17,* 349–363.

Elfenbein, H. A., & Ambady, N. (2002). On the universality and cultural specificity of emotion recognition: A meta-analysis. *Psychological Bulletin, 128,* 203–235.

Ellis, L., & Blanchard, R. (2001). Birth order, sibling sex ratio, and maternal miscarriages in homosexual and heterosexual men and women. *Personality and Individual Differences, 30,* 543–552.

Faber, S. (1981). *Identical twins reared apart.* London: Blackwell.

Fay, R. E., Turner, C. F., Klassen, A. D., & Gagnon, J. H. (1989). Prevalence and patterns of same-gender sexual contact among men. *Science, 243,* 338–348.

Fitton, A., & Heel, R. C. (1990). Clozapine: A review of its pharmacological properties and therapeutic use for schizophrenia. *Drugs, 40,* 722–747.

Flegal, K. M., Carroll, M. D., Ogden, C. L., & Curtin, L. R. (2010). Prevalence and trends in obesity among US Adults, 1999-2008. *JAMA: Journal of the American Medical Association, 303,* 235-241.

Ford, K., & Norris, A. E. (1997). Effects of interviewer age on reporting of sexual and reproductive behavior of Hispanic and African American youth. *Hispanic Journal of Behavioral Sciences, 19,* 369–376.

Foster, G. D., Wyatt, H. R., Hill, J. O., McGuckin, B. G., Brill, C., Mohammed, B. S., et al. (2003). A randomized trial of a low-carbohydrate diet for obesity. *New England Journal of Medicine, 348,* 2082–2090.

Fox, W. M. (1982). Why we should abandon Maslow's Need Hierarchy Theory. *Journal of Humanistic Education and Development, 21,* 29–32.

Fredrickson, B. L. (2001). The role of positive emotions in positive psychology: The broaden-and-build theory of positive emotions. *American Psychologist, 56,* 218–226.

Fredrickson, B. L., & Joiner, T. (2002). Positive emotions trigger upward spirals toward emotional well-being. *Psychological Science, 13,* 172–175.

Freedman, M. R., King, J., & Kennedy, E. (2001). Popular diets: A scientific review. *Obesity Research, 9,* 1S–40S.

Freud, S. (1910). The origin and development of psychoanalysis. *American Journal of Psychology, 21,* 181–218.

Fridlund, A. J. (1994). *Human facial expression: An evolutionary view.* San Diego, CA: Academic Press.

Friedman, B. H. (2009). Feelings and the body: The Jamesian perspective on autonomic specificity of emotion. *Biological Psychology.* doi: 10.1016/j.biopsycho.2009.10.006.

Friedman, M. I. (1991). Metabolic control of calorie intake. In M. T. Friedman, M. G. Tordoff, & M. R. Kare (Eds.), *Chemical senses.* (pp. 19-38). New York: Marcel Dekker.

Friedman, M. I., Tordoff, M. G., & Ramirez, I. (1986). Integrated metabolic control of food intake. *Brain Research Bulletin, 17,* 855–859.

Gangestad, S. W., Thornhill, R., & Garver, C. E. (2002). Changes in women's sexual interests and their partners' mate-retention tactics across the menstrual cycle: Evidence for shifting conflicts of interest. *Proceedings of the Royal Society of London Series B, Biological Sciences, 269,* 975–982.

Ganis, G., Kosslyn, S. M., Stose, S., Thompson, W. L., & Yurgelun-Todd, D. (2003). Neural correlates of different types of deception: An fMRI investigation. *Cerebral Cortex, 13,* 830–836.

Ganis, G., Morris, R. R., & Kosslyn, S. M. (2009). Neural processes underlying self- and other-related lies: An individual difference approach using fMRI. *Social Neuroscience, 4,* 539–553.

Garcia, J., Ervin, F. R., & Koelling, R. A. (1966). Learning with prolonged delay of reinforcement. *Psychonomic Science, 5,* 121–122.

Garcia, J., & Koelling, R. (1966). Relation of cue to consequence in avoidance learning. *Psychonomic Science, 4,* 123–124.

Garrido, E., Masip, J., & Herrero, C. (2004). Police officers' credibility judgments: Accuracy and estimated ability. *International Journal of Psychology, 39,* 254–275.

Gilbert, D. T. (2007). *Stumbling on happiness.* New York: Vintage.

Gladwell, M. (1998, February 2). The Pima paradox. *New Yorker,* 44–57.

Goldstein, M. D., & Strube, M. J. (1994). Independence revisited: The relation between positive and negative affect in a naturalistic setting. *Personality and Social Psychology Bulletin, 20,* 57–64.

Grammer, K. (1990). Strangers meet: Laughter and nonverbal signs of interest in opposite-sex encounters. *Journal of Nonverbal Behavior, 14,* 209–236.

Granhag, P. A., & Strömwall, L. A. (2001). Deception detection: Interrogators' and observers' decoding of consecutive statements. *Journal of Psychology: Interdisciplinary and Applied, 135,* 603–620.

Gray, J. R. (2001). Emotional modulation of cognitive control: Approach-withdrawal states double-dissociate spatial from verbal two-back task performance. *Journal of Experimental Psychology: General, 130,* 436–452.

Gray, J. R., Braver, T. S., & Raichle, M. E. (2002). Integration of emotion and cognition in the lateral prefrontal cortex. *Proceedings of the National Academy of Sciences of the United States of America, 99,* 4115–4120.

Gray, P. B., Kahlenberg, S. M., Barrett, E. S., Lipson, S. F., & Ellison, P. T. (2002). Marriage and fatherhood are associated with lower testosterone in males. *Evolution and Human Behavior, 23,* 193–201.

Grice, J. W., & Seely, E. (2000). The evolution of sex differences in jealousy: Failure to replicate previous results. *Journal of Research in Personality, 34,* 348–356.

Grimshaw, G. M., Adelstein, A., Bryden, M. P., & MacKinnon, G. E. (1998). First-language acquisition in adolescence: Evidence for a critical period for verbal language development. *Brain and Language, 63,* 237–255.

Gross, J. J. (2001). Emotion regulation in adulthood: Timing is everything. *Current Directions in Psychological Science, 10,* 214–219.

Gross, J. J. (2002). Emotion regulation: Affective, cognitive, and social consequences. *Psychophysiology, 39,* 281–291.

Hall, D. T., & Nougaim, K. E. (1968). An examination of Maslow's need hierarchy in an organizational setting. *Organizational Behavior and Human Performance, 3,* 12–35.

Hamann, S., & Mao, H. (2002). Positive and negative emotional verbal stimuli elicit activity in the left amygdala. *Neuroreport: For Rapid Communication of Neuroscience Research, 13,* 15–19.

Hamer, D. H., Hu, S., Magnuson, V. L., Hu, N., & Pattatucci, A. M. (1993). A linkage between DNA markers on the X chromosome and male sexual orientation. *Science, 261,* 321–327.

Harris, C. R. (2000). Psychophysiological responses to imagined infidelity: The specific innate modular view of jealousy reconsidered. *Journal of Personality and Social Psychology, 78,* 1082–1091.

Harris, C. R. (2002). Sexual and romantic jealousy in heterosexual and homosexual adults. *Psychological Science, 13,* 7–12.

Harris, J. R. (1998). *The nurture assumption: Why children turn out the way they do.* New York: Free Press.

Helson, H. (1964). *Adaptation-level theory: An experimental and systematic approach to behavior.* New York: Harper & Row.

Herman, C. P., Roth, D. A., & Polivy, J. (2003). Effects of the presence of others on food intake: A normative interpretation. *Psychological Bulletin, 129,* 873–886.

Hill, J. O., & Peters, J. C. (1998). Environmental contributions to the obesity epidemic. *Science, 280,* 1371–1374.

Hohman, G. W. (1966). Some effects of spinal cord lesions on experienced emotional feelings. *Psychophysiology, 3,* 143–156.

Insel, T. R. (2000). Toward a neurobiology of attachment. *Review of General Psychology, 4,* 176–185.

Izard, C. E. (1971). *The face of emotion.* New York: Appleton-Century-Crofts.

James, W. (1884). What is emotion? *Mind, 9,* 188–205.

Kagan, J. (1994). On the nature of emotion. *Monographs of the Society for Research in Child Development, 59,* 7–24, 250–283.

Kahneman, D., Krueger, A. B., Schkade, D. A., Schwarz, N., & Stone, A. A. (2004). A survey method for characterizing daily life experience: The day reconstruction method. *Science, 306,* 1776–1780.

Kalivas, P. W., & Nakamura, M. (1999). Neural systems for behavioral activation and reward. *Current Opinion in Neurobiology, 9,* 223–227.

Keltner, D., & Haidt, J. (2001). Social functions of emotions. In T. J. Mayne & G. A. Bonanno (Eds.), *Emotions: Current issues and future directions* (pp. 192–213). New York: Guilford Press.

Keltner, D., & Shiota, M. N. (2003). New displays and new emotions: A commentary on Rozin and Cohen (2003). *Emotion, 3,* 86–91.

Kenrick, D.T., Griskevicius, V., Neuberg, S. L., & Schaller, M. (2010). Renovating the pyramid of needs: Contemporary extensions built upon ancient foundations *Perspectives on Psychological Science, 5,* 292–314.

Kim, M., & Kim, H. (1997). Communication goals: Individual differences between Korean and American speakers. *Personality and Individual Differences, 23,* 509–517.

Kondo, T., Zakany, J., Innis, J. W., & Duboule, D. (1997). Of fingers, toes and penises. *Nature, 390,* 185–198.

Kozel, F. A., Padgett, T. M., & George, M. S. (2004). A replication study of the neural correlates of deception. *Behavioral Neuroscience, 118,* 852–856.

Kozel, F. A., Revell, L. J., Lorberbaum, J. P., Shastri, A., Elhai, J. D., Horner, M. D., et al. (2004). A pilot study of functional magnetic resonance imaging brain correlates of deception in healthy young men. *Journal of Neuropsychiatry and Clinical Neurosciences, 16,* 295–305.

Kruglanski, A. W., & Webster, D. M. (1996). Motivated closing of the mind: "Seizing" and "freezing." *Psychological Review, 103,* 263–283.

Laird, J. D. (1974). Self-attribution of emotion: The effects of expressive behavior on the quality of emotional experience. *Journal of Personality and Social Psychology, 29,* 475–486.

Laird, J. D. (1984). The real role of facial response in the experience of emotion: A reply to Tourangeau and Ellsworth, and others. *Journal of Personality and Social Psychology, 47,* 909–917.

Lang, P. J. (1994). The varieties of emotional experience: A meditation on the James-Lange theory. *Psychological*

Review (Special Issue: The Centennial Issue), 101, 211–221.

Lang, P. J. (1995). The emotion probe: Studies of motivation and attention. *American Psychologist, 50,* 372–385.

Lang, P. J., Bradley, M. M., Cuthbert, B. N. (1990). Emotion, attention, and the startle reflex. *Psychological Review, 97,* 377–395.

Lange, C. (1887). *Uber gemuthsbewegungen.* Leipzig: Theodor Thomas.

Larsen, J. T., McGraw, A. P., & Cacioppo, J. T. (2001). Can people feel happy and sad at the same time? *Journal of Personality and Social Psychology, 81,* 684–696.

Larson, J. A. (1932). *Lying and its detection: A study of deception and deception tests.* Chicago: University of Chicago Press.

Lazarus, R. S. (1984). On the primacy of cognition. *American Psychologist, 39,* 124–129.

LeDoux, J. E. (1996). *The emotional brain: The mysterious underpinnings of emotional life.* New York: Simon & Schuster.

Lepper, M. R., Greene, D., & Nisbett, R. E. (1973). Undermining children's intrinsic interest with extrinsic reward: A test of the "overjustification" hypothesis. *Journal of Personality and Social Psychology, 28,* 129–137.

LeVay, S. (1991). A difference in hypothalamic structure between heterosexual and homosexual men. *Science, 253,* 1034–1037.

LeVay, S., & Hamer, D. (1994). Evidence for a biological influence in male homosexuality. *Scientific American, 270,* 44–49.

Levenson, R. W., Ekman, P., & Friesen, W. V. (1990). Voluntary facial action generates emotion-specific autonomic nervous system activity. *Psychophysiology, 27,* 363–384.

Levin, R. J. (1994). Human male sexuality: Appetite and arousal, desire and drive. In C. R. Legg & D. Booth (Eds.), *Appetite: Neural and behavioral bases* (pp. 127–164). New York: Oxford University Press.

Levin, R. S. (1980). The physiology of sexual function in women. *Clinics in Obstetrics and Gynaecology, 7,* 213–252.

Levine, A. S., & Billington, C. J. (1997). Why do we eat? A neural systems approach. *Annual Review of Nutrition, 17,* 597–619.

Lewis, A. R., Zinbarg, R. E., & Durbin, C. E. (2010). Advances, problems, and challenges in the study of emotion regulation: A commentary. *Journal of Psychopathology and Behavioral Assessment, 32,* 83–91.

Linley, P. A., Harrington, S., & Garcea, N. (Eds.). (2010). *Oxford handbook of positive psychology and work.* New York: Oxford University Press.

Linley, P. A., & Joseph, S. (2004). Positive change following trauma and adversity: A review. *Journal of Traumatic Stress, 17,* 11–21.

Linner, B. (1972). *Sex and society in Sweden.* New York: Harper Colophon.

Lu, L. (1999). Personal or environmental causes of happiness: A longitudinal analysis. *Journal of Social Psychology, 139,* 79–90.

Lu, L., Shih, J. B., Lin, Y. Y., & Ju, L. S. (1997). Personal and environmental correlates of happiness. *Personality and Individual Differences, 23,* 453–462.

Lykken, D. T. (1959). The GSR in the detection of guilt. *Journal of Applied Psychology, 43,* 385–388.

Lykken, D. T. (1960). The validity of the guilty knowledge technique: The effects of faking. *Journal of Applied Psychology, 44,* 258–262.

Lykken, D., & Tellegen, A. (1996). Happiness is a stochastic phenomenon. *Psychological Science, 7,* 186–189.

Lyubomirsky, S. (2001). Why are some people happier than others? The role of cognitive and motivational processes in well-being. *American Psychologist, 56,* 239–249.

Mann, S., Vrij, A., & Bull, R. (2004). Detecting true lies: Police officers' ability to detect suspects' lies. *Journal of Applied Psychology, 89,* 137–149.

Markham, R., & Wang, L. (1996). Recognition of emotion by Chinese and Australian children. *Journal of Cross-Cultural Psychology, 27,* 616–643.

Markland, D., & Tobin, V. J. (2010). Need support and behavioural regulations for exercise among exercise referral scheme clients: The mediating role of psychological need satisfaction. *Psychology of Sport and Exercise, 11,* 91–99.

Markovits, C. (2003). *The un-Gandhian Gandhi: The life and afterlife of the Mahatma.* London: Anthem Press.

Maslow, A. H. (1970). *Motivation and personality* (2nd ed.). New York: Harper & Row.

Masters, W. H., & Johnson, V. E. (1966). *Human sexual response.* Boston: Little, Brown.

McClelland, D. C., & Atkinson, J. W. (1953). *The achievement motive.* New York: Appleton-Century-Crofts.

McClelland, D. C., Koestner, R., & Weinbereger, J. (1989). How do self-attributed and implicit motives differ? *Psychological Review, 96,* 690–702.

McDougall, W. (1908/1960). *Introduction to social psychology.* New York: Barnes & Noble.

McFadden, D., & Pasanen, E. G. (1999). Spontaneous otoacoustic emissions in heterosexuals, homosexuals, and bisexuals. *Journal of the Acoustical Society of America, 105,* 2403–2413.

McKenna, R. J. (1972). Some effects of anxiety level and food cues on the eating behavior of obese and normal subjects: A comparison of the Schachterian and psychosomatic conceptions. *Journal of Personality and Social Psychology, 22,* 311–319.

McKnight, J., & Malcolm, J. (2000). Is male homosexuality maternally linked? *Psychology, Evolution and Gender, 2,* 229–239.

Meston, C. M., & Frohlich, P. F. (2000). The neurobiology of sexual function. *Archives of General Psychiatry, 57,* 1012–1030.

Mikulincer, M. (1994). *Human learned helplessness: A coping perspective.* New York: Plenum.

Miller, L. C., Putcha-Bhagavatula, A., & Pedersen, W. C. (2002). Men's and women's mating preferences: Distinct evolutionary mechanisms? *Current Directions in Psychological Science, 11,* 88–93.

Miller, W. B., Pasta, D. J., MacMurray, J., Chiu, C., Wu, H., & Comings, D. E. (1999). Dopamine receptor genes are associated with age at first sexual intercourse. *Journal of Biosocial Science, 31,* 43–54.

Morgan, C. J., LeSage, J. B., & Kosslyn, S. M. (2009). Types of deception revealed by individual differences in cognitive abilities. *Social Neuroscience, 4,* 554–569.

Murphy, F. C., Nimmo-Smith, I., & Lawrence, A. D. (2003). Functional neuroanatomy of emotions: A meta-analysis. *Cognitive, Affective and Behavioral Neuroscience, 3,* 207–233.

Myers, D. G. (2000). The funds, friends, and faith of happy people. *American Psychologist, 55,* 56–67.

Nader, K., Bechara, A., & van der Kooy, D. (1997). Neurobiological constraints on behavioral models of motivation. *Annual Review of Psychology, 48,* 85–114.

Nanda, S. B. R. (1987). *Mahatma Gandhi: His life in pictures.* Delhi: Central Electric Press. Retrieved June, 2005, from http://www.mkgandhi.org/bio5000/birth.htm

Nathawat, S. S., Singh, R., & Singh, B. (1997). The effect of need for achievement on attributional style. *Journal of Social Psychology, 137,* 55–62.

Neel, R. G., Tzeng, O. C., & Baysal, C. (1986). Need achievement in a cross-cultural contact study. *International Review of Applied Psychology, 35,* 225–229.

Nemeroff, C., & Rozin, P. (1989). "You are what you eat": Applying the demand-free "impressions" technique to an unacknowledged belief. *Ethos, 17,* 50–69.

Niedenthal, P. M., Brauer, M., Halberstadt, J. B., & Innes-Ker, A. H. (2001). When did her smile drop? Facial mimicry and the influences of emotional state on the detection of change in emotional expression. *Cognition and Emotion, 15,* 853–864.

Niles, S. (1998). Achievement goals and means: A cultural comparison. *Journal of Cross-Cultural Psychology, 29,* 656–667.

Nilsson, T., Ericsson, M., Poston, W. S. C., Linder, J., Goodrick, G. K., & Foreyt, J. P. (1998). Is the assessment of coping capacity useful in the treatment of obesity? *Eating Disorders: The Journal of Treatment and Prevention, 6,* 241–251.

Nisbett, R. E. (1972). Hunger, obesity, and the ventromedial hypothalamus. *Psychological Review, 79,* 433–453.

Ochsner, K. N., & Gross, J. J. (2005). The cognitive control of emotion. *Trends in Cognitive Sciences, 9,* 242–249.

Öhman, A. (2002). Automaticity and the amygdala: Nonconscious responses to emotional faces. *Current Directions in Psychological Science, 11,* 62–66.

Olds, J., & Milner, P. (1954). Positive reinforcement produced by electrical stimulation of septal area and other regions of rat brain. *Journal of Comparative and Physiological Psychology, 47,* 419–427.

Olsson, A., & Phelps, E. A. (2004). Learned fear of "unseen" faces after Pavlovian, observational, and instructed fear. *Psychological Science, 15,* 822–828.

Overmeier, J. B., & Seligman, M. E. P. (1967). Effects of inescapable shock upon subsequent escape and avoidance responding. *Journal of Comparative and Physiological Psychology, 63,* 28–33.

Oyserman, D., Coon, H. M., & Kemmelmeier, M. (2002). Rethinking individualism and collectivism: Evaluation of theoretical assumptions and meta-analyses. *Psychological Bulletin, 128,* 3–72.

Panksepp, J. (1998). *Affective neuroscience: The foundations of human an animal emotions.* London: Oxford University Press.

Panksepp, J. (2005). Affective consciousness: Core emotional feelings in animals and humans. *Consciousness and Cognition: An International Journal, 14,* 30–80.

Paul, T., Schiffer, B., Zwarg, T., Krüger, T. H. C., Karama, S., Schedlowski, M., et al. (2008). Brain response to visual sexual stimuli in heterosexual and homosexual males. *Human Brain Mapping, 29,* 726–735.

Pedersen, W. C., Miller, L. C., Putcha-Bhagavatula, A. D., & Yang, Y. (2002). Evolved sex differences in the number of partners desired? The long and short of it. *Psychological Science, 13,* 157–161.

Penton-Voak, I. S., & Perrett, D. I. (2000). Female preference for male faces changes cyclically: Further evidence. *Evolution and Human Behavior, 21,* 39–48.

Peterson, C. (2000). The future of optimism. *American Psychologist, 55,* 44–55.

Phan, K. L., Wager, T., Taylor, S. F., & Liberzon, I. (2002). Functional neuroanatomy of emotion: A meta-analysis of emotion activation studies in PET and fMRI. *NeuroImage, 16,* 331–348.

Phan, K. L., Wager, T., Taylor, S. F., & Liberzon, I. (2004). Functional neuroimaging studies of human emotions. *CNS Spectrums, 9,* 258–266.

Pinker, S. (1994). *The language instinct: How the mind creates language.* New York: Morrow.

Pinker, S. (1997). *How the mind works.* New York: Norton.

Pinker, S. (2002). *The blank slate: The modern denial of human nature.* New York: Viking Press.

Plotkin, H. (1997). *Evolution in mind: An introduction to evolutionary psychology.* Cambridge, MA: Harvard University Press.

Plutchik, R., & Kellerman, I. (Eds.). (1980). *Emotion: Theory, research, and experience: Vol. 1. Theories of emotion.* New York: Academic Press.

Poston, W. S. C., Ericsson, M., Linder, J., Nilsson, T., Goodrick, G. K., & Foreyt, J. P. (1999). Personality and the prediction of weight loss and relapse in the treatment of obesity. *International Journal of Eating Disorders, 25,* 301–309.

Prinz, J. (2008). Embodied emotions. In W. G. Lycan & J. Prinz (Eds.), *Mind and cognition: An anthology* (3rd ed., pp. 839–849). Malden, MA: Blackwell Publishing.

Quigley, K. S., Barrett, L. F., & Weinstein, S. (2002). Cardiovascular patterns associated with threat and challenge appraisals: A within-subjects analysis. *Psychophysiology, 39,* 292–302.

Rankinen, T., Pérusse, L., Weisnagel, S. J., Snyder, E. E., Chagnon, Y. C., & Bouchard, C. (2002). The human obesity gene map: The 2001 update. *Obesity Research, 10,* 196–243.

Ravussin, E., & Bouchard, C. (2000). Human genomics and obesity: Finding appropriate target drugs. *European Journal of Pharmacology, 410,* 131–145.

Regan, P. C. (1996). Rhythms of desire: The association between menstrual cycle phases and female sexual desire. *Canadian Journal of Human Sexuality, 5,* 145–156.

Reid, J. E. (1947). A revised questioning technique in lie-detection tests. *Journal of Criminal Law and Criminology, 37,* 542–547.

Reisenzein, R., Meyer, W., & Schützwohl, A. (1995). James and the physical basis of emotion: A comment on Ellsworth. *Psychological Review, 102,* 757–761.

Rice, G., Anderson, C., Risch, N., & Ebers, G. (1999). Male homosexuality: Absence of linkage to microsatellite markers at Xq28. *Science, 284,* 665–667.

Richards, J. M. (2004). The cognitive consequences of concealing feelings. *Current Directions in Psychological Science, 13,* 131–134.

Richards, J. M., Butler, E. A., & Gross, J. J. (2003). Emotion regulation in romantic relationships: The cognitive consequences of concealing feelings. *Journal of Social and Personal Relationships, 20,* 599–620.

Richards, J. M., & Gross, J. J. (2000). Emotion regulation and memory: The cognitive costs of keeping one's cool. *Journal of Personality and Social Psychology, 79,* 410–424.

Robinson, S. J., & Manning, J. T. (2000). The ratio of the 2nd to 4th digit length and male homosexuality. *Evolution and Human Behaviour, 21*, 333–345.

Rolland, R. (1924). *Mahatma Gandhi*. London: Swarthmore.

Rolls, B. J., Rowe, E. A., Rolls, E. T., Kingston, B., Megson, A., & Gunary, R. (1981). Variety in a meal enhances food intake in man. *Physiology and Behavior, 26*, 215–221.

Rolls, E. T., & Cooper, S. J. (1974). Connection between the prefrontal cortex and pontine brain-stimulation reward sites in the rat. *Experimental Neurology, 42*, 687–699.

Rosenkranz, M. A., Jackson, D. C., Dalton, K. M., Dolski, I., Ryff, C. D., Singer, B. H., et al. (2003). Affective style and in vivo immune response: Neurobehavioral mechanisms. *Proceedings of the National Academy of Sciences of the United States of America, 100*, 11148–11152.

Ross, C. E. (1995). Reconceptualizing marital status as a continuum of social attachment. *Journal of Marriage and the Family, 57*, 129–140.

Rozin, P., Ashmore, M., & Markwith, M. (1996). Lay American conceptions of nutrition: Dose insensitivity, categorical thinking, contagion, and the monotonic mind. *Health Psychology, 15*, 438–447.

Rozin, P., & Fallon, A. (1986). The acquisition of likes and dislikes for foods. In National Research Council et al. (Eds.), *What is America eating? Proceedings of a symposium*. Washington, DC: National Academies Press.

Rozin, P., Lowery, L., & Ebert, R. (1994). Varieties of disgust faces and the structure of disgust. *Journal of Personality and Social Psychology, 66*, 870–881.

Russell, J. A. (2003). Core affect and the psychological construction of emotion. *Psychological Review, 110*, 145–172.

Russell, J. A., Bachorowski, J. A., & Fernández-Dols, J. M. (2003). Facial and vocal expressions of emotion. *Annual Review of Psychology, 54*, 329–349.

Ryan, R. M., & Deci, E. L. (2000). Self-determination theory and the facilitation of intrinsic motivation, social development, and well-being. *American Psychologist, 55*, 68–78.

Sagie, A., Elizur, S., & Hirotsugu, Y. (1996). The structure and strength of achievement motivation: A cross-cultural comparison. *Journal of Organization Behavior, 17*, 431–444.

Sargent, P. A., Sharpley, A. L., Williams, C., Goodall, E. M., & Cowen, P. J. (1997). 5-HT-sub (2C) receptor activation decreases appetite and body weight in obese subjects. *Psychopharmacology, 133*, 309–312.

Schachter, S., & Singer, J. (1962). Cognitive, social and physiological determinants of emotional state. *Psychological Review, 69*, 379–399.

Schaefer, S. M., Jackson, D. C., Davidson, R. J., Aguirre, G. K., Kimberg, D. Y., & Thompson-Schill, S. L. (2002). Modulation of amygdalar activity by the conscious regulation of negative emotion. *Journal of Cognitive Neuroscience, 14*, 913–921.

Schiffman, S. S., Graham, B. G., Sattely-Miller, E. A., & Warwick, Z. S. (1999). Orosensory perception of dietary fat. *Current Directions in Psychological Science, 7*, 137–143.

Schyns, P. (1998). Crossnational differences in happiness: Economic and cultural factors explored. *Social Indicators Research, 43*, 3–26.

Seligman, M. E., & Csikszentmihalyi, M. (2000). Positive psychology: An introduction. *American Psychologist, 55*, 5–14.

Seligman, M. E. P., & Pawelski, J. O. (2003). Positive psychology: FAQs. *Psychological Inquiry, 14*, 159–163.

Sheldon, K. M., Ryan, R., & Reis, H. T. (1996). What makes for a good day? Competence and autonomy in the day and in the person. *Personality and Social Psychology Bulletin, 22*, 1270–1279.

Simon-Thomas, E. R., Role, K. O., & Knight, R. T. (2005). Behavioral and electrophysiological evidence of a right hemisphere bias for the influence of negative emotion on higher cognition. *Journal of Cognitive Neuroscience, 17*, 518–529.

Slimp, J. C., Hart, B. L., & Goy, R. W. (1978). Heterosexual, autosexual and social behavior of adult male rhesus monkeys with medial preoptic-anterior hypothalamic lesions. *Brain Research, 142*, 105–122.

Small, D. M., Zatorre, R. J., Dagher, A., Evans, A. C., & Jones-Gotman, M. (2001). Changes in brain activity related to eating chocolate: From pleasure to aversion. *Brain, 124*, 1720–1733.

Solomon, R. L., & Corbit, J. D. (1974). An opponent-process theory of motivation: I. Temporal dynamics of affect. *Psychological Review, 78*, 3–43.

Soper, B., Milford, G. E., & Rosenthal, G. T. (1995). Belief when evidence does not support the theory. *Psychology and Marketing, 12*, 415–422.

Spangler, W. D. (1992). Validity of questionnaire and TAT measures of need for achievement: Two meta-analyses. *Psychological Bulletin, 112*, 140–154.

Stack, S., & Eshleman, J. R. (1998). Marital status and happiness. *Journal of Marriage and the Family, 60*, 527–536.

Stallone, D. D., & Stunkard, A. J. (1994). Obesity. In A. Frazer & P. B. Molinoff (Eds.), *Biological bases of brain function and disease* (pp. 385–403). New York: Raven Press.

Stephan, W. G., Stephan, C. W., & de Vargas, M. C. (1996). Emotional expression in Costa Rica and the United States. *Journal of Cross-Cultural Psychology, 27*, 147–160.

Stevens, L. E., & Fiske, S. T. (1995). Motivation and cognition in social life: A social survival perspective. *Social Cognition, 13*, 189–214.

Stokes, J. P., Damon, W., & McKirnan, D. J. (1997). Predictors of movement toward homosexuality: A longitudinal study of bisexual men. *Journal of Sex Research, 34*, 304–312.

Strack, F., Martin, L. L., & Stepper, S. (1988). Inhibiting and facilitating conditions of the human smile: A nonobtrusive test of the facial feedback hypothesis. *Journal of Personality and Social Psychology, 54*, 768–777.

Strömwall, L. A., Granhag, P. A., & Jonsson, A. (2003). Deception among pairs: "Let's say we had lunch and hope they will swallow it!" *Psychology, Crime and Law, 9*, 109–124.

Stunkard, A. J. (1982). Anorectic agents lower a body weight set point. *Life Science, 30*, 2043–2055.

Sulloway, F. J. (1997). *Born to rebel*. New York: Vintage.

Sulloway, F. J. (1999). Birth order. In M. A. Runco & S. R. Pritzken (Eds.), *Encyclopedia of creativity* (Vol. 1, pp. 189–202). San Diego, CA: Academic Press.

Tafarodi, R. W., & Swann, W. B., Jr. (1996). Individualism-collectivism and global self-esteem: Evidence for a cultural trade-off. *Journal of Cross-Cultural Psychology, 27*, 651–672.

Taris, T. W. (2000). Dispositional need for cognitive closure and self-enhancing beliefs. *Journal of Social Psychology, 140*, 35–50.

Tecott, L. H., Sun, L. M., Akana, S. F., Strack, A. M., Lowenstein, D. H., Dallman, M. F., et al. (1995). Eating disorder and epilepsy in mice lacking 5-HT2C serotonin receptors. *Nature, 374*, 542–546.

Tinker, J. E., & Tucker, J. A. (1997). Motivations for weight loss and behavior change strategies associated with natural recovery from obesity. *Psychology of Addictive Behaviors, 11*, 98–106.

Tomaka, J., Blascovich, J., Kibler, J., & Ernst, J. M. (1997). Cognitive and physiological antecedents of threat and challenge appraisal. *Journal of Personality and Social Psychology, 73*, 63–72.

Tomkins, S. S. (1962). *Affect, imagery, consciousness: Vol 1. The positive affects*. New York: Springer-Verlag.

Tracy, J. L., & Robins, R. W. (2004). Show your pride: Evidence for a discrete emotion expression. *Psychological Science, 15*, 194–197.

Trivedi, N., & Sabini, J. (1998). Volunteer bias, sexuality, and personality. *Archives of Sexual Behavior, 27*, 181–195.

Trivers, R. (1972). Parental investment and sexual selection. In B. Campbell (Ed.), *Sexual selection and the descent of man, 1871–1971* (pp. 136–179). Chicago: Aldine.

Tugade, M. M., & Fredrickson, B. L. (2004). Resilient individuals use positive emotions to bounce back from negative emotional experiences. *Journal of Personality and Social Psychology, 86*, 320–333.

Valins, S. (1966). Cognitive effects of false heart-rate feedback. *Journal of Personality and Social Psychology, 4*, 400–408.

Vrana, S. R. & Lang, P. J. (1990). Fear imagery and the startle-probe reflex. *Journal of Abnormal Psychology, 99*, 181–189.

Vrana, S. R., Spence, E. L., & Lang, P. J. (1988). The startle probe response: A new measure of emotion? *Journal of Abnormal Psychology, 97*, 487–491.

Vrij, A. (2004). Why professionals fail to catch liars and how they can improve. *Legal and Criminological Psychology, 9*, 159–181.

Vrij, A., & Mann, S. (2001). Telling and detecting lies in a high-stake situation: The case of a convicted murderer. *Applied Cognitive Psychology, 15*, 187–203.

Wager, T. D., Phan, K. L., Liberzon, I., & Taylor, S. F. (2003). Valence, gender, and lateralization of functional brain anatomy in emotion: A meta-analysis of findings from neuroimaging. *NeuroImage, 19*, 513–531.

Wahba, M. A., & Bridwell, L. G. (1976). Maslow reconsidered: A review of research on the need hierarchy theory. *Organizational Behavior and Human Decision Processes, 15*, 212–240.

Waite, L. J., Luo, Y., & Lewin, A. C. (2009). Marital happiness and marital stability: Consequences for psychological well-being. *Social Science Research, 38*, 201–212.

Weerasinghe, J., & Tepperman, L. (1994). Suicide and happiness: Seven tests of the connection. *Social Indicators Research, 32*, 199–233.

Weiner, B., & Kukla, A. (1970). An attributional analysis of achievement motivation. *Journal of Personality and Social Psychology, 15*, 1–20.

Whalen, P. J., Rauch, S. L., Etcoff, N. L., McInerney, S. C., Lee, M. B., & Jenike, M. A. (1998). Masked presentations of emotional facial expressions modulate amygdala activity without explicit knowledge. *Journal of Neuroscience, 18*, 411–418.

Williams, T. J., Pepitone, M. E., Christensen, S. E., Cooke, B. M., Huberman, A. D., Breedlove, N. J., et al. (2000). Finger length patterns and human sexual orientation. *Nature, 404*, 455–456.

Wise, R. A. (1996). Addictive drugs and brain stimulation reward. *Annual Review of Neuroscience, 19*, 319–340.

Wise, R. A. (2004). Dopamine, learning and motivation. *Nature Reviews Neuroscience, 5*, 483–494.

Woods, S. C., Schwartz, M. W., Baskin, D. G., & Seeley, R. J. (2000). Food intake and the regulation of body weight. *Annual Review of Psychology, 51*, 255–277.

Yeomans, M. R., & Gray, R. W. (1997). Effects of naltrexone on food intake and changes in subjective appetite during eating: Evidence for opioid involvement in the appetizer effect. *Physiology and Behavior, 62*, 15–21.

Zalla, T., Koechlin, E., Pietrini, P., Basso, G., Aquino, P., Sirigu, A., et al. (2000). Differential amygdala responses to winning and losing: A functional magnetic resonance imaging study in humans. *European Journal of Neuroscience, 12*, 1764–1770.

References: **Personality**

Adler, A. (1933/1964). *Social interest: A challenge to mankind*. New York: Capricorn Books.

Ahadi, S., & Diener, E. (1989). Multiple determinants and effect size. *Journal of Personality and Social Psychology, 56,* 398–406.

Ajzen, I. (2002). Perceived behavioral control, self-efficacy, locus of control, and the theory of planned behavior. *Journal of Applied Social Psychology, 32,* 665–683.

Allport, G. W. (1937). *Personality: A psychological interpretation*. New York: Holt.

Alonzo, M., & Aiken, M. (2004). Flaming in electronic communication. *Decision Support Systems, 36*(3), 205–221.

Anastasi, A. (1988). *Psychological testing* (6th ed.). New York: Macmillan.

Angleitner, A., Riemann, R., & Strelau, J. (1995, July 15–19). *A study of twins using the self-report and peer-report NEO-FFI scales*. Paper presented at the seventh meeting of the International Society for the Study of Individual Differences, Warsaw, Poland.

Archer, J. (2004). Sex differences in aggression in real-world settings: A meta-analytic review. *Review of General Psychology, 8,* 291–322.

Azar, B. (1995). Timidity can develop in the first days of life. *APA Monitor, 26*(11), 23.

Ball, S. A. (2002). Big Five, alternative five, and seven personality dimensions: Validity in substance-dependent patients. In P. T. Costa Jr. & T. A. Widiger (Eds.), *Personality disorders and the five-factor model of personality* (2nd ed., pp. 177–201). Washington, DC: American Psychological Association.

Bandura, A. (1977). Self-efficacy: Toward a unifying theory of behavior change. *Psychological Review, 84,* 191–215.

Bandura, A. (2004). Health promotion by social cognitive means. *Health Education and Behavior, 31,* 143–164.

Berenbaum, S. A. (1999). Effects of early androgens on sex-typed activities and interests in adolescents with congenital adrenal hyperplasia. *Hormones and Behavior, 35,* 102–110.

Bergeman, C. S., Plomin, R., Pederson, N. L., McClearn, G. E., & Nesselroad, J. R. (1990). Genetic and environmental influences on social support: The Swedish Adoption/Twin Study of Aging (SATSA). *Journal of Gerontology: Psychological Sciences, 45,* P101–P106.

Bond, M., Gardiner, S. T., Christian, H., & Sigel, J. J. (1983). Empirical study of self-rated defense styles. *Archives of General Psychiatry, 40,* 333–338.

Borman, W. C., Hanson, M. A., & Hedge, J. W. (1997). Personnel selection. *Annual Review of Psychology, 48,* 299–337.

Bouchard, T. J., Jr. (2004). Genetic influence on human psychological traits: A survey. *Current Directions in Psychological Science, 13,* 148–151.

Bowlby, J. (1973). *Attachment and loss: Vol. 2. Separation: Anxiety and anger*. London: Hogarth Press.

Brown, I., Jr., & Inouye, D. K. (1978). Learned helplessness through modeling: The role of perceived similarity in competence. *Journal of Personality and Social Psychology, 36,* 900–908.

Bruggemann, J. M., & Barry, R. J. (2002). Eysenck's P as a modulator of affective and electrodermal responses to violent and comic film. *Personality and Individual Differences, 32,* 1029–1048.

Brussoni, M. J., Jang, K. L., Livesley, W. J., & MacBeth, T. M. (2000). Genetic and environmental influences on adult attachment styles. *Personal Relationships, 7,* 283–289.

Buda, R., & Elsayed-Elkhouly, S. M. (1998). Cultural differences between Arabs and Americans: Individualism-collectivism revisited. *Journal of Cross-Cultural Psychology, 29,* 487–492.

Buss, A. H. (1995). *Personality: Temperament, social behavior, and the self*. Needham Heights, MA: Allyn & Bacon.

Buss, A. H., & Plomin, R. (1984). *Temperament: Early developing personality traits*. Hillsdale, NJ: Erlbaum.

Buss, D. M. (1995). Psychological sex differences: Origins through sexual selection. *American Psychologist, 50,* 164–168.

Butcher, J. N., & Rouse, S. V. (1996). Personality: Individual difference and clinical assessment. *Annual Review of Psychology, 47,* 87–111.

Canli, T., Zhao, Z., Desmond, J. E., Kang, E., Gross, J., & Gabrieli, J. D. E. (2001). An fMRI study of personality influences on brain reactivity to emotional stimuli. *Behavioral Neuroscience, 115,* 33–42.

Carver, C. S., Meyer, B., & Antoni, M. H. (2000). Responsiveness to threats and incentives expectancy of recurrence and distress and disengagement: Moderator effects in early-stage breast cancer patients. *Journal of Consulting and Clinical Psychology, 68,* 965–975.

Carver, C. S., & White, T. L. (1994). Behavioral inhibition, behavioral activation, and affective responses to impending reward and punishment: The BIS/BAS scales. *Journal of Personality and Social Psychology, 67,* 319–333.

Caspi, A. (2000). The child is father of the man: Personality continuities from childhood to adulthood. *Journal of Personality and Social Psychology, 78,* 158–172.

Castellà, J., & Pérez, J. (2004). Sensitivity to punishment and sensitivity to reward and traffic violations. *Accident Analysis and Prevention, 36,* 947–952.

Cattell, R. B. (1943). The description of personality: Basic traits resolved into clusters. *Journal of Abnormal and Social Psychology, 38,* 476–506.

Cattell, R. B., Eber, H. W., & Tatsuoka, M. M. (1970). *Handbook for the Sixteen Personality Factor Questionnaire (16PF)*. Champaign, IL: Institute for Personality and Ability Testing.

Center, D. B., Jackson, N., & Kemp, D. (2005). A test of Eysenck's antisocial behavior hypothesis employing 11–15-year-old students dichotomous for PEN and L. *Personality and Individual Differences, 38,* 395–402.

Cervone, D. (2005). Personality architecture: Within-person structures and processes. *Annual Review of Psychology, 56,* 423–452.

Chess, S., & Thomas, A. (1996). *Temperament: Theory and practice*. New York: Brunner/Mazel.

Church, T. A., & Katigbak, M. S. (2000). Trait psychology in the Philippines. *American Behavioral Scientist, 44,* 73–94.

Cloninger, R., Svarkic, D. M., & Prysbeck, T. R. (1993). Psychobiological model of temperament and character. *Archives of General Psychiatry, 50,* 975–990.

Collins, N. L. (1996). Working models of attachment: Implications for explanation, emotion, and behavior. *Journal of Personality and Social Psychology, 71,* 810–832.

Corr, P. J., & Kumari, V. (1997). Sociability/impulsivity and attenuated-dopaminergic arousal: Critical flicker/fusion frequency and procedural learning. *Personality and Individual Differences, 22,* 805–815.

Corr, P. J., Pickering, A. D., & Gray, J. A. (1995). Sociability/impulsivity and caffeine-induced arousal: Critical flicker/fusion frequency and procedural learning. *Personality and Individual Differences, 18,* 713–730.

Costa, P. T., & McCrae, R. R. (1995). Primary traits of Eysenck's P-E-N System: Three- and five-factor solutions. *Journal of Personality and Social Psychology, 69,* 308–317.

Costa, P. T., McCrae, R. R., & Dye, D. A. (1991). Facet scales for agreeableness and conscientiousness: A revision of the NEO Personality Inventory. *Personality and Individual Differences, 12,* 887–898.

Costa, P. T., Terracciano, A., & McCrae, R. R. (2001). Gender differences in personality traits across cultures: Robust and surprising findings. *Journal of Personality and Social Psychology, 81,* 322–331.

Cravens-Brown, L. M. (2003). Eysenck and antisocial behavior: An analysis of the associations between personality styles and problems with conduct (Hans J. Eysenck). *Dissertation Abstracts International. B. The Physical Sciences and Engineering, 64*(2), 958B.

Dabbs, J. M., Jr., Riad, J. K., & Chance, S. E. (2001). Testosterone and ruthless homicide. *Personality and Individual Differences, 31,* 599–603.

Dabbs, J. M., Jr., Strong, R., & Milun, R. (1997). Exploring the mind of testosterone: A beeper study. *Journal of Research in Personality, 31,* 577–587.

Davidson, R. J. (1992a). Emotion and affective style: Hemispheric substrates. *Psychological Science, 3,* 39–43.

Davidson, R. J. (1992b). A prolegomenon to the structure of emotion: Gleanings from neuropsychology. *Cognition and Emotion, 6,* 245–268.

Davidson, R. J. (2001). Toward a biology of personality and emotion. *Annals of the New York Academy of Sciences, 935,* 191–207.

Davis, D., Shaver, P. R., & Vernon, M. L. (2003). Physical, emotional, and behavioral reactions to breaking up: The roles of gender, age, emotional involvement, and attachment style. *Personality and Social Psychology Bulletin, 29,* 871–884.

Diehm, R., & Armatas, C. (2004). Surfing: An avenue for socially acceptable risk-taking, satisfying needs for sensation seeking and experience seeking. *Personality and Individual Differences, 36,* 663–677.

Digman, J. M. (1990). Personality structure: Emergence of the five-factor model. *Annual Review of Psychology, 41,* 417–440.

Dozier, M., & Kobak, R. R. (1992). Psychophysiology in attachment interviews: Converging evidence for deactivating strategies. *Child Development, 63,* 1473–1480.

Draycott, S. G., & Kline, P. (1995). The Big Three or the Big Five—The EPQ-R vs the NEO-PI: A research note, replication and elaboration. *Personality and Individual Differences, 18,* 801–804.

Eagly, A. (1987). *Sex differences in social behavior: A social-role interpretation*. Hillsdale, NJ: Erlbaum.

Eagly, A. H. (1995). The science and politics of comparing women and men. *American Psychologist, 50,* 145–158.

Ebstein, R. P., Benjamin, J., & Belmaker, R. H. (2002). Behavioral genetics, genomics, and personality. In R. Plomin, J. C. DeFries, I. W. Craig, & P. McGuffin (Eds.), *Behavioral genetics in the postgenomic era* (pp. 365–388). Washington, DC: American Psychological Association.

Ebstein, R. P., Novick, O., Umansky, R., Priel, B., Osher, Y., Blaine, D., et al. (1996). Dopamine D4 receptor (D4DR) exon III polymorphism associated with the human personality trait of Novelty Seeking. *Nature Genetics, 12,* 78–80.

Entwisle, D. R. (1972). To dispel fantasies about fantasy-based measures of achievement motivation. *Psychological Bulletin, 77,* 377–391.

Ernst, C., & Angst, J. (1983). *Birth order: Its influence on personality*. Berlin: Springer-Verlag.

Exner, J. E. (1974). *The Rorschach: A comprehensive system*. Oxford: Wiley.

Exner, J. E., Jr. (2002). A new nonpatient sample for the Rorschach Comprehensive System: A progress report. *Journal of Personality Assessment, 78,* 391–404.

Eysenck, H. J. (1979). The conditioning model of neurosis. *Behavioral and Brain Sciences, 2,* 155–199.

Eysenck, H. J. (1992). Four ways five factors are *not* basic. *Personality and Individual Differences, 13,* 667–673.

Eysenck, H. J. (1993). The structure of phenotypic personality traits: Comment. *American Psychologist, 48,* 1299–1300.

Eysenck, S. B. G., & Eysenck, H. J. (1967). Salivary response to lemon juice as a measure of introversion. *Perceptional and Motor Skills, 24,* 1047–1053.

Feingold, A. (1994). Gender differences in personality: A meta-analysis. *Psychological Bulletin, 116,* 429–456.

Fox, N. A., Henderson, H. A., Marshall, P. J., Nichols, K. E., & Ghera, M. M. (2005). Behavioral inhibition: Linking biology and behavior within a developmental framework. *Annual Review of Psychology, 56,* n.p.

Fraley, R. C., Garner, J. P., & Shaver, P. R. (2000). Adult attachment and the defensive regulation of attention and memory: Examining the role of preemptive and postemptive defensive processes. *Journal of Personality and Social Psychology, 79,* 816–826.

Fraley, R. C., & Shaver, P. R. (1997). Adult attachment and the suppression of unwanted thoughts. *Journal of Personality and Social Psychology, 73,* 1080–1091.

Freese, J., Powell, B., & Steelman, L. C. (1999). Rebel without a cause or effect: Birth order and social attitudes. *American Sociological Review, 64,* 207–231.

Freud, S. (1937/1964). Analysis terminable and interminable. In J. Strachey (Ed. and Trans.), *The standard edition of the complete psychological works of Sigmund Freud* (Vol. 23, pp. 209–253). London: Hogarth Press.

Freud, S. (1938). *The basic writings of Sigmund Freud*. New York: Modern Library (Random House).

Fulker, D. W., Eysenck, S. B., & Zuckerman, M. (1980). A genetic and environmental analysis of sensation seeking. *Journal of Research in Personality, 14,* 261–281.

Funder, D. C. (2001). *The personality puzzle* (2nd ed.). New York: Norton.

Funder, D. C., & Colvin, C. R. (1991). Explorations in behavioral consistency: Properties of persons, situations,

and behaviors. *Journal of Personality and Social Psychology, 60,* 773–794.
Garb, H. N., Wood, J. M., Lilienfeld, S. O., & Nezworski, M. T. (2002). Effective use of projective techniques in clinical practice: Let the data help with selection and interpretation. *Professional Psychology: Research and Practice, 33,* 454–463.
Gilligan, C. (1982). *In a different voice.* Cambridge, MA: Harvard University Press.
Goldberg, L. R. (1981). Language and individual differences: The search for universals in personality lexicons. In L. Wheeler (Ed.), *Review of personality and social psychology* (Vol. 2, pp. 141–165). Beverly Hills, CA: Sage.
Goodwin, R. D., & Gotlib, I. H. (2004). Gender differences in depression: The role of personality factors. *Psychiatry Research, 126,* 135–142.
Gray, J. A. (1982). Précis of the neuropsychology of anxiety: An enquiry into the functions of the septohippocampal system. *Behavioral and Brain Sciences, 5,* 469–534.
Gray, J. A. (1987). Perspectives on anxiety and impulsiveness: A commentary. *Journal of Research in Personality, 21,* 493–509.
Gray, J. A. (1991). The neuropsychology of temperament. In J. Strelau & A. Angleitner (Eds.), *Explorations in temperament: International perspectives on theory and measurement* (pp. 105–128). New York: Plenum Press.
Graziano, W. G., Jensen-Campbell, L. A., & Sullivan-Logan, G. M. (1998). Temperament, activity, and expectations for later personality development, *Journal of Personality and Social Psychology, 74,* 1266–1277.
Haier, R. J., Robinson, D. L., Braden, W., & Williams, D. (1984). Evoked potential augmenting-reducing and personality differences. *Personality and Individual Differences, 5,* 293–301.
Hansenne, M., Pinto, E., Pitchot, W., Reggers, J., Scantamburlo, G., Moor, M., et al. (2002). Further evidence on the relationship between dopamine and novelty seeking: A neuroendocrine study. *Personality and Individual Differences, 33,* 967–977.
Hartshorne, H., & May, M.A. (1928). *Studies in deceit.* New York: Macmillan.
Hazan, C., & Shaver, P. R. (1987). Romantic love conceptualized as an attachment process. *Journal of Personality and Social Psychology, 52,* 511–524.
Heath, A. C., & Martin, N. G. (1990). Psychoticism as a dimension of personality: A multivariate genetic test of Eysenck and Eysenck's Psychoticism construct. *Journal of Personality and Social Psychology, 58,* 11–121.
Heaven, P. C. L., Newbury, K., & Wilson, V. (2004). The Eysenck psychoticism dimension and delinquent behaviours among non-criminals: Changes across the lifespan? *Personality and Individual Differences, 36,* 1817–1825.
Heine, S. J., & Buchtel, E. E. (2009). Personality: The universal and the culturally specific. *Annual Review of Psychology, 60,* 369–394.
Henley, N. M. (1977). *Body politics: Power, sex, and non-verbal communication.* Englewood Cliffs, NJ: Prentice Hall.
Heponiemi, T., Keltikangas-Järvinen, L., Puttonen, S., & Ravaja, N. (2003). BIS/BAS sensitivity and self-rated affects during experimentally induced stress. *Personality and Individual Differences, 34,* 943–957.
Hoffman, L. W. (1991). The influence of the family environment on personality: Accounting for sibling differences. *Psychological Bulletin, 110,* 187–203.
Hofstede, G., & McCrae, R. R. (2004). Personality and culture revisited: Linking traits and dimensions of culture. *Cross-Cultural Research: The Journal of Comparative Social Science, 38,* 52–88.
Holden, C. (1980). Identical twins reared apart. *Science, 207,* 1323–1328.
Horvath, P., & Zuckerman, M. (1993). Sensation seeking, risk appraisal and risky behavior. *Personality and Individual Differences, 14,* 41–52.
Hui, C. H., & Triandis, H. C. (1986). Individualism-collectivism: A study of cross-cultural researchers. *Journal of Cross-Cultural Psychology, 17,* 225–248.
Hur, Y., & Bouchard, T. J., Jr. (1997). The genetic correlation between impulsivity and sensation seeking traits. *Behavior Genetics, 27,* 455–463.
Idemudia, S. E. (1997). Are people in prisons offenders or patients? The Eysenck three-factor personality trait explanation. *IFE Psychologia: An International Journal, 5,* 162–184.
Jenkins, J. M., Rasbash, J., & O'Connor, T. G. (2003). The role of the shared family context in differential parenting. *Developmental Psychology, 39,* 99–113.
Jerome, E. M., & Liss, M. (2005). Relationships between sensory processing style, adult attachment, and coping. *Personality and Individual Differences, 38,* 1341–1352.
Johnson, S. L., Turner, R. J., & Iwata, N. (2003). BIS/BAS levels and psychiatric disorder: An epidemiological study. *Journal of Psychopathology and Behavioral Assessment, 25,* 25–36.
Johnson, W., Bouchard, T. J., Jr., Krueger, R. F., McGue, M., & Gottesman, I. I. (2004). Just one g: Consistent results from three test batteries. *Intelligence, 32,* 95–107.
Joseph, J. (2001). Separated twins and the genetics of personality differences: A critique. *American Journal of Psychology, 114,* 1–30.
Judge, T. A., Erez, A., Bono, J. E., & Thoresen, C. J. (2002). Are measures of self-esteem, neuroticism, locus of control, and generalized self-efficacy indicators of a common core construct? *Journal of Personality and Social Psychology, 83,* 693–710.
Kagan, J. (1989). Temperamental contributions to social behavior. *American Psychologist, 44,* 668–674.
Kagan, J., Reznick, J. S., & Snidman, N. (1988). Biological bases of childhood shyness. *Science, 240,* 167–171.
Kamins, M. L., & Dweck, C. S. (1999). Person versus process praise and criticism: Implications for contingent self-worth and coping. *Developmental Psychology, 35,* 835–847.
Karon, B. J. (2000). The clinical interpretation of the Thematic Apperception Test, Rorschach, and other clinical data: A reexamination of statistical versus clinical prediction. *Professional Psychology: Research and Practice, 31,* 230–233.
Kasch, K. L., Rottenberg, J., Arnow, B. A., & Gotlib, I. H. (2002). Behavioral activation and inhibition systems and the severity and course of depression. *Journal of Abnormal Psychology, 111,* 589–597.
Katigbak, M. S., Church, A. T., & Akamine, T. X. (1996). Cross-cultural generalizability of personality dimensions: Relating indigenous and imported dimensions in two cultures. *Journal of Personality and Social Psychology, 70,* 99–114.
Katigbak, M. S., Church, A. T., Guanzon-Lapena, M., Angleles, C., Annadaisy, J., & del Pilar, G. H. (2002). Are indigenous personality dimensions culture specific? Philippine inventories and the five-factor model. *Journal of Personality and Social Psychology, 82,* 89–101.
Kendler, K. S., Neale, M. C., Kessler, R. C., Heath, A. C., & Eaves, L. J. (1992). The genetic epidemiology of phobias in women: The interrelationship of agoraphobia, social phobia, situational phobia and simple phobia. *Archives of General Psychiatry, 49,* 273–281.
Kenrick, D. T., & Funder, D. C. (1988). Profiting from the controversy: Lessons from the person-situation debate. *American Psychologist, 43,* 23–34.
Lennon, R., & Eisenberg, N. (1987). Gender and age differences in empathy and sympathy. In N. Eisenberg & J. Strayer (Eds.), *Empathy and its development* (pp. 195–217). New York: Cambridge University Press.
Lensvelt-Mulders, G., & Hettema, J. (2001a). Analysis of genetic influences on the consistency and variability of the Big Five across different stressful situations. *European Journal of Personality, 15,* 355–371.
Lensvelt-Mulders, G., & Hettema, J. (2001b). Genetic analysis of autonomic reactivity to psychologically stressful situations. *Biological Psychology, 58,* 25–40.
Lesch, K. P. (2003). Neuroticism and serotonin: A developmental genetic perspective. In R. Plomin, J. C. DeFries, et al. (Eds.), *Behavioral genetics in the postgenomic era* (pp. 389–423). Washington, DC: American Psychological Association.
Lilienfeld, S. O., Wood, J. M., & Garb, H. N. (2000). The scientific status of projective techniques. *Psychological Science in the Public Interest, 1,* 27–66.
Livesley, W. J., Jang, K. L., & Vernon, P. A. (2003). Genetic basis of personality structure. In T. Millon & M. J. Lerner (Eds.), *Handbook of psychology: Personality and social psychology* (Vol. 5, pp. 59–83). New York: Wiley.
Loehlin, J. C. (1992). *Genes and environment in personality development.* Newbury Park, CA: Sage.
Loehlin, J. C., Horn, J. M., & Willerman, L. (1981). Personality resemblance in adoptive families. *Behavior Genetics, 11,* 309–330.
Lott, B. (1996). Politics or science? The question of gender sameness/difference. *American Psychologist, 51,* 153–154.
Lykken, D., & Tellegen, A. (1996). Happiness is a stochastic phenomenon. *Psychological Science, 7,* 186–189.
Lykken, D., Bouchard, T. J., Jr., McGue, M., & Tellegen, A. (1993). Heritability of interests: A twin study. *Journal of Applied Psychology, 78,* 649–661.
Lynn, R., & Martin, T. (1997). Gender differences in extraversion, neuroticism, and psychoticism in 37 nations. *Journal of Social Psychology, 137,* 369–373.
Lyons, M. J., Goldberg, J., Eisen, S. A., True, W., Tsuang, M. T., Meyer, J. M., et al. (1993). Do genes influence exposure to trauma: A twin study of combat. *American Journal of Medical Genetics (Neuropsychiatric Genetics), 48,* 22–27.
Magnusson, D. (2003). The person approach: Concepts, measurement models, and research strategy. *New Directions in Child Adolescent Development, 101,* 3–23.
Mardaga, S., & Hansenne, M. (2009). Do personality traits modulate the effect of emotional visual stimuli on auditory information processing? *Journal of Individual Differences, 30,* 28–34.
Markus, H. R., & Kitayama, S. (1991). Culture and the self: Implications for cognition, emotion, and motivation. *Psychological Review, 98,* 224–253.
Mastandrea, S., Bartoli, G., & Bove, G. (2009). Preferences for ancient and modern art museums: Visitor experiences and personality characteristics. *Psychology of Aesthetics, Creativity, and the Arts, 3,* 164–173.
Matthews, G., & Amelang, M. (1993). Extraversion, arousal theory and performance: A study of individual differences in the EEG. *Personality and Individual Differences, 14,* 347–363.
Matthews, G., & Gilliland, K. (1999). The personality theories of H. J. Eysenck and J. A. Gray: A comparative review. *Personality and Individual Differences, 26,* 583–626.
McCrae, R. H., & Costa, P. T., Jr. (1987). Validation of the five-factor model of personality across instruments and observers. *Journal of Personality and Social Psychology, 52,* 81–90.
McCrae, R. H., & Costa, P. T., Jr. (1997). Personality trait structure as a human universal. *American Psychologist, 52,* 509–516.
McCrae, R. H., Costa, P. T., Jr., DelPilar, G. H., Rolland, J. P., & Parker, W. D. (1998). Cross-cultural assessment of the five-factor model: The revised NEO personality inventory. *Journal of Cross-Cultural Psychology, 29,* 171–188.
McGue, M., & Lykken, D. T. (1992). Genetic influence on the risk of divorce. *Psychological Science, 3,* 368–373.
Meyer, G. J. (2002). Exploring possible ethnic differences and bias in the Rorschach Comprehensive System. *Journal of Personality Assessment, 78,* 104–129.
Meyer, G. J., & Archer, R. P. (2001). The hard science of Rorschach research: What do we know and where do we go? *Psychological Assessment, 13,* 486–502.
Michalski, R. L., & Shackelford, T. K. (2002). An attempted replication of the relationships between birth order and personality. *Journal of Research in Personality, 36,* 182–188.
Mikulincer, M., & Horesh, N. (1999). Adult attachment style and the perception of others: The role of projective mechanisms. *Journal of Personality and Social Psychology, 76,* 1022–1034.
Mikulincer, M., & Orbach, I. (1995). Attachment styles and repressive defensiveness: The accessibility and architecture of affective memories. *Journal of Personality and Social Psychology, 68,* 917–925.
Mischel, W. (1984). Convergences and challenges in the search for consistency. *American Psychologist, 39,* 351–364.
Mischel, W. (2004). Toward an integrative science of the person. *Annual Review of Psychology, 55,* 1–22.
Mischel, W., & Shoda, Y. (1995). A cognitive-affective system theory of personality: Reconceptualizing situations, dispositions, dynamics, and invariance in personality structure. *Psychological Review, 102,* 246–268.
Modell, J. (1996). Family niche and intellectual bent. [Review of *Born to Rebel* by F. J. Sulloway]. *Science, 275,* 624.
Moskowitz, D. S. (1993). Dominance and friendliness: On the interaction of gender and situation. *Journal of Personality, 61,* 387–409.
Muris, P., & Meesters, C. (2002). Attachment, behavioral inhibition, and anxiety disorder symptoms in normal adolescents. *Journal of Psychopathology and Behavioral Assessment, 24,* 97–106.

Newman, L. S., Duff, K. J., & Baumeister, R. F. (1997). A new look at defensive projection: Thought suppression, accessibility, and biased person perception. *Journal of Personality and Social Psychology, 72,* 980–1001.

Niedenthal, P. M., Brauer, M., Robin, L., & Innes-Ker, H. (2002). Adult attachment and the perception of facial expression of emotion. *Journal of Personality and Social Psychology, 82,* 419–433.

Nye, R. D. (1992). *Three psychologies: Perspectives from Freud, Skinner, and Rogers.* Pacific Grove, CA: Brooks/Cole.

O'Connor, T. G., Marvin, R. S., Rutter, M., Olrick, J. T., & Britner, P. A. (2003). Child-parent attachment following early institutional deprivation. *Development and Psychopathology, 15,* 19–38.

Olson, J. M., Vernon, P. A., Harris, J. A., & Jang, K. L. (2001). The heritability of attitudes: A study of twins. *Journal of Personality and Social Psychology, 80,* 845–860.

Paunonen, S. V. (1998). Hierarchical organization of personality and prediction of behavior. *Journal of Personality and Social Psychology, 74,* 538–556.

Paunonen, S. V., & Ashton, M. C. (1998). The structured assessment of personality across cultures. *Journal of Cross-Cultural Psychology, 29,* 150–170.

Paunonen, S. V., Haddock, G., Forsterling, F., & Keinonen, M. (2003). Broad versus narrow personality measures and the prediction of behaviour across cultures. *European Journal of Personality, 17,* 413–433.

Paunonen, S. V., Zeidner, M., Engvik, H. A., Oosterveld, P., & Maliphant, R. (2000). The nonverbal assessment of personality in five cultures. *Journal of Cross-Cultural Psychology, 31,* 220–239.

Pederson, N. L., Plomin, R., McClearn, G. E., & Friberg, L. (1988). Neuroticism, extraversion and related traits in adult twins reared apart and reared together. *Journal of Personality and Social Psychology, 55,* 950–957.

Phillips, K., & Matheny, A. P., Jr. (1995). Quantitative genetic analysis of injury liability in infants and toddlers. *American Journal of Medical Genetics (Neuropsychiatric Genetics), 60,* 64–71.

Pinkerman, J. E., Haynes, J. P., & Keiser, T. (1993). Characteristics of psychological practice in juvenile court clinics. *American Journal of Forensic Psychology, 11,* 3–12.

Plomin, R., & Bergeman, C. S. (1991). The nature of nurture: Genetic influences on "environmental" measures. *Behavioral and Brain Sciences, 14,* 373–427.

Plomin, R., DeFries, J. C., McClearn, G. E., & Rutter, M. (1997). *Behavioral genetics* (3rd ed.). New York: Freeman.

Prescott, C. A., Johnson, R. C., & McArdle, J. J. (1991). Genetic contributions to television viewing. *Psychological Science, 2,* 430–431.

Rebollo, I., Herrero, Ó., & Colom, R. (2002). Personality in imprisoned and non-imprisoned people: Evidence from the EPQ-R. *Psicothema, 14,* 540–543.

Reif, A., & Lesch, K. (2003). Toward a molecular architecture of personality. *Behavioural Brain Research, 139,* 1–20.

Roberti, J. W., Storch, E. A., & Bravata, E. A. (2004). Sensation seeking, exposure to psychosocial stressors, and body modifications in a college population. *Personality and Individual Differences, 37,* 1167–1177.

Roberts, B. W., Caspi, A., & Moffitt, T. E. (2001). The kids are alright: Growth and stability in personality development from adolescence to adulthood. *Journal of Personality and Social Psychology, 81,* 670–683.

Rohde, P. A., Atzwanger, K., Butovskayad, M., Lampert, A., Mysterud, I., Sanchez-Andres, A., et al. (2003). Perceived parental favoritism, closeness to kin, and the rebel of the family: The effects of birth order and sex. *Evolution and Human Behavior, 24,* 261–276.

Rotter, J. B. (1966). Generalized expectancies for internal versus external control of reinforcement. *Psychological Monographs, 80* (1, Whole No. 609).

Roysamb, E., Harris, J. R., Magnus, P., Vitterso, J., & Tambs, K. (2002). Subjective well-being: Sex-specific effects of genetic and environmental factors. *Personality and Individual Differences, 32,* 211–223.

Rubin, K. H., Burgess,·K. B., & Coplan, R. J. (2002). Social withdrawal and shyness. In P. K. Smith & C. H. Hart (Eds.), *Blackwell handbook of childhood social development* (pp. 330–352). Malden, MA: Blackwell Publishers.

Saggino, A. (2000). The Big Three or the Big Five? A replication study. *Personality and Individual Differences, 28,* 879–886.

Sagi, A., Koren-Karie, N., Gini, M., Ziv, Y., & Joels, T. (2002). Shedding further light on the effects of various types and quality of early child care on infant-mother attachment relationship: The Haifa Study of Early Child Care. *Child Development, 73,* 1166–1186.

Sagi, A., van Ijzendoorn, M. H., Scharf, M., Joels, T., Mayseless, O., & Aviezer, O. (1997). Ecological constraints for intergenerational transmission of attachment. *International Journal of Behavioral Development, 20,* 287–299.

Salmon, C. A. (1998). The evocative nature of kin terminology in political rhetoric. *Politics and the Life Sciences, 17,* 51–57.

Salmon, C. A. (1999). On the impact of sex and birth order on contact with kin. *Human Nature, 10,* 183–197.

Salmon, C. A., & Daly, M. (1998). Birth order and familial sentiment: Middleborns are different. *Evolution and Behavior, 19,* 299–312.

Saroglou, V., & Fiasse, L. (2003). Birth order, personality, and religion: A study among young adults from a three-sibling family. *Personality and Individual Differences, 35,* 19–29.

Scarr, S., & McCartney, K. (1983). How people make their own environments: A theory of genotype-environment effects. *Child Development, 54,* 424–435.

Seuling, B. (1976). *The loudest screen kiss and other little-known facts about the movies.* New York: Doubleday.

Shaver, P. R., & Hazan, C. (1994). Attachment. In A. L. Weber & J. H. Harvey (Eds.), *Perspectives on close relationships* (pp. 110-130). Boston: Allyn & Bacon.

Shields, S. A. (1987). Women, men, and the dilemma of emotion. In P. Shaver & C. Hendrick (Eds.), *Sex and gender* (pp. 229–250). Newbury Park, CA: Sage.

Shoda, Y., & LeeTiernan, S. (2002). What remains invariant? Finding order within a person's thoughts, feelings, and behaviors across situations. In D. Cervone & W. Mischel (Eds.), *Advances in personality science* (pp. 241–270). New York: Guilford Press.

Siegel, D. J. (1999). *The developing mind: Toward a neurobiology of interpersonal experience.* New York: Guilford Press.

Silverman, L. (1976). Psychoanalytic theory: The reports of my death are greatly exaggerated. *American Psychologist, 31,* 621–637.

Skinner, B. F. (1953). *Science and human behavior.* New York: Macmillan.

Skinner, N. F. (2003). Birth order effects in dominance: Failure to support Sulloway's view. *Psychological Reports, 92,* 387–388.

Snidman, N., Kagan, J., Riordan, L., & Shannon, D. C. (1995). Cardiac function and behavioral reactivity during infancy. *Psychophysiology, 32,* 199–207.

Stelmack, R. M. (1990). Biological bases of extraversion: Psychophysiological evidence. *Journal of Personality, 58,* 293–311.

Stoolmiller, M. (1999). Implications of the restricted range of family environments for estimates of heritability and nonshared environment in behavior-genetic adoption studies. *Psychological Bulletin, 125,* 392–409.

Strom, S. (2000, January 4). Tradition of equality fading in new Japan. *New York Times.*

Sulloway, F. J. (1996). *Born to rebel: Birth order, family dynamics, and creative lives.* New York: Vintage.

Tellegen, A., Lykken, D. T., Bouchard, T. J., Wilcox, K. J., Segal, N. L., & Rich, S. (1988). Personality similarity in twins reared apart and together. *Journal of Personality and Social Psychology, 54,* 1031–1039.

Tesser, A., Whitaker, D., Martin, L., & Ward, D. (1998). Attitude heritability, attitude change and physiological responsivity. *Personality and Individual Differences, 24,* 89–96.

Tidwell, M. O., Reis, H. T., Shaver, P. R. (1996). Attachment, attractiveness, and social interaction: A diary study. *Journal of Personality and Social Psychology, 71,* 729–745.

Triandis, H. C., Bontempo, R., Villareal, M. J., Asai, M., & Lucca, N. (1988). Individualism and collectivism: Cross-cultural perspectives on self-ingroup relationships. *Journal of Personality and Social Psychology, 54,* 323–338.

Triandis, H. C., McCusker, C., & Hui, C. H. (1990). Multimethod probes of individualism and collectivism. *Journal of Personality and Social Psychology, 59,* 1006–1020.

Twenge, J. M. (1997). Changes in masculine and feminine traits over time: A meta-analysis. *Sex Roles, 36,* 305–325.

Twenge, J. M. (2000). The age of anxiety? Birth cohort change in anxiety and neuroticism, 1952–1993. *Journal of Personality and Social Psychology, 79,* 1007–1021.

Twenge, J. M. (2001a). Birth cohort changes in extraversion: A cross-temporal meta-analysis, 1966–1993. *Personality and Individual Differences, 30,* 735–748.

Twenge, J. M. (2001b). Changes in women's assertiveness in response to status and roles: A cross-temporal meta-analysis, 1931–1993. *Journal of Personality and Social Psychology, 81,* 133–145.

Twenge, J. M., & Campbell, S. M. (2008). Generational differences in psychological traits and their impact on the workplace. *Journal of Managerial Psychology, 23,* 862–877.

Twenge, J. M., Zhang, L., & Im, C. (2004). It's beyond my control: A cross-temporal meta-analysis of increasing externality in locus of control, 1960– 2002. *Personality and Social Psychology Review, 8,* 308–319.

van Ijzendoorn, M. (1995). Adult attachment representations, parental responsiveness, and infant attachment: A meta-analysis on the predictive validity of the Adult Attachment Interview. *Psychological Bulletin, 117,* 387–403.

Vazire, S., & Gosling, S. D. (2004). e-Perceptions: Personality impressions based on personal Websites. *Journal of Personality and Social Psychology, 87,* 123–132.

Waller, N. G., Kojetin, B. A., Bouchard, T. J., Jr., Lykken, D. T., & Tellegen, A. (1990). Genetic and environmental influences on religious interests, attitudes, and values: A study of twins reared apart and together. *Psychological Science, 1,* 138–142.

Waller, N. G., & Shaver, P. R. (1994). The importance of non-genetic influences on romantic love styles: A twin family study. *Psychological Science, 5,* 268–274.

Watson, J. B. (1913). Psychology as a behaviorist views it. *Psychological Review, 20,* 158–177.

Weisskirch, R. S., & Murphy, L. C. (2004). Friends, porn, and punk: Sensation seeking in personal relationships, Internet activities and music preference among college students. *Adolescence, 39,* 189–201.

Westen, D. (1998). The scientific legacy of Sigmund Freud: Toward a psychodynamically informed psychological science. *Psychological Bulletin, 124,* 333–371.

Westen, D. (1999). The scientific status of unconscious processes: Is Freud really dead? *Journal of the American Psychoanalytic Association, 47*(Suppl.), 1–45.

Wiesbeck, G. A., Mauerer, C., Thome, J., Jakob, F., & Boening, J. (1995). Neuroendocrine support for a relationship between "novelty seeking" and dopaminergic function in alcohol-dependent men. *Psychoneuroendocrinology, 20,* 755–761.

Wiggins, J. S. (1992). Have model, will travel. *Journal of Personality, 60,* 527–532.

Wood, J. J., McLeod, B. D., Sigman, M., Hwang, W., & Chu, B. C. (2003). Parenting and childhood anxiety: Theory, empirical findings, and future directions. *Journal of Child Psychology and Psychiatry, 44,* 134–151.

Wood, J. M., Lilienfeld, S. O., Nezworski, M. T., & Garb, H. N. (2001). Coming to grips with negative evidence for the comprehensive system for the Rorschach: A comment on Gacono, Loving, and Bodholdt; Ganellen; and Bornstein. *Journal of Personality Assessment, 77,* 48–70.

Wood, J. M., Nezworski, M. T., Garb, H. N., & Lilienfeld, S. O. (2001). Problems with the norms of the comprehensive system for the Rorschach: Methodological and conceptual considerations. *Clinical Psychology: Science and Practice, 8,* 397–402.

Yang, K., & Bond, M. H. (1990). Exploring implicit personality theories with indigenous or imported constructs: The Chinese case. *Journal of Personality and Social Psychology, 58,* 1087–1095.

Zane, N. W. S., Sue, S., Hu, L., & Kwon, J. H. (1991). Asian-American assertion: A social learning analysis of cultural differences. *Journal of Counseling Psychology, 38,* 63–70.

Zhengyan, W., Huichang, C., & Xinyin, C. (2003). The stability of children's behavioral inhibition: A longitudinal study from two to four years of age. *Acta Psychologica Sinica, 35,* 93–100.

Zuckerman, M. (1979). *Sensation seeking: Beyond the optimal level of arousal.* Hillsdale, NJ: Erlbaum.

Zuckerman, M. (1989). Personality as a third dimension: A psychobiological approach. *Personality and Individual Differences, 10,* 391–418.

Zuckerman, M. (1994). *Behavioral expressions and biosocial bases of sensation seeking.* New York: Cambridge University Press.

Zuckerman, M. (2003). Biological bases of personality. In T. Millon & M. J. Lerner (Eds.), *Handbook of psychology: Personality and social psychology* (Vol. 5, pp. 85–116). New York: Wiley.

Zuckerman, M., & Cloninger, C. R. (1996). Relationships between Cloninger's, Zuckerman's, and Eysenck's dimensions of personality. *Personality and Individual Differences, 21,* 283–285.

Zuckerman, M., Joireman, J., Kraft, M., & Kuhlman, D. M. (1999). Where do motivational and emotional traits fit within three factor models of personality? *Personality and Individual Differences, 26,* 487–504.

Zuckerman, M., & Kuhlman, D. M. (2000). Personality and risk-taking: Common biosocial factors. *Journal of Personality, 68,* 999–1029.

Zuckerman, M., Kuhlman, D. M., & Camac, C. (1988). What lies beyond E and N? Factor analyses of scales believed to measure basic dimensions of personality. *Journal of Personality and Social Psychology, 54,* 96–107.

Zweigenhaft, R. L. (2002). Birth order effects and rebelliousness: Political activism and involvement with marijuana. *Political Psychology, 23,* 219–233.

References: Psychology Over the Life Span

Aartsen, M. J., van Tilburg, T., Smits, C. H. M., & Knipscheer, K. C. P. M. (2004). A longitudinal study of the impact of physical and cognitive decline on the personal network in old age. *Journal of Socfial and Personal Relationships, 21,* 249–266.

Adolph, K. E. (2000). Specificity of learning: Why infants fall over a veritable cliff. *Psychological Science, 11,* 290–295.

Ainsworth, M. D. S., Blehar, M. C., Waters, E., & Wahl, S. (1978). *Patterns of attachment: A psychological study of the Strange Situation.* Hillsdale, NJ: Erlbaum.

Akhtar, N., & Tomasello, M. (1996). Two-year-olds learn words for absent objects and actions. *British Journal of Developmental Psychology, 14,* 79–93.

Albert, M. S., & Moss, M. B. (1996). Neuropsychology of aging: Findings in humans and monkeys. In E. L. Schneider, J. W. Rowe, T. E. Johnson, N. J. Holbrook, & J. H. Morrison (Eds.), *Handbook of the biology of aging* (4th ed.). (pp. 217–233). San Diego, CA: Academic Press.

Allemand, M., Zimprich, D., & Martin, M. (2008). Age differences in five personality domains across the life span. *Developmental Psychology, 44,* 758–770.

Almli, C. R., Ball, R. H., & Wheeler, M. E. (2001). Human fetal and neonatal movement patterns: Gender differences and fetal-to-neonatal continuity. *Developmental Psychobiology, 38,* 252–273.

Anglin, J. M. (1993). Vocabulary development: A morphological analysis. *Monographs of the Society for Research in Child Development, 58*(10, Serial No. 238).

Anisman, H., Zaharia, M. D., Meaney, M. J., & Merali, Z. (1998). Do early-life events permanently alter behavioral and hormonal responses to stressors? *International Journal of Developmental Neuroscience, 16,* 149–164.

Arnett, J. (1992). Reckless behavior in adolescence: A developmental perspective. *Developmental Review, 12,* 339–373.

Arnett, J. J. (1999). Adolescent storm and stress, reconsidered. *American Psychologist, 54,* 317–326.

Arterberry, M. E., & Yonas, A. (2000). Perception of three-dimensional shape specified by optic flow by 8-week-old infants. *Perception and Psychophysics, 62,* 550–556.

Association of SIDS and Infant Mortality Programs. (2002). *Infant sleep positioning and SIDS.* Retrieved from http://www.asip1.org/isp.html

Avorn, J., & Langer, E. (1982). Induced disability in nursing home patients: A controlled trial. *Journal of the American Geriatrics Society, 30,* 397–400.

Bahrick, L. E., Moss, L., & Fadil, C. (1996). Development of visual self-recognition in infancy. *Ecological Psychology, 8,* 189–208.

Baillargeon, R. (1993). The object concept revisited: New directions in the investigation of infants' physical knowledge. In C. E. Granrud (Ed.), *Visual perception and cognition in infancy* (pp. 265–315). Hillsdale, NJ: Erlbaum.

Baillargeon, R. (2004). Infants' physical world. *Current Directions in Psychological Science, 13,* 89–94.

Baird, A., Kagan, J., Gaudette, T., Walz, K., Hershlag, N., & Boas, D. (2002). Frontal lobe activation during object permanence: Data from near-infrared spectroscopy. *NeuroImage, 16,* 1120–1126.

Bakermans-Kranenburg, M. J., van Ijzendoorn, M. H., & Kroonenberg, P. M. (2004). Differences in attachment security between African-American and white children: Ethnicity or socio-economic status? *Infant Behavior and Development, 27,* 417–433.

Baldock, M. R. J., Berndt, A., & Mathias, J. L. (2008). The functional correlates of older drivers' on-road driving test errors. *Topics in Geriatric Rehabilitation, 24,* 204–223.

Ball, K., Berch, D. B., Helmers, K. F., Jobe, J. B., Leveck, M. D., Marsiske, M., et al. (2002). Effects of cognitive training interventions with older adults: A randomized controlled trial. *Journal of the American Medical Association, 288,* 2271–2281.

Baltes, P. B. (1987). Theoretical propositions of life-span developmental psychology: On the dynamics between growth and decline. *Developmental Psychology, 23,* 611–626.

Banks, M. S., & Bennett, P. J. (1988). Optical and photoreceptor immaturities limit the spatial and chromatic vision of human neonates. *Journal of the Optical Society of America, 5,* 2059–2079.

Beilin, H. (1996). Mind and meaning: Piaget and Vygotsky on causal explanation. *Human Development, 39,* 277–286.

Bell, J. H., & Bromnick, R. D. (2003). The social reality of the imaginary audience: A ground theory approach. *Adolescence, 38,* 205–219.

Berg, S. (1996). Aging, behavior, and terminal decline. In J. E. Birren & K. W. Schaie (Eds.), *Handbook of the psychology of aging* (4th ed., pp. 323–337). New York: Academic Press.

Berghella, V., Buchanan, E., Pereira, L., & Baxter, J. K. (2010). Preconception care. *Obstetrical and Gynecological Survey, 65,* 119–931.

Berko, J. (1958). The child's learning of English morphology. *Word, 14,* 150–177.

Beyers, J. M., & Loeber, R. (2003). Untangling developmental relations between depressed mood and delinquency in male adolescents. *Journal of Abnormal Child Psychology, 31,* 247–266.

Bhatt, R. S., & Bertin, E. (2001). Pictorial cues and three-dimensional information processing in early infancy. *Journal of Experimental Child Psychology, 80,* 315–332.

Birren, J. E., Riegel, K. F., & Morrison, D. F. (1962). Age differences in response speed as a function of controlled variations of stimulus conditions: Evidence of a general speed factor. *Gerontologia, 6,* 1–18.

Blanck, H. M., Marcus, M., Tolbert, P. E., Rubin, C., Henderson, A. K., Hertzberg, V. S., et al. (2000). Age at menarche and Tanner stage in girls exposed *in utero* and postnatally to polybrominated biphenyl. *Epidemiology, 11,* 641–647.

Bochner, S., & Jones, J. (2003). *Child language development: Learning to talk.* London: Whurr.

Bontempo, D. E., & D'Augelli, A. R. (2002). Effects of at-school victimization and sexual orientation on lesbian, gay, or bisexual youths' health risk behavior. *Journal of Adolescent Health, 30,* 364–374.

Bornstein, M. H., DiPietro, J. A., Hahn, C. S., Painter, K., Haynes, O. M., & Costigan, K. A. (2002). Prenatal cardiac function and postnatal cognitive development: An exploratory study. *Infancy, 3,* 475–494.

Bornstein, M. H., Tal, J., Rahn, C., Galperin, C. Z., Pêcheux, C-G, Lamour, M., et al. (1992). Functional analysis of the contents of maternal speech to infants of 5 and 13 months in four cultures: Argentina, France, Japan, and the United States. *Developmental Psychology, 28,* 593–603.

Bosworth, H. B., & Siegler, I. C. (2002). Terminal change in cognitive function: An updated review of longitudinal studies. *Experimental Aging Research, 28,* 299–315.

Botwinick, J. (1984). *Aging and behavior: A comprehensive integration of research findings.* New York: Springer.

Bowlby, J. (1969). *Attachment and loss: Vol. 1. Attachment.* New York: Basic Books.

Brach, J. S., Simonsick, E. M., Kritchevsky, S., Yaffe, K., & Newman, A. B. (2004). The association between physical function and lifestyle activity and exercise in the health, aging and body composition study. *Journal of the American Geriatrics Society, 52,* 502–509.

Brooks-Gunn, J., Graber, J. A., & Paikoff, R. L. (1994). Studying links between hormones and negative affect: Models and measures. *Journal of Research on Adolescence, 4,* 469–486.

Brown, B. (1999). Optimizing expression of the common human genome for child development. *Current Directions in Psychological Science, 8,* 37–41.

Brown, B. B., Clasen, D., & Eicher, S. (1986a). Perceptions of peer pressure, peer conformity dispositions, and self-reported behavior among adolescents. *Developmental Psychology, 22,* 521–530.

Brown, B. B., Lohr, M. J., & McClenahan, E. L. (1986b). Early adolescents' perceptions of peer pressure. *Journal of Early Adolescence, 6,* 139–154.

Browne, C. A., Colditz, P. B., & Dunster, K. R. (2000). Infant autonomic function is altered by maternal smoking during pregnancy. *Early Human Development, 59,* 209–218.

Bryan, R. N., Wells, S. W., Miller, T. J., Elster, A. D., Jungreis, C. A., Poirier, V. C., et al. (1997). Infarctlike lesions in the brain: Prevalence and anatomic characteristics at MR imaging of the elderly—Data from the Cardiovascular Health Study. *Radiology, 202,* 47–54.

Buchanan, C. M., Eccles, J., & Becker, J. (1992). Are adolescents the victims of raging hormones? Evidence for activational effects of hormones on moods and behavior at adolescence. *Psychological Bulletin, 111,* 62–107.

Burton, L. M. (1990). Teenage childbearing as an alternative life-course strategy in multigeneration Black families. *Human Nature, 1,* 123–143.

Burton, L. M. (1996). Age norms, the timing of family role transitions, and intergenerational caregiving among aging African American women. *The Gerontologist, 36,* 199–208.

Busse, E. W. (1969). Theories of aging. In E. W. Busse & E. Pfeiffer (Eds.), *Behavior and adaptation in later life* (pp. 11–32). Boston: Little, Brown.

Caldera, Y. M., & Sciaraffa, M. A. (1998). Parent-toddler play with feminine toys: Are all dolls the same? *Sex Roles, 39,* 657–668.

Cameron-Faulkner, T., Lieven, E., & Tomasello, M. (2003). A construction based analysis of child directed speech. *Cognitive Science, 27,* 843–873.

Campos, J. J., Langer, A., & Krowitz, A. (1970). Cardiac responses on the visual cliff in prelocomotor human infants. *Science, 170,* 196–197.

Carey, S. (1978). The child as word learner. In J. Bresnan, G. Miller, & M. Halle (Eds.), *Linguistic theory and psychological reality* (pp. 264–293). Cambridge, MA: MIT Press.

Carstensen, L. L. (1991). Socioemotional selectivity theory: Social activity in life-span context. In K. W. Schaie & M. P. Lawton (Eds.), *Annual review of gerontology and geriatrics* (Vol. 11, pp. 195–217). New York: Springer.

Carstensen, L. L. (1992). Social and emotion patterns in adulthood: Support for socioemotional selectivity theory. *Psychology and Aging, 7,* 331–338.

Carstensen, L. L., & Charles, S. T. (1998). Emotion in the second half of life. *Current Directions in Psychological Science, 7,* 144–149.

Carstensen, L. L., Gottman, J. M., & Levenson, R. W. (1995). Emotional behavior in long-term marriage. *Psychology and Aging, 10,* 140–149.

Carstensen, L. L., Pasupathi, M., Mayr, U., & Nesselroade, J. R. (2000). Emotional experience in everyday life across the adult life span. *Journal of Personality and Social Psychology, 79,* 644–655.

Case, R. (1977). Responsiveness to conservation training as a function of induced subjective uncertainty, M-space, and cognitive style. *Canadian Journal of Behavioral Sciences, 9,* 12–25.

Case, R. (1978). Intellectual development from birth to adulthood: A neo-Piagetian approach. In R. S. Siegler (Ed.), *Children's thinking: What develops?* (pp. 37–71). Hillsdale, NJ: Erlbaum.

Case, R. (1992a). *The mind's staircase.* Hillsdale, NJ: Erlbaum.

Case, R. (1992b). The role of the frontal lobes in the regulation of cognitive development. *Brain and Cognition, 20,* 51–73.

Cerella, J. (1990). Aging and information-processing rate. In J. E. Birren & K. W. Schaie (Eds.), *Handbook of the psychology of aging* (3rd ed., pp. 201–221). San Diego, CA: Academic Press.

Chapman, J. K. (2000). Developmental outcomes in two groups of young children: Prenatally cocaine exposed and noncocaine exposed: Part 2. *Infant-Toddler Intervention, 10,* 81–96.

Cheour-Luhtanen, M., Alho, K., Sainio, K., Rinne, T., & Reinikainen, K. (1996). The ontogenetically earliest discriminative response of the human brain. *Psychophysiology, 33,* 478–481.

Chess, S., & Thomas, A. (1987). *Know your child.* New York: Basic Books.

Chomsky, N. (1959). A review of B. F. Skinner's *Verbal Behavior. Language, 35,* 26–58.

Chomsky, N. (1972). *Language and mind.* New York: Harcourt Brace.

Chumlea, W. C., Schubert, C. M., Roche, A. F., Kulin, H. E., Lee, P. A., Himes, J. H., et al. (2003). Age at menarche and racial comparisons in U.S. girls. *Pediatrics, 111,* 110–113.

Clark, E. V. (1983). Meanings and concepts. In P. H. Mussen (Ed.), *Handbook of child psychology: Vol. 3. Cognitive development* (pp. 787–840). New York: Wiley.

Clark, E. V. (1993). *The lexicon in acquisition.* Cambridge: Cambridge University Press.

Claxton, L. J., Keen, R., & McCarty, M. E. (2003). Evidence of motor planning in infant reaching behavior. *Psychological Science, 14,* 354–356.

Clifford, D. B. (2000). Human immunodeficiency virus-associated dementia. *Archives of Neurology, 57,* 321–324.

Clopton, N. A., & Sorell, G. T. (1993). Gender differences in moral reasoning: Stable or situational? *Psychology of Women Quarterly, 17,* 85–101.

Cole, M. (1990). Cognitive development and formal schooling: The evidence from cross-cultural research. In L. C. Moll (Ed.), *Vygotsky and education* (pp. 89–110). New York: Cambridge University Press.

Cole, M., & Wertsch, J. V. (1996). Beyond the individual-social antinomy in discussions of Piaget and Vygotsky. *Human Development, 39,* 250–256.

Coleman, P., & Flood, D. (1986). Dendritic proliferation in the aging brain as a compensatory repair mechanism. *Progress in Brain Research, 70,* 227–236.

Colombo, J., & Mitchell, D. W. (2009). Infant visual habituation. *Neurobiology of Learning and Memory, 92,* 225–234.

Colombo, J., & Richman, W. A. (2002). Infant timekeeping: Attention and temporal estimating in 4-month-olds. *Psychological Science, 13,* 475–479.

Comings, D. E., Muhleman, D., Johnson, J. P., & MacMurray, J. P. (2002). Parent-daughter transmission of the androgen receptor gene as an explanation of the effect of father absence on age of menarche. *Child Development, 73,* 1046–1051.

Cooper, M. L., Wood, P. K., Orcutt, H. K., & Albino, A. (2003). Personality and the predisposition to engage in risky or problem behaviors during adolescence. *Journal of Personality and Social Psychology, 84,* 390–410.

Cooper, R. P., Abraham, J., Berman, S., & Staska, M. (1997). The development of infants' preference for motherese. *Infant Behavior and Development, 20,* 477–488.

Cornelius, M. D., & Day, N. L. (2000). The effects of tobacco use during and after pregnancy on exposed children. *Alcohol Research and Health, 24,* 242–249.

Costa, P. T., Jr., Herbst, J. H., McCrae, R. R., & Siegler, I. C. (2000). Personality at midlife: Stability, intrinsic maturation, and response to life events. *Assessment, 7,* 365–378.

Costa, P. T., & McCrae, R. R. (1988). Personality in adulthood: A six-year longitudinal study of self-reports and spouse ratings on the NEO personality inventory. *Journal of Personality and Social Psychology, 54,* 853–863.

Costela, C., Tejedor-Real, P., Mico, J. A., & Gilbert-Rahola, J. (1995). Effect of neonatal handling on learned helplessness model of depression. *Physiology and Behavior, 57,* 407–410.

Cotman, C. (1990). The brain: New plasticity/new possibility. In R. N. Butler, M. R. Oberlink, & M. Schechter (Eds.), *The promise of productive aging: From biology to social policy* (pp. 70–84). New York: Springer.

Craik, F. I. M., Anderson, N. D., Kerr, S. A., & Li, K. Z. H. (1995). Memory changes in normal aging. In A. D. Baddeley, B. A. Wilson, & F. N. Watts (Eds.), *Handbook of memory disorders* (pp. 211–241). New York: Wiley.

Craik, F. I., & McDowd, J. M. (1987). Age differences in recall and recognition. *Journal of Experimental Psychology: Learning, Memory, and Cognition, 13,* 474–479.

Damasio, A. (1994). *Descartes' error: Emotion, reason, and the human brain.* New York: Avon Books.

Dar, Y., & Kimhi, S. (2001). Military service and self-perceived maturation among Israeli youth. *Journal of Youth and Adolescence, 30,* 427–448.

Davis, B. E., Moon, R. Y., Sachs, H. C., & Ottolini, M. C. (1998). Effects of sleep position on infant motor development. *Pediatrics, 102,* 1135–1140.

Dean, W., Morgenthaler, J., & Fowkes, S. W. (1993). *Smart drugs: II. The next generation: New drugs and nutrients to improve your memory and increase your intelligence (Smart Drug Series, Vol. 2).* Petaluma, CA: Smart Publications.

Deary, I. J., Whiteman, M. C., Starr, J. M., Whalley, L. J., & Fox, H. C. (2004). The impact of childhood intelligence on later life: Following up the Scottish mental surveys of 1932 and 1947. *Journal of Personality and Social Psychology, 86,* 130–147.

De Beni, R., & Palladino, P. (2004). Decline in working memory updating through ageing: Intrusion error analyses. *Memory, 12,* 75–89.

DeCasper, A. J., & Fifer, W. P. (1980). On human bonding: Newborns prefer their mothers' voices. *Science, 208,* 1174–1176.

Dehaene-Lambertz, G., & Dehaene, S. (1994). Speed and cerebral correlates of syllable discrimination in infants. *Nature, 370,* 292–295.

de la Chica, R. A., Ribas, I., Giraldo, J., Egozcue, J., & Fuster, C. (2005). Chromosomal instability in amniocytes from fetuses of mothers who smoke. *Journal of the American Medical Association, 293,* 1212–1222.

Demetriou, A., Christou, C., Spanoudis, G., & Platsidou, M. (2002). The development of mental processing: Efficiency, working memory, and thinking. *Monographs of the Society for Research in Child Development, 67,* vii–154.

de Muinck Keizer-Schrama, S. M. P. F., & Mul, D. (2001). Trends in pubertal development in Europe. *Human Reproduction Update, 7,* 287–291.

de Villiers, P. A., & de Villiers, J. G. (1992). Language development. In M. H. Bornstein & M. E. Lamb (Eds.), *Developmental psychology: An advanced textbook* (3rd ed., pp. 337–418). Hillsdale, NJ: Erlbaum.

Diamond, L. M., & Dube, E. M. (2002). Friendship and attachment among heterosexual and sexual-minority youths: Does the gender of your friend matter? *Journal of Youth and Adolescence, 31,* 155–166.

Dick, F., Bates, E., Wulfeck, B., Utman, J. A., Dronkers, N., & Gernsbacher, M. A. (2001). Language deficits, localization, and grammar: Evidence for a distributive model of language breakdown in aphasic patients and neurologically intact individuals. *Psychological Review, 108,* 759–788.

DiPietro, J. A., Costigan, K. A., & Gurewitsch, E. D. (2003). Fetal response to induced maternal stress. *Early Human Development, 74,* 125–138.

DiPietro, J. A., Hodgson, D. M., Costigan, K. A., Hilton, S. C., & Johnson, T. R. B. (1996). Fetal neurobehavioral development. *Child Development, 67,* 2553–2567.

Dodge, K. A., & Pettit, G. S. (2003). A biopsychosocial model of the development of chronic conduct problems in adolescence. *Developmental Psychology, 39,* 349–371.

Dominey, P. F., & Dodane, C. (2004). Indeterminacy in language acquisition: The role of child directed speech and joint attention. *Journal of Neurolinguistics, 17,* 121–145.

Eder, R. A. (1989). The emergent personologist: The structure and content of 3-, 5-, and 7-year-olds' concepts of themselves and other persons. *Child Development, 60,* 1218–1228.

Elkind, D. (1967). Egocentrism in adolescence. *Child Development, 38,* 1025–1034.

Elkind, D., & Bowen, R. (1979). Imaginary audience behavior in children and adolescence. *Developmental Psychology, 15,* 33–44.

Ellis, B. J., Bates, J. E., Dodge, K. A., Fergusson, D. M., Horwood, L. J., Pettit, G. S., et al. (2003). Does father absence place daughters at special risk for early sexual activity and teenage pregnancy? *Child Development, 74,* 801–821.

Elman, J. L., Bates, E. A., Johnson, M. H., Karmiloff-Smith, A., Parisi, D., & Plunkett, K. (1996). *Rethinking innateness: A connectionist perspective on development.* Cambridge: MIT Press.

Epstein, H. T. (1980). EEG developmental stages. *Developmental Psychobiology, 13,* 629–631.

Erikson, Erik H. (1950). Childhood and society. Erikson, E. H. (1950). Childhood and society. New York: W. W. Norton & Co.

Eskenazi, B. (1993). Caffeine during pregnancy: Grounds for concern? *Journal of the American Medical Association, 270,* 2973–2974.

Eskenazi, B., Stapleton, A. L., Kharrazi, M., & Chee, W. Y. (1999). Associations between maternal decaffeinated and caffeinated coffee consumption and fetal growth and gestational duration. *Epidemiology, 10,* 242–249.

Farroni, T., Csibra, G., Simion, F., & Johnson, M. H. (2002). Eye contact detection in humans from birth. *Proceedings of the National Academy of Sciences of the United States of America, 99,* 9602–9605.

Feigenson, L., & Halberda, J. (2004). Infants chunk object arrays into sets of individuals. *Cognition, 91,* 173–190.

Fernald, A., Taeschner, T., Dunn, J., Papousek, M., Boysson-Bardies, B., & Fukui, I. (1989). A cross-language study of prosodic modifications in mothers' and fathers' speech to infants. *Child Development, 64,* 637–656.

Field, T., Schanberg, S., Scarfidi, F., Bauer, C., Vega-Lahr, N., Garcia, R., et al. (1986). Tactile/kinesthetic stimulation effects on preterm neonates. *Pediatrics, 77,* 654–658.

Field, T. M. (1998). Touch therapy effects on development. *International Journal of Behavioral Development, 22,* 779–797.

Field, T. M., Woodson, R., Greenberg, R., & Cohen, D. (1982). Discrimination and imitation of facial expressions by neonates. *Science, 218,* 179–181.

Finlay, F. O., Jones, R., & Coleman, J. (2002). Is puberty getting earlier? The views of doctors and teachers. *Child: Care, Health and Development, 28,* 205–209.

Fleischman, D. A., Wilson, R. S., Gabrieli, J. D. E., Bienias, J. L., & Bennett, D. A. (2004). A longitudinal study of implicit and explicit memory in old persons. *Psychology and Aging, 19,* 617–625.

Floyd, R. L., Rimer, B. K., Giovino, G. A., Mullen, P. D., & Sullivan, S. E. (1993). A review of smoking in pregnancy: Effects on pregnancy outcomes and cessation efforts. *Annual Review of Public Health, 14,* 379–411.

Fox, C. H. (1994). Cocaine use in pregnancy. *Journal of the American Board of Family Practice, 7,* 225–228.

Fozard, J. (1990). Vision and hearing in aging. In J. E. Birren & K. W. Schaie (Eds.), *Handbook of the psychology of aging* (3rd ed., pp. 150–170). San Diego: Academic Press.

Fraley, R. C., & Spieker, S. J. (2003). Are infant attachment patterns continuously or categorically distributed? A taxometric analysis of strange situation behavior. *Developmental Psychology, 39,* 387–404.

Freeman, J. H., Jr., & Nicholson, D. A. (2001). Ontogenetic changes in the neural mechanisms of eyeblink conditioning. *Integrative Physiological and Behavioral Science, 36,* 15–35.

Fried, P. A., & Makin, J. E. (1987). Neonatal behavioral correlates of prenatal exposure to marijuana, cigarettes, and alcohol in a low risk population. *Neurobehavioral Toxicology and Teratology, 9,* 1–7.

Fried, P. A., & Watkinson, B. (2000). Visuoperceptual functioning differs in 9- to 12-year-olds prenatally exposed to cigarettes and marihuana. *Neurotoxicology and Teratology, 22,* 11–20.

Friedler, G. (1996). Paternal exposures: Impact on reproductive and developmental outcome: An overview. *Pharmacology, Biochemistry and Behavior, 55,* 691–700.

Fung, H. H., Carstensen, L. L., & Lang, F. R. (2001). Age-related patterns in social networks among European Americans and African Americans: Implications for socioemotional selectivity across the life span. *International Journal of Aging and Human Development, 52,* 185–206.

Gabrieli, J. D. E. (1996). Memory systems analyses of mnemonic disorders in aging and age-related diseases. *Proceedings of the National Academy of Sciences of the United States of America, 93,* 13534–13540.

Galanaki, E. (2001). The "imaginary audience" and the "personal fable" in relation to risk behavior and risk perception during adolescence. *Psychology: The Journal of the Hellenic Psychological Society, 8,* 411–430.

Gelman, R. (1972). Logical capacity of very young children: Number invariance rules. *Child Development, 43,* 75–90.

Gerhardstein, P., Adler, S. A., & Rovee-Collier, C. (2000). A dissociation in infants' memory for stimulus size: Evidence for the early development of multiple memory systems. *Developmental Psychobiology, 36,* 123–135.

Gesell, A., & Thompson, H. (1938). *The psychology of early growth including norms of infant behavior and a method of genetic analysis.* New York: Macmillan.

Gibson, J. J., & Walk, R. D. (1960). The "visual cliff." *Scientific American, 202,* 64–71.

Giedd, J. N. (2008). The teen brain: Insights from neuroimaging. *Journal of Adolescent Health, 42,* 335–343.

Gilligan, C. (1982). *In a different voice.* Cambridge, MA: Harvard University Press.

Goodfellow, P. N., & Lovell-Badge, R. (1993). SRY and sex determination in mammals. *Annual Review of Genetics, 27,* 71–92.

Gottfredson, M. R., & Hirschi, T. (1990). *A general theory of crime.* Stanford, CA: Stanford University Press.

Gould, E., Tanapat, P., Hastings, N. B., & Shors, T. J. (1999). Neurogenesis in adulthood: A possible role in learning. *Trends in Cognitive Sciences, 3,* 186–192.

Gould, R. (1978). *Transformations.* New York: Simon & Schuster.

Grant, I., Marcotle, T. D., Heaton, R. K., & HNRC Group, San Diego, CA, USA. (1999). Neurocognitive complications of HIV disease. *Psychological Science, 10,* 191–195.

Greene, K., Krcmar, M., Rubin, D. L., Walters, L. H., & Hale, J. L. (2002). Elaboration in processing adolescent health messages: The impact of egocentrism and sensation seeking on message processing. *Journal of Communication, 52,* 812–831.

Grimshaw, G. M., Adelstein, A., Bryden, M. P., & MacKinnon, G. E. (1998). First-language acquisition in adolescence: Evidence for a critical period for verbal language development. *Brain and Language, 63,* 237–255.

Gross, J. J., Carstensen, L. L., Pasupathi, M., Tsai, J., Goetestam Skorpen, C., & Hsu, A. Y. C. (1997). Emotion and aging: Experience, expression, and control. *Psychology and Aging, 12,* 590–599.

Gutchess, A. H., Welsh, R. C., Hedden, T., Bangert, A., Minear, M., Liu, L. L., et al. (2005). Aging and the neural correlates of successful picture encoding: Frontal activations compensate for decreased medial-temporal activity. *Journal of Cognitive Neuroscience, 17,* 84–96.

Guttmann, C. R. G., Jolesz, F. A., Kikinis, R., Killiany, R. J., Moss, M. B., Sandor, T., et al. (1998). White matter changes with normal aging, *Neurology, 50,* 972–978.

Harlow, H. F. (1958). The nature of love. *American Psychologist, 13,* 573–685.

Hauser, M. (1996). *The evolution of communication.* Cambridge, MA: MIT Press.

Havinghurst, R. (1953). *Human development and education.* New York: Longmans, Green.

Hawkins, J. R. (1994). Sex determination. *Human Molecular Genetics, 3,* 1463–1467.

Herbst, J. H., McCrae, R. R., Costa, P. T., Jr., Feaganes, J. R., & Siegler, I. C. (2000). Self-perceptions of stability and change in personality at midlife: The UNC Alumni Heart Study. *Assessment, 7,* 379–388.

Herman-Giddens, M. E., Wang, L., & Koch, G. (2001). Secondary sexual characteristics in boys: Estimates from the National Health and Nutrition Examination Survey III, 1988–1994. *Archives of Pediatric Adolescent Medicine, 155,* 1022–1028.

Hertzog, C., & Schaie, K. W. (1988). Stability and change in adult intelligence: 2. Simultaneous analysis of longitudinal means and covariance structures. *Psychology and Aging, 3,* 122–130.

Hoffman, M. L. (2000). *Empathy and moral development: Implications for caring and justice.* New York: Cambridge University Press.

Hooper, C. J., Luciana, M., Conklin, H. M., & Yarger, R. S. (2004). Adolescents' performance on the Iowa gambling task: Implications for the development of decision making and ventromedial prefrontal cortex. *Developmental Psychology, 40,* 1148–1158.

Hooper, F. H., Hooper, J. O., & Colbert, K. K. (1984). *Personality and memory correlates of intellectual functioning: Young adulthood to old age.* Basel: Karger.

Hu, W. (1990, November 2–3). *The pragmatic motivation behind the use of the inverted sentence in the Beijing dialect.* Paper presented at the Midwest Conference on Asian Affairs, Bloomington, IN.

Hu, W. (1995). Verbal semantics of presentative sentences. *Yuyan Yanjiu (Linguistic Studies), 29,* 100–112.

Huen, K. F., Leung, S. S., Lau, J. T., Cheung, A. Y., Leung, N. K., & Chiu, M. C. (1997). Secular trend in the sexual maturation of southern Chinese girls. *Acta Paediatrica, 86,* 1121–1124.

Ivy, G., MacLeod, C., Petit, T., & Markus, E. (1992). A physiological framework for perceptual and cognitive changes in aging. In F. I. M. Craik & T. A. Salthouse (Eds.), *The handbook of aging and cognition* (pp. 273–314). Hillsdale, NJ: Erlbaum.

Jadack, R. A., Hyde, J. S., Moore, C. F., & Keller, M. L. (1995). Moral reasoning about sexually transmitted diseases. *Child Development, 66,* 167–177.

Jaffee, S., Caspi, A., Moffitt, T. E., Belsky, J., & Silva, P. (2001). Why are children born to teen mothers at risk for adverse outcomes in young adulthood? Results from a 20-year longitudinal study. *Development and Psychopathology, 13,* 377–397.

James, L. E., Burke, D. M., Austin, A., & Hulme, E. (1998). Production and perception of "verbosity" in younger and older adults. *Psychology and Aging, 13,* 355–367.

Johansson, B., Hofer, S. M., Allaire, J. C., Maldonado-Molina, M. M., Piccinin, A. M., Berg, S., et al. (2004). Change in cognitive capabilities in the oldest old: The effects of proximity to death in genetically related individuals over a 6-year period. *Psychology and Aging, 19,* 145–156.

Johnson, M. H. (2001). Functional brain development in humans. *Nature Reviews Neuroscience, 2,* 475–483.

Johnson, S. L., Turner, R. J., & Iwata, N. (2003). BIS/BAS levels and psychiatric disorder: An epidemiological study. *Journal of Psychopathology and Behavioral Assessment, 25,* 25–36.

Johnson, W., McGue, M., & Krueger, R. F. (2005). Personality stability in late adulthood: A behavioral genetic analysis. *Journal of Personality, 73,* 523–551.

Johnston, L. D., O'Malley, P. M., & Bachman, J. G. (1994). *National survey results on drug use from the Monitoring the Future study, 1975–1993* (NIH Publication No. 94-3810). Washington, DC: U.S. Government Printing Office.

Jones, N. A., Field, T., & Davalos, M. (1998). Massage therapy attenuates right frontal EEG asymmetry in one-month-old infants of depressed mothers. *Infant Behavior and Development, 21,* 527–530.

Jusczyk, P. W. (1995). Language acquisition: Speech sounds and phonological development. In J. L. Miller & P. D. Eimas (Eds.), *Handbook of perception and cognition: Vol. 11. Speech, language, and communication* (pp. 263–301). Orlando: Academic Press.

Kac, G., Auxiliadora de Santa Cruz Coelho, M.., & Velasquez-Melendez, G. (2000). Secular trend in age at menarche for women born between 1920 and 1979 in Rio de Janeiro, Brazil. *Annals of Human Biology, 27,* 423–428.

Kaplowitz, P. B., Slora, E. J., Wasserman, R. C., Pedlow, S. E., & Herman-Giddens, M. E. (2001). Earlier onset of puberty in girls: Relation to increased body mass index and race. *Pediatrics, 108,* 347–353.

Karpov, Y. V., & Haywood, H. C. (1998). Two ways to elaborate Vygotsky's concept of mediation. *American Psychologist, 53,* 27–36.

Kaufman, M. H. (1997). The teratogenic effects of alcohol following exposure during pregnancy, and its influence on the chromosome constitution of the pre-ovulatory egg. *Alcohol and Alcoholism, 32,* 113–128.

Kay, D. A., & Anglin, J. M. (1982). Overextension and underextension in the child's expressive and receptive speech. *Journal of Child Language, 9,* 83–98.

Keith, P. M., & Schafer, R. B. (1991). *Relationships and well-being over the life stages.* New York: Praeger.

Keller, A., Ford, L. H., & Meacham, J. A. (1978). Dimensions of self-concept in preschool children. *Developmental Psychology, 14,* 483–489.

Kempermann, G., & Gage, F. H. (1999). Experienced-dependent regulation of adult hippocampal neurogenesis: Effects of long-term stimulation and stimulus withdrawal. *Hippocampus, 9,* 321–332.

Kempermann, G., Kuhn, H. G., & Gage, F. H. (1998). Experience-induced neurogenesis in the senescent dentate gyrus. *Journal of Neuroscience, 18,* 3206–3212.

Kiffel, C., Campanella, S., & Bruyer, R. (2005). Categorical perception of faces and facial expressions: The age factor. *Experimental Aging Research, 31,* 119–147.

Kisilevsky, B. S., Hains, S. M. J., Jacquet, A. Y., Granier-Deferre, C., & Lecanuet, J. P. (2004). Maturation of fetal responses to music. *Developmental Science, 7,* 550–559.

Kisilevsky, B. S., & Low, J. A. (1998). Human fetal behavior: 100 years of study. *Developmental Review, 18,* 1–29.

Kitchener, R. F. (1996). The nature of the social for Piaget and Vygotsky. *Human Development, 39,* 243–249.

Kleemeier, R. W. (1962). Intellectual changes in the senium. *Proceedings of the American Statistical Association, 1,* 290–295.

Kochanska, G., DeVet, K., Goldman, M., Murray, K., & Putman, S. P. (1994). Maternal reports of conscience development and temperament in young children. *Child Development, 65,* 852–868.

Kodituwakku, P. W. (2009). Neurocognitive profile in children with fetal alcohol spectrum disorders. *Developmental Disabilities Research Reviews, 15,* 218–224.

Koga, H., Yuzuriha, T., Yao, H., Endo, K., Hiejima, S., Takashima, Y., et al. (2002). Quantitative MRI findings and cognitive impairment among community dwelling elderly subjects. *Journal of Neurology, Neurosurgery and Psychiatry, 72,* 737–741.

Kohlberg, L. (1969). Stage and sequence: The cognitive-developmental approach to socialization. In D. S. Goslin (Ed.), *Handbook of socialization theory and research* (pp. 347–480). Chicago: Rand McNally.

Krause, N. (2004). Stressors arising in highly valued roles, meaning in life, and the physical health status of older adults. *Journals of Gerontology: Series B. Psychological Sciences and Social Sciences, 59B,* S287–S291.

Kuhl, P. K., Williams, K. A., Lacerda, F., Stevens, K. N., & Lindblom, B. (1992). Linguistic experience alters phonetic perception in infants by 6 months of age. *Science, 255,* 606–608.

Kuller, L. H., Ives, D. G., Fitzpatrick, A. L., Carlson, M. C., Mercado, C., Lopez, O. L., et al. (2010). Does Ginkgo biloba reduce the risk of cardiovascular events? *Circulation: Cardiovascular Quality and Outcomes, 3,* 41–47.

Kunz, G., Beil, D., Deiniger, H., Einspanier, A., Mall, G., & Leyendecker, G. (1997). The uterine peristaltic pump. Normal and impeded sperm transport within the female genital tract. *Advances in Experimental Medicine and Biology, 424,* 267–277.

Lafuente, M. J., Grifol, R., Segarra, J., Soriano, J., Gorba, M. A., & Montesinos, A. (1997). Effects of the Firstart method of prenatal stimulation on psychomotor development: The first six months. *Pre- and Peri-Natal Psychology Journal, 11,* 151–162.

Lang, F. R., & Carstensen, L. L. (2002). Time counts: Future time perspective, goals, and social relationships. *Psychology and Aging, 17,* 125–139.

Langer, E. J., & Rodin, J. (1976). The effects of choice and enhanced personal responsibility for the aged: A field experiment in an institutional setting. *Journal of Personality and Social Psychology, 34,* 191–198.

Lansford, J. E., Sherman, A. M., & Antonucci, T. C. (1998). Satisfaction with social networks: An examination of socioemotional selectivity theory across cohorts. *Psychology and Aging, 13,* 544–552.

Lapsley, D. K. (1990). Egocentrism theory and the "new look" at the imaginary audience and personal fable in adolescence. In R. M. Lerner, A. C. Petersen, & J. Brooks-Gunn (Eds.), *The encyclopedia of adolescence* (pp. 281– 286). New York: Garland.

Lapsley, D. K., Jackson, S., Rice, K., & Shadid, G. (1988). Self-monitoring and the "new look" at the imaginary audience and personal fable: An ego-developmental analysis. *Journal of Adolescent Research, 3,* 17–31.

Larson, R., & Richards, M. H. (1994). *Divergent realities: The emotional lives of mothers, fathers, and adolescents.* New York: Basic Books.

Laursen, B., Coy, K. C., & Collins, W. A. (1998). Reconsidering changes in parent-child conflict across adolescence: A meta-analysis. *Child Development, 69,* 817–832.

Lemme, B. H. (1995). *Development in adulthood.* Needham Heights, MA: Allyn & Bacon.

Lester, B. M. (2000). Prenatal cocaine exposure and child outcome: A model for the study of the infant at risk. *Israel Journal of Psychiatry and Related Sciences, 37,* 223–235.

Levitt, A. G., & Wang, Q. (1991). Evidence for language-specific rhythmic influences in the reduplicative babbling of French- and English-learning infants. *Language and Speech, 34,* 235–249.

Levitt, M. J., Weber, R. A., & Guacci, N. (1993). Convoys of social support: An intergenerational analysis. *Psychology and Aging, 8,* 323–326.

Levy, B., Ashman, O., & Dror, I. (1999–2000). To be or not to be: The effects of aging stereotypes on the will to live. *Omega: Journal of Death and Dying, 40,* 409–420.

Li, S. C., Lindenberger, U., Hommel, B., Aschersleben, G., Prinz, W., & Baltes, P. B. (2004). Transformations in the couplings among intellectual abilities and constituent cognitive processes across the life span. *Psychological Science, 15,* 155–163.

Li, S. C., Lindenberger, U., & Sikström, S. (2001). Aging cognition: From neuromodulation to representation. *Trends in Cognitive Science, 5,* 479–486.

Light, L. (1991). Memory and aging: Four hypotheses in search of data. *Annual Review of Psychology, 42,* 333–376.

Liu, D., Diorio, J., Tannenbaum, B., Caldji, C., Francis, D., Freedman, A., et al. (1997). Maternal care, hippocampal glucocorticoid receptors, and hypothalamic-pituitary-adrenal responses to stress. *Science, 277,* 1659–1662.

Lobaugh, N. J., Cole, S., & Rovet, J. F. (1998). Visual search for features and conjunctions in development. *Canadian Journal of Experimental Psychology, 52,* 201–212.

Long, J. M., Mouton, P. R., Jucker, M., & Ingram, D. K. (1999). What counts in brain aging? Design-based stereological analysis of cell number. *Journals of Gerontology: Series A. Biological Sciences and Medical Sciences, 54A,* B407–B417.

Lou, H. C., Hansen, D., Nordentoft, M., Pryds, O., Jensen, F., Nim, J., et al. (1994). Prenatal stressors of human life affect fetal brain development. *Developmental Medicine and Child Neurology, 36,* 826–832.

Luna, B. (2004). Algebra and the adolescent brain. *Trends in Cognitive Sciences, 8,* 437–439.

Luna, B., Garver, K. E., Urban, T. A., Lazar, N. A., & Sweeney, J. A. (2004). Maturation of cognitive processes from late childhood to adulthood. *Child Development, 75,* 1357–1372.

Lunzer, E. A. (1978). Formal reasoning: A reappraisal. In B. Z. Presseisen, D. Goldstein, & M. H. Appel (Eds.), *Topics in cognitive development: Vol. 2. Language and operational thought* (pp. 47–76). New York: Plenum.

Lyons, E. A., & Levi, C. S. (1994). Sperm are not like salmon: Altered myometrial contractility is significant in unexplained infertility rates. *Radiology, 193[P],* 144.

Maccoby, E. E. (1988). Gender as a social category. *Developmental Psychology, 26,* 755–765.

Maccoby, E. E. (1990). Gender and relationships: A developmental account. *American Psychologist, 45,* 513–520.

Maccoby, E. E. (1991). Gender and relationships: A reprise. *American Psychologist, 46,* 538–539.

Maccoby, E. E., & Jacklin, C. N. (1987). Gender segregation in childhood. In H. W. Reese (Ed.), *Advances in child development and behavior* (Vol. 20, pp. 239–288). New York: Academic Press.

Malina, R. M., & Bouchard, C. (1991). *Growth, maturation, and physical activity.* Champaign, IL: Human Kinetics.

Marcus, G. F., Vijayan, S., Rao, S. B., & Vishton, P. M. (1999). Rule learning by 7-month-old infants. *Science, 283,* 77–80.

Marica, J. E. (1993). The status of the statuses: Research review. In J. E. Marica, A. S. Waterman, D. R. Matteson, S. L. Archer, & J. L. Orlofsky (Eds.), *Ego identity: A handbook for psychosocial research* (pp. 22–41). New York: Springer.

Markson, L., & Bloom, P. (1997). Evidence against a dedicated system for word learning in children. *Nature, 385,* 813–815.

Martin, C. L., & Ruble, D. (2004). Children's search for gender cues: Cognitive perspectives on gender development. *Current Directions in Psychological Science, 13,* 67–70.

Masataka, N. (1996). Perception of motherese in a signed language by 6-month-old deaf infants. *Developmental Psychology, 32,* 874–879.

Maynard, R. A. (Ed.). (1996). *Kids having kids: A Robin Hood Foundation special report on the costs of adolescent childbearing.* New York: Robin Hood Foundation.

McAdams, D. P., & de St. Aubin, E. (1992). A theory of generativity and its assessment through self-report, behavioral acts, and narrative themes in autobiography. *Journal of Personality and Social Psychology, 62,* 1003–1015.

McAdams, D. P., de St. Aubin, E., & Logan, R. L. (1993). Generativity among young, midlife, and older adults. *Psychology and Aging, 8,* 221–230.

McAdams, D. P., Reynolds, J., Lewis, M., Patten, A. H., & Bowman, P. J. (2001). When bad things turn good and good things turn bad: Sequences of redemption and contamination in life narrative and their relation to psychosocial adaptation in midlife adults and in students. *Personality and Social Psychology Bulletin, 27,* 474–485.

McArdle, J. J., Ferrer-Caja, E., Hamagami, F., & Woodcock, R. W. (2002). Comparative longitudinal structural analyses of the growth and decline of multiple intellectual abilities over the life span. *Developmental Psychology, 38,* 115–142.

McBride, J. (1999). *Steven Spielberg: A biography.* New York: Da Capo.

McCrink, K., & Wynn, K. (2004). Large-number addition and subtraction by 9-month-old infants. *Psychological Science, 15,* 776–781.

McGraw, M. B. (1943). *The neuromuscular maturation of the human infant.* New York: Columbia University Press.

McLean, D. E., Hatfield-Timajchy, K., Wingo, P. A., & Floyd, R. L. (1993). Psychosocial measurement: Implications for the study of preterm delivery in Black women. *American Journal of Preventive Medicine,* 9(6, *Suppl),* 39-81.

Meaney, M. J., Mitchell, J. B., Aitken, D. H., Bhatnagar, S., Bodnoff, S. R., Iny, L. J., et al. (1991). The effects of neonatal handling on the development of the adrenocortical response to stress: Implications for neuropathology and cognitive deficits in later life. *Psychoneuroendocrinology, 16,* 85–103.

Meltzoff, A. N., & Moore, M. K. (1977). Imitation of facial and manual gestures by human neonates. *Science, 198,* 75–78.

Menyuk, P., Liebergott, J. W., & Schultz, M. C. (1995). *Early language development in full-term and premature infants.* Hillsdale, NJ: Erlbaum.

Merrick, E. N. (1995). Adolescent childbearing as career "choice": Perspective from an ecological context. *Journal of Counseling and Development, 73,* 288–295.

Miller, J. M., Boudreaux, M. C., & Regan, F. A. (1995). A case-control study of cocaine use in pregnancy. *American Journal of Obstetrics and Gynecology, 172,* 180–185.

Morgane, P. J., Austin-LaFrance, R., Bronzino, J., Tonkiss, J., Diaz-Cintra, S., Cintra, L., et al. (1993). Prenatal malnutrition and development of the brain. *Neuroscience and Biobehavioral Reviews, 17,* 91–128.

Mori, H., Kamada, M., Maegawa, M., Yamamoto, S., Aono, T., Futaki, S., et al. (1998). Enzymatic activation of immunoglobulin binding factor in female reproductive tract. *Biochemical and Biophysical Research Communications, 246,* 409–413.

Murata, K., Weihe, P., Renzoni, A., Debes, F., Vasconcelos, R., Zino, F., et al. (1999). Delayed evoked potentials in children exposed to methylmercury from seafood. *Neurotoxicology and Teratology, 21,* 343–348.

Nagy, Z., Westerberg, H., & Klingberg, T. (2004). Maturation of white matter is associated with the development of cognitive functions during childhood. *Journal of Cognitive Neuroscience, 16,* 1227–1233.

Naito, T., & Lipsitt, L. P. (1969). Two attempts to condition eyelid responses in human infants. *Journal of Experimental Child Psychology, 8,* 263–270.

Nelson, K. (1981). Individual differences in language development: Implications for development and language. *Developmental Psychology, 17,* 170–187.

Nevid, J., Rathus, S., & Rubenstein, H. (1998). *Health in the new millennium.* New York: Worth.

Nilsson, L., & Hamberger, L. (1990). *A child is born.* New York: Delacorte.

Nowakowski, R. S. (1987). Basic concepts of CNS development. *Child Development, 58,* 568–595.

Owens, L., Shute, R., & Slee, P. (2000). "I'm in and you're out ..." Explanations for teenage girls' indirect aggression. *Psychology, Evolution and Gender, 2,* 19–46.

Pascual-Leone, J. (1970). A mathematical model for the transition rule in Piaget's developmental stages. *Acta Psychologia, 32,* 301–345.

Payne, D. L. (1992). *Pragmatics of word order flexibility.* Amsterdam: John Benjamins.

Petersen, A. C., Compas, B. E., Brooks-Gunn, J., Stemmler, M., Ey, S., & Grant, K. E. (1993). Depression in adolescence. *American Psychologist, 48,* 155–168.

Petitto, L. A., & Marentette, P. F. (1991). Babbling in the manual mode: Evidence for the ontogeny of language. *Science, 251,* 1493–1496.

Piaget, J. (1969). *The mechanisms of perception* (G. N. Seagrim, Trans.). New York: Basic Books.

Pinker, S. (1994). *The language instinct: How the mind creates language.* New York: Morrow.

Pinker, S. (1999). *Words and rules: The ingredients of language.* New York: Basic Books.

Pollack, H. A. (2001). Sudden infant death syndrome, maternal smoking during pregnancy, and the cost-effectiveness of smoking cessation intervention. *American Journal of Public Health, 91,* 432–436.

Porter, R. H., Makin, J. W., Davis, L. B., & Christensen, K. M. (1992). An assessment of the salient olfactory environment of formula-fed infants. *Physiology and Behavior, 50,* 907–911.

Pressman, E. K., DiPietro, J. A., Costigan, K. A., Shupe, A. K., & Johnson, T. R. B. (1998). Fetal neurobehavioral development: Associations with socioeconomic class and fetal sex. *Developmental Psychobiology, 33,* 79–91.

Pujol, R., Lavigne-Rebillard, M., & Uziel, A. (1990). Physiological correlates of development of the human cochlea. *Seminars in Perinatology, 14,* 275–280.

Puka, B. (Ed.). (1994). *Kohlberg's original study of moral development.* New York: Garland.

Qin, Y., Carter, C. S., Silk, E. M., Stenger, V. A., Fissell, K., Goode, A., et al. (2004). The change of the brain activation patterns as children learn algebra equation solving. *Proceedings of the National Academy of Sciences of the United States of America, 101,* 5686–5691.

Quinn, P. C., Bhatt, R. S., Brush, D., Grimes, A., & Sharpnack, H. (2002). Development of form similarity as a Gestalt grouping principle in infancy. *Psychological Science, 13,* 320–328.

Raag, T., & Rackliff, C. L. (1998). Preschoolers' awareness of social expectations of gender: Relationships to toy choices. *Sex Roles, 38,* 685–700.

Radvansky, G. A. (1999). Aging, memory, and comprehension. *Current Directions in Psychological Science, 8,* 49–53.

Räikkönen, K., Pesonen, A. K., Järvenpää, A. L., & Strandberg, T. E. (2004). Sweet babies: Chocolate consumption during pregnancy and infant temperament at six months. *Early Human Development, 76,* 139–145.

Rakic, P. (1975). Timing of major ontogenetic events in the visual cortex of the rhesus monkey. In N. Buchwald & M. Brazier (Eds.), *Brain mechanisms in mental retardation* (pp. 3–40). New York: Academic Press.

Ratliff-Schaub, K., Hunt, C. E., Crowell, D., Golub, H., Smok-Pearsall, S., Palmer, P., et al. (2001). Relationship between infant sleep position and motor development in preterm infants. *Journal of Developmental and Behavioral Pediatrics, 22,* 293–299.

Raz, N., Gunning, F. M., Head, D., Dupuis, J. H., McQuain, J. M., Briggs, S. D., et al. (1997). Selective aging of human cerebral cortex observed in vivo: Differential vulnerability of the prefrontal gray matter. *Cerebral Cortex, 7,* 268–282.

Resnick, S. M., Pham, D. L., Kraut, M. A., Zonderman, A. B., & Davatzikos, C. (2003). Longitudinal magnetic resonance imaging studies of older adults: A shrinking brain. *Journal of Neuroscience, 23,* 3295–3301.

Rest, J. R. (1979). *Development in judging moral issues.* Minneapolis: University of Minnesota Press.

Reznick, S. J., & Goldfield, B. A. (1992). Rapid change in lexical development in comprehension and production. Developmental Psychology, 28, 406–413.

Roberts, B. W., & DelVecchio, W. F. (2000). The rank-order consistency of personality traits from childhood to old age: A quantitative review of longitudinal studies. *Psychological Bulletin, 126,* 3–25.

Robinson, L. C. (2000). Interpersonal relationship quality in young adulthood: A gender analysis. *Adolescence, 35,* 775–784.

Rodier, P. (1980). Chronology of neuron development. *Developmental Medicine and Child Neurology, 22,* 525–545.

Rodin, J., & Langer, E. J. (1977). Long-term effects of a control-relevant intervention with the institutionalized aged. *Journal of Personality and Social Psychology, 35,* 897–902.

Rosen, A. C., Prull, M. W., Gabrieli, J. D. E., Stoub, T., O'Hara, R., Friedman, L., et al. (2003). Differential associations between entorhinal and hippocampal volumes and memory performance in older adults. *Behavioral Neuroscience, 117,* 1150–1160.

Rosenberg, M. (1979). *Conceiving the self.* New York: Basic Books.

Rosenheim, M. K., & Testa, M. F. (Eds.). (1992). *Early parenthood and coming of age in the 1990s.* New Brunswick, NJ: Rutgers University Press.

Rovee-Collier, C. (1997). Dissociations in infant memory: Rethinking the development of implicit and explicit memory. *Psychological Review, 104,* 467–498.

Rowe, J. W., & Kahn, R. L. (1998). *Successful aging.* New York: Pantheon.

Roy, R., Benenson, J. F., & Lilly, F. (2000). Beyond intimacy: Conceptualizing sex differences in same-sex relationships. *Journal of Psychology, 134,* 93–101.

Rush, A. N., Robinette, B. L., & Stanton, M. E. (2001). Ontogenetic differences in the effects of unpaired stimulus preexposure on eyeblink conditioning in the rat. *Developmental Psychobiology, 39,* 8–18.

Saffran, J. R. (2001). Words in a sea of sounds: The output of infant statistical learning. *Cognition, 81,* 149–169.

Salthouse, T. A. (1991a). Cognitive facets of aging well. *Generations, 15,* 35–38.

Salthouse, T. A. (1991b). *Theoretical perspectives on cognitive aging.* Hillsdale, NJ: Erlbaum.

Salzman, C. D., & Fusi, S. (2010). Emotion, cognition, and mental state representation in amygdala and prefrontal cortex. *Annual Review of Neuroscience,* 33, 173–202.

Saxe, G. B. (1988). Candy selling and math learning. *Educational Research. 17,* 14–21.

Schacter, D. L. (1996). *Searching for memory: The brain, the mind, and the past.* New York: Basic Books.

Schaie, K. W., Willis, S. L., & Caskie, G. I. L. (2004). The Seattle longitudinal study: Relationship between personality and cognition. *Aging, Neuropsychology, and Cognition, 11,* 304–324.

Sears, R., Maccoby, E., & Levin, H. (1957). *Patterns of child rearing.* New York: Harper & Row.

Seith, R. (2000). *Back sleeping may delay infant crawling.* CWK Network. Retrieved from http://www.kidsmd. comTipsheets/21_may2301/crawling.html

Semenov, L. A., Chernova, N. D., & Bondarko, V. M. (2000). Measurement of visual acuity and crowding effect in 3–9-year-old children. *Human Physiology, 26,* 16–20.

Shibahara, H., Shigeta, M., Toji, H., & Koyama, K. (1995). Sperm immobilizing antibodies interfere with sperm migration from the uterine cavity through the fallopian tubes. *American Journal of Reproductive Immunology, 34,* 120–124.

Shulman, S., Elicker, J., & Sroufe, L. A. (1994). Stages of friendship growth in preadolescence as related to attachment history. *Journal of Social and Personal Relationships, 11,* 341–361.

Simcock, G., & Hayne, H. (2002). Breaking the barrier? Children fail to translate their preverbal memories into language. *Psychological Science, 13,* 225–231.

Singer, L. T., Arendt, R., Minnes, S., Farkas, K., Salvator, A., Kirchner, H. L., et al. (2002a). Cognitive and motor outcomes of cocaine-exposed infants. *Journal of the American Medical Association, 287,* 1952–1960.

Singer, L. T., Salvator, A., Arendt, R., Minnes, S., Farkas, K., & Kliegman, R. (2002b). Effects of cocaine/polydrug exposure and maternal psychological distress on infant birth outcomes. *Neurotoxicology and Teratology, 24,* 127–135.

Singh, V. N. (1995). Human uterine amylase in relation to infertility. *Hormone and Metabolic Research, 27,* 35–36.

Sireteanu, R. (2000). Texture segmentation, "pop-out," and feature binding in infants and children. In C. Rovee-Collier & L. P. Lipsitt (Eds.), *Progress in infancy research* (Vol. 1, pp. 183–249). Mahwah, NJ: Erlbaum.

Small, B. J., & Bäckman, L. (2000). Time to death and cognitive performance. *Current Directions in Psychological Science, 6,* 168–172.

Small, B. J., Fratiglioni, L., von Strauss, E., & Backman, L. (2003). Terminal decline and cognitive performance in very old age: Does cause of death matter? *Psychology and Aging, 18,* 193–202.

Smith, D. E., Roberts, J., Gage, F. H., & Tuszynski, M. H. (1999). Age-associated neuronal atrophy occurs in the primate brain and is reversible by growth factor gene therapy. *Proceedings of the National Academy of Sciences of the United States of America, 96,* 10893–10898.

Snedeker, J., Geren, J., & Shafto, C. (2007). Starting over: International adoption as a natural experiment in language development. *Psychological Science, 18,* 79–87.

Snitz, B. E., O'Meara, E. S., Carlson, M. C., Arnold, A. M., Ives, D. G., Rapp, S. R., et al. (2009). Ginkgo biloba for preventing cognitive decline in older adults: A randomized trial. *Journal of the American Medical Association, 302,* 2663–2670.

Sommer, F. G., & Ling, D. (1970). Auditory testing of newborns using eyeblink conditioning. *Journal of Auditory Research, 10,* 292–295.

Spelke, E. S. (1991). Physical knowledge in infancy: Reflections on Piaget's theory. In S. Carey & R. Gelman (Eds.), *The epigenesis of mind: Essays on biology and cognition* (pp. 133–169). Hillsdale, NJ: Erlbaum.

Spelke, E. S., Breinlinger, K., Jacobson, K., & Phillips, A. (1993). Gestalt relations and object perception: A developmental study. *Perception, 22,* 1483–1501.

Spelke, E. S., Breinlinger, K., Macomber, J., & Jacobson, K. (1992). Origins of knowledge. *Psychological Review, 99,* 605–632.

Sroufe, L. A., & Fleeson, J. (1986). Attachment and the construction of relationships. In W. W. Hartup & Z. Rubin (Eds.), *Relationships and development* (pp. 51–71). Hillsdale, NJ: Erlbaum.

Stern, P. C., & Carstensen, L. L. (Eds.). (2000). *The aging mind: Opportunities in cognitive research.* Washington, DC: National Academies Press.

Stoel-Gammon, C., & Otomo, K. (1986). Babbling development of hearing-impaired and normally hearing subjects. *Journal of Speech and Hearing Disorders, 51,* 33–41.

Streissguth, A. P., Barr, H. M., Bookstein, F. L., Sampson, P. D., & Olson, H. C. (1999). The long-term neurocognitive consequences of prenatal alcohol exposure: A 14-year study. *Psychological Science, 10,* 186–190.

Streissguth, A. P., Barr, H. M., Sampson, P. D., Darby, B. L., & Martin, D. C. (1989). IQ at age 4 in relation to maternal alcohol use and smoking during pregnancy. *Developmental Psychology, 25,* 3–11.

Sullivan, R. (1999, June). Dad again. *Life,* 66–68.

Suomi, S. J. (2003). Gene-environment interactions and the neurobiology of social conflict. *Annals of the New York Academy of Sciences, 1008,* 132–139.

Susser, E., Neugebauer, R., Hoek, H. W., Brown, A. S., Lin, S., Lanovitz, D., et al. (1996). Schizophrenia after prenatal famine: Further evidence. *Archives of General Psychiatry, 53,* 25–31.

Swanson, K., Beckwith, L., & Howard, J. (2000). Intrusive caregiving and quality of attachment in prenatally drug-exposed toddlers and their primary caregivers. *Attachment and Human Development, 2,* 130–148.

Takahashi, K. (1990). Are the key assumptions of the "Strange Situation" procedure universal? A view from Japanese research. *Human Development, 33,* 23–30.

Tanner, J. M. (1990). *Foetus into man* (2nd ed.). Cambridge, MA: Harvard University Press.

Tarabulsy, G. M., Bernier, A., Provost, M. A., Maranda, J., Larose, S., Moss, E., et al. (2005). Another look inside the gap: Ecological contributions to the transmission of attachment in a sample of adolescent mother-infant dyads. *Developmental Psychology, 41,* 212–224.

Tardif, T., Fletcher, P., Liang, W., Zhang, Z., Kaciroti, N., & Marchman, V. A. (2008). Baby's first ten words. *Child Development, 44,* 929–938.

Tavares, C. H., Haeffner, L. S., Barbieri, M. A., Bettiol, H., Barbieri, M. R., & Souza, L. (2000). Age at menarche among schoolgirls from a rural community in Southeast Brazil. *Cad Saude Publica, 16,* 709–715.

Teilmann, G., Juul, A., Skakkebaek, N. E., & Toppari, J. (2002). Putative effects of endocrine disrupters on pubertal development in the human. *Best Practice and Research Clinical Endocrinology and Metabolism, 16,* 105–121.

Tentori, K., Osherson, D., Hasher, L., & May, C. (2001). Wisdom and aging: Irrational preferences in college students but not older adults. *Cognition, 81,* B87–B96.

Thatcher, R. W. (1994). Cyclic cortical reorganization: Origins of human cognitive development. In G. Dawson & K. W. Fischer (Eds.), *Human behavior and the developing brain* (pp. 232–266). New York: Guilford.

Thelen, E. (1995). Motor development: A new synthesis. *American Psychologist, 50,* 79–95.

Thelen, E., & Ulrich, B. D. (1991). Hidden skills: A dynamic systems analysis of treadmill stepping during the first year. *Monographs of the Society for Research in Child Development, 56*(1, Serial No. 223).

Thomas, A., & Chess, S. (1977). *Temperament: Theory and practice.* New York: Brunner/Mazel.

Thompson, P. M., Giedd, J. N., Woods, R. P., MacDonald, D., Evans, A. C., & Toga, A. W. (2000). Growth patterns in the developing brain detected by using continuum mechanical tensor maps. *Nature, 404,* 190–193.

Toppari, J., & Juul, A. (in press). Trends in puberty timing in humans and environmental modifiers. *Molecular and Cellular Endocrinology.*

Trevethan, S. D., & Walker, L. J. (1989). Hypothetical versus real-life moral reasoning among psychopathic and delinquent youth. *Development and Psychopathology, 1,* 91–103.

Tsai, J. L., Levenson, R. W., & Carstensen, L. L. (2000). Autonomic, subjective, and expressive responses to emotional films in older and younger Chinese Americans and European Americans. *Psychology and Aging, 15,* 684–693.

Tsekhmistrenko, T. A., Vasil'eva, V. A., Shumeiko, N. S., & Vologirov, A. S. (2004). Quantitative changes in the fibroarchitectonics of the human cortex from birth to the age of 12 years. *Neuroscience and Behavioral Physiology, 34,* 983–988.

Vaillant, G. (1977). *Adaptation to life.* Boston: Little, Brown.

Vartanian, L. R. (2001). Adolescents' reactions to hypothetical peer group conversations: Evidence for an imaginary audience? *Adolescence, 36,* 347–380.

Ventura, S. J. (2009, May). *Changing patterns of nonmarital childbearing in the United States* (NCHS Data Brief 18). Hyattsville, MD: National Center for Health Statistics.

Vogel, G. (1997). Cocaine wreaks subtle damage on developing brains. *Science, 278,* 38–39.

Vurpillot, E. (1968). The development of scanning strategies and their relation to visual differentiation. *Journal of Experimental Child Psychology, 6,* 632–650.

Vygotsky, L. S. (1978). *Mind in society: The development of higher mental processes.* Cambridge, MA: Harvard University Press. (Original works published 1930, 1933, 1935)

Vygotsky, L. S. (1934/1986). *Thought and language* (A. Kozulin, Trans.). Cambridge, MA: MIT Press.

Walker, L. J. (1995). Sexism in Kohlberg's moral psychology? In W. M. Kurtines & J. L. Gewirtz (Eds.), *Moral development: An introduction* (pp. 83–107). Boston: Allyn & Bacon.

Walster, E., Walster, G. W., & Berscheid, E. (1978). *Equity: Theory and research.* Needham Heights, MA: Allyn & Bacon.

Wark, G. R., & Krebs, D. L. (1996). Gender and dilemma differences in real-life moral judgment. *Developmental Psychology, 32,* 220–230.

Weaver, I. C. G., Cervoni, N., Champagne, F. A., D'Alessio, A. C., Sharma, S., Seckl, J. R., et al. (2004). Epigenetic programming by maternal behavior. *Nature Neuroscience, 7,* 847–854.

Weinstock, M. (1997). Does prenatal stress impair coping and regulation of hypothalamic-pituitary-adrenal axis? *Neuroscience and Biobehavioral Reviews, 21,* 1–10.

Weiss, R. S. (1986). Continuities and transformations in social relationships from childhood to adulthood. In W. W. Hartup & Z. Rubin (Eds.), *Relationships and development* (pp. 95–110). Hillsdale, NJ: Erlbaum.

Wheeler, M. D. (1991). Physical changes of puberty. *Endocrinology and Metabolism Clinics of North America, 20,* 1–14.

White, T. G. (1982). Naming practices, typicality, and underextension in child language. *Journal of Experimental Child Psychology, 33,* 324–346.

Wise, P. M., Krajnak, K. M., & Kashon, M. L. (1996). Menopause: The aging of multiple pacemakers. *Science, 273,* 67–70.

Witt, S. D. (1997). Parental influence on children's socialization to gender roles. *Adolescence, 32,* 253–259.

Yazigi, R. A., Odem, R. R., & Polakoski, K. L. (1991). Demonstration of specific binding of cocaine to human spermatozoa. *Journal of the American Medical Association, 266,* 1956–1959.

Zaharia, M. D., Kulczycki, J., Shanks, N., Meaney, M. J., & Anisman, H. (1996). The effects of early postnatal stimulation on Morris water-maze acquisition in adult mice: Genetic and maternal factors. *Psychopharmacology, 128,* 227–239.

Zentner, M. R., & Kagan, J. (1998). Infants' perception of consonance and dissonance in music. *Infant Behavior and Development, 21,* 483–492.

Zimmer, E. Z., Fifter, W. P., Young-Ihl, K., Rey, H. R., Chao, C. R., & Myers, M. M. (1993). Response of the premature fetus to stimulation by speech sounds. *Early Human Development, 33,* 207–215.

References: Stress, Health, and Coping

Abraham, H. D. (1983). Visual phenomenology of the LSD flashback. *Archives of General Psychiatry, 40,* 884–889.

Abrams, L. R., & Jones, R. W. (1994, August). *The contribution of social roles to psychological distress in businesswomen.* Paper presented at the 102nd annual convention of the American Psychological Association, Los Angeles, CA.

American Psychiatric Association. (2000). *Diagnostic and statistical manual of mental disorders* (4th ed., text revision). Washington, DC: Author.

Anch, A. M., Bowman, C. P., Mitler, M. M., & Walsh, J. K. (1988). *Sleep: A scientific perspective.* Englewood Cliffs, NJ: Prentice Hall.

Andersen, B. (1997, July). Psychological interventions for individuals with cancer. *Clinician's Research Digest, 16*(Suppl.), 1–2.

Anderson, C. A., & Bushman, B. J. (1997). External validity of "trivial" experiments: The case of laboratory aggression. *Review of General Psychology, 1,* 19–41.

Anderson, V. L., Levinson, E. M., Barker, W., & Kiewra, K. R. (1999). The effects of meditation on teacher perceived occupational stress, state and trait anxiety, and burnout. *School Psychology Quarterly, 14,* 3–25.

Arana, G. W., & Rosenbaum, J. F. (2000). *Handbook of psychiatric drug therapy.* Philadelphia: Lippincott Williams and Wilkins.

Aranda, M. P., & Knight, B. G. (1997). The influence of ethnicity and culture on the caregiver stress and coping process: A socio-cultural review and analysis. *Gerontologist, 37,* 342–354.

Bachen, E. A., Manuck, S. B., Cohen, S., Muldoon, M. F., Raible, R., Herbert, T. B., et al. (1995). Adrengergic blockage ameliorates cellular immune responses to mental stress in humans. *Psychosomatic Medicine, 57,* 366–372.

Barefoot, J. C., Dahlstrom, W. G., & Williams, R. B. (1983). Hostility, CHD incidence, and total mortality: A 25-year follow-up study of 255 physicians. *Psychosomatic Medicine, 45,* 59–63.

Barefoot, J., Dodge, K., Peterson, B., Dahlstrom, W., & Williams, R. (1989). The Cook-Medley Hostility Scale: Item content and ability to predict survival. *Psychosomatic Medicine, 51,* 46–57.

Barger, L. K., Cade, B. E., Ayas, N. T., Cronin, J. W., Rosner, B., Speizer, F. E., et al. (2005). Extended work shifts and the risk of motor vehicle crashes among interns. *New England Journal of Medicine, 352,* 125–134.

Baron, R. A., & Richardson, D. (1994). *Human aggression* (2nd ed.). New York: Plenum.

Barsky, A. J., Saintfort, R., Rogers, M. P., & Borus, J. F. (2002). Nonspecific medication side effects and the nocebo phenomenon. *Journal of the American Medical Association, 287,* 622–627.

Barth, J., Schumacher, M., & Herrmann-Lingen, C. (2004). Depression as a risk factor for mortality in patients with coronary heart disease: A meta-analysis. *Psychosomatic Medicine, 66,* 802–813.

Bastien, C. H., Morin, C. M., Ouellet, M., Blais, F. C., & Bouchard, S. (2004). Cognitive-behavioral therapy for insomnia: Comparison of individual therapy, group therapy, and telephone consultations. *Journal of Consulting and Clinical Psychology, 72,* 653–659.

Baumeister, R. F., & Boden, J. M. (1998). Aggression and the self: High self-esteem, low self-control, and ego threat. In R. G. Geen & E. Donnerstein (Eds.), *Human aggression: Theories, research, and implications for social policy* (pp. 111–137). San Diego, CA: Academic Press.

Baumeister, R. F., Smart, L., & Boden, J. M. (1996). Relation of threatened egotism to violence and aggression: The dark side of high self-esteem. *Psychological Review, 103,* 5–33.

Beck, R., & Fernandez, E. (1998). Cognitive-behavioral therapy in the treatment of anger: A meta-analysis. *Cognitive Therapy and Research, 22,* 63–74.

Beevers, C. G., & Meyer, B. (2004). Thought suppression and depression risk. *Cognition and Emotion, 18,* 859–867.

Benedetti, F., Pollo, A., Lopiano, L., Lanotte, M., Vighetti, S., & Rainero, I. (2003). Conscious expectation and unconscious conditioning in analgesic, motor, and hormonal placebo/nocebo responses. *Journal of Neuroscience, 23,* 4315–4323.

Berkman, L. F., & Syme, S. L. (1979). Social networks, host resistance, and mortality: A nine year follow-up study of Alameda Country residents. *American Journal of Epidemiology, 109,* 186–204.

Berkowitz, L. (1998). Affective aggression: The role of stress, pain, and negative affect. In R. G. Geen & E. Donnerstein (Eds.), *Human aggression: Theories, research, and implications for social policy* (pp. 49–72). San Diego, CA.: Academic Press.

Berkowitz, L., & Harmon-Jones, E. (2004). Toward an understanding of the determinants of anger. *Emotion, 4,* 107–130.

Berman, J. D., & Straus, S. E. (2004). Implementing a research agenda for complementary and alternative medicine. *Annual Review of Medicine, 55,* 239–254.

Berson, D. M., Dunn, F. A., & Takao, M. (2002). Phototransduction by retinal ganglion cells that set the circadian clock. *Science, 295,* 1070–1073.

Bishop, G. D. (1994). *Health psychology: Integrating mind and body.* Boston, MA: Allyn and Bacon.

Blascovich, J., & Tomaka, J. (1996). The biopsychosocial model of arousal regulation. *Advances in Experimental Social Psychology, 28,* 1–51.

Blazer, D. G., & Wu, L. (2009). The epidemiology of at-risk and binge drinking among middle-aged and elderly community adults: National Survey on Drug Use and Health. *The American Journal of Psychiatry, 166,* 1162–1169.

Blumenthal, J. A., Babyak, M., Wei, J., O'Connor, C., Waugh, R., Eisenstein, E., et al. (2002). Usefulness of psychosocial treatment of mental stress-induced myocardial ischemia in men. *American Journal of Cardiology, 89,* 164–168.

Boivin, D. B., Czeisler, C. A., Dijk, D., Duffy, J. F., Folkard, S., Minors, D. S., et al. (1997). Complex interaction of the sleep-wake cycle and circadian phase modulates mood in healthy subjects. *Archives of General Psychiatry, 54,* 145–152.

Bosch, J. A., Brand, H. S., Ligtenberg, A. J. M., Bermond, B., Hoogstraten, J., & Nieuw Amgerongen, A. V. (1998). The response of salivary protein levels and S-IgA to an academic examination are associated with daily stress. *Journal of Psychophysiology, 12,* 384–391.

Brannon, L. (1996). *Gender: Psychological perspectives.* Needham Heights, MA: Simon and Schuster.

Brody, J. (1998, April 6). Dealing with sleep deprivation. *International Herald Tribune,* p. 9.

Brosschot, J. F., & Thayer, J. F. (2003). Heart rate response is longer after negative emotions than after positive emotions. *International Journal of Psychophysiology, 50,* 181–187.

Brummett, B. H., Mark, D. B., Siegler, I. C., Williams, R. B., Babyak, M. A., Clapp-Channing, N. E., et al. (2005). Perceived social support as a predictor of mortality in coronary patients: Effects of smoking, sedentary behavior, and depressive symptoms. *Psychosomatic Medicine, 67,* 40–45.

Brunner, D. P., Dijk, D. J., Tobler, I., & Borbely, A. A. (1990). Effect of partial sleep deprivation on sleep stages and EEG power spectra: Evidence for non-REM and REM sleep homeostasis. *Electroencephalography and Clinical Neurophysiology, 75,* 492–499.

Buckalew, L. W., & Ross, S. (1981). Relationship of perceptual characteristics to efficacy of placebos. *Psychological Reports, 49,* 955–961.

Budney, A. J., Hughes, J. R., Moore, B. A., & Vandrey, R. (2004). Review of the validity and significance of cannabis withdrawal syndrome. *American Journal of Psychiatry, 161,* 1967–1977.

Bushman, B. J. (1988). The effects of apparel on compliance: A field experiment with a female authority figure. *Personality and Social Psychology Bulletin, 14,* 459–467.

Bushman, B. J. (1998). Threatened egotism, narcissism, self-esteem, and direct and displaced aggression: Does self-love or self-hate lead to violence? *Journal of Personality and Social Psychology, 75,* 219–229.

Bushman, B. J., Baumeister, R. F., & Phillips, C. M. (2001). Do people aggress to improve their mood? Catharsis beliefs, affect regulation opportunity, and aggressive responding. *Journal of Personality and Social Psychology, 81,* 17–32.

Bushman, B. J., Bonacci, A. M., van Dijk, M., & Baumeister, R. F. (2003). Narcissism, sexual refusal, and aggression: Testing a narcissistic reactance model of sexual coercion. *Journal of Personality and Social Psychology, 84,* 1027–1040.

Bushman, B. J., & Cooper, H. M. (1990). Effects of alcohol on human aggression: An integrative research review. *Psychological Bulletin, 107,* 1–14.

Bushman, B. J., & Wells, G. L. (1998). Trait aggressiveness and hockey penalties: Predicting hot tempers on the ice. *Journal of Applied Psychology, 83,* 969–974.

Cajochen, C., Knoblauch, V., Wirz-Justice, A., Kräuchi, K., Graw, P., & Wallach, D. (2004). Circadian modulation of sequence learning under high and low sleep pressure conditions. *Behavioural Brain Research, 151,* 167–176.

Cannon, W. B. (1942). Voodoo death. *American Anthropologist, 44,* 169–181.

Carney, R. M., Freeland, K. E., Veith, R. C., Cryer, P. E., Skala, J. A., Lynch, T., et al. (1999). Major depression, heart rate, and plasma norepinephrine in patients with coronary heart disease. *Biological Psychiatry, 45,* 458–463.

Carver, C. S., Scheier, M. F., & Weintraub, J. K. (1989). Assessing coping strategies: A theoretically based approach. *Journal of Personality and Social Psychology, 56,* 267–283.

Centers for Disease Control. (2009). *Obesity: Halting the epidemic by making health easier/at a Glance 2009.* Retrieved November 7, 2009, from http://www.cdc.gov/nccdphp/publications/AAG/pdf/obesity.pdf

Christensen, K. A., Stephens, M. A. P., & Townsend, A. L. (1998). Mastery in women's multiple roles and well-being: Adult daughters providing care to impaired parents. *Health Psychology, 17,* 163–171.

Chung, C. K., & Pennebaker, J. W. (2008). Variations in the spacing of expressive writing sessions. *British Journal of Health Psychology, 13,* 15–21.

Claar, R. L., & Blumenthal, J. A. (2003). The value of stress-management interventions in life-threatening medical conditions. *Current Directions in Psychological Science, 12,* 133–137.

Clark, D. M., Ball, S., & Pape, D. (1991). An experimental investigation of thought suppression. *Behaviour Research and Therapy, 29,* 253–257.

Clay, R. (1995). Working mothers: Happy or haggard? *The APA Monitor, 26*(11), 1, 37.

Cohen, J. D., Peristein, W. M., Braver, T. S., Nystrom, L. E., Noll, D. C., Jonides, J., et al. (1997). Temporal dynamics of brain activation during a working memory task. *Nature, 386,* 604–608.

Cohen, S., & Herbert, T. B. (1996). Health psychology: Psychological factors and physical disease from the perspective of human psychoneuroimmunology. *Annual Review of Psychology, 47,* 113–142.

Cohen, S., & Wills, T. (1985). Stress, social support and the buffering hypothesis. *Psychological Bulletin, 98,* 310–357.

Colado, M. I., O'Shea, E., & Green, A. R. (2004). Acute and long-term effects of MDMA on cerebral dopamine biochemistry and function. *Psychopharmacology, 173,* 249–263.

Compas, B. E., Haaga, D. A. F., Keefe, F. J., Leitenberg, H., & Williams, D. A. (1998). Sampling of empirically supported psychological treatments from health psychology. *Journal of Consulting and Clinical Psychology, 66,* 89–112.

Coren, S. (1996). *Sleep thieves: An eye-opening exploration into the science and mysteries of sleep.* New York: Free Press.

Crick, F., & Mitchison, F. (1983). The function of dream sleep. *Nature, 304,* 111–114.

Crick, F., & Mitchison, G. (1986). REM sleep and neural nets. *Journal of Mind and Behavior, 7,* 229–250.

Crick, N. R., & Grotpeter, J. K. (1995). Relational aggression, gender, and social-psychological adjustment. *Child Development, 66,* 710–722.

Cuomo, A. (2009). Relationship between depression, cardiovascular disease, and healthcare costs in female patients. *Primary Psychiatry, 16,* 13.

Curtin, J. J., Patrick, C. J., Lang, A. R., Cacioppo, J. T., & Birbaumer, N. (2001). Alcohol affects emotion through cognition. *Psychological Science, 12,* 527–531.

Dahloef, P., Norlin-Bagge, E., Hedner, J., Ejnell, H., Hetta, J., & Haellstroem, T. (2002). Improvement in neuropsychological performance following surgical treatment for obstructive sleep apnea syndrome. *Acta Oto-Laryngologica, 122,* 86–91.

D'Angelo, B., & Wierzbicki, M. (2003). Relations of daily hassles with both anxious and depressed mood in students. *Psychological Reports, 92,* 416–418.

Dannon, P. N., Lowengrub, K., Amiaz, R., Grunhaus, L., & Kotler, M. (2004). Comorbid cannabis use and panic disorder: Short term and long term follow-up study. *Human Psychopharmacology, 19*(2), 97–101.

David, J. P., & Suls, J. (1999). Coping efforts in daily life: Role of Big Five traits and problem appraisals. *Journal of Personality, 67,* 265–294.

Davis, C., Ralevski, E., Kennedy, S. H., & Neitzert, C. S. (1995). The role of personality factors in the reporting of side effect complaints to moclobemide and placebo. *Journal of Clinical Psychopharmacology, 15,* 347–352.

Davis, M. C., Matthews, K. A., & McGrath, C. E. (2000). Hostile attitudes predict elevated vascular resistance during interpersonal stress in men and women. *Psychosomatic Medicine, 62,* 17–25.

Degarrod, L. N. (1990). Coping with stress: Dream interpretation in the Mapuche family. *Psychiatric Journal of the University of Ottawa, 15,* 111–116.

DeLongis, A., Coyne, J. C., Dakof, G., Folkman, S., & Lazrus, R. S. (1982). Relationship of daily hassles, uplifts, and major life events to health status. *Health Psychology, 1,* 119–136.

Dhume, V. G., Agshikar, N. V., & Diniz, R. S. (1975). Placebo-induced side effects in healthy volunteers. *Clinician, 39,* 289–290.

Dickerson, S. S., & Kemeny, M. E. (2002). Acute stressors and cortisol responses: A theoretical integration and synthesis of laboratory research. *Psychological Bulletin, 130,* 355–391.

DiGiuseppe, R., & Tafrate, R. C. (2003). Anger treatment for adults: A meta-analytic review. *Clinical Psychology: Science and Practice, 10,* 70–84.

Dill, P. L., & Henley, T. B. (1998). Stressors of college: A comparison of traditional and nontraditional students. *Journal of Psychology, 132,* 25–32.

Dinges, D., Pack, F., Williams, K., Gillen, K., Powell, J., Ott, G., et al. (1997). Cumulative sleepiness, mood disturbance, and psychomotor vigilance performance decrements during a week of sleep restricted to 4–5 hours per night. *Sleep, 20,* 267–277.

Dodge, K. A., & Newman, J. P. (1981). Biased decision-making processes in aggressive boys. *Journal of Abnormal Psychology, 90,* 375–379.

Dornelas, E. A. (2008). *Psychotherapy with cardiac patients: Behavioral cardiology in practice.* (pp. 103–123). Washington, D.C.: American Psychological Association.

Drid, M. D., Raybaud, F., De Lunardo, C., Iacono, P., & Gustovic, P. (1995). Influence of the behavior pattern on the nocebo response of healthy volunteers. *British Journal of Clinical Pharmacology, 39,* 204–206.

Eagly, A. H., & Steffen, V. J. (1986). Gender and aggressive behavior: A meta-analytic review of the social psychological literature. *Psychological Bulletin, 100,* 309–330.

Eaker, E. D., Pinsky, J., & Castelli, W. P. (1992). Myocardial infarction and coronary death among women: psychosocial predictors from a 20-year follow-up of women in the Framingham Study. *American Journal of Epidemiology, 135,* 854–864.

Earle, T. L., Linden, W., & Weinberg, J. (1999). Differential effects of harassment on cardiovascular and salivary cortisol stress reactivity and recovery in women and men. *Journal of Psychosomatic Research, 46,* 125–141.

Edwards, M. R. (2007). The role of husbands' supportive communication practices in the lives of employed mothers. *Marriage and Family Review, 40,* 23–46.

Egbert, L. D., Battit, G. E., Welch, C. E., & Barlett, M. K. (1964). Reduction of postoperative pain by encouragement and instruction of patients. *New England Journal of Medicine, 270,* 825–827.

Epstein, R., Chillag, N., & Lavie, P. (1998). Starting times of school: Effects on daytime functioning fifth-grade children in Israel. *Sleep: Journal of Sleep Research and Sleep Medicine, 21,* 250–256.

Erickson, K., Drevets, W., & Schulkin, J. (2003). Glucocorticoid regulation of diverse cognitive functions in normal and pathological emotional states. *Neuroscience and Biobehavioral Reviews, 27,* 233–246.

Evans, G. W. (2003). A multimethodological analysis of cumulative risk and allostatic load among rural children. *Developmental Psychology, 39,* 924–933.

Fawzy, F. I., Kemeny, M. E., Fawzy, N. W., Elashoff, R., Morton, D., Cousins, N., et al. (1990). A structured psychiatric intervention for cancer patients: II. Changes over time in immunological measures. *Archives of General Psychiatry, 47,* 729–735.

Ferketich, A. K., Schwartzbaum, J. A., Frid, D. J., & Moeschberger, M. L. (2000). Depression as an antecedent to heart disease among women and men in the NHANES I study. National Health and Nutrition Examination Survey. *Archives Internal Medicine, 160,* 1261–1268.

Fischer, C., Hatzidimitriou, G., Wlos, J., Katz, J., & Ricaurte, G. (1995). Reorganization of ascending 5-HT axon projections in animals previously exposed to recreational drug 3,4-methelenedioxymetham-phetamine (MDMA, "Ecstasy"). *Journal of Neuroscience, 15,* 5476–5485.

Flaten, M. A., Simonsen, T., & Olsen, H. (1999). Drug-related information generates placebo and nocebo responses that modify the drug response. *Psychosomatic Medicine, 61,* 250–255.

Folkman, S., & Moskowitz, J. T. (2004). Coping: Pitfalls and promise. *Annual Review of Psychology, 55,* 745–774.

Food and Drug Administration. (2007). Retrieved December 4, 2009, from http://www.fda.gov/downloads/Drugs/DrugSafety/ucm085908.pdf

Forbes, E. J., & Pekala, R. J. (1993). Psychophysiological effects of several stress management techniques. *Psychological Reports, 72,* 19–27.

Francis, M. E., & Pennebaker, J. W. (1992). Putting stress into words: The impact of writing on physiological, absentee, and self-reported emotional well-being measures. *American Journal of Health Promotion, 6,* 280–286.

Frasure-Smith, N., Lesperance, F., Juneau, M., Talajic, M., & Bourassa, M. G. (1999). Gender, depression, and one-year prognosis after myocardial infarction. *Psychosomatic Medicine, 61,* 26–37.

Freud, S. (1900/1958). *The interpretation of dreams.* New York: Basic Books.

Geiser, F., Meier, C., Wegener, I., Imbierowicz, K., Conrad, R., Liedtke, R., et al. (2008). Association between anxiety and factors of coagulation and fibrinolysis. *Psychotherapy and Psychosomatics, 77,* 377–383.

Giancola, P. R., Josephs, R. A., Parrott, D. J., & Duke, A. A. (2010). Alcohol myopia revisited: Carlify aggression and other acts of disinhibition through a distorted lens. *Perspectives in Psychological Science, 5,* 265–278.

Gick, M. L., & Thompson, W. G. (1997). Negative affect and the seeking of medical care in university students with irritable bowel syndrome. *Journal of Psychosomatic Research, 43,* 535–540.

Gidron, Y., Davidson, K., & Bata, I. (1999). The short-term effects of a hostility-reduction intervention on male coronary heart disease patients. *Health Psychology, 18,* 416–420.

Goldstein, A. (1994). *Addiction: From biology to drug policy.* New York: Freeman.

Goldstein, D. S. (1995). *Stress, catecholamines, and cardiovascular disease.* New York: Oxford University Press.

Goldstein, D. S., & McEwen, B. (2002). Allostasis, homeostats, and the nature of stress. *Stress: International Journal on the Biology of Stress, 5,* 55–58.

Goode, E. (1999, November 2). New clues to why we dream. *New York Times,* p. D1.

Goodwin, R. D., Davidson, K. W., & Keyes, K. (2009). Mental disorders and cardiovascular disease among adults in the United States. *Journal of Psychiatric Research, 43,* 239–246.

Grant, B. F., & Dawson, D. A. (1997). Age at onset of alcohol use and its association with DSM-IV alcohol abuse and dependence: Results from the National Longitudinal Alcohol Epidemiologic Survey. *Journal of Substance Abuse, 9,* 103–110.

Grant, B. F., Stinson, F. S., Dawson, D. A., Chou, S. P., Dufour, M. C., Compton, W., et al. (2004). Prevalence and co-occurrence of substance use disorders and independent mood and anxiety disorders: Results from the National Epidemiologic Survey on Alcohol and Related Conditions. *Archives of General Psychiatry, 61,* 807–816.

Green, A. R., Cross, A. J., & Goodwin, G. M. (1995) Review of the pharmacology and clinical pharmacology of 3, 4-methylenedioxymethamphetamine (MDMA or "Ecstasy"). *Psychopharmacology, 119,* 247–260.

Grilly, D. (1994). *Drugs and human behavior* (2nd ed.). Boston: Allyn and Bacon.

Gross, J., & Levenson, R. W. (1997). Hiding feelings: The acute effects of inhibiting negative and positive emotion. *Journal of Abnormal Psychology, 106,* 95–103.

Grossarth-Maticek, R., Eysenck, H. J., Boyle, G. J., Heeb, J., Costa, C. D., & Diel, I. J. (2000). Interaction of psychosocial and physical risk factors in the causation of mammary cancer, and its prevention through psychological methods of treatment. *Journal of Clinical Psychology, 56,* 33–50.

Gruber, A. J., Pope, H. G., Hudson, H. I., & Yurgelun-Todd, D. (2003). Attributes of long-term heavy cannabis users: A case control study. *Psychological Medicine, 33,* 1415–1422.

Hahn, R. A. (1995). *Sickness and healing: An anthropological perspective.* New Haven, CT: Yale University Press.

Hahn, R. A. (1997). The nocebo phenomenon: Scope and foundations. In A. Harrington (Ed.), *The placebo effect: An interdisciplinary exploration* (pp. 56-76). Cambridge, MA: Harvard University Press.

Hahn, R. A. (1999). Expectations of sickness: Concept and evidence of the nocebo phenomenon. In I. Kirsch (Ed.), *How expectancies shape experience* (pp. 333–356). Washington, DC: American Psychological Association.

Haney, M., Ward, A. S., Comer, S. D., Foltin, R. W., & Fischman, M. W. (1999). Abstinence symptoms following smoked marijuana in humans. *Psychopharmacology, 141,* 395–404.

Hardy, J. D., & Smith, T. W. (1988). Cynical hostility and vulnerability to disease: Social support, life stress, and physiological response to conflict. *Health Psychology, 7,* 447–459.

Hart, K. E., & Hope, C. W. (2004). Cynical hostility and the psychosocial vulnerability model of disease risk: Confounding effects of neuroticism (negative affectivity) bias. *Personality and Individual Differences, 36,* 1571–1582.

Hecker, M., Chesney, M. N., Black, G., & Frautsch, N. (1988). Coronary-prone behaviors in the Western Collaborative Group Study. *Psychosomatic Medicine, 50,* 153–164.

Henry, J. P. (1977). *Stress, health, and the environment.* New York: Springer-Verlag.

Hobson, J. A. (1989). *Sleep.* New York: Scientific American Library.

Hobson, J. A. (1995). *Sleep.* New York: Scientific American Library.

Hobson, J. A., & McCarley, R. W. (1977). The brain as a dream state generator: An activation-synthesis hypothesis of the dream process. *American Journal of Psychiatry, 134,* 1335–1348.

Hochschild, A. (1989). *The second shift: Working parents and the revolution at home.* New York: Viking.

Hockemeyer, J., & Smyth, J. (2002). Evaluating the feasibility and efficacy of the self-administered manual-based stress management intervention for individuals with asthma: Results from a controlled study. *Behavioral Medicine, 27,* 161–172.

House, J., Landis, K., & Umberson, D. (1988). Social relationships and health. *Science, 241,* 540–545.

Ingledew, D. K., Hardy, L., & Cooper, C. L. (1997). Do resources bolster coping and does coping buffer stress? An organizational study with longitudinal aspect and control for negative affectivity. *Journal of Occupational Health Psychology, 2,* 118–133.

Inman, D. J., Silver, S. M., & Doghramji, K. (1990). Sleep disturbance in post-traumatic stress disorder: A comparison with non-PTSD insomnia. *Journal of Traumatic Stress, 3,* 429–437.

Ironson, G., Wynings, C., Schneiderman, N., Baum, A., Rodriguez, M., Greenwood, D., et al. (1997). Posttraumatic stress symptoms, intrusive thoughts, loss, and immune function after Hurricane Andrew. *Psychosomatic Medicine, 59,* 128–141.

Jacobs, G. D., Pace-Schott, E. F., Stickgold, R., & Otto, M. W. (2004). Cognitive behavior therapy and pharmacotherapy for insomnia: A randomized controlled trial and direct comparison. *Archives of Internal Medicine, 164,* 1888–1896.

Jewett, D. L., Fein, G., & Greenberg, M. H. (1990). A double-blind study of symptom provocation to determine food sensitivity. *New England Journal of Medicine, 323,* 429–433.

Johnson, J., Noel, N., & Sutter-Hernandez, J. (2002). Alcohol and male acceptance of sexual aggression: The role of perceptual ambiguity. *Journal of Applied Social Psychology, 30,* 1186-2000.

Kanner, A. D., Coyne, J. C., Schaefer, C., & Lazarus, R. S. (1981). Comparison of two modes of stress management: Daily hassles and uplifts versus major life events. *Journal of Behavioral Medicine, 4,* 1–39.

Karacan, I., Goodenough, D. R., Shapiro, A., & Starker, S. (1966). Erection cycle during sleep in relation to dream anxiety. *Archives of General Psychiatry, 15,* 183–189.

Karlamangla, A. S., Singer, B. H., McEwen, B. S., Rowe, J. W., & Seeman, T. E. (2002). Allostatic load as a predictor of functional decline: MacArthur studies of successful aging. *Journal of Clinical Epidemiology, 55,* 696–710.

Kiecolt-Glaser, J. K., & Glaser, R. (2002). Depression and immune function: Central pathways to morbidity and mortality. *Journal of Psychosomatic Research, 53,* 873–876.

Kiecolt-Glaser, J., Glaser, R., Strain, E., Stout, J., Tarr, K., Holliday, J., et al. (1986). Modulation of cellular immunity in medical students. *Journal of Behavioral Medicine, 9,* 5.

Kiecolt-Glaser, J. K., Marucha, P. T., Malarky, W. B., Mercado, A. M., & Glaser, R. (1995). Slowing of wound healing by psychological stress. *Lancet, 346,* 1194–1196.

King, A. C., Oman, R. F., Brassington, G. S., Bliwise, D. L., & Haskell, W. L. (1997). Moderate-intensity exercise and self-rated quality of sleep in older adults: A randomized controlled trial. *Journal of the American Medical Association, 277,* 32–37.

Klerman, E. B., Davis, J. B., Duffy, J. F., Dijk, D., & Kronauer, R. E. (2004). Older people awaken more frequently but fall back asleep at the same rate as younger people. *Sleep: Journal of Sleep and Sleep Disorders Research, 27,* 793–798.

Klinkenborg, V. (1997, January 5). Awakening to sleep. *New York Times Magazine,* 26.

Knox, S. S., Weidner, G., Adelman, A., Stoney, C. M., & Ellison, R. C. (2004). Hostility and physiological risk in the National Heart, Lung, and Blood Institute Family Heart Study. *Archives of Internal Medicine, 1642,* 2442–2448.

Kohler, P. F., Rivera, V. J., Eckert, E. D., Bouchard, T. J., Jr., & Heston, L. L. (1985). Genetic regulation of immunoglobulin and specific antibody levels in twins reared apart. *Journal of Clinical Investigation, 75,* 883–888.

Kolata, G. (1997, January 14). Which comes first: Depression or heart disease? *New York Times,* p. C1.

Koob, G. F., & Le Moal, M. (2008). Addiction and the brain antireward system. *Annual Review of Psychology, 59,* 29–53.

Kop, W. J. (2003). The integration of cardiovascular behavioral medicine and psychoneuroimmunology: New developments based on converging research fields. *Brain, Behavior and Immunity, 17,* 233–237.

Koster, E. H. W., Rassin, E., Crombez, G., & Näring, G. W. B. (2003). The paradoxical effects of suppressing anxious thoughts during imminent threat. *Behaviour Research and Therapy, 41,* 1113–1120.

Kubzansky, L. D., & Kawachi, I. (2000). Going to the heart of the matter: Do negative emotions cause coronary heart disease? *Journal of Psychosomatic Research, 48,* 323–337.

Lacks, P., & Morin, C. M. (1992). Recent advances in the assessment and treatment of insomnia. *Journal of Consulting and Clinical Psychology, 60,* 586–594.

Lakey, B., & Heller, K. (1988). Social support from a friend, perceived support, and social problem solving. *American Journal of Community Psychology, 16,* 811–824.

Landrigan, C. P., Rothschild, J. M., Cronin, J. W., Kaushal, R., Burdick, E., Katz, J. T., et al. (2004). Effect of reducing interns' work hours on serious medical errors in intensive care units. *New England Journal of Medicine, 351,* 1838–1848.

Lazarus, R. S., & Folkman, S. (1984). *Stress, appraisal, and coping.* New York: Springer.

Leccese, A. P. (1991). *Drugs and society: Behavioral medicines and abusable drugs.* Englewood Cliffs, NJ: Prentice Hall.

Leproult, R., Copinschi, G., Buxton, O., & Van Cauter, E. (1997). Sleep loss results in an elevation of cortisol levels the next evening. *Sleep, 20,* 865–870.

Leproult, R., Van Reeth, O., Byrne, M. M., Sturis, J., & Van Cauter, E. (1997). Sleepiness, performance, and neuroendocrine function during sleep deprivation: Effects of exposure to bright light or exercise. *Journal of Biological Rhythms, 12,* 245–258.

Levy, S. M., Herberman, R. B., Lippman, M. N., & d'Angelo, T. (1987). Correlation of stress factors with sustained depression of natural killer cell activity and predicted prognosis in patients with breast cancer. *Journal of Clinical Oncology, 5,* 348–353.

Levy, S. M., Herberman, R. B., Maluish, A. M., Schlien, B., & Lippman, M. (1985). Prognostic risk assessment in primary breast cancer by behavioral and immunological parameters. *Health Psychology, 4,* 99–113.

Levy, S. M., Lee, J., Bagley, C., & Lippman, M. (1988). Survival hazards analysis in first year recurrent breast cancer patients: Seven-year follow-up. *Psychosomatic Medicine, 50,* 520–528.

Linley, P. A., & Joseph, S. (2004). Positive change following trauma and adversity: A review. *Journal of Traumatic Stress, 17,* 11–21.

Lisspers, J., Sundin, Ö., Öhman, A., Hofman-Bang, C., Rydén, L., & Nygren, A. (2005). Long-term effects of lifestyle behavior change in coronary artery disease: Effects on recurrent coronary events after percutaneous coronary intervention. *Health Psychology, 24,* 41–48.

Lockley, S. W., Cronin, J. W., Evans, E. E., Cade, B. E., Lee, C. J., Landrigan, C. P., et al. (2004). Effect of reducing interns' weekly work hours on sleep and attentional failures. *New England Journal of Medicine, 351,* 1829–1837.

Lowe, P. (1999, May 2). Alike and different. *Denver Post.* p. A1.

Luce, G. G. (1971). *Biological rhythms in human and animal physiology.* New York: Dover.

Luckow, A., Reifman, A., & McIntosh, D. N. (1998, August). *Gender differences in coping: A meta-analysis.* Poster session presented at the 106th Annual Convention of the American Psychological Association, San Francisco, CA.

Maas, J. B. (1998). *Power sleep.* New York: Harper Perennial.

Madden, K. S. (2003). Catecholamines, sympathetic innervation, and immunity. *Brain, Behavior and Immunity, 17,* S5–S10.

Maier, K. J., Waldstein, S. R., & Synowski, S. J. (2003). Relation of cognitive appraisal to cardiovascular reactivity, affect, and task engagement. *Annals of Behavioral Medicine, 26,* 32–41.

Manuck, S. B., Cohen, S., Rabin, B. S., Muldoon, M. F., & Bachen, E. A. (1991). Individual differences in cellular immune response to stress. *Psychological Science, 2,* 111–115.

Martin, R. A., & Dobbin, J. P. (1988). Sense of humor, hassles, and immunoglobulin A: Evidence for a stress-moderating effect of humor. *International Journal of Psychiatry in Medicine, 18,* 93–105.

Marucha, P. T., Kiecolt-Glaser, J. K., & Favagehi, M. (1998). Mucosal wound healing is impaired by examination stress. *Psychosomatic Medicine, 60,* 362–365.

McEwen, B. S. (1998). Stress, adaptation, and disease: Allostasis and allostatic load. In S. M. McCann, J. M. Lipton, E. M. Sternberg, et al. (Eds.), *Annals of the New York Academy of Sciences: Neuroimmunomodulation: Molecular aspects, integrative systems, and clinical advances* (Vol. 840, pp. 33–44). New York: New York Academy of Sciences.

McEwen, B. S. (2000). Allostasis and allostatic load: Implications for neuropsychopharmacology. *Neuropsychopharmacology, 22,* 108–124.

McEwen, B. S. (2003). Mood disorders and medical illness: Mood disorders and allostatic load. *Biological Psychiatry, 54,* 200–207.

McEwen, B. S., Biron, C. A., Brunson, K. W., Bulloch, K., Chambers, W. H., Dhabhar, F. S., et al. (1997). The role of adrenocorticoids as modulators of immune function in health and disease: Neural, endocrine and immune interactions. *Brain Research Review, 23,* 79–133.

McEwen, B. S., & Schmeck, H. M., Jr. (1994). *The hostage brain.* New York: Rockefeller University Press.

McEwen, B. S., & Wingfield, J. C. (2003). Response to commentaries on the concept of allostasis. *Hormones and Behavior, 43,* 28–30.

McIntyre, K. P., Korn, J. H., & Matsuo, H. (2008). Sweating the small stuff: How different types of hassles result in the experience of stress. *Stress and Health: Journal of the International Society for the Investigation of Stress, 24,* 383–392.

McKnight-Eily L. R., Liu, Y., Perry, G. S., Presley-Cantrell, L. R., Strine, T. W., Lu, H., et al. (2009). Perceived insufficient rest or sleep among adults—United States, 2008. *Morbidity and Mortality Weekly Report, 58,* 1175–1179. Retrieved October 31, 2009, from http://www.cdc.gov/mmwr/preview/mmwrhtml/mm5842a2.htm#tab1

Mednick, S., Nakayama, K., & Stickgold, R. (2003). Sleep-dependent learning: A nap is as good as a night. *Nature Neuroscience, 6,* 697–698.

Miller, G. E., Dopp, J. M., Stevens, S. Y., & Fahey, J. L. (1999). Psychosocial predictors of natural killer cell mobilization during marital conflict. *Health Psychology, 18,* 262–271.

Miller, N. E. (1959). Liberalization of basic S-R concepts: Extensions to conflict behavior, motivation, and social learning. In S. Koch (Ed.), *Psychology: A study of science* (Vol. 2). (pp. 196-292). New York: McGraw-Hill.

Miller, T. Q., Smith, T. W., Turner, C. W., Guijarro, M. L., & Hallet, A. J. (1996). A meta-analytic review of research on hostility and physical health. *Psychological Bulletin, 119,* 322–348.

Moller, J., Theorell, T., de Faire, U., Ahlbom, A., & Hallqvist, J. (2005). Work related stressful life events and the risk of myocardial infarction. Case-control and case-crossover analyses within the Stockholm Heart Epidemiology Programme (SHEEP). *Journal of Epidemiological Community Health, 59,* 23–30.

Morf, C. C., & Rhodewalt, F. (2001). Unraveling the paradoxes of narcissism: A dynamic self-regulatory processing model. *Psychological Inquiry, 12,* 177–196.

Morling, B., Kitayama, S., & Miyamoto, Y. (2003). American and Japanese women use different coping strategies during normal pregnancy. *Personality and Social Psychology Bulletin, 29,* 1533–1546.

Moser, M., Lehofer, M., Hoehn-Saric, R., McLeod, D. R., Hildebrandt, G., Steinbrenner, B., et al. (1998). Increased heart rate in depressed subjects in spite of unchanged autonomic balance. *Journal of Affective Disorders, 48,* 115–124.

Mroczek, D. K., & Almeida, D. M. (2004). The effect of daily stress, personality, and age on daily negative affect. *Journal of Personality, 72,* 355–378.

Muehlenhard, C. L., & Linton, M. A. (1987). Date rape and sexual aggression in dating situations: Incidence and risk factors. *Journal of Counseling Psychology, 34,* 186–196.

Nasby, W., Hayden, B., & DePaulo, B. M. (1979). Attributional bias among aggressive boys to interpret unambiguous social stimuli as displays of hostility. *Journal of Abnormal Psychology 89,* 459–468.

National Admissions to Substance Abuse Treatment Services, November 2001, funded by the Substance Abuse and Mental Health Service Administration, DHHS.

National Center for Health Statistics. (2009). Health, United States, 2009: With Special Feature on Medical Technology. Library of Congress Catalog Number 76–641496. Retrieved May 14, 2010 from http://www.cdc.gov/nchs/data/hus/hus09.pdf#063.

National Institute on Drug Abuse. (1998). Slide Teaching Packet I, for Health Practitioners, Teachers and Neuroscientists. Section III: Introduction to Drugs of Abuse: Cocaine, Opiates (Heroin) and Marijuana (THC).

National Institute on Drug Abuse. (2003). *InfoFax: Drug Addiction treatment methods.* Retrieved from http://www.drugabuse.gov/infofax/treatmeth.html

National Institute on Drug Abuse. (2004, September). *NIDA InfoFacts: Crack and cocaine.* Retrieved August 2005 from http://www.drugabuse.gov/DrugPagesCocaine.html

National Institute on Drug Abuse. (2007). *NIDA InfoFacts: MDMA (Ecstasy).* Retrieved November 7, 2009, from http://www.nida.nih.gov/InfoFacts/ecstasy.html

National Sleep Foundation. (2002). *"Sleep in America" poll.* Retrieved from http://www.sleepfoundation.org2002poll.html

National Sleep Foundation. (2004). *Sleep in America poll* Retrieved August 13, 2005, from http://www.sleepfoundation.org/hottopicsindex.php?secid=16&id=143

National Sleep Foundation. (2005). *Sleep in America poll* Retrieved October 26, 2009, from http://www.sleepfoundation.org/sites/default/files/2005_summary_of_findings.pdf

National Sleep Foundation. (2008). *Sleep in America poll* Retrieved October 25, 2009, from http://www.sleepfoundation.org/article/press-release/longer-work-days-leave-americans-nodding-the-job

National Sleep Foundation. (2009). *Sleep in America poll* Retrieved October 25, 2009, from http://www.sleepfoundation.org/sites/default/files/2009%20POLL%20HIGHLIGHTS.pdf

Nelson, C. B., Heath, A. C., & Kessler, R. C. (1998). Temporal progression of alcohol dependence symptoms in the U.S. household population: Results from the National Comorbidity Survey. *Journal of Consulting and Clinical Psychology, 66*(3), 474–483.

Newcomer, J. W., Selke, G., Melson, A. K., Hershey, T., Craft, S., Richards, K., et al. (1999). Decreased memory performance in healthy humans induced by stress-level cortisol treatment. *Archives of General Psychiatry, 56,* 527–533.

NIH Technology Assessment Panel. (1996). Integration of behavioral and relaxation approaches into the treatment of chronic pain and insomnia. *Journal of the American Medical Association, 276*, 313–318.

Norton, T. R., Gupta, A., Stephens, M. A. P., Martire, L. M., & Townsend, A. L. (2005). Stress, rewards, and change in the centrality of women's family and work roles: Mastery as a mediator. *Sex Roles, 52*, 325–335.

O'Connor, D. B., & Shimizu, M. (2002). Sense of personal control, stress and coping style: A cross-cultural study. *Stress and Health: Journal of the International Society for the Investigation of Stress, 18*, 173–183.

Odgers, C. L., Caspi, A., Nagin, D., Piquero, A. R., Slutske, W. S., Milne, B., et al. (2008). Is it important to prevent early exposure to drugs and alcohol among teens? *Psychological Science, 19*, 1037–1044.

Ornish, D., Scherwitz, L. W., Billings, J. H., Gould, K. L., Merritt, T. A., Sparler, S., et al. (1998). Intensive lifestyle changes for reversal of coronary heart disease. *Journal of the American Medical Association, 280*, 2001–2007.

Ouimette, P. C. (1997). Psychopathology and sexual aggression in nonincarcerated men. *Violence and Victims, 12*, 389–395.

Overmeier, J. B. (2002). On learned helplessness. *Integrative Physiological and Behavioral Science, 37*, 4–8.

Pacak, K., & Palkovits, M. (2001). Stressor specificity of central neuroendocrine responses: Implications for stress-related disorders. *Endocrine Review, 22*, 502–548.

Páez, D., Velasco, C., & González, J. L. (1999). Expressive writing and the role of alexythimia as a dispositional deficit in self-disclosure and psychological health. *Journal of Personality and Social Psychology, 77*, 630–641.

Park, C. L., & Fenster, J. R. (2004). Stress-related growth: Predictors of occurrence and correlates with psychological adjustment. *Journal of Social and Clinical Psychology, 23*, 195–215.

Park, D. C., Polk, T. A., Park, R., Minear, M., Savage, A., & Smith, M. R. (2004). Aging reduces neural specialization in ventral visual cortex. *Proceedings of the National Academy of Sciences of the United States of America, 101*, 13091–13095.

Parker, G. B., Hilton, T. M., Walsh, W. F., Owen, C. A., Heruc, G. A., Olley, A., et al. (2009). "Timing is everything: The onset of depression and acute coronary syndrome outcome": Erratum. *Biological Psychiatry, 65*, 449.

Patel, S., Cravatt, B. F., & Hillard, C. J. (2005). Synergistic interactions between cannabinoids and environmental stress in the activation of the central amygdala. *Neuropsychopharmacology, 30*, 497–507.

Patterson, T. L., Semple, S. J., Shaw, W. S., Yu, E., He, Y., Zhang, M. Y., et al. (1998). The cultural context of caregiving: A comparison of Alzheimer's caregivers in Shanghai, China and San Diego, California. *Psychological Medicine, 28*, 1071–1084.

Pengilly, J. W., & Dowd, E. T. (1997). *Hardiness and social support as moderator of stress in college students*. Paper presented at the annual convention of the Association for the Advancement of Behavior Therapy, Miami Beach, FL.

Pennebaker, J. W. (1989). Confession, inhibition and disease. In L. Berkowitz (Ed.), *Advances in experimental social psychology* (Vol. 22, pp. 211–244). New York: Academic Press.

Pennebaker, J. W., Colder, M., & Sharp, L. K. (1990). Accelerating the coping process. *Journal of Personality and Social Psychology, 58*, 528–537.

Pennebaker, J. W., & Francis, M. E. (1996). Cognitive, emotional, and language processes in disclosure. *Cognition and Emotion, 10*, 601–626.

Perna, F. M., Antoni, M. H., Baum, A., Gordon, P., & Schneiderman, N. (2003). Cognitive behavioral stress management effects on injury and illness among competitive athletes: A randomized clinical trial. *Annals of Behavioral Medicine, 25*, 66–73.

Peters, A., Von Klot, S., Heier, M., Trentinaglia, I., Hörmann, A., Wichmann, H. E., et al. (Cooperative Health Research in the Region of Augsburg Study Group). (2004). Exposure to traffic and the onset of myocardial infarction. *New England Journal of Medicine, 351*, 1721–1730.

Peters, M. L., Godaert, G. L. R., Ballieux, R. E., & Heijnen, C. J. (2003). Moderation of physiological stress responses by personality traits and daily hassles: Less flexibility of immune system responses. *Biological Psychology, 65*, 21–48.

Petersen, R. C. (1977, July). Marihuana research findings: 1976. Summary. *NIDA Research Monograph, 14*, 1–37.

Petersen, R. C. (1979). Importance of inhalation patterns in determining effects of marihuana use. *Lancet, 31*, 727–728.

Peterson, C., Park, N., Pole, N., D'Andrea, W., & Seligman, M. E. P. (2008). Strengths of character and posttraumatic growth. *Journal of Traumatic Stress, 21*, 214–217.

Petrie, K. J., Booth, R. J., & Pennebaker, J. W. (1998). The immunological effects of thought suppression. *Journal of Personality and Social Psychology, 75*, 1264–1272.

Petrie, K. J., Booth, R. J., Pennebaker, J. W., Davison, K. P., & Thomas, M. G. (1995). Disclosure of trauma and immune response to a hepatitis B vaccination program. *Journal of Consulting and Clinical Psychology, 63*, 787–792.

Petrovic, P., Kalso, E., Petersson, K. M., & Ingvar, M. (2002). Placebo and opioid analgesia—Imaging a shared neuronal network. *Science, 295*, 1737–1740.

Phillips, D. P., & Smith, D. G. (1990). Postponement of death until symbolically meaningful occasions. *Journal of the American Medical Association, 263*, 1947–1951.

Phillips, D. P., Van Voorhees, C. A., & Ruth, T. E. (1992). The birthday: Lifeline or deadline. *Psychosomatic Medicine, 54*, 532–542.

Phillips, S. D., & Imhoff, A. R. (1997). Women and career development: A decade of research. *Annual Review of Psychology, 48*, 31–59.

Pietromonaco, P. R., Manis, J., & Frohardt-Lane, K. (1986). Psychological consequences of multiple social roles. *Psychology of Women Quarterly, 10*, 373–381.

Pihl, R. O., Paylan, S. S., Gentes-Hawn, A., & Hoaken, P. N. S. (2003). Alcohol affects executive cognitive functioning differentially on the ascending versus descending limb of the blood alcohol concentration curve. *Alcoholism: Clinical and Experimental Research, 27*, 773–779.

Pleis, J. R., Lucas, J. W., & Ward, B. W. (2009). Summary health statistics for U.S. adults: National Health Interview Survey, 2008. National Center for Health Statistics. *Vital Health Statistics 10*, 242.

Räikkönen, K., Matthews, K. A., Flory, J. D., & Owens, J. F. (1999). Effects of hostility on ambulatory blood pressure and mood during daily living in healthy adults. *Health Psychology, 18*, 44–53.

Reuter, M. (2002). Impact of cortisol on emotions under stress and nonstress conditions: A pharmacopsychological approach. *Neuropsychobiology, 46*, 41–48.

Roberts, A. H., Kewman, D. G., Mercier, L., & Hovell, M. (1993). The power of nonspecific effects in healing: Implications for psychosocial and biological treatments. *Clinical Psychology Review, 13*, 375–391.

Rojas, I. G., Padgett, D. A., Sheridan, J. F., & Marucha, P. T. (2002). Stress-induced susceptibility to bacterial infection during cutaneous wound healing. *Brain, Behavior and Immunity, 16*, 74–84.

Romero, L., & Sapolsky, R. (1996). Patterns of ACTH secretagog secretion in response to psychological stimuli. *Journal of Neuroendocrinology, 8*, 243–258.

Rosengren, A., Hawken, S., Ôunpuu, S., Sliwa, K., Zubaid, M., Almahmeed, W. A., et al. (2004). Association of psychosocial risk factors with risk of acute myocardial infarction in 11119 cases and 13648 controls from 52 countries (the INTERHEART study): Case-control study. *Lancet, 364*, 953–962.

Rosenzweig, P., Brohler, S., & Zipfel, A. (1993). The placebo effect in healthy volunteers: Influence of experimental conditions on the adverse events profile during phase I studies. *Clinical Pharmacological Therapy, 54*, 579–583.

Rutledge, T., Reis, S. E., Olson, M., Owens, J., Kelsey, S. F., Pepine, C. J., et al. (2004). Social networks are associated with lower mortality rates among women with suspected coronary disease: The National Heart, Lung, and Blood Institute-Sponsored Women's Ischemia Syndrome Evaluation Study. *Psychosomatic Medicine, 66*, 882–888.

Ryska, T. A. (1998). Cognitive-behavioral strategies and precompetitive anxiety among recreational athletes. *Psychological Record, 48*, 697–708.

Sapolsky, R. M. (1992). *Stress, the aging brain, and the mechanisms of neuron death*. Cambridge, MA: MIT Press.

Sapolsky, R. M. (1996). Why stress is bad for your brain. *Science, 273*, 749–750.

Sapolsky, R. M. (1997). *Why zebras don't get ulcers*. York: Freeman.

Schweiger, A., & Parducci, A. (1981). Nocebo: The psychologic induction of pain. *Pavlovian Journal of Biological Science, 16*, 140–143.

Scott, B., & Melin, L. (1998). Psychometric properties and standardised data for questionnaires measuring negative affect, dispositional style and daily hassles: A nationwide sample. *Scandinavian Journal of Psychology, 39*, 301–307.

Seeman, R. E., Berkman, L. F., Blazer, D., & Rowe, J. W. (1994). Social ties and support and neuroendocrine function: The MacArthur studies of successful aging. *Annals of Behavioral Medicine, 16*, 95–106.

Seeman, T. E. (2000). Health promoting effects of friends and family on health outcomes in older adults. *American Journal of Health Promotion, 14*, 362–370.

Seeman, T. E., Singer, B. H., Rowe, J. W., Horwitz, R. I., & McEwen, B. S. (1997). Price of adaptation—Allostatic load and its health consequences: MacArthur studies of successful aging. *Archives of Internal Medicine, 157*, 2259–2268.

Selye, H. (1976). *The stress of life*. New York: McGraw-Hill.

Shapiro, A. K. (1964). Factors contributing to the placebo effect: Their significance for psychotherapy. *American Journal of Psychotherapy, 18*, 73–88.

Shapiro, A. K., & Morris, L. A. (1978). The placebo effect in medical and psychological therapies. In S. L. Garfield & A. E. Bergin (Eds.), *Handbook of psychotherapy and behavior change: An empirical analysis* (2nd ed.). (pp. 369–410). New York: Wiley.

Shapiro, D. H., Jr., Schwartz, C. E., & Astin, J. A. (1996). Controlling ourselves, controlling our world: Psychology's role in understanding positive and negative consequences of seeking and gaining control. *American Psychologist, 51*, 1213–1230.

Sheehy, R., & Horan, J. J. (2004). Effects of stress inoculation training for 1st-year law students. *International Journal of Stress Management, 11*, 41–55.

Sheese, B. E., Brown, E. L., & Graziano, W. G. (2004). Emotional expression in cyberspace: Searching for moderators of the Pennebaker disclosure effect via email. *Health Psychology, 23*, 457–464.

Shepherd, M. (1993). The placebo: From specificity to the non-specific and back. *Psychological Medicine, 23*, 569–578.

Sinha, B. K., Willson, L. R., & Watson, D. C. (2000). Stress and coping among students in India and Canada. *Canadian Journal of Behavioral Sciences, 32*, 218–225.

Smith, C. A., & Kirby, L. D. (2000). Consequences require antecedents: Toward a process model of emotion elicitation. In J. P. Forgas (Ed.), *Feeling and thinking: The role of affect in social cognition* (pp. 83–106). New York: Cambridge University Press.

Smyth, J. M., Stone, A. A., Hurewitz, A., & Kaell, A. (1999). Effects of writing about stressful experiences on symptom reduction in patients with asthma or rheumatoid arthritis. *Journal of the American Medical Association, 281*, 1304–1329.

Solms, M. (1997). *The neuropsychology of dreams: A clinico-anatomical study*. Mahwah, NJ: Erlbaum.

Speisman, J. C., Lazarus, R. S., Mordkoff, A., & Davison, L. (1964). Experimental reduction of stress based on ego-defense theory. *Journal of Abnormal and Social Psychology, 68*, 367–380.

Steele, C., & Josephs, R. A. (1990). Alcohol myopia: Its prized and dangerous effects. *American Psychologist, 45*, 921–933.

Stephens, M. A. P., Franks, M. M., Martire, L. M., Norton, T. R., & Atienza, A. A. (2009). Women at midlife: Stress and rewards of balancing parent care with employment and other family roles. In K. Shifren (Ed.), *How caregiving affects development: Psychological implications for child, adolescent, and adult caregivers* (pp. 147–167). Washington, DC: American Psychological Association.

Sterling-Smith, R. S. (1976). *A special study of drivers most responsible in fatal accidents* (Summary for Management Report, Contract DOT HS 310-3-595). Washington, DC: Department of Transportation.

Stickgold, R. (1998). Sleep: Off-line memory reprocessing. *Trends in Cognitive Science, 2*, 484–492.

Stickgold, R., Malia, A., Maguire, D., Roddenberry, D., & O'Connor, M. (2000). Replaying the game: Hypnagogic images in normals and amnesics. *Science, 290*, 350–353.

Stickgold, R., Rittenhouse, C. D., & Hobson, J. A. (1994). Dream splicing: A new technique for assessing thematic coherence in subjective reports of mental activity. *Consciousness and Cognition: An International Journal, 3*, 114–128.

Stickgold, R., Whidbee, D., Schirmer, B., Paqtel, V., & Hobson, J. A. (2000). Visual discrimination task improvement: A multi-step process occurring during sleep. *Journal of Cognitive Neuroscience, 12,* 246–254.

Strike, P. C., Magid, K., Brydon, L., Edwards, S., McEwan, J. R., & Steptoe, A. (2004). Exaggerated platelet and hemodynamic reactivity to mental stress in men with coronary artery disease. *Psychosomatic Medicine, 66,* 492–500.

Suarez, E. C., Kuhn, C. M., Schanberg, S. M., Williams, R. B., Jr., & Zimmermann, E. A. (1998). Neuroendocrine, cardiovascular, and emotional responses of hostile men: The role of interpersonal challenge. *Psychosomatic Medicine, 60,* 78–88.

Suarez, E., & Williams, R. (1989). Situational determinants of cardiovascular and emotional reactivity in high and low hostile men. *Psychosomatic Medicine, 51,* 404–418.

Tacón, A. M., Caldera, Y. M., & Ronaghan, C. (2004). Mindfulness-based stress reduction in women with breast cancer. *Families, Systems and Health, 22,* 193–203.

Tangrea, J. A., Adrianza, M. E., & Helzer, W. E. (1994). Risk factors for the development of the placebo adverse reactions in a multicenter clinical trial. *Annals of Epidemiology, 4,* 327–331.

Tarter, R. E., Jones, B. M., Simpson, C. D., & Vega, A. (1971). Effects of task complexity and practice on performance during acute alcohol intoxication. *Perceptual and Motor Skills, 33,* 307–318.

Taylor, S. E. (2007). Social support. In H. S. Friedman & R. C. Silver (Eds.), *Foundations of health psychology* (pp. 145–171). New York: Oxford University Press.

Taylor, S. E., Klein, L. C., Lewis, B. P., Gruenewald, T. L., Gurung, R. A. R., & Updegraff, J. A. (2000). Biobehavioral responses to stress in females: Tend-and-befriend, not fight-or-flight. *Psychological Review, 107,* 411–429.

Taylor, S. E., Lewis, B. P., Gruenewald, T. L., Gurung, R. A. R., Updegraff, J. A., & Klein, L. C. (2002). Sex differences in biobehavioral responses to threat: Reply to Geary and Flinn (2002). *Psychological Review, 109,* 751–753.

Taylor, S. W., Repetti, R. L., & Seeman, T. (1997). Health psychology: What is an unhealthy environment and how does it get under the skin? *Annual Review of Psychology, 48,* 411–447.

Tedlock, B. (1992). The role of dreams and visionary narratives in Mayan cultural survival. *Ethos, 20,* 453–476.

Thomaes, S., Bushman, B. J., Stegge, H., & Olthof, T. (2008). Trumping shame by blasts of noise: Narcissism, self-esteem, shame, and aggression in young adolescents. *Child Development, 79,* 1792–1801.

Timmerman, I. G. H., Emmelkamp, P. M. G., & Sanderman, R. (1998). The effects of a stress-management training program in individuals at risk in the community at large. *Behaviour Research and Therapy, 36,* 863–875.

Tingey, H., Kiger, G., & Riley, P. J. (1996). Juggling multiple roles: Perceptions of working mothers. *Social Science Journal, 33,* 183–191.

Tucker, P. (2003). The impact of rest breaks upon accident risk, fatigue and performance: A review. *Work and Stress, 17,* 123–137.

Twenge, J. M., & Campbell, W. K. (2003). "Isn't it fun to get the respect that we're going to deserve?" Narcissism, social rejection, and aggression. *Personality and Social Psychology Bulletin, 29,* 261–272.

Twisk, J. W. R., Snel, J., Kemper, H. C. G., & van Mechelen, W. (1999). Changes in daily hassles and life events and the relationship with coronary heart disease risk factors: A 2-year longitudinal study in 27–29-yr-old males and females. *Journal of Psychosomatic Research, 46,* 229–240.

Van Cauter, E., Leproult, R., & Plat, L. (2000). Age-related changes in slow wave sleep and REM sleep and relationship with growth hormone and cortisol levels in healthy men. *Journal of the American Medical Association, 284,* 861–868.

Varker, K. A., Terrell, C. E., Welt, M., Suleiman, S. Thornton, L., Andersen, B. L., et al. (2007). Impaired natural killer cell lysis in breast cancer patients with high levels of psychological stress is associated with altered expression of killer immunoglobin-like receptors. *Journal of Surgical Research, 139,* 36–44.

Volkow, N. D., Chang, L., Wang, G., Fowler, J. S., Franceschi, D., Sedler, M. J., et al. (2001). Higher cortical and lower subcortical metabolism in detoxified methamphetamine abusers. *American Journal of Psychiatry, 158,* 383–389.

Waber, R. L., Shiv, B., Carmon, Z., & Ariely, D. (2008). Commercial features of placebo and therapeutic efficacy. *Journal of the American Medical Association, 299,* 1016–1017.

Wager, T. D., Rilling, J. K., Smith, E. E., Sokolik, A., Casey, K. L., Davidson, R. J., et al. (2004). Placebo-induced changes in fMRI in the anticipation and experience of pain, *Science, 303,* 1162–1167.

Walker, M. P., & Stickgold, R. (2004). Sleep-dependent learning and memory consolidation. *Neuron, 44,* 121–133.

Washburne, C. (1956). Alcohol, self and the group. *Quarterly Journal of Studies on Alcohol, 17,* 108–123.

Watson, D., & Hubbard, B. (1996). Adaptation style and dispositional structure: Coping in the context of the five-factor model. *Journal of Personality, 64,* 737–774.

Wegner, D. M. (1989). *White bears and other unwanted thoughts: Suppression, obsession, and the psychology of mental control.* New York: Viking/Penguin.

Wegner, D. M., Schneider, D. J., Carter, S. R., & White, T. L. (1987). Paradoxical effects of thought suppression. *Journal of Personality and Social Psychology, 53,* 5–13.

Wenzlaff, R. M., & Luxton, D. D. (2003). The role of thought suppression in depressive rumination. *Cognitive Therapy and Research, 27,* 293–308.

Werner, C., Brown, B., & Altman, I. (1997). Environmental psychology. In J. W. Berry, M. H. Segall, & C. KagitÁibasi (Eds.), *Handbook of cross-cultural psychology: Vol. 3. Social behavior and applications* (pp. 255–290). Needham Heights, MA: Allyn & Bacon.

White, J. M., & Ryan, C. F. (1996). Pharmacological properties of ketamine. *Drug and Alcohol Review, 15,* 145–155.

Williams, R., Barefoot, J., Califf, R., Haney, T., Saunders, E., Pryor, D., et al. (1992). Prognostic importance of social and economic resources among patients with angiographically documented coronary artery disease. *Journal of the American Medical Association, 267,* 520.

Wilson, R. I., & Nicoll, R. A. (2001). Endogenous cannabinoids mediate retrograde signalling at hippocampal synapses. *Nature, 410,* 588–592.

Zakowski, S., Hall, M. H., & Baum, A. (1992). Stress, stress management, and the immune system. *Applied and Preventative Psychology, 1,* 1–13.

References: Psychological Disorders

Abramson, L. Y., Seligman, M. E., & Teasedale, J. D. (1978). Learned helplessness in humans: Critique and reformulation. *Journal of Abnormal Psychology, 87,* 49–74.

Akiskal, H. S. (1996). The prevalent clinical spectrum of bipolar disorders: Beyond DSM–IV. *Journal of Clinical Psychopharmacology, 16*(Sûppl. 1), 4S–14S.

Altshuler, L. L., Bartzokis, G., Grieder, T., Curran, J., & Mintz, J. (1998). Amygdala enlargement in bipolar disorder and hippocampal reduction in schizophrenia: An MRI study demonstrating neuroanatomic specificity. *Archives of General Psychiatry, 55,* 663–664.

Altshuler, L., Bookheimer, S., Proenza, M. A., Townsend, J., Sabb, F., Firestine, A., et al. (2005). Increased amygdala activation during mania: A functional magnetic resonance imaging study. *American Journal of Psychiatry, 162,* 1211–1213.

American College Health Association. (2008). *National College Health Assessment. 5.* Retrieved January 10, 2010, from http://www.acha-ncha.org/docs/ACHA-NCHA_Reference_Group_ExecutiveSummary_Fall2008.pdf

American Psychiatric Association. (1994). *Diagnostic and statistical manual of mental disorders* (4th ed.). Washington, DC: Author.

American Psychiatric Association. (2000). *Diagnostic and statistical manual of mental disorders* (4th ed., text revision). Washington, DC: Author.

Andersen, A. E., & DiDomenico, L. (1992). Diet vs. shape content of popular male and female magazines: A dose response relationship to the incidence of eating disorders? *International Journal of Eating Disorders, 11,* 283–287.

Andreasen, N. C., Nasrullah, H., Dunn, V., Olson, S., Grove, W., Erhardt, J., et al. (1986). Structural abnormalities in the frontal system in schizophrenia. *Archives of General Psychiatry, 43,* 136–144.

Andreasen, N. C., Nopoulos, P., O'Leary, D. S., Miller, D. D., Wassink, T., & Flaum, M. (1999). Defining the phenotype of schizophrenia: Cognitive dysmetria and its neural mechanisms. *Biological Psychiatry, 46,* 908–920.

Andreasen, N. C., Rezai, K., Alliger, R., Swayze, V., Flaum, M., Kirchner, P., et al. (1992). Hypofrontality in neuroleptic-naïve patients and in patients with chronic schizophrenia: Assessment with xenon-133 single proton emission computed tomography and the Tower of London. *Archives of General Psychiatry, 49,* 943–958.

Angst, J. (1998). The emerging epidemiology of hypomania and bipolar II disorder. *Journal of Affective Disorders, 50,* 143–151.

Antony, M. M., & Barlow, D. H. (2002). Specific phobias. In D. H. Barlow (Ed.), *Anxiety and its disorders* (2nd ed., pp. 380–417). New York: Guilford Press.

Arlas, E., Anderson, R. S., Kung, H. C., Murphy, S. L., & Kochanek, K. D. (2003). Deaths: Final data for 2001. National Vital Statistics Reports. National Center for Health Statistics, Centers for Disease Control and Prevention, U.S. Department of Health and Human Services. DHHS Publication No. (PHS) 2001-1120 PRS 03-0436. Retrieved from http://www.cdc.gov/nchsabout/major/dvs/mortdata.htm; pdf file nvsr52_09p9.pdf

Auden, W. H. (1989). *Van Gogh: A self-portrait.* New York: Marlowe.

Barbarich, N. (2002). Is there a common mechanism of serotonin dysregulation in anorexia nervosa and obsessive compulsive disorder? *Eating and Weight Disorders, 7,* 221–231.

Beck, A. T. (1967). *Depression: Causes and treatment.* Philadelphia: University of Pennsylvania Press.

Beck, A. T., Emery, G., & Greenberg, R. L. (1985). *Anxiety disorders and phobias: A cognitive perspective.* New York: Basic Books.

Beck, J. G., Ohtake, P. J., & Shipherd, J. C. (1999). Exaggerated anxiety is not unique to CO_2 in panic disorder: A comparison of hypercapnic and hypoxic challenges. *Journal of Abnormal Psychology, 108,* 473–482.

Becker, A. E., Burwell, R. A., Herzog, D. B., Hamburg, P., & Gilman, S. E. (2002). Eating behaviours and attitudes following prolonged exposure to television among ethnic Fijian adolescent girls. *British Journal of Psychiatry, 180,* 509–514.

Bilukha, O. O., & Utermohlen, V. (2002). Internalization of Western standards of appearance, body dissatisfaction and dieting in urban educated Ukrainian females. *European Eating Disorders Review, 10,* 120–137.

Black, D. W., Noyes, R., Goldstein, R. B., & Blum, N. (1992). A family study of obsessive-compulsive disorder. *Archives of General Psychiatry, 49,* 362–368.

Blackburn, S., Johnston, L., Blampied, N., Popp, D., & Kallen, R. (2006). An application of escape theory to binge eating. *European Eating Disorders Review, 14,* 23–31.

Blais, M. A., Hilsenroth, M. J., & Castlebury, F. D. (1997). Psychometric characteristics of the Cluster B personality disorders under DSM-III-R and DSM-IV. *Journal of Personality Disorders, 11,* 270–278.

Blumer, D. (2002). The illness of Vincent van Gogh. *American Journal of Psychiatry, 159,* 519–526.

Booij, L., & Van der Does, A. J. W. (2007). Cognitive and serotonergic vulnerability to depression: Convergent findings. *Journal of Abnormal Psychology, 116,* 86–94.

Bouton, M. E., Mineka, S., & Barlow, D. H. (2001). A modern learning theory perspective on the etiology of panic disorder. *Psychological Review, 108,* 4–32.

Bowman, E. S., & Nurnberger, J. I. (1993). Genetics of psychiatry diagnosis and treatment. In D. L. Dunner (Ed.), *Current psychiatric therapy* (pp. 46–56). Philadelphia: Saunders.

Breiter, H. C., Rauch, S. L., Kwong, K. K., Baker, J. R., Weisskoff, R. M., Kennedy, D. N., et al, (1996). Functional magnetic resonance imaging of symptom provocation in obsessive-compulsive disorder. *Archives of General Psychiatry, 53,* 595–606.

Bremner, J. D., Vythilingam, M., Vermetten, E., Southwick, S. M., McGlashan, T., Nazeer, A., et al. (2003). MRI and PET study of deficits in hippocampal structure and function in women with childhood sexual abuse and posttraumatic stress disorder. *American Journal of Psychiatry, 160,* 924–932.

Breslau, N., Kessler, R. C., Chilcoat, H. D. Schultz, L. R., Davis, G. C., & Andreski, P. (1998). Trauma and posttraumatic stress disorder in the community: The 1996 Detroit Area Survey of Trauma. *Archives of General Psychiatry, 55,* 626–632.

Brown, A. S., Cohen, P., Harkavy-Friedman, J., & Babulas, V. (2001). Prenatal rubella, premorbid abnormalities, and adult schizophrenia. *Biological Psychiatry, 49,* 473–486.

Brown, A. S., van Os, J., Driessens, C., Hoek, S. W., & Susser, E. S. (1999). Prenatal famine and the spectrum of psychosis. *Psychiatric Annals, 29,* 145–150.

Brownell, K. D., & Rodin, J. (1992). *Medical, metabolic, and psychological effects of weight cycling.* Unpublished manuscript.

Buka, S. L., Goldstein, J. M., Seidman, L. J., Zornberg, G. L., Donatelli, J. A., Denny, L. R., et al. (1999). Prenatal complications, genetic vulnerability, and schizophrenia: The New England Longitudinal Studies of Schizophrenia. *Psychiatric Annals, 29,* 151–156.

Bulik, C. M. (2005). Exploring the gene-environment nexus in eating disorders. *Journal of Psychiatry & Neuroscience, 30,* 335-339.

Bulik, C. M., Tozzi, F., Anderson, C., Mazzeo, S. E., Aggen, S., & Sullivan, P. F. (2003). The relation between eating disorders and components of perfectionism. *American Journal of Psychiatry, 160,* 366–368.

Butzlaff, R. L., & Hooley, J. M. (1998). Expressed emotion and psychiatric relapse: A meta-analysis. *Archives of General Psychiatry, 55,* 547–552.

Cannon, T. D. (1997). On the nature and mechanisms of obstetric influences in schizophrenia: A review and synthesis of epidemiologic studies. *International Review of Psychiatry, 9,* 387–397.

Casbon, T. S., Burns, A. B., Bradbury, T. N., & Joiner, T. E., Jr. (2005). Receipt of negative feedback is related to increased negative feedback seeking among individuals with depressive symptoms. *Behaviour Research and Therapy, 43,* 485–504.

Coplan, J. D., Goetz, R., Klein, D. F., Papp, L. A., Fyer, A. J., Liebowitz, M. R., et al. (1998). Plasma cortisol concentrations preceding lactate-induced panic: Psychological, biochemical, and physiological correlates. *Archives of General Psychiatry, 55,* 130–136.

Cornblatt, B., Obuchowski, M., Schnur, D. B., & O'Brien, J. (1997). Attention and clinical symptoms in schizophrenia. *Psychiatric Quarterly, 68,* 343–359.

Coyne, J. C. (1976). Toward an interactional description of depression. *Psychiatry, 39,* 28–40.

Coyne, J. C., & Downey, G. (1991). Social factors in psychopathology: Stress, social support, and coping processes. *Annual Review of Psychology, 42,* 401–425.

Coyne, J. C., Kessler, R. C., Tal, M., Turnbull, J., Wortman, C., & Greden, J. (1987). Living with a depressed person: Burden and psychological distress. *Journal of Clinical and Consulting Psychology, 55,* 347–352.

Crowe, R., Noyes, R., Pauls, D., & Slyman, D. (1983). A family study of panic disorder. *Archives of General Psychiatry, 40,* 1065–1069.

Crowther, J. H., Kichler, J. C., Shewood, N. E., & Kuhnert, M. E. (2002). The role of familial factors in bulimia nervosa. *Eating Disorders: The Journal of Treatment and Prevention, 10,* 141–151.

Culbertson, F. M. (1997). Depression and gender: An international review. *American Psychologist, 52,* 25–31.

Dauncey, K., Giggs, J., Baker, K., & Harrison, K. (1993). Schizophrenia in Nottingham: Lifelong residential mobility of a cohort. *British Journal of Psychiatry, 163,* 613–619.

Davidson, R. J., Pizzagalli, D., Nitschke, J. B., & Putnam, K. M. (2002). Depression: Perspectives from affective neuroscience. *Annual Review of Psychology, 53,* 545–574.

DeMann, J. A. (1994). First person account: The evolution of a person with schizophrenia. *Schizophrenia Bulletin, 20,* 579–582.

Dohrenwend, B. P., Levav, I., Shrout, P. E., Schwartz, S., Naveh, G., Link, B. G., et al. (1992). Socioeconomic status and psychiatric disorders: The causation-selection issue. *Science, 255,* 946–952.

Dolan, B. (1991). Cross-cultural aspects of anorexia nervosa and bulimia: A review. *International Journal of Eating Disorders, 10,* 67–79.

Druss, B. G., Schlesinger, M., & Allen, H. M., Jr. (2001). Depressive symptoms, satisfaction with health care, and 2-year work outcomes in an employed population. *American Journal of Psychiatry, 158,* 731–734.

Eakin, E. (2000, January 15). Bigotry as mental illness or just another norm. *New York Times,* p. A21.

Ehlers, A., Mayou, R. A., & Bryant, B. (1998). Psychological predictors of chronic posttraumatic stress disorder after motor vehicle accidents. *Journal of Abnormal Psychology, 107,* 508–519.

Eley, T. C., Deater-Deckard, K., Fombone, E., Fulker, D. W., & Plomin, R. (1998). An adoption study of depressive symptoms in middle childhood. *Journal of Child Psychology and Psychiatry and Allied Disciplines, 39,* 337–345.

Ellman, L. M. (2008). Pre- and perinatal factors in the neurodevelopmental course of schizophrenia: Neurocognitive and clinical outcomes. *Dissertation Abstracts International: Section B: The Sciences and Engineering, 69*(1), 673B.

Fairburn, C. G., Cooper, Z., Doll, H. A., & Davies, B. A. (2005). Identifying dieters who will develop an eating disorder: A prospective, population-based study. *American Journal of Psychiatry, 162,* 249–255.

Fairburn, C. G., Stice, E., Cooper, Z., Doll, H. A., Norman, P. A., & O'Connor, M. E. (2003). Understanding persistence in bulimia nervosa: A 5-year naturalistic study. *Journal of Consulting and Clinical Psychology, 71,* 103–109.

Ferrier, S., & Brewin, C. R. (2005). Feared identity and obsessive-compulsive disorder. *Behaviour Research and Therapy, 43,* 1363–1374.

Field, A. E., Camargo, C. A., Jr., Taylor, B., Berkey, C. S., & Colditz, G. A. (1999). Relation of peer and media influences to the development of purging behaviors among preadolescent and adolescent girls. *Archives of Pediatric Adolescent Medicine, 153,* 1184–1189.

Field, T., Hernandez-Reif, M., & Diego, M. (2006). Risk factors and stress variables that differentiate depressed from nondepressed pregnant women. *Infant Behavior and Development, 29,* 169–174.

Foa, E. B., Steketee, G., & Olasov-Rothbaum, B. O. (1989). Behavioral/cognitive conceptualization of post-traumatic stress disorder. *Behavior Therapy, 20,* 155–176.

Forbush, K., Heatherton, T. F., & Keel, P. K. (2007). Relationships between perfectionism and specific disordered eating behaviors. *International Journal of Eating Disorders, 40,* 37–41.

Frank, E., Gonzalez, J. M., & Fagiolini, A. (2006). The importance of routine for preventing recurrence in bipolar disorder. *American Journal of Psychiatry, 163,* 981–985.

Freeman, H. (1994). Schizophrenia and city residence. *British Journal of Psychiatry, 164*(Suppl. 23), 39–50.

Gabbard, G. O. (1990). *Psychodynamic psychiatry in clinical practice.* Washington, DC: American Psychiatric Press.

Garfinkel, P. E., Goldbloom, D., David, R., Olmsted, M. P., Garner, D. M., & Halmi, K. A. (1992). Body dissatisfaction in bulimia nervosa: Relationship to weight and shape concerns and psychological functioning. *International Journal of Eating Disorders, 11,* 151–161.

Garner, D. M. (1997). Psychoeducational principles in treatment. In D. M. Garner & P. E. Garfinkel (Eds.), *Handbook of treatment for eating disorders* (2nd ed.). New York: Guilford Press.

Gater, R., Tansella, M., Korten, A., Tiemens, B. G., Mavreas, V. G., & Olatawura, M. O. (1998). Report from the World Health Organization collaborative study on psychological problems in general health care. *Archives of General Psychiatry, 55,* 405–413.

Geddes, J. R., & Lawrie, S. M. (1995). Obstetric complications and schizophrenia: A meta-analysis. *British Journal of Psychiatry, 67,* 786–793.

Gilmore, J. H., Sikich, L., & Lieberman, J. A. (1997). Neuroimaging, neurodevelopment, and schizophrenia. *Child and Adolescent Psychiatric Clinics of North America, 6*(2), 325–341.

Goff, D. C., & Coyle, J. T. (2001). The emerging role of glutamate in the pathophysiology and treatment of schizophrenia. *American Journal of Psychiatry, 158,* 1367–1377.

Goldstein, J. M., Goodman, J. M., Seidman, L. J., Kennedy, D. N., Makris, N., Lee, H., et al. (1999). Cortical abnormalities in schizophrenia identified by structural magnetic resonance imaging. *Archives of General Psychiatry, 56,* 537–547.

Goodwin, F. K., & Ghaemi, S. N. (1998). Understanding manic-depressive illness. *Archives of General Psychiatry, 55,* 23–25.

Gorman, J. M., Liebowitz, M. R., Fyer, A. J., & Stein, J. (1989). A neuroanatomical hypothesis for panic disorder. *American Journal of Psychiatry, 146,* 148–161.

Gottesman, I. I. (1991). *Schizophrenia genesis: The origins of madness.* New York: Freeman.

Gottesman, I. I., & Moldin, S. O. (1998). Genotypes, genes, genesis, and pathogenesis in schizophrenia. In M. F. Lenzenweger & R. H. Dworkin (Eds.), *Origins and development of schizophrenia: Advances in experimental psychopathology* (pp. 5–26). Washington, DC: American Psychological Association.

Green, M. F., Kern, R. S., Braff, D. L., & Mintz, J. (2000). Neurocognitive deficits and functional outcome in schizophrenia: Are we measuring the "right stuff"? *Schizophrenia Bulletin, 26,* 119–136.

Green, M. F., Nuechterlein, K. H., Breitmeyer, B., & Mintz, J. (1999). Backward masking in unmedicated schizophrenic patients in psychotic remission: Possible reflection of aberrant cortical oscillation. *American Journal of Psychiatry, 156,* 1367–1373.

Grimes, K., & Walker, E. F. (1994). Childhood emotional expressions, educational attainments, and age at onset of illness in schizophrenia. *Journal of Abnormal Psychology, 103,* 784–790.

Gunewardene, A., Huon, G. F., & Zheng, R. (2001). Exposure to westernization and dieting: A cross-cultural study. *International Journal of Eating Disorders, 29,* 289–293.

Guthrie, R. M., & Bryant, R. A. (2005). Auditory startle response in firefighters before and after trauma exposure. *American Journal of Psychiatry, 162,* 283–290.

Gyulai, L., Abass, A., Broich, K., & Reilley, J. (1997). I-123 lofetamine single-photon computer emission tomography in rapid cycling bipolar disorder: A clinical study. *Biological Psychiatry, 41,* 152–161.

Halmi, K. (1995). Basic biological overview of eating disorders. In F. E. Bloom & D. J. Kupfer (Eds.), *Psychopharmacology: The fourth generation of progress.* New York: Raven Press.

Halmi, K. (1996). The psychobiology of eating behavior in anorexia nervosa. *Psychiatry Research, 62,* 23–29.

Hare, R. D. (1993). *Without conscience: The disturbing world of the psychopaths among us.* New York: Pocket Books.

Heinssen, R. K., Perkins, D. O., Appelbaum, P. S., & Fenton, W. S. (2001). Informed consent in early psychosis research: NIMH workshop, November 15, 2000. *Schizophrenia Bulletin, 27,* 571–584.

Hemsley, D. R. (1994). Perceptual and cognitive abnormalities as the bases for schizophrenic symptoms. In A. S. David & J. C. Cutting (Eds.), *The neuropsychology of schizophrenia* (pp. 97–116). Hillsdale, NJ: Lawrence Erlbaum Associates.

Hierholzer, R., Munson, J., Peabody, C., & Rosenberg, J. (1992). Clinical presentation of PTSD in World War II combat veterans. *Hospital and Community Psychiatry, 43,* 816–820.

Horwath, E., & Weissman, M. M. (2000). The epidemiology and cross-national presentation of obsessive-compulsive disorder. *Psychiatric Clinics of North America, 23,* 493–507.

Hsee, C. K., Elaine, H., Carlson, J. G., & Chemtob, C. (1990). The effect of power on susceptibility to emotional contagion. *Cognition and Emotion, 4*(4), 327–340.

Hughes, J. R. (2005). A reappraisal of the possible seizures of Vincent van Gogh. *Epilepsy and Behavior, 6,* 504–510.

Insel, T. R. (1992). Toward a neuroanatomy of obsessive-compulsive disorder. *Archives of General Psychiatry, 49,* 739–744.

Jacobi, C., Hayward, C., de Zwaan, M., Kraemer, H. C., & Agras, W. S. (2004). Coming to Terms With Risk Factors for Eating Disorders: Application of Risk Terminology and Suggestions for a General Taxonomy. *Psychological Bulletin, 130,* 19-65.

Jamison, K. R. (1993). *Touched with fire: Manic-depressive illness and the artistic temperament.* New York: Free Press.

Jamison, K. R. (1995). *An unquiet mind: A memoir of moods and madness.* New York: Vintage Books.

Jang, K. L., Vernon, P. A., & Livesley, W. J. (2001). Behavioural-genetic perspectives on personality function. *Canadian Journal of Psychiatry, 46,* 234–244.

Jansen, A., Nederkoorn, C., & Mulkens, S. (2005). Selective visual attention for ugly and beautiful body parts in eating disorders. *Behaviour Research and Therapy, 43,* 183–196.

Jenike, M. (1984). Obsessive-compulsive disorder: A question of a neurologic lesion. *Comprehensive Psychiatry, 25,* 298–304.

Johnson, S. L., & Miller, I. (1997). Negative life events and time to recovery from episodes of bipolar disorder. *Journal of Abnormal Psychology, 106,* 449–457.

Johnson, S. M., & Roberts, J. E. (1995). Life events and bipolar disorder: Implications from biological theories. *Psychological Bulletin, 117,* 434–449.

Joiner, T. E. (1994). Contagious depression: Existence, specificity to depressed symptoms, and the role of reassurance seeking. *Journal of Personality and Social Psychology, 67,* 287–296.

Joseph, S., Williams, R., & Yule, W. (1995). Psychosocial perspectives on post-traumatic stress disorder. *Clinical Psychology Review, 15,* 515–544.

Judd, L. L., Akiskal, H. S., Maser, J. D., Zeller, P. J., Endicott, J., Coryell, W., et al. (1998). A prospective 12-year study of subsyndromal and syndromal depressive symptoms in unipolar major depressive disorders. *Archives of General Psychiatry, 55,* 694–700.

Kagan, R. M., & Reid, W. J. (1986). Critical factors in the adoption of emotionally disturbed youths. *Child Welfare, 65,* 63–73.

Kaniasty, K., & Norris, F. H. (1992). Social support and victims of crime: Matching event, support, and outcome. *American Journal of Community Psychology, 20,* 211–241.

Kaniasty, K. Z., Norris, F. H., & Murrell, S. A. (1990). Received and perceived social support following natural disaster. *Journal of Applied Psychology, 20,* 85–114.

Karkowski, L. M., & Kendler, K. S. (1997). An examination of the genetic relationship between bipolar and unipolar illness in an epidemiological sample. *Psychiatric Genetics, 7,* 159–163.

Katz, J., Beach, S. R. H., & Joiner, T. E. (1999). Contagious depression in dating couples. *Journal of Social and Clinical Psychology, 18*(1), 1–13.

Katz, J., & Joiner, T. E., Jr. (2001). The aversive interpersonal context of depression: Emerging perspectives on depressotypic behavior. In R. M. Kowalski (Ed.), *Behaving badly: Aversive behaviors in interpersonal relationships* (pp. 117–147). Washington, DC: American Psychological Association.

Kavanagh, D. J. (1992). Recent developments in expressed emotion in schizophrenia. *British Journal of Psychiatry, 148,* 601–620.

Kaye, W. H. (1995). Neurotransmitters and anorexia nervosa. In K. D. Brownell & C. G. Fairburn (Eds.), *Eating disorders and obesity: A comprehensive handbook* (pp. 255–260). New York: Guilford Press.

Kaye, W. (2008). Neurobiology of anorexia and bulimia nervosa. *Physiology and Behavior, 94,* 121–135.

Keane, T. M., Zimering, R. T., & Caddell, J. M. (1985). A behavioral formulation of post-traumatic stress disorder in Vietnam veterans. *Behavior Therapist, 8,* 9–12.

Kendler, K. S., & Diehl, S. R. (1993). The genetics of schizophrenia: A current genetic-epidemiologic perspective. *Schizophrenia Bulletin, 19,* 87–112.

Kendler, K. S., Gardner, C. O., & Prescott, C. A. (1999). Clinical characteristics of major depression that predict risk of depression in relatives. *Archives of General Psychiatry, 56,* 322–327.

Kendler, K. S., Jacobsen, K. C., Myers, J., & Prescott, C. A. (2002). Sex differences in genetic and environmental risk factors for irrational fears and phobias. *Psychological Medicine, 32,* 209–217.

Kendler, K. S., Myers, J., Prescott, C. A., & Neale, M. C. (2001). The genetic epidemiology of irrational fears and phobias in men. *Archives of General Psychiatry, 58,* 257–265.

Kendler, K. S., Neale, M. C., Kessler, R. C., Heath, A. C., & Eaves, L. J. (1992). The genetic epidemiology of phobias in women: The interrelationship of agoraphobia, social phobia, situational phobia and simple phobia. *Archives of General Psychiatry, 49,* 273–281.

Kessler, R. C., Berglund, P., Demler, O., Jin, R., Koretz, D., Merikangas, K. R., et al. (2003). The epidemiology of major depressive disorder: Results from the National Comorbidity Survey Replication (NCS-R). *Journal of the American Medical Association, 289,* 3095–3105.

Kessler, R. C., Chiu, W. T., Demler, O., & Walters, E. E. (2005). Prevalence, Severity, and Comorbidity of 12-Month DSM-IV Disorders in the National Comorbidity Survey Replication. *Archives of General Psychiatry, 62,* 617-627.

Kessler, R. C., & Frank, R. G. (1997). The impact of psychiatric disorders on work loss days. *Psychological Medicine, 27,* 861–873.

Kessler, R. C., Stein, M. B., & Berglund, P. (1998). Social phobia subtypes in the National Comorbidity Survey. *American Journal of Psychiatry, 155,* 613–619.

Kim, J.-H., & Lennon, S. J. (2007). Mass media and self-esteem, body image, and eating disorder tendencies. *Clothing and Textiles Research Journal, 25,* 3–23.

King, L. A., King, D. W., Fairbank, J. A., Keane, T. M., & Adams, G. A. (1998). Resilience-recovery factors in post-traumatic stress disorder among female and male Vietnam veterans: Hardiness, postwar social support, and additional stressful life events. *Journal of Personality and Social Psychology, 74,* 420–434.

Klein, D. F. (1993). False suffocation alarms, spontaneous panics, and related conditions: An integrative hypothesis. *Archives of General Psychiatry, 50,* 306–317.

Kleinknecht, R. A., & Lenz, J. (1989). Blood/injury fear, fainting and avoidance of medical treatment: A family correspondence study. *Behaviour Research and Therapy, 27,* 537–547.

Koren, D., Norman, D., Cohen, A., Berman, J., & Klein, E. M. (2005). Increased PTSD risk with combat-related injury: A matched comparison study of injured and uninjured soldiers experiencing the same combat events. *American Journal of Psychiatry, 162,* 276–282.

Krieger, S., Lis, S., & Gallhofer, B. (2001). Cognitive subprocesses and schizophrenia: A reaction time decomposition. *Acta Psychiatrica Scandanavia Supplement, 104,* 18–27.

Kuehner, C. (2003). Gender differences in unipolar depression: an update of epidemiological findings and possible explanations. *Acta Psychiatrica Scandinavica, 108,* 163-174.

Kulhara, P., & Chakrabarti, S. (2001). Culture and schizophrenia and other psychotic disorders. *Psychiatric Clinics of North American, 24,* 449–464.

Kuperberg, G., & Heckers, S. (2000). Schizophrenia and cognitive function. *Current Opinion in Neurobiology, 10,* 205–210.

Kushner, M., Riggs, D., Foa, E., & Miller, S. (1992). Perceived controllability and the development of posttraumatic stress disorder (PTSD) in crime victims. *Behaviour Research and Therapy, 31,* 105–110.

Laruelle, M., Kegeles, L. S., & Abi-Dargham A. (2003). Glutamate, dopamine, and schizophrenia: From pathophysiology to treatment. *Annals of the New York Academy of Sciences, 1003,* 138–158.

LeDoux, J. E. (1996). *The emotional brain: The mysterious underpinnings of emotional life.* New York: Simon & Schuster.

Lee, A. M., & Lee, S. (1996). Disordered eating and its psychosocial correlates among Chinese adolescent females in Hong Kong. *International Journal of Eating Disorders, 20,* 177–183.

Lee, S. (1996). Clinical lessons from the cross-cultural study of anorexia nervosa. *Eating Disorders Review, 7*(3), 1.

Lewinsohn, P. M., Allen, N. B., Seeley, J. R., & Gotlib, I. H. (1999). First onset versus recurrence of depression: Differential processes of psychosocial risk. *Journal of Abnormal Psychology, 108,* 483–489.

Li, D., Chokka, P., & Tibbo, P. (2001). Toward an integrative understanding of social phobia. *Journal of Psychiatry and Neuroscience, 26,* 190–202.

Liotti, M., Mayberg, H. S., McGinnis, S., Brannan, S. L., & Jerabek, P. (2002). Unmasking disease-specific cerebral blood flow abnormalities: Mood challenge in patients with remitted unipolar depression. *American Journal of Psychiatry, 159,* 1830–1840.

Livesley, W. J. (1998). Suggestions for a framework for an empirically based classification of personality disorder. *Canadian Journal of Psychiatry, 43,* 137–147.

Lubin, A. J. (1972). *Stranger on the earth: Vincent van Gogh.* New York: Da Capo Press.

Lyon, H. M., Startup, M., & Bentall, R. P. (1999). Social cognition and the manic defense: Attributions, selective attention, and self-schema in bipolar affective disorder. *Journal of Abnormal Psychology, 108,* 273–282.

Macklin, M. L., Metzger, L. J., Litz, B. T., McNally, R. J., Lasko, N. B., Orr, S. P., & Pitman, R. K. (1998). Lower precombat intelligence is a risk factor for posttraumatic stress disorder. *Journal of Consulting and Clinical Psychology, 66,* 323–326.

MacPhillamy, D. J., & Lewinsohn, P. M. (1974). Depression as a function of levels of desired and obtained pleasure. *Journal of Abnormal Psychology, 83,* 651–657.

Maher, B. A. (1966). *Principles of psychopathology: An experimental approach.* New York: McGraw-Hill.

McGuffin, P., Katz, R., Aldrich, J., & Bebbington, P. (1988). The Camberwell Collaborative Depression Study. II. Investigation of family members. *British Journal of Psychiatry, 152,* 766–774.

McNally, R. J., & Shin, L. M. (1995). Association of intelligence with severity of posttraumatic stress disorder symptoms in Vietnam combat veterans. *American Journal of Psychiatry, 152,* 936–938.

McNeil, T. F., Cantor-Graae, E., & Weinberger, D. R. (2000). Relationship of obstetric complications and differences in size of brain structures in monozygotic twin pairs discordant for schizophrenia. *American Journal of Psychiatry, 157,* 203–212.

Mednick, S. A., Gabrielli, W. F., & Hutchings, B. (1984). Genetic factors in criminal behavior: Evidence from an adoption cohort. *Science, 224,* 891–893.

Millet, B., Leclaire, M., Bourdel, M. C., Loo, H., Tezcan, E., & Kuloglu, M. (2000). Comparison of sociodemographic, clinical and phenomenological characteristics of Turkish and French patients suffering from obsessive-compulsive disorder. *Canadian Journal of Psychiatry, 45,* 848.

Mills, T. C., Paul, J., Stall, R., Pollack, L., Canchola, J., Chang, Y. J., et al. (2004). Distress and depression in men who have sex with men: The Urban Men's Health Study. *American Journal of Psychiatry, 161,* 278–285.

Modell, J., Mountz, J., Curtis, G., & Greden, J. (1989). Neurophysiologic dysfunction in basal ganglia/limbic striatal and thalamocortical circuits as a pathogenetic mechanism of obsessive-compulsive disorder. *Journal of Neuropsychiatry, 1,* 27–36.

Monroe, S. M., & Depue, R. A. (1991). Life stress and depression. In J. Becker & A. Kleinman (Eds.), *Psychosocial aspects of depression* (pp. 101–130). Hillsdale, NJ: Erlbaum.

Moran, P. (1999). The epidemiology of antisocial personality disorder. *Social Psychiatry and Psychiatric Epidemiology, 34,* 231–242.

Mortensen, P. B., Pedersen, C. B., Westergaard, T., Wohlfahrt, J., Ewald, H., Mors, O., et al. (1999). Effects of family history and place and season of birth on the risk of schizophrenia. *New England Journal of Medicine, 340,* 603–608.

Mowrer, O. H. (1939). A stimulus-response analysis of anxiety and its role as a reinforcing agent. *Psychological Review, 46,* 553–565.

Mulvany, F., O'Callaghan, E., Takei, N., Byrne, M., Fearson, P., & Larkin, C. (2001). Effect of social class at birth on risk and presentation of schizophrenia: Case control study. *British Medical Journal, 323,* 1398–1401.

Nemeroff, C. J., Stein, R., Diehl, N. S., & Smilach, K. M. (1994). From the Cleavers to the Clintons: Role choices and body orientation as reflected in magazine article content. *International Journal of Eating Disorders, 16,* 167–176.

Nigg, J. T., & Goldsmith, H. H. (1994). Genetics of personality disorders: Perspectives from personality and psychopathology research. *Psychological Bulletin, 115,* 346–380.

Nolan, S. A., & Mineka, S. (1997, November). Verbal, nonverbal, and gender-related factors in the interpersonal consequences of depression and anxiety. Presented at the annual meeting of the Association for the Advancement of Behavior Therapy, Miami Beach, FL.

Nolen-Hoeksema, S. (1987). Sex differences in unipolar depression: Evidence and theory. *Psychological Bulletin, 101,* 259–282.

Nolen-Hoeksema, S. (2000). The role of rumination in depressive disorders and mixed anxiety/depressive symptoms. *Journal of Abnormal Psychology, 109,* 504–511.

Nolen-Hoeksema, S., & Morrow, J. (1993). Effects of rumination and distraction on naturally occurring depressed mood. *Cognition and Emotion, 7,* 561–570.

Nuechterlein, K. H. (1991). Vigilance in schizophrenia and related disorders. In S. R. Steinhauer, J. H. Gruzelier, & J. Zubin (Eds.), *Neuropsychology, psychophysiology, and information processing* (pp. 397–433). New York: Elsevier Science.

Nutt, D. J. (2008). Relationship of neurotransmitters to the symptoms of major depressive disorder. *Journal of Clinical Psychiatry, 69*(Suppl. E1), 4–7.

Ogloff, J. R. P. (2006). Psychopathy/antisocial personality disorder conundrum. *Australian and New Zealand Journal of Psychiatry, 40,* 519-528.

Ozer, D. J., Best, S. R., Lipsey, T. L., & Weiss, D. S. (2003). Predictors of posttraumatic stress disorder and symptoms in adults: A meta-analysis. *Psychological Bulletin, 129,* 52–73.

Papp, L. A., Klein, D. F., & Gorman, J. M. (1993). Carbon dioxide hypersensitivity, hyperventilation, and panic disorder. *American Journal of Psychiatry, 150,* 1149–1157.

Papp, L. A., Martinez, J. M., Klein, D. F., Coplan, J. D., Norman, R. G., Cole, R., et al. (1997). Respiratory psychophysiology of panic disorder: Three respiratory challenges in 98 subjects. *American Journal of Psychiatry, 154,* 1557–1565.

Parker, G., Cheah, Y. C., & Roy, K. (2001). Do the Chinese somatize depression? A cross-cultural study. *Social Psychiatry and Psychiatric Epidemiology, 36,* 287–293.

Patel, V., Abas, M., Broadhead, J., Todd, C., & Reeler, A. (2001). Depression in developing countries: Lessons from Zimbabwe. *British Medical Journal, 322,* 482–484.

Pato, M. T., Pato, C. N., & Pauls, D. L. (2002). Recent findings in the genetics of OCD. *Journal of Clinical Psychiatry, 63,* 30–33.

Patterson, G. R., DeBaryshe, B. D., & Ramsey, E. (1989). A developmental perspective on antisocial behavior. *American Psychologist, 44,* 329–335.

Penn, D. L., Corrigan, P. W., Bentall, R. P., Racenstein, J. M., & Newman, L. (1997). Social cognition in schizophrenia. *Psychological Bulletin, 121,* 114–132.

Peterson, C., & Seligman, M. E. (1984). Causal explanations as a risk factor for depression: Theory and evidence. *Psychological Review, 91,* 347–374.

Plehn, K., & Peterson, R. A. (2002). Anxiety sensitivity as a predictor of the development of panic symptoms, panic attacks, and panic disorder: A prospective study. *Journal of Anxiety Disorders, 16,* 455–474.

Polivy, J., & Herman, C. P. (1993). Etiology of binge eating: Psychological mechanisms. In C. G. Fairburn & G. T. Wilson (Eds.), *Binge eating: Nature, assessment, and treatment* (pp. 173–205). New York: Guilford Press.

Pollock, V. E., Briere, J., Schneider, L., Knop, J., Mednick, S. A., & Goodwin, D. H. (1990). Childhood antecedents of antisocial behavior: Parental alcoholism and physical abusiveness. *American Journal of Psychiatry, 147,* 1290–1293.

Post, R. M. (1992). Transdirection of psychosocial stress into the neurobiology of recurrent affective disorder. *American Journal of Psychiatry, 149,* 999–1010.

Poulton, R., & Menzies, R. G. (2002). Non-associative fear acquisition: A review of the evidence from retrospective and longitudinal research. *Behaviour Research and Therapy, 40,* 1227–1249.

Quay, H. C. (1965). Psychopathic personality as pathological stimulus-seeking. *American Journal of Psychiatry, 122,* 180–183.

Rachman, S. (1997). A cognitive theory of obsessions. *Behaviour Research and Therapy, 35,* 793–802.

Rauch, S. L., Jenike, M. A., Alpert, N. M., Baer, L., Breiter, H. C. R., Savage, C. R., et al. (1994). Regional cerebral blood flow measured during symptom provocation in obsessive-compulsive disorder using oxygen 15–labeled carbon dioxide and positron emission tomography. *Archives of General Psychiatry, 51,* 62–70.

Rauch, S. L., van der Kolk, B. A., Risler, R. E., Alpert, N. M., Orr, S. P., Savage, C. R., et al. (1996). A symptom provocation study of posttraumatic stress disorder using positron emission tomography and script-driven imagery. *Archives of General Psychiatry, 53,* 380–387.

Rauch, S. L., Whalen, P. J., Shin, L. M., McInerney, S. C., Macklin, M. L., Lasko, N. B., et al. (2000). Exaggerated amygdala response to masked facial stimuli in posttraumatic stress disorder: A functional MRI study. *Biological Psychiatry, 47,* 769–776.

Regier D. A., & Kaelber, C. T. (1995). The Epidemiologic Catchment Area (ECA) program: Studying the prevalence and incidence of psychopathology. In M. T. Tsuang, M. Tohen, & G. E. P. Zahner (Eds.), *Textbook in psychiatric epidemiology* (pp. 133–157). New York: John Wiley & Sons.

Rende, R., & Plomin, R. (1992). Diathesis-stress models of psychopathology: A quantitative genetic perspective. *Applied and Preventative Psychology, 1,* 177–182.

Resnick, H. S., Kilpatrick, D. G., Dansky, B. S., Saunders, B., & Best, C. L. (1993). Prevalence of civilian trauma and posttraumatic stress disorder in a representative national sample of women. *Journal of Consulting and Clinical Psychology, 61,* 984–991.

Rosenberg, R. S., & Kosslyn, S. M. (2011). *Abnormal psychology.* New York: Worth.

Roskill, M. (1963). *The letters of Vincent van Gogh.* London: William Collins.

Rouillon, F. (1997). Epidemiology of panic disorder. *Human Psychopharmacology: Clinical and Experimental, 12*(Suppl. 1), S7–S12.

Ruscio, A. M., Brown, T. A., Chiu, W. T., Sareen, J., Stein, M. B., & Kessler, R. C. (2008). Social fears and social phobia in the USA: Results from the National Comorbidity Survey Replication. *Psychological Medicine, 38,* 15–28.

Šagud, M., Mihaljevic-Peleš, A., Pivac, N., Muck-Šeler, D., Šimunovic, I., & Jakovljevic, M. (2008). Genetics of schizophrenia in the context of integrative psychiatry. *Psychiatria Danubina, 20,* 364–368.

Salkovskis, P. M., Wroe, A. L., Gledhill, A., Morrison, N., Forrester, E., Richards, C., et al. (2000). Responsibility attitudes and interpretations are characteristic of obsessive–compulsive disorder. *Behaviour Research and Therapy, 38,* 347–372.

Salkovskis, P. M., & Forrester, E. (2002). Responsibility. In R. O. Frost, & G. Steketee (Eds.), *Cognitive approaches to obsessions and compulsions: Theory, assessment, and treatment* (pp. 45–61). Amsterdam, Netherlands: Pergamon/Elsevier Science Inc.

Saxena, S., & Rauch, S. L. (2000). Functional neuroimaging and the neuroanatomy of obsessive-compulsive disorder. *Psychiatric Clinics of North America, 23,* 563–586.

Schachter, S., & Latané, B. (1964). Crime, cognition, and the autonomic nervous system. In D. Levine (Ed.), *Nebraska Symposium on Motivation* (Vol. 12, pp. 221–273). Lincoln: University of Nebraska Press.

Schmidt, N. B., Lerew, D. R., & Jackson, R. J. (1997). The role of anxiety sensitivity in the pathogenesis of panic: Prospective evaluation of spontaneous panic attacks during acute stress. *Journal of Abnormal Psychology, 106,* 355–364.

Schmidt, N. B., Lerew, D. R., & Jackson, R. J. (1999). Prospective evaluation of anxiety sensitivity in the pathogenesis of panic: Replication and extension. *Journal of Abnormal Psychology, 108,* 532–537.

Schrof, J. M., & Schultz, S. (1999, March 8). Melancholy nation. *U.S. News and World Report,* 56–63.

Scott, J., Stanton, B., Garland, A., & Ferrier, I. N. (2000). Cognitive vulnerability in patients with bipolar disorder. *Psychological Medicine, 30,* 467–472.

Segrin, C., & Dillard, J. P. (1992). The interactional theory of depression: A meta-analysis of the research literature. *Journal of Social and Clinical Psychology, 11*(1), 43–70.

Shalev, A. Y., Peri, T., Brandes, D., Freedman, S., Orr, S. P., & Pitman, R. K. (2000). Auditory startle response in trauma survivors with posttraumatic stress disorder: A prospective study. *American Journal of Psychiatry, 157,* 255–261.

Shalev, A. Y., Sahar, T., Freedman, S., Peri, T., Glick, N., Brandes, D., et al. (1998). A prospective study of heart rate response following trauma and the subsequent development of posttraumatic stress disorder. *Archives of General Psychiatry, 55,* 553–559.

Shin, L. M., Kosslyn, S. M., McNally, R. J., Alpert, N. M., Thompson, W. L., Raush, S. L., et al. (1997). Visual imagery and perception in posttraumatic stress disorder: A positron emission tomographic investigation. *Archives of General Psychiatry, 54,* 233–241.

Shin, L. M., Orr, S. P., Carson, M. A., Rauch, S. L., Macklin, M. L., Lasko, N. B., et al. (2004). Regional cerebral blood flow in the amygdala and medial prefrontal cortex during traumatic imagery in male and female Vietnam veterans with PTSD. *Archives of General Psychiatry, 61,* 168–176.

Siegel, M., Brisman, J., & Weinshel, M. (1988). *Surviving an eating disorder: Strategies for family and friends.* New York: Harper and Row.

Silverstein, M. L. (2007). Descriptive psychopathology and theoretical viewpoints: Dependent, histrionic, and antisocial personality disorders. In *Disorders of the self: A personality-guided approach* (pp. 145–170). Washington, DC: American Psychological Association.

Skaer, T. L., Sclar, D. A., & Robison, L. M. (2008). Trend in anxiety disorders in the USA 1990–2003. *Primary Care and Community Psychiatry, 13,* 1–7.

Smeets, M. A. M., Smit, F., Panhuysen, G. E. M., & Ingleby, J. D. (1997). The influence of methodological differences on the outcome of body size estimation studies in anorexia nervosa. *British Journal of Clinical Psychology, 36,* 263–277.

Solomon, D. A., Keller, M. B., Leon, A. C., Mueller, T. I., Lavori, P. W., Shea, M. T., et al. (2000). Multiple recurrences of major depressive disorder. *American Journal of Psychiatry, 157,* 229–233.

Somers, J. M., Goldner, E. M., Waraich, P., & Hsu, L. (2006). Prevalence and incidence studies of anxiety disorders: A systematic review of the literature. *Canadian Journal of Psychiatry, 51,* 100–113.

Stark-Wroblewski, K., Yanico, B. J., & Lupe, S. (2005). Acculturation, internalization of western appearance norms, and eating pathology among Japanese and Chinese international student women. *Psychology of Women Quarterly, 29,* 38–46.

Stein, A., Woolley, H., Senior, R., Hertzmann, L., Lovel, M., Lee, J., et al. (2006). Treating disturbances in the relationship between mothers with bulimic eating disorders and their infants: A randomized, controlled trial of video feedback. *American Journal of Psychiatry, 163,* 899–906.

Steketee, G., & White, K. (1990). *When once is not enough: Help for obsessive-compulsives.* Oakland, CA: New Harbinger.

Stewart, W. F., Ricci, J. A., Chee, E., Hahn, S. R., & Morganstein, D. (2003). Cost of lost productive work time among US workers with depression. *Journal of the American Medical Association, 289,* 3135–3144.

Stice, E., Presnell, K., & Spangler, D. (2002). Risk factors for binge eating onset in adolescent girls: A 2-year prospective investigation. *Health Psychology, 21,* 131–138.

Strakowski, S. M., Adler, C. M., & DelBello, M. P. (2002). Volumetric MRI studies of mood disorders: Do they distinguish unipolar and bipolar disorder? *Bipolar Disorders, 4,* 80–88.

Striegel-Moore, R. H. (1993). Etiology of binge eating: A developmental perspective. In C. G. Fairburn & G. T. Wilson (Eds.), *Binge eating: Nature, assessment, and treatment* (pp. 144–172). New York: Guilford Press.

Strober, M. (1995). Family-genetic perspective on anorexia nervosa and bulimia nervosa. In C. G. Fairburn & K. Brownell (Eds.), *Comprehensive textbook of eating disorders and obesity* (pp. 212–218). New York: Guilford Press.

Sullins, E. S. (1991). Emotional contagion revisited: Effects of social comparison and expressive style on mood convergence. *Personality and Social Psychology Bulletin, 17*(2), 166–174.

Tafarodi, R. W., & Smith, A. J. (2001). Individualism-collectivism and depressive sensitivity to life events: The case of Malaysian sojourners. *International Journal of Intercultural Relations, 25,* 73–88.

Tandon, R., Keshavan, M. S., & Nasrallah, H. A. (2008). Schizophrenia, "just the facts": What we know in 2008. 2. Epidemiology and etiology. *Schizophrenia Research, 102,* 1–18.

Telch, M. J., Lucas, J. A., & Nelson, P. (1989). Nonclinical panic in college students: An investigation of prevalence and symptomatology. *Journal of Abnormal Psychology, 98,* 300–306.

Tennant, C. (2002). Life events, stress and depression: A review of the findings. *Australian and New Zealand Journal of Psychiatry, 36,* 173–182.

Thompson, J. K., & Stice, E. (2001). Thin-ideal internalization: Mounting evidence for a new risk factor for body-image disturbance and eating pathology. *Current Directions in Psychological Science, 10,* 181–183.

Tiernari, P. (1991). Interaction between genetic vulnerability and family environment: The Finnish adoptive family study of schizophrenia. *Acta Psychiatrica Scandinavica, 84,* 460–465.

Torgersen, S. G. (1983). Genetic factors in anxiety disorders. *Archives of General Psychiatry, 40,* 1085–1089.

Torrey, E. F. (1988). *Nowhere to go: The tragic odyssey of the homeless mentally ill.* New York: Harper & Row.

True, W. R., Rice, J., Eisen, S. A., Heath, A. C., Phil, D., Goldberg, J., et al. (1993). A twin study of genetic and environmental contributions to liability for posttraumatic stress symptoms. *Archives of General Psychiatry, 50,* 257–264.

Tsai, G., & Coyle, J. T. (2002). Glutamatergic mechanisms in schizophrenia. *Annual Review of Pharmacology and Toxicology, 42,* 165–179.

Tsuchiya, K. J., Agerbo, E., & Mortensen, P. B. (2005). Parental death and bipolar disorder: A robust association was found in early maternal suicide. *Journal of Affective Disorders, 86,* 151–159.

Tucker, G. J. (1998). Putting DSM-IV in perspective. *American Journal of Psychiatry 155*(2), 159–161.

Twenge, J. M. (2000). The age of anxiety? Birth cohort change in anxiety and neuroticism, 1952–1993. *Journal of Personality and Social Psychology, 79,* 1007–1021.

Tyrka, A. R., Waldron, I., Graber, J. A., & Brooks-Gunn, J. (2002). Prospective predictors of the onset of anorexic and bulimic syndromes. *International Journal of Eating Disorders, 32,* 282–290.

Urbszat, D., Herman, C. P., & Polivy, J. (2002). Eat, drink, and be merry, for tomorrow we diet: Effects of anticipated deprivation on food intake in restrained and unrestrained eaters. *Journal of Abnormal Psychology, 111,* 396–401.

Vajk, F. C., Craighead, W. E., Craighead, L. W., & Holley, C. (1997, November). Risk of major depression as a function of response styles to depressed mood. Poster presented at the annual meeting of the Association for the Advancement of Behavior Therapy, Miami Beach, FL.

van den Heuvel, O. A., van de Wetering, B. J., Veltman, D. J., & Pauls, D. L. (2000). Genetic studies of panic disorder: A review. *Journal of Clinical Psychiatry, 61,* 756–766.

Vanderlinden, J., Grave, R. D., Vandereycken, W., & Noorduin, C. (2001). Which factors do provoke binge-eating? An exploratory study in female students. *Eating Behaviors, 2,* 79–83.

Vehmanen, L., Kaprio, J., & Loennqvist, J. (1995). Twin studies on concordance for bipolar disorder. *Psychiatria Fennica, 26,* 107–116.

Ventura, J., Nuechterlein, K. H., Lukoff, D., & Hardesty, J. P. (1989). A prospective study of stressful life events and schizophrenic relapse. *Journal of Abnormal Psychology, 98,* 407–411.

Vermetten, E., & Bremner, J. D. (2002). Circuits and systems in stress. I. Preclinical studies. *Depression and Anxiety, 15,* 126–147.

Wahlbeck, K., Forsén, T., Osmond, C., Barker, D. J. P., & Eriksson, J. G. (2001). Association of schizophrenia with low maternal body mass index, small size at birth, and thinness during childhood. *Archives of General Psychiatry, 58,* 48–52.

Walder, D., Walker, E., & Lewine, R. J. (2000). The relations among cortisol release, cognitive function and symptom severity in psychotic patients. *Biological Psychiatry, 48,* 1121–1132.

Walker, E. F., & Diforio, D. (1997). Schizophrenia: A neural diathesis-stress model. *Psychological Review, 104,* 667–685.

Walker, E. F., Grimes, K. E., Davis, D., & Smith, A. (1993). Childhood precursors of schizophrenia: Facial expressions of emotion. *American Journal of Psychiatry, 150,* 1654–1660.

Walker, E. F., Savoie, T., & Davis, D. (1994). Neuromotor precursors of schizophrenia. *Schizophrenia Bulletin, 148,* 661–666.

Walker, E., Kestler, L., Bollini, A., & Hochman, K. M. (2004). Schizophrenia: Etiology and course. *Annual Review of Psychology, 55,* 401–430.

Weinstock, M. (1997). Does prenatal stress impair coping and regulation of hypothalamic-pituitary-adrenal axis? *Neuroscience and Biobehavioral Reviews, 21,* 1–10.

Weissman, M. M., Bland, R. C., Canino, G. J., Greenwald, S., Hwu, H., Lee, C. K., et al. (1994). The cross national epidemiology of obsessive compulsive disorder: The Cross National Collaborative Group. *Journal of Clinical Psychiatry, 55*(3, Suppl.), 5–10.

Weissman, M. M., Bruce, M. L., Leaf, P. J., Florio, L., & Holzer, C. (1991). Affective disorders. In L. N. Robins & D. A. Regier (Eds.), *Psychiatric disorders in America* (pp. 53–80). New York: Free Press.

Weissman, M. M., Wickramaratne, P., Nomura, Y., Warner, V., Verdeli, H., Pilowsky, D. J., et al. (2005). Families at high and low risk for depression: A 3-generation study. *Archives of General Psychiatry, 62,* 29–36.

Welberg, L. A., & Seckl, J. R. (2001). Prenatal stress, glucocorticoids and the programming of the brain. *Journal of Neuroendocrinology, 2,* 113–128.

Wender, P. H., Kety, S. S., Rosenthal, D., Schulsinger, F., Ortmann, J., & Luhde, I. (1986). Psychiatric disorders in the biological and adoptive families of adopted individuals with affective disorders. *Archives of General Psychiatry, 43,* 923–929.

World Health Organization. (2008). *The global burden of disease: 2004 update.* Geneva: Author.

Wurtzel, E. (1995). *Prozac nation: A memoir.* New York: Riverhead.

Yehuda, R. (2002a). Clinical relevance of biologic findings in PTSD. *Psychiatric Quarterly, 73,* 123–133.

Yehuda, R. (2002b). Post-traumatic stress disorder. *New England Journal of Medicine, 346,* 108–114.

Zlotnick, C. (1999). Antisocial personality disorder, affect dysregulation and childhood abuse among incarcerated women. *Journal of Personality Disorders, 13,* 90–95.

Zoccolillo, M., Price, R., Ji, T., & Hwu, H. (1999). Antisocial personality disorder: Comparisons of prevalence, symptoms, and correlates in four countries. In P. Cohen, C. Slomkowski, & L. N. Robins (Eds.), *Historical and geographical influences on psychopathology* (pp. 249–277). Mahwah, NJ: Erlbaum.

Zornberg, G. L., Buka, S. L., & Tsuang, M. T. (2000). Hypoxic-ischemia-related fetal/neonatal complications and risk of schizophrenia and other nonaffective psychoses: A 19-year longitudinal study. *American Journal of Psychiatry 157,* 196–202.

References: Treatment

Adams, S. J., & Pitre, N. (2000). Who uses bibliotherapy and why? A survey from an underserviced area. *Canadian Journal of Psychiatry, 45*, 645–649.

Agency for Health Care Policy and Research. (1999). *Newer antidepressant drugs are equally as effective as older-generation drug treatments, research shows* (AHCPR Publication No. 99-E013). Rockville, MD: Author.

Alexander, F., & French, T. (1946). *Psychoanalytic theory.* New York: Ronald Press.

American Psychiatric Association. (2000). Practice guideline for the treatment of patients with major depressive disorder (revision). *American Journal of Psychiatry, 157*(Suppl.), 1–45.

Anderson, I. M. (2000). Selective serotonin reuptake inhibitors versus tricyclic antidepressants: A meta-analysis of efficacy and tolerability. *Journal of Affective Disorders, 58*, 19–36.

Antonuccio, D. O., Danton, W. G., & DeNelsky, G. Y. (1995). Psychotherapy versus medication for depression: Challenging the conventional wisdom with data. *Professional Psychology: Research and Practice, 26*, 574–585.

Arcelus, J., Whight, D., Langham, C., Baggott, J., McGrain, L., Meadows, L., et al. (2009). A case series evaluation of the modified version of interpersonal psychotherapy (IPT) for the treatment of bulimic eating disorders: A pilot study. *European Eating Disorders Review, 17*, 260–268.

Ballus, C. (1997). Effects of antipsychotics on the clinical and psychosocial behavior of patients with schizophrenia. *Schizophrenia Research, 28*, 247–255.

Barak, A., Hen, L., Boniel-Nissim, M., & Shapira, N. (2008). A comprehensive review and a meta-analysis of the effectiveness of Internet-based psychotherapeutic interventions. *Journal of Technology in Human Services, 26*, 109–160.

Barbui, C., Espositro, E., & Cipriani, A. (2009). Selective serotonin reuptake inhibitors and risk of suicide: A systematic review of observational studies. *CMAJ, 180*, 291–297.

Barkham, M., & Shapiro, D. A. (1990). Brief psychotherapeutic interventions for job-related distress: A pilot study of prescriptive and exploratory therapy. *Counseling Psychology Quarterly, 3*, 133–147.

Baxter, L. R., Schwartz, J. M., Bergman, K. S., Szuba, M. P., Guze, B. H., Mazziota, J. C., et al. (1992). Caudate glucose metabolic rate changes with both drug and behavior therapy for obsessive-compulsive disorder. *Archives of General Psychiatry, 49*, 681–689.

Beck, A. T. (1967). *Depression: Causes and treatment.* Philadelphia: University of Pennsylvania Press.

Beutler, L. E., Machado, P. P., & Neufeldt, S. A. (1994). Therapist variables. In A. E. Bergin & S. L. Garfield (Eds.), *Handbook of psychotherapy and behavior change* (4th ed., pp. 229–269). New York: Wiley.

Blatt, S. J., Zuroff, D. C., Bondi, C. M., & Sanislow, C. A., III. (2000). Short- and long-term effects of medication and psychotherapy in the brief treatment of depression: Further analyses of data from the NIMH TDCRP. *Psychotherapy Research, 10*, 215–234.

Bleiberg, K. L., & Markowitz, J. C. (2005). A pilot study of interpersonal psychotherapy for posttraumatic stress disorder. *American Journal of Psychiatry, 162*, 181–183.

Bloom, B. L. (1997). *Planned short-term psychotherapy: A clinical handbook* (2nd ed.). Boston: Allyn & Bacon.

Bolton, P., Bass, J., Neugebauer, R., Verdeli, H., Clougherty, K. F., Wickramaratne, P., et al. (2003). Group interpersonal psychotherapy for depression in rural Uganda: A randomized controlled trial. *Journal of the American Medical Association, 289*, 3117–3124.

Buchkremer, G., Klingberg, S., Holle, R., Schulze-Moenking, H., & Hornung, W. P. (1997). Psychoeducational psychotherapy for schizophrenic patients and their key relatives or care-givers: Results of a 2-year follow-up. *Acta Psychiatrica Scandinavica, 96*, 483–491.

Chambless, D. L., & Gillis, M. M. (1993). Cognitive therapy of anxiety disorders. *Journal of Consulting and Clinical Psychology, 61*, 248–260.

Chambless, D. L., & Steketee, G. (1999). Expressed emotion and behavior therapy outcome: A prospective study with obsessive-compulsive and agoraphobic outpatients. *Journal of Consulting and Clinical Psychology, 67*, 658–665.

Clark, L. F., & Collins, J. E. (1993). Remembering old flames: How the past affects assessments of the present. *Personality and Social Psychology Bulletin, 19*, 399–408.

Colom, F., Vieta, E., Martinez, A., Jorquera, A., & Gasto, C. (1998). What is the role of psychotherapy in the treatment of bipolar disorder? *Psychotherapy and Psychosomatics, 67*, 3–9.

Crits-Christoph, P. (1992). The efficacy of brief dynamic psychotherapy: A meta-analysis. *American Journal of Psychiatry, 149*, 151–158.

Dannon, P. N., Dolberg, O. T., Schreiber, S., & Grunhaus, L. (2002). Three and six-month outcome following courses of either ECT or rTMS in a population of severely depressed individuals—Preliminary report. *Biological Psychiatry, 51*, 687–690.

DeRubeis, R. J., Hollon, S. D., Amsterdam, J. D., Shelton, R. C., Young, P. R., Salomon, R. M., et al. (2005). Cognitive therapy vs. medications in the treatment of moderate to severe depression. *Archives of General Psychiatry, 62*, 409–416.

Eisler, I., Simic, M., Russell, G. F. M., & Dare, C. (2007). A randomised controlled treatment trial of two forms of family therapy in adolescent anorexia nervosa: A five-year follow-up. *Journal of Child Psychology and Psychiatry, 48(6)*, 552-560.

Elkin, I., Shea, M. T., Watkins, J. T., Imber, S. D., Sotsky, S. M., Collins, J. F., et al. (1989). National Institute of Mental Health Treatment of Depression Collaborative Research Program: General effectiveness of treatments. *Archives of General Psychiatry, 46*, 971–982.

Ellis, A. (1957). Rational psychotherapy and individual psychology. *Journal of Individual Psychology, 13*, 38–44.

Ellis, A. (1994a). Rational emotive behavior therapy approaches to obsessive-compulsive disorder (OCD). *Journal of Rational-Emotive and Cognitive Behavior Therapy, 12*, 121–141.

Ellis, A. (1994b). The treatment of borderline personalities with rational emotive behavior therapy. *Journal of Rational-Emotive and Cognitive Behavior Therapy, 12*, 101–119.

Emmelkamp, P. M. G. (2004). Behavior therapy with adults. In M. J. Lambert (Ed.), *Bergin and Garfield's handbook of psychotherapy and behavior change* (5th ed., pp. 393–446). New York: Wiley.

Emmelkamp, P. M. G., Bruynzeel, M., Drost, L., & Van Der Mast, C. A. P. G. (2001). Virtual reality treatment in acrophobia: A comparison with exposure in vivo. *CyberPsychology and Behavior, 4*, 335–339.

Emmelkamp, P. M. G., Kloek, J., & Blaauw, E. (1992). Obsessive-compulsive disorders. In P. H. Wilson (Ed.), *Principles and practice of relapse prevention* (pp. 213–234). New York: Guilford Press.

Emmelkamp, P. M. G., Krijn, M., Hulsbosch, A. M., de Vries, S., Schuemie, M. J., & van der Mast, C. A. P. G. (2002). Virtual reality treatment versus exposure in vivo: A comparative evaluation in acrophobia. *Behaviour Research and Therapy, 40*, 509–516.

Epstein, C. M., Figiel, G. S., McDonald, W. M., Amazon-Leece, J., & Figiel, L. (1998). Rapid rate transcranial magnetic stimulation in young and middle-aged refractory depressed patients. *Psychiatric Annals, 28*, 36–39.

Eranti, S. V., & McLoughlin, D. M. (2003). Changing use of ECT: Author's reply. *British Journal of Psychiatry, 183*, 173.

Febbraro, G. A. R. (2005). An investigation into the effectiveness of bibliotherapy and minimal contact interventions in the treatment of panic attacks. *Journal of Clinical Psychology, 61*, 763–779.

Febbraro, G. A. R., & Clum, G. A. (2008). Self-regulation theory and self-help therapies. In P. L. Watkins & G. A. Clum (Eds.), *Handbook of self-help therapies* (pp. 59–76). New York: Routledge/Taylor & Francis Group and Erlbaum.

Fergusson, D., Doucette, S., Glass, K. C., Shapiro, S., Healy, D., Hebert, P., et al. (2005). Association between suicide attempts and selective serotonin reuptake inhibitors: Systematic review of randomised controlled trials. *British Medical Journal, 330*, 396.

Figiel, G. S., Epstein, C., McDonald, W. M., Amazon-Leece, J., Figiel, L., Saldivia, A., et al. (1998). The use of rapid-rate transcranial magnetic stimulation (rTMS) in refractory depressed patients. *Journal of Neuropsychiatry and Clinical Neurosciences, 10*, 20–25.

Finn, J., & Banach, M. (2000). Victimization online: The down side of seeking services for women on the Internet. *CyberPsychology and Behavior, 3*, 243–254.

Fiorentine, R. (1999). After drug treatment: Are 12-step programs effective in maintaining abstinence? *American Journal of Drug and Alcohol Abuse, 25*, 93–116.

Floyd, M., Scogin, F., McKendree-Smith, N. L., Floyd, D. L., & Rokke, P. D. (2004). Cognitive therapy for depression: A comparison of individual psychotherapy and bibliotherapy for depressed older adults. *Behavior Modification, 28*, 297–318.

Foa, E. B., Liebowitz, M. R., Kozak, M. J., Davies, S., Campeas, R., Franklin, M. E., et al. (2005). Randomized, placebo-controlled trial of exposure and ritual prevention, clomipramine, and their combination in the treatment of obsessive-compulsive disorder. *American Journal of Psychiatry, 162*, 151–161.

Fournier, J. C., DebRubeis, R. J., Hollon, S. D., Dimidjian, S., Amsterdam, J. D., Shelton, R. C., et al. (2010). Antidepressant drug effects and depression severity: A patient-level meta-analysis. *Journal of the American Medical Association, 303*, 47–53.

Francis, J. R., & Aronson, H. (1990). Communicative efficacy of psychotherapy research. *Journal of Consulting and Clinical Psychology, 58*, 368–370.

Freud, S. (1900/1958). *The interpretation of dreams.* New York: Basic Books.

Garfield, S. L., & Bergin, A. E. (1994). Introduction and historical overview. In A. E. Bergin & S. L. Garfield (Eds.), *Handbook of psychotherapy and behavior change* (4th ed., pp. 3–18). New York: Wiley.

Gaster, B., & Holroyd, J. (2000). St. John's wort for depression: A systematic review. *Archives of Internal Medicine, 160*, 152–156.

Geddes, J. R., Freemantle, N., Mason, J., Eccles, M., & Boynton, J. (2000). SSRIs versus alternative antidepressants in depressive disorder. *Cochrane Database System Review (2)*, CD001851.

George, M. S., Lisanby, S. H., & Sackheim, H. A. (1999). Transcranial magnetic stimulation: Applications in neuropsychiatry. *Archives of General Psychiatry, 56*, 300–311.

Glass, R. M. (2001). Electroconvulsive therapy: Time to bring it out of the shadows. *Journal of the American Medical Association, 285*, n.p.

Glynn, S. M. (1990). Token economy approaches for psychiatric patients: Progress and pitfalls over 25 years. *Behavior Modification, 14*, 383–407.

Goldstein, M. J. (1992). Psychosocial strategies for maximizing the effects of psychotropic medications for schizophrenia and mood disorder. *Psychopharmacology Bulletin, 28*, 237–240.

Gorman, J. M., & Kent, J. M. (1999). SSRIs and SNRIs: Broad spectrum of efficacy beyond major depression. *Journal of Clinical Psychiatry, 60*(Suppl. 4), 33–39.

Gould, R. A., Otto, M. W., & Pollack, M. H. (1995). A meta-analysis of treatment outcome for panic disorder. *Clinical Psychology Review, 15*, 819–844.

Greenberg, J. R., & Mitchell, S. A. (1983). *Object relations in psychoanalytic theory.* Cambridge, MA: Harvard University Press.

Greenberg, R. P., & Fisher, S. (1989). Examining antidepressant effectiveness: Findings, ambiguities and some vexing puzzles. In S. Fisher & R. P. Greenberg (Eds.), *The limits of biological treatments for psychological distress* (pp. 1–37). Hillsdale, NJ: Erlbaum.

Gregory, R. J., Schwer Canning, S., Lee, T. W., & Wise, J. C. (2004). Cognitive bibliotherapy for depression: A meta-analysis. *Professional Psychology: Research and Practice, 35*, 275–280.

Grunes, M. S., Neziroglu, F., & McKay, D. (2001). Family involvement in the behavioral treatment of obsessive-compulsive disorder: A preliminary investigation. *Behavior Therapy, 32*, 803–820.

Gunnell, D., Saperia, J., & Ashby, D. (2005). Selective serotonin reuptake inhibitors (SSRIs) and suicide in adults: Meta-analysis of drug company data from placebo controlled, randomised controlled trials submitted to the MHRA's safety review. *British Medical Journal, 330*, 385–388.

Haaga, D. A., & Davison, G. C. (1989). Slow progress in rational-emotive therapy outcome research: Etiology and treatment. *Cognitive Therapy and Research, 13*, 493–450.

Helms, J. E., & Cook, D. A. (1999). *Using race and culture in counseling and psychotherapy: Theory and process.* Needham Heights, MA: Allyn & Bacon.

Henry, W. P., Strupp, H. H., Schacht, T. E., & Gaston, L. (1994). Psychodynamic approaches. In A. E. Bergin & S. L. Garfield (Eds.), *Handbook of psychotherapy and behavior change* (4th ed., pp. 467–508). New York: Wiley.

Higgenbotham, H. N., West, S., & Forsyth, D. (1988). *Psychotherapy and behavior change: Social, cultural and methodological perspectives.* New York: Pergamon.

Hollon, S. D., & Beck, A. T. (1994). Cognitive and cognitive-behavioral therapies. In A. E. Bergin & S. L. Garfield (Eds.), *Handbook of psychotherapy and behavior change* (4th ed., pp. 428–466). New York: Wiley.

Hollon, S. D., DeRubeis, R. J., Shelton, R. C., Amsterdam, J. D., Salomon, R. M., O'Reardon, J. P., et al. (2005). Prevention of relapse following cognitive therapy vs. medications in moderate to severe depression. *Archives of General Psychiatry, 62,* 417–422.

Hollon, S. D., & Shelton, R. C. (2001). Treatment guidelines for major depressive disorder. *Behavior Therapy, 32,* 235–258.

Husain, M. M., Rush, A. J., Fink, M., Knapp, R., Petrides, G., Rummans, T., et al. (2004). Speed of response and remission in major depressive disorder with acute electroconvulsive therapy (ECT): A consortium for research in ECT (CORE) report. *Journal of Clinical Psychiatry, 65,* 485–491.

Janicak, P. G., Dowd, S. M., Martis, B., Alam, D., Beedle, D., Krasuski, J., et al. (2002). Repetitive transcranial magnetic stimulation versus electroconvulsive therapy for major depression: Preliminary results of a randomized trial. *Biological Psychiatry, 51,* 659–667.

Kasper, S., & Resinger, E. (2001). Panic disorder: The place of benzodiazepines and selective serotonin reuptake inhibitors. *European Neuropsychopharmacology, 11,* 307–321.

Kazdin, A. E. (1994). Methodology, design, and evaluation in psychotherapy research. In A. E. Bergin & S. L. Garfield (Eds.), *Handbook of psychotherapy and behavior change* (4th ed., pp. 19–71). New York: Wiley.

Kho, King Han; VanVreeswijk, Michiel Floris; Murre, Jaap M.J. (2006). A Retrospective Controlled Study into Memory Complaints Reported by Depressed Patients After Treatment with Electroconvulsive Therapy and Pharmacotherapy or Pharmacotherapy Only. *The Journal of ECT, 22,* 199-205.

Kiropoulos, L. A., Klein, B., Austin, D. W., Gilson, K., Pier, C., Mitchell, J., et al. (2008). Is internet-based CBT for panic disorder and agoraphobia as effective as face-to-face CBT? *Journal of Anxiety Disorders, 22,* 1273–1284.

Kirsch, I., & Lynn, S. J. (1999). Automaticity in clinical psychology. *American Psychologist, 54,* 504–515.

Kirsch, I., & Sapirstein, G. (1998). Listening to Prozac but hearing placebo: A meta-analysis of antidepressant medication. *Prevention and Treatment, 1,* Article 0002a.

Kirsch, I., Scoboria, A., & Moore, T. J. (2002). Antidepressants and placebos: Secrets, revelations, and unanswered questions. *Prevention and Treatment, 5,* n.p.

Kitzmann, K. M. (2000). Effects of marital conflict on subsequent triadic family interactions and parenting. *Developmental Psychology, 36,* 3–13.

Klein, E., Kreinin, I., Chistyakov, A., Koren, D., Mecz, L., Marmur, S., et al. (1999). Therapeutic efficacy of right prefrontal slow repetitive transcranial magnetic stimulation in major depression: A double-blind controlled study. *Archives of General Psychiatry, 56,* 315–320.

Kleinman, A. (1978). Clinical relevance of anthropological and cross-cultural research: Concepts and strategies. *American Journal of Psychiatry, 135,* 427–431.

Klosko, J. S., Barlow, D. H., Tassinari, R., & Cerny, J. A. (1990). A comparison of alprazolam and behavior therapy in treatment of panic disorder. *Journal of Consulting and Clinical Psychology, 58,* 77–84.

Knekt, P., Lindfors, O., Härkänen, T., Välikoski, M., Virtala, E., Laaksonen, M. A., et al. (2008). Randomized trial on the effectiveness of long- and short-term psychodynamic psychotherapy and solution-focused therapy on psychiatric symptoms during a 3-year follow-up. *Psychological Medicine, 38,* 689–703.

Kohut, H. (1977). *The restoration of self.* New York: International Universities Press.

Lam, A. G., & Sue, S. (2001). Client diversity. *Psychotherapy: Theory, Research, Practice, Training, 38,* 479–486.

Lam, R. W., Bartley, S., Yatham, L. N., Tam, E. M., & Zis, A. P. (1999). Clinical predictors of short-term outcome in electroconvulsive therapy. *Canadian Journal of Psychiatry, 44,* 158–163.

Lambert, M. J. (1983). Introduction to assessment of psychotherapy outcome: Historical perspective and current issues. In M. J. Lambert, E. R. Christensen, & S. S. DeJulio (Eds.), *The assessment of psychotherapy outcome* (pp. 3–32). New York: Wiley-Interscience.

Lehman, A. F., & Steinwachs, D. M. (1998). Translating research into practice: The Schizophrenia Patients Outcome Research Team (PORT) Treatment Recommendations. *Schizophrenia Bulletin, 24,* 1–10.

Leichsenring, F. (2001). Comparative effects of short-term psychodynamic psychotherapy and cognitive-behavioral therapy in depression: A meta-analytic approach. *Clinical Psychology Review, 21,* 401–419.

Leichsenring, F. (2009). Applications of psychodynamic psychotherapy to specific disorders: Efficacy and indications. In G. O. Gabbard (Ed.), *Textbook of psychotherapeutic treatments* (pp. 97–132). Arlington, VA: American Psychiatric Publishing.

Leichsenring, F., Rabung, S., & Leibing, E. (2004). The efficacy of short-term psychodynamic psychotherapy in specific psychiatric disorders: A meta-analysis. *Archives of General Psychiatry, 61,* 1208–1216.

Leichsenring, F., Salzer, S., Jaeger, U., Kächele, H., Kreische, R., Leweke, F., et al. (2009). Short-term psychodynamic psychotherapy and cognitive-behavioral therapy in generalized anxiety disorder: A randomized, controlled trial. *American Journal of Psychiatry, 166,* 875–881.

Leuchter, A. F., Cook, I. A., Witte, E. A., Morgan, M., & Abrams, M. (2002). Changes in brain function of depressed subjects during treatment with placebo. *American Journal of Psychiatry, 159,* 122–129.

Lin, K.-M. (2010, January 12). Addressing both instrumental and symbolic effects of treatment. *Psychiatric Times.* Retrieved January 21, 2010, from http://www.psychiatrictimes.com/display/article/10168/1505053

Linden, M., Zubraegel, D., Baer, T., Franke, U., & Schlattmann, P. (2005). Efficacy of cognitive behaviour therapy in generalized anxiety disorders. *Psychotherapy and Psychosomatics, 74,* 36–42.

Maletzky, B. M. (2004). The first-line use of electroconvulsive therapy in major affective disorders. *Journal of ECT, 20,* 112–117.

Malik, N., Kingdon, D., Pelton, J., Mehta, R., & Turkington, D. (2009). Effectiveness of brief cognitive-behavioral therapy for schizophrenia delivered by mental health nurses: Relapse and recovery at 24 months. *Journal of Clinical Psychiatry, 70,* 201–207.

Marks, I. (1997). Behaviour therapy for obsessive-compulsive disorder: A decade of progress. *Canadian Journal of Psychiatry, 42,* 1021–1027.

Martinez, C., Rietbrock, S., Wise, L., Ashby, D., Chick, J., Moseley, J., et al. (2005). Antidepressant treatment and the risk of fatal and non-fatal self harm in first episode depression: Nested case-control study. *British Medical Journal, 330,* 389–393.

Mitchell, J. E., Halmi, K., Wilson, G. T., Agras, W. S., Kraemer, H., & Crow, S. (2002). A randomized secondary treatment study of women with bulimia nervosa who fail to respond to CBT. *International Journal of Eating Disorders, 32,* 271–281.

Nakatani, E., Nakgawa, A., Ohara, Y., Goto, S., Uozumi, N., Iwakiri, M., et al. (2003). Effects of behavior therapy on regional cerebral blood flow in obsessive-compulsive disorder. *Psychiatry Research: Neuroimaging, 124,* 113–120.

Otto, M. W., Gould, R. A., & Pollack, M. H. (1994). Cognitive-behavioral treatment of panic disorder: Considerations for the treatment of patients over the long term. *Psychiatric Annals, 24,* 307–315.

Otto, M. W., Smits, J. A. J., & Reese, H. E. (2005). Combined psychotherapy and pharmacotherapy for mood and anxiety disorders in adults: Review and analysis. *Clinical Psychology: Science and Practice, 12,* 72–86.

Paquette, V., Lévesque, J., Mensour, B., Leroux, J. M., Beaudoin, G., Bourgouin, P., et al. (2003). "Change the mind and you change the brain": Effects of cognitive-behavioral therapy on the neural correlates of spider phobia. *NeuroImage, 18,* 401–409.

Pretorius, N., Arcelus, J., Beecham, J., Dawson, H., Doherty, F., Eisler, I. et al., (2009). Cognitive-behavioural therapy for adolescents with bulimic symptomatology: The acceptability and effectiveness of internet-based delivery. *Behaviour Research and Therapy, 47,* 729-736.

Prien, R. F., & Kocsis, J. H. (1995). Long term treatment of mood disorders. In F. E. Bloom & D. J. Kupfer (Eds.), *Psychopharmacology: The fourth generation of progress* (pp. 1067–1080). New York: Raven Press.

Ramirez, M., III. (1999). *Multicultural psychotherapy: An approach to individual and cultural differences* (2nd ed.). Needham Heights, MA: Allyn & Bacon.

Rivas-Vazques, R. A. (2001). Antidepressants as first-line agents in the current pharmacotherapy of anxiety disorders. *Professional Psychology: Research and Practice, 32,* 101–104.

Rivera-Arzola, M., & Ramos-Grenier, J. (1997). Anger, ataques de nervios, and la mujer puertorriquena: Sociocultural considerations and treatment implications. In J. G. Garcia & M. C. Zea (Eds.), *Psychological interventions and research with Latino populations.* (pp. 125–141). Boston, MA: Allyn & Bacon.

Rosenbaum, J. F., Arana, G. W., Hyman, S. E., Labbate, L. A., & Fava, M. (2005). *Handbook of psychiatric drug therapy* (5th ed.). Philadelphia: Lippincott Williams and Wilkins.

Roth, A., & Fonagy, P. (2005). *What works for whom: A critical review of psychotherapy research* (2nd ed.). New York: Guilford Press.

Rothbaum, B. O., Anderson, P., Zimand, E., Hodges, L., Lang, D., & Wilson, J. (2006). Virtual reality exposure therapy and standard (in vivo) exposure therapy in the treatment of fear of flying. *Behavior Therapy, 37,* 80–90.

Rothbaum, B. O., Hodges, L., Anderson, P. L., Price, L., & Smith, S. (2002). Twelve-month follow-up of virtual reality and standard exposure therapies for the fear of flying. *Journal of Consulting and Clinical Psychology, 70,* 428–432.

Rothbaum, B. O., Hodges, L., Smith, S., Lee, J. H., & Price, L. (2001). A controlled study of virtual reality exposure therapy for the fear of flying. *Journal of Consulting and Clinical Psychology, 68,* 1020–1026.

Sackeim, H. A., Devanand, D. P., & Nobler, M. S. (1995). Electroconvulsive therapy. In F. E. Bloom & D. J. Kupfer (Eds.), *Psychopharmacology: The fourth generation of progress* (pp. 1123–1141). New York: Raven Press.

Schwartz, J. M., Stoessel, P. W., Baxter, L. R., Martin, K. M., & Phelps, M. E. (1996). Systematic changes in cerebral glucose metabolic rate after successful behavior modification treatment of obsessive-compulsive disorder. *Archives of General Psychiatry, 53,* 109–113.

Sensky, T., Turkington, D., Kingdon, D., Scott, J. L., Scott, J., Siddle, R., et al. (2000). A randomized controlled trial of cognitive-behavioral therapy for persistent symptoms in schizophrenia resistant to medication. *Archives of General Psychiatry, 57,* 165–172.

Shapira, B., Tubi, N., Drexler, H., Lidsky, D., Calev, A., & Lerer, B. (1998). Cost and benefit in the choice of ECT schedule: Twice versus three times weekly ECT. *British Journal of Psychiatry, 172,* 44–48.

Sifneos, P. E. (1992). *Short-term anxiety-provoking psychotherapy: A treatment manual.* New York: Basic Books.

Skinner, B. F. (1953). *Science and human behavior.* New York: Macmillan.

Stanley, M. A., & Turner, S. M. (1995). Current status of pharmacological and behavioral treatment of obsessive-compulsive disorder. *Behavior Therapy, 25,* 153–186.

Starker, S. (1988). Psychologists and self-help books: Attitudes and prescriptive practices of clinicians. *American Journal of Psychotherapy, 42,* 448–455.

Sue, S., Zane, N., & Young, K. (1994). Research on psychotherapy with culturally diverse populations. In A. E. Bergin & S. L. Garfield (Eds.), *Handbook of psychotherapy and behavior change* (4th ed., pp. 783–820). New York: Wiley.

Sullivan, H. S. (1953). *The interpersonal theory of psychiatry.* Oxford: Norton.

Szegedi, A., Kohnen, R., Dienel, A., & Kieser, M. (2005). Acute treatment of moderate to severe depression with hypericum extract WS 5570 (St John's wort): Randomised controlled double blind non-inferiority trial versus paroxetine. *British Medical Journal, 330,* 503.

TADS Team. (2007). The Treatment for Adolescents with Depression Study (TADS): Long-term effectiveness and safety outcomes. *Archives of General Psychiatry, 64,* 1132–1144.

Talbot, N. L., & Gamble, S. A. (2008). IPT for women with trauma histories in community mental health care. *Journal of Contemporary Psychotherapy, 38,* 35–44.

Thase, M. E., & Jindal, R. D. (2004). Combining psychotherapy and psychopharmacology for treatment of mental disorders. In M. J. Lambert (Ed.), *Bergin and Garfield's handbook of psychotherapy and behavior change* (5th ed., pp. 743–766). New York: Wiley.

Tillman, J. G., Oberwager, K., & Agar, K. (2010, January 13–17). *Research publications in three psychoanalytic journals, 2001–2008.* Paper presented at the annual meeting of the American Psychoanalytic Association, New York, NY.

Tohen, M., & Grundy, S. (1999). Management of acute mania. *Journal of Clinical Psychology, 60*(Suppl. 5), 31–34.

Van Noppen, B., & Steketee, G. (2003). Family responses and multifamily behavioral treatment for obsessive-compulsive disorder. *Brief Treatment and Crisis Intervention, 3,* 231–247.

Vieweg, R., & Shawcross, C. R. (1998). A trial to determine any difference between two and three times a week ECT in the rate of recovery from depression. *Journal of Mental Health (UK), 7,* 403–409.

Voth, H. M., & Orth, M. H. (1973). *Psychotherapy and the role of the environment.* New York: Behavioral Press.

Walach, H., & Maidhof, C. (1999). Is the placebo effect dependent on time? A meta-analysis. In I. Kirsch (Ed.), *How expectancies shape experience* (pp. 321–332). Washington, DC: American Psychological Association.

Waldron, V. R., Lavitt, M., & Kelley, D. (2000). The nature and prevention of harm in technology-mediated self-help settings: Three exemplars. *Journal of Technology in Human Services, 17,* 267–293.

Whittal, M. L., Agras, W. S., & Gould, R. A. (1999). Bulimia nervosa: A meta-analysis of psychosocial and pharmacological treatments. *Behavior Therapy, 30,* 117–135.

Wilson, G. T., & Fairburn, C. G. (2002). Treatments for eating disorders. In P. E. Nathan & J. M. Gorman (Eds.), *A guide to treatments that work* (2nd ed., pp. 559–592). London: Oxford University Press.

Wilson, G. T., & Fairburn, C. G. (2007). Treatments for eating disorders. In P. E. Nathan & J. M. Gorman (Eds.), *A guide to treatments that work* (3rd ed., pp. 579–609). New York: Oxford University Press.

Winnicott, D. W. (1958). *Collected papers: Through paediatrics to psychoanalysis.* London: Tavistock.

Winzelberg, A., & Humphreys, K. (1999). Should patients' religiosity influence clinicians' referral to 12-step self-help groups? Evidence from a study of 3,018 male substance abuse patients. *Journal of Consulting and Clinical Psychology, 67,* 790–794.

Wolpe, J. (1997). Thirty years of behavior therapy. *Behavior Therapy, 28,* 633–635.

Wyatt, R. J., Green, M. F., & Tuma, A. H. (1997). Long-term morbidity associated with delayed treatment of first admission schizophrenic patients: A re-analysis of the Camarillo State Hospital data. *Psychological Medicine, 27,* 261–268.

Wykes, T., Steel, C., Everitt, B., & Tarrier, N. (2008). Cognitive behavior therapy for schizophrenia: Effect sizes, clinical models, and methodological rigor. *Schizophrenia Bulletin, 34,* 523–537.

Zane, N., Hall, G. C. N., Sue, S., Young, K., & Nunez, J. (2004). Research on psychotherapy with culturally diverse populations. In M. J. Lambert (Ed.), *Bergin and Garfield's handbook of psychotherapy and behavior change* (5th ed., pp. 805–821). New York: Wiley.

References: Social Psychology

Aguiar, P., Vala, J., Correia, I., & Pereira, C. (2008). Justice in our world and in that of others: Belief in a just world and reactions to victims. *Social Justice Research, 21(1)*, 50–68.

Aldag, R. J., & Fuller, S. R. (1993). Beyond fiasco: A reappraisal of the groupthink phenomenon and a new model of group decision processes. *Psychological Bulletin, 113*, 533–552.

Allport, G. (1954). *The nature of prejudice.* Oxford: Addison-Wesley.

Allyn, J., & Festinger, L. (1961). The effectiveness of unanticipated persuasive communications. *Journal of Abnormal and Social Psychology, 62*, 35–40.

Almendros, C., Carrobles, J. A., & Rodríguez-Carballeira, Á. (2007). Former members' perceptions of cult involvement. *Cultic Studies Review, 6*, 1–20.

Anderson, C. A. (1983). Abstract and concrete data in the perseverance of social theories: When weak data lead to unshakable beliefs. *Journal of Experimental Social Psychology, 19*, 930–1108.

Anderson, C. A., Lepper, M. R., & Ross, L. (1980). Perseverance of social theories: This role of explanation in the persistence of discredited information. *Journal of Personality and Social Psychology, 39*, 1037–1049.

Arkes, H. R., & Tetlock, P. E. (2004). Attributions of implicit prejudice, or "Would Jesse Jackson 'fail' the Implicit Association Test?" *Psychological Inquiry, 15*, 257–278.

Aronson, E., & Osherow, N. (1980). Cooperation, prosocial behavior, and academic performance: Experiments in the desegregated classroom. *Applied Social Psychology Annual, 1*, 163–196.

Aronson, E., & Patnoe, S. (1997). *The jigsaw classroom: Building cooperation in the classroom* (2nd ed.). New York: Addison-Wesley Longman.

Asch, S. E. (1951). Effects of group pressure upon the modification and distortion of judgment. In H. Guetzkow (Ed.), *Groups, leadership, and men* (pp. 177–190). Pittsburgh, PA: Carnegie.

Asch, S. E. (1955). Opinions and social pressure. *Scientific American, 193*, 31–35.

Bandura, A. (1999). Moral disengagement in the perpetration of inhumanities. *Personality and Social Psychology Review, 3*, 193–209.

Bargh, J. A., Chen, M., & Burrows, L. (1996). Automaticity of social behavior: Direct effects of trait construct and stereotype activation on action. *Journal of Personality and Social Psychology, 71*, 230–244.

Bargh, J. A., & McKenna, K. Y. A. (2004). The Internet and social life. *Annual Review of Psychology, 55*, 573–590.

Bargh, J. A., McKenna, K. Y. A., & Fitzsimons, G. M. (2002). Can you see the real me? Activation and expression of the "true self" on the Internet. *Journal of Social Issues, 58*, 33–48.

Baron, R. A., & Byrne, D. (1997). *Social psychology* (8th ed.). Needham Heights, MA: Allyn & Bacon.

Batson, C. D. (1998). Altruism and prosocial behavior. In D. T. Gilbert, S. T. Fiske, & G. Lindzey (Eds.), *The handbook of social psychology* (4th ed., pp. 282–316). New York: McGraw-Hill.

Batson, C. D. (2010). Empathy-induced altruistic motivation. In M. Mikulincer & P. R. Shaver (Eds.), *Prosocial motives, emotions, and behavior: The better angels of our nature* (pp. 15–34). Washington, DC: American Psychological Association.

Batson, C. D., Bolen, M. H., Cross, J. A., & Neuringer-Benefiel, H. E. (1986). Where is the altruism in the altruistic personality? *Journal of Personality and Social Psychology, 50*, 212–220.

Baumeister, R. F., Stillwell, A., & Wotman, S. R. (1990). Victim and perpetrator accounts of interpersonal conflict: Autobiographical narratives about anger. *Journal of Personality and Social Psychology, 59*, 994–1003.

Baxter, J. S., Macrae, C. N., Manstead, A. S. R., Stradling, S. G., & Parker, D. (1990). Attributional biases and driver behavior. *Social Behaviour, 5*, 185–192.

Beaman, A., Barnes, P., Kletz, B., & McQuirk, B. (1978). Increasing helping rates through information dissemination: Teaching pays. *Personality and Social Psychology Bulletin, 4*, 406–411.

Bearak, B. (1997, March 29). Time of puzzles, heartbreak binds relatives left behind. *New York Times*, p. 1.

Beck, A. T. (1967). *Depression: Causes and treatment.* Philadelphia: University of Pennsylvania Press.

Berscheid, E. (2006). Searching for the meaning of "love." In R. J. Sternberg & K. Weis (Eds.), *The new psychology of love* (pp. 171–183). New Haven, CT: Yale University Press.

Berscheid, E., & Reis, H. T. (1998). Attraction and close relationships. In D. T. Gilbert, S. T. Fiske, & G. Lindzey (Eds.), *The handbook of social psychology* (4th ed., pp. 193–281). New York: McGraw-Hill.

Bierhoff, H. W., Klein, R., & Kramp, P. (1991). Evidence for the altruistic personality from data on accident research. *Journal of Personality, 59*, 263–280.

Blakemore, S., Winston, J., & Frith, U. (2004). Social cognitive neuroscience: Where are we heading? *Trends in Cognitive Sciences, 8*, 216–222.

Blass, T. (1999). The Milgram Paradigm after 35 years: Some things we now know about obedience to authority. *Journal of Applied Social Psychology, 29*, 955–978.

Bobo, L. (1983). Whites' opposition to busing: Symbolic racism or realistic group conflict? *Journal of Personality and Social Psychology, 45*, 1196–1210.

Bodenhausen, G. V., Kramer, G. P., & Susser, K. (1994). Happiness and stereotypic thinking in social judgment. *Journal of Personality and Social Psychology, 66*, 621–632.

Bohm, J. K., & Hendricks, B. (1997). Effects of interpersonal touch, degree of justification, and sex of participant on compliance with a request. *Journal of Social Psychology, 137*, 460–469.

Bond, R., & Smith, P. B. (1996). Culture and conformity: A meta-analysis of studies using Asch's (1952b, 1956) line judgment task. *Psychological Bulletin, 119*, 111–137.

Breckler, S. J. (1984). Empirical validation of affect, behavior, and cognition as distinct components of attitude. *Journal of Personality and Social Psychology, 47*, 1191–1205.

Brehm, J. W. (1956). Post-decision changes in the desirability of alternatives. *Journal of Abnormal and Social Psychology, 52*, 384–389.

Brewer, M. B., & Brown, R. J. (1998). Intergroup relations. In D. T. Gilbert, S. T. Fiske, & G. Lindzey (Eds.), *The handbook of social psychology* (4th ed., pp. 554–594). New York: McGraw-Hill.

Brewer, M. B., & Miller, N. (1984). Beyond the contact hypothesis: Theoretical perspectives on desegregation. In N. Miller & M. B. Brewer (Eds.), *Groups in contact: The psychology of desegregation* (pp. 281–302). Orlando: Academic Press.

Brown, J. D., & Rogers, R. J. (1991). Self-serving attributions: The role of physiological arousal. *Personality and Social Psychology Bulletin, 17*, 501–506.

Burnstein, E. (1982). Persuasion as argument processing. In H. Brandstatter, J. H. Davis, & G. Stocker-Krechgauer (Eds.), *Group decision making* (pp. 103–124). London: Academic Press.

Bushman, B. J. (1984). Perceived symbols of authority and their influence on compliance. *Journal of Applied Social Psychology, 14*, 501–508.

Bushman, B. J. (1988). The effects of apparel on compliance: A field experiment with a female authority figure. *Personality and Social Psychology Bulletin, 14*, 459–467.

Buss, D. M. (1989). Sex differences in human mate preferences: Evolutionary hypotheses tested in 37 cultures. *Behavioral and Brain Sciences, 12*, 1–49.

Buss, D. M. (1999). *Evolutionary psychology: The new science of the mind.* Boston: Allyn & Bacon.

Byrne, D. (1971). *The attraction paradigm.* New York: Academic Press.

Cacioppo, J. T., Petty, R. E., Losch, M. E., & Kim, H. S. (1986). Electromyographic activity over facial muscle regions can differentiate the valence and intensity of affective reactions. *Journal of Personality and Social Psychology, 50*, 260–268.

Carlo, G., Okun, M. A., Knight, G. P., & de Guzman, M. T. (2005). The interplay of traits and motives on volunteering: Agreeableness, extraversion and prosocial value motivation. *Personality and Individual Differences, 38*, 1293–1305.

Cialdini, R. B. (1994). Interpersonal influence. In N. S. Shavitt & T. C. Brock (Eds.), *Persuasion: Psychological insights and perspectives* (pp. 195–218). Boston: Allyn & Bacon.

Cialdini, R. B., & Goldstein, N. J. (2004). Social influence: Compliance and conformity. *Annual Review of Psychology, 55*, 591–621.

Cialdini, R. B., & Trost, M. R. (1998). Social influence: Social norms, conformity, and compliance. In D. T. Gilbert, S. T. Fiske, & G. Lindzey (Eds.), *The handbook of social psychology* (4th ed., pp. 151–192). New York: McGraw-Hill.

Cialdini, R. B., Vincent, J. A., Lewis, S. K., Catalan, J., Wheeler, D., & Darby, B. L. (1975). Reciprocal concessions procedure for inducing compliance: The door-in-the-face technique. *Journal of Personality and Social Psychology, 31*, 206–215.

Collins, M. A., & Zebrowitz, L. A. (1995). The contributions of appearance to occupational outcomes in civilian and military settings. *Journal of Applied Social Psychology, 25*, 129–163.

Cooper, J. (1998). Unlearning cognitive dissonance: Toward an understanding of the development of dissonance. *Journal of Experimental Social Psychology, 34*, 562–575.

Cramer, R. E., Schaefer, J. T., & Reid, S. (1996). Identifying the ideal mate: More evidence for male–female convergence. *Current Psychology: Developmental, Learning, Personality, Social, 16*, 157–166.

Crawford, M., Stark, A. C., & Renner, C. H. (1998). The meaning of Ms.: Social assimilation of a gender concept. *Psychology of Women Quarterly, 22*, 197–208.

Dalbert, C., & Yamauchi, L. (1994). Belief in a just world and attitudes toward immigrants and foreign workers: A cultural comparison between Hawaii and Germany. *Journal of Applied Social Psychology, 24*, 1612–1626.

Darley, J. M., & Latané, B. (1968). Bystander intervention in emergencies: Diffusion of responsibility. *Journal of Personality and Social Psychology, 10*, 202–214.

Darley, J. M., & Latané, B. (1970). Norms and normative behavior: Field studies of social interdependence. In J. Macauley & L. Berkowitz (Eds.), *Altruism and helping behavior* (pp. 83–101). New York: Academic Press.

Delany, S. L., Delany, A. E., & Hearth, A. H. (1993). *Having our say: The Delany sisters' first 100 years.* New York: Delta.

DeSteno, D., Dasgupta, N., Bartlett, M. Y., Cajdric, A. (2004). Prejudice from thin air: The effect of emotion on automatic intergroup attitudes. *Psychological Science, 15*, 319–324.

Devine, P. G., & Monteith, M. J. (1993). The role of discrepancy-associated affect in prejudice reduction. In D. M. Mackie, & D. L. Hamilton, (Eds.), *Affect, cognition, and stereotyping: Interactive processes in group perception* (pp. 317–344). San Diego, CA: Academic Press.

Dew, A. M., & Ward, C. (1993). The effects of ethnicity and culturally congruent and incongruent non-verbal behaviors on interpersonal attraction. *Journal of Applied Social Psychology, 23*, 1376–1389.

Dobson, R. (2002, May 11). Broadcast of star's colonoscopy puts up screening by 20%. *British Medical Journal, 324*, 1118.

Dovidio, J. F. (2000). Racism. In A. E. Kazdin (Ed.), *Encyclopedia of psychology* (Vol. 6, pp. 497–501). Washington, DC: American Psychological Association.

Dovidio, J. F., Evans, N., & Tyler, R. B. (1986). Racial stereotypes: The contents of their cognitive representations. *Journal of Experimental Social Psychology, 22*, 22–37.

Dovidio, J. F., Piliavin, J. A., Gaertner, S. L., Schroeder, D. A., & Clark, R. D., III. (1991). The arousal: Cost-reward model and the process of intervention: A review of the evidence. In M. S. Clark (Ed.), *Prosocial behavior* (pp. 86–118). Thousand Oaks, CA: Sage.

Downing, J. W., Judd, C. M., & Brauer, M. (1992). Effects of repeated expressions on attitude extremity. *Journal of Personality and Social Psychology, 63*, 17–29.

Eagly, A. H., & Carli, L. (1981). Sex of researchers and sex-typed communications as determinants of sex differences in influence-ability: A meta-analysis of social influence studies. *Psychological Bulletin, 90*, 1–20.

Eagly, A. H., & Chaiken, S. (1998). Attitude structure and function. In D. T. Gilbert, S. T. Fiske, & G. Lindzey (Eds.), *The handbook of social psychology* (4th ed., pp. 269–322). New York: McGraw-Hill.

Eagly, A. H., & Wood, W. (1999). The origins of sex differences in human behavior: Evolved dispositions versus social roles. *American Psychologist, 54*, 408–423.

Eisenberg, N., Guthrie, I. K., Cumberland, A., Murphy, B. C., Shepard, S. A., Zhou, Q., et al. (2002). Prosocial development in early adulthood: A longitudinal study. *Journal of Personality and Social Psychology, 82,* 993–1006.

Eisenberg, N., Miller, P. A., Schaller, M., Fabes, R. A., Fultz, J., Shell, R., et al. (1989). The role of sympathy and altruistic personality traits in helping: A reexamination. *Journal of Personality, 57,* 41–67.

Emerson, M. O., Kimbro, R. T., & Yancey, G. (2002). Contact theory extended: The effects of prior racial contact on current social ties. *Social Science Quarterly, 83,* 745–761.

Epley, N., & Dunning, D. (2000). Feeling "holier than thou": Are self-serving assessments produced by errors in self- or social prediction? *Journal of Personality and Social Psychology, 79,* 861–875.

Fazio, R. H., Chen, J., McDonel, E. C., & Sherman, S. J. (1982). Attitude accessibility and the strength of the object-evaluation association. *Journal of Experimental Psychology, 18,* 339–357.

Feather, N. T. (1996). Social comparisons across nations: Variables relating to the subjective evaluation of national achievement and to personal and collective. *Australian Journal of Psychology, 48,* 53–63.

Fehr, B., Sprecher, S., & Underwood, L. G. (Eds.). (2008). *The science of compassionate love: Theory, research, and applications.* New York: Wiley-Blackwell.

Feingold, A. (1990). Gender differences in effects of physical attractiveness on romantic attraction: A comparison across five research paradigms. *Journal of Personality and Social Psychology, 59,* 981–993.

Festinger, L., & Carlsmith, J. M. (1959). Cognitive consequences of forced compliance. *Journal of Abnormal and Social Psychology, 58,* 203–210.

Fiske, S. (1998). Stereotyping, prejudice, and discrimination. In D. T. Gilbert, S. T. Fiske, & G. Lindzey (Eds.). *The handbook of social psychology* (4th ed., pp. 357–411). New York: McGraw-Hill.

Fiske, S. T. (2002). What we know about bias and intergroup conflict, the problem of the century. *Current Directions in Psychological Science, 11,* 123–128.

Ford, M. T., Heinen, B. A., & Langkamer, K. L. (2007). Work and family satisfaction and conflict: A meta-analysis of cross-domain relations. *Journal of Applied Psychology, 92,* 57–80.

Freedman, J. L., & Fraser, S. C. (1966). Compliance without pressure: The foot-in-the-door technique. *Journal of Personality and Social Psychology, 4,* 195–202.

Gaertner, S. L., Dovidio, J. F., Anastasio, P. A., Bachman, B. A., & Rust, M. C. (1993). The common in-group identity model: Recategorization and the reduction of in-group bias. In W. Stroebe & M. Hewstone (Eds.), *European review of social psychology* (Vol. 4, pp. 1–26). London: Wiley.

Galanter, M. (2000). Cults. In A. E. Kazdin (Ed.), *Encyclopedia of psychology* (Vol. 2, pp. 380–382). Washington, DC: American Psychological Association.

Gangestad, S. W. (1993). Sexual selection and physical attractiveness: Implications for mating dynamics. *Human Nature, 4,* 205–235.

Gerteis, J., & Savage, M. (1998). The salience of class in Britain and America: A comparative analysis. *British Journal of Sociology, 49,* 252–274.

Gesy, L. J. (Ed.). (1993). *Today's destructive cults and movements.* Huntington, IN: Our Sunday Visitor Publications.

Gibson, J. T. (1991). Training people to inflict pain: State terror and social learning. *Journal of Humanistic Psychology, 31,* 72–87.

Gilbert, D. T. (1995). Attribution and interpersonal perception. In A. Tesser (Ed.), *Advanced social psychology* (pp. 99–147). New York: McGraw-Hill.

Gilbert, D. T. (2002). Are psychology's tribes ready to form a nation? *Trends in Cognitive Sciences, 6,* 3.

Gilbert, D. T., & Hixon, J. G. (1991). The trouble of thinking: Activation and application of stereotypic beliefs. *Journal of Personality and Social Psychology, 60,* 509–517.

Glennon, F., & Joseph, S. (1993). Just world belief, self-esteem, and attitudes towards homosexuals with AIDS. *Psychological Reports, 72,* 584–586.

Goethals, G. R., Cooper, J., & Naficy, A. (1979). Role of foreseen, foreseeable, and unforeseeable behavioral consequences in the arousal of cognitive dissonance. *Journal of Personality and Social Psychology, 37,* 1179–1185.

Goethals, G. R., & Zanna, M. P. (1979). The role of social comparison in choice shifts. *Journal of Personality and Social Psychology, 37,* 1469–1485.

Graziano, W. G., Habashi, M., Sheese, B., & Tobin, R. M. (2007). Agreeableness, empathy, and helping: A person X situation perspective. *Journal of Personality and Social Psychology 93,* 583-599.

Grusec, J. E., Davidov, M., & Lundell, L. (2002). Prosocial and helping behavior. In P. K. Smith & C. H. Hart (Eds.), *Blackwell handbook of childhood social development* (pp. 457–474). Malden, MA: Blackwell Publishers.

Guadagno, R. W., Asher, T., Demaine, L. H., & Cialdini, R. B. (2001). When saying yes leads to saying no: Preference for consistency and the reverse foot-in-the-door effect. *Personality and Social Psychology Bulletin, 27,* 859–867.

Guéguen, N., & De Gail, M. (2003). The effect of smiling on helping behavior: Smiling and Good Samaritan behavior. *Communication Reports, 16,* 133–140.

Guerin, B. (1993). *Social facilitation.* Paris: Cambridge University Press.

Hafer, C. L., & Choma, B. L. (2009). Belief in a just world, perceived fairness, and justification of the status quo. In J. T. Jost, A. C. Kay, & H. Thorisdottir (Eds.), Series in political psychology. Social and psychological bases of ideology and system justification (pp. 107–125). NY: Oxford University Press.

Haney, C., Banks, W. C., & Zimbardo, P. G. (1973). Interpersonal dynamics in a simulated prison. *International Journal of Criminology and Penology, 1,* 69–97.

Haney, C., & Zimbardo, P. G. (1976). Social roles and role-playing: Observations from the Stanford prison study. In E. P. Hollander & R. G. Hunt (Eds.), *Current perspectives in social psychology* (4th ed., pp. 266–274). New York: Oxford University Press.

Harkins, S., & Szymanski, K. (1989). Social loafing and group evaluation. *Journal of Personality and Social Psychology, 56,* 934–941.

Harkins, S. G., & Petty, R. E. (1982). Effects of task difficulty and task uniqueness on social loafing. *Journal of Personality and Social Psychology, 43,* 1214–1229.

Hastie, R., & Kameda, T. (2005). The robust beauty of majority rules in group decisions. *Psychological Review, 112,* 494–508.

Hastorf, A. H., & Cantril, H. (1954). They saw a game: A case study. *Journal of Abnormal and Social Psychology, 49,* 129–134.

Hatfield, E., & Sprecher, S. (1986). Men's and women's preferences in marital partners in the United States, Russia, and Japan. *Journal of Cross-Cultural Psychology, 26,* 728–750.

Hazan, C., & Shaver, P. R. (1990). Love and work: An attachment-theoretical perspective. *Journal of Personality and Social Psychology, 59,* 270–280.

Heatherton, T. F. (2004). Introduction to special issue on social cognitive neuroscience. *Journal of Cognitive Neuroscience, 16,* 1681–1682.

Heatherton, T. F., Macrae, C. N., & Kelley, W. M. (2004). What the social brain sciences can tell us about the self. *Current Directions in Psychological Science, 13,* 190–193.

Hedges, C. (1997, November 26). Bosnia's factions push their versions of war into the history books. *International Herald Tribune, 5.*

Hewstone, M., Rubin, M., & Willis, H. (2002). Intergroup bias. *Annual Review of Psychology, 51,* 575–604.

Hoeksema-van Orden, C. Y. D., Gaillard, A. W. K., & Buunk, B. P. (1998). Social loafing under fatigue. *Journal of Personality and Social Psychology, 75,* 1179–1190.

Hovland, C. I., & Weiss, W. (1951). The influence of source credibility on communication effectiveness. *Public Opinion Quarterly, 15,* 635–650.

Ilies, R., Wilson, K. S., & Wagner, D. T. (2009). The spillover of daily job satisfaction onto employees' family lives: The facilitating role of work-family integration. *Academy of Management Journal, 52,* 87–102.

Isenberg, D. J. (1986). Group polarization: A critical review and meta-analysis. *Journal of Personality and Social Psychology, 50,* 1141–1151.

Jackson, J. W. (1993). Realistic group conflict theory: A review and evaluation of the theoretical and empirical literature. *The Psychological Record, 43,* 395–413.

Jacobs, R. C., & Campbell, D. T. (1961). The perpetuation of an arbitrary tradition through several generations of a laboratory microculture. *Journal of Abnormal and Social Psychology, 62,* 649–648.

Janis, I. L. (1982). *Victims of groupthink* (2nd ed.). Boston: Houghton Mifflin.

Johnston, L. C., & Macrae, C. N. (1994). Changing social stereotypes: The case of the information seeker. *European Journal of Social Psychology, 24,* 581–592.

Kaplan, M. F. (1987). The influencing process in group decision making. In C. Hendrick (Ed.), *Review of personality and social psychology* (Vol. 8, pp. 189–212). Newbury Park, CA: Sage.

Karau, S. J., & Williams, K. D. (1993). Social loafing: A meta-analytic review and theoretical integration. *Journal of Personality and Social Psychology, 65,* 681–706.

Karuza, J., & Carey, T. O. (1984). Relevance preference and adaptiveness of behavioral blame for observers of rape victims. *Journal of Personality, 52,* 249–262.

Kassin, S. M., & Wrightsman, L. S. (1981). Coerced confessions, judicial instruction, and mock juror verdicts. *Journal of Applied Social Psychology, 11,* 489–506.

Kelley, H. H. (1972). Attribution in social interaction. In E. E. Jones, D. E. Kanouse, H. H. Kelley, R. E. Nisbett, S. Vahns, & B. Weiner (Eds.), *Attribution: Perceiving the causes of behavior.* (pp. 1-26). Morristown, NJ: General Learning Press.

Kelley, H. H., & Michela, J. L. (1980). Attribution theory and research. *Annual Review of Psychology, 31,* 57–501.

Kiesler, C. A., & Kiesler, S. B. (1969). *Conformity.* Reading, MA: Addison-Wesley.

Kilham, W., & Mann, L. (1974). Level of destructive obedience as a function of transmitter and executant roles in the Milgram obedience paradigm. *Journal of Personality and Social Psychology, 29,* 696–702.

Kirchler, E., & Davis, J. H. (1986). The influence of member status differences and task type on group consensus and member position change. *Journal of Personality and Social Psychology, 51,* 83–91.

Kunda, Z., & Oleson, K. C. (1995). Maintaining stereotypes in the face of disconfirmation: Constructing grounds for subtyping deviants. *Journal of Personality and Social Psychology, 68,* 565–579.

Lambert, A. J. (1995). Stereotypes and social judgment: The consequences of group variability. *Journal of Personality and Social Psychology, 68,* 388–403.

Latané, B., Williams, K., & Harkins, S. (1979). Many hands make light the work: The causes and consequences of social loafing. *Journal of Personality and Social Psychology, 37,* 822–832.

Lerner, M. J. (1980). *The belief in a just world: A fundamental illusion.* New York: Plenum Press.

Leventhal, G. S., Singer, R., & Jones, S. (1965). The effects of fear and specificity of recommendation upon attitudes and behavior. *Journal of Personality and Social Psychology, 2,* 20–29.

Levine, J. M., & Moreland, R. L. (1998). Small groups. In D. T. Gilbert, S. T. Fiske, & G. Lindzey (Eds.), *The handbook of social psychology* (4th ed., pp. 415–469). New York: McGraw-Hill.

Li, N. P., Bailey, J. M., Kenrick, D. T., & Linsenmeier, J. A. W. (2002). The necessities and luxuries of mate preferences: Testing the tradeoffs. *Journal of Personality and Social Psychology, 82,* 947–955.

Lieberman, M. D., Ochsner, K. N., Gilbert, D. T., & Schacter, D. L. (2001). Attitude change in amnesia and under cognitive load. *Psychological Science, 12,* 135–140.

Lipkus, I. M., & Siegler, I. C. (1993). The belief in a just world and perceptions of discrimination. *Journal of Psychology, 127,* 465–474.

Lorenzo-Hernandez, J. (1998). How social categorization may inform the study of Hispanic immigration. *Hispanic Journal of Behavioral Sciences, 20,* 39–59.

Losch, M., & Cacioppo, J. (1990). Cognitive dissonance may enhance sympathetic tonus, but attitudes are changed to reduce negative effect rather than arousal. *Journal of Experimental Social Psychology, 26,* 289–304.

Lydon, J. E., Jamieson, D. W., & Zanna, M. P. (1988). Interpersonal similarity and the social and intellectual dimensions of first impressions. *Social Cognition, 6,* 269–286.

Macrae, C. N., Bodenhausen, G. V., Milne, A. B., & Jetten, J. (1994). Out of mind but back in sight: Stereotypes on the rebound. *Journal of Personality and Social Psychology, 67,* 808–817.

Major, B., & O'Brien, L. T. (2005). The social psychology of stigma. *Annual Review of Psychology, 56,* 393–421.

McKenna, K. Y. A., Green, A. S., & Gleason, M. E. J. (2002). Relationship formation on the Internet: What's the big attraction? *Journal of Social Issues, 58,* 9–31.

Mealey, L., Bridgestock, R., & Townsend, G. C. (1999). Symmetry and perceived facial attractiveness: A monozygotic co-twin comparison. *Journal of Personality and Social Psychology, 76,* 151–158.

Mickelson, K. D., Kessler, R. C., & Shaver, P. R. (1997). Adult attachment in a nationally representative sample. *Journal of Personality & Social Psychology, 73,* 1092–1106.

Milgram, S. (1963). Behavioral study of obedience. *Journal of Abnormal and Social Psychology, 67,* 371–378.

Milgram, S. (1965). Some conditions of obedience and disobedience to authority. *Human Relations, 18,* 57–76.

Milgram, S. (1974). *Obedience to authority: An experimental view.* New York: Harper & Row.

Miller, A. G., Collins, B. E., & Brief, D. E. (1995). Perspectives on obedience to authority: The legacy of the Milgram experiments. *Journal of Social Issues, 51,* 1–19.

Miller, M. G., & Ross, M. (1975). Self-serving biases in attribution of causality: Fact or fiction? *Psychological Bulletin, 82,* 313–325.

Miller, N., Maruayama, G., Beaber, R. J., & Valone, K. (1976). Speed of speech and persuasion. *Journal of Personality and Social Psychology, 34,* 615–624.

Miller, T. W., Veltkamp, L. J., Kraus, R. F., Lane, T., & Heister, T. (1999). An adolescent vampire cult in rural America: Clinical issues and case study. *Child Psychiatry and Human Development, 29,* 209–219.

Monteith, M. J. (1996). Affective reactions to prejudice-related discrepant responses: The impact of standard salience. *Personality and Social Psychology Bulletin, 22,* 48–59.

Montoya, R. M., & Horton, R. S. (2004). On the importance of cognitive evaluation as a determinant of interpersonal attraction. *Journal of Personality and Social Psychology, 86,* 696–712.

Moreland, R. L., & Zajonc, R. B. (1982). Exposure effects in person perception: Familiarity, similarity, and attraction. *Journal of Experimental Social Psychology, 18,* 395–415.

Morris, M. W., & Peng, K. (1994). Culture and cause: American and Chinese attributions for social and physical events. *Journal of Personality and Social Psychology, 67,* 949–971.

Morris, W., & Miller, R. (1975). The effects of consensus-breaking and consensus preempting partner on reduction in conformity. *Journal of Experimental Social Psychology, 11,* 215–223.

Ochsner, K. N., & Lieberman, M. D. (2001). The emergence of social cognitive neuroscience. *American Psychologist, 56,* 717–734.

Olczak, P. V., Kaplan, M. F., & Penrod, S. (1991). Attorneys' lay psychology and its effectiveness in selecting jurors: Three empirical studies. *Journal of Social Behavior and Personality, 6,* 431–452.

O'Sullivan, C. S., & Durso, F. T. (1984). Effects of schema-incongruent information on memory for stereotypical attributes. *Journal of Personality and Social Psychology, 47,* 55–70.

Park, J. H., & Schaller, M. (2005). Does attitude similarity serve as a heuristic cue for kinship? Evidence of an implicit cognitive association. *Evolution and Human Behavior, 26,* 158–170.

Park, S., & Catrambone, R. (2007). Social facilitation effects of virtual humans. *Human Factors, 49,* 1054–1060.

Parkinson, B., & Simons, G. (2009). Affecting others: Social appraisal and emotion contagion in everyday decision making. *Personality and Social Psychology Bulletin, 35,* 1071–1084.

Parks, M. R., & Roberts, L. D. (1998). "Making MOOsic": The development of personal relationships on line and a comparison to their off-line counterparts. *Journal of Social and Personal Relationships, 15,* 517–537.

Penner, L. A., Dovidio, J. F., Piliavin, J. A., & Schroeder, D. A. (2005). Prosocial behavior: Multilevel perspectives. *Annual Review of Psychology, 56,* n.p.

Perdue, C. W., Dovidio, J. F., Gurtman, M. B., & Tyler, R. B. (1990). Us and them: Social categorization and the process of intergroup bias. *Journal of Personality and Social Psychology, 59,* 475–486.

Perlow, L., & Weeks, J. (2002). Who's helping whom? Layers of culture and workplace behavior. *Journal of Organizational Behavior, 23,* 345–361.

Pettigrew, T. F. (1969). Racially separate or together? *Journal of Social Issues, 24,* 43–69.

Pettigrew, T. F. (1981). Extending the stereotype concept. In D. L. Hamilton (Ed.), *Cognitive processes in stereotyping and intergroup behavior* (pp. 303–331). Hillsdale, NJ: Erlbaum.

Petty, R. E., & Cacioppo, J. T. (1986). The elaboration likelihood model of persuasion. In L. Berkowitz (Ed.), *Advances in experimental social psychology* (Vol. 19, pp. 123–205). New York: Academic Press.

Petty, R. E., & Wegener, D. T. (1998). Attitude change: Multiple roles for persuasion variables. In D. T. Gilbert, S. T. Fiske, & G. Lindzey (Eds.), *The handbook of social psychology* (4th ed., pp. 323–390). New York: McGraw Hill.

Postmes, T., Spears, R., & Cihangir, S. (2001). Quality of decision making and group norms. *Journal of Personality and Social Psychology, 80,* 918–930.

Powell, M. C., & Fazio, R. H. (1984). Attitude accessibility as a function of repeated attitudinal expression. *Personality and Social Psychology Bulletin, 10,* 139–148.

Priester, J. R., & Petty, R. E. (1995). Source attributions and persuasion: Perceived honesty as a determinant of message scrutiny. *Personality and Social Psychology Bulletin, 21,* 637–654.

Rabinowitz, F. E., Sutton, L., Schutter, T., Brow, A., Krizo, C., Larsen, J., et al. (1997). Helpfulness to lost tourists. *Journal of Social Psychology, 137,* 502–509.

Richmond, L. J. (2004). When spirituality goes awry: Students in cults. *Professional School Counseling, 7,* 367–375.

Romero, A. A., Agnew, C. R., & Insko, C. A. (1996). The cognitive mediation hypothesis revisited: An empirical response to methodological and theoretical criticism. *Personality and Social Psychology Bulletin, 22,* 651–665.

Rosenthal, A. M. (1964). *Thirty-eight witnesses.* New York: McGraw-Hill.

Ross, L., Greene, D., & House, P. (1977). The false consensus effect: An egocentric bias in social perception and attribution processes. *Journal of Experimental Social Psychology, 13,* 279–301.

Rouhana, N. N., & Bar-Tal, D. (1998). Psychological dynamics of intractable ethnonational conflicts: The Israeli-Palestinian case. *American Psychologist, 53,* 761–770.

Rubin, Z. (1970). Measurement of romantic love. *Journal of Personality and Social Psychology, 16,* 265–273.

Ruiter, R. A. C., Abraham, C., & Kok, G. (2001). Scary warnings and rational precautions: A review of the psychology of fear appeals. *Psychology and Health, 16,* 613–630.

Rustemli, A., Mertan, B., & Ciftci, O. (2000). In-group favoritism among native and immigrant Turkish cypriots: Trait evaluations of in-group and out-group targets. *Journal of Social Psychology, 140,* 26–34.

Rynes, S. L., Gerhart, B., & Parks, L. (2005). Personnel psychology: Performance evaluation and pay-for-performance. *Annual Review of Psychology, 56,* 561–600.

Saletan, W. (2004, May 12). Situationist ethics: The Stanford Prison Experiment doesn't explain Abu Ghraib. *Slate Magazine.* Retrieved on June 10, 2010 from http://slate.msn.com/id/2100419

Sanbonmatsu, D. M., & Fazio, R. H. (1990). The role of attitudes in memory-based decision making. *Journal of Personality and Social Psychology, 59,* 614–622.

Schacter, D. L. (1996). *Searching for memory: The brain, the mind, and the past.* New York: Basic Books.

Schmitt, B. H., Gilovich, T., Goore, N., & Joseph, L. (1986). Mere presence and social facilitation: One more time. *Journal of Experimental Social Psychology, 22,* 242–248.

Seta, J. J., & Seta, C. E. (1992). Increments and decrements in mean arterial pressure as a function of audience composition: An averaging and summation analysis. *Personality and Social Psychology Bulletin, 18,* 173–181.

Shanab, M. E., & Yahya, K. A. (1977). A behavioral study of obedience in children. *Journal of Personality and Social Psychology, 35,* 530–536.

Shaver, P. R., & Hazan, C. (1994). Attachment. In A. L. Weber & J. H. Harvey (Eds.), *Perspectives on close relationships.* (pp. 110-130). Boston: Allyn & Bacon.

Sherif, M., Harvey, O. J., White, B. J., Hood, W. R., & Sherif, C. W. (1961). *Intergroup conflict and cooperation: The robber's cave experiment.* Norman, OK: University Book Exchange.

Simon, L., Greenberg, J., & Brehm, J. (1995). Trivialization: The forgotten mode of dissonance reduction. *Journal of Personality and Social Psychology, 68,* 247–260.

Singer, M. T. (1995). Cults: Implications for family therapists. In R. H. Mikesell et al. (Eds.), *Integrating family therapy: Handbook of family psychology and systems theory* (pp. 519–527). Washington, DC: American Psychological Association.

Singer, M. T., & Lalich, J. (1995). *Cults in our midst.* San Francisco: Jossey-Bass.

Slater, M., Antley, A., Davison, A., Swapp, D., Guger, C., Barker, C., et al. (2006). A virtual reprise of the Stanley Milgram obedience experiments. *PLoS ONE, 1*(1), e39.

Snyder, M. (1984). When belief creates reality. In L. Berkowitz (Ed.), *Advances in experimental social psychology* (Vol. 25, pp. 67–114). San Diego, CA: Academic Press.

Snyder, M. (1992). Motivational foundations of behavioral confirmation. In M. P. Zanna (Ed.), *Advances in experimental social psychology* (Vol. 18, pp. 248–306). New York: Academic Press.

Snyder, M., & Ickes, W. (1985). Personality and social behavior. In G. Lindzey & E. Aronson (Eds.), *Handbook of social psychology* (3rd ed., Vol. 2, pp. 883–947). New York: Random House.

Speed, A., & Gangestad, S. (1997). Romantic popularity and mate preferences: A peer-nomination study. *Personality and Social Psychology Bulletin, 23,* 928–935.

Sprecher, S., Aron, A., Hatfield, E., Cortese, A., Potapova, E., & Levitskaya, A. (1994). Love: American style, Russian style and Japanese style. *Personal Relationships, 1,* 349–369.

Sternberg, R. J. (1986). A triangular theory of love. *Psychological Review, 93,* 119–135.

Sternberg, R. J. (1988). *The triangle of love.* New York: Basic Books.

Stürmer, S., Snyder, M., & Omoto, A. M. (2005). Prosocial emotions and helping: The moderating role of group membership. *Journal of Personality and Social Psychology, 88,* 532–546.

Tajfel, H. (1982). *Social identity and intergroup relations.* Cambridge: Cambridge University Press.

Tal-Or, N., & Papierman, Y. (2007). The fundamental attribution error in attributing fictional figures' characteristics to the actors. *Media Psychology, 9,* 331–345.

Tesser, A. (1993). The importance of heritability of psychological research: The case of attitudes. *Psychological Review, 100,* 129–142.

Thornhill, R., & Gangestad, S. W. (1993). Human facial beauty: Averageness, symmetry, and parasite resistance. *Human Nature, 4,* 237–269.

Tidwell, M. O., Reis, H. T., Shaver, P. R. (1996). Attachment, attractiveness, and social interaction: A diary study. *Journal of Personality and Social Psychology, 71,* 729–745.

Trivers, R. (1972). Parental investment and sexual selection. In B. Campbell (Ed.), *Sexual selection and the descent of man, 1871–1971* (pp. 136–179). Chicago: Aldine.

Trivers, R. (1985). *Social evolution.* Menlo Park, CA: Benjamin/Cummings.

Tsang, J. (2002). Moral rationalization and the integration of situational factors and psychological processes in immoral behavior. *Review of General Psychology, 6,* 25–50.

van Boven, L., White, K., Kamada, A., & Gilovich, T. (2003). Intuitions about situational correction in self and others. *Journal of Personality and Social Psychology, 85,* 249–258.

Van Swol, L. M. (2009). Extreme members and group polarization. *Social Influence, 4,* 185–199.

Varma, A. (2000). Impact of watching international television programs on adolescents in India. *Journal of Comparative Family Studies, 31,* 117–126.

Walker, I., & Crogan, M. (1998). Academic performance, prejudice, and the Jigsaw Classroom: New pieces of the puzzle. *Journal of Community and Applied Social Psychology, 8,* 381–393.

Waller, N. G., & Shaver, P. R. (1994). The importance of non-genetic influences on romantic love styles: A twin family study. *Psychological Science, 5,* 268–274.

Walsh, Y. (2001). Deconstructing "brainwashing" within cults as an aid to counselling psychologists. *Counselling Psychology Quarterly, 14,* 119–128.

Weiner, B. (1980). A cognitive (attribution) emotion-action model of motivated behavior: An analysis of judgments of help-giving. *Journal of Personality and Social Psychology, 39,* 186–200.

West, L. J. (1980). Persuasive techniques in contemporary cults. In M. Galanter (Ed.), *Cults and new religious movements* (pp. 165–192). Washington, DC: American Psychiatric Press.

Wheeler, L., & Kim, Y. (1997). What is beautiful is culturally good: The physical attractiveness stereotype has different content in collectivistic cultures. *Personality and Social Psychology Bulletin, 23,* 795–800.

Whyte, Glen (2000). Groupthink. In A. E. Kazdin (Ed.), Encyclopedia of psychology (Vol. 4, pp. 35-38). Washington, DC: American Psychological Association.

Wilder, D. A., Simon, A. F., & Faith, M. (1996). Enhancing the impact of counter-stereotypic information: Dispositional attributions for deviance. *Journal of Personality and Social Psychology, 71*, 276–287.

Williams, C. N. (2003). America's opposition to new religious movements: Limiting the freedom of religion. *Law and Psychology Review, 27*, 171–182.

Wolf, N. (1991). *The beauty myth*. New York: Anchor/Doubleday.

Wyer, N. A., Sherman, J. W., & Stroessner, S. J. (2000). The roles of motivation and ability in controlling the consequences of stereotype suppression. *Personality and Social Psychology Bulletin, 26*, 13–25.

Zajonc, R. B. (1968). Attitudinal effects of mere exposure. *Journal of Personality and Social Psychology, 9*(2, Pt. 2), 1–27.

Zimbardo, P. G. (2004, May 9). Power turns good soldiers into "bad apples." *Boston Globe*. Retrieved on June 2, 2006 from http://www.boston.com/news/globeeditorial_opinion/oped/articles/2004/05/09

Zimbardo, P. G., Maslach, C., & Haney, C. (2000). Reflections on the Stanford Prison Experiment: Genesis, transformations, consequences. In T. Blass (Ed.), *Obedience to authority: Current perspectives on the Milgram paradigm* (pp. 193–237). Mahwah, NJ: Erlbaum.

References: Appendix

Doheny, M. (1993). Effects of mental practice on performance of a psychomotor skill. *Journal of Mental Imagery, 17*(3–4), 111–118.

Driskell, J., Copper, C., & Moran, A. (1994). Does mental practice enhance performance? *Journal of Applied Psychology, 79*(4), 481–492.

Druckman, D., & Swets, J. A. (Eds.). (1988). *Enhancing human performance: Issues, theories, and techniques.* Washington, DC: National Academies Press.

Huff, D. (1954). *How to lie with statistics.* New York: Norton.

Kosslyn, S. M. (2006). Graph design for the eye and mind. New York: Oxford University Press.

Prather, D. C. (1973). Prompted mental practice as a flight simulator. *Journal of Applied Psychology, 57,* 353–355.

Vieilledent, S., Kosslyn, S. M., Berthoz, A., & Giraudo, M. D. (2003). Does mental simulation of following a path improve navigation performance without vision? *Cognitive Brain Research, 16,* 238–249.

White, A., & Hardy, L. (1995). Use of different imagery perspectives on the learning and performance of different motor skills. *British Journal of Psychology, 86*(2), 169–180.

Woolfolk, R. L., Parrish, M. W., & Murphy, S. M. (1985). The effects of positive and negative imagery on motor skill performance. *Cognitive Therapy and Research, 9,* 335–341.

Index

Page references followed by "f" indicate illustrated figures or photographs; followed by "t" indicates a table.

1

12-Step programs, 462, 585
16PF, 293, 565

A

ABCDEF technique, 454
Abilities
  uniquely human, 57
Abnormal behavior
  diathesis-stress models of, 583
  historical views of, 282
Abnormality
  biopsychosocial model, 407-408
  culture and, 402
  defined, 401
  defining, 400-401
  models of, 405
Abstinence violation effect, 431
Abstract reasoning, 342, 387
Abstract thinking
  intelligence as, 224, 557
Academic achievement
  parental influence on, 573
  risk behavior and, 570
Accessing stored information, 161
Accidents
  in middle childhood, 581
Accommodation
  in cognitive development, 357
Acetylcholine
  memory and, 47, 349-350
Achievement
  IQ and, 219
Achievement motive, 563
Achromatopsia, 545
Acquiescence, 293
Acquisition in classical conditioning, 123
Acronyms, 186
Acrophobia, 517, 585
Action potential
  properties of, 40, 43, 533, 541
Activational effects, of hormones, 569
Activation-synthesis hypothesis, 377, 527, 576
Active interaction, 72, 527
Active searching, 100
Actualization needs, 265
Acute stressor, 361, 527
Adaptation
  happiness and, 561-562
  hedonic, 561
Adaptation phase, 363, 537
Adaptation-level theory, 561-562
Addiction
  and culture, 575
  classical conditioning and, 549-550
Addictive behavior
  psychopathology and, 563
Ader, Robert, 131
Adjustment disorder
  stressors and, 576
Adolescence
  adolescent egocentrism, 346
  and moral development, 571
  attachment in, 573
  autonomy, 352
  brain development in, 571
  conflicts with parents, 348
  egocentrism, 346, 570-571
  egocentrism in, 570
  emotional development during, 318
  formal operations, 346
  growth spurt, 344

identity, 346, 404, 555
  imaginary audience, 346, 569
  information processing in, 569
  intellectual changes in, 571
  moral development, 341-342, 571-573
  moral development of, 342
  peer pressure, 569
  personal fable, 346-348, 571
  physical development, 318
  physiology of, 545
  pregnancy in, 347
  psychosocial development, 352-353
  psychosocial stages in, 352
  secular trend, 571
  self-concept in, 571
  sleep and, 404
  teenage pregnancy, 347, 570
Adolescence(ents)
  cognitive changes in, 571
  depression and, 556
  suicide and, 347
Adolescent egocentrism, 346
Adolescents
  aggression in, 565
  depression in, 585
  eating disorders and, 466
Adult attachment style, 310-311, 566
Adult attachment styles, 312, 491, 565
Adult development
  basic concepts of, 572
Adulthood
  generativity, 352-353, 572
  intimacy and, 311
  late adulthood, 571
  memory, changes in, 570
  midlife, 570-572
  parenthood and, 572
  perception and cognition in, 318, 569
  physical changes, 573
  successful aging, 572
Adulthood, middle
  burnout, 575
Advertising
  classical conditioning in, 128
  how it works, 129
  psychology and, 550-552
Aesthetic needs, 265
Affective disorders, 557
Affirming the consequent, 212, 527
African Americans
  age of menarche, 570
  grandparents, 355, 490
  IQ scores and, 230
  IQ tests, 219-220, 556
  locus of control and, 309
  longevity, 354, 391
  school achievement, 559
  teen mothers, 348, 571
African Americans/blacks
  IQ scores, 218-220
African-Americans
  and higher education, 558
  and smoking, 559
  and teenage pregnancy, 570
  anxiety disorders and, 416
African-Americans/blacks
  IQ scores
    group differences, 228-229, 559
Afterimages
  color, 91
Age
  and expertise, 555
  and health, 232, 351
  and self-esteem, 349
  schizophrenia and, 425, 583
Age and aging
  and suicide, 410, 585

cognitive changes, 571
  generativity and, 572
Age at onset
  of anorexia nervosa, 428, 581
  of bipolar disorder, 414, 582
  of bulimia nervosa, 428
  of eating disorders, 430-432, 581-584
  of obsessive-compulsive disorder, 581
  of panic disorder, 415, 464, 581
  of schizophrenia, 422-427, 581-584
Age norms, 569
Age ranges, 326
Age/aging
  dreams and, 579
Age-related changes
  in cognitive function, 569
  in taste, 112
Aggression
  amygdala and, 256, 561
  and biology, 313, 571
  and sexual selection, 564
  dopamine and, 388, 566
  empathy and, 566
  entertainment media and, 550
  environmental influences on, 565
  in adolescence, 348, 562
  personality traits and, 578
  rape and, 577
  shyness and, 313
  situational determinants, 579
  spanking and, 549
  substance abuse and, 347, 386, 577
Aging
  and brain, 544
  influences on brain, 544
  intelligence and, 351
  secondary, 348, 571
  successful, 319, 571-572
  wisdom and, 573
Agonist, 80, 544
Agonists, 49, 543
Agoraphobia
  without panic, 416
AIDS (Acquired immunodeficiency syndrome)
  prenatal development and, 323
Alarm phase, 362, 527
Alarm system, 416
Alcohol
  fetal alcohol spectrum disorder, 322
  genetics and, 544
  mental retardation and, 235, 531, 558
  use and abuse, 385
Alcohol abuse and dependence
  genetic factors in, 424, 583-584
  in adolescents, 565
alcohol consumption
  thought suppression and, 575
Alcohol myopia, 387-388, 527, 576
Alcohol use
  date rape and, 577
Alcohol use/abuse
  placebo effect in, 394, 578
Alcoholics Anonymous (AA), 462
Alcoholism/alcohol abuse
  myopia, 387-388, 576
Alfred Binet, 216
Algebra, 208, 345, 572
All-nighters, 376-377
All-or-none law, 45, 527
Allostasis, 363, 576-577
Allostatic load, 363-364, 527, 576-577
Alternative and complementary therapies
  acupuncture, 114, 364, 545
Alternative five, 299, 565
Alzheimer's disease
  early-onset, 544
Alzheimer's disease

hippocampus and, 173, 350, 543
Alzheimer's disease
    neuropathology of, 553
Alzheimer's disease
    symptoms of, 389, 410, 583
Ambien, 379
Ambiguous figure, 97
Ambiguous figures, 93
American Psychiatric Association, 385-386, 402-404,
        466-467, 550
Ames, Adelbert, 95
Ames room, 95
Amistad, 318
Amnesia
    anterograde, 182-183, 527
    implicit memory in, 551-552
    infantile, 183-184
    infantile amnesia, 183-184
    retrograde, 183, 537, 551
Amphetamine psychosis, 389
Amphetamines
    characteristics of, 527
    types of, 60, 385-386, 527
Amusia, 543
Amygdala
    emotions and, 278, 413
    in depression, 411-413
    in panic, 417, 581
    in schizophrenia, 581-584
    removal of, 418, 550
Anal stage, 284
Analgesics, 386, 534
Analogical problem solving, 556
Anal-retentive personality, 287
Analytic intelligence, 224
Analyzing data, 30
Androgen insensitivity syndrome, 273
Anger
    managing, 461
Animals
    Big Five traits and, 576
    cognition and, 127, 279, 561
    communication among, 77, 532
Animal(s)
    emotions in, 60, 260, 557
Animals
    intelligence of, 555
    language acquisition in, 562
    learning by, 152
Anomalous cognition, 114
Anorexia nervosa
    perfectionism and, 582
    treatment of, 466, 582
Antagonists, 49-50
Antianxiety medications, 459
Anticipatory nausea, 131-132, 549
Antidepressant drugs
    atypical, 457-458, 543
Antidepressants
    MAOIs, 458
Antipsychotics (neuroleptics)
    for schizophrenia, 585-586
Antisocial personality disorder (APD)
    causes of
        genetic influences, 591
Antisocial personality disorder (ASPD)
    alcohol use and, 559
    developmental perspective on, 583
Anxiety
    comorbidity of, 582
    heart disease and, 371, 532
    immune system and, 368
    twin studies, 303, 552
Anxiety disorders
    agoraphobia as, 586
    and psychotherapy, 552
    biological influences, 282
    cognitive perspectives on, 572
    specific phobia, 418, 538
    types of
        obsessive-compulsive disorder, 47, 404, 450
        panic disorder, 415-416, 448, 576
Anxious attachment, 311
Anxious attachment style, 311
Anxious-ambivalent style, 491
Appetizer effect, 268, 564
Applied psychologist, 40
Applied psychologists, 15, 527
Appraisal performance

theories of emotion, 248, 563
Approach emotions, 248
Approach–approach conflict, 366, 527
Approach–avoidance conflict, 367, 527
Aptitude, 556
Archetypes, 286
Arguments
    definition, 210, 559
Aronson, Joshua, 233
Arousal
    drives and, 262
    low level of, 264, 299
    misattribution of, 251, 534
Arousal response
    autonomic nervous system in, 543
    in phobias, 418
Arousal theory, 262, 566
Articulatory loop, 160
Artificial intelligence, 557
Artificial selection
    in animals, 563
Asia, Asians/Asian-Americans
    and emotional expression, 255
Asian Americans
    osteoporosis, 349
    therapy and, 468, 576
Asians/Asian-Americans
    and alcohol, 381, 570
Aspartame (NutraSweet), 112
Assessment
    diagnosis and, 581
    psychosocial, 567
Associative learning, 121, 169, 544
Astronauts, 113
Atkinson, Richard, 158
Atkinson-Shiffrin model, 553
Atmospheric perspective, 95
Attachment
    love relationships as, 490
    separation anxiety, 339
    threats and, 565
Attachment relationships
    disorganized/disoriented, 339
    resistant, 339, 488
Attachment styles
    combinations, 356, 434
Attachment theory
    pros and cons of, 115
Attention
    sleep deprivation and, 376
    working memory and, 259, 350
Attention deficit/hyperactivity disorder (ADHD)
    in adults, 583
Attention problems, 47
Attentional blink, 101, 527, 545-547
Attentional processes
    selective attention, 99, 544
Attention-deficit/hyperactivity disorder
    diagnosis of, 55, 415, 461, 544
Attention-deficit/hyperactivity disorder (ADHD), 47
Attitude accessibility, 590-591
Attitudes
    affective component, 507
    classical conditioning of, 549
    correctness, 505
    media and, 550
Attitudes and attitude change
    persuasive communications, 589
Attraction
    romantic attraction, 590
Attribution
    of harm, 532
Attributions
    blaming the victim, 488
Audition
    disorders, 534-535, 545
Auditory acuity
    in infants, 567
Auditory canal, 105
Auditory cues, 104
Auditory hallucinations, 390, 410
Auditory information, 108, 566
Auditory scene analysis, 107, 545
Auditory sensation, 82, 532
Auditory sensory memory, 158
authority
    and compliance, 589
    compliance and, 589
Autobiographical memories

childhood amnesia
    explanations for, 572
Automatic processes, 170-171
Autonomic nervous systems, 131-132
Average children, 236
Aversive conditioning
    conditioned taste aversion, 130
Avoidance conditioning, 549
Avoidance learning, 124, 528, 549
Avoidance–avoidance conflict, 367, 528
Avoidant coping, 382
Avoidant coping strategies, 382
Avoidant personality disorder, 433-434
Avoidant style, 310-311, 491
Axel, Richard, 110

B

B cell, 369, 528
B cells, 368
Babbling, 330, 571-573
Babinski reflex, 324
Backward conditioning, 123, 549
Backward pairing, 123
Baillargeon, Renee, 337
Bantu, 545
Bard, Philip, 250
Barn owls, 108
Barrymore, Drew, 182
BAS, 297
Basal ganglia
    in classical conditioning, 527-528
    in OCD, 420
Base-rate rule, 213, 528
Basic-level names, 207
Bechterev, Vladimir, 124
Behavior
    and hormones, 59
    and neurotransmitters, 172, 298, 407
    and stress, 288, 347, 406-407, 569
    automatic, control of, 61, 534
    brain structures and, 65, 298
    during puberty, 62
    genetic influences on, 544
    influencing situations
        Stanford Prison Experiment, 493-494, 591
    prison study, 506, 590
    social influence on, 480
Behavior therapies
    based on classical conditioning, 450
    based on operant conditioning, 470
    exposure therapies, 586
    operant conditioning and, 134, 437
Behavior therapist, 449, 582
Behavior therapy
    phases of, 21, 82-83, 122, 236, 274, 319
    systematic desensitization, 129, 450-451, 539
Behavioral disengagement, 382
Behavioral perspective
    mood disorders and, 557
Behavioral theories
    of mood disorders, 528, 584
Behavioral therapies, 442, 586
Behavioral treatment
    for anxiety disorders, 459
    for panic disorder, 437, 463, 582
Behavior(s)
    classically conditioned, 122, 172, 531
    hypnosis and, 177, 551
    in early infancy, 547
    social situations and, 297
Beliefs
    genetics of, 270
Bell curve
    for IQ scores, 219
Bell-shaped curve, 511, 535
Belongingness needs, 265
Benzodiazepine drugs
    panic disorder and, 471, 586
Berthold, Arnold, 273
Between-group differences, 228-229
Bias
    disconfirmation, 590
    in signal detection, 85, 528
    performance evaluation and, 591
    positive emotion, 576
    response bias, 31, 271-272, 537
    social desirability, 293, 538
Biased sample, 272
Biases